Dictionary of Literary Biography

1 *The American Renaissance in New England,* edited by Joel Myerson (1978)

2 *American Novelists Since World War II,* edited by Jeffrey Helterman and Richard Layman (1978)

3 *Antebellum Writers in New York and the South,* edited by Joel Myerson (1979)

4 *American Writers in Paris, 1920-1939,* edited by Karen Lane Rood (1980)

5 *American Poets Since World War II,* 2 parts, edited by Donald J. Greiner (1980)

6 *American Novelists Since World War II, Second Series,* edited by James E. Kibler Jr. (1980)

7 *Twentieth-Century American Dramatists,* 2 parts, edited by John MacNicholas (1981)

8 *Twentieth-Century American Science-Fiction Writers,* 2 parts, edited by David Cowart and Thomas L. Wymer (1981)

9 *American Novelists, 1910-1945,* 3 parts, edited by James J. Martine (1981)

10 *Modern British Dramatists, 1900-1945,* 2 parts, edited by Stanley Weintraub (1982)

11 *American Humorists, 1800-1950,* 2 parts, edited by Stanley Trachtenberg (1982)

12 *American Realists and Naturalists,* edited by Donald Pizer and Earl N. Harbert (1982)

13 *British Dramatists Since World War II,* 2 parts, edited by Stanley Weintraub (1982)

14 *British Novelists Since 1960,* 2 parts, edited by Jay L. Halio (1983)

15 *British Novelists, 1930-1959,* 2 parts, edited by Bernard Oldsey (1983)

16 *The Beats: Literary Bohemians in Postwar America,* 2 parts, edited by Ann Charters (1983)

17 *Twentieth-Century American Historians,* edited by Clyde N. Wilson (1983)

18 *Victorian Novelists After 1885,* edited by Ira B. Nadel and William E. Fredeman (1983)

19 *British Poets, 1880-1914,* edited by Donald E. Stanford (1983)

20 *British Poets, 1914-1945,* edited by Donald E. Stanford (1983)

21 *Victorian Novelists Before 1885,* edited by Ira B. Nadel and William E. Fredeman (1983)

22 *American Writers for Children, 1900-1960,* edited by John Cech (1983)

23 *American Newspaper Journalists, 1873-1900,* edited by Perry J. Ashley (1983)

24 *American Colonial Writers, 1606-1734,* edited by Emory Elliott (1984)

25 *American Newspaper Journalists, 1901-1925,* edited by Perry J. Ashley (1984)

26 *American Screenwriters,* edited by Robert E. Morsberger, Stephen O. Lesser, and Randall Clark (1984)

27 *Poets of Great Britain and Ireland, 1945-1960,* edited by Vincent B. Sherry Jr. (1984)

28 *Twentieth-Century American-Jewish Fiction Writers,* edited by Daniel Walden (1984)

29 *American Newspaper Journalists, 1926-1950,* edited by Perry J. Ashley (1984)

30 *American Historians, 1607-1865,* edited by Clyde N. Wilson (1984)

31 *American Colonial Writers, 1735-1781,* edited by Emory Elliott (1984)

32 *Victorian Poets Before 1850,* edited by William E. Fredeman and Ira B. Nadel (1984)

33 *Afro-American Fiction Writers After 1955,* edited by Thadious M. Davis and Trudier Harris (1984)

34 *British Novelists, 1890-1929: Traditionalists,* edited by Thomas F. Staley (1985)

35 *Victorian Poets After 1850,* edited by William E. Fredeman and Ira B. Nadel (1985)

36 *British Novelists, 1890-1929: Modernists,* edited by Thomas F. Staley (1985)

37 *American Writers of the Early Republic,* edited by Emory Elliott (1985)

38 *Afro-American Writers After 1955: Dramatists and Prose Writers,* edited by Thadious M. Davis and Trudier Harris (1985)

39 *British Novelists, 1660-1800,* 2 parts, edited by Martin C. Battestin (1985)

40 *Poets of Great Britain and Ireland Since 1960,* 2 parts, edited by Vincent B. Sherry Jr. (1985)

41 *Afro-American Poets Since 1955,* edited by Trudier Harris and Thadious M. Davis (1985)

42 *American Writers for Children Before 1900,* edited by Glenn E. Estes (1985)

43 *American Newspaper Journalists, 1690-1872,* edited by Perry J. Ashley (1986)

44 *American Screenwriters, Second Series,* edited by Randall Clark, Robert E. Morsberger, and Stephen O. Lesser (1986)

45 *American Poets, 1880-1945, First Series,* edited by Peter Quartermain (1986)

46 *American Literary Publishing Houses, 1900-1980: Trade and Paperback,* edited by Peter Dzwonkoski (1986)

47 *American Historians, 1866-1912,* edited by Clyde N. Wilson (1986)

48 *American Poets, 1880-1945, Second Series,* edited by Peter Quartermain (1986)

49 *American Literary Publishing Houses, 1638-1899,* 2 parts, edited by Peter Dzwonkoski (1986)

50 *Afro-American Writers Before the Harlem Renaissance,* edited by Trudier Harris (1986)

51 *Afro-American Writers from the Harlem Renaissance to 1940,* edited by Trudier Harris (1987)

52 *American Writers for Children Since 1960: Fiction,* edited by Glenn E. Estes (1986)

53 *Canadian Writers Since 1960, First Series,* edited by W. H. New (1986)

54 *American Poets, 1880-1945, Third Series,* 2 parts, edited by Peter Quartermain (1987)

55 *Victorian Prose Writers Before 1867,* edited by William B. Thesing (1987)

56 *German Fiction Writers, 1914-1945,* edited by James Hardin (1987)

57 *Victorian Prose Writers After 1867,* edited by William B. Thesing (1987)

58 *Jacobean and Caroline Dramatists,* edited by Fredson Bowers (1987)

59 *American Literary Critics and Scholars, 1800-1850*, edited by John W. Rathbun and Monica M. Grecu (1987)

60 *Canadian Writers Since 1960, Second Series*, edited by W. H. New (1987)

61 *American Writers for Children Since 1960: Poets, Illustrators, and Nonfiction Authors*, edited by Glenn E. Estes (1987)

62 *Elizabethan Dramatists*, edited by Fredson Bowers (1987)

63 *Modern American Critics, 1920-1955*, edited by Gregory S. Jay (1988)

64 *American Literary Critics and Scholars, 1850-1880*, edited by John W. Rathbun and Monica M. Grecu (1988)

65 *French Novelists, 1900-1930*, edited by Catharine Savage Brosman (1988)

66 *German Fiction Writers, 1885-1913*, 2 parts, edited by James Hardin (1988)

67 *Modern American Critics Since 1955*, edited by Gregory S. Jay (1988)

68 *Canadian Writers, 1920-1959, First Series*, edited by W. H. New (1988)

69 *Contemporary German Fiction Writers, First Series*, edited by Wolfgang D. Elfe and James Hardin (1988)

70 *British Mystery Writers, 1860-1919*, edited by Bernard Benstock and Thomas F. Staley (1988)

71 *American Literary Critics and Scholars, 1880-1900*, edited by John W. Rathbun and Monica M. Grecu (1988)

72 *French Novelists, 1930-1960*, edited by Catharine Savage Brosman (1988)

73 *American Magazine Journalists, 1741-1850*, edited by Sam G. Riley (1988)

74 *American Short-Story Writers Before 1880*, edited by Bobby Ellen Kimbel, with the assistance of William E. Grant (1988)

75 *Contemporary German Fiction Writers, Second Series*, edited by Wolfgang D. Elfe and James Hardin (1988)

76 *Afro-American Writers, 1940-1955*, edited by Trudier Harris (1988)

77 *British Mystery Writers, 1920-1939*, edited by Bernard Benstock and Thomas F. Staley (1988)

78 *American Short-Story Writers, 1880-1910*, edited by Bobby Ellen Kimbel, with the assistance of William E. Grant (1988)

79 *American Magazine Journalists, 1850-1900*, edited by Sam G. Riley (1988)

80 *Restoration and Eighteenth-Century Dramatists, First Series*, edited by Paula R. Backscheider (1989)

81 *Austrian Fiction Writers, 1875-1913*, edited by James Hardin and Donald G. Daviau (1989)

82 *Chicano Writers, First Series*, edited by Francisco A. Lomelí and Carl R. Shirley (1989)

83 *French Novelists Since 1960*, edited by Catharine Savage Brosman (1989)

84 *Restoration and Eighteenth-Century Dramatists, Second Series*, edited by Paula R. Backscheider (1989)

85 *Austrian Fiction Writers After 1914*, edited by James Hardin and Donald G. Daviau (1989)

86 *American Short-Story Writers, 1910-1945, First Series*, edited by Bobby Ellen Kimbel (1989)

87 *British Mystery and Thriller Writers Since 1940, First Series*, edited by Bernard Benstock and Thomas F. Staley (1989)

88 *Canadian Writers, 1920-1959, Second Series*, edited by W. H. New (1989)

89 *Restoration and Eighteenth-Century Dramatists, Third Series*, edited by Paula R. Backscheider (1989)

90 *German Writers in the Age of Goethe, 1789-1832*, edited by James Hardin and Christoph E. Schweitzer (1989)

91 *American Magazine Journalists, 1900-1960, First Series*, edited by Sam G. Riley (1990)

92 *Canadian Writers, 1890-1920*, edited by W. H. New (1990)

93 *British Romantic Poets, 1789-1832, First Series*, edited by John R. Greenfield (1990)

94 *German Writers in the Age of Goethe: Sturm und Drang to Classicism*, edited by James Hardin and Christoph E. Schweitzer (1990)

95 *Eighteenth-Century British Poets, First Series*, edited by John Sitter (1990)

96 *British Romantic Poets, 1789-1832, Second Series*, edited by John R. Greenfield (1990)

97 *German Writers from the Enlightenment to Sturm und Drang, 1720-1764*, edited by James Hardin and Christoph E. Schweitzer (1990)

98 *Modern British Essayists, First Series*, edited by Robert Beum (1990)

99 *Canadian Writers Before 1890*, edited by W. H. New (1990)

100 *Modern British Essayists, Second Series*, edited by Robert Beum (1990)

101 *British Prose Writers, 1660-1800, First Series*, edited by Donald T. Siebert (1991)

102 *American Short-Story Writers, 1910-1945, Second Series*, edited by Bobby Ellen Kimbel (1991)

103 *American Literary Biographers, First Series*, edited by Steven Serafin (1991)

104 *British Prose Writers, 1660-1800, Second Series*, edited by Donald T. Siebert (1991)

105 *American Poets Since World War II, Second Series*, edited by R. S. Gwynn (1991)

106 *British Literary Publishing Houses, 1820-1880*, edited by Patricia J. Anderson and Jonathan Rose (1991)

107 *British Romantic Prose Writers, 1789-1832, First Series*, edited by John R. Greenfield (1991)

108 *Twentieth-Century Spanish Poets, First Series*, edited by Michael L. Perna (1991)

109 *Eighteenth-Century British Poets, Second Series*, edited by John Sitter (1991)

110 *British Romantic Prose Writers, 1789-1832, Second Series*, edited by John R. Greenfield (1991)

111 *American Literary Biographers, Second Series*, edited by Steven Serafin (1991)

112 *British Literary Publishing Houses, 1881-1965*, edited by Jonathan Rose and Patricia J. Anderson (1991)

113 *Modern Latin-American Fiction Writers, First Series*, edited by William Luis (1992)

114 *Twentieth-Century Italian Poets, First Series*, edited by Giovanna Wedel De Stasio, Glauco Cambon, and Antonio Illiano (1992)

115 *Medieval Philosophers*, edited by Jeremiah Hackett (1992)

116 *British Romantic Novelists, 1789-1832*, edited by Bradford K. Mudge (1992)

117 *Twentieth-Century Caribbean and Black African Writers, First Series*, edited by Bernth Lindfors and Reinhard Sander (1992)

118 *Twentieth-Century German Dramatists, 1889-1918*, edited by Wolfgang D. Elfe and James Hardin (1992)

119 *Nineteenth-Century French Fiction Writers: Romanticism and Realism, 1800-1860*, edited by Catharine Savage Brosman (1992)

120 *American Poets Since World War II, Third Series*, edited by R. S. Gwynn (1992)

121 *Seventeenth-Century British Nondramatic Poets, First Series,* edited by M. Thomas Hester (1992)

122 *Chicano Writers, Second Series,* edited by Francisco A. Lomelí and Carl R. Shirley (1992)

123 *Nineteenth-Century French Fiction Writers: Naturalism and Beyond, 1860-1900,* edited by Catharine Savage Brosman (1992)

124 *Twentieth-Century German Dramatists, 1919-1992,* edited by Wolfgang D. Elfe and James Hardin (1992)

125 *Twentieth-Century Caribbean and Black African Writers, Second Series,* edited by Bernth Lindfors and Reinhard Sander (1993)

126 *Seventeenth-Century British Nondramatic Poets, Second Series,* edited by M. Thomas Hester (1993)

127 *American Newspaper Publishers, 1950-1990,* edited by Perry J. Ashley (1993)

128 *Twentieth-Century Italian Poets, Second Series,* edited by Giovanna Wedel De Stasio, Glauco Cambon, and Antonio Illiano (1993)

129 *Nineteenth-Century German Writers, 1841-1900,* edited by James Hardin and Siegfried Mews (1993)

130 *American Short-Story Writers Since World War II,* edited by Patrick Meanor (1993)

131 *Seventeenth-Century British Nondramatic Poets, Third Series,* edited by M. Thomas Hester (1993)

132 *Sixteenth-Century British Nondramatic Writers, First Series,* edited by David A. Richardson (1993)

133 *Nineteenth-Century German Writers to 1840,* edited by James Hardin and Siegfried Mews (1993)

134 *Twentieth-Century Spanish Poets, Second Series,* edited by Jerry Phillips Winfield (1994)

135 *British Short-Fiction Writers, 1880-1914: The Realist Tradition,* edited by William B. Thesing (1994)

136 *Sixteenth-Century British Nondramatic Writers, Second Series,* edited by David A. Richardson (1994)

137 *American Magazine Journalists, 1900-1960, Second Series,* edited by Sam G. Riley (1994)

138 *German Writers and Works of the High Middle Ages: 1170-1280,* edited by James Hardin and Will Hasty (1994)

139 *British Short-Fiction Writers, 1945-1980,* edited by Dean Baldwin (1994)

140 *American Book-Collectors and Bibliographers, First Series,* edited by Joseph Rosenblum (1994)

141 *British Children's Writers, 1880-1914,* edited by Laura M. Zaidman (1994)

142 *Eighteenth-Century British Literary Biographers,* edited by Steven Serafin (1994)

143 *American Novelists Since World War II, Third Series,* edited by James R. Giles and Wanda H. Giles (1994)

144 *Nineteenth-Century British Literary Biographers,* edited by Steven Serafin (1994)

145 *Modern Latin-American Fiction Writers, Second Series,* edited by William Luis and Ann González (1994)

146 *Old and Middle English Literature,* edited by Jeffrey Helterman and Jerome Mitchell (1994)

147 *South Slavic Writers Before World War II,* edited by Vasa D. Mihailovich (1994)

148 *German Writers and Works of the Early Middle Ages: 800-1170,* edited by Will Hasty and James Hardin (1994)

149 *Late Nineteenth- and Early Twentieth-Century British Literary Biographers,* edited by Steven Serafin (1995)

150 *Early Modern Russian Writers, Late Seventeenth and Eighteenth Centuries,* edited by Marcus C. Levitt (1995)

151 *British Prose Writers of the Early Seventeenth Century,* edited by Clayton D. Lein (1995)

152 *American Novelists Since World War II, Fourth Series,* edited by James and Wanda Giles (1995)

153 *Late-Victorian and Edwardian British Novelists, First Series,* edited by George M. Johnson (1995)

154 *The British Literary Book Trade, 1700-1820,* edited by James K. Bracken and Joel Silver (1995)

155 *Twentieth-Century British Literary Biographers,* edited by Steven Serafin (1995)

156 *British Short-Fiction Writers, 1880-1914: The Romantic Tradition,* edited by William F. Naufftus (1995)

157 *Twentieth-Century Caribbean and Black African Writers, Third Series,* edited by Bernth Lindfors and Reinhard Sander (1995)

158 *British Reform Writers, 1789-1832,* edited by Gary Kelly and Edd Applegate (1995)

159 *British Short-Fiction Writers, 1800-1880,* edited by John R. Greenfield (1996)

160 *British Children's Writers, 1914-1960,* edited by Donald R. Hettinga and Gary D. Schmidt (1996)

161 *British Children's Writers Since 1960, First Series,* edited by Caroline Hunt (1996)

162 *British Short-Fiction Writers, 1915-1945,* edited by John H. Rogers (1996)

163 *British Children's Writers, 1800-1880,* edited by Meena Khorana (1996)

164 *German Baroque Writers, 1580-1660,* edited by James Hardin (1996)

165 *American Poets Since World War II, Fourth Series,* edited by Joseph Conte (1996)

166 *British Travel Writers, 1837-1875,* edited by Barbara Brothers and Julia Gergits (1996)

167 *Sixteenth-Century British Nondramatic Writers, Third Series,* edited by David A. Richardson (1996)

168 *German Baroque Writers, 1661-1730,* edited by James Hardin (1996)

169 *American Poets Since World War II, Fifth Series,* edited by Joseph Conte (1996)

170 *The British Literary Book Trade, 1475-1700,* edited by James K. Bracken and Joel Silver (1996)

171 *Twentieth-Century American Sportswriters,* edited by Richard Orodenker (1996)

172 *Sixteenth-Century British Nondramatic Writers, Fourth Series,* edited by David A. Richardson (1996)

173 *American Novelists Since World War II, Fifth Series,* edited by James R. Giles and Wanda H. Giles (1996)

174 *British Travel Writers, 1876-1909,* edited by Barbara Brothers and Julia Gergits (1997)

175 *Native American Writers of the United States,* edited by Kenneth M. Roemer (1997)

176 *Ancient Greek Authors,* edited by Ward W. Briggs (1997)

177 *Italian Novelists Since World War II, 1945-1965* edited by Augustus Pallotta (1997)

178 *British Fantasy and Science-Fiction Writers Before World War I,* edited by Darren Harris-Fain (1997)

179 *German Writers of the Renaissance and Reformation, 1280-1580,* edited by James Hardin and Max Reinhart (1997)

180 *Japanese Fiction Writers, 1868-1945,* edited by Van C. Gessel (1997)

181 *South Slavic Writers Since World War II,* edited by Vasa D. Mihailovich (1997)

Documentary Series

1 *Sherwood Anderson, Willa Cather, John Dos Passos, Theodore Dreiser, F. Scott Fitzgerald, Ernest Hemingway, Sinclair Lewis*, edited by Margaret A. Van Antwerp (1982)

2 *James Gould Cozzens, James T. Farrell, William Faulkner, John O'Hara, John Steinbeck, Thomas Wolfe, Richard Wright*, edited by Margaret A. Van Antwerp (1982)

3 *Saul Bellow, Jack Kerouac, Norman Mailer, Vladimir Nabokov, John Updike, Kurt Vonnegut*, edited by Mary Bruccoli (1983)

4 *Tennessee Williams*, edited by Margaret A. Van Antwerp and Sally Johns (1984)

5 *American Transcendentalists*, edited by Joel Myerson (1988)

6 *Hardboiled Mystery Writers: Raymond Chandler, Dashiell Hammett, Ross Macdonald*, edited by Matthew J. Bruccoli and Richard Layman (1989)

7 *Modern American Poets: James Dickey, Robert Frost, Marianne Moore*, edited by Karen L. Rood (1989)

8 *The Black Aesthetic Movement*, edited by Jeffrey Louis Decker (1991)

9 *American Writers of the Vietnam War: W. D. Ehrhart, Larry Heinemann, Tim O'Brien, Walter McDonald, John M. Del Vecchio*, edited by Ronald Baughman (1991)

10 *The Bloomsbury Group*, edited by Edward L. Bishop (1992)

11 *American Proletarian Culture: The Twenties and The Thirties*, edited by Jon Christian Suggs (1993)

12 *Southern Women Writers: Flannery O'Connor, Katherine Anne Porter, Eudora Welty*, edited by Mary Ann Wimsatt and Karen L. Rood (1994)

13 *The House of Scribner, 1846–1904*, edited by John Delaney (1996)

14 *Four Women Writers for Children, 1868–1918*, edited by Caroline C. Hunt (1996)

Yearbooks

1980 edited by Karen L. Rood, Jean W. Ross, and Richard Ziegfeld (1981)

1981 edited by Karen L. Rood, Jean W. Ross, and Richard Ziegfeld (1982)

1982 edited by Richard Ziegfeld; associate editors: Jean W. Ross and Lynne C. Zeigler (1983)

1983 edited by Mary Bruccoli and Jean W. Ross; associate editor: Richard Ziegfeld (1984)

1984 edited by Jean W. Ross (1985)

1985 edited by Jean W. Ross (1986)

1986 edited by J. M. Brook (1987)

1987 edited by J. M. Brook (1988)

1988 edited by J. M. Brook (1989)

1989 edited by J. M. Brook (1990)

1990 edited by James W. Hipp (1991)

1991 edited by James W. Hipp (1992)

1992 edited by James W. Hipp (1993)

1993 edited by James W. Hipp, contributing editor George Garrett (1994)

1994 edited by James W. Hipp, contributing editor George Garrett (1995)

1995 edited by James W. Hipp, contributing editor George Garrett (1996)

1996 edited by Samuel W. Bruce and L. Kay Webster, contributing editor George Garrett (1997)

Concise Series

Concise Dictionary of American Literary Biography, 6 volumes (1988-1989): *The New Consciousness, 1941-1968; Colonization to the American Renaissance, 1640-1865; Realism, Naturalism, and Local Color, 1865-1917; The Twenties, 1917-1929; The Age of Maturity, 1929-1941; Broadening Views, 1968-1988.*

Concise Dictionary of British Literary Biography, 8 volumes (1991-1992): *Writers of the Middle Ages and Renaissance Before 1660; Writers of the Restoration and Eighteenth Century, 1660-1789; Writers of the Romantic Period, 1789-1832; Victorian Writers, 1832-1890; Late Victorian and Edwardian Writers, 1890-1914; Modern Writers, 1914-1945; Writers After World War II, 1945-1960; Contemporary Writers, 1960 to Present.*

Dictionary of Literary Biography® • Volume One Hundred Eighty-One

South Slavic Writers Since World War II

Dictionary of Literary Biography® • Volume One Hundred Eighty-One

South Slavic Writers Since World War II

Edited by
Vasa D. Mihailovich
University of North Carolina at Chapel Hill

A Bruccoli Clark Layman Book
Gale Research
Detroit, Washington, D.C., London

Advisory Board for
DICTIONARY OF LITERARY BIOGRAPHY

John Baker
William Cagle
Patrick O'Connor
George Garrett
Trudier Harris

Matthew J. Bruccoli and Richard Layman, Editorial Directors
C. E. Frazer Clark Jr., Managing Editor
Karen Rood, Senior Editor

Printed in the United States of America

Published simultaneously in the United Kingdom
by Gale Research International Limited
(An affiliated company of Gale Research)

The paper used in this publication meets the minimum requirements
of American National Standard for Information Sciences–Permanence
Paper for Printed Library Materials, ANSI Z39.48-1984. ∞ ™

This publication is a creative work fully protected by all applicable copyright laws, as well as by misappropriation, trade secret, unfair competition, and other applicable laws. The authors and editors of this work have added value to the underlying factual material herein through one or more of the following: unique and original selection, coordination, expression, arrangement, and classification of the information.

All rights to this publication will be vigorously defended.

Copyright © 1997 by Gale Research
835 Penobscot Building
Detroit, MI 48226

All rights reserved including the right of reproduction in
whole or in part in any form.

Library of Congress Cataloging-in-Publication Data

South Slavic writers since World War II / edited by Vasa D. Mihailovich.
   p. cm.–(Dictionary of literary biography; v. 181)
"A Bruccoli Clark Layman book."
Includes bibliographical references and index.
ISBN 0-7876-1070-4 (alk. paper)
1. Authors, Southern Slavic–20th century–Biography. 2. Slavic literature, Southern–20th century–History and criticism. I. Mihailovich, Vasa D. Series.
PG564.S684 1997
891.8'1'009–dc21   97-18810
[B]   CIP

---

10 9 8 7 6 5 4 3 2 1

Contents

Plan of the Series xiii
Introduction xv

Ivan Aralica (1930–) 3
Aldijana Šišić

Matija Bećković (1939–) 9
Aleksandar Petrov

Mirko Božić (1919–) 16
Ljerka Debush

Miodrag Bulatović (1930–1991) 21
E. D. Goy

Kole Čašule (1921–) 29
Thomas Eekman

Živko Čingo (1935–1987) 36
Savo Cvetanovski

Branko Ćopić (1915–1984) 41
Nicholas Moravcevich

Dobrica Ćosić (1921–) 48
Vasa D. Mihailovich

Vladan Desnica (1905–1967) 54
Cynthia Simmons

Blaga Dimitrova (1922–) 59
Cleo Protokhristova

Dimitŭr Dimov (1909–1966) 64
Cleo Protochristova

Danijel Dragojević (1934–) 70
Aida Vidan

Andrej Hieng (1925–) 75
Peter Scherber

Drago Ivanišević (1907–1981) 78
Dasha Čulić Nisula

Drago Jančar (1948–) 84
Helga Glušič

Slavko Janevski (1920–) 91
Milne Holton

Vjekoslav Kaleb (1905–1997) 97
Maria B. Malby

Nikolay Khaytov (1919–) 104
Thomas Eekman

Boris Khristov (1945–) 114
Raia Kuncheva

Danilo Kiš (1935–1989) 119
Tomislav Z. Longinović

Blaže Koneski (1921–1993) 125
Christina Kramer

Ciril Kosmač (1910–1980) 132
Helga Glušič

Kajetan Kovič (1931–) 137
Henry R. Cooper Jr.

Ivan V. Lalić (1931–1996) 142
Francis R. Jones

Mihailo Lalić (1914–1992) 150
Branko Popović

Mateja Matevski (1929–) 158
Milne Holton

Marijan Matković (1915–1985) 165
Ellen Elias-Bursać

Dragoslav Mihailović (1930–) 170
Radmila J. Gorup

Slavko Mihalić (1928–) 177
Ellen Elias-Bursać

Branko Miljković (1934–1961) 182
Anita Lekić

Vera Mutafchieva (1929–) 187
Roumiana Deltcheva

Rajko Petrov Nogo (1945–) 197
Bogdan Rakić

Slobodan Novak (1924–) 205
Aldijana Šišić

Contents

Vesna Parun (1922-) 210
Dasha Čulić Nisula

Milorad Pavić (1929-) 215
Tomislav Z. Longinović

Konstantin Pavlov (1933-) 222
Cleo Protokhristova

Miodrag Pavlović (1928-) 226
Bernard Johnson

Borislav Pekić (1930-1992) 233
Bogdan Rakić

Aleksandar Petrov (1938-) 242
Krinka Vidaković

Valeri Petrov (1920-) 251
Nikita Nankov

Vasko Popa (1922-1991) 258
Anita Lekić

Aleksandar Popović (1929-1996) 264
Edward J. Czerwinski

Yordan Radichkov (1929-) 270
Lyubomira Parpulova-Gribble

Stevan Raičković (1928-) 275
Anita Lekić

Radoy Ralin (1923-) 281
Nikita Nankov

Tomaž Šalamun (1941-) 288
Michael Biggins

Petar Šegedin (1909-) 295
Cynthia Simmons

Slobodan Selenić (1933-1995) 300
Nadežda Obradović

Meša Selimović (1910-1982) 307
Thomas J. Butler

Ljubomir Simović (1935-) 314
Dubravka Juraga

Ivan Slamnig (1930-) 321
Thomas Eekman

Milivoj Slaviček (1929-) 327
Aida Vidan

Antun Šoljan (1932-1993) 332
Ellen Elias-Bursać

Aco Šopov (1923-1982) 337
Graham W. Reid

Emiliyan Stanev (1907-1979) 341
Cleo Protokhristova

Goran Stefanovski (1952-) 346
George Mitrevski

Gregor Strniša (1930-1987) 355
Tom Lozar

Dragutin Tadijanović (1905-) 361
Dasha Čulić Nisula

Dimitŭr Talev (1898-1966) 366
Ivan Ruskov

Veno Taufer (1933-) 373
Marko Juvan

Aleksandar Tišma (1924-) 381
Dubravka Juraga

Dubravka Ugrešić (1949-) 388
E. Celia Hawkesworth

Dane Zajc (1929-) 393
Marija Mitrović

Vitomil Zupan (1914-1987) 399
Peter Scherber

Books for Further Reading 405
Contributors 407
Cumulative Index 411

Plan of the Series

... Almost the most prodigious asset of a country, and perhaps its most precious possession, is its native literary product — when that product is fine and noble and enduring.

Mark Twain*

The advisory board, the editors, and the publisher of the *Dictionary of Literary Biography* are joined in endorsing Mark Twain's declaration. The literature of a nation provides an inexhaustible resource of permanent worth. We intend to make literature and its creators better understood and more accessible to students and the reading public, while satisfying the standards of teachers and scholars.

To meet these requirements, *literary biography* has been construed in terms of the author's achievement. The most important thing about a writer is his writing. Accordingly, the entries in *DLB* are career biographies, tracing the development of the author's canon and the evolution of his reputation.

The purpose of *DLB* is not only to provide reliable information in a convenient format but also to place the figures in the larger perspective of literary history and to offer appraisals of their accomplishments by qualified scholars.

The publication plan for *DLB* resulted from two years of preparation. The project was proposed to Bruccoli Clark by Frederick C. Ruffner, president of the Gale Research Company, in November 1975. After specimen entries were prepared and typeset, an advisory board was formed to refine the entry format and develop the series rationale. In meetings held during 1976, the publisher, series editors, and advisory board approved the scheme for a comprehensive biographical dictionary of persons who contributed to North American literature. Editorial work on the first volume began in January 1977, and it was published in 1978. In order to make *DLB* more than a reference tool and to compile volumes that individually have claim to status as literary history, it was decided to organize volumes by topic, period, or genre. Each of these freestanding volumes provides a biographical-bibliographical guide and overview for a particular area of literature. We are convinced that this organization—as opposed to a single alphabet method—constitutes a valuable innovation in the presentation of reference material. The volume plan necessarily requires many decisions for the placement and treatment of authors who might properly be included in two or three volumes. In some instances a major figure will be included in separate volumes, but with different entries emphasizing the aspect of his career appropriate to each volume. Ernest Hemingway, for example, is represented in *American Writers in Paris, 1920-1939* by an entry focusing on his expatriate apprenticeship; he is also in *American Novelists, 1910-1945* with an entry surveying his entire career, as well as in *American Short-Story Writers, 1910-1945, Second Series* with an entry concentrating on his short stories. Each volume includes a cumulative index of the subject authors and articles. Comprehensive indexes to the entire series are planned.

The series has been further augmented by the *DLB Yearbooks* (since 1981) which update published entries and add new entries to keep the *DLB* current with contemporary activity. There have also been *DLB Documentary Series* volumes which provide biographical and critical source materials for figures whose work is judged to have particular interest for students. One of these companion volumes is entirely devoted to Tennessee Williams.

We define literature as the *intellectual commerce of a nation:* not merely as belles lettres but as that ample and complex process by which ideas are generated, shaped, and transmitted. *DLB* entries are not limited to "creative writers" but extend to other figures who in their time and in their way influenced the mind of a people. Thus the series encompasses historians, journalists, publishers, book collectors, and screenwriters. By this means readers of *DLB* may be aided to perceive literature not as cult scripture in the keeping of intellectual high priests but firmly positioned at the center of a nation's life.

*From an unpublished section of Mark Twain's autobiography, copyright by the Mark Twain Company

Plan of the Series

DLB includes the major writers appropriate to each volume and those standing in the ranks behind them. Scholarly and critical counsel has been sought in deciding which minor figures to include and how full their entries should be. Wherever possible, useful references are made to figures who do not warrant separate entries.

Each *DLB* volume has an expert volume editor responsible for planning the volume, selecting the figures for inclusion, and assigning the entries. Volume editors are also responsible for preparing, where appropriate, appendices surveying the major periodicals and literary and intellectual movements for their volumes, as well as lists of further readings. Work on the series as a whole is coordinated at the Bruccoli Clark Layman editorial center in Columbia, South Carolina, where the editorial staff is responsible for accuracy and utility of the published volumes.

One feature that distinguishes *DLB* is the illustration policy–its concern with the iconography of literature. Just as an author is influenced by his surroundings, so is the reader's understanding of the author enhanced by a knowledge of his environment. Therefore *DLB* volumes include not only drawings, paintings, and photographs of authors, often depicting them at various stages in their careers, but also illustrations of their families and places where they lived. Title pages are regularly reproduced in facsimile along with dust jackets for modern authors. The dust jackets are a special feature of *DLB* because they often document better than anything else the way in which an author's work was perceived in its own time. Specimens of the writers' manuscripts and letters are included when feasible.

Samuel Johnson rightly decreed that "The chief glory of every people arises from its authors." The purpose of the *Dictionary of Literary Biography* is to compile literary history in the surest way available to us–by accurate and comprehensive treatment of the lives and work of those who contributed to it.

The *DLB* Advisory Board

Introduction

During World War II, Yugoslavia was the battlefield of many-sided wars, including the internal war between its nations and a politically inspired civil war between the nationalists and communists. Understandably, little of good literature could be written or published. Aside from a few writers and works, most of that literature is evaluated today from almost exclusively a historical point of view.

After World War II all South Slavic writers found themselves in a totally different situation from that before the war. Both Yugoslavia and Bulgaria embraced the communist system at the end of the war, not so much by free will as by the dictates of the victorious partisan forces in Yugoslavia and by the Soviet army in Bulgaria. Writers were expected to accept the new regime—in fact, they were ordered to accept it. As in Russia after the revolution of 1917, in Yugoslavia and Bulgaria the entire way of life changed overnight. Those writers accused of collaboration with the enemy were liquidated; some fought for the communist regime while others willingly embraced it; others felt they had to accept it in order to survive; some writers were prevented from publishing; and a small number found it necessary to emigrate. The moribund ideas of socialist realism were to become the undisputed law of the literary life in the first three postwar years. Literature, like every other walk of life, became a servant of political exigencies.

All that changed in Yugoslavia in 1948, when the country was expelled from the Soviet bloc of nations. Yugoslav communists, led by Josip Broz Tito, deserve credit for standing up to Stalin, which was made possible primarily because the struggle that brought them to power was mostly of their own making (with significant help from the Western allies, to be sure). This new political climate ushered gradual changes in other walks of life, including literature.

Until then, the atmosphere of tight controls, of prescribed themes and methods, and of unabashed glorification of the so-called People's War of Liberation and the building of a new society along communist lines was dominant. The writers who between the wars expounded leftist, if not openly communist, ideas were cleverly giving the tone. Many writers who were hoping to empty their drawers of manuscripts written during the war were eventually convinced that a new era had arrived to stay. Some prominent interwar writers (Ivo Andrić, Miroslav Krleža, Veljko Petrović, Vladimir Nazor, France Bevk, Prežihov Voranc, Alojz Gradnik) welcomed the change and became active in the new society. A certain number refused to cooperate and to appear in print, while several well-known writers were declared enemies and liquidated. Thus, despite the efforts of some new, politically engaged writers, the new epoch in Yugoslav literature was still represented by the already established authors. Through this, literature preserved the continuity, which, in turn, prevented Yugoslav literatures from becoming totally subservient to the establishment and, somewhat later, enabled a freer and saner atmosphere to prevail.

It was Ivo Andrić who gave the breath of life to the new period in literature with his three novels, *The Bridge on the Drina, The Chronicle of Travnik* and *Miss (The Woman from Sarajevo)*. However, great as they were, they were somewhat anachronistic at the time. Dealing with the distant past, they contain not a single line of praise for the recent victory over the national enemies. For this was the general tenor of the new literature: the extolling of the heroic deeds of the guerrilla forces and their leadership. In this respect Yugoslav literatures came close to emulating the official dogma of Soviet literature—socialist realism.

Other works at this time were meant to do just that, especially in poetry. But, not surprisingly, aside from Andrić's novels and a few successful poems and stories, not many great works appeared. The established prewar writers, aside from lending their name and prestige, produced little of good new literature. Even those works, officially sanctioned and fostered, which tried to varnish reality and to show life not as it is but as it ought to be, were artistic failures. For some reason, socialist realism never took real hold among Yugoslav writers, except among those more politically than artistically minded.

Then came the year 1948 and the fateful break with the Soviet Union. The impact of this epochal event in the cultural circles was commensurate to that in other walks of life. Since the cultural developments normally move more cautiously and do not show immediate symptoms, it took writers another year or two to call for action. After the first stirring and demands for change, the struggle between the "old" and the "new" forces quickly developed into a full-fledged cultural war. This was best manifested in 1952 at the writers' congress, with the venerable writer Miroslav Krleža giving the tone by demanding freedom of creativity. The opposing forces were composed of the defenders of the status quo, called the realists, and the challengers, labeled the modernists because of their advocacy of greater freedom, above all the freedom to experiment. To be sure, by the label realists the modernists did not always have socialist realism in mind, and, conversely, the realists did not always label the modernists reactionary, decadent, and removed from reality. It would be a mistake, therefore, to assume that the fronts were always clearly drawn or that the realists were exclusively the supporters of the regime whereas the modernists, in their opposition to the existing literary situation, were always opposing the entire political system. In both camps were those who believed that the nature of state government should not be questioned at all and that the controversy should be confined to artistic matters. The fact that some of the leading figures of the interwar leftist, procommunist surrealistic movement (Marko Ristić, Aleksandar Vučo, Oskar Davičo) were among the modernists certainly gave the lie to the realists' argument that the modernists were decadent, irresponsible, or even hostile to the new order. There was indeed an irony in this reversal of roles. Between the wars, the surrealists were the forerunners of the wrecking crew whose task was to undermine and eventually bring down the bourgeois order of the monarchy. For this purpose they used the most ruthless methods, attacking the very foundations of bourgeois "conservative" and "reactionary" morality. After the war the surrealists rose again, this time against their own brethren, whose path they helped to clear, indeed of whose cloth they themselves were made. But if there was an irony in the new situation, the surrealists were certainly consistent. And while they were destructive in their previous efforts, they were now playing a constructive role in bringing about the relaxation of tension and a considerable amount of freedom in artistic creativity by the end of the 1950s.

The struggle reached its climax in 1955. The realists, gathered around the magazine *Savremenik* (Contemporary), defended their positions ineptly, relying more on the support from party officials than on the force of their arguments. Their view was that literature must, first of all, serve society, that society is governed by immutable Marxist laws, and that any deviation from the straightforward, socially tinged depiction of reality represents a malignant growth of formalism, aestheticism, etc. The modernists, gathered around the magazine *Delo* (Action), refuted these views as undemocratic, constrictive, and stale. They demanded the abolition of dictates by the authorities, a greater freedom of creativity, and, above all, freedom to experiment.

Generally speaking, the struggle was most keenly felt in Serbia and Slovenia, while Croatia was relatively calm at the time. Belgrade bore the brunt of the battles due, undoubtedly, to the centralization of the state. Although there were some non-Serbs writing in Belgrade, it was primarily the Serbs who initiated and carried the battle and suffered the consequences most acutely. This in no way implies that writers of other nationalities were indifferent to the issues at stake or docilely supporting the status quo.

Toward the end of the controversy, about the middle of the 1950s, a new note was injected by the so-called second generation of postwar writers (Vasko Popa, Miodrag Pavlović, Stevan Raičković, Branko Miljković, Miodrag Bulatović, Vesna Parun, Slavko Mihalić, Milivoj Slaviček, Cene Vipotnik, Ciril Zlobec, Andrej Hieng, and others). The struggle ended in the triumph of the modernists, expressed not through wild celebration and vendetta, but through a somber, deeply satisfying enjoyment of the hard-won freedom.

Since that battle, the situation on the Yugoslav literary scene has been characterized by a steady growth of freedom, by a steady influx of extremely gifted writers, and by total opening to the world. Every now and then the authorities would attempt to assert their might in prosecuting and even jailing some writers, but by and large the writers have been able to develop and express themselves with a great amount of freedom.

The war in the former Yugoslavia in the first half of the 1990s has had repercussions among the writers as well. Even before the country was split into several independent entities, the writers fought their own war among themselves. The monolithic Union of Yugoslav Writers foreshadowed the deep division among the nationalities by the demands of the Croatian and Slovene writers in the late 1980s that it be disbanded, which eventually took place in 1990. The writers went their own nationalistic ways, and individual literatures function today as totally independent bodies. In reality this is how it has been ever since Yugoslavia was created in 1918 and re-created in 1945. It should be pointed out that there is no Yugoslav literature as such; this term is used for expedience only. After 1990, even the pretext of unity was dropped. Due to the cruelty of the third Balkan War, the chances are that they will not be considered as one again, which is how it should be, after all.

None of this struggle existed in Bulgaria from 1944, when the Soviet army "liberated" the country, until the early 1990s, when, with the fall of communism in the Soviet Union, for the first time in almost five decades the Bulgarian writers were free to express themselves according to their own artistic dictates. Until that time, generally speaking, Bulgarian post–World War II literature was weaker in comparison to any period in the preceding centuries. Drastic political and social changes dictated by the communist regime led to a noticeable drop in the quality of literature, though it was not lacking in quantity. Of all South Slavic literatures, the Bulgarian suffered the most from the imposition of political dictates. Nevertheless, in addition to scores of writers of limited skills who tried to give life to the moribund method of socialist realism, others managed to preserve their dignity and to produce works of redeeming quality. Among these are Blaga Dimitrova (1922–), Atanas Dalchev (1904–), Dimitur Talev (1898-1966), Emiliyan Stanev (1907-1979), Anton Donchev (1930–), Pavel Vezhinov (1914–), Nikolay Khaitov (1919–), and Yordan Radichkov (1929–). The fortitude of these writers was rewarded by recent developments in Bulgaria and by the rejection of political controls in literature after almost half a century of ideological bondage. It is too early to tell whether the political changes will lead to total rejuvenation of literary life, but it seems that a better future is in store for Bulgarian literature.

Thanks to Krleža, Croatian literature after World War II escaped the clutches of socialist realism. The present-day situation is marked by freedom of expression, a wide-open relationship with world literatures, and the sophistication that comes from a rich tradition of the preceding accomplishments. Ranko Marinković (1913-), Jure Kaštelan (1919-1990), Vesna Parun (1922-), Mirko Božić (1919-), and Slavko Mihalić (1928-), among others, lead the long list of accomplished writers and rising talents. The developments in the early 1990s led to the fulfillment of a cherished dream of total independence from "Yugoslav" association.

It was not until after World War II that the Macedonians were allowed to exist as a separate nation (within the Republic of Yugoslavia, to be sure) and to publish unhindered in their own language. The adoption of a Western Macedonian dialect around Prilep as an official literary language, formulated by a leading poet and scholar, Blaže Koneski, and others, enabled the writers to write in one language for the first time. In a relatively short time since, Macedonian literature has been able not only to make up for lost time, but also to produce works that have attracted the world's attention and admiration. Having bypassed, of necessity, entire periods and movements, such as Romanticism, realism, symbolism, and others, the writers have been able to get in step with modern trends in world literature quickly and remarkably well.

The lion's share in this endeavor belongs to the brothers Dimitrije (1810-1862) and Konstantin Miladinov (1830-1862), Kosta Kočo Racin (1908-1943), Blaže Koneski (1921-1993), Slavko Janevski (1920-), and Aco Šopov (1923-1982), who in their early works proved that Macedonian writers were equal to their peers in Yugoslavia. Racin published in 1939 the first book of modern poetry, *Beli mugri* (White Dawns), and Janevski the first Macedonian novel, *Selo zad sedumte jaseni* (The Village behind the Seven Aspens, 1953), while the books of verse by Koneski and Šopov were of decisive influence in the further development of Macedonian poetry. These writers were joined later by new generations of poets, fiction writers, and playwrights, such as the poets Bogumil Gjuzel (1939-), Vlada Urošević (1934-), and Radovan Pavlovski (1937-); the fiction writers Georgi Abadžiev (1910-1963), Yordan Leov (1920-), Simon Drakul (1930-), and Živko Čingo (1935-1987); and the playwrights Kole Čašule (1921-), and Goran Stefanovski (1952-). The vibrancy of the ever-increasing number of new writers is typical of a young literature, even if their roots go back centuries. Indicative of this vitality is the renowned "Struga Poetry Evenings," which every summer gathers writers from all over the world at the Lake of Ohrid for the celebration of poetry.

The Second World War, with all its implications and changes for the peoples of Yugoslavia, initially brought about a new wind in Serbian literature—socialist realism. It lasted only a short time, however, due to further political changes. From 1948 on, Serbian literature was pretty much free to follow its own designs and tendencies. It was preceded by three novels of Ivo Andrić (1892-1975), all published in 1945. Their sweeping portrayal of the diverse peoples of Bosnia and the artistic creation of characters earned Andrić the Nobel Prize in 1961–the only South Slav writer to be so honored. He was followed by many accomplished writers, first by those who had their beginnings in the previous period and then by postwar writers who continued in the tradition of Serbian literature but also changed it for the better. Among many noteworthy authors, several have become internationally known: Vasko Popa (1922-1991), Miodrag Pavlović (1928-), and Ivan V. Lalić (1931-) in poetry; and Dobrica Ćosić (1921-), Meša Selimović (1910-1982), Danilo Kiš (1935-1989), and Milorad Pavić (1929-) in fiction. Their ranks are being strengthened by a steady stream of newcomers. The present-day literature in Serbia is characterized by openness, despite sporadic political restrictions; by sophistication and cosmopolitanism; and by a desire to transcend local boundaries. It may be too early to pass the final judgment on the achievements of the contemporary generation, but it would be correct to say that they have already moved Serbian literature ahead by several leaps in comparison to the previous generations.

Most of the Slovene interwar authors continued to be active after World War II. After a short and abortive experiment with socialist realism, they opened up to the world influences. Today, in keeping step with other literatures, Slovenes employ a wide array of approaches accompanied by genuine talent and sophistication. Poetry is the dominant genre, and poets such as Edvard Kocbek (1904-1981), Dane Zajc (1929-), Gregor Strniša (1930-1987), Veno Taufer (1933-), and Tomaž Šalamun (1941-), despite being different in many respects, all contribute to the profile of a literature whose high quality is internationally recognized.

As in the first volume of the South Slav literatures, individual literatures have been arranged alphabetically in order to forestall the potential accusation of nationalistic bias. Within literatures the authors have also been arranged alphabetically, although a chronological arrangement could have been used as well. The selection of the authors is based on their generally recognized reputation as recorded in literary histories. The inclusion or exclusion of some authors may be debatable, but those represented in this volume have all left their marks on the respective literatures and exerted strong influence on other writers. The choice of contributors has been dictated by their availability outside of the countries involved. Qualified scholars abroad have been by and large preferred to native scholars, for practical and other reasons. Although a good number of the contributors are themselves native of South Slavic countries, their spending most of their adult life abroad has enabled them to acquire fresh vistas in analyzing the writers without neglecting the traditional approach. They have arrived at their opinions mostly on their own rather than by depending heavily on secondary sources. As is customary with the *DLB* series, they have concentrated on the lives and works rather than engaging in abstract discussions. Special attention has been given to the bibliographic material because in many instances the writers under discussion are presented here for the first time to the English-speaking world. Following the established practice of the series, the first editions are listed chronologically under Books, and translations, if any, are listed after original works; those interested in a complete list of translations into English should consult the all-encompassing bibliographies compiled by Vasa D. Mihailovich and Mateja Matejić (Columbus, OH: Slavica, 1984, and supplements). In some instances, works in lesser genres are listed under Other and Periodical Publications. Secondary sources, where available, are listed under Letters, Bibliographies, and Biographies, as well as under References. The latter has concentrated on the most important sources, to avoid cluttering; those published in English have been listed exhaustively, while those in the respective languages, which are often inaccessible to the outside readers, have been restricted for practical reasons to the most outstanding ones. Finally, a Papers section is listed whenever known; the war conditions in the Balkans in the first half of the 1990s, however, sometimes made it difficult to ascertain where the papers are deposited.

For a list of translations of primary works into English and a chronology of important events, authors, and works, see *DLB 147: South Slavic Writers before World War II.*

The editor is grateful to the contributors for their labor of love, without which the volume would have been very difficult to complete. Similarly, gratitude is expressed to the publishers for their understanding and highly professional work, especially in obtaining necessary information and illustrations under rather difficult conditions due to the war.

It is hoped that this volume, along with *DLB 147,* will help in informing the general public in the English-speaking world about South Slav literatures, which until now have been known outside of their respective countries only to a small circle of specialists. It is also hoped that these volumes will lead to additional endeavors toward the same goal, so that eventually the achievements of these writers will receive their well-deserved due in the family of world literature.

—*Vasa D. Mihailovich*

PRONUNCIATION GUIDE

a	f*a*ther or m*o*ther
e	w*e*ll or s*e*t
i	s*ee*k or s*i*ck
o	g*o* or b*a*ll
u	bl*ue* or t*oo* or p*u*t
j	*y*ell or bo*y*
lj	mi*lli*on or bri*lli*ant
nj	ca*ny*on or *n*ew
dj, ǵ	resi*due*
c	ca*ts*
ć, ḱ	*tu*ne
č	chur*ch*
š	*sh*e
ž	plea*su*re
dž	*Ge*orge
h	Ba*ch*
ŭ	*ea*rth

All other letters are pronounced the same way as in English. Some of the examples above are approximations because sometimes there are no exact equivalents in English.

Acknowledgments

This book was produced by Bruccoli Clark Layman, Inc. Karen L. Rood is senior editor for the *Dictionary of Literary Biography* series. Kenneth Graham was the in-house editor.

Administrative support was provided by Ann M. Cheschi and Brenda A. Gillie.

Bookkeeper is Joyce Fowler.

Copyediting supervisor is Jeff Miller. The copyediting staff includes Phyllis A. Avant, Patricia Coate, Christine Copeland, Thom Harman, and William L. Thomas Jr.

Editorial associate is L. Kay Webster.

Layout and graphics staff includes Marie L. Parker and Janet E. Hill.

Office manager is Kathy Lawler Merlette.

Photography editors are Julie E. Frick and Margaret Meriwether. Photographic copy work was performed by Joseph M. Bruccoli.

Production manager is Samuel W. Bruce.

Software specialist is Marie L. Parker.

Systems manager is Chris Elmore.

Typesetting supervisor is Kathleen M. Flanagan. The typesetting staff includes Pamela D. Norton and Patricia Flanagan Salisbury. Freelance typesetters include Melody W. Clegg and Delores Plastow.

Walter W. Ross, Steven Gross, and Mark McEwan did library research. They were assisted by the following librarians at the Thomas Cooper Library of the University of South Carolina: Linda Holderfield and the interlibrary-loan staff; reference-department head Virginia Weathers; reference librarians Marilee Birchfield, Stefanie Buck, Stefanie DuBose, Rebecca Feind, Karen Joseph, Donna Lehman, Charlene Loope, Anthony McKissick, Jean Rhyne, Kwamine Simpson, and Virginia Weathers; circulation-department head Caroline Taylor; and acquisitions-searching supervisor David Haggard.

Tom Ložar received help in his research from Dr. Katarina Bogataj-Gradišnik and Professor Marko Kranjec of Ljubljana, as well as from Thea Skinder-Strniša.

George Mitrevski was aided by a grant from the International Research & Exchange Board (IREX), with funds provided by the Andrew W. Melon Foundation, the National Endowment for the Humanities, and the U.S. Department of State. None of these organizations is responsible for the views expressed.

The following contributors were helpful beyond their own contributions: Thomas Butler, Henry R. Cooper, Jr., Helga Glušič, Radmila Gorup, E. Celia Hawkesworth, Miran Hladnik, W. Milne Holton, Nikita Nankov, Aleksandar Petrov, Cleo Protochristova, and Bogdan Rakić.

Dictionary of Literary Biography® • Volume One Hundred Eighty-One

South Slavic Writers Since World War II

Dictionary of Literary Biography

Ivan Aralica
(10 September 1930 -)

Aldijana Šišić
University of London

BOOKS: *Svemu ima vrijeme* (Zagreb: Zora, 1967);
A primjer se zvao Laudina (Split: Matica hrvatska-Split, 1969);
Filip (Zadar: Matica hrvatska-Zadar, 1970);
Konjanik (Zagreb: Naprijed, 1971);
Ima netko siv i zelen (Zagreb: Nakladni zavod Matice hrvatske, 1977);
Opsjene paklenih crteža (Zagreb: Znanje, 1977);
Psi u trgovištu (Zagreb: Znanje, 1979);
Put bez sna (Zagreb: Znanje, 1982);
Duše robova (Zagreb: Znanje, 1984);
Graditelj svratišta (Zagreb: Znanje, 1986);
Okvir za mržnju (Zagreb: Znanje, 1987);
Asmodejev šal (Zagreb: Znanje, 1988);
Tajna sarmatskog orla (Zagreb: Znanje, 1989);
Majka Marija (Zagreb: Znanje, 1991);
Zadah ocvalog imperija (Zagreb: Znanje, 1991);
Pir ivanjskih krijesnica (Zagreb: Znanje, 1992);
Sokak triju ruža (Zagreb: Znanje, 1992);
Spletanje i raspletanje čvorova (Zagreb: Znanje, 1993);
Knjiga gorkog prijekora (Zagreb: Znanje, 1994).

SELECTED PERIODICAL PUBLICATIONS–
UNCOLLECTED: *Oluje u tihom ozračju*, Revija, nos. 2, 3 (1967);
Nevjernik, Mogucnosti, nos. 8, 9 (1967).

Ivan Aralica

With his compassionate understanding of ethical turmoil in the lives of ordinary men and his aspiration to search for a connection between the individual and society, Ivan Aralica is widely regarded as the greatest living writer in Croatian literature. In a writing career that has spanned more than thirty years he has written thirteen novels and three volumes of short stories as well as three collections of political essays and analyses. Aralica's career can be traced from the days when his books were appreciated only as the work of a regional author until he gained acceptance from critics and readers as the most widely read contemporary writer in Croatia.

Aralica was born on 10 September 1930, the son of Filip and Pera Aralica. Born in Promina, a part of Dalmatinska Zagora, young Aralica attended elementary school in his native village of Puljani. He left Puljani for Drniš and Knin to complete his secondary-school education.

Graduating in 1953 at the Teachers Training College in Knin, he began his professional life as a teacher in the villages of Ocestovo and Crno in Dalmatinska Zagora. At the age of twenty-six Aralica published his first story, "Smokva" (The Fig, 1956), in the magazine *Prosvjeta* (Education) and then continued to publish essays, stories, and short novels in different magazines and literary journals. At the same time, while still working as a teacher, he enrolled as a part-time student at the University of Zadar in the Department of South Slavonic Languages and Literatures. In 1961, on completing his studies, Aralica moved to Zadar to work as a high-school teacher and later, from 1964, he served as director at the Teachers Training College in Zadar. However, he continued to write for various newspapers and magazines, and in 1965 he became a member of the editorial board of the magazine *Zadarska revija* (Zadar Review).

In 1967, when he was thirty-seven years old, Aralica published his first book, a collection of stories, *Svemu ima vrijeme* (All in Good Time). The majority of the stories—such as "Školjka" (Shell), where a daughter brings her father and herself before a firing squad through a series of unfortunate incidents, or "Raskol" (Schism), which follows the tragic journey of a soldier fleeing from the death penalty—are concerned with war themes and the human potential to face fear, death, or murder. In the story "Križ" (The Cross), in which an old man, Čuka, searches for the stone that will remain as indestructible evidence of his existence after his death, the author articulates for the first time his thoughts about human mortality. Already known through his literary work published in numerous magazines and journals, Aralica and his book of fourteen stories received considerable attention from the literary establishment. This was a time when Croatian literature was dominated by modernist writers who embraced a more philosophical approach to literature. They adopted the paradigms of modern aesthetics following in the footsteps of Franz Kafka, James Joyce, William Faulkner, and Albert Camus and distanced themselves from any sociocritical engagement. But Aralica did not belong to these groups, which gathered around the journals *Krugovi* (Circles) and *Razlog* (Reason). Viewing modernism as a possible tool for the termination of Croatian literature and insisting that overvaluation of modern European writers undermined Croatian literature itself, he persisted in his commitment to critical realism and its regional flavor. Zadar, Knin, Promina, and the rural people of the Dalmatian region were the inspiration for Aralica's writing. Their existence and survival, daily problems, and dilemmas about personal and collective morality were the author's predicaments, too. This is why his later books—*A primjer se zvao Laudina* (And the Example Was Named Laudina, 1969), *Filip* (Philip, 1970), and *Konjanik* (The Rider, 1971)—were seen as the work of a traditional writer exploring previously examined space. Although Aralica received the Zadar Award for his novel *Filip,* he was generally regarded at this stage of his career merely as an author whose concept of literature was outside the dominant discourse.

Nevertheless, such judgments did not discourage Aralica, and he continued to deliver his work to different journals, mostly *Mogućnosti* (Possibilities) and *Revija* (Review). Here Aralica published his short novels, *Nevjernik* (An Infidel, 1967) in *Mogućnosti* and *Oluje u tihom ozračju* (Storms in the Stillness, 1967) in *Revija*. Gradually his work appeared in other publications such as *Riječka revija, Republika, Kolo, Telegram, Bagdala, Ljetopis Matice Hrvatske, Letopis Matice Srpske,* and *Forum*. In 1968 Aralica was accepted as a full member of *Društvo hrvatskih književnika* (Society of Croatian Writers). Within the practice of the existing political system, the positions of headmaster and president of the sub-committee of Matica Hrvatska in Zadar (since 1966), as well as his activities at the editorial board of *Zadarska revija,* inevitably led to his involvement in the Croatian political scene. But as he committed himself to the duties of editor of *Zadarska revija* in 1971, many people in Croatia were marked as "political dissidents" during the political movement known as the "Croatian spring" or "Maspok." They were expelled from the Communist Party in the belief that they were aiming to destroy brotherhood and unity as well as the political stability of the Socialist Federal Republic of Yugoslavia. By the word that was passed among party leaders many politicians, scientists, artists, journalists, and writers were banned from public appearances. Among them, Aralica was banished from the Croatian political scene and expelled from his position as representative in the House of Counties of the Socialist Republic of Croatia, which he had held since 1969. This political fiasco and the actions of the communist leaders made Aralica's life extremely difficult. On the other hand, some critics today believe that this expulsion was the reason that he became more respected in the eyes of his readers as a symbol of resistance to a repressive political system.

After the failure of Maspok, Aralica lived in Zadar with his wife, Ružica Škorić (a teacher), his daughter, Gorana, and son, Tomislav, working as a teacher at the Pedagogical High School. He continued to write, restricted in his activities and prevented from full involvement in public life but still faithful to the ordinary people of his native Dalmatia. Challenging the survival of human freedom under pressure from the norms of society, he published the novel *Ima netko siv i zelen* (There is Someone Gray and Raw) and a volume of short stories, *Opsjene paklenih crteža* (Illusions of Infernal Sketches), in 1977. Once again the connection between an individual and society is the main concern of the author's work.

The last years of the 1970s, as his novel *Psi u trgovištu* (Dogs in the Market-town, 1979) went to press, marked the final days of Aralica's marginal status and a widening acceptance from his critics and readers. Exploiting the chronicles of Franciscan friars and diaries of travelers from the various parts of the Ottoman Empire and the West as the fundamental source of data for his novels, Aralica focused on the historical novel to express his admiration for patriarchal principles and ethics. Presenting both positive and negative experiences from the past, he praised traditional values and the notion of the patriarchal collective. These themes remain dominant through all of Aralica's historical novels, which suggests that his disagreement with the concept of modernism is based not only on a belief that modernism had discouraged the creativity of Croatian writers, but also on his general understanding of life and his admiration for traditional values.

Psi u trgovištu received the INA Award, and the following novels–*Put bez sna* (Dreamless Journey, 1982), *Duše robova* (The Souls of Slaves, 1984), *Graditelj svratišta* (The Inn-Builder, 1986), and *Asmodejev šal* (The Scarf of Asmodeus, 1988)–earned critical approval for Aralica as one of the classics of mainstream Croatian literature. The historical trilogy (*Put bez sna, Duše robova,* and *Graditelj svratišta*), together with the novel *Asmodejev šal,* describes the struggle, survival, and life of Croats from Rama during their migration toward the West and through the historical events in the period between the seventeenth and nineteenth centuries. It begins in the seventeenth century in a place where people of different cultures, religions, and customs inhabit the same land. In *Put bez sna,* the first novel of the trilogy, the story is focused on an average man in the leading role and historical personalities in supporting roles; Aralica dramatizes the fate of

Title page of Aralica's novel Psi u trgovištu *(Dogs in the Market-town, 1979)*

Croatians as the pressure from clashes between the Ottoman Empire and Venetian Dalmatia mounts. The destiny of the Grabovac family is followed and, at the same time, with convincing attention to authentic detail, the author introduces his readers to the different cultures, religions, and customs of the people living together in this part of the world. Aralica had explored historical themes in his earlier writings, too, but here he achieves genuine artistic vision through his sense of historical detail, understanding of religion, familiarity with folk traditions, knowledge of old crafts, and skillful use of language.

The second novel of the trilogy, *Duše robova,* explores the world of different cultures and the need for an atmosphere of mutual respect for other ideas and ideals. Here, by tracing the destiny of Matija Grabovac, Aralica follows the fate of the second generation of Croats from Rama at the beginning of the eighteenth century. The new clashes between the Ottomans and the Venetians drive Matija into warfare against the Turks. By refusing to sell his slave–a Muslim soldier given to him as a war trophy–and setting him free instead, Matija Grabovac breaks the law and finds himself in trouble. At the end, after a series of unfortunate events make Matija a fugitive for a second time, he becomes disillusioned with life, and Aralica again introduces thoughts about human mortality:

> Life should be loved as we love a big nothing, an all embracing nothing. The meaning of everything we have is filled with the senselessness of all things given to us to possess. Out of nothing will come nothing, everything we have will be lost, everyone we love will vanish, but what will remain forever is the fact that we do possess and we do love, that we are possessed and we are loved, that what we build is temporary and destructible. That is how we build houses, establish families, it is how we hold fast to our nation—out of nothingness comes nothing, but nothing in everything is all we have and without it we cannot live.

The futility and finality of individual existence is a constant theme in Aralica's work. The grave is one of the symbols that is always present in the novels to remind the reader of the final reality. On the other hand, the only survivors are monuments that appear in Aralica's writings as witnesses of a cultural and collective identity preserved during difficult times. This was one of the conclusions in the third novel in Aralica's trilogy, the memoirs of Jakov Grabovac, titled *Graditelj svratišta*. The work is set around 1808, when Dalmatia, occupied by Austria after the fall of Venice, was given to Napoleon. The novel centers around the construction of an inn on Turija (for the use of Napoleon's troops), but it also explores the economic and political struggle of Croatians while the inn is being built. A prophecy, an enigma that needs to be resolved, serves as the basic frame for all further developments in the novel, which are accompanied by Jakov's reflections of the past. Once again Aralica presents the wisdom of the common people, wisdom that has grown out of their historical experience.

Many critics believe that Aralica's writing was transformed by his traumatic experiences with "The System," the communist domination of his country, and that these difficult experiences were in part the reason his historical trilogy shifted his position away from the margins of Croatian literature. At the same time, external reasons influenced the change of Aralica's status, notably the publicity accompanying the awards he received: the Ksaver Šandor Djalski Prize (1981) for *Put bez sna*, and both the Goran Prize (1985) and the Award of the Miroslav Krleža Foundation (1985) for *Duše robova*. Additional publicity was given to the script for the film *Život sa stricem* (Life with Uncle) based on Aralica's novel *Okvir za mržnju* (Framework for Hatred, 1987), directed by Krsto Papić. Aralica wrote this saga about the first years following World War II a year after he became an associate member of the Yugoslav Academy of Science and Art in 1986. In this work he describes the postwar age as being one of disease, lice, and food aid from America; it was also the period when orders that were not to be questioned came from only one place, "The Top." Writing about the faith of Martin Kujundzic, a scholar at the Teachers Training College in Knin, Aralica spoke out critically about an aggressive period in which peasants were put under pressure and strongly "advised" to join collectives. If they decided differently, as Kujundzic's family did, they faced difficulties and were treated as obstructions to the development of socialism. In a similar position himself because of his political stance, Aralica used this novel to criticize directly the system whose authoritative power encouraged the development of mediocrities whose only aim was personal success. Aralica's next novel, *Tajna sarmatskog orla* (The Secret of the Sarmatian Eagle, 1989), suggested a radical dualism with two chief principles—good and evil—as the central foundation of Bolshevism and brought the writer still more publicity. Furthermore, because he continued to favor loyalty to the nation above the urban and cosmopolitan elements in literature, Aralica was assured an even wider acceptance by his readers at a time of radical changes and growing dissatisfaction with the political system in the former Yugoslavia in general.

The collapse of communism in the former Yugoslavia at the end of the 1980s and the subsequent development of a multiparty system and political freedom brought, among other things, a pardon for many people who had been labeled political dissidents in the past. One of them was Aralica, who at this stage concentrated more on writing political essays and analyses, publishing them mainly in the daily newspaper in Zagreb, *Vjesnik* (Herald). A collection of these writings, written between December 1990 and April 1991, was later published under the title *Zadah ocvalog imperija* (The Stench of the Decaying Empire, 1991) in the year when Aralica moved from Zadar to Zagreb. As the war erupted in Croatia, Aralica focused primarily on political circumstances, not only as a writer but as a politician as well. Once again he stepped onto the political scene, this time as a member of the parliament and the vice president of the House of Counties in the newly born state of Croatia. His writing continued, but it engaged only in observing the present situation, the war in Croatia and later in Bosnia and Herzegovina. Aralica's articles and stories about the war for independence were regularly published in the daily newspaper in Split, *Slobodna Dalmacija* (Free Dalmatia), and later in collections under the titles *Pir ivanjskih krijesnica* (The Wedding of The Midsummer Glow Worms, 1992) and *Sokak triju ruža* (The Street of Three Roses, 1992).

In 1991 Aralica returned to fiction, publishing another novel on a contemporary theme, *Majka Marija* (Mother Marija). In the novel a rich Croatian émigré, Mate Vodopija, returns to the motherland at the end of the 1980s to regain the pieces of land given away by his aunt, Mother Marija. Attempting to reclaim all the land, he exposes the people who deceived Mother Marija in their quest for her land. Aralica once again describes the suffering of people who find themselves in conflict with the communist system, but through his characters he also indicates who and what exemplifies a direct danger to the national culture and identity of the new Croatia. The threat is associated with a lack of respect for religion and tradition, a lack of attachment to one's roots. Danger is also posed by hypocrites, human greed, and people who are, like Ante Opančar, prepared to abuse the collective and to sell out the nation to make a profit for themselves. Aralica wrote this novel when the question of national identity was becoming one of the most important issues in the lives of the majority of Croatians. It was also a time when political changes enabled postwar émigrés to return to Croatia. Aralica himself has been in direct contact with communities of Croatian émigrés living and working abroad. In 1992 and 1993 he went on a tour with *Hrvatsko narodno Kazalište* (the Croatian National Theater), visiting the United States, Canada, Australia, and South Africa. Returning to Croatia, Aralica wrote a series of articles about the perceptions and feelings he experienced during these visits; he published the articles in *Slobodna Dalmacija* from December 1992 to May 1993 and incorporated in them descriptions of the lives, attitudes, needs, and hopes of his hosts during his travels. These texts were included in a new edition of political essays and analyses, also published in 1993 and titled *Spletanje i raspletanje cvorova* (The Tying and Untying of Knots).

In 1994 Aralica published his latest novel,

Title page of the second novel in Aralica's historical trilogy

Knjiga gorkog prijekora (A Book of the Bitter Reproach), returning to his favorite form, the historical novel. The story about the adolescence of Elizabeth Kotromanić, the daughter of the Bosnian, Ban Stjepan, who lived in Zadar in the fourteenth century when the city was under Venetian rule, is also a story full of similarities to the situation in present-day Croatia. Once again Aralica places his characters in the middle of a psychological storm and confronts them with decisions to be made or the consequences of their earlier choices. They are individuals in the sense that they have different appearances, different personalities, and different jobs, but they are always bearers of collective feelings, firmly attached to their roots and possessing a firm religious training.

Some of Aralica's current reviewers see him as a "Catholic writer," because of the visible presence of the Catholic faith in all his novels. Aralica himself believes that the Roman Catholic religion has played an important political role in the lives of all Croatians; in his opinion the church represents a nucleus around which Croatians have developed and preserved their traditions and culture not only in difficult times but also in peacetime as well. It would seem appropriate to believe that this notion is the origin of

Aralica's writing of the film *Gospa* (Mother of God, 1994), directed by Jakov Sedlar and financed by Hollywood. Even though the film has divided critics in Croatia, Aralica may be seen in it once again as being true to his own concept of art. As a writer he has continually advocated his own concept of the relation between literature and society, and in the end Aralica has emerged not only as a novelist of the consciousness and conscience of his time and his people but as a classic of Croatian literature as well.

Interviews:

Miljenko Žagar, "Nisam zakrabuljeni pripovjedač," *Naša knjiga*, 2 (October 1982): 10–13;

Stanko Bašić, "Generacija bez šansi," *Fokus* (December 1989);

Ante Ivković, "Ne tražim ispriku," *Večernji list* (January 1990).

References:

Branimir Donat, "Candide iz Promine," in his *Brbljiva sfinga* (Zagreb: Znanje, 1978), pp. 126–129;

Donat, "Socijalni patolog," in his *Brbljiva sfinga* (Zagreb: Znanje, 1978), pp. 130–132;

Željko Ivanković, "Portret mržnje," *Život*, 5 (1987): 670–673;

Cvjetko Milanja, "Didaktički o suvremenosti," *Oko* (1987);

Josip Pavičić, "Književni krov Ivana Aralice," in Aralica's *Majka Marija* (Zagreb: Znanje, 1993), pp. 291–300;

Ranko Risojević, "Hroničar i zastupnik," *Život*, 9 (1986): 327–329;

Josip Šentija, "Beletristička povijesna studija," *Naša knjiga*, 19–20 (1986): 35–37;

Velimir Visković, "Araličin povratak suvremenosti," *Danas*, 257 (May 1987): 43–44;

Visković, "Individua, nacija, povijest," in Aralica's *Svemu ima vrijeme* (Sarajevo: Svjetlost, 1990), pp. 7–35;

Visković, "Morlačka saga," *Danas*, 239 (September 1986): 38–39;

Tomislav Wruss, "Točka gledišta u romanu i stajalište u politici," *Qvorum*, 1–2 (1987).

Matija Bećković
(29 November 1939 -)

Aleksandar Petrov
University of Pittsburgh

BOOKS: *Vera Pavladoljska* (Belgrade: Ovako, 1962);

Metak lutalica (Belgrade: Prosveta, 1963);

Tako je govorio Matija (Belgrade: Prosveta, 1965);

Dr. Janez Paćuka o medjuvremenu (Novi Sad: Matica srpska, 1969);

Če, tragedija koja traje, by Bećković and Dušan Radović (Belgrade: Bećković & Slobodan Mašić, 1970);

Reče mi jedan čoek (Belgrade: Prosveta, 1970);

Medja Vuka Manitoga (Belgrade: Srpska književna zadruga, 1976);

Lele i kuku (Belgrade: Prosveta, 1978);

Dva sveta (Belgrade: Prosveta, 1980);

Poeme (Belgrade: Srpska književna zadruga, 1983);

Kaža (Belgrade: Srpska književna zadruga, 1988);

Služba Svetom Savi (Šabac: Glas crkve, 1988);

Čiji si ti, mali? (Belgrade: BIGZ, 1989);

Ono i ono (Novi Sad: Dnevnik, 1995);

Ceracemose jos (Podgorica: Oktoik, 1996).

Collections: *Izabrane pesme i poeme* (Belgrade: BIGZ, 1989);

Sabrana dela, 6 volumes (Belgrade & Nikšić: Srpska književna zadruga/BIGZ/Univerzitetska riječ, 1990).

Editions in English: *Ché: A Permanent Tragedy,* translated by Drenka Willen (New York: Harcourt Brace Jovanovich, 1970);

Poems, translated by Charles Simic, in *Contemporary Yugoslav Poetry,* edited by Vasa D. Mihailovich (Iowa City: University of Iowa Press, 1977), pp. 206-208;

Poems, translated by Momčilo Selič, in *Relations,* 5-6 (1978): 36-40;

Poems, translated by Mario Suško and E. J. Czerwinski, in *Slavic and East European Arts,* 1, no. 1 (1982): 30-43;

Poems, translated by Selič, in *Relations,* 2-3 (1984): 30-56;

Poems, translated by Charles Simic and Momčilo Selić, in *Serbian Poetry from the Beginnings to the Present,* edited by Milne Holton and Mi-

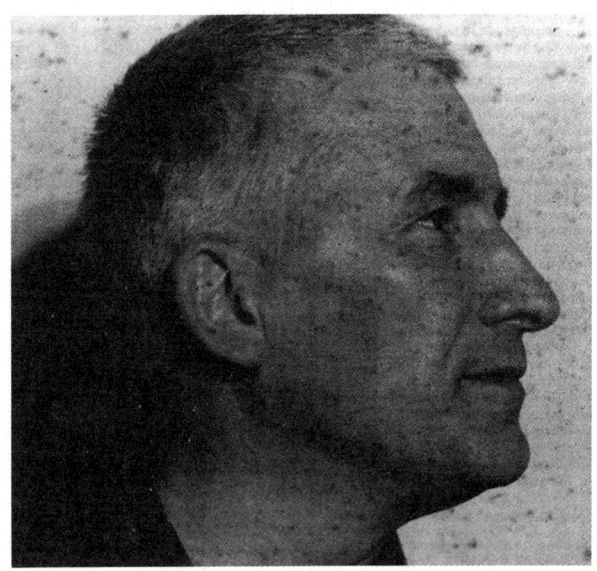

Matija Bećković (Snimio: Vican Vicanović)

hailovich (New Haven: Yale Center for International and Area Studies, 1988), pp. 377-380.

Writers after World War II were faced with a question: How should they write after the horrors of Hiroshima and the holocaust in Europe? There was no universal answer, and there could be none. The question contained another question just as essential: How should writers live after all that had happened? The poetics of the second half of the twentieth century were based by and large on the poets' answers to these questions. Matija Bećković, who experienced the war catastrophe as a child, asked himself, especially as a mature poet, a basically similar though not identical question: How should he live and write not only after the horrible war crimes (perpetrated on his people as well) but also after the triumph of communist dictatorships at the end of the war, even in his own country, and on at least one half of the globe? The question was that much harder because he saw in the victory something other poets did not: the end of the world. One of his poems, written after the fall of communism, is explicit even in its title, "Bio je smak sveta" (It Was the Doomsday). Bećković's later poetry begins basically with this realization, resulting in a conviction that no one will write poetry any more. And what poets write or will write is not the same as the poetry written before the end of the world. Similarly, neither is life in the meantime the same as that before God's punishment or after God's salvation. Thus, Bećković is a poet of the absurdity of existence and, at the same time, a poet with a firm belief in salvation; a poet of antipoetry, or poetry of the absurd; and a poet of the gate of the primeval secret, one who places hope in its promised and merciful absolution.

Bećković was born on 29 November 1939 in Senta. His life, as well as that of his family, changed drastically before he was two years old. The events of those days formed one of the basic thematic nuclei of his poetry and were a deep source of his rather tragic inspiration, which is nevertheless accompanied by his nearly omnipresent humor. His father, Vuk Bećković, a royalist officer, escaped capture in World War II by going with his family to a Montenegrin village, Velje Duboko. In this village, with its intriguing name meaning "Big Deep," which one can take now as a symbol of the poet's imagination, Bećković was in a sense conceived for the second time, this time as a poet of Velje Duboko, of Montenegro, and of the entire Serbian nation, yet in terms wider than those limited nationally and geographically—much later, of course. Without Velje Duboko, Bećković would not be currently known and revered as one of the leading Serbian poets of the second half of the twentieth century.

At the end of the war Bećković's father and four of Bećković's brothers were killed by the communists, who considered them "enemies of the people" because of their participation on the royalist, *chetnik* side. Even the burial site of Bećković's father is unknown. Bećković finished elementary school in his father's native village. His mother, Zorka, a war widow, regarded by the communists as a widow of a war traitor, decided to leave the village, and thus the migrations began. Bećković started high school in Kolašin. Running from the stigma of the cast-out, which the poet describes in his poems, his mother left Montenegro altogether. Bećković continued his education in the Croatian city of Slavonski Brod. Neither could the family stay in Croatia for long. They moved to Serbia, where Bećković completed high school in Valjevo.

Bećković published his first verses in high school and his first book in 1962, the latter in a bibliophile edition with only one long poem, "Vera Pavladoljska." The poem was dedicated to and named for the love of his youth, who later became his wife. The following year he published his first collection, *Metak lutalica* (Roaming Bullet, 1963). His early poetry contains little that is directly critical or polemical. It radiates, more than anything else, a powerful energy of imagination, and it glitters with great linguistic invention. It also exudes a fiery faith in the power of poetry. According to Bećković, poetry must use means available only to it; as he says, "Only the telepathic connections are still working." The young poet resembled Orpheus, whose song brings nature around him into ecstasy: "Water under the earth boils like glass"; "subterranean crystals gush like rods"; "a violet in the air is audible." Poetry transforms its creator as well: "I make ink out of my heart and write." But there is a verse with another message: a poet must, if need be, talk "through his back" if someone wants to shut his mouth. At that time, it seemed that no one wanted to do that. The roaming bullet, conjured by the title of the collection (and alluding to the family wound that seems to invite another bullet) luckily seems to be diverted through the poet's magic.

But Bećković's poetry, despite the Orphic inspiration and the surrealistic influence, was also a poetry of this world, as attested by the following verses in "Malen'kaia Verochka" (Little Vera):

> When I first saw her I said:
> This is how a capital looks
> Without lights when she closes her eyes.
> The only virgin that bears children
> That woman tall as a metro
> And beautiful as if non-existent
> Her room was annihilated by scents
> She used make-up and combed her hair
> And that is all she did for poetry.

What Vera Pavladoljska did for poetry she did with her great sensuality, expressed through her scents, her movements, her lips, and the way she wore her hair; and her appearance brought on a renewal of sensual love poetry. Yet the poet emphasizes her virginity, conjuring an indirect comparison with the immaculate Virgin-Mother. He also emphasizes her purity: "I was born with more impurity than she had in her life." Such an image of a woman in poetry is traditional, yet it occurs in a new context and with new means of expression. But Bećković brought much more than the revival of sensuality to poetry: he brought about the revival of poetic language. His language is free, everyday, and understandable. Its communication is not encumbered by the many hyperboles and paradoxes; on the contrary, they make it easier and even more natural. Besides, the poet uses images supplied not only by nature ("write to me, flower") but also by modern civilization, as in the above poem, in which he mentions the metro and a kiss delivered by phone.

The next book by Bećković, *Tako je govorio Matija* (So Spake Matija, 1965), extends the first in many ways, but its basic tone is different. The title—paraphrasing Friedrich Nietzsche's *Also Sprach Zarathustra* (translated as *Thus Spake Zarathustra*, 1883-1891)—evokes the image of a prophet, implying that these poems would be uniquely prophetic. At least one poem was undoubtedly so, "Poeziju više niko neće pisati" (No One Will Write Poetry Any More). The poem is a polemic with all those who, from Lautréamont to Bertolt Brecht and Branko Miljković, believed that eventually everyone will write poetry. Prophesying exactly the opposite, Bećković also carries on a polemic with himself. Did he not maintain in the previous book that he will speak even with his back? Another poem in this book expresses his need for speech, yet this poem has its double in the poem about the need to be silent. In fact, doubt about the power of poetry now becomes dominant: all that the poets used to sing—nature, great ideas and hopes, even grand words such as *freedom*—will desert poetry, according to Bećković. And poems, abandoned and disappointed, will turn against their creators. Is the cutting edge of this doubt turned toward the poet voicing it? Did Bećković feel that with this book he had said everything he had to say, or that he had reached his pinnacle, that he himself was facing the decision whether or not to write any more poetry? These questions can easily be answered affirmatively.

In *Tako je govorio Matija*, however, there was an additional motif from the previous book in the metaphor of a bullet seeking the poet's forehead. Feelings of love, also present here, could not suppress this threatening foreboding. The bullet is no longer the incarnation of the omnipresent, abstract death. To the bullet is added a realization of the presence of a persecutor who sometimes appears in different guises and sometimes remains unrecognizable. This feeling of persecution is connected with the theme of incarceration. Even the poem "Kad bih znao da bih se ponosno držao" (If I Knew I'd Bear Myself Proudly) is, in a way, prophetic. As if he had had a presentiment of facing judges, the poet tries to find an answer to the question of whether or not he would preserve his dignity during such a confrontation (or possibly torture).

Bećković's foreboding was not groundless. In the mid 1960s he had become not only a recognized poet but also a high-profile public figure. He was successful as an author of television plays, which enabled him to reach a wide audience, and dramatizations of his texts were performed in theaters across the country. At the same time he increasingly manifested another extraordinary side of his talent—his humor. His closest friends knew him to be one of the wittiest Serbian writers of any time, and others soon recognized this side of him. He applied his talent for puns, irony, derision, and satire to the conditions and problems of Yugoslav society, contributing to various satiric and humorous publications and earning his living in this manner for years. To be sure, he was essentially forced into this way of earning an income because his family history and his increasingly provocative writings, which met with official protest, effectively closed the doors to most alternative means of employment. It seemed that he had found the answer to his poetic dilemma—he did not want to remain silent any longer to what was happening around him. Those in power were no longer willing to accept silently the fact that a son of a so-called traitor and so-called enemy of the people was acquiring fame in a society that he was deriding but which was admiring and glorifying him. Bećković's fame grew steadily; as it did, the attacks on him multiplied and the opportunities for public appearances dwindled. Even his father's name was used increasingly in the attacks on the poet. His father's role in World War II as an "enemy of the people" was also magnified, leading the witty Bećković to say that if he ever received the Nobel Prize, the significance of his father would surely equal that of Adolf Hitler (against whom his father rebelled).

It looked at that time as though Bećković's prophecy that he would not write poetry any longer would be fulfilled. In the second half of the 1960s and the beginning of the 1970s, two nonpoetic books appeared: *Dr. Janez Paćuka o medjuvremenu* (Dr. Janez Paćuka about the Interval

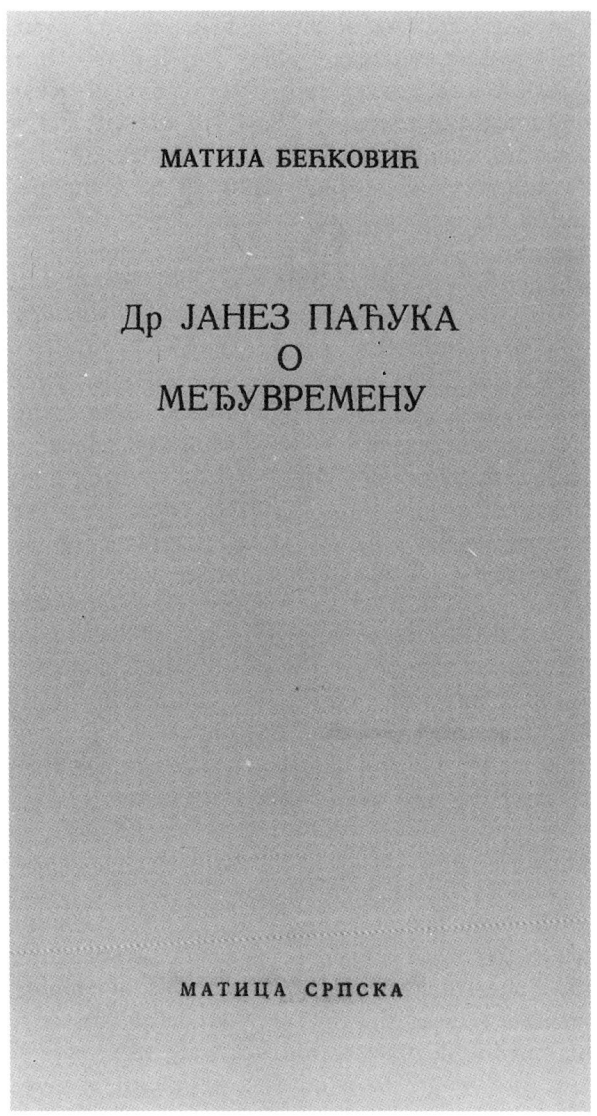

Title page of Dr. Janez Paćuka o medjuvremenu (Dr. Janez Paćuka about the Interval Period, 1969), a series of satiric articles

Period, 1969) and *Če, tragedija koja traje* (1970; translated as *Che: A Permanent Tragedy*, 1970), which he wrote with Dušan Radović. The character of Dr. Janez Paćuka was intended to show that it was not the poet who expressed critical views about the society but some fictitious character. Because Bećković was soon convinced that such a mask did not fool anybody, Dr. Janez disappeared from the subsequent editions. Bećković's satiric articles were brilliant. Nothing wittier had been written about the communist period in Yugoslavia in half a century of its existence, and hardly any other writing carried a sharper sting. His articles about freedom and the misuse of democracy belong to every anthology of texts about the unmasking of the communist deceit.

The text of "O mladima" (About Youth, 1968) is perhaps the most interesting. The end of the 1960s was a time of student unrest in Belgrade and elsewhere. In June 1968 the students bluntly told the icons of the communist ideology that they had betrayed the ideology by which they were still swearing. The paradox of the student movement was that the students were rebelling in the name of that betrayed ideology in whose truth they still believed. Although an open enemy of that ideological "truth," in all its possible variants, Bećković sided with the young and, in the style of Emile Zola, wrote a fierce indictment of the old revolutionaries.

During the politically charged summer of 1968, the Belgrade journal *Delo* (Action), which was also devoted to the "young Marx," contained *Che: A Permanent Tragedy*. The play was named after one of the revolutionary idols of the student youth, Che Guevara, who was seen as a leader who was neither corrupted nor consumed by power; but the tragedy was written not to glorify the ideology whose saint and martyr Che was, but rather to place that ideology, along with the idea of a revolution, on the stage of the theater of the absurd. After the fall of communism and the civil wars that followed, some of the dialogue about heroism and about justice and injustice sounds even more topical now than it did at the time it was written:

> Heroes never believe in programs.
> All they believe in is heroism,
> which is nothing but a lack of solutions...
> Heroes are hungry for injustice.
> The heroes of one nation
> are the criminals of another...
> Injustice is more natural than justice.
> It's always there, while justice must be invented.
> And justice is only the name plastered over a new injustice.
> (translation by Drenka Willen)

The next book by Bećković, *Reče mi jedan čoek* (A Man Told Me, 1970), provides some explanations about his prophecy of the end of poetry. This book signifies the end of writing—at least temporarily—of one type of poetry and the beginning of another. This collection of long poems, written in the dialect of his father's region, reveals a radically different Bećković. The word *new* hardly fits this book, though, except in the sense that it is a poetic novelty. With this local and dialectic poetry Bećković returned to the old sources of Serbian and Montenegrin patriarchal tradition and to the forgotten layers of people's linguistic memory. Bećković discovered for himself and poetry lovers a gold mine of inspiration. The book was enormously successful and was reprinted five times in two years.

During the 1970s two more books of this kind appeared, *Medja Vuka Manitoga* (The Border of the Crazy Vuk, 1976) and *Lele i kuku* (Wailing, 1978), forming a trilogy with *Reče mi jedan čoek*. Aside from several poems in which contemporary everyday language of Montenegro predominates, all others are written in an archaic dialect that is still used in some of the towns and villages of the region. Yet the trilogy is modern not only because the poet did not seek refuge in the patriarchal consciousness and dialect, but because he did not regard these merely as relics of the past. He recognized patriarchal consciousness, even in its degenerate form, in the present as well, especially in the ideology of local communism, which pretended to represent the future of mankind. Within the Montenegrin context he presented the patriarchal consciousness as an "inherited" trait of the national being. In the process he created a collective mythic voice of astounding energy and invention.

Bećković's modernity is manifested also in the fact that he presents the dramatic scenes of his poems, otherwise of epic proportions, more as comedies than tragedies. In his works tragedy turns into comedy while preserving its tragic accents even by changing linguistic codes. Tragedy in a dialect also has a comic effect. In the language of his characters and in the way that they use that language, Bećković's work has essential similarities with the comedy of the absurd. He has pointed at his kinship with the playwrights Eugène Ionesco and Samuel Beckett.

Bećković did not wish to neglect the old, but he could not pass up the opportunity to create the new. The critics noticed his connection with perhaps the greatest Serbian poet of the nineteenth century, Petar II Petrović Njegoš. Bećković does not hide, even in his poems, the connection with his teacher. Along with dramatic monologues and dialogues—not to mention the obvious connection with epic poetry (at least in the length of the poems)—Bećković follows Njegoš also in the basic verse form of Serbian oral poetry, the decasyllabic verse. Further emulating Njegoš, he uses the proverb as a model of expression. Bećković's trilogy echoes Njegoš's lament for Montenegro. Of all the genres of folk poetry, Bećković prefers the lament. But his lament is in two voices, regularly separated by ironic distance. The mocking voice was not alien to Njegoš either, although it did not serve the same function in his work. In Bećković that voice is directed more at his own people than at foreign people. It appears as the "false bottom" of the majority of voices in his dramatic poems. The voice of the mocker has helped Bećković, following in his teacher's path, to create works of exceptional originality and great value.

The poems in the trilogy are mostly in the form of monologues, sometimes dialogues. The voices of his characters are not the poet's voice, nor are their worldviews his. Bećković even tries to convince the reader that the poetry of this trilogy was not written but found, not new or just created but something that "has existed forever." "Therefore," as he says in a note in the third volume of the trilogy, "it does not belong to us, but we belong to it." Still, he was the director, scenographer, costume designer, and cameraman in this only seemingly ancient drama of the absurd. And as a poet of great linguistic prowess, he discovered various layers and codes in the dialect, emphasizing especially the features from the "lower" and "secondary" strata, which are and are not the language of the absurd. In exploring this dialect he found his most effective instrument for seeing his homeland from its less known, almost forbidden side. In the resulting form that resembles the epic poem, what finally emerged is in fact more a farce than an epic. But even this farce is not only a farce. The best description of this trilogy would be the one formulated by Elizar Meletinsky, the connoisseur of Russian myths who called James Joyce's *Ulysses* (1922) "the incarnation of myth and its travesty."

The idea of the end of the world is essential to these poems. Everything that could happen to mankind has already happened; everything that had to be written is already written; the best nations have disappeared, and those that were the worst have become the best. Bećković develops this idea locally: Montenegro has died or is dying; there are no longer the real Montenegrins; only the Montenegrin mountains have remained. This trilogy, too, can be called the poetry of the "interval," which is the title of his essays.

It is alien to Bećković to name phenomena and things. He has said often that for the community he is bringing to the stage, language is the repository of the greatest secret. His characters use language in a manner commensurate with such a secret. In this relationship they often bring matters to the level of the absurd because they are afraid that, depriving language of secre-

Matija Bećković (Snimio: Zoran Tatar)

tiveness, they may see their own lives as absurd. Bećković uses this method, and as a result some critics called the language in these poems the "language of mystification." For Bećković, and for his characters, too, it was necessary to speak so that others do not completely understand what is meant by the linguistic expressions, and to speak so that the poems would be published and the poet would not suffer the political consequences. In so doing while following the language mannerisms of his heroes, Bećković made a virtue out of necessity. One of his methods for covering up is the use of pronouns, as seen in the poem "Bez nidje nikoga" (Without Anybody Anywhere), in which the central pronoun *it* stands for the existing evil, but what that evil is is left to the reader to figure out (possible interpretations are many).

In the 1980s Bećković published several more books of poetry and essays as well as many reprints and selections from his work. Among these new books *Kaža* (A Tale, 1988) stands out; the book has its roots in the same "world beyond world," the town of Velje Duboko. Perhaps the most ambitious of his books, it is based on a tale, as the title indicates; it should be pointed out that the particular word for tale (*kaža*) was almost out of circulation before Bećković used it.

The tale is actually an anecdote. After a devastating war a woman and her children are left without any kin. Plagued by extreme misery and poverty, she seeks advice from the village teacher. Himself poor and hungry, he advises her to take up quackery and fortune-telling. The new "business" thoroughly changes her life. She proceeds to acquire wealth as well as power over people. Both she and her children are guaranteed eternal gratitude and remembrance by the society. The tale about the false happiness of the people spreads and multiplies, resembling a cancerous, that is, fatal disease; this process provides the real theme of the central "Kaža o Čminti" (Tale about Čhminta) and all the other tales in the six cycles of several thousand verses. Bećković also introduces here a first-person narrator who reveals the tenor of his tale's theme in the first verse, "I am afraid to tell this story."

Kaža differs from Bećković's earlier works in its pronounced apocalyptic vision of evil. The focus shifts from the interval of Dr. Janez Paćuka to doomsday. Perhaps in the 1980s Bećković could call things by their real names after "Čhminta's death," after democratization in Yugoslavia, and after Tito, one possible interpretation of the identity of Čhminta, had left the scene. The world that *Kaža* presents is dominated by absolute evil. But the shadow of the frightening and omnipresent evil does not cover all horizons. The spark of good gleams somewhere, in the narrator, too, even when at the end he introduces himself with monastic modesty as one who possesses "the evil mind," a "darkened heart," and a "small stature among people." That spark of good is, according to Bećković, of divine origin and bears witness to the Creator's existence. With this clear road sign, the poet avers that salvation can be attained through spiritual discipline, which in its ultimate and higher form has an ascetic character.

By the 1980s and 1990s Bećković had come to be regarded by a large majority of the public in Serbia as a first-rate poet. He became a corresponding member of the Academy of Sciences and Arts in 1983 and ten years later a regular member. He has received many national awards and was the president of the Union of Serbian Writers from 1988 to 1992. At present he lives in Belgrade, where he works as a freelance writer.

References:

Milovan Danojlić, "Zavičaj pesme," *Letopis Matice srpske,* 147, no. 1 (1971): 87–96;

Dušan Jović, "Znakovna slojevitost *Kaže o Čminti* Matije Bećkovića," *Književna kritika,* 18, no. 3 (1987): 107–114;

Nikola Koljević, "Lelek rovačkog sebra," *Književnost,* 33 (1978): 1906–1913;

Steven Kordić, "Njegoš i Matija: tragedija i komedija istog ili jedno celo," *Književnost,* 46 (1991): 1536–1554;

Dragan Lakićević, "Tri poeme Matije Bećkovića," *Savremenik,* 25 (1979): 454–471;

Miodrag Petrović, "Velika poema Matije Bećkovića," *Književna kritika,* 21, no. 3-4 (1990): 127–154;

Branko Popović, "Neprolazna mudrost naivne reči," in his *Umetnost i umeće* (Belgrade: Prosveta, 1977), pp. 151–175;

Slobodan Rakitić, "Poetry as the Language Sublimation of a Myth," *Relations,* 2 (1977): 80–85;

Ljubomir Simović, "Epske poeme Matije Bećkovića," in his *Duplo dno* (Belgrade: Prosveta, 1983), pp. 237–251;

Simović, "Group Self-Protrait with Čminta," *Relations,* no. 2 (1988): 56–61;

Momir Vojvodić, "Dramatični trenuci u poemama Matije Bećkovića," *Književna kritika,* 8, no. 4 (1977): 82–95;

Pavle Zorić, "Matija Bećković," in his *Vrhovi* (Belgrade: Srpska književna zadruga, 1991), pp. 117–140.

Mirko Božić
(21 September 1919 -   )

Ljerka Debush
Harvard University

BOOKS: *Drame* (Zagreb: Novo pokoljenje, 1950);
Kurlani, gornji i donji (Zagreb: Mladost, 1952);
Novele (Zagreb: Prosvjeta, 1953);
Neisplakani (Zagreb: Zora, 1955);
Ljuljaška u tužnoj vrbi (Belgrade: Nolit, 1957);
Svilene papuče (Zagreb: Naprijed, 1958);
Zapisi usputni (Split: Mogućnosti, 1975);
Colonnello (Zagreb: Mladost, 1975);
Bomba (Zagreb: Mladost, 1976);
Tijela i duhovi (Zagreb: Znanje, 1981);
Slavuji i šišmiši (Zagreb: Znanje, 1990).
Collection: *Odabrana djela,* 4 volumes (Zagreb: Matica hrvatska, 1970).

TELEVISION: *Čovik i po,* RTV Zagreb, 1974.

RADIO: *Bubnjevi,* RTV Zagreb, 1963.

OTHER: *Hrvatski književni jezik u svjetlu izmjene Ustava socijalističke Republike Hrvatske* (Split: Marksistički Centar, 1973).

Mirko Božić

Mirko Božić belongs to a generation of Croatian writers who appeared on the literary scene immediately following World War II. While most of those writers actively sought new modes of expression, Božić remained more of a traditionalist. He also belongs to a group of writers who fought during World War II with the partisans of Josip Broz Tito. No other writer, however, pursued such an active political career after the war as Božić climbing all the rungs of the Yugoslav Communist Party up to its central committee. Finally, Božić is also one of many writers from the Dalmatian rural regions of Zagora, a poor, isolated, backward area where the peasants struggle daily for survival and the townspeople lead a petit bourgeois existence. In his writings Božić managed to capture in a unique and forceful way not only the conflicts, problems, and obsessions of the people from Zagora, but also their vitality and strength in the face of adversity. He developed a highly individual style, full of neologisms and syntagmas bursting with connotations. These elements came most strongly to the fore in his first, and best, novel, *Kurlani, gornji i donji* (The Kurlans, Upper and Lower, 1952).

Božić was born on 21 September 1919 in Sinj, a small town in the Dalmatian hinterland marked by many contrasts. Sinj was home to a large military garrison of the newly formed Kingdom of Serbs, Croatians, and Slovenes. It also had an old Franciscan monastery and the Church of Our Lady of Sinj, the destination of countless pilgrimages. Many villages were scattered in the inhospitable, rugged, arid mountains surrounding Sinj, where their frequently famished inhabitants farmed minuscule plots of land and hauled water from remote springs. In the town itself a well-established middle class led a comfortable existence. As the son of a civil servant, Božić grew up in this middle-class milieu. His mother, née Obradović, was from Montenegro.

Božić attended elementary school and high school (1925–1938) in his hometown. He started writing love poetry at the age of seventeen but soon tried his hand at epigrams and satiric verse. While still in high school he wrote two short satiric plays, *Napad iz vazduha* (Air Raid) and *Moderni suci* (Modern Judges). Both were staged by an amateur theatrical company in Sinj. In 1938 Božić moved to Belgrade to study law. He later transferred to the University of Zagreb but was prevented from graduating when World War II engulfed Yugoslavia in 1941. He immediately returned to his native Sinj. During the next two years he secretly collaborated with Tito's partisans, and in 1943 he joined their ranks. During the war years he wrote several short one-act plays and his first complete play, *Majka zaklinje* (Mother Implores). The first postwar years Božić spent in Split, where he founded and ran a puppet theater. He was also an opera singer in the Split national theater, thus fulfilling a youthful dream of having a career in music. In 1947 he moved to Rijeka to become the secretary of the national theater located there. During the next few years he wrote several plays with war themes: *Most* (The Bridge, 1947), *Devet gomolja* (Nine Potatoes, 1949), *Povlačenje* (Retreat, 1949), and *Skretnica* (The Turn Off, 1950). In 1952 Božić became the head of the drama department of the Croatian National Theater in Zagreb. Up to that time, except for one short story published in the daily newspaper *Vjesnik* (Herald) in 1945, (*Protivnica* [Opponent]), Božić had written only for the stage. But the 1950s turned out to be a decade of fiction. In 1952 he published his first novel, *Kurlani, gornji i donji*. One year later his collection of short stories, *Novele* (Novellas), was published, followed in 1955 by *Neisplakani* (Tears Unshed), the second part of a planned trilogy about the Kurlans. In 1957 his play *Ljuljaška u tužnoj vrbi* (A Swing in the Weeping Willow) was produced. In 1958 Božić published a short novel, *Svilene papuče* (Silk Slippers), which he later rewrote as a stage play. Conversely, the piece *Djevojka i hrast* (The Girl and the Oak) was first written for the stage (in 1955) but was later revised and published as a short story.

In 1961 Božić wrote his best-known play, *Pravednik* (An Innocent Man). Between 1965 and 1969 Božić was the general manager of the Croa-

Dust jacket for Božić's novel about the Kurlan family

tian National Theater. During his tenure the neo-baroque theater building was completely renovated. Throughout the 1960s and 1970s he was active politically as he rapidly rose through the Communist Party ranks. He served as vice president of the Croatian Parliament between 1971 and 1974 and as a member of the Croatian presidency between 1974 and 1978, when he became a member of the Central Committee of the Yugoslav Communist Party. In 1975 he became a full-fledged member of the Yugoslav Academy of Arts and Sciences. He was the editor of several literary periodicals, such as *Kulturni radnik, Literatura, Književnik,* and *Telegram*. In the period when he was most active both in running the Croatian National Theater and in the political arena, Božić published little. He wrote a radio play, *Bubnjevi* (Drums) in 1963 and in 1974 a television series, *Čovik i po* (A Man and a Half). He rewrote the script of the first episode of this series into a

Title page for Božić's collected plays

short novel, which came out in 1975 under the title *Colonnello* (The Colonel). In the same year he also published *Zapisi usputni* (Notes in Passing), a collection of essays and comments written between 1965 and 1974 on contemporary cultural and literary events. In 1976 another novel *Bomba* (The Bomb), followed. The third part of the trilogy about the Kurlans, *Tijela i duhovi* (Bodies and Souls), appeared in 1981, twenty-nine years after the first part and twenty-six years after the second. It received a prestigious literary prize from the Belgrade weekly *NIN* as the best novel of the year. Božić's most recent novel is *Slavuji i šišmiši* (Nightingales and Bats), published in 1990. Božić presently lives in Zagreb.

Although he started his literary career as a playwright and spent most of his working life in the theater, Božić is best known for his novels, particularly the Kurlan trilogy. The Upper and Lower Kurlans of the eponymous first novel are the inhabitants of two villages in the vicinity of Sinj. The patriarchs of the two villages are brothers: Silvestar Kurlan in the somewhat richer lower village and Mrkan Kurlan in the desperately poor upper one. The two brothers and their families are constantly feuding over a little piece of land that the older Silvestar sees as his birthright and the younger Mrkan regards as a bequest from their father. The conflict reaches a climax when a donkey belonging to the Upper Kurlans wanders into the Lower Kurlans' vineyard and nibbles on a few vines. Silvestar files a lawsuit against his brother for damages.

Within the framework of this conflict Božić depicts the way of life in the Dalmatian hinterland. The place is almost untouched by civilization; the illiterate peasants live in abject poverty; their joys in life are few; and their future is bleak. The men are stubborn, hotheaded, and proud. The women, powerless and deprived, work themselves to exhaustion or even death. They are expected to marry early, bear sons, toil without respite, and never complain. There are three prominent female characters in the novel: Andjelija from the Upper Kurlans, wife of Filip, who, after a first stillborn son, has another son but never recovers from childbirth and dies after a few years; the widow Perka, who has an illegitimate son by Andjelija's husband and is destroyed by feelings of guilt; and Gara, Silvestar's daughter, who also has an illegitimate son.

The dominant organizing principle of the novel is the pairing of opposites: the Upper and Lower Kurlans, the upper and lower social strata, the town and the village. The novel has two parts: Carnival and Procession. Although the carnival is essentially a secular feast and the procession is a church celebration of a religious holiday, the two events are remarkably similar. Everybody participates in them: the rich and the poor, the townspeople and the peasants, men and women, plaintiffs and defendants, politicians and voters. For one day their dreary, boring lives are interrupted. From this day they expect some solution to a problem, a prayer to be granted, a score to be settled, or a debt to be paid. But all is in vain. After the feast life goes on essentially unchanged. Perka prays for the health of her child but, pushed by the mob, falls and crushes her son to death. The retarded Berleša dresses up as a bear, and the children get to beat him with a rod. Filip whacks the "bear" in a futile attempt to vent his frustrations. Alcohol, blood, and sweat flow, and the masses go wild. Božić is at his best in describing the carnival and the carnivalesque aspects of life in the town.

The Kurlans' lawsuit continues unresolved through the second novel, *Neisplakani*. Božić uses the protracted legal process as the background for contrasting the world of the urban bourgeoisie with the peasant world. The issue of the damaged vineyard has assumed grotesque proportions. Like a curse, it marks the fates of individuals. The feud between the Kurlans is more bitter than ever, and the knot that binds them is more and more tangled. Božić leads his characters through a series of dramatic episodes: Andjelija dies in her sleep; Andrija from the Lower Kurlans stabs his cousin Filip over a girl; and Perka loses her mind. In the town the election process is rigged; the wife of the main candidate loses all hope of a positive change in her life and struggles to keep up appearances; and the bureaucrats continue exploiting the illiterate peasants. And yet the peasants and the townspeople differ only superficially. In essence, they are all slaves to their temperaments, lust, envy, and greed. A third social group emerges in the novel—young Marxist revolutionaries. They are incessantly persecuted and interrogated by the police.

Several studies have been written about Božić's style and language, particularly in these two novels. A skillfully nuanced use of various linguistic registers is one of the main tools of Božić's realism. The peasants speak in local dialect, in terse sentences, while the townspeople pepper their speech with Latin and Italian phrases. Aptly crafted neologisms abound. The intensity of emotions, the gravity of deeds, and the starkness of the scenery all have correlates in syntax, derivatives, and word order.

Božić's third novel in chronological order is *Svilene papuće*, published in 1958. In it Božić turns away completely from the Kurlan milieu to contemporary urban life. The tragic love story between a young ballet dancer, Rina Baldi, and a violin virtuoso, Karlo Menoti, unfolds over the period of only a few days. The third protagonist of the drama is Karlo's possessive and manipulative mother. The triangular tension creates several simultaneous conflicts. One emerges from the jealousy of the mother and her almost demonic attempts to keep her son for herself even if it means destroying his happiness. Another conflict arises from Karlo's internal tension between an unresolved Oedipal complex (manifested in his inability to free himself from his mother) and his extreme narcissism. His love for Rina is an innocent puppy love, not the passionate kind she craves. She therefore vacillates between a tender affection for Karlo and a passion she has for a former lover whose child she now carries. Various objects that the characters have or give as gifts are endowed with strong sexual symbolism. Karlo's extremely valuable violin can be seen as his umbilical cord. As the events unravel, he first breaks a string on it and finally destroys it completely. The mother gives Rina a pair of silk ballet slippers, a symbol of virginity and sexuality to the mother: after a few uses they are ready to be discarded. The mother manipulates her son's sexuality too: she leaves the house key and money for the prostitute that she hires for him. Although the events in the story reach a climax, they are not resolved completely, and the three protagonists remain both villains and victims.

Over the next fifteen years Božić did not publish any new major works. He was intensely occupied by his political and party duties and by running the theater. He did, however, write essays, comments, and reviews of contemporary cultural and political events, and he gave speeches and interviews. These were all published in book form in 1975.

In 1974 Božić returned to his favorite theme of life in the Dalmatian hinterland. In a screenplay for a ten-part television series, *Čovik i po*, he portrays the peasants as partisans in World War II. He later developed the basic ideas from this series in his next novel, *Colonnello* (1975). An elderly Italian colonel gets lost in the woods and is captured by the partisans. The partisans' commissar, Pipe, immediately concocts a plan to trade the fascist for five truckloads of badly needed food and arms. Using the local priest as a mediator, he quickly strikes a deal with the Italians. On their way to the agreed-upon meeting place for the swap the partisans manage to lose the colonel. Faced with the dilemma of whether he should trick the enemy and grab the loot or keep his word, Pipe astounds both friend and foe by his admission that he has nothing to trade. Pipe again appears in Božić's next novel, *Bomba*, in which an enemy bomb lands near the village but does not explode. Pipe decides to disable it and reuse the explosive to blow up a bridge. After many comic scenes and dialogues, the partisans finally disable the bomb, only to find that it is filled with sand—a trick of the Italian antifascist saboteurs. The partisans can be consoled only by the fact that these saboteurs are, ultimately, on their side.

The third part of the Kurlan trilogy *Tijela i duhovi*, came out in 1981. The events take place during World War II, and the external happenings are echoed in the internal struggles and conflicts of the characters. The war has brought out the best and the worst in people. The personal feuds between the Kurlans are not forgotten but are pushed into the background by the menace of German aggressors. Božić portrays the events in a series of memorable episodes: an innocent man is slain in a case of mistaken identity; Gara's son suffers a tragic death, but she manages to escape and survive; and Andrija executes his own brother. The novel is divided into eleven chapters, each named after a particular character. The author alternates between third- and first-person narrative, assigning the first person to the captured German officer. Through oppositions of "us" and "them," the enemy and the defenders, the domestic and the foreign, and the old and the new, Božić expounds his philosophy of life and man: the past is indelible; it lives in and with the individual; she or he cannot perceive it objectively; and those who live in a particular time are its least reliable witnesses.

In his latest novel, *Slavuji i šišmiši,* Božić again moves into the urban milieu of the postwar period. Drawing heavily from his personal experience as both a theater manager and a Communist Party official, he uses a theatrical setting as a stage on which various roles are acted out. All characters, both inside and outside the theater, wear masks. They play their roles according to the requirements of the Communist Party, the society, or the workplace. Not surprisingly, Božić is more interested in what is happening behind the masks. The protagonist walks a tightrope by trying to reconcile his conscience with the party ideology. The year is 1947, when the war is still an immediate, tangible past. A clash within the theater management is ostensibly about hiring an opera singer who has the voice of a nightingale but a grotesquely obese body. She is Italian, and she also performs in Croatian territories in the then-disputed Zone B. In those days this made her at least suspicious, if not an outright enemy. When she is not hired, all Italian and some Croatian musicians resign from the orchestra. Because of this, a young party official is executed and his family is told a false story about his heroic death. The horrible purges of 1948 are thus foreshadowed. The novel ends on a somewhat sentimental note, with the protagonist rediscovering his love for his wife.

Božić cuts an imposing figure in post–World War II Croatian literature. His communist beliefs have left an indelible mark on his oeuvre and certainly have helped his career in the former communist Yugoslavia. Božić is at his strongest in works in which he explores archetypal conflicts, such as those between man and nature, between man as builder and man as destroyer, and between feuding brothers, or that of fratricide. He succeeded in capturing the spirit of his native region and the atmosphere of many turbulent years.

Bibliography:

M. Selaković, "Mirko Božić," in *Leksikon pisaca Yugoslavije,* volume 1 (Novi Sad: Matica Srpska, 1972), pp. 318–321.

References:

Miloš Bandić, "Kurlanski besni čvor," in his *Vreme romana* (Belgrade: Prosveta, 1958);

Nada Barac, "Dva romana Mirka Božića," *Krugovi,* 6-7 (1956);

Vatroslav Kalenić, "Nekoliko problema uz jezik dvaju romana Mirka Božića," *Književnik,* 8 (1960): 112–119;

Slobodan Novak, "Lirski roman Mirka Božića, Kurlani," *Krugovi,* 7 (1952): 564–569;

Vlatko Pavletić, "Odlomak bijede i kontinuitet primitivizma," in his *Sudbina automata* (Zagreb, 1955);

Pavletić, "Stil i jezik Mirka Božića," *Stvaranje,* 7-8 (1953);

Gajo Peleš, "Inoviranje klasičnog postupka," in his *Poetika suvremenog jugoslavenskog romana* (Zagreb: Naprijed, 1966), pp. 41–54;

Petar Šegedin, "*Kurlani*–roman Mirka Božića," *Republika,* 9 (1954): 725–729; 10 (1954): 813–816;

Šime Vučetić, "Književnik Mirko Božić," *Forum,* 37, 1-2 (1979): 5–24;

Vučetić, "Mirko Božić and His Work," *Most,* 4 (1980): 13–22;

Vučetić, "Mirko Božić, Izabrana djela," in his *Pet stoljeća hrvatske književnosti,* volume 147 (Zagreb: Matica hrvatska, 1980).

Miodrag Bulatović
(20 February 1930 - 15 March 1991)

E. D. Goy
Cambridge University

Miodrag Bulatović

BOOKS: *Djavoli dolaze* (Belgrade: Nolit, 1955);

Vuk i zvono (Zagreb: Zora, 1958);

Crveni petao leti prema nebu (Zagreb: Naprijed, 1958);

Heroj na magarcu (Belgrade: *Savremenik*, nos. 1-12, 1964; Rijeka: Otokar Keršovani, 1967);

Godo je došao (*Savremenik*, nos. 10-12, 1965; no. 1, 1966);

Najveća tajna sveta (Belgrade: Srpska književna zadruga, 1971);

Ljudi sa četiri prsta (Belgrade: BIGZ, 1975);

Rat je bio bolji (Belgrade: Prosveta, 1977);

Peti prst (Belgrade: BIGZ, 1977);

Jahač nad jahačima (Belgrade & Ljubljana: Partizanska knjiga, 1980);

Gullo Gullo (Belgrade: Prosveta, 1983);

Godo je došao i druge drame, 2 volumes (Belgrade: DBR International Publishing, 1994).

Edition: *Sabrana dela*, 7 volumes (Belgrade: Prosveta, 1982).

Editions in English: "A Tale of Happiness and Unhappiness," translated by E. D. Goy, *Atlantic Monthly* (December 1962): 131-134; translated by Mario Suško and Edward J. Czerwinski as "A Story of Happiness and Unhappiness," *Slavic and East European Arts*, 2, no. 2 (1984): 47-54;

"The Lovers," translated by Goy, *Evergreen Review*, 6, no. 27 (1962): 60-74; translated by Alec Brown in *New Writers*, volume 2 (London: Calder, 1962), pp. 55-73;

The Red Cockerel Flies to Heaven, translated by Goy (London: Weidenfeld & Nicolson, 1962); translated by Goy as *The Red Cock Flies to Heaven* (New York: Geis, 1962);

A Hero on a Donkey, translated by Goy (London: Secker & Warburg, 1966);

"A Fable," an excerpt of *Vuk i zvono* translated by Goy, in *New Writing from Yugoslavia*, edited by Bernard Johnson (Baltimore: Penguin, 1970), pp. 198-210;

The War Was Better, translated by B. S. Brusar, adapted by Michael Wolfert (New York: McGraw-Hill, 1972);

"Stop the Danube," translated by Srdjan Bogosavljević, *Relations*, no. 12 (1983): 21-43;

"Apples of Fire," translated by Mladen Jovanović, *Zavičaj*, 35, no. 9-10 (1988): 38-40.

Miodrag Bulatović was one of the most interesting and original of the writers who arose in Serbia during the 1950s and 1960s. His best works are of lasting value and typify the upsurge in prose writing, and of literature generally, after

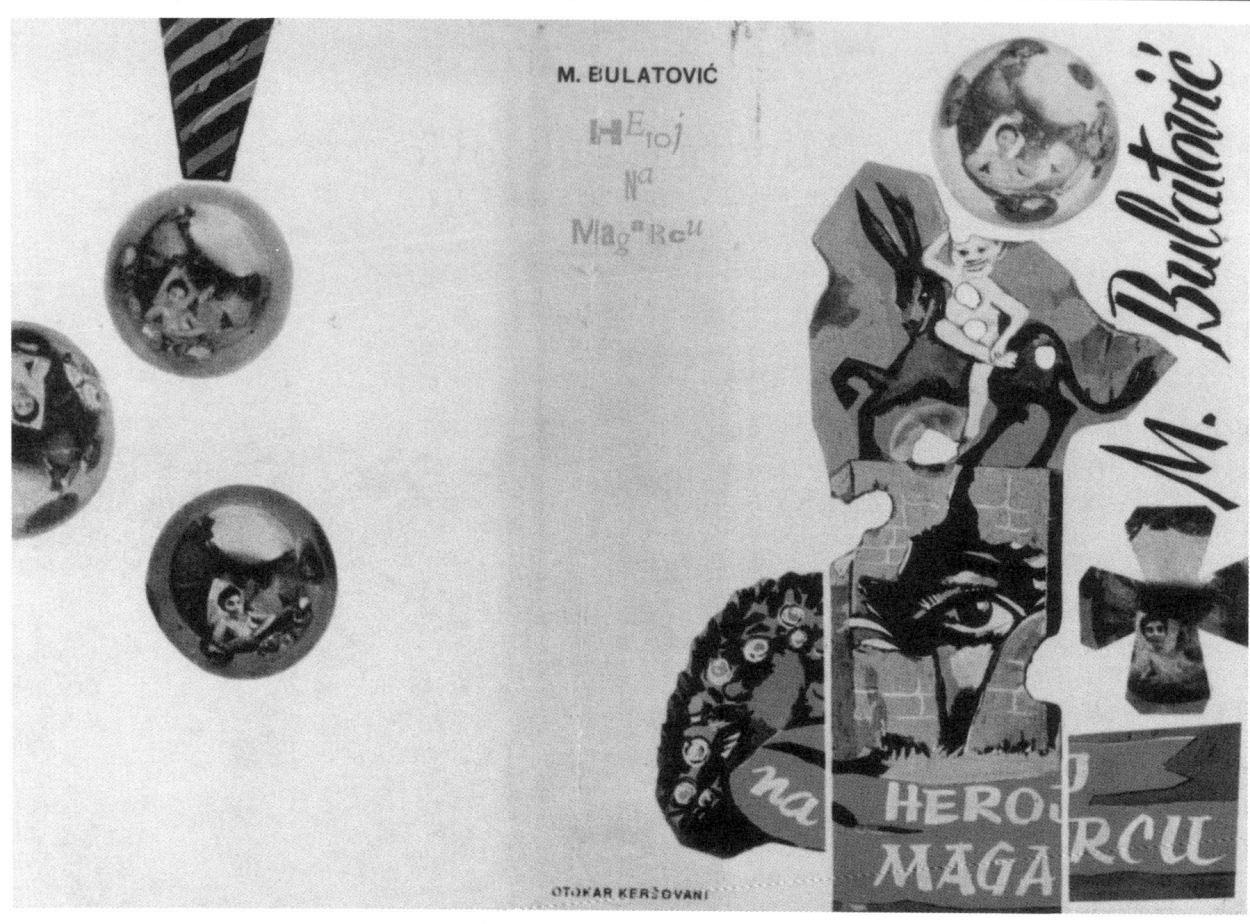

Dust jacket for Bulatović's satiric novel translated as A Hero on a Donkey *(1964)*

Yugoslavia's break with Joseph Stalin in 1948 and the gradual relaxation of the dictatorship of ideology over literature.

Miodrag Bulatović was born in 1930 in the village of Okladi near the ancient town of Bijelo Polje, now in northern Montenegro but originally in the twelfth century the capital of Hum (the ancient Hercegovina), which was ruled by Miroslav, the brother of Stefan Nemanja; the town was the place where the monk Gligorije produced the renowned *Miroslavljevo evandelije* (The Miroslav Gospel) around 1180 and where Miroslav's Church of Saint Peter still exists. Bijelo Polje on the river Lim was the background for most of Bulatović's writings and the center of his inner world.

On 18 March 1940 Bulatović suffered a traumatic event when, as a boy of eleven, holding his father's hand, he witnessed his father's murder. Bulatović's uncle simply walked up to them and shot the father dead. The young Bulatović was so disturbed that he set fire to the murderer's house. The event left him with a form of epilepsy from which he never completely recovered.

During World War II Bulatović experienced his country's chaos and fear, the Italian occupation, the conflicts between the Chetniks, the Muslims, and the partisans, and the constant struggle against starvation. At the end of the war he ran away to Belgrade, where his aunt, the wife of the uncle who had killed Bulatović's father who had joined the partisans, was an official in an institute for orphans of the war; from her the young Bulatović received regular meals and some education. Before the war an uncle engaged in trade with Marseilles had promised the boy's father to take him into his firm and had given him a textbook of the French language. Just when Bulatović began studying the language is not clear, but as a mature man he spoke French fluently. He also learned Russian and was profoundly attracted to the works of Nikolai Gogol and Fyodor Dostoyevsky. (He once stated that Gogol's laughter was not laughter but a desperate giggle.) Bulatović believed that life was a struggle against a world that was essentially fire, murder, and hatred. There was no room for optimism, and Bulatović was fascinated with literature and the need (and delight) of expressing the human predicament in what was a living hell. In 1955 he published his first book of short stories, *Djavoli dolaze* (The Devils are Coming), which immediately affirmed him as an original and important writer. The rest of his life was spent as a professional writer. He married the daughter of a well-known Slovene professor and had three children, living most of the time in Ljubljana. He was an eccentric character and a fighter against the life that he found so cruel. He loved his car and driving yet never obtained a driver's license. Ironically, this was tolerated in communist Yugoslavia, although it would never have been permitted in a democracy. His behavior was self-affirmatory, a bold challenge to a hostile world. He quickly realized the need for recognition, and his energy in publishing his works made him one of the most translated authors of modern Yugoslav literature. His works would not have been translated had they not possessed the originality and beauty that at least the early works possess. That he is still not well known in the world at large may perhaps be attributed to the fact that in the English-speaking world at least, there is little interest in translated works. In Yugoslavia, Bulatović was awarded the prize of the Association of Serbian Writers in 1958 and the NIN Prize for the novel of the year in 1975.

The appearance of the seven short stories comprising the volume *Djavoli dolaze* caused some shock and even revulsion to critics brought up on the ideals of so-called realism, resulting in criticism that those who wrote it and who are still alive would doubtless prefer to forget. The stories convey a sadomasochism yet also a great tenderness. The volume's epigraph from the Book of Job is expressive. Typical is the story "Exit from the Circle," in which a scorpion is placed in a circle of burning straw so it will sting itself to death. The crippled boy who watches its death hates it because it has killed his sister, yet the narrator sees it, first, as a strange little being:

> We saw the scorpion—short and rosy-red like a bird-cherry, with claws like pincers.
> When it caught sight of us it became alarmed. It circled. Then it fingered a wisp of straw with its pincer and was still.
> Does it know we're going to kill it?
> It knows.
> I don't know myself why I said this.

In the conclusion the narrator identifies with the scorpion: "And I wander the world, seeking some cursed thing or another. I weep and grow grey. Yet never can I find the exit from the circle."

Perhaps, of all the stories, the most striking is "Ljubavnici" (The Lovers), which certainly shocked some contemporary critics. Bulatović succeeds in creating the individual who accepts the world for what it is and the Other for just another object. To reject feeling is to avoid pain and suffering. (Narcissism naturally leads to necrophilia—where the Other is object and thus free to be used.) The narrator's wife, Olya, is treated with possessive indifference. The dominant tone is carried by the use of the terms *normal* and *usual*. Olya's death and, indeed, everything else are merely "normal" for the narrator. For him poetry and suffering are only a sickness. A passing interest in airplanes is the same as love.

> The next morning Olya was stiff. She looked quite normal. Her hand lay alongside her head. Clenched and yellow, it resembled a worm.... I stood beside the window and looked at her!

The narrator ends as a blind beggar and is perfectly happy. "I cannot suffer, but liquid matter oozes up in my eye-sockets when I recall how your lips rotted and fell apart." Has existence been reduced to an objective and detached awareness or has self-encapsulation not entirely succeeded?

The world is a world of suffering, and the individual is crucified between the fear of the Other and the need of the Other. The intimate essence of individuality is, perhaps, property, no matter how small. The threat to the individual is those who will take that property. The theme of taking, be it the crippled boy's kid or Muharem's cockerel in *Crveni petao leti prema nebu* (1958; translated as *The Red Cockerel Flies to Heaven*, 1962)—this is the source of fear and the harshest awareness of the existence of the Other. What one most treasures will be taken away. The story "Priča o sreći i nesreći" (A Tale of Happiness and Unhappiness) deals, rather ludicrously, with an insane man's love of a tie that his grandfather or his father had given him.

> Has anyone seen a boy with a tie?
> —What, is that your tie, man?
> —Why, we're looking for that tie too—people said.
> I rushed and stopped others:
> —No, we're looking for him too.

The theme is an essential image of the state of individual being.

In 1958 Bulatović published *Vuk i zvono* (The Wolf and the Bell), which is a novel in form but which presents each chapter as a separate incident. The theme is again the confrontation of the individual and the life which is a fire that burns throughout the novel. It is both the fire of war and destruction and the fire of purity. The individual in the mass is a reduction to vision and curiosity—the inhabitants of a prison/asylum vie with one another for a view of what is taking place. The soldiers rob the crippled boy of his goat. The man hides in a kiosk, only to die. The beetle falls from the prison window, and the little Mullah lies crushed and dying on the minaret. All are spectators in one sense. In another they desire the comfort of the Other. Even sadism and the act of taking may be an inverted form of love. Yet, if man be a tragic horror, he is also the bearer of light and love. If not he, then who? In Bulatović's view, all people are on the dusty road that leads nowhere. As he writes, "We are in great danger and so we huddle together, when one is in great misfortune, one must have someone to whom one can tell one's lies and to whom one may confide the terror that has crept beneath one's skin."

Always, vision is dominant. The beetle, as it falls, sees an inverted vision of the world. "He fell diagonally, his head down to the left. He saw the slanted walls of the great building where he had been since he could remember. He saw the sky, with its flame, stood on end." The beetle is the image of individual being. It is the size of a man's thumbnail. "In the world of people nobody paid it any attention, but this did not anger it, for it knew that this was unimportant. In any case it depended on people for the crumbs they dropped. It knew that one day it would be crushed underfoot. Yet it did not fear death, only the pain of death." Existence is a chaos of fire, a burning jungle that the individual may neither conquer nor escape. To withdraw is a choice tragically negated by the need for the Other as a condition of being, of expression. The need to exist is the need for the Other, and this is the affirmation of one's individual being. Thus, even the robbers and the rapists, in their inverted approach to connection, are also angels. Their acts are a simplistic—and desperate?—form of the need for the Other.

In 1958 Bulatović published his finest work, the novel *Crveni petao leti prema nebu*. It is dominated by torrid heat and activity, in which the central theme is that of the consumptive Muharem who, invited by a stranger to meet in town for a drink, decides to sell his dearest possession, his red cockerel, to be able to return the stranger's hospitality. In a small area various events take place, all in sight of each other. There is a wedding feast with riotous guests; two Muslim grave-diggers with the body of a girl search in vain for her family grave; meanwhile old Ilija, paralyzed by a stroke, yearns to tell Muharem that he is the son for whom he searched for many years yet never dared to tell him. Between this wind the dry, dusty road and the river Lim. On a rise by the river sit the two tramps, Petar and Jovan, tormented by hunger and a desire for the Other that will end in a fantasy of the one eating the other. For them being is to travel the road till they reach the sea, urinate in it, and then return to repeat the journey. Like time the road winds on, just as the river ripples on its way. The whole is united by the cloud of dandelion seed blown in her birth pangs by Mad Mara, the eternal victim of rape who casts her offspring into the river. This will, at the end of the novel, be supplemented by the cries of the red cockerel and the shower of blood and feathers that obliterates the sun that spins like a sick spider.

The central event is the taking of Muharem's cockerel by the drunken wedding guests. Muharem is beaten, and the cockerel flies up to be shot and then, as birds sometimes do when wounded in the lungs, soars upward in a convulsive death throe that deluges the entire scene. Muharem then staggers away; passing the two grave-diggers, he is led to touch the breasts of the dead girl, an act that fills him with shame. The shame comes from the fact that it is not the real connection with the Other that he sought. Thus, when Petar and Jovan invite him to join them in their eternal journeying, he refuses, for the individual feels the need to live life, rather than to avoid it. That Petar and Jovan pass by the wedding feast, with its mass of food for the taking, suggests a rejection of the life that draws Muharem, but the situation is fraught with contradiction, as is human existence itself. They too desire to connect. They recognize the cockerel as the cockerel that crows in their breasts.

The novel resembles a naive village painting, or rather, a painting by Marc Chagall or even Pieter Brueghel. Its use of hyperbole and its very naiveté have a force and freshness that make it a work of outstanding quality. The cru-

Dust jacket for a translation of Rat je bio bolji, *1977*

elty is offset by a tenderness that transcends the action. Thus Mad Mara calls to Muharem:

> "Come up here to me."
> "How?" Muharem asked.
> "It'd be nice" Mara's dark figure replied from the hill, "Where I am is where you should be."
> "I'm not sure I can ... whether I could become a man there ... and there's another thing, I've ... "
> "We're brother and sister," Mad Mara said tenderly, "For we both want to live a thousand years."
> "I can't come," Muharem said hoarsely. "Not for anything. I'm defiled and evil."
> "What of it," Mad Mara said. "There's a lot of flowers here and down there on the road there aren't any at all. Can't you see?"
> "I see, but what's the use," Muharem said sadly. "I'd come if I weren't what I am."

The breaking of tension from extreme cruelty and violence to a relief of gentleness and humanity is reminiscent of the cathartic pauses in Dostoyevsky.

These are the truly original and successful of Bulatović's works, in which he appears as a creative and original force, powerful in its naive directness. In the early 1960s Bulatović traveled abroad and spent a considerable amount of time in Paris. Just as his early love for the works of Gogol is fully understandable, so it is not surprising that his acquaintance with the writing of Samuel Beckett should have resulted in the play *Godo je došao* (Godot Has Come). It was not published in its original language in book form until 1994, but it was serialized in *Savremenik* (Contemporary) in 1965–1966 and published in German translation as early as 1966. In 1970 it was performed in translation by a group of Cambridge students at the Edinburgh Festival. The strange play is hardly plagiarism, since its theme is rather a completion of Beckett's play than an imitation. If Beckett's tramps are forever waiting for Godot's arrival, Bulatović sees Godot's arrival as no great event. He is just a small, happy baker who is willing to supply the goods of his trade but otherwise has little more to contribute. It seems to affirm Ludwig Feuerbach's statement that the essence of man is man's highest essence. On the other hand, the play is a parody of Beckett, and, as such, its originality does not quite overcome its original.

During the 1960s Bulatović was occupied

with a novel that clearly expanded the naive and personal nature of his earlier works into a critique of war and human tragedy. In other words, what had been portrayed as direct, if symbolic, experience is now expanded into the portrayal of a universal statement. During the late 1960s Bulatović recounted the idea and many of the episodes of the new novel to his friends, including the author of this article. One's impression at the time was of a new and exciting work, though with, perhaps, the reservation that a work created so often in the writer's mind might prove rather different when it was written down on paper. The novel in question, *Heroj na magarcu* (*A Hero on a Donkey*, 1966) appeared in 1967 (after having been serialized in *Savremenik* in 1964) and was widely translated. It achieved some fame because it was judged harshly by many Titoist critics, who saw in it a possible denigration of the partisans and their leader.

The novel differs from *Crveni petao leti prema nebu* in that it is less intimately lyrical; it also applies hyperbolic realism to a satire on war and politics. The term *satire* is only vaguely applicable to the earlier works, but here it is directly so. Bulatović said that the idea for the novel occurred to him when, walking through a wood near Bijelo Polje, he found a rusty Italian mess tin with a name scratched on it. The theme of the novel is that war and pornography are parallel expressions of the same human aspiration to impose upon others. They are the crudest forms of self-affirmation. Sex and power both serve as confirmations of the ego. Thus the Italian general, Besta, who never goes anywhere without a pair of woman's knickers and other items of female underwear in his luggage, remarks: "Militarily we have lost the war but, sexually, we have won it." The impact of this is perhaps lessened by an element of moral judgment from the author, whose alter ego, Maj. Antonio Peduto, apologizes at the end of the novel for the behavior of his division. Peduto, the narrator of the story, is also writing a novel titled *The Time of Shame,* the subtitle of the actual novel. He is observing as well as participating in action that burgeons with characters—the soldier Paolone, Brambilla, Marika the prostitute, and Salvatore, the sentry who waits in vain for relief and whose rifle grows to immense proportions. The hyperbole is crude. The right ear of the spy, Mustafa Agić, grows to the size of a trumpet.

The main character is the Montenegrin Gruban Malić, whose name suggests what he is: a crude, vulgar little man. He runs a wineshop and sells pornography but at the same time spreads a boastful rumor that he is an agent of the Partisan 501st Army, a hyperbole in itself. "Yes," Malić says triumphantly, "I've broken with my old negative life and begun to think and dream of mankind's highest ideals." There is a Gogolesque theme of vulgarization here. Indeed, it is hard to be sure to what degree Malić is actually real rather than a mere literary image. Peduto calls him his favorite metaphor. His move to "ideals" is a move from selling contraceptives to dealing in lies and boasting. Malić's boastful defiance of the Italians is treated with humorous contempt. Malić is the embodiment of the ordinary man whose ambitions are crude, and the more idealistic they become, the more grotesque they are. At the end of the novel Malić is arrested and brought back to the town on a donkey. The reference is as clear as it is ambiguous.

The theme of a work of literary art is really of little importance in itself; the question is never really "What?," but "How?" *Heroj na magarcu* is full of humor, action, surrealistic imagery, and sex; it also provides a sensitive depiction of human suffering and innocence. Yet, compared with the earlier works, the novel is a failure. It lacks the lyrical intonations without which its personages become puppetlike. The obscene army songs of the guitarist Augusto Napolitano do not compensate for the loss of magic.

If Bulatović is to be believed, he spent a great deal of time researching this novel. One is tempted to think that this may have been part of the difficulty. One may think of the second volume of Gogol's *Dead Souls* (1842), in which the novel ends with a sense of its not being entirely achieved. In 1968, the year after the publication of Bulatović's *Heroj na magarcu,* the sequel to the novel appeared, *Rat je bio bolji* (translated as *The War Was Better,* 1972). The main characters are much the same. Antonio Peduto continues to act as observer, while Malić, more unreal and hyperbolic than ever, looms as a constantly recurring figure. Peduto, with his pet tortoise (mistress?), escapes from the burning Montenegro on a ship that is bombed and machine-gunned from a plane piloted by Malić. Before they escape they see the arrival of the American troops in Montenegro. The people are drowned in a shower of condoms and chocolate bars. Peduto and his companions travel to Venice, Rome, and Paris, where General Besta appears as the rather poetic proprietor of a brothel. Malić reappears on his donkey as a shadowy figure who is reminiscent of Tito and other dictators visiting abroad. The theme is that the vulgarity and pornography of *Heroj na magarcu,* unrestrained by war, now dominate a world that lacks even the purifying fire of fear and action. Pure satire, this novel includes such characters as Lady Agatha Christlie, Angus McPurdy, and Sir Stanley Gordon Clumsy. But it is too long and makes for tedious reading. Indeed, its best achievement is its sexual provocativeness. Other than this, it is a clumsy afterthought to *Heroj na magarcu.* The novel's deficiencies led to its being far less widely translated than the earlier works.

The shift from existential experience to political and social satire was not a happy one. The idea that the common individual's aspirations have little to do with anything but instinctive self-affirmation in terms of whatever ideas are dominant at the time, reinforced by the sexual urge, is interesting, as is its corollary, that this alone will ever, in one idiom or another, dominate human history; but its artistic expression lacks the impact of earlier, more concentrated works. In 1975, after Bulatović had published nothing for several years, his novel *Ljudi sa četiri prsta* (The People with Four Fingers) appeared. Its satire narrowed now to the merely political, the novel recounts the Mafia-like activities of the Ustasha-dominated Croatian nationalists among the Gastarbeiter in Austria and Germany. Despite its element of truth, it is pure nationalistic and even socialistic propaganda, carrying no artistic impact. The work is almost a poor self-imitation. For example, the great black sow that plans all in the background, like some evil deity, fails to frighten. That the novel was awarded the NIN prize may have resulted simply from the fact that it pleased some of the "old guard" in literary circles. For the sake of Bulatović's reputation it is best forgotten. Its sequel, *Peti prst* (The Fifth Finger, 1977), is very much in the same vein. In 1983 Bulatović produced yet another novel of about the same quality: *Gullo Gullo.* The word *gullo* is the Latin name for the wolverine, or glutton, a voracious member of the weasel family, and in this novel refers to the barbaric capitalist. The theme of the exploitation of the world by corrupt power does not provide the artistic justification for what is little more than yet another pulp novel. Miroslav Krleža's 1919 novella "Hodorlahomor the Great" is a far more intelligent and artistically vital performance.

These later works by Bulatović should not detract from an appreciation of his true stature as a writer. His was a fresh and original genius, and his early works are among the best produced

Miodrag Bulatović

in postwar Yugoslavia. They may rank with Mihailo Lalić's *Lelejska gora* (The Mountain of Leleja, 1962), Radomir Konstantinović's *Čisti i prljavi* (The Pure and the Defiled, 1958), Meša Selimović's *Tvrdjava* (The Fortress, 1970), and Vladan Desnica's *Proljeća Ivana Galeba* (The Springtimes of Ivan Galeb, 1957). That his genius seemed to exhaust itself is nothing new or strange in the world of literature; one has only to think of Gogol or the later Leo Tolstoy. It is for his early works, up to and including *Crveni petao leti prema nebu,* that Bulatović will long be remembered.

Bibliography:

Živorad P. Jovanović, "Bulatović, Miodrag," *Leksikon pisaca Jugoslavije,* volume 1, edited by Živojin Boškov and others (Novi Sad: Matica srpska, 1972), pp. 383–385.

References:

Miloš I. Bandić, "Zatočenici patnje, ognja i drumova," *Književnost,* 15, no. 4 (1960): 314–323;

Milorad Djurić, "U svetu ljubavi Miodraga Bulatovića," introduction to Bulatović's, *Najveća tajna sveta* (Belgrade: Srpska književna zadruga, 1971), pp. vii–xli;

Petar Džadžić, *"Vuk i zvono,"* in his *Kritike i ogledi* (Belgrade: Srpska književna zadruga, 1973), pp. 77–81;

E. D. Goy, "The Novel and Stories by Miodrag Bulatović," *Review* (London), no. 7 (1968): 584–617;

Dragan Jeremić, "Miodrag Bulatović ili Kako se izmiriti sa svetom," in his *Prsti nevernog Tome* (Belgrade: Nolit, 1965), pp. 298–320;

Miodrag Jurišević, "Bulatović, vitez tužnoga lika," *Književnost,* no. 8 (1968): 179–193;

Vasa D. Mihailovich, "The Eerie World of Miodrag Bulatović," *Slavic and East European Journal,* 12, no. 3 (1968): 323–329;

Borislav Mihajlović-Mihiz, "Miodrag Bulatović, *Djavoli dolaze,*" in his *Književni razgovori* (Belgrade: Srpska književna zadruga, 1971), pp. 201–205;

Predrag Palavestra, "Čudnovati svet Miodraga Bulatovića," *Letopis Matice srpske,* 394, no. 5 (1964): 432–440;

Svetlana Velmar-Janković, "Poezija patnje," in her *Savremenici* (Belgrade: Prosveta, 1967), pp. 149–169;

Radovan Vučković, "Tragikomični i marionetski svet Miodraga Bulatovića," *Savremenik* (June 1972): 554–564;

Clas Zilliacus, "Three Times Godot: Beckett, Brecht, Bulatović," *Comparative Drama,* no. 4 (1970): 3–17.

Kole Čašule
(12 March 1921 -)

Thomas Eekman
University of California, Los Angeles

BOOKS: *Prvite dni* (Skopje: Nopok, 1950);
Naroden heroj Strašo Pindžur (Skopje: Ilinden, 1950);
Raskazi (Skopje: Koco Racin, 1953);
Vejka na vetrot (Skopje, 1957);
Crnila (Skopje: Kultura, 1962);
Drami (Skopje: Kultura, 1967);
Partitura za eden Miron (Skopje: Misla, 1968);
Proza 1945-1967 (Skopje, 1968);
Igra ili Socijalistička Eva (Skopje: Misla, 1969);
Prostum (Skopje: Misla, 1970);
Premreže (Skopje: Kultura, 1977);
Žitolub (Skopje: Kultura, 1977);
Trilogija (Skopje: Misla, 1980);
Vomjazi (Skopje: Misla, 1981);
Imela (Skopje: Misla, 1982);
Gorčila (Skopje: Misla, 1983);
Kanadski fragmenti (Skopje: Našna kniga, 1985);
Zapisi za nacijata i literaturata (Skopje: Misla, 1985);
Novi zapisi (Skopje: Naša kniga, 1989);
Proza; Gorčila; Konzulski pisma (Skopje: Kultura, 1990);
Makedonski dilemi (Skopje: Makedonska kniga, 1992).

Edition: *Odbrani dela*, 8 volumes to date (Skopje: Kultura, 1978-).

Editions in English: "A Macedonian Girl," translated by Allan McConnell, in *The Big Horse and Other Stories of Modern Macedonia* (Columbia: University of Missouri Press, 1974), pp. 43-56;
"Compatriots," translated by McConnell, *Macedonian Review*, 5 (1975): 305-314;
Darkness, translated by Ilija Čašule in *Five Modern Yugoslav Plays*, edited by Branko Mikasinovich (New York: Cyrco Press, 1977), pp. 267-322;
"The Whirlpool," translated by Ilija Čašule, *Scena*, no. 7 (1984): 194-211.

PLAY PRODUCTION: *Zadruga*, Skopje, Makedonski Narodni Teatr, 1950.

Kole Čašule

Kole Čašule is a prolific Macedonian novelist and playwright who is also a prominent Macedonian activist and patriot. His early writings, published in extracts in magazines when he was a student, were part of a movement among young Macedonian writers to write poetry and prose in their own language. Čašule is one of the initiators of contemporary Macedonian literature and a pioneer particularly in the field of drama, to which he devoted himself almost exclusively in the years from 1950 to 1970.

Čašule was born on 12 March 1921 in Prilep, Macedonia, the son of a high-school teacher. During his high-school years in Prilep and Bitola and his later study of medicine, from 1938 to 1941, at Belgrade University, he became a convinced and dedicated Macedonian patriot and communist, although in recent years he seems to have become disillusioned by communism. He started writing when he was an adolescent; later he stated that "I remember my first steps into literature as a linguistic adventure. As a national demonstration." When he read one of his stories to the literary club of Bitola High School, a story with dialogue in the Macedonian language, the literature teacher, a Serb, became angry, and Čašule was almost expelled from school. He vowed never to write again in Serbian or Bulgarian, only in Macedonian.

After Nazi Germany attacked and occupied Yugoslavia in 1941, Čašule joined the partisan resistance and took part in the Prilep uprising of October 1941. He was arrested, sentenced to hard labor for life, and spent two years, from 1942 to 1944, in prison in Skopje, then under Bulgarian occupation. In 1944 he escaped and rejoined the partisans. After the war Čašule was active as a journalist and writer in the newly established Socialist Federal Republic of Yugoslavia, in which Macedonia became one of the six republics; he also worked for the Communist Party and participated in public functions. From 1947 to 1950 he was managing director of the Macedonian People's Theater in Skopje; from 1950 to 1952 he was the director of the Vardar Film Company. He then worked as a Yugoslav consul in Toronto, Canada, from 1953 to 1955. This first assignment abroad enabled him to learn English and to read widely; it also inspired him to write *Kanadski fragmenti* (Canadian Fragments, 1985) and *Konzulski pisma* (Consular Letters, 1990). Čašule founded various magazines, one of which was the literary-sociopolitical magazine *Razgledi* (Views), of which he served as the main editor from 1957 to 1962. He also spent approximately ten years as a Yugoslav ambassador in Bolivia, Peru, and Brazil. From the early 1970s on he was mainly active as a novelist and functionary in the world of letters in the Macedonian capital, Skopje. He won several Macedonian literary prizes and was elected chairman of the presidium of the Yugoslav Writers Union. He resigned from this position in 1985 when a conflict broke out at the Writers' Congress in Novi Sad between Čašule, who advocated an avowedly political attitude and a political activism for writers, and some members who rejected this objective. This affair proved somewhat detrimental to his reputation; however, with new literary works he established his position as one of the foremost writers of prose in Macedonian literature. Most of his work is at least partly autobiographical and marked by his strong sociopolitical convictions, which does not detract from its intrinsic literary values.

All the stories in *Prvite dni* (The First Days, 1950) are stories about war and liberation in which the Bulgarians are the enemies and the partisans and the Macedonian people are the heroes. "Denot" (The Day), for example, published in the first issue of the new Macedonian literary magazine *Nov den* (The New Day), is the first story Čašule wrote. It portrays a mother who lost her son in the battle for Skopje and heroically resigns herself to his death. The title story depicts a group of intrepid young people involved in secret, anti-Bulgarian activity; in a final scene, both touching and somewhat sentimental, the central hero, Krste, says good-bye to his mother and his girlfriend. Two stories tell about prisoners who, despite beatings and torture, refuse to reveal the names of fellow partisans. Dimitar Mitrev has observed: "Sharp, schematic opposition of the positive and negative (the well-known black-and-white technique) is the foremost distinctive mark in all the stories by this author."

Čašule's first play to be performed was *Zadruga* (The Collective Farm), performed in Skopje in the 1950–1951 season. It dramatizes the process of collectivization in a Macedonian village. Much more successful was a play that is set in the United States, *Vejka na vetrot* (A Twig in the Wind, 1957). In this play a Macedonian emigrant has returned to his homeland and finds a girl who, although much younger than he, is willing to marry him and follow him back to the United States. The Macedonian man had previously married an American woman and has a son from that marriage. Čašule brings these three characters together in a conflict that he works out psychologically and that ends with the young woman's tragic death. In the foreign environment she feels "like a twig, torn loose by the wind and only with its bark still attached to the branch." The ideological and historical-political elements are rather subdued in this play.

However, they return in full strength in *Crnila* (Darkness, 1962). The setting is Sofia in 1921, where Macedonian political refugees gather; the question that dominates them (well known also in Russian literature) is whether those who share a common cause may legitimately liquidate someone considered an enemy of the cause. The group decides that killing the rejected member is warranted, and the murder is carried out. By the end of the play it is clear that hatred and fanaticism lead inevitably to more senseless deaths.

The drama is based on an event that occurred in 1921, when the Macedonian revolutionary Djorče Petrov was killed in Sofia. Again, this play has an ethical thesis and strong national, political, and historical references.

Vitel (The Whirlpool, 1967) deals with the people and problems of Čašule's own time and with the moral and political questions of his country, but, as Miodrag Drugovac observes, "the theme of *The Whirlpool* is so universal that it could refer to another time period and to a different national and social environment." The play presents a confrontation between the Prisoner and the Investigator; the latter tries to prove that the prisoner is a traitor. In the end he has to bow before the prisoner's strength of character. Some fantastic elements enliven the action. A pronounced social and political perspective also characterizes the drama *Ostavka na eden karipski minister za vantrešni raboti ili dostaga na samiot vrv od najvisokata vlast* (The Dismissal of a Caribbean Minister of the Interior or the Attainment of the Very Summit of the Highest Power).

Partitura za eden Miron (A Musical Score for One Miron, 1968) is obviously a satire of the Soviet system. There are no acts, but two parts. In the first part two strange figures, Miron and Kiron, appear; they move mechanically and rigidly. Miron talks lengthily about the greatness of the Leaders, and he worships their portraits that are displayed, especially the portrait of Kain, until Kiron informs him that Kain has disappeared, the victim of an international conspiracy. The perpetrator has been caught, and Miron is assigned to investigate the incident. The assault had actually taken place some time ago, but a man who exactly resembles Kain has played Kain's role as leader since that time. At the hearing, where the pseudo-Kain appears before Miron, everything is comical and cynical. Kain pretends to agree to all of Miron's ridiculous, unproved accusations; he "plays the game" and gives lively details of his "crime." In an interpolated scene Kain I, resuscitated, and Kain II have a conversation. In the second part, Kain II, realizing his case is hopeless, wants the trial to be over as quickly as possible, and he is ready to sign his death sentence; but unexpectedly Kiron reappears and declares it was all a mistake. He offers Kain "a billion excuses"; recognizes Kain as the true, great Leader; and acts humbly, even slavishly toward him. Then comes the climax: Kain is hanged anyway, and his corpse is seen lying in front of his largest portrait. Kiron reads an official announcement that says, in effect: the enemies of our State, our Society, our Leadership and our bright future have killed our great Leader, Thinker and Statesman. It is a suggestive play that could not help but impress the public in dictatorial times.

Prostum (Resistance, 1970), his debut as a novelist, was a success. In it the young Gorčin ("The Bitter One"), is introduced; he is an autobiographical hero who occurs in several of Čašule's works of fiction. The work is a cleverly constructed, polyphonic modern novel that is also a historical novel: in Gorčin's mind pass various episodes from the Macedonian past, which is marked by wars, uprisings, and inhuman actions. These episodes are brought to life in a rich, subtly variegated, sometimes emotional language. The next long novel, *Premreže* (Blur or Opacity, 1977), actually two volumes in one, evokes the period between World War I and World War II, "twenty-three years of Serbian occupation," as the author calls it. The entire action takes place in 1941, but by way of memories, flashbacks, and dialogues a whole period of Macedonian history is revived. Interestingly, the novel consists of lengthy letters or reports by a Bulgarian functionary who is sent to Prilep to supervise the police and, notably, to study the files in which communist activities are reported. *Premreže* is a book about Prilep, and it portrays many aspects of life between the two wars, particularly political life and the secretly flourishing communist movement. "As you see," writes the letter writer to his anonymous addressee,

> at least it's not dull here. Everything around me is a challenge. A challenge to what exactly, I don't know. How do I find out: why did Geščv [his superior] select just me for Prilep? . . . There is something humiliating in my status here. As a matter of fact: what am I? A liberator? A son of the glorious Bulgarian nation, as General Mikhov, who came to Macedonia, told all of us a few days ago, that finally has lived to the day of its unification? Are we at home here? Is one at home in his brother's house?

In June 1941 the German army "liberated" Macedonia from the Serbs; although the supreme command remained German, the Bulgarian army then marched in, formally occupying the area, followed by the Bulgarian police and Bulgarian teachers whose task it was to erase the differences between Bulgarian and Macedonian, which is a South Slavic language closer to Bulgarian than to Serbian. The letter writer has long conversations with various colorful inhabitants of the town, among them historical personalities such as the well-known, Prilep-born Bulgarian novelist, Dimitar Talev (1898–1966), who states: "Prilep is complicated. . . . It is unusual, because it is unpredictable. . . . It can be great and dwarfish. Open and with wolves' teeth that dig in a person without his knowing why and when it happened." According to one interlocutor, "our historical antennas up to now have been directed exclusively towards the act of destruction! After all, in all our Macedonian history we haven't had anything but destruction! That's why we are so talented, so imaginative, so creatively productive when it comes to destroying!" He adds that "all that is creative, revolutionary, talented, spiritually rich in Prilep finds itself in the communist ranks." There is also a discussion between the Bulgarian and his German chief in which he attempts to argue that the Bulgarian presence in Macedonia is not an occupation, but a liberation.

Chapter 13 consists entirely of a dialogue between the "me" who is the letter writer and the Prilep citizen and communist, Katrin, who is extremely taciturn, often does not answer "my" questions, and clearly tries to remain uncommitted. In this part of the book Čašule uses a stylistic device present in several later works: very short sentences, and often single words, are put on separate lines, presumably to give each word extra weight. The dialogue with Katrin is interrupted by short texts in italics, which include dialogues between the narrator and his superior, Geshev, and a fragment from a police dossier. Chapter 15 consists of the letter writer's dream. After much introspection he concludes: "I find myself at the funeral of my conscience."

Part II begins with the radio announcement that Germany has attacked the Soviet Union. There are evaluations of the European political situation, and there is also a lot of introspection by the letter writer; his love life is not neglected either. His memories of Marija Pop-Peeva expand to a novella within the novel. Then there is a segment about a Danail Krapčev, a Macedonian from Sofia whom the writer of the letters knows and whose activity leads him to remark: "In the Bulgarian government, army, economy, industry, trade, banking, diplomacy, church, science, culture—everywhere a Macedonian is at the helm!" He also notes that "All our national traumas are of Macedonian origin! All our national tragedies are because of Macedonia!" At the end of the texts some Bulgarian orders and instructions are printed. The letter writer is shocked; he tells his mistress: "This morning I received instructions to burn villages, Evdokija! To fire! To kill prisoners." Čašule does not continue the story up to October of the same year, when a Macedonian uprising against the occupants started, in which the Prilep communists played a prominent role.

Čašule wrote the novel *Imela* (Swoon, 1982) mainly during his stay in Brazil in 1980 and 1981. It is also narrated in the first person, but the narrator here is the presumably autobiographical Gorčin. The action starts with the German invasion and bombing of Belgrade. Gorčin is among the soldiers who are on a train to Skopje, and he has to take a suitcase to a certain address in that city (obviously a party order). Before the crammed-full train left Belgrade he was asked by somebody to sit with a French diplomat's wife and child on their way to Thessaloníki. There are digressions about Gorčin's student life in Belgrade and his political involvement. The adventurous trip (the train is being machine-gunned) ends shortly before the train reaches Skopje: supposedly, army trains are blocking the tracks. Gorčin makes his way, in the face of great difficulties, with the young Frenchwoman and her child to the Skopje railroad station and manages to put them on a train that is leaving for Thessaloníki. Gorčin reflects extensively about the country's situation, his own situation, and his discussions with his father. The latter's warnings notwithstanding, he reports as a volunteer to the military authorities; but the officer on duty, noticing that he is a communist, tells him he will be arrested and helps him escape. Gorčin's experiences include meetings and confrontations in Skopje (including one with the man to whom he had to deliver the suitcase), and there are flashbacks about his life in Belgrade, including his love life. During a machine-gun attack on Skopje, Gorčin flees to the graveyard and spends some time there. A family friend, Azman, comes and enthusiastically shows Gorčin and his father a pamphlet saying that the Germans have liberated Macedonia from the Serbian yoke; he asks them to sign a document and says that, with their help, an independent Macedonia can be built; but Gorčin and his father refuse to sign. When a representative of a "National Committee" delivers a speech, calling for friendship with the Germans, Gorčin shouts him down and expounds his view of a world revolution; but then he is shouted down by people who ask: does he want bloodshed and destruction?

The sudden appearance of the young wife of the French diplomat is a climactic point: the Germans have forced the train back to Skopje.

Gorčin is elated, and yet thinks of various reasons not to take her home (for one, he knows she is Jewish). When he later goes to the people she and her child were living with, he gets a good-bye note: she has left with a group of black marketeers who promised to hustle her across the Albanian border. This development does not destroy Gorčin, nor does it end the novel; he next receives a party order to leave for Prilep and there follow more of his political, sometimes philosophical, considerations and effusions, mostly in connection with the war in southeastern Europe, the "Balkan notturno," or Balkan night. Čašule continues in this work his habit of putting inserted texts in italics.

Gorčila (Bitter Things, 1983) can hardly be called a novel: it is a transition to a more modernist, avant-garde type of prose. What is new is also the Eastern Orthodox religious element in this book. It consists of short texts in italics, each on its own page, headed by a day of the week, sometimes a church holiday. Only gradually does one discover that there is a narrative line connecting these texts, which are written in short, laconic sentences. Some texts are more or less philosophical, like this one: "I find a sense in everything, except in human life. This will be the truth about the expulsion from paradise: that we live without sense. Cains to ourselves. Jealousy and hatred are our joys. There is no way out. Not even in death." Next to such somber pages are light, even comic scenes, for example, when the narrator wants to call his newborn baby Danail; but the priest declines. It is impossible. He has a list of names sanctioned by the state; all other names are forbidden.

> Only those. The rest is anti-state. I protest: it is my right to name my child the way I want. There is no right, answers the priest. "There isn't. There is the state. If it's not right with you, change your state." I understood what he meant. Oh Macedonia.

What returns regularly is the narrator's distrust of the word, of people's talk. "Silence is truth. Only silence is. The word is a conspiracy against others. Hell. My living wound, my word."

These texts are followed by some forty pages of "Documents." It appears that the man who sought freedom to give his child the name he wanted is now requesting that his own name be changed, apparently for no other reason than to establish his freedom. The priest Pop tries to dissuade him, but finally gives in and prays: "May now Your Grace and Your Reverence judge and adjudicate, there is nobody else to blame but me, servant of God—I'm waiting for justice with an open heart, impatiently, because the demons in this town, like that Čašule [Kole Čašule's father], are guileful and powerful, children of the evil one." Then follow official documents about the name change. Later it appears that, a week after the name change was formalized, the man with the new name died; according to an official telegram and a police report it was "suicide in mental derangement." A doctor's report confirms that he had a disturbed mind. There is a denouncement that warns against "Macedonia-minded communists and students."

Kanadski fragmenti (Canadian Fragments) is totally different in its character and setting. The narrator-protagonist is a recent immigrant looking for a job in Toronto; the "old country" he came from is never mentioned, but it is presumably Macedonia, and his wife is still there. There are three fragments. The first recounts the immigrant's vagaries: he gets drunk in a pub, ends up in jail, is released, gets involved with a woman, and has two companions (one of whom speaks in a humorous mixture of Macedonian and English). "She," the nameless woman he cared for, dies from a heart attack, and the narrator has difficulty in persuading the police that he did not kill her. At the police station he is offered a job as a police informer, but he refuses. After he receives a letter from his wife asking him to sever all ties with her, he commits suicide.

The second fragment is a third-person narrative. The main character first came illegally to Italy and later managed to enter Canada as a "DP" (displaced person). Here the plot begins. The Yugoslav king is supposed to visit Canada from England; secret agents have arrived to prepare the visit and eliminate possible assailants. The central character is among the suspects; he decides to expose himself voluntarily to the interrogation (and tortures?) of the agents (who are assisted by the Federal Bureau of Investigation and the Royal Canadian Mounted Police) rather than try to hide. The suspense is palpable as he enters the room where they ordered him to go; he knows there will be tortures and has a lethal pill under his tongue. His thoughts are rendered suggestively. Later he wakes up from a sleep to find that there have been no tortures; instead he is given orders to be at the airport when the king arrives and flourish a Chetnik flag. An important role in this narrative, actually a short novel, is played by his girlfriend, as her thoughts and her viewpoint are also rendered.

The third fragment, titled "Konzulski noki" (A Consul's Nights), also deals with the king's visit. The first-person narrator is a consul of the Yugoslav Socialist Republic who has to face thousands of hostile Serbian Chetniks and Croatian Ustaše now living in Canada; he gets many threatening phone calls. He drives with his wife to the airport to watch, from a hidden corner, the arrival of King Peter II. It is clear that the whole visit is a failure: the king is a nonentity, and the press pays almost no attention to him. In a final "Consular Night" the consul is called to a police station because an immigrant who looks like a Yugoslav has committed suicide; he also talks to a former Macedonian, "Tom Buick," now a restaurant owner, who tells his story.

The "Consul's Letters," published in the 1990 volume of prose, are actually part of the *Kanadski fragmenti*. These twelve letters—some of them extremely long—are written by a consul from a southeastern European country who is in Toronto and writing to another consul, whom he hardly knows but whom he designates as his confidant. From his letters it becomes increasingly clear that he is not only a fearful person but a paranoiac. He speaks in great detail about himself, his past and present, and the world. He confesses that after World War II he was appointed an investigator in a small Yugoslav town, Novo Mesto. This was in fact an immoral job. His justification is: "We were deeply convinced that, to establish somebody's guilt, it was sufficient that we believed in it. We did not need evidence." He claims he knows from experience that "innocence, purity, honesty don't exist!" He shows himself to be a skeptic, a hypochondriac, and a defeatist. Increasingly afraid and suspicious, he at last starts to suspect even his wife and to spy on her. The FBI is, he is certain, behind everything and constantly after him. In his homeland his chief, a man named Victor, once ordered him to liquidate a young woman who was a party member and, on weak grounds, was suspected of disloyalty to the party. The narrator followed his orders and killed her; later her innocence was established. This experience (in letters six through eight) evidently contributed to the consul's paranoia. Letter nine is written by his wife, who has found out to whom he is writing all these epistles. "Andrey is ill, Mr. consul. He does not distinguish, in his illness, between what is the truth and what he imagines it to be." There follow texts of telegrams and a newspaper item reporting that "the consul of the republic Blatvia" apparently had lost control of his steering wheel, the car capsized and caught fire, and he, his wife, and two daughters were killed. The name of his country, revealed only now, is that of one of the two imaginary countries, Blitva and Blatvia, immortalized by the prominent Croatian writer Miroslav Krleža in his novel *Banket u Blitvi* (Banquet in Blitva, 1938–1939).

Čašule has also written two volumes of nonfiction, *Zapisi za nacijata i literaturata* (Notes About the Nation and Literature, 1985) and *Novi zapisi* (New Notes, 1989), and more volumes are expected. An indefatigable publicist, polemicist, and speaker at various congresses, he nearly always treats the subject of Macedonia. When he writes or speaks about the Macedonian language or literature, he does so not as a linguist or literary specialist, but as a militant politician, a prominent activist of the Yugoslav League of Communists, fervently defending the Macedonian cause, notably against "Great-Bulgarian chauvinism." When the Greek authorities begin actions against the Aegean Macedonians, he attacks Greece, too. Some of his articles contain interesting autobiographical material. The first volume also contains his "Ten Prose Miniatures" (in fact, only nine are printed), nonrealistic lyrical texts, and poems in prose from 1955, for which he was attacked by the communist press; however, he replied that he was still a communist and a patriot. His "Attempt at a Profile of a Certain Criticism" (1962) is his first essay that is nonpolitical: it deals with literary issues, such as the debate about realism versus modernism. Of special interest is "A Long Journey Into Light," an essay about Eugene O'Neill, with whom he became acquainted and who supposedly had a great impact on him, especially his playwriting. O'Neill is the only author whose influence he ever acknowledged. The second volume contains more articles, speeches, interviews, theses for conferences, and diary fragments, mostly from the 1980s. The incident of his abdication as chairman of the presidium of the Yugoslav Writers Union takes up much room in this volume. There is an interview for Radio Skopje in 1982, in which he speaks revealingly about himself and literature. Repeatedly he points to his wife, Vandža, as his great helper.

Čašule is a prolific writer who, while maintaining his deep social and political convictions, has evolved from a socialist-realist fiction writer and dramatist to an author who uses modern technical and stylistic devices and methods. He has also evolved from being a devoted communist and Stalinist to being a satirist who warns against totalitarian regimes and the police state.

Interview:

Radovan Popović, "Yugoslav Dramatists Speaking," *Scena,* no. 2 (1979): 123-130.

Bibliographies:

T. Sazdov, "Čašule, Kole," in *Leksikon pisaca Jugoslavije,* volume 1 (Novi Sad: Matica srpska, 1972), pp. 484-485;

"Kole Čašule," in *Jugoslovenski kniževni leksikon* (Novi Sad: Matica srpska, 1984), p. 111;

Vasa D. Mihailovich and Mateja Matejić, *A Comprehensive Bibliography of Yugoslav Literature in English 1593-1980* (Columbus, Ohio: Slavica, 1984), p. 57; *First Supplement* (1988), pp. 32.

References:

A. Aleksijev, "*Gradskiot sat,* nov dramski potfat na Kole Čašule," *Sovremenost,* 16, no. 3 (1966): 258-262;

Milan Djurčinov, *Nova makedonska kniževnost 1945-1980* (Belgrade: Nolit, 1988);

Miodrag Drugovac, *Istorija na makedonskata kniževnost, XX vek* (Skopje: Misla, 1990);

Drugovac, "Raskazite na Kole Čašule," in *Povoeni makedonski pisateli,* volume 1 (Skopje: Naša kniga, 1986), pp. 366-371;

Makedonska kniževnost (Belgrade: Prosveta, 1968)—includes contributions by Dimitar Mitrev and J. Boškovski;

Makedonska kniževnost vo kniževnata kritika, volume 3 (Skopje, 1973), pp. 360-388, 518-519;

Mateja Matevski, "Aktuelni simboli upateni kon idninata," *Razgledi,* 10, no. 5 (1968): 640-645;

Matevski, "Dolgi godini na *Crnila,*" *Razgledi,* 10, no. 6 (1968): 735-739;

Matevski, "Kole Čašule, *Vitel,*" *Razgledi,* 9, no. 9 (1968): 1089-1092;

Tome A. O. Sazdov, *Makedonska kniževnost* (Zagreb: Školska knjiga, 1991);

Vele Smilevski, ed., *Makedonskiot raskaz* (Skopje: Makedonska kniga, 1990);

Gane Todorovski, "Čitajki go Čašule," in his *Makedonska kniževnost vo XX vek* (Skopje: Naša kniga, 1990).

Živko Čingo
(13 August 1935 - 1987)

Savo Cvetanovski
University of Skopje

BOOKS: *Paskvelija* (Skopje: Kultura, 1962);
Nova Paskvelija (Skopje: Kultura, 1965);
Semejstvoto Ogulinovci (Skopje: Kočo Racin, 1965);
Strikovite vodenici (Skopje: Misla, 1966);
Srebrenite snegovi (Skopje: Nova Makedonija, 1966);
Požar (Skopje: Makedonska kniga, 1970);
Golemata voda (Skopje: Makedonska kniga, 1971);
Kengurski skok (Skopje: Makedonska kniga, 1979);
Prikazni od Paskvel (Skopje: Misla, 1988);
Al (Skopje: Makedonska kniga, 1989);
Babadžan (Skopje: Naša kniga, 1989);
Bunilo (Skopje: Misla, 1989);
Grob za dušata (Skopje: Kultura, 1989);
Drami (Skopje: Kultura, 1992).

Editions in English: "From's Daughter," translated by Michael Samilov, in *New Writing in Yugoslavia,* edited by Bernard Johnson (Baltimore: Penguin, 1970), pp. 320-326;
"The Estranged" *Macedonian Review,* 1 (1971): 118-124;
"The Medal," translated by Allan McConnell, in *The Big Horse and Other Stories of Modern Macedonia,* edited by Milne Holton (Columbia: University of Missouri Press, 1974), pp. 71-78;
"Father," translated by Michael Seraphinoff, *Short Story International,* no. 40 (1983): 155-164;
"Spirit in the House," translated by Mario Suško and Edward J. Czerwinski, *Slavic and East European Arts,* 2, no. 2 (1984): 65-72.

Živko Čingo is one of the most distinguished and talented men of letters in modern Macedonian literature, the author of many significant short stories, novels, and plays. His works have been scrutinized by critics and literary theoreticians. In this attempt to evaluate his overall creative output from a literary and aesthetic perspective, the true dimensions of his opus will be established.

Živko Čingo

Čingo was born on 13 August 1935 in Velgošti, a village near Ohrid, southern Macedonia, to a working-class family. He completed elementary school in his native village and high school in Ohrid. He studied literature at the University of Skopje, graduating in 1959. He spent a year as an instructor at a teachers' school in Ohrid and then became a journalist and an editor for cultural programming at Radio and TV Skopje. He was an assistant at the Folklore Institute in Skopje and spent some time in specialization in Bulgaria. In 1962 he began publishing short stories, both for adults and children, and continued contributing to all leading Macedonian literary magazines until his death in 1987 at the age of fifty-two. Some of his works have been published posthumously, and some were left unfinished. In his last years Čingo participated in the political life of Macedonia, having been elected a representative in the Macedonian parliament.

Beginning with his books of short stories, *Paskvelija* (Land of Pasquelia, 1962) and *Nova Paskvelija* (New Pasquelia, 1965), and continuing with his other short-story collections, plays, and his masterpiece, the novel *Golemata voda* (Big Waters, 1971), Čingo showed a definite progress and deepening in the themes, content, and techniques of his work. He also produced, along with his philosophy of life, a particular Čingonian poetics. When the body of his literary work is examined and the chief aspects of his poetics are synthesized, several dominant characteristics and tendencies emerge.

Čingo's view of life and world, as the prominent Macedonian critic Milan Gjurčinov points out, is largely under the spell of Albert Camus's "tragic idealism," a phrase that summarized Camus's understanding of humanity and its destiny. Gjurčinov and other critics (in particular, Slobodan Micković) argue that Čingo's humanism is the highest value and component of his writing. An analysis of Čingo's works, however, reveals that the author applied the doctrine of the ancient Stoics to almost every short story, play, and novel. More precisely, one is aware that Čingo incorporates in his writings the three fundamental Stoic ideals: the correct understanding of values, the relevance of values to human conduct and the sustaining of values, and self-consciousness. The first ideal pertains to Čingo's characters' efforts to understand nature and to live in conformity with its laws. The second ideal, that of relevance, refers to the individual's knowledge that what he experiences is inevitable and thus he must sustain it. The ideal of self-consciousness relates to Čingo's characters' capacity for inner peace and self-control over feelings, whether pleasant or painful. Consequently, the humanism of Čingo's characters in the two "Pasquelias" is expressed in a somewhat hyperbolic but lucid, meditative, and dreamlike recollection, with much pathos and some morbidity, but altogether sincerely and emotionally, with maximum precision of expression. Čingo ultimately achieves a synthetic composition in which his eloquence and wisdom fuse into an inseparable artistic whole.

Čingo's stories, like those of Slavko Janevski, are knitted together by elements of the Latin American literary style sometimes referred to as "magic realism." But much of his fiction precedes the Latin American works that exhibit the features of magic realism. It is therefore more likely that Čingo was influenced in this aspect of his style by the works of William Faulkner, which were widely translated into Macedonian and which were Čingo's favorite literature. Literary critics have confirmed the debt of Latin American fiction writers to the work of Faulkner. The debt is particularly evident in the fiction of Gabriel García Marquez and Mario Vargas Llosa, whose works have, in turn, influenced recent American and European writers. In the interview "La Novela en America Latina" (The Novel in Latin America) in *Imagen y Literatura* (1968), Marquez and Llosa acknowledged being influenced by Faulkner's method, judging it more effective than the European or Spanish models for telling about the Latin American reality.

Indeed, some of the fundamental characteristics of magic realism are forcefully expressed in Čingo's fiction in an intensely personal manner that conveys his inner convictions, beliefs, dreams, and ideals. His writings contain a myriad of details about the reality that Macedonians faced after World War II, out of which he creates new, personal images of the world that in his fiction is as much real as it is imaginative. One finds several further characteristics: an understanding of man as a mysterious being surrounded by a real world; a tragic sense of defeat; a subjective experience of time that may lose its real dimensions and acquire a personal, unpredictable rhythm that intermingles individual, collective, and historical time; a penetration of reality for the purpose of its destruction in order to present not only its sensual and objective sides, but also its hidden dimension, its double meaning and secret side; and a style of expression that is both popular and learned, vulgar and elaborate. These elements are most illustrative in Čingo's masterpiece, *Golemata voda,* which is set in a children's dormitory immediately after World War II and presents a picture of a hellish existence. *Golemata voda* was later dramatized under the title *Sidot vodata* and subsequently made into a movie directed by Branko Stavrov.

From another point of view, Čingo, like Slavko Janevski and William Faulkner, is a regional writer, although his region is an imaginary one: the Paskvelia county invokes that of Janevski's Kukulino and Faulkner's Yoknapatawpha. But Čingo does not provide his imaginary locale with much detail, nor does he present its historical continuity and unity or its complete social status and structure. Nevertheless, he uses

Title page of Čingo's novel Golemata voda
(Big Waters, 1971)

history and the social and political system of postwar Macedonia as the milieu for his narration. At the same time, he is critical of the social and political structures, especially the collectivization of land, the monolithic socialist system, and the state and local bureaucracy, which all devastate people's physical existence and their moral and psychological dignity. Perhaps for this reason, Čingo's prose dwells both on erotic passion and cruelty and also on the connection between the two. But where Ernest Hemingway's cult of violence is uninhibited, almost innocent, and Faulkner's is twisted and melancholy, Čingo's cult of cruelty is socially and politically connected. In essence Čingo portrays his major characters as being from two social classes: the rural peasantry and the newly sprung bureaucrats. Above all, he uses his imaginary county (in real life, the county of Ohrid) as a physical and spiritual locale that enhances his narrative action and his myths and that creates a background against which to portray strong or weak characters. Thus, the imaginary Paskvelija is the source of the symbolism of his ideas, of his metaphors and other figures of speech, and of the metamorphosis of his characters. His Paskvelija is carefully and authentically planned and presented with all the features of a real geographical location, with its topography and landscapes, with precise description of the local villages and houses and of the people, their professions, the manners and habits of their daily lives, situated in a milieu that reveals their ideological, social, religious, moral, and emotional views and reactions. Čingo's chief interest, however, is not merely to depict the local atmosphere and the manners of the characters but rather to present their personal and psychological motivations. Accordingly, Čingo's writing may be defined as a kind of literature of regionalism, while his method of presentation is much closer to that of rural naturalism.

Čingo's narration is enriched by the archaic folklore tradition of his region, mythological heritage, and his intercontinental intellectualism. Closely related to these is Čingo's use of the principles of carnivalization and the grotesque. As Gjurčinov points out, "It is not so difficult to perceive in [some] of Čingo's works a net of numerous polarities: high/low, elevated/banal, humane/evil, comic/tragic, etc." Čingo uses myths, legends, fables, proverbs, and other folklore materials and mythological traditions to promulgate his points of view; to guess at the meaning of life and death; to account for natural phenomena; to chronicle historical events and the actions of his heroes; to give concrete expression to something deep and primitive in human nature; and to present it in a stirring narrative at once familiar and strange.

Whether Čingo's narratives draw from history and fact or from contemporary social and political life, all of them contain fictional elements. Thus, the author weaves fictional episodes about historical and social characters and about contemporary life and its settings not only to make his fiction interesting and entertaining, but also to make it instructive, edifying, persuasive, and exciting. The imaginative elaboration of incidents and the ability to create the qualities of real persons are especially evident in the story "Lazarevo pismo" (Lazar's Letter) and in the novel *Babadžan* (1989).

Čingo's fiction, particularly the short stories of *Paskvelija* (to the end of 1958), epitomized the clash of the former literature of the dogmatic Marxist and Zhdanovite type and the new, modern literary approaches. The Zhdanovite doctrine of socialist realism, imposed on the Macedonian writers and artists, was subservient to political goals. Slogans celebrating the socialistic organization of farmland and of the peasants were glorified, as were the "prosperous and great achievements" in agriculture; the brilliant future of socialism was acclaimed as the only road to progress, as Vlada Urošević stresses. Čingo, like many of his contemporaries, felt the emptiness of these slogans and phrases. Consequently, his fiction was once deemed erratic by Marxist literary critics. The official slogans and the "big words" that echoed at officially organized mass meetings acquired a pathetic tone and sounded absurd in the contexts of Čingo's fiction and plays. Most importantly, Čingo's works exposed those ideas with irony, so that they seemed unsubstantial and built upon principles rooted in abstract speculations, not real-life experiences. Čingo's works, therefore, are anti-utopian if, as Urošević points out, one accepts the socialist idea of an Arcadia or idyll in the Macedonian agricultural regions, which is not evident in the Paskvelija stories. Čingo's writings thus greatly helped Macedonian writers gradually to free themselves from political considerations and the dogmatic literary directives of socialist realism. At the same time, writers responded favorably to works written primarily for their artistic merits. Čingo, obviously enough, was one of the fiercest fighters for the liberalized literary trends that would permit genuinely artistic achievements.

Čingo's characters, although diverse, tend to fall into clearly defined groups. There are "flat" or static characters, conformists who represent the prevailing sociopolitical system and who are depersonalized in their ideas and thinking–for example, Olivera Strezoska and Briton Jakovleski in *Golemata voda* and Filip in *Al* (1989). There are also the initiated, "rounded" characters who, unable to adapt to the system, create their own dreamworld of liberty, called the Senterlion Hill (Kejten and Lem in *Golemata voda* and Baba Likirija in *Al*). Nevertheless, Čingo sympathizes with both types of characters even while rejecting their responses to life. The two points of view thus represent a two-dimensional, interrelated narration, as seen in Lem's occasionally narrating in both dimensions. There is no manifestation of the polarities of the evil and good characters in Čingo's works, although the author leans toward the good ones. He counterposes the wall of nonfreedom created by the system with goodness, happiness, and belief in the individual's capacity to create inner peace and freedom. The characters with such attitudes represent the unfailing intuition, the sensibility, and the gift of sympathy that for Čingo were the supreme human qualities that give a person the intensity and radiant power that illuminates the darkness of conformists like lightning. The conformists could not be sympathetic characters. Their anxiety and loneliness and their need for admiration and sympathy are not enough to humanize their intransigent positivism, selfishness, and brusquerie.

The essentials of Čingo's style derived from three chief sources: from his experiences as a journalist; from Macedonian folk tales; and from the influence of those authors whom he read avidly, particularly Isaac Babel, Maksim Gorky, Bret Harte, Ernest Hemingway, and William Faulkner. As a journalist for the daily newspaper *Nova Makedonia* (New Macedonia), Čingo learned to write succinctly, to avoid superfluous adjectives and adverbs, and to pack maximum content into the minimum space. Čingo said in his interview with Petar T. Boškovski (in the introduction to Čingo's book, *Požar* [Fire, 1970]) that from his early childhood he had an opportunity to hear from his father, "who was regarded as one of the best folk tale narrators and singers of songs in the country," many stories and all kinds of "sayings about life . . . [which] were particularly powerful, clear, told in an understandable, distinctive language, so that at once the pain of the people about whom he was talking was embedded in your soul." Indeed, the debt of Čingo's style to folk literature was pointed out by the Macedonian critics Dimitar Mitrev, Gjurčinov, Urošević, Miodrag Drugovac, Boškovski, and Micković, who stress that his narrative idiom, although inherited, is powerful and uniquely personal. The result is, as Urošević points out: "When we read Čingo's short stories we very often have an impression that we are present at an oral storytelling. The enthusiasm of the narration, the sentence intonation, the stream of the mythos, all that resonates in Čingo's works with the acoustic of the spoken word, which enriches us with its oral syntax."

However, as Micković rightfully notes, Čingo's "inspiration sources are closely connected with his artistic ennobling" of the folktale, the short story, and everyday speech. Thus, there is a stylistic synthesis of the three sources of influence. Nevertheless, the most typical examples of Čingo's fiction–*Paskvelija* and *Golemata voda*–are written in two alternating styles. First, there is the highly condensed description and narration that is written in the flowing chain of images suggestive of free verse. The second style is characterized by terse dialogue, almost bare of comment and full of conversational blind alleys and non sequiturs. It is through alternating these two styles that Čingo avoids either monotony or overt subversiveness in his treatment of social classes.

Čingo's plays, of which the last three—*Rabotnici* (Workers), *Pod otvoreno nebo* (Under Clear Skies), and *Surati*—have not yet been produced, represent his engagé texts; they are vivisections of contemporary people and of the social life in which they are bound to live. There is genuine artistic courage in Čingo's plays, which speak of truth and wisdom, of the human talent for prophetic visions, and of nightmarish reactions that destroy health and shorten life. Against the demonic power of destruction, Čingo raises his voice in the name of human dignity.

Bibliography:
Haralampije Polenaković, "Živko Čingo," in *Leksikon pisaca Jugoslavije,* volume 1 (Novi Sad: Matica srpska, 1972), pp. 496–497.

References:
Petar T. Boškovski, *Ogledi i kritiki* (Skopje: Misla, 1978);

Miodrag Drugovac, *Povoeni makedonski pisateli,* volume 2 (Skopje: Naša kniga, 1986);

Drugovac, "Živko Čingo," in his *Contemporary Macedonian Writers* (Skopje: Macedonian Review, 1976), pp. 173–181;

Hristo Georgievski, *Poetikata na makedonskiot raskaz* (Skopje: Misla, 1985);

Milan Gjurčinov, *Makedonski pisateli* (Skopje: Misla, 1969);

Gjurčinov, *Opredeluvanja* (Skopje: Kultura, 1969);

Gjurčinov, *Sovremena makedonska kniževnost* (Skopje: Misla, 1983);

Vera Janeva, *Metafora na otugjuvanjeto* (Skopje: Makedonska kniga, 1982);

Makedonska kniževnost vo Kniževnata kritika, volume 5 (Skopje: Misla, 1974)—includes studies by Gjurčinov, Boškovski, and Vlada Urošević;

Slobodan Micković, *Tolkuvanja* (Skopje: Misla, 1973);

Micković, *Vreme na pesnata* (Skopje: Naša kniga, 1983);

Micković, *Zbor i razbor: Poetikata na Živko Čingo* (Skopje: Naša kniga, 1990);

Dimitar Mitrev, *Ogledi i kritiki,* volume 3 (Skopje: Naša kniga, 1970);

Vele Smilevski, ed., *Makedonskiot raskaz* (Skopje: Makedonska kniga, 1990)—includes studies by Micković, Georgi Stardelov, and Urošević;

Georgi Stardelov, *Megju literaturata i život* (Skopje: Kultura, 1981);

Vlada Urošević, *Mrež za neulovivoto* (Skopje: Makedonska kniga, 1980);

Urošević, *Vrsnici* (Skopje: Misla, 1971);

Živko Čingo: Obid za budenje (Skopje: Misla, 1982)—includes studies by Gjurčinov, Micković, Milošević, Boškovski, and Urošević.

Branko Ćopić
(1 January 1915 - 26 March 1984)

Nicholas Moravcevich
University of Illinois at Chicago

BOOKS: *Pod Grmečom* (Belgrade: Geca Kon, 1938);

Borci i bjegunci (Belgrade: Geca Kon, 1939);

U carstvu leptirova i medveda (Belgrade: Geca Kon, 1939);

Planinci (Belgrade: Srpska književna zadruga, 1940);

Ognjeno radjanje domovine (Slobodna teritorija Hrvatske: Mi mladi, 1944);

Priče partizanke (Sarajevo: Riječ antifašističke omladine Bosne i Hercegovine, 1944);

Pjesme pionirke (Zagreb: Prosvjeta, 1945);

Bojna lira pionira (Zagreb: Prosvjeta, 1945);

Rosa na bajonetima (Zagreb: Prosvjeta, 1946);

Sveti magarac (Belgrade: Jež, 1946);

Ratnikovo proljeće (Belgrade & Zagreb: Novo pokoljenje, 1947);

Vratolomne priče (Zagreb: Novo pokoljenje, 1947);

Surova škola (Belgrade: Novo pokoljenje, 1948);

Armija odbrana tvoja (Belgrade: Prosveta, 1948);

Ljudi s repom (Belgrade: Savez udruženja novinara, 1949);

Ježeva kuća (Belgrade: Novo pokoljenje, 1949);

Prolom (Belgrade: Prosveta, 1952);

Ljubav i smrt (Belgrade: Srpska književna zadruga, 1953);

Priče ispod zmajevih krila (Belgrade: Dečja štampa, 1953);

Doživljaji mačka Toše (Belgrade: Dečja knjiga, 1954);

Doživljaji Nikoletine Bursaća (Sarajevo: Svjetlost, 1956);

Gluvi barut (Belgrade: Prosveta, 1957);

Orlovi rano lete (Sarajevo: Narodna prosveta, 1957);

Ne tuguj, bronzana stražo (Sarajevo: Svjetlost, 1958);

Gorki med (Belgrade: Srpska književna zadruga, 1959);

Deda Trišin mlin (Sarajevo: Veselin Masleša, 1960);

Magareće godine (Sarajevo: Veselin Masleša, 1960);

Slavno vojevanje (Sarajevo: Veselin Masleša, 1961);

Branko Ćopić

Bitka u zlatnoj dolini (Sarajevo: Veselin Masleša, 1963);

Stihovi (Rijeka: Otokar Keršovani, 1963);

Osma ofanziva (Belgrade: Prosveta, 1964);

Bašta sljezove boje (Belgrade: Srpska književna zadruga, 1970);

Delije na Bihaću (Sarajevo: Svjetlost, 1975);

12.xii.1939. uveče (Belgrade: BIGZ, 1994).

Collections: *Odabrana djela Branka Ćopića,* 6 volumes (Rijeka: Otokar Keršovani, 1964);

Sabrana djela, 12 volumes (Belgrade & Sarajevo: Prosveta, Svjetlost and Veselin Masleša, 1964);

Sabrana dela Branka Ćopića, 14 volumes, jubilee edition (Belgrade & Sarajevo: Prosveta, Svjetlost, Veselin Masleša, 1978).

Editions in English: "An Awkward Companion," translated by Vida Janković, in *Death* *of a Simple Giant and Other Stories,* edited by Branko Lenski (New York: Vanguard, 1965), pp. 17–22;

"The Bearleader's Last Journey," translated and edited by Svetozar Koljević, in *Yugoslav Short Stories* (London: Oxford University Press, 1966), pp. 342–353;

"Love and Jealousy," translated by Donald Davenport, *Literary Review,* 11, no. 2 (1967/1968): 187–192;

"Cruel Heart," translated by Branko Mikasinovich, in *Introduction to Yugoslav Literature,* edited by Mikasinovich, Vasa D. Mihailovich, and Dragan Milivojevich (New York: Twayne, 1973), pp. 240–246;

"The Election of Comrade Sokrat," translated by Branko Mikasinovich, in *Modern Yugoslav Satire,* edited by Mikasinovich (Merrick, N.Y.: Cross-Cultural Communication, 1979), pp. 44–48;

"The Gypsies Turned to Stone," translated by Mihailovich; thirteen poems, translated by William Tribe, *Books in Bosnia and Herzegovina,* 4, no. 6 (1985): 393–409.

A poet, short-story writer, novelist, and prolific writer of children's books, Branko Ćopić is one of the most diverse and most popular Serbian authors of the post–World War II period. Thematically, he is a distinct regionalist, for his native Bosnian Krajina is the favorite locale of his prose, a terra firma that he leaves only to follow his sturdy peasant countrymen on their disparate wartime and postwar migrations and resettlements. Yet, his authorial message is universal and enlivened with profound truths about the tenor of life in his native land both during the wartime popular struggle for survival and the postwar social upheavals engendered by the country's rapid socialization.

Ćopić was born on 1 January 1915 into a peasant family in the hamlet of Hašani in western Bosnia. Having completed grade school in his native village and his secondary-school education in Bihać, Banja Luka, Sarajevo, and Karlovci, he attended the University of Belgrade, graduating from its Faculty of Philosophy in 1940. The following year Yugoslavia was drawn into World War II. After the country's speedy collapse and dismemberment by the Axis powers, Ćopić, then a young leftist intellectual, joined the popular uprising in the Bosnian Krajina that eventually became the communist-led partisan resistance movement. He remained in the partisan forces to the end of the war, working first as a political commissar of the combat detachment of the Podgrmeč region, later in the cultural and propaganda sphere of the partisan resistance, and finally as a correspondent for various Communist publications, including the party's official newspaper *Borba* (Struggle). In the early postwar period he was the chief editor of the youth paper *Pionir* (Pioneer) (1944–1949); during the remaining years of his life, until his death on 26 March 1984, he lived and worked in Belgrade as a professional writer.

In 1928, while still in secondary school, Ćopić wrote a short prose composition under the pseudonym "Braco," and it was published in the periodical *Venac* (Wreath). His first short story, signed with his own name and titled "Smrtno ruvo Soje Čubrilove" (Burial Clothing of Soja Čubrilova), appeared in 1936 in the literary supplement of the newspaper *Politika.* His later work was printed in almost all the important Yugoslav literary papers and periodicals, but the newspaper *Politika* remained his true literary home.

In the initial prewar period of his literary activities, Ćopić's most important works were his three collections of short stories, *Pod Grmečom* (Under the Grmeč Mountain, 1938), *Borci i bjegunci* (Fighters and Fugitives, 1939), and *Planinci* (The Mountaineers, 1940). In these three collections Ćopić describes the routine and the vicissitudes of poor rural life in his native Krajina region. Its population, known for its hardy individualism, feistiness, and tenacity, was split into three faiths—Eastern Orthodox, Muslim, and Roman Catholic—and condemned to a perpetually uneasy coexistence exacerbated by centuries of mutual intolerance and mistrust. Atmospherically these stories from village life have much in common with the manner in which the dreary human existence in this same region was depicted fifty years earlier by Petar Kočić.

But Ćopić is more lyrical than his illustrious predecessor; his peasants are more oppressed by the monotony and loneliness of their rural semiwilderness than Kočić's; thus, they tend to be passive dreamers who bear their ordeals with a meekness and sorrow unknown by Kočić's tempestuous, testy mountaineers. For that reason all Ćopić's stories from these collections, despite the wide variety of themes and subjects they introduce, are similar in tone and composition. In all of them destiny places an immeasurably heavy load on their subjects, and the central character, whether a boy, vagrant, church deacon, conjurer, or ordinary peasant, usually fervently yearns to run away to become someone grander or different. However, hopelessly blocked by the cruelty of destiny and his abject poverty, he remains where he is, forever pinned down, disgruntled, and unhappy. Though Ćopić depicts such characters with an almost childlike tenderness and is full of empathy and sorrow for their intractable condition, he offers them no relief at the end, except through an occasional whiff of gentle humor that alleviates some of the darkest hues of their demise.

As a partisan during World War II, Ćopić abruptly replaces his prewar lyrical tenderness and soulfully passive empathy for his poor, rural compatriots with an energetic and essentially epic glorification of the individual and collective effort in the great popular struggle against the invaders and their local minions. His wartime poetry from the collection *Ognjeno radjanje domovine* (Fiery Birth of the Homeland, 1944) breathes with the vitality and folkloric simplicity of the old Serbian popular oral poetry, on the one hand, and the defiance and polemical fervor of the poetic tirades of the Soviet futurists, on the other. While the poetry in this collection occasionally suffers from ideologically motivated outbursts of pathos, the two poems "Pjesma mrtvih proletera" (Song of the Fallen Proletarians) and "Grob u žitu" (A Grave in the Wheat Field) are notable for their exceptional blend of lyric and epic motifs and their profound sincerity and directness of expression.

In his collection of verse *Ratnikovo proljeće* (Warrior's Spring, 1947), Ćopić finds himself in the new age of his country's postwar recovery, in which he is an enthusiastic and active participant: with an exceptionally mellow lyricism he recollects the horrendous costs of the struggle for liberation and vows his and the younger generation's resolve to remain worthy of those whose supreme wartime sacrifices made the new beginnings possible.

In the early postwar period much of Ćopić's creative energy and fervor went into his collections of poetry and prose for children, a domain in which he stands supreme among his contemporaries. His interest in literature for children started in the prewar period with his collection of stories *U carstvu leptirova i medveda* (In the Kingdom of Butterflies and Bears, 1939), in which the world of the Bosnian forest comes alive with plants, animals, birds, and fishes shepherded by the forces of nature in an idyllic domain of sun-drenched tranquillity and peace. All Ćopić's heroes in this book speak a common language and coexist in perfect harmony, which the author presents with a childlike spontaneity and a complete absence of didacticism. The intensity of the war experiences, however, compels him to change his manner of addressing his young audience. Having witnessed the struggle and shared the sufferings of both old and young in the vortex of war, he introduces stories about the war in his works intended for children, and he develops a different attitude toward young readers. Now he addresses children as equals and includes them as such in all sorts of wartime activities pursued by their elders. They undertake their responsibilities in the popular uprising with exemplary enthusiasm and bravery, and the enormity of their trust in the righteousness of the sacred cause of liberation is all the more poignant because it emanates from the depths of their naive idealism. Ćopić endows the valiant deeds of his child-heroes with all the heroic attributes given the exploits presented in legends and fairy tales, so that the young heroes will serve as examples of the purest patriotism for his young readers. In these works partisan fighters and the peasants who help them are imbued with the most noble traits imaginable, while the invaders and their minions are painted in the darkest colors of perfidy and inhumanity. Thus, the contemporary historical truths are simplified and most often conveyed in the style of a fairy tale or fable.

In his postwar prose and verse for children on themes other than the war, Ćopić did not limit himself to subjects with realistic content. Yet, despite a wide range of subjects treated and the author's considerable skill in versification and storytelling, many of these works, particularly those about the peacetime economic recovery and childrens' everyday lives at home or school, suffer from their propagandistic underlining of socialist values and aspirations. Such heavy-handedness appears, for example, in the verse collection *Armija odbrana tvoja* (The Army, Your Defense, 1948), in which the agitprop intent far outstrips artistic value. An exception is the verse collection of forest fables, *Ježeva kuća* (Porcupine's House, 1949), in which Ćopić returns to nature to introduce children to a great assembly of forest dwellers from the animal and plant worlds. In contrast to his prewar emphasis on harmony in such a milieu, Ćopić now presents a more balanced view of the natural inhabitants by endowing them with a whole scale of human characteristics that at times produces considerable discord. The undisputed hero of this domain is the porcupine Ježurka Ježić, who wins the reader's sympathy by his unshakable integrity and touching love for his home. Simplicity in the plot and character development of these fables assures that the intended allegorical meanings are inescapable and that the young reader's imagination is given free rein.

Though Ćopić's poetry and prose works for

children are extremely heterogeneous in their themes and form, all are imbued with his aim to enrich the realities of life, replete with hard and unpleasant things, with the hopes and desires engendered by the imagination. Thus the commonplace hardships that can embitter childhood are to some extent softened in these pieces by the hope that the future will bring more joy and satisfaction. Moreover, Ćopić's prose and verses for children are endowed with a special sense of humor that depends not so much on the comical situations that show human shortcomings and faults as it does on the sheer cheerfulness with which the writer perceives commonplace human reality. His steady good cheer and optimism win young readers over by appealing to their natural joy in life and laughter. Only in some instances, largely in the stories and poems set in wartime, when he desires to indoctrinate his young readers about the character of the wartime enemy, does the writer turn to mockery, derision, and jeering that is aimed at the defects or inhumanity of the enemy. Since the real-life examples of contemptible behavior were plentiful during World War II, some of Ćopić's portraits of enemies may certainly be justified, but his occasional tendency to exaggerate lessens the overall artistic value of such pieces.

Ćopić's earliest attempt to create a long prose work for adult readers was his novel *Prolom* (Breakthrough, 1952), in which he shows his native region in the flames of the popular uprising against the invaders and their native-born puppets. Conceived in the epic manner of Leo Tolstoy and Mikhail Aleksandrovich Sholokhov, this work is structurally divided into three parts. The first concentrates on the early days of the uprising, when the establishment of the Croat fascist regime under German occupation unleashes a reign of terror against the largely peaceful Serbian population of rural Podgorina, provoking the wrath of these people. The second delineates the ideological segmentation of that struggle into the nationalist- and communist-led insurrectionist factions, which eventually leads to the vicious civil war between the *Chetniks* and the partisans. The third part of *Prolom* depicts the sufferings and growth of the Communist-led insurrectionist forces that eventually dominate the region and convert their initial uprising into a full-fledged revolutionary struggle that aims at the complete change of the country's prewar social and political order.

Although the broad masses of the brutally mistreated Serbian rural population in the territory of the Croatian fascist state are the real, collective hero of this panorama of the revolutionary struggle, their most finely delineated representative is Todor Bokan, a hardy young man from a village. Caught in the vortex of the wartime atrocities, Todor at first rebels because of his sheer survival instinct but later matures into a conscious revolutionary fighter, one who, by overcoming his sense of isolation and loneliness, not only becomes comfortable in the mass liberation movement but in fact becomes ready to lead it. Thus, the spiritual transformation of the young Todor parallels the structural flow of the novel's action and the author's underlying political message.

Ćopić's next major prose work is the short-story collection *Doživljaji Nikoletine Bursaća* (Adventures of Nikoletina Bursać, 1956), in which the thematic unity is provided by the personality of the hero, Nikoletina. He is shown to be physically strong but kind-hearted, epically brave but somewhat awkward, and verbally curt but emotionally pure and extremely stable. He is a young peasant from Krajina who, through his participation in the partisan-led popular uprising, grows both as a person and as an ideologically enlightened individual. Together with his assistant and sidekick, Jovica Jež, Nikoletina, who is at first the detachment's valiant machine gunner, later a squad and platoon leader, and finally the company commander, heroically endures the countless peripeties of the guerrilla war, emerging from each crisis stronger and more dedicated. His final brave sacrifice of his life in the liberation struggle gradually transforms him into a legendary figure who continues to inspire those whose duty is to complete the great task of liberation and the rebuilding of a better life. Both the epic and the ideological elements in Nikoletina's portrait are enriched by a strong element of humor that softens both these elements and makes Nikoletina a more appealing character. Ćopić's emphasis on the elemental optimism and cheerfulness in Nikoletina's personality makes these stories appealing to adolescents as well.

The novel *Gluvi barut* (Deaf Gunpowder, 1957) is a thematic, compositional, and chronological sequel to *Prolom*. Its subject is also the popular uprising in Krajina, but the added dimension, in which lies the essence of the author's intent, is the depiction of the conflicting tendencies within the leadership of the partisan movement and the eventual popular rejection of the radical revolutionary strategies and tactics used by some communist leaders in an attempt to convert the popular liberation struggle into a full-fledged communist revolution. The conflict in this work is provided by juxtaposing the different conceptions of the revolutionary struggle and dramatizing the results of different practices. Three leading characters of the novel, the commander of the partisan detachment, Tigar, his political commissar, Vlado, and the commander's deputy, Captain Radekić, represent those different ideological positions. Their profound differences in handling both the armed struggle and the populace within the partisan-controlled territory emanate from their divergent ideological stances, their social background, and their individual psychological profiles. The detachment commander, Tigar, is a seasoned fighter who has been tempered by his prewar communist activities and his participation in the Spanish Civil War. His character traits of fearlessness, boundless energy, and abiding love for his comrades, set side by side with his cutting cruelty and hatred toward all enemies of the revolution, are the result of his lifelong psychological striving to compensate for his small stature and his frailty as a child. He is a dogmatist stamped by the internationalism rooted in his Spanish experiences. This actually harms him when he has to promote revolution in a struggle carried out almost entirely by the ideologically undeveloped masses of poor peasants, with whom he has nothing in common. Equally dogmatic, but for different reasons, is his political commissar, Vlado, a young student full of bookish revolutionary ideas and overwhelmed by personal vanity. His desperate attempts to emulate Tigar turn him into a caricature of a revolutionary and, through his brutal deeds, even into a destroyer of the revolution.

Opposed to these two is Radekić, a native of the region who, by great personal effort, became an officer in the prewar royal army, though he was never quite accepted as an equal because of his peasant origins. Nonetheless, the army service gave him valuable military experience, and his social background provides him with a visceral knowledge of the local peasantry; it inspires their trust as well. He, too, has accepted the communist ideology, but he has no pre-tailored models; moreover, he has the practical awareness that he must work patiently with the rural masses to help them understand concepts broader than that of the armed defense of their homes and villages. Representing the idea of a more relaxed and humanistically sensitive path to the revolution, Radekić is the true representative of the author's point of view in this novel because he is a partisan leader who, by adapting to the specific realities of the local struggle, can at the same time lead the masses of peasants in battle and help them overcome their ideological limitations without alienating them.

The third human component in this novel is that of the rural masses whom the revolutionaries try to convert to their ideas but who stubbornly hold to their tribalism, religious traditions, and ancestral prejudices. This amorphous mass of people could be either cruel or magnificent because it carried both the light of change and the darkness of inertia, and it is a representative of the dark forces within those aggrieved masses who, at the end of the novel, kills Tigar just when he has perceived the extent of his mistakes and resolved to correct them. But behind him remains his child, born after his wartime love affair with the beautiful, tender, and wanderlust-touched young woman named Janja. Thus the novel's additional message appears to be that love is the rectifier of cruel wartime dogmatism and the only real redeemer of a person's death.

Ćopić downplays some of the ideological content of the novel by the humor that is produced, mainly by the exploits of the two sly peasant idlers, Jovandeka Babić and Stanko Veselica; by plundering, these two always find ways, even in the most difficult wartime situations, to reap some small benefits for themselves. These two characters are the heroes of Ćopić's next novel, *Ne tuguj, bronzana stražo* (Don't Grieve, You Bronze Sentry, 1958), which depicts, in a succession of short sketches, the postwar life of the Krajina settlers in the rich lowlands of Banat, on the lands that before the war belonged to the ethnic Germans who have now been expelled from the country because of their collaboration with the German occupiers. The work is again imbued with Ćopićian humor: occasionally ironic, often good-natured, but mostly lyrical and mellowly sad. Indirectly the novel has a serious dimension as well, but the main authorial tendency is to overlay with humor both the situations and the characters of this new peacetime phase of the country's revolutionary ferment. The action of the novel flows horizontally rather than in depth. Reality is stylized and both comically and poetically elevated so that its rough and cruel basis is hardly felt. The Krajina settlers rename their new village Bursaćevo after their already legendary wartime hero, Nikoletina Bursać, and they erect a bronze monument to him. Placed in the center of the village, it stands as an enduring warning against the small peacetime betrayals of their traditional, epic way of life. As a symbol of their hardy, warrior past and of ascetic faithfulness to the ideals of liberation, the monument also glaringly contrasts with the villagers' soft beddings and their tendency to be idle or to indulge in petty affairs. At the same time, its presence stimulates their nostalgia for their mountains and a less complicated former life that is gone forever. This novel is notably less realistic than Ćopić's earlier ones; the potential seriousness of its theme is diluted by its thick overlay of humor and lyricism. At its conclusion it appears that even the long-gone Nikoletina Bursać may reappear; the rumor has spread that he has somehow survived the war and is searching for his elderly mother. But this rumor is left unconfirmed, and Ćopić ends his chronicle of the settlers' life on an optimistic note that is justifiable only in a fairy tale.

The problem of adjustment is also the theme of Ćopić's next novel. However, in this work, *Osma ofanziva* (The Eighth Offensive, 1964), the authorial scrutiny is not upon the poor Krajina mountaineers resettled on the fertile fields of Banat but upon their more distinguished brothers whom the partisans' victory had brought onto the streets of the nation's capital, Belgrade. Having advanced during the war as ardent fighters, the heroes of this cluster of Ćopić's stories are now peacetime functionaries of the new regime. What keeps them in touch with one another is that all of them are from the same Krajina village, and thus can share their nostalgia for their ancestral rural roots, which the drab reality of their new urban existence and their innate unsuitability for bureaucratic life and tasks magnify into a dream of paradise lost. They are the pyrrhic victors who in various ways are realizing that they are actually victims of their own success. Formally, this work resembles Ćopić's earlier, thematically united story collections. Offering many sketches in which a cluster of characters (such as Stojan Starčević, Pepo Bandić, Dragija Dragan, and Djeja Starčević) suffer through their personality crises, Ćopić describes their predicaments with a mixture of realistic, humorous, lyrical, and satiric details.

Ćopić's satiric stance toward the postwar communist bureaucracy in this work hearkens back to earlier attempts in his writing to define some of the new problems of the Yugoslav postwar socialist society. For example, in a satiric sketch, "Jeretička priča," published in 1950, he introduced the theme of the estrangement of the country's new socialist elite from the masses. That well-meaning sketch, criticized by many Communist Party leaders soon after its publication, led to severe party reprimands of Ćopić and eventually to his expulsion from the League of Communists. Although at first he held his own and continued to write according to his own conscience, his ideological clash with the party gradually worsened despite his popularity as a writer both at home and abroad. His personal dismay about this clash was enormous. It resulted, by the mid 1970s, in his chronic depression, his nervous breakdown, and a series of mostly unsuccessful treatments in psychiatric hospitals.

However, before Ćopić's mental health deteriorated, he produced two more significant works. The first was a collection of stories, *Bašta sljezove boje* (Garden of Mallow Color, 1970), in which he assembled a cluster of autobiographical tales about his family and people from his native region during the years from World War I to the end of the 1960s. In these lyrical and humorous pieces the picture of a special world emerges, one in which the author's ability to conjure up the naive wonder of childlike visions of reality is intertwined with his skill in drawing upon the philosophical syntheses produced by the wisdom of old age. The stories, in which the flowering colors of the medicinal mallow plant assume symbolic significance, present a broad panoply of rural life in which the harshness of the commonplace reality is constantly tempered by the lyrical and fairy-tale meanderings of the narrator's imagination and mellow humor.

Ćopić's last important work, the novel *Delije na Bihaću* (Heroes in the Assault on Bihać, 1975), is his attempt to dress even the realities of wartime in the mantle of a lyrical fairy tale, replete with comedic tones. The unifying element in this collection of stories is the partisan siege and taking of the town of Bihać, which the author uses as a locus for the resurrection of a multitude of characters from his earlier works. By mixing real historical personages with literary characters, Ćopić gave this book the qualities of both a legend and a humorous folktale in which everything exists simultaneously on both a mimetically real and fantastically unreal level. Amid the heat and thunder of the battle, his swashbuckling partisan heroes act with an indestructible reserve of optimism and humor. Their enemies are like marionettes that fight and fall with an almost predestined certainty, and what destroys them is not so much the shells and bullets of the valiant attackers as it is the buoyancy of spirit and the humorous ease with which the attackers manifest their spiritual superiority, drawn from the great ideal of the revolution triumphant, over their opponents.

After the publication of *Delije na Bihaću*, Ćopić's already-fragile mental condition worsened, and he had to be hospitalized. The psychiatric treatments at first brought some improvements, but these were followed by deeper and more lasting depressions during which he refused even to speak. In March 1984, while convalescing at his home, he left his apartment ostensibly to take a stroll through Belgrade; instead, he went to the Sava River bridge, from which he jumped to his death.

Although Ćopić lived and wrote in an era of enormous political and literary upheavals in his country, he always championed a down-to-earth, commonplace realism, sometimes tempered by humor and lyricism and sometimes by satire and wit. Initially an idealistic believer in the righteousness of the communist cause, he gradually became one of the leading literary dissidents of his generation when he perceived the extent of the postwar betrayal of those egalitarian ideals that led his simple, sturdy Krajina peasants to become the heroes of the liberation and reconstruction struggle. The profundity of his realism and his innate understanding of the common man (which made him the nation's most popular author of his time) are equally appreciated today. Even more appreciated by both the contemporary literary establishment and the reading public is his brave criticism of the crude excesses of the postwar communist order. Its total moral and material collapse less than a decade after Ćopić's suicide is the best proof that he, both as a writer and as a person, was a visionary.

Interview:

Branko Letić, "Knjige pišem u jednom dahu: Razgovor s Brankom Ćopićem," *Književnost*, 66, no. 9 (1978): 1545-1554.

Bibliographies:

B. Novaković and Ž. P. Jovanović, "Ćopić, Branko," in *Leksikon pisaca Jugoslavije*, volume 1 (Novi Sad: Matica Srpska, 1972), pp. 528-536;

Voja Marjanović, "Branko Ćopić: A Bio-Bibliography," *Books in Bosnia and Herzegovina*, 4, no. 6 (1985): 413-414.

References:

Miloš I. Bandić, "Tužna i vedra pričanja od srca srcu o miru i o ratu: Pripovedanje Branka Ćopića," *Književnost*, 24, no. 1 (1957): 67-74;

Milovan Danojlić, "Glas iz detinjstva," *Letopis matice srpske*, no. 6 (1971): 661-673;

Nikola Disopra, "Smijeh mitraljesca golubijeg srca," *Mogućnost*, no. 9 (1956): 697-702;

Djuro Gavela, "Jedan darovit mlad pripovedač," *Politika*, 26 May 1938, p. 14;

Zoran Gavrilović, "Prolom," *Revija*, 1 (11 December 1952), p. 12;

Velibor Gligorić, "Branko Ćopić," in his *Ogledi i studije* (Belgrade: Prosveta, 1959), pp. 269-270;

Gligorić, "Seljaci u revoluciji," *Savremenik*, 7, no. 1 (1958): 89-94;

Muris Idrizović, ed., *Kritičari o Ćopiću* (Sarajevo: Svjetlost, 1981);

Jovan Jakšić, *Drugovanje sa Brankom Ćopićem* (Belgrade: Književni klub "Branko Ćopić," 1994);

Dragan Jeremić, "Poslednji čin revolucije," *Borba*, 24, no. 5 (1964): 10;

Jeremić, "Veliko detinjstvo Branka Ćopića," *Politika*, 5, no. 1 (1974);

Raško Jovanović, "Branko Ćopić, *Osma ofanziva*," *Književnost*, 9, no. 9 (1964): 225-228;

Vuk Krnjević, "A Narrator of the Collective Soul," *Books in Bosnia and Herzegovina*, 4, no. 6 (1985): 391-392;

Skender Kulenović, "Prijateljstvo poezije i poezija prijateljstva," introduction to Ćopić's *Stihovi* (Rijeka: Otokar Keršovani, 1963);

Slavko Leovac, *Branko Ćopić, svetlo i tamno* (Sarajevo: Džepna knjiga, 1957);

Vojislav Marjanović, *Pripovedačka proza Branka Ćopića* (Sarajevo: Svjetlost, 1982);

Russell McCaskie, "The Writer under Socialism: Branko Ćopić's Heresy," *Australian Slavonic and East European Studies*, 2, no. 2 (1988): 111-133;

Borisav Mihajlović-Mihiz, "Branko Ćopić u *Bašti sljezove boje*," in his *Književni razgovori* (Belgrade: Srpska književna zadruga, 1971), pp. 130-140;

Milosav Mirković, "Ćopićev sunčani svet," *Književne novine*, 18, no. 10 (1957): 6;

Dragoslav Nikolić-Micki, "Branko Ćopić: The Tragic Lyre of Mirth," *Review*, no. 1 (1974): 38-39;

Boško Novaković, "Prvi roman Branka Ćopića," *Letopis matice srpske*, 371 (1953): 362-371;

Sima Pandurović, "Mladi pesnik i pripovedač Bosne," *Politika*, 1, no. 7 (1939): 8;

Borisav Pavić, "Branko Ćopić: Ježeva kuća," *Književnost*, 10, no. 5 (1950): 502-504;

Vlastimir Petković, "Branko Ćopić, *Bašta sljezove boje*," *Književnost*, 52, no. 5 (1970): 487-488;

Vlado Popović, "Poezija Branka Ćopića," *Republika*, 4, no. 10 (1948): 883-889.

Dobrica Ćosić
(29 December 1921 -)

Vasa D. Mihailovich
University of North Carolina

BOOKS: *Daleko je sunce* (Belgrade: Prosveta, 1951);

Koreni (Belgrade: Prosveta, 1954);

Deobe, 3 volumes (Belgrade: Prosveta, 1961);

Bajka (Belgrade: Prosveta, 1966);

Vreme smrti, 4 volumes (Belgrade: Prosveta, 1972-1979);

Vreme zla, 3 volumes *(Grešnik, Otpadnik,* and *Vernik)* (Belgrade: BIGZ, 1985-1990);

Vreme vlasti, volume 1 (Belgrade: BIGZ, 1996).

Editions in English: *Far Away Is the Sun,* translated by Muriel Heppell and Milica Mihajlovic (Belgrade: Jugoslavija, 1963);

Into the Battle, translated by Heppell (New York: Harcourt Brace Jovanovich, 1978);

A Time of Death, translated by Heppell (New York: Harcourt Brace Jovanovich, 1978);

Reach to Eternity, translated by Heppell (New York: Harcourt Brace Jovanovich, 1980);

South to Destiny, translated by Heppell (New York: Harcourt Brace Jovanovich, 1981).

OTHER: *Sedam dana u Budimpešti* (Belgrade: Borba, 1957);

Akcija (Belgrade: Prosveta, 1964);

Moć i strepnje (Belgrade, n.p., 1971);

Stvarno i moguće (Rijeka: Otokar Keršovani, 1983);

Srpsko pitanje–demokratsko pitanje (Belgrade: NIN, 1992).

Dobrica Ćosić

Dobrica Ćosić is primarily a novelist, although he has also written political essays. Throughout his literary career he has been fascinated by the forces that have molded, influenced, and decided the fate of his countrymen in the Serbian state of the former Yugoslavia. In particular, he has attempted to show the effect that two world wars have had on his native land. Because Ćosić has always been politically oriented, it was natural for him to turn to historical and social themes once he discovered his artistic bent. He was one of the first postwar novelists in Yugoslavia to broach sensitive subject matter, not so much by describing such subjects as by finding the real motives behind the actors and their actions in a period of tragic events. From World War II, in which he directly participated, he moved back to World War I, searching for the links between them. By tracing the rise and fall of two families who appear in almost all of his novels, he presents a powerful saga of Serbian society in its passing from a primitive stage of development in the late nineteenth century into the modern era. A pronounced artistic acumen has added a mark of excellence to his works. Ćosić's articles on sociopolitical themes express his views on various ideological, political, and cultural problems that have preoccupied him his entire adult life. They shed some light on his novels as well, but, for the most part, these essays reflect preoccupations that are mainly outside the subjects of his novels.

Ćosić was born on 29 December 1921 in Velika Drenova, a village in central Serbia. While he was attending an agricultural school, he was exposed to socialist literature; his acceptance into the Communist Youth League in 1938 led to his expulsion from school. In World War II he participated on the side of the partisans as a political commissar. After the war he held several official positions, becoming a member of the parliament and a director of the venerable *Srpska književna zadruga* (Serbian Literary Society). With the publication of his first novel, *Daleko je sunce* (1951; translated as *Far Away Is the Sun*, 1963), he moved to the front rank of young Serbian writers. His fame grew with every new novel, as did his dissatisfaction with political developments in his country. He began to call for more freedom, became a leading dissident, and as a consequence was stripped of all his posts and duties. Thereafter, he worked as a freelance writer while leading the fight for greater democratic freedom. In 1991 he was elected president of the restructured state of Yugoslavia, but was soon outmaneuvered by his former communist comrades and ousted from his post. He continues to write as a private citizen.

Ćosić emerged from the war as a proud victor, full of hopes for a better future and ready for further sacrifices. This desire to help in building a better life for his fellow human beings undoubtedly spurred him to his first literary efforts. As he grew as a writer, however, another desire became even stronger—to tell the truth in an artistic fashion, regardless of consequences. *Daleko je sunce,* although based on actual events and largely autobiographical, is a skillfully written war novel with a fast-moving plot, believable action, and well-developed characters. Its refreshing quality is reflected in its objectivity, a feature unusual in history written by victors. To be sure, the partisan struggle is still glorified; the leading characters at times display the superhuman powers and the instinctive ability to separate right from wrong that are characteristic of socialist realist heroes; and the enemy is all evil. However, there is also a willingness to admit that heroes may sometimes be wrong. By taking such an attitude, the author shows his awareness of the complexity of the situations in which the warring sides often found themselves. He also appears willing to admit that, even though the correctness of the partisan cause was never in doubt, individual actions and decisions were not always above reproach. The novel's restrained tone and traditional realistic manner, as well as its originality, are features that made *Daleko je sunce* a popular success when it appeared.

Ćosić's second novel, *Koreni* (Roots, 1954), begins a series of novels that present the development of Serbian society in the twentieth century. The story in *Koreni* goes back to the last decade of the nineteenth century. The main character, a strong-willed, rebellious, and stubborn peasant, Aćim Katić, is driven by his often-expressed desire to see the creation of a just, democratic society among the Serbian peasants, who for centuries had been ruled mainly by their primitive impulses. Accordingly, he sends his younger son to be educated in France. When his son refuses to return to his native village upon graduation and joins a political party that opposes his father's, the true nature of Aćim Katić is revealed. Deeply hurt by his son's betrayal, he manifests in his grief and anger a frustrated will to dominate everyone and everything around him, as well as his hidden fear of defeat by both men and fate. He marries his sterile older son to a strong peasant woman and arranges for her to produce a child with the help of a virile neighbor. At the end of the novel the powerfully created characters and their destinies remain uncertain, to be taken up again in later works. Ćosić tells this stark peasant tale in a highly lyrical and experimental style that fits the dark, naturalistic atmosphere of the life of Serbian peasants at the turn of the century. This departure from the rather simple realism of the first novel reveals not only his preoccupation with social and political matters but also his search for a truly artistic idiom, a search that has been apparent throughout his work.

With *Deobe* (Divisions, 1961), Ćosić resumes his exploration of a mode of human behavior that has fascinated him from the beginning—war. Returning to the period of World War II, he takes up many themes he had explored earlier in *Daleko je sunce*: bravery under the most trying conditions; the struggle of a small nation against an overpowering enemy; the bearing of the brunt of that struggle by peasants who are reluctant to fight away from their homes; the corruption of the existing order; and the weaknesses and the sins of the enemy. But while in the former novel the war struggle is seen from the vantage point of the partisans, in *Deobe* the point of view shifts to the opposing side, the *Chetniks,* a nationalist force that is fighting both the Germans and the partisans. The *Chetniks'* point of view is used mainly to discredit them. In this sense *Deobe* is much less objective than any other novel by Ćosić. The *Chetniks* are maligned while the partisans, seen only in the distant background, show their moral superiority. Ćosić's subjectivity, however, can be explained by his desire to understand why the *Chetniks* committed the cruel acts attributed to them and whether they could have behaved differently. The author grapples with other questions: Why do human beings commit bestial acts of horror? Why is hatred so deep that it destroys reason? Can the descendants of those same people comprehend and believe many years later that such acts were, and even could be, committed by humans? Thus, the aim of the author in this novel is not the objective depiction of the civil war, but rather the attempt to penetrate the way of thinking of the people responsible for war. Seen from this angle *Deobe* attains, despite its shortcomings, a more universal significance than that perceived on a first reading.

Unfortunately Ćosić offers few satisfactory answers. As the war drags on and the inhumanity intensifies to alarming proportions, he becomes more philosophical about the issues. He is convinced that war leads to utter demoralization, total chaos, and despair. Everybody feels compelled to fight everybody else; hatred permeates everything; and all are killers. The eye-for-an-eye principle becomes dominant. Even though Ćosić attributes most of these aberrations to the enemies of the partisans, the realization grows that more is involved than the struggle for social, political, and ideological causes and a better future. On the one hand, the war has moved inward into the hearts and souls of the participants. On the other, the signs of people's resignation and helplessness are increasingly visible in statements such as, "It's war.... We are guilty because we are humans and because we are alive." There is even a hint that war is a total mystery. Descendants of the characters from *Koreni* reappear in later works, though in somewhat secondary roles. Ćosić again experiments with style, mostly by using the cinematic technique of many quick shots and flashbacks; he also employs spare description, frugal punctuation, and a choruslike, impersonal character who is a kind of Everyman on his descent into Hell. The multiple voices of the chorus symbolize the universality of the tragedy portrayed in the novel. In this sense *Deobe* is an important step toward the mature style of Ćosić's final works.

Ćosić's next novel, *Bajka* (Fairy Tale, 1966), is his only novel not based fully on realistic events. It is nevertheless a repository of his ideas about the same problems depicted in his more-realistic works. In a thinly veiled allegory about a mythical state, the author attempts to visualize the future on the basis of developments in the present. In this respect *Bajka* is also an anti-utopian novel. It is not easy to penetrate the allegorical and symbolic framework of this "fairy tale." Moreover, Ćosić's desire to modernize his expression—a process begun in *Koreni*—makes it more difficult to follow the already thin main thread. Action and plot, however, are not as important to the author as is his examination, in a semiessayistic, pseudophilosophical fashion, of the underpinnings of the events depicted in his earlier works (as well as in his later ones, as it turns out). Ćosić's obsession with endless strife among human beings—above all, with war as its most drastic manifestation—is the moving force in this work. The result is a complex vision of Man's endeavor to forge his own destiny, his successes and failures, and his belief, almost a fanatic faith, that the ideal of a better humanity can indeed be realized. At the end of the novel, Man is still looking at a shimmering quartz stone lying on the river bottom. That, however, does not dampen his enthusiasm and faith, for he vows to continue his search for a better future. *Bajka* is, therefore, more a testimony to man's determination to achieve his goal of a perfect society than a criticism of the shortcomings of the present world. In this sense the author's humanistic views lift his vision above the horizon of everyday concerns. The examples of Adolf Hitler and Joseph Stalin as equal partners in their efforts to dehumanize people, which Ćosić analyzes at length, serve as warnings of what could happen if vigilance and hope are abandoned.

From 1972 to 1979 Ćosić published a four-volume novel, *Vreme smrti* (translated as *A Time of Death,* 1978), about the fate and struggle of the Serbian nation in World War I. The novel adheres closely to the historical facts and chronological order of events enveloping the small state of Serbia in World War I: it presents a short prewar scene; the outbreak of the war; the initial defeats and the ensuing military and

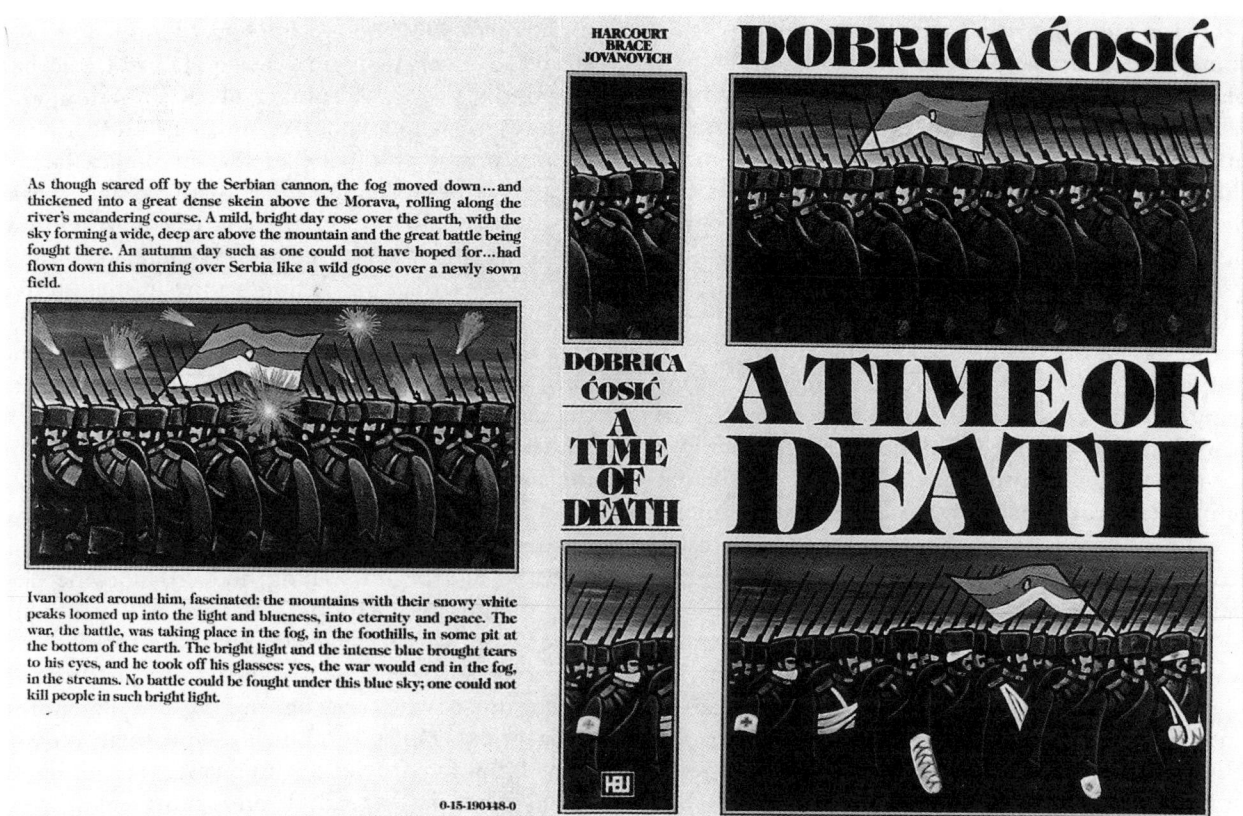

Dust jacket for a translation of Ćosić's four-volume novel about the fate of Serbia in World War I

moral victories; the crushing, though not final, defeat in 1915; the superhuman retreat through the snow-covered mountains; and finally the rescue of the survivors on the Albanian seashore. Yet it is not so much the subject matter, monumental though it may be, that lends the novel epic proportions; rather, it is Ćosić's approach to the theme, his flair for the dramatic and his skill in shaping characters, actions, and situations, and, above all, his understanding of the little man who carries the heaviest burden in any war. His concentration on the little man now becomes the trademark of Ćosić as a writer.

War as the most fateful behavior of human beings, the theme that continues to rivet Ćosić's attention, is the most important focus of this novel. The fact that in the title itself the author implicitly links war with the only certain reality, death, signals his ongoing obsession with the fact of war. The characters in *Vreme smrti* offer a variety of opinions about war and what makes people wage war, not all of which, to be sure, can be attributed to the author himself. The view of war that a character holds in Ćosić's novels depends largely on the social background and position of that character. The old peasant leader in *Koreni*, Aćim, expresses a conservative, peasant's view when he advises his grandson against deserting: "Go with people, son. One has no better road." His son Vukašin, a politician and opposition leader educated in France, has a much more sophisticated notion of war, as befits a highly educated intellectual: "War," he says, "is the only time when we work for history and acquire respect through suffering and dying." For the crafty political leader of the country, war is a supreme test of statesmanship and of the stamina of the people. A high commanding officer expresses a loathing for war. Considering himself to be the greatest coward, he continually insists that Serbia fights only for survival and, therefore, right and justice are on its side. A young socialist has his misgivings, believing that Serbia can be saved only through a revolution, yet even he fights on bravely.

Ćosić's characters frequently express their opinions about the war and its cataclysmic upheaval. For some the war is a great equalizer that unmasks everything and shames people even more than it kills them; it is a terrible illness that will eventually conquer all. As the disaster brings on more misery, suffering, and death, some people become more philosophical, seeing war as something older and more eternal than human beings, a phenomenon that reveals essential truths about the violent nature of existence; others, less stout-hearted, seem to falter under the weight of the calamity. Peasants and city dwellers, leaders and simple soldiers alike are disappointed in their allies and in civilization in general. They believe that small nations never win a war forever, and that the deck is always stacked against them. For them Europe is a criminals' hunting ground, a thieves' bazaar where politics has a field day, where all restraints are removed and participants therefore have the right to use any and all means, so that murderers kill murderers. All of these opinions can be summed up in the often-repeated phrase "War is hell!" This sentiment is echoed by all participants, from generals to foot soldiers.

As most of the characters agree that the war is a calamity, they seem also to agree about the reasons for it, concurring that the war, cruel and unjust as it is, must be endured because the alternative is even worse. Death becomes unimportant as everyone's will to survive is put to the sternest test. This iron will is expressed through the commanding officer, General Mišić. Himself of peasant stock, unpretentious and down-to-earth, he repeats time and again the reason that Serbia must fight on and endure even beyond what seems humanly possible: "Ours is a peasant army, defending its home and children.... When one fights for survival, he has the right to do anything.... Only the sacrifices made for one's survival are not in vain." Most of the characters accept this simple reasoning and endure more than they believe they are capable of enduring. Even the young Socialist changes his thinking and becomes more stoic, as he is often brought to the brink of death as a sacrifice.

Using General Mišić as his vehicle, Ćosić expresses his own conclusions about the nature of war. If in *Daleko je sunce* he condones war primarily for the sake of an idea and in *Deobe* he has no answer for the incomprehensible cruelty of people, in *Vreme smrti* he finds that war may be justified, even if in only one case: in self-defense and the struggle for survival. He has found a perfect example for such a justification in the death struggle of his small nation against seemingly insurmountable odds. He does so not from chauvinistic impulses, but because he has decided that every person, through his nation, has the right and even the obligation to defend his dignity and liberty. It must be added that it is not so much biological survival that Ćosić has in mind as it is the survival of a nation and society in which liberty, justice, and human dignity prevail. He believes that in such a fateful struggle human beings must display high moral qualities, because only then is life worth living and only then does freedom become necessary. He believes that his nation values justice above freedom, that war is won and lost in the soul, and that the victor's bravery is not always the most important thing. Furthermore, barbarism in the name of freedom is a sign of military despair, while bravery for the sake of one's survival is the highest act of moral rectitude.

In his magnum opus Ćosić found the answer to the question that had plagued him since he had begun writing, indeed, since he had begun thinking. Although people will probably never stop warring and committing atrocities and inflicting suffering, war acquires its justification when those who are fighting it are defending themselves against annihilation—and then, only if they fight for freedom and justice at the same time. This is the final and most significant message of *Vreme smrti* and of Ćosić's entire opus. Through it, Ćosić seems to have found peace with himself as far as his feelings about his nation's past are concerned. His country's more recent history, on the other hand, is a matter with which he comes to grips in his later work. Many qualities make *Vreme smrti* an exceptional novel, in addition to its epic theme and its treatment of fundamental moral issues. The book shows the maturing of the author's style, which is apparent in his control of the plot and the characters, his skillful description of war scenes (without glorifying heroic deeds or dwelling on war's gruesome aspects), and his modernistic blend of narration, dialogue, and documentary material.

In Ćosić's equally ambitious novel, the trilogy *Vreme zla* (A Time of Evil, 1985–1990), he deals with a dilemma from his own past—his participation in the communist movement. Shifting the scene to the late 1930s and to World War II, he continues the saga of the Katić family and concentrates on the internecine struggle among the communists that eventually destroys the idealism of many of their young followers. In the first volume, *Grešnik* (The Sinner, 1985), the main characters pass through a painful crisis of belief and identity; this leads to a catharsis that dissolves relationships between husbands and wives, parents and children, and friends. This experience is repeated in the second volume,

Otpadnik (The Apostate, 1986), in which the emphasis shifts to the real source of tragedy—the centers of the communist world, Moscow and Stalin. After witnessing the senseless sacrifice of countless like-minded idealists, the protagonist, Bogdan Dragović, pays the ultimate price for his naiveté and for his belief in the "god that failed." Ćosić avoids the pitfalls to which fiction that includes political and ideological subject matter is liable; he does so by lifting the narrative to the high artistic level that he had already achieved in his previous works. Moreover, *Vreme zla* has overtones that make it appear to be a work of personal catharsis, which lends it a genuine pathos. Whether the author has been able to purge himself fully of the naive idealism of his past is difficult to say, and it is certainly inconsequential to the evaluation of his literary opus. His latest novel once again confirms Ćosić to be one of the most powerful among contemporary Serbian writers, a position accorded him by both readers and critics. His literary influence, however, has not been large, perhaps because of his unique personal experiences and his distinctive approach to literature.

Bibliography:
Živorad P. Jovanović, "Dobrica Ćosić," in *Leksikon pisaca Jugoslavije,* volume 1 (Novi Sad: Matica srpska, 1972), pp. 546–550.

Biographies:
Nikola Drenovac, "Dobrica Ćosić," in his *Pisci govore* (Belgrade: Grafos, 1964), pp. 83–90;

Slavoljub Djukić, *Čovek u svom vremenu: Razgovori sa Dobricom Ćosićem* (Belgrade: Filip Višnjić, 1989).

References:
Miloš Bandić, *Dobrica Ćosić* (Belgrade: Rad, 1968);

Miroslav Egerić, "The Novel as a Subjective Epopee: The Last Book of *Time of Death,*" *Relations,* 1 (1986): 25–38;

Egerić, "Roman kao subjektivna epopeja," *Delo,* 18 (1972): 951–967;

Zoran Gavrilović, "*Vreme smrti*: Nadsmislovi istorije," *Književna kritika,* 8 (1977): 22–35;

Muriel Heppel, "Dobrica Ćosić and the Yugoslav Idea," *South Slav Journal,* 7, nos. 1–2 (1984): 2–12;

Slavko Leovac, "Romani Dobrice Ćosića," *Izraz,* 9 (1965): 229–241;

Vasa D. Mihailovich, "Aspects of Nationalism in Dobrica Ćosić's Novel *A Time of Death*: Chauvinism or Sincere Patriotism?" *World Literature Today,* 60 (1986): 413–416;

Mihailovich, "War in the Works of Dobrica Ćosić," *Serbian Studies,* 3, nos. 1–2 (1984–1985): 27–34;

Nicholas Moravcevich, "The Portrait of Nichola Pašić in Dobrica Ćosić's novel *Vreme smrti,*" *Serbian Studies,* 5, no. 4 (1990): 21–30;

Predrag Palavestra, "*Koreni* Dobrice Ćosića," *Letopis Matice srpske,* 375 (1955): 260–268;

Slobodan Selenić, "Čovek traži djavola," *Delo,* 13 (1967): 281–299;

George Vid Tomashevich, "Ćosić's Novels *The Sinner* and *The Apostate*: Revolutionary Hopes and Disappointments," *South Slav Journal,* 10, no. 4 (1987–1988): 14–25;

Vitomir Vuletić, "O kompoziciji *Vremena smrti,*" *Letopis Matice srpske,* 420 (1977): 456–486.

Vladan Desnica
(7 September 1905 – 4 March 1967)

Cynthia Simmons
Boston College

BOOKS: *Zimsko ljetovanje* (Zagreb: Zora, 1950);
Olupine na suncu (Zagreb: Matica hrvatska, 1952);
Proljeće u Badrovcu (Belgrade: Prosveta, 1955);
Slijepac na žalu (Zagreb: Društvo književnika Hrvatske, 1956);
Tu, odmah pored nas (Novi Sad: Matica srpska, 1956);
O pojmovima "tipa" i "tipičnoga" i njihovoj neshodnosti na području estetike (Zagreb: Univerzum, 1957);
Proljeća Ivana Galeba (Sarajevo: Svjetlost, 1957);
Fratar sa zelenom bradom (Zagreb: Mladost, 1959);
Izbor pripovjedaka (Zagreb: Školska knjiga, 1966);
Zimsko ljetovanje: Pripovijesti, Pet stoljeća hrvatske književnosti, volume 17 (Zagreb: Zora Matica hrvatska, 1968).

Collection: *Sabrana djela Vladana Desnice,* 4 volumes (Zagreb: Prosvjeta, 1974).

Editions in English: "Derelicts in the Sun" (fragment), translated by Petar Mijušković, in *Some Yugoslav Novelists,* volume 2 (Belgrade: Jugoslovenska knjiga, 1956), pp. 21–25;
"Mr. Pink's Soliloquy," translated by Mijušković, in *Some Yugoslav Novelists,* volume 3 (Belgrade: Committee for Foreign Cultural Relations, 1957), pp. 39–46; translated in *Death of a Simple Giant and Other Modern Yugoslav Stories,* edited by Branko Lenski (New York: Vanguard, 1965), pp. 271–281;
Springtimes of Ivan Galeb (fragment), translated by Petar Mijušković as *Springtimes of Ivan Galeb* (fragment), in *Some Yugoslav Novelists,* volume 4 (Belgrade: Committee for Foreign Cultural Relations, 1959), pp. 55–77;
"Tale of the Friar with the Green Beard," translated by Olga Humo, in *Death of a Simple Giant and Other Modern Yugoslav Stories,* pp. 283–290;
"The Visit," translated by Branko Brusar, *Bridge,* 5/6 (1967): 5–13; translated by Celia Williams, *Bridge,* 23/24 (1970): 66–75;

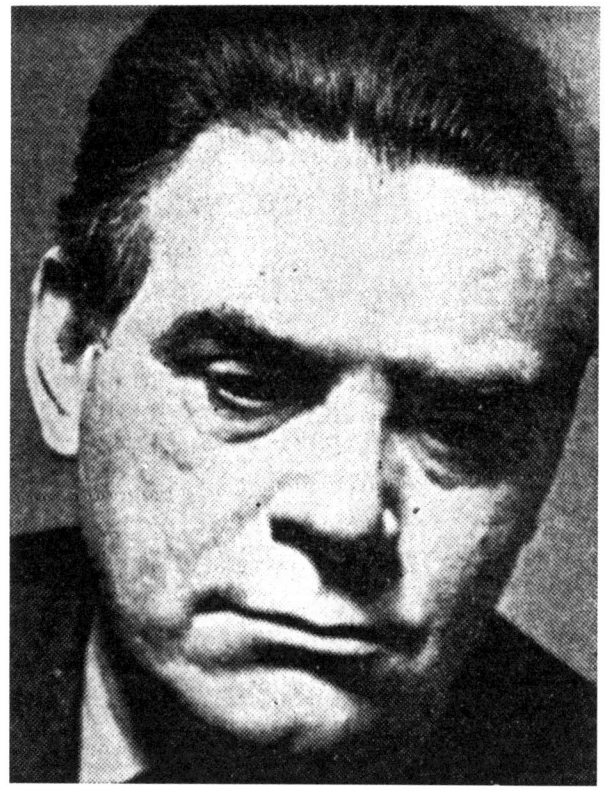

Vladan Desnica

"Farewell," translated by Alan Ferguson, *BC Review,* 3, no. 6 (1976): 4–7;
"Justice," translated by E. D. Goy, in *New Writing in Yugoslavia,* edited by Bernard Johnson (Harmondsworth, U.K.: Penguin, 1979), pp. 83–86;
Springtime in the Life of Ivan Galeb, translated by Srebrenka Kunek-Huljev, *Most,* 1–2 (1981): 46–57.

TRANSLATIONS: Benedetto Croce, *Eseji iz estetike* (Split: Kadmos, 1938);
Ignazio Silone, *Kruh i vino* (Zagreb: Glas rada, 1952);

Leo Tolstoy, *Pripovijesti,* "Poslije plesa" (Zagreb: Matica hrvatska, 1952), pp. 263–274;

Lionello Venturi, *Od Giotta do Chagalla* (Zagreb: Mladost, 1952);

Marcel Aym, *Priče mačke na grani* (Zagreb: Mladost, 1963);

Croce, *Književna kritika kao filozofija* (Belgrade: Kultura, 1969).

The prose and poetry of Vladan Desnica constitute a vital link in a long line of works by writers such as Vladimir Nazor, Dinko Šimunović, Petar Šegedin, Vjekoslav Kaleb, and Ranko Marinković that succeeds in capturing the essence of life in their time in the villages and towns of Dalmatia. His writing, like that of Šegedin and Marinković, embodied and introduced to the national literature narrative techniques (interior monologue, the unreliable narrator, and so forth) that reveal the preoccupation in the modern era with human psychology and the human ability to cope with ever-more-rapid social changes. Like some of these writers, Desnica also contributed to the cultural and political life of his country as it changed shape and changed names. Yet Desnica holds a special position among his colleagues when viewed from the perspective of the late twentieth century: he was the only Serb among them. Desnica inherited a legacy of leadership among the Croatian Serbs, and in postwar Yugoslavia he claimed membership in the doomed fraternity of Yugoslav writers.

Desnica was born on 7 September 1905 in the Adriatic coastal town of Zadar. He was descended on both his mother's and father's sides of the family from prominent and well-respected ancestors. His father, Dr. Uroš Desnica, was a distinguished lawyer with a doctor of law degree from the University of Vienna. Active politically, he struggled against Italian and Austrian influence in Dalmatia. Uroš Desnica was in fact carrying on the tradition of political leadership established by his own father, Vladimir Desnica, a landowner and president of the Obrovac municipality. Desnica's grandfather Vladimir held the latter post for thirty years, attending the Imperial Council in Vienna and aiding the Herzegovinians in the uprising of 1875. In 1905 Desnica's father, Uroš, and grandfather Vladimir signed the Zadar resolution that paved the way for the Croato-Serbian coalition.

When Desnica's grandfather Vladimir married Olga Janković, he allied the Desnica family with a noble line that traced its heritage to the famous sirdar Stojan Janković. Olga's father, Count Ilija Janković, was a well-educated man, an admirer of Voltaire, and a deist. He was also a Slavophile who attended the Pan-Slav Congress in Moscow in 1867. When he died in 1874, the last male descendant of the family, Vladimir Desnica inherited the Janković castle and estate in Islam Grčki, near Zadar, and Ilija Janković's role in the political and cultural life of northern Dalmatia. The sense of responsibility and at times, no doubt, burden of such a heritage were instilled in Uroš and later in his own son, Vladan. Vladan Desnica did not live to see the family castle in Islam Grčki, filled with art and artifacts, some dating back centuries, burned to the ground in the recent Balkan War. Desnica's daughter and other family members live still in Zagreb, Croatia.

Desnica began both his elementary and high-school education in Zadar, but his course of study was interrupted twice: for two years during World War I he was educated on the family estate; and when Zadar fell to Italian rule, he continued his education in Split and Šibenik. He graduated from the classical gymnasium in Šibenik in 1924. Desnica studied law in Zagreb and Paris, earning his degree from the law faculty in Zagreb in 1930. His first position was in the state legal office in Split, where he remained until the outbreak of World War II. In 1941 he was sent by the Italian occupation forces to Zadar to work as a translator. He left Zadar in 1943 to take refuge in Islam Grčki. From there he made his way in 1944 to freed territory and in 1945 to Zagreb. Desnica worked in Zagreb as the head of the legal division of the Ministry of Finance until 1950, when he left this post to be a professional writer.

Desnica's heritage of civic responsibility was complemented by an exposure to the arts that was a prerequisite of his family's position in society. His parents and their circle discussed literature and music as well as politics. Desnica studied voice and music composition (fourteen of his compositions have been copyrighted), and he made a thorough study of both national and foreign literatures. Among foreign writers, he admired Stendhal and Gustave Flaubert. He found a kindred spirit, however, in Leo Tolstoy. A common theme in the works of both authors is the search for a philosophical and spiritual acceptance of death. Even more important, Desnica no doubt considered Tolstoy the embodiment of what he considered to be the writer's responsibility to *očovječenje čovjeka* (humanize the human), a position that he expressed in interviews and in

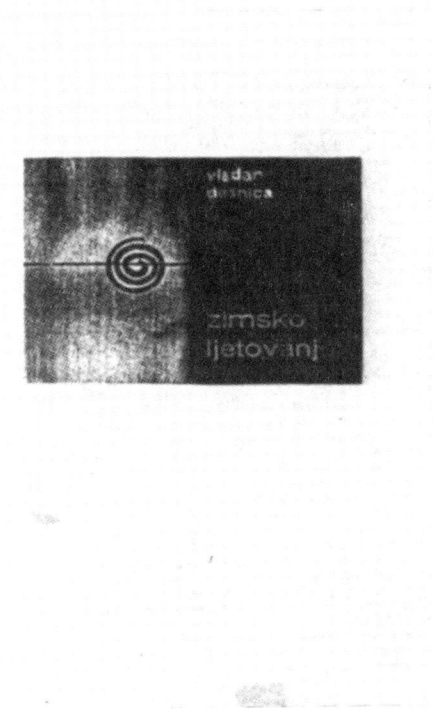

Dust jacket for Desnica's first novel, which describes a group of people uprooted during World War II

his fiction. He may also have sympathized with Tolstoy's aristocratic heritage and the weight of noblesse oblige.

Desnica was a writer of broad taste and education. He studied philosophy and attended the meetings of the Philosophical Society of Zagreb. He knew Latin, Italian, French, Greek, and Russian, and he translated into his native language significant works of foreign literature and criticism. Desnica was not only a gifted writer, but also a leading intellectual of his time.

Desnica is best known for his two novels. The first one, *Zimsko ljetovanje* (A Wintertime Summer Holiday, 1950), established him as a mature writer. The novel embodies a social (and spatial) confrontation that figures in his other novel and in many of the short stories—that of town versus village, or urban versus provincial. It describes the experiences during World War II of a group of tradespeople from Zadar (a bookbinder, a barber, a merchant, a seamstress, and an accountant) and their families who flee the town when it comes under bombardment. They make their way to the village of Smiljevci, having already realized the power of the instinct for survival: they pass by the rubble of bombed-out dwellings even though they know that the inhabitants are trapped below. Their first impressions of the village serve to confirm their preconceptions of "peasant filth, shrewdness, and readiness to gain from another's misfortune." Yet gradually, although they continue to refer to the villagers as "beasts," their attitudes change from disgust to something like pity and compassion. In Smiljevci the townspeople learn the basics of survival and hear a story told as only the villagers can tell it. Their resignation is short-lived, however. When the Zadar barber's daughter is killed by the pig that belongs to the family's host in Smiljevci, all are in shock. The pig's owner, Ican, wonders why the townspeople were not aware that pigs could eat humans. The townspeople wonder at Ican's sympathy for the pig and at a God who could create such a man. Shocking events aside, the underlying theme of this novel is exile. The townspeople are exiles who are forced to live with people in many ways quite unlike themselves. Read in the context of the breakup of the former Yugoslavia, *Zimsko ljetovanje* bears more relevance to the reality of its homeland now than at any other time since its publication at the end of World War II.

Many consider *Proljeća Ivana Galeba* (1957, translated as *The Springtimes of Ivan Galeb*, 1959) Desnica's masterpiece. It is an exemplary piece of modern fiction, a sprawling novel in which the action is limited to the ruminations of the physically bound but intellectually liberated protagonist. This work takes place in the subgenre of what might be termed the "literature of incarceration." As in many such narratives, a narrator who is physically confined in some way discovers the epiphany, or epiphanies, that can occur when one is freed to live a life of the spirit or mind. Ivan Galeb, a violinist, spends many months in the hospital after an accident that has maimed his hand, ruined his career, and threatened his survival. Torn from what most would consider a normal life and living only marginally, he ponders the boundaries of existence and the relationship between sensation and reason. He considers his predilection for light over shadow to be an instinctual, and perhaps even primordial, reflex that seems to have influenced the process of logical reasoning. He perceives in the seeming lack of routine of Sundays an internal rhythm and increased intensity that predate its biblical, and then logical, delineation as a day of rest.

Desnica gives greatest rein in this novel to his preoccupation with death and nonbeing. Galeb's revelations, one may assume, are Desnica's own. As the narrator gives himself over to childhood memories, he comes to realize that infirmity is like old age just before death. One returns to life's beginning, which is, like life's end, more significant than life's middle span. The latter is a period of egotism and striving for self-gratification that stifles the sense of cosmic connection that the human being senses at the beginning and at the end of life. Infirmity, like death, reconnects one with birth, nonbeing, and the cycle of life. Galeb, as a writer (and spokesman for the author) is quite clear on this idea: "Death is essentially the singular theme of the writer"; "It is the only thing that *really* happens to us in life"; (because?) "Death is that which consecrates things." Desnica is a writer who is convinced of a metaphysical order in the universe. Galeb's dream of death as a "light at the end of the tunnel" (in this novel, the light at the end of a shady path) recalls Tolstoy's "Death of Ivan Ilich," a story that Desnica greatly admired. The narrator's preference for light over shadow and his wish to die on a sunny day one can interpret as his, and no doubt Desnica's, sense of the transcendent. At the end of *Proljeća Ivana Galeb,* the narrator leaves the hospital. It is another of his springs, and he is a changed man. His aspirations are simple: to enjoy the (sun)light and to make some contribution to the "humanization of the human."

Desnica wrote thirty-two short stories. Fifteen were published in the first collection, *Olupine na suncu* (Derelicts in the Sun, 1952). Twelve of these were reprinted in *Proljeće u Badrovcu* (Springtime in Badrovac, 1955) along with three new stories. The collection published just the next year, *Tu, odmah pored nas* (Here Just Beside Us, 1956), is comprised of the three new additions to *Proljeće u Badrovcu* and thirteen new stories. Only one story not previously published is found in *Fratar sa zelenom bradom* (The Friar with the Green Beard, 1959). It is interesting that despite the reshuffling and republishing of Desnica's short works, they form in each arrangement a cohesive whole. They share various themes with the two novels (and are on occasion worked into the larger works)—for example, provincial life in Dalmatia, the hardships of war, and the psychological effects of the fragmentation and possible alienation of urban existence in the modern era. Several of them belong to the canon of Croatian short fiction.

When "Pravda" (Justice) was published in 1951, it bore the subtitle "Street Scene." The description in the first paragraph of a woman being mercilessly beaten by a man immediately calls to mind a similarly disturbing scene, the horse-beating incident in Fyodor Dostoyevsky's *Crime and Punishment* (1866). The narrator's rationalization for why he should not intercede reminds one of the reasoning of Dostoyevsky's hero for justification for his violent attack on a defenseless person. Desnica's story is the more modern one not only chronologically but philosophically as well. Desnica's tale ends ambiguously with the narrator asking: "Who could figure the just stand in such a situation?" There is no overriding absolutist morality according to which, as in Dostoyevsky's novel, each human being is responsible for the other, no matter what. Ultimate justice in the story is represented only by a policeman—"official justice." A truly modern fiction, "Pravda" is left open-ended. The reader can only surmise what Desnica's views were in the postwar era about a society in which justice might be simultaneously relative and official.

In "Solilokvoji gospodina Pinka" (Soliloquies of Mr. Pink, 1955), the contemplations of an isolated individual bring none of the enlightenment experienced by Desnica's character, Ivan Galeb. Mr. Pink is a lonely bachelor whose lack of connectedness to life has left him ultimately fearful. In his "conversations" with himself he imagines what possible accidents may have led to a puzzling event (his radio playing when he returns home) or may lead in the future to some unforeseen disaster. His cogitation is pathological. It seems that Mr. Pink cannot recall such "springs" in his life, as could Ivan Galeb, that reassured him that, even if there is such a thing as an accident, life itself is not one of them.

"Priča o fratru sa zelenom bradom" (translated as "Tale of the Friar with the Green Beard," 1965) is another story of loneliness and neurotic behavior that may stem from a person's social isolation. This tale is told in the third person, but there is reason to analyze the story as an *erlebte Rede* (first-person narrative); one senses that the narrator shares the protagonist's paranoia and that perhaps they share the same consciousness. The protagonist is haunted by a seemingly harmless dream of a friar with a green beard. He becomes obsessed with the dream, or, more precisely, with the dreaming of the dream or thinking about the dreaming of the dream. The protagonist struggles to overpower an endless chain of associations that inevitably bring him back to the dream, but in the end he succumbs to his own cerebration. "Priča o fratru sa zelenom bradom" has the effect of a case study that unnerves "healthy" readers because the illness in the story seems so threatening; each individual must deal privately with the subconscious and with the wanderings of the conscious mind.

The relevance of Desnica's subjects to the postwar era and the novelty, both stylistically and thematically, with which he often treated them was well recognized by both the reading public and his fellow writers. He received three major awards in recognition of his talent: in 1951, from the Union of Croatian Writers, for *Olupine na suncu;* in 1957, again from the Union of Croatian Writers, for *Tu, odmah pored nas;* and in 1958 the Matica srpska "Zmajeva" award for *Proljeća Ivana Galeba.* Desnica's ambiguous position among his colleagues is revealed in his recognition by both Croatian and Serbian organizations. He undoubtedly viewed his position as one on the "frontier" and representative of a growing membership of Yugoslav writers. In fact, his position was more often politically marginal. These awards take on even greater meaning, for in reality he received them *despite* his "cultural diversity."

Bibliography:

Z. P. Jovanović, "Vladan Desnica," in *Leksikon pisaca Jugoslavije,* volume 1 (Novi Sad: Matica srpska, 1972), pp. 604–607.

References:

Miloš Bandić, "Proleće i olupine," *Književnost,* 3 (1956): 268–271;

Milica E. Banjanin, "The Short Stories of Vladan Desnica," *Florida State University Slavic Papers,* 2 (1967): 74–80;

Komnen Bećirović, "Vladan Desnica. Un slave méditerranéen," *Revue de Paris,* 77 (January 1960): 62–65;

Henryk Bereza, "Vladan Desnica: Niespokojne Wiosny," *Twórczość,* 16, no. 12 (1960): 139–142;

Fadil Bukić, "Strukture romana *Proleća* Ivana Galeba," *Putevi,* 6 (1968): 526–537;

Zoran Gluščević, "Psihoanalitički doživljaj vremena i prostora," *Književna kritika,* 2 (1970): 6–42;

Nikola Ivanisin, "O Desnicinom romanu *Zimsko ljetovanje,*" *Zadarska revija,* 1 (1968): 40–64;

Dubravko Jelčić, "Pripovjedačka umjetnost Vladana Desnice," *Izraz,* 12 (1965): 1167–1187;

Živko Jeličić, "Dvije knjige Vladana Desnice," in his *Lica i autori* (Zagreb: Kultura, 1953), pp. 101–130;

Dragan Jeremić, "Vladan Desnica," in his *Prsti nevernog Tome* (Belgrade: Nolit, 1965), pp. 152–176;

Marijan Jurković, "Tuga i nada jedne proze," *Savremenik,* 10 (1956): 363–371;

Slobodan Kalezić, *Sjenke i stvari: Struktura pripovjedaka Vladana Desnice* (Titograd: Pobjeda, 1978);

Nikica Kolumbić, "Poezija Desnicina romana *Zimsko ljetovanje,*" *Zadarska revija,* 1 (1958): 14–28;

Stanko Korać, *Svijet, ljudi i realizam Vladana Desnice* (Belgrade: Srpska Književna zadruga, 1972);

Radovoje Mikić, *Proleća Ivana Galeba Vladana Desnice* (Belgrade: Zavod za udžbenike i Nastavna sredstva, 1985);

Božo Milačić, "Skrivena poezija," in his *Suze i zvijezde* (Zagreb: N.I.P., 1956), pp. 95–116;

Vojislav Nikčević, "Poetika Vladana Desnice," *Izraz,* 7 (1969): 98–110;

Vlatko Pavletić, "Djelom do istine ili osmišljena zbiljnost beletrističkih proza Vladana Desnice," in his *Djelo u zbilji: Eseji i analize* (Zagreb: Naprijed, 1971), pp. 205–251;

Miloje Petrović, "Filozofske ideje u književnom djelu Vladana Desnice," *Stvaranje,* 7–8 (1967): 868–883;

Nikola R. Pribić, "The Motif of Death in Vladan Desnica's Prose," in *American Contributions to the Eighth International Congress of Slavists, Zagreb and Ljubljana, September 3–9, 1978,* volume 1, edited by Victor Terras (Columbus, Ohio: Slavica, 1978), pp. 644–656;

Čedo Prica, "Desnica kao pripovjedač," *Krugovi,* 5 (1957): 412–423;

"Vladan Desnica," *Yugopress Weekly Features,* 2 (1958): 8–10.

Blaga Dimitrova
(2 January 1922 -)

Cleo Protokhristova
University of Plovdiv, Bulgaria

BOOKS: *Stikhove za vozhda* (Sofia: Bŭlgarski pisatel, 1950);

S Nazŭm Khikmet v Bŭlgaria. Pŭtepis (Sofia: Bŭlgarski pisatel, 1952);

Pesni za Rodopite (Sofia: Profizdat, 1954);

Na otkrito. Stikhotvoreniya (Sofia: Bŭlgarski pisatel, 1956);

Do utre. Lirika (Sofia: Bŭlgarski pisatel, 1959);

Liyana. Poema (Sofia: Narodna mladezh, 1959);

Svetŭt v shepa. Stikhotvoreniya (Sofia: Bŭlgarski pisatel, 1962);

Ekspeditsiya kŭm idniya den. Kiricheski poemi (Sofia: Narodna kultura, 1964);

Obratno vreme. Stikhotvoreniya (Sofia: Bŭlgarski pisatel, 1965);

Pŭtuvane kŭm sebe si. Roman (Sofia: Narodna mladezh, 1965);

Osŭdeni na lyubov. Stikhotvoreniya (Sofia: Narodna mladezh, 1967);

Otklonenie. Roman (Sofia: Bŭlgarski pisatel, 1967);

Migove. Poeziya (Sofia: Bŭlgarski pisatel, 1968);

Strashniya sŭd. Roman-pŭtepis (Sofia: Narodna kultura, 1969);

Ime. Stikhove (Varna: Dŭrzhavno izdatelstvo, 1971);

Lavina. Roman-poema (Plovdiv: Khristo G. Danov, 1971);

Impulsi. Izbrana poeziya (Sofia: Bŭlgarski pisatel, 1972);

Podzemno nebe. Vietnamski dnevnik 72 (Sofia: Partizdat, 1972);

Kak. Stikhotvoreniya (Sofia: Narodna mladezh, 1974);

Mladostta na Bagryana i neynite spŭtuitsi, by Dimitrova and Yordan Vasilev (Plovdiv: Khr. G. Danov, 1975);

Dni cherni i beli. Elisaveta Bagryana-nabyudeniia i razgovori, by Dimitrova and Vasilev (Sofia: Nauka i izkustvo, 1975);

Gong. Stikhotvoreniya (Sofia: Narodna mladezh, 1976);

Zabraneno more. Poema (Varna: G. Bakalov, 1976);

Prostranstva. Stikhotvoreniya (Sofia: Bŭlgarski pisatel, 1980);

Litse. Roman (Sofia: Bŭlgarski pisatel, 1981);

Izbrani tvorbi, 2 volumes (Sofia: Bŭlgarski pisatel, 1982);

Glas. Stikhove (Plovdiv: Khr. G. Danov, 1985);

Labirint. Stikhotvoreniya (Sofia: Bŭlgarski pisatel, 1987);

Otvŭd lyubovta. Lyubovna lirika (Sofia: Narodna mladezh, 1987);

Mezhdu. Stikhotvoreniya (Sofia: Bŭlgarski pisatel, 1990);

Tranzit. Poema (Sofia: K. Kadiĭski, 1990);

Predizvikatelstva. Politicheski etiŭdi (Sofia: Institut po kultura, 1991);

Klyuch. Poemi (Varna: Galaktika, 1991);

Noshten dnevnik. Stikhove. 1988-1992. (Sofia: I. K. Nov Zlatorog, 1992);

Otsam i otwŭd. Silueti na priyateli (Sofia: Kotar, 1992);

Pomen za Topolata (Sofia: Kotar 88, 1992);

Hobiada: Hobioda za Hobimoda (Sofia: Kotar 88, 1992);

Ctikhove (Sofia: Sofia Press, 1993);

Uraniya, Roman (Sofia: Tsuyat, 1993);

I Pak Otnachalo, Stikhove, 1993-94 (Sofia: Nov Zlatorog, 1994);

Do Rŭba, Stikhotvoreniya, 1994-95 (Sofia: Universitetsuo Izdatelstvo St. Kliment Okhridski, 1996);

Cherna Kotka v Tunela: Zagadki, Dogadki (Sofia: Otvoreno Obshtestvo 1996);

Raznoglasitsi. Eseta (Sofia: Universitetsko Izdatelstvo St. Kliment Okhridski, 1996);

Gluharcheto (Sofia: Nov Zlatorog, 1996).

Editions in English: *Journey to Oneself,* translated by Radost Pridham (London: Cassell, 1969);

Because the Sea Is Black: Poems of Blaga Dimitrova, selected and translated by Niko Boris and Heather McHugh (Middletown, Conn.: Wesleyan University Press, 1989).

Blaga Dimitrova is one of the most significant contemporary Bulgarian poets. An independent person and artist, she cannot easily be grouped with others in what is for convenience called a "poetic generation." With her collections of poems, several novels and plays, and many articles and essays, she is widely read in Bulgaria and has a prominent international reputation. At the same time, Dimitrova is one of the most outstanding personalities in contemporary Bulgarian social and political life. An author of strong moral concern, she creates works that are predominantly reflexive, but the intellectual quest in them is never allowed to overwhelm the artistic vision. A dominant characteristic of her *ars poetica* is her confidence in the Word—its magic, its creative potentials, and its ability to build up its own universe that coexists with reality.

Blaga Nikolova Dimitrova was born on 2 January 1922 in Byala Slatina into a family of intellectuals. Most of her childhood was spent in Veliko Tŭrnovo. Her first poems were published in the journal *Bŭlgarska rech* (Bulgarian Speech) in 1938. Later, while a student in Sofia, she was published in the journals *Prometey* (Prometheus), *Uchenicheski podem* (Students' Progress), and *Izkustvo i kritika* (Art and Criticism), and in the newspaper *Literaturen zhivot* (Literary Life). During her school years she studied piano with Professor Andreĭ Stoyanov. In 1941 Dimitrova graduated from the Classical High School in Sofia and enrolled in the Slavic Department of the University of Sofia "St. Kliment Okhridski." During the war years in 1944–1945 she visited the front, wrote poems, and took part in the Volunteer Workers' Movement. She did postgraduate work in Moscow at the Maksim Gorky Institute for Literature, where she defended her Ph.D. thesis on Vladimir Mayakovski, "Mayakovsky and Bulgarian Poetry."

From 1950 to 1955 Dimitrova was an editor for the journal *Septemvri* (September). She also spent the two years from 1952 to 1953 on construction projects in the Rhodopa Mountains. Her experience there and the reminiscences from this period found expression in the collection *Pesni za Rodopite* (Songs of the Rhodopa Mountains, 1954) and later in the novel *Pŭtuvane kŭm sebe si* (Journey to Oneself, 1965). During the 1950s several more collections of her poems were published; with her strong consciousness of civic duty, she expressed her attitude toward all the significant events in her homeland. Her early verse is rather stiff in its declarative style, but she later overcame this rigidness. The first collec-

Title page for Dimitrova's Dni Cherni i beli *(1975), a study of the Bulgarian poet Elisaveta Bagryana*

TRANSLATIONS: Aleksandŭr Tvardovskiy, *Vasiliy T'orkin* (Sofia: Bŭlgarska Rabotnicheska Partiya [komunisti], 1946);

Adam Mickiewicz, *Pan Tadeucz* (Sofia: Narodna kultura, 1959);

Homer, *Iliada,* by Dimitrova and Aleksandur Milev (Sofia: Narodna kultura, 1969);

Edit Södergran, *Prŭstenut na vechnostta,* by Dimitrova and Antoaneta Primatarova-Milcheva (Sofia: Narodna kultura, 1984);

Iosten Sjöstrand, *Chuvam pulsirasht vsemir,* by Dimitrova and Primatarova-Milcheva (Sofia: Narodna kultura, 1984);

Wislawa Szymborska, *Obmislyam sveta* (Sofia: Narodna kultura, 1989).

tion showing her development was *Do utre* (Until Tomorrow, 1959), in which the poems reveal an intimate female world of personal experiences and private feelings. The same year her translation of *Pan Tadeusz* by Adam Mickiewicz was published.

In 1962 Dimitrova worked as an editor for the publishing house of Bŭlgarski pisatel and later was affiliated with the publisher Narodna kultura. A collection of her poems from this period, *Svetŭt v shepa* (1962), includes poems that contain her impressions from her trips to Paris and Rome, the cycle "Glas ot nebeto" (A Voice from Heavens). *Obratno vreme* (1965) manifests the shift to a predominantly reflexive poetry, with poems that represent her attempt to realize her place in the world, to come to terms with the vast dimensions of the universe, and to find a female approach to eternal issues.

In 1965 her novel *Pŭtuvane kŭm sebe si* appeared. Both its form and contents were surprising considering the rather strict norms followed by fiction at the time. The novel recounts the experiences of a young woman at a construction project in the mountains and offers a deep insight into her personal feelings, thoughts, and development. It also eliminates the traditional patterns of plot: its focus is the intimate world of the young woman, and the novel becomes a lyrical meditation on love and on the female approach to the real world. Among its best pages are those about love and anxiety. Her next novel, *Otklonenie* (Detour, 1967), follows the same pattern. It is an account of an unfulfilled love, of a strong, spontaneous passion that is destroyed by social and political demands. The story of the young lovers is told from the perspective of their meeting years after their romantic experiences. Both novels may be regarded as narrative adaptations of poetic inspiration; it is easy to trace in them an intricate network of self-referential allusions to the author's poems.

Dimitrova visited Vietnam several times during the war in Southeast Asia. Three of her books—the collection of poems *Osŭdeni na lyubov* (Condemned to Love, 1967), the novel-travelogue *Strashniya sŭd* (Judgment Day, 1969), and the Vietnam diary *Podzemno nebe* (Underground Sky, 1972)—grew out of her experiences in that country. Far-off Vietnam became a part of her private life—she adopted a Vietnamese girl, Ha, who appears as a character in these works. *Strashniya sŭd* conveys the horrors and anxieties of the contemporary world that are provoked by the Vietnam War. During the same period Dimitrova collaborated with Aleksandur Milev on a translation of Homer's *Iliad,* published in 1969.

The novel *Lavina* (Avalanche, 1971) represents an important stage in the poet's artistic development. It is an account of an actual tragic incident in which a group of young mountaineers meet their deaths in the snow. Keeping within the scheme of documentary narration, the author depicts the paths followed by each of the sixteen men and women up to the moment of their last climb. But she goes beyond the factual plane into the realm of philosophical reasoning about the issues of life, juxtaposing what may be considered the "everyday" morals of human relations, love and friendship, and duty and responsibility to more abstract, existential problems.

Dimitrova's next collection, *Kak* (How, 1974), is marked by its intellectual sophistication. Here she reaches to the kernel of words to explore the secrets of their designations and thus to gain control of a language that is capable of expressing the complexity of existence. So the paradoxes in her thoughts find their verbal equivalents. The poet reflects on the transformations wrought by time and the fundamental values of a human being's individual choices; in her view, hesitation in making choices becomes a form of persistence. The collection suggests a serene confidence in the durability of human insights, which in a way overcome death. The poem "Ako" (If) offers a brilliant image, full of tragic enlightenment, of the way that an individual may pass out of the world unnoticed.

Collaborating with her husband, the literary critic and scholar Yordan Vasilev, whom she married in 1967, Dimitrova worked on a large-scale study of the great Bulgarian poet Elisaveta Bagryana. The main part of it was published in 1975 in two separate volumes that offer a profound insight into Bagryana's life and poetry. The book also portrayed a generally denied and widely forgotten image of Bulgarian cultural life during the first decades of the twentieth century, a portrait deliberately misinterpreted by communist propaganda and severely attacked by official critics.

The next year *Gong* (Gong), a volume that includes works written between 1956 and 1975, was published. In this selectively compiled retrospective, previously published poems are juxtaposed with the framework of the two poetic cycles written in the early to mid 1970s, "Second Life" and "Alternative," which confront the issues of life and death. The earlier poems thus acquire new meanings, and the entire collection functions both as a meditation upon the preciousness of existence and as a call for humanity, wisdom, and tolerance.

In 1981, after many years of censorship, the novel *Litse* (Face) was published. It presents the difficult and painful sobering of a former fighter for communist ideas in the face of the monstrosities of the new society. The main character, Bora Naydenova, in her mid thirties, is a professor of Marxism who has dedicated her life entirely to political activity. She leads a strange life, simultaneously in the reality of endless engagements and in the world of her memories of Andrey, the man whom she once loved, with whom she shared the risks of the struggle and who was later killed. The encounter with Kiril Argirov, a student who has just been expelled from the university for political reasons, brings a change in her rather monotonous existence. She offers to shelter the student in her own apartment. As a result of the moral and intellectual conflict between them, Bora starts to see life around her in a different way. Their relationship develops into unexpected but overwhelming love, leading to a climax in which, as in the moment of recognition in Greek tragedy, Bora realizes what the narrator, and therefore the reader, has known from the beginning—that Kiril had taken part in the execution of Andrey. The novel offers an honest, unadorned picture of the so-called socialist society, of its evils, its people's apathy and fears, and the manner in which it deforms every human soul.

The multiplicity of semantic perspectives in *Litse* is enriched by the presence of an unconventional character—an India-rubber plant that becomes the "ideal spectator." Thus, an intrinsically lyric and ironic tone is brought into the narrative. Written over a period of many years, the novel gives expression to some of the most essential themes and motives in the author's poetry: the problem of moral choice and individual responsibility and the theme of the human face as a symbol of personality (several of her poems are similarly titled: "Face," "Self-portrait," "Face to Face," "Self-portrait under Water"). Having situated the events in the late 1950s, the writer also incorporates into the plot realities from Bulgarian life during the next decades. Thus, the story powerfully depicts not only "temporary faults" (a cliché used by communist propaganda), but also the inherent vices of socialist society. The novel was received with hostility and was sanctioned by the official critics but became an underground masterpiece among the reading public.

Since the 1960s Dimitrova has increasingly developed her own recognizable style, but it was in the 1980s that she attained her highest poetic achievements. Starting with *Prostranstva* (Expanses, 1980), her best works, charged with concentrated intellectual and spiritual energy, began to appear. In these the poet makes her way into the complexity of existence, contemplating the fundamental concepts of space and time and the paradox in the oppositions between the individual and the cosmos, life and death, dream and reality, and memories and the present. Themes that gained further expression in her poetry during this period include the human being in the world, conveyed in a markedly antianthropocentric perspective; human vulnerability; and memory as one's most precious possession and as a sanctuary for human identity. The collection *Glas* (Voice, 1985) is titled—characteristically for Dimitrova—with one of the key words in her poetry; the voice is a metaphor of one's personal presence, moral choices, and social position. There is sound reason to claim that the voice serves also as a sign of the poet's own artistic and social image, as a voice of reason and justice in defense of human values. "The Ballad of the Stake" is the expressive core of the collection. There a concrete event, the torching of a famous artist's studio, is interpreted in the context of abstract issues such as the social and moral role of art, art's might and vulnerability, and its incompatibility with intolerance and violence.

The collection *Labirint* (Labyrinth, 1987) continues the poet's quest for the meaning of human existence and the true dimensions of its dramas. The dominant image of the labyrinth in the title expresses the paradoxes of life and the intrinsic equation between existence and identity. It also functions as a specific summing up for the poet. A recurrent motif in the collection is time and its irreversibility. As in her earlier works there are coinages and plays upon words that reveal new and unexpected semantic nuances in what appeared to be conventional and fixed meanings. A remarkable achievement is the narrative poem "Slŭnchogledi" (Sunflowers), placed in the center of the book; it presents an allegorical account of the calamities experienced by the Bulgarian people in their social and political history. By means of the main multidimensional metaphor, which conveys various semantic potentialities, the poet offers a deep insight into her compatriots' fate. During the decade of the 1980s

Dimitrova also translated several books, and for her translations from Swedish she was awarded the Lundkvist Prize in Stockholm.

The collection *Mezhdu* (Between, 1990) concerns the dramatic changes in Bulgarian life in recent years. Motifs characteristic of Dimitrova reappear–the poet gives an interpretation of her own name, discovering in it unlimited meanings; she contemplates her path in life and reveals at the same time the unexpected dimensions of fundamental moral concepts. The poet questions again the schematic ideas of what is essential and arbitrary in human existence. In poems such as "In the Jungle" and "Face to Face" she analyzes the complexity of interpersonal relations. The narrative poem "Chasovnikovata kula" (The Clock Tower) recapitulates the poet's ideas about the irrational, antihuman, even absurd nature of social and political life in Bulgaria since 1944.

The most significant among her latest books, which include volumes of political essays and memoirs about friends, is the collection of narrative poems *Klyuch* (The Key, 1991). The title symbolizes the quest for a solution to the essential issues of life (and its enigmas)–love, science, and art. The poet scrutinizes her own experience to find an explanation for a nagging hesitation that she observes in her own life. Leading images in the collection are the home and the road, which are conceived as fundamental, ontological categories. Most of these poems express the tension between the individual and the universe and develop a lyric impulse to break the borders of the self and penetrate the immensity of the universe, entering into its rhythm and eternity.

Having long displayed dignity and courage in her determined opposition to the totalitarian system, Dimitrova became by the early 1990s one of the most outstanding leaders of the democratic opposition. She was among the founders of the Club for Democracy and other opposition groups. For this reason she and her husband were subjected to continuing surveillance by the organs of state security. In October 1991 she was elected a deputy in the parliament, and in January 1992 she became vice president of the Republic of Bulgaria. She was also awarded the Herder Prize for poetry in May 1992. She also engaged in various governmental and social activities, among them the leadership of the Bulgarian department of the Open Society foundation. In the early and mid 1990s she took part in many international meetings and conferences (in Paris, London, Newark, Washington, Krakow, and Berlin) on human rights, on the social and cultural futures of Europe, and on the course of development in East European countries. Dimitrova not only contributes to the best achievements of contemporary Bulgarian literature, but she also offers, through her public image, an essential representation of Bulgaria's current political emancipation.

Interview:

Lyubomira Parpulova, "Istinskoto e estestveno. Razgovor s Blaga Dimitrova," *Bŭlgarski folklor*, no. 2 (1980): 40-52.

References:

Minko Benchev, "Za kategorichnata izyava na talanta i za sŭvestta, koyato obvinyava," *Septemvri*, 12 (1972): 217;

Lyuben Georgiev, "Strashniyat sŭd na sŭvestta," *Literaturna mis*, 1, no. 3 (1970): 54-62;

Svetlozar Igov, "Prozata na Blaga Dimitrova," in his *Groznite pateta* (Sofia: Bŭlgarski pisatel, 1989), pp. 180-186;

Bozhidar Kunchev, "Klyuchut, bez koyto ne mozhem," *Bŭlgarska kniga*, 2 (1992): 48-49;

Rozaliya Likova, "Ot konkretniya fakt do filosofskoto obobshtenie. Poeziyata na Blaga Dimitrova prez 80-te godini," *Plamŭk*, 10 (1988): 141-148;

Elena Mikhaylova, "Kinematografichni urotsi. Publitsistichnata proza na Blaga Dimitrova," *Septemvri*, 3 (1974): 205-210;

Atanas Natev, "Kakvinata na poeticheskoto mislene," *Septemvri*, 4 (1975): 180-192;

Zdravko Petrov, "Blaga Dimitrova," in his *Profili na sŭvremennitsi* (Sofia: Bŭlgarski pisatel, 1973), pp. 142-156;

Atanas Svilenov, "Dramata da zhiveesh istinski," *Plamŭk*, 2 (1975): 168-172;

Petŭr Uvaliev, "Khigiena na dukha," *Vsyaka nedeya*, 1 (1990): 42-45;

Petŭr Velchev, "Blaga Dimitrova," *Literaturna misŭl*, 1 (1982): 113-121;

Toncho Zhechev, "Na praga," in his *Kriticheski dnevnik* (Sofia: Bŭlgarski pisatel, 1987), pp. 146-153.

Dimitŭr Dimov
(25 June 1909 - 1 April 1966)

Cleo Protokhristova
Plovdiv University, Bulgaria

BOOKS: *Poruchik Bents* (Sofia: Bratya Miladinovi, 1938);

Osŭdeni dushi (Sofia: Khemus, 1945);

Tyutyun (Sofia: Narodna kultura, 1951; revised and enlarged edition, Sofia: Narodna kultura, 1954);

Zheni s minalo: Satira v 4 deystviya (Sofia: Bŭlgarski pisatel, 1961).

Editions and Collections: *Sŭbrani sŭchineniya*, 6 volumes (Sofia: Bŭlgarski pisatel, 1966-1967);

Sŭchineniya, 5 volumes (Sofia: Bŭlgarski pisatel, 1974-1975).

PLAY PRODUCTIONS: *Zheni s minalo*, Sofia, Naroden teatŭr na mladezhta, 25 March 1959;

Vinovniyat, Pernik, Boyan Danovski, October 1960;

Pochivka v Arko Iris, Sofia, Naroden teatŭr na mladezhta, 9 January 1964.

MOTION PICTURE: *Tyutyun*, screenplay by Dimov, Studia za igralni filmi, Sofia, 1962.

SELECTED PERIODICAL PUBLICATIONS-
UNCOLLECTED: "Sevastopol, 1913," *Literaturen glas*, no. 476 (15 May 1940): 1-4; republished as "Shpionkata," *Mir*, 48 (March 1942): 12468-12470;

"Karnaval," *Literaturen glas*, no. 543 (February 1942): 1-6;

"Subtropichni bregove. Vpechatleniya," *Mir*, 48 (September 1942): 12623-12630;

"Zadushna nosht v Sevilya," *Septemvri*, no. 1 (September 1949): 57-71;

"Anatomŭt Da Kosta," *Nasha rodina*, no. 8 (1955): 9-13;

Tyutyun, Literaturen stsenariy. Kinoizkustvo, no. 7 (1956): 3-46; no. 8 (1956): 3-44;

Vinovniyat, Teatŭr, no. 5 (1961): 82-112;

Dimitŭr Dimov

Pochivka v Arko Iris, Septemvri, no. 11 (1963): 3-106.

Dimitŭr Dimov is among the most outstanding authors and popular novelists in Bulgarian literature. He established in his native literary tradition a modern style marked by genuine psychological insight, intellectual depth and sophistication, and a rare feeling for dramatic conflicts and the subtleties of language. The critic Krŭstyo Kuyumdzhiev has called Dimov "a poet and philosopher of the tragic," and he is considered to be the originator of a new tradition in Bulgarian fiction.

Dimov was born on 25 June 1909 in Lovech, Bulgaria, to Todor Dimov and Vesa Kharizanova. His father was a soldier, and his mother was particularly interested in literature and greatly influenced her son's intellectual development. Before the child was two years old, the family moved to Dupnitsa. In this town "Misho" (the nickname used by friends and relatives all his life) spent his early childhood and first school years. The beautiful surroundings influenced his imagination and later provided the background for his fictional world. The main occupation of the people in the town was the production of tobacco, and this fact played an important role in the creation of Dimov's major work, the novel *Tyutyun* (Tobacco, 1951). When Dimov was four years old his father, an officer, was killed in the Second Balkan War. In 1918 Dimov's mother married Rusi Genev, also a soldier, who later became a tobacco expert and provided his stepson with valuable information about the world of tobacco production. This world served both as the actual background for Dimov's novel and also as an emblem for the dramatic events in the novel.

The next year Dimov's family settled in Sofia. There Dimov graduated from the First Boys' High School in 1928 and enrolled in the University of Sofia, "St. Kliment Okhridski." After a year of studying law he moved to the school of veterinary medicine, from which he graduated in 1934. Until 1939 he worked as a veterinarian in the village of Vaksevo, in the county of Sofia, and in Khezha; he also worked as a microbiologist at the veterinary-bacteriological laboratory in Burgas. During this period he confided to his best friend, Boris Koychev, that he was writing a novel. Before trying to write and publish a single story, Dimov faced the challenge of a genre as difficult as the novel. He rewrote the work several times before delivering it to the publishing house.

In 1938 the novel was published under the title *Poruchik Bents* (Lieutenant Bents). It presents events from the last years of World War I and thus falls into the category of war fiction, which was well represented in Bulgarian literature of the 1920s and 1930s. Rather than taking the conventional approach of describing battles and the misery of war, Dimov centered his story around the emotional experiences of his protagonist, Bents—a German military doctor working at a hospital in a small town in Southern Bulgaria. In a circle of German and Bulgarian officers who spend their evenings in shallow talk and playing cards, Bents meets Elena Petrasheva, the daughter of a late Bulgarian general and a French woman, an exceptionally beautiful and intelligent woman who has already seen several men who were attracted to her meet with catastrophe. A German aviator, infatuated with her, is killed in an air raid, and an Austrian colonel, her former fiancé, perishes in the war. Falling in love with her, Bents neglects his duties as a doctor and as an officer, deserts from the army, and finds himself in the rear of the Allied Forces. Witnessing the next affair of Elena with a French officer, Bents commits suicide.

The novel explores the intimate relations between the characters in a manner strongly influenced by the ideas of Sigmund Freud, Friedrich Nietzsche, and Henri-Louis Bergson, as well as by the works of Octave Mirabeau, whom Dimov greatly admired. Elena Petrasheva is presented as a "fatal woman," an overwhelming manifestation of the subconscious; her character is marked also by certain melodramatic overtones. Bents himself is seen primarily as a moral failure. The plot is organized around the extraordinary personal conflicts of the characters and their rather pathological relationships.

In 1939 Dimov became an assistant professor of domestic-animals anatomy at the School of Veterinary Medicine. It is likely that he began at this time to work on a novel describing the life of the Bulgarian bourgeoisie, a work that he never completed. The main character of this novel is Adamov—a young, intelligent, good-looking man of small means who is engaged to a smart, pleasant girl. He then meets the fatal Adriana, who is rich, provocatively sophisticated, extremely attractive, and eager to seduce him. Most of Dimov's critics share the opinion that "Adamov" (the work is also known by the title "Roman bez zaglavie"—A Novel without a Title) is an initial version of the novel *Tyutyun*. Despite the fact that many significant similarities between the two works can be found—the downfall of three generations of Bulgarian bourgeoisie; the characters of Adamov and Boris Morev; and the motivations and actions of the female characters—it seems unlikely that this critical view is accurate.

In January 1943 Dimov received a scholarship to the Ramon y Cajal Institute in Madrid, where he specialized in the histology of nerves until March 1944. Returning to Bulgaria he was

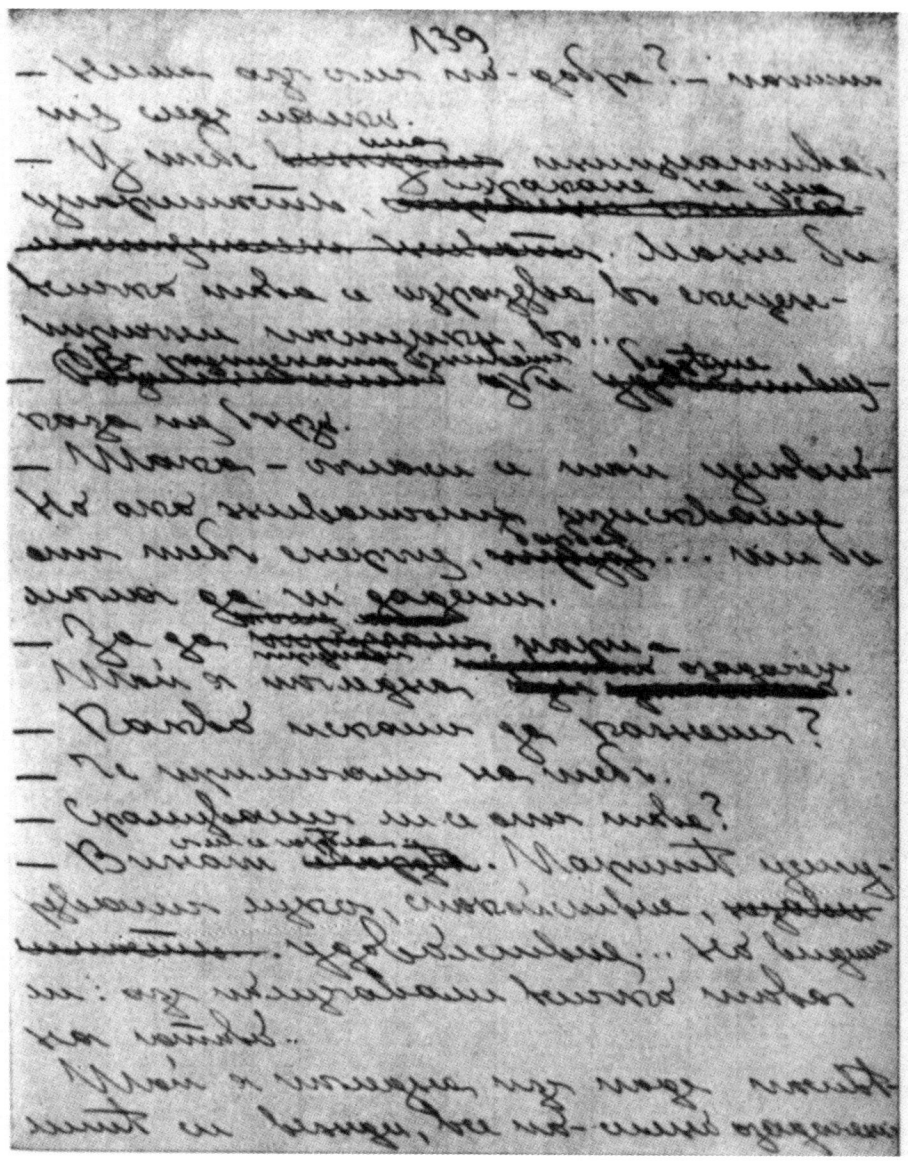

Manuscript page from Dimov's "Adamov," also known by the title "Roman bez zaglavie," an unfinished novel written in the 1930s

mobilized and served in the Aegean area until September 1944. In 1945 his second novel, *Osŭdeni dushi* (Damned Souls), was published. Its title is an expressive metaphor of the drama related in the novel; it is also symptomatic of Dimov's work in general. The idea of "damned souls" is essential to his conceptualization of human personality, and whatever his plots, his characters inevitably bear the sign of damnation.

The action of *Osŭdeni dushi* is set in Spain in the 1930s, during that country's civil war. Fani Horn is the central character, an English aristocrat, young and beautiful, bored and spoiled, who is traveling in search of excitement. She falls in love with a Jesuit monk, Rikardo Eredia, who has an overwhelming personality and who irresistibly impresses her. A supporter of the fascist rebels, Eredia organizes a lazaretto for typhus patients in Pehya Ronda, where, led by her passion, Fani follows him. But all her efforts to seduce him fail. The agony of her love coincides with the destruction of the typhus camp, during which Eredia is killed. Although the main concern of the narrative is the emotional experience of the two leading characters, the development of the plot is subordinated to a distinct ideological design that presents the clash between the world of the reactionaries and the world of the republican forces, culminating in the symbol of the fire in which the camp disappears.

The plot of the novel is carefully structured. Starting with a prologue, when Fani, already a morphine addict, is staying at a hotel in Madrid with Rikardo's brother, an international scoundrel, the narrative reveals retrospectively, and by a shift in the point of view, the drama experienced by Fani and Eredia. In *Osŭdeni dushi* Dimov seems to continue the artistic manner demonstrated in his first novel–his preference for extraordinary characters and striking events, his interest in the idea of the fatal woman, and his exploration of extreme emotions and their destructive power. What is new in this novel are the wider social perspective of the drama and the Spanish theme, which was to play a central role in his work.

Still, *Osŭdeni dushi* is a work without precedent in Bulgarian literature. It belongs to a tradition of philosophical and analytical prose that is incompatible with the predominantly descriptive style characteristic of Bulgarian prose writers. For this reason the novel was not adequately evaluated when it was first published. Later critics achieved a better understanding of its specific and unique style. It was characterized as a "novel-metaphor" by Boris Delchev and by Tonco Zhechev as "an essay, unfolded into a novel." Krŭstyu Kuyumdzhiev, one of the best interpreters of Dimov, finds *Osŭdeni dushi* to be a masterly work, a new stage in the development of the Bulgarian novel. In 1975 a successful screen version of the novel appeared using the same title, with a screenplay by Vŭlo Radev, who also directed the movie.

The occurrence of the Spanish theme in the novel was no accident. From his early youth Dimov was fascinated by the Hispanic world and dreamed of traveling to South America. When he chose the profession of veterinarian, he did so hoping to practice it in Argentina. For years he studied Spanish (ironically characterizing it in a letter to a friend as a "useless language") and attended lectures on Spanish literature at the university. The opportunity to do research in Madrid was a dream come true. Spain appears in his travel writings–"Yanuarska prolet" (A January Spring, 1946), "Kastilska zima" (A Castillian Winter, 1946), "Kukha Ispaniya" (Hollow Spain, 1946), and "San Sebastian" (1949)–in "Zadushna nosht v Sevilya" (A Stuffy Night in Sevilla, 1949), which he considered his best short story, and later in the play *Pochivka v Arko Iris* (A Rest in Arko Iris, 1963).

In 1946 Dimov became an associate professor at the School of Agriculture in the University of Plovdiv. From 1949 until 1952 he was an associate professor at the Academy of Agriculture in Sofia, and in 1953 he became a professor of anatomy, embryology, and histology. Meanwhile, Dimov's literary preoccupations continued. He wrote his travel essays about Spain and a couple of short stories. In 1953, invited by Pablo Neruda, he made a trip to Chile that resulted in the short story "Anatomŭt Da Kosta" (The Anatomist Da Kosta, 1955), a work full of autobiographical reminiscences. Most of the time after 1946, though, Dimov devoted to the novel he had been working on since 1946, *Tyutyun*.

The novel *Tyutyun* is Dimov's most significant work. It depicts a panorama of life in Bulgaria from the beginning of the 1930s to the end of World War II. The events take place in a small town in south Bulgaria, then in Sofia, and later in different places, sometimes outside Bulgaria. Involved in the plot are Bulgarian tobacco industry monopolists, representatives of a German tobacco concern, workers, peasants, and communists. The plot is fueled by the conflict between the two opposing worlds. One world is that of the tobacco company, Nikotiana, represented by its heads, Papa Pier, Torosyan, Barutchiev, and Boris Morev. The other world is personified by the communists Pavel Morev (brother of Boris); Lila and Varvara; the partisan commander, Shishko; and the intelligent Maks Eshkenazi. The collapse of the social system is embodied in the personal fates of the main characters, Irina, a doctor; Boris; and Kostov and von Geier, both company executives. A central and specific position in this configuration of characters is reserved for the company itself, Nikotiana–a symbolic but nevertheless real and overwhelming presence that determines the fate of the people involved with it, a threatening force that attracts and destroys its victims very much as does the poison nicotine, alluded to in the name of the company.

The plot of *Tyutyun* focuses mainly on Boris and Irina. Boris is the typical nouveau riche character, ambitious and willful, who gains a high social position at the cost of his moral and emotional degradation. Irina is the most complex and dramatic personality in the novel. As a young woman she had fallen in love with Boris, a minor clerk at Nikotiana at the time, but she loses him when he marries Maria, the boss's daughter. Years later, when Boris is a high-ranking company official and his wife is insane and suffering from an incurable illness, he and Irina meet again and become lovers. Eventually

Dimitŭr Dimov with his wife, Lili Dimova, and daughter Teodora in 1964

their lives become dominated by the interests of the company, and Irina, urged by Boris, sells herself out. A decisive step in this downfall is her becoming a mistress of von Geier. The moral decay of Irina and Boris coincides with the end of the war, when, after the death of Boris, whom she had married, Irina kills herself.

The novel was an instant and enormous success and was widely read and discussed by the public. Its nomination for a Dimitrov's prize (the highest award in Bulgaria at the time) was the occasion for intense discussion by professional critics, some of whom accused the author of ideological errors. The dramatic progress of this discussion, the escalation of negative reactions, and the twist in the critics' attitude after an editorial in the newspaper *Rabotnichesko delo,* an organ of the Communist Party, convey in a unique manner the atmosphere of dogmatism and anxiety in Bulgarian society that was characteristic of the period. Dimov was forced to revise the novel. He decided to enlarge the parts describing the characters of communists, especially Lila and Pavel, as antipodes to Irina and Boris. The second edition was published in 1954 and was reprinted many times as a standard edition. Not until 1992 could the reading public see the original version again. The materials concerning the discussion and the revision of the novel were published as a book in 1992, with the title *Sluchayat Tyutyun 1951–1952* (The Case of "Tyutyun"). The novel was also made into a movie by Nikola Korabov that was released in October 1962 and was enormously popular.

In the 1950s Dimov began writing for the theater. His first play was *Zheni s minalo* (Women with a Past, 1959), in which he presents a world of personal intrigues and moral corruption that is seen as an unsurmounted relic of the past. *Vinovniyat* (The Guilty One, 1960) repeats the same conceptual scheme. The main theme is love, interpreted in opposition to personal and social depth. The characters are typical for Dimov—intellectuals with subtle and varied emotional reactions. Dimov's most successful dramatic work was *Pochivka v Arko Iris* (1963), inspired by the heroic actions of the civil war in Spain. In a dynamic and tragic collision, the communist ideal is claimed to present an alternative to the morals of the Spanish aristocrats and the destructive fervor of the anarchists. Against the background of the civil war the intense, almost hectic action of the play is seen in a series of dramatic snapshots; the passionate encounter of the aristocrat, Ines Montero, and the captain of the communist battalion, Estanislao Bravo, a Bulgarian volunteer, is presented in a form similar to the traditional Spanish *Cante hondo*—the desperate song of love and death in which both subjects are exalted. The beautiful love story is counterpoised against the disasters of the war. The unbelievability of the characters' motivations, reactions, and attitudes is explicitly discussed in the play and considered to be a manifestation of what is supposedly a peculiarity of the Spanish national character: that people in Spain live as if they were in a dream.

In 1964 Dimov was elected chairman of the Union of Bulgarian Writers. He then initiated the first meeting of Balkan writers in May 1964, traveled extensively (to the Soviet Union and Greece in 1965, to Romania in 1966), and wrote articles, essays, and criticism. On 1 April 1966, while in Bucharest organizing the second meeting of Balkan writers, he died suddenly from a cerebral stroke. On his desk were left various unfinished works, the most significant of which was "Akhilesova peta" (Achilles' Heel), a novel that is markedly autobiographical. Its protagonist is a writer who is unable to carry out a project, planned for years, to write a biography of the celebrated revolutionary Yane Sandanski, who was the aunt of Dimov's mother.

Dimov was an extremely creative individual, a writer who introduced exotic colors and romantic ecstasy into the national literature of the 1940s and 1950s and provided the most impressive representation of the tragic, inextricable contradictions in the human soul, as well as the terrifying destructive power of human passions. Dimov's work presents remarkable artistic achievements, among which is his masterpiece, *Tyutyun*, considered one of the best novels in Bulgarian literature.

Biographies:

Ekaterina Ivanova, *Stranitsi ot zhizneniya i tvorcheskiya pŭt na Dimitŭr Dimov* (Sofia: Nauka i izkustvo, 1981);

Neli Dospevska, *Poznatiyat i nepoznat Dimitŭr Dimov* (Sofia: Profizdat, 1985);

Lyuben Georgiev, *Dimitŭr Dimov. Zhivot i tvorchestvo* (Sofia: Narodna prosveta, 1985).

References:

Albert Benbasat and Anna Svitkova, *Sluchayat Tyutyun 1951–1952* (Sofia: Kliment Okhridski, 1992);

Petŭr Dinekov, "Pŭrvite romani na Dimitŭr Dimov," in his *Literaturni obrazi* (Sofia: Narodna kultura, 1956), pp. 279–288;

Lyuben Georgiev, *Dimitŭr Dimov. Monografiya* (Sofia: Bŭlgarski pisatel, 1981);

Svetlozar Igov, "Raztsvet na epicheskiya roman," *Septemvri*, 1 (1981): 200–219;

Ekaterina Ivanova, *Dimitŭr Dimov, Avtor, vreme i geroi* (Sofia: Narodna prosveta, 1985);

Krŭstyo Kuyumdzhiev, *Dimitŭr Dimov, Monografiya* (Sofia: 1987);

Valeri Stefanov, "Rimskiyat pŭt (metaforizatsiya na bolestta v romana *Tyutyun*)," in his *Literaturnata institutsiya* (Sofia: Anubis, 1995), pp. 177–190;

Panteley Zarev, *Dimitŭr Dimov* (Sofia: Bŭlgarski pisatel, 1972);

Tonco Zhechev, "Dimitŭr Dimov i roman na osudenite dushi; Tyutyun ili zaveshtanieto na Dimitŭr Dimov," in his *Bŭlgarskiyat roman sled Deveti septemvri* (Sofia: Nauka i izkustvo, 1980), pp. 24–32, 51–68;

Zhechev, ed., *Dimitŭr Talev, Svetoslav Minkov, Dimitŭr Dimov v spomenite na sŭvremennitsite si* (Sofia: Bŭlgarski pisatel, 1974).

Danijel Dragojević
(28 January 1934 -)

Aida Vidan
Harvard University

BOOKS: *Kornjača i drugi predjeli* (Split: Pododbor Matice hrvatske, 1961);
U tvom stvarnom tijelu (Zagreb: Naprijed, 1964);
Svjetiljka i spavač (Zagreb: Naprijed, 1965);
Nevrijeme i drugo (Zagreb: Studentski centar Sveučilišta u Zagrebu, 1968);
Bijeli znak cvijeta (Zagreb: Privately printed, 1969);
O Veronici, Belzebubu i kucanju na neizvjesna vrata (Zagreb: Kolo, 1970);
Četvrta životinja (Zagreb: Naprijed, 1972);
Prirodopis (Zagreb: Studentski centar Sveučilišta u Zagrebu, 1974);
Izmišljotine (Zagreb: Naprijed, 1976);
Razdoblje karbona (Zagreb: Centar za kulturnu djelatnost SSO Zagreb, 1981);
Rasuti teret (Belgrade: Nolit, 1985);
Zvjezdarnica (Zagreb: Hrvatska Sveučilišta naklada, 1994);
Cvjetni trg (Zagreb: Durieux, 1994).

Editions in English: Selection translated by Vasa D. Mihailovich and Ronald Moran, in *The Bridge*, nos. 19-20 (1970): 79-82;
Selection in *New Writing in Yugoslavia*, edited by Bernard Johnson, translated by Jovan Hristić and Johnson (Baltimore: Penguin, 1970), pp. 78-82;
Selection in *Contemporary Yugoslav Poetry*, edited by Mihailovich, translated by Mihailovich and Moran (Iowa City: University of Iowa Press, 1977), pp. 194-197;
"The True Lovers," "Autumn," and "A Map," translated by Mihailovich, in *The Bridge*, no. 3 (1982): 57-58.

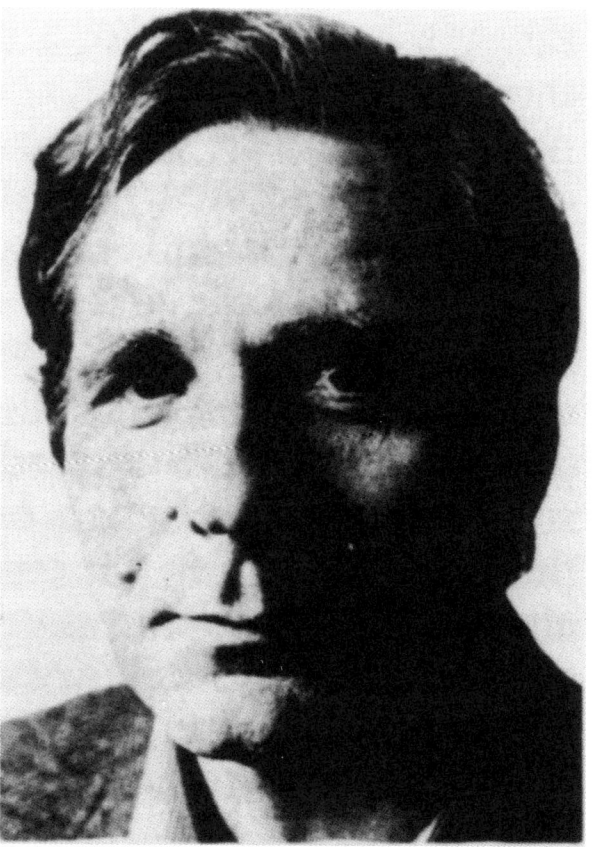

Daniel Dragojević

Although uniformly recognized as one of the most talented poets of Croatian postwar literature, Danijel Dragojević has not become a widely known public personality. Rather, he has decided to let his poetry speak for him. The high quality of his works, apparent in his first collection published in 1961, has remained a constant throughout his career. More than any of his contemporaries he has shown a profound interest in prose-as-poetry, continually experimenting and redefining this genre over several decades. The highly individualized tone of his works is simultaneously philosophical and lyrical, addressing many of the crises of humanity in the twentieth century.

Dragojević was born on 28 January 1934 in Vela Luka on the island of Korčula in the Adriatic Sea. He finished high school in Dubrovnik and obtained his bachelor's degree in art history at the College of Philosophy, University of Zagreb. His first verses were published in 1956 in the publication *Mogućnosti* from Split. In addition to poetry Dragojević started in the 1960s publishing essays and monographs on painters and sculptors, concentrating primarily on twentieth-century artists. He has also worked for Radio Zagreb.

Dragojević's first book, *Kornjača i drugi predjeli* (The Tortoise and Other Regions, 1961), was inspired by the ancient philosopher Zeno's appreciation of paradox, as well as by his respect for the tortoise's persistence. In this remarkable collection of poems in prose, particularly intriguing is the fourth chapter, a cycle in which the viewpoint is that of a tortoise. The views of the lyric persona/tortoise are saturated with Zeno-like paradoxes. Many critics have pointed out that paradox seems to be the crux of both Dragojević's expression and his perception of the world. As Ivo Frangeš defines Dragojević's approach in his entry on the poet in *Povijest hrvatske književnosti* (History of Croatian Literature, 1987), "If the paradox is outside of us, it is perhaps within us as well." One should perceive, claims Frangeš, it as something turned inside out, or reversed, which reveals the world as *mundus inversus*. Paradox in turn becomes the only way to depict reality in poetry. However, this is not only a poetry of colliding extremes, but also of refined and profound lyricism. A few lines from the twenty sixth prose poem in "The Tortoise" cycle illustrate this point:

> My path will no longer outwit me. It is enough for me to bite into the root and sweeten my tamed insides, it is enough for me to rejoice in all the connections that are harmonious and all the connections that spend death on harmony. Now I wonder: why, my soul, you adorned yourself with questions. I stretch my head to the wind and clouds, but my feet have been for a long time already on the ground: in that union shines my peace.

More than perhaps in any other of Dragojević's collections, here the elements of the Mediterranean landscape are given particular prominence and are quite often used as a point of orientation for the poet's perception of the world. In his poem "Prepoznavanja" (Recognitions), from the same collection, he clearly states that "On the island, throughout my childhood I thought that the sea was the beginning and the end." Even in those instances in which details associated with the islands of the Adriatic are not explicitly named, one can frequently derive them from oblique or metaphorical references. Dragojević's early poems are saturated with salty winds, ripe grapes, white stones, masts, water, and knotty olive trees, to which are ascribed almost mystical qualities. In spite of their philosophical orientation, and the weighty questions they often pose, these verses are full of bright colors and light, testifying thereby to the poet's celebration of life.

The poem after which his next collection was named, "U tvom stvarnom tijelu" (In Your Real Body), had been published in Dragojević's first book, announcing in that way the main thematic orientation of his next project, which came out in 1964. Mediterranean motifs are still ubiquitous in the fifty short prose poems that comprise this book; however, instead of philosophical quests the young poet turns now to the exploration of love themes. These are undeniably among the most sensual lines ever written by Dragojević. The title poem has been recognized as containing some of the most refined images in contemporary Croatian love poetry:

> Always prudent enough to turn toward all the sides of the world that exist, always expansive enough to reconcile all imaginary moments and moments under foot, you heal me of the diseases of heaven and earth and remain my vigil-keeper over the three degrees of deceptive inner faces in the course of the day.... I recall you, your head entered straight from the morning into my hands and cleansed them of everything they had been touching.... I watch you this evening with my blind vision as you send to me the ray of birth.

Svjetiljka i spavač (The Lamp and the Sleeper, 1965), as Dragojević's next collection is called, reveals an attempt to concentrate on everyday details and situations that, though expressed from an individual perspective, contain universal human experiences. Such a thematic choice does not prevent Dragojević from posing existential questions and looking for eternal truths.

Significant in his book *Nevrijeme i drugo* (Bad Weather and Other Things, 1968) is the first appearance of verse poems in the oeuvre of this talented author. Dragojević's stylistic experimentation further brings out both the unique semantic playfulness of his language and its exceptional reflective quality. This is particularly obvious in a poem such as "Ako se jednom" (If Once), in which the poet, with somewhat religious overtones, wonders about the realization of man's eternal dreams. Dragojević achieves the figure of paradox not only by juxtaposing totally opposed elements in a syntagma, but also by means of the

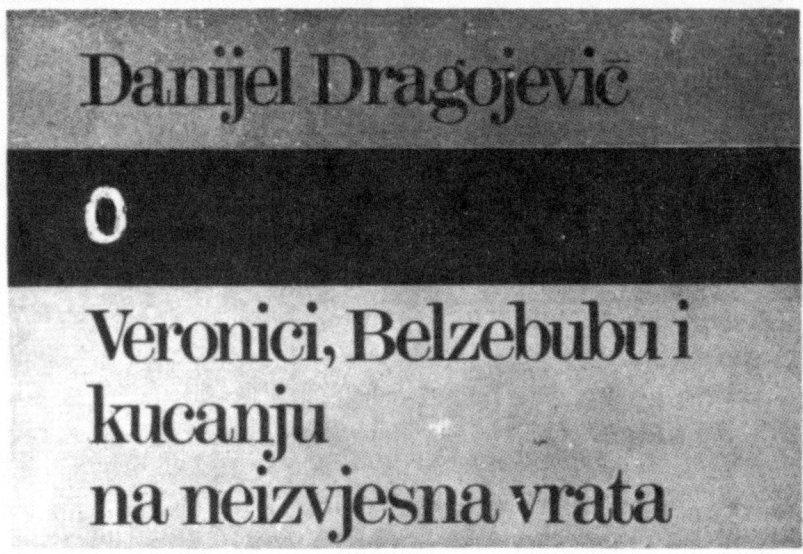

Dust jacket for a collection of Dragojević's critical and philosophical essays written in the 1970s

unexpected switching of linguistic codes and levels in neighboring lines. As soon as the reader selects one avenue of perception, as Frangeš points out, he is redirected and confronted with a new code and a new possibility of understanding the material. Because paradox is the predominant figure appearing in Dragojević's poetry, the rules that operate in it can be compared with the logic of the world observed in a set of reflecting mirrors. This type of logic guides both one's perception of physical appearances and shapes one's mental processes. Dragojević, for example, sees falling as rising reversed; for him, jumping down turns out to be jumping up, as is the case in his poem "Težina" (Weight), from *Četvrta životinja* (The Fourth Animal, 1972).

This "model of the reversed world," to use Vlatko Pavletić's words from his 1985 article in *Forum*, "Visoki napon Dragojevićevih pjesama" (The High Tension of Dragojević's Poems), a model that Dragojević so frequently employs, violates conventional expression and makes the reader pause for a moment before the unexpected meaning. Such an approach allows for the possibility of viewing the world from an uncustomary perspective, thereby questioning at the same time the quality and types of relations that exist in it. Dragojević is known for creating in his poems sets of surprising images and leaps in thought, the goal of which is not a clearly defined message but a series of associations that in many instances remain ambiguous or even have an oneiric quality. In the untitled prose poem from the collection *Kornjača i drugi predjeli,* one can find, for example, the following dreamlike images:

> Behind every color we look at there is yet another, completely different one.... Behind every color the wolf with a weary cloak, perhaps, climbs alone up the slope of the hill while behind his back, opulently like the river, the darkness comes on.

Symbolism in Dragojević's verses is for the most part grounded in a visual quality that many critics have associated with Surrealism in painting. Since Dragojević was trained as an art historian with a particular interest in twentieth-century art, it is not surprising that he reserves such a prominent place in his poetry for the visual dimension.

"Dragojević has learned from the Surrealists how to strike a bright poetic spark by reversing relations or by uniting extremes, i.e., by the semantic coalescing of paradigmatically distanced and different levels," writes Pavletić in his 1985 article. The truth of this statement is particularly evident if one considers the ending of the poem "Četvrta životinja, životinja od vremena" (The Fourth Animal, the Animal of Time), from the collection bearing the same title: "and when (at the beginning, end, in the middle) you don't know / what is happening with you, then she, that reflective night / rhymes the tip of its tail and our head." Dragojević's tendency to place semantically loaded but disparate units in juxtaposition results in an abundance of connotative possibilities. These colliding motifs invariably take the reader aback with their unusual and striking combinations, for which it is sometimes difficult to decide whether they belong to the realm of fantasy or of a peculiarly viewed reality.

In his two collections of essays from the 1970s, *O Veronici, Belzebubu i kucanju na neizvjesna vrata* (On Veronika, Beelzebub and Knocking on a Precarious Door, 1970) and *Izmišljotine* (Fabrications, 1976), Dragojević, although operating in a completely different genre, succeeds in many ways in applying some of the principles that are typical of his poetry. The paradoxes of twentieth-century existence and thought remain as central topics in these essays. From expressing his opinion on such burning issues as the writer's engagement in social and political issues, to analyzing the logic and meaning behind a colloquial expression or a work of art, Dragojević discusses a variety of topics with equal ease and competence. His erudition and his keen sense of perception are accompanied in these essays with an exceptional lyric sensibility and a desire to search for ultimate meanings. References to William Shakespeare, Franz Kafka, Karl Marx, Salvador Dali, François de La Rochefoucauld, Ludwig Wittgenstein, Ivan Meštrović, and John Cage, to mention but a few, testify to the breadth of Dragojević's intellectual interests. Although not the first writer to experiment with the boundaries of the essay in Croatian literature, Dragojević undeniably made one of the most interesting contributions to it in the past few decades, creating almost single-handedly the subgenre of the poetic essay.

Mediterranean motifs recur throughout Dragojević's oeuvre, though in his more-recent collections they are outnumbered by those with urban content. It is interesting that in some cases he even manages to fuse the two groups, as in his poem on Dubrovnik, "Grad" (The City), from *Zvjezdarnica* (Astronomical Observatory, 1994). Here, however, the stress is placed predominantly on the specific historical and cultural details pertaining to Dubrovnik, rather than on a generalized urban experience. In some of his other city poems one recognizes that the place in question is Zagreb. Dragojević's experience of urban life is not necessarily burdened with a sense of melancholy or painted only in subdued colors. Although these lines abound in buses, streets, telephone booths, and city hustle, there is no trace of alienation or rejection in them. Dragojević is able to capture and convey a different type of awareness than that apparent in his "southern poems," one that concentrates on the beauty of a simple moment, one containing a narrative potential. Such are his poems "Jutarnji trg" (A Morning Square), "Proročanstvo" (Prophesy), and "Zvijezda tamnopute žene" (The Star of a Dark-Skinned Woman) from *Zvjezdarnica,* which are grounded in simple observations of facts by the lyric persona with speculations on past and future events, all skillfully interwoven in the visual sketches.

Dragojević has never shown an interest in the sound quality of his poems. Their main potential and power lie in the strings of unusual visual images and the poet's philosophical impulse. In reviews of Dragojević's collections it is often mentioned that he tends to make an impact on the reader more by means of an oblique suggestion than by a realistic presentation. Critics praise his vivid perception, stressing, however, that the disconnected and disparate images it often produces may sometimes bring the poem to the border of dissolution. This is particularly the case with those poems that primarily consist of a series of oneiric expressive units held together only by a sudden turn of phrase at the end. On the other hand, some see in this a possibility for a wider field of connotations and a more profound symbolism that arise precisely because of the loose connection of the poem's semantic units.

The range of themes in Dragojević's poetry is exceptionally broad: he can pose his questions as skillfully in a poem on a button as in one that deals with the concept of a divine entity. However, ultimately it is the visual and verbal tension that becomes the main subject in his poems. A detailed scholarly treatment of this "poetry of the eye" or "poetry of paradox" would help one reach a better understanding of the innovations it brought about and of its place in the history of Croatian literature. It can be stressed already at this point, though, that Dragojević has not only revived the prose poem and poetic essay, but has enriched them with elements these genres did not previously have in Croatian literature. As Frangeš points out, Dragojević learned the style of his poetic prose from the greatest of masters, Charles Baudelaire and Arthur Rimbaud; thus, in his works, just as in those of the two French poets, "the erudition nourishes the emotion and the emotion ennobles the erudition."

References:
Branko Bošnjak, "Kozmički prezent iskustva. O

poeziji Danijela Dragojevića," *Republika,* no. 7-8 (1975): 808-818;

Ivo Frangeš, *Povijest hrvatske književnosti* (Zagreb & Ljubljana: Nakladni zavod Matice hrvatske Cankarjeva založba, 1987), pp. 402-403, 446;

Neven Jurica, "Razdoblje carbona," *Most,* nos. 1-2 (1982): 200-201;

Tomislav Ladan, "Izmedju homiletike i hermetike," in his *Pjesništvo. Pjesme. Pjesnici* (Zagreb: August Cesarec, 1976), pp. 154-159;

Jasmina Lukić, "Slike neba i pejsaži zemlje," *Republika,* nos. 5-6 (1995): 194-196;

Zvonko Maković, *Četvrta životinja, Books Abroad,* 48 (1974): 183;

Maria Malby, *O Veronici, Belzebubu: kucanju na neizvjesna vrata, Books Abroad,* 45 (1971): 541;

Igor Mandić, "Mantija feljtonizma," in his *101 kratka kritika* (Zagreb: August Cesarec, 1977), pp. 22-24;

Mandić, "Pjesme ljudskog interesa," in his *101 kratka kritika* (Zagreb: August Cesarec, 1977), pp. 294-296;

Zvonimir Mrkonjić, "Razdoblje karbona," *Republika,* nos. 2-3 (1982): 146-147;

Mrkonjić, *Suvremeno hrvatsko pjesništvo (razdioba)* (Zagreb: Kolo, 1971), pp. 143-147;

Vlatko Pavletić, "Visoki napon Dragojevićevih pjesama," *Forum,* nos. 4-5 (1985): 841-856;

Nikica Petrak, "Rasuti teret," *Most,* no. 1 (1986): 82;

Andriana Škunca, "Poetika paralelnih svjetova," *Republika,* nos. 1-2 (1987): 173-177.

Andrej Hieng
(17 February 1925 -)

Peter Scherber
University of Göttingen

BOOKS: *Novele treh,* by Hieng, Lojze Kovačič, and France Bohanec (Maribor: Obzorja, 1954);
Usodni rob (Maribor: Obzorja, 1957);
Planota (Ljubljana: Cankarjeva založba, 1961);
Gozd in pečina (Ljubljana: Slovenska matica, 1966);
Burleska o Grku (Maribor: Obzorja, 1969);
Cortesova vrnitev (Maribor: Obzorja, 1969);
Gluhi mož na meji (Maribor: Obzorja, 1969);
Osvajalec (Maribor: Obzorja, 1971);
Orfeum (Maribor: Obzorja, 1972);
Lažna Ivana (Maribor: Obzorja, 1973);
Čarodej (Ljubljana: Cankarjeva založba, 1976);
Izgubljeni sin (Maribor: Obzorja, 1976);
Nori malar (Maribor: Obzorja, 1979);
Večer ženinov (Maribor: Obzorja, 1979);
Obnebje metuljev (Ljubljana: Mladinska knjiga, 1980);
Možje na meji, edited by Bohanec (Ljubljana: Mladinska knjiga, 1980);
Zakladi gospe Berte (Maribor: Obzorja, 1983);
Čudežni Feliks (Ljubljana: Mladinska knjiga, 1993).

TELEVISION: *Gluhi mož na meji,* RTV Ljubljana, 1969;
Nori malar, RTV Ljubljana, 1978;
Dež v Piranu, RTV Ljubljana, 1983;
Mark in Antonij, RTV Ljubljana, 1985.

RADIO: *Cortesova vrnitev,* RTV Ljubljana, 1968;
Krvava ptica, RTV Ljubljana, 1979.

Andrej Hieng

The literary career of Andrej Hieng began when his short stories and novellas started appearing in the mid 1950s; his work immediately provoked a lively interest and appreciation among both the critics and public because of his highly innovative prose style. At the end of the 1960s he turned to dramatic writing, especially for the mass media. His radio and television plays were a formative influence on the development of Slovene work in these media, and some of these plays were translated and performed in other European languages. Although he was a professional stage director and his plays were being published, Hieng did not limit himself to his work in the theater; after 1966 he became increasingly successful as a novelist. He has never been a social realist or humanist (in the sense of the leading literary trend of the 1940s and 1950s), and he cannot be called a socialist writer. His liberal and cosmopolitan style, with its references to the great heritage of twentieth-century prose fiction by such writers as William Faulkner, James Joyce, Marcel Proust, and Thomas Mann, proved to be a remarkable stimulus to Slovene literature after World War II. Hieng may be called an erudite poet, an excellent stylist, and an imaginative narrator in one.

Hieng was born in Ljubljana on 17 February 1925. His father was a bank director and his mother a trader, and he grew up in a well-ordered, upper-middle-class family that provided him with a broad range of literary and cultural stimuli. He started school in Ljubljana in 1932 and completed the gymnasium in 1944, shortly before the end of World War II. In the years from 1939 to 1944 he published two short stories in a youth journal, one of which won an award. After World War II Hieng was required to perform military service from 1946 to 1948 in Zagreb. Although from early youth he had wanted to be a writer, he decided in 1949 to study stage directing at the Academy of Dramatic Arts in Ljubljana. He worked as a director from 1951 to 1953 at the theater in Kranj (Upper Carniolia) and from 1953 to 1960 in Celje (Lower Styria). He married in 1961 and also began working as a freelance writer.

With his semifictional "Študije o nenavadnih značajih" (Studies about Unusual Characters, 1949–1950), he bravely entered the literary scene in the uncertain postwar times, making clear that he would not yield to the literary and political demands of the ruling cultural elite. He simultaneously set a high artistic standard for the literary milieu; so, despite the protests of cultural leaders, his works continued to be read for their indisputable quality and their aesthetic innovations. Two novellas that Hieng wrote were published in 1954, followed three years later by his first collection of short prose, *Usodni rob* (Fateful Edge, 1957). In 1961 his second collection, *Planota* (Plateau), was published, and his writing achieved wide acceptance among the public. The most common traits of his short prose are his preference for unusual characters and his decisions to throw his characters into chaotic realities where they live as strangers who are unable to adapt to those realities. In the late 1950s and early 1960s Hieng also had several jobs in film, working as a director for Viba Film, a Slovenian company, and writing scenarios and adapting literary works for the screen. In the 1960s, when he was considered a master of short prose, he surprised his public by writing his first novel, *Gozd in pečina* (Wood and Cave, 1966). It is a novel about an artist and is full of narrative lines that are woven together in tales about different speakers, and enriched with dreams and suggestive remembrances.

In 1968 Hieng wrote the radio play *Cortesova vrnitev* (The Return of Cortes). It was the first part of a tetralogy, the so-called Spanish cycle, in which he intended to stress recent, actual problems of his contemporaries—problems relating to revolution, power, ethics, and morality—while setting them in remote times and places. He describes the disappointment of the principal character, Don Francisco, that the Spanish conquest in America did not result in a better world that was pleasing in the sight of God. He had hoped that the conqueror Hernán Cortés's return from Spain would undo the negative consequences of the gold rush, but this hope was not fulfilled. Hieng also wrote a television play, *Burleska o Grku* (The Burlesque of the Greek, 1969), that shows the Greek painter El Greco living in Spain in the early seventeenth century as a seeker of God. Another painter, Francisco Goya, is the subject of the television play *Gluhi mož na meji* (The Deaf Man at the Frontier, 1969). Hieng completed his Spanish cycle with the drama *Osvajalec* (The Conqueror, 1971). In this play, a kind of summary of his themes, he focused on the classic conflict between father and son, thereby exploring a virulent problem of the 1970s—the understanding of revolution. For Baltasar, the son, revolution has to be a permanent and ever-changing process. Don Felipe, the father and conqueror, who fell out of favor with the rulers of Spain, tends to rest and enjoy the fruits of his labor. With *Osvajalec* Hieng gained recognition throughout Yugoslavia; he also won the award named after the Croatian artist and man of the theater, Branko Gavella.

Hieng titled his next play *Izgubljeni sin* (The Prodigal Son, 1976); it is a "melodrama" that developed the traditional biblical theme of the prodigal son, which was also popular in Slovene literature. Because of its complex, hermetic, and opaque plot, the work was scarcely noticed by critics or the public. Another melodrama, *Večer ženinov* (Evening of the Grooms, 1979), is situated, like his later drama *Zakladi gospe Berte* (The Treasures of Mrs. Berta, 1983), in a milieu of lower-middle-class people in contemporary Slovenia; it reworks the myth of *Lepa Vida* (Beautiful Vida), one of the typical themes in Slovene literature, used earlier by France Prešeren, Ivan Cankar, Srečko Kosovel, and many others. Both the television play about Jožef Petkoušek, *Nori malar* (The Mad Painter, 1978), and the radio play *Krvava ptica* (The Bloody Bird, 1979) are dramatic works that lead thematically back to Hieng's historical plays of the Spanish cycle.

Hieng's second novel, published in 1972, was *Orfeum* (Orpheus). It bears the subtitle "Poročilo o nekem gledališču" (Report about a Theater), which carries a double meaning: the novel is about a theater in a Slovene province, but it is also a discourse about the contemporary drama in general. It shows the intellectual debates in the theater and about the theater but relates in a parallel plot the story of the narrator's mother, Mila, during her severe illness that leads to her death. The critic Taras Kermauner called Hieng a "classical existentialist" and the novel itself a "grotesquerie about style and anarchy." This novel expresses in a unique manner the zeitgeist and intellectual spirit of the 1970s. In the novel *Čarodej* (The Sorcerer, 1976), set in a Slovene town at the end of the nineteenth century, Hieng again contrasted two parallel narratives: one about the trader Kotnik, with his disordered family affairs governed by violation and unhindered authority; and another about a chain of events in one of the town's inns, events that are only loosely connected with the main scenario of the novel.

A rare formal experiment is Hieng's novel *Obnebje metuljev* (Horizon of Butterflies, 1980), which incorporates the three-act drama *Slavolok* (The Triumphal Arch); in this work Hieng follows his own tradition of collating two texts into one literary entity. The contrast of both texts is intended and balanced: the drama interprets and opens the prose fiction and yet does not destroy the integrity of the surrounding novel. Later Hieng returned to the time and setting of his former Spanish cycle. The main character in *Obnebje metuljev* is a Spanish nobleman who lives in Caracas at the end of the eighteenth century, some years before the liberation of the Spanish colonies in Latin America took place. At the end of the novel he retires to Trieste, a city and port of rising prosperity in the Slovene Karst region. *Čudežni Feliks* (Wondrous Felix, 1993) is Hieng's latest novel. Planned as the first book of a trilogy, the novel is set in prewar Slovenia, which is threatened and encircled by aggressive dictatorships in Italy, Germany, and even Yugoslavia itself. The protagonist is Felix, a sixteen-year-old boy of Jewish descent; using his diaries and his point of view, Hieng develops a fictional world that is heading toward disaster. For this novel Hieng won the Kresnik Award in 1994.

Hieng's literary awards have affirmed his standing among both the literary public and the critics. In 1967 *Cortesova vrnitev* won the Slovene contest for radio plays; in 1968 it also won the Yugoslav contest for radio plays. In 1967 Hieng's first novel, *Gozd in pečina*, won a Prešeren Award, and in 1971 Hieng won the Župančič Award of the city of Ljubljana. Some of his works have been translated, primarily into east European languages, although some of his novellas and plays have been translated into English and other European languages as well. Although his oeuvre is not yet complete, Hieng is considered to be one of the outstanding talents of postwar Slovene drama and fiction, a writer whose stature is comparable to that of his literary contemporaries Vitomil Zupan and Rudi Šeligo.

Interviews:

Branko Hofman, *Pogovori s slovenskimi pisatelji* (Ljubljana: Cankarjeva zalozba, 1978), pp. 55–68;

France Pibernik, *Čas romana* (Ljubljana: Cankarjeva založba, 1980), pp. 53–88;

Milan Dekleva, "Biti mlad v postaranem svetu," *Dnevnik* (2 July 1994): 12;

Ciril Zlobec, *Sobodnost*, 43 (March 1995): 779–797.

Bibliography:

F. Dobrovoljc: "Hing (Hieng), Andrej," in *Leksikon pisaca Jugoslavije*, volume 2 (Novi Sad: Matica Srpska, 1979), pp. 382–383.

References:

Helga Glušič-Krisper and Matjaž Kmecl, "Proza," in *Slovenska književnost 1945–1965*, volume 1 (Ljubljana: Slovenska matica, 1967), pp. 326–331;

Andrej Inkret, *Spomini na branje* (Maribor: Obzorja, 1977);

Taras Kermauner, *Družbena razveza* (Ljubljana: Cankarjeva založba, 1982);

Kermauner, "Groteska o stilu in anarhiji," in *Zgodba o živi zdajšnjosti* (Maribor: Obzorja, 1975), pp. 92–120;

Kermauner, "Uvod v novejšo slovensko prozo," *XXX. Seminar slovenskega jezika, literature in kulture* (Ljubljana: Univerza v Ljubljani, 1994), pp. 263–285;

Kermauner, *Vračanje mita v sodobni slovenski dramatiki* (Ljubljana: Partizanska knjiga, 1988);

Božica Kitičič, *Literarna ustvarjalnost Andreja Hienga* (Ljubljana: Slovenska matica, 1980);

Jože Pogačnik, "Twentieth Century Slovene Literature," *Le livre slovène*, 1 (1989): 1–189;

Pogačnik, *Zgodovina slovenskega slovstva*, volume 8: *Eksistencializem in strukturalizem* (Maribor: Obzorja, 1972), pp. 178–186;

Dimitrij Rupel, *Branje* (Maribor: Obzorja, 1973);

Malina Schmidt, "Konstante Hiengove dramatike," *Sodobnost*, 22 (1974): 263–272;

Borut Trekman, "Mnogoplastnost Hiengove proze," *Sodobnost*, 24 (1976): 1067–1073.

Drago Ivanišević
(10 February 1907 - 1 June 1981)

Dasha Čulić Nisula
Western Michigan University

BOOKS: *Zemlja pod nogama* (Zagreb: A. Čelap, 1940);
Kotarica stihova (Zagreb: Novo pokoljenje, 1951);
Turica (Zagreb: Savez amaterskih kazališta i kazališnih društava Hrvatske, 1956);
Dnevnik (Zagreb: Lykos, 1957);
Ljubav u koroti (Antiantigona) (Belgrade: Stožer, 1958);
Mali libar (Zagreb: Rad JAZU, 1959);
Karte na stolu (Zagreb: Zora, 1959);
Jubav (Zagreb: Lykos, 1960; enlarged edition, 1975);
Srž (Novi Sad: Matica srpska, 1961);
Poezija (Zagreb: Znanje, 1964);
Split (Belgrade: Jugoslavija, 1966);
Igra bogova ili pustinje ljubavi (Novi Sad: Matica srpska, 1967);
Glasine (Zagreb: Naprijed, 1969);
Da sam ptica (Zagreb: Školska knjiga, 1970);
Vrelo vrelo bez prestanka (Zagreb: Matica hrvatska, 1970);
Od blata jabuka (Zagreb: August Cesarec, 1971);
Pismo mrtvoj ljubavi '73 ili Feljton (Zagreb: Encyclopaedia moderna, 1973);
Mali, ne maline (Zagreb: Mladost, 1973);
Historija (Zagreb: August Cesarec, 1974);
Ljubav (Zagreb: Matica hrvatska, 1977);
Čovjek (Zagreb: Biblioteka Vid Bože Biškupića, 1978);
Čovjeku riječ (Zagreb: Grafički zavod Hrvatske, 1980);
Druga sloboda (Zagreb: Mladost, 1981).
Collection: *Izabrana Djela,* Pet stoljeća hrvatske književnosti, no. 125 (Zagreb: Matica hrvatska, 1981).
Editions in English: Poems, translated by Vasa D. Mihailovich, *Bridge,* nos. 19-20 (1970): 16-17; *Bridge,* no. 4 (1987): 46-49;
Poems, translated by Mihailovich, *Mundus Artium,* 4, no. 2 (1971): 42-43;
Poems, translated by Ellen Elias-Bursać, *Matica,* 21, no. 9 (1975): 38;

Drago Ivanišević

Poems, translated by Gregor McGregor, *Bridge,* no. 50 (1976): 59-60;
Poems, translated by Peter Kastmiller, *Bridge,* no. 12 (1985): 113-117.

PLAY PRODUCTION: *Ljubav u koroti ili Antiantigona,* Zagreb, Croatian National Theater, 1957.

TRANSLATIONS: André Gudem, *Put u Kongo,* translated by Ivanišević and Dragan Težak (Zagreb, 1934);

Iz stare kineske lirike (Zagreb: Rudolf Grbić, 1942);

Moj Ungaretti (Zagreb: Rudolf Grbić, 1942);

Pablo Neruda, *Kronika, Republika,* no. 9 (1947);

Knjiga pjesama Frederika García Lorke (Zagreb: Zora, 1950);

Carlo Goldoni, *Mirandolina* (Zagreb, 1950);

Crnačka poezija (Sarajevo: Narodna prosvjeta, 1956);

Osvaldo Ramos, *Riječ u vremenu,* translated by Ivanišević, A. Stipčević, and Š. Vučetić (Zagreb: Zora, 1969);

Otajna Hrvatska, translated by Ivanišević and Giuseppe Ungaretti (Rim, 1969);

Paul Éluard, *Ljubav poezija* (Split, 1970);

Amerika (Zagreb, 1973);

Natália Correa, *Zemlja iskrsla iz mora* (Zagreb, 1974).

When Drago Ivanišević died in 1981 at the age of seventy-four, he had been writing poetry for more than fifty years. He had also been painting, creating the first Surrealistic paintings in Croatian art, for nearly the same length of time. But recognition for this multitalented writer came late. His first published collection of poetry appeared in 1940, when he was thirty-three; the first public exhibit of his paintings was in 1970, when he was sixty-three. An overall evaluation of his work and the contributions he made as a poet, translator, and artist has yet to be made; but his experimentations in poetry and painting, as well as his translations of French, Spanish, and Italian poets, have unquestionably had an inspiring effect on many poets and artists in postwar Croatia.

A comparativist by training, a polyglot by necessity, and an artist by nature, Ivanišević was born in the multilingual port town of Trieste on 10 February 1907. He was the eldest child of wine merchants, Mate and Tomica, from the Poljica region in Dalmatia. In Trieste his first three years of schooling were in an Italian school, while he was also studying the Croatian and the Slovenian languages at the local South Slavic Hall. In 1916, during World War I, when his father fled from the Austrian front, he repeated the third year, in a German school, and then the fourth year in Zenica. In 1918, back in Trieste, he studied the first half of the school year in a naval high school; the second half he finished at a school in Sušak. In the fall of 1919 Ivanišević enrolled in a classical gymnasium in Split. By then his education was already firmly rooted in a multilingual experience.

In Split in 1925, he published his first poems in *Hrvatska sloga* (Croatian Unity). The following year he graduated from high school and attended the University of Belgrade, the only university that offered studies in comparative literature. There he also began to develop an interest in theater. Later that year he visited Paris, where he was introduced to the major literary and artistic trends of the time. This trip determined the course of his future development. Thereafter, he returned to Paris intermittently from 1926 to 1939; it was in Paris that Ivanišević first began to paint.

Completing his studies in French language and comparative literature in 1930, Ivanišević traveled to Italy, where he attended lectures in Rome and Florence. The next year he attended the University of Munich, then moved to Padova, where he continued his work in comparative literature, focusing on Latin, Spanish, Russian, and Czech studies. In 1931 his work culminated in a doctoral thesis on Dante Alighieri, "La fortuna di Dante nella letteratura serbocroata" (Dante's Fate in Serbo-Croatian Literature). By the end of 1932 he had also completed his army service in Mostar, where he befriended Antun Motika, a professor of Surrealist art, benefiting greatly from his association with a man who had a keen artistic sensibility and a professional knowledge of art.

Back in Zagreb in 1933, the poet spent several years as a high-school teacher and continued to publish his work in *Hrvatska revija* (Croatian Review), *Savremenik* (Contemporary), and *Dani i ljudi* (Days and People), the best literary journals of the period. From 1936 to 1938 he resided again in Paris, where he devoted his time to the three loves of his life: poetry, painting, and theater—probably in that order. In 1939, just before the outbreak of World War II, he became the director and cofounder of the Acting School of the Croatian National Theater in Zagreb. The following year he published his first collection of poetry, *Zemlja pod nogama* (Earth Beneath the Feet, 1940).

This collection not only came relatively late in Ivanišević's life, but it was also ill-timed because it appeared in the year just before the war swept into Yugoslavia, when most people were occupied with other issues. The collection, therefore, did not receive the kind of attention it deserved. If it had, Ivanišević's readers and colleagues would have realized that this collection offered something completely different from the kind of poetry they had been used to reading and writing. The collection was close to what the European Surrealists were doing, reflecting Ivanišević's familiarity with their work. Unfortunately, inasmuch as he was the only poet in Zagreb circles who accepted Surrealism (up to a point), no one else was able fully to understand and appreciate his work. Surrealism was as yet unrecognized, and the collection was thought to be bizarre. Himself influenced by the musicality of Spanish verse, by Italian hermetists, and by the Imagists, Ivanišević resisted overflowing emotional lyrics and preferred concentrated, precisely phrased poetic expression.

In his first collection the most significant works are the first three poems in prose, written in Dubrovnik in 1930. They are "Jutro" (Morning), "Podne" (Noon), and "Večer i noć" (Evening and Night), and they constitute the main sources of modernity in Croatian poetry. Poems in prose were the favorite form for Surrealists, revealing the uses of free association and the spontaneity of automatic writing. With this book Ivanišević widened the scope of Croatian poetic expression and anticipated what was to come twenty years later. However, it was obvious from the response to this first collection that his poetry would not attract wide public interest.

Once the war broke out and writers began to follow the revolutionary spirit in a neorealist style, Surrealistic innovations were crushed. Ivanišević's play with Surrealism was judged to be decadent and destructive. Because of this negative response, Ivanišević, like many other poets in Croatia, lost his lyric voice and began to devote his energies to translating. He translated the French poets Guillaume Apollinaire and Paul Éluard, the Spanish poets Federico García Lorca and Pablo Neruda, and the Italian poet Giuseppe Ungaretti. In 1938, for his work at the Sorbonne and his professor's exam in Belgrade, he wrote "Marcel Proust—sa vie et son oeuvre" (Marcel Proust: His Life and His Work). In 1942 he published his translations from the Italian, *Moj Ungaretti* (My Ungaretti), and from the French, *Iz stare kineske lirike* (From Old Chinese Lyrics). His translations of Lorca, under the title *Knjiga pjesama* (A Book of Poems), published in Zagreb in 1950, had an especially profound influence on the younger poets of the time who had already accepted Lorca's work as authentically modern poetry.

Besides translating, Ivanišević also engaged in producing theater. During the Nazi occupation of the country, he joined the Partisans in 1944 and was transferred to the liberated Glina to serve as director of the Central Theater and leader of the Partisan Acting School. At the end of the war in 1945, he returned to Zagreb, where he was named director of the newly established Acting School. In 1950 he became an assistant professor at the Zagreb Academy of Theater Arts, and in 1951 he became president of the Union of Amateur Theater Groups of Croatia. From 1956 until his retirement in 1960 he was the distinguished professor at the Zagreb Academy of Theater Arts.

The publication of Ivanišević's translation of Lorca in 1950 and Tin Ujević's translation of Walt Whitman in 1951 helped to create the new journal *Krugovi* (Circles). This journal, published in 1952 in the postwar political atmosphere, is associated with the ultimate breakup of the dogmatic, utilitarian trend in literary circles. The journal featured experimentation in Surrealism and supported individualism and art for art's sake. With this, the doors to free and modern literary creativity opened. Ivanišević, himself silent for almost two decades, published his second volume of poetry, *Dnevnik* (Diary), in 1957. In the same year he directed his own play, *Ljubav u koroti ili Antiantigona* (Love in Mourning, or Antiantigone), at the Croatian National Theater in Zagreb; the play was published the following year.

Besides translating and working in theater during the war years, Ivanišević also turned to writing in the Chakavian dialect spoken in his native Dalmatia. He wrote some of his gentlest love poetry in this dialect. His Chakavian verse, *Kotarica stihova* (A Basket of Verse), a collection of poetry for children, came out in 1951. Another collection in Chakavian, *Mali libar* (A Little Book), was published in 1959. In the same year Ivanišević published his first collection of short stories, *Karte na stolu* (Cards on the Table).

The following decade was highly productive for Ivanišević, who published five collections of poetry. He opened the decade with the publication of *Jubav* (Love) in 1960, a collection in Chakavian dialect, later enlarged and republished in 1975. Verse in Chakavian was particularly attractive to Ivanišević because it offered him the kind of musicality he sought. One notices his Surrealistic flights, humorous verse, and play with language in this dialect, as is true for his verse in standard literary Shtokavian. He demonstrated, however, that Chakavian is not an inferior dialect, and that any topic may be treated in this dialect. However, his best poems are tied to village life, domestic scenes, and close family relations. In Chakavian, Ivanišević returned to the happy days of his childhood, when in Trieste, in a family room, he first listened to his mother's native speech. Another of his collections, *Srž* (Core), appeared in 1961, and still another in 1964, *Poezija* (Poetry). *Srž* contains some of the most lyrical poems Ivanišević had published to that time. The main characteristic of his poetry is its changeability or its continual disintegrations of form. As soon as he adopts one form, he breaks it, a practice that gives his poetry an unusual freshness.

In the early 1960s Ivanišević also worked as an honorary secretary for the Association of Croatian Writers and served on the Yugoslav Publishing Council for foreign books. In addition, he worked as an editor for the publishing house Znanje and served as the president of the Poljica Association. He received the Golden Wreath Award for his work in 1961 and the Silver Star merit awards for 1962 and 1963.

Two more collections of poetry came out in the late 1960s: *Igra bogova ili pustinje ljubavi* (Gods' Play, or the Deserts of Love, 1967); and *Glasine* (Rumors, 1969), a collection of satiric poems for which the poet won the Goran Award. Almost all the poems in *Igra bogova* were written after those in the collection *Srž*. The collection is divided into six sections and includes drawings done by the author, signed with one of his pseudonyms, Albert Jordan. Many poems in this collection deal with the cities Ivanišević visited or lived in, such as Paris and Zagreb. Included also are his well-known poems "Jasenovac" and "Tinove metamorfoze" (Tin's Metamorphoses), and also a poem about the civil rights leader Medgar Evers (slain in 1963), under the title "U spomen Medgara Eversa" (In Remembrance of Medgar Evers). These are mature and serious poems, somewhat longer and more traditional in composition; they are less lyrical and more rationally and intellectually formulated. Many climax with one strong line at the end of the poem.

Glasine is a collection that contains all the types of poems Ivanišević included in his poetic practice: a few are in the Chakavian dialect; there are epigrams and satiric poems; and there are poems that feature the wordplay for which Ivanišević is known. Some poems, such as "A Quella Donna," employ both Croatian and Italian. Ivanišević is also known for his short poems.

In this collection there are many, including a one-line poem, "Tišina" (Silence), with a single word below the title "Srnče" (Young Buck). "Metafizika I" (Metaphysics I) contains three lines: "Dvije muhe kruže uokolo ožičane lampe / Jutro / Dvije muhe" (Two flies circle around a wire-lamp / Morning / Two flies). It appears that by the end of the 1960s Ivanišević found his old self, and in the sixth decade of his life became once again young and creative. In the next decade he truly found his own expression and was full of passion, creative energy, and the love of art.

In 1970 Ivanišević published two collections of poetry: a collection of verse for children, *Da sam ptica* (If I Were a Bird) and *Vrelo vrelo bez prestanka* (Spring, Endless Spring). There is no postscript to this edition, and the introduction by Jure Kaštelan, in line with his dislike for lengthy talk about poetry, is one page long. Kaštelan notes that Ivanišević's work seems amazingly fresh, as if he were at the beginning of his career. Though late maturity is rare among poets, Ivanišević was now writing his best poetry. He was a virtuoso with words and expressions. His desire for life, in spite of declining health, made him passionate and tireless in the search for new expressions. For him, to live is the same as to create. Kaštelan sees each of his poems as an incessant challenge: the bigger the misunderstanding, the better the comprehension.

Though there are poems from 1970 in this collection, there are also Ivanišević's classics from the previous decades, such as poems from the war, "Čitajući jednu kinesku knjigu" (Reading a Chinese Book) and "Trideset i četvrti rođendan" (Thirty-fourth Birthday); there is the line in "Deset tisuća razapetih na brdu Ararat" (Ten Thousand Crucified on the Hill of Ararat) that reads: "Čuješ li sirenu, metni masku na lice!" (If you hear a siren, put on a mask!). There are poems in the Chakavian dialect from the *Jubav* collection, and poems that are bi- and trilingual, employing Croatian, Italian, and Japanese, as in "Absurd sentimentalnosti ili jačajmo se humorom" (The Absurdity of Sentimentality, or, Let's Strengthen with Humor).

In 1970 Ivanišević held his first solo art exhibit in the Gallery Inex in Zagreb from 2 March until 16 March. His translations of Éluard were published as *Ljubav poezija* (Love Poetry). In the following year Ivanišević continued his art exhibits in Studio Forum in Zagreb and published his next volume of poetry, *Od blata jabuka* (An Apple of Mud). Awards for poetry that year include the

Cavaliere ufficiale award from Italy, the Goran Award, and the Ark of Marko Marulić Award. In 1973 he published a long poem titled *Pismo mrtvoj ljubavi '73 ili Feljton* (Letter to a Deceased Love '73, or, Satire) and another collection of poetry for children, *Mali, ne maline* (Little Boy, Not Raspberries).

Besides his poetry, Ivanišević also published translations from Spanish in 1973 and a book of translations from Portuguese, Natália Correa's *Zemlja iskrsla iz mora* (Land Resurrected from the Sea) in 1974. In that year his poetry collection *Historija* (History) appeared, and he continued his art exhibits in Zagreb, Split, and Osijek. In 1975 he was elected to the Yugoslav Academy of Arts and Sciences. The following year he was named the Founder Fellow of the International Academy of Poets, Cambridge, England. He held another exhibit from 10 February to 28 February 1977 in Zagreb in Salon Schira. His last collection of poetry, *Čovjeku riječ* (A Word to Man), was published in 1980; his last art exhibit was in May 1981 in Zagreb.

Ivanišević's work shows both domestic and foreign influences. There are traces of Augustin "Tin" Ujević and Antun Branko Šimić, but these influences, as well as those of the Imagists and the French Surrealists, basically gave Ivanišević an impetus for work and creativity. Whatever he adopted from these movements and admired in individual artists, he adopted in his own way and re-created as something authentically his own. In fact, he never joined an artistic school or movement. Whatever he embraced he embraced because his own disposition and training led him to do so. After all, Ivanišević was first of all a polyglot, a linguist, and as such was primarily interested in the word itself and in the sound of language, which led to his interest in the musical Chakavian dialect. It is no wonder that rhythm is often the most important element in his poems.

As a comparativist trained in Italian, French, and Spanish, he also translated from Modern Greek, Catalan, Rumanian, German, and Russian. Translations from these languages appeared mostly in anthologies such as *Antologija svjetske lirike* (An Anthology of World Poetry), *100 najvećih djela svjetske književnosti* (100 Greatest Works in World Literature), *100 pjesnika svijeta* (100 World Poets), *Antologija ljubavne poezije* (An Anthology of Love Poetry), *Umro od ljubavi* (Died from Love), and others. His interest in the theater attests again to his focus on the sound and the use of language, and Ivanišević's attraction to Surrealism can probably be attributed to the playing with language in which the Surrealists were interested. Furthermore, whatever Ivanišević could not say in one language, he said in another. Finally, what he could not say in words, he painted. Thus emerges an all-encompassing relationship among the three disciplines in which he worked: literature, theater, and art.

Ivanišević's early poems, those written before World War II, tend to be longer than his later poems. In fact, he began his career publishing poems in prose in 1925. With the publication of his war poems in 1957 and his subsequent collections, his verse became shorter and more intense. Some critics believe that the poet's strength lies in the short format, where everything is reduced to the minimum number of words necessary to carry a message.

Ivanišević's poems can certainly be called economical. He uses only as many words as he needs to suggest his subject. His poems are rhythmically rather than semantically ordered. Thus, rhythm and imagery are dominant, and because of this feature, his poems seem open-ended. The author suggests; he never tells. The meaning is reduced to essential words that are rhythmically associated. In these short poems two or three strong lines at the end of the poem usually epitomize its meaning. They can be detached from the previous lines and still constitute the essence of the poem in a haikulike, connotative structure. A good example of such a structure is the ending of Ivanišević's poem "Amfora": "and I ask myself why / my fear / oh sleeping amphora"; and there are two haikulike, independent, highly connotative lines at the end of the poem "Naranča" (Orange): "in the wreck shines an orange / which will disappear with me." This type of poetic structure is common in Ivanišević, who, earlier than anyone else in his country, knew and imitated haiku.

Another characteristic of Ivanišević's poetry is the repetition of sounds, then words, and even whole lines. Playing with sound is used, for example, in the poem "Fiordaliza," where the sound for the substantive suffix *-iza* (like Mona*liza*) finds its variants in Par*iza*, kr*iza*, and paral*iza*. Repetition of sounds, words, and lines is characteristic of Ivanišević's poetry. Initially this repetition produces an emphasis and calls attention to itself. It then produces a kind of expectation on the part of the reader, just enough so that the author can produce a variant of it, that is, betray the expectation by startling the reader and offering a surprise ending in the line or at the end of a stanza or poem. What Ivanišević does is to produce a constant pattern and then vary it. A combination of words and line repetition occurs in a poem such as "A Quella Donna," a bilingual (Italian and Croatian) poem. Ivanišević is also a master of the use of anaphora and anadiplosis. He often repeats the same word vertically, reducing it in each line by one letter, as in the poem "Tako biva": "Kolovrat / olovrat / lovrat / ovrat / vrat / rat / at / t." He does the same horizontally, reducing the line by a word in horizontal succession, as in the poem "Rastvaranje jednog stiha Vitezslava Nezvala" (translated as "The Dissolution of One Verse by Vitezslav Nezval"):

Nothing can help you, no nothing can help you
Nothing can help you, no, nothing can help
Nothing can help you, no, nothing can. . . .

Ten years before his death, the poet began to promote his works in the visual arts. Apparently he had something to say that he had never said in poetry. His last exhibit in Zagreb in 1981 consisted of sculptures and drawings. Besides exhibiting in Zagreb, Split, and Rijeka, he held shows in Osijek, Varaždin, Sisak, Dubrovnik, Komiža, and Hvar. At these showings Ivanišević at times showed more attachment to some of his small drawings than he did toward many of his poems and books.

Of the paintings first exhibited in 1970, the most interesting are the six Surrealistic paintings from 1936 to 1938. The oldest is *San* (Dream) from 1936. Then come two from 1937, *Hommage à Breton* and *Hommage à Éluard*. Some show the clear, visible influence of Georges Braque and Pablo Picasso. Two paintings from 1938 are *Hommage à Krleža* and *Između noći i dana* (Between Night and Day). In later exhibits, the poet Ivanišević, as the artist Albert Jordan, presented drawings from his mythology, at the center of which is a woman-monster with the head of a bird.

Nevenka Bezić-Božanić notes that, although poets usually write about artistic works, Ivanišević drew his verse. The ties between poetry and art over time became stronger and stronger. As he grew older, he returned to painting, which he had explored in high school and to which he had thought he would devote his life. He drew on paper with pencils and on canvas with paint; and he used clay to make sculptures. His art is totally unconventional and spontaneous, and manifests a remarkable freshness. All his drawings and sculptures reveal the artist's inner self, his view of the world and the joy of life. But in spite of all his interests and occupations, this multitalented man remained at heart a poet.

Bibliography:
M. Žeželj, "Ivanišević, Drago," in *Leksikon pisaca Jugoslavije,* volume 2 (Novi Sad: Matica srpska, 1979), pp. 482–483.

References:
Nevenka Bezić-Božanić, "Dva zapisa o Dragi Ivaniševiću," *Mogućnosti,* 28 (1981): 635–637;

Srećko Diana, "Iskustvo ali i ljubav. Marginalije uz izabrane pjesme Drage Ivaniševića *Ljubav,*" *Mogućnosti,* 25 (1977): 705–710;

Milivoje Marković, "Bura mladosti i rezignacija starosti," in *Iskušenja poezije: savremeni hrvatski pesnici* (Belgrade: Narodna knjiga, 1981), pp. 103–138;

Nedjeljko Mihanović, *Drago Ivanišević, 1907–1981* (Zagreb: Jugoslavenska akademija znanosti i umjetnosti, 1989);

Zvonimir Mrkonjić, "Drago Ivanišević, pjesnik od vremena," *Izraz,* 22 (1957): 471–474;

Vlatko Pavletić, "Drago Ivanišević," in *Drago Ivanišević: Izabrana djela* (Zagreb: Matica hrvatska, 1981), pp. 7–34;

Pavletić, "Ivaniševića poetika medju nadrealizma i ulipoizma," *Izraz,* 22 (1977): 96–123;

Pavletić, "Tri odlomka o Ivaniševiću," *Mogućnosti,* 26 (1979): 429–447;

Boško Petrović, "Reč o Dragi Ivaniševiću," *Letopis Matice srpske,* 421 (1977): 639–643;

Saša Vereš, "Ruže ruža u grču i neprebolu: na marginama poezije Drage Ivaniševića," in *Poezija* (Zagreb: Znanje, 1964), pp. 207–220.

Drago Jančar
(13 April 1948 -)

Helga Glušič
University of Ljubljana, Slovenija

BOOKS: *Romanje gospoda Houžvičke* (Maribor: Založba Obzorja, 1971);

Petintrideset stopinj (Maribor: Založba Obzorja, 1974);

Galjot (Murska Sobota: Pomurska založba, 1978);

O bledem hudodelcu (Ljubljana: Mladinska knjiga, 1978);

Blodniki: Disident Arnož in njegovi, Razseljena oseba, Nenavadni dogodki v Kotu (Maribor: Založba Obzorja, 1982);

Severni sij (Murska Sobota: Pomurska založba, 1984);

Sproti (Trst: Založništvo tržaškega tiska, 1984);

Smrt pri Mariji Snežni (Ljubljana: Mladinska knjiga, 1985);

Veliki briljantni valček (Ljubljana: Cankarjeva založba, 1985);

Triptih o Trubarju (Maribor: Založba Obzorja, 1986);

Tri igre: Dedalus, Klementov padec, Zalezujoč Godota, edited by Andrej Inkret (Ljubljana: Mladinska knjiga, 1988);

Terra incognita (Klagenfurt & Celovec: Wieser, 1989);

Poročilo iz devete dežele (Klagenfurt & Celovec: Wieser, 1991);

Razbiti vrč (Ljubljana: Mihelač, 1992);

Disput, Adam Michnik: Drago Jančar (Klagenfurt & Celovec: Wieser, 1992);

Erinnerungen an Jugoslawien (Klagenfurt & Celovec: Hermagoras, 1992);

Pogled angela (Ljubljana: Mihelač, 1992);

Posmehljivo poželenje (Klagenfurt & Celovec: Wieser, 1993);

Der Sprung von der Liburnia (Klagenfurt & Salzburg: Wieser, 1993);

Augsburg in druge resnične pripovedi (Ljubljana: Mihelač, 1994);

Halštat, (Klagenfurt & Celovec: Wieser, 1994);

Egiptovski lonci mesa (Ljubljana: Mihelač, 1995).

Drago Jančar

Editions in English: "Death at Mary-of-the-Snows," translated by Mario Suško and Edward J. Czerwinski, *Slavic and East European Arts,* 2, no. 2 (1984): 99–108;

Terra incognita, translated by Anne Czech, *Pen International,* 37, no. 1 (1987): 59–65;

The Great Brilliant Waltz, translated by Czech and Peter Perhonis, *Scena,* no. 11 (1988): 195–200;

Stakeout at Godot, Scena Theater, Washington, D.C. (1988);

The Great Brilliant Waltz, Scena Theater, Washington, D.C. (1989).

PLAY PRODUCTIONS: *Sojenje Johanu Otu,* edited by T. Partljič, Maribor, Drama SNG, 11 April 1979;

Disident Arnož in njegovi, Ljubljana, Drama SNG, 22 January 1982;

Veliki briljantni valček, Ljubljana, Drama SNG, 6 March 1985;

Dedalus, Ljubljana, Drama SNG, 6 May 1988;

Vsi tirani mameluki so hud konec vzeli ali Lex moralis Primoža Trubarja, Ljubljana, Mestno gledališče Ljubljansko, 9 October 1986;

Klementov padec, Ljubljana, Mestno gledališče Ljubljansko, 15 March 1988;

Dedalus, Ljubljana, Drama SNG, 6 May 1988;

Zalezujoč Godota, Ljubljana, Drama SNG, 17 February 1989;

Halštat, Trst, Slovensko stalno gledališče, 1994.

MOTION PICTURES: *Razseljena oseba,* screenplay by Jančar, Viba film, Ljubljana, 1982;

Heretik, screenplay by Jančar, Viba film, Ljubljana, 1986.

TELEVISION: *Nenavadni dogodki v Kotu,* script by Jančar, RTV Ljubljana, 1981;

Trubar, script by Jančar, serial, RTV Ljubljana, 1986.

RADIO: *Izpoved hudodelca,* script by Jančar, Radio Ljubljana, 1988;

Zalezujoč Godota, script by Jančar, Radio Maribor, 1993.

TRANSLATIONS: Borisav Višinski, *Mavrica* (Murska Sobota: Pomurska Založba, 1977);

Borisav Stanković, *Tri drame: Koštana, Tašana Jovča,* with an introduction by Jančar (Maribor: Založba Obzorja, 1980);

Jordan Plevneš, *Erigon* (Nova Gorica: Primorsko dramsko gledališče, 1983).

As a novelist, short-story writer, playwright, and essayist, Drago Jančar is a central figure in contemporary Slovenian literature. In the past twenty years his writing has revealed an artistic power of formulating and expressing ideas that reach far beyond the spiritual and cultural sphere of his native Slovenia, thereby making his work accessible to a large and varied audience.

Jančar was born on 13 April 1948 in Maribor, Slovenija, to Anton Jančar, a technical supervisor in an automobile factory, and Rozalija Trantura. In 1970 Jančar earned a degree from the law college in Maribor. As a student he was editor in chief, executive, and cultural editor of the student magazine *Katedra*. In 1970 he married Olga Čerič, director of the theater festival Boršikovo srečanje in Maribor; the couple has one daughter. From 1971 to 1974 Jančar worked as a journalist for the Maribor daily *Večer;* in 1975 he was sentenced to one year in prison for writing so-called enemy propaganda, but after three months he was released. In 1978 Jančar became a freelance writer and moved from Maribor to Ljubljana, where he became stage director at the Viba Film Company. Since 1980 he has been secretary and editor at the Slovenska matica publishing house in Ljubljana.

Jančar's first notable literary success came with the novel *Galjot* (The Galley Slave, 1978). In this work Jančar abandoned the experimental prose of his earlier novel, *Petintrideset stopinj* (Thirty-five Degrees, 1974), and his short-story collections, *Romanje gospoda Houžvičke* (The Pilgrimage of Mr. Houžvička, 1971) and *O bledem hudodelcu* (About the Pale Sinner, 1978); in *Galjot* he turned instead to the traditional form of the historical novel, specifically choosing the form of an adventure novel. Although the novel is set in the picturesque seventeenth century in central Europe, the fate of its hero, Johan Ot, also reflects the destiny of modern man. The narrative evokes a time of stormy changes in the social, political, and religious spheres, a time when all the signs of transition mixed together with moral decay and spiritual decadence. Relating the story of both an individual and an era, the novel portrays the dynamic disharmony in a community, pitting authorities against the human crowd. These two factions, in spite of their differences, are capable of an ambivalent symbiosis. In contrast to them stands Ot, a passive, speculating observer who, because of his objective distance, appears in all situations to be dangerous to the community.

Galjot is a story about human restlessness and the desire for a full life, escape and the quest for solutions, overpowering weakness, and the yearning for freedom. As Jančar writes: "The galley slave held wide expanses within his chest. The entire crazy and chaotic world, all its intelligent and non-intelligent dimensions warred within this body covered with scars. But see: he survived all deaths." The narration is a fireworks of dynamic descriptions of states and spaces that not only shape the life-journey of Johan Ot but also frame the world, as it is formulated in folk superstitions and interwoven with mythological and historical elements. This world is described

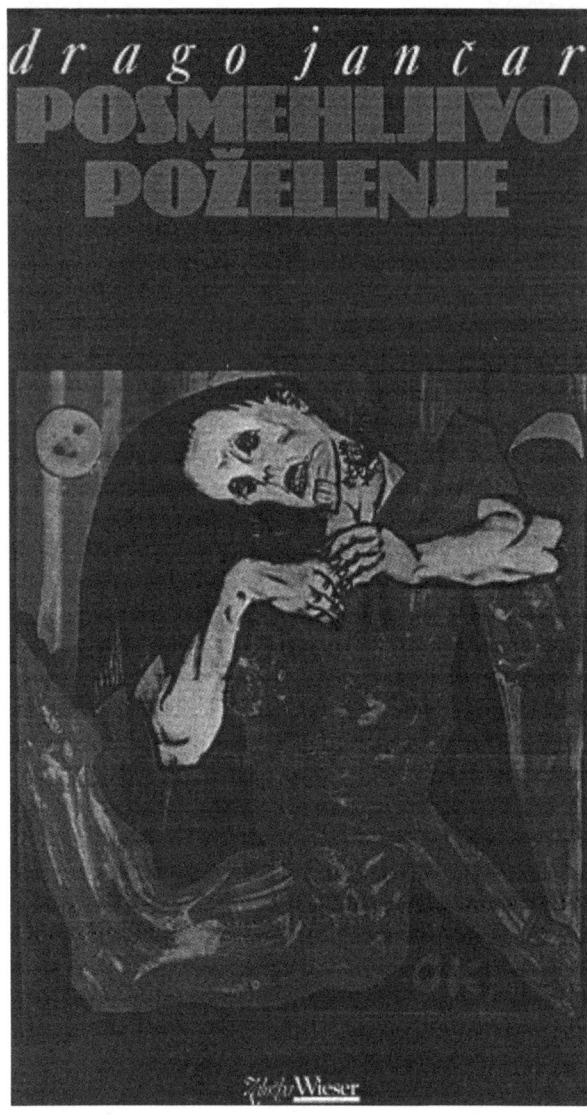

Dust jacket for Jančar's 1993 novel, inspired by his experiences in the United States

with a contemporary ironic attitude and a melodious lyricism that relates the story of the future. Although the galley man's story is determined by the events of the seventeenth century, this presentation of the past and the formulation of the destiny of the main hero reflect the story of any historically exposed time. Present-day man, or Everyman, could not survive without being ironic, poetic, or fantastic. Three editions of *Galjot* have been published in Slovenia, and it has been translated into ten languages (German, Hungarian, Polish, Macedonian, Serbian, Czech, Russian, Dutch, Cossack, and White Russian).

Jančar's second novel, *Severni sij* (Aurora Borealis, 1984), centers around events in the Slovenian city of Maribor before World War II. It is a story about a stranger who, during an extremely tense time filled with predictions of a great slaughter, arrives with a covert mission, knowing a secret that contains a germ of his approaching insanity. The narration reveals a disintegrating human consciousness that, during decadent enjoyment, unconsciously expects a forecasted catastrophe. The form of the novel introduces a few experiments into Jančar's oeuvre, primarily on two levels: the levels of the objective narration and that of the subjectivism of the central literary figure, Erdman, the stranger in the city. Erdman is interested in anthropology (especially as it explores racial theory), occultism, and mysticism (insofar as it offers an explanation of the aurora borealis and explores the esoteric elements of experience); he is also involved in social, political, and erotic affairs.

The objective narrative level of the specific time and space, that is, prewar Maribor, is recorded in "documentary" chapters that serve as a frame for Erdman's first-person narration. These chapters contain not only descriptions of the city but also several stories set in the bourgeois environment and among the semiproletariat, with psychological portraits of individuals; these portraits also evoke the psychology of the social milieu. Each segment is part of the mosaic of the central story. The narrative technique differs greatly from the documentary sections, including such diverse subjects as an anthropological study of the shape of the human head and the explanation of the aurora borealis to wartime scenes from Maribor, police records on a double murder, and a psychiatric report on Erdman. The narrative is broken several times by a reverse-time perspective that relates a future story involving certain characters (explaining what happens to them during the war and afterward) and by authorial interruptions in the form of commentaries. Not only in the stories about the future but also in the end of Erdman's story there is the comment: "But Erdman, he has no more to say."

The two interlocking narrative levels contain one of the most important messages of the novel: its anticipation of world catastrophe (with consciously included causes of this cataclysm). This premonition about the all-encompassing disintegration of values and the impossibility of rational forecasting is contained chiefly in Erdman's story about his own consciousness, about not being conscious of one's own identity and intentions or about one's own emotional state. Erdman's story is filled with dramatic symbols: a sphere, a ball, a globe, security in a mother's lap, and dream visions growing from fear and uncertainty. The appearance of the bloody red evening, with the aurora borealis spanning the sky over the mob, confirms the ill omens foretelling the coming catastrophe. In the plot this foreshadowing is confirmed by a double murder and Erdman's insanity, which symbolically conveys the idea of the "pulsation of that gigantic world heart" with "a magnetic needle... and this needle now only slightly quivers." *Severni sij* is a novel whose inner dynamics and intertwining of documentary and superrealistic elements make it a stirring narrative. This impact is created primarily by the consistently formulated sense of premonition, the force of which is driven by fragmented actions and experiential restraint in which resignation alternates with irony, thus creating the experience of emotional pain and the realization, as Jančar writes, "that evil is a necessary cleavage in perfection." The novel has been published in two editions in Slovenia and has been translated into German, Croatian, Dutch, and Russian.

After almost a decade during which Jančar wrote shorter prose works and essays, his third novel appeared, *Posmehljivo poželenje* (Derisive Desire, 1993), inspired by Jančar's experiences as a Fulbright fellow in New York and New Orleans in 1985. The novel, presently being translated into English, German, and Polish, relates the story of Gregor Gradnik and his stay in New Orleans. Gradnik experiences an environment that challenges him as "an invisible observer, inaudible listener, and an ignorant know-it-all." The novel opens with the dream of a plane flight as well as with the image of the creation of the text that Gradnik is writing. The awakening of the hero signals his entrance into an entirely alien world that reflects both itself and Gradnik. The mirroring creates the perspective of an observer of an exotic place, exotic faces, and exotic ideas who becomes acquainted with a picturesque side of human beings in a world palpitating to a southern rhythm.

"I am an observer.... I observe what has been happening to me here, in the other part of the world," Gradnik says while he confronts his landlord and again as he explores the university, the city's architecture, its nightlife, and the outlines of human fates. His companion on this journey is also the sum of his life's influences, ranging from the literary works of Tennessee Williams, Thomas Mann, and Franz Kafka to his personal, emotional, and creative experiences. In its reflection of the lively panoramas and its jovial, sad, sometimes violent, sometimes indifferent cast of characters, Gradnik's story contains a mixture of his astonishment and uncertainty spiced with a large dose of irony. Most of his ironical references relate to formulations about the established ideas of the United States of America, which at first burden the narration considerably. Later these critical evaluations give place to the hero's self-analysis, in which self-irony and melancholy meet.

Posmehljivo poželenje is a novelized essay on melancholy. The narration is filled with a dense reflection of the environment, characterized by elementary external signs: intensive colors, human beings, music, and conversational and behavioral styles. The shock arising from the recognition that there is a specifically American way of thinking, which enhances Gradnik's feelings of alienation and powerlessness regarding surrounding events, leads to his surrender to eroticism and drinking. There is a strong social sense present in the descriptions of marginal individuals who alternately awaken sympathy, uncertainty, or even disgust in the main character. The depth of these feelings is also a sign of a strong inclination on the author's part toward the vulnerable. The mosaic of the novel is also filled with a love story that is accompanied by the doubt and hate that Gradnik's imminent departure engenders. The narrative levels are bound by melancholy as the theme of a study, which in scholarly language attempts to discover the origin of the otherwise unclear moods that accompany the main character at work, in artistic and literary company, in love, and in his growing inner resistance toward "being an alien." Gradnik's resistance causes homesickness and creates apparitions of his homeland, his mother, and his Slovene-ness, mockingly accompanied by "melancholic devils," which refers to a specific national characteristic.

Descriptions and impressions alternate with ironic scholarly passages about melancholy; the novel includes charts and a picture of the human body with critical points marked. The combination of objectivity and subjectivity leads to the unfolding of Gradnik's story. His stay in the United States ends in an entanglement of contradictory feelings, of being either moved and shocked or defensively derisive. A rendezvous with his wife and the news of his mother's death complement his vision of a return to the environment of childhood, to his roots, to a dimension of timelessness and boundless space that allows the hero to accept all the impressions coming from the surrounding world.

Jančar's short stories develop thematically and ideologically along the same lines as his novels, but they allow him to experiment with other stylistic techniques. In his short stories, which do not necessarily have a short-story structure, he adapts the narrative form to his intuitive understanding of human destiny. At the center of his collections of short stories—*Romanje gospoda Houžvičke; O bledem hudodelcu; Smrt pri Mariji Snežni* (1985, translated as "Death at Mary-of-the-Snows," 1984); *Pogled angela* (The Look of an Angel, 1992); and *Augsburg in druge resnične pripovedi* (Augsburg and Other True Stories, 1994)—is a man with evil and violence within himself. The stories contain fierce scenes of uncontrollable instincts, nonsensical but fatally determined and tragic deaths, and a causal interconnection of times, places, and deeds. In these connections reason cannot explain the causes for a situation where, as Jančar writes in *Pogled angela,* two understandings of "history and civilisation [meet], the one that man recorded, developed, and systemized, and the other operating according to an automated mechanism; one that is the reason of the world and its centre, and the other that is the automatic will of the world, and man's dark, always accompanying shadow."

The motifs characteristic of Jančar's short-story writing are principally connected with death, which is often represented by symbolic signs that lead to the realization of a destiny that happens after dark premonitions. The stories are written in an expressive and poetic language, the most powerful tool of Jančar's prose. His short stories are also characterized by dramatic, surprising turns that propel the events to thrilling, meaningful climaxes. Perhaps the most outstanding among the stories are "Smrt pri Mariji Snežni" and "Augsburg," which won the European Award for Short Fiction in Arnsberg, Germany, in 1994 and has been translated into German and English. Foreign anthologies also contain the following short stories by Jančar: "Noč nasilja" (The Night of the Violence), "Ogenj" (The Fire), "Pogled angela," "Dve sliki" (Two Pictures), and "Aithiopika."

In the center of his most prominent short story, "Augsburg," there are scenes about recent changes in the European political and national map. In its last part the author writes: "There is a slight insanity going over the Continent." The story reveals the meaning of an ironically conjectured narrative framework that contains scenes of wild evil and the absurd pretexts by which mankind gives sense to his actions. The main character is a man traveling through chaos who anticipates and recognizes above all the absurdity of this world as he approaches the city of Augsburg. He enters through a network of civilizational knots and barriers into an ironical and also unrealizable ideal world that is described in an ancient travelogue. As the narrator observes, "It is not easy to arrive to Augsburg. We know that already." The trip symbolizes the ambivalent feelings of the present moment, of "going into Europe." This world has not changed from the times of the humanist and skeptic Michel de Montaigne; therefore Jančar's storyteller concludes his narration by saying: "We are now in Augsburg. In 1580. When we have gained enough sleep, we will continue our dreams."

Jančar's literary success in Slovenia and in international literary circles has resulted in productions of his plays, which include *Disident Arnož in njegovi* (Dissident Arnož and his Followers, 1982); *Nočni prizori* (Night Scenes, 1987); *Triptih o Trubarju* (Triptych about Trubar, 1986); *Veliki briljantni valček* (The Great Brilliant Waltz, 1985); *Klementov padec* (Klement's Fall, 1988); *Dedalus* (1989); *Zalezujoč Godota* (Stakeout at Godot, 1989); *Halštat* (Hallstatt, 1994); and *Dvoboj* (The Duel, 1992), an adaptation of a story by Anton Chekhov. Three of these plays were very successful abroad: *Zalezujoč Godota* and *Veliki briljantni valček* were acclaimed in Austria, the United States, Hungary, Macedonia, Bulgaria, Croatia, and Serbia, and *Halštat* was enthusiastically received in Italy and Austria. Jančar also wrote two film scripts, *Razseljena oseba* (Displaced Person, 1982) and *Heretik* (Heretic, 1986), and two television scripts and two radio plays. His dramatic texts explore history, politics, war, political or social systems, and human destiny, and Jančar particularly focuses on man's persecution and flight. He wrestles with the issues of morality and freedom, dissension, the will to power, and self-determination. By filtering reality through his playful imagination, he represents insoluble traumas of humankind from an ironic perspective.

The play *Veliki briljantni valček* attracted much attention. Andrej Inkret, a critic and commentator, calls it "a drama of metaphor and paradox." Its setting is an institution called Freedom Liberates, where people cannot be what they want and consequently become what the institution requires them to be. "The paradox of Jančar's metaphor lies in the fact that a man must until the very end remain enslaved and caught in a wish," Inkret writes. Jančar's dramatic heroes are split within themselves. In their contradictory state of freedom and dependency, they lose their identity; they are insane, and their insanity is a metaphor for human imperfection. Specialists in metaphor, as the doctors and the employees of the institution are called, convert the imperfect human beings. They direct and manipulate them; they do away with their individual imperfection and split state and reconstitute them into uniform, empty people. The irony of "liberation" and "treatment" in this madhouse is what motivates the dramatic action. At one point a gradual equalizing of the employees (the "specialists in metaphor") and the objects of their treatment happens. All are a part of an uncontrollable, blanketing system whose executive authority is metaphorically represented in the terrifying character of Volodja, the attendant. The final scene is flooded with a melody by Frédéric Chopin that connects the real world to the magic world and represents harmony and truly redeeming freedom. Inkret's comment on the play compares it with Djordje Jovanovic's play *Norci* (The Fools, 1970) and Ken Kesey's novel *One Flew Over the Cuckoo's Nest* (1962), which was later made into a film by Milos Forman. This similarity is especially apt with regard to the central hero, the history professor Simon Veber, alias the Polish rebel Drohojowsky, who swings in his identity between the two faces of his ego.

Halštat, Jančar's eleventh theater piece, is a play in four acts with an epilogue. It can be considered a comedy with the noble mission of a work of art that plays with serious things and mocks them. This is a theater of inner confrontations between reality and imagination, between the seen and the created in a piece of art. The reality of events, as in Luigi Pirandello's work, is relativized and is not formulated directly in a critical message; rather, it is a vivid, surprising intertwining of a rational plan and an amicable joke. The setting is an abandoned mine in which two archaeologists, Habilis and Anastazija, excavate precious archaeological findings that will make them world famous. The place abounds in bones and jewelry. Three other characters are Jula, Nela, and Honza, the tramp who causes the entanglement of the action with his naive and yet wise interventions. This comedy builds its humor by contrasting the aesthetically superior (history, science, and humanity) with the profane (tramps, a lost young woman, drinking, homelessness, and primitive sex). Humorous scenes and dialogues

Dust jacket for a collection of Jančar's writings, including novels, short stories, and essays

reveal serious things in an almost grotesque way, with allusions to the bones of the dead and to concentration camps. The contrast can be seen in the language used. For instance, the superior speech of the archaeologist is opposed to the tramp's common talk, which is mixed with intellectualisms that make the dialogue especially humorous.

The text contains allusions to present-day Slovenia and political life in general through its explorations of such subjects as excavating bones, digging into the past, and antagonisms between the Left and the Right. These are, however, only tiny parts of a humorous encounter between two worlds, the seeming versus the real or the acted versus the true: the stupidly priggish, smart, and rough, on one hand, versus the jovial, free, clever-minded, and, above all, mocking, on the other, as represented in the emotional, doggishly tame Honza. The language in *Halštat* is part of a witty, surprisingly dynamic dialogue: it reflects the metamorphoses of the protagonists and characterizes them in scenes that balance the intellectual and instinctive elements in the heroes. The dialogue illuminates the social, ethical, and personal roles of the characters. This contemporary comedy has the power to mock and provoke with jesting playfulness.

As president of the Slovenian P.E.N. Center from 1987 to 1991, Jančar established important connections with members of European literary associations. In 1988 he stayed in Germany for three months on a scholarship for writers. Political changes in Europe during these years inspired his essays, which primarily present his views on literature and on the Slovenian nation, its past and present, and its relation to political events. He also presents his views about the problems connected with the rise of a new democracy after a historical period in which two nondemocratic political systems were in place. Jančar's essays are characterized by their picturesqueness and the author's personal freedom. Using suggestive metaphors, he seeks the spiritual essence of contemporary man in his social reactions. Because of his political independence he can even foresee the direction toward which the present tends. As an extremely refined humanist and a convincing artist, he records his observations about the radical changes that have been taking place in Slovenia and Europe. In the late 1990s Jančar seems to be at the peak of his creative power. He has received several Slovene literary awards for his fiction, dramatic works, and essays. His writing also has an enthusiastic following among readers and critics around the world, and he is, after Ivan Cankar and Ciril Kosma, the Slovenian author most frequently translated abroad. In 1995 Jančar was honored by membership in SAZU, the Slovenian Academy of Science and Art.

Interview:

Nela Malečkar, "Drago Jančar: 'Ko se nasanjamo, bomo spali naprej,'" *Razgledi,* 17 (September 1994): 4–9.

References:

Helga Glušič, "Drago Jančar in odprtost samobitnosti," *Seminar slovenskega jezika, kulture in literature,* 28 (1992): 91–96;

Glušič, "Jančarjev roman Galjot," *Seminar slovenskega jezika, kulture in literature,* 20 (1984): 179–185;

Andrej Inkret, "Jančarjeve tri komedije," introduction to *Tri igre* (Ljubljana: Mladinska knjiga, 1988), pp. 277–304;

Inkret, "A Tragicomedy of Daedalus, Builder of a Socialist Prison," *Scena,* 12 (1989): 23–28;

Inkret, "Zgodovinski roman o veliki drajni in o strašnem samotnem begu," introduction to *Galjot* (Ljubljana: Mladinska knjiga, 1984), pp. 355–363;

Inkret, "Tujci, disidenti in blodniki," introduction to *Galjot* (Maribor: Založba Obzorja, 1980), pp. 403–439, 440–441;

Klaus Detlef Olof, "Drago Jančar," IDE, Informationen zur Deutschedidaktik, 4 (Wien & Klagenfurt, 1991): 45–57.

Slavko Janevski
(11 January 1920 -)

Milne Holton
University of Maryland

BOOKS: *Krvava niza* (Skopje: Kultura, 1945);
Pesni, by Janevski, Aco Šopov, Blaže Koneski, Gogo Ivanovski, and Lazo Karovski (Skopje: Glaven odbor na narodnata mladina na Makedonija, 1946);
Pioneri, pionerki, bubački, i šumski dzverki (Skopje: Državno knigoizdatelstvo na Makedonija, 1946);
Pruga na mladosta (Skopje: Glaven odbor na narodnata mladina na Makedonija, 1946);
Raspeani bukvi (Skopje: Državno knigoizdatelstvo na Makedonija, 1946);
Milion džinovi: Prikazni za Petgodišnot plan (Skopje: Nopok, 1948);
Pesni: (1944-1948) (Skopje: Državno knigoizdatelstvo na Makedonija, 1948);
Sneško (Skopje: Nopok, 1948);
Egejska barutna bajka (Skopje: Nopok, 1950);
Ulica (Skopje: Državno knigoizdatelstvo na Makedonija, 1950);
Lirika (Skopje: Kočo Racin, 1951);
Selo zad sedumte jaseni (Skopje: Kočo Racin, 1952); revised as *Stebla* (Skopje: Kultura, 1965);
Šećerna prikazna (Skopje: Detska radost, 1952);
Klovnovi i luģe (Skopje: Kočo Racin, 1955);
Dve Marii (Skopje: Kočo Racin, 1956);
Leb i kamen (Skopje: Kočo Racin, 1957);
Mesečar (Skopje: Kočo Racin, 1958);
Karamba Baramba (Skopje: Kočo Racin, 1959);
Marsovci i gluvci (Skopje: Kočo Racin, 1959);
Gorčlivi legendi (Skopje: Kočo Racin, 1962);
Siromaviot črni Džo (Skopje: Kočo Racin, 1962);
Temni kažuvanja, with Kiril Kamilov and Meto Jovanovski (Skopje: Kočo Racin, 1962);
I bol i bes (Skopje: Kočo Racin, 1964);
Evanģelie po Itar Pejo (Skopje: Kočo Racin, 1966);
Gluvi komandi (Skopje: Misla, 1966);
Tančarka na dlanka (Belgrade: Prosveta, 1966);
Pesni (Skopje: Makedonska kniga, Detska radost, 1967);
Crni i žolti (Skopje: Makedonska kniga, 1968);
Kainavelija (Skopje: Makedonska kniga, 1968);

Slavko Janevski

Itar Pejo Kainaveliski (Skopje: Naša kniga, 1969);
Najgolemiot kontinent (Skopje: Naša kniga, 1969);
Tvrdoglavi (Skopje: Naša kniga, 1969);
Vojnik dva metra v zemja (Skopje: Misla, 1969);
Baram, Baram, Barambaš (Skopje: Naša kniga, 1970);
Omarnini (Skopje: Nova Makedonija, 1972);
Plaketa na poezija: bibliofilsko izdanie (Skopje: Centar za kultura i informacie, 1975);
Kovčeg (Skopje: Naša kniga, 1976);
Okovano jabolko (Skopje: Misla, 1979);
Astropeus (Skopje: Makedonska kniga, 1980);
Gorčinovci: izbor (Skopje: Makedonska kniga, Misla, 1980);

Zmejovi za igra (Skopje: Makedonska kniga, 1983);
Legionite na Sveti Adofonis (Skopje: Kultura, Makedonska kniga, Misla, 1984);
Čekajki čuma (Skopje: Kultura, Makedonska kniga, Misla, 1984);
Kučeško raspetie (Skopje: Kultura, Makedonska kniga, Misla, 1984);
Umetničkoto bogastvo na Makedonija, by Janevski, Kosta Bojadžievski, Blagoja Drnkov, Kiril Bilbilovski, and Risto Šapkar (Skopje: Makedonska kniga, 1984);
Devet Kerubinovi vekovi (Skopje: Kultura, 1986);
Decata od svetot (Skopje: Detska radost, 1987);
Pesji sumi (Skopje: Misla, 1988);
Čudotvorci (Skopje: Makedonska kniga, 1988);
Rulet na sedum brojki (Skopje: Misla, 1989).

Collections: *Izabrana dela,* 9 volumes (Skopje: Naša kniga, 1969–1971);
Odbrani raskazi (Skopje: Kultura, 1980);
Odbrani pesni (Skopje: Misla, 1982);

Editions in English: Poems in *Reading the Ashes: An Anthology of the Poetry of Modern Macedonija,* edited by Milne Holton and Graham W. Reid (Pittsburgh: University of Pittsburgh Press, 1977), pp. 12–20;
The Bandit Wind, translated by Charles Simic (Takoma Park: Dryad Press, 1991); bilingual.

OTHER: *Bitovoto i istoriskoto vo makedonskata umetnička proza: materijali od naučniot sobir održan vo Skopje na 10 i ll maj 1983 godina,* edited by Janevski, Vasil Iljoski, and Mateja Matevski (Skopje: Makedonska akademija na naukite i umetnostite, 1986).

Slavko Janevski's beginnings as a poet and the recognition of the language in which he composed his poems were almost simultaneous. His language, Macedonian, was spoken by the South Slavs of the Pirin Mountains and the Vardar region from Thessaloníki to Skopje; it had been used as a literary language since at least the second half of the nineteenth century, but it was not recognized as such until 7 July 1945. On that date it was acknowledged as the official language of the law courts and schools of the new Macedonian Socialist Republic, one of Josip Broz Tito's five Socialist Federated Republics of Yugoslavia. The Macedonian Socialist government remained in power for forty-five years until a vote for independence separated it from Yugoslavia in 1990.

With the recognition of the Macedonian language came the assertion that its literature was the most recent of the modern European literatures (and in the minds of some, also the most ancient, in a sense, since Macedonian was historically the language most closely related to Old Church Slavic). As has often been the case in the Slavic world, the claim of legitimacy as a modern language for Macedonian was based upon the existence of a literature written in that language. In this case that literature was in the early stages of development in the postwar years. So it is not insignificant that it was also in 1945, when Janevski was a young Partisan writer, that his first collection of poems appeared in Skopje.

From the outset, postwar Macedonian writers had two directions in which to look. As socialist realists in a Marxist regime they could celebrate a postrevolutionary future; as Macedonians (especially after Tito's 1948 break with Joseph Stalin and the success of the Modernists in their confrontation with Belgrade Ždanovites in the 1950s) they could establish their identity by looking back to their own past and traditions. This backward look led them eventually, as it led their Serbian neighbors, not only to the literary nationalists of the nineteenth century but also to the Slavic peoples who had stood with Rome beneath the walls at Salonika, who had shared the glory of the Byzantines and the Nemanjids, and who had suffered under Turkish rule.

Janevski, one of Macedonia's most celebrated poets and novelists, began his career by looking in both directions. Born to an itinerant worker family in Skopje on 11 January 1920, he attended the gymnasium in Niš and then began his higher education in mechanical engineering at a technical school; World War II interrupted his education, and his family moved to Belgrade. There he passed the early years of the German occupation. In early May of 1944 he made his way to Macedonia to join the Partisans in the Balkan mountains. Later he served in Agitprop in Skopje and as an editor of Pionir Press, where he was responsible for the publication of one hundred thousand copies of the text which helped to codify the Macedonian literary language.

Janevski also wrote poetry during the war. Afterward, in 1945, he published *Krvava niza* (Bloody String of Pearls), one of the first collections of poems to appear in Macedonian. His first important recognition came the next year, when his poems appeared, with those of Aćo Šopov, Blaže Koneski, Gogo Ivanovski, and Lazo Karovski, under the title *Pesni* (Poems). Partly as

Title page of Janevski's 1980 book Astropcus

a result of this book, Janevski, Šopov, and Koneski came to be regarded as the fathers of modern Macedonian literature. Janevski followed his postwar career in publishing and journalism, first as an editor with several early postwar Macedonian magazines, including *Horizon,* an early literary review, then with *Nova Makedonija* (New Macedonia), the Skopje daily. He continued to write poetry and other collections followed: *Pruga na mladosta* (Railtracks of Youth) with Šopov in the next year, *Pesni: (1944–1948)* in 1948, *Raspeani bukvi* (Singing Beech Trees), which won the Vladi Prize in a Yugoslav competition in the same year, *Egejska barutna bajka* (Egean Dynamite Fairy Tale) and the now greatly admired *Ulica* (Street) in 1950, and *Lirika* (Lyrics) in 1951.

As is evident from these early collections, Janevski's poetic intentions were lyrical from the beginning. The poems were conceived to be sung and therefore to become part of the long and honored Macedonian tradition of singing. In Janevski's early poems, sailors, bandits, monks, even the sultan himself, all sing. Moreover, as Janevski knew, words that are sung change and gain meanings, and make other words generate new strangenesses, new beauties, and new terrors. It is important to poets interested in origins, like Janevski, to find the roots of their poetry in that singing.

In 1947 Janevski returned to war—this time the war with Greece. He spent six months in the fighting near Strumica. On his return to Skopje, Janevski turned his attention to fiction. In 1952 he completed a war novel, first titled *Selo zad sedumte jaseni* (Village Beyond Seven Ash Trees), revised and republished three years later in a somewhat darker version as *Stebla Selo zad sedumte jaseni* (Treetrunks: Village Beyond Seven Ash Trees), which has been generally recognized as the first novel in the Macedonian language and which brought him significant recognition. It was followed by *Klovnovi i luǵe* (Clowns and Fools, 1955); *Dve Marii* (Two Marias, 1956); *Mesečar* (Sleepwalker, 1958), which won the 11 October Prize of 1959; and then, after the Skopje earthquake of 1963, *I bol i bes* (Pain and Rage, 1964) and *Tvrdoglavi* (The Stubborn Ones, 1969). Unlike the poetry, the novels were written in a realistic tradition, although they hardly manifested the faith of the conventional socialist realist. But it is interesting to note that the first shape manifested by Janevski's fiction bore little resemblance to the fanciful and the increasingly Surrealist images that emerged even in the early poetry.

While Janevski as a new novelist was assisting the birth of Macedonian fiction, he was also establishing the viability of its literature through his leadership role in the nascent publishing and media industries in a Skopje that was emerging after the earthquake as a major modern city. Janevski sponsored talented younger Macedonian writers such as Meto Jovanovski, Mateja Matevski, and Vlada Urošević, and he continued to write his own poetry. *Lirika* was published in 1951, followed by *Leb i kamen* (Bread and Stone, 1957) and *Marsovci i gluvci* (Martians and the Deaf, 1959). By the early 1960s Janevski was becoming increasingly prominent in Macedonian letters and was gaining importance throughout Yugoslavia. He traveled widely during those years and made a long journey from Egypt across Asia to Japan in 1965. His *Gorčlivi legendi* (Bitter Legends, 1962) described those travels. In 1966 *Evanǵelie po Itar Pejo* (The Gospels According to Old Pejo), probably Janevski's best-known collection of poems, appeared; it was centered around the persona of the sly old peasant who has become one of the most familiar voices in Macedonian poetry. In these poems Janevski moves beyond his earlier lyrics; he demonstrates an increasing metaphorical subtlety and concerns himself now with the historical subjects that were becoming important to other modernist Yugoslav poets such as Miodrag Pavlović in Belgrade and Veno Taufer in Ljubljana. Janevski's new poems also displayed bold and sometimes bizarre imagistic experiments and established him as one of Macedonia's most original and compelling, and indeed most difficult, new poets. By the late 1960s Janevski was clearly one of Macedonia's dominant literary presences, both in its literary politics and in its poetry and fiction; on 18 August 1966 he was inducted into the Macedonian Academy of Arts and Sciences.

Two more strikingly original collections of poems, *Gluvi komandi* (Deaf Commands, 1966) and *Kainavelija* (Land of Cains and Abels, 1968), appeared shortly thereafter. Perhaps Janevski's most interesting poems are found in these two books; they teem with strange creatures reminiscent of the paintings of Hieronymus Bosch, creatures composed of bits and pieces of men, animals, and inanimate objects. As is manifest in his *Itar Pejo Kainaveliski* (Old Pejo, the Son of Cain), the second of the Pejo collections that appeared in 1969, the presiding spirit continues to be a peasant trickster of a sensibility that is in some ways similar to the sensibility in the trickster tales in American literature. Carl Jung spoke of the trickster as a "collective shadow figure," and certainly Pejo had now emerged as such for Macedonian readers.

"It was light then, and yet it was dark," the American Indian storyteller has it. For Janevski's poetry as well, history is at its base a creation myth, an account of the origins of the tribe. There was once a time when earth and heaven, gods and men, were not yet separated, when all things were a part of all things, when all beings could change and make many different kinds of appearances. Once upon a time each part of the universe mirrored all others. It is this time that Janevski seems to seek. As Janevski says of his peasant trickster-protagonist at one point, "Sly Pejo dangles his legs from heaven's scythe." It was Janevski's collection of such primal poems, *Crni i žolti* (Black and Yellow), that won the Struga Poetry Evenings Prize of 1968.

One of Janevski's remarkable poetic sequences in the late 1960s is "Anatomija" (Anatomy) in *Vojnik dva metra v zemja* (A Man Two Meters Tall), another collection of poems published in 1969. Here is to be found another kind of mythmaking; beginning in anatomical specifics, these poems probe, as it were, the psychic potential of each body part. Out of this process narratives are generated. Janevski is here an anthropologist of the anatomy, perhaps more aptly a necromancer of the body. In these poems he finds himself in the company of other twentieth-century phenomenologist poets and fabulists—of the Surrealists, of Francis Ponge, and of Janevski's contemporary from Belgrade, Vasko Popa.

Janevski continued to advance a successful career that established his prominence in publishing, journalism, and other media. Like much of the Macedonian economy, the burgeoning literary industry in Skopje was heavily supported by the Yugoslav government in the late 1960s, 1970s, and 1980s, and Janevski was an increasingly powerful voice both locally and in Belgrade. He traveled to the United States and Australia in the 1980s and wrote in *Nova Makedonija* about that journey and about many other matters, both literary and political. He continued to publish realistic fiction, although some of these narratives were not without an experimental and at times a historical dimension. *Omarnini* (Humidity) appeared in 1972, *Kovčeg* (Treasure Chest) in 1976, *Čekajḱi čuma* (Awaiting Plague) in 1984, and in 1986 *Devet Kerubinovi vekovi* (Nine Centuries of Cherubs), a work of nearly five hundred pages. All these were widely noted. There were new collections of poems as well. In 1979 *Okovano jabolka* (Plated Apple) won prizes at the Struga Poetry Evenings, the 13 November Prize awarded by the city of Skopje, and the Racin Prize. *Zmejovi za igra* (Dragons for Play) appeared in 1983, another collection generated by the visit to China eighteen years earlier. In 1986 his trilogy of novels, *Mirakuli na grožomorata* (Miracles of Horror), won the Krleža Prize, one of the most important literary honors in the former Yugoslavia.

Janevski has also written several children's books and film scenarios, and he has worked—since 1972—not only as a scenarist but as a director and a producer of films in his home city of Skopje. At the Pula Film Festival in 1974 his scenario for the Macedonian film, *Volčja noḱ* (Night of the Wolf), was honored, and the German Democratic Republic awarded him a prize for *Katastrofa, stradanja, nadežu* (Catastrophe, Suffering, Hope).

More recently Janevski has engaged in another kind of writing. In 1984 Makedonska kniga presented a celebratory edition of Macedonian medieval art, *Umetničkoto bogatstvo na Makedonija* (Religious Art in Macedonia), with a distinguished team of editors, scholars, and photographers. Janevski was chosen to write the text. Again in 1986 the Macedonian Academy chose Janevski and Mateja Matevski to present its historical catalogue for a celebratory exhibition of Macedonian literature, *Bitovoto i istoriskoto vo makedonskata umetnička proza: materijali od naučniot sobir održan vo Skopje na 10 i 11 maj 1983 godina* (Tradition and History in Macedonian Literary Prose: Materials from the Scholarly Meeting Held in Skopje, 10-11 May 1983). Janevski's selection to work on these books is an indication of the high opinion in which he is held by his compatriots.

Janevski's career in writing and publishing has spanned six decades, from the inception of his nation and the recognition of its language to the present era. During that time he has been one of Macedonia's most productive and most honored writers in almost every imaginable literary genre—fiction, poetry, travel writing, as well as in film. His work has been translated into many languages—not only into the Serbo-Croatian, Slovenian, Albanian, Hungarian, and Turkish of the former Yugoslav peoples, but also into Italian, Russian, German, Romanian, Bulgarian, Polish, Czech, Ukrainian, and Esperanto. A collection of his poems in English, *The Bandit Wind*, translated by Charles Simic, the first of a series of translations of Macedonian poets, appeared in the United States in 1991.

Janevski's importance and his accomplishments have been recognized throughout the former Yugoslav nations. His collected works, *Izabrana dela*, appeared in eight volumes in Macedonian and Serbo-Croatian in 1969 and 1971 and in ten volumes in 1976. In his extraordinarily productive career Janevski has proved to be one of the most active and valuable poets and leaders of the literary life of his nation.

Bibliographies:
Slavko Janevski, *Izbrana dela,* volume 9 (Skopje: Naša kniga, 1977);
M. Isajloska and M. Izotova, "Janevski, Slavko," *Leksikon pisaca Jugoslavije,* volume 2 (Novi Sad: Matica Srpska, 1979), pp. 535-537.

Biographies:
Miodrag Drugovac, *Kniga za Janevski* (Skopje: Makedonska kniga, 1971);
Radivoje Pešić, *Slavko Janevski* (Belgrade: Rad, 1968).

References:

Ante Čolak, "Književni profil Slavka Janevskog," *književnost,* 8 (1961): 202–207;

Miodrag Drugovac, "The Literary Works of Slavko Janevski," *Macedonian Review,* 3 (1973): 56–64;

Drugovac, "Slavko Janevski," in his *Contemporary Macedonian* (Skopje: Macedonian Review, 1976), pp. 51–64;

Milan Ǵurčinov, "Temi i razgovori za luǵeto," in his *Kritički svedoštva 1953–1973* (Skopje: Kultura, 1976), pp. 26–33;

Radomir Ivanović, "Myth, Space and Time in the Novels of Slavko Janevski," *Macedonian Review,* 10 (1980): 177–195;

Ivanović, *Poetika Slavka Janevskog* (Kraljevo: Slovo, 1989);

Aldo Kliman, "Raskažuvačkata proza na Slavko Janevski," *Sovremenost,* 26, 4–5 (1976): 125–132;

Zlatko Kramarik, *Novi experimentum Macedonicum* (Skopje, 1989);

Kramarik, *Romanite na Slavko Janevski* (Skopje: Makedonska kniga, 1987);

Dimitar Mitrev, "Vrz opusot na Slavko Janevski," in his *Kritiki i ogledi* (Skopje: Misla, 1969), pp. 70–94;

Georgi Stardelov, "Čovekoviot bol i bes," "Eden svet vo dva romana," in his *Svetovi* (Skopje: Misla, 1969), pp. 68–73, 89–97;

Stardelov, *Experimentum Macedonicum* (Skopje: Naša kniga, 1983).

Vjekoslav Kaleb
(27 September 1905 - 13 April 1996)

Maria B. Malby
East Carolina University

BOOKS: *Na kamenju* (Zagreb: Matica hrvatska, 1940);

Izvan stvari (Zagreb: Suvremena biblioteka, 1942);

Brigada (Zagreb: Zora, 1945);

Novele (Zagreb: Zora, 1946, 1947);

Trideset konja (Zagreb: Novo pokolenje, 1947);

Kronika dana (Zagreb, 1949);

Poniženе ulice (Zagreb: Zora, 1950);

Pripovijetke (Zagreb: Matica hrvatska, 1951);

Divota prašine (Zagreb: Mladost, 1954);

Bijeli kamen (Zagreb: Kultura, 1954);

Smrtni zvuci (Sarajevo, 1957);

Nagao vjetar (Zagreb: Matica hrvatska, 1959);

Ogledalo (Belgrade: Prosveta, 1962);

Pripovijetke (Zagreb, 1963);

Luk i strijela (Zagreb, 1963);

Bez mosta (Zagreb: Mladost, 1986);

Sveti govor (Zagreb, 1994).

Editions and Collections: *Odabrana djela*, 6 volumes (Zagreb, 1969);

Izabrane novele (N.p., 1971).

Editions in English: *Glorious Dust,* translated by Zora G. Depolo (London: Lincolns-Prager, 1960);

"The Guest," *Yugoslav Short Stories,* edited by Svetozar Koljević (London: Oxford University Press, 1966), pp. 290-299;

"The Arch of Triumph," translated by Donald Davenport, *Literary Review,* 11 (1967-1968): 167-172;

"A Stick for a Stroll," translated by Celia Williams, *Bridge,* nos. 23-24 (1970): 76-84;

"A Cane on a Stroll," translated by Vasa D. Mihailovich, *Bridge,* nos. 1-2 (1985): 45-51;

The Wonder of Dust, translated by Slobodan Drenovac, *Bridge,* no. 3 (1985): 41-99; no. 4 (1985): 41-103.

Vjekoslav Kaleb is a towering figure among contemporary Croatian writers, one whose impressive body of work includes fifty-seven short stories and novellas, three novels (one of which

Vjekoslav Kaleb

was rewritten under a different title), screenplays, poems, articles, essays, manuals, and translations. Some critics believe that his place of honor among Croatian writers was secured by the appearance of two of his earliest stories: "Odlazak Perušine" (The Departure of Perušina, 1938) and "Gost" (The Guest, 1940). Actually these and several other stories, published in various newspapers and journals, did not make an impact immediately, but they soon captivated readers and critics alike in collections titled *Na kamenju* (On the Stone, also referred to as On Stones and On the Rocks, 1940) and *Izvan stvari* (Outside of

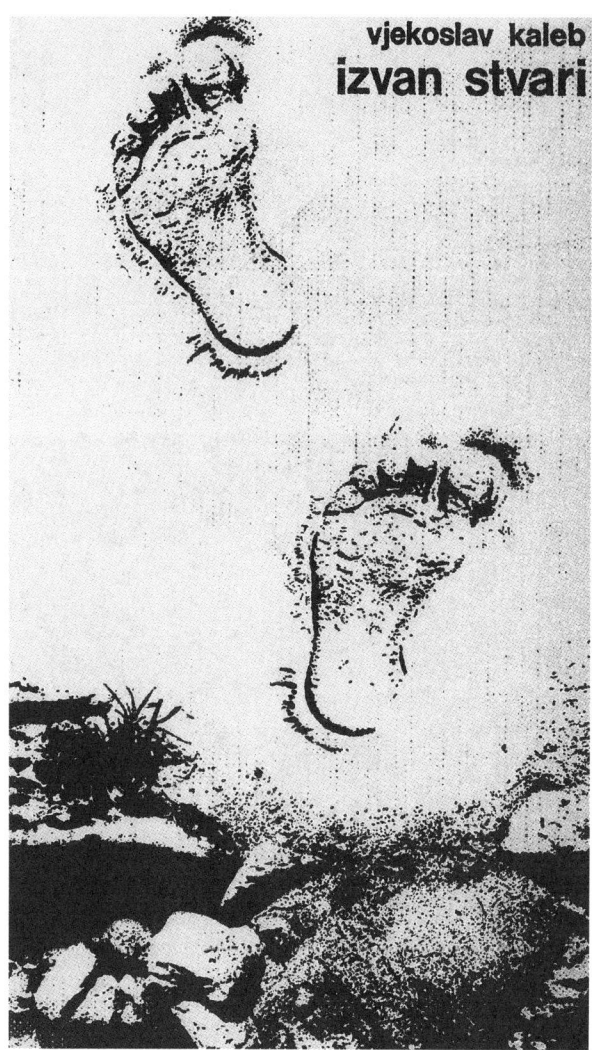

Title page of Kaleb's 1942 collection of short stories

Things, also referred to as Outside Things and Beyond the Affair, 1942). Many critics still consider these two volumes of short stories and novellas Kaleb's best. Readers seem to agree, since these early stories, with various new additions, were repeatedly reprinted under new titles such as *Novele* (Novellas, 1946 and 1947), *Pripovijetke* (Stories, 1951), and *Ogledalo* (Mirror, 1962). In 1969, under the supervision of the author, these two collections, in a much expanded form, were published as part of the six-volume *Odabrana djela Vjekoslava Kaleba* (Selected Works of Vjekoslav Kaleb).

Kaleb's early stories, which catapulted the unknown, thirty-five-year-old writer to success, present with great simplicity, yet great accuracy, the lives of the peasants of his native Dalmatia and the hinterland known as Dalmatinska zagora, where he held teaching posts in local schools.

Kaleb stepped into the courtyards and the huts of the poor to evoke a backward world that has hardly changed in more than a thousand years. He depicts men, women, and children huddled with animals on mud floors—dirty, diseased, and above all hungry. Avoiding pathos, yet with obvious empathy and the precision of a sculptor chiseling stone, he carves out reliefs of wretched lives. It was in fact the actual stone that emerged from the parched, barren soil of the Zagora that was responsible for much of the suffering. On it nothing could grow, and no animal, with the exception of a few sheep, could graze.

Kaleb was born on 27 September 1905 in Tijesno (Tisno in the local "Ikavian" dialect), a small town located partly on the coastal mainland and partly on the island of Murter, near Šibenik. The Kalebs were not poor, but they worked hard for their living. Vjekoslav's father, Ivan (Ive in the local dialect), had a small grocery store that sold bread baked daily by Vjekoslav's mother, Cvita, born Olivari. The father's honesty was so well known that it gave rise to a saying: "Honest like Ive Kaleb." The last name Kaleb derives from a nickname given in that region to children with very light, "white" hair. There were six children in the Kaleb family, three sons and three daughters. The author remembers his great-grandmother Jerka, who died in her ninety-fourth year "with all her teeth intact." He learned that his great-grandfather Ive was killed by an Austrian policeman because he was protesting heavy land taxation imposed by the Austrian government then in control of Dalmatia. The Kaleb land was passed on to children and grandchildren, all of whom worked on it with a hoe. The mark of their "wealth" was an adequate supply of bread and a horse-drawn cart that took the family into the field. Many others had to walk. Even in the 1990s Kaleb continues to visit each year the homestead he inherited from his parents and his grandparents Šime and Petra Kaleb.

From 1912 to 1918 Kaleb attended the local elementary school in Tijesno. After he completed the sixth grade, his father took him to Zadar to study at a teachers' school. When Italy annexed Zadar in 1922, Kaleb was sent to the teachers' school in Belgrade. After a year he transferred to Šibenik, where he graduated in 1924 from a school once closed by the Italians. The same year he married Antica and started his teaching career in various hamlets throughout the Dalmatian Zagora. In his free time he indulged in two passions: hunting and painting. Painting had begun to fascinate Kaleb while he was still a child. He taught himself how to paint and later applied several times for a scholarship at the Art Academy in Zagreb. After several rejections, he gave up this dream at age thirty but continued to paint. In 1986 his paintings were exhibited in Zagreb, and his name is now officially listed among Croatian painters.

In 1936 Kaleb secured a position in Šibenik, a coastal town with a population of twenty thousand. There he began writing stories and novellas based on anecdotes that he had heard personally or that had been reported to him by his wife when they lived in the hinterland. The family, which now included a son and a daughter, lived on the author's small salary, half of which was spent on rent. The situation improved in 1940 after the publication of *Na kamenju*. Sudden literary fame helped Kaleb relocate to Zagreb, where he received a job in the Department of Education. Kaleb continued to write and from 1941 to 1943 was a student at the Higher Pedagogical Institute in Zagreb. In 1943 he received his first literary prize for *Izvan stvari*, and he joined the partisans, the fighters against Nazi occupation. Although in his second collection of short stories Kaleb no longer exclusively depicts peasant lives but incorporates town dwellers and intellectuals as well, his observations and themes essentially remain the same.

Although they have often compared Kaleb to Luigi Pirandello, Anton Chekhov, and even Leo Tolstoy, critics seem to have missed the most obvious parallelism, that between Kaleb and Ivan Turgenev. Like Turgenev, Kaleb often disguises himself as a hunter passing through little hamlets and creating unique verbal pictures of various incidents. Since what he sees is mostly quite distressing, the author's view of life is pessimistic. As in Turgenev, humanity is seen as a little speck of dust in an endless sequence of time that leads ultimately into nothingness, struggling against all sorts of menacing forces symbolized by the night. Thus people live in constant fear, surrounded by beautiful, at times dangerous, but always indifferent nature. This indifference is reflected in the cold, bluish moon and stars at night in the stories "Noć" (Night, 1940) and "Izmetu dana i noći" (Between Day and Night, 1940). The hearts of Kaleb's protagonists, who are at the mercy of elements and always hungry, are closed. His characters do not–they cannot–believe in God. If they go to church, they do so out of habit and to show off their new used clothes ("Cikina ženidba" [Ciko's Wedding], 1940) or to make an irreverent gesture at the altar, like Mate after he loses both wife and daughter to a flu epidemic, in "Matin obračun" (Mate's Revenge, 1940).

The settings of Kaleb's stories and novellas are often places in extremis. His men are deprived of masculinity, and the women are deprived of femininity. They feel alone in a cruel world in which, oddly enough, animals have at times human qualities that humans have lost. But an animal may also turn into a menacing force, as does a pig who bites off a portion of a child's hand in "Na kamenju," a short story that gave its title to the collection. This story, more than any other, illustrates the tragedy of people living "on stones." Not having any land to cultivate, too hungry, and, therefore, too lethargic to hire themselves as laborers somewhere else, Kazo and Loja lie in the sun drifting in and out of sleep. The author often focuses on the word *san*, meaning both "sleep" and "dream." He sees humankind in general as constantly alternating between the two states of sleep and awareness. Lethargy notwithstanding, however, Loja repeatedly steals money from her stepson Trajo, who is deaf and mute. In order to buy a cap so he can feel like a man he works in a distant factory. Loja abuses her own two children after discovering that they have eaten the last bits of corn flour in the house, and she takes pride in helping bleed to death a twin girl born to a neighbor. It seems poetic justice when Trajo slits Loja's throat at the end of the story.

Even the lowliest of the low, Kaleb observes, have an inborn desire to distinguish themselves in some way. So Loja feels important after committing her murderous act. She too has to validate her existence, awful and perverted as the means may be. There are many more such examples. In the story "Odlazak Perušine" (Perusina's Departure, 1940) the father accompanying his son to the train for Zagreb, where he is to learn a trade, boasts to anyone willing to listen that he has outfitted the boy with good, used clothes. He wants his son to be proud of his father, but even more, he needs to feel proud of himself. In "Lojko" (1940) a rich man kills a poor man's dog for having stolen a prey shot by his master yet claimed by the rich man. The "little man" confronts the wrongdoer, but rather than striking him, he cries out: "I am a far better man than you!" The beggar in "Prosjak" (Beggar, 1940) feels that he is doing something useful when he recites his litanies to earn alms. Likewise, the woman who gives him a cup of water basks in the glory of her Samaritan act. A young man in "Marač nije umro" (Marač Did Not Die, 1940) sings in praise of old man Marač, but he is mainly interested in exhibiting his voice. Mara, an old maid in "Veselje u raju" (Merrymaking in Paradise, 1942), whose bridegroom dies shortly after their wedding, feels important as his widow. Ironically, her lifelong dream was to be his wife. Lastly, in "Gost," a story included in most anthologies and translations of Croatian literature, a peasant family is proud for having been "chosen" by a gentleman's dog to come uninvited to their home, eat their food, and sleep on their bed. Before leaving, the dog urinates on their threshold. This scene is not only sarcastic but also symbolic. It shows what, according to Kaleb, his protagonists and people in general get from life.

While some of Kaleb's characters accept the cruel play of fate in a passive way, others rebel. They become violent, and at times, they kill. Trajo kills his stepmother, and Marko stabs Šime in "Usput" (Along the Way, 1942), not just because of an old family feud but because Šime had snatched up a piece of land Marko had wanted to buy and because Šime had once courted his wife. Ciko in "Cikina ženidba" comes close to killing his common-law wife when he realizes that she does not intend to sign over her property to him. Not only the poor, but even intellectuals can be prone to violence. The nameless painter in "Izvan stvari" has the impulse to "shove the teeth into the mouth" of the woman who was once his great love. Unlike most novellas in Kaleb's early collections, which are marked by clarity, the meaning of this work is slightly obscure. It is, after all, as its title says, "outside of things." Critics have stated that this was the beginning of a new phase in Kaleb's creativity. According to them the author began aiming toward a more modern approach to writing and started experimenting with abstract techniques. Others accept this simply as an alternate method seen in many other writers. They point out that, even when he is writing in his usual manner, Kaleb never creates plots and therefore the endings of his stories are always open questions, in a Chekhovian fashion. Of course, when he describes the outer world, the strokes of his paintbrush are more firm than when he paints a person's inner world with all its intangible dimensions. The penchant for analyzing the human soul came to the fore in the second phase of Kaleb's post–World War II writing.

Among the products of Kaleb's early period there are works that have a rather mellow quality. A true cameo among them is "Susret" (An Encounter, 1940), in which the mutual attraction between a teacher and a pupil is described. Because of Kaleb's strange habit of referring to a young woman as *djevojčica* (young girl), not *djevojka* (young woman), this story has so far been misunderstood. Critics see in it the teacher's yearning merely for the beauty and innocence that the girl represents. The main characters' few moments in each other's proximity clearly reveal, however, erotic undertones, albeit of the subtlest and purest kind. Love is generally absent in Kaleb's works. Few wives and mothers tend to their families' needs. Thus love is inferred rather than portrayed. In "Susret," Kaleb created the only circumstance in his entire opus with a palpable atmosphere of love.

The novella "U stakleniku" (In the Glasshouse, 1942) has clearly autobiographical elements. It contains a young teacher's reminiscences about his own painful schooling. Quiet and shy, Jakov was often the butt of his classmates' jokes and often was unjustly punished by an exceptionally ignorant and cruel teacher. Like so many in a similar situation, he becomes increasingly withdrawn, developing a contemplative nature. Perhaps this was a necessary evil that eventually produced a writer with a gift for observation and introspection.

A few of the early stories have an eerie quality. The reader gets glimpses into local folklore, quackery, and the characters' sense of the supernatural in such stories as "Između dana i noći" and "Špirkan u kući" (Špirkan at Home, 1942). In the former, villagers at a wake, waiting for the dawn, afraid of the dead and the cold, stormy night, become a portrait of humanity as a whole. According to Kaleb, people carry on in spite of their pain and fears. They receive no rewards except the small victories representing daily survival. Something inside of them propels them to move always forward, for their known routines are preferable to that which will follow: nothingness.

Humor is also present at times in Kaleb's dark world. Little Perušina's amazement at city houses whose staircases he must climb is genuinely amusing. So is his father's speech, filled with misused and mispronounced words. In "Sat" (The Watch, 1940) a peasant pays in advance for the repair of his watch in order to impress the watchmaker from the city. After realizing that he has been duped, he goes after the repairman with a gun in his pocket, never meaning, however, to fire it. Even more tragicomic is Grandfather Martin in the 1940 story by the same title, who has designs on his grandson's fiancée and later wife. Like all his other stories, these show Kaleb's remarkable talent for noticing the unusual in the usual and depicting it with carefully selected words. Kaleb rations his words, almost mimicking his protagonists' laconic speech. When given in its original dialect, this speech consists of monosyllabic, untranslatable utterances both comical and somewhat sad.

In 1943 Kaleb moved to Otočac in the liberated territory, where he worked in the cultural division of the National Antifascist Liberation Council of Yugoslavia. From there he eventually moved to Livno and the islands of Hvar and Vis. In January 1944 he was evacuated with other partisans to El Shat, Egypt. After the end of World War II in 1945, Kaleb returned to Zagreb, where he worked as editor of the journal *Republika* (1945–1950), wrote a cultural column for *Naprijed* (Forward), and became secretary of the publishing house Matica hrvatska and artistic director for the Jadran Film Company. He also became a member of the Union of Croatian Writers, serving in 1956 as president of this organization.

In the postwar period new publications of Kaleb's early stories appeared under the title *Novele*. The 1947 edition contains a new story, also published separately in 1947, titled "Trideset konja" (Thirty Horses). This title refers to the horsepower in a motor supposed to keep a mill running. Idle during the war, the mill is reopened by party officials in a coastal town. A comic situation arises when a good-for-nothing fellow and his hand-picked crew start running the mill in a haphazard way. Their incompetence and arrogance form the plot of this story, the best written by Kaleb in the style of socialist realism. Like so many Yugoslav writers, Kaleb attempted to write, in the first phase of his postwar period, according to precepts of Soviet literary dogmas, and he lost his way. *Brigada* (Brigade, 1945), a collection of stories, earned its author the prize of the Committee for Art and Culture of Yugoslavia, but it is considered a failure. Most likely inspired by real-life occurrences, its heroic men, women, and children and their utterly evil enemies create a credibility gap no literary work can afford.

Also weak artistically is Kaleb's first novel, *Ponižene ulice* (Humiliated Streets, 1950), a novel he later rewrote and published under a new title, *Poniženi grad* (Humiliated City, 1969). Both versions lack artistic qualities. The city and the streets are those of Zagreb during the war. The main male character, Ivan Butko, an odd character, walks, thinks, and talks, introducing the reader to Nazi sympathizers and their opponents during the tragic war years. In his odyssey Butko lands first in a hospital, then in a woman's room, then in a territory liberated by partisans, and finally in a Zagreb prison, which destination would be followed most likely by a lineup before a firing squad. If he were not such a cardboard figure, one might feel sorry for this supposedly true "man from the underground." He is a schoolteacher but never teaches; he is a husband but has no family life; he is drawn to various women but only makes passes at them. Throughout the novel he sneers at the reactionary elements in town, mutters provocative curses, and associates with some revolutionaries but is incapable of making a commitment to them.

Title page of Kaleb's 1954 novel, translated as Glorious Dust, *about partisan resistance fighters in World War II*

Pripovijetke (Stories, 1951) incorporates several new works but is basically a collection of previously published stories and novellas. Two of the new ones, "Malena ali . . ." (Little but . . . , 1951) and "Ogledalo" (Mirror, 1951), illustrate once again the human need to be important. If his efforts in promoting himself fail, such a man becomes violent, like the shoemaker who boasts of having an English book on his nightstand, which he pretends to read in the first story. The boy in the second story attracts a crowd with the magic of his mirror, but when children tire of it, he breaks the mirror to recapture the attention he had lost.

In 1954 Kaleb's second novel, *Divota prašine* (published as *Glorious Dust,* 1960, also referred to as The Wonder of Dust, The Beauty of Dust, and The Marvel of Dust), was published. It was another instant success, clearly showing that the second phase of Kaleb's postwar period had begun. This novel was translated into many languages and earned Kaleb a prize from the Yugoslav Writers' Union and from the Yugoslav Publishers Association. Considered one of the best novels based on the partisan warfare in Yugoslavia, this odyssey of a young man–the "Naked One"–and a "Boy," is a powerful account of hardships that are followed by triumph. Separated from their battalion during an offensive, the two soldiers must rejoin their comrades or die. Tortured by cold and hunger, they move through beautiful but dangerous mountains encountering both friends and foes. The dialogue between the boy and the man who is wearing only a leather coat is, at times, implausible, but the realistic and naturalistic descriptions of the protagonists' struggle for survival are a clear reflection of personal experiences during the war. The continuous motion of these heroes symbolizes humanity's progress toward goals that may or may not be reached. In this case, the men are met and carried off by a procession of women going to a victory celebration. The finale is in sharp contrast to the rest of the novel, which is devoid of tendentiousness.

Kaleb's third novel, *Bijeli kamen* (White Stone or White Rock), was published in 1954, but it was actually written before his second novel. Once again, the author returned to the stones of his native Dalmatia, here under Italian occupation during the war. Both realistic and symbolic, this novel portrays a peasant sculptor, Strane, who in spite of the atrocities of war keeps creating beauty out of blocks of the white stone that surrounds him. Like a true artist, he lives in his own world, isolated and alone. The two women in the novel, his understanding wife, Cvita, and their mutual friend, Naste, are in the background, playing supporting roles. Unless seen as a symbol of the eternal feminine, an ideal needed by the artist, Naste's role is baffling. The childlike naiveté of this young woman is an irritant to critics, yet it manages to dispel sexual overtones. All the main characters lose their lives in the end, but the author shows examples of humaneness amid much enemy brutality. This novel was also widely translated, and it received the City of Zagreb Prize.

A new collection of short stories and novellas, *Smrtni zvuci* (Deadly Sounds, or Deathly Sounds), was published in 1957. It contains some works marked by psychological realism and others marked by a high degree of symbolism, abstract musings in the form of inner monologues that lead to the realm of the absurd. The unifying theme of these works is death. Narrated either in the first or third person, the stories often have a nameless protagonist, referred to as "the poet," "the guest," "the head," "she," or "he." At times it is hard to grasp the meaning of the story, especially when Kaleb announces at the end that it was all a dream, as he does in "Paučina" (The Cobweb). Other stories resemble essays about the sham of a so-called civilization that promotes warfare, depletes natural resources, and creates noise pollution as well. Such stories are "Tehnika" (Technology) and "Meki putovi" (Soft Paths). The most symbolic is "Trijumfalna vrata" (Triumphal Gate), with its dreamlike setting in which the narrator opens imaginary gates to save a donkey from a circus owner's panther, grazing in the same yard. In trying to rescue the donkey, the narrator almost becomes a victim himself, all of which reflects Kaleb's perception of life. Many stories deal with the war theme, but they are much more sophisticated than those of Kaleb's early postwar period. In "Štap u šetnji" (A Stick for a Walk), a father whose son died in the war meets a train every day in the hope of seeing his son again. His concern about the safety of the little children for whom "others have died" is heartwarming. In "Suze vola" (Tears of an Ox) oxen become human as they submit to slaughter, knowing that they have to die so that the partisans can live. The onetime prisoner in "Zarobljenik" (Prisoner) is now a madman enjoying the safety of his room with bars on the windows where those who make war cannot enter. The story that gave its title to the collection describes a barber whose hobby is music, a pleasure denied him by his wife. He plans either to kill her with the harsh sounds of his flute or transform her with melodious notes. When his strategies fail, his resentment toward his wife intensifies.

The last collection of Kaleb's novellas appeared in 1959. It is titled *Nagao vjetar* (Sudden

Wind). The title refers to a callous husband's words when his wife Mlade and baby come to live with him in Zagreb, where he works in a car factory. With a great deal of patience and hard work, Mlade manages to turn her husband around and save the marriage. This relapse into socialist realism, evident also in "Pogled s prozora" (A View from the Window), is surprising, as is the inclusion here of "Trideset konja." Only the fourth novella in this collection, "Dolazak na vodu" (At the Waterhole), is original, albeit tediously long. It is an allegory of humankind's inability to transcend its prehistoric origins. This collection was reprinted and enlarged in 1969.

Although all of Kaleb's works appeared again in 1969, many in a much expanded format, most critics agree that his best stories can be found in *Pripovijetke* and *Ogledalo*. A smaller collection of *Pripovijetke* appeared in 1963, followed by the publication of the entire opus in 1969. Since then Kaleb has written many articles about the Croatian language and some political treatises. These were collected under the title *Sveti govor* (Sacred Speech) and published in 1994. Kaleb has adapted some of his short stories into screenplays, and his most recent novel, *Bez mosta* (Without a Bridge), about which little is known abroad, was published in 1986. A handful of his poems were published in the quarterly *Republika* in 1994. They reiterate many of the themes already introduced in Kaleb's prose. While he amazed the reading public with his early stories about his native region, Kaleb in his later works paved the road for an entire generation of Croatian postmodernist writers. For his life's work, translated into twenty languages, Kaleb received the Vladimir Nazor Prize for literature.

Bibliography:

M. Radojičić and S. Tišma, "Kaleb, Vjekoslav," in *Leksikon pisaca Jugoslavije,* volume 3 (Novi Sad: Matica srpska, 1997), pp. 26–29.

References:

V. Čeklić, "Proza Vjekoslava Kaleba," *Dometi,* 1 (1968): 27–40;

Tode Čolak, "Vjekoslav Kaleb," in his *Portreti,* volume 2 (Belgrade: Sloboda, 1976), pp. 117–156;

Thomas Eekman, *Thirty Years of Yugoslav Literature (1945–1975)* (Ann Arbor: Michigan Slavic Publications, 1978), pp. 54–59;

Ante Kadić, "Vjekoslav Kaleb," *Journal of Croatian Studies,* no. 20 (1979): 102–110;

Milivoje Marković, "Trajanje kamena i sna: Vreme, ljudi i dogadjaji u prozi Vjekoslava Kaleba," *Putevi,* 9 (1963): 64–92;

Vlatko Pavletić, "Analiza i konstrukcija: Pristup Kalebovim novelama," *Republika,* 18, nos. 2-3 (1962): 49–59;

Čedo Prica, "Vjekoslav Kaleb: *Bijeli kamen,*" *Republika,* 11, no. 8 (1955): 625–629;

Ivan Slamnig, "Suvremeni prozaici," in *Panorama hrvatske književnosti XX stoljeća,* by Pavletić (Zagreb: Stvarnost, 1965), pp. 625–628;

Emil Štampar, "Književni put prozaika Vjekoslava Kaleba," *Slavistička revija,* 16 (1968): 505–534;

Miroslav Vaupotić, *Hrvatska suvremena književnost/Contemporary Croatian Literature* (Zagreb: Croatian P.E.N. Club Centre, 1966), pp. 110–113;

Pavle Zorić, "Sivi pejsaž Vjekoslava Kaleba," *Savremenik,* 5 (1959): 859–874.

Nikolay Khaytov
(15 September 1919 -   )

Thomas Eekman
University of California, Los Angeles

BOOKS: *Gorski razkazi* (Sofia: Profizdat, 1956);
Supernitsi (Sofia: Bŭlgarski pisatel, 1957);
Prez vekovete (Sofia: Nauka i izkustvo, 1958);
Minaloto na selo yavrovo (Sofia: BAN, 1958);
Iskritsi ot ognishteto (Sofia: Narodna mladezh, 1959);
Razbulena Rodopa (Sofia, 1960);
Pisma ot pushtinatsite (Sofia: Bŭlgarski pisatel, 1960);
Zheni khaydutki (Sofia: NSOF, 1962);
Smolyan (Tri vŭrkha v srednorodopskata istoriya) (Sofia: NSOF, 1962);
Proizshestvie v gorata (Sofia: Nauka i izkustvo, 1963);
Zaklyuchena prolet (Sofia: Nauka i izkustvo, 1963);
Po zemyata (Sofia: Bŭlgarski pisatel, 1963);
Devin (Sofia: NSOF, 1964);
Matei Preobrazhenski-Mitkaloto (Sofia: NSOF, 1964);
Asenovgrad v minaloto (Sofia: Nauka i izkustvo, 1965);
Moyata pesen, moyat gryakh (Sofia: Nauka i izkustvo, 1965);
Shumki ot gabŭr (Sofia: Narodna mladezh, 1965);
Selo Manastir, Smolyansko (Sofia: NSOF, 1965);
Rodopski vlastelini (Sofia: NSOF, 1965; enlarged edition, Plovdiv: Khr. G. Danov, 1974);
Gorski trevogi (Sofia: Bŭlgarski pisatel, 1966);
Kucheta; Lodka v gorata; Pŭteki (Sofia: Komitet po kultura i izkustvo, 1966);
Lamyata (Sofia: Bŭlgarski pisatel, 1967; Sofia: Otechestvo, 1970; enlarged, 1977);
Divi razkazi (Plovdiv: Khr. G. Danov, 1967; revised, 1969);
Khayduti (Sofia: Narodna mladezh, 1968);
Iskritsi ot ognishteto (Sofia: Bŭlgarski pisatel, 1968);
Sharena sol (Sofia: Nauka i izkustvo, 1968);
Rodopskite komiti razkazvat (Sofia: NSOF, 1972);
Peruanski zapiski (Sofia: Profizdat, 1975);
Publitsistika (Sofia: Bŭlgarski pisatel, 1975);
Bodlivata roza (Sofia: OF, 1975);
Razkazi s opashki (Sofia: Bŭlgarski pisatel, 1976);

Nikolay Khaytov (photo by Iliana Gentcheva)

Nadnikvane v sŭkrovenoto (Varna: G. Bakalov, 1977);
Zhivotvorniyat izvor (Sofia: Profizdat, 1979);
Khvurkatoto korito (Plovdiv: Khr. G. Danov, 1979);
Zhelyaznata gora (Sofia: Narodna mladezh, 1980);
Magiosnikŭt ot Breze (Sofia: Profizdat, 1980);
Vŭlshebnoto ogledalo (Sofia: OF, 1981);
Za tvorchestvoto (Varna: G. Bakalov, 1982);
Razkazi i eseta (Sofia: Bŭlgarski pisatel, 1984);
Piesi (Sofia: Bŭlgarski pisatel, 1986).

Editions and Collections: *Izbrani proizvedeniya*, 2 volumes (Sofia: Bŭlgarski pisatel, 1979);
Izbrani proizvedeniya (Sofia: Bŭlgarski pisatel, 1989).

Edition in English: *Wild Tales*, translated by Michael Holman (London: Peter Owen, 1979).

Nikolay Khaytov is one of the most highly respected figures in Bulgarian cultural life in the last third of the twentieth century and the contemporary Bulgarian writer best known by readers outside Bulgaria. His principal claim to fame is his 1967 collection of short stories, *Divi razkazi* (translated as *Wild Tales*, 1979); his oeuvre also includes many other short stories as well as sketches, other prose writings (but no novels), several plays, and journalistic pieces and essays in many periodicals and newspapers, only a small part of which has been collected and republished in his *Izbrani proizvedeniya* (Selected Works, 1979, 1989).

Khaytov was born into a poor Bulgarian peasant family on 15 September 1919. The family lived in Yavrovo, near Plovdiv. Khaytov's mother was illiterate, and he and his two brothers had to struggle for an education. He did go to school and was, after passing an exam, admitted to high school, but, due to the family's poverty, he was unable to attend school. Many details from the early years of his life are known from his "Autobiography," written in 1975. When his father became ill, Khaytov had to support himself, and from age fourteen he worked at many jobs, including apprenticing in a flour shop (which he left because he could not get along with the owner), waiting tables, and working as a hotel bellhop in Plovdiv. In 1935 he returned to his home village, where he worked on the land and was also employed as an unemployment relief worker. He was obliged to stop working because of a hernia and prepared himself for admission to high school; then he worked again for the unemployment relief as a street paver during the summer of 1936, until he fell ill. He finally enrolled in high school in nearby Asenovgrad; while attending school he had various jobs because his parents were unable to pay his living expenses. After graduation he enrolled in Sofia University, where he majored in pedagogy, but lack of financial resources obliged him to quit school and return to Asenovgrad.

There he found a job in a seed-drying operation run by the department of forestry. With the money he saved he returned to Sofia after ten months and in 1940 enrolled in the university again, majoring in forestry. Although he had a job at the same time in a bakery, he managed to graduate in three years. In June 1943 he started a year of practice in various forestry testing stations. Two years of army service followed; then, in 1946, he was appointed forester-verderer; after a year he was promoted to the post of director of forestry service.

In the meantime, while still in military service, Khaytov had become a member of the Bulgarian Communist Party, which no doubt helped him in his career, although it also brought him trouble. In December 1950 an article appeared in the communist newspaper *Rabotnichesko delo* (Workers' Affairs) under the heading "Sabotage by a Specialist," in which Khaytov was attacked (by, as it was learned later, the treasurer of the forestry service, with whom Khaytov had had several conflicts). He was fired, as a disciplinary measure, for "not cooperating with the local social organizations." He was also expelled from the Communist Party. When investigated, the accusations in the newspaper article proved to be false, and in 1951 Khaytov was appointed manager of another forestry department.

However, in 1954 he was fired again, because an action was brought against him for transgressions at his job; this time the charges appeared more serious: he was sentenced to eight years in prison, and all his possessions were confiscated. However, the sentence was never confirmed by the authorities in Sofia, and it was eventually revoked. But Khaytov was unemployed for three years. As he writes in his autobiography, "As an expelled party member I had to remain lower than the grass and quieter than a fly in order to exist, but my character is peppery, it often happens that I get myself into ill-considered conflicts and have to bear the consequences."

When an acquaintance asked him to write a text for forestry workers, Khaytov wrote eighteen pages on forestry problems, advancing some "theses," and the text was printed. This gave him, for the first time, the idea of writing in order to make a living. Thus, he gradually became a journalist and a fiction writer. In 1956 his first unassuming little book, *Gorski razkazi* (Forest Tales), appeared, followed in 1957 by a volume of sketches and stories, *Supernitsi* (Rivals). In 1959 he became a member of the Bulgarian Writers' Union. His name appeared increasingly in the press, including *Rabotnichesko delo,* and the Communist Party eventually acknowledged that his expulsion in 1950 was unjustified. He was

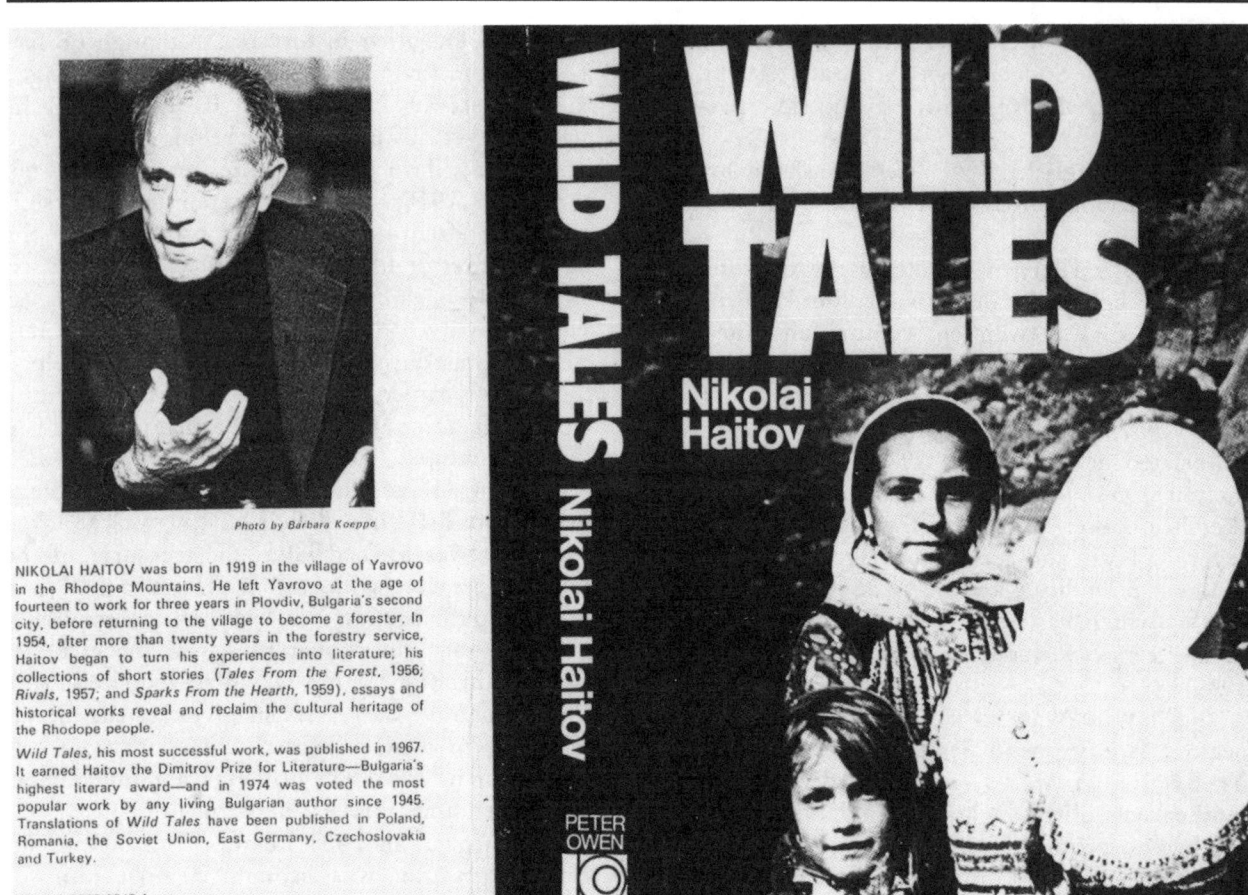

Dust jacket for the English translation of Khaytov's Divi razkazi, his 1967 collection of stories about life in Bulgarian villages

then rehabilitated, and he became a "candidate member" again. However, he was at that time going through divorce proceedings. He was notified that he could aspire to become a full-fledged member of the party only if he desisted from the divorce. When he refused to stop the divorce proceedings, he was expelled again, in 1961, and has remained *bezpartien* (a nonparty member) since then. In 1957 Khaytov joined a new magazine, *Narodna kultura* (People's Culture), first as a contributor, then as an editor. In 1965 he became editor in chief of the new monthly *Rodopi* (Rhodope), a position he held for many years. During the 1960s he worked as an independent journalist and writer. He published several more books of short stories, sketches, essays, and travelogues.

The great turning point in Khaytov's career was 1967, the year his *Divi razkazi* appeared. The book won rave reviews from both the critics and the public; Khaytov won the 1969 George Dimitrov Prize; practically every other year a new edition was published; and the book was translated into at least twenty languages. By this time the political and literary establishment had accepted him: he received the "Red Banner of Labor" award (also in 1969, on his fiftieth birthday) and in 1972 the title Meritorious Cultural Worker. He became a member of the executive board of the Writers' Union and chairman of the "Creative Fund" of the Union; he also accepted other public roles, becoming a deputy in the Sofia City Council and chairman (1975–1977) of the Town Assembly for Art and Culture.

The adjective *divi* (wild) in the book's title does not refer to the artistic form or the literary genre: the stories are not avant-garde; neither does it reveal much about the contents, the events described. Rather it indicates that the narrators and the protagonists belong to a special category of Bulgarians–the inhabitants of the Rhodope Mountains, of villages and small towns in this remote and desolate part of the country that Khaytov, through his work as a forester, knew well and painted with love and understanding. Some of the stories take place in the heroic past of these freedom-loving people, some in

Khaytov's own time, among people (mostly men) the author must have known.

To enhance the liveliness of his tales he often uses first-person narration, as he does in the first of the series, "When Men Were Men," which starts with the characteristic words: "I was a right daredevil in my young days." This "daredevil" tells how he once helped a neighbor kidnap a girl and marry her; her brother opposed them and defended the girl, which resulted in all kinds of adventures, during which the girl "fought like fury." The bridegroom turned out not to be very strong or heroic; but the brother also fled. Finally the couple were married—only to go back, after a few weeks, to the priest and request a divorce.

In "Retraining" the narrator is urged by his friend Yumar to accompany him and help him with sheep insemination. They go to a beautiful mountain area where an impressive ram is brought to a ewe; he dances and jumps around her, and the two men catch the sperm, which seems enough to inseminate "not fifty, but five hundred ewes." Their conversation while they are resting under the stars is rendered in the English translation by Michael Holman, like all the dialogues in the book, in the Yorkshire dialect, which gives it some pseudo-*couleur locale*. The narrator advises his friend to go back to his wife, whom he has deserted, and be nice to her. Yumar does so and returns the next morning, elated. The next day the narrator of the story goes to the mayor of their village and asks him whether he ties his wife to the bed; although the answer is negative ("No need!"), it is stated that "all the men in this village either tie their wives to the bed or snarl at them." The narrator confesses: "It makes my old heart bleed when I think that in making love our folk are worse than cattle." The mayor agrees to organize a "Retraining Scheme" for men "up at the sheepfolds." That is, says the narrator, finishing his story, "what I'm working at now."

"When the World Stopped Wearing Baggy Breeches" is told by a shoemaker who is forced out of business because the slippers he used to make have gone out of fashion. He even tries to drown himself. When a friend plans to leave for the United States, the shoemaker plans to do the same but decides instead to open a beer pub; to his great delight, the money flows in so that he is able to hire a seamstress to make a dress for his wife.

"Fear" is enacted in the wild forests: the "I" of the story is ordered to go to Karakouz, where the forest warden has disappeared:

> In the small Muslim village I only meet the hodja, who offers me a bed in a room of a primitive mosque. During the night I am disturbed by a constant noise, I even fire my revolver, but the noise goes on. The next day it turns out it was caused by a badger; but it took me weeks to get over the panic.

In "A Tree with No Roots" the narrator is an older man living with his son and daughter-in-law, who both have busy jobs. He comes straight from a small village and is not used to city life, which is the source of various comical situations: he does not like the canned food they are eating and the huge quantities of mayonnaise they use, whereas the daughter-in-law complains that he stinks when he eats garlic; essentially, he feels "caught up in this golden cage." Finally the old man gets a piece of land from the cooperative, on which he works hard. He protests to his son: "Nature doesn't have retired foxes.... Ever heard of retired eagles?... Eagles die on the wing." He decides to write a note to his son and go back to the country.

In "A Forest Spirit" there is a forest warden, Metyu, from the times ("in your grandfather's day") when a warden had to be an intrepid person in these parts, "czar, police chief and Allah as well." He caught unauthorized tree cutters, but he also helped good people. However, tax collectors, police, excise men, and wood merchants start coming to the forest. Two policemen even arrest Metyu, imprison him, and torture him, but he manages to escape: "There's one boss in this forest!" The police do not give up their intention to eliminate him, and Metyu is forced to flee. Afterward the beautiful forest is gradually ravaged and desecrated, and the majestic trees are chopped, burned, and stolen "till only these lean and hungry hills were left." But at night Metyu could still be heard calling, frightening people. This is one of the stories in which Khaytov shows himself as an environmentalist in a time when few people were concerned about the natural environment.

The story "You Never Can Tell" (in the original, "A Bedeviled World") is also written in first person. The narrator was sent with the sheep into the mountains from age five onward; he still has bloodshot eyes from the heavy smoke in the hut where he spent the nights. Once a bear chased him; he was injured, but rescued, and has limped ever since. He tells about fights with other shepherds and with gypsies. When his father-in-law refuses to share his sheep with him, he takes vengeance by killing all his bees and throwing the hives into the river. Then he starts to buy sheep and sell them across the border, which proves to be a lucrative business.

However, his dealer on the Greek side not only disappears without paying him but turns out to be a spy, and the narrator is arrested. After some time he is released, and that is the end of his story, except that the unruly shepherd has a married son. When the son's young wife flees to her village, the son is so depressed that he sets fire to his own house, wanting to forget her and his home, thereby showing that he is of the same temperament as his father.

The story "Ibryam-Ali" is about another daredevil, a farmhand who becomes a feared robber, on whose head thousands of levs are placed; he is a good singer too. When for some time no one has seen him, people believe he has died, and they breathe more freely, but suddenly he turns up again, attacking and killing a shepherd. The narrator (a shepherd) sees him at night: Ibryam-Ali forces him to give him a ram, which they roast, and they have a friendly conversation. Later the rumor that he is dead resurfaces, but one day the narrator is at the train station when Ibryam-Ali joins him, disguised by a black beard—he had for some time lived in Greece. When the men in the village pub start singing his favorite song, he cannot help taking the lead, and then everybody recognizes him, whereupon Ibryam-Ali orders a bottle of wine for each person present. At the end Ibryam-Ali is shot dead. The village teacher comments: "He was tough and he was terrible, but that song was stronger still."

"The Little Black Bird" is an expanded anecdote about a whistling black bird in a cage; the bird is finally killed and buried by the whole village. "Getting Wed" is another story about a forced marriage. A girl, Hatta, runs away from her wedding and comes to the narrator; she and he go to his village to be joined in marriage by the *hodja;* in the meantime the bridegroom and his wedding guests, a wild pack, come rushing, "daggers in their teeth." A duel takes place, not between the bridegroom and the narrator, but between the bridegroom and the narrator's uncle. The latter wins and then claims the bride for himself. The narrator runs off and hides in the woods; later he returns home, planning to kill both his uncle and Hatta, but he never does.

"Paths" is the story of a naive but honest, work-loving older man who is laying footpaths in the woods just because he loves them and because "This old life of ours wouldn't be worth much without beauty, would it?" This particular story reflects the Soviet socialist realistic idealization of labor and simple people's goodness. Another typical "wild tale" is "The Seed of the Dervishovs," in which the narrator tells that he was forced to marry as a boy of almost fourteen years; but the bride's two brothers ran away with her and gave her to a friend in exchange for a couple of billy goats. He remarried soon thereafter, but he kept longing for his first wife. He visited her when her husband became ill, and he carried wood for her; however, the husband had not passed out, as the narrator expected he would, and the narrator becomes frustrated.

Among the stories not translated in the English edition is "Bukova glava" (Beech Head), centered around a village church, a stolen icon, and other church valuables that have disappeared; it is a light story but certainly not complimentary toward the Orthodox Church and clergy.

"Koziyat rog" (The Goat's Horn), because of its film version, became perhaps Khaytov's best-known work. It starts: "This bloody history also begins with violence." Deli Mustafa has raped the attractive wife of Karaivan. When her husband comes home, he finds her deranged and takes her to a monastery to have her cured, but she dies after a short time. Karaivan burns his house and leaves with his ten-year-old daughter to the mountains, where they live for ten years in a winter cabin. One day the rapist is found dead, pierced with a goat's horn, but nobody thinks of Karaivan anymore. Then more killings occur. When Turkish policemen come to the winter cabin, they see the demented, giggling Karaivan and leave. More murders are reported, and the goat horn used as a weapon causes general consternation.

At a village festivity a maiden appears who unintentionally drops a goat horn. The police come, but she throws herself from a rock, and Karaivan escapes. Soon thereafter a man shows up at a nearby monastery and asks to be admitted as a laborer; soon he becomes sick and dies. From his confession the priest hears Karaivan's story and then divulges it. The reader learns details about the man's crimes. It turns out that he had educated and trained his daughter as if she were a boy. Once, when he found out she had tender feelings for a man, he killed that man. At the end the narrator states that he heard this bloody story from a monk.

The motion picture made from this story, one of the six tales in *Divi razkazi* that served as

Nikolay Khaytov

the base for films, had much success, both in Bulgaria and abroad. It received the Silver Hugo Prize in Chicago and eight other international awards. "The Goat's Horn" was both the most popular and the most acclaimed Bulgarian movie; it was also the cheapest to produce and took the least time (forty-eight days) to finish.

From the many short stories not included in *Divi razkazi,* a few of the most noteworthy deserve mention. "Kalinkiniti chanove" (Kalinka's Bells) is a variation of the international legendary motif of the incarcerated (immured) woman. Before Kalinka dies, she begs her husband to cast her silver necklace and make it into bells for his sheep so that he will always be reminded of her. One day the son, who is the narrator, and his twin brother wait for their father somewhere in the mountains; their dog comes to them and they find the father, who is injured. He stammers: "The bells ... they grabbed them.... Run!" The brothers hunt and overtake the thieves, kill one, and get the bells back. They return home with their wounded father, who soon passes away. The melted necklace, symbolizing the mother's soul, has been rescued.

In "*Gola sŭvest*" (A Clean Conscience), a somewhat longer story, the narrator tries hard to keep a clean conscience and be immune to bribery and to the political and business manipulations in which everybody, even the priest and the doctor, appear to be involved. He carries out a symbolic action: he announces a funeral, brings a casket to the church, then takes it to the graveyard and opens it—there is only a (political) "calendar" in it. In a speech he declares that all politicians are "people given to briberies and violence, from the prime minister to the last ranger!"

"Angel voivoda" (The Chieftain Angel) is a typical folktale told in a language replete with Turkish and obsolete words about the young Angel, his adventures, and fights with the Turks. He becomes a *khaidut, haidutin* (rebel, freedom fighter) who always has his bagpipe with him and who gains such a reputation that songs are sung about him. Suddenly he disappears (this is in 1847—the story contains some dates that lend it the appearance of authenticity). It turns out he is in one of the Orthodox monasteries on the Athos Peninsula, waiting to be accepted as a monk. "Where there is sin, there should be repentance," he argues. He is being trained as a monk and everything is satisfactory, but he misses his bagpipe. A week before his ordination he goes to a fair, where he hears a song about himself, the courageous *khaidut*; he cannot resist the strong feelings this evokes in him, and he becomes a gang leader again (this supposedly actually happened in 1863). More adventures follow until, at age fifty-five, he feels there have been enough adventures. The song about him survives, and through it he enters "the realm of eternity." The story is presented as Khaytov's rendition of true historical facts; no sources are mentioned.

Parts of Khaytov's more contemplative texts also have a narrative element. In "Krai selo" (Close to the Village) from the series "Iz planinata" (In the Mountains), for example, the narrator tells how his uncle urged him not to sit with books, but to walk, and he does, meeting various village people and animals and enjoying natural scenes, including a ravine and a grave mound. He visits the ruins of an old fortress that has a view of the whole Plovdiv plain. He reminisces about Uncle Naso, who has lived somewhere in the forest. "Although he always walked with an axe, nobody ever saw him using it: he only collected dry wood. He believed the forest had a *saibi* [master] whom he didn't want to upset.... He was a master of finding mouse depositories of nuts, but he would take only half of it, never the whole stock."

In the next series, "Kŭm vŭrkha" (To the Summit), there is "Ashovitsa," supposedly a story an uncle told the narrator as a boy, but it is presented here in the form of a literary text. The central hero is Kara Asan, who is induced by a "blood sucker," a landowner, to ignite and burn a large piece of virgin forest so that his cattle could graze there. Asan feels a deep pain and regret when the trees burn and the forest animals perish. His niece, Ashe, meets her death in a storm; the uncle buries her there, and the place is still called Ashovitsa. "Chovekut, koito nadvi" (The Man Who Overcame) is more of an adventure story. The narrator is obviously in a higher position now, a full-fledged forester. He orders an overseer to cut down a beech tree, but the overseer, Marinski, ignores the order. Later he lets a substitute do the job, and a cartridge is found, hidden in the core of the tree. Then Marinski's story is told: A man called Isein once had to show a Turk, Tosun Bey, the way through the forest, and he noticed the latter had a *kemer,* or belt, in which money was carried. When he later learned the Turk had died, he looked and looked for the money that he assumed was hidden in the woods, but he searched in vain. He told Marinski this before his death. Once Marinski discovered by accident a hole in a beech tree but could not investigate it because a surveying brigade was working close by. Marinski dreams about the money and what he could do with it (build a house with a balcony), but each time he wants to fell the beech he is hindered and prevented from doing the job. Finally he gives up: "Let Tosun Bey's belt go to hell!"

"Magyosnikŭt ot Breze" (The Magician from Breza), in the same series, is a story told to the narrator by a hodja. The story has a double frame. When the main character is able to help some parents arrange the marriage of their son to the girl they want him to marry, he gets the reputation of being a magician and does all he can to maintain that reputation. The girl in question has received an amulet from him. But he has bad feelings when he learns she has been unfaithful and has been killed by her husband. He does not understand Allah, who is supposed to be good and just. This induces him to ask the Mufti to be released as a hodja.

Khaytov wrote nine plays (plus four puppet theater plays), of which the best known is the triptych *Pŭteki* (Paths), *Lodka v gorata* (A Boat in the Forest), and *Kucheta* (The Dogs), all one-act plays. The first is a comedy, a dialogue based on the story of the same title, between the Director and Vlashko, the man who loves to make trails in the woods without compensation. In the end the Director chases him away under the pretext that Vlashko demands too much by way of a pension. The second play is also a dialogue, this time between the ranger, Marin, and the young woman, Gina, whom he catches cutting tobacco stakes. She has a child but is unmarried; he, it turns out, is divorced. A rather lively conversation ensues, with bickerings, conflicts, and misunderstandings that are eventually resolved. There is a discussion about the situation of the sexes in the countryside: Gina remarks, "The men eat and drink and rest. They don't die easily. A man's paradise—that's what our village is. And they don't divorce.... The village women make the money and the men don't let them go." Their dialogue is interspersed with sexual remarks and allusions. Then they quarrel again. He says he has to report that she has been cutting tobacco stakes, which is forbidden—but he helps her carry them. After a while they rest; they talk again, imagining they are in a boat at sea—and finally they embrace.

Kucheta has three characters: Uncle Nacho, sitting in his shepherd's hut; Buzata (The Cheek), another shepherd who comes to tell him that the authorities demand that Nacho kill his dogs (there is a resolution limiting the number of dogs, and extra or unplanned dogs have to be immediately destroyed, but Nacho protests—he has only two dogs for five hundred sheep); and the "Zootechnician," an authoritative bureaucrat who insists on execution of the resolution. He even tries to kill one of the dogs, but they pull at his arm, so he misses. Angry and threatening, he exits but returns even more furious that the order has not been acted upon. Buzata threatens him with his revolver and attempts to force him to confess—he is known for his disreputable behavior. But the Zootechnician strikes the revolver out of Buzata's hand, brandishes it, and even shoots, but the revolver is empty. Now Buzata triumphs again; however, he hands over some patrons to the Zootechnician and tells him to fire, calling him names. Finally, he strikes the weapon out of the Zootechnician's hands and boxes him on his ears, whereupon the Zootechnician leaves again, riding his moped. Nacho and Buzata then leave for a village meeting, where they will have to testify. They reassure each other: "A human is a human!"

Of Khaytov's nonfiction writings, *Asenovgrad v minaloto* (Asenovgrad in the Past, 1965) is a 440-page historical survey, a solid scholarly work on the origin and history of a town close to Khaytov's native village, located twenty kilometers southeast of Plovdiv, where the Asenitsa River leaves the Rhodope Mountains and flows into the Thracian plain. It was a medieval fortress and settlement originally named Stanimaka. The book is illustrated and contains information about the economy, growth, folklore, way of life, and physiognomy of the town. *Shumki ot gabŭr* (Leaves of the Hornbeam, 1965) is a collection of essays, articles, and memories. The first piece consists of evocations of nature, reflections about nature, and a comparison of several mountain ranges in Bulgaria. In the second, Khaytov writes about the hornbeam leaves that work "a small, but beneficial miracle; they transform the rebellious forest noises into a *song.*" The next text is called "Khalishta" (Blankets); it deals with blankets as a folkoric art. They are unpainted in the houses of Christian shepherds (because Muslim freebooters would confiscate anything beautiful and colorful), but they are painted with interesting motifs and patterns in Islamic houses. Khaytov describes various kinds of blankets and mentions his trips in search of beautiful ones and his conversations with women. He concludes: "For the woman from Rhodope, who lives her life without holidays, the blanket is a holiday. Her pride. Her triumph. It spreads the glory of her hands."

There is also an essay about the richness of the Bulgarian language as spoken by country folk; he praises those who tell folktales. "Detskite ochi" (Children's Eyes) is about the difference between early memories and reality when one visits one's native village. In "Oruzhenostsi na slovoto" (Protectors of the Word) the subject is old chronicles and the monk chroniclers who left their notes that have been preserved in libraries and museums from the thirteenth to the nineteenth centuries. Khaytov provides many quotations that have been somewhat modernized to make them understandable. As the monk Visarion wrote: "The grass withers and flowers fall off, but the word remains from generation to generation." In "Gergiovden" (Saint George's Day) the author discusses the spring festivities that exist in every civilization, from heathen times (when "a single God was not yet invented") to the present. The wishes and prayers for the new spring and summer season were later directed to Saint George; however, "in essence, Christianity has nothing in common with this holiday." In the Rhodope region it is not celebrated in church, but in the open. "What has this great joy in common," he asks, "with the gloom of God's temple, the incense smell of the Christian liturgy, the skinny faces of saints and the vague allusions to the hereafter?... The force of Saint George's Day overcame even the fanaticism of Islam."

There are more contributions that focus on folk beliefs and traditions. The second part of the book is called "Dokumentatsiya," but it is not much different in character from the first part. "Dobraluk" is a description of the village of that name; it is a typical Rhodope village consisting of some two hundred houses, but it has a long history and can boast of two-thousand-year-old Thracian remnants. It has a population of Christians and Bulgarian Muslims. It was long neglected and disadvantaged; until the 1950s there was no school, telephone service, water, electricity, or radio. The first truck reached Dobraluk in 1959. In 1961, so the author concludes in an optimistic tone, "darkness is forever chased out of Dobraluk by 100 watt electric suns. The desolate wilderness is a memory." In the same optimistic mood he writes "The Radio and the Two Peasant Women," in which the two women talk about and are bewildered by the phenomenon of radio. There are a few articles in reportage style, including conversations with workers. More interesting for the Western reader is "Posledna duma" (The Last Word), which begins: "Comrades judges! Comrade public prosecutor!" and ends: "Copied from the judicial protocols by Nikolai Khaytov." The defendant tells his judges that he is normal, not crazy, as his lawyer tries to present him—he knows what he is doing and takes full responsibility for his act: he has damaged eighty-seven motorbikes in Sofia. The noise of a motorcycle rivals that of a jet plane, he argues. He could not sleep in his apartment on one of the Sofia boulevards, so he started to slash tires and to hammer on bikes, which gave him a good feeling. He turned to the city council and wrote to the newspapers—all in vain. Now he hopes he will stay in prison quite some time because here he can sleep quietly.

"Izkarvaite kozite, khe-e-ei!" (Drive out the Goats, Heeey!) is a reminiscence from his native Yavrovo. Every morning before sunrise the goatherd used to shout three times, waking up the goats and the whole village, and then all who owned goats would take their goats to the goatherd. The rest of the text is a eulogy of the goat, notwithstanding its harmfulness from an environmental point of view, a fact with which Khaytov must have been familiar. Statistically it is established, he writes, that most of the people who live to be one hundred or more live in the mountains, where goat buttermilk and goat cheese are the traditional fare. Goats were domesticated more than ten thousand years ago, long before cows and sheep.

"Za razzhivyavaneto" (For Living One's Life to the Full) is a plea for frugality. Humans spoil themselves in many ways, and civilizations have collapsed as a result of luxury. Lao-tzu, Confucius, Buddha, and other wise men all called for moderation; the Bulgarians survived five centuries of Ottoman rule because they were forced to live a hard life and knew no luxuries. Not by "living to the full," warns Khaytov, but by work and abstinence will the nation and humanity survive. In the section "Dushata na lesa" (The Soul of the Forest) there are typical environmental pieces such as "Monologŭt na posledniya" (Monologue of the Last One), declaimed by the last tree that is left (because it is crooked). "Thus I was able to survive all of them, to witness that here, on these devastated grounds and bare rocks, once upon a time there was a forest...."

Khayduti (The Outlaws, 1968) is a series of four extended historical essays. In his introduction, "Khaiduts–Legend and Reality," Khaytov attempts to correct various misconceptions about the Bulgarian rebels and presents an overview of their history in which he stresses that women played heroic roles as well. "Khaiduting," he concludes, "is a historical phenomenon, that rehabilitates the Bulgarian, fallen into [Turkish] bondage." "The Chieftain Chavdar and the Banner Bearer Lalush" is a vividly narrated text, adapted from a historical source, about the two heroes, Chavdar and Lalus, with dialogues and lines quoted from heroic songs. Probably Khaytov also used as a source the Bulgarian epic folk songs, of which a great many have been preserved. The next essay, "The Chieftain Chakŭr," begins: "While Chavdar and Lalush are, to a large extent, the products of a legend, an inspired legend, a myth–Chakŭ the Chieftain from Bamokov is a true historical person." The years 1848, 1851, and 1854 are mentioned. Chakŭ, nicknamed "the Baron of Samokov," was a heroic fighter who perished as a result of "An Insidious Murder" (the title of the last chapter). "Chieftain Rumena" tells about a female *khaidut* born in 1829. When she is twelve, an attempt is made to convert her to the Turkish way of life. Her father arranges an early marriage to prevent her from falling into Turkish hands again: at sixteen she marries a twenty-two-year-old man. Various events show that "she was not only courageous, but had a boldness bordering on insanity." Khaytov based his rendering of this legendary life on several sources. The remaining three texts, "Chieftain Angel," "Mitkaloto," and "Captain Petko the Chieftain" (a text of 140 pages, divided into subchapters), are all in the same vein.

In *Bodlivata roza* (The Prickly Rose, 1975), Khaytov speaks once more as a moralist and an environmentalist. There are cultural-philosophical musings and reasonings and expatiations on the horrors of air pollution and urbanization, but there are also pieces about his Rhodope, the mountains and forests, and on nature in general. He writes:

> Green nature is not something neutral to man, he is, when he enters it or is confronted with it, constantly enveloped by nature's field of force or radiance and he bathes in the waves of that almost imperceptible vibration.... Thousands of years of experience have demonstrated that this radiation is not simply munificent, not just wholesome, but absolutely essential to a normal development of a human being and to his/her health.... At least for myself I can say that the impact of green nature is pretty much bewitching.

Khaytov is important in Bulgaria as a born storyteller, a prominent writer of nonfiction, an efficient essayist, the apostle of the neglected Rhodope region, and the first Bulgarian environmentalist. He has also written travelogues, descriptions and histories of towns, books for children, diaries, and radio and television plays.

Interviews:

R. Trifonov, "Pri korenita na zhivota," *Pogled*, no. 18 (1967);

S. Velikov, "Sreshti i razgovori s Nikolay Khaytov," *Septemvri*, no. 8 (1969).

Bibliography:

Rechnik na bŭlgarskata literatura, volume 3 (Sofia: BAN, 1982), pp. 519–522.

References:

D. Asenov, "Mezhdu ocherka i raskaza," *Septemvri*, no. 10 (1957);

P. Dinekov, "Folklorut i tvorchestvoto na Nikolay Khaytov i Yordan Radichkov," *Bŭlgarski folklor*, no. 7 (1977);

K. Elenkov, "S tsvetovete na nadezhdata," *Septemvri*, no. 9 (1979);

M. Georgiev, "Vŭzvrashtane kŭm dumata," *Septemvri*, no. 8 (1960);

E. Karanfilov, "Kniga za dushata na Rodopa," *Plamŭk*, no. 6 (1965);

S. Khadzhikosev, "Visshiat zhivot na natsiata," *Otechestven front* (9 October 1981);

L. Kirova, "Nikolay Khaytov," *Rodna rech*, no. 2 (1969);

O. Markova, "Prozorets kŭm natsionalniya kharakter," *Kinoizkustvo*, no. 7 (1976);

G. Nedelchev, "Zhanrova forma i poeticheski sintaksis na Khaytovite *Divi razkazi*," *Ezik i literatura*, no. 4 (1975);

Z. Nedkov, "Drugiyat Khaytov," *Plamŭk*, no. 11 (1974);

"Polemika za knigata na N. Khaytov *Divi razkazi*," *Literaturna misŭl*, nos. 2, 3, 6 (1974);

S. Sultanov, "Misli za poetikata na Nikolay Khaytov," *Plamŭk*, no. 10 (1971);

S. Svilenov, "Nikolay Khaytov i bŭlgarskoto kino," *Plamŭk*, no. 9 (1979);

P. Zarev, "Tvorchestvoto na Nikolay Khaytov," *Plamŭk*, no. 1 (1975);

T. Zhechev, "Nikolay Khaytov i dukhŭt na Rodopite," *Rodopi*, no. 2 (1968).

Boris Khristov
(14 August 1945 –)

Raia Kuncheva
Institute of Literature, Sofia

BOOKS: *Vecheren trompet. Stichotvoreniya* (Varna: G. Bakalov, 1977);

Chesten krŭst (Varna: G. Bakalov, 1982);

Bashtata na yaitseto (Plovdiv: Khristo G. Danov, 1987);

Slyapoto kuche. Dolinata na obuvkite (Varna: G. Bakalov, 1990);

Smŭrtni petna (Sofia: Bŭlgarski pisatel, 1990).

Editions in English: *The Wings of the Messenger*, selected works translated by Roland Flint, Betty Grinberg, and Lyubomir Nicolov (Sofia: Petrikov, 1991);

Dumi & grafiti. Words & Graphite, translated by Flint and Grinberg (Varna: Andina, 1991);

Dumi vŭrkhu drugi dumi. Words on Words, translated by Flint, Grinberg, and Nicolov (Sofia: Petrikov, 1991);

Cherni bukvi vŭrkhu cheren list. Black Letters on a Black Page, translated by Flint and Grinberg (Sofia: LUKE, 1997).

OTHER: *Bŭlgarska lirika*, edited by Khristov (Sofia: Petrikov, 1994);

Bŭlgarski razkazi, edited by Khristov (Sofia: LUKE, 1995);

Narodni ustni pismena, edited by Khristov (Sofia: LUKE, 1995).

Boris Khristov's writing speaks to the tragedy of the human condition, particularly as that tragedy unfolds in the spiritual and political slavery suffered under communist regimes. His poetry and prose contrast sharply with the ideologically charged, semi-official art that was encouraged for decades by the Bulgarian government. Khristov's art is essentially the exploration of a question: how can a person live in an unfree world and protect himself as an individual? In his answer the poet focuses on personal life and the language in which all that is expressed makes it into a psychological character sketch, one created by body gestures, actions, and sensations, in images and symbols that are often archetypal. The theme of hopelessness and the individual's resistance to it results in a narrative of human life that is interlaced with metaphor, analogy, and a sense of the grotesque. Lyricism transforms that personal confession about the world's disintegration and humanity's self-destruction; it opens a new ground for the kind of existence that resists the forces of stagnation.

Boris Khristov was born on 14 August 1945 in the village of Crapets in the region of Radomir. His childhood and adolescence coincided with the cruelest era of the totalitarian Bulgarian state. After World War II that state imposed collectivism on its people, rejected the idea of personal freedom, dispossessed the peasants of their land, and forced Soviet-style industrialization in a traditionally agrarian country. All these actions provoked profound changes in people's consciousness. In this period of mass political repression, thousands of innocent people found themselves in jails and interment camps. The country's spiritual, intellectual, and economic elite was physically destroyed. The church was also subjected to repression. For decades to come literature and the arts were relegated to being nothing more than a means of propaganda for the communist regime. Such a reality was a prerequisite for the dramatic and tragic motifs in Khristov's work. Regardless of the political and spiritual stagnation of the time, the poet developed as an internally free man, finding support and solace in his art and his defiant individualism.

Khristov's childhood was profoundly marked by the loss of his father and his two sisters. His father died in an accident in the mines of the town of Pernik when the poet was only a year old. Thus, death and country life became his constant themes, the subjects from which he starts and to which he always returns. He finished elementary and high school in Pernik, a little town near Sofia, the capital, and graduated in

Bulgarian philology at the University of Veliko Tŭrnovo. He then held different jobs that included being a teacher, a journalist, and an editor of literary magazines. Having inherited musical talent from his mother, he played various folk instruments and for a short time made his living with his trumpet (the key word of his first book of verse). Although he remained close to the natural life of the countryside and although different forms of folk and ethnic art attracted him, his work does not show the explicit influence of such elements. He preferred small towns and rural life to life in the large cities, with their paralyzing restrictions. He also developed a love for jazz, which the communist authorities considered a decadent art.

His first book of verse, *Vecheren trompet. Stichotvoreniya* (Evening Trumpet, 1977), was rejected by the major publishing houses. Socialist realism continued to be the official aesthetic of the regime, in spite of its episodically declared intention of liberalizing the arts. The emotions and thoughts of Bulgarian artists had to be contained within the framework of this doctrine, and every differing point of view regarding the problems of human existence was looked upon with hostility and criticized ideologically. Khristov's book was eventually published by a provincial publishing house.

Once published, the verses impressed readers, and Khristov rapidly became one of the most celebrated and beloved Bulgarian poets. This popularity has both an artistic and a social import, because Khristov's poetry illuminates such human realities as depression in the face of death, solitude, the sense of the futility of life, and barbed-wire fences; it also bristles with the resistance of a rebel. The dead world of nothingness, which for many of his readers echoes their own sense of paralyzing emptiness, is confronted by the dynamism of overcoming oneself and the strength represented by meeting the difficulties of life with resistance. Each of Khristov's works is inspired by the memory of some particular insight about the essence of life and death, a moment when one discovers for oneself a new stoicism.

His childhood, in which he knew both death and love, his youth, with its perpetual expectation of something about to happen in the town, his later acceptance of solitude and his overcoming it by means of poetry—all these experiences shaped and informed *Vecheren trompet. Stichotvoreniya*, which became a book about the mastery of suffering and provided a declaration of the poet's credo. For Khristov, a person creates his own world, and in Khristov's world the main character is the lonely individual; the landscape for that individual is symbolized by his sleeping under the burning sun. His second book of verse, *Chesten krŭst* (Cross My Heart, 1982), plumbs deeper into and enlarges upon the human problems explored in the first; it is charged with a social, moral, and aesthetic nonconformism.

Khristov's confession is not an aim in itself, although for many readers he is precisely the poet who has discovered the language of harsh realities. His first book follows the creation of the personal "ego" and, respectively, that of Khristov's world, figuratively and dramatically. The second book expresses the fortitude required to face the absurd alone. Poems such as "Stenata" (The Wall) and "Samoletŭt zakŭsniava" (The Plane Is Late) convey tragic conclusions about doomed people in the closed world of the so-called socialist countries. In the latter poem Khristov writes:

> In neighboring airports, from which barbed wire
> keeps us, planes take off every second, they
> batter the skies. And, utterly hopeless, we tear up
> our tickets, to wait for the night, compliant as cows.
>
> Probably the plane will come, and, like an angel appear,
> men grown old will start after it, the wings bent,
> but I myself will no longer be—my head by then
> will be a cricket's house, furnished with pebbles.

But at the same time that they address political realities, Khristov's images turn into symbols of human existence. Metaphysical problems enter his work with a skepticism characteristic of the end of the twentieth century. The spirit is a "winged wolf" that kills "the lamb of God," but the body is only pain and permanent travail, as it is in "Tyalo" (Body):

> Vicious with weakness—like the blind mouse,
> which sucks at the hard nipple of a hazelnut, it
> walks under the rain and writes on the wet streets:
> "Live like a bird—die like a dog."

The last verse provides a key expression in the first of Khristov's novellas, *Slyapoto kuche* (The Blind Dog, 1990). The intertextual links between Khristov's poetry and prose are not so much deliberate as they are a consequence of the fact that everything he wrote in any genre represents images or dramatic visions, insights in the process of gaining self-consciousness. The metaphor and the symbols are the means of naming the logically unnameable.

A strong motif in the second book of verse is that of the human being who has reached the end of his strength and is in a collision with an infinity—either of desire, of a dream, or of art. Khristov reinterprets the biblical motif of guilt, creating visions of human self-destruction. The personal existential situation projects itself on a cosmic level, while his mythological imagery combines with concrete psychological and physical details. The enlarging of consciousness continues by images that acquire archetypal contents. Woman is the eternal temptress ("Zhenata Maria" [The Woman Maria]); the world of the dead is not terrible, and one shall descend there down the ropes of rain and be seated at the eternal dinner table ("Kambanata" [The Bell]). "Pesenta na mravkite" (The Song of the Ants) is a vision of anonymous resistance. In the first book Khristov expressed the depression he experienced in the closed space of his native country. After his journey to the United States in 1981 to participate in the International Writers Program of the University of Iowa, he outlined in his second book the parabola of his return, creating the image of the modern Odysseus and the feeling of belonging to a definite place, tradition, or memory. In *Chesten krŭst*, again by using mythic references, the poet's personal feelings are projected through images from the Christian tradition. A striking feature of Khristov's artistry is that his works achieve meanings on the sensory-object level, the emotional level, and the spiritual level.

In that context, the question of the sense of one's life and the sense of writing verse arises. According to Khristov, life and poetry, in his experience, undergo strange reciprocal transformations. Poetry helps him rescue himself from the stupidity in the world, but it is also written to relieve the pain of others, and it will always connect him with people. Art is itself a form of life, and, if circumstances are against it, art is simply impossible—that is actually a principal theme of Khristov's. In "Chesten krŭst," the only lyric poem, which provides the title for the book, the poet describes his refusal to write verse anymore because in the world of lies and compulsion he wants to save poetry as truth and as an expression of personal freedom. Khristov's attitude toward poetry is as serious as his attitude toward life, and he will not permit art to be manipulated. This declared personal responsibility turns his poetry into something more than literature. The words *Chesten krŭst* (cross my heart) mean, "I swear before God," but once spoken they represent a personal standpoint. In fact, after *Chesten krŭst* Khristov did not publish verse for a long time and turned to writing prose instead. At a time when he was already recognized as one of the most significant poets of contemporary Bulgarian literature, he refused, in a categorical gesture of accusation, to publish verses.

During the 1980s he worked in a movie studio, and a cinematographer's point of view can be detected in his prose. He wrote screenplays for feature, documentary, and cartoon films—*Smŭrtta na zaeka* (The Death of the Rabbit, 1981), *Bashtata na yaitseto* (The Father of the Egg, 1990), *Korabŭt* (The Ship, 1983), and *Gorgonata* (The Gorgon, 1994). Some of his screenplays were banned. In 1982 his novella *Slyapoto kuche* was published in the journal *Sŭvremennik* (The Contemporary). The following year it was published as a separate book, but on orders from the State Security Service the entire edition was destroyed; it was not published again until 1990. In the libraries—including the largest, the National Library in Sofia—*Chesten krŭst* and *Slyapoto kuche* were on the forbidden list and were locked in a special collection until 1989.

Even when he changes from poetry to short fiction, Khristov creates a world that is recognizably his. His characters are outcasts from society, among whom is Lazar Vekhtosharia (a secondhand dealer), a man who speaks with a bird perched on his shoulder while walking the streets to collect clothes, and who had been well known as a tailor. When Lazar prepares himself for death, he does not want to leave anything behind in which he has put all of himself. He does not even want others to repeat words that he had once spoken. But his words and his image remain in the hearts of his friends, who try, unsuccessfully, to bury him. The short novel is constructed by juxtaposing two worlds—the world of outsiders and the world of state institutions with their artificial rituals and ideological obtuseness. Khristov presents the narrative in a satirical-grotesque light.

Dolinata na obuvkite (The Valley of the Shoes) was published in periodicals in 1988 (in 1990 both this novella and *Slyapoto kuche* were published in one volume). Yorgo and Leta are in a mental hospital. Rejected by "the normal persons," they are the only ones who can save themselves by love and deserve to remain on earth to create a new kind of person. Yorgo is obsessed by the idea that he is a spaceman, and so reality is seen through one of the myths of the communist regime. Yorgo rejects the life in which brutality besieges human existence on all sides. Little Yorgo had felt that rejection while still in his mother's womb. Then he experiences the shame of undressing in public and shuts himself in a heroic-individualist illusion of himself, from which love returns him to life. Making love and the launching of a rocket into outer space are joined in a metaphor of the miracle of love.

Khristov's fiction does not use the traditional narrative technique that encourages the reader to identify psychologically with characters in the story. At the same time, satire, irony, and the grotesque do not embrace his vision of the world totally. To them Khristov opposes the poetic quality, and each of his prose works is a new discovery of a hidden and unexpected world of beauty. The atmosphere of the poetic quality absorbs the stupidity, desolation, and cruelty of a kind of society that is well known and painful to the reader.

In 1987 Khristov's novel *Bashtata na yaitseto* was published. This is a strange book whose unconventional genre is a challenge to the reader. In this narrative absolutely everything is personified—both organic and inorganic nature, the animal kingdom and the sea world, birds and stones, people and statues—all are connected to and dependent upon each other. Obviously the author's message warns of the catastrophic damage that human beings cause to the natural world, but the so-called ecological theme by no means exhausts the meanings of the story. In the last chapter the author tells how every living being leaves the earth and goes back to the sea, but the novel does not depict a utopian road to safety. The wars in the novel are strange, too—an image of a huge bird is projected against the sky; the monuments that people have created turn against them. The total militarization of the state, the recruiting of the entire population as informants for the State Security, a society that cannot exist without enemies and looks for them among the unborn—all these convey a sad truth about the contemporary age. The book was published before the change of the political regime, but in the whirlwind of the fast-changing scene the author managed to speak of the monuments of the so-called socialist realism, about the erecting of monuments of "state men" during their lifetime, and of creators condemned to the interment camps because of their art.

The inclusion of these realities in a fantasy world, where everything is moving in the game of an all-pervading vitalism, creates a new kind of vision, one that enables the reader to observe from a distance humanity and the world it is creating. The story is told from the point of view of a thinking observer who is both alienated from society and yet sympathetic, like an investigator of some natural species. The story does not achieve its impact by showing characters whose actions are psychologically motivated. In that sense *Bashtata na yaitseto* is a novel without characters. Instead of structuring reality, Khristov prefers to convey his themes through the level of chaotic meetings and associations of different substances, of different forms of nature. This is not an anthropocentric world simply because the world of the novel has no center. Thus, one discovers once more in the principle of the narration itself the effect of Khristov's metaphor in which the borders of separate categories have been removed.

While the titles of the short novels *Slyapoto kuche* and *Dolinata na obuvkite* have their own keys to interpretation, hinted at in the works themselves, the title of *Bashtata na yaitseto* is left open for different interpretations. In his poetry, as in his prose, Khristov uses symbols that have various layers of meanings but, included in a concrete context and without losing their multiplicity of meanings, still have a plastic, almost tangible impact. One of the characters in the novel is the ornithologist Tilza.

The main character in the next work, *Smŭrtni petna* (Death Spots, 1990), bears the same name, Tilza. He is a projection of the author's personality. After the books of poetry, after the novellas and the novel, here, by means of autobiographical material that is narrated in the third person, one meets again and in a new way the personality of the author. Actually, this work, which combines Khristov's innovations in verse and prose, outlines the human condition. In his typical mythological-conventional style the author presents his life as an ascent of the Peak, at the age of thirty-three, and the descent into the Valley, where death is.

Like the characters in the other stories, Tilza is also an outsider in his own way. He refuses to live the life of the others because he has chosen a creator's solitude. Pain gives birth to verse, and he begins the search for pain. Two temporal worlds alternate in the course of the narrative, and, if the road to death begins with the descent from the Peak, the beginning of Tilza's life goes back to his father's funeral. It is to that death that he constantly reverts when he feels guilty for turning his mother's suffering into poetry and when he realizes that the demands of art make him seem cruel to those who love him. In an all-permissive world Tilza continues to experience the suffering of being on the border between Good and Evil, finding them inextricably mixed. Khristov writes about humanity as it proceeds to an ever-deepening self-destruction, when the qualitites that make humans human seem to be preserved solely by being conscious of and experiencing their loss. Death spots are signs of the destruction—of human beings and of nature. To express his misgivings and create the warning signs of self-destruction, Khristov creates a metaphorical story that is written in prose passages that alternate with three-line poems.

Khristov wrote verse in tercets from the end of the 1960s to the 1980s, but he published these works a decade later in *Dumi & grafiti* (Words & Graphite, 1991), *Dumi vŭrkhu drugi dumi* (Words on Words, 1991), and *Cherni bukvi vŭrchu cheren list* (Black Letters on a Black Page, 1997). These works are neither impressions nor poetical aphorisms nor metaphorical fragments. Khristov's three-line poems express meaning in a highly condensed form that has to be extended by the reader's imagination and power of reflection. They contain a few words enveloped in the silence of a white sheet of paper, where each of the tercets is accompanied by a visible image, in graphics by Yana Levieva and Anri Koulev.

At the beginning of the 1990s Khristov created several anthologies—some of Bulgarian lyric poetry and some of Bulgarian short stories. His lasting interest in folklore throughout the years resulted in his selecting material for the anthologies, *Bŭlgarska lirika* (Bulgarian Lyrics, 1994), *Bŭlgarski razkazi* (Bulgarian Short Stories, 1995), and *Narodni ustni pismena* (Folk Writings, 1995). Khristov was invited to attend many poetry recitals in different countries—in the United States (San Francisco, New York, Washington, and cities in Kansas), Canada, India, England, Germany, and Greece. He participated in the Wheatland Foundation Conference on Literature in San Francisco. Khristov is a member of the Board of Managers of the Open Society Foundation and an editor at the review *Lettre International*. His works have been published in English, German, Russian, Hindi, Italian, and other languages.

References:

Rositsa Dimcheva, "Baladno-satirichni motivi v poeziyata na Boris Khristov," *Sŭvremennik*, 20, no. 2 (1992): 310-321;

Dimcheva, "Stihŭt na Boris Khristov," *Ezik i literatura*, 48, no. 1 (1993): 84-92;

Rumyana Koycheva, "Ot poeziya kŭm beletristika," *Plamŭk*, nos. 10-12 (1990): 118-120;

Bozhidar Kunchev, *Edin byal list, edno pero* (Sofia: Narodna mladezh, 1981), pp. 224-234;

Kunchev, "Iskam da kapna od moite sŭlzi," *Narodna mladezh*, no. 202 (26 August 1977); p. 4;

Kunchev, *Pogled kŭm poeziyata* (Sofia: Bŭlgarski pisatel, 1990), pp. 197-222;

Rozaliya Likova, "No da vŭrvim sega, nadezhdo moya . . ." *Septemvri*, no. 9 (1989): 220-231;

Likova, "Protsesi na intenzifikatsiya na poeticheskoto sŭznanie," in her *Poeziya na sedamdesette i osemdesette godini* (Sofia: Bŭlgarska akademiya na naukite, 1994), pp. 176-190;

Ivan Radev, *Predhodnitsi i sŭvremennitsi* (Sofia: Bŭlgarski pisatel, 1984), pp. 78-89;

Radev, *S belega na vremeto* (Sofia: Narodna mladezh, 1980), pp. 226-264;

Radoy Ralin, "V tozi poet ne mozhem da se izlŭzhem," *Trud* (12 October 1977): 4-238;

Ivan Stankov, *Smŭrt ne mozhe da ima. V liricheskiya svyat na Boris Kristov* (Veliko Tŭrnovo: Slovo, 1996), p. 200;

Valeri Stefanov, "V zemnata gradina," *Septemvri*, no. 7 (1990): 250-252;

Evelina Stefanova, "Sŭotnoshenie na grazhdanskoto i nravstveno-filosofskoto nachalo v poeziyata na 60-te i 70-te godini: Nablyudeniya vŭrkhu tvorchestvoto na Lyubomir Levchev, Ivan Tsanev i Boris Khristov," *Literaturna misŭl*, no. 7 (1987): 49-60;

Stela Stoyanova, "Dikhotomiyata dukhovno-telesno i problemŭt za slovoto v poeziyata na Boris Khristov," *Plamŭk*, 37, nos. 11-12 (1993): 109-114;

Petŭr Velchev, "Kak schte zhiveya s toya skitnik sŭrtseto," *Septemvri*, no. 4 (1979): 222-231;

Velchev, *Pogled vŭrkhu poeziyata* (Sofia: Narodna mladezh, 1979), pp. 165-213;

Aleksandŭr Yordanov, "Roman za alternativite," *Septemvri*, no. 11 (1988): 250-253;

Yordanov, *V syankata na dumite* (Sofia: Bŭlgarski pisatel, 1989), pp. 149-153;

Nikolay Zvezdanov, "A da zvŭnya pri udar samo—kato kamertona," *Narodna kultura*, no. 12 (25 March 1983): 7.

Danilo Kiš
(22 February 1935 – 29 October 1989)

Tomislav Z. Longinović
University of Wisconsin–Madison

BOOKS: *Mansarda, Psalam 44* (Belgrade: Kosmos, 1962);

Bašta, pepeo (Belgrade: Prosveta, 1965);

Rani jadi (Belgrade: Nolit, 1969);

Peščanik (Belgrade: Prosveta, 1972);

Po-etika (Belgrade: Nolit, 1972);

Po-etika II (Belgrade: Ideje, 1974);

Grobnica za Borisa Davidoviča (Belgrade & Zagreb: BIGZ/Liber, 1976);

Mansarda (Belgrade: Slovo ljubve, 1977);

Čas anatomije (Belgrade: Nolit, 1978);

Enciklopedija mrtvih (Belgrade: Prosveta, 1985);

Lauta i ožiljci (Belgrade: BIGZ, 1994);

Skladište (Belgrade: BIGZ, 1995).

Edition: *Sabrana dela,* 14 volumes (Belgrade: BIGZ, 1995).

Editions in English: *Garden, Ashes,* translated by William L. Hannaher (New York: Harcourt Brace Jovanovich, 1975);

A Tomb for Boris Davidovich, translated by Duška Mikić-Mitchell (New York: Harcourt Brace Jovanovich, 1978);

The Encyclopedia of the Dead, translated by Michael Henry Heim (New York: Farrar, Straus & Giroux, 1989);

Hourglass, translated by Ralph Manheim (New York: Farrar, Straus & Giroux, 1990);

Homo poeticus—Essays and Interviews, edited by Susan Sontag, translated by Michael Henry Heim, Manheim, and Francis R. Jones (New York: Farrar, Straus & Giroux, 1995).

Danilo Kiš

Danilo Kiš is the most important writer to emerge in Serbia and Yugoslavia since the 1960s. After Ivo Andrić and Miloš Crnjanski, Kiš can be regarded as the most important Serbian writer of the twentieth century within the modernist and postmodernist orientation. The publication of his politically controversial novel *Grobnica za Borisa Davidoviča* (The Tomb for Boris Davidovich, 1976) and the resulting scandal in Serbian and Yugoslav public life left a permanent mark on the literary establishment and decisively influenced younger authors who began writing in the mid 1970s. The work of Kiš has also gained recognition outside of Yugoslavia, making him one of the most important writers of East-Central Europe alongside Milan Kundera, György Konrád, and Czeslaw Milosz.

Danilo Kiš was born on 22 February 1935 in the town of Subotica, a Serbian province of Vojvodina, near the Yugoslav-Hungarian border. His father, Eduard, a Hungarian Jew, was employed as an inspector of the Yugoslav railways. His mother, Milica (née Dragićević), was a Montenegrin Serb who stayed at home and took care of Danilo and his sister, Danica. During World War II Eduard Kiš was deported to a German concentration camp, where he later perished. Later in life Danilo Kiš discovered that his father was once committed to the mental hospital in Kovin, before the war, for the treatment of alcoholism and anxiety neurosis. This fact was crucial for Kiš's depiction of the father in the works from his "family cycle." During the war Milica Kiš took the children to Hungary, where Danilo completed his elementary school education from 1941 to 1944.

After the war ended, the family moved to Cetinje, in the Yugoslav republic of Montenegro, where Kiš attended grammar school until graduation in 1954. There he published his first short story, "Juda" ("Judas"), in *Omladinski list* (The Youth Newspaper) in 1953. After graduation Kiš moved to Belgrade, where he entered the university in the newly opened department of comparative literature and completed his studies in 1958. He worked part-time at the Center for the Theory of Literature and Art in Belgrade after finishing his graduate work in 1960. He was later employed as a lecturer in Serbo-Croatian at the French universities in Strasbourg (from 1963 to 1964), Bordeaux, and Lilles (from 1973 to 1976).

Biography plays a crucial role in Kiš's novelistic poetics, though not in the trivial sense of recounting the details of one's life. On the contrary, following the theory of Victor Šklovsky, he treats autobiographical data as "raw material for the shaping of plot" (*Čas anatomije* [The Anatomy Lesson, 1978]). This means that the author uses a few images or details from the past and tries to fit them into a more universal novelistic meditation on human destiny. In the case of Kiš, the crucial event that continually haunts his life is the deportation of his father to the Nazi death camp in 1942. The three prose works that comprise the so-called family cycle reflect on the horrors of war that were engraved in the memory of the seven-year-old boy.

Rani jadi (Early Sorrows, 1969) is a collection of short stories about the Sam family; although published after *Bašta, pepeo* (1965; translated as *Garden, Ashes*, 1975), it was written before it. The title hints at the influence of a less-than-happy childhood on the character of the narrator-protagonist, Andreas Sam. The stories are about Andreas's first innocent infatuation with a girl ("Verenici"–Betrothed), his sad friendship with a dog ("Dečak i pas"–A Boy and a Dog), bed-wetting ("Priča od koje se crveni"–A Story Which Makes You Blush), and, inevitably, his father's senseless death in the concentration camp ("Iz baršunastog albuma"–From a Velvet Album). Most of the images in these short stories are derived from the chaos of wartime Europe: the reader sees desperate, rain-soaked soldiers wandering through the Pannonian plains, the animals who suffer from human cruelty, and a hypersensitive boy who is puzzled and horrified by the violence of the war. The destiny of the Sam family continues to be the central theme of the other two books from the family cycle, *Bašta, pepeo* and *Peščanik* (1972; translated as *Hourglass*, 1990). There is a strong sense of isolation and solitude in this collection, symbolized in the name of the family; in Serbo-Croatian the word *sam* means alone, lonely, or solitary.

Bašta, pepeo is the second book in the family cycle, devoted to the memory of Eduard Sam, the narrator's father. Using the lyric style that evokes the lethargic beauty of Central European provinces, Kiš introduces Eduard Sam as the somewhat crazed genius who tries to construct a global railway timetable. The book is fragmentary in organization, ironic in tone, and rich in grotesque details from the narrator's childhood. It represents an imaginative attempt at reconstructing the world of childhood as seen through the prism of Andreas Sam, Kiš's alter ego. The work is permeated with the sense of the loss and tragedy that the European Jewry suffered at the hands of the German and Hungarian Nazis. A particularly touching scene in *Bašta, pepeo* describes the father's confrontation with Hungarian peasants who suspect that his prolonged walks in the forest are a sure sign of collaboration with the Allies. They believe that he is hiding a radio station under a tree and one day surround him while he is taking a nap under it. The scene ends with a demonstration of the father's gift of rhetoric, during which he persuades the peasants not to lynch him by proving that the alleged radio station is in fact an old, rusty stove. Since Kiš was a brilliant student of comparative literature at the University of Belgrade while he wrote these works, the echoes of William Faulkner, early James Joyce, and especially Bruno Schulz are evident in his work. In both of these first two volumes of the family cycle the narrator uses the first-person point of view to recount the events from the past that disturb and obsess him.

In the last book of the cycle, *Peščanik*, the point of view changes from first to third person. Andreas Sam is entirely absent as a character, and Eduard Sam is present only in the initials E. S. The facts about the father's madness and alcoholism from the previous two books are repeated and elaborated with acute attention to detail. The tone of the book changes from the biting but still laughable irony of the earlier works to the heavy and somber atmosphere of mourning for the dead father. Kiš's style becomes influenced by the "objectivism" of the French new novel, which makes the prose style of *Peščanik* opaque and rather hermetic. Kiš received the prestigious NIN Literary Award for this work in 1972.

The central metaphor of the novel revolves around the image of the hourglass that, in textbooks on psychology, is sometimes used to illustrate the relationship between foreground and background in visual perception. The subject first perceives the white figure of the hourglass on the black background, until his or her perception is reoriented and he or she notices the two black human profiles forming the two symmetrical sides of the hourglass. The illustration of this perceptual illusion appears on page 15 of the original edition, as the narrator announces his desire to get closer to and merge with E. S. in a perpetual motion of perception from the foreground to the background. Since the simultaneous access to the profiles and the hourglass is impossible, the book can only offer an illusion of understanding the other, who remains inaccessible in the realm of death and forgetfulness.

The hourglass symbolizes the ultimate tragedy of human existence confronted with the inevitable passage of time and a loss of memory. The final chapter of the book, which Kiš calls "the table of contents," is a letter that his real father had written before being deported to the concentration camp. The letter is posited as a key to understanding the hermetic text that precedes it. Every sentence of the letter is a starting point for the narrator's meditation on the most trifling circumstances of the event that the sentence describes. For example, the letter mentions the fact that the father had bought some pork sausages and intestines for the children and his wife to celebrate Easter. This fact is followed in the letter by an intriguing sentence: "But fate is a dog and gobbled it all up." Kiš devotes an entire section of the book to an attempt to decipher the meaning of this sentence. He describes an imaginary duel between his father and a pack of wild dogs, in which E. S. uses a kilo of pork he bought to escape from them. Such ostensibly trivial statements in the letter are starting points for each of the *Peščanik* chapters.

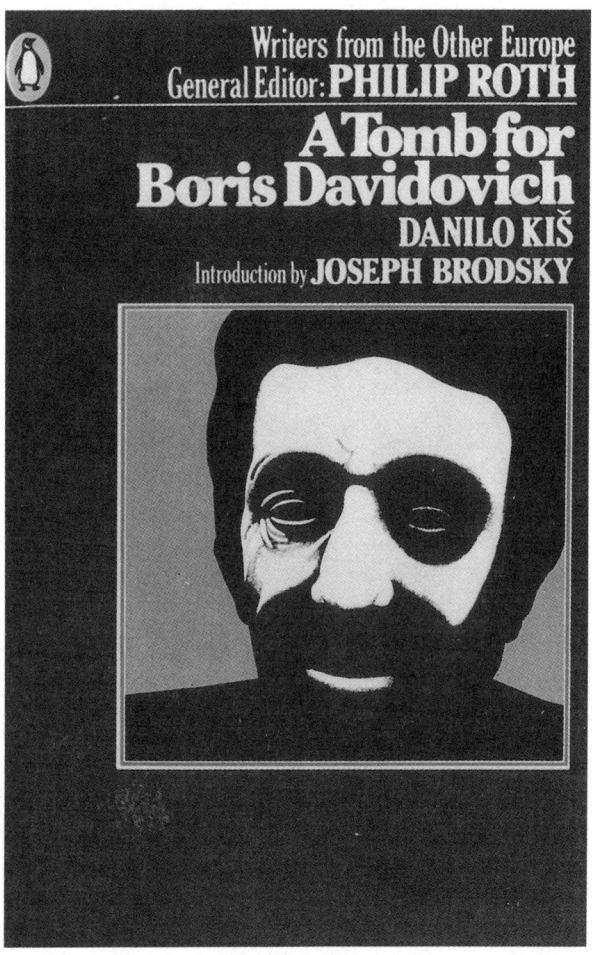

Title page of the translation of Grobnica za Borisa Davidoviča, Kiš's 1976 novel about the sufferings of Russian and European revolutionaries under Stalinism during the 1930s

Kiš calls this novelistic technique the "literature of the fact," an imaginative and often unconventional mode of narration that, while presenting a highly defamiliarized novelistic universe, nevertheless differs from fantastic literature. According to Kiš, the usual technique of fantastic literature is the invention of an alternative, make-believe universe based on nonsense and imagination. In 1984 he remembered: "My mother read novels until she was twenty when, not without regret, she realized that novels are 'invented' and rejected them once and for all. Her aversion to 'mere inventions' is also latent in my writing." Although Kiš's poetics is dominated by the belief in a magical horizon that somehow connects all events in the universe, that connection is derived from historical "documentation" and experience and not from the "mere invention" of literary imagination. The facts Kiš borrows from his life in the family cycle and from

Title page of Kiš's 1972 novel, Peščanik, *which explores the destiny of the Sam family*

historiography in his latter works are the foundation for his novelistic poetics. "The conviction that fantasy is the sister of lie, and therefore dangerous, results in his [Andrić's] poetics which rejects 'the laughable textures of imagination as a shameful deception,'" Kiš said while accepting the Ivo Andrić Literary Award in 1984. The paradoxical "truthfulness of the literary creation" would remain the guiding idea of his prose until Kiš's death in 1989.

This "factual" method was applied successfully in Kiš's best-known work, *Grobnica za Borisa Davidoviča*. Subtitled "Seven Chapters of the Common Narrative," this book formally represents a border between a novel and a collection of short stories. Besides the fact that the same characters reappear in different chapters of the book, the thematic unity of the work is guaranteed by the horrifying fate of Russian and European revolutionaries at the hands of the Stalinist Comintern in the 1930s. To present his theory of evil in fictional form, Kiš amply borrowed historiographic and biographical data from the works of Roy Medvedev, Karlo Štajner, and Aleksandr Solzhenitsyn about the world of Soviet labor camps known under the name *Gulag*.

In the central chapter, "The Magic Card Dealing," the narrator meditates on the revolutionary inversion of values and the creation of a Gulag-like social system that favors the manipulative criminal over the idealistic intellectual. The unleashed, reawakened power of the criminal mind destroys the codes of humanist ethics derived from the Judeo-Christian moral imperatives. The respect for individual life is replaced by the improbable code of criminal morality, which is represented by the sign of the Devil in the card game played by the inmates in the Gulag. The stakes in the game are the lives of political prisoners, revolutionary idealists who were purged by the Stalinists from the Soviet society because they were not ready to lie, kill, and steal in the name of the revolution.

Although *Grobnica za Borisa Davidoviča* never explicitly mentions Yugoslavia, its Communists, or their youthful Stalinist sins, the text exploded like a bomb in Belgrade literary circles when it appeared in 1976. Those in charge of the political correctness of literature, or "literary gangsters" as Kiš called them, began to sound their alarm as soon as the book was published in Zagreb. What probably touched a nerve was the work's implicit critique of every ideology (including the Yugoslav brand of so-called "self-management" socialism) that allowed the criminal element of society to rise to the top by destroying the ethical standards of civil moral codes. Since Kiš's attack on Stalinism was within the permissible limits of the officially sanctioned literary freedom, the literary guardians of political correctness had to invent another pretext for the assault. Therefore, Kiš was accused of plagiarism because he used the material of other authors in his work. This accusation, however laughable it seemed to Kiš and to other intellectuals who were sensing the arrival of the postmodern condition (which treats originality as no more than a catchword for the naive), stirred up the fiercest literary debate in Yugoslavia since World War II. The anti-Kiš camp included the novelists Miodrag Bulatović and Branimir Šćepanović, university professor Dragan Jeremić, and a journalist, Dragoljub Golubović-Pižon.

Golubović-Pižon opened the campaign by publishing the "evidence" of plagiarism six months after the publication of *Grobnica za Borisa Davidoviča*. It consisted of an article denouncing Kiš as a "reproductive" and not an "original" literary artist and two photocopies from Roy Medvedev's *Stalinism* and Louis Réau's *Russian Art*. The article alleged that Kiš copied entire paragraphs from the two books without acknowledgment. Kiš responded in the next issue of the same newspaper, *Oko* (Eye), treating Golubović-Pižon as an ignoramus acting on orders from the more powerful representatives of the Belgrade literary establishment. Another round of articles was exchanged between Golubović and Kiš before the true culprits of the scandal joined in the polemic.

Dragan Jeremić, a professor of aesthetics at Belgrade University and a man who controlled a multitude of literary institutions and awards committees, wrote an article denouncing Kiš and his defenders, which included the most prominent literature professors from Belgrade and Zagreb, such as Nikola Milošević and Predrag Matvejević. To counter the pressure from the literary establishment in Belgrade, Kiš's defenders awarded him Goran's Literary Award for the best novel in 1976. The fierce polemic continued for almost a year and then slowly died out until 1978, when Kiš published his theoretical tour-de-force, *Čas anatomije*, and reopened the wounds that had never fully healed. Dragoljub Golubović took Kiš to court for slander during the same year. The trial turned into a farce and a major embarrassment for the plaintiff after the judge dismissed all charges against Kiš.

Čas anatomije is probably the best work in the area of critical theory written in Yugoslavia in the socialist period. It demonstrates Kiš's erudition as well as his ability to do away with the phantoms of socialist realism and nationalism that have dominated the practice of literary criticism ever since World War II. It represents not only a defense of *Grobnica za Borisa Davidoviča* against the guardians of national literature, but also an acute insight into the literary autobiography of the writer. Kiš explains his relationship to Judaism, his admiration for Jorge Luis Borges and Arthur Koestler, and his scorn for nationalism and the provincial brand of culture it is bound to produce. He also directly polemicizes with Jeremić, Šćepanović, Bulatović, and others who organized the campaign against him. The response from the opposing camp was overwhelming and took the polemic well into 1979.

The result of the whole affair was Kiš's decision to leave the country and make his home in Paris. He visited Belgrade and Yugoslavia occasionally but was never entirely at home there after the scandal. The scandal actually worked in favor of *Grobnica za Borisa Davidoviča*, which was translated into more than ten languages and brought its author international prestige. Together with Milan Kundera of Czechoslovakia and György Konrád of Hungary, Kiš came to be regarded by the Parisian critics as one of the main exponents of the so-called Central European style. When asked to explain the qualities of this style, Kiš defined it as "ironic lyricism" and added that it is perhaps created by the combination of the Slavic and Hungarian propensity for pathos, spiced with a Jewish sense of irony.

The title of the last book published during his lifetime, *Enciklopedija mrtvih* (1985; translated as *The Encyclopedia of the Dead*, 1989), can be read as an omen of Kiš's premature death in 1989. The book is permeated with his awareness of the impending end, since he was aware while he was working on the manuscript that he was sick with lung cancer. The nine stories that comprise this collection are of uneven quality, with the title story (also published in *The New Yorker* in July 1982 as "The Encyclopedia of the Dead") probably being the best. Kiš says in the postscript of the original edition: "All stories in this book are to a greater or lesser degree influenced by a theme that I would like to call metaphysical; from the song of Gilgamesh, the question of death is one of the most obsessive themes in literature." From the fictionalized destiny of the Russian-Jewish poet Osip Mandelstam to the genealogical archives of the Mormons kept in the deserts of Utah, Kiš attempts to provide a poetic elaboration for the topic of human mortality with his usual blend of irony, wit, and erudition.

The female protagonist of the title story travels to Sweden on a scholarly research trip and discovers a volume in a local library that turns out to be a universal history of all the dead that once lived on Earth. She quickly looks up the life of her recently deceased father. The rest of the story is a poetic summary of that entry, supplemented with an authorial meditation on the nature of the entire encyclopedia. The reader discovers that the individual entries recount everything that is particular to the dead person, leaving the abstract and generalized history of one's life aside. "History is for the Book of the Dead a collection of human destinies, a totality of ephemeral events. Accordingly, it records every activity, every thought, every creative breath; every coordinate is entered into the register, every shovel plunged into the dirt, every movement that has removed the brick from the ruin." The aim of this encyclopedia is directly opposed to the project of history, which ignores the particular in favor of the universal. The most startling detail in the story is the magical connection established between the shape of the flowers that the protagonist's father paints during the last years of his life and the shape of the tumor that finally kills him. As the narrator reveals this similarity, she wakes up from a dream, managing to tell the reader that the last glimpse at the book in her dream revealed that the moment in which her father started painting the flowery motifs coincided with the development of the first cancerous cells in his body. This last statement is obviously related to Kiš's own position, since he wrote this story as he began to suffer from his own deadly disease.

Kiš's premature death in 1989 impoverished the cultural life of Yugoslavia as well as that of the international literary scene. It is uncanny that his preoccupation with death as a literary theme materialized in his case with such unmerciful immediacy and horror. With Andrić and, more recently, Milorad Pavić, Kis remains one of the rare Yugoslav writers who has earned a place of honor among the world-renowned literary figures.

Interviews:

Karen Rosenberg, "An Interview with Danilo Kiš," *Formations*, 5, no. 2 (1989): 46–51;

Michael March, "Danilo Kiš Interviewed," *Normal*, 4 (1990): 4.

Bibliography:

Z. Marinac & Z. Malbaša, "Kiš, Danilo," in *Leksikon pisaca Yugoslavije*, volume 3 (Novi Sad: Matica srpska, 1987), pp. 140–150.

References:

Marianna D. Birnbaum, "History and Human Relationships in the Fiction of Danilo Kiš," *Cross Currents*, 8 (1989): 346–360;

David Bynum, "Philosophical Fun and Merriment in the First Fiction of Danilo Kiš," *Serbian Studies*, 2, no. 4 (1984): 3–20;

Norbert Czarny, "Imaginary–Real Lives: on Danilo Kiš," *Cross Currents*, 3 (1984): 279–284;

Jovan Delić, *Književni pogledi Danila Kiša* (Belgrade: Prosveta, 1993);

Thomas Eekman, *Yugoslav Literature (1945–1975)* (Ann Arbor: Michigan Slavic Publications, 1978), pp. 272–273;

Branko Gorjup, "Danilo Kiš: From 'Enchantment' to 'Documentation,'" *Canadian Slavonic Papers*, 29, no. 4 (1987): 387–394;

Dragan Jeremić, *Narcis bez lica* (Belgrade: Nolit, 1981);

Boro Krivokapić, *Treba li spaliti Danila Kiša?* (Zagreb: Globus, 1980);

Tomislav Z. Longinović, *Borderline Culture* (Fayetteville: University of Arkansas Press, 1993);

Dušan Martinović, ed., *Izmedju Cetinja i Panonskog potopa* (Cetinje: CNB Djurdje Crnojević, 1993);

Predrag Matvejević, "Danilo Kiš: *Encyclopedia of the Dead*," *Cross Currents*, 7 (1988): 337–349;

Mirjana Miočinović, *Gorki talog iskustva* (Belgrade: BIGZ, 1991);

Matt F. Oja, "Fictional History and Historical Fiction: Solzhenitzyn and Kiš as Exemplars," *History and Theory*, 27 (1988): 111–124;

Petar Pijanović, *Proza Danila Kiša* (Podgorica: Oktoih, 1992);

The Review of Contemporary Fiction [articles by and about Kiš], 15, no. 1 (1994): 97–208;

Serge Shishkoff, "Košava in a Coffee Pot: or a Dissection of a Literary Cause Célèbre," *Cross Currents*, 6 (1987): 340–371;

Milivoj Srebro, "Semantizacija forme u romanima Danila Kiša," *Književna kritika*, 14, no. 3 (1983): 107–120;

Velimir Visković, "Radjanje paralelne istorije," *Politika* (29 October 1983);

Edmund E. White, "Danilo Kiš: The Obligation of Form," *Southwest Review*, 71 (1986): 363–377.

Blaže Koneski
(19 December 1921 - 7 December 1993)

Christina Kramer
University of Toronto

BOOKS: *Mostot* (Skopje: Kultura, 1945);

Makedonskata literatura i makedonskiot literaturen jazik (Skopje: Kultura, 1945);

Po povod najnoviot napad na našjit jazik (Skopje: Zemski odbor na NR Makedonija, 1945);

Zbirka na makedonski pesni (Skopje: Državno knigoizdatelstvo na Makedonija, 1945);

Zemjata i ljubovta (Skopje: Državno knigoizdatelstvo na Makedonija, 1948);

Makedonski pravopis so pravopisen rečnik, by Koneski and Krum Tošev (Skopje: Državno knigoizdatelstvo na Makedonija, 1950);

Gramatika na makedonskiot literaturen jazik, part I (Skopje: Državno knigoizdatelstvo na Makedonija, 1952);

Za makedonskiot literaturen jazik (Skopje: Kočo Racin, 1952);

Pesni (Skopje: Kočo Racin, 1953);

Gramatika na makedonskiot literaturen jazik, part II (Skopje: Prosvetno delo, 1954);

Vezilka (Skopje: Kultura, 1955; revised and enlarged, Skopje: Kultura, 1961);

Lozje (Skopje: Kočo Racin, 1955);

Istorija na makedonskiot jazik (Skopje: Kočo Racin, 1965);

Makedonskiot jazik vo razvojot na slovenskite jazici (Skopje: Kultura, 1968);

Jazikot na makedonskata narodna poezija (Skopje: Makedonska akademija na naukite, 1971);

Zapisi (Skopje: Makedonska kniga, 1974);

Stari i novi pesni (Prilep: Stremež, 1979);

Češmite (Skopje: Makedonska kniga, 1987);

Poslanie (Skopje: Kultura, 1987);

Crkva (Skopje: Misla, 1988);

Dnevnik po mnogu godini (Skopje: Makedonska kniga, 1988);

Zlatovrv (Skopje: Makedonska kniga, 1989);

Seizmograf (Skopje: Misla, 1989).

Editions and Collections: *Izbrani dela vo sedum knigi* (Skopje: Kultura, 1967);

Blaže Koneski

Izbrani dela vo sedum knigi, second expanded jubilee edition (Skopje: Kultura/Makedonska kniga / Misla: Naša kniga, 1981);

Sobrani pesni (Skopje: Makedonska kniga, 1987).

Editions in English: Poems, by various translators, in *Reading the Ashes,* edited by Milne Holton and Graham W. Reid (Pittsburgh: University of Pittsburgh Press, 1977), pp. 3-11;

Poems, by various translators, in *Contemporary Yugoslav Poetry,* edited by Vasa D. Mihailovich (Iowa City: University of Iowa Press, 1977), pp. 48-51;

Poems: Blaže Koneski, translated by Andrew C. Harvey and Anne Pennington (London: Andre Deutsch, 1979); *Pesni–Poems* (Skopje: Makedonska kniga / Struga: Struški večeri na poezijata, 1981);

Poetry, translated by Harvey and Pennington (Skopje: Macedonian P.E.N. Centre, 1983);

Poems, selected and translated by Ewald Osers, in *Contemporary Macedonian Poetry* (London: Forest Books / Skopje: Kultura, 1991), pp. 11–21;

Poems, translated by Graham W. Reid, *Macedonian Review*, 24, no. 3 (1994): 230–234.

OTHER: *Makedonskata literatura vo 19 vek*, selected with an introductory essay by Koneski (Skopje: Državno knigoizdatelstvo na Makedonija, 1950);

Skazni i storenija, Marko Cepenkov, edited by Koneski (Skopje: Kočo Racin, 1954);

Rečnik na makedonskiot literaturen jazik, 3 volumes, edited by Koneski (Skopje: Institut za makedonski jazik, 1961–1966);

Tekstovi za vežbi po istorija na makedonskiot jazik (Skopje: Katedra za južnoslovenski jazici, 1965);

Makedonski tekstovi 10-20 vek, compiled by Koneski and Olivera Jašar-Nasteva (Skopje: Sojuz na društvata za makedonski jazik i literatura, 1966);

Od istorijata na jazikot na slavenskata pismenost vo Makedonija (Skopje: Makedonska kniga, 1975);

"Macedonian," in *The Slavic Literary Languages: Formation and Development,* edited by Alexander Schenker and Edward Stankiewicz (New Haven: Yale University Press, 1980), pp. 53–63.

It is impossible to imagine postwar Macedonian intellectual life without the contributions of Blaže Koneski. He played a pivotal role in the codification of the standard Macedonian literary language, in the development of modern Macedonian literature, and in the establishment of those institutions that promote an active intellectual community, and he was widely recognized internationally as the leading figure in postwar Macedonian letters. His contributions as a linguist, scholar, and writer fundamentally shaped the development of the Macedonian language and the direction of Macedonian poetry. Critics have tried to assess which aspect of Koneski's work is primary–that of Koneski the wise, cerebral poet, or that of Koneski the linguist, who, reflecting on his writing of *Istorija na makedonskiot jazik* (The History of the Macedonian Language, 1965), writes:

> My work was going unexpectedly well. Every morning I went outside after breakfast and across a rapid stream, I set off to a nearby pine grove. There I found a fallen tree trunk, just right for sitting on, I set my note book on my right knee and wrote. This book of mine was written in the outdoors, in the fresh air, in the clear forest, with the intoxicating smell of grass and pine. I hope that something of this pure beauty has been passed on to it.

Clearly both aspects of Koneski's works are conjoined. It is the poet who endows his scholarly writing with unexpected grace and clarity, while it is the scholar who endows the poetry with historical references and reflection. In all of Koneski's writing it is the place, Macedonia, whose imprint is felt. Koneski is clearly a poet and scholar whose views were shaped by the history, folklore, and people of his country.

Koneski was born on 19 December 1921 in the village of Nebregovo, where he lived until his family moved to the town of Prilep when he was eight years old. In his later work Koneski felt indebted to those early years in the village. In a 1974 interview that Koneski gave to the newspaper *Politika,* he remarked:

> What could I have heard then in those 6-7 years in the village? Folk traditions lived strongly, most clearly in songs, stories, legends. That tradition was an inseparable part of life: no event took place without those old folk songs, legends, fables, proverbs.... At home my father's mother, Dunavka, who knew an unbelievable number of songs and stories, gave me special attention. In her lived that inexhaustible folk tradition of story-telling and singing. Those songs and stories of hers undoubtedly created a deep influence on me.

In Prilep Koneski completed elementary school and junior high school, then attended high school from 1934 to 1939 in Kragujevac, Serbia. He began writing poetry when he was ten, and his school poems, written in Serbo-Croatian, were published in 1938. The following year, 1939, Koneski began writing in Macedonian, and that year is considered the start of his literary work. After completing high school Koneski studied languages and literature in Belgrade, completing his studies in Sofia, Bulgaria, in 1944. At this time he was a consultant to the Macedonian National Theater in Skopje, and beginning in 1945, he served on the editorial board of the satiric journal *Osten* (Goad). He was soon thrust into prominence through his participation in the committee that codified the Macedonian literary language. Although the youngest member of the commission, Koneski is largely credited with shaping the modern standard language that

Dust jacket for a 1979 translation of Koneski's poems

came into official use in the Republic of Macedonia in 1945.

In 1945 his poem "Mostot" (The Bridge) was published. While current opinion is critical of the poem's overly patriotic and declamatory style, a style reminiscent of Vladimir Mayakovski, the work is recognized as an important contribution to the development of poetry in the immediate postwar era. Koneski himself was never fully satisfied with the poem and revised it several times, publishing it in modified forms in various anthologies of his poetry. The poem, a mosaic comprising seven sections of varying length and meter, is a key example of the socialist aesthetic typical of Macedonian writing from 1945 through the early 1950s. Critics saw in the poem glimpses of the future great poet but recognized that the piece itself is not one of Koneski's great works. Part 6, the longest in the cycle, "Skaznata na stariot majstor" (The Story of the Old Master), is narrated by a father who tells the story of his son, a soldier who died defending the bridge. In the father's call to other young men to follow the example of his son and rebuild the bridge, Koneski employs the folk motif of a bridge made strong through human sacrifice: "Blood lies in its foundation. And such a structure neither can time destroy nor storm diminish."

Koneski makes frequent references to folk traditions and motifs. Throughout his career he published anthologies of and critical works about Macedonian folk tradition. Koneski's interest in, and debt to, folk lyrics is evident in the form and imagery of his poems, poems that allude to folk heroes, dances, and embroidery. His first anthology of folk stories was published in 1945 and again in 1986 in an expanded edition, serving as a testament to Koneski's lifelong interest in folk tradition. A selection of these folk lyrics was translated into English in 1978 by Andrew Harvey and Anne Pennington under the title *Songs from Macedonia*.

In 1948 Koneski published his first collection of lyric poems, aptly titled *Zemjata i ljubovta* (Land and Love). This collection, like the poem

Blaže Koneski

"Mostot," belongs to the immediate postwar period in Macedonian literature. Thematically the poems still resonate with references to the war and the rebuilding in its aftermath. In particular one can cite the poems "Teškoto" (The Heavy Dance), "Ilinden ski melodii" (Ilinden Melodies) and "Pesnata" (The Song). The theme of separation, loss, and rejuvenation after the war expressed in the closing stanzas of "Mostot" is echoed in poems such as "Pismo" (Letter), in which a friend composes a letter to his close friend who has died in the war, ending with the verse: "To me you are not dead. In my memory you will live always. And even today I can be your true friend."

Koneski's commitment to his country, his people, and the role of the poet—a theme that recurs throughout his work—is seen in lines such as the following from "Proletna pesna" (Spring Song):

And now when my song ripens,
I know to whom I'll tell it—
to my people, who fervently sing,
who sing in the starry night.

In this first collection it is the poem "Teškoto" that has received the greatest literary acclaim. The poem, written in 1946, recalls an incident that took place in 1942. In that year the People's Council (Narodni Sobor) was held, and the dance, *teško oro,* was danced without music. Folk motifs, the sound of native instruments, and the dance itself all serve as strong symbols of the tragedy of the Macedonian nation and the centuries of its foreign domination. "Teškoto" is typical of Koneski's use of everyday images to convey universal themes. Love of country is also evident in the frequent allusions to specific locations in Macedonia: Ohrid, Dojran, Karaorman. Koneski's works are rooted in Macedonian soil and tradition. As one critic commented, everywhere in this volume is affirmed Koneski's remark that he always thought of himself as a man who just left the shore of oral poetic tradition.

In 1948 Koneski also published a short work titled "Po povod najnoviot napad na našjot jazik" (Answers to the Most Recent Attack on Our Language) and a verse translation of Petar Petrović Njegoš's poem "Gorski vijenac" (The Mountain Wreath). Koneski's ability to combine the work of a linguist, poet, editor, and translator is already evident at this early stage of his career.

During the 1950s Koneski published two more volumes of poetry, *Pesni* (Poems, 1953) and *Vezilka* (Embroideress, 1955); a collection of short stories, *Lozje* (Vineyard, 1955); *Gramatika na makedonskiot literaturen jazik* (Grammar of the Macedonian Literary Language, part I, 1952, part II, 1954); and together with Krum Tošev, *Makedonski pravopis so pravopisen rečnik* (Orthographic Dictionary of Macedonian, 1950). At this time Koneski was a member of the Macedonian language department of the University of Kiril and Methody in Skopje, where he later served as chair of the Department of Yugoslav Languages, dean of the Faculty of Philosophy from 1952 to 1953, and rector of the university from 1968 to 1970.

Pesni (Poems) appeared in 1953. These lyric poems belong to the so-called intimate phase in Macedonian poetry that began in the early part of the decade as writers began to seek themes beyond the war experience. This collection was hailed by the critics for its simple style, which nonetheless conveyed an intimate sense of the Macedonian land, legends, and humanity seeking its place within historical events. These poems have in common with his earlier work frequent references to the landscape. Once again the poems belong in Macedonia. Not only are there poems set in specific locations, such as "Skopje," "Kalemegdan," and "The Kumanovo Bend," but there are also poems titled "Rž" (Rye), "Mak" (Poppy), and "Pčenica" (Grain). In this collection, too, are several dialogue poems such as "Srebda so Žinzifov" (Meeting with Žinzifov), "Raku-vanje" (Handshake), and "Racin and Nedelkovski." Through these poems Koneski seeks a continuity with earlier Macedonian writers. Both here and in his later poetic works Koneski successfully marries old motifs with new poetic forms and rejuvenates old folkloric genres by merging them with the present. One of Koneski's great contributions here and elsewhere is the recognition of his debt as a Macedonian writer to folk tradition while revitalizing that tradition through contemporary genres. Koneski has been praised for his poems about children, which possess an intimate and delicate understanding of the relationship between grown-up and child. This ability to treat personal themes without excessive sentimentality is evident in the poem of this collection dedicated to his daughter, "Igra co dete" (Game with a Child).

While Koneski was composing his own poetic works in the early 1950s, he also published many translations into Macedonian of world literature, including the poems of Heinrich Heine, "Lirsko intermeco" (Lyrical Intermezzo), published in Macedonian in 1952; Shakespeare's "Otelo" (Othello), published in 1953; and the poetry of Aleksander Blok, with whom Koneski felt a special affinity, as is evident in his own cycle of poems, (To the Unknown), which appeared in *Pesni*. Other nonpoetic works that appeared during this period include the second edition of *Makedonska literatura vo 19 vek* (Macedonian Literature in the Nineteenth Century, 1950)—a short overview and texts—and a volume of stories by the nineteenth-century folklorist Marko Cepenkov, *Skazni i storenija* (Stories and Other Works), edited by Koneski and published in 1954.

Two significant works appeared in 1955: *Lozje,* a volume of short stories, and *Vezilka,* a collection of poems. *Lozje* is recognized by critics as a major contribution to Macedonian fiction. While the stories do not have the grace of the poems and the compositions are of unequal quality, their publication marked a turn away from socialist realism and war themes and turned the focus on to the lives of ordinary people. Each of the ten stories captures the pathos of everyday disappointments: a young painter not represented in an exhibit, a child's hope for a pair of new shoes dashed when he again receives second-hand ones, the death of a family member. The collection expanded the thematic possibilities of Macedonian prose, which had, prior to its appearance, focused on the war and postwar patriotism. Critics believe that *Lozje* not only remains one of the most successful works in the development of Macedonian prose but is even more powerful when read in a contemporary context. This collection of Koneski's stories remains a seminal contribution to postwar Macedonian writing and it seems today, perhaps, more relevant and readable than when it first appeared.

Vezilka, the collection of poems that first appeared in 1955 and again in an expanded edition in 1961, solidified Koneski's growing stature as the leading poet of the postwar generation. In this volume, two of the main thematic motifs of Koneski's verse are developed further: the use of external landscape to express inner emotion and the use of Macedonian myths and legends to connect Macedonians with their past. The intertwining of such legends with the present is evident from the opening stanzas of the title poem "Vezilka":

> Embroideress, tell how the
> simple and strict Macedonian song is born.
> From the heart which
> carries on a nighttime monologue
> in sleepless excitement?
> Pull two threads from the heart,
> the one black and the other red,
> The one awakens terrible sorrows,
> the other longing both bright and insatiable.

Some critics, for example, Georgi Stardelov in *Portreti i Profili* (Portraits and Profiles, 1987) and *Odzemanje na silata* (Breaking of Strength, 1990), consider this collection of poems to be a turning point in postwar Macedonian poetry not only for the new poetic tendencies of the 1950s but as one of the most significant contributions during the last thirty years. In particular, the cycle of poems "Sterna," which appeared in the expanded second edition, is viewed as one of Koneski's masterworks. The poems in the cycle, "Odzemanje na silata," "Sterna," and "Markov monastir" (Prince Marko's Church), treat motifs presented in folktales, but they do so here in a powerful, modern poetic form with imagery that is menacing and insistent. Andrew Harvey and Anne Pennington, in their introduction to *Zapisi* (Notes, 1974), write:

> As a writer in Macedonian Koneski has the privilege to inherit a rich folk tradition and to inherit

this with the kind of immediacy which a Western writer, brought up in a more urban culture and one that has almost completely lost touch with its rural past, finds difficult to comprehend.... he takes an old figure and an old story and uses both in a thoroughly modern way; in both "Sterna" and "Prince Marko's Church" he achieves, with quick force, what other modern Europeans have been far more prolix about–a representation of the moral and intellectual plight of the modern artist.

The decade of the 1960s was an active one for Koneski as both a scholar and linguist. Between the years 1961 and 1965 Koneski was president of the Union of Yugoslav Writers. In addition to being appointed a corresponding member of the Yugoslav Academy of Arts and Sciences in 1962, the Serbian Academy of Arts and Sciences in 1963, and the Slovenian Academy of Arts and Sciences in 1968, Koneski also became the president of the Macedonian Academy of Arts and Sciences at its founding in 1967, a position he held until 1975.

The first volume of the three-volume Macedonian dictionary, *Rečnik na makedonskiot jazik,* edited by Koneski, appeared in 1962. The second volume was published in 1965, and the third in 1966. This dictionary of the Macedonian language, with Serbo-Croatian glosses, was republished in one volume in 1986. At the time of this reprinting it was noted that, although the Macedonian lexicon has been greatly enriched since the 1960s, this dictionary, with its seventy thousand entries, remains an unsurpassed reference work.

In his collection of prose sketches, *Dnevnik po mnogu godini* (A Diary of Many Years, 1988), Koneski includes a sketch on the 1963 Skopje earthquake. This personal account relates how Koneski, then working on his book on the historical phonology of Macedonian and planning a trip to South America, learned of the earthquake and made his journey back to Macedonia. Together with descriptions of the harsh realities of the tragedy and his personal loss, Koneski also mentions how the files for the Macedonian dictionary were saved and how the university community regrouped. It is a tribute to the spirit of the scholars working in Skopje that so much was produced in the early part of that decade as the city was rebuilt around them.

Istorija na makedonskiot jazik (The History of the Macedonian Language) was published in 1965. This work, too, has been widely hailed as a major contribution not only to Macedonian studies but more broadly to the general literature on the history and development of the Slavic languages.

After a decade in which Koneski's major work was outside the field of poetry he published a new collection of poems, *Zapisi,* in 1974. Thematically this small collection of poems is connected to his earlier works: the poems treat themes of love, country, and parting. The reappearance of Koneski as poet met with critical success. Many poems in this collection were later translated into English in the collection *Poems* by Harvey and Pennington. This collection was followed by the collection *Stari i novi pesne* (Old and New Poems), in 1979.

In the 1980s Koneski again turned his talents again to poetry. The publication of a second jubilee edition of Koneski's collected works, *Izbrana dela vo sedum knigi* (Selected Works in Seven Volumes, 1981), was followed by the publication in the late 1980s of six volumes of poetry and the collection of prose sketches *Dnevnik po mnogu godini,* published in 1988. The latest volumes of Koneski's poetry, *Česmite* (The Fountains, 1987), *Poslanie* (Epistle, 1987), *Crkva* (Church, 1988), *Zlatovrv* (Golden Summit, 1989), and *Seizmograf* (1989), are intensely personal and reflective poems on aging, love, and Macedonia. While little criticism has yet been written on these, there is little doubt that many of these poems will prove to be some of the most significant of the poet's career.

Koneski's multifaceted role in Macedonian letters is widely recognized. For those who know Koneski mainly through his linguistic work, his poetry is often startling in its transparency and delicacy, coupled with its bitterness and power. Through his poetry Koneski has set himself firmly in the place, Macedonia, as one voice among the long history of Macedonian voices; yet his work transcends the small borders of the Republic of Macedonia. The opening poem in *Crkva,* when related to the period of destruction in the former republics of Yugoslavia, helps convey how intimately one may be touched by the loss of those places intimate in our memories:

May that hour be damned when they told me
that the church in Nebregovo was destroyed!
It was as if then a thousand laments keened
in me as if from a dark underground they had
    emerged.

Koneski died on 7 December 1993, leaving behind the legacy of a pioneer and widely acknowledged as one of the most important writers in Macedonian literature. The following poem "Vo parkot" (In the Park), from the collection *Zlatovrv* (1989), typifies the personal nature of Koneski's later poems:

Wait for me until I return.
Find a good place to sit down.
Conversation isn't important.
We could just sit quietly.
It is still warm,
Though the sun is setting.
It is still light,
Though the darkness comes.

Bibliographies:

Ljiljana Ristevska, "Prilog kon bibliografijata na trudovite na Blaže Koneski," *Razgledi* (1981): 85–101;

Ristevska, "Bibliografia na trudovite na akademiot Blaže Koneski," *Makedonski jazik,* 32–33 (1982): 1–20;

Garth Terry, *Blaže Koneski: A Bibliography* (Nottingham: Astra Press, 1983);

Mileva Milev and Ristevska, "Koneski, Blaže," in *Zbornik vo čest na Blaže Koneski* (Skopje: Univerzitet Kiril i Metodij, 1984), pp. 3–28; *Leksikon pisaca Jugoslavije,* volume 3 (Novi Sad: Matica srpska, 1987), pp. 232–236.

References:

Milorad R. Blečić, *Blaže Koneski: Portret pesnika* (Belgrade: Novo delo, 1986);

Ivonne Burns, "Blaže Koneski: The Right Man in the Right Place at the Right Time," *Makedonski jazik,* 32–33 (1981–1982): 75–83;

Miodrag Drugovac, "Blaže Koneski," in his *Contemporary Macedonian Writers* (Skopje: Macedonian Review, 1976);

Ksenija Gavriš, "Blaže Koneski," *Macedonian Review,* 1, no. 2 (1971): 226–234;

Radomir Ivanović, *Govor pun darova* (Nikšić: Univerzitetska riječ, 1988);

Ivanović, *Poetika Blaža Koneskog* (Belgrade: Partizanska knjiga, 1982);

Anita Lekić, "The Perils of Articulation: A Reading of 'Sterna,'" *Macedonian Review,* 18, no. 1 (1988): 65–68;

Mateja Matevski, "The Poetry of Blaže Koneski," in *Blaže Koneski: Poetry,* edited by Georgi Stardelov (Skopje: Macedonian P.E.N. Centre, 1983), pp. 5–12;

Slobodan Micković, *Poetskite idei vo poezijata na Blaže Koneski* (Skopje: Naša kniga, 1986);

Anne Pennington and Andrew Harvey, "Blaže Koneski," *Macedonian Review,* 1, no. 1 (1971): 56–70;

Hristo Poljanski Andonov, "The Historiographic Thought of Blaže Koneski," *Macedonian Review,* 14, no. 1 (1984): 88–95;

Petar Širilov, "Portrait: Blaže Koneski," *Macedonian P.E.N.,* 3, no. 1 (1975): 4–6;

Mile Tomić, *Jazikot vo literaturnite dela na Blaže Koneski* (Skopje: Institut za makedonski jazik, 1977).

Ciril Kosmač
(29 September 1910 - 28 January 1980)

Helga Glušič
University of Ljubljana, Slovenija

BOOKS: *Sreča in kruh* (Ljubljana: Državna založba Slovenije, 1946);
Pomladni dan (Ljubljana: Prešernova družba, 1953);
Iz moje doline, Novele, edited by Bojan Štih (Ljubljana: Mladinska knjiga, 1958);
Očka Orel (Ljubljana: Cankarjeva založba, 1964);
Balada o trobenti in oblaku (Ljubljana: Cankarjeva založba, 1964); republished, edited by Helga Glušič (Ljubljana: Mladinska knjiga, 1968);
Tantadruj (Ljubljana: Cankarjeva založba, 1964);
V gaju življenja, Novele, edited by Ivan Bizjak (Ljubljana: Mladinska knjiga, 1972);
Sreča in lepota, edited by Bohanec (Ljubljana, Zagreb & Trst: Partizanska knjiga/Spektar-Založništvo tržaškega tiska, 1972);
Izbrannoe (Moskva: Progress, 1976);
Medvejke (Ljubljana: Mladinska knjiga, 1981);
Proze, edited by Glušič (Novi Sad: Matica Srpska, 1981);
Prazna ptičnica, introduction by Glušič (Ljubljana: Cankarjeva založba, 1988).
Collections: *Izbrano delo,* 3 volumes, edited by Franček Bohanec (Ljubljana: Mladinska knjiga, 1970);
Izabrana proza, edited by Ivan Cesar (Zagreb: Skolska knjiga, 1974).
Editions in English: *A Day in Spring,* translated by F. S. Copeland (London: Lincolns-Prager, 1959);
"Luck," translated by Elza Jereb and Alasdair MacKinnon, *Le livre slovène,* 1 (1963-1964): 81-87;
"Death of a Simple Giant," translated by Cordia Kveder, in *Death of a Simple Giant and Other Modern Yugoslav Stories,* edited by Branko Lenski (New York: Vanguard, 1965), pp. 137-188;
"The Caterpillar," translated by Svetozar Kolijevic, in *Yugoslav Short Stories,* edited by Kolijevic (London: Oxford University Press, 1966), pp. 305-320;

Ciril Kosmač

"Tantadruj," translated by Milica Hrgovic, *Review,* no. 3 (1974): 39-40.

MOTION PICTURES: *Na svoji zemlji,* Slovenski knjižni zavod, 1949;
Balada o trobenti in oblaku, by Kosmač and France Štiglic, Triglav Film, 1961;
Tistega lepega dne, Triglav Film, 1962.

TELEVISION: *Tantadruj,* TV Slovenija, 1994.

RADIO: *Balada o trobenti in oblaku,* edited by Mitja Mejak, Radio Ljubljana, 1963;
Tantadruj, edited by Mejak, Radio Ljubljana, 1966.

Ciril Kosmač is an outstanding master of the short story who created his own version of a frame story containing a narrative based on memories from his richly varied life. His fiction, composed primarily in the form of short stories, was first sparked by his experiences in 1929 in an Italian fascist jail, by his subsequent flight to exile, and by his long absence from his native region. This absence led to the creation of his only novel, *Pomladni dan* (1953; translated as *A Day in Spring,* 1959). His narration is characterized by emotional and moral force when he describes the fascist terror in the Slovenian Littoral, which after the treaty of Rapallo in 1920 fell under Italian authority. He also describes events during World War II in this same region of Slovenia. Kosmač is especially effective in portraying village characters who are nonconformists or eccentrics and he often uses such characters to express metaphorically his own views on civilization, especially his view that so-called civilized life obliterates humanity's emotional and moral integrity.

Kosmač was born on 29 September 1910, in Slap ob Idrijci, Slovenia, near the Italian border. His parents, Franc Kosmač and Marija Trušnovec, were farmers who had four children. Kosmač's father was also an organist who organized the cultural life in the village; his mother was a gifted folk-story teller. Kosmač attended school in Gorica, where he studied at a commercial school, and in Tolmin, where he obtained his elementary school degree. Because he joined the national rebellion movement against fascism (Trst-Istra-Gorica-Reka, which combines the names of four places in Slovenia and Croatia), he was imprisoned by the Italian authorities, first in Gorica, then in Koper, and then for one year in Rome in the Regina Coeli jail, from 1929 to 1930. There he began the early sketches that he later wove into his first literary fragments. In Trieste in 1930, at the first court trial of those who had rebelled against fascism, Kosmač was pardoned on the basis of being the youngest accused. He was allowed to return home, but he was required to be under police surveillance–a condition that led him to flee to neighboring Yugoslavia. He started publishing his prose in immigrant magazines such as *Istra* and *Jadranski kalendar* that had been started by immigrants from the Primorsko region. The prose is characterized by its evocation of melancholic moods and its expressions of a longing for freedom and justice.

Soon after his arrival in Ljubljana, the cultural center of Slovenia, Kosmač met other writers who accepted him as a friend, not only because they were sympathetic to his difficult cir-

Title page for a translation of Pomladni dan, *Kosmač's 1953 novel, which pairs love stories from World War I and World War II*

cumstances but also because they delighted in his witticisms and his talent as a storyteller, which he had inherited from his mother. His father hoped that Kosmač would write about the interesting real-life stories from his home valley; his father's hope was the topic of the fragment titled "Pot v Tolmin" (The Road to Tolmin, 1953). In the years he spent in Ljubljana, Kosmač's works were also published in the chief literary magazines, *Ljubljanski zvon* and *Sodobnost*. Critics soon noticed the dramatic tone in his short stories and their engagement with social issues. They were enthusiastic about his short story "Hiša št. 14" (The House No. 14, 1934), written in the style of modern social realism. The majority of his texts from that period deal with the theme of imprisonment and with portraits of his home village. In 1938 he obtained a grant from the French government to study in Paris, where he remained until the German occupation of the city during World War II.

Kosmač worked for a while at the Yugoslav diplomatic mission in Paris; then he moved to Marseilles in May 1940, and by 1942 to London, where he worked for the Slovene program of the BBC, the British Broadcasting Corporation. In 1944 he traveled across Egypt to Bari, Italy, where he joined the partisans. Later he returned home to Slovenia, where he became editor of the newspaper *Slovenski poročevalec* from 1944 to 1946, and of the weekly *Tovariš*. He also worked for a time as a stage director at the Triglav Film Company and wrote the screenplay for the first Slovene film, *Na svoji zemlji* (On the Land of My Own, 1949). In 1946 Kosmač married Stana Brajnik. By the 1950s he began devoting himself completely to writing, and it was during this period that he wrote his best prose. During a short stay in the monastery of Pleterje he wrote his long short story, *Balada o trobenti in oblaku* (The Ballad of the Trumpet and the Cloud, 1964). In 1954 he moved to Portorož, a resort along the Adriatic coast, where he lived until his death in Ljubljana on 28 January 1980. As a member and president of the Slovene, and for a short time also the Yugoslav Writers' Association, Kosmač traveled throughout Europe and also to Brazil. In 1961 he became a member of SAZU, the Slovenian Academy of Science and Art.

Kosmač's short-story writing is characterized by a plenitude of dramatic actions, through which he celebrates the strong humanistic ideals of national and individual freedom. The ideal of personal freedom is connected with descriptions of his home village and its inhabitants. Settings beyond this circle can hardly be found in his writing. Frequent characters who appear in his short stories are village rebels (or eccentrics), courageous old men, and simple people who are resolutely moral and full of folk wisdom and dreams of happiness. Even Kosmač's earliest short stories reflect the attitude of one who has been tempered by events; the focus of his stories is narrow so that he can specifically examine a general truth about life, one that he has filtered through his own experience. In his short stories "Gosenica" (The Caterpillar), "Sreča" (The Happiness), and "Kruh" (The Bread), Kosmač achieves an effective union of the traditional short-story form (frame story) and an individual message. He also fully develops the meani-g of his many symbols, through which happiness is directly connected with unhappiness: a caterpillar symbolizes the fight for existence, for survival, whereas bread is a symbol of something that, by itself, does not suffice for survival because it does not meet the human need for love and spiritual nourishment.

These short stories express Kosmač's specific understanding of the world. He formulated his perceptions in anecdotal forms, playfully using the simple logic of folk wisdom. His views on life show a deep understanding of both the weakness and power of human beings, not only in ethical but also in emotional spheres. Kosmač, who considers the incapacity for emotional reaction the greatest human handicap, decides again and again in favor of the weak in regard to social issues, in favor of the strong in ethical and emotional conflicts, and above all in favor of those people who are sympathetic and understanding. Nevertheless, his texts do not appear moralistic because they are characteristically accompanied by an ironic and humorous kind of meditation. In this way he counters the emotional tensions and pathos in the fates of his characters. By reining in his own passions and controlling the emotional outbursts of the heroes of his stories, he manages to retain an impression of spontaneity, even of seeming carelessness, that gives his short stories a more dramatic effect. The distinctive tone of Kosmač's work also results from a confrontation between his realistic and romantic approaches to his material, between his stance as an objective observer and a passionate humanist. In describing the bitterness and sadness of people's experiences he expresses a will to overcome bitterness, a will to life, a will to gain command over tragedy and one's own weaknesses.

Two additional features in Kosmač's writing are notable: his emphasis on the romantic and subjective aspects of experience; and the intrusion of the imaginary world into the objective, logical course of the narration. In the early stories fantastic elements appear only as fragmentary motifs, as they do in the fragment "Zlato" (The Gold), while in later works these elements expand in accordance with the development of Kosmač's creative process and the inner structure of the short story, as in "Balada o trobenti in oblaku." Through his artistry and creativity, Kosmač expresses in his imaginary worlds not only interesting spiritual states but also the buried, secretive powers of nature. But these spiritual and natural dimensions also challenge him to create a new metaphor for human destiny. In his narratives Kosmač explores the destiny of his characters by presenting their particular experiences of love and death.

His novel *Pomladni dan,* which is the most explicit exploration of his characters' fates, relates the narrator's return home to the stories of his valley, particularly to two love stories that unite the memories of World War I and World War II. The story from World War I details the tragic love between a local woman and an Austrian lieutenant, both of whom commit suicide; the other story focuses on the daughter of the woman in the first story and portrays the love between her and an Italian partisan from World War II. This story nearly repeats the first when the Italian partisan accidentally shoots and kills himself, but in this story the woman survives, along with the infant daughter born to her and the partisan. Nostalgic memories from Kosmač's youth, which convey the writer's attachment to his home, provide the background for the two stories. The novel powerfully depicts the suffering, death, and loneliness that war causes, but it also celebrates the beauty of life and conveys a devotion to the memories of the way of life that existed before the wars.

In *Balada o trobenti in oblaku* death is also the central theme. This long short story with several narrative strands is probably the most prominent of Kosmač's works. Its central character is Peter Majcen, a writer who decides to write about a hero from World War II. Majcen plans to write about a courageous old man who decided to give his life to save the lives of a group of wounded partisans. However, another person from the world of the writer enters the narrative; functioning as the moral opposite of the writer's fictional hero, this character is a weak, unethical, irresponsible person, full of despair. The story dramatizes the confrontation of the three characters: the writer, his hero, and his hero's opposite, and reality and fantasy intertwine by an associative narrative technique. In the end the power of Majcen's fictional hero surpasses not only his weak, counterpoint character but also that of the writer himself, who becomes helpless in his creative process as he ceases to be the authorial constructor of the story. The old man who is the hero eventually destroys his opposite, who, under moral pressures from his own past, commits suicide. The solution to this complicated narrative plot construction, and the rather complicated ethical problem, led Kosmač into a creative crisis. For a while he interrupted the work, which was being published in installments. When he continued the story, he accompanied it with an introduction, explaining to readers that he had chosen one of the possible endings of the story. Several variants remain in manuscript. In fact, *Balada o trobenti in oblaku* is in other ways Kosmač's most anguished work. Its narrative abounds with open questions, uncertainties, venturing into unknown regions, and torments suffered by the creator of a literary work; it is full of images that grow through association into creative, secretive, symbolic allegories. These allegories, with the writer's other stylistic features, reveal the tragedy of human weakness in the face of momentous, potentially fatal decisions in which one man intervenes in the fate of another.

The somberness of *Balada* probably reflects a crisis in Kosmač's life. The work that followed it, after the author had moved to the Mediterranean town of Portorož, is the tragicomic "Tantadruj," published in 1959 in the periodical *Naša sodobnost.* "Tantadruj" tells the story of a man who is a village eccentric and who has decided to die. Death becomes his one and only goal. According to the introduction, the story has its source in folk tradition; here, however, the originally happy story that was told by Kosmač's mother turns into a bitter story about the way people who are different are excluded from established social structures. This story defends these individuals' right to their own yearnings and their own ways of life, which result in the diversity and heterogeneousness of society. Several stories by Kosmač are forerunners of "Tantadruj," confirming his interest in characters who are unusual either emotionally, socially, or intellectually. In this story Tantadruj's stubborn goal of finding the right way to die, a way that will be accepted by both the church and the law, leads him through many trials in the various places where people gather: at the fair, where Tantadruj collects bells for martyrs; in a pub, where he sits in a hidden place with other people who are also different; and at the cemetery, where he wants to be buried but cannot be because he must live and suffer until he deserves his death. For punishment, the village outcasts are made to leave their village, and they disperse to other valleys. The story ends with an epilogue in which two views of the world meet: the frozen future of the civilized world with a mankind that is numb; and the playful world of the originals, those who in their creative fantasies can look forward not only to life, but even to death.

To express both the value of the human will to live and the beauty of moral deeds is perhaps the main goal of Kosmač's art. In his narrative prose beauty is associated with emotions and memories, with the loveliness of one's home, with a sensitive comprehension of the world as a whole, and with secret listenings to unpronounced and unpronounceable thoughts and feelings. The condensed and precise linguistic form of Kosmač's style often makes the final meaning of his writings elusive; because he was not a didactic writer, his stories are evocative rather than explicit in their designs. His world of ideas is built vertically: it possesses both the high dimension of fantasy and the rootedness of folk wisdom, a storehouse of knowledge that crystallizes centuries of practical thinking, possesses a specific logic, and contains insights, messages, and instructions for living one's life and meeting one's fate. Kosmač was convinced this wisdom could not be invalidated.

Kosmač is considered one of the most prominent Slovene writers of the twentieth century. Not only is his writing admired for its stylistic polish, but his short stories form a complex whole that, in the judgment of some contemporary critics, represents work that is among the finest fiction in modern Slovene literature.

Bibliography:

F. Dobrovoljc, "Kosmač, Ciril," in *Leksikon pisaca Jugoslavije,* volume 3 (Novi Sad: Matica Srpska, 1987), pp. 272-276.

Biography:

David S. Denton, "The Life and Works of Ciril Kosmač," dissertation, Nottingham University, 1984.

References:

Ivan Cesar, *Poetika pripovedne proze Cirila Kosmača* (Ljubljana & Koper: Mladinska knjiga/Lipa, 1981);

Helga Glušič, "Neznani Ciril Kosmač," introduction to *Prazna ptičnica* (Ljubljana: Cankarjeva založba, 1988), pp. 141-157;

Glušič, *Pripovedna proza Cirila Kosmača, Razvoj motivike in načini njenega oblikovanja* (Ljubljana: Slovenska matica, 1975);

Boris Paternu, "Kosmačevo pripovedništvo med arhaiko in modernizmom," introduction to *Pomladni dan* (Ljubljana: Mladinska knjiga, 1985), pp. 315-355;

Jože Pogačnik, "Proletni dan," *Književna istorija,* 5 (1972): 642-671;

N. Vagapova, "Čelovek na svoej zemle," in *Izbrannoe* (Moskva: Progress, 1976), pp. 5-17;

Franc Zadravec, "Umetnička proza Cirila Kosmača," *Nova obzorja,* 16 (1963): 132-145, 235-253.

Papers:

All papers and manuscripts of Ciril Kosmač are held at the family archive.

Kajetan Kovič
(21 October 1931 -)

Henry R. Cooper Jr.
Indiana University

BOOKS: *Pesmi štirih*, by Kovič, Ciril Zlobec, Janez Menart, and Tone Pavček (Ljubljana: Slovenski knjižni zavod, 1953; republished, with an afterword by Mitja Mejak: Ljubljana: Cankarjeva založba, 1988);

Prezgodnji dan (Koper: Primorska založba Lipa, 1956);

Korenine vetra (Ljubljana: Cankarjeva založba, 1961);

Franca izpod klanca (Ljubljana: Mladinska knjiga, 1963);

Ogenjvoda (Ljubljana: Cankarjeva založba, 1965);

Ne bog, ne žival (Maribor: Obzorja, 1965);

Zlata ladja (Ljubljana: Mladinska knjiga, 1969);

Tekma, ali kako je arhitekt Nikolaj preživel konec tedna (Maribor: Založba Obzorja, 1970);

Vetrnice: Izbrane pesmi (Ljubljana: Državna založba Slovenije, 1970);

Moj prijatelj Piki Jakob (Ljubljana: Borec, 1972);

Pesmi (Ljubljana: Partizanska knjiga, 1973);

Mala čitanka (Maribor: Obzorja, 1973);

Maček Muri (Ljubljana: Mladinska knjiga, 1975);

Labrador (Ljubljana: Cankarjeva založba, 1976);

Pesmi, by Kovič, Dane Zajc, and Gregor Strniša (Ljubljana: Mladinska knjiga, 1976);

Zgodnje zgodbe (Ljubljana: Mladinska knjiga, 1978);

Križemkraž (Ljubljana: Mladinska knjiga, 1980);

Zmaj Direndaj (Ljubljana: Mladinska knjiga, 1981);

Pesmi (Ljubljana: Državna založba Slovenije, 1981);

Pajacek in punčka (Ljubljana: Mladinska knjiga, 1984),

Iskanje Katarine (Ljubljana: Mladinska knjiga, 1987);

Dežele (Ljubljana: Cankarjeva založba, 1988);

Poletje (Maribor: Obzorja, 1990);

Križemkraz: Zgodnje pesmi, zgodnje zgobe in se malo macje godbe (Ljubljana: Mladinska kniga, 1991);

Kajetan Kovič

Sibirski ciklus: In druge pesmi raznih let (Ljubljana: Mihelač, 1992);

Letni časi: Izbrane pesmi, with afterword by Vid Snoj and bibliography (Ljubljana: Mladinska knjiga, 1992);

Lovec (Ljubljana: Litterapicta, 1993);

Pot v Trento: Prizori iz navadnega življenja Franca M. (Murska Sobota: Pomurska založba, 1994);

Profesor domišljije: Ljubljanska zgobda (Ljubljana: Mihelac, 1996).

Editions in English: Poems, translated by various translators in *Modern Poetry in Transla-*

tion, no. 8 (1970): 9-10;

Poems in *Contemporary Yugoslav Poetry,* edited by Vasa D. Mihailovich, translated by various translators (Iowa City: University of Iowa Press, 1977), pp. 80-84;

The Clown and the Little Girl, translated by Branka Javornik and Martin Cregeen (Ljubljana: Mladinska knjiga, 1984);

Poems, translated by Tom Lozar, in *Prisoners of Freedom: Contemporary Slovenian Poetry,* edited by Aleš Debeljak (Santa Fe, N.M.: Pedernal, 1994).

TRANSLATIONS: Gustav Krklec, *Lirika,* translated by Kovič and others (Ljubljana: Državna založba Slovenije, 1959);

Paul Eluard, *Nepretrgana pesem* (Ljubljana: Državna založba Slovenije, 1966);

Alois Hergouth, *Sladka gora* (Maribor, 1967);

Rainer Maria Rilke, *Pesmi* (Ljubljana: Mladinska knjiga, 1968);

Georg Trakl, *Trakl* (Ljubljana: Mladinska knjiga, 1971);

Vladimir Holan, *Noč s Hamletom* (Ljubljana: Državna založba Slovenije, 1972);

Stevan Raičković, *Balada o zgodnjem večeru* (Ljubljana: Državna založba Slovenije, 1973);

Endre Ady, *Kri inzlato,* by Kovič and Jože Hradil (Murska Sobota: Pomurska založba, 1977);

Eluard (Ljubljana: Mladinska knjiga, 1978);

Ady, *Ady* (Ljubljana: sMladinska knjiga, 1980);

Alois Hergouth, *Mesec med jablanami: Iz mojega življenja* (Murska Sobota: Pomurska založba, 1983);

Sandor Weöres, *Boben in ples,* by Kovič and Hradil (Ljubljana: Državna Založba Slovenije, 1983);

Miklos Radnoti, *Razglednice,* by Kovič and Hradil (Ljubljana: Državna založba Slovenije, 1984);

Hergouth, *Obkrožanje noči* (Maribor: Založba Obzorja, 1986);

Raičković, *Mlin na veter* (Ljubljana: Mladinska knjiga, 1988);

Rilke, *Rilke* (Ljubljana: Mladinska kniga, 1988);

France Prešeren, *V tujem jeziku napisal sem knjigo: Prešernove nemške pesmi* (Ljubljana: Cankarjeva založba, 1989);

Stefan George, *Stefan George* (Ljubljana: Mladinska knjiga, 1995).

Kajetan Kovič has been an important, productive, and successful Slovene writer from his first major appearance in print in 1953. Though the field of Slovene poetry is remarkably crowded for such a small nation (which has some two million inhabitants in all), Kovič has set himself apart by composing short, lucid verse that is often both rhythmic and rhymed. He has avoided ideology, eluded labeling, and maintained a distinctive and recognizable poetic voice. With his 1994 novel, *Pot v Trento: Prizori iz navadnega življenja Franca M.* (The Road to Trent: Scenes from the Commonplace Life of Franc M.), by far the longest item in his corpus, he added something new to his repertory: a memoir of sorts that covers more than half a century of his family's history. It is rich with detail and appears to be deeply personal, and in both regards it resonates quite differently from most of his previous writing.

Kovič was born on 21 October 1931 in Maribor, Slovenia's second-largest city, near the Austrian border. He was too young to take part in World War II, which in the Yugoslav lands ran from April 1941 to early 1945. But he was not too young to remember the war, though it would take him an unusually long time (for a Yugoslav *litterateur*) to write about it. His education took place while his country was passing through conditions of bewildering turmoil and diversity: from the disintegration of royal Yugoslavia to annexation into the Third Reich, then Stalinist communization, and finally the Titoist schism between Yugoslavia and the Soviet Union and the ensuing relaxation of the Soviet grip. Kovič completed a degree in comparative literature at the university in Ljubljana in 1956 and worked as a newsman and editor until, in 1986, he became editor in chief of the *Državna založba Slovenije* (the State Publishing House of Slovenia), the nation's most important press. He published his first poem as a sixth-grader in 1947, and his first translations (from the German of Rainer Maria Rilke) in 1953. In the ensuing four decades Kovič has maintained a consistently steady output of poetry, prose, and works for children as well as scholarly and popular articles on literary topics. In 1964 he won the Levstik Award, in 1965 the Prežih Award, in 1967 the Award of the Prešeren Fund, and in 1978 the most prestigious literary prize in Slovenia, the Prešeren Award. He was admitted as a corresponding member of the Slovene Academy of Sciences and Arts in 1991 and in 1995 was elevated to the rank of full member.

One of the high points of Kovič's career occurred early with the appearance in 1953 of *Pesmi štirih* (A Foursome's Poems), the product of his attempt with three other young poets—Ciril

Zlobec, Janez Menart, and Tone Pavček—to produce an anthology that challenged and changed postwar Yugoslav literary policies. Kovič's were the first poems in the collection (though the authors were not arranged by alphabetical order), and his work was more fully represented than that of his colleagues, perhaps because he so successfully set the tone. The whole collection is, as one critic put it, emblematic of the poetic generation to come. The first poem, "Bela pravljica" (White Tale), epitomizes both Kovič's contribution and the volume as a whole:

> Crisscross the world go footprints,
> crisscross the world tracks through snow.
> God knows who went before me,
> God knows who comes behind me.
>
> All roads are eternally old,
> all go in the direction of death.
> For all at the beginning is birth,
> every step is eternally new.
>
> Crisscross the world go footprints,
> crisscross the world tracks through snow.
> One among them is mine,
> on it snow falls and falls.

The past and the present are evoked here; the future is studiously avoided. The time line is inverted in the second stanza (first old, then new, first death, then birth); progress disappears; and introspection and circumspection prevail. There is a hint of religion and a dose of resignation. White predominates (after green, Kovič's favorite color). The rhythm is regular (trochaic tetrameter), and the repetitions, like the refrain of a song, are characteristic. Critics have come to regard this collection, and particularly this poem, as quintessential in Kovič's work: he has always been a poet of memory, distance, and sonority.

As a poet, Kovič was in his most productive phase in the quarter-century following his debut. Some see his first two collections, in *Pesmi štirih* and his first solo volume, *Prezgodnji dan* (Too Early a Day, 1956), as notable for their intimate quality and their opposition to the postwar literature of revolution and socialist reconstruction. While he did not lapse into existentialism or neo-expressionism, popular in Slovenia and elsewhere at the time, critics do note a change of tone—bolder metaphors, greater anxiety, and more irrational expressions—in the two volumes from the 1960s, *Korenine vetra* (The Roots of the Wind, 1961) and *Ogenjvoda* (Firewater, 1965). The poet himself stressed in an interview with Branko Hofman in 1976 that the very titles of these collections were intended to evoke the synthesis of contradictions, which in his poetry he hoped would lead not to the disharmony and chaos he detected in the literary (and real) world around him, but to a new sense of wholeness, integrity, and relationship despite the realities of the world.

Two features of Kovič's poetry that all critics have noted are its strict adherence to poetic rules, whether of meter or rhyme or structure, unequaled in modern Slovene poetry, and the beauty of the poetic language. This nearly classical orderliness and eloquence are well evidenced in his most highly regarded volume, *Labrador* (1976), for which he won the Prešeren Award two years later. Putting sense above reason and heart over mind, Kovič tells impossible time in "Bezgove ure" (The Elderberry Hours), explores mysterious landscapes in "Labrador" and "Dežela nerojenih" (The Land of the Unborn), sings ballads of forbidden love in "Želja po sestri" (Desire for the Sister), and ends at the beginning in "Genesis," and "Adam in Eva" (Adam and Eve). The revelations here are, however, heavily veiled: the poet is very private. For all the virtuosity of their technique and the seeming simplicity of their language, one sees through these brief lyrics darkly. Overarching this volume, and indeed all of Kovič's poetry, is a gentle but pervasive air of resigned agnosticism, as if he were a modern Marcus Aurelius contemplating this century's version of the decline of humanity.

Kovič's prose, on the other hand, is more limpid, with flashes of humor, richness of detail, and lightness of language that set it apart from his poetry. In his earliest novellas, *Ne bog, ne žival* (Neither God nor Beast, 1965) and *Tekma, ali kako je arhitekt Nikolaj preživel konec tedna* (The Contest, or How Nicholas the Architect Survived the Weekend, 1970), urban life is well embodied: characters, eat, drink, dance, smoke (incessantly), and copulate (occasionally). Though he has been quoted, in the 1976 interview, to the effect that "I do not like to let people get close," a certain autobiographical note seems evident in much of Kovič's prose writings. *Mala čitanka* (The Little Reader, 1973), for example, is partly a memoir. Kovič's work over the years has shown both an increasing orientation toward prose and an ever-greater readiness for self-revelation, as amply demonstrated in his weightiest work, *Pot v Trento*.

On the backside of the title page of this 379-page work is the following advisement: "In this book all the personages, including the author

Kajetan Kovič

too, are merely fruits of the imagination." Yet this piece of alleged fiction reads as if it is the deeply felt, lovingly recollected personal history of Kovič's maternal uncle: his loves, fights, friendships, wars, intoxications, hangovers, fortunes, and misfortunes are told in great detail, both in the third person and in the first, by a narrator hard to distinguish from Kovič himself. The author plays with his readers by leading them around in circles of time and space. The opening chapter, "Prolog," is set in 1983, some twenty years after Uncle Franc's death. The narrator is on the road to the northern Italian city of Trent, where in 1916 Franc fell in love with an Italian woman whom the narrator hopes to meet but fails to locate. The final chapter, "Epilog," follows upon Uncle Franc's death (again!) and details the narrator's second trip to Trent in 1993, when he succeeds in locating the beloved, never-forgotten Enrica. In between is the story of Franc's "everyday" life, though in many ways it was quite extraordinary too, and the telling of it is as rich as was the life itself. Indeed, that seems to be the point: anchored between two points of "contact with reality," that is, the two trips to Trent, the tale of Franc is really the application of the narrator's "mind and heart to ancient shades," as he says. Kovič successfully makes literature out of life—a thickly textured novel out of memoirs and memories. No wonder, then, that he gives the warning at the outset: the "fruits of his imagination" look so real that the reader might be tempted to swallow them.

Kovič's work for children, which includes both poetry and prose, has enjoyed a success quite independent of his reputation as a serious poet and novelist. Two books, *Moj prijatelj Piki Jakob* (My Friend Piki Jakob, 1972), a collection of short tales, and *Maček Muri* (Muri, the Tom Cat, 1975), a fable, have been reissued many times and translated into other languages. Also, Kovič's only work to be translated fully into English (though there are many translations of individual poems) is the children's fable *Pajacek in punčka* (*The Clown and the Little Girl*, 1984). Kovič has claimed in print that he wrote his first work for children in 1952 to finance his education. He continues to favor the genre, however, because in the twentieth century literature for children can be esteemed on a par with literature for adults.

Kovič's translations have also won high praise in Slovenia. Perhaps because he comes from a part of Slovenia that is closely connected to German-speaking lands, he has worked with writers such as the Austrians Rilke (1875-1926) and Georg Trakl (1887-1914), and more recently the German Stefan George (1868-1933). He seems to have a particular affinity for the Austrian poet Alois Hergouth (1925-), who, though born of Slovene parents, grew up in a German-language environment near Graz and only later in his life discovered his Slavic roots. Perhaps the biggest challenge for a translator, given both the texts and those who have previously attempted them, was Kovič's translation into Slovene in 1989 of the poems that Slovenia's national poet, Francè Prešeren (1800-1849), originally wrote in German. Kovič has also tried his hand at closely related Serbo-Croatian, translating both the Croatian Gustav Krklec (1899-1977) and the Serbian Stevan Raičković (1928-). He has worked with Czech, French, Hungarian, and Russian as well.

Because of his early start, his steady production, and his long, ongoing career Kovič cuts a larger figure in postwar Slovene literature than has perhaps been acknowledged. He has not been ignored by the critics; on the contrary, each new book of his is duly noted and soon reviewed in the press, and every literary history accords him at least a couple of paragraphs, if not pages. At the same time, however, neither monographs nor specific studies have yet been done about him; thus, the most recent scholarly treatment of his novel, by a serious and competent analyst of Slovene literature, contains not a single reference to another scholarly work. In time this shortcoming will likely be remedied; in the meantime the poet who has also flexed his literary muscles as a successful novelist may well provide critics and scholars with substantially more about which to write.

Interviews:

France Pibernik, *Med tradicijo in modernizmom: Pričevanja o sodobni poeziji* (Ljubljana: Slovenska matica, 1978), pp. 199–212;

Branko Hofman, *Pogovori s slovenskimi pisatelji* (Ljubljana: Cankarjeva založba, 1978), pp. 139–154;

Marjeta Novak Kajzer, *Kako pišejo* (Ljubljana: Mihelač, 1993), pp. 33–40;

Nela Malečkar, *Expressing the Beauty of the World* (Ljubljana: Domus, 1993) pp. 72–75;

Darja Pavlič, "Intervju: Kajetan Kovič, 'Edina pot k bralcu je pot k sebi,'" *Literatura*, 23, no. 5 (1993): 35–42.

Bibliographies:

Živojin Boškov, F. Dobrovoljc, and others, eds., *Leksikon pisaca Jugoslavije*, volume 3 (Novi Sad: Matica srpska, 1987), pp. 359–362;

Janko Kos and Ksenija Dolinar, eds., *Slovenska književnost* (Ljubljana: Cankarjeva založba, 1996), pp. 222–223.

References:

Mikolaj Dutsch, "Kajetan Kovič: Das lyrische Werk," in *Kindlers Neues Literatur Lexikon*, volume 9, edited by Rudolf Radler (Munich: Kindler, 1990), pp. 710–712;

Thomas Eekman, *Thirty Years of Yugoslav Literature (1945–1975)* (Ann Arbor: Michigan Slavic Publications, 1978), pp. 308–309;

Helga Glušič, "Inventura senc v panonskem taktu," *Razgledi: časopis za umetnost, družbo in humanistiko*, no. 23 (9 December 1994): 36–37;

Monika Kalin, "Motiv drevesa v poeziji avtorjev *Pesmi štirih*," *Jezik in slovstvo*, 36, no. 7–8 (1990–1991): 211–219;

Taras Kermauner, "Humanistična resignacija (Premišljevanje ob prvih pesniških zbirkah Kajetana Kovičov, ob *Pesmi štirih* in *Prezgodnjem dnevu*)," *Slavistična revija*, 16 (1968): 535–588;

Kermauner, "Prodoba in sla," *Sodobnost*, 25 (1977): 66–74;

Janko Kos, *Pregled slovenskega slovstva* (Ljubljana: Državna založba Slovenije, 1979), pp. 392–393;

Kos, *Primerjalna zgodovina slovenske literature* (Ljubljana: Partizanska knjiga, 1987), p. 251;

Sveta Lukić, *Contemporary Yugoslav Literature: A Sociopolitical Approach*, edited by Gertrude Joch Robinson, translated by Pola Triandis (Urbana: University of Illinois Press, 1971), pp. 73–77;

Mitja Mejak, "Marginalije ob liričnem jubileju," *Sodobnost*, 20 (1973): 313–317;

Marija Mitrović, *Pregled slovenačke književnosti* (Sremski Karlovci & Novi Sad: Izdavačka knjižarnica Zorana Stojanovića, 1995), p. 324;

Boris Paternu, "Kovič, Kajetan," in *Enciklopedija Slovenije*, volume 5, edited by Marjan Javornik and others (Ljubljana: Mladinska knjiga, 1991), pp. 342–343;

Paternu, *Pogledi na slovensko književnost: Študije in razprave*, volume 2 (Ljubljana: Partizanska knjiga, 1974), pp. 335–338;

Jože Pogačnik and Franc Zadravec, *Zgodovina slovenskega slovstva* (Maribor: Založba Obzorja, 1973), pp. 518–527;

Brane Senegačnik, "Med poetiko in poezijo: Esej o poeziji Kajetana Koviča, napisan ob zbirki *Poletje*," *Literatura*, 19, no. 1 (1993): 58–67;

Jože Snoj, "Prispodoba brez primerjave: Ob izboru pesmi Kajetana Koviča," *Sodobnost*, 22 (1974): 606–618;

Miran Štuhec, "Kovičeva pot od zafrkljivosti do temeljne bivanjske resnice," *Sobodnost*, 44 (1996): 102–108;

Franc Zadravec, "Poetika in stil Kovičevega romana *Pot v Trento*," *Slavistična revija*, 43, no. 1 (1995): 25–37.

Ivan V. Lalić
(8 June 1931 – 28 July 1996)

Francis R. Jones
University of Newcastle

BOOKS: *Bivši dečak* (Zagreb: Lykos, 1955);
Vetrovito proleće (Zagreb: Društvo književnica Hrvatske, 1956);
Velika vrata mora (Belgrade: Nolit, 1958);
Melisa (Zagreb: Lykos, 1959);
Argonauti i druge pesme (Zagreb: Naprijed, 1961);
Vreme, vatre, vrtovi (Novi Sad: Matica srpska, 1961);
Čin (Belgrade: Prosveta, 1963);
Krug (Belgrade: Nolit, 1968);
Izabrane i nove pesme (Belgrade: Srpska književna zadruga, 1969);
Kritika i delo (Belgrade: Nolit, 1971);
Smetnje na vezama (Belgrade: Srpska književna zadruga, 1975);
O poeziji dvanaest pesnika (Belgrade: Slovo ljubve, 1980);
Strasna mera (Belgrade: Nolit, 1984);
Pesme, selected, with an introductory essay, by S. Velmar-Janković (Belgrade: Prosveta, 1987; second enlarged edition, Belgrade: Prosveta, 1995);
Vizantija (Čačak: Gradska biblioteka, 1987);
Pismo (Belgrade: Srpska književna zadruga, 1992; second edition, Belgrade: Srpska književna zadruga, 1993);
Četiri kanona (Belgrade: Srpska književna zadruga, 1996).

Editions in English: *Four Yugoslav Poets,* translated by Charles Simic (Northwood Narrows, N.H.: Lillabulero, 1970);
Fire Gardens, selected and translated by C. W. Truesdale and Simic (New York: New Rivers Press, 1970);
The Works of Love, selected and translated, with an introductory essay, by Francis R. Jones (London: Anvil, 1981);
Last Quarter, selected and translated by Jones (London: Anvil/Turret, 1987);
The Passionate Measure, translated, with an introductory essay, by Jones (London: Anvil, 1989; Dublin: Dedalus, 1989);

Ivan V. Lalić

Roll Call of Mirrors, selected and translated by Simic (Middletown, Conn.: Wesleyan University Press, 1989);
A Rusty Needle, edited and translated, with an introductory essay, by Jones (London: Anvil, 1996);
Fading Contact, translated, with an introductory essay, by Jones (London: Anvil, 1997).

RADIO: *Majstor Hanuš,* LMS, 1965.

RECORDING: *CD Poets 2,* translations by Jones, read by Lalić, with other poets, London, Bellew, 1995.

TRANSLATIONS: K. Acz, *Pesme umesto tišine*

(Belgrade: Prosveta, 1965);
Sandor Weöres, *Preobraženja* (Novi Sad: Forum, 1965);
Antologija moderne francuske lirike (Belgrade: Prosveta, 1966);
Pierre Jean Jouve, *Pesme* (Belgrade: Prosveta, 1967);
Friedrich Hölderlin, *Odabrana dela*, selected and translated by Lalić (Belgrade: Nolit, 1969);
Antologija moderne američke poezije, selected and translated by Lalić and Branka Lalić (Belgrade: Prosveta, 1972);
Alfred Bosquet, *Beleške za jednu samoću* (Kragujevac: Bagdala, 1972);
Walt Whitman, *Vlati trave* (Belgrade: BIGZ, 1974);
Antologija nemačke lirike XX veka, edited by Lalić and B. Zivojinović, translated by Lalić and others (Belgrade: Nolit, 1976);
T. S. Eliot, *Izabrane pesme*, with an introductory essay by Lalić (Belgrade: BIGZ, 1978);
Jaroslav Seifert, *Izabrane pesme*, selected and translated by Lalić and J. Ribnikar (Belgrade: Srpska književna zadruga, 1984);
Charles Simic, *Avenija Amerika* (Vršac: Književna opština Vršac, 1992);
David Gascoyne, *Pesme* (Novi Sad: Matica srpska, 1993);
Christopher Marlowe, *Tamerlan Veliki*, translated by Lalić and B. Lalić (Belgrade: Srpska književna zadruga, 1995).

In recent years Ivan V. Lalić has gained an international reputation as one of the major poets of the former Yugoslavia. His poetic quest into the nature of time, culture, and human perception combines a startling clarity of images and a thoughtful, highly crafted, lucid diction that places him firmly in the tradition of European and American modernism, in which he is acknowledged to be one of Europe's masters.

Lalić was born into a cultured family in Belgrade on 8 June 1931; his father, Vlajko, was a journalist, and his grandfather Isidor Bajić had been a celebrated composer. Half a century later, in 1983, a BBC interviewer asked Lalić how he had found his poetic voice. "My childhood and boyhood in the war marked everything I ever wrote as a poem or poetry," Lalić replied, leaning forward to pick up *Izabrane i nove pesme*, the definitive selection of his early verse, compiled in 1969. He opened this book to the first poem, "Zardjala igla" (A Rusty Needle), also the opening poem of his first book, *Bivši dečak* (Once a Boy, 1955). This poem, he explained, was the foundation-stone of his whole poetic oeuvre. Accordingly, *A Rusty Needle* became the title of my English version of *Izabrane i nove pesme*, from which all translations quoted here are taken.

Lalić's family built a second home on the slopes of Mount Maljen, a few hours south of Belgrade; the mountain air, they felt, would build up the young Ivan's weak health. In "Zardjala igla" Lalić tells of his happy childhood summers spent there, secure in his mother's love:

> Then I came to love the night, to love it for the wind teased
> Through the dark needles of the pines, and the rapping of the
> Shutter at the window of the solid house, whose foundations
> Are all that remain, and the green rust of weeds.
> When the wind was gone, the crickets remained,
> And my mother's breath, rightwards in the dark,
> Tepid and gentle. I sank into sleep as if into soapy water,
> Quickly, softly, without a ripple on the surface.

Soon war brought a harsh coming of age. Trapped in the city, Lalić saw many school friends perish, especially in the Allied air raids of Easter 1944. "Zardjala igla" relates how, out of this trauma, Lalić's poetic duty was born—the duty to pit fragile human memory against the destruction that is the human condition:

> Did they really come of age in an instant, just
> Before they crumpled like poppies under the scree
> Of rubble, their eyes full of fear and dust,
> Dumbstruck, for this was not what they wanted?
> I don't know. But I remained, to grow on
> With their gaze in the nape of my neck, like
> A rusty needle just under the skin; but also, slowly,
> To come to love the night and her soft stars again.

To remember, to record—to search for an image that might last beyond the constant destruction of the present instant—is one of Lalić's key poetic tasks.

One means of memory that he explores in depth is culture. To Lalić culture is a network of threads that link one not only back to a personal and collective past but outward, to a wider geographic space than that of one's birth. Thus, although he was born in Serbia, lived in Belgrade, and wrote in Serbian, Lalić is anything but a narrowly Serbian poet, a fact particularly important to bear in mind in the wake of the murderous nationalistic rivalries that infested the former Yugoslavia in the early 1990s.

For one thing, Lalić can also claim a Croatian heritage. In 1946, at the age of fifteen, he moved to Zagreb, the Croatian capital. Zagreb was the scene of two events that became decisive for his poetry: "the early death of my mother, compensated for by the crazy luck of meeting a girl who was to return my love and become my wife and muse in the same person," as Lalić wrote in a letter to the author of this article. In Zagreb he also finished high school in 1949 and then studied law at the university. His first verses were published here. Significantly, in view of Lalić's acknowledged debt to wider European as well as native influences, his first published work was a translation—of Arthur Rimbaud's "Le bâteau ivre" (The Drunken Boat), which appeared in the journal *Književnost* (Literature) in 1951. Lalić, who was interested in translation throughout his artistic career, produced Serbian-language versions (sometimes in collaboration with Branka, his wife) of Christopher Marlowe, Walt Whitman, T. S. Eliot, Friedrich Hölderlin, and other poets, as well as anthologies of German, French, Hungarian, and American poetry.

In 1955 the first volume of Lalić's own verse, *Bivši dečak*, was published. Lalić graduated the same year but did not enter the legal profession; instead, he joined Radio Zagreb, where he eventually became an editor. By 1961 Lalić's poetic reputation was becoming established: five volumes of his poetry had been published, and he had won the first two of many awards, *Tribine mladih* in 1960 and the *Zmaj* prize in 1961. In 1961 Lalić also returned to Belgrade to begin the first of two appointments as general secretary of the Yugoslav Writers' Union. In 1964 he became an editor at the Jugoslavija publishing house. By 1969 Lalić had eight original volumes to his name. All, however, are out of print and hard to find, as a result of a deliberate decision by Lalić, who preferred readers to use the 1969 edition of *Izabrane i nove pesme* as the definitive, winnowed-out guide to his earlier verse.

His early poems, the best of which (or most of the best) are indeed preserved in *Izabrane i nove pesme*, show three features that became his trademark: his easy, human, accessible tone; his use of elemental images such as sun, wind, fire, and sea; and, to paraphrase a British reviewer, his blazing successes of metaphor. In "Glas koji peva u vrtovima" (A Voice Singing in Gardens), for example, he writes:

> As for the dead, whom I am afraid
> To ask in case they know much, too much,
> They do not notice us as they concentrate on
> Carefully dismantling their former fates,
> Like watchmakers.

Themes are wide-ranging. Some poems, such as "Glas koji peva u vrtovima," describe vivid, metaphysical quests that foreshadow the more measured searchings of Lalić's maturity; in others, scenes from classical or national history have a compelling existential depth that takes them beyond mere genre sketches. In the celebrated poem "Smederevo," which is about the last bastion of the medieval Serbian state, the soldiers in the fortress, awaiting its inevitable overthrow by the Ottoman invader, produce echoes of the Chinese T'ang dynasty poets writing home from a distant, hostile frontier:

> We wait, and twenty-four towers wait with us,
> Exposed to time as to the rain, all of us together.
> I think we will never be forgotten, we who watch
> From the last citadel on the right bank of the river,
> Although we will not turn to stone beneath the towers;
> It is enough that we are the ones who wait, who strain our ears
> For the echo of a thousand hooves growing in the night
> Beneath the indifferent stars.

Other topics are personal: love or the happiness of childhood, broken off by the deaths of friends and his mother and sought again through memory. There are also explorations of literary themes and characters—Orpheus, in several poems; Ophelia, in a poem, "Ofelia," that has stronger echoes of Rimbaud's "Le bâteau ivre" than it does of William Shakespeare's Hamlet or Sir John Everett Millais's painting of Ophelia.

> Slow your progress: bridges quiver,
> Sails are bathed in the heat of the sun.
> Death in your flesh, the gurgling river
> Beneath you: is your suffering done?

In much of this early work there is a strong formal streak, as in the rhyming couplets just quoted. In his own country Lalić is recognized as a supreme master of poetic form. This, however, is a somewhat double-edged compliment. In a country where the book-buying public likes its verse to be lyrical and impassioned, and where much of the poetry establishment has espoused a rather arid avant-gardism, there has been a tendency in the popular mind to categorize Lalić as a rather Parnassian formalist. Such categorization does injustice to his work, for even in his own country, his impressive array of literary prizes (seven national literary awards by 1992) provides evidence for the wide recognition of his poetic talent. Lalić himself, however, would be the first to admit that he aims for a lasting, universal quality in his verse and to assert that he does not merely follow literary fashions. As he once said to this author: "When some were playing the peasant flute, and others the saxophone, I just sat and played my cello."

He was alluding here to the conflict between the bucolic, party-line traditionalists and the avant-garde writers during the struggle for freedom from Communist Party control over literature in the early 1950s. The struggle was won by the avant-garde, not because of the quality of their polemic, but because of their poetry—especially that of Vasko Popa, the atavistic surrealist. The lifting of party control over literature, however, released a surge of creative talent in all genres, not only in avant-garde poetry: Lalić, reaching his poetic stride in the late 1950s, is one of the leading poetic representatives of this gifted "second generation."

Occasionally, in meeting the demands and temptations of rhyme and meter in his earlier formal verse, Lalić risks detracting from the clarity of diction, image, and underlying message, although the risk equally often pays off. His fondness for formal fireworks, together with his tendency to create rich, densely layered images, also seen in some of his earlier verse, reached its culmination in the book *Melisa* in 1959, which was abridged to a cycle in *Izabrane i nove pesme*. This is a set of hexameter sonnets about Melissa, a woman torn to pieces, so Greek legend has it, because she refused to reveal the secrets of Demeter's mysteries; the grateful goddess turned her into a swarm of bees as a result. In "1: Pčele" (1: Bees) Lalić writes:

> Blood the colour of summer, whose humming lingers
> All afternoon, dripping from blades of light
> Beyond my sight, as I break my dirty fingers
>
> On the hideous bulk of your wall, till these
> Torn hands bear fruit, my speechless words grow white
> As milk, as your body, Melissa, turning to bees.

After *Melisa*, however, Lalić turned from rhymed verse for many years, a decision that marked a watershed in his work. The blank verse of his poetic maturity, which builds on the strengths of his early blank verse, is that of a poet of European stature. In language lucid as crystal, with images more powerful for being used more sparingly and coherently, he combines the sensual and the intellectual with a skill unmatched by any of his contemporaries. This com-

Dust jacket for a translation of Strasna mera, *Lalić's 1984 collection of poems, which strikes a note of foreboding about the future of Yugoslavia*

bination, with its echoes of the great European and American modernists such as T. S. Eliot or William Butler Yeats, and especially the Mediterranean poets such as George Seferis or Eugenio Montale, to whom Lalić feels the closest kinship, earned Lalić international recognition as one of the leading postwar poets of the former Yugoslavia.

His poems of the 1960s have a single, distinctive voice; they are humane, easy, and warm, yet they pull no intellectual punches. His love poetry, for example, describes personal experience not from above, as would a Parnassian, or from within, as would a lyricist, but from underneath, thereby revealing universal levels deeper than that of the personal. In "Četiri psalma" (Four Psalms), for instance, he writes:

> I'll make you a land;
>   a pure plain
> Where a mountain grows from glistening orchards,
> In keeping, like a movement in a beautiful dream;

With one decisive breath, like a glassblower
Who, before the fire, recalls a beauty
He has not learnt.

The most striking feature in Lalić's work is his joy in the visual. His verse blazes with the Franciscan elements of wind, fire, sun, earth, and, most of all, the sea. For many years Lalić, his wife, Branka, and their two sons, Vlajko and Marko, spent their summers in Rovinj, a town on the western coast of the Istrian Peninsula, just across the Adriatic from Venice and Ravenna. If asked, Lalić categorized himself not as a Serb or Yugoslav but a Mediterranean poet; whether describing the sea or not, his verse is drenched with a Mediterranean luminosity. In "Inventar mesečine" (Inventory of Moonlight), for instance, he writes:

A garden turned in compassion towards the sea
And steeped in the blue anaesthetic of afternoon shadows;
The old lace of light, yellowing and frayed,
And the sea's fire between the trees.

To Lalić the Mediterranean is more than a geographical landscape (or seascape, perhaps); it is a cultural one. The Mediterranean and its daughter seas, the Adriatic and the Aegean, are routes of cultural transmission through time as well as space. It was along these sea routes that the harsh clarity of the desert religions of the Near East merged with the easy animism of Greece and Rome to form European culture.

Izabrane i nove pesme culminates in two masterly cycles specially written for this volume. These two cycles about two ancient Mediterranean cities, one of them, Dubrovnik, surviving miraculously intact, and the other, Byzantium, vanquished and sacked, explore his own and Yugoslavia's double heritage—a heritage that then seemed to be his country's richness rather than its undoing.

The first cycle, "Dubrovnik, zimska priča" (Dubrovnik, a Winter's Tale), looks to the Latin and Catholic West. The city-state of Dubrovnik, the epicenter of Croatia's literary and cultural golden age in the seventeenth century, was the lens through which the art and values of the Italian Renaissance were focused onto the South Slav lands. The opening poem, "Putnik pred Dubrovnikom, januara" (Traveler Before Dubrovnik, January), pictures a city that is beyond time:

A stone garland wreathed around
The smooth forehead of the centuries, without a wrinkle
Betraying an effort of memory,
                    and islands
At anchor, strong points of immobility,
Green in the slow silver of the ebbing tide.

The second cycle looks to the East, to the Greek classical and Orthodox heritage: Byzantium was a cultural wellspring as significant for Serbia as the Adriatic renaissance city-states were for Croatia. The cycle "O delima ljubavi, ili Vizantija" (Of the Works of Love, or Byzantium) describes the city's last siege and fall to the Ottoman Turks in 1453. But Lalić's Byzantium also has universal meaning as a complex symbol of the destruction that eventually faces even the wisest, most beautiful human creations. The agonized historian in "Plač letopisca" (Lament of the Chronicler) says:

Alas o city, sandcastle on the beach!
Hear the rising of the wave and the rustle of absurdity
Lacing its edge, as it passionlessly erases our marks;
Who may complete the manuscript, this book which emptiness
Flicks through with fingers of flame?

The year 1975 marked the beginning of Lalić's second appointment as general secretary of the Yugoslav Writers' Union. It was also the year that *Smetnje na vezama* appeared (translated as *Fading Contact,* from which the quotations here are taken). This jewel of a collection continues the trends set in the 1960s. What makes it one of his most accomplished works is the way in which the surface mood and visual impact of personal experience and historical events are perfectly balanced by a more explicit search for what wider meaning, if any, the experiences and events may have. Thus *Smetnje na vezama* looks into both the personal meaning of memory and what culture, or heritage, means to those who carry the torch forward. On the one hand, the beauty and wisdom of the past may survive miraculously intact, like Dubrovnik in the previous volume. Now, in the cycle "Atos u pet pevanja" (Athos in Five Songs), the poet travels to Mount Athos in Greece, the epicenter of the Orthodox faith; here history, personal memory, and the present moment merge. The opening poem "Dafni" (Daphne) relates that

the real reason for coming is loyalty
To an image wedded a second ago, to a word
Unspoken in the briefness of memory
But whispered
In a future which brushes my cheeks
And parts the new leaves of the old plane trees

With the fingers of the same sea-wind
On this terribly real shore.

But even if survival is the exception and destruction the rule, destruction is never total, as the superb cycle "Mnemosina" (Mnemosyne), addressed to the Greek goddess of memory, mother of all the muses, relates. The dead live on in memory:

There's no clean future: space stays infected
With the fever of signs, the germ of remembering-
And a mother's kiss
Transmits the saving disease.

And the random shards of the past, whether personal or cultural, are not only one's sole hope of eternity, but they also give meaning to one's brief existence: "Our task is to remember, to deliver blows; / The task of the peach is to blossom." In *Smetnje na vezama* Lalić also explores the nature of human perception: the relationship between the world, the seer, and the fixing of what is seen in memory. Which is more real, Lalić asks: the event as it occurs or its fixing in memory? Perhaps memory is what makes the fleeting real, as he muses in these lines from "Zimsko more" (Winter Sea):

We walk down the path towards the shore
Between yesterday's images, real only today
In our speech, where spirits
Touch like leaves in the wind.

But in the end one lives not in history but in the here and now which must be constantly and joyously affirmed, as it is in these lines from "Vizantija VIII, ili Hilandar" (Byzantium VIII, or Chilandar):

    you must enter at the proper hour, filled
With love for the visible:
               for stone, brick, lead,
Towers, verandas, galleries, cupolas,
The silver foil of afternoon sun
On the thin glass of windows, for a shadow
Climbing, like oil up a wick, straight up the cypress
In the close, paved with stone
And wild mallow.

This affirmation is each person's duty—and especially the poet's, as is made clear in the closing of "Na putu za Esfigmen" (On the Way to Esphigmenou) from the Athos cycle:

The real effort is still to come,
Courage which perhaps begins
With the choice of the exact image,

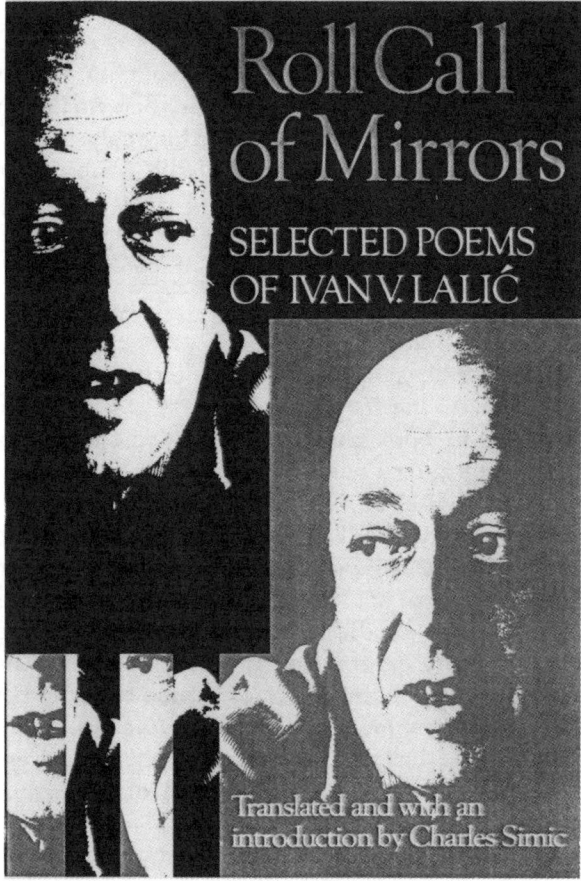

Dust jacket for a 1989 translation of Lalić's poems

                       with the touch
Of fingers feeling the edge of the remembered
In disbelief, like the edge of a wound[.]

Smetnje na vezama also looks at personal themes. But there is a dark undercurrent to many of these poems: insomnia, despair, considerations of suicide, the ever-encroaching void. Here too, however, links are made between personal experience and its wider significance. Read twenty years later, for example, the poem "Emisija" (Broadcast), with its "fading contact" that gave the book its title, seems to show an uncanny foresight into the fate of Lalić's homeland. Lalić writes:

    the voice isn't getting through,
We remember half sentences, but the context is so unclear,
The broadcast is vitally important,
They say, the last before a long, long night
Without love,
And no one can recall now
How the contact first started to fade.

But the answer, Lalić says, is not to surrender to

the void, but to keep broadcasting, to keep scanning the ether for messages from the past—from memory. In "Pismo Džonu Berimenu na vest o njegovoj smrti" (Letter to John Berryman on Hearing the News of his Death), his reply to Berryman's advocation of suicide, Lalic writes:

> Your courage is that of the prodigal; I
> Respect it, but choose to admire the courage
> Of those prepared to keep on giving answers
> Even when the lips that question are silent.

In 1979, at the end of his term as general secretary of the Yugoslav Writers' Union, Lalić returned to book publishing, this time with the Nolit publishing house, where he stayed until his retirement in 1993. His next major work of poetry appeared in 1984, *Strasna mera,* translated as *The Passionate Measure* (1989), from which the quotations here are taken. *Strasna mera* marks another change of direction in Lalić's work. The tone is more restrained, the images mellower, and the lines of thought more complex. Though culture and memory still exist as themes, there are no more historical tableaux: in the rudderless drift into disaster of the Yugoslavia of the 1980s, it is the present, not the past, that is under threat from an ominous, indifferent enemy. According to the opening poem, "Poslednja četvrt" (Last Quarter): "the century is waning fast, making for / The delta, headlong down the slope." This despair, as in the previous volume, also has echoes on the personal level. But there are other concerns, those of a mature middle age: taking stock and looking back, but also looking forward to what still has to be done, preserving the memories that still must be set against the forgetting, and in "Rovinjski kvartet: 4" (Rovinj Quartet: 4), keeping

> Faithfulness in returning to places we love,
> To a razed centre, and the star
> Over the empty ruins, over the sea.

And in the eponymous poem "Prostori nade" there are still "Spaces of Hope" to set against the despair:

> a lilac garden,
> A street in Florence, a morning room,
> A sea smeared with silver before the storm,
> Or a starless night lit only
> By the book on the table.

During the 1980s Lalić's reputation, already assured at a national level, gained an international dimension. By the mid 1990s book-length editions of his verse had appeared in six languages, including English (in the United States, the United Kingdom, and Ireland), French, Italian, Polish, Hungarian, and Macedonian; individual poems had appeared in journals and anthologies in more than twenty languages. Lalić has had seven solo volumes of poetry published in English alone. National awards, including the coveted Branko Miljkovic Prize of 1985 for *Strasna mera,* were complemented by international prizes: the Hungarian *Pro litteris hungaricis* in 1970, and, from the United States, the Thornton Wilder Prize in 1990. *The Passionate Measure* was awarded Britain's European Poetry Translation Prize of 1991, and a selection from *A Rusty Needle* (together with verses by the Croatian poet Drago Štambuk) was runner-up in the British Comparative Literature Association's 1994 Translation Awards.

Rather than resting on his laurels, Lalić continued developing. *Pesme* of 1987 contains, besides a selection of earlier poems, a new cycle of sonnets written in strict rhyme and meter. This cycle, "Deset soneta nerodjenoj kćeri" (Ten Sonnets to an Unborn Daughter), formed the kernel of Lalić's last collection, *Pismo* (Script) of 1992. With *Pismo,* Lalić returned to mine the formalist style of his youth; all the poems use strict syllabic meters, and most have complex rhyme schemes. This book remains untranslated, apart from my own, formally faithful draft of the first "Sonnet to an Unborn Daughter," in which Lalić writes:

> All that nothing keeps concealed, lies unseen
> Like untouched ore, and shares its scintillation;
> All that has no existence, might still have been,
> Or does exist, outside predestination.
>
> And in the ore a ring: to wed the presence
> Of what isn't with a known reality;
> The ore seethes with lava's incandescence
> As the unlived yearns for temporality.

As this extract shows, *Pismo* has a musing, reflective, complex tone similar to that of *Strasna mera.* It formidably combines the mature image-building and thematic skills of *Strasna mera* with the formal craftsmanship of his early rhymed verse; on the other hand, it is perhaps less immediately accessible than the blank verse of the late 1960s and 1970s.

By the early 1990s Lalić had gained international recognition as his country's—the former Yugoslavia's—leading living poet. *Pismo* alone had been awarded three national prizes. Yet these years brought a double personal trauma. Lalić's elder son, while yachting from Venice to Rovinj (two key, numinous places in Lalić's poetry), was caught in a freak storm and drowned. Then came the vicious Serb-Croat war, leaving its aftermath of hatred and mistrust. Lalić, as a Serb, even though his wife is Croatian, was unable to spend the summers in his beloved Rovinj, as he had done for decades.

Lalić's last work, *Četiri kanona* (Four Canons), published in 1996, shows only indirect traces of the personal and political scars revealed in Lalić's letters to the present author. In this work he revives the *kanon*, a Byzantine cycle of verse meditations upon a predetermined set of biblical texts. This choice of form, however, might be seen as an attempt to seek a past order amidst the present chaos that surrounded him; and although many of the meditations are dark and brooding, the predominant theme is that of a search for grace in the incomprehensibility of the divine will, for "spaces of hope" in the darkness. In "Pvri kanon 2" (First Canon 2), for example, he writes:

> Take me away, wind, into that black light,
> Where a blind man dimly glimpses a tiny flame
> Like a star at the bottom of a well:
> Someone there is rehearsing grace
> In the long, drawn-out night of the soul,
> In a desert land, and in the waste howling wilderness.

In July 1996, at the height of his poetic powers, Lalić suddenly became ill and died of heart failure. Obituaries in many different countries confirmed that he was a poet of European rather than merely local stature. Though Lalić's work inevitably bears traces of the political and intellectual climate of the times through which he lived, it is rooted not in the specific but in the universal concerns of humanity: the nature of time, culture, and perception, and the thin threads of love and memory that link them together.

Interviews:

Graham Fawcett, "The Works of Love: the Poetry of Ivan V. Lalić," BBC Radio 3, 1984;

Slobodan Zubanović and Mihailo Pantić, "Ivan V. Lalić," in their *Deset pesama–deset razgovora* (Novi Sad: Matica srpska, 1992), pp. 73-93.

References:

Bernard Johnson, "Ivan V. Lalić," in *Contemporary World Poets* (London: St. James Press, 1992);

Francis R. Jones, "Ivan V. Lalić and Drago Štambuk: Poems," *Comparative Criticism*, 16 (1994): 105-125;

Jones, "The Rose Whose Scent Is Time: The Poetry of Ivan V. Lalić," *Tracks*, 2 (1982): 31-34;

Branko Mikasinovich, "Ivan V. Lalić, a Serbian 'Modern Traditionalist'," Proceedings: Pacific Northwest Conference on Foreign Languages, edited by Walter C. Kraft (Corvallis: Oregon State University, 1972): 217-221;;

Radivoje Mikić, "Štajejače: vidljivo ili nevidljivo," in his *Jezik poezije* (Belgrade: BIGZ, 1990), pp. 19-36;

Milica Nikolić, *Mare Mediterraneum Ivana V. Lalića* (Belgrade: Slobodan Mašić, 1996);

Aleksandar Petrov, "O smetnjama, o vezama," in his *Poezija danas* (Belgrade: Vuk Karadžic, 1980), pp. 96-102.

Mihailo Lalić
(7 October 1914 – 30 December 1992)

Branko Popović
Teachers' School, Belgrade

BOOKS: *Staze slobode* (Cetinje: Narodna knjiga, 1948);
Izvidnica (Belgrade: Prosveta, 1948);
Izabrane pripovijetke (Cetinje: Narodna knjiga, 1950);
Svadba (Belgrade: Prosveta, 1950);
Tri dana (Zagreb: Zora, 1950);
Osveta Martoloza (Cetinje: Pobjeda, 1951);
Prvi snijeg (Belgrade: Prosveta, 1951);
Na Tari (Belgrade: Narodna knjiga, 1952);
Usput zapisano (Belgrade: Novo pokolenje, 1952);
Zlo proljeće (Belgrade: Novo pokolenje, 1953);
Raskid (Cetinje: Narodna knjiga, 1955; revised, Belgrade: Nolit, 1969);
Tajne bistrih voda (Belgrade: Narodna knjiga, 1955);
Na mjesečini (Novi Sad: Matica srpska, 1956);
Lelejska gora (Belgrade: Nolit, 1957; revised, 1962, revised, 1990);
Hajka (Belgrade: Nolit, 1960);
Posljednje brdo (Belgrade: Nolit, 1967);
Gosti (Belgrade: Srpska književna zadruga, 1967);
Proza (Belgrade: Jugoslavia, 1967);
Pusta zemlja (Belgrade: Prosveta, 1968);
Pramen tame (Belgrade: Prosveta, 1970);
Ratna sreća (Belgrade: Nolit, 1973);
Zatočnici (Belgrade; Nolit, 1976);
Svitanje (Titograd: Pobjeda, 1976);
Dokle gora zazeleni (Belgrade: Nolit, 1982);
Gledajući dolje na drumove (Belgrade: Nolit, 1983);
Prelazni period: dnevnik posmatrača (Belgrade: Nolit, 1988);
Odlučan čovek (Belgrade: Rad, 1990);
Tamara (Belgrade: Srpska književna zadruga, 1992);
Prutom po vodi (Novi Sad: Dnevnik, 1992);
Opraštanja nije bilo (Belgrade: Srpska književna zadruga, 1994);
Epistolae seniles (Belgrade: Srpska književna zadruga, 1995).

Editions and Collections: *Sabrana dela* (Belgrade: Nolit, 1976);

Mihailo Lalić

Izabrana dela, 10 volumes (Belgrade: Nolit, 1981).

Editions in English: *The Wailing Mountain,* translated by Drenka Willen (New York: Harcourt, Brace & World, 1965).

Mihailo Lalić, author of twelve novels, is one of the greatest Serbian novelists. Although he also wrote poetry, criticism, reportage, travelogues, screenplays, and plays, he acquired his reputation from his novels and short stories. His novels, four of which—*Lelejska gora* (1957, translated as *The Wailing Mountain,* 1965), *Ratna sreća* (War Fortune, 1973), *Hajka* (Chase, 1960), and

Zlo proljeće (Evil Spring, 1953)—are of seminal value, honor not only Serbian but European literature.

Lalić was born on 7 October 1914 into a peasant family in Trepča, Montenegro. He lost both parents before he started school. The experience of being a lonely village orphan and the psychological anxiety of being a motherless child left an indelible impression on his sensibility and solidified his determination to direct his literary efforts to the liberation of the socially deprived and, in general, those oppressed and endangered by the cataclysm of war. The writer attended elementary school in his native Trepča from 1921 to 1925 and high school in Berane from 1925 to 1933. In high school he joined a group of Marxist students; his study of law at the University of Belgrade from 1931 to 1941 was interrupted by periodic imprisonments as a member of the Communist Party, which he had joined in 1935.

According to his autobiographical notes, *Epistolae seniles* (Letters in Old Age), published posthumously in 1995, in which he describes his "childhood, boyhood and youth," Lalić wrote nothing before moving to Belgrade to study. Only after his twentieth year did he begin publishing stories, poems, reviews, and reportage in newspapers and literary journals. Ideologically and aesthetically he advocated social literature and was active in the circle of young writers on the literary Left, whose model was the Russian writer Maksim Gorky. Politically he identified himself in demonstrations against the monarchy with other Marxist-oriented students; he was arrested three times and served a six-month sentence for his "anti-state rebellion" and struggle against the dictatorial regime. During the prewar period he published about thirty shorter literary pieces (not counting the reportage), but from all of that he included only a few poems and three somewhat revised short stories in his first book, *Staze slobode* (Paths of Liberty, 1948). His early literary works, from 1935 to 1945, are considered the productions of a neophyte and are usually referred to only to describe a stage in his development.

Lalić was born at the beginning of World War I and began his literary career on the eve of World War II. He participated in the antifascist struggle at the beginning and end of World War II, spending the middle part of the war in prisoner-of-war camps in Kolašin and Salonika. Because every generation of Lalić's ancestors had suffered the tragic consequences of wars, whether fighting against Turks, Austrians, Germans, it is

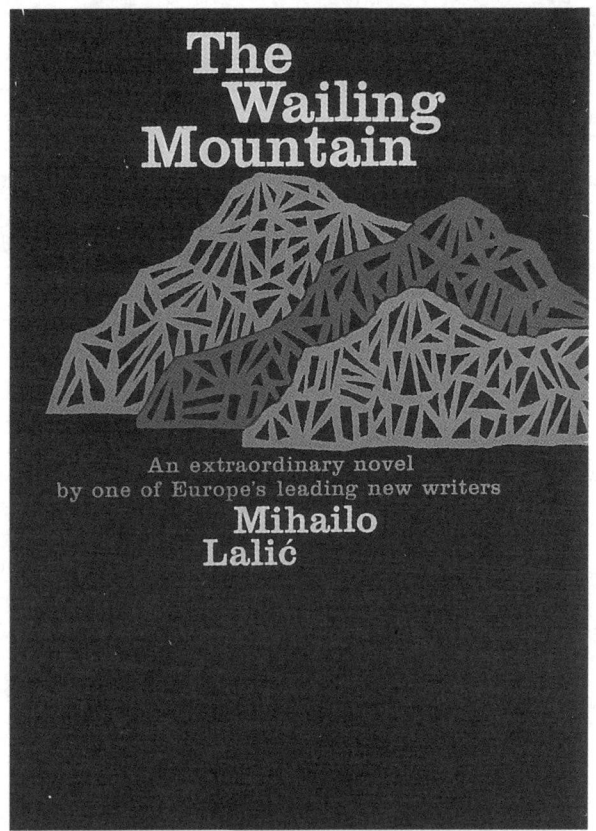

Dust jacket for a translation of Lelejska gora, *Lalić's novel about a partisan fighter in World War II*

understandable that in almost every narrative—naive or artistic—about his ancestors the theme of war predominates. That is the way it was in Serbian epic poetry, in the poetry of the greatest Serbian poet, Petar Petrović Njegoš, and so the war-struck fate of his people, particularly of his immediate homeland, Montenegro, is reflected in Lalić's narratives as well.

Although Lalić dwells on the emotional and moral destruction left in the wake of war more than on the war itself, his entire opus could be named after the title of one of his novels, *Ratna sreća*, which means "war fortune." In the context of Lalic's work, the word *fortune* acquires a wide spectrum of connotative meanings: expected but unrealized happiness, false happiness, the temporary fortune of a victor, and, most often, the bitter-ironic antipode of happiness—war "un-fortune." From this thematic perspective, Lalić is perhaps the best Serbian depicter of war. In his works, the surviving warriors are defeated victors. The vast number of war victims and the failure to accomplish the ideals fought for and suffered for in war show that war conquers the victors as well as the vanquished and transforms them into unfortunate warriors. Nevertheless, Lalić continues the epic tradition of hero worship and the branding of traitors in the wars of liberation. In this respect he follows the poetics of the folk epic songs, but he gives subtler nuances and deeper motivations to the actions of the protagonists in the war dramas.

At the end of the war Lalić found himself on the victorious side. He belonged to the partisans, who were of the republican communist persuasion and whom the Allied antifascist coalition supported not only in the struggle against the German and Italian occupiers but, at the end of the war, in the civil war against the monarchists, the so-called *chetniks*. The partisans led a twofold war from 1941 to 1945: against the occupiers and against the monarchists. They were fighting for a revolutionary change of power. In most of his works Lalić depicts this inner, civil component of the war in Montenegro. In the process his visibly autobiographical narrator does not hide his sympathy for the partisans, whom he considers the liberators of the people from both the occupiers and the domestic "social exploiters." Only in the last phase of his creativity, especially in his last three books, did Lalić become critical of the "deviant" Communists, that is, as he says, "the monsters with the red card," who betrayed the author's youthful idealism and admiration for the morally exemplary fighters for the egalitarian utopia.

As soon as World War II ended, the thirty-year-old writer found employment in the cultural section of the newspaper *Pobjeda* (Victory) in Cetinje. There, with two local poets, he founded and edited a literary journal, *Stvaranje* (Creation), in which he published his stories and poems. In Cetinje he also started a family. At the end of 1946 Lalić moved to Belgrade and worked first as an editor, then as a reporter for the daily *Borba* (Struggle). His reportorial activity resulted in a travelogue, *Usput zapisano* (Written Down on the Road, 1952). In 1955 he tried to live as a freelance writer, but he soon became an editor in the publishing house of Nolit (New Literature), where he worked until his retirement in 1965.

In Belgrade he became more actively engaged in literary creativity. In Cetinje in 1948 he published his poems in *Staze slobode,* and in Belgrade he published a book of short stories, *Izvidnica* (Reconnaissance), the same year. Both books received awards—the poetry won the Republican Award, and the short stories won the Federal Award. *Staze slobode* consists of poems written before and during the war, but the majority were published here for the first time. As the critic Aleksandar Petrov interprets Lalić's first and only book of poetry:

> For the most part Lalić's poetry is in the spirit of Yugoslav interwar social poetry. Even in the intimate poems of predominantly personal, gloomy, and melancholic disposition the poet expresses sentiments awakened by the realization of human misery, hunger, misfortune, expiations. While in some poems the feelings of anxiety, helplessness and sorrow dominate, . . . in many others such feelings are expressions of the poet's rebellion, and so his poetry has the task to engage people in the struggle against social injustice. . . . Clearly, the esthetic value of these poems was not the poet's first concern.

Critics generally either glossed over Lalić's poetry or judged it of little value. The author understood this reaction as a signal that he should abandon poetry and dedicate himself to prose, which was lauded even in his first book. However, judging by the many excellent lyrical passages in his prose work—pictures of nature and imaginative dream sequences—it seems that Lalić prematurely lost his poetic confidence. Studying the mature phase of his fiction, critics may likely conclude that the best qualities of Lalić's narration are found in his narrative passages of great poetic beauty.

The first book of Lalić's short stories, with its symbolic title *Izvidnica* (Reconnaissance) was a reconnoitering trip into the art of short-story telling. Although much later, primarily in his novels, the writer reaches the refinement of epic narrative, Lalić even here exhibited the qualities of a superb storyteller. The critic Velibor Gligorić evaluated *Izvidnica* in the following words: "Lalić showed in *Izvidnica* already that he is a born storyteller. His narration overpowers with full-blooded vitality and with the plot development that is intense in its inner burning, with lively characterization, excellent language, and passionate empathy in events and characters."

Full recognition for Lalić was not achieved until 1950, with his novel *Svadba* (Wedding). The first reviewer of *Svadba,* the influential critic Milan Bogdanović, ranked the novel among "the few best novels our postwar literature has produced," emphasizing the depth of penetration into the nature of humanity and the narrative power to bear witness truthfully, through the pandemonium, to the outside world at war. Bogdanović observes that "When he encounters the dark spots and black holes in the characters on the good side, Lalić does not close his eyes and gloss over them." About Lalić's style Bogdanović says, "His is one of the most vigorous styles we have. In Lalić's style imagination knows of no respite; metaphor, that is, picture, affects you sometimes so boldly that it almost looks 'modernistic'.... That is why his style is modern in the real sense, a style of our times."

Svadba ushers in a cycle of novels (*Svadba, Zlo proljeće, Raskid,* and *Lelejska gora*) in which the author appears as a strong, competent witness to and participant in the wartime events about which he writes with an added autobiographical motivation. *Svadba,* a product of the celebratory climate of the victors, lights the dark horizons of a wartime prison that is described with the serenity acquired only at the time of writing. A talented immediacy, originality, and vitality—a poetic freshness beneath the "naive" composition form—break through in the still relatively uncultivated form. This early, neophyte novel takes its honorable place at the beginning of a series of novels that surpass *Svadba* in their artistic qualities.

After the youthful triumph of his first novel, Lalić published *Izabrane pripovijetke* (Selected Stories, 1950); a collection of short stories, *Prvi snijeg* (The First Snow, 1951); a travelogue, *Usput zapisano*; and several separate short stories. Thereafter, Lalić went for a year-long period of study in Paris (1953–1954). There he wrote the novel *Zlo proljeće,* in which, from the perspective of the wartime spring of 1941 and the capitulation of Yugoslavia to the German fascists, he depicts his unhappy childhood and the unfortunate war experiences of his people in the past. Two motifs are intertwined in the novel: the motif of a dead beloved and the motif of a homeland struck dead by the war.

From the aesthetic point of view, *Zlo proljeće* represents an important turn. From this novel on begins the "high school," so to speak, of the artistry of Lalić's novels. If *Svadba* manifested his talent, *Zlo proljeće* reveals a tamed disquiet and lyric melancholy. The rhetoric and the immediacy of the open scenery in *Svadba* are replaced by the subdued tones of the memory of a lost love and lost freedom. One gets the impression that *Svadba* was written by a warrior who had not yet laid down his weapons and uniform, and *Zlo proljeće* by an artist hurt by war. The fact that Lalić wrote *Zlo proljeće* in Paris has some connection with the sudden aesthetization of all the formal aspects of a novel. He does not embrace the notion of *l'art pour l'art* (art for art's sake) and the other fashionable empty methods of the contemporary French novel, but he extends his field of observation, cultivates his expression, and plans to perfection the relationship of the key structural units of the novel. In this novel Lalić demonstrates that the first-person narrative style is best suited for the narration with autobiographical admixtures; he introduces here the method of intertwining the temporal planes; and finally, the novelistic "career" of Lalić's most important character, Lado Tajović, begins with this novel. The critic Borislav Mihajlović, who had spent time with Lalić in Paris, was the first reader of *Zlo proljeće* and enthusiastically described the novel as:

> A rhetorical burst out of Lalić which I have anticipated as a possibility for a long time but which started flowing in a wide course only in this novel, unhindered, destined for a distant journey. The passionate language and its strength and poetry Lalić raised in places to a height seldom reached in our literature. There is something primeval, deep-rooted in his narration. It was Montenegro that spoke through with its wisdom of an age-old talented narrator in the scenes in which nothing is a spectacle, but everything is color and scent, and the word is resolute, right, and at the right time.

With a group of writers of related ideological and aesthetic orientation (including Velibor Gligorić, Branko Ćopić, Erih Koš, and Dušan Kostic), Lalić started in 1955 a literary magazine, *Savremenik* (Contemporary). It was the defensive gesture of a group of realists against the challenging, aggressive step of an opposing group of writers gathered around a modernist journal, *Delo* (Act). Although he participated passionately in the confrontations between the realists and the modernists, Lalić, through his strength as a talented and original writer and through his powerful creative energy and discipline, benefited from both groups. From the realists he inherited his solid moorings in the historically identifiable social reality as well as his striving to extend the powerful tradition of epic poetry, traced clearly by folk epic poetry and Njegoš, so as to remain a treasury of the spiritual values of the people, a select "historical memory" of the liberating and moral feats of the people. From the modernists he acquired a passion to master new expressive forms and techniques, as well as an aspiration to reach creative perfection and, especially, to widen his field of observation while depicting the inner depths of his characters. In *Zlo proljeće* Lalić already treats with equal care that which really

Dust jacket for Lalić's 1970 novel, Pramen tame

happens to his heroes and that which he dreams, imagines, or hallucinates about, and what he considers a sound or a demented mind. In Lalić traditional realism loses its bordering "shores" and becomes what Roger Garraudi calls "realism without shores"—"integral realism," for the integral picture of all spiritual and situational states of a modern person.

Between 1950 and 1960 Lalić published five novels, including, in addition to *Svadba* and *Zlo proljeće: Raskid, Lelejska gora,* and *Hajka.* The first versions of *Raskid* and *Lelejska gora* narrow the thematic field around the protagonists, concentrating on a much shorter time period and a narrower circle of problems concerning the protagonists so that they almost become the novels of personalities. From the external, large, and visible plans in the preceding novels, Lalić turns here to the observation of the inner life, to the artistic "filming" of the more complex psychological states of the protagonists. Both novels offer a psychological analysis of the reactions of solitary men surrounded by the enemy. It can be said that the heroes of these novels—Doselić in *Raskid and Lado Tajović* in *Lelejska gora*—are two branches of the same ideological and fighting trunk. The morally unbending branch (Doselić) breaks; the more flexible, morally adaptable one (Tajović) only bends under the blows of a storm that is as powerful as he is. Both novels represent two difficult choices for escaping the entangling war misfortunes of the isolated partisans. On a general plane two concepts of humanity's moving toward the revolutionary change of the world are offered along with two versions of moral behavior during that movement. Neither of these modernistically laid-out novels pleased the author in their first versions. *Raskid,* in which Lalić depicts the captivity of Niko Doselić and his return to the partisans, was not highly regarded by any critic. Lalić was personally sensitive to this still-fresh theme, especially because of the clear biographical connection between him and the protagonist of this novel. On the other hand, the change in literary method (toward the inner observation of the hero) could not help but reveal the tentativeness of its exploratory phase. These were, after all, works (including the first, unpublished version of *Hajka*) of Lalić's transient, reorienting creative phase.

The novel *Hajka* comes as a crown of that reorientation. It is the first of Lalić's novel written in two versions (which would later become almost his creative rule). In *Hajka* the tendency toward a psychological analysis of characters reaches maturity and completion. Here all the artistic lessons from his previous work are utilized in a fortunate union, making *Hajka* a significant turning point in Lalić's development. Structurally, *Hajka* is among the most complex of Lalić's novels. Here, in almost equal fashion, about twenty characters from four different camps are followed: a group of occupying officers organizes two groups of local police servants to chase several isolated partisans. Only a first-class artist could control such a disparate and broad narrative and subjugate it to the central plan and simultaneously avoid the limitations of a detective story. By avoiding creating a story that merely describes the changing scenery of a chase, and by saturating the plot with a plethora of participants and situations, but revealing the key points with a "moving camera" technique that shows minutely sensitive, emotional, most often premortal flickers, Lalić shows his mastery of a highly functional narrative method and a complex expressive technique. *Hajka* represents the most important step in Lalić's development as a novelist.

The novel, however, did not mark the end of the writer's creative growth. The second version of *Lelejska gora* (1962)—twice as large as the first—confirms that. The critics are almost unanimous: In *Lelejska gora* Lalić created not only his best novel but one of the best written in Serbian. For the second version he was awarded the prestigious Njegoš Award. After his great success with the revised versions of *Hajka* and *Lelejska gora*, Lalić fundamentally reworked *Raskid* in 1969 and then began a definitive stylistic revision of all his earlier significant works. In his short stories he even changed titles; with his novels he kept the original titles but changed chapter titles. There are few writers in world literature who have revised and perfected their works with such persistence and in such scope as Lalić. With every new "final" edition, he made emendations. So, for the latest edition of *Lelejska gora* (1990) Lalić reworked an entire chapter. To justify such interminable changes, Lalić said, "A published work represents only a tolerable form of imperfection."

As in *Zlo proljeće*, Lado Tajović is both the protagonist and the narrator in *Lelejska gora*. The classical motif of an isolated hero (who is a contemporary variant of Odysseus or Robinson Crusoe) is presented here. Tajović would rejoin the society with an impaired identity. The Leleja story ought to be read on at least two large planes: as a "novelistic history" of an isolated rebel in Montenegro during World War II and as a contemporary story about existential and ethical problems of a lone individual anywhere. The problem is how to live a solitary and lonely life. The partisan Tajović separates himself from his group in the mountain wilderness and is surrounded and chased by both the occupiers and the chetniks. *Lelejska gora* is envisaged as a novel of a threefold trial: existential, ideological, and moral. Tajović's resilience in the face of isolation, loss of freedom, and difficult living conditions is tested again and again. To survive as an individual, he perishes as a man. Tajović himself offers a diagnosis of the ultimate, corrosive effect of loneliness on his personality: "I am not a traitor ... but I am everything else: a liar, a thief, a womanizer. A murderer too ... only I don't want to be a traitor, that is taboo." He does not betray the ultimate ideas of the communist movement, but he betrays the morality of a fighter for a better world, for which the ideological saints will not forgive him.

Lelejska gora was written during the heyday of the philosophy of existentialism. Jean-Paul Sartre said, "Hell—that is in others." Tajović was raised in a collectivist spirit. Happiness, according to his ideological schooling, moved from a happy society to a happy individual, not the other way around. Individualism seemed to Lalić also as "a fatigue from morality, from the readiness for sacrifice, from belonging to a collective, from altruism." Can a lone man be enough of a man? Through Tajović's painful experience as an endangered individual, the author sees loneliness from a general, cosmic, and ontological plane. As Tajović says, "The mountain peaks have surrounded us.... I sense the essence of this planet that makes its way through emptiness, as a nag gone mad from loneliness." He is saying that loneliness is a universal evil. The general phenomenon of loneliness caught Tajović in the hell of Leleja wilderness. (*Lelejska gora* should be interpreted literally as "the wailing mountain.") To carry out the "social experiment," Lalić has banned Tajović to the Leleja Mountain, ergo, to hell. The Leleja is a damned area built on the principle of antihome, in which an individual cannot survive as a responsible and morally consistent being.

The name *Leleja* has several meanings. Leleja does not exist geographically, but it can be recognized by descriptions as a mountain complex near the author's home. On the first symbolic level *Lelejska gora* represents Montenegro—the small, isolated state that has bloodily resisted conquerors for centuries. At the time of writing the novel (1956-1957), it may represent also the isolated Yugoslavia that had separated from the Eastern socialist community but had not succeeded in joining the West. Finally, on the basis of the earlier quotation from Tajović that the planet has "gone mad from loneliness," *Lelejska gora* symbolizes planetary, universal loneliness and alienation. Therefore, the Leleja region is a metaphorical symbol for the apocalyptic destruction of a lonely man who is abandoned by God and has surrendered to the devil's will, in a small corner of Chaos and Hell, which in a microcosm becomes a reflection of cosmic destiny. Being lost in the roadlessness of the Leleja Mountain is a condition symbolic of planetary loneliness, a sign of ontological omission and perdition in a homeless universe. Through the second component of his lonely destiny, Tajović personifies the alienated split of the modern individual and the devilishness of his alienation, a manic person in collision with both the society and himself.

In this novel Lalić risked monotony in the use of monologues. He cleverly personifies Ta-

Mihailo Lalić

jović's doubts, anxieties, hallucinations, and craving for a partner and conversation in the form of a devil. The psychological situation not only allows but demands a fellow loner, even if invented. The devil is the product of Tajović's split soul, a bitter remedy against loneliness—his defense mechanism. The devil changes his forms, shapes, and roles: now he is Tajović's examiner, now his confessor, but always his critic, a correcting component of his disturbed consciousness. At the end Tajović identifies with the devil, becomes himself a devil, and behaves toward others like a devil. The devil is Tajović's negative double. However, the figure is also an excellent *poetic* device in the novel, one that illuminates the other side of reality, an active reverse side of a being, a shadow which, without being material, cna easily achieve anything it desires.

Lalić is a novelist who never ceased to be a poet. His fiction possesses three important features of poetry: a pronounced orderly form, a picturesque and symbolic speech, and an uncanny freedom of imagination. Because of a felicitous combination of orderliness and freedom, picturesqueness and inventiveness, *Lelejska gora* is an embodied poem in prose, one that employs the strengths of both forms—poem and novel.

The novel *Raskid* is the last juncture in the development of Lalić's novelistic art, its completing link, aesthetically. It was a long journey from the ideological straightforwardness of *Svadba,* the lyrical melancholy of *Zlo proljeće,* and the poetic complexity of *Hajka* and *Lelejska gora* to the complex simplicity of *Raskid.* In it the central accent moves thematically and temporally to the past, from the microanalysis of the emotional vibrations of individuals to the macroanalysis of the collective being of Montenegrins. The confrontation of two eras, begun in *Zlo proljeće*—the times of the narrator's youth and of the two world wars—makes possible a dialogue in the two "films" in slow motion, to ascertain the role of the past in the present and unravel the "rules" that governed the tragic events in the past and continue to govern them in the present. By choosing a neutral narrator, Lalić frees himself from a pronounced subjectivity and speaks with the calm, mature, somewhat ironic voice of a wise man who intertwines his memoirs from World War I with his diary notes from World War II. The narration is devoid of any ideological exclusivity (against which the author was not immune in his previous works) and free of the romantic view of the heroic past; it proceeds in a voice free of poetic ornamentation

Ratna sreća (1973) is the first and best volume in the tetralogy that also includes *Zatočnici* (Captives, 1976), *Dokle gora zazeleni* (Till the Mountain Turns Green, 1982), and *Gledajući dolje na drumove* (Looking Down at the Roads, 1983). Even though they do not match all the artistic qualities of *Ratna sreća,* the other volumes of the tetralogy were written in the critical, objective, and unassuming style of the first volume; together they aspire to be the novelized history of a half-century of war and of other tragedies in Montenegro.

Before *Ratna sreća* Lalić published a book of new short stories, *Posljednje brdo* (The Last Hill, 1967), and a novel about an antihero, *Pramen tame* (A Patch of Darkness, 1970). After the tetralogy Lalić published two novels, *Odlučan čovek* (A Resolute Man, 1990) and *Tamara* (1992), and two volumes of a diary, *Prelazni period* (A Transitional Period, 1988) and *Prutom po vodi* (Striking the Water With a Switch, 1992). He also prepared a collection of short stories, *Opraštanja nije bilo* (There Was No Forgiving, 1994), and a brief autobiographical work, *Epistolae seniles,* both published posthumously.

The last works by Lalić are written with

the stylistic maturity, the skeptical-ironic tone, and the objectivity of *Ratna sreća,* but the critical stance is drastically altered. In these novels and short stories (also, partially, in the diary prose), Lalić for the first time turns his critical cutting edge directly and sharply against the Communists. Contrary to his earlier works, he offers rigorous criticism of the revolution by choosing Communists as negative heroes. To be sure, Lalić does not undermine the utopian (and his own erstwhile humanitarian) foundations of the revolution, but he criticizes the actions of the "socialist" distorters and describes the damage done to the revolution by its immoral activists.

Lalić's basic aspiration as an artist was to bear witness truthfully and eloquently to the moral achievements and failures of a man in the most difficult war situations of this century, always with his eye on existential, ethical, anthropological, and universal implications. War dominates Lalić's prose. To qualify for Lalić's narration, a hero has to be on "the height of the tragic fall." Wars are the repetitive tragedy of history. History imposed itself on Lalić as "the teacher of tragic permanence." Those who understand the dark side of history meet it with greater strength when it recurs; this observation is a part of the poetics and the philosophy of Lalić. The objective critic, if he concentrates on aesthetic values and puts aside his, and the author's, ideological biases, will likely rank Lalić's best novels (especially his polysemous *Lelejska gora*) among the seminal artistic accomplishments of the contemporary era.

Interviews:

Nikola Drenovac, "Mihailo Lalić," *Pisci govore* (Belgrade: Grafos, 1965), pp. 271–280;

Rade Nikolić, "Poznanstva: Razgovor sa Mihailom Lalićem," *Stremljenja,* 4 (1963): 325–330.

Bibliographies:

Dobrilo Aranitović and Branko Popović, "Bibliografija," *Stvaranje,* no. 1 (1984): 109–172;

Popović, "Lalić, Mihailo," *Leksikon pisaca Jugoslavije,* volume 3 (Novi Sad: Matica srpska, 1987), pp. 576–584.

References:

Miloš I. Bandić, *Mihailo Lalić–povest o ljudskoj hrabrosti* (Titograd: Grafički zavod, 1965);

"Djelo Mihaila Lalića," *Stvaranje,* 3 (1975): 385–473 [17 articles];

R. Djukić, "Vizija revolucije u Lalićevom književnom delu," *Stremljenja,* 1 (1960): 253–261;

Radomir Ivanović, *Pisanje kao sudbina: Poetika Mihaila Lalića* (Priština: Jedinstvo, 1994);

Ivanović, *Romani Mihaila Lalića* (Belgrade: Narodna knjiga, 1974);

Dragan M. Jeremić, "Mihailo Lalić ili borba protiv animalizacije čoveka," *Savremenik,* 18 (1963): 501–518;

Kritičari o Mihailu Laliću (Belgrade: Nolit, 1984);

Mihailu Laliću u počast, edited by Čedo Vuković (Titograd: CANU, 1984) [29 articles and poems];

Božo Milačić, "U životu i snovima: O prozi Mihaila Lalića," *Izraz,* 1, no. 2 (1957): 103–116;

"O djelu Mihaila Lalića," *Glasnik CANU,* 13 (1995);

Ilija Pavićević, *Poetika vremena i prostora u Lalićevim romanima* (Nikšić: Univerzitetska riječ, 1987);

Aleksandar Petrov, "Mihailo Lalić," in *Mihailo Lalić* (Belgrade: Jugoslavija, 1967), pp. 5–37;

Popović, *Romansijerska umetnost Mihaila Lalića* (Belgrade: Vuk Karadžić, 1972);

Nikola R. Pribić, "Mihailo Lalić: A Modern Yugoslav Novelist," *Balkan Studies,* 10 (1969): 208–209;

Radojica Tautović, *Nesporazumi oko Mihaila Lalića* (Belgrade: Novela, 1984);

Pavle Zorić, "Tema hajke u književnom delu Mihaila Lalića," *Letopis Matice srpske,* 390 (1962): 160–170.

Papers:

Lalić's papers are held by his widow, Milena Lalić, and the executor of his legacy is Branko Popović.

Mateja Matevski
(13 March 1929 -)

Milne Holton
University of Maryland

BOOKS: *Doždovi* (Skopje: Kultura, 1956);
Ramnodenica (Skopje: Kultura, 1963);
Praznična romansa (Skopje: Misla, 1966);
Zalez (Skopje: Misla, 1969);
Perunika (Skopje: Kultura, 1976);
Krug (Skopje: Kultura, 1976);
Lipa (Skopje: Makedonska kniga, 1980);
Glas (Skopje: Misla, 1984);
Ragane na tragedijata (Skopje: Makedonska kniga, 1985);
Poezija (Skopje: Misla, 1986);
Bitovoto i istoriskoto vo makedonskata umetnička proza: materijali na naučniot sobir održan vo Skopje na 10 i 11 maj 1983 godina, by Matevski, Vasil Iljoski, and Slavko Janevski (Skopje: Makedonska akademija na naukite i umetnostite, 1986);
Drama i teatar: ogledi, kritiki i prikazi (Skopje: Misla, 1987);
Podgotovki za patuvanje (Skopje: Makedonska kniga, 1987);
Od tradicijata kon idninata: ogledi, kritiki i prikazi za literatura (Skopje: Misla, 1987);
20 godini Makedonska akademija na naukite i umetnostite: 1967-1987, by Matevski, Krum Tomovski, and Miloš Miloševski (Skopje: Makedonska akademija na naukite i umetnostite, 1988);
Kliment Ohridski i ulogata na Ohridskata kniževnata škola vo razvitokot na slovenskata prosveta, by Matevski, Blaže Koneski, and Dimče Kočo (Skopje: Makedonska akademija na naukite i umetnostite, 1989);
Slobodata i stremežot za sloboda vo makedonskata literatura: naučen sobir, by Matevski, Aleksandar Spasov, and Georgi Stardelov (Skopje: Makedonska akademija na naukite i umetnostite, 1990);
Oddalečuvanje (Skopje: Makedonska kniga, 1990);
Crna kula (Skopje: Makedonska kniga, 1992);
Maski (Skopje: Makedonska kniga, 1992);

Mateja Matevski

Zavevane (Skopje: Makedonska kniga, 1996).
Editions in English: Poems, translated by various translators in *Reading the Ashes: An Anthology of the Poetry of Modern Macedonia,* edited by Milne Holton and Graham W. Reid (Pittsburgh: University of Pittsburgh Press, 1977), pp. 57-67;
Poems, translated by Charles Simic and Vasa D. Mihailovich in *Contemporary Yugoslav Poetry,* edited by Mihailovich (Iowa City: University of Iowa Press, 1977), pp. 146-150;
Poems, translated by Louis Bourne in *Equivalences,* no. 14 (1987): 9-45;
Footprints of the Wind, translated by Ewald Osers (Boston & London: Forest Press, 1988).

Mateja Matevski is a central figure in the second generation of Macedonian poet-intellectuals who came to maturity with their nation in the 1950s and shaped the main directions of its contemporary literature. The founding generation of Macedonian poets who came before them–that of Blaže Koneski and Aco Šopov–had fought the battles for modernism beside their Serbian colleagues and against the Ždanovite Realists of the early Socialist days. Now a second generation, university poets educated after the war, brought a new complexity, an informed literacy, and a heightened symbolic complexity to that literature. Poets such as Radovan Pavlovski shaped Macedonian natural imagery to new surrealistic power; Gane Todorovski and Vlada Urošević brought contemporary and urban subjects into the poetry, but it would be Bogomil Gjuzel and especially Matevski who would bring that poetry to a new formal and referential awareness, a sense of form, and a consciousness in composition perhaps necessary to gain for it the high regard that it now enjoys in the world. Thus, Matevski and his colleagues did much to shape the directions and the impact of Macedonia's and Yugoslavia's modern literatures both in the years of Josip Broz Tito and in the difficult years of Macedonia's rebirth as an independent nation in the 1990s.

Matevski was born in Istanbul on 13 March 1929 into a Macedonian family that had recently immigrated to that city. Soon after his birth the family returned to western Macedonia, then a remote province of the Kingdom of the Serbs, Croatians, and Slovenes, formed after World War I and shortly to become the first Yugoslav state under a Serbian king. Matevski spent his childhood and the war years in the western Macedonian town of Gostivar. Then, after World War II, during which he joined in the Resistance, he studied Yugoslav literature at the University of Skopje, newly established in the new Yugoslavia under Tito. Excelling in his studies, he spent the year of 1962–1963 in Paris on a French government fellowship to study French theater, and it was then that he formed his first liaison with the French literary culture, which has remained important to him throughout his career.

Since his university years his working career has been varied. Matevski has taught in Macedonian schools, and he has served as an editor of various publications, including *Mlada literatura* (Young Literature) and *Razgledi* (Panorama). After 1963 he worked in radio and television, rising to the position of director general of radio and television in the 1970s. He also served as president of the Macedonian Committee for Foreign Cultural Relations and continued in that post into the years of Macedonian independence. Matevski is a professor of drama at the University of Skopje and a member of the Macedonian Academy of Arts and Sciences, an institution of which he has written a history and for which he served as secretary in the department of arts. A leader in the literary community of Skopje, Matevski is one of the founders of the International Poetry Evenings, an important international poetry festival held each summer in Struga on Lake Ohrid.

Matevski began writing poetry in 1950 and gained an international reputation early, with his poems appearing in France in an anthology of Macedonian poetry as early as 1959. He has also translated poetry from French (André Freneau), Spanish (Federico García Lorca and Pablo Neruda), Italian (Ivan Minatti), Russian (Aleksandr Pushkin), Serbo-Croatian, Slovenian, and Albanian. Matevski's own poetry has been translated into many languages. He has also written as a critic and literary historian. His criticism has been collected in *Bitovoto i istoriskoto vo makedonskata umetnička proza* (Tradition and History in Macedonian Literary Prose, 1986) and in *Drama i teatar* (Drama and Theater, 1987). His contribution to *Slobodata i stremežot za sloboda vo sovremenata makedonska literatura* (Freedom and the Aspiration for Freedom in Contemporary Macedonian Literature, 1990) and his study of medieval Slavonic literature in *Kliment Ohdridski i ulogata na Ohridskata kniževnata škola vo razvitokot na slovenskata prosveta* (Kliment of Ohrid and the Role of the Ohrid Literary School in the Development of Slavic Literacy, 1989) are two significant examples.

Over the years Matevski has been the recipient of various literary awards, including the Special Prize for Mediterranean Literature in Palermo, the Blaise Cendrars Prize in France, and the Prize of the International Poetry Meetings in Yverndon, Switzerland. He is also the recipient of the French Legion d'Honneur. Matevski lives in Skopje, where he continues to be active in Macedonian cultural life.

His first collection of poems, *Doždovi* (Rains), appeared in Skopje in 1956. The earliest poems appear at first reading deceptively simple. Apparently generated from the impulse toward natural realism so prevalent in Balkan poetry, a

Dust jacket for Lipa, Matevski's 1980 collection of poems

poem such as "Zvona" (Bells) seems at first to bear only representational intent.

Ringing somewhere, somewhere far,
The sounds are wind waves
In the fugitive grass.

Ringing somewhere: sharp, steady, soft;
All else is deaf; only the beat
Bounds on the wrought rim.

But then the poem turns its attention to subjective experience and presents not the sound of the bells itself but the poet's emotion provoked by that sound, imbuing the poem with a certain symbolist character:

Ringing somewhere, hurl me in air;
Fly through the rung cage,
Deafly and helplessly.

Ringing somewhere: like a child I ring, sing,
Everything's locked, I sound spellbound,
Hang on the sound.

This symbolic resonance moves the poem to more-profound considerations of experience—to the nature of memory and of time before it returns the reader or listener to the security of present reality itself:

Ringing somewhere, strike me, brave, tamed,
Time strike my memory,
Rude and so greedy.

Ringing somewhere: long hence but now,
Everything aches. Sky, let me down
With the grass. I know sound.

—translation by Milne Holton and Graham W. Reid (in *Reading the Ashes: An Anthology of the Poetry of Modern Macedonia*, 1977)

Other early poems more clearly present Matevski's memories of his western Macedonian youth in the Gostivar region. "Topola" (The Poplar), also from *Doždovi*, takes an element from a typical Macedonian landscape, but again the argument leads the poem well beyond its apparent Balkan realism to considerations about isolation and relationship that are infinitely more profound and that seem rather like the works of Rainer Maria Rilke in their exploitation of image:

Green fountain-jet balanced in silence
sadly erect and peacefully upright

Children crumble
the nests of sounds
and yet it's so hopelessly alone

Lean, support yourself, you innocent
on the wind's shoulder
Don't bend, rise up for one brief glance
across that uneven
tall
waving meadow of houses

Then awake the gorge
from its red grasses:
they remember the soil
that gave you birth[.]

—translation by Ewald Osers (in *Footprints of the Wind*, 1988)

The title sequence of Matevski's first collection of poems, *Doždovi,* is dominated by sharply sensory images, especially sound images (sound images are a hallmark of Matevski's poetry). But here this imagery is employed in a devolving metaphor that in its opening to meaning takes one deeper into the mind of the poet. Here the metaphoric association of the sound of rain with that of hoofbeats determines the structure of the first poem of the sequence, an anticipatory section titled "Strav" (Fear):

> Now come the sluggish, come the exhausted horses of space
> the far and foreboding murmur of the forgotten tongue
> Clip-clopping unceasingly, alone before the closed windows,
> muffled clip-clopping, blunted legs without horseshoes,
> on you, earth, slippery, loamy, calm earth[.]

Once again the direction of the poem is toward speculation, a speculation on origins.

> Where, O where,
> you compact dough of rain and earth?
> O man, me,
> stone in the hands, and in the eyes, mud.

After a second section titled "Pesna" (Song), which opens the metaphor to a second association, that of the rain/hoofbeats to the uncontrollable impulse of the imagination, the poem closes imaginatively upon the image of the hoofbeat itself, repeating Matevski's opening line of "Fear" to open the final section, "Konji" (Horses), and to generate a remarkable closure for the sequence:

> Now come the sluggish, come the exhausted horses of space
> (pale rains, pathless and mute)
> before the palms of my hands on the window.
>
> Feed, I say, feed yourselves, horses! sweating
> and wet from the warm vapor filtering
> from the loins of the night.
>
> Playfully whinny, make me cry out for joy,
> spring, bird with forgotten wings,
> goat-leg dancer, tired and exhausted mare,
> through my window spring
> together and back again
> and ever without ceasing
> under the shadowy brightness of space.
>
> —translation by Bogomil Gjuzel and Howard Erskine-Hill (in *Reading the Ashes*, 1977)

The imagistic vigor of the poem is not atypical of the poetry that was being written in Macedonia in the 1960s and early 1970s—one thinks of poets such as Radovan Pavlovski and perhaps Bogomil Gjuzel. But Matevski's care in construction, his intellectual and structural control of metaphor, which will be seen again in later sequences like *Lipa* (The Lime Tree, 1980), is perhaps unique, something unusual for a poetry written in a newly formed literary language. There was little question that poetry of this order in a first collection promised much for Macedonian poetry, now hardly in its second generation as a viable presence in European literature.

Yet Matevski's second collection, more abstractly titled *Ramnodenica* (Equinox, 1963)—the opposition of light and darkness implied in its title established a theme for the collection—showed significant sophistication and maturity even beyond the first. Here the poems were generated less out of the traditional rural realism that had become conventional, almost obligatory among the Macedonian poets of the 1950s and 1960s. Matevski showed early a boldness to risk independence from such popularistic conceits.

In the title poem of the collection, a part of which follows, the reader is asked to share, not a recognition of rural experience with the poet but a meditative recognition, a moment of synthetic awareness, a pure act of the mind, which is generated out of the absence of sensory provocation. Indeed, the silence that provokes the poem is resolved in a metaphor of light that invokes imaginatively a world not of rural Macedonia but of an étude of Aleksandr Scriabin:

> This is an hour of calm, a quiet hour
> an idyll of days and nights like a folding of hands
> The sky soft on the stretched body of the plain
> Now is the hour when nothing happens
> as if the world didn't breathe as if the rain didn't pour
> a dream enclosed in the dark of a hazelnut
> a stone forgotten under the body of a hill
> Now is the instant when wheat is harvested
> when the chimney does not smoke nor the road resound
> Man lies beneath the body of the sun
> distilled into nothing by its shadows
> This is the total moment: the balance of black and white[.]
>
> —translation by Carolyn Kizer and Reid (in *Reading the Ashes*, 1977)

In the late 1960s and during the 1970s Matevski established his reputation as a major Macedonian poet. *Praznična romansa* (Holiday Song) appeared in 1966, his first collection in a recognized series, and *Zalez* (Sunset) in 1969. *Perunika* (Iris) and *Krug* (Circle) appeared in 1976, and it was in the same period that Matevski's poems were being translated, first in Italian (*Nebbie e tramonti*, 1969), then in Serbian (*Pesni-Pesme*, 1974), Slovene (*Poezija*, 1975), and Albanian (*Balade për kohën*, Ballad of Time, 1976).

From its beginning Matevski's poetry engaged major subjects. What he came to refer to as "the trap of time," one's inevitable engagement in the continuity of experience, became a recurrent theme. The theme manifests itself in poems specific to particular seasons of the year, poems often arranged in seasonal patterns in the early volumes. One such poem is "Balada za vremeto" (Ballad of Time), employed as the title poem in the Albanian language collection of Matevski's poetry. This reflective autumn poem proceeds from a theme of entry into continuity, here the "ballad" of time, because the poem is again a poem of sound. But it is the refrain of retrospection that establishes the poem's final balance:

> I listen to time dying
> Beside the falling leaves
> and the frost nipping at hands
> how far did I get
>
> Time dies in all that is born
> and there is always less and less of me
> even if by a step
>
> Autumn is rich in dreams
> if sometimes sad
> in the receding waters
> there is no sailing
>
> The rich November fogs
> what do the rivers nurse them with
> In their shallow waters
> how far shall I get
>
> I listen to time dying
>
> From autumn in the cold
> one fruit is left
> that asks with blue lips
> where shall I get to[.]

—translation by Kizer and Reid (in *Reading the Ashes,* 1977)

Matevski's poetry darkened in the 1970s and 1980s and frequently began to assume an autobiographical and even narrative form. It was in 1980 that a distinguished collection, *Lipa,* appeared. The title sequence of poems in that collection, a memorial poem, can be offered as an example. Again the sequence consists of three poems and is structured very much like the earlier "Rains."

The sequence describes the cutting down of a tree that the speaker had known since childhood; it presents the event in three parts: the decision to destroy life, the act of the destruction of the tree, and the recognition of the consequences of that act. It opens flatly:

> When I decided to cut it down
> while I was still deciding
> my forehead was bedewed with hailstones
> my heart beat in my throat
> for parting wasn't easy
> feeling my contemporary the one I grew up with
> whom I watched from a tender shoot to a full-grown trunk[.]

The reader is provoked by Matevski's symbolic intentions: is the poem really meant to be political–as early as 1980–or is the discourse of wider and less provocative reference? But, as in the poetry of his Serbian contemporary, Vasko Popa (who was writing similar, if somewhat less provocative, poetry at the time), Matevski's poem does not betray its political implication. Rather it pursues an entirely personal course.

The middle section describes subjectively the act of violent destruction itself ("the branches began to drop off and the leaves to fall / and the sap was mingling with tears and sweat"), and the third section moves to consequences–the broadened and deepened vision, the intensified awareness of the destructive speaker, but also a surrealistic and yet curiously intimate sense both of alienation and of companionship with his victim:

> I'm lying in the grass gazing at summer clouds
> to where my glances used to run up through the lime-tree's
>   shade . . .
> All is quiet and calm while we two are lying
> two trunks cut down two objects in pain two dried up springs
> not visited by birds nor cradled by song
> Because in cutting down the tree I cut myself in half
> turning my body my hand into a corpse
> no longer stumbling down the road of smoke
> And on the grass's edge I'm watched by the reproach of veins
> with a linden fragrance
> about the house and summer[.]

—translation by Osers (in *Footprints of the Wind,* 1977)

A poem like this lends Matevski's poetry the richest levels of meaning.

Perhaps Matevski's most important later collection is *Ragane na tragedijata* (The Birth of Tragedy, 1985), which was translated into French as *Naissance de la tragedie* and published by Editions St. Germain des Pres in 1986. The volume gives evidence of many directions, one of which is manifest in simplified, hardened, rather more suggestively political poems after the manner of Popa and his English disciple, Ted Hughes, the best example being a poem called "Nož" (Knife). Another is found in several travel poems: "Kalendarot na Aztekite" (Aztec Calendar) and "Montesuma" (Montezuma), or a set of poems under the subtitle of "Švedska zima" (Swedish Winter), or another set subtitled "Noć nad Njujork" (Night in New York), all of which reflect Matevski's experiences on official trips abroad during the late 1970s and 1980s. But perhaps the most important direction is found in the collection's opening section, a set of classically oriented poems of the genre of much of the important South Slavic poetry of the 1970s and 1980s, the mythic and classically oriented works of poets as diverse as Miodrag Pavlović, Jovan Hristić, and Ivan V. Lalić of Belgrade and Veno Taufer of Ljubljana.

One of these poems from the opening section of *Ragane na tragedijata* is a somewhat retrospective and valedictory poem committed to a mythic analogy that has been exploited not only by Taufer and Hristić but by poets as early as Alfred Tennyson, but Matevski's poem is uniquely developed; apparently it has remained special to him. Matevski's poems here are self-referential; two "thematic" poems, "Kod temata za Ikar" (On the Theme of Ikarus) and "Kod temata za Orfei" (On the Theme of Orpheus) had earlier appeared in *Zalez* and had provoked a no less impressive four-part poem titled "Barajki bregot"("Seeking the Shore").

Here the first poem, "Kod temata za Ulis" (On the Theme of Ulysses), which seems at first reading a rather conventional, perhaps even a Browningesque dramatic monologue, is a distinguished example of its genre. It opens in a moment of return:

> To return from far away
> after created after perfected horror
> as if from outer space
> from orbiting through darkness
>   through emptiness
>   . . .
> into another that awaits you
> like love[.]

From that image of spatial emptiness a remarkable metaphor is devolved:

> The sea no longer obediently roars
> under your oar
> but sea-monsters and sharp rocks on the shore
> still lie in wait
> Only the surf of unextinguished hope of youth
> whips up our blood
> sets the course of stars

Mateja Matevski

> And you move you move but with one roar in your mind
> discovering yourself in space
> having lost your way in your own sea of dreams
> as in a wood
> while a sweet shudder of the unknown
> runs over the sea's skin[.]

Again, this remarkably sounded poem closes, first upon the act of singing, and finally, as in "Equinox," upon the image of light:

> Your mind which knows that to travel
> is better than to arrive
> unlocks the word's closed cages
> and a song is born
> And when after so many oars and voices drowned
> in the treacherous waters
> the dawn settles on your face
> with white hand drawing the long-sought space
> upon your forehead
> know then that it is time[.]

—translation by Osers (in *Footprints of the Wind*, 1988)

Matevski's poetry, as such examples show, has earned a considerable presence in South Slavic, and even in European poetry. His sense of poetic order and control, his keen perception, his deep feeling, his clear comprehension, and his craftsmanship serve as standards for his contemporaries and successors in Macedonia and abroad. But what is perhaps more important to his country's literature, Matevski's poetry gives evidence of the fact that its creator is one upon whom, as Henry James once said, nothing is lost.

References:

Kiril Bujukliev, "Zborot vo presret na mugrata," *Razgledi,* nos. 1-2 (1982): 95-99;

Mirella Colarieti, "A colloquio con Mateja Matevski: Poeta della natura che parla all'uomo: Riflessioni sulla giovane letteratura macedone," *Balcanica: Annuaire de lumetnička Institut des Etudes Balkaniques,* 4, nos. 3-4 (December 1985): 55-67;

Branko Cvetkovski, "Simbiozata na vizuelnoto i auditivnoto: Niz primeri od poezijata na Mateja Matevski," *Razgledi,* no. 6 (1984): 606-615;

Ion Deaconescu, "The Phonotext of Troubled Waters or the World's Loose Ground," *Macedonian Review,* 15, no. 3 (1985): 316-327;

Ljupčo Dimitrovski, "Vo semantičkoto jadro na *Lipa* od Mateja Matevski–obid za tolkuvanje," *Razgledi,* no. 6 (1982): 498-512;

Milan Djurčinov, "A Poet of the Modern World," *Macedonian Review,* 2 (1972): 223-229;

Miodrag Drugovac, "Mateja Matevski," in his *Contemporary Macedonian Writers* (Skopje: Macedonian Review, 1976), pp. 117-128;

Blaže Kitanov, *Od pejzažot kon čovekot niz poetskiot svet i izraz na Mateja Matevski* (Skopje: Makedonska kniga, 1987);

Eftim Kletnikov, "Ponorot na tradičnoto čuvstvuvanje na vremeto," *Razgledi,* nos. 1-2 (1986): 79-85.

Marijan Matković
(21 September 1915 - 31 July 1985)

Ellen Elias-Bursać
Harvard University

BOOKS: *Iz mraka u svjetlo* (Zagreb: Privately printed, 1936);
Dramaturški eseji (Zagreb: Matica hrvatska, 1949);
Dvije dramske epizode (Zagreb: Glas Rada, 1949);
Dva eseja iz hrvatske dramaturgije (Zagreb: Zora, 1950);
Pieter Bruegel (Zagreb: Zora, 1950);
Koraci: dramska epizoda (Belgrade: Novo pokolenje, 1951);
Prometej (Zagreb: Glas Rada, 1952);
Na kraju puta (Zagreb: RAD JAZU #301, 1954); *Pozorišni život,* 1 (1955); *Na kraj na patot* (Skopje: Kočo Racin, 1956);
Igra oko smrti (Zagreb: Zora, 1955);
Antologija hrvatske drame od Marina Držića do Miroslava Krleže, 2 volumes (Belgrade: Nolit, 1958);
Vašar snova (Novi Sad: Sterijino pozorje, 1959);
I bogovi pate (Zagreb: Zora, 1962);
Američki triptih (Zagreb: Mladost, 1974);
Marijan Matković: Drame, eseji, Californija-Zephyr (Pet stoljeća Hrvatske književnosti, Zagreb: Zora & Matica Hrvatska, 1976);
Ikari bez krila (Zagreb: Nakladni zavod MH, 1977);
Ogledi i ogledala (Zagreb: Mladost, 1977);
Miroslav Krleža (Paris: UNESCO, 1977);
Razgovori i pogovori: o pjesnicima, slikarima i odlascima (Zagreb: Znanje, 1985).
Editions in English: "Hercules" (excerpt), translated by Frank Lambasa, *Most/The Bridge,* 3-4 (1979): 146-155.

PLAY PRODUCTIONS: "Slučaj maturanta Wagnera," Zagreb, Hrvatsko narodno kazalište, 2 December 1935;
"Na kraju puta," Osijek, Hrvatsko narodno kazalište, 28 November 1954;
"Vašar snova," Zagreb, Zagrebačko dramsko kazalište, 28 January 1958;
"Heraklo," Zagreb, Hrvatsko narodno kazalište, 1 February 1958;

"Prometej," Rijeka, Narodno kazalište "Ivan Zajc," 31 January 1959;
"Karmine" and "Krizantem," performed with the shared title "Zatvoreni krug," Zadar, Narodno kazalište, 27 September 1959;
"Ahilova baština," Zagreb, Hrvatsko narodno kazalište, 15 February 1961;
"Ranjena ptica," Zagreb, Hrvatsko narodno ka-

zalište, 23 January 1966;

"Snjegović," Zagreb, Hrvatsko narodno kazalište, 6 March 1967;

"Tigar," Zagreb, Zagrebačko dramsko kazalište, 17 October 1969;

"General i njegov lakrdijaš," Zagreb, Hrvatsko narodno kazalište, 14 February 1970;

"Klitemnestra," Karlovac, Dramski studio Karlovac, 7 October 1974.

SELECTED PERIODICAL PUBLICATIONS–UNCOLLECTED: "General i njegov lakrdijaš," *Forum*, 9–10 (1969): 537–605;

"Trojom uklete: Helena, Andromaha, Klitemnestra," *Forum*, 1–3 (1972): 969–1005;

"Stope na stazi," *Forum*, 1–3 (1982): 500–544; 4–6 (1982): 1021–1067; 7–9 (1982): 525–578; 10–12 (1982): 1028–1093; 10–12 (1983): 913–959;

"Izmetu neba i zemlje," *Forum*, 12 (1985): 102–105;

"Osječko predavanje," *Forum*, 5–6 (1986): 521–539.

Marijan Matković was one of the most prolific playwrights in twentieth-century Croatian literature. A member of the generation that followed Miroslav Krleža, he served as a bridge between Krleža's vision of theater and modern, more exploratory dramatic forms. Matković is best known for his plays (he wrote more than twenty), but he also wrote essays on many subjects, including theater, poetry, painting, and travel. He was also a crucial figure in the functioning of several key cultural institutions, particularly the Yugoslav Academy of Arts and Sciences.

Matković was born in Karlovac on 21 September 1915, but he spent his childhood in Zagreb, where he earned his degree in law at Zagreb University in 1941. As a student he traveled widely throughout Europe, studying art history and literature in Vienna and Paris; he later felt that this period of travel and study constituted his true education. During the years immediately after World War II he held several prominent positions in major cultural institutions: he was head of the culture and art department of Radio Zagreb from 1945 to 1946, literary secretary for the publishing house of Nakladni zavod Hrvatske (1946–1949), and director of the Croatian National Theater (1949–1953). He was one of the cofounders of the Dubrovnik Summer Festival in 1950 and director of its drama program from 1970 to 1974. He was artistic director of Zagreb Film from 1959 to 1964.

At the age of thirty Matković was elected to the Yugoslav Academy of Arts and Sciences and served for many years as secretary of the Academy Section for Contemporary Literature (1954–1978). From 1974 to his death in 1985 he was director of the Academy Institute for Literature and Theater; he edited nineteen volumes of academy publications dedicated to contemporary literature, an anthology of Croatian drama in 1958, and two volumes of essays on Miroslav Krleža (one in 1963, the other in 1973). He was editor in chief of the journal *Forum*, a publication of the academy, in 1962 and 1963, and then for twenty more years, from 1966 to 1985. When he died in 1985, he was survived by his widow, son, and grandson.

Matković's appreciation for complexity gave him the qualities he needed both for excellent playwriting and for his dextrous steering of Croatian cultural institutions through difficult times. His plays, particularly the first cycle, *Igra oko smrti* (Dance around Death, 1955), show the strong influence of Krleža and August Strindberg. Matković was a progressive playwright who was sympathetic to socialism. His first writing for the theater was the work of a rebel; a stubborn, questioning streak persists throughout his life. Despite whatever political difficulties they might be facing, writers in disfavor with the authorities recall Matković as someone willing to publish their work in *Forum*.

Matković started writing for the theater as a student at a gymnasium, or college preparatory school, in the spring of 1934. When he was nineteen he submitted his first play anonymously to the director of the Croatian National Theater. The three-act play, "Slučaj maturanta Wagnera" (The Case of Matriculator Wagner, 1935), follows the predicament of Emil Wagner, who, about to graduate from the gymnasium, is told to leave his school because of his unexcused absences and his insolence to his teachers. He is a rebellious young man, incensed by his repressive upbringing, drawn to communist ideals, but unable to stand up to his family and strike out on his own. He and his friend Rikard debate the plight of young people trapped in their ambitious families; Rikard tries to convince Emil to make a clean breast of the situation to his parents. Emil, however, cannot bring himself to do so, and the play ends when his parents are informed by the police that Emil has thrown himself off a bridge into the Sava River.

"Slučaj maturanta Wagnera" was performed in 1935 amid raging controversy. Demonstrations were held on opening night by progressive gymnasium students who supported the play, but reactionary forces in Croatia banned it from the stage after only four performances. Matković's reputation was so damaged by the scandal that, shortly thereafter, when he submitted to the theater two more plays ("Bučarovi slave," The Bučars Celebrate, and "Prije katastrofe," Before the Catastrophe), they were rejected; nothing remains of them but their titles. Despite the ban on performing "Slučaj maturanta Wagnera" in Zagreb, it was performed by amateurs in Karlovac and Sušak in the following years. In October 1937 "Slučaj maturanta Wagnera" was translated into Czech by B. Mavlikova and performed in Prague. Matković submitted two more plays to the Croatian National Theater in the late 1930s: "Karmine" (The Wake) in 1938 and "Njegova žrtva" (His Victim) that same year, but again his plays were rejected. He did, however, publish a book of verse, *Iz mraka u svjetlo* (From Darkness into Light, 1936), which the author has described as "narrative rhetoric."

Matković's first plays comprise the cycle *Igra oko smrti*, published in 1955. It includes two long plays and eight short plays: "Slučaj maturanta Wagnera," "Karmine," "Rub zbilje" (The Edge of Reality), "Smrt njegove ekselencije" (The Death of His Excellency), "Smrt u kući" (Death in the House), "Bezimena" (Nameless), "Krizantem" (Chrysanthemum), "Koraci" (Steps), "Trojica" (The Trio), and "Na kraju puta" (At the End of the Road), all revolving around the same cast of characters, members of Zagreb's bourgeoisie. The plays follow the characters from their teenage years in "Slučaj maturanta Wagnera" to the parts they play in the Independent State of Croatia in World War II in the final play of the cycle, "Na kraju puta" (1954). While "Slučaj maturanta Wagnera" is Matković's favorite, "Na kraju puta" is the most acclaimed of Matković's plays. It premiered in Croatia, in Zagreb and Osijek, and in Serbia and Slovenia in the same year, 1954. In the following years it was performed in Split and Rijeka in Croatia, in Bitola and Štip in Macedonia, and in Sombor in Serbia.

The play describes, through flashbacks, the roles of its protagonists (several of whom first appear in "Slučaj maturanta Wagnera"), in World War II; the play's dramatic tension arises from the question of what precisely was their relationship to the partisans and the fascists, a relationship that unfolds in considerable subtlety in

Scene from a 1958 production of Matković's Heraklo

the course of the play. The portrayal of entwined political alliances and personal loyalties is given far more complex and intriguing treatment than such subjects were generally accorded in the immediate postwar period.

Matković's second cycle of plays was based on classical myth. The trilogy *I bogovi pate* (The Gods, Too, Suffer, 1962) includes "Heraklo" (Hercules, 1958), "Prometej" (Prometheus, 1959), and "Ahilova baština" (Achilles' Legacy, 1961). The boldest and most popular of the three was "Heraklo," which depicts Hercules as a cantankerous, rheumatic old man obsessed with proving to the world that he is not the titanic warrior of the myth, the great figure embodied in a statue of him, which he keeps trying to have destroyed. No one, however, not even his wife, seems prepared to accept his reality, and each of the actions he takes to prove his point is distorted by the poets, who, blind and therefore dependent on the interpretations of others, rework each event to sustain the Hercules myth. The play was first performed in Zagreb in 1958 and later staged in Belgrade, Split, Poland, Czechoslovakia, and West Germany. It has been translated into English by Frank Lambasa; it has also been translated into French, German, Italian, Polish, Hungarian, and Greek.

Matković wrote one more play based on classical mythology: "Trojom uklete" (Accursed by Troy, 1972), which includes three one-act sections: "Helena" (Helen), "Andromaha" (Andromache), and "Klitemnestra" (Clytemnestra).

He is best known for the plays based on myths and for his first cycle, *Igra oko smrti*. He did, however, write seven plays on contemporary themes: "Vašar snova" (Market of Dreams, 1958), "Ranjena ptica" (Wounded Bird, 1966), "Snjegović" (Snowman, 1967), "Premijera (Opening Night, 1967), "Na palubi" (On Deck, 1969), "Tigar" (Tiger, 1969), and "Jationov san" (Jation's Dream, 1973), which appeared in the volume *Ikari bez krila* (Icaruses without Wings, 1977). Several of his other plays have been published only in periodicals. Beyond the Strindberg/Krležian structure of his earliest plays, he explores other theatrical models, and several of his plays show the influences of Jean-Paul Sartre, Albert Camus, George Bernard Shaw, and Jean Giraudoux.

The most controversial of Matković's plays is "General i njegov lakrdijaš" (The General and His Fool, 1969), the only play he based explicitly on Croatian national mythology. It takes place in the sixteenth century. An actor from Dubrovnik, Miha, speaking a jumble of phrases and jargon from Renaissance Dubrovnik literature, saves the life of a military commander, Gašo Alapić, during the siege of Siget, when Nikola Zrinski, the legendary Croatian hero, is killed. Miha hopes to use Alapić's military skills to free Dubrovnik from the stranglehold of its aristocracy. Alapić, however, devotes himself instead to defending the aristocracy and suppressing the peasant rebellion led by Matija Gubec in Zagreb and Zagorje, championing the very interests that Miha had hoped to subvert. In a compelling scene Zrinski, the hero of Croatian history, orchestrates the end of the siege and also his imminent demise. In a detailed treaty with the Turks, he includes the provision that, in return for his head on a stake, his scribe will survive the siege to record to Zrinski's satisfaction his place in history.

Of the reception of this play Matković commented, in "Osječko predavanje" (The Osijek Lecture, 1986): "Writing about myth, its ironization, no matter how mild, is not without danger as I realized about ten years ago when the play 'General i njegov lakrdijaš' opened. Every contemporary myth has its fanaticized believers, who without any sense of irony, cannot forgive the undedicated if he trespasses on their reserve of unshaken dedication." If anything, intolerance for a playful ironic approach to the sacrosanct mythical figures of Croatian history has grown in the years since Croatia seceded from Yugoslavia, and it has burdened the reception of Matković's plays, particularly "General i njegov lakrdijaš."

In 1982 and 1983 Matković published a series of excerpts from his diaries, "Stope na stazi" (Footsteps on the Path), starting with entries from 1980 when Josip Broz Tito died and not long after when Krleža, Matković's most important model in literature, died. The entries on Krleža's death are interesting for Matković's descriptions of the controversies that then erupted over Krleža's critical writing. An unfinished play Matković was writing for the Croatian National Theater, "Izmedu neba i zemlje" (Between Heaven and Earth, 1985), was published immediately after Matković's death. It appeared in *Forum*, along with "Osječko predavanje" (1986), the transcript from a lecture Matković gave in Osijek on 19 March 1980. In an informal exchange of questions Matković comments on his work, saying about his own rebellious nature:

> "Slučaj maturanta Wagnera" and all my early, lost plays were written in that fever, a protest against that world in which I found myself, against my will. An expression of crisis and my lack of compass in the world, in the society I was born to. To this day I still feel a certain lack of compass, I am still better at asking questions than giving answers, but back then, long ago—this was much more severe, more acute, more grotesque.

Of his mission as a writer, he noted:

> I did not choose this world, none of those of us who walk upon it did, it was imposed upon us. We found ourselves here against our will like the blades of grass in a meadow who would certainly, if asked, prefer another death to being mown by a scythe.... But I love the fact that this world has allowed me to fight for freedom. Alone and with those who share my views. A freedom which I will never completely realize, but that matters less. Freedom, after all, is only a possibility. I would like my writing to be understood and accepted precisely that way: as the documents of a man who strode and stumbled, fell and got back up, but prevailed on a path on which he created freedom amid a pervasive lack of freedom.

As an intellectual committed throughout his life to progressive politics, Matković had to defend himself against detractors who suggested that he was able to publish his plays and hold his jobs only because he complied with the Yugoslav socialist regime. His only defense against these claims is the quality inherent in all that he wrote and did—in his complex, critical plays; his thoughtful, thorough essays and studies; and his insightful guidance as an editor. Matković took the models Krleža provided in his cycle about the Glembaj family and explored further ways to portray society on the stage. Later playwrights were more radical than Matković in their theatrical experimentation, but they would have found it harder to experiment had they not had the solid foundation that Matković had built in Croatian dramatic literature.

Interviews:
Vlatko Pavletić, "Respekt pred neispisanim papirom," *Pozorišni život,* 10 (1959);
Petar Šegedin, "Razgovor povodom izvodjenja drame 'General i njegov lakrdijaš' u Hrvatskom narodnom kazalištu," *Kritika,* 11 (1970).

Bibliographies:
Branko Hećimović, "Bibliografija," *Marijan Matković: Drame, eseji, California-Zephyr,* 'Pet stoljeća Hrvatske književnosti' (Zagreb: Matica hrvatska & Zora, 1976), pp. 29-32;
Kronika (Zagreb: Zavod za književnost i teatrologiju JAZU, no. 31, 1985).

References:
Darko Gašparović, "Od Matkovićeva 'Herakla' Heretika," in his *Artaudova vizija kazališta* (Zagreb: Centar za kulturu Narodnog sveučilišta grada, 1974);
Branko Hećimović, "Marijan Matković," in *Marijan Matković: Drame, eseji, California-Zephyr* 'Pet stoljeća Hrvatske književnosti' (Zagreb: Matica hrvatska & Zora, 1976), pp. 7-32;
Hećimović, "Napomena za drugo izdanje" and "Bilješka o piscu," in Matković's *Igra oko smrti* (Zagreb: Globus, 1986), pp. 409-414;
Hećimović, "Sudionik vremena," in Matković's *Razgovori i pogovori* (Zagreb: Znanje, 1985), pp. 5-7;
Slavko Leovac, "Dramatičar Marijan Matković," *Izraz,* 3 (1959);
Ljubomir Maraković, "Dramska kronika ("Slučaj maturanta Wagnera")," *Hrvatska straža* (11 January 1936);
Vlado Matarević, "Heraklo na vašaru snova ili Iluzije i mit anti-heroizma," *Izraz,* 5 (1958);
Vlado Obad, "Matkovićev *General i njegov lakrdijaš* u kontekstu evropske drame," in *Krležini dani u Osijeku* (Osijek & Zagreb: HNK, Pedagoški fakultet-HAZU, 1993);
Obad, "Ratanje 'Herakla' Marijana Matkovića," *Znak,* 2-3 (1972);
Vojmil Rabadan, "Dva Sigeta i jedna istina," *Kritika,* 14 (1970): 720-726;
Darko Suvin, "Heraklijada ili Mit za čovjeka," in his *Dva vida dramaturgije* (Zagreb: Studentski centar Sveučilišta Zagrebu, 1964), pp. 83-87.

Papers:
The author's papers are held by his family.

Dragoslav Mihailović
(17 November 1930 -   )

Radmila J. Gorup
Columbia University

BOOKS: *Frede, laku noć* (Novi Sad: Matica srpska, 1967);
Kad su cvetale tikve (Novi Sad: Matica srpska, 1968);
Petrijin venac (Belgrade: Srpska književna zadruga, 1975);
Čizmaši (Belgrade: Srpska književna zadruga, 1983);
Uhvati zvezdu padalicu (Belgrade: Srpska književna zadruga, 1983);
Uvodjenje u posao. Drame (Belgrade: Narodna knjiga, 1983);
Goli otok, volume 1 (Belgrade: Politika, 1990);
Lov na stenice (Belgrade: BIGZ, 1993);
Gori Morava (Belgrade: Srpska književna zadruga, 1994);
Goli otok, volumes 2-3 (Belgrade: BIGZ/Srpska književna zadruga, 1995).
Collections: *Dela Dragoslava Mihailovića,* 6 volumes (Belgrade: BIGZ/Srpska književna zadruga/Prosveta, 1984);
Dela Dragoslava Mihailovića, 7 volumes (Belgrade: Politika, 1990).
Editions in English: *When the Pumpkins Blossomed,* translated by Bernard Johnson, in *The New Writing in Yugoslavia* (Harmondsworth, U.K.: Penguin, 1970), pp. 168-178;
When the Pumpkins Blossomed, translated by Drenka Willen (New York: Harcourt Brace Jovanovich, 1971);
"The Traveler," translated by Olga Shaskevich and Alfred Pasqualucci, *Colorado Quarterly,* 20, no. 3 (1972): 331-338;
"Freedom," translated by Maja Samolov, *Relations* (1976): 125-136;
"The Guest," translation by M. Lazić, *Relations,* 4 (1977): 13-25;
"Ruffians, Horses and Peasants," translated by Dragan Monašević, *Relations,* 2 (November 1981): 69-79;
"The Traveller," translated by Sanja Gligorijević, in *The Serbian Short Story 1950-1982,* by Radivoje Mikić, *Relations,* 4 (Winter 1984): 111-130;
"General," translated by Mateja Andronov, *Most,* 19, no. 85 (1984): 10-17;
"The Dog," translated by Cristina Pribićević, *Relations,* 1 (Spring 1985): 39-42;
"A Dog," translated by Mladen Jovanović, *Zavičaj,* no. 36 (1989): 348-349.

Dragoslav Mihailović

In the 1960s Serbian fiction writers started to modernize their writing and to follow the modern trends in European literature. A new brand of Yugoslav aestheticism emerged in which literature became its own theme. Attempts to go beyond this aestheticism were many. One of the few writers successful in this difficult test was Dragoslav Mihailović, now recognized as one of the most accomplished authors of postwar Serbian fiction.

Mihailović was born on 17 November 1930 in Ćuprija, a small provincial town southeast of Belgrade. His mother, Ljubica Todorović, a seamstress, died when Dragoslav was two years old. His father, Branko, a small merchant and tavern owner, died in 1948, leaving his teenage son an orphan. Mihailović finished the last two years of high school supported by the town municipality. In the fall of 1949 he entered the University of Belgrade, studying in the Department of Yugoslav Literature and Serbo-Croatian Language. The year 1950 was an especially difficult one for Mihailović. Only nineteen years old, he was afflicted with tuberculosis; he was also charged with committing subversive activities against the state, arrested, and imprisoned. This experience left an indelible mark on Mihailović both as a man and as an artist.

He was kept for several months in the investigative prisons of Ćuprija, Kragujevac, and Belgrade before being sent to the infamous political prison camp at Goli otok. Released in 1952, Mihailović returned to his native Ćuprija and later moved to Belgrade. In both towns he worked at odd jobs from which he was repeatedly dismissed because of his time in prison. During that period his jobs included working as a baker and a clerk, and working in an army mess hall, a sugar mill; as a copywriter in a title company, a packer, an egg salesman, an impresario of a traveling circus, and as a journalist for a small newspaper published for the Yugoslav guest workers abroad.

In 1957 Mihailović finished his studies at the University of Belgrade. The same year *Ježev kalendar* (Hedgehog's Calendar) published his first written work, a short humorous story titled "Pismo" (A Letter). Mihailović continued to write short stories and publish them in the literary journal *Letopis Matice srpske* (Chronicle of Matica srpska).

His story "Gost" (The Guest) appeared in *Letopis Matice srpske* in 1959. In the story Mihailović chose to depict a commonplace situation—life in an ordinary bachelor's room. The "guest" is a mouse that the man kills at the end. Everything is ordinary: the disorder of a bachelor's room, the behavior of an ordinary mouse, and the feeling of loneliness. However, the artistic quality of the story triumphs over the banality of the theme. The final image in the story, in which the mouse is flushed down the toilet with a drop of blood on its mouth, announces the major future themes of Mihailović's prose: suffering, compassion, and loneliness.

Only when Serbian literature reestablished a link with the prewar literature and its classics, Ivo Andrić and Miloš Crnjanski, was the reading audience ready to appreciate stories such as "The Guest." The story was included in Mihailović's first collection of short stories, which was published in 1967. Titled *Frede, laku noć* (Good Night, Fred), the collection immediately affirmed Mihailović as a serious author. In the more-liberal 1960s the book was received with high acclaim and awarded the prestigious Belgrade October Prize.

Frede, laku noć consists of six stories, previously published individually: "Gost," "Lilika," "Frede, laku noć," "Putnik" (Traveler), "Boginje" (Measles), and "O tome kako je ostala fleka" (How the Spot Got There), each a masterpiece in its own right, each containing in germ the major themes of Mihailović's opus and written in the technique Mihailović adopted in his acclaimed novels, *Kad su cvetale tikve* (1969; translated as *When the Pumpkins Blossomed,* 1970) and *Petrijin venac* (Petrija's Wreath, 1975). The stories are told in the technique of *skaz*, the confessional narrative in the first-person singular. An additional feature, present in particular in the story "Boginje," is the dialectical and colorful speech of the protagonist, which foreshadows another characteristic of Mihailović's later prose, his artistic use of regional language. The stories in *Frede, laku noć* tell of the tragic destinies of ordinary people: the young mother in the German prison camp who knows that she is doomed and desperately tries to save her infant son born in the prison; the sad life of the unloved and abused girl, Lilika; or the mentally disturbed teenage resistance fighter who became a willing executioner.

The 1968 publication of Mihailović's short novel *Kad su cvetale tikve* was a literary event. It moved both readers and critics and was an overwhelming success. At the time a group of Serbian writers, including Živojin Pavlović, Borislav Pekić, Mirko Kovač, Vidosav Stevanović, and Milisav Savić, was active on the literary scene, writing in a realistic style that came to be known as "stvarnosna proza" (a prose of reality). The writing of Mihailović added an extraordinary ex-

Dragoslav Mihailović

pressiveness to the realistic style and represented a qualitative change.

As he does in the short stories, the author treats in *Kad su cvetale tikve* a simple and a contemporary topic. The hero of the novel, Ljuba Sretenović, nicknamed "Champion," is a former boxer who failed to have a successful career, a tragic figure from the outskirts of Belgrade. His destiny is shaped by forces that he does not comprehend and cannot control. The narration is vivid, direct, and dynamic without moral or philosophical reflections. Yet, under the surface of their ordinary existences, the lives of Ljuba and those around him assume the quality of truly human tragedy. The first-person narration enables the author to detach himself from his hero and allows the protagonist to express himself without an intermediary, both by his words and his actions. That gives the story its authenticity. The language of the hero is the slang of tough young men living in the outskirts of Belgrade, somewhat primitive but highly expressive and totally in harmony with the reality depicted. This authentic language empowers the realistic style of Mihailović. The epigraph of the novel is "Deprived of our glory, in great humiliation we stand, led by the forces to where we do not wish to go"; while not compatible with the limited perspectives of the main protagonist, it is very much in line with the broad scope of the central theme: the powerful forces of destiny present not only in the hero's environment but also within himself.

In Sweden the middle-aged Ljuba Sretenović recalls his adulthood, his early successes in boxing, the political turmoil of 1948, the suffering of his father and brother, his quarrel with the underworld figure Stole, his trouble with the authorities, the deaths of his sister and mother, and, with that, the loss of home. When he avenged the death of his sister and had to leave the country, he broke the ties with the only environment in which he was able to exist. The exile to a foreign country condemns Ljuba to defeat and loneliness. He bears it stoically, but never finds peace and happiness.

The novel is written in a confessional style. Afflicted with incurable nostalgia, Ljuba relives tragic events of his life. He preserves his emotions and his colorful language, but he narrates the events from his life without pathos. Another characteristic of *Kad su cvetale tikve* is Mihailović's novel use of language, both in its relationship to the reality it depicts and to literature. He continued with the technique of skaz adopted in *Frede, laku noć*.

Mihailović wrote a play based on this novel, and the Yugoslav Drama Theater in Belgrade staged it in the fall of 1969. After only five performances the production was cancelled by the intervention of the leading political figures of the time. Marshall Tito himself criticized the play during a public speech on 25 October of that year. For nine years the novel *Kad su cvetale tikve* was out of print, and its copies were removed from many libraries in the country; the play was not staged again for fourteen years. In 1984, when it was staged by the National Theater in Belgrade, some of those responsible for its removal in 1969, including Tito, were dead, and the staging proceeded without a problem. This play, as well as the other plays written on the basis of Mihailović's short stories, were performed frequently in all the Yugoslav republics and abroad.

He continued to publish in the literary journals *Savremenik* (Contemporary), *Vidici* (Horizons),

Zora (Dawn), *Književna reč* (Literary Word), and *Duga* (Rainbow). His short story "Treće proleće Svete Petronijevića" (The Third Spring of Sveta Petronijević), published in *Zora* in 1968–1969, and "Barabe, konji i gegule" (Ruffians, Horses and Peasants), which appeared in *Savremenik* in 1970, were highly praised by the critics. *Kad su cvetale tikve,* along with some stories from *Frede, laku noć* were translated into English and many other foreign languages. Since 1971 Mihailović has dedicated himself exclusively to writing. In 1974 he was a guest lecturer at the University of Poitier in France.

In 1975 his second novel, *Petrijin venac,* appeared. Another overwhelming success, it was awarded the Ivo Andrić Prize, the literary award established after the death of the Nobel Prize winner Andrić. The novel was later translated into several foreign languages.

Consisting of five parts, *Petrijin venac* is the life story of an uneducated woman, told in her native dialect, with which Mihailović had been familiar since his childhood. Just as it is in *Kad su cvetale tikve,* the life of the protagonist, Petrija, is filled with tragic events caused both by the social and political circumstances and by her own human condition. Her narration presupposes an unidentified addressee to whom she is retelling her life story while constantly offering him cigarettes, coffee, and plum brandy. She views old photographs with him and expects, even demands from him, compassion and understanding. Petrija takes an avid interest in the affairs of her invisible companion. She is terrified that she might remain alone and forget how to speak with people. In this way she protects herself from loneliness and keeps in touch with her fellowman. This technique, which also engages the reader, is an important characteristic of Mihailović's fiction.

Petrija sees both the sad and happy events in her life through the prism of popular superstitions that help her to accept her tragic destiny. All in one breath she talks about the beneficial influence of water drinking, childbearing, witches, charms, soothsayers, mercury poisoning, her husband's death, and the real and the imaginary. Old and alone, eking out a bare existence, Petrija retains her abilities. She is still able to love and hate, to forgive and take revenge. She still distinguishes the good from the evil, and, above all, she feels compassion toward those who suffer. Witnessing the decay of the region in which she lives, a poor mining section of Serbia, Petrija broadens that observation to include her entire nation and the whole time in which she lives. Petrija is even able to make fun of herself, and her humor alleviates to some extent the tragic feeling of the story.

The second collection of short stories by Mihailović, *Uhvati zvezdu padalicu* (Catch a Falling Star), was published in 1983. Most of the stories of this collection were published earlier in literary journals. The stories are told against the definite geographical and historical backdrop of central Serbia. They are told in the now-distinctive narrative manner characteristic of Mihailović, most of them in the first-person singular and in the distinctive dialect of the Resava-Morava region of Serbia.

Again the protagonists are nonheroic individuals; they are either ordinary people or at the bottom of the social ladder. Thanks to Mihailović's narrative skill, they are transformed into convincing characters, vital and tragic souls. In the existence of each of these people there arrives a fateful moment that changes the course of their lives. In the case of Sveta Petronijević, the protagonist of the story "Treće proleće Svete Petronijevića," this is the moment when the young and promising police investigator discovers that his superior officer had an affair with the wife of a prisoner during his investigation. This, for the times a rather trivial matter, makes Sveta bitter and unwilling to pursue his career. His life changes radically. All the stories of this collection depict the trying life of post–World War II Yugoslavia, filled with human tragedies but also with human nobility and compassion.

Mihailović's third novel, *Čizmaši* (Boots), was published in 1983, as was *Uvotenje u posao* (Introduction into Business), which contains three plays: *Kad su cvetale tikve, Protuve piju čaj* (Tramps Are Drinking Tea), and *Uvotenje u posao*. The novel *Čizmaši* was awarded the NIN Prize and was voted best book of the year. It is a collage of fictional and documentary prose. The documentary fragments, which chronicle certain events from the tragic past of Yugoslavia, sound as a warning of things to come. *Čizmaši* continues the narrative device present in *Kad su cvetale tikve* and *Petrijin venac*. The male protagonist of *Čizmaši,* the uneducated junior sergeant Žika the Wolf, is, like Petrija, telling his life story to an imaginary addressee. However, he is a less heroic figure than Petrija and more picaresque in character.

With the exception of documentary fragments that are interwoven into the romanesque structure of *Čizmaši,* the novel is written in the first-person singular. It has two long segments as well as a third shorter one. The first two are written from the point of view of the character who lives in the 1970s and retells the life of Žika as a young man and a military enlistee. The third part looks both to the past and to the future, as Žika the Wolf, at the time an old man, summarizes his life.

According to the author, *Čizmaši* was conceived as the first volume of a trilogy. However, Mihailović found that the technique of skaz, while ideal to add an expressive quality to a shorter fictional composition, did not lend itself well to long fiction. As the author explains in his letter to Robert Hodel, he felt fatigue at the end of the first volume and was unable to continue searching for new expressive words. Whether and when the other two volumes will be finished is unclear. Both the protagonist Žika and another major character of *Čizmaši*, the regiment colonel Čiča Miljković, appear as characters in other stories. The chronological gap that exists between the first two parts of *Čizmaši* and the third part is filled by one chapter of *Petrijin venac* titled "The Celestial Musicians," in which Žika the Wolf is a character.

By the time his third novel was published, Mihailović was one of the most widely read and respected authors in the country. He became an associate member of the Serbian Academy of Arts and Sciences in 1981 and a permanent member seven years later. In 1984 his collected works appeared in six volumes. That same year he wrote the award-winning screenplay *Vijetnamci* (Vietnamese).

Critics, as well as readers, wondered why an author who was able to depict suffering in others in such a sublime way, and who himself suffered a great deal, would not write autobiographical prose. The answer came in 1990, when Mihailović published a long book of documentary prose based on his experience in the prison camp in Goli otok. *Goli otok* is a testimony to the suffering of those accused of sympathizing with the Soviet Union after Tito's break with Joseph Stalin in 1948. Two more volumes of the book appeared in 1995.

Mihailović returned to the theme of the prison-camp experience, with his collection of short stories *Lov na stenice* (Hunting the Bedbugs), published in 1993. It is a collection of masterfully executed short stories reminiscent of the style of *Kad su cvetale tikve* and Mihailović's earlier short stories. It continues the theme documented in *Goli otok*—suffering in the prison camp in the 1950s. In the nine stories of this volume Mihailović furthers his analysis of the concept of evil, which fills each page of the book.

While the stories of the political prison camps were no longer a novelty, Mihailović's prose in this collection brings a new dimension to both the human tragedy of the political persecution. The stories bear witness to humanity's downfall into crime and brutality and its ascension to nobility and salvation. The characters in the stories, whether victims or perpetrators, are rendered skillfully. Constantly the theme of the stories is suffering in all forms. Both the prison inmates and the guards suffer. In a dramatic and moving way Mihailović depicts a political system that used the most brutal way to eliminate those who did not share the regime's convictions. The reader is constantly confounded by the ever-increasing brutality present in fellow human beings and can clearly see the consequences such measures will have on the country and on generations of its citizens. Mihailović repeatedly conveys a bewilderment that the reader often shares: How was it possible to submit human beings to such cruelty in the name of an ideology?

Perhaps one of the most successful works on the subject of the political prison camps, *Lov na stenice* is at the same time full of both bitterness and philosophical calm, something only a temporal distance of almost fifty years could allow. When the survivors meet their torturers, they always see that the latter have met with their punishment. In the final balance the victims are the moral victors and the tortured never wish to change their lot with the torturers. Burdened by guilty consciences, the former prosecutors and guards are afraid that their crimes will be revealed. The stories exhibit a gallery of convincing characters such as police officer Slavko Glumac, the Russophile; Sveta "the French"; Krsta Nikezić, nicknamed "Aznavour"; and others—all real people who bear witness to the events described.

The stories are written in Mihailović's distinctive technique, the first-person singular. In addition to the pain and suffering present in each story, the reader feels the author's eagerness to document evil in the time that marked his life and that of his country while those who witnessed it were still living. The reader does not feel a desire for revenge on the part of the narrator. Rather, the feeling is that the stories deserve to be told to preserve the memory of the defeated and humiliated and to expose the evil of that period so that it cannot be repeated.

The novel *Gori Morava* (The Morava is Burning), published in 1994, is, like *Lov na stenice*, autobiographical, and, like all other works by Mihailović, it deals with the theme of suffering. The novel has three parts, each consisting of a score or more vignettes: "Bajanje od glave" (Soothsaying), "Divizijska muzika u glavnoj ulici" (Military Music on the Main Street), and "Čija to duša ovuda tumara" (Whose Soul Is Wandering Around Here). The first two parts represent recollections of people, events, and situations from the provincial town in which the narrator lived. The third part depicts the return of the narrator to the place of his childhood, some two decades later, now marked by his experiences in life.

The author returns to the scenes of his childhood and adulthood as the young boy retells, without bitterness or anger, the story of a life full of deprivation. The goodness of the child transcends adversity. In the child's world, all good is answered by good, and that is why the illness and subsequent death of his loving Uncle Dragi are incomprehensible to him and remain wrapped in mystery. Those around him speak about death as if it were something ordinary and unavoidable. The little boy often stresses his inability to understand what is happening around him, coming to the conclusion that "one cannot understand anything in this world." This limitation does not prevent him, however, from uncovering and commenting on the tragic events. The story of Kalina the dog is a moving story about the sunset of life, when old age becomes an unsupportable burden.

Even though the child does not understand the illness of his uncle Dragi, he vividly describes it from the point of view of a child. He shows tenderness toward the woman he calls Mother, who turns out to be his aunt. Toward his estranged father, an impractical man who suffers a great deal, he always preserves an emotionally neutral attitude. Prepared for by the death of Kalina at the end of the second part, the third part furthers the theme of dying. The narrator, now grown up, finds that his destiny is shaped by things both present and past, experiences and people no longer with him, and the unhappy souls that wander by the Morava River.

Filled with melancholy and nostalgia, the stories are populated with successful and diverse characters who were a part of the young narrator's life, part of a lost world. Such are the old woman, Velika, the protectress of the boy, who sees all children's games through the metaphor of the Great War (World War I); the gentle aunt the boy takes for his mother; the stern and unhappy father; the loving grandfather; the sweet Uncle Dragi; the colorful Maksim Pizdić; and the dog, Kalina.

Even though the author avoids openly making references to them, his passing remarks are sufficient to conjure up images of both world wars, which shaped the lives of those close to the narrator. *Gori Morava* is replete with descriptions of the customs of people in a small town: their folk laments, soothsaying, and fortune-telling. Always present in the background is the theme of death and suffering.

Mihailović lives in Belgrade, where he continues to write and publish. His works possess compelling powers of evocation, dramatic tension, and an autochthonic style. He conjures up visible and invisible throbs of human destiny. He is a modern realist in a higher form of realistic fiction, in the sense formulated by Fyodor Dostoyevsky. His prose style transcends both fashionable and traditional forms, while his narrative style employs both modern and traditional narrative devices. By presenting the lives of ordinary people in brilliant dialogues in the colorful language of regional and social registers, which he employs as stylistic devices, and creating a gallery of unforgettable characters, Mihailović reflects an entire period in his work. Critic Stevan Grubač describes Mihailović's fiction as the literature from which one ages fast and could become gray overnight.

Interviews:

Mirko Miloradović, "Moja literarna filozofija vodi najdirektnije poreklo iz moga naroda," *Politika* (22 October 1967);

Vidosav Stevanović, "Stil je nešto drugo," *Književna reč*, 2 (12 March 1973): 10-11;

Boro Krivokapić, "Bio sam nadvladan," *NIN*, 35 (22 January 1984): 27-29.

Bibliographies:

"Bibliografija Dragoslava Mihailovića," *Godišnjak SANU*, 88 (1982): 302-311;

"Bibliografija," in Mihailović's *Frede, laku noć* (Belgrade: Politika, 1990), pp. 193-241.

References:

Miloš Bandić, "Retorika i proza: jezik kao postojbina sveta," in *Savremena proza* (Belgrade: Nolit, 1973), pp. 789-800;

Bandić, "Roman i romansijeri u godini 1968: Slobodan Novak, Slobodan Selenić, Dragoslav

Mihailovi," *Letopis Matice srpske,* 403, no. 3 (1968): 320-336;

Snežana Brajović, "O gornjoj i donjoj kući: *Uhvati zvezdu padalicu,*" *Književnost,* 76, no. 12 (1983): 2060-2065;

Petar Džadžić, "Novi talas," in his *Kritike i ogledi* (Belgrade: Srpska književna zadruga, 1973), pp. 146-150;

Miroslav Egerić, "Bekstvo kao kritika života," *Delo,* 16, no. 2 (1970): 217-231;

Zoran Gluščević, "Životna zbitija jednog podnarednika: *Čizmaši,*" *Književnost,* 78, no. 8-9 (1984): 1502-1512;

Robert Hodel, *Betrachtungen zum Skaz bei N. S. Leskov und Dragoslav Mihailović* (Bern: Peter Lang, 1994);

Srba Ignjatović, "Postupak i značenje u priči *Frede, laku noć,*" *Književna reč,* no. 290 (10 December 1986): 8-9;

Vladeta Janković, "Dramski tekst i odgovornost pozorišne kritike: Polemika povodom drame *Protuve piju čaj* Dragoslava Mihailovića," *Književnost,* 67, no. 6 (1979): 1061-1067;

Janković, "O dramama Dragoslava Mihailovića," in Uvotenja v posao (Belgrade: Narodna knjiga, 1983), pp. 201-213;

Ljubiša Jeremić, "Mihailović, Between Perdition and Recognition, post facto: *The Works of Dragoslav Mihailović* (Belgrade: BIGZ/Srpska književna zadruga/Prosveta, 1984)," *Relations,* no. 1 (1985): 77-80;

Jeremić, "Tale of Suffering and Mercy: On Dragoslav Mihailović's *Petrijin venac,*" *Relations,* no. 9-10 (1979): 79-86;

Danilo Kiš, "*Petrijin venac* Dragoslava Mihailovića," *Književna reč,* no. 64 (10 January 1976): 4;

Božo Koprivica, "Jedan životopis ispunjen stradanjima i patnjom," *Književna kritika,* 7, no. 2 (1976): 81-85;

Ivan V. Lalić, "Nemogućnost jednog povratka na Dušanovac: *Kad su cvetale tikve,*" *Književnost,* 48, no. 5 (1969): 520-523;

Čedomir Mirković, "Čoveku je potrebno nadanje: *Kad su cvetale tikve* Dragoslava Mihailovića," in his *Zmajev znak na koricama* (Belgrade: Srpska književna zadruga, 1992), pp. 190-195;

Predrag Palavestra, *Posleratna srpska književnost* (Belgrade: Prosveta, 1972), pp. 316-318;

Petar Pijanović, "Nepouzdano pripovedanje Dragoslava Mihailovića," *Književnost,* 74, no. 10 (1982): 1458-1482;

Pijanović, "The Realism of Dragoslav Mihailović," *Književna reč,* no. 2-3 (1982): 41;

Vladislava Ribnikar, "Kmetnost vripovedanja," *Književna reč,* no. 50 (1976);

Milivoj Srebro, "Struktura *Petrijinog venca,*" *Književna istorija,* 12, no. 48 (1980): 601-633;

Nikolaj Timčenko, "Nekoliko napomena o posleratnoj srpskoj književnosti," *Savremenik,* 21, no. 12 (1975): 475-500;

Djordjije Vuković, "Književni jezik i savremeni roman," *Treća program,* 2, no. 41 (1979): 111-128.

Slavko Mihalić
(16 March 1928 -)

Ellen Elias-Bursać
Harvard University

BOOKS: *Komorna muzika* (Zagreb: Privately printed, 1954);
Put u nepostojanje (Zagreb: Lykos, 1956);
Početak zaborava (Zagreb: Zora, 1957);
Darežljivo progonstvo (Zagreb: Lykos, 1959);
Godišnja doba (Zagreb: Privately printed, 1961);
Ljubav za stvarnu zemlju (Zagreb: Zora, 1964);
Jezero (Belgrade: Prosveta, 1966);
Posljednja večera (Zagreb: Kolo, 1969);
Vrt crnih jabuka (Zagreb: Razlog, 1972);
Krčma na uglu–Krčma na voglu [parallel edition in Croatian and Slovenian, Slovene translations by Ciril Zlobec] (Trieste: Založba tržaškega tiska / Koper: Založba Lipa, 1974);
Petrica Kerempuh u starim i novim pričama (Zagreb: Školska knjiga, 1975);
Klopka za uspomene (Zagreb: Znanje, 1977);
Pohvala praznom džepu (Zagreb: Liber, 1981);
Tihe lomače (Zagreb: Naprijed, 1985);
Iskorak (Zagreb: Naprijed, 1987);
Ispitivanje tišine (Ljubljana: Mladinska kniga, 1990)–contains "Antologija 100 pjesama" and "Mozartova čarobna kočija";
Zavodnička šuma (Zagreb: Meandar, 1992);
Baršunasta žena (Zagreb: Meandar, 1993);
Karlovački diptih (Karlovac: Matica hrvatska, 1995).
Collections: *Izabrane pjesme* (Zagreb: Matica hrvatska, 1966);
Izabrane pjesme (Zagreb: Matica hrvatska, 1980);
Atlantida (Belgrade: Prosveta, 1982);
Izabrane pjesme (Zagreb: Naprijed, 1988);
Približavanje oluje, izbor izdjela, Zagreb: Skolska kniga, 1996).
Editions in English: *Atlantis: Selected Poems 1953-1982,* translated by Charles Simic and Peter Kastmiler (Greenfield Center, N.Y.: Greenfield Review, 1983);
Black Apples: Selected Poems 1954-1987, translated by Bernard Johnson (Toronto: Exiled Editions, 1989); expanded as *Orchard of Black Apples: Selected Poems 1954-1990* (Zagreb: Erasmus Naklada, 1994).

Slavko Mihalić

OTHER: *Iskrišta u tmini,* edited by Mihalić (Zagreb: Lykos, 1957);
Antologija hrvatske poezije dvadesetog stoljeća, selected by Mihalić, Antun Šoljan, and Josip Pupačić (Zagreb: Znanje, 1966);
Novi hrvatski pjesnici, edited by Mihalić (Split: Vidici, 1968);
La poesie croate des origines a nos jours, edited by Mihalić and Ivan Kušan (Paris: Seghers, 1972);

"Orfejeva oporuka," *Forum*, 4–5 (April–May 1973);

Novata hrvatska poezija, edited by Mihalić and Gane Todorovski (Skopje, 1973);

Antologija hrvaške poezije, edited by Mihalić and Ciril Zlobec (Ljubljana: Cankarjeva založba, 1975).

The year 1928, an important year in Croatian poetry, marks the beginning of a new generation of poets with Slavko Mihalić, born that year; Josip Pupačić, also born in 1928; Vlado Gotovac, born in 1930; Irena Vrkljan (1930); Ivan Slamnig (1930); and Antun Šoljan (1932). These groundbreakers and pathfinders, joined by Vesna Parun and Nikola Milićević (both born in 1922), have spent their lives balancing their works between hope and despair, between themes that explore the life of the individual and those that probe the life of the social order. Their tug-of-war has taken them from World War II through the Cold War and on to the new Balkan wars as they define, each time anew, the dynamic of the modern intellectual and his or her relationship and responsibilities to society.

The poet Charles Simic has said of Mihalić's generation that they "survived an epoch of unimaginable violence." After living his teenage years during World War II, Mihalić was coming of age in 1948, a young man of twenty, when Joseph Stalin's attempt at eliminating the postwar Yugoslav leadership backfired and Josip Broz Tito used Stalin's threat to entrench further his own position as head of the country. The conflict and ensuing repression in Yugoslavia in the late 1940s and early 1950s were a clear lesson in complexity and relativity for Mihalic's generation and propelled them into an intellectual life marked by a pessimistic or perhaps skeptical sophistication. Mihalić in an interview in 1969 has described how this coming of age in this period affected his work:

> At first my writing was a search, much service done to beauty and wisdom ... until one day when I stepped back and wondered why fate was making more and more brazen demands on us while taking such bad care of me ... I had to set words free of their lyrical cages so they could revive their strength in freedom[.]

The strongest poets of the period between the two world wars, controversial extrovert Miroslav Krieža and cosmic introvert Tin Ujević, had been writers of grandiose pretension and scope who fancied themselves the guiding lights of their artistic and political communities. The postwar generation shrank from this inflated sense of self, preferring instead to champion the tangible, the world within arm's reach, the realities close at hand.

The mission of Mihalić's generation thereby became the defense of the individual, and in this respect their choice of the vernacular, of everyday speech, of the commonplace, was their most powerful weapon. As Mihalić put it:

> Unexpected meanings were at every turn, things long underrated were waiting in lines. The same was true of words. Many floated up from the depths where they had been exiled by a barren lyrical shallowness. Sanctified human speech, the speech with which one is born, one loves and one dies—gave poetry not only a new meaning for words, but new and more passionate harmonies, rhythms. This was a splendid moment when it seemed as if anything was possible in poetry[.]

And for Mihalić, a pathfinder from his youth, if something was not possible, he would try to make it so. If no publisher would take his poetry, he would publish it himself. If there was no literary magazine to his taste, he would start one.

Mihalić was born in Karlovac on 16 March 1928 to Stjepan Mihalic and his wife Zlata, neé Milčić. Stjepan Mihalic was a writer and his wife an actress. During Mihalic's secondary school years at the Karlovac gymnasium he wrote and drew and attended the Karlovac music conservatory to study the cello and flute. He also started a school newspaper, the first of many publishing ventures he was to undertake. In 1947 he graduated and moved from Karlovac to Zagreb, where he found work from 1947 to 1951 as a reporter for *Borba* (Struggle), a leading newspaper. In this transition period he relinquished his ambitions of becoming a painter and resolved instead to devote himself to writing; he enrolled as a student in the Humanities faculty of Zagreb University. In 1952, while a student there, he started the literary magazine *Tribina* (Stage), which came out in only two numbers.

Mihalić worked for several Zagreb periodicals as a reporter. In 1954 he started his own publishing company, Lykos, the first book published being his own first volume of poetry, *Komorna muzika* (Chamber Music), that same year. His Lykos poetry series became a respected institution, a key forum for poetry; Lykos under his guidance also organized the first festivals of poetry in postwar Yugoslavia. *Književna tribina* (Literary Stage), a literary journal active from 1959 to 1960, was yet another offshoot of his publishing venture. Mihalić worked as well for several years for *Telegram,* a Zagreb literary and cultural periodical, as technical editor.

In 1964, with six volumes of poetry in print and already enthroned as one of the leading poets of his generation, Mihalić was elected executive secretary of the Association of Writers of Croatia, and that same year he was appointed general secretary of the Yugoslav Writers' Association, an umbrella organization to represent internationally the individual writers' associations of each republic. In this capacity he inaugurated *The Bridge* in 1966, a journal published under the auspices of the Writers' Association of Croatia and committed to translating Croatian literature into other languages; here he served as editor in chief until 1971. During his tenure the Association of Writers of Croatia also initiated the ongoing tradition of the Zagreb International Literary Talks, an event held every other year to bring together writers and scholars of Croatian literature from Croatia and abroad.

Over the years since *Komorna muzika* appeared in 1954, Mihalić published nearly a volume of poetry every other year and received many literary awards. The titles of these books suggest his dominant themes: *Put u nepostojanje* (A Journey into Nonexistence, 1956), *Početak zaborava* (The Beginning of Oblivion, 1957), *Darežljivo progonstvo* (Generous Exile, 1959), *Godišnja doba* (The Seasons of the Year, 1961), *Ljubav za stvarnu zemlju* (Love for the Real Earth, 1964), *Jezero* (The Lake, 1966), and *Posljednja večera* (The Last Supper, 1969). The underlying questions asked in these volumes relate to fear, defeat, pain, freedom, love, and death. The framework in which these issues are explored is that of Existentialism. The language is emphatically ordinary, the symbols elementary, such as water, the seasons, bread. The arsenal used is unrhymed verse with a concise, pregnant form of eight, twelve, sixteen, or sometimes twenty lines; several of the poems are unrhymed sonnets. Mihalić has only a few long poems.

The poem/song duality of the word *pjesma,* which can mean either poem or song, is essential to Mihalić's verse; several of his poems carry music-related names: some are ballads, such as "Suzdržana balada" (Restrained Ballad) or "Prognana balada" (Exiled Ballad); others are romances, which are also balladlike folk songs, such as "Romanca" (Romance) and "Romanca o djevojci u luci na prozoru" (A Romance about a Girl in a Harbor by a Window). There are yet

Cover for the 1966 edition of Mihalić's selected poems

other references to music: "Rapsodija" (Rhapsody), "Pastorala" (Pastoral), "Étude," "Eine kleine Nachtmusik" (A Little Night Music), "Requiem," "Mala fuga" (Little Fugue), "Karlovačka simfonija" (Karlovac Symphony), and "Kantata o kavi."

In defining the role of the poet and how he or she should respond to the repression and destruction of modern society, Mihalić, a poet of action and defiance, is articulate. "I acknowledge only those critics, or rather those writers, who with me (or I with them, it makes no difference) take part in the tragic drama of the human cosmic exception."

When the poetry of Mihalić first appeared in *Komorna muzika* in 1954, it seemed already mature, fully formed. It seemed that he waited until he was fully ready to publish. The twelve poems in the sixteen-page chapbook that introduced him to his readership are still considered some of his finest work. "Metamorfoza" (Metamorphosis) from this collection exists in several English versions (Janko Lavrin's, Bernard Johnson's, and Peter Kastmiler's). Here is the first stanza of Kastmiler's translation–"I would like to know from where / this emptiness comes, so that I / can change myself into a clear lake / where the bottom can be seen, but without fish"—as an illustration of Mihalić's earliest Existentialist-oriented work focused on defeat and emptiness.

The masterful contrasts resulting from Mihalić's overlay of abstract and colloquial, his juxtaposition of wry humor and pain, set the stage in "Približavanje oluje" (An Approaching Storm) for a couple's hasty retreat from a romantic tryst:

> I tell you, life's really much simpler
> Here's the first drop, the whirlwind is close behind
> Button your dress, look, even the flowers are closing
> I couldn't forgive myself if something happened to you now
> Of course my memory of this spot will be sacred forever
> But look lively please and don't look back.
>
> —translation by Bernard Johnson (in *Black Apples: Selected Poems 1954–1987*, 1989)

Antun Šoljan characterizes the Mihalić of this period as a born poet, one whose own poetic speech in his own language comes to him naturally. The melody of his verse merges with the flow of his language. He is a meticulous poet in building his phrase, and his is a current poetry, contemplative yet not abstract. His is a profoundly personal experience of the world.

Vesna Krmpotić, when weighing where Mihalić's poetry stands on a scale between defeat and hope, decided that he had chosen defeat as his leitmotif: "The underlying sense of this poetry is defeat. Defeat everywhere and defeat always. Defeat is the fate of this poet."

The topography of Croatian culture dramatically changed in the late 1960s and early 1970s. Faced with growing insistence in cultural and political spheres from all around Yugoslavia to democratize, Tito's government was faced with the dilemma that it must either resign or repress, and it chose the latter. Waves of repression spread throughout Yugoslavia, hitting Croatia in 1971. This turnaround came at a time of some of the most exciting literary production seen in postwar Croatia and indeed in all of Yugoslavia. It is hardly surprising, therefore, that these years effected a change in Mihalić's writing.

In his poems of the 1970s and later, Mihalić shifted from the world of the individual to the concrete realities of his street, city, republic, country, and continent. His earlier commitment to eluding suggestion of, or reference to, local detail underwent a change; in Mihalić's poetry of the 1970s and 1980s one finds instead a search for the coordinates of what makes the here and now what it is. In "Vrt crnih jabuka" (Orchard of Black Apples), he writes:

> Good evening, unknown land
> that hides its tracks so well.
> Your each and every dweller
> a fine destroyer. Now I know,
> you summon him yourself.
>
> —translation by Bernard Johnson (in *Black Apples: Selected Poems 1954–1987*, 1989)

This new stage suggests Mihalić's conviction that grave times have come. Always a man of action, one to take his social and cultural responsibility seriously, Mihalić's gradual swings from *I* to *you* and *we*, from the no-man's-land of his earlier writing to Zagreb, Croatia, and Europe, constitute his call for a sober, more grounded articulation. "Majstore, ugasi svijeću" (Master, Blow Out the Candle) in 1977 conveys both his assessment of the times and his commitment to his vocation:

> Master, blow out the candle, somber days are coming.
> Better count the stars at night, sigh for lost youth.
> Your disobedient words might bite through the leash.
> Plant onions in your garden, chop wood, clean out the attic.
> It's better that no one sees your eyes full of wonder.
> That's how your craft is: there's nothing you can pass over in silence.
> If you can't stand it and some night again pick up the pen,
> Master, be sensible, don't bother with prophesy.
> Try to write the names of the stars instead.
> The times are serious, nothing is forgiven to anyone.
> Only clowns know the way you might pull through:
> They cry when they feel like laughing and laugh when cries rip their faces.
>
> —translation by Charles Simic and Peter Kastmiler (in *Atlantis: Selected Poems 1953–1982*, 1983)

Everyday speech is no longer only present in these poems in individual lines of verse, but it permeates the way the lines are interconnected.

Mihalić incorporates the Existential questions of the individual that occupied him in the 1950s and 1960s into a broader exploration of the individual's position in and influence on society. This turn toward empirical reality in Mihalić's poetry is first suggested before the political turbulence of the 1970s in the collection *Jezero* in 1966; by *Vrt crnih jabuka* (1972; translated as *Black Apples: Selected Poems 1954–1987*, 1989) it is in greater evidence, and it reaches full expression with *Klopka za uspomene* (A Trap for Memories, 1977).

Titles of poems, such as those in *Pohvala praznom džepu* (Praise to an Empty Pocket, 1981), demonstrate his articulation of geographic coordinates: "Ilica, kad se napokon spusti kiša" (Ilica, When It Finally Rains), "U proljeće na Kvaternikovu trgu" (In Spring on Kvaternik Square), and "U tramvaju" (In the Tram).

Of this collection of poems Vasa D. Mihailovich says, "It is hard not to perceive Mihalić's poetry as a gloomy monologue of a lost soul. Yet the very fact that he is telling us about his plight is an indication of a desire to find a way out. A careful reader should be able to hear not only faint calls for help but also expressions of an obdurate conviction that help is possible after all."

Along similar lines, also probing for the balance between Slavko Mihalić's role as onlooker or action-taker, Vuk Krnjević describes the poet in his foreword to *Atlantida* (Atlantis, 1982): "Mihalić, therefore, is a poet who does not strive for anything, who does not urge, who does try with his poems to prolong inner life by seeing it only for what it is: a struggle with total vulnerability. Mihalić's poems are not a solace but testimony. And this testimony is a provocation of defeat."

In her review of *Tihe lomače* (Quiet Fires, 1985), Maria Malby touches again on this balance:

> Mihalić has no answers, no solutions. He simply reaches out to a fellow human who cannot find "the door" and if he does, wonders why "the door leads into birdcages . . . in spite of his melancholy, there is hope that on that day when we all reach the" "hollow" in which "one world stops and the other starts" we shall understand.

In *World Literature Today* (Summer 1991) critic Zdenko Novački describes Mihalić as a "skeptic rather than a pessimist; he wants things to turn out for the best but knows too much to believe they will."

Adriana Škunca finds the crux of Mihalić's poetry in his use of irony and paradox. Paradox breathes life into his images. She admires his purity of expression, the precision and density with which he creates his images, the complexity of his poetic fabric, and the variety of his textual givens. Neven Jurica sees a balance struck between despair and hope in Mihalić's verse. For if Mihalić's poetry is a testimony to the metaphysical depression of futility, in its real and vital dimension it is also a testimony to the great variety of human behavior. The very possibility of that variety returns the problem to a far deeper speculative level, because each variety of behavior is founded in the realm of freedom. And this reciprocally imposes upon the individual the alternative of choice. Zvonimir Mrkonjić speaks of Mihalić's poetry as the fullest metaphor for freedom in contemporary Croatian poetry. Mihalić, he says, is not so much a poet of freedom as he is freedom's tool. In the phenomenology of freedom as delineated by Mihalić's poems, this is its ultimate final expression: to speak out and let that freedom be fulfilled.

A poet of paradox and irony, wry yet deadly serious, always exploring new ways to strike his own balance between despair and hope, Mihalić, who has always been a pathfinder, has never failed his readership in his commitment to integrity. He has walked the tightrope of honesty in times of repression and has survived to provide an example for the poets of his generations and the generations who followed. His poetry has been well translated into English, both because his style is accessible to English and because his excellence as a poet has attracted good translators. With Charles Simic and Peter Kastmiler's *Atlantis: Selected Poems 1953-1982* and Bernard Johnson's *Orchard of Black Apples: Selected Poems 1954-1990* English readers can begin to appreciate Mihalić's qualities as a poet and his significance in Croatian literature.

Interview:

Ante Stamać and Slavko Mihalić, "Slavko Mihalić" (with V. Zuppa and others), *Telegram*, 10, no. 496 (31 October 1969): 9-13.

References:

Bernard Johnson, "Slavko Mihalić," *Most*, 4 (1987): 25-30;

Zvonimir Mrkonjić and others, "U fokusu kritike," *Republika*, 9-10 (September-October 1986): 1020-1043;

Vlatko Pavletić, *Klopka za naraštaje: Kontrapunkt eqzistencije u poeziji Slavica Mihailica* (Zagreb: Naprijed, 1987);

Pavletić, "Slavko Mihalić," in *Slavko Mihalić* (Zagreb: Matica hrvatska, 1980);

Antun Šoljan, "Uvod u čitanje Mihalićevih pjesama," *Forum* (1974): 326, 329-330.

Branko Miljković

(29 January 1934 - 11 February 1961)

Anita Lekić
State University of New York at Stony Brook

BOOKS: *Uzalud je budim* (Belgrade: Omladina, 1957);

Poreklo nada (Zagreb: Lykos, 1960);

Vatra i ništa (Belgrade: Prosveta, 1960); *Vatra i ništa: Pesme,* with an introduction by Petar Džadžić (Belgrade: Prosveta, 1968);

Pesme, edited by Džadžić (Belgrade: Brazde, 1965; revised edition, Belgrade: Prosveta, 1968);

Kritike (Niš: Gradina, 1972);

Orfičko zaveštanje: Pesme (Niš: Gradina, 1972);

Prevodi (Niš: Gradina, 1972);

Dok budeš pevao, with an afterword by Muharem Pervić (Belgrade: Rad, 1981);

Poezija, edited with an introduction by Džadžić (Belgrade: Prosveta, 1981).

Collection: *Sabrana dela,* edited by Dimitrije Milenković and others, 4 volumes (Niš: Gradina, 1972).

Editions in English: Poems, translated by Charles Simic and Aleksandar Nejgebauer in *Stony Brook,* no. 1-2 (1968): 114-115;

Seven poems, translated by Simic, Vasa D. Mihailovich, and Charles David Wright in *Four Yugoslav Poets,* edited by Simic (Northwood Narrows, N.H.: Lillabulero Press, 1970);

Poems, translated and edited by Bernard Johnson in *New Writing in Yugoslavia* (Baltimore: Penguin, 1970), pp. 240-242;

Poems, edited by Mihailovich, in *Contemporary Yugoslav Poetry* (Iowa City: University of Iowa Press, 1977), pp. 151-157;

Five poems, translated by Karolina Udovički in *Relations,* no. 2-3 (1984): 1-3;

Seven poems, translated by Bogdana Gagrica Bobić, in *Relations,* no. 2 (1985): 41-45;

Poems, translated by John Matthias and Vladeta Vuckovich, in *Translation,* 14 (1985): 304-306;

Four poems translated by Matthias and Vuckovich in *Margin,* no. 2 (1987): 57-59;

Branko Miljković

Poems, translated by various translators in *Serbian Poetry from the Beginnings to the Present,* edited by Milne Holton and Mihailovich (New Haven: Yale Center for International and Area Study, 1988), pp. 348-352.

Branko Miljković, whose meteoric poetic career left an indelible mark on contemporary Serbian poetry, was a leading representative of a generation of poets who emerged on the Yugoslav literary scene in the mid 1950s. Miljković rose to prominence in the wake of the literary confrontations that marked the definitive demise of postwar socialist realism in Yugoslavia. Miljković and his contemporaries quickly bloomed in the new literary climate. Theirs was a generation that had been nurtured on modern French, English, and Russian poetry. Well-read and actively involved in literary translation, Miljković's generation of poets created a newly cerebral poetry, characterized by extreme erudition and intellectualism, a poetry essentially aimed at literary and critical circles.

Miljković was born in Niš, Serbia, on 29 January 1934. He was a child when World War II broke out, and the tragic vision of life that strongly permeates his poetry may have had its roots in the traumatic experiences of a childhood disrupted by the war years. As a child Miljković witnessed two massacres, experiences that probably contributed to his pronounced fascination and preoccupation with death in his poetry. He began writing poetry in his teens, and in secondary school, as president of the school's literary club, he was regarded as a catalytic figure who brought together many talented young poets. He is generally credited with having awakened new interest, not only among his classmates, but also among his townspeople, in poetry readings and other literary events that he successfully organized and to which he drew large audiences. A diligent student, he made rapid strides in learning French and Russian, and before long was translating poetry from both tongues into Serbo-Croatian. He published his first poem in a Niš journal in 1951 and his first translations in 1952.

In 1953 Miljković moved to Belgrade, perhaps feeling that the provincialism of Niš would thwart his poetic development, and studied philosophy at Belgrade University. With the help of a major literary figure, Oskar Davičo, then editor of the literary journal *Delo,* Miljković published his first cycle of poems, "Uzalud je budim" (I Wake Her in Vain), in 1955. Two years later his first volume of poetry appeared in print under the same title. The reviews were on the whole favorable, and Miljković, already regarded as a highly promising poet, won further critical acclaim when *Smrću protiv smrti* (Death Against Death), a joint collection of poems on patriotic themes by Miljković and Blažo Šćepanović, followed in 1959. In 1960 Miljković published two new collections, *Poreklo nada* (The Origins of Hope) and *Vatra i ništa* (Fire and Nothing). That same year he received the prestigious October Award of the City of Belgrade for *Vatra i ništa.* Although critics were divided on the respective merits of the two books, his talent was never in dispute, and his oeuvre had already propelled him to a foremost position among his contemporaries. In 1961 a special edition of his poems from an earlier volume, *Smrću protiv smrti,* lavishly illustrated by artist Radomir Stević-Ras, was published under the title *Krv koja svetli* (Radiant Blood).

At a time when no one could have foreseen anything but a bright future for the poet, Miljković moved from Belgrade to Zagreb, where he accepted a position as cultural affairs editor for Radio Zagreb. A few months later, between 11:00 PM and 12:00 AM on 11 February 1961, and only a few days after his twenty-seventh birthday, Miljković hanged himself from a tree in a copse outside Zagreb. The reason for his suicide remains unknown; the news was received with shock and grief by his friends, critics, and the public. The poet's death was variously attributed to disappointment with his work or to an unhappy love affair; these explanations, however, remain no more than speculation.

An incident in the last weeks of Miljković's life sheds some light on his state of mind preceding his suicide. On 27 January 1961, sixteen days before he took his own life, Miljković addressed a letter to *Duga* (Rainbow), a Belgrade periodical, disowning every volume he had written and renouncing the award he had received: "I want it known that I have made a clean break with everything I've scribbled over these past few years." Several days later Miljković evidently had a change of heart, asking *Duga* to withdraw his statement from publication. His request could not be fulfilled, since the issue had been published already, and his statement of renunciation was interpreted as a somewhat capricious and reckless gesture.

After the poet's death, his close friend and critic Petar Džadžić published a wide selection of Miljković's poems in an edition titled *Pesme* (1965). Džadžić's introduction to the collection, "Branko Miljković ili neukrotiva reč" (Branko Miljković, or The Untamable Word), constituted the first exhaustive critical analysis of Miljković's work. The study won Džadžić the October Award of the City of Belgrade, and it continues to be regarded as the authoritative commentary on Miljković's work.

Miljković's collected works, *Sabrana dela,* were published in four volumes in 1972. This comprehensive edition contains all of Miljković's known published and unpublished works. The first volume consists of his four published collections of verse; the second includes all other poems not included within these collections; the third comprises his translations of thirty-two Russian, French, and other poets; and the fourth is a compilation of essays on Yugoslav and foreign poets and on poetry in general. A book that may be regarded as a supplement to Miljković's collected works, *Branko Miljković u književnoj kritici*

Dust jacket for Branko Miljković u književnoj kritici, which includes selected reviews of the poet's work

(Branko Miljković in Literary Criticism), consisting of some fifty selected reviews of his work, appeared in 1973.

Miljković's generation had not participated directly in bringing down the vulnerable structure of socialist realism. In theoretical and practical experience, this heterogeneous assemblage had been fledgling and, as it reached maturity, the main literary showdown was over. Well-read and actively involved in literary translation, the young poets produced an innovative poetry designed to appeal to the mind rather than the heart. The new intellectualism in poetry had one inescapable adverse consequence. It limited the audience to those who were qualified to wade through its often esoteric waters. Since Miljković had studied pure philosophy, it is not surprising that philosophical rigidity often overshadows and fetters the poetic resonance of his symbols. But as far as technique is concerned, the poet's work marks a return to the strict and highly demanding classical forms that had been all but relegated to obscurity by most poets. One of the characteristic qualities of Miljković's poetry is its consummate artistry. The sonnet and other long-forgotten traditional forms were restored and endowed with a new brilliance. The extreme care Miljković devoted to his poems testifies to the importance he attached to refinement in form. Miljković continually sought to create the masterfully chiseled poetic forms that he believed were the true prerequisites of his craft.

For some time after his death Miljković was idolized and, inevitably, this made critical scrutiny of his poetry difficult. More recent criticism has sought to reassess and provide a more objective evaluation of the poet's actual position in postwar Serbian poetry. And yet, despite some unfavorable critiques of his work, Miljković's prestige has not diminished but has in fact increased. Almost every poem Miljković wrote, regardless of whether it has achieved a standard of excellence as a whole, contains lines of anthological value. From the considerably large body of poetry that he left behind, critics tend to agree in their selection of some twenty poems as exceptional achievements. Although his work has been subjected to renewed critical scrutiny, one should not disregard the poet's age when his four volumes were published. Miljković's development as an artist from his first published poem in 1951 to his death in 1961 justifies the assumption that had he lived longer, his exceptional creative potential would certainly have found brilliant expression in his maturity.

Several themes recur in Miljković's finest poems and, indeed, throughout his corpus. In his 1981 introduction to an edition of Miljković's poetry, which constitutes a well-written, sympathetic, and yet critical approach that does not fail to point out Miljković's shortcomings, Džadžić pinpoints the obsessive themes that plagued the poet:

> the drama of his anxiety, the emptiness in existence and in the world, the cold presence of The Untamable Word, the fire of hope with which verse blazes . . . the impudent threat of nothingness, the subdued call of life barely penetrating through the steel armor of the poet's isolation, the need to be part of and to ceremonially plunge into the world, the lure of the chasm that the night opens and the day fails to close.

Miljković is at his best when he articulates these themes through both an emotive and an intellectual prism. But his predilection for both philosophy and poetry occasionally proved deleterious. Miljković often stood, and sometimes crossed, the narrow threshold separating the two in order to enter a world of highly abstruse symbols. Crossing this edge, on occasion, yielded unhappy results—a purely cerebral, abstract poetry, devoid of imagery and symbolic resonance. And yet, time and again, the poet in Miljković braved abstraction to create what Džadžić described in his 1981 edition as "poems which timidly stretch out their hands over the very flame of life . . . poems which ultimately cast off their spiritual insulators to reveal bare flesh, flesh exposed to all the changes of suffering, the flesh of pain."

One of the most striking features of Miljković's poetry is the frequency of its anticipatory insights. Throughout his poems are lines of pure premonition, point-blank forecasts of his own end. These intuitive moments are not just a feature of his later poetry but are present from its beginnings. In "Triptych for Eurydice," for example, the poet typically voices his preoccupation with death: "Faceless, barehanded, I journey with death in my mind." The most striking single example of an entire prophetic poem that foreshadows Miljković's own end is "Goran," devoted to the young Croatian poet, Ivan Goran Kovačić, who perished in World War II. This poem, part of a cycle titled "Seven Dead Poets," written five years before Miljković's death, is a chilling prophecy of the exact manner in which the poet was to commit suicide: "In these obscure woods enveloped in black / The tree too said don't. O my white-flooded morn / I leave you my name for I can't go back."

From the beginning, the "prince of poets," as Džadžić calls him, was a poet of death. "Like spring forgetful of its time to bloom," Miljković wrote in "Goran," "I now lie dead at the north of the world." The thin line marking the boundary where eternal emptiness begins held an irrepressible fascination for him, menacing and yet continually beckoning him forward. A major symbol pervading Miljković's work is the nether world as the abode of death. His poetry does not soar, but plunges deep into the earth, seeking an Orphean world of nonexistence. In this underground realm, "blind and ghastly," Miljković sought his true poems. The figure of Orpheus and his doomed quest for Eurydice represent principal motifs in Miljković's work. The poet alone, he believed, is endowed with powers that enable him to gain entry into the underworld. Miljković's quest for what Džadžić terms "the untamable word" led him repeatedly to these subterranean regions. His work abounds in images of descent, with return always a tenuous prospect.

In an early poem dedicated to Croatian poet Augustin "Tin" Ujević, Miljković voices his anguish before a world in which death blooms like a flower: "O why are we so alone, so weak and frail / While around its death the world spins and turns / Beneath the ground an evil silence blooms." The poet's work was ultimately an immense effort to subdue and curb the menacing lure of death. But Miljković never forgot the precarious line along which a poet treads, regarding it as a disease to which he himself could succumb.

Miljković began his poetic career with an almost fanatic conviction that the inherent power of words could retrieve and bring to life the underlying, lost reality of the world. "Poetry is frozen in words like electrons in an atom. The word must be smashed and its emotive power released," he wrote in an essay published by Džadžić in the 1981 edition of *Poezija*. Words merely designate; in poetry they must be forced to recapture the secret, vital spirit of things, to reawaken the dormant, true meaning of the reality they conceal. The path Miljković chose to prevent the diffusion of his poems was linguistic compression and the confinement of words within a rigid form.

Miljković favored the neglected sonnet form above all other rhyme schemes because it exacted the greatest degree of artistic agility and demanded the poet's total subordination to the requirements of the poem. "Resorting to strict poetic forms is characteristic of consummate artists only. A poor poet dares not take upon himself such a grave responsibility. Preciseness, the complete subordination of words to the idea and the idea to the form of a poem is a devilish task," he wrote, as quoted in the 1981 edition by Džadžić. But Miljković was not preoccupied with poetic form alone. His constant reflections on the potentials and limitations of poetry permeate his work. About two-thirds of the body of his poetry is devoted, explicitly or implicitly, to the nature of poetry itself.

Miljković eventually began to feel that his words and poetry were becoming unbridled and escaping his control. He believed that there was a point at which poems would become self-sufficient, casting off and renouncing their author. The more he wrote, the more convinced he grew that his poems were stronger than he and that it was his work, in fact, that was slowly consuming him. In the end Miljković could not resist the overpowering signification of his words. In a letter addressed to Džadžić a month before his death and published in the 1981 edition of *Poezija,* Miljković wrote:

> Now my poems seek my head. No one can any longer reconcile them to me.... [The most dangerous thoughts] have run amuck and assault me with raving fury. If I could only escape the things I have said! I live in the greatest alarm. I am afraid to speak, to write. Every word could kill me.... My poetry has now lost its value and turned into my fiercest foe.

The protective mechanism of poetry through which the poet had always sought to control his sense of isolation and anxiety no longer functioned. But for his readers Miljković left behind a poetry of great intellectual refinement, consummate skill, and true artistic passion.

Bibliographies:

Gojko M. Tešić, "Bio-bibliografska gradja o Branku Miljkoviću, I deo," *Književna istorija,* 25 (1974): 155-165;

Tešić, "Bio-bibliografska gradja o Branku Miljkoviću, II deo," *Književna istorija,* 26 (1974): 343-396.

References:

Mića Danojlić, "Simboli suštine," *Delo,* 11 (1960): 1295-1300;

Petar Džadžić, "Branko Miljković or The Untamable Word," *Relations* (1975): 34-35;

Džadžić, introduction to *Branko Miljković: Poezija* (Belgrade: Prosveta, 1981), pp. 5-92;

Miroslav Egerić, *Srećna ruka. Ogledi o srpskim pesnicima i kritičarima* (Belgrade: Srpska književna zadruga, 1979), pp. 187-201;

Dragoslav Grbić, "Prilaženje vatri," *Gradina,* 4 (1981): 300-309;

E. Celia Hawkesworth, "The Potent Word: The Poetry of Branko Miljković," *Slavonic and East European Review,* 54, no. 4 (1976): 527-537;

Dragan M. Jeremić, "Branko Miljković ili pesnik u traganju za smislom," *Savremenik,* 4 (1962): 287-299;

Milan Komnenić, introduction to *Branko Miljković. Vatra i ništa,* edited by Dimitrije Milenković and Vice Petrović (Niš: Gradina, 1972), pp. 11-83;

Dimitrije Milenković, "Miljkovićevo orfičko zaveštanje," *Gradina,* 4 (1981): 166-170;

Sava Penčić, ed., *Branko Miljković u književnoj kritici* (Niš: Gradina, 1973);

Aleksandar Petrov, "Orphean Inspiration in Recent Serbian Poetry," *Literary Quarterly,* no. 2 (1966): 156-170;

Vidosav Petrović, "Sećanja na Branka Miljkovića ili pesnikov uzlet," *Gradina,* 4 (1981): 154-165;

Stevan Tontić, "Tragično u poeziji Branka Miljkovića," *Letopis Matice srpske,* 6 (1971): 650-658.

Vera Mutafchieva
(28 March 1929 -)

Roumiana Deltcheva
University of Alberta

BOOKS: *Ranni vûstanija protiv turskoto vladichestvo* (Sofia: Izdatelstvo na Natsionalnija sûvet na Otechestvenija front, 1960);
Goljamata borba (Sofia: Natsionalen sûvet na Otechestvenija front, 1961);
Kûrdzhalijsko vreme (Sofia: Nauka i izkustvo, 1962);
Agrarnite otnoshenija v Osmanskata imperija prez XV-XVI v. (Sofia: BAN, 1962);
Gabrovo: Istoricheski ocherk (Sofia: Natsionalen sûvet na Otechestvenija front, 1963);
Povest za dobroto i zloto (Sofia: Natsionalen sûvet na Otechestvenija front, 1963);
Da se znae!... (Sofia: Natsionalen sûvet na Otechestvenija front, 1964);
Letopis na smutnoto vreme: Roman v dve chasti (Sofia: Natsionalen sûvet na Otechestvenija front, 1965-1966);
Sluchajat Dzhem (Sofia: Natsionalen sûvet na Otechestvenija front, 1967);
Sur l'état du système des timars des XVIIc-XVIIIc siècles, by Mutafchieva and Str. A. Dimitrov (Sofia: Editions de l'Académie bulgare des sciences, 1968);
Poslednite Shishmanovtsi (Sofia: Narodna mladezh, 1969);
I Klio e muza (Plovdiv: Khristo G. Danov, 1969);
Ritsarjat (Sofia: Narodna mladezh, 1970);
Geroika (Sofia: Profizdat, 1972);
Protsesût 1873 (Levski pred sûda): Ese (Plovdiv: Khristo G. Danov, 1972);
Belot na dve rûtse (Sofia: Bûlgarski pisatel, 1973);
Bogomili: Istoricheski razkazi za detsa (Sofia: Narodna mladezh, 1974);
Zhelezni stûpki: Istoricheski razkazi za detsa (Sofia: Narodna mladezh, 1974);
Povest s dvojno dûno (Sofia: Voenno izdatelstvo, 1974);
Alkiviad Malki (Sofia: Natsionalen sûvet na Otechestvenija front, 1975);
Alkiviad Veliki (Plovdiv: Khristo G. Danov, 1976);

Vera Mutafchieva

Kûrdzhalijsko vreme: Izsledvane (Sofia: Nauka i izkustvo, 1977);
Kniga za Sofronij (Sofia: Voenno izdatelstvo, 1978);
Izbrani tvorbi: Alkiviad Malki i Alkiviad Veliki (Sofia: Bûlgarski pisatel, 1979);
Predrecheno ot Pagane: Istoricheski roman za junoshi (Sofia: Otechestvo, 1980);

187

Obraz nevûzmozhen: Mladostta na Rakovski (Sofia: Voenno izdatelstvo, 1983);
Bombite (Sofia: Voenno izdatelstvo, 1985);
Sûedinenieto pravi silata (Sofia: Otechestvo, 1985);
Belijat svjat: Pûtepisi (Sofia: Voenno izdatelstvo, 1987);
Az, Anna Komnina (Sofia: Khemus, 1991);
V sjankata na Azija: Zavladjavane na Bûlgarija ot osmantsite. (Sofia: Slovo D, 1992);
Osmanska sotsialno-ikonomicheska istorija: Izsledvanija (Sofia: BAN, 1993);
Reaktsii: Publitsistika (Sofia: Universitetsko izdatelstvo "Kliment Okhridski," 1995).

Editions in English: *Bulgaria's Past,* by Mutafchieva and Nikolai Todorov, translated by Georgina Yates (Sofia: Sofia Press, 1969);
Agrarian Relations in the Ottoman Empire in the 15th and 16th Centuries (Boulder, Colo.: East European Monographs, 1988).

OTHER: *Turski izvori za bûlgarskata istorija, Seriij XV-XVI v,* edited by Mutafchieva and B. Tsvetkova, volume 1 (Sofia: BAN, 1964);
Rumelijski delnitsi i praznitsi ot XVIII v. (Sofia: BAN, 1978);
Dokladi: krûgli masi: Pûrvi mezhdunaroden kongres po bûlgaristika 23/5-3/6/1981, edited by Mutafchieva, Dimitûr Angelov, and Tsvetana Georgieva (Sofia: BAN, 1982).

SELECTED PERIODICAL PUBLICATIONS—UNCOLLECTED: "Kûm vûprosa za polozhenieto na vojnushoto naselenie." *Izvestija na Dûrzhavnata biblioteka,* "Vasil Kolarov" (Sofia, 1952);
"Edin prinos ot zakona za vojnutsite ot Nikopolskija i Silistrenskija sandzhak," *Izvestija na Dûrzhavnata biblioteka,* "Vasil Kolarov," (Sofia, 1953), pp. 267–273;
"Feodalnata renta, prisvojavana ot lennija dûrzhatel v Osmanskata imperija s ogled na nashite zemi prez XV–XVI v.," dissertation, *Izvestija na Instituta za bûlgarska istorija* (Sofia: BAN, 1957), pp. 163–204;
"Kûm vûprosa za chiflitsite v Osmanskata imperija prez XIV-XVII v.," *Istoricheski pregled,* 17 (1958): 34–57;
"Za sûstojanieto na spakhilûka prez XV–XVI v.," *Istoricheki pregled,* 3 (1959): 32–63;
"Otkupvaneto na dûrzhavnite prikhodi v Osmanskata imperija prez XV–XVII v. i razvitieto na parichnite otnoshenija," *Istoricheski pregled,* 1 (1960): 40–74;
"Za prilozhenieto na robskija trud v osmanskoto stopanstvo prez XV-XVI v.," *Sbornik, posveten na Marin Drinov,* special issue of *Izvestija na Instituta za bûlgarska istorija* (Sofia: BAN, 1960), pp. 505–519;
"Kategorii feodalno zavisimo naselenie v nashite zemi pod turska vlast prez XV-XVI v.," *Izvestija na Instituta za bûlgarska istorija* (Sofia: BAN, 1960), pp. 57–93;
"Kûm vûprosa za sûstava i oblika na osmanskata feodalna klasa prez XV-XVI v.," *Istoricheski pregled,* 6 (1961): 46–80;
"Novi osmanski dokumenti za vakûfite v Bûlgarija pod turska vlast," *Izvestija na dûrzhavnite arkhivi,* 6 (1962): 269–274;
"Za roljata na vakûfa v gradskata ikonomika na Balkanite pod turska vlast prez XV-XVI v.," *Izvestja na Instituta za bûlgarska istorija* (Sofia: BAN, 1962), pp. 121–145;
"Feodalnite razmiritsi v Severna Trakija prez kraja na XVIII i nachaloto na XIX v.," *Paisij Khilendarski i negovata epokha* (Sofia: BAN, 1962);
"Kûm vûprosa za statuta na bûlgarskoto naselenie v Chepinskoto korito i pod osmanska vlast," *Rodopski sbornik,* 1 (1965): 115–127;
"K voprosu o zemevladenii v Sirii XIV–XVI vv.," *Vizantiiskii vremennik,* 4 (1965);
"Feodalnite razmiritsi v Severna Bûlgarija v kraja na XVIII i nachaloto na XIX v. i tjakhnoto otrazhenie vûv Vlakhija," by Mutafchieva and Al. Vianu, *Bûlgaro-rumûnski vrûzki i otnoshenija prez vekovete,* 1 (1965): 193–251;
"Die Wakfe im Karaman (XV–XVI Jahrhundert)," *Etudes balkaniques,* 1 (1975);
"Osnovni problemi v izuchavaneto na vakûfa kato chast ot sotsialno-ikonomicheskata struktura na Balkanite pod osmanska vlast (XV–XIX v.)," *Studia balkanica,* 14 (1979): 90–126;
"Drugite," *Literaturen forum,* 26 (1–7 July 1992): 1, 5;
"Otmalko dostojnstvo–vpechatlenija ot Petija panair na femistichnata kniga, 24–28 June 1992, Amsterdam." *Literaturen forum,* 32 (12–18 August 1992): 1, 6;
"Chuzhdoto," *Literaturen forum,* 31 (4–10 August 1993): 1, 5;
"Ako iskash da bûdesh shtastliv, bûdi!" *Literaturen forum,* 49 (8–14 December 1993): 1, 4;
"Ezikût ni obednja kato naroda: Izkazvane, napraveno po vreme na razgovora za sûvremennija bûlgarski ezik, 12 Jan. 1994, BAN." *Literaturen forum,* 6 (9–11 February 1994);

"Krajat na [khudozhnitsite Boris i Slavka] Denevi: Iz *Spomeni ne za izdavane*." *Literaturen forum*, 7 (16–22 February 1994): 1, 5;

"Paraleli na istorijata–Iberija i Balkanite." *Literaturen forum*, 18 (11–17 May 1994): 1, 6;

"Obida i strakh obuslavjat obraza na 'drugija,'" *Kontinent*, 230 (7 October 1994): 10;

"Belijat svjat II: Ploshtadi," *Kontinent*, 254 (4 November 1994): 27;

"Kûrdzhalijsko vreme," *Literaturen forum*, 38 (9–15 November 1994): 1, 3.

With her early historical investigations, her literary production, and her active political stance, especially after the profound changes that affected her country in 1989, Vera Mutafchieva is one of the most committed intellectuals of contemporary Bulgaria. She has implemented in practice the idea of the writer's duty to be a leader in the cultural progress of the nation, a role that emerged in the periods that she has vividly represented with her literary talent and knowledge of history. In both her historical novels and her contemporary fiction, Mutafchieva has portrayed women as major and multidimensional characters, and she has delved deeply into the complex social and political issues of gender. She has also engaged in various literary experiments in narrative technique. The strong interest in her historical analyses and literary production is confirmed by the many reprints of her historical monographs, essayistic prose, and novels. Her works have been translated into twelve languages, including Russian, Czech, Slovak, Polish, Hungarian, Romanian, Turkish, English, French, and German.

Vera Mutafchieva was born in Sofia on 28 March 1929, the daughter of Peter Mutafchiev, one of the most renowned Bulgarian historians of the first half of the twentieth century. Mutafchieva's mother, Nadezhda Trifonova, was also a historian. Mutafchieva herself finished her degree in history at the University of Sofia in 1951. She worked as a research assistant in the Department of Orientalism at the Cyril and Methodius National Library from 1950 to 1955. During the years 1955–1958 she was a graduate student of Ottoman history at the History Institute of the Bulgarian Academy of Sciences. In 1958 she defended her Ph.D. dissertation on "Feodalnata renta, prisvojavana ot lennija dûrzhatel v Osmanskata imperija s ogled na nashite zemi prez XV–XVI v." (Feudal Taxes in the Ottoman Empire during the Fifteenth–Sixteenth Centuries). In 1977 she completed her postdoctoral study on *Kûrdzhalijsko vreme* (The Time of the Kûrdzhali), a topic that had interested her since her student years. In 1958 Mutafchieva became a research associate at the Institute of Balkan Studies and in 1966 a senior research associate. Mutafchieva was the director of the Center for Ancient Languages and Cultures at the Committee for Culture (1978–1980) and the director of the Bulgarian Research Center in Austria (1980–1982). From 1979 to 1991 she worked at the Literature Institute at the Bulgarian Academy of Sciences; in 1991–1992 she worked at the Center for Demographic Studies; and since 1992 she has been a professor at the History Institute. She is also deputy chair of the Bulgarian Academy of Sciences, a position she has held since 1993. Mutafchieva also headed the Agency for Bulgarians Abroad in 1991.

Mutafchieva was a member of the Union of Bulgarian Writers from 1967 to 1995. From 1982 to 1986 she served on the union's executive council, heading the section on prose. In the 1990s she became one of the founding members of an alternative Writers' Alliance. Mutafchieva received various awards during different periods of her literary career: the Bulgarian Writers' Union Award in 1978; the Gottfried von Herder Award in 1980; the Gueorgui Dimitrov Award in 1981; in 1986 the award of the city Sofia; and the John Panitsa Award for journalistic integrity and professionalism in 1995.

Mutafchieva's career as a writer began as early as 1952 with studies and monographs on Bulgarian history during the Turkish domination, specifically the agrarian relations during the Ottoman Middle Ages. In the 1950s she published many historical articles. At the same time, she was mastering literary craftsmanship, writing the essays that appeared a decade later under the title *I Klio e muza* (Clio Is a Muse, Too, 1969). Her first book of historical writing appeared in 1960; her first literary book came out in 1961.

According to the writer's own admissions, she became a historian not so much out of love for the discipline per se, but out of duty toward her father. Having originally selected architecture and literature as her principal interests at the university, Mutafchieva changed her mind after learning that a new program in Ottoman civilization was being introduced that year. In the course of her studies Mutafchieva also began work at the National Library, where she gained access to new, unprocessed documents and sources about life and socioeconomic relations in

Bulgarian society during the centuries of Turkish domination. In the years when Mutafchieva was receiving her training as a historian specializing in Ottoman studies, the methodology of the discipline was undergoing serious changes. Until that time the primary sources for investigation included various historical narratives, Turkish chronicles, writings by European travelers, and legislative acts of the Ottoman rulers. The enormous quantity of archives from the times of the Ottoman Empire remained outside the historians' focus of attention. Mutafchieva's work as an assistant at the National Library exposed her to a tremendous wealth of documents and information; these she not only researched to make her original contribution to Bulgarian historiography, but they also became the factual foundation for the majority of her subsequent literary oeuvre.

As Mutafchieva states in an interview in *Sûvremennik* in 1979, her involvement with Ottoman studies was prompted from the beginning by literary intentions. This premise underlies her literary début, *Letopis na smutnoto vreme* (Chronicle of the Times of Turbulence, 1965–1966). The novel presents a panoramic depiction of Bulgarian life during the violent times of anarchy in the Turkish Empire at the end of the eighteenth and the beginning of the nineteenth centuries. This is the so-called time of the *kûrdzhali*—the ruthless bands of rebels who took advantage of the chaos in the empire and were not answerable to any authority. They pilfered, pillaged, and killed indiscriminately, notorious for their ruthlessness and brutality and feared even more than the Ottoman rulers themselves. This period in Bulgarian history is also treated in Mutafchieva's monograph of the same title and in *Kniga za Sofronij* (A Book about Sofronij, 1978).

Letopis na smutnoto vreme is a literary work that is original in its attempts to approach the theme not only from the point of view of Ottoman scholarship but also through a specifically Bulgarian perspective. The novel illustrates certain features that define Mutafchieva's highly original and innovative narrative technique. Unlike the traditional approach to historical subject matter manifested in the writings of Paisij Khilendarski, Zakhari Stojanov, and Ivan Vazov, Mutafchieva rejects the romantic pathos, exoticism, and purely entertaining, adventurous quality of historical events. She opts for a deeper, philosophical treatment of the topic. One of her major objectives is the establishment of continuity between past and present: the recontextualization of past events and the tracing of their implications for the current social and political reality. Thus, Mutafchieva reinterprets the essence of the historical novel as a genre, investing in it a broader content in which the author may present his or her own views, defend his or her original theses, and look for eternal issues that are concurrent with the present. In this framework, Mutafchieva's narrative technique manifests a high degree of the Brechtian *Verfremdungs-Effekt* (alienation effect)—she intentionally aims at destroying the effect of empathy and involvement on the part of readers in favor of an emotionally detached, yet philosophical rationalization of the depicted events and portrayed characters. Their active participation is engaged in the process of interpretation.

In her narrative Mutafchieva incorporates original documents from the Turkish archives, which until then had remained beyond the interest of historical investigations. Moreover, the novel presents a thesis that at the time was vehemently rejected by historians and gained recognition only toward the end of the 1970s: despite the brutality and suffering the anarchy in the Turkish political organization caused, it nonetheless objectively played a positive role in the defining of the national consciousness and the revival of the Bulgarian nation. Mutafchieva situates her events within a broader context—against the background of the historical events taking place in Europe during that period: the French Revolution, Napoleon's rise, the Russo-Turkish wars, and the intricate diplomatic plots regarding the decaying Ottoman Empire.

Bulgarian literary scholars and critics have designated *Letopis* a "roman-epopeia," an epic novel, one characterized by large spatial and temporal parameters, the intertwining of a multitude of plots, and the portrayal of historical figures and fictional characters, aiming at the rendition of a kaleidoscopic picture of life in a time long past. Mutafchieva introduces five different plot lines, which deal with different social and political strata in the Turkish Empire. Thus, the novel presents the tragic fates of Sultan Selim III; the kûrdzhali leader Kara Feizi; the autonomous ruler Osman Pazvanoglu, a Muslimized Slav who rose in the Ottoman administration; and the Bulgarian Stano Mukhtar and his children. By presenting dozens of characters and their individual fates in a period of violence and anarchy, Mutafchieva not only reconstructs a vast panorama of the historical past, but also poses many issues of continuing significance. The reader is simultaneously confronted with the problems of the "enlightened ruler" desperately trying to save the status quo, the tragic desperation of the outwardly ruthless kûrdzhali leader, the irrational rebellion of the autonomous despot, and the diverse possibilities of the Bulgarians at this crucial moment of their history.

After the death of Stano Mukhtar, killed by Muslimized Bulgarians, his strong, patriarchal family falls apart. One of his sons, Stojan, becomes attracted to the big city, illustrating the slow emergence of the bourgeoisie and the gradual process of class differentiation in Bulgarian society. The second son, Pûrvan, devastated by the murder of his wife, becomes a *khajdutin*, a guerrilla fighter, and goes to the mountains. The fate of Dobri, Stano's youngest son, is of particular importance since it introduces another prominent theme of the novel—the role and activity of the intellectual in times of ordeal. Overwhelmed by the desire for knowledge, Dobri decides to pursue the life of a *prosvetitel* (educator). Mutafchieva's fictional character meets the historically authentic priest Stojko Vladislavov (Bishop Sofronij Vrachanski), one of the most important figures in the Bulgarian national revival, and becomes his closest disciple and companion. The author constructs the figure of Sofronij on the basis of his autobiographical manuscript, *Zhitie i stradanija greshnago Sofronija* (The Life and Sufferings of the Sinful Sofronij, 1861), part of which is incorporated in the text in the form of a letter. Sofronij is portrayed through a realistic prism as a sickly and vulnerable man, yet at the same time intelligent, persevering, and infallible in his pursuit of higher purposes.

This Bakhtinian treatment of the creative personality through his or her deeds and the problem of the guiding role of the intellectual are constantly foregrounded in Mutafchieva's works. They provide one of the thematic links among her varied literary output. This topic is present not only in *Letopis*, but also in her later novels, *Sluchajat Dzhem* (The Cem Affair, 1967), *Poslednite Shishmanovtsi* (The Last of the Shishmans, 1969), the *Alkiviad* dilogy (1975, 1976) *Az, Anna Komnina* (I, Anna Comnena, 1991), as well as in the biographical sketches *Kniga za Sofronij* and *Obraz nevûzmozhen: Mladostta na Rakovski* (Impossible Image: The Youth of Rakovski, 1983). In each case Mutafchieva textualizes the intellectual biography of a concrete historical figure whose main task was not only creative activity, but even more so the active strife toward the preservation and dissemination of the cultural artifacts resulting from it.

There is no doubt that with her first novel Mutafchieva secured for herself a significant place among the contemporary Bulgarian writers. The success of the epic can be judged purely statistically by the number of reprints *Letopis* has undergone over the years. At the same time Mutafchieva received the admiration and recognition of her colleagues in the genre. Canonized writers such as Stojan Zagorchinov, Emilian Stanev, and the chronicler Simeon Radev praised her highly. Her contemporaries, Anton Donchev and Gencho Stoev, also credit her for her innovations in the treatment and philosophical rationalization of historical subject matter. According to many Bulgarian literary scholars, Mutafchieva's *Letopis*, with Donchev's *Vreme razdelno* (Time of Ordeal, 1964) and Stoev's *Tsenata na zlatoto* (The Price of Gold, 1965) mark one of the peaks in the development of the Bulgarian historical novel.

Mutafchieva's second novel, *Sluchajat Dzhem*, is both reminiscent of and radically different from *Letopis*. Thematically, it sheds light on the political and diplomatic relations between the Ottoman Empire and the European powers during the fifteenth century. Structurally, the epic vastness and immediacy of the events are replaced by a more individualized and subjective narrative style that has Sultan Cem as the central protagonist. The novel's aim is not so much to present minute descriptions and massive scenes but rather a psychological, multilayered inquiry into the relationship between the individual and history. The focal point of the author's investigation is the tragic fate of Cem, brother of Bayezid II, whose rule extends only for eighteen days after the death of his father, Mehmed. Unable either to avoid his brother's conspiracy against him or to secure his power as sultan, Cem is forced to flee to the island of Rhodes, which is held by Christian missionaries. This marks the beginning of his thirteen long years of exile. The novel follows his personal story as hostage to the West European powers whose efforts to use him as a spearhead of a new crusade expedition against Istanbul ultimately prove unsuccessful. At the same time it presents an insightful commentary on the social and political processes taking place in the West and the East. In this context the Balkan Peninsula, with its mediating position, becomes a tangential arena of intersection between the two. This novel is in a way Mutafchieva's most "cosmopolitan" work: the "Bulgarian theme" is only indirectly approached through the more immediate conflicts between the European great powers and the Ottoman Empire, which in the fifteenth

Dust jacket for Mutafchieva's Alkiviad Veliki, a historical novel about Alcibiades

century not only possesses but demonstrates enormous expansionist vitality. In the novel the East-West conflict is depicted from a generalizing philosophical perspective, as the juxtaposition between two irreconcilable cultural antipodes.

Compared to *Letopis*, *Sluchajat Dzhem* is a much more polemical work. While on one level the author exploits a fascinating plot line, on another the narrative is suppressed in favor of a more argumentative exposition that conveys Mutafchieva's personal position as a historian. She claims unequivocally:

> Let's assume that the "Eastern question" does not begin with Russia's expansion towards the warm seas and the efforts of the West to stop it, but with the efforts of that same West to stop the development of the European East by abandoning it, even subjecting it to many centuries of suffering. Never again—as during the Cem affair—was the liberation of the newly conquered Balkans so achievable. Yet, the West missed this opportunity not by accident.

Although referring to the medieval times, these conclusions sound unexpectedly relevant not only regarding the recent past of Eastern Europe but also for the situation in the Balkans in the 1990s.

The composition of the novel is structured as a trial investigation. The author constructs a multiperspectival narrative in which the testimonies of the participants in the events at the end of the fifteenth century are presented before the judgment of history. This original approach, reminiscent of Bernard Shaw's *St. Joan* (1923), gives a polyphonic quality to the work and necessarily involves the reader in active participation and evaluation of the multitude of points of view presented. Mutafchieva rejects the superior position of the omniscient narrator who must carry the responsibility for the validity of the text. The character of Cem is constructed gradually, through the different stories recounting his life in Rhodes, Savoy, and Rome. The episodes of Cem's many attempts to organize his escape, his desperation, and his revived hope possess many of the features of the adventure novel; yet they are interspersed with sections of meditative and philosophical generalizations functionally motivated by the selected testimonial structure. In the course of the narrative Cem's gradual degradation is traced. His transformation from an enterprising monarch, a talented poet, and a fascinating hero into a resigned victim, a flaneur with no goals, and a wretched antihero is depicted with a great degree of plausibility and psychological depth.

The novel preserves its unity through the primary—the fictional poet Saadi, Cem's only companion and confidant during the years of exile and wandering. In the subplot describing the relationship between Cem and Saadi, Mutafchieva returns to the problem of the role of the intellectual and his or her duty to civilization. The dichotomy between ruler and intellectual resurfaces with further implications in Mutafchieva's controversial novel *Az, Anna Komnina*, in which similar issues are complicated by the introduction of the issue of gender.

With *Poslednite Shishmanovtsi* Mutafchieva once again delves into more immediate Bulgarian subject matter, though it is set against a broader European context. The novel focuses on the tragic lives of the last two Bulgarian medieval czars, Ivan-Shishman and Ivan-Aleksandûr, before the fall of the independent Bulgarian state under Turkish domination at the end of the twelfth century. On its publication the novel received mixed reviews in which Mutafchieva was praised for her skills and knowledge as a historian, yet criticized for what was considered to be her positive portrayal of Ivan-Aleksandûr. To evaluate Mutafchieva's innovativeness in this work, one must be aware that her Ivan-Aleksandûr goes against the traditional historical and literary image of this last medieval ruler. One of the most complex and interesting Bulgarian czars is practically destroyed by the Bulgarian national writer Ivan Vazov in his drama *Kŭm propast* (Toward the Abyss, 1910). In the play Ivan-Aleksandûr is simplistically presented as an idle drunkard, an irresponsible monarch, the main cause for the fall of the Bulgarian kingdom. This false view of the czar had persisted in the decades following the play. Mutafchieva is the first writer who attempts to rehabilitate and to search for deeper insights concerning individual and collective responsibility in times of crisis.

In her novels Mutafchieva is always engaged in a dialogic relationship with her readers. She not only believes in their active response to the subject matter but also in their capacity for association and generalization. This belief in her contemporary readers' ability to decipher her specific interpretation of history is present in *Ritsarjat* (The Knight, 1970). The novel reinforces the author's intention to treat the historical subject matter from the perspective of modernity. Rejecting an idealized view of the past and focusing on the complexities of life, Mutafchieva presents a picture of the Crusades and knighthood. Yet, again the medieval setting is only a background for human conflicts and dramatic episodes, an original starting point for associations that refer the reader to more-immediate occurrences in modern history.

Mutafchieva's preference for a contemporary reevaluation of history and its recontextualization in modernity underlies the diversity of her literary activity. In this sense it is difficult to find a clear-cut definition for the genre of some of her prose works, such as *I Klio e muza, Geroika* (Heroism, 1972), *Protsesût 1873* (The Trial of 1873, [1972]), or *Kniga za Sofronij*. They represent a synthetic blend of narration, argumentation, and description. The essayistic prose of *Geroika* marks the author's transition from historical subject matter to more-contemporary thematics. Reflecting upon the drastic changes in Bulgarian society of the 1960s, Mutafchieva goes beyond the collective in her attempt to penetrate and understand the motivation of individual human conduct. Moreover, in *Geroika* she sketches the character of a Bulgarian female type who becomes the central protagonist in her next novel, *Belot na dve rûtse* (Belote for Two, 1973). *Belot* is the name of a French card game.

Belot is one of Mutafchieva's most controversial and experimental works. Set in socialist Bulgaria, the novel portrays the modern emancipated woman who has risen above the restrictive conventions and norms previously imposed upon her by society. Recent reevaluations of the work have defined it as a detailed analysis of the "anatomy of love." The female protagonist is in certain respects autobiographical, not so much in terms of concrete details, but more in terms of a global overlapping in worldview between author and heroine. The two protagonists in the book possess the characteristics of general types of modernity; hence, Mutafchieva's implementation of the avant-garde technique of leaving them unnamed: throughout they remain simply as the Woman and the Man. In narrative technique the novel is constructed as one long interior monologue and displeased the critics of the 1970s with its overtly individualistic subject matter. Another original aspect of the work is the author's intentional use of "trebling," reminiscent of the structure of fairy tales and indirectly referring the reader to Christian ideology. Thus, in analyzing the "woman's soul," Mutafchieva traces its development in three concrete time spans—adolescence, youth, and maturity. This composition is mirrored in the novel's epilogue, which depicts three possible solutions for the expectedly unhappy love story. The choice of such an ambivalent ending, coupled with the free-flowing interior monologue, emphasizes Mutafchieva's idea at the core of the work, that the woman's narrative as Other is much more complex and enduring than is suggested by official decrees and impersonal manifestos.

After the publication of *Belot na dve rûtse* Mutafchieva was accused of glamorizing the "irrational-biological aspect of the love at first sight" syndrome and of choosing "free love" over marital love based on respect and stability. According to some critics, the author contrasts the sexes and suggests that in terms of spiritual and moral qualities males are inferior. This was inadmissible in a society that formally had long resolved the issue of women's emancipation. For Mutafchieva, however, while from a jurisdictional point of view equality may be a legal fact, the Bulgarian woman is still in a position of subordination. This unprivileged position is manifested in literature by the fact that, apart from a few exceptions, the woman's function in the Bulgarian narrative is to reinforce a main idea that is embodied in a male protagonist. In general the female is hardly ever a protagonist; she rarely has her own conflicts and challenges to overcome, and she is treated merely as the bearer of traditional patriarchal values such as faithful, sacrificial love.

In this context it is obvious why *Belot* created such a stir. Until that novel Mutafchieva had always centered her plots around larger-than-life male heroes whose position as leaders remained unchallenged. This work is crucial in Mutafchieva's literary production for various reasons: her focus on modernity, her experimentation with narrative technique, her postmodernist approach to the story with the introduction of an open, multifarious ending. It also marks another dominant theme in the writer's works, namely, the venturing into the sphere of feminism. While feminist problematics are given a strong political treatment in many of her newspaper articles (as in "Ima neshto gnilo ne samo v Danija, ami izobshto" [Something Is Rotten Not Only in the State of Denmark, but in General, 1994]), in her novels Mutafchieva manages to state and defend her theses through the more subtle mechanisms of artistic representation.

A strong feminist stance is taken in Mutafchieva's more recent novel *Az, Anna Komnina*, which presents one of the most fascinating women in Byzantine history through the viewpoint of the female gaze in a society of dominant male values. Once again Mutafchieva demonstrates her skepticism toward official historiography and aims at a consistent debunking of reigning mythologies. Both thematically and compositionally, the novel is reminiscent of *Sluchajat Dzhem*. At the center of her story Mutafchieva places Anna, daughter of Emperor Alexius Comnenus and author of the fifteen-volume *Alexiad* (1148), which chronicles the sequence of events in the second half of the eleventh and the beginning of the twelfth century in Byzantium. The Comnenian dynasty was the last to attempt to stop the general decay in Byzantium under the relentless attacks of the Ottoman invaders from the East, and it was successful in this endeavor for nearly a century. Anna received a good education in literature, philosophy, history, and geography. She married Nicephorus, the leader of Bryennium, and joined her mother, the empress Irene, in a vain effort to persuade her father to disinherit his son, John II, in favor of Nicephorus. Later on, after John's accession to the throne, she was again unsuccessful in her conspiracy against her brother. After the plot was discovered, Anna forfeited her property and retired to a convent, where she wrote the *Alexiad*. As a historical document, this work provides a panoramic picture of religious and intellectual activities within the empire, reflecting the Byzantine conception of imperial office.

In *Az, Anna Komnina*, Anna's character is revealed polyphonically, through seventeen multi-perspectival monologues by Anna's mother, her two grandmothers, her nanny, and the protagonist herself. The novel polemicizes with the *Alexiad*'s official rendition of history and presents the chronicled events from the position of the woman as a voiceless Other. Mutafchieva adopts a postmodernist narrative technique with a high degree of conventionality. Each of the multiple narrators knows what the other woman has said or is about to tell. Anna comments on many of her texts in the *Alexiad* and many later evaluations of the period are achronically incorporated. Having once established this specific convention, however, *Az, Anna Komnina* presents the reader with a wealth of information about the hidden, private side of history, about life in Constantinople, and about Anna's personal drama and that of her contemporaries.

Similar to Cem, Anna realizes the cynicism and mediocrity that infects politics, but unlike him, she manages to comprehend this much earlier. Having found high ideals and beauty only in the world of art, Anna finds it easier to renounce the ambitions for the throne and dedicate herself to the Word instead. Together with the other two female protagonists, Anna Dalasena and Empress Irene, Anna's conduct in Mutafchieva's novel raises several gender issues. These women not only succeed in imitating the manner of male conduct in the corridors of power, but they surpass the males in the degree of manipulativeness and abuse of the resources and myths of power. By introducing multiple narrative voices that recount the same historical events, the author not only relativizes the story and the history, but she also achieves a higher degree of introspection. This approach is a characteristic feature of her style in general: she refuses to moralize or present an unequivocal straightforward perspective; her aim is not to preach. Rather she constantly provokes and questions the world she reconstructs by permeating it sometimes with benevolent irony and sometimes with shattering resonances of tragic absurdism.

The convergence between contemporary and historical subject matter finds an original synthesis in Mutafchieva's *Alkiviad* dilogy, which focuses on individualism as a worldview and a socioethical position and the permissible limits in the individual's conduct, set against two chronotopically distinct epochs: antiquity and modernity. The two novels, *Alkiviad Malki* (Alcibiades the Little, 1975) and *Alkiviad Veliki* (Alcibiades the Great, 1976), demonstrate Mutafchieva's attitude toward the phenomenon of "Alcibiadism"—the duplicitous intellectual game of manipulation and betrayal—recurring in various historical periods. The theme finds its formal manifestation in the double format and the specific poetics based on an inverted temporal marker: from the contemporary mutation back to the ancient prototype. The dilogy develops the idea of the individual obsessed with a mania for grandeur (Alcibiades the Great) and his transformation into a modern Alcibiades the Little. Unlike his ancient model, Alcibiades the Little is faced with the impossible task of playing alone against society and counting on his ability to manipulate it.

The difference between the two protagonists is reflected in the structures of each novel. The author presents the story of Alcibiades the Great by means of stylistic exuberance and rhetorical grandiloquence. True to her artistic credo, Mutafchieva does not portray a flat, one-dimensional character; rather, with the unfolding of the plot she traces the protagonist's evolution. Alcibiades emerges as a complex figure, full of inner contradictions. He is a man of contrasting traits: he is an extraordinarily gifted and fearless strategist and warrior, yet his boundless narcissism and egoism turn him into a traitor. The story of the modern Alcibiades, on the other hand, manifests a different kind of communicative quality, something like an informal dialogue among reader, witness, and victims. In terms of genre it resembles a composite between a psychological survey and a criminal investigation. The implications of the text suggest that the contemporary mutant presents a much more serious danger because of his greater abilities to metamorphose and multiply in an era of technological and scientific breakthroughs. With its greater immediacy of subject matter, *Alkiviad Malki* was received with mixed feelings by the ideologically biased literary critics at the time.

Bombite (The Bombs, 1985) is an autobiographical novel in which Mutafchieva relives her wartime experiences; it marks the continuity in the author's interest in a more philosophical and anthropological subject matter in which the key concept changes from "history" to "life." The same universality and variability are found in the collection of essays called *Belijat svjat: Pûte pisa* (This World, 1987). Constructed as a travelogue, the book follows the author's perceptions of the world, which lead her to polydirectional recollections and rationalizations of accumulated emotions. In some respects this is the most optimistic work of Mutafchieva's oeuvre.

Mutafchieva's name is also connected to what for many critics and scholars is the best Bulgarian film and the greatest box-office success in that country: *Khan Asparukh* (shown in the United States under the title *The Glory of Khan;* 1981, directed by Ljudmil Stajkov). The film was released in 1981 to commemorate the thirteen-hundredth anniversary of the foundation of the Bulgarian state. Mutafchieva wrote the script for the film based on her 1980 novel *Predrecheno ot Pagane* (Pagane's Prophesy). For this project and for her overall creative achievements, she received the prestigious Gottfried von Herder Award in 1980 and the Georgi Dimitrov Award a year later. Mutafchieva's 1985 novel *Sûedinenieto pravi silata* (Unity Breeds Power) was also reworked from a script for a film project that was never produced.

After the major political changes in Bulgaria that started in 1989, Mutafchieva has been an active commentator on the dynamic processes in society. She has given many interviews and participated in various panels, discussing the present state of Bulgarian culture and the prospects for the future. According to the author herself, this may be viewed as her journalistic period—a statement confirmed by the fact that Mutafchieva was the recipient in 1995 of the first John Panitsa Award, recently instituted to honor high achievements in the fields of mass media and investigative journalism.

Over the years of her long and prolific career, both as a historian and as a writer of fiction, Mutafchieva has succeeded in preserving her close connection to and popularity with her readers. In spite of the ambiguous and often implicitly negative reviews she has been given by some scholars, who have criticized her often controversial treatment of historical and contemporary subject matter, her complex characters struggling with their internal contradictions, and her detached, questioning, and often highly subjective narrative style, her books have always attained the status of best-sellers in Bulgaria. In the mid 1990s, when she subordinated her career as a writer to devote herself to the more immediate changes in Bulgarian society, Mutafchieva continues to be an influential presence on the Bulgarian intellectual scene.

Interviews:

Atanas Svilenov, "Pri Vera Mutafchieva: intervju s Atanas Svilenov," *Sûvremennik,* 4 (1979): 167–188;

"Na ureda za mûchenija e otnovo inteligentsijata," *Demokratsija,* 103 (1 May 1992);

"Praznikût na Sv. sv. Kiril i Metodij e povod da pogovorim za bûlgarskata kultura i otseljavaneto na natsijata," *Anteni,* 20 (20 May 1992): 8;

"I Petûr Pûrvi, i Akhmed Treti . . ." *Kultura,* 32 (7 August 1992): 4;

"Khvûrlikh se vûv vodata bez dûno," *Literaturen forum,* 39 (30 September–6 October 1992): 3;

"Istorijata ne se povtarja," *Literaturen vestnik,* 9 (8–14 March 1993): 3;

"Iska mi se da vjarvam, che podir desetiletie bûlgarite shte bûdat po-drugi," *Trud,* 98, 29 (April 1993): 1, 5;

"Naj-dobre e Zapadût da ni zabravi, dokato se opravim sami," *168 chasa,* 39 (27 September 1993): 41;

"Bûdeshteto na SBP? Anketa," *Literaturen forum,* 47 (24–30 November 1993): 1, 3;

"Gladki, kamo li ednoposochni pûtishta v naukata ne sa zapomneni," *Demokratsija,* 232 (10 October 1994): 13;

"Ima neshto gnilo ne samo v Danija, ami izobshto," *Literaturen forum,* 43 (14–20 December 1994): 1, 3.

References:

Todor Abazov, "Antologija na vûtorga," *Literaturen front,* 29 (19 July 1973);

Maja Atanasova, "Pûtishta kûm sveta," *Vek 21,* 10 (8–13 March 1995): 10;

Sabina Beljaeva, "Istoricheskite romani na Vera Mutafchieva," *Plamûk,* 2 (1972);

Beljaeva, "Vera Petrova Mutafchieva," in her *Rechnik po nova bulgarska literatura (1878–1992)* (Sofia: Khemus, 1994), pp. 243–245;

Svoboda Bûchvarova, "S eruditsija i darba," *Plamûk,* 7 (1968): 79–82;

Vikhren Chernokozhev, "Istorijata kato metafora," *Literaturen forum,* 39 (30 September–6 October 1992): 3;

N. Davidov, "Osmisljane na istorijata," *Literaturen front,* 2 (4 January 1968);

S. Dimitrov, "Bûlgarski ucheni: Profesor Vera Mutafchieva," *Vekove,* 6 (1988): 69–75;

Magda Karabelova-Panova, "Intelektualnostta kato samopoznanie-nabljudenija vûrkhu tvorchestvoto na Vera Mutafchieva," *Plamûk,* 6 (1989): 152–158;

Stojan Karolev, "Realizûm i romantizûm v istoricheskija roman," *Literaturen front,* 45 (3 November 1966);

Simeon Khadzhikosev, "Tvorets s originalna fizionomija," *Septemvri,* 3 (1979): 234–244;

Lilija Kirova, "S tûrseshta misûl–Vera Mutafchieva na 50 godini," *Plamûk,* 3 (1979): 145–147;

Elka Konstantinova, "Retsenzija za istoricheskite eseta na Vera Mutafchieva," *Septemvri,* 5 (1970): 233–234;

Konstantinova, "Stranstvuvashtijat ritsar na Vera Mutafchieva," *Septemvri,* 5 (1972): 238–241;

Konstantinova, "Sûvremenni razmisli vûrkhu istorijata," *Septemvri,* 5 (1972): 235–237;

Rozalija Likova, "Chovekût i vremeto v edin istoricheski roman," *Narodna kultura,* 33 (13 August 1966);

Likova, "Novi momenti v sûvremennata beletristika," *Literaturna misûl,* 1 (1966): 55–81;

Zdravko Nedkov, "Obshta tsel, razlichni pûtishta," *Trakija,* 3 (1973): 69–72;

Aleksandûr Panov, "Skepsisût kato pozitsija i metod," *Literaturen forum,* 39 (30 September–6 October 1992): 3;

Ivan Popivanov, "Kontseptsii i tvorchesko prevûplûtjavane," *Literaturen front,* 25 (22 June 1972);

Z. Popzlatev, "Letopis na smutnoto vreme," *Slivensko delo,* 106–107 (4 September 1965);

Emilija Prokhaskova, "Letopis na smutnoto vreme," *Plamûk,* 7 (1965): 107–108;

Prokhaskova, "Za Apostola, revoliutsijata, analogiite i drugi njakoi neshta," *Septemvri,* 3 (1973): 232–239;

Ognjan Saparev, "Kakvo ima otvûd dumite," *Septemvri,* 8 (1973): 239–241;

Krumka Sharova, "Prof. D-r Vera Mutafchieva–uchenijat i tvoretsût," *Istoricheski pregled,* 6 (1989): 62–66;

Ljudmila Stojanova, "Predizvikatelstvata na novija prochit i Sluchajat Dzhem," *Literaturen forum,* 33 (18–24 August 1993): 1, 5;

Atanas Svilenov, "Prisûstvieto na silnata lichnost," *Literaturen front,* 15 (12 April 1979): 3;

Toncho Zhechev, "Nov roman na Vera Mutafchieva," *Letopisi,* 2 (1992): 11–13.

Rajko Petrov Nogo
(13 May 1945 -)

Bogdan Rakić
Indiana University

BOOKS: *Zimomora* (Sarajevo: Svjetlost, 1967; enlarged edition, Sarajevo: Svjetlost, 1969);

Zverinjak (Sarajevo: Svjetlost, 1972);

Jesi li živ (Sarajevo: Veselin Masleša, 1973);

Bezakonje (Belgrade: Prosveta, 1977);

Rodila me tetka koza (Sarajevo: Svjetlost, 1977);

Planina i počelo (Belgrade: Slovo ljubve, 1978);

Obilje i rasap materije: O poeziji Skendera Kulenovića (Sarajevo: Svjetlost, 1978);

Koliba i tetka koza (Kragujevac: Svetlost, 1981–1982);

Zimomora (Belgrade: Srpska književna zadruga, 1984; enlarged edition, Belgrade: Srpska književna zadruga & BIGZ, 1987);

Na kraju milenija (Sarajevo: Veselin Masleša, 1987);

Na Vukovoj stazi (Kragujevac: Svetlost, 1987);

Lazareva subota (Belgrade: Srpska književna zadruga, 1989);

Lazareva subota i drugi dani (Podgorica: Oktoih, 1993);

Na kapijama raja (Belgrade: Srpska književna zadruga, 1994).

Collection: *Lirika* (Belgrade: BIGZ, 1995).

Editions in English: Poems, translated by Alan McConnell-Duff, *Relations*, 1 (1969): 67–68;

Poems, translated by Vera Tošić, *Relations*, 2–3 (1984): 99–102;

Poems, translated by Svetozar Koljević and Andrew Harvey, *Relations*, 2 (1986): 33–39.

OTHER: Aleksa Šantić, *Pjesme,* edited by Nogo (Belgrade: Slovo ljubve, 1981);

Ćamil Sijarić, *Priče kod vode,* edited by Nogo (Belgrade: Srpska književna zadruga, 1982);

Skender Kulenović, *Soneti i poeme,* edited by Nogo (Sarajevo: Veselin Masleša, 1983);

Srpske junačke pjesme, edited by Nogo (Belgrade: BIGZ, 1987);

Branko Ćopić, *Poezija i proza,* 1–4, edited by Nogo (Belgrade: BIGZ & Prosveta, 1987);

Rajko Petrov Nogo (photo by Olga Milović)

Jovan Dučić, *Poezija,* edited by Nogo (Belgrade: BIGZ, 1995).

Rajko Petrov Nogo made an unusual and loud entry into Serbian poetry in the second half of the 1960s: he announced, as it were, his arrival on the stage with a microphone. The frequent guest of many public recitals of poetry and many television shows, Nogo spoke with the hoarse, disillusioned voice of a social outcast who grew up in a provincial orphanage and was not inclined to mince his words. The time was propitious for this kind of rhetoric: 1968, with its international wave of youth protest, was at hand, and a trend of nonconformist, somewhat exhibitionist, but also self-ironic engagé poetry had been on the rise in Yugoslavia, with Matija Bećković and Branislav Petrović its major representatives in Belgrade. Nogo belonged to the circle around the popular, semidissident Sarajevo poet Duško Trifunović, who liked to refer to his protegés as "the young, spiritual maniacs," destined "to rule the world, until they grow up." Nogo later remarked that he was fortunate never to rule anything, but he could not help growing up, which had even more fortunate consequences for his poetry. The initial bitterness never completely disappeared from it, although the mature Nogo considerably lowered his voice. However, the turning point in his development was the discovery of tradition, which for him–in T. S. Eliot's words in "Tradition and the Individual Talent"–did not imply just an "archeological reconstruction" of the past. Rather, it helped Nogo recreate his sense of artistic identity through the projection of his own experience into different mythical, religious, folkloric, and pantheistic settings. This process of amalgamation became Nogo's artistic trademark and can be seen in his imagery, in the formal elements of his poems, and in his language. It was this interplay of the past and the present, the ancestral and the personal, that eventually established Nogo's reputation as one of the leading Serbian poets in the 1980s and 1990s.

Nogo was born on 13 May 1945, in a shingle-roof cabin in the mountain village of Borija in Herzegovina, a region well known for its outlaws and heroic songs. According to family tradition, the Nogos (formerly called the Rašovićs) originally came from Montenegro and belonged to the large clan of the Kuči, whose most distinguished member was Marko Miljanov, the celebrated nineteenth-century Serbian writer and warrior. Rajko's father, Petar, was a farmer who cherished the traditional art of epic singing and played the *gusle* (a one-string instrument) and bagpipe. Driven by poverty, he left for the United States before World War I. In 1914, although officially an Austro-Hungarian citizen, he returned to volunteer for the Serbian army. Petar died a poor man in 1954 at the age of seventy. The sparkling memories of the heroic past and the national myths captured in Serbian epic poetry, along with hereditary asthma and the later adopted patronymic, were all that Rajko inherited from his father.

Nogo's mother, Stana, née Domazet, also came from a family of rebels: her two brothers were killed fighting the Nazis during World War II. Their feats were praised in a folk song, and a monument erected to their memory stands in the Herzegovinian town of Ljubinje. Much younger than her husband, Stana died in a Sarajevo hospital a year before him; her family never found out where she was buried.

Nogo, nine years old, and his older brother Radovan were first put into an orphanage in the small city of Trebinje; a year later they were sent to the even more provincial Nevesinje. After he had finished elementary school in the Nevesinje orphanage, Nogo moved to Sarajevo. He began to publish poetry and short prose pieces in various literary journals in 1963. His talent was soon recognized: he met Trifunović, began his lessons in irony and political heresy, was introduced to a wider circle of readers, and soon became a well-known figure in the Sarajevo artistic and Bohemian circles. It was not long before Nogo was ready for his first collection of poems.

As Thomas Eekman has noted, the diction of *Zimomora* (The Chills, 1967) is "a bit too loud" and its manner of expression a bit "too plain." But it also contains some of the crucial elements of Nogo's later work and is therefore invaluable for the full appreciation of his development. The "loud" diction basically results from Nogo's adolescent feeling of revolt: in "Moj slučaj" (My Case), for example, he describes himself as "lousy and malicious and eternally against everything." Other poems offer a rather comprehensive list of things that get on the poet's nerves. In this respect, his reference to the sophisticated intellectualism prevailing in contemporary poetry as "mellifluous concerts of eunuchs" is typical in his poem "Zapis za blijedu, za ovu bijedu" (An Inscription Regarding This Miserable Pallor). But Nogo's anger often conceals a deeper feeling of anxiety before the alien and unfriendly world. This sense of fear and unease is conveyed by the title of the collection. It is significant that the exposure to cold has remained one of Nogo's obsessive motifs. In general *Zimomora* indicates that Nogo's scorn for the social establishment and its conventions at this point was not generated by any kind of adverse ideological attitude; it rather developed from his acute feeling of uprootedness and bitterness at being a rejected outsider and "no one's child" ("Rajkovanje," Rajkoing–the title refers to his first name). This is the first sign of the peculiar bipolarity typical of Nogo's poetry; his aggressiveness is often counterbalanced by marked lyric undertones that reveal the presence of a delicate, vulnerable personality under the harsh mask of a rebel.

A similar paradox can be observed in Nogo's approach to form. With his strong preference for rhymed and metered verse, Nogo looked like a surprisingly cantabile rebel. The

Dust jacket for Nogo's Lirika, the 1995 edition of his collected poems

confrontation and mingling of the contrasts are also visible in his manipulation of language. Although some critics introduced Nogo as a kind of belated, Serbian Robert Burns and stressed his "rural idiom," a closer examination reveals that these "rural" phrases often border on urban slang and that Nogo is at his best when he welds lexical items belonging to mutually exclusive registers: both rural and urban, literary and political, modern and obsolete. In any case *Zimomora* is a collection of highly communicative poems; the communicativeness has remained a major characteristic of Nogo's poetry.

But the general impression left by *Zimomora* is one of an immediacy that is sometimes obtrusive. Rebellious or lyric, the young Nogo is always deeply and openly personal. The resulting sense of enormous poetic intensity is a clear outcome; on the other hand, many poems show more of the poet than his poetry. Nogo's true potential, which he fully developed later, is revealed in those occasional moments of transcendence in which he translates his bitter personal experience into the purer and more comprehensive language of metaphors and symbols without depriving them of the intensity of the original emotions. The perfect example of this transcendence is Nogo's "Suncokret" (Sunflower), in which the poet's longing for light and warmth is presented through a symbolic image, while the necessary artistic distance is established with a touch of subtle irony:

You couldn't find a greater fool...

Neck bent with that weight—
Weak prop for a mad head
Blind with sun
Crazy for light—
Like a monk scanning the stars
Dying of loneliness
(while swallows nest along his arms)
Staring downstream into the stars.
Even as he goes white, dried by grief,
His vast head bending shyly nearer his heart,
Even as his many small pupils fall out
He goes on
Like in May

Stubbornly dreaming of the sun.

You couldn't find a greater fool.

    —translation by Svetozar Koljević and Andrew Harvey
        (in *Relations*, 2 [1986]: 35)

In June 1968, a year after *Zimomora* was published, a series of student protests broke out in Yugoslavia. Nogo distinguished himself by delivering passionate speeches from the roof of the College of Liberal Arts building in Sarajevo; he was as noisy a political orator as he was a poet. The consequences of his short political career were twofold. His file with the political police began to grow, as some prominent members of the Communist Party expressed a rather uncommon and—unfortunately for Nogo—lasting interest in his artistic and other activities. On the other hand, Nogo learned an important lesson about political oppression, and his adolescent revolt "against everything" became (and remained) much more focused.

After he graduated from the University of Sarajevo in 1968 with a degree in Yugoslav literature, Nogo became secretary of the Association of Writers of Bosnia-Herzegovina; then he took the position of editor in the Sarajevo publishing house Veselin Masleša. His second collection of poems, *Zverinjak* (Bestiary), appeared in 1972. Fifteen years later he humorously explained that he decided to write about animals because "the more [he] got to know men, the more [he] preferred beasts." The book has an Aesopian dimension, as some of the poems resemble fables dealing with contemporary psychology of political power, but it also focuses on nature in a more literal meaning of the word. It seems that the disappointments Nogo experienced after 1968 (as well as the lyric side of his artistic sensibility) directed him toward nature at a time when he was trying to embrace something vital and meaningful in a world becoming even more alien and oppressive. Nogo sees nature as characterized by a certain innate purity, but he primarily shows it as biologically elemental, life-inspiring, and—unlike "civilization"—devoid of moral pretensions.

Another important characteristic of *Zverinjak* is its radical change of tone and method of presentation. The adolescent noise is gone; the anger is turned into subtle irony and even self-irony; lines are perfectly polished and balanced; images are highly stylized; and there is no trace of the "too plain" manner of presentation, the main source of critical objections to *Zimomora*.

And yet the essential Nogo with his typical intensity and defiant attitude is still there. The change is probably best illustrated by the concluding poem, "Iz pazuva boga" (From the Armpit of God), which capitalizes on the triumph of subtlety over roughness:

When the earth
opens up its womb
to speak forth
it will be a dry time
in the rocky waste
and from the armpit of god
then just for spite
by none awaited
beautiful out of reach
ever ready to face its doom
a thorn
will shine
itself surpassed
by its bloom.

    —translation by Stephen M. Dickey

In 1970 Nogo began to write literary criticism for the Sarajevo review *Odjek* (Echo). These texts, published in book form under the title *Jesi li živ* (Are You Still Alive, 1973), sparked a political controversy and caused Nogo many nonliterary problems that culminated in his being severely beaten by police agents. But the controversial aspects aside, the book is interesting primarily because it offers valuable glimpses into Nogo's artistic beliefs.

Writing about the importance of tradition in poetry, Nogo argues that modern poets must turn to "myths and tradition" since they live in an age characterized by the "general eclipse of ideas." In the "search for identity and spirituality" they inevitably trade "private symbols for universal ones." Consequently, the language of poetry becomes "richer and more communicative" because it not only conveys the "emotions" of an individual but also becomes comprehensive or "referential" in the process. "Poetry is a subjective interpretation of the universe," Nogo writes. "Therefore tradition is necessary to give it the convincing objectivity, which protects it from modern skepticism." However, any glorification of the past must be avoided: "The past is just an organic part in the artistically complete world of poetry; a poem may be permeated with the past, but it should remain modern."

Nogo's next collection, *Bezakonje* (Lawlessness, 1977), clearly reflects these views. The book sums up his long discontent with the outside world in an image of metaphysical darkness, generated by grotesque political oppression. But Nogo's main intention was not just to expose the modern horrors of absolute power, of which he himself had unpleasant and recent firsthand experience. Rather than that, Nogo tried in *Bezakonje* to learn how to protect himself, to find something that could help him mentally endure and emotionally survive the constant pressure. As in *Zverinjak*, nature again comes to the rescue. But Nogo also discovered something even more precious: the ancient, rich treasury of Serbian myths, with their traditional symbols and poetic imagery of epic songs, which contain the entire cultural memory of the Serbs. Thus he confronted the chaos and meaninglessness of contemporary history with the implicit orderliness and healing powers of culture and tradition. But he also went a step further: he presented this sharp clash of sense and non-sense in the restrained, elegant form of the Petrarchan sonnet. Like those mythical symbols and traditional poetic images with which he shielded himself against the chaos of the modern age, the strict rules and undisturbed order of the sonnet form could also offer protection against the outside chaos. One of his finest poems, the sonnet "Zrelo žito vilov dole bosioče plavi" (O Ripe Wheat, Vilov Valley, Blue Sweet Basil), perfectly illustrates this process:

> O ripe wheat, Vilov valley, sweet blue basil,
> Don't despise me, take me, hide me in the grasses,
> O sister water, give me back your soft eyes,
> With which mountains and rivers began to see.
>
> O beasts, birds, tadpoles, ants, do not run,
> I've kept words for you in my cruel head,
> I'm standing in the world like a scarecrow in a field,
> Like a lightning rod's tip where misfortune strikes.
>
> My white nerves are burning, the old frost of my soul,
> Let your chlorophyll save me, let it keep laser beams
> In the steady hand of a mafia hit-man from burning
>   through me.
>
> If your vegetable soul can save anything at all,
> If there's any more saving for this black head of mine,
> O golden wheat, nettle, and sweet blue basil.

—translation by Stephen M. Dickey

Nogo wrote this sonnet immediately after the episode with the police agents: it was a radical illustration of the "lawlessness" of the age in which the instruments of political oppression are equated with the "steady hand of the mafia hit-man." In despair, he turned to the few remaining images from his childhood: the Vilov valley is the place where Nogo's father had his hut. Nature also seems to offer some hope of protection: the destructive "laser beams" can be neutralized by the life-giving "chlorophyll," which is backed by "beasts," "birds," "tadpoles," "ants," "golden wheat," "sweet blue basil," and "sister water." The last three images, however, are formulaic and belong to the stock of Serbian traditional poetry. The invocation of tradition brings Nogo a new and powerful ally, but the ready-made phrases, used time and again in various epic songs, also activate numerous associations, and Nogo's language suddenly becomes much more "referential" as it begins to resound with past voices. The sonnet form functions here in the same manner—it represents a link, a continuation of an ancient, meaningful tradition into the present day. This, in fact, is a process of relativization: Nogo's individual experience, associated with pantheistic and traditional images and cast into a highly stylized poetic form, finally becomes "universal."

However, the "lawlessness" did not reign only in Nogo's poetry—the political pressure on him persisted, and he was eventually forced to leave Sarajevo for Belgrade, which was politically more liberal; there he became the editor in the BIGZ publishing house in 1982. He wrote criticism, prepared a few widely acclaimed editions of a variety of works of Serbian literature, and published several volumes of his own selected poetry. However, after his Sarajevo experiences Nogo needed a period of spiritual recuperation. Therefore his next collection, *Lazareva subota* (Lazarus's Day, 1989), came out a full twelve years after *Bezakonje*.

In *Lazareva subota* Nogo continued to link the present with the past, although he changed both the tone and the subject matter considerably. Adopting the plaintive rhythms of a ballad, and combining them with simple rhymed quatrains and couplets of an ordinary folk song, he turned to the memories of his childhood: his mother's illness and attempted suicide, his father's desperation and death, his own frantic efforts as a child to understand what was going on around him. Nogo indicated that his primary intention was "to recreate that ruined hut from Borija with every single line of the collection"; this endeavor is clearly visible in the poem "Listovi vječnog kalendara" (Pages of the Eternal Calendar), which describes the disintegration of the

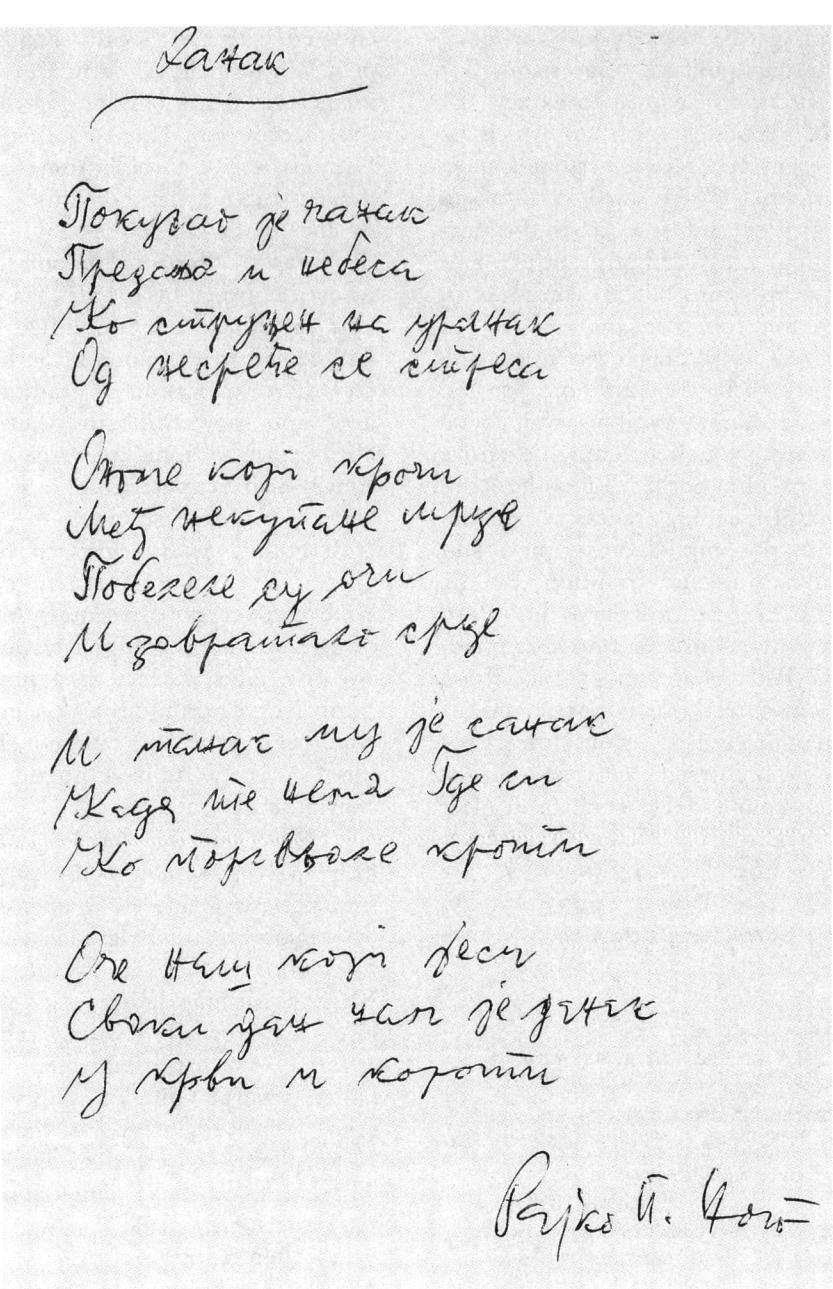

Manuscript for Nogo's "Danak" (from his 1994 collection Na kapijama raja)

family after his mother's death. The poem's tragic sense of life is also one of the major characteristics of the entire collection:

> Of late our mother's health has failed
> Our old house leans on crooked walls,
> And, every leaf a torn-off page,
> The calendar eternal has begun to fall
>
> On All Saints' Eve a weasel birthed
> Out in the yard—the time was wrong
> Winged orphans rose above the earth
> The valley echoed a bagpipe's song
>
> Saints Dmitri's and George's days are lost
> From the empty pages of our book
> Our basil flowers are cloaked in frost
> And cobwebs drape the cauldron-hook.
>
> —translation by Stephen M. Dickey

The frequent references to religious motifs indicate that Nogo wanted to establish some other important links. The central part of the collection, which deals with his personal memories, is introduced and concluded by two shorter cycles, focused on the biblical legend of the resurrection of Lazarus, and on the most important event in Serbian medieval history, the Battle of Kosovo in 1389, in which Serbian Prince Lazar Hrebeljanović chose the "heavenly kingdom," that is, death, rather than Turkish vassalage. Evoking Christian myths with the events from his early childhood—Lazarus's Day happened to be his father's *slava,* the most important religious holiday for a Serbian family—Nogo established an associative link between his family's traditions and biblical legends. But in his interpretation the biblical Lazarus also became identified with the historical Prince Lazar, the Serbian national symbol of the victory of the moral will over historical realities. In this way the whole collection acquired the quality of archetypal and collective experience, which in fact characterized the heroic songs and family rituals that Nogo remembered from his childhood.

Nogo's last collection *Na kapijama raja* (At the Gates of Eden, 1994) is marked by the return to the sonnet form and the frequent recurrence of religious motifs. Considering the enormity of the contemporary chaos and tragedy in the lands of the former Yugoslavia, with which the collection largely deals, its formal strictness and characteristic imagery seem appropriate to anyone who is familiar with Nogo's poetics. The "Eden" from the title poem is presented as a highly ambiguous religious concept: its associations range from the "heavenly kingdom" of Prince Lazar to the promises of the communist social paradise in the 1950s. It also functions as a bitter comment regarding the tragedy of the early 1990s. But in general, in *Na kapijama raja,* religion has assumed the protective role played by tradition in *Bezakonje.* However, as the concluding poem, "Kraj nametne gromile" (At the Burial Mound), clearly shows, this religion is much older and even more comprehensive than Christianity. The poem is an epitaph for Nogo (the solemn atmosphere of the entire collection is underlined by the inclusion of four more epitaphs and two prayers in sonnet form):

> Where our house used to be, a forest grew up overnight,
> Not a forest but a church, its vault the starry sky,
> From the highest mountain to the Istanbul highway,
> From the newlyweds' graveyard to the Giaour's tomb,
> Through gorges and ravines, through chasms and thickets,
> Where the black-robed raven's caw is still a chant,
> In that wide churchyard the burial mounds are mass-graves,
> They glow on the horizon when the sky darkens,
> I, too, was an altar boy in the Vilov valley,
> On snow-crowned trees there shines a cross of frost,
> Do not say it is the wind, that is a liturgy
> Sung by brotherhoods of pines and sisterhoods of firs.
>   At the burial mound, when light shines from above,
>   You can read: Here lieth a sinful scribe, formerly Rašović by name.

—translation by Stephen M. Dickey

The reaching out toward tradition and the past is stressed by the introduction of the family's old name—Rašović. Religion is not approached as a form of fixed dogma but as an ideal of pantheistic and spiritual unity. Therefore Christian symbols merge with pagan and pantheistic images, with memories of the lost home, with the symbolic geography and the tragic history of Nogo's native Herzegovina. In this light these fourteen lines may be taken to represent the poetic sum of Nogo's entire life, experience, and all of his spiritual and artistic endeavors.

"Poetry is not a turning loose of emotion, but an escape from emotion; it is not the expression of personality, but an escape from personality," wrote Eliot. This is why the adoption of tradition—mythical, religious, pantheistic—had such fortunate consequences for Nogo, whose artistic imagination and creative impulses depend so much upon his personal memories and immediate emotional reactions. It was literally Eliot's "historical sense" that enabled Nogo "to continue to be a poet beyond his twenty-fifth year." On the other hand, Nogo has always strongly resembled that "foolish" sunflower of his, who stubbornly keeps dreaming "of the sun," despite everything. There are many moments of a funeral atmosphere in *Na kapijama raja,* but the threshold of death can be perceived in this book as an attempt to regain the lost primal purity of human life—or a shred of its meaning beyond actual historical fate. For this quest, it seems that tradition has offered Nogo the most promising chance of success.

Bibliography:
Mira Miljanović, "Bibliografija," *Život,* 37, nos. 9–10 (1988): 34–40.

References:
Thomas Eekman, *Thirty Years of Yugoslav Literature* (Ann Arbor: University of Michigan Press, 1978), pp. 304–305;

Nikola Koljević, "Čarna bezakonja Rajka P. Noga: Portreti bosanskohercegovačkih pisaca," *Život,* 37, no. 9-10 (1988): 3-16;

Svetozar Koljević, "Nogova čarna bezakonja," in *Putevi reči* (Sarajevo: Svjetlost, 1978), pp. 207-223;

Koljević, "O dozivanju reči," in Nogo's *Na kapijama raja* (Belgrade: Srpska književna zadruga, 1995), pp. 59-70;

Mihajlo Pantić, "A Lyrical Narrator," *Relations,* 1-2 (1995): 207-209;

Novica Petković, "Dva Lazara," Rajko Petrov Nogo, *Lazareva subota* (Belgrade: Srpska književna zadruga, 1990), pp. 47-64;

Petković, "Lično i predačko iskustvo u poeziji Rajka Noga," *Letopis Matice srpske,* 5 (1979): 871-885;

"Dva Lazara," Rajko Petrov Nogo, *Lazareva subota* (Belgrade: Srpska književna zadruga, 1990), pp. 47-64;

Marko Vešović, "Bilješke o poeziji Rajka Petrova Noga," *Književnost,* 40, no. 7-8 (1985): 1425-1449.

Slobodan Novak
(3 November 1924 -)

Aldijana Šišić

BOOKS: *Glasnice u oluji* (Zagreb: Novo pokoljejenje, 1950);
Iza lukobrana (Zagreb: Zora, 1953);
Izgubljeni zavičaj (Split: Pododbor Matice hrvatske, 1955);
Trofej, by Novak and Stjepan Perović (Zagreb: Lyksos, 1960);
Tvrdi grad (Zagreb: Zora, 1961); republished as *Novele* (Belgrade: Prosveta, 1962);
Mirisi, zlato i tamjan (Zagreb: Nakladni zavod Matice hrvatske, 1968);
Izvanbrodski dnevnik (Zagreb: Biblioteka, 1976).
Editions: *Izgubljeni zavičaj i dvanaest novela* (Zagreb: Znanje, 1980);
Sabrana djela, 6 volumes (Zagreb: Globus, 1990).
Edition in English: *Gold, Frankincense and Myrrh*, translated by Celia Hawkesworth (Zagreb: Most/The Bridge, 1991).

PLAY PRODUCTIONS: *Strašno je znati*, 1962;
Mirisi, zlato i tamjan, adapted for the stage by Božidar Violić, Zagreb, Theater Zagreb, 1974–1994.

RADIO: *Strašno je znati*, Radio Zagreb, 1961–1966;
Trofej, Radio Zagreb, 1964;
Majstore, kako vam je ime?, Radio Zagreb, 1966;
Zakrivljeni prostor, Radio Zagreb, 1969;
Školjka šumi, Radio Zagreb, 1975;
Redukcija, Radio Zagreb, 1983;
Zakrivljeno vrijeme, Radio Zagreb, 1984;
Hlap, Radio Zagreb, 1988;
Samotnik, Radio Zagreb, 1995.

The literary opus of Slobodan Novak is not large, but it is one of exceptional quality. His work includes poetry, short stories, novels, and dramatic texts as well as many essays and critical articles printed in various newspapers and literary journals. With only a few published volumes, Novak's work ranks among the highest accomplishments of contemporary Croatian literature.

Slobodan Novak

Slobodan Novak was born on 3 November 1924 in Split to Duje Novak, a caterer, and his wife, Marija, née Smoje. After his mother's early death Novak moved to one of the Adriatic islands, Rab, where he spent his childhood living with his aunt. After completing elementary school Novak returned to Split to continue his schooling in the Catholic Seminary and state high school. When World War II broke out and the Italian forces occupied Dalmatia, Novak's education was interrupted. Once again he left Split, this time for Sušak, near Rijeka, where he completed his secondary education and, after graduation, joined the National Liberation Movement forces (Partisans) in 1943.

Novak began to write in high school and continued during the period between 1943 and 1945, submitting his work to war newspapers. With the end of the war and demobilization he moved to Zagreb, and in 1945 he registered as a student. In the years leading to his degree from the Philosophical Faculty of the University of Zagreb, Novak was involved in the work of *Student-*

ski list (Student News), in which he published poems, essays, and criticism. In 1948, with the help of his friends, Novak launched, cofounded, and edited the literary periodical *Izvor* (The Source), which provided a forum for the writings of younger Croatian authors. Novak contributed articles to *Izvor,* although lyric verse was his primary form of expression as a young man.

Novak's first collection of poems, *Glasnice u oluji* (Harbingers in the Storm), was published in 1950. In the same year he became a member of Društvo hrvatskih književnika (Society of Croatian Writers). When in 1951 *Izvor* ceased publication, Novak continued to work as an editor and journalist, launching a new literary journal in Zagreb the following year called *Krugovi* (Circles). This journal became one of the central organs of a group of young Croatian writers who continued the ideas of modernism. Distancing themselves from predetermined dogmatic attitudes, Novak and his colleagues gathered around *Krugovi* and embraced freedom of expression and an appreciation of literature for its own sake. With their work coming increasingly close to the contemporary literature of Western Europe, contributors to this literary magazine, later known as "krugovaši," influenced and established the future of a new approach to Croatian literature. In addition to Novak, *Krugovi* was edited by Antun Šoljan, Zvonimir Golob, Vlatko Pavletić, Josip Barković, Nikola Milićević, and Josip Pupačić. They were selective in choosing articles for the magazine but were also open to a variety of high-quality writing. In addition, the magazine contained many essays and reviews by new authors as well as contributions by established Croatian writers. *Krugovi* also included a substantial number of translations from European writers such as T. S. Eliot, Virginia Woolf and Boris Pasternak. At this stage of his career, as he continued to write for *Krugovi* and the Zagreb newspaper *Vjesnik* (The Herald), Novak may be described as mostly a journalist and a poet. Together with two other Croatian poets, his good friends and colleagues Milićević and Pavletić, Novak published a second collection of verse, *Pjesme* (Poems), in 1953. In this volume Novak's own poems were gathered under the title *Iza lukobrana* (Behind the Breakwater).

The following years were a turning point for Novak, who began to explore prose as a new form of expression. During the period between 1952 and 1954 he published fragments of prose in the literary journals *Krugovi* and *Republika*. Novak's first volume of short novellas, *Izgubljeni zavičaj* (Lost Homeland), was independently published in 1955, the year he became director of drama at the Croatian National Theater in Split. In five related narrative studies containing a considerable number of autobiographical elements seen through the eyes of a child, Novak shares with his readers a lyrical pastoral story about a prewar childhood spent on an island. When, after World War II, the young man returns to the island of his childhood in the uniform of a warrior, searching for forgotten memories and his lost homeland, Novak also shares with his readers the pain that comes with broken hopes, unfulfilled love, and disillusion. The home is lost; the loved ones are dead; and the narrator leaves the island.

Containing no political references, Novak's book was warmly welcomed by critics, particularly because it came at a time when there was a determined movement to break away from patriotic, folk-oriented literature. Some critics believe that with *Izgubljeni zavičaj* Novak became the first Croatian writer in this period to dare to write prose without an ideological dimension. Novak opened a new door for a whole generation of like-minded writers by writing a novel without focusing on partisan-derived or partisan-condoned themes at a time when Croatian authors were freeing themselves from the prescribed dogmas of socialist realism. Ultimately, *Izgubljeni zavičaj* proved to be one of the last lyrical pastoral stories in Croatian literature, as new contemporary forms were about to be explored.

Toward the end of the 1950s and at the beginning of the 1960s Novak worked as an editor at the literary journal *Mogućnosti* (Possibilities), the newspaper *Slobodna Dalmacija* (Free Dalmatia), and the publishing house *Lykos* and as a journalist at Radio Zagreb.

In 1961 he published his second volume of prose, *Tvrdi grad* (Unyielding City), which was republished in 1962 as *Novele* (Novellas). This was a collection of short stories written since 1952, some of which had already been published in various magazines. Continuing to write in the first person and again using autobiographical elements, Novak established a recognizable pattern in his writing. Depicting a series of life situations with realistic, rather than idealized, human beings as the main characters, he explored such themes as the life of a Catholic nun and the death of newborn children in *Badessa Madre Antonia* (Badessa Madre Antonia), possible ways of dying in *Treba umrijeti logično* (One Should Die in a Logical Manner), and an act of suicide and execution during wartime in *Dolutali metak* (Stray Bullet).

In the story *Na uzvišici* (On the Hill), dominated by the atmosphere of a graveyard which represents nothing other than an archive of dead names, the narrator witnesses the final truth about human life. United with the cemetery by his own mortality, he recalls victories and defeats in his own life. The scent of death and the atmosphere of graveyards can be found in Novak's later writings too. Together with the secrets of the human consciousness, the notion of mortality versus life became one of his main topics while he continued in his work to search for a full understanding of human existence. With this volume of stories Novak's central concerns became even clearer: the tragic consequences of the psychological damage caused by war and the distortion of human relationships in modern life. With the publication of *Tvrdi grad* Novak achieved immediate recognition, just as he had with his first book of prose. This collection of stories assured his standing in Croatian literature, demonstrating that the accomplishment of *Izgubljeni zavičaj* was not mere chance. Nevertheless, writing prose did not prevent Novak from exploring the world of drama.

At the beginning of the 1960s Novak published his first dramatic text, *Trofej* (Trophy, 1960), with Stjepan Perović as co-author. The same text was used to create a drama for Radio Zagreb in 1963. Novak's dramatic texts were often played on Radio Zagreb: *Strašno je znati* (It Is Terrible to Know) in 1961; *Majstore, kako vam je ime?* (Maestro, What Is Your Name?) in 1966; *Zakrivljeni prostor* (Crooked Space) in 1969; and *Školjka šumi* (Murmuring Shell) in 1975. *Zakrivljeni prostor* was performed on Radio Prague; *Strašno je znati* was adapted into a stage play in 1962; and the story "Dolutali metak" was adapted into a television play with the same title in 1964. At the Yugoslav Radio Television festival held in Novi Sad in 1966 Novak received the award for the best radio play, and two years later he won an international award in Prague.

For the last nineteen years of his working life, from 1964 through 1983, when he retired, Novak worked as an editor in the publishing houses Zora (Dawn) and Naprijed (Forward). During these years he published only two books, *Mirisi, zlato i tamjan* (1968; translated as *Gold, Frankincense and Myrrh*, 1991) and *Izvanbrodski dnevnik* (Off the Ship Diary, 1976). *Mirisi, zlato i tamjan* is the story of a retired former partisan who lives with his wife on one of the Adriatic islands and takes care of an old dying lady, Madona Markantunova. Surrounded by the scent of slow death, they live their lives to a rhythm dictated by the eighteen-day cycle of Madona's digestive system. In this atmosphere of living and dying, left alone with the old lady while his wife is away, the narrator begins his intellectual monodrama, daringly asking himself questions which convert his personal and intimate suffering into something more or less universal. The novel describes his state of mind as he is occasionally tempted to speed up the process of the old lady's death in order to free himself and live his own life. At other times, as he questions the meaning of his own existence, the old lady becomes the only worthy purpose left in his life. Additionally, *Mirisi, zlato i tamjan* reflects an observation of the new ways versus the old. The dying lady, Madona Markantunova, represents the old: she is a disturbing leftover from the prewar system. Nevertheless, witnessing the fading of moral and human values as the new system overcomes the old one, and using irony as his main form of expression, Novak offers a bitter perception of the new world, articulating the feelings of a whole generation of like-minded fellow writers:

> There isn't a trace of my illustrious ancestor in my present make-up, but neither are there any traces in us of what we ourselves were once, or of what we wanted. We were our own great forefathers; now we are our own degenerate posterity. Now you've begun to talk about all this as well, now you've seen that you are not my disciple, it will be easier for me to support this exile, and I shall possibly even begin to love Madonna in a way: because she is something that I dare to despise in the face of my past, that I dare to condemn and reject, that I dare to hate. That is why I must love her. As long as she lives, I shall feel directly that we have achieved something, that we have invested our youth in something, that we have destroyed something that threatened to fall on our heads. So, what's to be done? So, let's let Madonna live! Let her endure, for me to busy myself with her! Let that past vegetate on since it's so innocuous and piteous compared to the evils we ourselves created! She really is a monster; although she's partly our doing as well, but she's really a monster in her own right too, she's a very suitable object to embody much of what was poisoning mankind, what had to be wiped out, she's worthy of contempt, appropriate to justify the exploits of our heroic youth, everything we undertook in faith and sacrifice and work, even our rashness and presumptuousness and even our unintentional crimes!

For this novel Novak was awarded three of

Dust jacket for Novak's 1968 novel, Mirisi, zlato i tamjan, *which tells the story of a former partisan who cares for a dying old woman*

the most important literary prizes in the former Yugoslavia: the prize of the Croatian publisher Matica hrvatska (1968); one of the most distinguished awards of Yugoslav literary critics for the novel of the year, the NIN prize (1969); and the annual Croatian state award, the Vladimir Nazor Prize (1969). Also *Mirisi, zlato i tamjan* inspired the film producer Ante Babaja to produce a film in 1971 and Božidar Violić, a theater director, to adapt it into a play with the same title in 1974. The play was performed in the Theater Zagreb for twenty years (until 1994). Many critics commenting on Novak's work argue that the irretrievable loss of the homeland, ideals, and hopes in his first book of prose, *Izgubljeni zavičaj*, is the main reason for the endurance and growth of sarcasm in his writings. Novak's irony became strikingly strong in *Mirisi, zlato i tamjan,* but it reached its crescendo in *Izvanbrodski dnevnik*.

In this work the narrator's irony becomes not only an instrument for the process of observation, but also a perfect tool for the self-defense of a writer with no illusions left. Novak published this short novel after a long pause in his creative writing, eight years after *Mirisi, zlato i tamjan*. Although all of his writings include autobiographical elements, none of them said so much about his own ethical standpoint as *Izvanbrodski dnevnik*. In this book it becomes perfectly clear to the reader that Novak is an author with a stable set of moral values and beliefs. He is merciless in questioning himself and his role as a subject in "the system." Similarly, he shows no sympathy for others or for the system itself. The story is written in three chapters in which the narrator describes his journeys between the Island, the Mainland, and the Town and then back to the Island again. Perusing the world through the eyes of a patient from a mental hospital and using intense and powerful sarcasm, Novak clearly underlines his belief that no institution and no system but instead the human being should be the measure for everything. He expresses his awareness of the hidden ethical whirlpools inside the human mind and indicates his concern for the survival of human individuality.

Novak has not published any new books since 1976. Moreover, few later editions of his work or critical studies about him have been published. In 1980 Novak's first novel, *Izgubljeni zavičaj*, was reprinted together with some of his earlier stories under the title *Izgubljeni zavičaj i dvanaest novela* (Lost Homeland and Twelve Novellas). This was a new edition of some already published prose from the collection *Tvrdi grad*, but the story "Nacionalni park" (National Park) was published for the first time in this volume. This volume also contains the story "Crvena mrlja" (Red Mark), which was the result of cooperative work with Antun Šoljan. The story is the outcome of a friendly literary game between the two men. They agreed to write a story with the same title but from two different perspectives. In this way, twin stories were born. They were published for the first time in the journal *Forum* (1962). In 1983 Novak became a full member of the Croatian Academy of Science and Art, and he retired in the same year. Since then he has written four more radio plays that were performed on Radio Zagreb, including *Redukcija* (Reduction, 1983) and *Zakrivljeno vrijeme* (Crooked Time, 1984).

In 1990 all of Novak's writings were gathered in *Sabrana djela* (Collected Works). This six-volume collection contains previously independently published writings and three stories written and published in various magazines after 1983: "Riba Jonina" (A Fish Called Jona, 1986), "Hlap" (Lobster, 1986), and "Moje univerzijade" (My Universiade, 1987). Many writings in this edition are edited by Novak himself, and often the final texts differ from their originals. For instance, the story "Badessa Madre Antonia" is completely changed. In 1990, the same year that the *Sabrana djela* volumes were published, Novak was presented the Vladimir Nazor Prize for Life Achievement. In 1995 Novak published a novella, *Gospa od oprosta* (Mother of Forgiveness), in the journal of the Society of Croatian Writers, *Hrvatsko slovo* (Croatian Word) and the monologue *Samotnik* (Loner) in the journal *Forum*. His work has been published in Hungary, Germany, Czechoslovakia, Poland, Italy, Slovenia, and Great Britain, and individual texts have appeared in the United States, Holland, Russia, Bulgaria, and France.

Since he retired in 1983, Slobodan Novak has lived a quiet life with his wife Nada (née Nedeljković) and their two sons. They spend their time in Zagreb and Rab, the island of Novak's childhood that is reflected in so much of his work. By the complex body of work he has created, Novak has contributed immensely to Croatian literature and has rightfully become one of its most prominent writers.

References:

Josip Barković, "Nova stvarnost?," *Republika*, 6 (1961): 31;

Miroslav Beker, "Slobodan Novak: *Mirisi, zlato i tamjan*," *Croatica*, 7–8 (1976): 231–238;

Duško Car, "Zarobljenik u tvrdom gradu," *Književnik*, 26 (1961): 241–256;

Dalibor Cvitan, "Most ironičnog komentara," *Telegram*, 185 (1963): 5;

Branimir Donat, "Moralistički roman," in his *Brbljava sfinga* (Zagreb: Znanje, 1978), pp. 92–98;

Ivo Frangeš, *Povijest hrvatske književnosti* (Zagreb & Ljubljana: Nakla ni zavod Matice hrvatske Cankanjeva založba, 1987), pp. 404–407;

E. Celia Hawkesworth, "The Allegorical Significance of *Mirisi, zlato i tamjan*," *Sezione Slava*, 18 (1976): 109–127;

Boris Lukšić, "Roman antiideologije Slobodana Novaka," *Republika*, 2–3 (1969);

Igor Mandić, "Od pastorale do ironije," in his *Književnost i medijska kultura* (Zagreb: Nakla ni zavod Matice hrvatske, 1984), pp. 61–79;

Mandić, "Zlato Novakove proze," in his *Uz dlaku* (Zagreb: Mladost, 1970), pp. 174–176;

Tonko Maroević, "Ideologija priče," *Kolo*, 3 (1968);

Ranko Marinković, "Askeza prokušanog skeptika," in his *Nevesele oči kla una* (Zagreb: Globus, 1988), pp. 225–227;

Republika, special issue on Novak, no. 3–4 (1991);

Đuro Šnajder, "Traženje izgubljenog u osvojenom prostoru," in his *Uvod u najnoviju hrvatsku prozu* (Zagreb: Matice hrvatske, 1971), pp. 73–103.

Vesna Parun
(10 April 1922 -   )

Dasha Čulić Nisula
Western Michigan University

BOOKS: *Zore i vihori* (Zagreb: Društvo književnika Hrvatske, 1947);
Pjesme (Zagreb: Matica hrvatska, 1948);
Crna maslina (Zagreb: Društvo književnika Hrvatske, 1955);
Ropstvo (Belgrade: Nolit, 1957);
Vidrama vjerna (Zagreb: Zora, 1957);
Pusti da otpočinem (Sarajevo: Narodna prosvjeta, 1958);
Tuga i radost šume (Zagreb: Mladost, 1958);
Zec mudrijan (Sarajevo: Svjetlost, 1958);
Koralj vraćen moru (Zagreb: Naprijed, 1959);
Ti i nikad (Zagreb: Lykos, 1959);
Patka Zlatka (Zagreb: Lykos, 1959);
Kornjačin oklop (Zagreb: Naša djeca, 1960);
Jao jutro (Belgrade: Prosveta, 1963);
Vjetar Trakije (Zagreb: Zora, 1964);
Pjesme (Zagreb: Matica hrvatska, 1964);
Gong (Zagreb: Naprijed, 1966);
Mačak Džingiskan i Miki Trasi (Zagreb: Spektar, 1968);
Miki Trasi i baba Pim-Bako (Zagreb: Vlastita naklada, 1968);
Mačak na mjesecu (Zagreb: Vlastita naklada, 1969);
Ukleti dažd (Zagreb: Zrinski, 1969);
Miki-slavni kapetan (Zagreb: Školska knjiga, 1970);
Sto soneta (Čakovac: Zrinjski, 1972);
I prolazim životom (Belgrade: Nolit, 1972);
Stid me je umrijeti (Zagreb: August Cesarec, 1974);
Olovni golub (Belgrade: Slovo ljubve, 1975);
Apokaliptičke basne (Belgrade: Prosveta, 1976);
Ljubav bijela kost (Zagreb: Suria, 1978);
Salto mortale: 1975-1981 (Zagreb: Sveučilišna naklada Liber, 1981);
Grad na Durmitoru (Nikšić: Univerzitetska riječ, 1988);
Krv svjedoka (Banjaluka: Glas, 1988);
Kasfalpirova zemlja: soneti (Belgrade: Književne novine, 1989).
Editions and Collections: *Konjanik* (Zagreb: Školska knjiga, 1961);
Bila sam dječak (Zagreb: Naprijed, 1963);

Vesna Parun (photograph by Dragutin Dumančić)

Otvorena vrata (Belgrade: Prosveta, 1968);
Izabrane pesme (Belgrade: Srpska književna zadruga, 1979);
Šum krila-šum vode (Zagreb: Mladost, 1981);
Vesna Parun: Izabrana djela (Zagreb: Nakladni zavod Matice hrvatske, 1982);

Pod muškim kišobranom (Zagreb: Globus, 1987);

Izabrana djela Vesne Parun, selected and arranged by Vlatko Pavletić (poetry) and Karmen Milačić (prose and drama), 9 volumes (Zagreb: Mladost, 1988-1990).

Editions in English: Poems in *The Bridge,* translated by Vasa D. Mihailovich, Ronald Moran, Maria Malby, and R. A. Ford, 19-20 (1970): 31-36;

Poems in *Contemporary Yugoslav Poetry,* edited by Mihailovich, Moran, and Malby (Iowa City: University of Iowa Press, 1977), pp. 42-47;

Poems in *Contemporary East European Poetry,* edited by George Emery, translated by Peter Kastmiller (Ann Arbor: Ardis, 1983), pp. 354-361;

Poems in *Most,* translated by Vesna Dye and Kastmiller, 1-2 (1985): 98-112; 4 (1985): 147-152;

Selected Poems of Vesna Parun, selected and translated by Dasha Culic Nisula (University Center, Mich.: Green River Press, 1985).

PLAY PRODUCTIONS: *Marija i mornar,* Zadar, Narodno kazalište, October 1959; second version in Zagreb, Hrvatsko narodno kazalište, 19 April 1961;

Nasmiješih se i pođoh dalje, Belgrade, Theater of Poetry, 1968;

Mačak Džingiskan i Miki Trasi, Zagreb, Zagrebačko kazalište mladih, 1 February 1971;

Večernja zvijezda ili žena sam, Zagreb, Theater ITD, 1978;

Magareći otok, Zagreb, Hrvatsko narodno kazalište, 20 June 1979;

Apokaliptičke basne, based on the book of poetry by the same name, Zagreb, Theater of Poetry "Goranovo proljeće," June 1982;

Škola za skitnice, Zagreb, Malo kazalište Trešnjevka, 26 September 1983;

U Zlarinu na rtu Bučini, Šibenik, Narodno kazalište, 19 June 1988.

RADIO: *Marija i mornar,* Radio Zagreb, 1962;

Apsirt, brat Medejin, Radio Zagreb, 1969;

Tri morske pustolovke, Radio Belgrade, 1971;

Srce od bumbara, Radio Zagreb, 1971;

Zlarinska rapsodija, Radio Zagreb, 1977;

Miki Trasi i Hijena SSS, Radio Zagreb, 1983;

Slike iz Nenine stale, Radio Zagreb, 1985;

Suncokret na pučini, Radio Zagreb, 1987.

OTHER: "Tragom Magde Isanos," sonnets from Romania by Parun and Radomir Andrić in *Karpatsko umiljenije* (Kruševac: Bagdala, 1971);

Penjo Penev: Poetry, translated from Bulgarian into Croatian by V. Parun (Zagreb: Mladost, 1971);

"Potres u gradu Kali," *Forum,* no. 1-2 (1979).

Vesna Parun is indisputably the grande dame of Croatian poetry. She, like other poets of the postwar period, was influenced by the outstanding figure of the prewar era, Tin Ujević, who stands at the threshold of pre- and postwar Croatian literature. In the subsequent period, the 1940s and 1950s, it was the work of Parun and Jure Kaštelan that determined the new course for modern poetry in Croatia. In her forty-year career Parun has published more than twenty collections of poetry, some ten books of poetry for children, many plays and radio dramas, journalistic prose, and translations from Slovenian and Bulgarian. Her own poetry has been translated into Bulgarian, English, French, German, Russian, Slovakian, and Slovenian. The breadth and depth of her poetry, and the deeply feminine perspective that she brought to it, make her the Anna Akhmatova of Croatian literature. She has received many prestigious literary awards, including the City of Zagreb Award, 1954; Vladimir Nazor Prize, 1959; Grigor Vitez Prize, 1968; Aleksa Šantić Prize, 1973; and the Zmaj and Goranov Vjenac Award.

Vesna Parun was born on the island of Zlarin near Šibenik on 10 April 1922; the early 1920s saw the birth of other important East European poets, such as Miroslav Holub, Blaže Koneski, Vasko Popa, and Aco Šopov. Parun attended grade school on the island of Vis and high school in Šibenik and Split. In 1932, at the age of ten, she published her first poem in "Andjeo Čuvar" (Guardian Angel). In 1940 she enrolled in the department of Romance languages at the University of Zagreb. During World War II her family lived in Sesvete, near Zagreb. It was from there that her brother went to fight with the partisans and never returned. The loss of her brother affected her profoundly, and the void that she has felt since then has inspired many poems, the most frequently named being "Mati čovjekova" (Mother of Man). After the war she studied again at the University of Zagreb, in the department of philosophy. Postwar reconstruction called for the participation of the whole society, and Parun did her part. While on an assignment to rebuild the Šamac-Sarajevo railroad in 1948, she contracted a severe case of ty-

Title page of Parun's 1966 collection of experimental poems

phus. Miraculously, she survived, and she has since lived and worked as a freelance writer in Zagreb.

Parun's first collection of poetry, *Zore i vihori* (Dawns and Storms), was published in 1947, one year after Anna Akhmatova had been viciously attacked by the Central Committee of the CPSU (Communist Party of the Soviet Union), expelled from the Soviet Writers' Union, and forbidden to publish. This incident is significant because it shows that Yugoslavia was still firmly under Soviet influence at that time. When Parun's first collection appeared, this fresh and exuberant volume was met with immediate criticism by the literary establishment. It was labeled "dark," "sick," "formalistic," and "decadent." By formalistic the official critical community had in mind any art that deviated from the form that was traditional and ideologically correct.

Parun gave the critics what they wanted the next year in her second collection, *Pjesme* (Poems, 1948). The collection consists of 125 poems without titles in traditional eleven-syllable lines in four-line stanzas. Parun then withdrew into a seven-year silence and a slow recovery from typhus. Upon regaining her health, she broke this silence with her third collection, *Crna maslina* (Black Olive Tree, 1955), two years after Joseph Stalin's death and seven years after the Yugoslav break with the Soviet Comintern.

Crna maslina represents for Parun a beginning, as did *Zore i vihori;* both collections contain the seeds of formal and thematic concerns that Parun continued to explore throughout her literary career. But in her third collection, which is just one of several in a cycle beginning with *Crna maslina,* Parun's poetry is more mature and her point of view quite firm. Together with Jure Kaštelan, who in the same year published his *Biti ili ne,* she, with her unconventional themes and style, called for the freeing of postwar poetry from conservative formalism.

The two poets responded to World War II in different ways. The darkness that befell the world became a part of Kaštelan's creative output. Parun, on the other hand, although scarred by the war in her own way, faced this darkness with the resilience of her own youth and blossoming femininity. While the world began to "enter" her "inharmoniously," she resisted by writing of the peaceful and harmonious world of nature and of the beauty that she knew in her childhood. Much of her poetry focuses on the sudden realization of danger and its infringement on the otherwise carefree and innocent life of a child.

Parun represents this disharmony, for example, as a bullet that hits a squirrel, or as a lamb that suddenly is lost without its mother. The theme of loss reappears in almost all of Parun's collections, but the nature of the loss varies. It may be the loss of innocence, love, a dear one, or youth. By enumerating these losses in her life, however, Parun seems to affirm life itself, for in them there is the confirmation that there are things of value in life to be lost. Because Parun's focus above all has been on human relationships, critics have called her the poet of love.

The four other collections that she published in the 1950s include: *Ropstvo* (Slavery, 1957), *Vidrama vjerna* (Faithful to Otters, 1957), *Koralj vraćen moru* (Coral Returned to Sea, 1959), and *Ti i nikad* (You and Never, 1959). While *Ropstvo* contains some of her longer poems, it is thematically and stylistically a further development of *Crna maslina*. *Vidrama vjerna* is also a continuation of *Crna maslina,* but this time the poet's use of shorter forms is more obvious. As with other volumes, she explores the human condition (albeit focusing on the condition of women), human relationships, and changes in these that occur over time. She depicts particularly traumatic or eventful moments in life, after which she somehow must reorient herself and continue down untrodden roads of life. Parun's own loss of childhood innocence, virginity, and love she takes as stages of human experience that, though painful, must be accepted.

Two years later the poet published *Koralj vraćen moru,* a collection that contains her most beautiful and authentic evocations of the Mediterranean landscape. In this collection Parun also demonstrates the ability to re-create moments in her past, and thereby re-create herself. She completed the circle of *Crna maslina* with her collection *Ti i nikad.* Her output was extraordinary during this phase, as if she had to pour out the accumulated thoughts of seven years of silence, leading to the production of five major collections in a decade.

In 1958 Parun published two collections of poetry for children, and she devoted the next four years to writing poetry and stories for children. Many of these were produced for radio. She then came out with *Jao jutro* (Woe, Morning, 1963), one of four volumes she produced in the 1960s. This is a collection of poems without punctuation, employing language that is simple but elliptical, imbued with a certain musical quality. In the next two collections, *Vjetar Trakije* (The Wind of Thrace, 1964) and *Gong* (Gong, 1966), Parun made an attempt at a new poetic expression. Both of these collections are considered her most uneven, seemingly due to her experimentation.

Realizing that she could not take a new path in her search for the absolute, Parun returned to her original poetic expression in *Ukleti dažd* (The Accursed Rain, 1969), her last collection of the 1960s. This volume contains her deepest understanding of the human condition. Although she has returned to an earlier style, she manages to point to her truths in a new way—something that only Parun can do. In her search for the absolute she continually evolved new solutions and new approaches while still using her tried-and-true voice and her themes of the past. Critics who miss this duality have wrongly accused her of being repetitious.

Over her career Parun used free verse as her dominant form of expression, but she was also a master of the sonnet. She displayed her ability in that classic form in several collections. Her sonnets from Romania titled "Tragom Magde Isanos" (On the Trails of Magda Isanos) in *Karpatsko umiljenije* (The Carpathian Charm) were published in 1971. The next year she followed up with the collection *Sto soneta* (A Hundred Sonnets, 1972). Unfortunately, she was again criticized for focusing on form. The volume was reviewed by one critic as "one hundred misses." Nevertheless, the collection has some of the best sonnets written in the Croatian language, one of them being "Molitva čovjeka koji je izgorio spasavajući pčele" (The Prayer of the Man Burned While Saving the Bees). Reflecting her desire that this collection be first of all musical, Parun dedicated it to the composer Vatroslav Lisinski.

In addition to these sonnets there are eighty-six more in *Olovni golub* (A Leaden Pigeon, 1975). Parun herself says that she has written some five hundred. Her musical command of the language places her among the four or five best sonnet writers in Croatian literature. Parun closes her cycle of sonnets with the collection *Ljubav bijela kost* (Love, a White Bone, 1978). Parun published three other collections in the 1970s. *I prolazim životom* (Passing through Life, 1972) came out in the same year as *Sto soneta.* In this volume she picks up and continues the thread begun in *Ukleti dažd,* matching the achievement of the earlier book. *Stid me je umrijeti* (I Am Ashamed to Die, 1974) rounds out the period of poetry for this decade.

The final collection in this decade, a collection of satiric poems, *Apokaliptičke basne* (Apocalyptic Fables, 1976), puzzled the critics. It appeared as if this collection had nothing to do with the previous ones. Yet, as Parun herself said in an interview with Vlatko Pavletić, "lyrics metamorphosize into satire." Poems for this book were produced for the stage under such titles as "Tales for Fools" and "Zoo for People from Adam to Judas." Parun points out that behind all these poems was an "attempt to prevent, via language, the process of separating man from the truth, society from human nature, and art from theory."

In the 1970s and 1980s Parun continued to write for the stage; she also picked up the sonnet form again. Her collection of ironic and satiric sonnets, *Salto mortale: 1975–1981* (Mortal Leap, 1981), consists of four cycles with a total of seventy-seven poems written between 1975 and 1981. At the suggestion of the Montenegrin poet

Vukman Otašević, to whom she had promised a collection of sonnets, she took one of her sonnets "Grad na Durmitoru" (A Tower on the Durmitor), from the above collection, and used it as the title for her next collection, eighty-five sonnets dedicated to Otašević, which was published in 1988.

Her last collection of sonnets in the 1980s was *Kasfalpirova zemlja: soneti* (Kasfalpir's Country, 1989), consisting of three cycles that she calls autobiographical narrative sonnets. The title of the collection is an acronym for the geological, trisymbolic chemical composition ($CaCO_3$ ZnS and FeS_2). Kasfalpir, as Parun calls this composition, does not exist; it is a natural fantasy, comprised of units of three stones and the syllables, *ka-sfal-pir*. Parun calls *kasfalpir* the spirit of isolation, deep in the center of the earth.

Thematically this is a complete cycle of poems, as *Crna maslina* and *Salto mortale* are. Parun calls this collection a lyrical dramatization of her life. She points out that poetry was not her goal here, only a means. These are unusual sonnets, and she calls them bastard sonnets. They are less poetry than narration or psychological reflections. They were written furiously, without stopping, in the summer of 1974 in her apartment in Dubrava, Zagreb. Parun wanted to communicate her experience in prose, something she wished she could write from the beginning of her career, but she always seemed to have been pulled by the poetic form.

Nevertheless, in the late 1980s Parun did publish two books of prose: *Pod muškim kišobranom* (Under a Male Umbrella, 1987) and *Krv svjedoka* (The Blood of Witnesses, 1988). The first collection consists of journalistic prose, fables, sketches, satire, speeches, and interviews; the second is a meditative book in which Parun addresses such topics as life and suffering, history and truth, and art and love.

From 1988 to 1990 the complete works of Parun, nine volumes, were published in Zagreb by Mladost. The volumes of poetry were arranged by Vlatko Pavletić, those of prose and drama by Karmen Milačić. Parun's talent as an artist is displayed on several covers of these volumes. Despite the publication of her complete works, careful study of Parun's oeuvre in the context of her own development in particular and of Croatian literature in general has yet to be made. Her position as the best and most prolific female poet of Croatian literature, however, is already established, and her influence on the younger generation of Croatian poets, especially women, is evident in the works of such poets as Irena Vrkljan, Neda Miranda Blažević, and Jagoda Zamoda. One finds echoes in Parun's work of the Bible, Augustin "Tin" Ujević, and traditional Croatian lyric poetry. Despite these influences, her poetry remains unique in Croatian literature. Parun views her work in part as an attempt to escape all categorizations and definitions. It seems that all along she has been writing but one single book, in one enormous endeavor that is still to be completed. Parun has herself predicted that "I will not find the bottom of my well."

References:

Ante Kadić, "Postwar Croatian Lyric Poetry," *American Slavic and East European Review*, 17 (1958): 509–529;

Ivan V. Lalić, "O poeziji Vesne Parun," *Književnost*, no. 10 (1979): 1549–1557;

Branko Maleš, "Kozmološki genetizam i naturalistički humanizam Vesne Parun," in his *Šum krila, šum vode* (Zagreb: Mladost, 1981), pp. 197–214;

Igor Mandić, "Sto promašaja," in *101 kratka kritika* (Zagreb: August Cesarec, 1977), pp. 206–208;

Nikola Milićević, "Vesna Parun," in his *Riječ u vremenu* (Zagreb: Mladost, 1981), pp. 143–164;

Berislav Nikpalj, "Hod matere čovjekove," in *Stih*, no. 2 (1976): 42–57;

Vlatko Pavletić, "Razgovori s Vesnom Parun," *Knijiževnost*, 75, nos. 10–11 (1983): 1870–1894;

Antun Šoljan, "Tragična ćutilnost Vesne Parun," *Delo*, 24, no. 12 (1978): 77–87.

Milorad Pavić
(15 October 1929 -)

Tomislav Z. Longinović
University of Wisconsin–Madison

BOOKS: *Vojislav Ilić (1860–1894)* (Belgrade: Prosveta, 1961);
Palimpsesti (Belgrade: Nolit, 1967);
"Zabavnik" Vuka Karadžića (Belgrade, 1969);
Istorija srpske književnosti baroknog doba: XVII i XVIII vek (Belgrade: Nolit, 1970);
Mesečev kamen (Belgrade: Nolit, 1971);
Vojislav Ilić i evropsko pesništvo (Novi Sad: Matica srpska, 1971);
Gavril Stefanović Venclović (Belgrade: Srpska književna zadruga, 1972);
Vojislav Ilić, njegovo vreme i delo (Belgrade: Prosveta, 1972);
Od Baroka do klasicizma (Belgrade: Nolit, 1973);
Gvozdena zavesa (Novi Sad: Matica srpska, 1976);
Jezičko pamćenje i pesnički oblik (Novi Sad: Matica srpska, 1976);
Konji svetog Marka (Belgrade: Prosveta, 1976);
Istorija srpske književnosti klasicizma i predromantizma (Belgrade: Nolit, 1979);
Ruski hrt (Belgrade: Slovo ljubve, 1979);
Nove beogradske priče (Belgrade: Nolit, 1981);
Duše se kupaju poslednji put (Novi Sad: Matica srpska, 1982);
Hazarski rečnik (Belgrade: Prosveta, 1984);
Istorija, stalež i stil (Novi Sad: Matica srpska, 1985);
Predeo slikan čajem (Belgrade: Prosveta, 1988);
Izvrnuta rukavica (Novi Sad: Matica srpska, 1989);
Unutrašnja strana vetra (Belgrade: Prosveta, 1991);
Poslednja ljubav u Carigradu (Belgrade: Prosveta, 1994);
Šešir od riblje kože (Belgrade: Draganić, 1995).
Collections: *Sabrana dela,* 7 volumes, edited by Vule Kznjević and Miloslav Mizković (Belgrade: Prosveta, 1990);
Sabrana dela Milorada Pavića, 10 volumes (Belgrade: Draganić, 10 volumes (Belgrade: Draganić, 1996).
Editions in English: *Dictionary of the Khazars,* translated by Christina Pribićević-Zorić (New York: Knopf, 1988);

Milorad Pavić (photograph by M. Djurka, The International Weekly, *Belgrade)*

A Short History of Belgrade, translated by Pribićević-Zoriù (Belgrade: Prosveta, 1990);
Landscape Painted with Tea, translated by Pribićević-Zorić (New York: Knopf, 1990);
The Inner Side of the Wind, or The Novel of Hero and Leander, translated by Pribićević-Zorić (New York: Knopf, 1993);
A Theater Menu, Forever and a Day, translated by Pribi-ćević-Zorić (Belgrade: Graficki atelje Dereta, 1997).

Milorad Pavić is a poet, a writer of fiction, a professor at the University of Belgrade and Novi Sad, and a historian of Serbian literature from the seventeenth through the nineteenth centuries. His work as a fiction writer went almost unnoticed for more than three decades until he earned worldwide popularity with the publication and subsequent translation into many languages of *Hazarski rečnik* (1984, translated as *Dictionary of the Khazars,* 1988). This book, subtitled "A Lexicon Novel in 100,000 Words," represents a daring literary experiment that examines the history of the lost Khazar tribe from the diverging perspectives of Christian, Moslem, and Jewish histo-

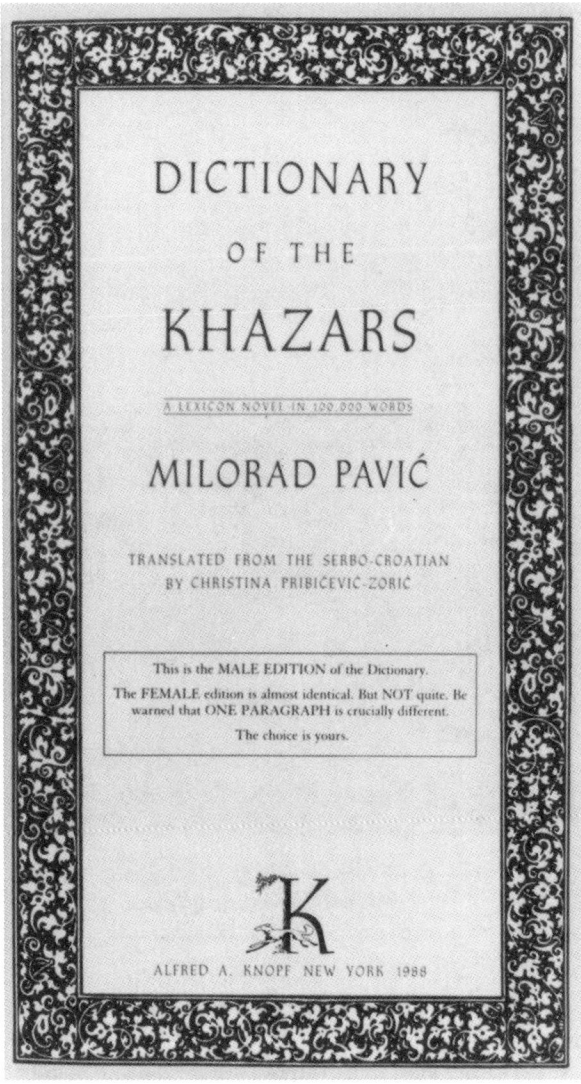

Title page for a translation of the "Male Edition" of Pavić's Hazarski rečnik

riography. His next novel, *Predeo slikan čajem* (1988, translated as *Landscape Painted with Tea*, 1990), is a formal experiment as well, in which Pavić attempts to construct a book that can be read like a crossword puzzle, both "across" and "down." These two innovative books, combined with Pavić's peculiar word usage, have earned him a place among the most widely read and most controversial contemporary literary figures.

Pavić has often stated that he has no biography, or rather that his biography is his bibliography. This statement reveals not only his dedication to writing and publishing but also his preference for metaphors, mystifications, and exaggerations that has become a trademark of his fiction. When interviewers ask when he started writing, Pavić routinely responds that he has been a writer for more than two hundred years.

He then adds that the Pavić family began to publish its first books in the eighteenth century and that one of his ancestors, Emerik Pavić, lived in Budim (Hungary) and wrote poems in *deseterac* (the traditional meter of the Serbian heroic epic) long before this form became fashionable among such giants of European Romanticism as Johann Gottfried von Herder; Johann Wolfgang von Goethe; George Gordon, Lord Byron; Adam Mitzkiewicz; and Aleksandr Pushkin. According to family legends, this line of literary creators extended right up to his own time and included Armin Pavić, a nineteenth-century literary historian and honorary member of the Serbian Academy of Sciences, and Nikola Pavić, a minor playwright and Milorad's uncle, who was considered one of the best representatives of Croatian poetry written in the *kajkavski* dialect.

Although biography is apparently marginal to Pavić's novels, which are permeated with flamboyant historical, mythological, and philosophical reflections, the author himself claims that his most celebrated novel, *Hazarski rečnik*, in fact represents his own autobiography. He explains this statement by invoking his family history. His ancestors were Orthodox Christian Serbs from Žumberk in Croatia. Around the year 1670 many Serbs in Croatia, including the Pavić family, were forcefully converted to Roman Catholicism. Pavić and his family later reconverted to the Orthodox faith, but the process of conversion, identity loss, and ultimately the disappearance of a people is the most significant idea behind *Hazarski rečnik*. The war in the former Yugoslavia in the 1990s and the destiny of the Serbs, who are once again forced to live dispersed throughout the emerging Balkan states, provide a fitting context for understanding the poetic underpinnings of this curious novel. An air of improbability and historical uncertainty has always played a dominant role in the life of the Serbian people; Pavić attributes their tragic sense of collective loss and their fear of disappearance from the face of the earth to his obsession with the topic of the Khazars, elaborated in *Hazarski rečnik*.

Milorad Pavić was born in Belgrade on 15 October 1929. His father was a sculptor and with his mother belonged to Soko, the famous athletic society founded by educated Slavs of the Austro-Hungarian Empire. His mother Vera (née Mihajlović), a professor of philosophy, was also an avid student of Serbian folklore and the South Slavic oral tradition. Pavić stresses the fact that his father deviated from the respected family tradition of becoming a writer. It seems that young

Milorad identified more with his uncle Nikola, a famous poet of the kajkavski dialect of Croatia. The decisive factor that prompted Pavić to embark upon a writing career was his first experience with a foreign language. Since many children in Belgrade learned French between World War I and World War II, Pavić and his sister begged their parents to find them a French teacher. "Breaking the shell of another language," as Pavić has called it, left a lasting impression on the young boy, causing an enormous sense of satisfaction. Only later did he realize that he had misunderstood many words but that this mistranslation was exactly what gave rise to his poetic impulse. Errors in translation placed familiar words in unfamiliar relationships, creating extraordinary metaphors. This experience decisively influenced the development of Pavić's style, with its extravagant metaphoric and synesthetic effects. In addition, most of his later works envision literature as a game of hide-and-seek between the writer and his implied reader. The reader is often called upon to abandon conscious control and labor through the text to decipher the hidden meanings of the narrative. There is something "mediumistic" about this approach to art, especially since Pavić often invokes the reader and emphasizes his or her power to create meanings and narratives out of the usually disjointed, fragmentary, and sometimes outrageous statements he makes in his books. The concept of shifting perspective, which the reader introduces with his or her set of cultural biases, plays a crucial role in the structural organization of his most popular literary works.

Pavić wrote some prose sketches during World War II while staying with his grandmother in Pančevo, a small town just north of Belgrade. His first serious literary attempts, however, came right after the war while he was a student in the Seventh Belgrade Grammar School. He became friends with two young colleagues, Djordje Olejnik and Nedeljko Nešić, who were also beginning to write their first poems. Inspired by this new friendship, Pavić wrote two prose pieces and put them on the school bulletin board. He later tried to publish them in the youth magazine *Mladost* (Youth) but without success, since the prevalent socialist realist orientation of the immediate postwar period in Yugoslavia demanded a literary style that would enforce the political program of the Communist Party. This failure to publish his first story and the general intolerance for the literary models that deviated from the socialist realist one resulted in Pavić's disappointment and withdrawal from the literary scene. He did not write any creative pieces for more than ten years, certain that the political climate would never change.

In the meantime, while a student of literature at the University of Belgrade, Pavić began to translate poetry. He published his first translation from Russian, parts of Pushkin's "Poltava," when he was only twenty years old. Aside from literature, he studied violin in the Belgrade Academy of Music but eventually had to abandon his love of this art for the sake of his career as a literary historian. As early as 1952 he published the entire "Poltava," and by 1954, while still a student, Pavić started publishing contributions in journals devoted to literary history. His main area of study was Serbian literature of the Baroque, Classical, and pre-Romantic eras, which marginalized him politically within the academic circles. For the state-controlled academia, literary history began with the Romantic movement, which the Communists considered the first revolutionary period in literature. Pavić's interest in earlier periods was considered "ideologically unsound," and he was forced to teach subjects outside his area of research.

During his long academic career the political climate became more liberal, and Pavić began to publish monographs, articles, and books in his area of scholarly expertise; he also published his first collections of poetry and, later, fiction. His writing was accepted with mixed blessings until the 1984 publication of *Hazarski rečnik*. His earlier prose works are stylistically close to the later ones. The characters that inhabit his literary universe are often portrayed as humanoid monsters whose body parts and social habits defy common sense and the logic of everyday reality. For example, the main character of the story "Jaje" (Egg) from the collection *Ruski hrt* (Russian Hound), published in 1979, is characterized in the following manner: "Eustahija Zorić, the student of the Romance Languages Department, broke an egg on her forehead that Sunday morning and ate it.... She had a single brow arched over her eyes and lived in the busiest part of Belgrade, in a room rented above 'Zlatno burence' in Prizrenska street where she kept a refrigerator full of French books and makeup." This enigmatic reality is constructed by the abundant exploitation of the Balkan mythological imagination, especially the Serbian one. Pavić stresses the fact that he enjoys traveling to the remotest villages, listening to the way common people speak, and recording their phrases in his

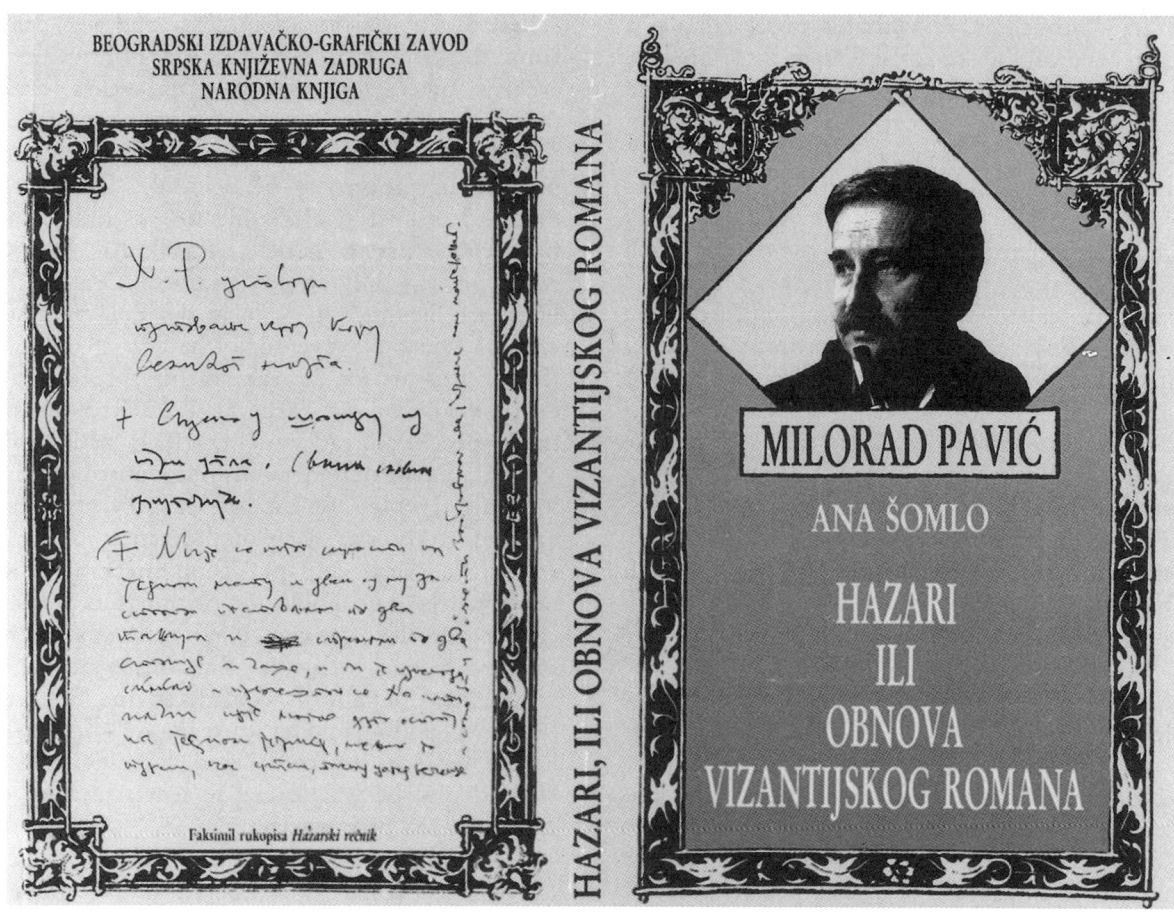

Dust jacket for Pavić's Hazarski rčnik, with a facsimile of a page from the manuscript

notebook. But the vernacular speech is only the starting point of his highly extravagant style, which defamiliarizes the language of the common people with a surreal sense of word and phrase choice.

Hazarski rečnik is the culmination of Pavić's effort to construct a universe that reflects the unusual reality of the Balkans. The book itself is not only an attempt to represent three versions of the same historical event simultaneously but also a daring experiment in book design and marketing. It is impossible to summarize precisely the narrative space opened up by the novel's unusual form. First of all, the book is sold in two versions, the male and the female, which differ in the content of one paragraph late in the book (page 293 in the English translation). This paragraph supposedly provides a totally different perspective on the reading of the entire novel. Secondly, the book is divided into three parts that are differentiated by the colors of their pages: red pages for the Christian version, yellow for the Jewish version, and green for the Moslem version of the destiny of the Khazars, a people who mysteriously disappeared from world history around the tenth century. Each of the books is written in encyclopedic form, with entries for both real and invented personalities and events, all of which are cross-referenced among the three parts. The reader can elect to read the book in a linear order or skip from entry to entry, using the novel as a reference manual. The architectonics of the "dictionary" is built around the tension between the differing versions of the Khazar story, narrated through a stylistic combination of historical facts and mythic inventions.

Pavić uses the scarcity of historical data on this eastern tribe to build his own marvelous world around it. The ruler of the warlike and nomadic tribe of Khazars, who bears the title of *kaghan,* decides to adopt that religion which would be the best for his people. He invites to his court Saint Cyril, a founder of Slavic literacy; Isaac Sangari, a rabbi, and Fababi Ibn Kora, the Islamic representative. They are each supposed to persuade the *kaghan* that their particular religion would be the best for the Khazars. The dispute among the three clerics about the benefits of their own civilization enters the novel as "The Khazar Polemic." The "dictionary" is structured around similar triads (Christian, Jewish, and Moslem) that cover the span from the eighth century to the twentieth century and establish loose narrative links between characters and events. These links are often based on dreams, reincarnations, and magical transportations of objects across eternal time and space. Besides the original participants in the polemic, there are the contemporary chroniclers Methodius, Judah Halevi, and Al-Bakri; the seventeenth-century students of the Khazar question, Avram Brankovich, Samuel Cohen, and Yusuf Masudi; and the twentieth-century scholars Dr. Isailo Suk, Dr. Dorothea Schultz, and Dr. Abu Kabir Muawia.

The latter three characters participate in a conference on "The Culture of the Black Sea Shores in the Middle Ages," which takes place in Istanbul in October 1982. Dr. Muawia is murdered in a hotel garden one day, and the reader has to go back several centuries through the maze of reincarnations and magical events to discover the culprit among the many demons who inhabit this book. The Christian demon, Nikon Sevast, is an icon painter who is suspected of being one of the devil's reincarnations; the Jewish one, Ephrosinia Lukarevich, has two thumbs on each hand and has black milk in her breasts; and the Islamic one, Yabir Ibn Akshany, has no shadow and leaves his grave as soon as he is buried. The work abounds with mythical creatures and magical connections that make this novel similar to a cabalistic treatise. The reader is prodded by the author to create order out of the chaotic narrative fragments by his constant promises that there is a higher meaning to the novel.

Pavić often expresses his conviction that the literary text has precedence over whatever one chooses to consider reality, and that, by means of metaphor, it actively participates in the creation of that reality. There is an abundance of entries that proliferate around the complex narrative skeleton, further displacing the reader's confidence in the stability of the universe. The reader is led astray on purpose as the narrator constantly assures him that there is an order underlying the chaos and that it is the reader's duty to discover it through his own, particular arrangement of the dictionary entries. "For the time being, *The Khazar Dictionary* is still just a heap of random letters, names and pseudonyms," says one of the protagonists. The task of the reader is mimicked in the novel by the secret sect of dream hunters who attempt to reconstruct Adam Cadmon, a cosmic man whose body corresponds to the text of the original edition of the *Khazar Dictionary*. Adam Cadmon is a metaphor of the imaginary order that dwells within the chaos of "random letters, names and pseudonyms" characteristic of the current version of *The Khazar Dictionary*. By placing the original and complete book in the past, Pavić liberates his present literary construction from any pressure of narrative coherence.

In his 1985 essay on the Khazar jar, Pavić offers his theory of the fantastic after surveying the history of the genre. First of all, the term he chooses to describe the performance of the fantastic writer is tied to the debunking of literary realism. Pavić offers a nonmimetic approach, redefining Plato's theory of mimesis by insisting that the fantastic must insert itself at the level of ideal forms, and, as in Byzantine literature (which lacks humanism and the Renaissance), embraces a monistic vision of the universe. Instead of mimesis, the new approach should be "a synthesis of poetic, documentary or even scientific texts with narrative prose." Pavić calls for total literature, one that does not compromise itself by contemplating what is taken as "material reality," but positions its narrative as a world before reality, using erudition to assemble an array of literary and extraliterary discourses into a nonmimetic novel. By refusing mimesis as a method of novelistic poetics, the writer produces a fantastic literature that posits a new world. That world blends Pavić's folkloric fantasy with the anxiety of history, calling into question every certainty from the past, while at the same time making obvious the unbearable burden of the past. Erudition is not used to enlighten or inform the reader; instead, it acts as an effect of history and replicates the narrative chaos out of which every reader is promised the possibility of carving out an imaginary labyrinth. This narrative construction emerges within the postmodern condition that resurrects a Baroque vision of the universe ruled by the unfathomable powers whose trappings remain forever inaccessible to humans. Yet, the secret order that Pavić posits beyond the narrative chaos invokes a medieval stability for which the Baroque yearned. The reader gets the impression that the author treats both reality and truth as concepts constructed by the dominant cultural paradigms of his day and age. This impression produces a sense of relativity and doubt in the validity of any universal, totalizing master narrative.

The second novel that has been widely translated, *Predeo slikan čajem,* is a similar attempt to avoid the linearity of narration. The book is envisioned as a crossword puzzle, and reading it "across" or "down" supposedly produces different interpretations of the destiny of Atanasije Svilar, a Belgrade architect who makes a fortune as the director of a chemical corporation in California. This book is even more fragmented in structure and extravagant in style. Its title is derived from the protagonist's habit of drawing landscapes on the covers of his notebooks with brushes dipped in tea. One of the most prominent landscapes is a depiction of the late Yugoslav president Josip Broz Tito's villa on the Adriatic island of Brioni. Svilar tries to pattern his life after this landscape, building an exact replica of Tito's villa in the Caribbean. He also imitates the lavish lifestyle of the late dictator, smoking Havana cigars and drinking Chivas Regal whiskey. Pavić uses these descriptions to implicitly criticize the "socialist" Yugoslav society by recounting the luxuries with which Tito surrounded himself. Besides its political content, *Predeo slikam čajem* invokes some of the philosophical ideas derived from Orthodox Christianity. According to Pavić, life in the Serbian Orthodox monastery on Mount Athos is divided between two groups of monks: *cenobytes,* who live in a community and are actively involved in the building of the material world, and *ideorhythmics,* who live in ascetic isolation and devote themselves exclusively to spiritual affairs. The book revolves around this idea in its explanation of historical cycles that are at one time dominated by one or the other type of social organization.

Unutrašnja strana vetra (1991; translated as *The Inner Side of the Wind, or The Novel of Hero and Leander,* 1993) is a story of two lovers who reach to each other across the gulf of centuries. It is based on the ancient myth of Hero and Leander, with two lovers from Belgrade in the leading roles. The book is again innovative in design: the reader can start reading the novel from either cover, one story being from Hero's and the other from Leander's point of view. One of the most symbolic gestures in the book is Leander's building of the church in Belgrade, which has been ravaged by the Austro-Turkish War, as a sign of humanity's triumph over the blind forces of destruction.

Pavić retired from his professorial post in 1992 and became actively involved in the public debate over the civil war in the former Yugoslavia. He emerged as a strong supporter of the right of Serbs to live in one state after the breakup of the Yugoslav federation. His views on the Yugoslav crisis are to a large extent replicated in his literary works. Pavić sees Serbs as the victims of the "new world order," which strengthens Western Christian (Catholic and Protestant) values and institutions at the expense of Eastern Orthodox Christianity and its culture. He claims that after the demise of Communism, Eastern Europe reverted to the old religious values. Since the Orthodox do not have a centralized clerical administration, like the Vatican, for example, they are in danger of being destroyed and assimilated (like the Khazars in his novel) by the Catholics, Protestants, and Moslems. He believes that the latter have been used by the West throughout history to annihilate the achievements of Byzantine culture. The Serbs, who are positioned on the western border of the Orthodox world, are the first to feel the aggression of the "new world order," and, as Pavić sees it, are again being singled out for genocide by the neighboring Catholic and Moslem nations. For him, the annihilation of the Serbian cultural heritage, the destruction of many Orthodox churches, libraries, and monuments in the current war, is just the beginning of the general destruction of a culture that has its roots in ancient Greece and has produced figures such as Fyodor Dostoyevsky, Eugène Ionesco, Ivo Andrić, and Nikos Kazantzakis. These unorthodox views have won Pavić a controversial reputation in European cultural circles, which generally expect a less nationalistic and more liberal position from their best-selling authors. Pavić continues to work on his scholarly and literary works, and he was nominated for the Nobel Prize in literature.

Interviews:

Miloš Jevtić, *Razgovori sa Pavićem* (Belgrade: Naučna kujiga, 1990);

Ana Šomlo, *Milorad Pavić: Hazari ili obnova vizantijskog romana* (Belgrade: BIGZ/Srpska književna zadruga/Narodna knjiga, 1990).

Bibliography:

Jasmina Mihailović, *Bio-bibliografija Milorada Pavića, 1949–1995* (Belgrade: Draganić, 1996), pp. 165–418.

References:

Robert Coover, "He Thinks the Way We Dream," *New York Times Book Review* (20 November 1988), pp. 15–20;

Jovan Delić, *Hazarska prizma* (Belgrade: Prosveta, 1991);

Kimberly A. Jastremski, "The Truth and Images of the Body in Pavić's *Dictionary of the Khazars* and Kiš's *A Tomb for Boris Davidovich*," *Serbian Studies*, 6, no. 1 (1991): 69–75;

Hans Robert Jauss, "Das Religionsgespräch oder: Figuren des Endes in Pavić's *Chasarischem Wörterbuch*," in *Poetik und Hermeneutik–Das Ende: Figuren einer Denkform* (Munich, 1996), pp. 388–396;

Ken Kalfus, "To Serbs With Love," *Village Voice Literary Supplement* (March 1992), pp. 22–23;

Književnost, 90 (1990): 1862–1945 [11 articles on Pavić];

Vasa D. Mihailovich, "The Parable of Nationhood," *World & I*, 3, no. 11 (1988): 378–383;

Jasmina Mihajlović, *Priča o duši i telu: Slojevi i značenja u prozi Milorada Pavića* (Belgrade: Prosveta, 1992);

Predrag Palavestra, "Abracadabra, a la Khazar," *World & I*, 3, no. 11 (1988): 384–389;

Charles Simic, "Balkan Bizzare," *World & I*, 3, no. 11 (1988): 390–397;

Jasmina Tešanović, *Kratka istorija jedne knjige; izbor napisa o romanu leksikonu u 100,000 reči Hazarski rečnik od Milorada Pavića* (Vršac: Književna opština Vršac, 1991);

Milorad Vučelić, "Unutrašnje granice moraju se promeniti," *Politika* (13 September 1991): 7–8.

Konstantin Pavlov
(2 April 1933 -)

Cleo Protokhristova
Plovdiv University

BOOKS: *Satiri* (Sofia: Bŭlgarski pisatel, 1960);
Stikhove (Sofia: Bŭlgarski pisatel, 1965);
Poyavyavane. Stikhove (Sofia: Fakel, 1989);
Agonia sladka. Stikhove (Sofia: Fakel, 1991);
Ubiystvo na spyasht chovek. Stikhove (Gabrovo: Ingraf, 1992);
Fyoni mŭti krŭgli rechni kamŭni. Tŭzhna prikazka (Vratsa: Budilnek, 1993);
Repetitsiya za gala tants (Sofia: Literaturen forum, 1995);
Spasenie (Sofia: Fakel, 1995).

Collections: *Stari neshta. Izbrani stikhove i kinostsenarii* (Sofia: Bŭlgarski pisatel, 1983);
Elegichen optimizŭm. Izbrano (Sofia: Fakel, 1993).

SELECTED PERIODICAL PUBLICATIONS—
UNCOLLECTED: *Spomen za bliznachkata*, Kinoizkustvo, 3 (1976): 69-104;
Chuy petela, Kinoizkustvo, (1976): 99-120;
Bez draskotina, Kinoizkustvo, 10 (1976): 88-120; 11 (1976): 87-120;
Byala magiya, Kinoizkustvo, 9 (1981): 91-120;
Seltseto, Kinoizkustvo, 7, (1987): 82-112; 8 (1987): 84-119;
Neshto vŭv vŭzdukha, Kinoizkustvo, 4 (1989): 99-120;
Persifedron, Literaturen vestnik, 45 (1990): 4-5;
Bunt v nedelya, Fakel, 1 (1995): 6-31.

Konstantin Pavlov is the most prominent contemporary Bulgarian poet and screenwriter, an author of a remarkably original style, and a person of strong individuality. He is among the few writers who dared to defend their personal and artistic independence during the time the totalitarian regime was in power. Because of his independence, he was not officially recognized, and his name was hardly mentioned except in a derogatory manner. Nevertheless, since his first books appeared, his popularity has been great. Although the poet could not publish his works for a long time, his poems were copied and read, and the most outstanding among his fellow poets have acknowledged his talent and moral superiority.

Konstantin Mirchev Pavlov was born on 2 April 1933 in the village Popovo (renamed Vitoshko in 1944 and later deserted) in the district of Sofia. His parents were simple people with little education, his father having never gone beyond his first year in school. The son, though, could read and write before he was three years old. In 1935-1936 the family moved to another village, Kurilo, where Pavlov attended elementary and secondary school. Later the family lived in Sofia. Pavlov's father died early, and from 1947 on Pavlov coped with problems and difficulties largely by himself. He was expelled from the Third Boys' High School in 1951, studied for some months in Pernik, and graduated in Pavlovo the next year. He started writing when he was about ten. His first poems were published in 1947 in the newspaper *Septemvriyche*. In 1952 he began his studies at Sofia University "St. Kliment Okhridski." He was interested in literature but studied law; he completed all the semesters and exams required for the general course but never graduated. According to his own statement, he was expelled from the university many times.

From 1955 to 1957 Pavlov concentrated on poetry and searching for his artistic identity. His poems appeared in various journals and newspapers such as *Literaturen front* (Literary Front), *Stŭrshel* (Hornet), *Plamŭk* (Flame), *Nasha rodina* (Our Country), and *Rodna rech* (Native Speech), as well as in poetry collections—*Smyana* in 1955 and 1956 and *Poeziya* (Poetry) in 1962. Meanwhile Pavlov had various occupations. He worked as an editor for Radio Sofia from 1957 to 1959, then for the publishing house Bŭlgarski pisatel from 1961 to 1962 and 1964 to 1965, for the newspaper *Literaturen front* in 1963, and in 1964 to 1965 for Multfilm Studio.

Pavlov's first book, *Satiri* (Satires), was published in 1960. Most of the poems included in its two parts had not been published earlier and shocked the official critics with their audacity and willfulness. "Stikhotvorenie za skotovŭdnata ferma na poeta" (A Poem to the Poet's Animal Farm), "Na edin predatel" (To a Traitor), and "Intsident" (An Accident) seemed especially provocative. "Otmŭshtenieto na mŭdrostta" (The Revenge of Wisdom) suggested the tendency toward grotesque writing that Pavlov developed later. Some of the poems presented themes that became ongoing for the poet—for example, "Slaveite peyat" (The Nightingales Are Singing).

Satiri was met with exceptional interest. The evaluations were extreme—only sporadically affirmative and more often negative. But even in favorable criticism the premonitory tone prevailed. A critical cliché for Pavlov was coined by Vassil Kolevski, who spoke of the poet's "Bohemian nihilistic attitude towards reality." To a great extent it foreshadowed the obstacles and ordeals for his future artistic career. In 1963 the poet took part in a discussion on satire organized by the journal *Septemvri*. His main concern was with the paradoxes of satire—namely, the necessity of being rejected and suppressed for its development and the danger of flourishing, lest "the satirist get fat." He compared satiric work to "the dwarf that the more you beat, the bigger it gets." Ironically enough, this formula was to be constantly applied to his work for the next three decades.

In 1965 his second book, *Stikhove* (Verses), was published, accompanied by a strange editorial note that said: "The publishing house Bŭlgarski pisatel is offering a book, peculiar and in certain sense disputable with the ideas of its author, ..." and later suggested that the book could provide matter for discussion about "certain tendencies in the development of some young Bulgarian poets." When it appeared, *Stikhove* was an impressive and challenging book. The first group of poems—the programlike "Declaratsiya" (Declaration), "Flotatsiya" (Flotation), "Pastoralno" (In a Pastoral Manner), "Masovo chudo" (Miracle En Masse), and "Alkhimitisi" (Alchemists)—directly attacked the current ideological dogmas and clichés and were not accepted officially. The rest of the verses—with poems such as "Kucheto Hektor" (The Dog Hektor), "Paradoks" (A Paradox), "Boleznena chuvstvitelnost" (Unhealthy Sensitivity), and "Edaipov Kompleks" (Oedipal Complex)—manifested a rather unconventional grotesque imagery that was interpreted too literally by most critics.

After the publication of *Stikhove* Pavlov fell into the silence that became emblematic for him. The figurative expression of that silence became "in the whale's womb," the metaphor used in the title of a poem that Pavlov published years later. He never found a permanent occupation. After the seven years from 1965 to 1972 in which he was constantly unemployed, Pavlov started working in 1973 as an editor and consultant in Bulgarian cinematography—a job he had intermittently until 1991. Throughout these years the poet was often prosecuted and fired from work because of his independent behavior and unconventional writing. During this period he also wrote for the cinema and the theater. His plays include *Tabu* (Taboo, 1968, co-authored with Stefan Tsanev); *Stari neshta* (Old Things, 1968); *Drevna tragediya* (Ancient Tragedy, 1970); *Bunt v nedelya* (Revolt on Sunday, 1971); and *Ptitsi* (Birds, 1971). His screenplays are *Nie ne se predavame* (We Do Not Give Up, 1962); *Ptitsi* (Birds, 1966, an animated film); *Danil* (Danil, 1967); *Provodnik* (Provodnik, 1967); *Alfons* (Alfonce, 1967); *Sofroniada,* 1968); *Dvama maystori* (Two Masters, 1973); *Selo v planinata* (A Village in the Mountain, 1973), a television script in six episodes; *Masovo chudo* (Miracle En Masse, 1974); *Spomen za bliznachkata* (Remembrance of the Twin Sister, 1977); *Chuy petela* (Listen to the Cock, 1978); *Byala magiya* (White Magic, 1980); and *Ilyuziya* (Illusion, 1980). Not all these writings were published or produced, but the movies that were made are considered representative of Bulgarian cinema: *Spomen za bliznachkata* (directed by Lyubomir Sharlandzhiev, 1976); *Chuy petela* (Stefan Dimitrov, 1978); *Ilyuziya* (Lyudmil Staykov, 1980); *Masovo chudo* (Ivan Pavlov, 1982); *Byala magiya* (Ivan Andonov, 1982); *Pamet* (Docho Bogzhakov, 1987); *Seltseto* (Ivan Terziev, 1987); *Bez draskotina* (Zako Kheskiya, 1989); and *Neshto vŭv vŭzdukha* (Petur Popzlatev, 1993).

The only poetry published during this long silence is a cycle of poems that appeared in the almanac *More* in 1981. In a poem titled "Intervyu v utrobata na kita" (An Interview in the Whale's Womb) he confessed that his silence was imposed. For all their autobiographical reminiscences, the poems of the cycle should not be taken literally. Works such as "Adaptatsiya" (Adaptation), "Bezkrayna poema" (An Endless Poem), and "Kŭsno e da bŭda razvratén" (It Is Too Late for Me To Get Corrupted) speak in the enigmas of a parable about the tragedy of artistic self-consciousness.

On Pavlov's fiftieth birthday a volume that includes most of the poems from the first two collections and the cycle from *More* was published as *Stari neshta* (Old Things, 1983). The poet waited six more years to see publication of his next book, for which he chose the telling title *Poyavyavane* (Appearance, 1989). With these poems Pavlov goes deeper into the painful and torturous process of a self-analysis that moves to the edges of existence. His quest for the truth beyond routine human relationships reaches to a vision that is intolerably repellent and even disgusting.

Pavlov's next collection, *Agonia sladka* (Agony Sweet, 1991), is similar to the previous one; at the same time, one can feel the profound transformation that has taken place. The issues of human life are seen in the double vision of someone who has experienced the encounter with nonexistence. The extraordinary wisdom achieved after this traumatic experience provides the poet with a feeling of limitless freedom.

The collection is transparently structured. Within the space between the introduction, titled "Skŭpi priyatelyu" (Dear Friend), and the three epilogues, the poems are grouped into three parts—"Malko predi tova" (A Little Bit before That), "Arkhaichen arkhiv" (Archaic Archive), and "Malko sled tova" (A Little Bit after That). The poems dwell on the moral and epistemological motivations of writing, the relationship between intimate emotional experience and the things that objectively exist (the two versions of "Plachat neshtata" [Things Are Crying]), placed in the first and the third part, and the relationship between art and reality, as in "Skulptor bez model" (A Sculptor Missing a Model). *Agonia sladka* offers a further step in the debunking of unquestioned values such as faith and generosity, national heroics, and folklore tradition. The book is also a parable-like reflection upon the social and psychological changes in Bulgaria after 1989 and discounts the fundamental ideological formulas that concern national history, political struggles, and glory and disgrace. Glory and disgrace are, in fact, the abstract poles of the collection. They pass from the introductory poem to the epilogues like a leitmotiv, along with many self-references that place the poems in the context of Pavlov's earlier work. A similar function is attributed to the images constantly demystifying death by travesty of the standard idea and suggestion for the supreme experience of its unattainability. Undoubtedly *Agonia sladka* represents an important and prolific step in the artistic development of the poet.

In 1992 Pavlov became head of Channel 1 of Bulgarian National Television for a short time. The same year he was awarded the poetry prize of the International Academy of Arts in Paris, and a collection of his poems, *Ubiystvo na spyasht chovek* (A Murder of a Sleeping Man), was published. This book marked a significant turn in Pavlov's poetics. Compared to his earlier works, the new poems demonstrate a return to simplicity of articulation, to more profound expressiveness, and to clarity and translucence. The first poem, "Bog obicha svoya sekretar" (God Loves His Secretary), which functions as a manifesto, introduces the main issues of the book—the inadequacy of words and the ultimateness of silence, the expressiveness of pauses, the anxiety of time, and the authenticity and nonauthenticity of poetry. The main dramatic conflict is between the unnamed experience, the suppressed, the poems never born, and the insufficient yet cherished poetic utterance. The poet develops further the fundamental issues of his work—social and political imitation, the substitution of values, and the relativity of moral criteria, now interpreted from a different perspective. A threatening alternative to the poet's martyred striving for the unattainable is the poetic mimicry, the falsity and hypocrisy, the imitation of reflections and feelings, and, most destructive of all, repetition and self-limitation, as in the poem "Tematichno razpyavane" (A Theme Becoming a Voice).

In 1993 Pavlov published the anthology *Elegichen optimizŭm* (Elegiac Optimism), with most of the poems from his earlier books (*Satiri, Stikhove, Poyavyavane,* and *Ubiystvo na spyasht chovek*) were included. Brought together, the poems written between 1955 and 1992 form an impressive image of the poet's rich and organic uniqueness. Another work in 1993 was *Fyoni mŭti krŭgli rechni kamŭni. Tŭzhna prikazka* (Fyoni Broods Round River Stones. A Sad Tale). Designed as a book for children, it recounts in an enigmatic manner a parable of man's hope and his inborn impulse to love. The tale is a sad recognition of the absurdity of expectations, of the invincible reciprocity of love and pain, of self-realization and suffering, and of despair in human existence.

Two recent books by Pavlov reproduce the atmosphere of existential and moral anxiety. In *Repetitsiya za gala tants* (A Rehearsal for a Gala Dance, 1995) and in *Spasenie* (Redemption, 1995), poems from *Poyavyavane, Agonia sladka, Ubiystvo na spyasht chovek* and even from the earliest collections, are republished with the addition of new works. Much like *Elegichen optimizŭm,* they have an exceptionally strong impact on the reader, dragging him into a world that seems both temptingly familiar and also threateningly alien and incomprehensible. Especially impressive is *Spasenie,* which is a collaboration with the artist Svetlin Russev, a longtime close friend of Pavlov's. The work is a kind of prayer for salvation—a prayer of Vanga (a Bulgarian prophetess), of humanity and goodness. Fragments from the frescoes painted by Svetlin Russev for the church built by Vanga do not simply illustrate the poems but create a secondary poetic plot by providing additional semantic and emotional interrelations between the poems. The whole book has the effect of a lamentation, a profound insight into the abyss of human tragedy.

Pavlov has had a strong impact on younger Bulgarian poets. In spite of his modesty and lack of vanity, he is regarded by many of them as a guru. He is loved and admired by his readers, and professional critics are also indebted to him. Although during the last years many articles and reviews have been written, his work has not yet been entirely and systematically studied. The challenge of Pavlov's private symbols and abracadabras, such as "something," "that," "Persifedron," "Fyoni," and "Oron," the bewildering enigmas of his verses, the capricious and grotesque vision, and the unpredictable metamorphoses of ideas and images, all need further interpretation. The most characteristic features of Pavlov's poetry are the coherence of its worldview, its startling imagery, and its articulateness and power. Confusing and sometimes embarrassing, harshly unconventional, destructive toward standard logical formulas, Pavlov's poetry offers at the same time an alternative to the misery and alienation of human life in its social and political realities.

Interview:

Konstantin Pavlov, *Intervyuta* (Sofia: Fakel, 1995).

References:

Rumen Bogomilov, "Ot satirata kum absurda," *Literaturen forum,* 28 (12 July 1990): 2;

Vikhren Chernokozhev, "Ironichnite antielegii na Konstantin Pavlov," in his *Bŭlgarskiyat smyak h. Ochertsi i portreti* (Sofia: Bŭlgarski pisatel, 1994), pp. 211-216;

Lyubomir Levchev, "Izkustvoto na proritsatelite" in his *Kazani dumi* (Varna: Knigoizdatelstvo Georgi Bakalov, 1983), pp. 179-185;

Rozaliya Likova, "Promeni v sŭvremennoto satirichno vizhdane," *Literaturen forum,* 50 (16-22 December 1992): 3;

Encho Mutafov, "Persifedron," *Septemvri,* 4 (1990): 232-239;

Prilep. Spisanie za literatura, Kyustendil, special issue on Pavlov, volume 1, no. 2 (1990);

Violeta Ruseva, "Krizata na izkaza—sriv na tsennosti," *Literaturen forum,* 10 (11-17 March 1992): 2;

Vanda Smokhovska-Petrova, "Misiyata na tsigularya, iztŭrval svoyata tsigulka," *Literaturen forum,* 50 (16-22 December 1992): 2;

Lyudmila Stoyanova, "Antipoeziyata na Konstantin Pavlov," *Literaturen forum,* 7 (14-20 February 1996): 1-3;

Katya Yaneva, "Dŭrzosta na satirika," *Septemvri,* 10 (1987): 207-217;

Toncho Zhechev, "Konstantin Pavlov kato yavlenie v nashata kultura," *Letopisi,* 2 (1992): 8-10.

Miodrag Pavlović
(28 November 1928 -)

Bernard Johnson
London School of Economics

BOOKS: *87 pesama* (Belgrade: Nolit, 1952, 1963; Gornji Milanovac: Dečje novine, 1979);
Stub sećanja (Belgrade: Novo pokoljenje, 1953);
Oktave (Belgrade: Nolit, 1956);
Most bez obala (Novi Sad: Matica srpska, 1956, 1983);
Rokovi poezije (Belgrade: Srpska književna zadruga, 1959);
Mleko iskoni (Belgrade: Prosveta, 1962);
Igre bezimenih (Belgrade: Prosveta, 1963);
Osam pesnika (Belgrade: Prosveta, 1964);
Velika Skitija (Sarajevo: Svjetlost, 1969);
Hododarje (Belgrade: Nolit, 1971);
Svetli i tamni praznici (Novi Sad: Matica srpska, 1971);
Velika Skitija i druge pesme (Belgrade: Srpska književna zadruga, 1972);
Dnevnik pene (Belgrade: Slovo ljubve, 1972);
Zavetine (Belgrade: Rad, 1976);
Karike (Kragujevac: Svetlost, 1977);
Pevanje na viru (Belgrade: Slovo ljubve, 1977);
Poetika modernog (Belgrade: Grafos, 1978);
Ništitelji i svadbari (Belgrade: BIGZ, 1979);
Vidovnica (Belgrade: Narodna knjiga, 1979);
Bekstva po Srbiji (Belgrade: Slovo ljubve, 1979);
Divno čudo (Belgrade: Nolit, 1982; Književne novine, 1989);
Zlatna zavada (Niš: Gradina, 1982);
Kina (Niš: Gradina, 1983);
Nova pevanja na viru (Belgrade: Centar za umetnost i kulturu RU, 1983);
Prirodni lik i oblik (Belgrade: Nolit, 1984);
Sledstvo (Belgrade: Srpska književna zadruga, 1985);
Poezija: i kultura (Belgrade: Prosveta, 1986);
Svetogorski dani i noći (Priština: Jedinstvo, 1987);
Govor o Ničem (Niš: Gradina, 1987);
Poetika žrtvenog obreda (Belgrade: Nolit, 1987);
Hram i preobraženje (Belgrade: Sfairos, 1989);
On (Novi Sad: Matica srpska, 1989);
Knjiga staroslovna (Belgrade: Srpska književna zadruga, 1989);

Miodrag Pavlović

Ulazak u Kremonu (Belgrade: Nolit, 1989);
Bezazlenstva (Valjevo: Milić Rakić, 1989);
Cosmologia profanata (Belgrade: Grafos, 1990);
Pesme o detinjstvu i ratovima (Belgrade: Srpska književna zadruga, 1992);
Eseji o srpskim pesnicima (Belgrade: Srpska književna zadruga, 1992);
Bitni ljudi (Belgrade: Prosveta, 1995).

Editions and Collections: *Izabrane pesme* (Belgrade: Rad, 1979);
Izabrana dela (Belgrade: Vuk Karadžić, 1981).

Editions in English: *The Conqueror in Constantinople,* translated by Joachim Neugroschel (New York: New Rivers, 1976);

Singing at the Whirlpool, translated by Barry Callaghan (Toronto: Exile Editions, 1983);

A Voice Locked in Stone, translated by Callaghan (Toronto: Exile Editions, 1985);

The Slavs Beneath Parnassus, translated by Bernard Johnson (London: Angel Books; Saint Paul: New Rivers, 1985);

Links, translated by Johnson (Toronto: Exile Editions, 1989; Leek: Aguila, 1989).

OTHER: *Antologija moderne engleske poezije,* edited by Pavlović and Svetozor Brkić (Belgrade: Nolit, 1957, 1975);

Antologija srpskog pesništva, edited by Pavlović (Belgrade: Srpska književna zadruga, 1964, 1969, 1973, 1979);

Pesništvo evropskog romantizma, edited by Pavlović (Belgrade: Prosveta, 1969, 1979);

Antologija lirske narodne poezije, edited by Pavlović (Belgrade: Vuk Karadžić, 1982).

Miodrag Pavlović was born in Novi Sad in 1928, but his parents moved to Belgrade the following year. He grew up in the Serbian capital, was educated there, and spent the war years of 1941–1945 under the German occupation that was followed by civil war and the establishment of Josip Broz Tito's communist regime. In the year 1948, which marked Tito's break with Joseph Stalin and the Soviet Union and the beginnings of Yugoslavia's independence from the Eastern bloc, Pavlović was twenty years old and beginning a course of medical studies; he completed his medical training and graduated in 1954. He then practiced as a doctor for several years before deciding to devote himself full time to a literary career. During his studies he had become fluent in the principal European languages, literatures, and philosophy. He began writing poetry when he was a student, and, although he has written short stories and plays as well, it is poetry that has remained his main preoccupation in both his creative and critical works.

Pavlović began publishing verse in 1951, and his first book, *87 pesama* (87 Poems) appeared in 1952, followed by *Stub sećanja* (Pillar of Memory) in 1953. At that time there were two dominant currents in Serbian poetry. One was the traditional and lyrical, which had become popular again after the suffering that people had experienced during the wartime occupation and the civil strife; this traditional lyricism was found particularly in the poetry of Desanka Maksimović and Stevan Raičković. The other current was the surrealist current found in the verse of Oskar Davičo and Dušan Matić, which had taken as its model the French surrealists of the interwar period. Both streams influenced Pavlović, as did the symbolism of the Serbian poet Momčilo Nastasijević, although the latter influence was not immediately apparent. Pavlović was a member of a small grouping of "modernists" who included another highly innovative poet, Vasko Popa.

Their poetry was radically different from what had gone before, and they were criticized and attacked by those traditionalists who advocated a social realist norm for literature similar to that in the Soviet Union. In fact 1953 was a crucial date in Yugoslavia for the emergence of literature that moved outside the political arena, but progress toward greater freedom of expression was slow at first. Pavlović's early poems were neither traditional nor socialist realist: they were concise, hermetic, and usually offered a single stark image presented in a direct and striking manner. Against the harsh background of his youth in wartime Belgrade and his clinical studies as a doctor, the poems produce a vivid impression on their readers, as in the stark realization of the universality of death in "Rekvijem" (Requiem):

> This time
> someone close has died . . .
>
> You feel
> the world has become lighter
> by one human brain[.]

Or in the symbolic violence of "Na smrt jedne kokoške" (Death of a Hen):

> A tethered hen
> hangs by a leg from the clouds
> headless
>
> Blood in the toilet bowl
>
> Hand in hand
> two knives
> are playing the piano[.]

Pavlović's next major book of verse was *Mleko iskoni* (Milk of Yore) in 1962. In the meantime he had become the drama director at the Belgrade National Theatre from 1960 to 1961, and from 1961 to 1984 he was a literary editor with the publishing house Prosveta. In 1978 he was elected to the Serbian Academy of Sciences. *Mleko iskoni* takes themes from classical antiquity and treats them from a highly original viewpoint,

Dust jacket for Osam pesnika, *Pavlović's 1964 collection of poems*

often with the ironic comment of a contemporary observer or participant. Pavlović's poetry became increasingly involved with the universality of myth, which he has always regarded as a kind of distilled essence of the ritual, cultural, and historical memories of an earlier civilization, preserved through the prism of popular narration and belief. So, for example, in "Običan čovek o stvaranju sveta" (An Ordinary Man on the Creation of the World), there is a striking comment on both religious and scientific beliefs about man's evolution, ending with an omnipresent commentator's ironic aside:

> It's hard to talk about it
> without book-learning.
> How can one trust memory when it wasn't yet created?
> . . . and then at last I saw my mother
> shrouded behind swamp-laden mists
> and for an instant at her flank
> my own image:
> under the wind's blows, thick as roots
> my skull half-open
> and the mottled bulge at the base of my brain,
> predicting a lengthy road for a painstaking craftsman.
> Yet you'd like to go straight to pure light
> like some grand gentleman.

In Pavlović's treatment of the myth of Odysseus, Odysseus himself looks upon his endless journeying as a means of delaying the passage of time before he must eventually return to his inescapable destiny:

> For me the sea is a vast expanse of sailing
> and the realm of Nothing upon it;
> my sky is forever clear
> and this darkness always means freedom . . .
> They say I'm a seafarer who's wandered off course,
> but that's not my secret:
> it's my way of saving myself from the earth!

Pavlović sees the civilization of ancient Greece as the birthplace and cradle for all of subsequent European civilization, but as he says in his short preface to *Pevanje na viru* (1977, translated as *Singing at the Whirlpool,* 1983) he believes in the transient nature of all civilizations, which seem to carry within them the seed both of their own rise and of their own destruction. If myths bear witness to the great events of former times, they must nevertheless be tempered by the nature of this transience: this view is at the base of much of Pavlović's ironic and original treatment of such themes.

It is often the comment and verdict of imagined contemporaries, observers of the events, given in today's matter-of-fact terms and language, that make the poems so striking: Orestes on the steps of the Acropolis is left bemused by the radical changes that have meant that he has been judged by the new system of the laws of men, as the power of the laws of the gods has ended:

> . . . and they went off somewhere inside
> and left me here in the dusk alone,
> to enthrone the crime on the spot.
> The time of violence has passed with the knife,
> now everything is short and simple:
> I've become a priest to a confused age.
> On the barehearted earth
> another man stands
> and not a single god.

Similarly, in "Stražar pred Atinom" (A Guard before Athens), only an aura of greatness remains about the town, but it must be preserved and passed on to later generations. As with others of Pavlović's poems of the second cycle, *Mleko iskoni, Velika Skitija* (Great Scythia, 1969), *Hododarje* (Pilgrimage, 1971), and *Svetli i tamni praznici*

(Light and Dark Holy Days, 1971), the poet's closeness to the visual arts, especially painting, is marked. In *Mleko iskoni,* for example, the poem "Radjanje Afrodite" (The Birth of Aphrodite) shows a clear reference to Sandro Botticelli's *Birth of Venus.*

Although Pavlović sees the transience of successive epochs as inevitable, each is continued by its successor: the South Slavs in the Balkans are the natural heirs to Greek culture, both in their own pagan traditions and by the transmission of Christianity through the Eastern Church and Byzantium. *Velika Skitija,* which is a pivotal work in Pavlović's opus, is concerned with this translation to the theme of Slav history and culture in the period of the medieval Serbian kingdom. The poet uses this background and its relation to Constantinople and the destruction of both by the advancing Turks as his focus. In 1389 the Serbs fought an inconclusive battle with the Turks at Kosovo in which the Serbian leader, Prince Lazar, and the Turkish sultan were both killed. After the eventual Turkish conquest of Serbia, Serbian tradition made of this battle a great defeat but a moral victory. Pavlović sees Kosovo through this tradition as an event of enormous symbolic importance, a turning point in the history of the nation, a watershed still seen by many Serbs as being as real and immediate as more contemporary events in their history.

But the poet alludes to the continuing and recurring universal nature of such themes as they are preserved in myths. So "Kći kneževa veze" (Prince's Daughter Weaving) refers to the Greek stories of Penelope and even Proserpine, and the group of poems directly concerned with Kosovo, "Govor uoči bitke" (Speech on the Eve of Battle), "Razgovor na bojnom polju" (Conversation on the Battlefield), "Kneževa večera" (Prince's Supper) and "Posečen knez se seća" (A Beheaded Prince Remembers), all continue the traditional parallel between Prince Lazar and Jesus Christ. On the eve of battle Lazar is offered the choice between the heavenly kingdom and martyrdom through defeat or victory and the earthly kingdom. He chooses the moral victory of the former, both for himself and for his people. Kosovo is a recurrent theme in Pavlović's poetry, just as it is in the large body of Serbian epic poetry that has been handed down orally through the gusla players for hundreds of years. In a similar manner, in the final section of *Velika Skitija,* Pavlović deals with the role of the poet as the sacred and continuing chronicler of his people's destiny, in a direct parallel with the folksingers' unbroken tradition.

The final book of this cycle, *Svetli i tamni praznici,* deals with biblical themes and images of Christ and of the saints and martyrs of the early Christian church, both real and stylized. There are also poems concerned with the universal themes of life and death, faith and persecution, and the transient nature of greatness. Pavlović again uses the semi-ironic, down-to-earth commentary style employed so effectively in *Mleko iskoni* and *Velika Skitija.* As with these earlier works, there are poems in the first person that refer to the poet's own role outside the time in which the poem is set. As with much of Pavlović's poetry, but especially in *Svetli i tamni praznici,* there is a direct connection between poetry and visual art—here the frescoes, icons, and illustrations of the liturgical works of the early church; these images also show the deep influence of symbolism on the poet and function on several different levels of meaning. One of the more general theme poems of this collection, and among Pavlović's best, is "Zmijobija" (Dragonslayer), which combines allusions to the recurrent hero, monster, and maiden myths, in particular that of Saint George, with the ironic treatment of a microcosm of nature and the eventual fragility of greatness:

> Every year he comes down from the mountain
> on a steed as white as the lily
> a dragonfly girded with a breastplate of iron
> and rises up before the silver veil that looks on him in tears.
> The scallop-shell of his palm touches the harp
> and the trembling lips of the prince's daughter.
> Then he goes out to the serpent
> which, as is known, has come
> out of some festering corner of the universe
> and whose strength is made up of the unity
> of a multitude of death in a hundred-headed monster.
> And so this knight of valor, with his beauty
> and with his lance, kills the abomination
> and a choir of maidens from on high
> sings to his glory.
> With his head on the dawn's shoulder
> he modestly goes on his way
> and sits down to rest in the narrow shade of a cedar.
> There he is set upon by spiders and their henchmen
> who tear his body into sheaves,
> taking his head with special care
> into their workshop to torture.
> And now at the sight of his life-springs—
> seek rhyme or reason in this world—
> he who severed the Tsar-Serpent's head,
> the favoured of the gods,
> can be dissolved in ant's acid.

The poems in this cycle established Pavlović as a major national poet who combined traditional themes with new forms and an entirely novel mode of contemporary, sometimes even colloquial expression. This modernist technique owes something to T. S. Eliot, a poet whom Pavlović greatly admires, but Pavlović's work has remained unquestionably Serbian in feeling, background, and atmosphere, despite its many larger dimensions. From the myths of his own background and the traditions of the Western world, Pavlović moved to the study of Eastern societies in his search for universal sources and parallels. He traveled widely, not only to the United States and Australia but also and notably to India and China, researching comparative mythology and the oral tradition; this research was to lead to an extensive use of universal myths relocated alongside South Slav variants in a new cycle of poems of epic inspiration and form, poems devoted to a symbolic interpretation of his people's destruction, a search for new beginning, and a final rebirth. This cycle contains *Apokalipsa* (Apocalypse), *Bekstva po Srbiji* (Flights through Serbia, 1979) and *Divno čudo* (A Divine Miracle, 1982).

The last and most interesting of these poems is divided into three sections: in the first, the motif of a feast as a symbol of battle and destruction, as seen in the Kosovo poems and in many poems of the Kosovo folklore cycle, is used, but in a wider context, "Gozba vekova na Rtnju" (The Feast of the Centuries at Rtanj). The second part, again based on symbols from mythology, "Mesečeva svadba" (The Wedding of the Moon), deals with the reconciliation of opposites, victory and defeat, heaven and earth, life and death. The third section, "Prelazak" (The Crossing), suggests the evolutionary redemption of humanity through the continuing cycles of death and rebirth. In the poem it is the poet himself who leads us through and explains the meaning of the poem's metaphysical themes, and it is his task to experience, record, and interpret the trials, tribulations, and eventual triumphant renaissance of his people. This is the role of the poet within the progress of civilization and society as Pavlović has always seen it, and he himself sees *Divno čudo* as a culminating work in his whole opus. It is a fine and unusually complex work.

The fourth cycle of Pavlović's poetry, although chronologically interleaved with the longer epic poems, is in complete contrast to it. His researches into the sources of universal tradition and his own belief in the poet's sacred role led him, logically, further back in time to search for the original source of poetry and a justification for his belief in ritual ceremonies as the origins of myth and, hence, poetry itself. This brought him into direct contact with anthropologists and their interpretations of archeological discoveries and artifacts. The chance discovery of an important Mesolithic settlement on the middle Danube at Lepenski vir in the early 1970s gave him further insight into humanity's early artistic and creative stirrings and rites taken from the river civilization with its apparent fish-god carvings and ritual objects.

It was almost as if the archaeological discovery of this Danube civilization came at just the right time to provide Pavlović with inspiration in a new but related direction. The books *Pevanje na viru, Nova pevanja na viru* (New Singing at the Whirlpool, 1983), *Karike* (Links, 1977), and *Zavetine* (Spells, 1976) are written from the viewpoint of these primitive people and the objects that surrounded them in nature. Again, the style is modern and the commentary ironic, but Pavlović has returned to the short format of his first poems, and they are often almost epigrammatic in structure. Pavlović sees an unbroken chain of development between these distant ancestors, their land, and their customs, and the present day—a chain that encompasses natural phenomena, the land, and human civilization. The traces of stylized ritual worship involving the recurring cycles of nature are transmitted through myth into poetry down the centuries. Pavlović's view of the combined role of poet as high priest, interpreter and prophet, guardian of essential mysteries of humanity's spiritual life, is nowhere better seen than in this fourth cycle of his work. This can be seen in the poem "Prorok" (Prophet) from *Pevanje na viru*:

> While others sleep
> he goes on striving
> he climbs up
> to where rain flows
> where others
> try to make out
> number and reason
> he weaves words
> he goes hungry
> beneath his roof-board
> his kin is dead
> where's that one of yours
> who's mad
> only a deer
> asks about him[.]

In addition to his creative writing, Pavlović has published definitive critical essays on nineteenth-century and modern Serbian and European poetry, including two important books:

Rokovi poezije (Poetic Timespans, 1959), which contains both general and specific essays, and *Osam pesnika* (Eight Poets, 1964), devoted to longer studies of individual poets. There have also been books concerned with the wider philosophic aspects of poetry, books such as *Poetika modernog* (Poetry of the Modern, 1978) and *Poezija i kultura* (Poetry and Culture, 1986) in which Pavlović has expounded his own carefully-conceived poetic theories.

Finally, Pavlović has compiled several important and influential anthologies. *Antologija moderne engleske poezije* (Anthology of Modern English Poetry), which Pavlović edited in conjunction with Svetozar Brkić, was first published in 1957. It was highly influential for the new attention it focused on the contemporary currents of English verse, much of which had not appeared in translation in Serbian before, and also, more specifically, on the poets that had strongly influenced Pavlović himself: William Butler Yeats, W. H. Auden and Eliot. It came at the time when the postwar generation of poets in Yugoslavia had begun to make its mark, and the book represents one of the final victories of the modernists against politically-controlled literary authoritarianism.

Antologija srpskog pesništva (Anthology of Serbian Verse), first published in 1964, also aroused some controversy initially but was quickly recognized for the merits of its editor's new interpretation of the course of Serbian poetry. Pavlović included many of the traditionally well-known Serbian poets and their frequently anthologized poems, but he also researched his theme in depth and brought to light many poets and poems previously unknown or not considered significant. The critics of the anthology were mainly those in the older generation who could not come to terms with this new interpretation of the development of Serbian poetry. By the time of the second edition in 1969 the anthology had achieved general acceptance as the definitive work of its kind and of its time. *Antologija lirske narodne poezije* (Anthology of Lyrical Folk Poetry), in which the editor shifts attention away from the better known epic folk verse tradition toward the somewhat neglected lyrical current, came out in 1982, when Pavlović was already acknowledged as a perceptive critic and authority on Serbian (and other) poetry.

Pavlović's verse has been translated into most European languages. Initially disadvantaged by the general inaccessibility of his language, his reputation as a talented and original poet of the

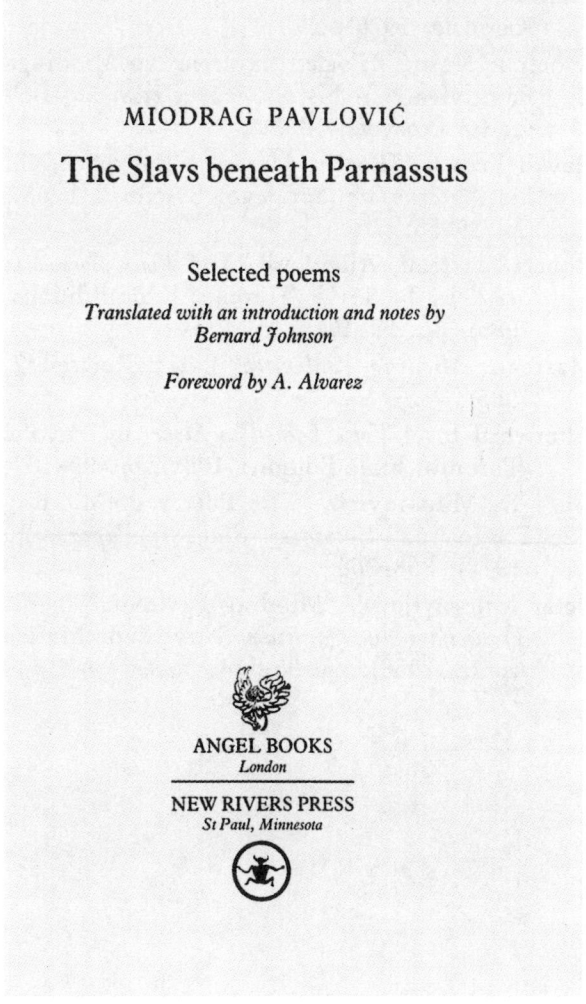

Dust jacket for a 1985 translation of selected poems by Pavlović

highest caliber has spread widely in the last decade. Had it not been for the recent political upheavals in Yugoslavia, he would certainly have been a strong candidate for a Nobel Prize.

References:

Časlav Djordjević, "The All-Seeing Eye of the Poet," *Relations,* 3-4 (1987): 71-85;

Djordjević, *Miodrag Pavlović, pesnik humanističke etike* (Kragujevac: Svetlost, 1974);

Zoran Gluščević, "Miodrag Pavlović," in his *Poezija i magija* (Belgrade: Prosveta, 1980);

Dragoslav Grbić, "Glas nad pustinjom," in his *Pet pesnika* (Belgrade: Nolit, 1963), pp. 73-92;

Bernard Johnson, Introduction to *The Slavs Beneath Parnassus* by Pavlović (London: Angel Books; Saint Paul: New Rivers, 1985), pp. 10-26;

Radoman Kordić, *Govor s dna* (Belgrade: Vuk Karadžić, 1976);

Zvonimir Kostić, "Pogled na pesništvo Miodraga Pavlovića," in his *Arhaično i moderno* (Belgrade: Prosveta, 1983);

Slavko Leovac, "Poezija Miodraga Pavlovića," in his *Metamorfoze* (Sarajevo: Svjetlost, 1965), pp. 35–55;

Robert Marteau, Afterword to *A Voice Locked in Stone,* by Pavlović (Toronto: Exile Editions, 1985), pp. 99–107;

Marteau, *Miodrag Pavlovitch* (Paris: Recueil 2, 1985);

Afterword to *A Voice Locked in Stone,* by Pavolić (Toronto: Exile Editions, 1985), pp. 99–107;

Vasa D. Mihailovich, "The Poetry of Miodrag Pavlović," *Canadian Slavonic Papers,* 20 (1978): 358–368;

Petar Milosavljević, "Miodrag Pavlović," in his *Tradicija i avangardizam* (Novi Sad: Matica srpska, 1968), pp. 95–114;

Zoran Mišić, "Sunčeva svetlost na stubu sećanja," in his *Reč i vreme* (Belgrade: Novo pokolenje, 1953), pp. 209–222;

Aleksandar Petrov, "Od parodije do apokalipse," *Savremenik,* 24 (1966): 285–303;

Bogdan A. Popović, *Epski raspon Miodraga Pavlovića* (Belgrade: Grafos, 1985);

Popović, "Three Principles of the Creative Universe: The Poetry of Miodrag Pavlović," *Relations,* 3 (1986): 41–63;

Ljubomir Simović, "Bitka na granici nestajanja: O poeziji Miodraga Pavlovića," *Književnost,* 54 (1972): 94–124;

Svetlana Velmar-Janković, "Poezija Miodraga Pavlovića," in her *Savremenici* (Belgrade: Prosveta, 1967), pp. 187–197;

Pavle Zorić, "Miodrag Pavlović," in his *Vrhovi* (Belgrade: Srpska književna zadruga, 1991), pp. 9–55.

Borislav Pekić
(4 February 1930 - 2 July 1992)

Bogdan Rakić
Indiana University

BOOKS: *Vreme čuda* (Belgrade: Prosveta, 1965);
Hodočašće Arsenija Njegovana (Belgrade: Prosveta, 1970);
Uspenje i sunovrat Ikara Gubelkijana (Belgrade: Slovo ljubve, 1975);
Odbrana i poslednji dani (Belgrade: Slovo ljubve, 1977);
Kako upokojiti vampira (Belgrade: BIGZ, Rad, Narodna knjiga, 1977);
Zlatno runo, 7 volumes (Belgrade: Prosveta, 1978–1986);
Besnilo (Zagreb: Liber, 1983);
1999 (Ljubljana & Zagreb: Cankarjeva založba, 1984);
Pisma iz tuđine (Zagreb: Znanje, 1987);
Godine koje su pojeli skakavci, volume 1 (Belgrade: BIGZ, 1987); volumes 2 and 3 (Belgrade: BIGZ / Priština: Jedinstvo, 1989–1990);
Atlantida, 2 volumes (Zagreb: Znanje, 1988);
Novi Jerusalim (Belgrade: Nolit, 1988);
Nova pisma iz tuđine (Zagreb: Mladost, 1989);
Poslednja pisma iz tuđine (Belgrade: Dereta, 1991);
Sentimentalna povest britanskog carstva (Belgrade: BIGZ, 1992);
Odmor od istorije, edited by Radoslav Bratić (Belgrade: BIGZ, 1993);
Graditelji (Belgrade: BIGZ, 1995).

Collection: *Odabrana dela Borislava Pekića,* 12 volumes (Belgrade: Partizanska knjiga, 1984).

Editions in English: *The Time of Miracles: A Legend,* translated by Lovett F. Edwards (New York: Harcourt Brace Jovanovich, 1976);
The Houses of Belgrade, translated by Bernard Johnson (New York: Harcourt Brace Jovanovich, 1978);
The Generals or Kinship-In-Arms, translated by Vidosava Janković, *Scena,* 13 (1990): 143–153.

PLAY PRODUCTIONS: *Generali ili srodstvo po oružju,* Belgrade, Atelje 212, 1971;

Borislav Pekić

U Edenu, na istoku, Belgrade, Atelje 212, 1971;
Kako zabavljati gospodina Martina, Belgrade, Krug 101, National Theater, 1971;
Kategorički zahtev, Titograd (Podgorica), National Theater of Montenegro, 1977;
Buđenje vampira, Belgrade, Belgrade Drama Theater, 1978;
Remek delo ili sudbina umetnika, Belgrade, National Theater, 1979;
Obešenjak, Skopje, National Theater of Macedonia, 1979;
Ko je ubio Lily Schwarckopf, Ljubljana, Student Cultural Center, 1980;
Razaranje govora, Belgrade, Belgrade Drama Theater, 1980;
Neka se zbude pismo, Belgrade, Atelje 212, 1993.

MOTION PICTURES: *Dan četrnaesti,* Lovćen film, 1960;
Ne diraj u sreću, by Pekić and Milo Dukanović, Lovćen film, 1961;
That Summer of White Roses, Maestro Film, Rajko Grlić, and Mladen Koceić, 1989;
Vreme čuda, Singidunum, Television Belgrade, Channel Four, and Metropolitan Pictures, 1990.

Danilo Kiš, Dragoslav Mihailović, and Borislav Pekić–the leading trio of probably the most talented generation of Serbian writers after World War II–radically changed the course of Serbian literature almost immediately after they made their debut in the mid 1960s. However, Pekić stands out even in this company, because his reputation is not based solely upon the aesthetic quality of his works. Not even erudite novelists like Kiš or Milorad Pavić roam with such ease through an enormous variety of cultures–Judaic, Byzantine, Ottoman, Greek, Serbian, Central and West European–and the most important historical periods from the early Christian era and the Middle Ages to the present, with occasional excursions even into the future. At the same time it was Pekić's thorough knowledge of the long tradition of European thought from Plato to Sigmund Freud and Martin Heidegger, together with his artistic affiliation with some of the most important writers in this century–Thomas Mann, James Joyce, Aldous Huxley, Samuel Beckett, George Orwell, and Aleksandr Solzhenitsyn–that greatly helped reintegrate Serbian literature into the major European trends after a decade-long dispute between the so-called realists and the modernists, who, despite their conflicting views about writing, belonged to the same school of Marxist aesthetics.

Pekić was also among the first to voice a deep sense of disillusionment with life in post–World War II Yugoslavia, but his criticism was not confined exclusively to the totalitarian aberrations of the system in his native country. His antidogmatism and animosity toward the contemporary vogue of cultural and political myth-making soon turned his works into a bitter assessment of modern civilization in general, targeting its mechanical patterns of living, materialistic obsessions, alienation, environmental problems, physical cruelties, and spiritual poverty. In this respect Pekić was a dissident of the most universal kind, and it is not surprising that in the late 1970s and early 1980s his works exercised a strong influence upon a whole generation of young Serbian intellectuals who had freed themselves of Marxist dogmas but were still reluctant to replace them mechanically with some of the ready-made myths of the Western world.

Pekić was born on 4 February 1930 in Podgorica, the present-day administrative center of Montenegro, in a well-to-do middle-class family. His father, Vojislav, was a high-ranking state official whose quiet, somewhat sarcastic disposition contrasted sharply with the ardent nationalism of his youthful years, when he had been a guerrilla fighter supporting the Serbian political cause in Macedonia. Pekić's mother, Ljubica, née Petrović, was a high-school teacher of mathematics; outwardly energetic and rational, she had a strong inclination toward painting. During Pekić's childhood the family frequently moved, following Vojislav's appointments to various positions in Novi Bečej, Mrkonjić Grad, Knin, and Cetinje. It was in Cetinje that eleven-year-old Borislav first showed his rebellious nature and had the first of his many unpleasant encounters with the police: he was briefly detained during the anti-German demonstrations of 27 March 1941. The family spent the years of the German occupation at Ljubica's estate in Bavanište in the Vojvodina region. They moved to Belgrade in 1944 after Josip Broz Tito's partisans liberated the city with Russian help and established their own government. Young Pekić experienced the blessings of freedom with a peculiar bitterness that was later occasionally reflected in his works: "That year I was deprived of one of the happiest of all human feelings–the feeling of being liberated, victorious, and triumphant–and I realized how poignant it is to be defeated in victory."

Pekić's problems with the new regime culminated in November 1948 when the police arrested him as a member of the Association of Democratic Youth of Yugoslavia, a well-organized, rather large anticommunist group that, in his words, raised the necessary funds "using both Robin Hood's and Lenin's methods." Pekić was in charge of ideology, propaganda, and the work of a secret printing shop. One of the group's escapades, in which a few typewriters and mimeographs were stolen from a government office, brought charges of "terrorism and armed rebellion" against him. The indictment also included "espionage in favor of one or more foreign powers." Pekić was sentenced to eight years, but the prosecution complained and he finally was sentenced to fifteen years.

The time that Pekić spent in prison decisively affected his life, ideas, and subsequent

Dust jacket for a translation of Pekić's 1965 novel, which offers a radical reinterpretation of biblical themes

writing career. He was released on probation in 1953, but the rough treatment that he received during the six months of pretrial investigation in Belgrade and the four and one-half years in the Sremska Mitrovica and Niš prisons undermined his health severely, and he became afflicted with tuberculosis. It was in prison that he began to write, although he insisted that his first attempts dated back to his elementary-school days in Knin when he wrote a diary after being urged by his mother to improve his handwriting. The reasons behind his prison diary were naturally quite different, as were the tools that he used: he scratched his observations on pieces of toilet-tissue with the tooth of a comb. But the most valuable possession with which he left the prison was the scheme of the genealogical tree of the fictitious Njegovan family; more than twenty-five years later, Pekić described their history in his seven-volume masterpiece, *Zlatno runo* (The Golden Fleece, 1978–1986), the novel that became the center of his artistic universe.

After he left prison Pekić studied psychology at the University of Belgrade. In 1958 he interrupted his studies and married Ljiljana Glišić, an architect whose father was executed by the Communists in 1944 and whose uncle was Milan Stojadinović, the influential prewar Yugoslav prime minister. The marriage, of course, did not improve his relations with the authorities. Their only daughter, Aleksandra, was born in 1959.

At this time Pekić began to work as a screenwriter. In 1961 the film *Dan četrnaesti* (The Fourteenth Day), based on his scenario, represented Yugoslavia at the Cannes Film Festival. He finally began to earn more money; but as he put it, this "improved [his] games of poker rather than [his] standard of living." At the same time Pekić was working on several of his future novels. The first of them, *Vreme čuda* (1965, translated as *The Time of Miracles: A Legend*, 1976), was published when he was thirty-five; it anticipated many of his later works both in its thematic preoccupations and in the manner of their treatment.

The novel is divided into two parts. The first, subtitled "The Time of Miracles," deals with the seven miracles that, according to the Gospel, Jesus Christ performed on his way to Jerusalem. The second part, subtitled "The Time of Dying," describes the deaths of four people, all related to Jesus' arrest and condemnation. In fact, each of the eleven stories offers a highly idiosyncratic reinterpretation of biblical motifs. The extent of Pekić's interference with the original may be illustrated by the concluding story, "Death at Golgotha," in which Simon of Cyrene is shown dying, crucified in Jesus' place while Jesus himself escapes with Mary Magdalene.

This radical distortion of biblical stories reveals one of the most prominent features of Pekić's art: its antimythical orientation, which resulted from his deep skepticism and uncompromising antidogmatism. But in *Vreme čuda* the Christian myth also becomes a vehicle for exposing the moral hypocrisy, cruelty, and futility of modern myths, especially those built around the Communists' ideal of their own promised land. It is not a coincidence that all the miracles that Pekić's Jesus worked eventually brought misfortunes to the people affected, and that Jesus—who is presented as a nondescript, ordinary man—acquired his prophetic stature only through their, not his, subsequent suffering. His disciples are likewise depicted as a group of ambitious, power-hungry opportunists and dogmatists, who "teach unasked and save without being entreated," and among whom the zealot Judas is particularly impressive for his striking resemblance to a Soviet political commissar in charge of both ideology and money. But Pekić's criticism of the supporters of the new egalitarian faith does not imply any idealization of their opponents. This is especially true of the story "Miracle at Bethany," in which the dead Lazarus is twice resurrected by Jesus only to be killed one more time by the Sadducees. Thus, he becomes a helpless victim for whom the two ideologically confronted parties engaged in proving the superiority of their respective teachings show equal disregard.

Vreme čuda reveals Pekić's other important artistic qualities as well. The variety of linguistic devices adapted for the purpose of characterization is amazing. They range from highly ornate imitations of the biblical diction of the apostles to expressions bordering on urban slang and the country vernacular used by minor characters. The inevitable flatness of the allegorical presentation is always counterbalanced by the enormous vividness of realistic details that almost give Pekić's descriptions of contemporary life in Palestine the semblance of a travelogue. And the implied irony makes this somber book surprisingly light. These features remained the hallmarks of Pekić's style throughout his career.

In 1964, seven months prior to the publication of *Vreme čuda,* Pekić went to the hospital with an extremely serious case of tuberculosis. After he left the hospital, he soon discovered that the short period of his relative affluence had ended. In search of material security, he became the editor of the influential literary review *Književne novine* (Literary Gazette) in 1968. Yugoslavia's tempestuous political events in that year helped him find an appropriate ending for his second novel, *Hodočašće Arsenija Njegovana* (1970, translated as *The Houses of Belgrade*, 1978) but further complicated his relations with the authorities. He used the Belgrade University students' march on the city in June 1968 as a symbolic illustration of a farcical repetition of revolutionary history that eventually killed his story's hero; at the same time, he was accused of being an ardent supporter of the students, although he did not at all share their radical Marxist ideology. Consequently, when he decided to leave Yugoslavia and move to England in 1970, he was not granted a passport and had to wait for a year before he could join his wife and daughter abroad.

Written in the form of the hero's last will, which is often interrupted by his lengthy reminiscences, *Hodočašće Arsenija Njegovana* is a novel that deals with another of Pekić's important subjects: alienation. The former well-to-do Belgrade landlord Arsenije Njegovan lives in self-imposed isolation, unaware of any social or political changes that have taken place in the twenty-seven years during which he has never left his apartment. When in June 1968 he finally decides to interrupt his seclusion in order to inspect some of the buildings he owns (or, because of the expropriation introduced by the Communists, he thinks he owns), his trip through the streets of Belgrade and the encounter with the student protesters trigger a series of misunderstandings that eventually cause his death. The mixture of comic and tragic elements gives the novel a touch of absurdist burlesque, both humorous and pessimistic, strongly resembling a Beckettian play performed on a typical Balkan stage.

The central problem concerning alienation is combined with several other issues such as Pekić's ironic treatment of ownership and his characteristic antidialectical vision of history. In one of his essays Pekić singled out "the will to possess" as one of the most powerful driving forces in our world, a phenomenon that inevitably influences even the "spiritual and moral side of man." Therefore Arsenije's devotion to his apartment buildings becomes more and more grotesque as he insists on giving them feminine names and finally develops feelings bordering on perverted sexuality for one of them. This preoccupation with material things was later to acquire proportions of a modern myth and become central in *Zlatno runo*. On the other hand, Pekić's skeptical view of history, which implies occasional changes of history's form but never of its substance (hinted at earlier in *Vreme čuda*), is shown through three decisive moments of Arsenije's life: the October Revolution, the anti-German demonstrations in March 1941, and the student unrest in Belgrade in 1968. Despite the timespan and apparent changes, the Communist ideological pattern remained virtually the same in all these events, and Arsenije's growing inability to understand what is going on is the only visible result that they have brought about.

In 1971 *Hodočašće Arsenija Njegovana* won the prestigious NIN literary award as the best Yugoslav novel of the year, and Pekić finally obtained his passport and left for Great Britain. In London he associated with the circle of dissident intellectuals (Desimir Tošić, Nenad Petrović, Vane Ivanović) around the journal *Naša reč* (Our Word), all of whom insisted on the necessities of democratic reforms in Yugoslavia, but he refused to write for their paper. Instead, he devoted his free time to his orchids. Nevertheless, the Yugoslav authorities considered him persona non grata, and in 1973 the publishing house Nolit cancelled—although not for long—the publication of three of his works that had already been accepted and paid for. One of them, the novel *Kako upokojiti vampira* (How to Get Rid of the Vampire, 1977), touched upon an entirely new subject.

Based in part on Pekić's experiences in prison, the novel offers an insight into the mechanisms of modern totalitarian logic and psychology. It tells the story of Konrad Rutkowski, a former SS *Obersturmführer* and Gestapo agent, now a professor of medieval history at the University of Heidelberg; the novel presents his endeavors both to justify and to renounce his Nazi past. His painful inner deliberations and his final acceptance of the Nazi ideology are described in twenty-six letters to his brother-in-law. But Rutkowski tries to reach a moral compromise with his past by exploiting some of the major currents of European philosophy. Therefore, the alleged editor of his manuscript, Borislav Pekić (himself an "ardent admirer of the tradition of European

Page from a journal Pekić kept in the 1960s (collection of Mrs. Borislav Pekić)

thought") connected each of the letters with well-known works by some of the most influential European thinkers: Plato, Augustine, René Descartes, John Locke, Immanuel Kant, Georg Wilhelm Friedrich Hegel, Karl Marx, Friedrich Nietzsche, Sigmund Freud, and Ludwig Wittgenstein. In Pekić's own words, this was necessary to show that the SS *Obersturmführer* Rutkowski, his ideology and the logic that he pursues, do not represent a deviation from, but rather a continuation of the "standard currents of European philosophical tradition; the 'molecular structure of Rutkowski's mind' simply resulted from a consistent radicalization of those currents." Pekić claimed that his intention was to show "that fascism or some related form of totalitarianism could again knock on our door." But he also indicated how thin is the line that separates the intellectual tradition of which Europe is so proud from some of the recent aberrant political ideologies. In this way Pekić questioned the ethical validity of the entire history of rational thinking; but he also hinted at the direction his writing was to take during the following decade.

In the 1970s Pekić also distinguished himself as one of the best contemporary Serbian dramatists. He always insisted, however, that he was a theatrical dilettante who began to write plays only because he felt "a psychological need for political involvement and action," but eventually "chose theater rather than open rebellion." He also claimed that his plays were like "garbage cans" in which he disposed of everything that would not fit into his novels. But critics were of a different opinion, and at least one of his plays, *Generali ili srodnost po oružju* (1969, translated as *The Generals or Kinship-In-Arms,* 1990) can be found in any anthology of Serbian drama of the period.

In 1978, after more than two decades of planning, researching, sketching, and developing, Pekić published the first volume of *Zlatno runo*. In its different aspects the novel can be compared to some of the most important works of modern European literature: like Joyce's *Ulysses* (1914–1921), it is based on and often follows the narrative patterns of classical myths; like Mann's *Buddenbrooks* (1901), it maps out a long family history; and like Huxley's *Point Counter Point* (1928), its inner tensions are created through a maze of conflicting perspectives. And yet, it is quite unique. One of the novel's obvious distinctions is its enormous scope and thematic complexity. *Zlatno runo* describes the wanderings of the generations of the Njegovans, Pekić's ironic version of the mythical Argonauts, and their quest for the Golden Fleece. The quest began in ancient times when the forefather of the clan left his homeland of Arcadia, fleeing the rage of a mythical Hercules; it ended in a fire on Christmas Eve, 1941, during a family gathering in their castle near Ljubljana in Slovenia. This span of time gave Pekić an opportunity to explore some of the most important events that shaped the political, social, and cultural map of the Balkans: from the battle at Adrianapolis in 1205 and the fall of Constantinople to the Turks in 1453, to the Austrian occupation of Belgrade in 1915 and the ominous signs of the approaching German invasion in 1941. Within this broad framework there is a narrower sphere of more particular interest: a turbulent period of Serbian history, lasting a little over a century, during which the country rose from a backwater Turkish province to an independent European state. Within this period there is yet another focus: on the origins, economic development, and final disintegration of the Serbian middle class. The choice of the Njegovans as the vehicle for showing these dramatic changes was not a random one. The Njegovans are not Serbs; they are Tzintzars, the progeny of one of the oldest peoples in the Balkans, who accepted the Serbian language, culture, and nationality but always kept themselves apart from their Serbian countrymen. Thus, Pekić was able to depict Serbian society from within; at the same time he established a significant critical distance from it. This was important, since one of Pekić's artistic intentions was to expose several Serbian national myths that were essential to the understanding of Serbian history and the national character. But his main target, and the novel's real focal point, in which all its diverse thematic aspects converge, is a more important and more universal myth. The family's ultimate goal, the Golden Fleece, is a symbol of the "will to possess." In fact, the history of the Njegovans is shown as the universal history of man's craving for wealth, with the triumph of material interests over spiritual values in its center. Bringing the problem of material interests to the foreground and making it a phenomenon of mythic importance, Pekić in fact turned *Zlatno runo* into an ironic comment regarding not only Serbia or the Balkans but the nature of all of modern civilization as well.

The complex idea of *Zlatno runo* is clearly reflected in its structure. Pekić addressed this point in a diary entry in 1963:

> I imagine the Njegovan saga as resembling a planetary system. One major book, like a sun, in its center ... Less important books, like planets, circle around that sun. They deal with certain periods from the long family history ... And around several planets, like their satellites, revolve smaller books, portraits or biographies of those Njegovans, who are only mentioned elsewhere, but who deserve a more detailed approach.

The seven-volume novel is in fact divided into five major parts, subtitled in appropriate business terms: The Account, The Business Venture, The Profit, The Lawsuit, and The Balance Sheet. Central to its first four parts, like a sun, is the story about Simeon, nicknamed "The Boss," the venerable head of the last generation of the Njegovans. More than a hundred years old, The

Boss epitomizes modern Serbian history and the development of the Serbian bourgeoisie. Since through him the objective historical perspective is reduced to an idiosyncratic vision, the whole story turns into a phantasmagoric grotesque that combines the elements of reality, myth, and family legends. Around "The Boss" revolve the "planets," or stories about other important Njegovans and the different periods in which they lived: Simeon "The Pilgrim," his philanthropic father and the only nonmaterialistic Njegovan; Simeon "The Wolf," his unscrupulous grandfather and the founder of the family firm; Simeon "The Greek," his unsuccessful great-grandfather and the crafty Balkan politician; Simeon of Sighet, an ancestor with uncommon artistic inclinations who lived in the sixteenth century; and other, even older Simeons. These lesser characters, usually buried deep in history, take the roles of the "satellites." Each of the characters' major features inspired Pekić to enlarge on different issues: philanthropy, business, politics, art, love, and family matters. The fifth, concluding part, which serves as a mythical framework for the previously described events, is a direct ironic reworking of the classical story about the search for the Golden Fleece and the Argonauts, who epitomize the sublime ideals of nonmaterialistic behavior. The important relativistic perspective, in which these ideals are shown in contrast to the base realities of life and often ridiculed, is provided by the only nondivine, materialistic member of the *Argo*'s crew, Noemis, a mirror reflection (even in name) of the modern Simeons and the actual progenitor of the Njegovans.

The narrative method is no less complex: the first-person accounts are combined with the objective third-person historical narration, lengthy monologues, stream-of-consciousness, dramatic dialogues, epistolary passages, "showing" and "telling" procedures, and the constant switches of points of view. Pekić explained the enormous variety of narrative techniques as "originating from the great number of different Simeons, the novel's real heroes, as well as from the disparity of historical periods in which the events take place." Indeed, in the huge and complicated structure of *Zlatno runo* there is nothing random or accidental: the book offers a model example of organic unity. But there is more than the sheer technical perfection that makes the reading of the unbelievable thirty-five hundred pages of one of the best contemporary Serbian novels a venture that is not undertaken exclusively by professionals. Not the least, it is Pekić's rare ability to keep the reader constantly wondering "what's going to happen next"–a gift that has almost completely disappeared among present day practitioners of highbrow literature.

At the age of fifty Pekić–who insisted that his life took different turns "at the beginning of each new decade"–became somewhat dissatisfied with his work. He claimed that his previous novels had brought him "nothing but disappointments," primarily because they dealt with "inherited models" of human history. The limited possibilities of the traditional concepts of historical time and space prevented them from reaching the "true reality of human condition," which in Pekić's opinion existed beyond these categories. Therefore, he felt that he eventually had "to touch a different universe, and create something entirely new." In fact, at that time he had already been collecting the material for a book about the lost island of Atlantis for a year, intending to give "a new, although poetical, explanation of the roots, development, and the end of our civilization." Despite the classical sources that inspired his anthropological interests, Pekić decided to project his new vision into the future and thus avoid the restrictions of the "historical models" with which he had inevitably to deal in his earlier reworkings of ancient myths. As a result, during the 1980s he produced three novels, each following the antiutopian tradition in its own way.

Besnilo (Rabies, 1983) was finished in 1981, at the time when Pekić was still searching for the "new reality" about which he wanted to write. Mixing elements of science fiction with political, detective, and metafiction (as if Pekić had been wantonly trying to show how he could manipulate different genres), *Besnilo* tells on its surface a story about an epidemic of rabies at Heathrow International Airport in London and its disastrous consequences. But in fact it offers an apocalyptic vision of the moral, intellectual, and environmental breakdown of modern civilization brought about by criminal irresponsibility of both politicians and genetic scientists, and it draws a paradoxical equation between the mutant rhabdovirus and man, according to which the deadly virus "destroys its natural environment with the same sly, cruel, sick arrogance with which man misuses and destroys his own."

Pekić's propensity for intellectual abstractions and generalizations found new possibilities of expression in *Besnilo*. In his short preface Pekić characteristically stated that his heroes–the Heathrow Airport officials–do not represent par-

Dust jacket for a translation of Pekić's Hodočašće Arsenija Njegovana, a novel about an encounter between an old man and student protesters in Belgrade in 1968

ticular individuals, but rather symbolize their "professional positions." He continued along similar lines in *Atlantida* (Atlantis, 1988), which he defined as an "anthropological epic, that does not deal with this or that man in particular, but with *homo sapiens* in general." This attempt at an "analysis of our *Indo-Mechanical civilization*, whose many aspects have never seemed really human," is based on a story about the millennium-long battle between the humanoid natives of the former Atlantis and the robots whom they had created in order to free themselves from the worries of everyday life. The idea of the clash is gradually developed on different levels, from the symbolic opposition of gold and iron (John Carver, the human hero, is shown as a man with "a golden tinge in his eyes," while his robotic counterpart, John Alden, has "eyes of iron"), to the comparison between basic principles of biology and cybernetics. Thus, the story turns into an allegory and almost ends with its inevitable black-and-white flatness. But Pekić gives its conclusion an ironic and relativistic twist: the victorious John Carver finally realizes how similar humanoids and androids have been in their development and how they applied similar strategies to achieve their respective goals. Moreover, he realizes that the very idea of progress of humanity is essentially corrupted, since "people created their history from the depths of evil within themselves," while "good is not based on any kind of development or chronology."

Although published four years before *Atlantida*, *1999* (1984) was originally planned as the concluding part of Pekić's antiutopian trilogy. It deals with the period following a nuclear war that supposedly destroys modern civilization in 1999. Trying to indicate the true nature of his vision rather than his artistic indebtedness, Pekić dedicated the novel to George Orwell; with the same intention he dedicated the individual chapters to Ray Bradbury, Aleksandr Solzhenitsyn, Clifford Simak, Isaac Asimov, and Aldous Huxley. In its different aspects, the novel describes a search for the humaneness that had disappeared from the earth long ago. This is the reason the last representative of the human race, the amateur archeologist Arno, is ready to idealize the life in a Siberian Gulag, where he discovered the bones of men and rats mixed together: to avoid misunderstandings that brought about the destruction of the former civilization, Arno himself has to live alone, and in his world "solitude is genetically inherited." The quest for humaneness is also carried out through the endeavors of perfected generations of robots to reach the human ideal. They discover it in the feeling of uncertainty (as opposed to certainty that is characteristic of androids), and, thus, another symbolic circle, so essential for Pekić's art, is closed. As a matter of fact, *1999* closes more than one circle as it ends with the same quotation from the Bible that Pekić chose as the motto for his first novel, *Vreme čuda:* "The thing that hath been, is that which shall be; and that which is done is that which shall be done: and there is no new thing under the sun."

Ironically, the biblical maxim perfectly suited Pekić's own life at the time. In the late 1980s, after the one-party political system had collapsed in Yugoslavia, he returned to Belgrade and finally became involved in politics as one of the prominent members of the Democratic Party. Exactly fifty years after his first clash with the police in 1941, Pekić again was beaten by security forces in 1991, during demonstrations organized in Belgrade by the united opposition against the ruling Socialists. The following year he again developed problems with his lungs; this time the problems proved fatal and he died of cancer in London, active both as a writer and as a public figure almost until the last day of his life.

Unlike so many critics of modern civilization, Pekić did more than simply denounce that civilization. A skeptic who rejected the idea of progress, a pessimist who considered the world "meaningless and accidental," he nevertheless occasionally offered not only his vision of how things are, but also of how they should be. These rare moments of transcendence—like the one in which Simeon "The Boss" realizes that his dead wife meant more to him than his money, and at least temporarily overcomes his real nature with his no-less-real grief—appear inspired by Pekić's defiant refusal to accept the very reality that he otherwise dealt with. "During our inevitable fall into nothingness we must never remain inert," he wrote. "Sisyphus must not give up pushing his rock uphill even if he knows that it will bounce down as soon as he reaches the top . . . The very secret of our existence may be in—pushing." It is not surprising, therefore, that Pekić considered "literature, or art in general, as one of many projections of the work of Sisyphus."

Interview:
Božo Koprivica, *Vreme reči* (Belgrade: BIGZ, 1993).

References:
Mateja Matejić, "The Art of Literary Adaptation: Andrić's *The Bridge on the Drina* and Pekić's *The Time of Miracles*," *Southeastern Europe*, 9, no. 1-2 (1982): 11-18;

Nikola Milošević, "Borislav Pekić i njegova mitomahija," *Književnost* 4-5, 6-7 (1984): 606-621; 939-955;

Predrag Palavestra, "Porodični roman kao istorijska fantazmagorija," *Književnost-kritika ideologije* (Belgrade: SKZ, 1991), pp. 204-237;

Petar Pijanović, *Poetika romana Borislava Pekića* (Belgrade: Prosveta/Dosije/Dečje novine/Oktoih, 1991);

Savremenik, special issue on Pekić, 7 (1979).

Aleksandar Petrov
(8 January 1938 -   )

Krinka Vidaković
University of Pittsburgh

BOOKS: *Razgovori s poezijom* (Novi Sad: Matica srpska, 1963);

U prostoru proze (Belgrade: Nolit, 1968);

Poetika ruskog formalizma (Belgrade: Prosveta, 1970);

Sazdanac (Belgrade: Nolit, 1971);

Poezija Crnjanskog i srpsko pesništvo (Belgrade: Vuk Karadžić, 1971; Nolit, 1988);

Brus (Belgrade: Narodna knjiga, 1978);

Poezija danas (Belgrade: Vuk Karadžić, 1980);

Krila i vazduh (Belgrade: Narodna knjiga, 1983);

Slovenska škola (Kruševac: Bagdala, 1985);

Poslednje Kosovo (Belgrade: Spectra, 1988);

Istočni dlan (Kruševac: Bagdala, 1992);

Srpski modernizam (Belgrade: Signature, 1996).

Editions in English: Poems, translated by Petrov and Denis Johnson, in *Modern Poetry in Translation*, 19–20 (1973): 62;

Poems, translated by Mark Strand and Krinka Vidaković, in *Contemporary East European Poetry*, edited by Emery George (Ann Arbor: Ardis / Oxford: Oxford University Press, 1983), pp. 381–383;

Poems, translated by Vidaković, Mark Strand, and Charles Simic, in *Serbian Poetry from the Beginnings to the Present*, edited by Milne Holton and Vasa D. Mihailovich (New Haven: Yale Center for International and Area Studies, 1988), pp. 387–389;

Poems, translated by L. Ikach and Luis Bourne, in *Poetry Miscellany*, no. 2 (1988): 50–55;

Poems, translated by Vidaković, Strand, and Aleksandar Nejgebauer, in *World Poets from Iowa*, edited by Tong-choon Shin (Seoul, South Korea: The Twelfth World's Poets' Congress, 1990), pp. 59–62;

Lady in an Empty Dress, translated by Richard Burns (London: Forest Books, 1990);

Sochi. Eroticism. Siberia, translated by various translators (Chattanooga, Tenn.: Poetry Miscellany, 1992).

Aleksandar Petrov

OTHER: *Poezija jugoslovenskih naroda 1945–1975,* edited by Petrov (Belgrade: Delo, 1975);

Antologija ruske poezije XVII–XX vek, edited by Petrov (Belgrade: Prosveta, 1977);

Poezija mladjih jugoslovenskih pesnika, edited by Petrov (Belgrade: Nolit, 1978);

New Serbian Poetry / La Nouvelle Poesie Serbe, edited by Petrov (Belgrade: Relations, 1978);

A Book for Bhopal: 13 Poets from Belgrade, edited by Petrov (Belgrade: Udruženje književnika Srbije/BIGZ, 1985);

Manje poznati Dučić / A Less Known Dučić, edited by Petrov (Trebinje, Pittsburgh, Belgrade: Signature, 1994).

When the Romanian literary journal *Transylvania* published a selection of Aleksandar Petrov's poems in 1988, the translator, Mircea Ivanescu, a distinguished Romanian poet and literary critic, gave a brief but comprehensive portrait of the Serbian writer:

> A poet of intellectual lyricism, an authentic and vibrant sensibility, who knows how to combine data from a biography dedicated to creativity with data pertaining to the specific culture of his country as well as to universal culture, this is the poet and literary critic Aleksandar Petrov. The selection in this issue presents him in a contemporary and universal lyrical landscape, as a unique voice of extraordinary originality and strength, as a truly important modern poet (his poems have been rendered into English by the outstanding American poet Charles Simic) and representative of the best of Yugoslav poetry. The creative spirit of that country, the beauty of its landscape and its people, are embodied in the beauty of A. Petrov's poems.

Petrov was born on 8 January 1935 in Niš, a city in eastern Serbia. His parents, Nikolai Petrov and Irina (née Karateyev) Petrov, were Russian emigrants who had fled Russia as teenagers because of the civil war that broke out with the October Revolution in 1917. Petrov's mother's family were Russian aristocrats in Saint Petersburg. When the revolution started, Irina was a student in the renowned Smolny Institute, a boarding school for girls from aristocratic families, founded by Catherine the Great in the eighteenth century. When Vladimir Lenin took over Saint Petersburg, Smolny was evacuated, and the school eventually moved to Yugoslavia. Petrov's father, Nikolai, was born in Vladikavkaz, a city in the Russian Caucasus. At the time of the revolution he was a young officer in the White Army. After being defeated by the Red Army, his company also found refuge in Yugoslavia. The lives and destinies of Petrov's parents play an important role in his literary work because they highlight issues that became important themes in his poetry: the fate of the individual marked by history and geography, the confrontation and integration of cultures, the changing of identities, the questioning of values, and the quest for meaning in a world continuously on the move in a gray zone of consciousness.

Petrov's earliest memories are of Belgrade, especially the German bombing of 6 April 1941, which marked the outbreak of World War II in Yugoslavia. The bombing was designed to hit not only military but also cultural targets—in particular, the Serbian National Library. The memories of the destruction—of the city, his house, and the library—returned many years later as in his poem "Nedelja. April. XX vek" (Sunday. April. Twentieth Century) from *Istočni dlan* (Easter Palm of the Hand, 1992). It is about the lives of books, some made of iron, others rusted, scarred, crippled, or buried:

> Some books are burnt.
> Ash in the clouds.
> Embers
> in the mouth.

The poem "Varšava. Jerusalim" (Warsaw. Jerusalem), from also *Istočni dlan,* deals with two Jewish brothers and a sister from Poland, all born in the same room but in different countries (as Warsaw changed hands between Russians, Germans, and Poles), and it is people who are burned:

> The sister did not have a son.
> She is the Eternal Virgin.
> Transparent as air.
> Air-borne. Like ash.

Both poems were written before the outbreak of the civil war in Yugoslavia in 1991, but they invoke an awareness of the horrors of war that would once again bring destruction to the Balkans.

In the late 1940s and the 1950s Petrov attended school in Belgrade. After a confrontation with the high school's Communists, he was expelled from all Yugoslav youth organizations and deprived of the benefits such status provided its members. It was at this time that he began writing poetry. His first poems, published in 1955, followed the new models proposed by modernist poets of the early postwar period. As a student of Yugoslav and comparative literature at the University of Belgrade, Petrov started publishing criticism on Yugoslav and foreign writers in *Savremenik* (Contemporary), a leading Serbian journal. In the 1960s he published several contributions in the field of criticism, his book of essays, *Razgovori s poezijom* (Talks with Poetry, 1963), and *U prostoru proze* (In the Realm of Prose, 1968), a study on modern Yugoslav prose writers. He returned to poetry during his army service from 1962 to 1963 when he began writ-

Title page for Petrov's Slovenska škola (1985), a book of poems written while he was teaching in the United States

ing a new kind of poetry quite different from his early writings.

Petrov's first book of poems, *Sazdanac* (a neologism that can be translated as "The Created One," 1971), was welcomed by the leading Serbian poetry critic, Zoran Mišić: "It is a poetry of a specific kind that is quite rare (at least in our literature), distinctly intellectual, clearly and coherently constructed. Unlike most poets we read today, Petrov has not offered us a collection of lyrical poems, but a book of modern, reflexive poems dealing with the old theme of the biblical *Job*, four cycles of poems in the unconclusive dialogue between man (*sazdanac*) and (God) *samosazdanac*." Other critics observed that this extraordinary book took a further step in the Serbian tradition of humorous and parodic poetry. No one in this tradition or any other has "written on God in such a way," Branko Popović wrote in 1971, adding that by the suggestive power of the poems, coupled with their innovative point of view, Petrov had produced poems "of anthological value." Popović drew attention to the creative approach to poetic language through a wide range of linguistic sources—the language of oral tradition (proverbs, sayings, curses), the language of religious ritual, colloquial speech, intellectual discourse, and surrealist innovations, all of which converge in "a poetic adventure of linguistic exploration and innovation." A relevant feature of this book not particularly stressed by critics is its close connection with the mainstream of the literature of the absurd and of the fantastic; Petrov's criticism in the same period deals with just this type of literature in writers such as Nikolay Gogol, Edgar Allan Poe, Fyodor Dostoyevsky, Franz Kafka, Samuel Beckett, and Eugène Ionesco. Petrov's questioning of God's ways is far more radical than Job's; it follows Dostoyevsky's line of thought (if there is no God, nothing is forbidden): if there is no Logos (God), then the world is a theater of the absurd. One would hardly expect such a position in the first book of a young poet if it were not a strong feature of modern literature to rely on irony to question traditional understandings of reality and to subject traditional poetic instruments to parodic recreation. As Mišić observed, the book deals with "the way of all flesh" (in Samuel Butler's words) but makes use of old-fashioned prosodic and versification models to convey an "original sensibility," a new imagery, and its underlying reflexive model.

In 1963 Petrov was given a permanent position in the Institute of Literature and Art (the major literary research center in Belgrade). Although he had been the best student in the Department of Yugoslav and Comparative Literature, he could not obtain a position at the university to teach contemporary literature because of his "unfavorable" political background (Petrov was never a Communist Party member). In the institute he engaged in another confrontation with Communist Party officials and was expelled from his job in 1967. However, he was reinstated following a public polemic and a court order, probably under the pressure of student demonstrations in Belgrade in 1968, and continued at the institute until 1991. As a scholar Petrov's main interest was in theoretical issues. His M.A. thesis in 1967 dealt with poetic elements in the prose works of the Serbian novelist and Nobel laureate Ivo Andrić (the thesis was published as part of *U prostoru proze*). Petrov's lengthy study on the poetics of Russian formalism (first published in sequels in the late 1960s) was included as an introduction to his anthology of formalist contributions *Poetika ruskog formalizma* (The Poetics of Russian Formalism, 1970). This book had an important impact since at that time few scholars (with the exception of Victor Erlich) had similar insights into formalist theory. The culmination of Petrov's theoretical research was his Ph.D. thesis at the University of Zagreb in 1971 on the poetry of Miloš Crnjanski, a key twentieth-century Serbian poet. *Poezija Crnjanskog i srpsko pesništvo* (The Poetry of Crnjanski and the Serbian Poetic Tradition, 1971) was awarded the Isidora Sekulić Prize, one of the most prestigious in Yugoslav literature.

In this period Petrov was participating in the activities of the Serbian and Yugoslav Writers' Association, which he had joined in 1964, and the International P.E.N., which he had joined in 1966. From 1965 to 1968 he was a member of the editorial board of the *Književne novine* (Literary Gazette), the main literary weekly published in Belgrade; from 1968 to 1972 he was editor in chief of *Književna istorija* (Literary History), which became the best scholarly journal in the field of literature. Petrov also continued his contributions to the field of criticism, writing almost exclusively about poetry. The publication of *Sazdanac*, his first collection of poems, and his excellent study on Crnjanski (both in 1971) placed him among the most outstanding writers and scholars of his generation. The following year he was invited to be a poet-in-residence at the International Writing Program at the University of Iowa. Petrov's experience in the United States was crucial in the evolution of his creative writing; it was also during his almost two-year stay in Iowa (1972–1974) that he completed most of the work on two important anthologies: *Poezija jugoslovenskih naroda 1945–1975* (The Poetry of the Yugoslav Peoples 1945–1975), a selection from contemporary Yugoslav poetry accompanied by a landmark study on this topic (published in 1975), and the two-volume bilingual *Antologija ruske poezije XVII–XX vek* (Anthology of Russian Poetry from the Seventeenth to the Twentieth Century, 1977), with a general introduction and detailed comments. In 1982 the Russian poet and Nobel laureate Joseph Brodsky commended Petrov's accomplishment: "A poet of considerable powers himself, Mr. Petrov is able to approach his material with the lucidity of [an] insider. The most comprehensive anthology of Russian poetry to date is for instance compiled by this man, a native of Yugoslavia, a visiting scholar to various American campuses, a literati in the old-fashioned sense of the word."

The book was declared an extraordinary cultural event in the Yugoslavia of those years. Petrov was among the first to edit a consistently designed anthology of Russian poetry from its beginnings to its most recent trends, and he stressed the contributions of underground poetry. He effected a complete reevaluation of Russian poetry according to modern principles, eliminating from his anthology many poets who had achieved renown under the Soviet regime and highlighting poets who were its victims—Osip Mandelstam and others. The importance of this anthology lay in Petrov's new approach that underlined the absurdist line of Russian poetry, evolving from the early nineteenth century and culminating in the Russian underground poetry of the communist period. Certain poets from this tradition had never been included in any anthology of Russian poetry, and some had never been published in book form. This bilingual anthology provoked a political scandal. During their visit to Belgrade several high-ranking Soviet party officials demanded that the anthology be banned, and even President Leonid Brezhnev protested during his meeting with the Yugoslav president, Josip Broz Tito. In a private letter to Yugoslav political officials Petrov managed to defend his anthology and evade the ban; however, the anthology was not reprinted. In the years after his return from Iowa to Belgrade, Petrov published two more anthologies—the bilingual (English/French) *New Serbian Poetry / La Nouvelle Poesie Serbe* (Belgrade, 1978) and *Poezija mladjih jugoslovenskih pesnika* (The Poetry of Young Yugoslav Poets, 1978), which has gone through nine editions since its first publication.

In the early 1970s Petrov began writing a new collection of poems that he nearly finished during his two years in Iowa from 1972 to 1974. The collection was published under the title *Brus* (Whetstone, 1978). This book revealed a new poetic dimension, although the hand of *Sazdanac* can be traced in the use of irony, humor, and the absurd. Two Serbian poets and critics, Dobroslav Smiljanić and Dragan Stojanović, stressed the modernity of Petrov's poetry. Stojanović indicated that the antimetaphysical position—of both modern poetry and Petrov's *Brus*—is typical of an epoch that is experiencing the collapse of its metaphysical structure, questioning itself, and reflecting on its own end.

Both critics elaborate on how this perspective affects poetic language. Certain poetic elements considered traditional are subjected to reinterpretation involving both preservation and change, with irony playing a crucial role. Irony, observed Stojanović, leads toward the multiplication of meanings and nuances, not merely the establishment of a countermeaning; however, it does not follow that it assumes a nihilistic position toward the semantics of the text, which assumes a relative quality. Irony, bitter sarcasm, mocking, simulacra, blasphemous language, and disruptive phrases result from a return to the "zero point" of language that, according to Smiljanić, writing in 1978, releases new and unpredictable poetic possibilities: "Each word is cut in two, doubled, bipolar and double-edged, each one bearing within a set of specific correlations and oppositions, double accents of unequal strength, fire and water at the same time."

Other aspects of *Brus* that Stojanović discussed are its eroticism and its confrontation with "another voice" that is defined by its opposition to poetry. For Petrov poetry is a way of reaching tangible reality, touching, exploring, feeling, and sensing it. Therefore, according to Stojanović, the body assumes an important role:

> Calling the world into the body, the movement of the world towards the body, this becomes a great theme. Poetry appears as a mediator between the world and the body, like a 'dress' on the body.... And when the body positions itself in the focus of attention, this opens a number of new questions. The first and most relevant ... is that of touching in all its forms.

As for the "other voice" opposed to poetry, Stojanović refers to Petrov's essay "Majstor i Margarita" (The Master and Margarita, 1974), in which the author explains the specific position of poetry. On the one hand, poetry yearns to belong to, and to become integrated into, society (figuratively speaking, a circle) in which it would assume meaning and responsibility and renounce absolute freedom. If poetry remains outside society, it is free but at the same time irrelevant. The position of poetry is that of a point orbiting on the edge of a circle, both inside and outside, relatively free and also capable of viewing the circle both from within and without. Although poetry makes nothing happen (as W. H. Auden has said) and cannot change the world from without, it can at least, in Petrov's words, "encourage the Revolution / of the red blood cells." In a world of "instrumentalized objectives," as Smiljanić put it, in which truth and beauty—which have no objectives outside themselves and are therefore "useless," "superfluous," and "dangerous"—have become utterly outdated ornaments, durable goods unable to compete with their ephemeral substitutes produced by the culture industry.

An interesting feature, not noted by these two meticulous critics, is the fact that the book is closely connected with Petrov's American experience. America is identified with modern civilization at the end of the present millennium. In "Poezija u staklenoj kocki" (Poetry in a Glass Cube), in *Brus,* the protagonist is poetry itself (accompanied by the poet), questioning its role in a world alien to it. Part of the imagery is derived from Petrov's visit to a major American insurance company, a modern glass building with a collection of modern paintings.

In "Kako je eksplodirala poezija" (How Poetry Exploded, 1978) nobody pays attention to poetry on the street, and nobody hears it: not even the shop windows show its reflection. Finally, in "Poezija u praznoj haljini" (Poetry in an Empty Dress, 1978) poetry is an ambiguously empty dress. The latter poem provided the title for two anthologies of Petrov's poetry: *La dama del vestido vacio* (Lady in an Empty Dress, 1988) and *Lady in an Empty Dress* (1990).

On his return to Yugoslavia Petrov continued writing criticism, focusing almost completely on poetry; he was the permanent contributor to the literary supplement of *Politika*. Two new books resulted from these activities: *New Serbian Poetry / La Nouvelle Poesie Serbe* and *Poezija danas* (Poetry Today, 1980), probably the best critical survey of current Serbian poetry, identifying its main features, literary predecessors, and international influences.

In 1980 Petrov was again in the United States, this time as a Fulbright Scholar, a visiting professor (teaching Russian and comparative literature), a guest lecturer (visiting at several universities, from Harvard and Columbia to Berkeley and UCLA), and a participant in academic conferences. During the 1980s he began working on a new poetic project that resulted in *Slovenska škola* (Slavic School, 1985). The title refers to Petrov's teaching experience in the United States. The relationship between professor and student became a specific topic in his poetry. Unlike in Europe, where poets are seldom university professors, many leading poets in America teach at universities and thereby establish a live contact with the future readers and writers of poetry. This situation seemed to Petrov a renewal of the ancient oral communication channel between the poet and his audience, albeit reduced to a small circle of chosen interlocutors and limited to campuses. Petrov was convinced that this communication played an important role in the revitalization of modern American poetry. This distinctive American situation (the lyric "I" is a university professor) is coupled with the Slavic aspect (topics of his lectures): the ancient and the new protagonists of Slavic culture who are immersed in a dynamic poetic world of changing time and space. Being a poet, critic, and professor provided Petrov with the specific perspectives of both insider and observer. Joseph Brodsky called Petrov "a born comparativist," a description that implies a multiplicity of perspectives, languages, cultures, and traditions.

Petrov's views and sensibility were shaped by his own genealogy, which connected him to Poland (where his mother was born), Saint Petersburg, the Caucasus, the Balkans, and the Far East. One of his mother's cousins, an immigrant in South America, Mihail Karateyev, had published (in Paris and Russia) several historical novels about the Karateyev family in the Middle Ages, when one of their ancestors married Tamerlane's granddaughter. Therefore, the motif of identity in *Slovenska škola* assumed an Asian aspect, one that Petrov continued to explore and develop in his poetic and scholarly works in the 1990s.

However, the most interesting aspect of *Slovenska škola* is its poetic technique. As the critic Novica Petković pointed out in his afterword to *Slovenska škola,* this technique is deliberately laid bare, so that the reader can follow both the poem and the poetic process from which it results, a process transforming facts (autobiographical, historical, and impersonal) into poetic facts. Petković indicates that Petrov's poems contain their own interpretation:

> It is like a merging of two different voices: that of the poet and that of the critic. In Petrov's poetry the poetic and the meta-poetic appear as two sides of the same coin. A surprising feature of Petrov's po-

Title page for Petrov's 1992 collection of poems, Istočni dlan, some of which deal with the breakup of Yugoslavia in the early 1990s

etry is the concurrent rendering of the metaphorical refractions and the comparison they are derived from. This enables him to give an insight into the poem as well as into the poet's workshop where it was made. This technique—a simultaneous view of the work itself, the work-in-progress, and the workshop—has become a preference of today's art. However, Petrov introduces it into contemporary Serbian poetry in an interesting manner. This technique begins with a selection of details given in their literal meaning, these are interrelated through analogy or some kind of contact (spacial, temporal), then there is a tropic or symbolic refraction, the initial material is transformed into metaphors and metonymies that are suspended in the air by poetic polysemia.

According to Petković, *Slovenska škola* is "an extraordinary book in many respects; a book which in Serbian poetry of today could and should be experienced as a valuable innovation." It might be added that it is also a book unlike Petrov's previous works: autobiographical and personal, but not at all sentimental; stripped of any kind of moralizing and antipathetic; and at the same time an acceptance of life with all its imperfections and ironic twists, tragedies and comedies, great historic events and epiphanies hidden in the everyday lives of common people.

In "Gutljaj entropije" (A Gulp of Entropy) Petrov describes a "Balkan Type of C without W" (a watercloset, restroom), a "bunker down the hall of my uncle's house," with a loophole window "opening on an alley of roses." It is the place where newspaper clippings—"Confusion of pages. Columns. Dates."—have an additional use in view of the toilet paper shortage. This is the scene where the death of reading occurs, where it disappears in entropy's warm gulp. It is also a place, like any other place on earth, where reality turns blindness into insight:

> In the late forties I did not read Pound.
> When the texture of New Criticism was coming apart
> I wore darned socks. Kicked a ball made of rags.
> Got indoctrinated with socialism.
> Was cured of children's diseases.
> I didn't knock out the wedge of artism with Williams' "Wedge."
> But I discovered a point of view.
> The yellow spot. Reality's dilated pupil.

–translated by Mark Strand and Krinka Vidaković

While Petrov was in the United States, his friend and fellow poet, Gojko Djogo, was arrested and accused of referring sarcastically in his collection of poems to Tito, the late Yugoslav president. Petrov returned briefly to Yugoslavia in 1981 to attend the trial and express his solidarity with the poet. When the latter was sent to serve his sentence in 1982, Petrov returned to Belgrade and became one of the organizers of the protests demanding the poet's freedom. Protest poetry readings held by the Yugoslav Writers' Association lasted eleven weeks, until Djogo was set free; but Petrov's dissident activity continued. These were the years when the writers' organization had moved into the forefront of the movement demanding the democratization of Yugoslavia and the introduction of a multiparty system. As a leader of this movement, Petrov was elected to the executive board of the Serbian Writers' Association (1983), then to the board of the Yugoslav Writers' Association (1985); he served as president of the former from 1986 to 1988 and acting president of the latter in 1987.

However, the early 1980s witnessed not only the rise of a democratic movement but also an intensification of ethnic confrontation and secessionist demands. Especially dramatic was the situation in Kosovo, where the conflict between the Albanian majority and Serb minority was reaching its culmination. This old confrontation had been evident in 1968 during Albanian demonstrations that demanded the status of a republic for Kosovo, secession, and union with Albania. When Petrov visited the region, he witnessed the pressure that produced the exodus of Serbs from Kosovo. He wrote a cycle of poems based on his insights, but in those years it was impossible to publish anything on this topic because of the deliberate media blackout on Kosovo imposed by the communist authorities. In the 1980s, as a leading official of the writers' organizations, Petrov defended the rights of both ethnic groups in Kosovo, but not the secessionist movements that were threatening to destroy the multicultural framework of Yugoslavia. Petrov wrote two more cycles of Kosovo poems and published the collection *Poslednje Kosovo* (The Last Kosovo, 1988) twenty years after the first poems had been written.

In this book Petrov effected a reevaluation of the Kosovo myth and stressed the Christian aspect of what he had called "the sacred story of the Serbian nation." Kosovo represents what Miguel de Unamuno y Jugo has called "the tragic sense of life." *Poslednje Kosovo* deals with a theme that has permeated the Serbian literary tradition since the fourteenth century, when the historic battle of Kosovo Field took place in 1389. The importance of this battle can hardly be underestimated since it marked the beginning of a five-century-long history of national subjugation, massive migration and exile, and economic, social, and cultural deterioration, all of which encouraged the cult of the memory of freedom and the hope in its return. During the Ottoman age and the period that followed (the reestablishment of Serbia, the liberation of Kosovo in 1912, and the first and second Yugoslavia), Kosovo remained a symbol with powerful cultural and political implications.

Even more important was Petrov's attempt to explain the Kosovo complex in the Serb cultural tradition and understand the causes of the new waves of tragedy in the 1990s in the so-called ethnic cleansing designed to produce ethnic purity in Kosovo. Furthermore, Petrov not only sought to understand the circumstances that were leading to the breakup of a multiethnic Yugoslavia but also to anticipate the consequences of that breakup. Vasa D. Mihailovich wrote that Petrov's approach was that of a modern poet: "In a series of apocalyptic visions, he recalls the symbolism of the ultimate sacrifice, but also the dangers to the very existence of the Kosovo legacy today."

The end of the 1980s marked the collapse of communism in the world, a process that coincided in the early 1990s with the disintegration of Yugoslavia. On the eve of the "death of the nation," the multiparty system was established in Yugoslavia. In April 1990 the newly founded democratic parties organized their first multiparty meeting in Belgrade in fifty years. The leaders of the opposition invited Petrov to chair this historic event. Although his commitment to the democratic movement in Yugoslavia had been continuous and fruitful, Petrov decided in 1990 to withdraw from politics and dedicate himself entirely to his creative and scholarly work. At the invitation of Hokkaido University he spent time from 1990 to 1991 in Sapporo, Japan, working on a research project in Slavic studies and writing poetry. As a major foreign poet Petrov was invited to give poetry readings and participate in other activities with Japanese writers. In Japan he continued writing poems in Serbian and in Russian, just as he had done many years before in Iowa City. Petrov's poetry was published in Japan in various journals and books.

For Petrov Japan was a door that opened to Asia. He was invited to neighboring countries to give poetry readings, lecture at universities, and participate in international conferences. During one of his trips to China and Inner Mongolia, Petrov wrote a cycle of poems called "Kineska Sreska," or "Chinese Notebook," which completed the collection *Istočni dlan*, begun in the mid 1980s. As English poet Richard Burns pointed out in the introduction to his 1990 translation of *La dama del vestido vacio*, the hand is one of Petrov's favorite images:

> A constantly recurring image in Alexander Petrov's poetry is the human hand: whether holding a car wheel, a book or a pen, chiselling in stone or tapping away at a typewriter, stroking, caressing or provoking, folded in prayer or outstretched, palms open, revealing the lifeline. The span of this hand is huge: from summer in Columbus, Ohio, to winter in Siberia; from Warsaw to William Carlos Williams, St. Petersburg to Ezra Pound, Harvard to Haley's Comet, Cleveland to the Caucasus, Jerusalem to Tsvetaeva, and Borges back to Belgrade. Vast areas and stretches of language are cunningly sliced up into staccato snippets, wrapped in connotative codes, sprinkled with associations, spiced with ambiguities, salted with erudition, and peppered with irony. Here collage is conscience and montage is memory. The recipe: self-criticism through world-questioning and world-criticism through self-questioning. A wry documentation of personal history all too disarmingly condenses that of millennia: exile and migration, emigration and hope. The heart is human. It beats in the Balkans.

The palm of the hand is not only a map of personal and collective lifelines. According to a traditional Serbian saying, it is the place where one guards the most precious treasure in the world: a drop of water. The poems in this book are "drops" of life on the palm of a hand identified with all the variations of the East: Eastern Europe (Belgrade, Warsaw, Russia, and Serbia); the Ancient East (Byzantium, Georgia, Armenia, and the Caucasus); the Holy East (Jerusalem); the natural East (Siberia); and the Far East (China and Japan). One of the poems is about Christopher Columbus: the conviction that the East would be reached by going west and the unpredictable discovery of a new continent. This can be understood as a metaphor of Petrov's creative process: the discovery of a new poetic land, reaching art through life, coming home by experiencing the world. Although this book continues developing the poetics of *Slovenska škola*, there is an urge (encouraged, perhaps, by the Eastern poetic tradition) to achieve extreme economy in language by combining utterly simple structures with complex images. A new theme presented in this book is the looming tragedy of the civil war in Yugoslavia, predicted in previous poems but witnessed and recorded in these.

In the second half of 1991 Petrov was active in the peace movement in Yugoslavia, but when he realized that peace would be shattered by the breakup of Yugoslavia, he went to the United States to continue his professional activities: poetry, research, and teaching. He was first a researcher at Ohio State University. Since 1993 he has taught Serbian culture, literature, and language at the University of Pittsburgh and has been editor of the Serbian language section of *American Srbobran* and its literary supplement (a bilingual edition, whose publication Petrov has renewed).

Petrov's reputation as a poet and scholar was fully confirmed in the early 1990s. In those years his poems were published in more than twenty languages. He is one of the few contemporary foreign writers to have three books published in Chinese: an anthology of his poems, *Descending Ladders of Light,* published both in Taipei (1992) and Beijing (1993) and a collection of essays, *The Poet's Space and Time* (1994) in Taiwan (as a bilingual edition in Chinese and English). Poets and critics around the world have written about Aleksandar Petrov as a modern, cosmopolitan, multifaceted intellectual (poet, critic, scholar, and teacher). When Petrov was invited to Taiwan to speak, the Chinese poetess Chang Shiang-hua wrote: "It was an epoch-making and revolutionary event for students of Chinese literature, and even for the whole of academia." Petrov's speech opened up "broad new horizons to the world." It could be said that opening new horizons is the main feature of Petrov's endeavor as poet and scholar.

References:

Zoran Djerić, "Slovenska škola poezije," *Letopis Matice srpske,* no. 9 (1985): 298–301;

Anna Edlinskaia, "Slavianskaia shkola, Poslednee Kosovo," *Sovremennaia khudozhestvennaia literatura za rubezhom* (September–October 1990): 5–23;

Milivoje Jovanović, "Uz jedan kulturni dogadjaj," *Književnost,* no. 3 (1978): 415–425;

Vasa D. Mihailovich, "Krila i vazduh," *World Literature Today,* 58 (1984): 441;

Mihailovich, "Poslednje Kosovo," *World Literature Today,* 63 (1989): 507;

Mihailovich, "Slovenska škola," *World Literature Today,* 60 (1986): 334–335;

Branko Mikasinovich, "Lady in an Empty Dress," *World Literature Today,* 65 (1991): 737;

Branko Popović, "Agonija postojanja pod sarkastičnom lupom," *Književnost,* no. 9 (1971): 275–282;

Popović, "Aleksandar Petrov," in his *Samosvest kritike* (Belgrade: Nolit, 1987), pp. 57–73;

Popović, "Poezija danas," *World Literature Today,* 55 (1981): 501;

Žarko Rošulj, "Krila i vazduh," *Delo,* no. 10 (1984): 149–152;

Rošulj, "The Poetic Subject in History," *Relations,* 2 (1985): 85–88;

Dobroslav Smiljanić, "Otisci poezije u podzemnom prolazu," *Književna reč,* no. 111 (25 November 1978): 13;

Dragan Stojanović, "Pesnik i azbuka," *Književna kritika,* 1 (1982): 36–42.

Valeri Petrov
(22 April 1920 -   )

Nikita Nankov
Indiana University

BOOKS: *Ptitsi kŭm sever,* as Asen Rakovski (Sofia: D [obromir] Chilingirov, 1938);

Kŭm polyusa, as Asen Rakovski (Sofia: D[obromir] Chilingirov, 1938);

Naroden sŭd (Sofia: BRP [k] / Mladezhka biblioteka, 1944);

Stikhotvoreniya (Sofia: Nauka i izkustvo, 1949);

Dnite, koito zhiveem (Sofia: Narodna mladezh, 1952);

Gost-geroy (Sofia: Narodna mladezh, 1953);

Tam na Zapad . . . (Sofia: Bŭlgarski pisatel, 1954);

Kniga za Kitay (Sofia: Bŭlgarski pisatel, 1958);

V mekata esen (Sofia: Bŭlgarski pisatel, 1961);

Poemi (Sofia: Bŭlgarski pisatel, 1962);

Kogato rozite . . . (Sofia: Bŭlgarski pisatel, 1965);

Afrikanski belezhnik (Sofia: Bŭlgarski pisatel, 1965);

Poemi (Sofia: Bŭlgarski pisatel / Biblioteka za uchenika, 1966); republished as *Poemi, stikhotvoreniya, satira* (n.p., 1987);

Dŭzhdvali–slŭntse gree (Sofia: Bŭlgarski pisatel, 1967);

Kato poglednesh nazad (Sofia: Narodna kultura, 1969);

Na smyakh (Sofia: Bŭlgarski pisatel, 1970);

Poeziya (Sofia: Bŭlgarski pisatel, 1973);

Byala prikazka (Sofia: Otechestvo, 1977);

Stikhotvoreniya i poemi (Sofia: Bŭlgarski pisatel, 1977);

Kopche za sŭn (Sofia: Otechestvo, 1978);

Meko kazano (Sofia: Otechestvo, 1980);

Palechko (Sofia: Bŭlgarski khudozhnik, 1981);

V lunnata staya (Sofia: Bŭlgarski khudozhnik, 1982);

Puk! (Sofia: Bŭlgarski khudozhnik, 1983);

Izbrani stikhove (Varna: Georgi Bakalov, 1984);

Poeziya (Sofia: Bŭlgarski pisatel, 1984);

Teatŭr, lyubov moya (Sofia: Repertoarna biblioteka, no. 13, 1984);

Pet prikazki (Sofia: Otechestvo, 1986);

Satirichni poemi (Sofia: Bŭlgarski pisatel, 1988);

Valeri Petrov

Neveroyatnite priklyucheniya na Sin Dyado, by Petrov and Khristo Ganev (Sofia: Khristo Botev, 1992).

Collections: *Izbrani proizvedeniya v dva toma* (Sofia: Bŭlgarski pisatel, 1980);

Izbrani proizvedeniya v dva toma (Sofia; Bŭlgarski pisatel, 1990);

Stikhotvoreniya. Tom prvi, Poemi. Tom vtori (Sofia: Khristo Botev, 1994);

Zhivot v stikhovi (Sofia: Khristo Botev, 1997).

TRANSLATIONS: William Shakespeare, *Komedii,* 2 volumes (Sofia: Narodna kultura, 1970–1971);

Shakespeare, *Tragedii,* 2 volumes (Sofia: Narodna kultura, 1973-1974);

Shakespeare, *Tragikomedii i romansi* (Sofia: Narodna kultura, 1976);

Shakespeare, *Istoricheski drami,* 2 volumes (Sofia: Narodna kultura, 1980-1981);

Shakespeare, *Soneti* (Sofia: Narodna izdatelstvo, 1992).

Valeri Petrov is one of the most talented and innovative Bulgarian writers in the period after World War II. He is also the most culturally sophisticated among his literary peers. The brilliant combination of imagination and erudition that manifested itself when Petrov was barely twenty paradoxically deferred full recognition of his achievements for some two decades. Between the 1940s and the 1960s Marxist critics were unable to appreciate the novelty of Petrov's work, which stands apart from and above the literary criteria of that time. Petrov is a poet, screenwriter, playwright, and translator; he writes for adults and children, and in all these fields he has made his mark. Petrov has been a lifelong adherent to the ideas of communism. The combination of his intellectual honesty, civic courage, and unselfishness in political matters represents one of the few instances in Bulgarian literature and culture after World War II of how creative fantasy and social ideals complement each other.

Valeri Petrov is the pen name of Valeri Nisim Mevorakh, a Bulgarian Jew who was born on 22 April 1920 in Sofia. His father, Nisim Mevorakh, who had studied in Switzerland, was a well-known lawyer, professor of law at the University of Sofia "St. Kliment Okhridski," ambassador to the United States, and an ardent lover of the arts. In the narrative poem "Sbogom, tate!" (Farewell, Dad!), a requiem for his adored parent, Petrov describes his father's idealistic moral stance as that of a "Don Quixote" or a "wrinkled child" and his intellectual style as a "brilliance of words and thought." Petrov's mother, Mariya Petrova, who also studied in Switzerland, was a widely read high-school teacher of French. In his family, which was close to the communist and leftist intellectuals, and later in the Italian School in Sofia, which Petrov finished in 1939, the young Valeri cultivated a lifelong taste for matters of culture. In school Petrov learned Italian, Latin, and German; in his family he was obliged to be familiar with French and Russian, and later he studied English by himself.

As a teenager enthusiastically encouraged by his father, Petrov unsuccessfully tried drawing and guitar-playing before turning to literature and creative writing. He read voraciously in several languages, participated in literary organizations, and, in collaboration with his father, wrote two juvenile novels that were never printed. At this time Petrov was influenced mainly by French and Russian poetry. He was published for the first time in the journal *Uchenicheski podem* (Pupils' Uplift) in 1936. He also contributed to the journal *Khorovod* (Khoro Leader). Petrov's first book, *Ptitsi kŭm sever* (Birds Flying North, 1938), was published with the help of his father's money and connections. It is a naive poem about the landing of the Russian scientist Oto Yul'evich Shmidt at the North Pole in 1937. The newspaper *Literaturen glas* (Literary Voice) characterized the book as a complete failure. In 1939 Petrov became a member of BONNS (Bŭlgarian Common People's Students Union), a university students' organization led by the Communist Party.

The early maturity of Petrov's talent shone in the works published, although some were censored, in the journal *Izkustvo i kritika* (Art and Criticism) between 1938 and 1943—especially the cycle "Noshti v Balkana" (Nights in the Balkan Mountains, 1940) and the narrative poem *Juvenes dum sumus* (1943). From 1940 to 1948 some of the highest poetic accomplishments of Petrov were written: the narrative poems *Detinstvo* (Childhood, 1940), *Palechko* (Tom Thumb, 1943), *Na pŭt* (On the Way, 1943), *Kray sin'oto more* (By the Blue Sea, 1941-1947), *Tavanski spomen* (Remembrance from the Attic, 1942-1948 [the poem circulated in manuscript and was published only in 1962]), and the cycles "Nezhnosti" (Endearments, 1940-1943), "Stari neshta malko po novomu" (Old Things Retold a Little Differently, 1945), "Mezhdu agitkite" (Between the Propaganda Plays, 1944-1946), "Pŭstri freski" (Motley Frescoes, 1946), and some others. These works constitute the pivots of Petrov's artistic view of life and poetics, to which he has remained faithful throughout his life and which, remodeled, are the bases of some of his best plays, film scripts, children's tales, satires, travelogues, and translations. The most striking feature of these early works is the freedom with which Petrov tackles traditional poetic themes, images, and values in both Bulgarian literature and culture in general. What is considered sacred and central there—the struggle for political freedom and social justice, the sublimity of heroic death, the national and communist ideals, and so on—is often parodied and allotted only a peripheral place by Petrov. His poetry, at its best, merrily plays with the inherited hierarchies of the Bulgarian cultural universe, and in this broadest sense it is antiauthoritative and liberating through laughter. Petrov not only writes parodies but, more importantly, perceives things parodically: again and again, with few words, he sketches discursive, genre, stylistic, or ideological patterns and exposes their pretenses to a monopoly on truth. Petrov's view of life balances the extremes through irony, detachment, and erudite skepticism. For him nothing is totally good or totally bad, completely elevated or completely vulgar, irrevocably tragic or irrevocably comic.

In Petrov's art all phenomena are in the making, their meaning is never completely revealed, they always hide unsuspected potential, and they can easily become their own opposites. This is an imaginative world of fluidity and change where no ultimate meanings and answers exist. Here every object speaks, literally, and this anthropomorphism is not solely a technique that makes a bridge to Petrov's works for children but, on a deeper level, also a polyphonic device that epitomizes his reluctance to underscore a single domineering voice. Petrov's poetry rests on ambivalent identifications and oppositions between the concrete (he is the supreme master of the minute, even bizarre, detail in Bulgarian poetry) and the infinite. This is why his works more often than not have symbolic connotations (which, however, under certain conditions become allegories verging on didacticism). Petrov, more consistently than any other Bulgarian poet after World War II, stands by the aesthetic self-sufficiency of the verbal artistic play; he is an unsurpassed demiurge of "storms of calambours," a superb formal craftsman, and one of the great innovators of Bulgarian rhyme. He, in fact, has published no unrhymed poems; his life-long love for rhymes is spelled out in the poem "Sbogom na rimata" (Farewell to the Rhyme). Petrov formulates three requirements for his rhymes, which are, in ascending importance: exactness, freshness, and expressiveness. It should be remembered that in the early 1950s poetic craftsmanship was a banner under which Marxist dogmatism was challenged.

Petrov graduated in 1944 with a degree in medicine from the University of Sofia "St. Kliment Okhridiski", but his medical career as a physician in the Rila Monastery lasted only briefly. From September 1944 to 1945 he worked at Radio Sofia. In 1945 Petrov participated in the Patriotic War as a military writer and an editor at *Shturmovak* (Stormtrooper), a satiric weekly. In the same year he became one of the founders of the major humorous and satiric newspaper in socialist Bulgaria, *Stŭrshel* (Hornet), a weekly, and from 1945 to 1962 (with some interruptions) he was an editor, a deputy chief editor, and a member of the board of editors. In 1947 he became a member of the Bulgarian Writers Union. Between 1947 and 1950 Petrov was a press attaché at the Bulgarian Legation in Rome. From 1961 to 1962 he was an editor at Bŭlgarski pisatel (Bulgarian Writer) publishing house.

Some of Petrov's early works were collected in his first mature book of poetry, *Stikhotvoreniya* (Poems, 1949), which had the misfortune of appearing in an epoch of rigorous conformity and bigotry. The verdict of the Marxist criticism was that the poet was guilty of incorrect ideological views, intellectual individualism, petit-bourgeois and decadent sentiments, and formalism. At one point Petrov thought that his artistic principles might indeed be wrong and his critics might have been right. The next two collections, *Dnite, koito zhiveem* (The Days We Live, 1952) and *Tam na Zapad . . .* (Over There, in the West . . . , 1954), testify to Petrov's efforts to conform to the literary standards of the time. The deplorable result was a poetry that satisfied his critics but not Petrov's muse; these works are not included in the later editions of his poetry, with the exception of the poem "Rimski ploshtadi" (The Squares of Rome, 1954). After this compromise he spent several years in a relative poetic silence, restoring his artistic self-confidence. During this period he traveled to China (1955) and published the travelogue *Kniga za Kitay* (A Book about China, 1958). Petrov's second travelogue is *Afrikanski belezhnik* (African Notebook, 1965), which tells about his six-month journey in Africa by invitation of UNESCO (United Nations Educational, Social, and Cultural Organization) from 1961 to 1962. These two works are undeservedly neglected by literary critics and historians. The openness of the travelogue genre enables Petrov, by means of his elegant, humorous, and knowledgeable prose, to demonstrate in a new form the freedom and unpredictability of his pen.

The poetic silence was broken by *V mekata esen* (In the Mild Autumn, 1961), Petrov's longest lyric work, containing some two thousand lines. He started writing it in late 1957 or early 1958, not intending to publish it. The renewed poetic labors began as a meditation on "personal and

Illustration from the cover of Petrov's first play, Kogato rozite tantsuvat *(When Roses Dance, 1961), which mixes verse and prose*

social problems which had gathered head" and an exploration of a new "poetic utterance and compositional method."

Compositionally, *V mekata esen* is built on loose associations that roam in all temporal, cultural, personal, and social dimensions, and thus do not allow the dominance of a single idea, mood, plot, or point of view. This kaleidoscopic poem contains many of the major themes of Petrov's work: the antifascist resistance, the debasement of the communist ideals in a communist dictatorship, the struggle for peace and social justice all over the globe, the split of the world during the Cold War, love, death, grief for the frustrated potential of goodness, the love felt by a husband and father, the work of the artist, pride in communist Bulgaria, the achievements of the Soviet Union in such fields as space technology, and the celebration of communist ideals. Typically for Petrov, the problems are presented as an argument between two equally possible and often witty oppositions: bookish knowledge versus immediate practical reality, the recognition of the talent and wisdom of old age versus the ambition of youth, insignificant everyday happenings versus events of universal importance, emotion versus reason, appearance versus essence, the poet versus the ordinary man, mortality versus immortality, formalistic poetry versus revolutionary poetry, and ordinary facts versus cultural erudition. Throughout the poem the lyrical narrator is self-reflective, self-critical, and self-ironic, so that even when he admires or curses the things he loves or hates the most, some ambiguous aloofness always exists, resulting in a surplus of meaning beyond what is directly stated.

V mekata esen was awarded first prize in poetry from the Bulgarian Writers Union in 1961 and the highest state award in communist Bulgaria, the Dimitrov Prize, in 1962. Petrov's triumphant poetic comeback had several sources: the dogmatic period in Bulgarian literature subsided with the political repudiation of the personality cult in the late 1950s and was superseded by more tolerant, if not more sophisticated, aesthetic criteria. The ending of the poem is a sincere and clever praise of communist Bulgaria, the Soviet Union, and the ideals of communism. *V mekata esen* is a work of impressive artistic energy that voices the indispensable characteristics of the intellectual climate in the country in the late 1950s. It does not openly confront the hierarchies of the communist culture of that time. Last, but not least, the regime had learned by that time to regulate culture not only through force but through awards as well.

The next poetic collection, *Dŭzhd vali–slŭntse gree* (It Rains and the Sun Shines, 1967), and the cycles " . . . A drugade i s drugi dvama" (. . . And Somewhere Else and with Two Other People, 1958–1964), "Za kucheta i kotki" (About Dogs and Cats, 1965–1973), "Chiponoso slŭntse" (Snub-Nosed Sun, 1975–1977), "Novi stikhove" (New Poems, 1963–1989), "Detski temi za golemi" (Children's Themes for Adults), and "Vŭzrast na srokovete" (Age of the Time Limits, 1989–1992) augment the themes, poetics, and artistic view of life in Petrov's poetry.

Petrov's interest in cinema helped him to live through the difficult period of his poetic career in the late 1940s and 1950s. During this time he started writing movie scripts, and from 1955 to 1968 and from 1977 to 1980, with some interruptions, he was an editor at *Studiya zaigralni filmi* (the feature film studios) of *Bŭlgarska dŭrzhavna kinematografiya* (the Bulgarian Cinematography State Trust). Petrov became an important catalyst for the coming-of-age of Bulgarian cinema. His screenplays fall into two groups: those about the antifascist resistance and those that deal with contemporary issues. The first category is comprised by *Na malkiya ostrov* (On the Small Island, 1958), which was directed by Rangel Vŭlchanov and won a special prize at the International Film Festival in Karlovi Vari, Czechoslovakia, in 1958; *Pŭrvi urok* (First Lesson, 1960), also directed by Vŭlchanov; *Vaskata* (Vaskata, 1964), which was directed by Borislav Sharaliev and won the Golden Dove Great Award for documentary and short films at the International Festival in Leipzig, East Germany in 1964; and *Otkŭde se znaem?* (Where Do We Know Each Other From?, 1974). The second group consists of *Tochka pŭrva ot dnevniya red* (Point One on the Agenda, 1956), directed by Boyan Danovski; *Slŭntseto i syankata* (The Sun and the Shadow, 1962), directed by Vŭlchanov; *Ritsar bez bronya* (A Knight without Armor, 1966), directed by Sharaliev; *S lyubov i nezhnost* (With Love and Tenderness, 1978), again directed by Vŭlchanov; *Edin snimachen den* (One Day of Filming, 1966), directed by Sharaliev; *Burya v chasha s vino* (A Storm in a Wine Glass, 1978); *Yo-kho-kho* (Yo-ho-ho!, 1981), directed by Zako Kheskiya; *Esenno slŭntse* (Autumn Sun, 1986); *and Stepni khora* (Steppe People, 1986). In the 1950s Petrov wrote scripts for animated cartoons as well, which included *Grŭmootvod* (Lightning-Conductor) and *Prikazka za borovoto klonche* (Tale about the Pine-Tree Twig). In 1995 Petrov was awarded a prize for lifelong achievements in cinema.

Petrov's interest in drama was spurred by his connections with some of the best young theater directors in the late 1950s and the early 1960s, grouped in the theater of the city of Burgas: Yuliya Ognyanova, Vili Tsankov, Leon Daniel, and Metodi Andonov. Petrov's first drama, *Kogato rozite tantsuvat* (When the Roses Dance, 1961), is a reworking of an unsuccessful poem. The play is a blend of verse (in the fantastic framework) and prose (in the realistic love episodes). The main characters are the Young Man and the Old Man, standing for the spirit of youth and the spirit of old age. In a symbolic, even somewhat allegorical fashion, they argue whether love is possible. The three acts of the play present three incomplete love stories: in youth, in middle age, and in old age, the suggestion being that love is always possible, though not always happy. The play was staged—not without resistance, because of its fantastic character and the taboos against speaking openly about love at that time—three years after it had been written: first in the theater of the city of Khaskovo and later in the Theater of Satire in Sofia. The driving force behind the work is Petrov's belief that "there must not be any canons on the stage; on it quite different forms or mixtures of forms should be played, provided they are written or blended in a talented way." This conviction, coupled with some techniques borrowed from circus and variety entertainment which challenged the theatrical stereotypes of the time and the desire to create in Bulgaria something that was already being done abroad, put this play on the level of the best of Petrov's poetry and screenplays. It was awarded second prize for dramaturgy at the Second National Review of Bulgarian Drama and Theater (1964). In Bulgarian theater history this work is often classified as a part of the so-called poetic or lyric drama wave in the 1960s, which promoted innovations in Bŭlgarian drama, after the era of Stalinist-type dogmatism, through staging plays by poets such as Ivan Peychev, Ivan Radoev, Bozidar Bozhilov, Georgi Dzhagarov, and Petrov. Petrov's other plays are: *Snyag* (Snow, 1968); *Chestna musketarska* (Upon My Musketeer's Word, 1977), a lyric re-writing of *The Three Musketeers* in which the four musketeers, somewhat Quixotic figures, are old but continue to fight and die one by one as they are attacked by the intrigues of the royal family and the cardinal, acting in an evil alliance. Another of Petrov's plays is *Teatŭr–lyubov moya!* (Theater—My Love!, 1981).

Petrov's first important satiric work is *Improvizatsiya* (Improvisation, 1962), co-authored with Radoy Ralin. The episodically structured play is an allegory of Nikita Khrushchev's and the Bulgarian regime's "thaw." Eskimos in their igloo are invited to come out because the spring has arrived. Taken in, they leave their shelter only to be met by a storm and cold weather. They return inside. This is repeated until the Eskimos no longer believe in the invitations and remain in the igloo when spring finally comes. The work was staged in the Satirical Theater in Sofia by Grisha Ostrovski and was a great success. The play was repeatedly attacked by the establishment press, and the co-authors immediately added new scenes to strike back. The performance, "an encyclopedia of dissent," according to Atanas Slavov, was stopped in 1963.

From 1965 to 1987 Petrov wrote fourteen narrative poems that can be defined as either humorous, satiric, or parodic. Some are collected in *Na smyakh* (For Fun, 1970). In these works Petrov's mordant wit informs his poetic virtuosity: they are ingenious genre, stylistic, and discursive parodies in which the writer's susceptibility to verbal playfulness reigns. These satires do not question the social order as a whole but only some of its deficiencies that impede the full blossoming of communist principles. *Khozhdenie po bukvite* (Walking Over the Letters, 1970), in the form of a medieval morality play, criticizes bureaucratic delay by presenting the life of Saint Cyril and Saint Methodius, the brothers who invented and spread the Slavic alphabet in the ninth century. *Balada za kontraadmirala* (A Ballad about the Rear-Admiral, 1970) parodies a historical chronicle of the defeat of the Spanish Armada in 1588 in order to uncover the corruption of the state apparatus and the fear of criticism. The fourteen poems, if interpreted as parodies, expose the manipulativeness of clichêd language, its wearing out as a communicative tool, and its role as a cause of stupidity and social apathy.

The eighteen-poem cycle "Za lichno polzvane" (For Private Use, written over the years from 1955 to 1989) appeared after the fall of communism; it is quite different from Petrov's previous "soft" satire. These poems, which had been kept hidden in the writer's drawer, rank among the best, most bitter, and angriest political satire written in Bulgarian, reminding one of the noble rage of Khristo Botev and Stoyan Mikhaylovski. In them Petrov directly—and with intellectual splendor—addresses "the domestic stench" (in "Tuk i otvŭd" [Here and Over There]) of communism: the idiocy, ignorance, corruption, and cruelty of officials; the servility and avarice of intellectuals; and the lack of civic courage, dignity, and ideals. Petrov demonstrated his own bravery when he refused to sign an official letter against Alexander Solzhenitsyn by the Bulgarian Writers Union and was expelled from the Communist Party; this case is portrayed in the poem "Chayat" (The Tea).

Neveroyatnite priklyucheniya na Sin Dyado (The Unbelievable Adventures of Blue Old Man, 1992), co-authored with Khristo Ganev, an outstanding radical leftist satirist and screenwriter, is a parodic epistolary novel that employs the political discourses after the fall of communism in order to expose conformism, political intolerance, and the efforts to restore obsolete political institutions in postcommunist Bulgaria.

Petrov's first work for children is the poem *Gost-geroy* (A Hero as a Guest, 1953), but his fame in this area rests on five tales in prose and verse written in the 1970s and the 1980s, some of which exist in literary, theatrical, and script versions. *Byala prikazka* (White Tale, 1977) and *Meko kazano* (Put Rather Delicately, 1980) are works with a moral: friendship and honesty require courage and are tested through hardships. *Kopche za sŭn* (A Button for Sleep, 1978) and *V lunnata staya* (In the Moonlight Room, 1982) are stories of pure imagination. *Puk!* (Crack!, 1983; titled *Morsko sin'o* [Navy Blue] in its musical form) has more complex messages: In growing older, one may lose his initial purity; and horrifying ugliness sometimes is a shield for a tender heart. In the era of perestroika *Puk!* enjoyed enormous popularity among children and parents alike. An explanation of its popularity may be found in the identity between the meaning of the tale and the belief in the period of perestroika that communism may find its true self by going back to its sources and that the outer deformities of the system hide an inner, frustrated humanitarian potential.

Petrov ranks among the most prominent Bulgarian translators. His translations of Gianni Rodari's poems for children and Rudyard Kipling's *Just So Stories,* as well as poetry from Russian, Italian, and English, graceful as they are, were still only a harbinger of Petrov's magnum opus in this realm—the translation of all of William Shakespeare's plays and sonnets. This work was inspired—as can be inferred from the cultural situation in the 1960s and from Petrov's poems "Nad prevodite" (Over the Translations), "Viy, otsŭzhdashti . . ." (You, Who Judge . . .), and "Nashe vreme" (Our Time)—by his striving for genuine accomplishment in an age of creative pettiness that was more concerned with how to serve the political elite than how to serve art. The labor on this project took some twenty years, and its scholarly quality was attested by Petrov's editor, Professor Marko Minkov, an internationally renowned Shakespearean scholar. The translations, comprising seven volumes that were published from 1970 to 1981 (not including the sonnets), won the Great Award of the Union of Bulgarian Translators and of the Press Committee (1975). Not enough critical work has been done on these translations, but some critics believe that Petrov renders Shakespeare's comedies better than the tragedies, historical plays, or romances. A comparison of Petrov's *Hamlet* with the classical translation of the play by Geo Milev, in 1917, at the zenith of Bulgarian symbolism, and with the original play shows that the Shakespearean imagery is more substantial than the ethereal imagery of the symbolist *Hamlet* of Milev but less substantial than Petrov's imagery, which is replete with concrete details.

Petrov has been and continues to be a member of many Socialist Party and professional institutions. He has received many awards and decorations for his contribution to literature, theater, film, and culture in general, among which are the title of Honored Cultural Worker in 1965 and the title of People's Artistic and Cultural Worker in 1977. These were the two highest artistic titles in communist Bulgaria. From 1990 to 1991 Petrov was a deputy to the Seventh Great National Assembly, chosen by the Bulgarian Socialist Party.

Petrov's artistic principles crystallized in his works of the 1940s and matured in his diverse accomplishments in the following decades. Petrov's work has enriched Bulgarian culture by its quest for tolerance and its intellectual sophistication, creative audacity, cheerfulness, independence from ideological dictatorship, and inner freedom that is not intimidated by questions that cannot be unambiguously answered.

Interviews:

Bŭlgarski pisateli za sebe si i za svoeto tvorchestvo, volumes 1 and 2 (Sofia: Bŭlgarski pisatel, 1970), pp. 128–130, 496–498; 236–246;

Chavdar Dobrev, *Lirichna drama* (Sofia: Nauka i izkustvo, 1973), pp. 375–376;

Atanas Svilenov, "Valeri Petrov," *Aprilski krŭgozori* (Sofia: Bŭlgarski pisatel, 1981), pp. 231–235.

References:

Svoboda Bŭchvarova, "Istini, kazani eksprompt . . . ," *Septemvri,* 1 (1963): 249–252;

Irma Dimitrova, *Ot homo ludens do govoreshtiya avtomat. Valeri Petrov i poetite ot 40-te godini* (Sofia: Universitetsko izdatelstvo "Sv. Kliment Okhridski," 1994);

Chavdar Dobrev, *Lirichna drama* (Sofia: Nauka i izkustvo, 1973), pp. 253–274;

Stoyan Karolev, "Na protivorechivi pozitsii," *Septemvri,* 1 (1949): 137–148;

Rozaliya Likova, *Valeri Petrov* (Sofia: Prosveta, 1994);

Rumyana Mileva, "Kharakterni cherti na dramaturgiyata na Valeri Petrov," *Literaturna misŭl,* 6 (1987): 45–53;

Nikita Nankov, "'Hamlet' i 'Khamlet': opit za stereo-chetene," *Literaturna misŭl,* 4 (1993): 148–165;

Isak Pasi, "Esteticheskiyat rakurs na khudozhnika," *Ezik i literatura,* 3 (1962): 87–90;

Petŭr Pondev, "Ot samotselnite lutaniya na individualizma kŭm realizŭm i zhizneutvŭrzhdavashta poeziya," *Izkustvo,* 8–9 (1949): 172–196;

Atanas Slavov, *The "Thaw" in Bulgarian Literature* (Boulder, Colo.: East European Monographs, 1981), pp. 92–98 and in passim;

Lyubomir Tenev, "Poeziya i dramaturgiya," *Plamŭk,* 12 (1961): 69–75;

Dimitŭr Tsolov, "Razmishleniya vŭrkhu kinodramaturgiyata na Valeri Petrov," *Literaturna misŭl,* 3 (1981): 61–78.

Vasko Popa
(29 June 1922 - 5 January 1991)

Anita Lekić
State University of New York, Stony Brook

BOOKS: *Kora* (Belgrade: Novo pokolenje, 1953);
Nepočin-polje (Novi Sad: Matica srpska, 1956);
Pesme (Belgrade: Srpska književna zadruga, 1965);
Sporedno nebo (Belgrade: Prosveta, 1968);
Pesme (Belgrade: Prosveta, 1968);
Pesme (Novi Sad: Srpska književna zadruga, 1971);
Uspravna zemlja (Belgrade: Vuk Karadžić, 1972);
Poezija (Sarajevo: Veselin Masleša, 1973);
Vučja so (Belgrade: Vuk Karadžić, 1975);
Živo meso (Belgrade: Vuk Karadžić, 1975);
Kuća nasred druma (Belgrade: Vuk Karadžić, 1975);
Pesme (Belgrade: BIGZ, 1978);
Rez (Novi Sad: Vojvodjanska Akademija nauka i umetnosti, 1982);
Pesme (Belgrade: Nolit, 1988).

Collection: *Dela,* 8 volumes (Belgrade: Nolit, 1980-1981).

Editions in English: *Selected Poems,* translated by Anne Pennington, introduction by Ted Hughes (Harmondsworth: Penguin, 1969);
The Little Box, translated, with an introduction by Charles Simic (Washington, D.C.: The Charioteer Press, 1970);
Earth Erect, translated by Pennington (London: Anvil Press, 1973; Iowa City: University of Iowa International Writing Program, 1973);
Collected Poems 1943-1976, translated by Pennington, with an introduction by Hughes (Manchester: Carcanet, 1978; New York: Persea Books, 1979);
The Blackbirds' Field: A Poem by Vasko Popa, translated by Pennington (Oxford: Mid-Day Publications, 1979);
Homage to the Lame Wolf: Selected Poems 1956-1975, translated, with an introduction by Simic (Oberlin: The Field Translation Series, 1979; revised, 1987);
"The Cut," translated by Pennington and Francis R. Jones, *Poetry World,* 1 (1986): 8-32.

OTHER: *Domentijan,* edited by Popa (Belgrade: Nolit, 1963);

Vasko Popa

Od zlata jabuka, edited by Popa (Belgrade: Prosveta, 1966, 1979); translated by Pennington and Andrew Harvey as *The Golden Apple* (London: Anvil Press, 1980);
Ponoćno sunce. Zbornik pesničkih snovidjenja, edited by Popa (Belgrade: Nolit, 1979);
Urnebesnik. Zbornik pesničkog humora, edited by Popa (Belgrade: Nolit, 1979).

PERIODICAL PUBLICATION: "Mala kutija," *Savremenik,* 30, no. 11-12 (1984): 7-18.

Vasko Popa is a poet of towering stature in contemporary Yugoslav literature. His poetic achievement—eight slim volumes of verse written over a period of thirty-eight years—has received extensive critical acclaim both in his native land and beyond, in Europe and the United States, where his works, which have been widely translated, have reached a remarkably diverse audience. His eight collections have been translated into English in their entirety, in different editions, by Anne Pennington in Great Britain and distinguished poet Charles Simic in the United States. Additionally, his collections have given rise to an extensive critical apparatus, including several books devoted exclusively to his poetry.

Popa, who often spent years working on a single book, was not a prolific poet; yet with each of his eight collections he channeled the development of contemporary poetry in Yugoslavia in new directions. His first book, *Kora* (Bark), was the cause of considerable turmoil in Yugoslav literary circles when it appeared in 1953. In an age dominated by socialist realism, it was a radically innovative work that boldly broke with established norms and conventions. Although its significance is somewhat obscured by the intrinsic values of Popa's later works, *Kora* merits an important place in literary history as a work that marked the advent of postwar modernism in Yugoslavia. All Popa's later collections met with a favorable if sometimes subdued critical response. With each new work, he surprised and at times perplexed critics and readers alike. Each collection lays out the terms of a new universe with ground rules to be mastered anew. This resistance to established practices is characteristic of Popa; he assiduously avoids the conventionalization of his own work.

Popa was born to a family of mixed Serbian and Romanian extraction on 29 June 1922 in Grebenac, a small Serbian village near the Yugoslav-Romanian border. The poet, who considered himself a Serb, lived in Belgrade most of his life and wrote his poetry exclusively in Serbo-Croatian. He attended elementary and secondary school in Vršac, a town in Vojvodina located some thirty kilometers from his place of birth. In 1940 he moved to Belgrade to study Romance languages and literatures. Because of the outbreak of World War II, he was forced to continue his education in Bucharest and Vienna. After the war he resumed his studies at the University of Belgrade, from which he was graduated in 1949 with a degree in French.

In secondary school Popa had held leftist views. His political affiliations led to his being interned for several months during the war in a German concentration camp in Bečkerek. In 1944 Popa joined the Communist Party. From 1948 to 1951 he worked as a journalist for Radio Belgrade and the journal *Književne novine* (Literary Gazette), and from 1951 to 1953 he served as secretary general of the Society for Yugoslav-French Cultural Cooperation. In 1954 he joined the prestigious Belgrade publishing house Nolit and remained as an editor for twenty-five years. During his career as a poet Popa was awarded many domestic literary awards. In 1968 he was the recipient of the Austrian State Award for European Literature. He was also a member in full standing of the Vojvodina Academy of Arts and Sciences and a corresponding member of both the Serbian Academy of Arts and Sciences and the Mallarmé Academy in Paris. Popa died in Belgrade on 5 January 1991.

His poems were first published in 1951 in the journals *Književne novine* and *Borba* (Struggle).

VASKO POPA

Collected Poems
1943-1976

translated by ANNE PENNINGTON

with an introduction by TED HUGHES

Carcanet/Manchester

Title page for a 1978 translation of Popa's free-verse poems, marking the advent of postwar modernism in Yugoslav poetry

His first collection, *Kora,* appeared in 1953. He subsequently published seven additional volumes of poetry: *Nepočin-polje* (Unrest-Field) in 1956; *Sporedno nebo* (Secondary Heaven) in 1968; *Uspravna zemlja* (Earth Erect) in 1972; *Vučja so* (Wolf Salt), *Živo meso* (Raw Flesh), and *Kuća nasred druma* (The House on the High Road) in 1975; and *Rez* (The Cut) in 1982. Many selections from his poetry have been published over the years. In 1980 Nolit printed Popa's first seven volumes of verse under the title *Dela* (Collected Works); the eighth volume, *Rez,* was published as part of the poet's collected works in 1981. Prior to his death Popa was working on his ninth collection, *Gvozdeni sad* (The Iron Garden), which remains unpublished. The eleven poems of *Mala kutija* (The Little Box), which were to constitute one of the cycles in this collection, were published in definitive form in 1984 in the journal *Savremenik* (Contemporary).

Popa's work is characterized by a continual breaking away from traditional forms of expression. He dispenses with accepted conventions and introduces subject matter previously ignored or judged unworthy of a literary work. In his singular mode of apprehending reality, he appears to disavow the existence of precursors. Nevertheless, interpreters of Popa's work have dwelled on his assimilation of various elements from the literary tradition. His debts to Surrealism and national folklore have been written on at length. The poet, however, projects a unique vision of the world even when he relies on earlier poetic developments. The familiar is always relentlessly defamiliarized in Popa's poetry.

Popa's poems never convey a sense of improvisation; as opposed to automatic writing, his poems strike the reader and critic as having been meticulously conceived and methodically executed. Popa started writing about two decades after the Surrealist movement, imported from France, flourished in Belgrade. This temporal distance allowed him to assume a critical stance toward the Surrealist legacy. He rejected the exuberance and impassioned revolt of Surrealism, while retaining throughout his work a predilection for the unusual juxtaposition of images. Like the Surrealists, Popa distanced himself from the traditional conventions of rhyme. All of his poems are written in free verse, and some of his earliest work included prose poetry. In the revised editions of his collections, however, Popa dispensed with prose poems. The prose texts were rearranged into lines of verse with certain phrases transposed and others excised altogether. The changes, which constitute an improvement, are noteworthy in that they represent tangible evidence of Popa's desire for concision, as well as his wish to retain the visual impact of poetry without its traditional or conventional adornments.

Because his poems are written in what he himself referred to as strictly free verse, Popa frequently resorts to repetition (of words, phrases, and lines, in their entirety or with slight variations) for thematic emphasis and as a formal device approximating the function of rhyme. A close reading of the poet's work shows that repetition of specific words and phrases, as well as images, is a constant with which the reader must continually reckon. Through repetition Popa ensures symmetry and binds the segments of his poems into tightly knit wholes. His poems abound in parallel although not quite identical syntactic constructions. The unfettered nature of free verse is offset by the following constraints Popa imposes upon his poems: syntactic repetition; elliptical modes of expression presented in stanzaic form; and cyclical organization, which establishes recognizable formal patterns and lends a certain narrative dimension to his poems. The poet eschews meditative, rambling modes of expression; in his work the palpable and tangible are always in the forefront. Popa's is a poetry continually concerned with the corporeality of word and image.

His collections are extremely cohesive in structure. The poet assembles his poems with a precise scheme in mind. He generally writes them in cycles and arranges the cycles linked by common themes into a book. Poems function as units within larger structures that, in turn, ensure the progression of the discourse of the work as a whole. In this manner Popa draws attention to the syntagmatic aspects of his work. His collections unfold. Although his poems are as a rule very short, it is the cycles that become the vehicles of narration.

One of the constants of Popa's work is the depersonalized nature of his poetry. The poet takes pains to absent himself from his own work. He does not dwell on the turmoils of the self. This rigorous objectification of his poetry may have been triggered early by a distaste for the confessional mode of poetry prevalent in the immediate postwar years. Following selected early poems in *Kora,* Popa abandons the sphere of intimate experiences and subjective emotions as subject matter inappropriate to his poetry. The subjective world is, instead, projected onto objects.

He animates the inanimate. The whole external world comes alive in his work. Human figures in general are conspicuously absent from the early volumes. The works that follow are often permeated by anonymous voices and choric presences.

Only in Popa's last collections does the first person pronoun reappear. But even as the poet reenters his work, he assumes a marginal position in his poems, which, in most instances, focus on figures other than himself. Positioning himself on the sidelines of his work, Popa discerns the immanence and poetic qualities of myth in the gestures, actions, and reflections of his contemporaries. The subjective consciousness is too restricted a subject for Popa, who is interested rather in the modalities of human existence. His poetry dwells on humanity's continual confrontation with annihilation. In his work there are essentially only two forces, man and death, locked in eternal combat. From his first book to his last, Popa circles around the void and gives it voice.

Popa reveals the essential aspects of the antagonistic relationship between the individual and the void. The confrontation is all-important and everything else incidental. Perhaps this is why his poetic landscapes are so stark and barren. Popa contemplates the world around him with the unjaded vision of a child. He looks at the world, in his own words, as "innocently as the first to set eyes on it and ruthlessly as the very last person to ever set eyes on it" (*Kora,* 1969). His utter absorption with the ways in which the individual resists the threat of nothingness is also reflected in the ascetic quality of his language, which dispenses with inessentials. Language is pared down to the level of formulae. The full severity of the struggle in which life is pitted against death is rendered in diction characterized by the most austere simplicity.

At the same time that Popa's poetry points to existential concerns, it endeavors to surmount and in effect deny the constraints ruling the individual's presence in time. The rudiments of this attempt may tentatively be traced to the poet's third collection, *Sporedno nebo* (1968). Acutely conscious of human finitude, Popa ponders the ways in which the individual may ultimately resist the flow of history. In his finest work, *Uspravna zemlja* (1972), devoted in its entirety to the most dramatic moments of national history, the vicissitudes of history are perceived as the manifestations of a vast cosmic design. In *Vučja so* (1975) historical time is entirely supplanted by mythic time.

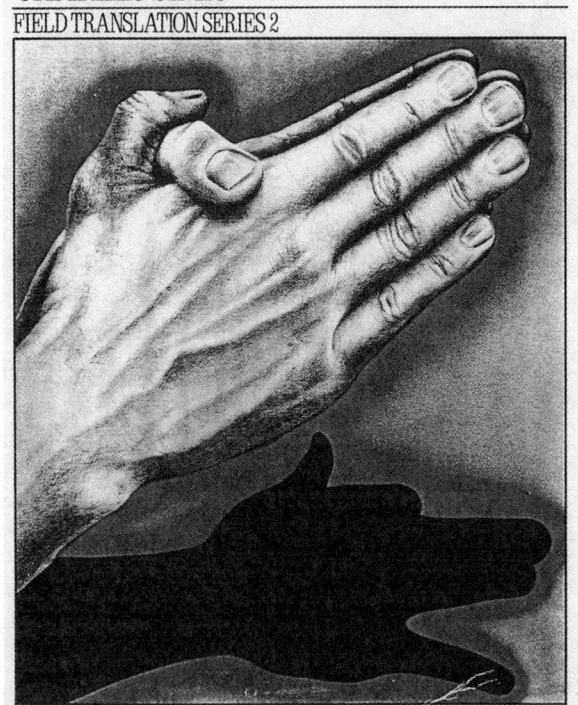

Cover for a translation of Vučja So, *Popa's 1975 collection of poems*

The circle, in Popa's early work a symbol of the oppressive presence of nonbeing, becomes in the later work a symbol of recurrence through which humanity conquers death. Time, invested with cyclicity, is held in abeyance. The thematic emphasis on eternal repetition is further reinforced by the cyclical organization of Popa's work, in which the opening and closing poems of individual cycles, as well as of entire books, link with and flow into each other. The conception of time as eternal recurrence in *Uspravna zemlja* and *Vučja so,* as well as the emphasis in both on transcendent models that humanity continually attempts to approximate in its conduct, are to a large extent analogous to the archaic experience of history as discussed by Mircea Eliade in *The Myth of the Eternal Return* and other works. Popa was well acquainted with Eliade's thought.

In his major works Popa turns to his nation's myths for inspiration. In *Uspravna zemlja* and *Vučja so* he resurrects the supreme gods of

Serbian paganism and employs them as archmodels to narrate and interpret the continuum of human existence through the vicissitudes of history. Concrete historical figures are also endowed with demiurgical powers and archetypal dimensions. In more recent works such as *Živo meso*, *Kuća nasred druma*, and *Rez*, the presence of the same primeval forces can be discerned in the secular world. For Popa, a reality more enduring than that of quotidian existence leaves its indelible inscription on the present.

The image of a celestial script recurs with striking frequency in Popa's work. Language possesses its own archetype, its own divine model. Popa's poems dwell on the strength and immediacy of the primeval "wolf howl" and ponder the enervation of a language that no longer signifies the presence but the absence of things. His work is exceptionally self-reflective. As it calls forth its own extraordinary worlds into being, his poetry meditates on the potentials and failures of the very medium of which it is born. This disaffection with the mediatory qualities of language is reflected in the brevity of Popa's poetry. Meaning is concentrated in as few words as possible; symbols and images assume the burden of words; the words that are accorded entry into his poems carry a tremendous charge. Bridging the gaps of silence surrounding them, they break free of the automatism that held them captive, assuming a dense, polysemous character.

Popa's eight collections represent eight stages of an artistic journey characterized by powerful creative ingenuity and innovative energy. The journey itself continually weaves its way around fundamental questions of human existence. At once simple and complex, transparent and opaque, the poet's work bears witness to the most profound realities. Popa meditates on the ways in which the individual creates himself in time and history. To existential dread and a tragic perception of existence he juxtaposes a vision of the limitless potentials of human freedom. His poetry celebrates human action and engagement as the means by which humanity asserts its freedom, denies the terrors of existence, and forges the course of its own destiny. Popa's subjects declare their insubordination to the imperatives of a hostile and irrational universe and revel in the liberty that such defiance offers. In Popa's work there is never despair, only rebellion and an extraordinary sense of human indomitability.

Conscious of humanity's estrangement from the world that lies beyond it, Popa bridges in his poetry the gap existing between the subjective consciousness and the external world. With compelling power his work penetrates to the otherness of the nonhuman world. The experience of that world is at once modern and archaic. Popa imbues the inanimate with a life of its own at the same time that he invests it with symbolic functions. Observed in its immanence, the objective world continually opens onto a transcendent dimension.

From one collection to another there is the evolution of an increasingly complex symbolic system. Popa draws on national tradition, history, myth, and alchemy, as well as on the vast repository of world culture for his material. He develops his own personal symbols but also exploits conventional symbols that he endows with new ranges of reference. He employs them for his own purposes and his own vision of the world while allowing them to retain their preexisting associations. At once familiar and strange, accessible and abstruse, his symbols are charged with immense power of resonance. Themselves the product of irreconcilable contradictions, they communicate a vision of the infinite tensions and ambiguities inherent in human existence.

Popa's poetry represents a reconciliation of antagonistic impulses, a synthesis of two opposing forces. Fond of paradox and the drama of antithesis, Popa creates poetry permeated by two distinct worldviews. On the one hand, it reflects the modern consciousness, with its alienated and fragmented experience of the world and, on the other, in its later stages, an archaic sense of the spiritual fullness of being. Pervading the poet's major works is a primitivist immersion in the totality of being, in which all things are measured in cosmic terms. Popa overcomes his preoccupation with death, evinced in the early works, by turning to the mythic past, to the preconscious creative impulse of humanity, where he finds firm anchorage.

The ambivalence of the Popian corpus and its duality are evident in the very areas of human experience to which the poet turns for inspiration, namely, history and myth. They testify to Popa's continuing absorption with the role of the individual human being in time as well as with the transcendent dimensions of human existence. His poetry resolves the antitheses of destruction and creation, finitude and duration, death and life. In his work the temporal and the transcendent coexist in fragile harmony, eternally opposing and complementing each other. A composite of the archaic and the modern vision of man and history, Popa's poetry sings of the unquellable energies of human existence and represents a testament to humanity's continual victory over time and death.

Bibliography:

Gojko Tešić, "Bibliografija Vaska Pope," *Ulaznica*, 44-45, no. 9 (1975): 114-121, 123-132.

References:

Ronelle Alexander, *The Structure of Vasko Popa's Poetry* (Columbus, Ohio: Slavica, 1985);

Alain Bosquet, "Vasko Popa ou lexorcisme populaire," in *Verbe et vertige, situations de la poésie* (Paris: Hachette, 1961), pp. 193-200;

Ivan V. Lalić, "Poezija Vaska Pope," *Književnost*, 50 (1970): 318-332;

Anita Lekić, *The Quest for Roots: The Poetry of Vasko Popa* (New York: Peter Lang, 1993);

Slavko Leovac, "Poezija Vaska Pope," in his *Metamorfoze* (Sarajevo: Svjetlost, 1965), pp. 56-73;

Vasa D. Mihailovich, "Vasko Popa," in *Critical Survey of Poetry: Foreign Language Series*, volume 3 (New York: Salem Press, 1984), pp. 1268-1274;

Zoran Mišić, "Poezija Vaska Pope," *Književnost*, 8 (1953): 546-557;

Karlo Ostojić, *Izmedju stvari i ništavila* (Belgrade: Prosveta, 1962);

Miodrag Pavlović, "Od kamena do sveta," in *Nepočin-polje*, by Vasko Popa (Belgrade: Prosveta, 1963), pp. 7-28;

Novica Petković, "Uvod u čitanje poezije Vaska Pope," in *Poezija*, by Vasko Popa (Sarajevo: Veselin Masleša, 1973), pp. 5-19;

Aleksandar Petrov, "Pesnički svet *Kore*," in *Kora*, by Vasko Popa (Belgrade: Nolit, 1969), pp. 7-46;

Petrov, "*Sporedno nebo* Vaska Pope," *Književna istorija*, 1 (1968): 887-923;

John Pilling, "Vasko Popa," *A Reader's Guide to Fifty Modern European Poets* (London: Heinemann, 1982), pp. 392-399;

Bogdan A. Popović, "Put ka univerzalnom," in *Pesme*, by Vasko Popa (Belgrade: Prosveta, 1968), pp. 5-24;

Nikolaj Timčenko, *Zapisi o pesniku: O poeziji Vaska Pope* (Kruševac: Bagdala, 1972);

Djordjije Vuković, "Ars Combinatoria," *Savremenik*, 10 (1975): 255-265.

Aleksandar Popović
(22 November 1929 – 9 October 1996)

E. J. Czerwinski
State University of New York, Stony Brook

BOOKS: *Sudbina jednog Čarlija* (Belgrade: Prosveta, 1964);
Čarapa od sto petlji, Drame (Belgrade: Prosveta, 1967);
Razvojni put Bore Šnajdera (Belgrade: Prosveta, 1967);
Mreščenje šarana i druge drame (Belgrade: Beogradski izdavačko-grafički zavod, 1986);
Bela kafa i druge drame (Belgrade: Srpska kniževna zadruga, 1992).
Editions in English: *Second Door Left*, translated by E. J. Czerwinski, *Drama and Theater*, 8 (Winter 1970): 101–118;
Kiss, Kiss translated by Czerwinski, *Slavic and East European Arts*, 2, no. 1 (Fall 1983): 6–27.

PLAY PRODUCTIONS: *Lyubinko i Desanka*, Belgrade, 1964;
Sablja Dimiskija, Belgrade, 1966;
Čarapa od sto petlji, Belgrade, 1967;
Razvojni put Bora Šnajdera, Belgrade, 1967;
Kape dole, Belgrade, Atelier 212, 1968;
Utva ptica zlatokrila, Belgrade, 1969;
Mreščenje šarana, Belgrade, 1986;
Bela kafa, Belgrade, 1992;
Ljubi, ljubi, Port Jefferson, New York, Slavic Cultural Center, 1978;
Ružičnjak, Belgrade, 1995;
Čarlama, zbogom, Belgrade, Atelier 212, May 1995;
Mrtva tačka, Belgrade, Zvezdara-teatar, 1995;
Tamna je noć, New York, La Mama Experimental Theater, 1995.

In 1970, in an interview at La Mama Theater in New York City, where his play *Druga vrata levo* (translated as *Second Door Left*, 1970) was having its American premiere, Aleksandar Popović almost mechanically enumerated the targets of his rage: "Bureaucracy, ignorance, greed, sham, and enemies of freedom." As if weighing the formidable opposition, he quietly declared: "I plan to battle all my life" (*Drama and Theater*,

Aleksandar Popović

VIII, no. 2, 1969–1970). A quarter century later Popović continued his combat with elusive adversaries. Until his death in 1996 he was Belgrade's Poet of the Streets and a constant warrior, confronting *vrazi* (devils) within Serbian society. He is also indisputably the best playwright that Serbia has produced during the past fifty years.

His genius lies neither in constructing unusual situations nor in creating outstanding characterizations that leap like Falstaff from the stage and take their place among the gallery of immortal literary personae. Rather, Popović's gift lies in writing superb dialogue supported often by a mere wisp of a plot. Only rarely, as in his children's plays and war dramas, such as *Jelena Ćetković*, does he allow plot and sequential action to stand in his way of shaping a typically Popovićean fairy-tale world.

His enormous talent has certain liabilities. For one, it is almost impossible to re-create his language in another tongue. For another, his subject matter, especially in his early plays, is often quite specific: One must be a Serb (perhaps even a resident of Belgrade—and a knowledgeable one at that), not simply a former Yugoslav (whether Croat, Slovene, or Macedonian) fully to appreciate Popović's work. But, perhaps even more important, one must be ready for the unexpected, to accept a play that is not quite a play, and to forgive a playwright his flights of fancy, destined at times to destroy illusion itself. His theater ("the New Theater," as he simply calls it) is not for those who expect profound messages or the traditional development of themes. It is for those who want to laugh, who are determined to laugh simply because laughter is good, and who find the present far more challenging and exciting than the past. It is for those who insist that they be spoken to on their own level and not be bored in the process.

Popović was born on 22 November 1929 in Belgrade, where he has spent his entire life as a freelance writer. Recognition came slowly and unexpectedly. In 1966, after having written a dozen plays that were produced in various theaters in Belgrade, Popović was surprised to find that neither he nor his plays were mentioned in the prestigious *Srpska drama* (Serbian Drama). Two years later, in 1968, he was acclaimed Yugoslavia's greatest playwright, and his play *Razvojni put Bore Šnajdera* (The Evolutionary Road of Bora the Tailor), was one of three invited to appear in New York's Lincoln Center. Mira Trailović, director and founder of Atelier 212, was instrumental in furthering Popović's career and chose his play for the American tour. It was the beginning of Popović's relentless effort to break the Serbian barrier and be accepted in the United States.

His desire for fame, combined with an innate obstinacy, became evident early in life. After World War II, at the age of eighteen, he worked at various jobs, first as a dockhand, then as a laborer building roads. His formal education did not extend beyond high school; he then educated himself through reading and observation. Throughout the lean years he found solace and a staunch supporter in his wife, Danica, the mother of his four daughters. It was she who convinced him to try his hand at writing in 1949, perhaps the most difficult period in his life. He became completely absorbed in his literary work. During that year he edited the first private paper (or broadside) in Yugoslavia, called *Zapisi* (Notes). After a half-dozen issues he stopped publishing.

A year later, in 1950, he brought out a controversial paper, *Crveno jeste* (The Red Truth), which provoked the authorities and resulted in his imprisonment, sporadically and with increasing severity from 1950 to 1955. After his final release from prison, he returned to manual labor, this time as a wall painter: "I was afraid I would end up like Hitler," Popović later joked. It was during this period, the most traumatic of his career, that he managed to get a job writing for radio, primarily programs for children. He used his own children as fictive personae.

In 1964, after eight years of writing hundreds of radio scripts, Popović wrote his first stage play, *Ljubinco i Desanka,* (Ljubinko and Desanka, 1964), which was read by chance by an actor friend, Mića Tomić. The latter was so impressed by the originality of the script that he persuaded fellow actors to produce it privately. Mira Trailović, director of the newly founded Atelier 212, offered her theater to the group. It marked the beginning of Popović's successful collaboration with the staff and actors of that theater.

He was not, however, an overnight success. Several critics dismissed him as a charlatan. Popović began to battle his detractors. The adverse criticism came from writers, directors, and critics who refused to understand what Popović was attempting to do. They were not attuned to his type of theater; but audiences were, and one play followed another, until in 1966 four plays were running in repertory at four different theaters in Belgrade.

Popović seemed to enjoy explaining his view of theater and insisted that he could describe his theater in one word—*freedom*. As he said in an interview in 1970:

> I am concerned with freedom, not only in the political-social sense of the word, but in the artistic sense as well. I don't want form to bind me, to hamper me. I want form to free me, to let me expand and let my audience expand with me.

Popović's theater is hard to define. Its nearest predecessors are burlesque and vaudeville, complete with low comedy, "dumb broads," and vulgarity, but with an artistic awareness and sophistication alien to that genre. Popović often crosses the line separating good taste from bad. His audiences not only accept but expect this; indeed, as pointed out by Serbian critics (Jovan Hristić among them), Serbs generally enjoy ribaldry. Curses flow spontaneously from the lips of even the prettiest and most innocent of heroines. But it is not pointless vulgarity. Where burlesque and vaudeville were designed solely for entertainment, Popović's theater is predicated on the idea that one learns better when one laughs. In most of his works he assails various venerated institutions and holds up his own broken mirror to Serbian nature. Nothing escapes his mockery: bureaucracy, the lack of understanding among people, the monotony of daily routine, the mechanization of life, daydreaming, capitalism, communism, and mindless sex. Before the breakup of Yugoslavia, he angrily denied charges of nationalism and regionalism that certain critics leveled at him. His response to these critics allowed him in his 1970 interview to express his position in world literature: "Every good writer is nationalistic and must write about what he knows best, what he loves, what he believes in. Of course I'm regional—Serbian—Yugoslav—just as much as Shakespeare was London—England—the world."

Time did not diminish Popović's impatience with his critics. He insisted that he was not simply a topical writer capitalizing on current events. Rather, he wrote about people's fundamental concerns. In great measure, Popović describes his plays quite accurately. He manages to capture moments from life, and like life, his plays sometimes trail off abruptly without apparent logic; sometimes they explode with revealing truths; and sometimes they seem to be out of sync with what has gone before. There is no real beginning, middle, or end; plot development, especially in his early plays, is nonexistent. Miodrag Pavlović, Serbia's eminent poet and critic, jokingly accused Popović of planting microphones and recorders in every home, coffeehouse, and powder room in Belgrade; in truth, the dialogue in his plays often pours forth without pattern, without any apparent reason, but with the rhyme and beat that only a people's poet, an artist like the ancient *guslar,* could capture—the vibrant tongue of a nation.

Spontaneous and free though it seems, his work is built on an intricate form. By his own admission, he was not always certain of what he wanted to create in his plays. It was only after completing his fourth play, *Čarapa od sto petlji* (A Stocking of a Hundred Loops), in 1967 that he found his métier: he called his future works "The New Theater." *Čarapa od sto petlji* and the plays that followed had certain elements in common: the presence of a plot (in most cases, quite unsubstantial) and a subtly constructed dramatic form that is almost seamless. Popović's growth as an artist can be elucidated by analyzing his three early plays: *Ljubinko i Desanka, Sablja Dimiskija* (The Damascus Sword, 1966), and *Razvojni put Bore Snajdera* (1967).

His first play, *Ljubinko and Desanka,* could very well have been performed on radio. It shows clear signs of Popović's strong ties to the spoken word. There is little action and scarcely any plot. Desanka and Ljubinko meet in the park and strike up a conversation. During the course of the action they find that they seem to know the same people and share similar experiences, yet they do not fall in love and live happily ever after. In a foreword to the play Popović explains the outcome: "Fate touches all. All are unhappy, those who have reached their goals and those who have not. Basically all people are the same—but that does not mean that they must fall in love." In the end Desanka leaves Ljubinko alone with another character, Spijalter, and exits with a guitar-playing character named August. The work is not so much a play as an exercise in scene writing.

There is no plot, in the conventional sense, and action is more cerebral ("my plays deal with relationships") than graphic or visual. The roots of Popović's theater are already here, and its antecedent—radio—is apparent. In fact Popović owes much more to his apprenticeship as a radio writer than he or his critics have discerned. His theater is for the ear and mind above all. All his characters speak wittily—poetically, as if they were the children of the same parents; they seem as ingenuous as Adam and Eve before the Fall. His characters are plunged in medias res, and the dialogue takes the place of overt action.

In *Sablja Dimiskija* Popović is still searching for a form to suit his artistic expression. The setting is more definite: a coffeehouse called The Damascus Sword, which at one time actually existed in Belgrade. But some of his later innovations are already present: his signature final line directed more or less at the audience ("Now we are shifting to the left!"); his helpless, pathetic characters ("because they're only human"); and his reliance on songs and music to hold the audience's interest ("a writer can't depend on wit alone"). It is a play that most critics found "too Serbian." Their criticism is well founded. The four girls (the Slavic equivalent of a chorus line) intermittently sing a bawdy ditty about "A Serbian Lass." The main characters—Rada, Rodja, and Inkiostro—resemble Eugene O'Neill's forlorn men in *The Iceman Cometh* (1946), except that they do not indulge in soul-searching soliloquies.

Popović never allows his characters to forget that they must, above all, entertain—each other and the audience.

Razvojni put Bore Snajdera is also plotless and lacks action. It is Popović's first "serious play," as he referred to it. In examining the values of his characters, he allows them to undergo something of a transformation. Having placed emphasis on the wrong things—sex and a higher standard of living—the characters effect a quantitative but not a qualitative change. At the end they have better clothes and more money but fail to make any significant moral changes. It is, as Popović points out, a change for the worse.

In *Čarapa od sto petlji* Popović reached a point in his artistic development where his philosophic and moral message found an ideal vehicle. Subtitled "A Farce in Memoriam," the play is rich in ritual and it was meant as a story of an underground man. But the play also deals with the issues of objective reality versus subjective reality and alienation versus solidarity—for Popović, the real human dilemmas. Velja-Agnes, a male character and a typical Popovićean hero, has both a masculine (Velja) and feminine (Agnes) name (the latter in memory of his dead mother). In the course of the five Memoriams, or entr'actes, the relations among the characters (Dragoljub, Flora, and Velja-Agnes) are developed. Although the play resembles a war of the sexes, it ultimately becomes an exploration of matters of the heart. Velja-Agnes's ritualistic death in Memoriam V, although comic on one level, is reminiscent of the death of an idealist like Don Quixote; it is a gentle chiding of those who ridicule and ultimately destroy the dreamer.

After *Čarapa od sto petlji* Popović continued to experiment, but he seemed to have found the ideal vehicle for his talent. By the time *Second Door Left* premiered at the La Mama Off-Broadway theater, he announced that he had found his way. Considered by most critics as one of the best plays written during what is considered his middle period, the play marked a turning point in Popović's search for his "New Theater." Earlier in his career and prior to *Second Door Left*, Popović relied heavily on sound value (not simply word value). His apprenticeship as a radio writer, especially of children's programs, left traces in all of his subsequent work. Because sounds (not necessarily "meaningful" ones) make up an important part of a child's domain, Popović, the father of four girls, relied a great deal on "sound images" in his plays. In writing for children, Popović felt, there was no need to bridge understanding and meaning with wordy transitions. As a result, Popović dispenses with tidy transitions in his plays. Scenes follow one another as in real life without rhyme or reason. Instead of transitions, Popović relies on metaphors, made up of "sound images," concrete detail, and sensual (more specifically, sexual) nuances. Nowhere is this more evident than in *Ljubi, ljubi* (translated as *Kiss, Kiss*), which premiered at the Slavic Cultural Center in Port Jefferson, New York in 1978. The play is ranked by most critics as the most ambitious and successful of Popović's middle period.

In his early plays, especially *Ljubinko and Desanka*, *Sablja Dimiskija*, and *Krmeći kas* (Piggy Trot, 1966), some critics accused Popović of writing "antiplays," works without plot and without apparent themes. These plays are certainly models of ambiguity. They almost defy plot summary because nothing really happens—that is, in the traditional sense of the unfolding of events. Instead Popović develops metaphors that usually run a page or two of dialogue. These metaphors form the action of the play. At the conclusion of a metaphor scene (similar to the traditional French scene, so far as structure is concerned), the characters participating in the dialogue usually exit (sometimes for no apparent reason) and other characters (or the same ones) enter and begin another metaphor scene. Seldom in these early works is there a group scene: even when several characters remain onstage (as, for example, in *Razvojni put Bore Šnajdera*, *Utva ptica zlatokrila* [The Gold-Winged Duck, 1969], or *Kape dole* [Hats Off, 1968]), there is no group conflict. Each character delivers his dialogue as if speaking to someone in the audience. Rarely do characters react to each other's dialogue. Popović prefers audience involvement, and his plays are an attempt to engage his audience.

Popović's dramatic technique is his greatest liability. His metaphors depend almost completely on sound, wordplay, and poetic nuances, the elements most difficult to capture and reproduce in another language. He is difficult for Serbian audiences; he is almost impossible for foreign audiences. Popović was aware that audiences find his plays perplexing. His response was that audiences should become like children and react accordingly to his plays. He cites *Second Door Left* as a play he wrote for those who refused to become children. Although containing recognizable elements present in Popović's earlier works, the play boasts something new: a well-defined plot that dictates action.

The plot of *Second Door Left* is a modern version of the revolt of God's angels. In Popović's handling of the story, God is One in Three Persons: Heavenly, the mother; Father, the father; and an ominous, wrathful, noxious unseen presence. Their children (Elmo, Dove, Bestman, Soda Water, Permonition, and Tantuz Lilliput) are the equivalents of God's angel helpers. The action takes place in a "syncopated dream of Paradise," and as Popović wryly adds—"by all means." Instead of the expected Hymn to God, Popović has the children-angels jump on huge jumping balls and sing a playfully raunchy ditty.

Popović regards *Second Door Left* as his paean to freedom. The children's attempts to "let fresh air come in from all four sides of the world," by giving birth to "one new life"—innocent, free of fear, born of love—is also a search for a future paradise in which everyone will live free and happy. Popović genuinely believed (prior to the dismemberment of Yugoslavia) that such a paradise could become a reality. During the heady days of the reign of Josip Broz Tito, it was possible to harbor such dreams. But his naiveté provoked criticism from his fellow artists and critics, who accused Popović of trying to "out-Lenin Lenin." His ingenuous fervor also accounts for the note of didacticism in almost all of his works.

But Popović's didacticism has roots in Jonathan Swift and Lewis Carroll rather than in socialist realism. His criticism topples all barriers: he has at various times attacked his countrymen's preoccupation with materialism and has ridiculed their lives filled with sham and self-deceit (especially in *Utva ptica zlatokrila*). He often openly criticized the defects in his country's political system in *Kape dole,* whose title could also be translated as "Down with the Communist Party." As a result, *Kape dole* was removed from the repertory of Atelier 212 after only two performances. The censor also set his sights on *Second Door Left,* which had to travel to New York for its premiere.

Not surprisingly, it is in *Second Door Left* that Popović makes his greatest indictment, chastising all of humanity, including Serbs. Having chosen a pompous theme, he managed to avoid pomposity and created a fairy-tale world. But instead of bunnies and turtles scurrying about the landscape, innocent, disturbed children jump on jumping balls and try to make sense of a world that refuses to grow up. Only Tantuz Lilliput, the microhero, penetrates into the evil created by his parents, Heavenly and Father. The drama involves his estrangement from his rebelling brothers and sisters and his eventual recognition that "one more new life" must be created in order to void the malevolent world of his parents. After his declaration, Popović's admonishing voice can be heard in the final lines of the play: "The performance is over, and now you can all go to your own homes quietly."

The play is subtitled "A Theatrical Benediction in Two Parts," and the stress on ritual is intentional. In his later plays the emphasis is placed heavily on the ritualistic aspect of daily life. Espousing materialism and declaring himself a believer in humanity, Popović nonetheless respects the Orthodox tradition and allowed his wife, Danica (a former ballerina), to celebrate the church's holy days. His passion for ritual and iconography (his collection includes Serbian, Macedonian, Russian, and Bosnian icons) is reflected in his work. Preferring primitive icons and art for their honesty and lack of guile, he has tried, by his own admission, to capture this spirit in his works.

After the death of his wife (from whom he was divorced), Popović continued his assault on political figures, institutions, and, above all, the human condition. His later works, from *Mrešćenje šarana* (The Spawning of Carps, 1986) to *Bela kafa* (Coffee with Milk, 1992), dig into the fabric of a country that has lost its bearings and is searching for redemption with honor. According to Jovan Hristić, Popović in the 1990s is creating some of the finest works of his career. It is as if Aristophanes had decided to write like Aeschylus. At age sixty-six, Popović had three plays premiere during the 1995 season: *Ružičnjak* (The Rose Garden); *Čarlama, zbogom* (Farewell, Liars), produced in May at Atelier 212; and *Mrtva tačka* (The Dead Spot), premiered at the newly founded theater, Zvezdara-teatar (Star Theater). His controversial antiwar play *Tamna je noć* (Dark Is the Night) premiered in New York at Ellen Stewart's La Mama Experimental Theater in September 1995.

Popović died on 9 October 1996. He found solace in the children's world that he created in his plays, a world sketched in black and white but illumined by myriads of rainbows. His optimism was a laser beam that strikes at the heart of man's conscience. In his work he is the Pied Piper of Serbia, singing his way into people's hearts, prodding them to change their ways and work for a better future. The legacy he created, hundreds of radio and television plays and serials and more than fifty stage plays, seems as prodigious and staggering as the man himself.

Interviews:

E. J. Czerwinski, "Interview with Aleksandar Popović at Theater La Mama," *Drama and Theater,* 8 (1970): 99-118;

"Playwrights Speaking," *Scena,* no. 4 (1981): 160-162.

References:

Duško Babić, *Pozorište iracionalnog* (Novi Sad: Matica srpska, 1988);

E. J. Czerwinski, "Aleksandar Popović: Belgrade's Poet of the Streets," *Books Abroad,* 43 (Summer 1969): 349-354;

Czerwinski, "Aleksandar Popović and Pop-Theater: Beyond the Absurd," *Comparative Drama,* 3 (Fall 1969): 168-175;

Czerwinski, "Aleksandar Popović: Sound-Images, Metaphor-Scenes and Audience-Involvement," *Modern Drama,* 15 (1971): 449-456;

Radoslav Lazić, "Force and a Half," *Scena,* no. 11 (1988): 40-42;

Sveta Lukić, *Savremena jugoslovenska literatura 1945-1965* (Belgrade: Prosveta, 1968), pp. 60-62;

Peter Marjanović, "Aleksandar Popović: The Development of Boris Taylor (1969)," *Scena,* no. 7 (1984): 237-242;

Mirjana Miočinović, "Predgovor," *Izabrane drame Aleksandra Popovića* (Belgrade: Nolit, 1987), pp. 5-29;

Miočinović, "Stage Action in the Plays of Aleksandar Popović," *Scena,* no. 3 (1980): 199-212;

Vladimir Stamenković, *Pozorište u dramatizovanom društvu* (Belgrade: Prosveta, 1987);

Mardi Valgemae, "Socialist Allegory of the Absurd: An Examination of Four East European Plays," *Comparative Drama,* 5 (1971): 44-52.

Yordan Radichkov
(6 October 1929 -)

Lyubomira Parpulova-Gribble
Ohio State University

BOOKS: *Gorda Stara planina* (Sofia: Narodna mladezh, 1956);

Sŭrtseto bie za khorata: Sotochinski razkazi (Sofia: Narodna mladezh, 1959);

Prosti rŭtse: Razkazi (Sofia: Narodna mladezh, 1961);

Obŭrnato nebe: Razkazi (Sofia: Narodna mladezh, 1962);

Planinsko tsvete: Razkazi (Sofia: Profizdat, 1964);

Sharena cherga: Razkazi za detsa (Sofia: Narodna mladezh, 1964; second enlarged edition, Sofia: Otechestvo, 1987);

Goreshto pladne: Razkazi (Sofia: Narodna mladezh, 1965);

Svirepo nastroenie: Razkazi (Sofia: Bŭlgarski pisatel, 1965);

Neosvetenite dvorove: Pŭtepis za Sibir (Sofia: Bŭlgarski pisatel, 1966);

Vodoley: Razkazi (Sofia: Narodna mladezh, 1967);

Kozyata brada: Noveli (Sofia: Bŭlgarski pisatel, 1967);

Vyatŭrŭt na spokoystvieto: Noveli (Sofia: Narodna mladezh, 1968);

Nie, vrabchetata: Razkazi za detsa (Sofia: Narodna mladezh, 1968);

Baruten bukvar: Razkazi (Sofia: Bŭlgarski pisatel, 1969);

Kozheniyat pŭpesh: Razkazi (Plovdiv: Khristo G. Danov, 1969);

Skalni risunki: Noveli (Sofia: Bŭlgarski pisatel, 1970);

Choveshka proza: Razkazi (Plovdiv: Khristo G. Danov, 1971);

Plyava i zŭrno: Razkazi (Sofia: Bŭlgarski pisatel, 1972);

Kak taka? Razkazi (Varna: G. Bakalov, 1974);

Malko otechestvo: Razkazi (Sofia: Dŭrzhavno voenno izdatelstvo, 1974);

Vsichki i nikoy: Roman (Sofia: Otechestven front, 1975);

Spomeni za kone: Noveli (Sofia: Bŭlgarski pisatel, 1975);

Shest malki matryoshki i edna golyama: Noveli (Varna: G. Bakalov, 1977);

Sumatokha. Yanuari. Lazaritsa: Piesi (Sofia: Bŭlgarski pisatel, 1978);

Prashka: Roman (Plovdiv: Khristo G. Danov, 1979);

Luda treva: Razkazi (Sofia: Bŭlgarski pisatel, 1980);

Malka severna saga (Sofia: Bŭlgarski pisatel, 1980);

Pedya zemya: Razkazi (Sofia: Profizdat, 1980);

Sumatokha. Yanuari. Lazaritsa. Opit za letene: Piesi (Sofia: Bŭlgarski pisatel, 1982);

Nezhnata spirala: Razkazi (Sofia: Bŭlgarski pisatel, 1983);

Po vodata: Noveli (Sofia: Narodna mladezh, 1983);

Verblyud: Razkazi i noveli (Varna: G. Bakalov, 1984);

Izpadnali ot karutsata na boga: Razkazi, groteski, miniatyuri (Sofia: BZNS, 1984);

Skakalets: Razkazi (Sofia: Profizdat, 1984);

Koshnitsi: Piesa (Sofia: Bŭlgarski pisatel, 1985);

Skandinavtsite: Razkazi (Sofia: Bŭlgarski pisatel, 1985);

Tenekienoto petle: Noveli (Sofia: Partizdat, 1985);

Noev kovcheg: Roman (Sofia: Bŭlgarski pisatel, 1988);

Khora i svraki: Razkazi (Sofia: Narodna mladezh, 1990).

Editions in English: *Hot Noon*, translated by Peter Tempest (Sofia: Sofia Press, 1972);

Lazarus Treed, translated by E. J. Czerwinski, *Slavic and East European Arts*, 5 (Summer 1987): 11-44.

MOTION PICTURES: *Goreshto pladne*, screenplay by Radichkov, Studiya za igralni filmi, 1966;

Privŭrzaniyat balon, screenplay by Radichkov, Studiya za igralni filmi, 1967;

Posledno lyato, screenplay by Radichkov, Studia za igralni filmi, 1974.

SELECTED PERIODICAL PUBLICATION–
UNCOLLECTED: "Obraz i podobie. Khronika: Piesa," *Sŭvremennik,* 14, no. 2 (1986): 11–44.

Yordan Radichkov is the most original fiction writer and playwright in Bulgarian literature in the second half of the twentieth century, one who has created works that are appreciated both within his country and abroad. The recognition of his talent, however, did not come easily. The difficulty in accepting his writing came partly from the inertia of the general reading public, whose taste had been formed by the norms and values of the traditional discourse, and partly from the fact that Radichkov's works did not comply with the rules of the so-called method of socialist realism, which many official literary critics tried to enforce. Initially the author had a relatively small but extremely enthusiastic group of admirers, mostly among the young generation. During the 1960s the number of people who began to appreciate his witty parodies, intricate grotesques, and colorful imagery grew rapidly. In the 1970s, although there were still readers who for various reasons had reservations about his manner of writing, Radichkov was already a celebrity and his name was a synonym for an avant-garde author.

Yordan Dimitrov Radichkov was born on 6 October 1929 in the village of Kalimanitsa, Mikhaylovgrad district. His father, Dimitŭr Traykov Radichkov, was a farmer and a mason. The writer's mother, Mladena Vasileva Filipova, from the neighboring village of Bistrilitsa, not only worked around the house and in the fields, but was also a midwife and practiced some folk medicine. In a 1978 interview for the magazine *Septemvri,* Radichkov said that he had lived in his village for twenty-two years. This is only partially true, because after finishing the school in Kalimanitsa he attended high school in the town of Berkovitsa, from which he graduated in 1947. Obviously the writer considers the year 1951, when he got a job as a regional correspondent for the newspaper *Narodna mladezh* (National Youth), the end of what one might call the village period in his life. A year later he was promoted to the position of editor in the same newspaper and moved to Sofia. He finished his journalistic career with the newspaper *Vecherni novini* (Evening News, 1955–1959). After several years on the Scenario Board of the Bulgarian Cinematography Company (1959–1962), Radichkov was appointed editor for *Literaturen front* (Literary Front, 1962–1969) and thus got directly involved with the institutions of literature. In 1962 he also became a member of the Union of Bulgarian Writers.

His first book is the collection of journalistic sketches *Gorda Stara planina* (The Proud Balkan Range, 1956), which the author himself does not consider as part of his literary works. The true beginning of Radichkov's literary career is *Sŭrtseto bie za khorata: Sotochinski razkazi* (The Heart Beats for the People: Stories from Sotochino, 1959). A remarkably productive writer, between 1961 and 1965 Radichkov published six new collections of short stories, namely, *Prosti rŭtse* (Simple Hands, 1961), *Obŭrnato nebe* (The Sky Upside Down, 1962), *Planinsko tsvete* (A Mountain Flower, 1964), *Sharena cherga* (A Multicolored Rug, 1964), *Goreshto pladne* (1965; translated as *Hot Noon,* 1972), and *Svirepo nastroenie* (Violent Mood, 1965). The first four books were written in a relatively traditional manner. The author pays special attention to detail. A strong lyrical current permeates the discourse, and the plot culminates in an intense dramatic conflict.

The traditional narrative style dominates *Sharena cherga* and *Goreshto pladne,* but there one also finds several unusual personifications, mythical images, and extensive deviations from the main plotline. All these features became the trademark of vintage Radichkov. Written for children, the former book provides the author with the opportunity to play with naive imagery and unconventional associations. For instance, a little boy tried to write, but the letter would not stay still: it would "raise its bottom," "wiggle between the lines" of the notebook, and "move its ear as if trying to chase a fly away." The results of these experiments were successfully employed later in the works intended for an adult audience. In "Goreshto pladne," the story that gives its name to the latter book, the small village river, so inviting and friendly at first, is seen as a mythical serpent when it threatens the life of a boy trapped in the foundations of a bridge. *Goreshto pladne* exhibits yet another characteristic of Radichkov's mature writing, namely, its disregard for the traditional literary genres. Its subtitle, *Razkazi,* means short stories, but the book actually includes three rather lengthy pieces (the other two being "Posledno lyato" [Last Summer] and "Privŭrzaniyat balon" [The Tied Balloon]) which many critics consider novelettes rather than short stories.

The book that fully displayed Radichkov's unique perception of the world was *Svirepo nastroenie.* The action in the stories, as in *Goreshto pladne*, takes place in Cherkazki, an imaginary village located in the western part of the Balkan Range, which is in the vicinity of Radichkov's native Kalimanitsa. However, Cherkazki is not an ordinary village but a surrealistic universe in which a pig is able to plow into the sky faster than Halley's comet ("Svirepo nastroenie"), a peasant's dog eats up his master and the story itself ("Kucheto zad karutsata" [The Dog Behind the Cart]), and a rifle fires and blows the village and its inhabitants into pieces ("Studeno" [Cold]). "Dŭrvoyadetsŭt" (The Woodworm), for example, is an absurd story about a house, a wolf, and a sheep that the author had inherited from his father. The house, renowned for its chimney through which the devil had once dropped in, was infested with woodworms. They wandered in their labyrinths inside the beams like the thoughts inside the head of the writer. Convinced that he had persuaded the wolf and the sheep to live in peace (the wolf even began to graze), the author during the night wrote the story about the new relations between the two animals. Following his father's advice, he used ink made with soot from the "devil's chimney." In the morning, the author saw two sheep in the meadow and for a moment thought that the wolf had turned into a sheep, but a peasant came and said that the sheep were his. In the meantime the woodworms had eaten through the construction of the house, and it collapsed. In a typical Radichkovian fashion, the text offers no indications as to how to interpret it. One possible explanation of the disappearance of the animals is that the wolf had eaten up the sheep and fled. The house demolished by the woodworms can be interpreted as a theory that cannot endure the pressure of critical thinking. The ink from the devil's chimney, used for the rosy story in which conflicts are solved regardless of the real situation, reminds one of the Stalinist version of socialist realism, which banned depicting any serious conflicts. The father himself may be an allusion to *tatko Stalin* (father Stalin), a common expression used during the 1950s to refer to the Soviet leader. And yet, there is nothing in the text that one may use as hard evidence proving that this interpretation was the one intended by Radichkov.

The elusive authorial intentions go beyond the level of elementary political precautions and become a distinctive aesthetic principle of Radichkov's writings. His narratives are open and can sustain several different interpretations, which is a typical feature of mythical discourse. Critics frequently talk about a mythological dimension in his works. However, they usually discuss not the principle itself but specific creatures that are either taken directly from Bulgarian folk demonology or created by the author. The mythopoeic trend is also present in all books published during the 1960s, namely, *Neosvetenite dvorove* (Unlit Courtyards, 1966), *Vodoley* (Aquarius, 1967), *Kozyata brada* (Goat's Beard, 1967), *Vyatŭrŭt na spokoystvieto* (The Wind of Calm, 1968), *Nie, vrabchetata* (We, the Sparrows, 1968), *Baruten bukvar* (The Gunpowder ABC Book, 1969), and *Kozheniyat pŭpesh* (The Leather Melon, 1969).

Neosvetenite dvorove, the first long travelogue written by Radichkov, resulted from his trip to the Soviet Union in 1965. It presents a highly original picture of the past and present Siberia, with its intriguing secrets and vast human and natural resources. The book became popular not only in Bulgaria but also in Europe (France, Finland, and especially Sweden, where it had four editions). *Nie, vrabchetata* was Radichkov's second book for children. The stories, however, are also of interest to the adults because of their finely crafted, naive style of narration. The humorous illustrations, drawn by Radichkov, are an additional asset to this work. *Baruten bukvar* was the book that attracted much attention by its unusual angle of presenting the armed antifascist resistance in Bulgaria. The hardliners were disturbed by the lack of explicit references to the role of the Communist Party and its ideology, while liberal critics defended the author, pointing out that his general attitude toward the resistance was positive and emphasizing the high literary quality of the works.

During the 1970s Radichkov continued to be highly productive. He published four collections of short stories: *Choveshka proza* (Human Prose, 1971), *Plyava i zŭrno* (Chaff and Grain, 1972), *Kak taka?* (How Come?, 1974), and *Malko otechestvo* (Small Fatherland, 1974), which included new works as well as some old pieces. The successful experiment with longer narrative forms from the previous decade was continued and expanded. The author published three collections of novelettes, *Skalni risunki* (Rock Drawings, 1970), *Spomeni za kone* (Memories about Horses, 1975), *Shest malki matryoshki i edna golyama* (Six Small Matryoshkas and a Big One, 1977), and two novels, *Vsichki i nikoy* (Everybody and No One, 1975) and *Prashka* (Sling, 1979). During this period Radichkov established himself as a playwright with *Sumatokha* (Commotion, published in 1978), *Yanuari: Zimna poema* (January: A Winter

Poem, 1973), *Lazaritsa: Piesa v 4 sezona* (Lazarus Treed: A Play in Four Seasons, 1978; translated as *Lazarus Treed,* 1987), and *Opit za letene* (An Attempt to Fly, 1982).

In all these works the author continues to explore the possibilities of the style, manner of composition, point of view, and strategies for interpretation typical of the dialogue of peasants and less educated urban dwellers. His texts of all genres are built by repetition of themes and images (with slight variations), unexpected associative links, wordplay, weak cause-and-effect connections between the episodes, and a mixture of centuries-old traditions with experiences from modern life. The characters are mostly Bulgarian peasants who have either migrated to the city or face the intrusion of modern civilization in their remote villages. Even in the capital city of Sofia elements of the Cherkazki mentality coexist with modern-day technology. For instance, one of the author's favorite images, the *tenets* (a spirit of a deceased person who lives and helps the living people), exists in these stories with the same rights as the visitors from outer space.

Radichkov's plays deserve a special mention. With the exception of *Zhelyaznoto momche* (Iron Boy, 1967), a play for children that did not attract much attention, they were all received with great enthusiasm both by the artistic elite and the general public. Their stagings were a success that was as great as it was unexpected, since the texts seemed to defy all rules of dramatic art. Perhaps there was some special affinity to theater hidden within the fiction writer that enabled him to produce these unique plays. This suggestion may not be far-fetched, considering that Radichkov's son, Dumitŭr, is a theater director and his daughter, Roza, is a drama critic.

A good example of the highly unconventional poetics of the plays is *Lazaritsa*. The entire play consists of the monologue of its only character, the peasant Lazar. He wanted to shoot his dog but missed, and the viewers first see him hiding from the angry animal in the branches of a wild pear tree. Lazar spends all four seasons in the tree contemplating his life. *Lazaritsa* illustrates two general trends that began to develop in Radichkov's writings during the 1970s. The first concerns the thematic scope of the works. Born and raised in close contact with nature, and a passionate hunter who has never lost touch with the wilderness, Radichkov became alarmed by the devastating changes in the environment in recent years. Consequently, the issue of the preservation of wildlife and nature becomes one of the prominent themes of his writings. The second trend is related mainly to the literary devices used. The author begins to use more markers to indicate the intended interpretation of the text, not that the works have been inundated by didactic lecturing or obtrusive allegories, but they are not as completely open as they were before.

During the 1970s Radichkov, although still an unorthodox and rather independent writer, received various signs of acceptance on the part of the literary establishment. For example, he was appointed as an adviser on the Council for Cultural Treasures (1971) and was awarded the title of honored cultural worker (1974). From 1986 to 1990 he served as deputy chairman of the Union of Bulgarian Writers. During the last two and one-half decades his talent also gained considerable recognition abroad. The writer was invited to Sweden in 1979; to Italy to receive the international prize for literature Grinzane Cavur, and to promote his books *Short Stories from Cherkazki* and *An Egg in January;* to Moscow, Warsaw, Prague, and Berlin (for premieres of his plays); and to Sweden, Italy, and Russia for roundtables discussing contemporary literature. He participated in the congresses of P.E.N. in Rio de Janeiro and San Marino, California. In 1984 the author and his wife, Suzi Markova Garti, traveled to the United States as guests of USIA, the United States Information Agency. In 1988 they spent a month in France at the invitation of the French Foreign Ministry.

The trip to Sweden inspired the travelogue *Malka severna saga* (A Small Northern Saga, 1980). The lyrical current in this book is stronger than in *Neosvetenite dvorove,* while the imagery is less exotic and surprising. The 1980s were as productive for Radichkov in terms of new book titles as the 1970s. The writer published five collections of short stories: *Luda treva* (Wild Grass, 1980), *Pedya zemya* (A Span of Land, 1980), *Nezhnata spirala* (The Tender Spiral, 1983), *Skakalets* (Grasshopper, 1984), and *Skandinavtsite* (Scandinavians, 1985); two books of novelettes, *Po vodata* (On the Water, 1983) and *Tenekienoto petle* (The Little Tin Rooster, 1985); and one novel, *Noev kovcheg* (Noah's Ark, 1988). *Verblyud* (1984), a collection of already published short stories and novelettes, presents a comprehensive view of Radichkov's mythopoeic and absurd grotesques. In *Izpadnali ot karutsata na boga* (Things That Have Fallen off God's Cart, 1984) the author has gathered shorter texts with a relatively clear message (especially in the second part of the book). The little story "Kato ptichki bozhii po dŭrvetata" (Like

God's Birds in the Trees), for example, implies that one must not deceive himself that environmental problems will be solved in some miraculous way. The plot is centered around an absurd event: the fish from the polluted rivers have migrated to the trees and continue to live happily, completely adjusted to the new environment. The author transforms the saying "to live like God's birds," which means "to live without worries," into an ironic metaphor. Radichkov also wrote one new play, *Koshnitsi* (Baskets, 1985), which was immediately staged and received positive reviews. In the literary magazine *Sŭvremennk* (1986, no. 2, 283-329) finally appeared *Obraz i podobie: Khronika* (Image and Likeness: A Chronicle), a play which for several years could not be published because of its thinly veiled criticism of totalitarian ideology. Radichkov's most recent collection of short stories, *Khora i svraki* (People and Magpies, 1990), presents some philosophical reflections about humanity and nature masterfully conveyed through his distinctive imagery and manner of narration. The author himself has illustrated the book with a series of naive drawings.

Although never published in a separate volume, the three motion-picture scenarios expand further the scope of Radichkov's literary production. They, like the plays, use some of the already existing stories. The first scenario is for the movie *Goreshto pladne,* directed by Zako Kheskiya. The premiere took place on 3 January 1966. The picture was awarded the Silver Plate, a prize given by the Swiss magazine *Cinema Internacionale* for innovative means of expression, and a Prize for Contemporary Cinematographic Expression at the Festival of Bulgarian Films in Varna in 1966. The second screenplay was for the movie *Privŭrzaniyat balon,* directed by Emil Vagenshtayn. Although its premiere was in 1967, for censorship reasons the picture was withdrawn and appeared in movie theaters only after 27 May 1990. The third screenplay was for *Posledno lyato,* directed by Khristo Khristov, which premiered 10 May 1974. This movie received the award for best foreign director at the International Movie Festival in Atlanta, Georgia, in 1974, a gold medal for best actor at the International Movie Festival in San Remo, Italy, in 1974, and the Special Prize of the Jury at the International Festival in Toulon, France, in 1975.

Radichkov is a major figure in Bulgarian literature. During the late 1960s there was a flood of short stories by younger writers imitating his distinctive narrative style. Gradually the tide subsided when it became clear that no one could rival the creator of Cherkazki. Although it is still too early to assess the full impact of Radichkov's works, it is clear that he has certainly established a new trend in the national literature, which no one, neither his fellow writers nor literary critics, will be able to ignore.

Interviews:

Atanas Svilenov, "Pri Yordan Radichkov," in his *Sŭbesednitsi* (Sofia: Bŭlgarski pisatel, 1975), pp. 219-266;

Lyubomira Parpulova, "Kladenetsŭt," *Bŭlgarski folklor,* 4 (1978): 45-54;

Parpulova, "Verblyud, divyachka krusha, Lazaritsi, dim i vinena prepaska," *Septemvri,* 8 (1978): 56-73;

"Reflections in Front of the Official Entrance to the City," translated and with an introduction by Roland Flint, *Delos,* 1 (Winter 1988-1989): 123-134.

References:

Petŭr Dinekov, "Yordan Radichkov," *Septemvri,* 10 (1979): 234-242;

Nikola Georgiev, "Prevrashteniyata na Nane Vute," *Septemvri,* 6 (1968): 216-235;

Elena Gyurkova, "Nyakoi printsipi na khudozhestvenata sistema na Radichkov v kinoto," *Kino i vreme,* 21 (1983): 117-153;

Encho Mutafov and Dimitŭr Staykov, *Yordan Radichkov: Literaturno-kriticheski ocherk* (Sofia: Bŭlgarski pisatel, 1986);

Boyan Nichev, "Radichkov i istoricheskata poetika na khudozhestvenata ni proza," *Sŭvremennik,* 16, no. 4 (1988): 410-418;

Lyubomir Tenev, "Piesite na Yordan Radichkov," *Septemvri,* 8 (1976): 175-199;

"Yordan Radichkov," in *A Biobibliographical Handbook of Bulgarian Authors,* edited by Karen L. Black, translated by Predrag Matejic (Columbus, Ohio: Slavica, 1981), pp. 322-324;

Toncho Zhechev, "Yordan Radichkov," *Septemvri,* 12 (1969): 200-206;

Nikolay Zvezdanov, *Neosvetenite dvorove na dushata: Yordan Radichkov* (Sofia: Nauka i izkustvo, 1987).

Stevan Raičković
(5 July 1928 -)

Anita Lekić
State University of New York, Stony Brook

BOOKS: *Detinjstva. Pesme* (Belgrade: Novo pokolenje, 1950);

Pesma tišine (Belgrade: Prosveta, 1952; revised edition, Belgrade: Srpska književna zadruga, 1981);

Balada o predvečerju (Belgrade: Nolit, 1955; revised edition, Belgrade: Nolit, 1973);

Veliko dvorište. Pripovetke za decu (Cetinje: Narodna knjiga, 1955; revised edition, Belgrade: Prosveta, 1963);

Kasno leto (Zagreb: Lykos, 1958);

Družina pod suncem. Pesme za decu (Belgrade: Prosveta, 1960);

Tisa (Belgrade: Prosveta, 1961);

Gurije. Poema za decu (Belgrade: Prosveta, 1962; revised, 1967, 1990);

Priča o slonu, o ostalima i o jednoj buvi na kraju. Pripovetka za decu (Belgrade: Sportska knjiga, 1962);

Pesme (Novi Sad: Matica srpska / Belgrade: Srpska književna zadruga, 1963; revised, 1978);

Kamena uspavanka. Pesme (Belgrade: Prosveta, 1963; revised, 1969);

Stihovi (Belgrade: Prosveta, 1964);

Prolazi rekom ladja (Novi Sad: Matica srpska, 1967);

Varke. Izbor pesama (Belgrade: Prosveta, 1968);

Zapisi o crnom Vladimiru. Poema (Belgrade: Privately printed, 1971);

Zapisi. Pesme (Subotica: Rukovet, 1971);

Krajcara i druge pesme. Pesme za decu (Belgrade: Žar ptica, 1971);

Pesme (Novi Sad: Matica srpska / Belgrade: Srpska književna zadruga, 1972);

Vetrenjača. Pesme za decu (Belgrade: Vuk Karadžić, 1974);

Male bajke. Pripovetke za decu (Belgrade: Srpska književna zadruga, 1974);

Pesme (Belgrade: Rad, 1977);

Beleške o poeziji (Novi Sad: Matica srpska, 1978);

Slučajni memoari (Belgrade: Prosveta, 1978);

Stevan Raičković

Tri pesme o Tisi (Čačak: Gradska biblioteka i SIZ kulture, 1979);

Pesme. Izbor pesama za decu (Sarajevo: Svjetlost, 1980);

Raičković. Pesme (Valjevo: Milić Rakić, biblioteka Pesnikovom rukom pisano, 1982);

Panonske ptice (Belgrade: BIGZ, 1988);

Monolog na Topli (Belgrade: Prosveta, 1988);

Svet oko mene (Belgrade: Srpska književna zadruga, 1988);

Pesme (Belgrade: Srpska književna zadruga, 1990);

Stihovi iz dnevnika 1985–1990 (Novi Sad: Matica srpska, 1990);

Dnevnik o poeziji (Belgrade: Narodna knjiga, 1990);

Suvišna pesma. Devet fragmenata o genocidu sa predgovorom i komentarima (Belgrade: Mala biblioteka Srpske književne zadruge, 1991);

Rane: kasne pesme (Belgrade: Narodna biblioteka Srbije-Srpska književna zadruga, 1996).

Editions and Collections: *Pesme. Izbor pesama za decu* (Sarajevo: Svjetlost, 1980);

Pjesme. Izbor pesama za decu (Sarajevo: Veselin Masleša, 1980);

Dela Stevana Raičkovića. Poezija i proza za decu i omladinu u četiri knjige [Veliko dvorište, Gurije, Male bajke, Vetrenjača] (Belgrade: BIGZ/Prosveta, 1982);

Dela Stevana Raičkovića. Sabrana poezija u šest knjiga [Pesma tišine, Balada o predvečerju, Kamena uspavanka, Kasno leto, Točak za mučenje, Slučajni memoari] (Belgrade: BIGZ/Prosveta, 1983).

Editions in English: "Awareness of Autumn," and "The Son of the Grass," translated by A. Lenarčič and Janko Lavrin, in *An Anthology of Modern Yugoslav Poetry,* edited by Lavrin (London: J. Calder, 1962), pp. 179–180; also in *Introduction to Yugoslav Literature,* edited by Branko Mikasinovich and others (New York: Twayne, 1973), pp. 263–265;

Poems, translated by Aleksandar Nejgebauer, *Relations,* no. 1-2 (1970): 10–12;

Poems, translated by Muriel Heppell, in *New Writing in Yugoslavia,* edited by Bernard Johnson (Baltimore, Md.: Penguin, 1970), pp. 76–77;

Poems, translated by various translators, in *Contemporary Yugoslav Poetry,* edited by Vasa D. Mihailovich (Iowa City: University of Iowa Press, 1977), pp. 52–56;

Poems, translated by Nejgebauer, *Relations,* no. 8 (1978): 13–18;

Poems, translated by Karolina Udovički, *Relations,* no. 10 (1983): 7–21;

Poems, translated by various translators, in *Serbian Poetry from the Beginnings to the Present,* edited by Milne Holton and Mihailovich (New Haven, Conn.: Yale Center for International Studies, 1988), pp. 312–317.

TRANSLATIONS: William Shakespeare, *Šekspir: Soneti,* verse rendition by Raičković on the basis of prose translations by Živojin Simić (Belgrade: Prosveta, 1966);

Šest ruskih pesnika: Blok, Ahmatova, Pasternak, Mandeljštam, Cvetajeva, Zabolocki (Belgrade: Kultura, 1970);

Deset ljubavnih soneta Frančeska Petrarke posvećenih Lauri (Belgrade: Privately printed, 1974);

Slovenske rime: Pasternak, Riljski, Kupala, Tuvim, Nezval, Novomjeski, Lorenc, Bagrjana, Gradnik, Koneski (Belgrade: Rad, 1976).

Stevan Raičković is a leading representative of intimate, lyric poetry in postwar Serbian literature. A prolific poet, Raičković emerged on the Yugoslav literary scene in the early 1950s with work that challenged the socialist realism dogma dominating the immediate postwar years. Raičković's rebellion against the prevalence of social and patriotic themes in vogue at the time assumed the form of lyric poetry focusing on the self and the sphere of personal, subjective emotions. In his formative years as a poet, Raičković never succumbed to mainstream influence. In the turbulent 1950s, as socialist realism was banished from the literary scene and replaced by an innovative, highly cerebral poetry whose methods grew increasingly refined, Raičković continued to be faithful to his own vision of poetry, its main features being unobtrusiveness, simplicity, and intimacy. Although Raičković began writing at the same time as two fellow major poets, Vasko Popa and Miodrag Pavlović, whose own work marked the advent of postwar modernism in Yugoslavia, throughout the next four decades he continued to be a supreme lyricist, his work consistently characterized by a melancholic tone, an enhanced subjectivity, and a strong devotion to nature.

Stevan Raičković was born in Neresnica, Serbia, on 5 July 1928. In his youth he experienced the full hardships of life in a country torn apart by World War II. Raičković's parents, both of whom were teachers, fled with their family from one town to another and eventually settled in Subotica. It was there that Raičković resumed his schooling and, in 1947, graduated from secondary school. Subsequently, he pursued his studies of Yugoslav literature in the philosophy department at Belgrade University. Raičković joined a leading Belgrade publishing house, Prosveta, as editor in 1959, retiring in 1980 after a twenty-year career. He has been a member of the Serbian Academy of Arts and Sciences since 1972.

Raičković began writing poetry during the war, and in 1945 he published his first poem, "Majka nad zavejanim uspomenama" (Mother amid Snowy Memories). Five more years were to elapse before his first volume of verse, *Detinjstva* (Childhoods), appeared in print in 1950. While he was studying in Belgrade, Raičković's halfhearted attempts to have his poems published in the journal *Mladost* proved futile. His work was rejected by the editors on the grounds that its tone was too somber and melancholy. Indeed, the elegiac quality of Raičković's poetry was completely at odds with the enthusiasm and didactic optimism of socialist realism.

Detinjstva first saw the light of day as a result of a chance meeting between Raičković and Oskar Davičo, an already established and widely respected poet; Davičo was also an editor at Novo pokolenje and was interested in introducing new, previously unpublished poets to the public. The manuscript was submitted to the publishers in 1948. However, partly because of technical problems involved in publishing the book and partly because of an understandable slowness on the publisher's part, the volume did not appear in print until two years later. To Raičković's disappointment, several poems he had been particularly fond of were omitted because of their alleged decadence and pessimism. Raičković's poetry continued to be greeted with a dose of suspicion for some time because of its introspective qualities and utter detachment from the political concerns of the day.

In the years that have since elapsed, Raičković has maintained an uninterrupted presence on the Yugoslav literary scene. He has published many volumes of poetry and stories for children and has written extensively about poets and poetry. His work has been translated into many languages, and Raičković has devoted much time and energy to translating other poets. He collaborated with Živojin Simić in translating William Shakespeare's sonnets (Simić translated the sonnets into Serbian, then Raičković rendered them into verse); he also translated the sonnets of Petrarch. Both projects exerted a decisive influence on the poet's later predilection for the sonnet form in his own poetry.

In addition to his poems and stories for children, his essays, and translations, Raičković's volumes of verse after *Detinjstva* include *Pesma tišine* (Song of Silence) in 1952; *Balada o predvečerju* (Ballad about Dusk) in 1955; *Kasno leto* (Late Summer) in 1958; *Tisa* (named after a river in Vojvodina that lingered in the poet's memories from childhood) in 1961; *Kamena uspavanka* (Stone Lullaby) and *Pesme* (Poems) in 1963; *Stihovi* (Verses) in 1964; *Prolazi rekom ladja* (A Boat Sails Down the River) in 1967; *Varke* (Illusions, 1968); *Zapisi o crnom Vladimiru* (A Testament to Black Vladimir) and *Zapisi* (Notes) in 1971; *Slučajni memoari* (Chance Memoirs, 1978); *Točak za mučenje* (The Rack, 1981); and *Suvišna pesma* (Superfluous Song) in 1991. Revised and augmented editions of these collections have been printed frequently over the years. In 1982 and 1983 two major Belgrade publishers published a collaborative ten-volume edition of Raičković's poetry and prose works. Raičković has received major literary awards for much of his work and through the years has commanded the attention of an ever-larger audience, enjoying wide popularity among readers and critics alike.

Raičković's oeuvre is a cloistered poetry of the soul's innermost recesses. His poems reflect his devotion to solitude, isolation, and silence, and he finds the ideal setting for these themes in nature. His poetry is primarily one of images, with nature always in the foreground. Poem after poem and collections as a whole sing nature's praises (an appropriate example is the collection titled *Tisa*, named after a river from Raičković's childhood). The elements of nature and landscapes—grass, trees, plants, stones, and rivers—are his basic motifs. They are symbols of a mood of unthreatened tranquillity that Raičković longs to regain and successfully projects in his poems. Perhaps the most striking quality of his poems is their pervasive stillness, beneath which lies an agonized perturbation of mind. In Raičković's work there are startling innovations or bold experimentation. His subdued tones seem designed to soothe any feelings of unease or anxiety that could be prompted by the content.

The extreme simplicity of Raičković's style is in harmony with the unassuming tone of his poems. Raičković does not experiment with language. He has a good ear for the spoken language and a pronounced inclination toward the vernacular in his work, and this trait has been subjected to some criticism. His preference for elision, in keeping with his primarily syllabic poetry, is felt by some critics to be appropriate to speech only. But the fact that Raičković enjoys a growing readership is to be attributed in large part to his unpretentious wording and the ease with which he presents themes that are far from simple.

Raičković has experimented with various poetic forms throughout his career and has shown himself equally adept at all. When he writes in free verse, he achieves a smooth and fluid style, enabling him to express fully his lyric qualities. Most of his poems, however, consist of quatrains and rhymed couplets. *Stihovi,* a collection devoted wholly to the poet's dialogue with his poems, is written entirely in couplets. Raičković's major translation project, the sonnets of Shakespeare, inevitably influenced his decision to write the fifty poems in his finest collection, *Kamena uspavanka,* in sonnet form. The poet has admitted that many years after the project was completed he continued to work under the influences of the sonnet form, writing the rhymed verses to which he had grown accustomed while translating Shakespeare. It is noteworthy that Raičković tends to resort to the rigidity of traditional poetic forms precisely when he gives voice to his most complex themes. The fixed constraints of traditional forms enable him to rein in his poems and rid them of any redundant elements that could dilute their force. In *Kamena uspavanka,* in which he worked within the strict confines of the sonnet form, Raičković has included two of his finest poems, "Pesma i smrt" (The Poem and Death) and "Kamena uspavanka."

For Raičković, poetry is an indispensable instrument in confronting and coming to terms with the transience of human life. Death is ever present in his work; it hovers ominously in the background even in his most tranquil and seemingly carefree poems. The capacity of poetry to come to grips with death is contemplated anew in every volume of his oeuvre. The poet continually carries on a dialogue with his poetry, exploring the full spectrum of possibilities that the poem offers as well as its limitations and shortcomings.

The poems of *Kamena uspavanka* give eloquent expression to Raičković's desire to escape the inevitable by arresting all motion and bringing the passage of time to a stop. The longing to immobilize painlessly every living thing by drawing a shroud of perpetual slumber over life reflects a deliberate revolt against destiny. This is the theme of "Pesma i smrt." The rhythm of the verses has been deliberately slowed down to suggest the arrest of all motion: "This poem may be likened to a valley / In which to aching stone a lone wolf turns." The longing to stop time from unfolding and to halt the process of continual decay is, however, futile. Not only is the poet unable to perceive clearly the path he follows, but he is powerless to resist the forces that lead him:

"And all I feel is a dark and heavy knell / Pull me slowly towards a distant tomb." It is precisely because "This poem has no sharp words to speak" and "no balms to ease the mind" that it is simultaneously poignant and ruthless. On the surface calm, imperturbable, and solemn, the poem bespeaks a tortured state of mind as the poet comes to accept the lot that awaits him.

Raičković feels a strong affinity for his poems. More than just companions, poems are welcome friends. But they must remain speechless, as speechless as the poet, in the face of suffering: "Come with me, my poem, quietly along the grass ... / No one but silence will accompany us," Raičković writes in "Najtiša" (The Quietest Poem), from *Pesma tišine*. He feels the world around him to be one of pain, suffering, and solitude, and he knows that both he and his poem can do nothing to overcome this inherent sorrow. The poet's only recourse is silence, a willful submission to and a conscious acceptance of the world as it is: "Long have I gazed at the silent stone. / Long have I watched the tree in agony: / It stands, solitary, with arms outstretched." A comforting note is struck by the strong sense of camaraderie between Raičković and his poem, for the poet's perception of life is shared by his work. Together they can bear their heavy burden, the pain of their knowledge, in the unperturbed and impassive setting of nature.

Raičković's poetry is often concerned with the problem of decoding the secret cipher of silence and mastering the primitive, inarticulate tongue of nature. The poet longs to merge with nature, but the long years of urban life have numbed him and deadened his senses. The sense of kinship with the poem vanishes in poems devoted to urban settings, where the focus is on the poet in the process of creating his poem. Instead of the quiet resignation that marks Raičković's earlier work, other poems convey a sense of self-recrimination: "No one's to blame / For the bird you bear within your breast," he writes in "Spavači" (The Sleeping), another poem from *Pesma tišine*. The poet now perceives that his poetry is the cause of his isolation; poetry is the invisible burden he alone must carry. The rest of the world is at peace, indifferent to the poet's existence. The acute sense of isolation hence also stems from the urban landscape in which the poet creates his work. He feels he has lost his sense of hearing and his powers of perception. But silence is not willing to embrace into its fold those who have consciously abandoned it. It mistrusts trespassers, and the poet feels like an intruder preyed upon by nature. The burden of the past and the weight of his struggle for survival in the city thwart his attempts at reconciliation with nature and deny him access to its silent language.

For Raičković, the origins of a poem are to be sought in shadowy, unreal, and inexpressible regions. But as the poem grows, so do its demands. It requires more than just work on its structure; it begins to feed on its author's suffering. After the poet devotes all that he has at his disposal—his memories, his yearnings, and long hours of toil—the poem begins to acquire a will of its own.

One of Raičković's major concerns is how to create a truly authentic and meaningful poem. A common thread linking the whole of the poet's oeuvre is his uninterrupted dialogue with his poems and his unwavering pursuit of a "pure" poem, a work that would dematerialize its author and exist as an independent phenomenon. A poem must concentrate within itself the very essence of life, as a brilliant flame blazing in a gulf of darkness. The poet feels his words are inadequate; they have lost their capacity to convey the precise meanings he seeks to express. Only words that are the actual embodiment of life can help Raičković face the impassive stare of death. Living, breathing words alone can give voice to the poet's anguish. In many of Raičković's poems the attempt to achieve mastery over words is perceived as futile, with the ideal poem remaining elusive. Silence is an undesired condition from which the poet wants to but cannot extricate himself, as the true poem of his life irreversibly drifts away.

For Raičković, as for his close friend and outstanding fellow poet Branko Miljković, retrieving the original force and meaning of words is of utmost importance. Words must possess their own reality, a reality transcending that of the poet himself. "Thus a poem steps forward before its readers, sufficient unto itself, as if it had always existed, or as if it had suddenly, thanks to some unaccountable laws, emerged alone in a bare, empty and unoccupied space," Raičković wrote in a 1974 essay, "Beleške o poeziji" (Notes on Poetry), published in the journal *Savremenik* (Contemporary).

Raičković's "Pesma trave" (Song of the Grass), from his collection *Pesma tišine,* is considered one of his most pessimistic poems—one that utterly negates the need for poetry. The poem can, however, be viewed as a courageous act of coming to terms with the tragic dimensions of human existence. The thought that the grass has weighs heavily on the poet: not only should the poem be abandoned as superfluous, but speech itself must be suppressed in favor of silence. In accepting the silence offered him by the grass, however, the poet is triumphant, because he is capable of making that silence sing. Confronting his own innermost depths, the poet comes to perceive the world beyond him with new eyes and in a new light, as a world in which a man is comparable to an ant—on the one hand, restless, striving, and ambitious, and, on the other, solitary, insignificant, and finite. In perceiving and describing this condition in his poetry, Raičković sings with a force that transcends the walls of silence.

Raičković's poetry as a whole reflects his desire to share that absolute and perpetual silence that has been Miljković's choice. Early on, Miljković understood this yearning for silence in Raičković's poetry as a dissatisfaction with the unrealized potential of words, implying the need for a revision of language that would reach to its beginnings. Raičković's silence, Miljković wrote as early as 1959 in an essay on the poet that appeared in *Izraz* (Expression), is the precursor of words as they were in the beginning—pure, unadulterated, and uncontaminated:

> The poem must be sought where it ceases to be and is replaced by nature, death, and silence. This ontological nonbeing of the poem constitutes its origins and essence.... What rest is for motion, silence is for the poem: not an absence of motion, but frozen, arrested motion; not the absence of a poem but the pure possibility of a poem.... The poem needs this total absence, this peace and silence, to be able to create itself on its own.

Sensitive poets, Miljković wrote, dream of wordless poems. But silence must be the point of departure. Silence must be voiced; it must be made audible. Miljković was an early admirer of Raičković's poetry of silence, and he correctly anticipated, several decades ago, the fulfillment of Raičković's poetic potential and his uninterrupted rise as a poet: "Growing now, hardly audible, like blades of grass, but stronger and more triumphant from day to day, is the poetry of Stevan Raičković." Raičković is now recognized as a leading representative of the lyric tradition in Serbo-Croatian poetry, as a poet who has best preserved and advanced the spirit of lyricism to new heights of excellence.

References:

Miloš I. Bandić, "Stevan Raičković: *Balada o*

predvečerju," *Književnost,* 24 (1957): 184–190;

Boško Bogetić, "Opsednutost bolom," *Savremenik,* 31 (1970): 478–480;

Zoran Gavrilović, "Pesnik tihog proticanja," *Savremenik,* 39 (1974): 12–16;

Djordje J. Janić, "Pesnik pred ilovačom," *Savremenik,* 55 (1982): 641–643;

Dragan M. Jeremić, "Pesnik, priroda i pesma. Zapisi prilikom ponovnog čitanja pesama Stevana Raičkovića," *Književne novine* (16 May 1976);

Vujadin Jokić, "The Metaphysics of the Soul: A Note on the Poetry of Stevan Raičković," *Relations,* no. 3 (1986): 85–95;

Ivan V. Lalić, "Iskušenje lirskog pevanja," *Letopis Matice srpske,* 399 (1967): 487–491;

Slavko Leovac, "Poezija Stevana Raičkovića," in his *Metamorfoze* (Sarajevo: Svjetlost, 1965), pp. 24–34;

Sveta Lukić, "Stevan Raičković: *Balada o predvečerju,*" *Delo,* 3 (1956): 321–327;

Branko Miljković, "Pesma i smrt. Marginalije o jednoj pesmi Stevana Raičkovića," *Izraz,* 6 (1959): 242–244;

Nikola Milošević, "Raičkovićeva 'složena jednostavnost,'" *Savremenik,* 39 (1974): 17–21;

Karlo Ostojić, "Stevan Raičković: Trenuci istine," *Letopis Matice srpske,* 412 (1973): 634–648;

Predrag Palavestra, "U krugu tradicije: Stevan Raičković," *Savremenik,* 22 (1965): 233–243;

Palavestra, "The Pastorale as the Lyrical Land of Happiness," *Relations,* nos. 9–10 (1979): 93–100;

Aleksandar Petrov, "Poetsko delo Stevana Raičkovića," *Savremenik,* 10 (1964): 103–108;

Bogdan A. Popović, "Permanentna supstanca," *Savremenik,* 25 (1967): 574–581;

Predrag Protić, "Izbor po srodnosti," *Savremenik,* 49 (1978): 119–121;

Svetlana Velmar-Janković, "Varijacije o smrti," *Književnost,* 53 (1971): 493–496;

Slobodan Zubanović and Mihajlo Pantić, "Stevan Raičković, 'O sjaj su samo vrata kraja,'" in their *Deset pesama-deset razgovora* (Novi Sad: Matica srpska, 1992), pp. 41–72.

Radoy Ralin
(22 April 1923 -)

Nikita Nankov
Indiana University

BOOKS: *Stikhotvoreniya* (Sofia: Narodna mladezh, 1949);
Chetirinadeset dni (Sofia: Politichesko upravlenie na voyskata, 1950);
Planinata se srina (Sofia: Bŭlgarski pisatel, 1954);
Voynishka tetradka (Sofia: Narodna kultura, 1955);
Strogo poveritelno (Sofia: Profizdat, 1956);
Istoriya s lŭv (Sofia: Profizdat, 1958);
Vtoro razhdane (Sofia: Profizdat, 1959);
Nepredvideni chuvstva (Sofia: Bŭlgarski pisatel, 1959);
Bezopasni igli (Sofia: Bŭlgarski pisatel, 1960);
Khalosni patroni (Sofia: Profizdat, 1961);
Vnimatelni feyletoni (Sofia: Bŭlgarski pisatel, 1963);
Lirika (Sofia: Bŭlgarski pisatel, 1965);
Lichen kontakt (Varna: Georgi Bakalov, 1965);
Molya, zapovyadayte (Sofia: Bŭlgarski pisatel, 1966);
Dukhŭt i vtoroto shishe (Sofia: Biblioteka Stŭrshel, 1967);
Lyuti chushki (Sofia: Bŭlgarski khudozhnik, 1968);
Esenni kŭpini (Sofia: Bŭlgarski pisatel, 1972);
Obstoyatelstva (Sofia: Bŭlgarski pisatel, 1973);
Vsichko mi govori (Sofia: Narodna mladezh, 1975);
Khlyab i portokali (Sofia: Bŭlgarski pisatel, 1975);
Nyama nachin, Khamlete! (Sofia: Biblioteka Stŭrshel, 1978);
Apostrofi (Sofia: Bŭlgarski pisatel, 1980);
Kharakteri khorski (Sofia: Biblioteka Stŭrshel, 1980);
Dyavolska teritoriya (Sofia: Biblioteka Stŭrshel, 1980);
Shte doyde deteto (Sofia: Profizdat, 1981);
Voyna i mir v tri stranitsi (Sofia: Biblioteka Stŭrshel, 1982);
Epigramki v ramki (Varna: Georgi Bakalov, 1983);
Ezopiada (Sofia: Bŭlgarski pisatel, 1987);
Kadrovikŭt Teofrast (Plovdiv: Khristo G. Danov, 1987);

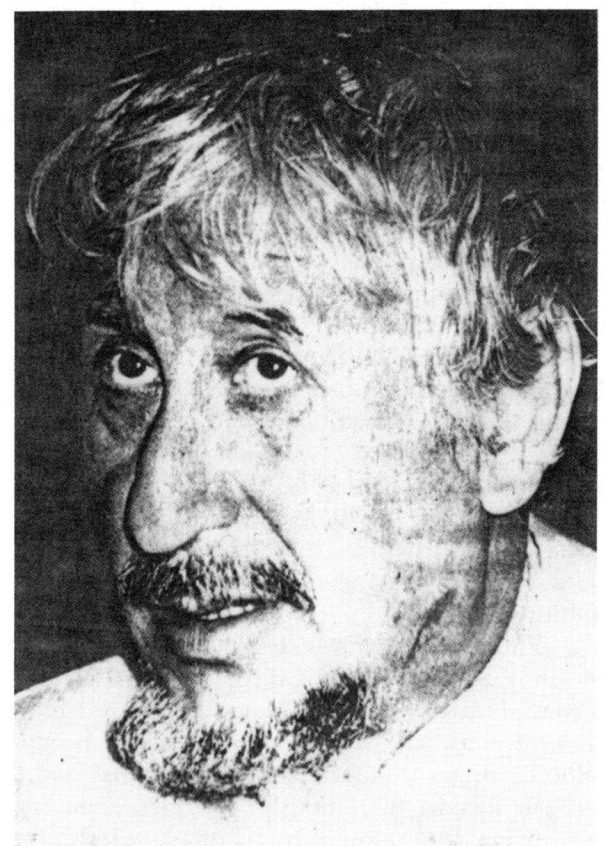

Radoy Ralin

Posleden ponedelnik (Sofia: Profizdat, 1988);
Koilo–galena treva (Sofia: Narodna mladezh, 1989);
Samoraslyatsi (Sofia: Bŭlgarski pisatel, 1989);
Sŭvremenna prikazka za zlatnata ribka (Sofia: Otechestvo, 1990);
Zlatnoto runo (Sofia: Plamŭk, 1990);
Aforizmi (Augsburg: Lyuk-Lück, 1993);
Eskimoski plazh (Sofia: Pelikan-Alfa, 1993);
Az sŭm Levski (Plovdiv: Khristo G. Danov, 1994);

Utesheniyata na Vasil Chertovenski (Sofia: Fakel, 1994).

Collection: *Izbrani tvorbi v dva toma* (Sofia: Bŭlgarski pisatel, 1984).

The status of Radoy Ralin in Bulgarian literature and culture is enviably paradoxical: his admirers greatly outnumber his readers. Ralin's political satire, coupled with his histrionics, have made him extremely popular even among people with no taste for literature, and his work has been given an extra luster by anecdotes about him, some of which are authentic and some of which are apocryphal. Ralin's creativity unites the lyrical poet with the satirist, a peculiarity that has confused many critics who approach Ralin either as a poet only or as an exclusively satiric writer. Last but not least, the evolution of Ralin's ideological commitments poses a question to the literary and cultural historians, because in him "verses and politics" are entwined, which means that his political preferences leave a direct mark on his work and public persona. Like many other Bulgarian intellectuals from his generation, Ralin was deeply influenced in his youth by communist ideals and activities. However, he grew increasingly skeptical of communism until, in the late 1980s and the early 1990s, his name became inseparable from the anticommunist forces in Bulgaria despite the fact that for decades he had been a devoted member of the Bulgarian Communist Party.

Radoy Ralin, whose actual name is Dimitŭr Stefanov Stoyanov, was born on 22 April 1923 in Sliven. This city near the Stara Planina Range is renowned as "the city of the one hundred captains," a name commemorating its merits in the struggle against the Turkish rule that dominated the region for nearly five hundred years from 1396 to 1878. Ralin takes pride in being a great-grandson of Captain Tan'o. Captain Tan'o was a follower of Vasil Levski, revered as a saint for his role in paving the way for Bulgarian liberation, and a friend of Stefan Karadzha, a legendary captain from Sliven. Ralin's father, Stefan Dimitrov, was a well-known printer, publisher, and bookseller who personally knew such outstanding figures in the international and Bulgarian communist movement as Georgi Dimitrov, Georgi Bakalov, and Dimitŭr Polyanov. At the age of nine Ralin became a member of a children's group, of RMS (The Workers' Youth Union), and learned about the social struggles of the proletariat in his home city. Ralin's first printed work is the poem "Esen" (Autumn), which appeared in 1931 in the children's newspaper *Izgrev* (Sunrise), published in Sliven. He studied in the Boys' High School "Dobri Chintulov" in Sliven (1936–1941). In 1938, as a member of RMS, he participated in the Communist Party's initiatives to use the legal provincial periodicals for its goals. During this time he carried on a correspondence with young leftist intellectuals. In July and August 1941 Ralin collaborated with the illegal bulletin *Istinata po antisŭvetskata voyna* (The Truth About the Anti-Soviet War), a project of RMS, of which only a few issues appeared. From 1941 to 1945 he studied law at the University of Sofia "St. Kliment Okhridski," and he became acquainted with many of the finest writers of his generation. Ralin was introduced to Nikola Vaptsarov, an outstanding communist poet who actively participated in the antifascist struggle during World War II, whom he semilegally sheltered in October and November 1941. In the fall of 1942 Ralin was arrested for his RMS activities, and in the police headquarters he conceived some of the poems later to be included in the cycle "Zapiski ot aresta" (Notes from the Detention).

Ralin's poems from 1940 to 1942 (some of which were banned by the fascist censors), appeared in a dozen or so periodicals and miscellanies; they echoed the poetics and themes of the revolutionary social Bulgarian poetry of Khristo Botev, Khristo Smirnenski, and Vaptsarov. The lyric hero is young and strong but choked by social passivity and injustice, so he makes rebellious gestures and appeals to his readers: "let us never get accustomed to the darkness" ("Vreme" [Time]), calling on them to struggle for a better life, and reminding them of the heroic past.

After 9 September 1944, when the pro-Soviet government of OF (Oteyectbeh Øpoht, or The Fatherland Front) took power in Bulgaria, Ralin, for three months, headed the Propaganda and Agitation Department of the Sliven District Fatherland Committee. Disagreements with some "revolutionary" actions of the committee led to his quitting, and he enrolled as a volunteer to fight against the Nazis. At the front he contributed to the newspapers *Frontovak* (Front Fighter) and *Chasovoy* (Sentry). He returned with a golden military cross and material for poems that constited his first mature work, the volume of poetry *Voynishka tetradka* (Soldier's Notebook, 1955).

After World War II Ralin settled in Sofia. In 1949 and 1950 he lived in Czechoslovakia. He participated in the youth festivals in Bucharest (1953) and Moscow (1947), and at the former he fell in love with an Italian woman, Laura, who became a recurrent topic and image in many of his works. In the following decades he held various editorial positions, the usual job for a professional writer in Bulgaria during socialism. Ralin worked for the magazine *Slavyani* (Slavs) from 1945 to 1946; for the newspapers *Literaturen front* (Literary Front) from 1946 to 1949 and from 1987 to 1990, *Stŭrshel* (Hornet) from 1952 to 1961 (he was dismissed from this paper for his criticism of the Communist regime), and *Literaturni novini* (Literary Gazette) from 1961 to 1963. He also worked in the Studiya za igralni filmi (Feature Film Studios) from 1963 to 1964 and in the Studiya za dokumentalni filmi (Documentary Film Studios) from 1964 to 1966, where he created the popular satiric movie series *Fokus* (Focus). He worked at the B˘lgarski pisatel (Bulgarian Writer) publishing house from 1967 to 1976, and in the Bŭlgarska Kinematografiya (Bulgarian Cinematography) from 1976 to 1987.

Since 1992 Ralin, together with his lifelong friend, the artist Boris Dimovski, and Kin Stoyanov, Ralin's elder son, has been publishing the satiric newspaper *Shtastlivets* (The Lucky One). Ralin has translated Russian, Czech, French, German, Hungarian, Greek, and Romanian poets. He wrote the scripts for more than a dozen feature, documentary, and animated cartoon movies, and the drama *Konferans* (The Text for the Entertainers, 1973). Among Ralin's several satiric plays, *Improvizatsiya* (Improvisation, 1962, in collaboration with Valeri Petrov) stands out. The book *Apostrofi* (Apostrophes, 1980) was awarded the national prize, Georgi Kirkov–Maystora, at the thirteenth Festival of Humor and Satire in Gabrovo, Bulgaria in 1981. Ralin is a member of the Bulgarian Writers' Union and an Honored Cultural Worker (1980), the second-highest artistic title given in socialist Bulgaria. In 1993 he became the first recipient of the award for satire, Rayko Aleksiev, for his lifelong achievements. Works by Ralin have been translated into many languages.

Ralin's first mature literary work appeared in 1955, the collection of poems titled *Voynishka tetradka* (Soldier's Notebook), which presents the experience of an ordinary soldier. Patriotic, communist, and humanistic rhetoric occasionally surfaces, but in some of the best poems, such as "Poet" (Poet), "Spomen" (Recollection), "Khudozhnikŭt" (The Painter), and "Grob na priyatel" (Grave of a Friend), the rhetoric is subverted by the development of the poetic theme. With its sober attitude toward war–which some critics in the mid 1950s castigated as "misunderstood realism," *Voynishka tetradka* follows the traditions of depicting military life set in Bulgarian literature by Dimcho Debelyanov and Yordan Yovkov.

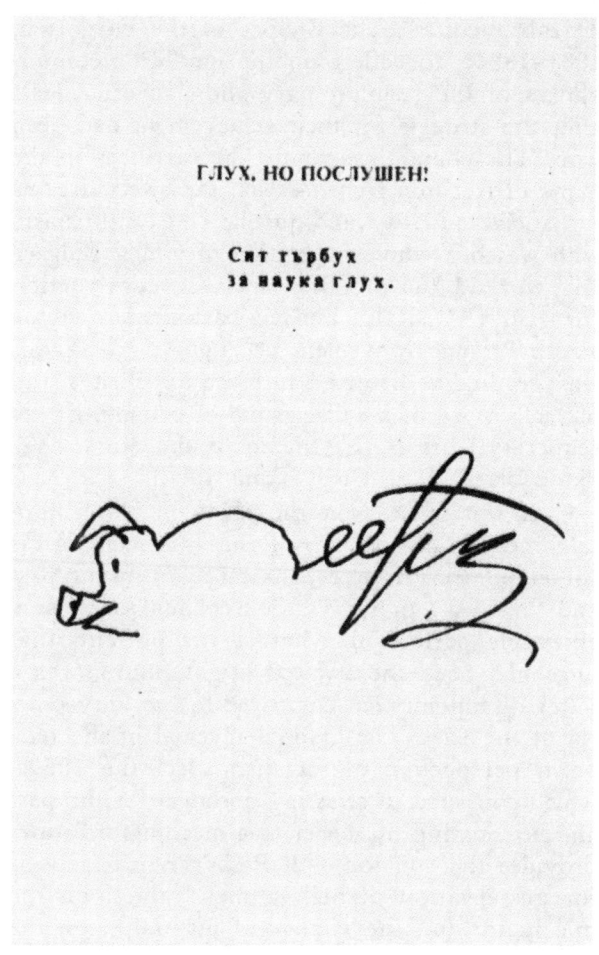

Cover of Ralin's satire Lyuti chushki *(Hot Peppers, 1968), with an illustration by Boris Dimonski. Because the pig's tail resembled the signature of a prominent public official, the book was banned.*

Ralin's next book of poetry, *Nepredvideni chuvstva* (Unforeseen Feelings, 1959), was warmly received and was awarded the prestigious annual prize of the Central Committee of DKMS (The Dimitrov's Communist Youth Union). Here and in his later volumes of poetry, *Lirika* (Lyric Poetry, 1965), *Esenni kŭpini* (Autumnal Blackberries, 1972), *Vsichko mi govori* (Everything Speaks to Me, 1975), *Khlyab i portokali* (Bread and Oranges, 1975), *Posleden ponedelnik* (Last Monday, 1988), *Koilo-galena treva* (Koilo–Caressed Grass, 1989), Ralin outlines several permanent poetic topics, the pivotal and the most multifaceted of which is the theme of the relationship between historical time and personal time. He, like many of his peers in the 1950s and 1960s, took up the tradition, set by Ivan Vazov with the cycle "Epopeya na zabravenite" (The Epopee of the Forgotten, 1881–1884), to reflect on the ignoble metamorphoses of the revolutionary and patriotic ideals after the struggle for their achievement had been won. The communist youth, the sacrifices in the name of freedom from fascism, the sweet dreams for social equality and justice, the enthusiasm with which a whole generation of young Bulgarians worked on the first socialist construction sites (in 1947 Ralin himself participated in the Youth Brigade Movement in Yugoslavia)–all this was gradually distorted into empty clichés and put in service of a small group of communist bureaucrats (this is the theme of the story "Velikoto utre!" [The Great Tomorrow!]).

In this sense, from the 1950s on, the historical time was perceived by Ralin and many of his contemporaries in a paradoxical manner: the past and the ideals of the youth were felt as an unachievable perfection, whereas the present, that once had been the awaited bright future, was a bitter disappointment compared to the lofty criteria of the past. The gradual reversal of the temporal perspective of socialism after the 1950s, which consisted in stressing nostalgia for the past and attenuating the belief in a meaningful future, provides the soil for both Ralin's lyrical appeals for preservation of high human values, on the one hand, and the vitality of his satire, on the other hand. This temporal reversal, which the "thaw" in the 1950s and 1960s and the *perestroika* in the 1980s delayed but proved unable to stop, is one explanation of Ralin's abandonment of the communist ideas in the late 1980s and the early 1990s. In this respect he is representative of the mental development of a whole generation of Bulgarian intellectuals. The theme of the inverted historical time is central for poems such as "Elegiya" (Elegy); "Balada za vrŭstnitsite na geroya" (A Ballad for the Peers of the Hero), where one reads that "the old age becomes our ideal"; "Balada za Zora" (A Ballad for Zora); "Vŭzdishka" (A Sigh); "Epizod" (An Episode); "Balada za Robert Peri" (A Ballad for Robert Perry); "Balada za ozhivyaveneto" (A Ballad for the Survival); and "Ogledalo" (Mirror).

In the early 1960s the inverted historical time in Ralin's poetry was counterbalanced by the theme of the private time of the individual: the passing of personal time is felt in these works as a maturation of manhood, as a readiness for giving birth and the joys of fatherhood. Ralin's poems "April" (April); "Poriv" (Impulse), which asserts that "There is nothing better than becoming a father"; "Na Kin" (To Kin); "Na Stefan" (To Stefan); "Santimentalna elegiya" (A Sentimental Elegy); "Novorodenite" (The Newly Born); "Urok po aritmetika" (A Lesson in Arithmetics); "Nasledstvo" (Heritage); and "Balada za bashtinstvoto" (A Ballad for Fatherhood) augment the somewhat exotic theme of fatherhood in Bulgarian literature with insights of rare sensitivity. The sophistication of this theme in Ralin comes also in works such as "Razminavane" (Passing Each Other) and "Balada za maychinstvoto" (A Ballad for Motherhood), which depict the experience of a divorced father who takes care of his two sons without their mother, and which are, perhaps, unparalleled in Bulgarian poetry.

The inverted historical time is counterbalanced in another respect as well: the expectations of a grandiose future and the nostalgia for the collective heroic past are superseded by a striving for a meaningful individual present. "I would like to be simple as breathing," the poet writes in "Yuri Gagarin 66" (Yuri Gagarin 66). "Molitva" (A Prayer), one of Ralin's highest poetic achievements, reads: "Freedom is like bread. Every day it is kneaded, baked, eaten up." This theme is also present in "Mŭlchalivo sŭglasie" (Tacit Consent), "Nay-posle:" (At Last:), "Khigiena" (Hygiene), "Predanostta na setivata" (The Devotion of the Senses), and "Prichinata" (The Reason).

Starting in the mid 1960s, the theme of private time in an individual's life takes on more somber overtones: elapsing time does not bring maturity and does not root one in the present but wears away; old age creeps upon one unawares; deeds are abortive; and one's destiny is physical and artistic impotence: "Umorata" (The Fatigue) reads, "We live in order to die. The fatigue is a rehearsal for death." This is also the poetic mood in "Epos" (Epos), "Elegiya po povod" (An Occasional Elegy), "Posleditsa" (A Consequence), "Starostta" (The Old Age), and "Dikilitash." In works such as "Balada za kraya" (A Ballad for the End), "Izsŭkhnalo dŭrvo" (Withered Tree), or "Chetvŭrta emblema" (Fourth Emblem), the problem is whether it is possible to die with dignity. In the context of this theme, *Koilo-galena treva,* a collection of love poems written between 1937 and 1987, exudes beautiful but tragically doomed nostalgia for youth and love.

Interlaced with the theme of the destructive private time is the theme of the limits of art and poetry: in a world of impending death where the past is no more, the future is impossible, and the present is meaningless, poetry is superfluous. Poetic gestures of resigning to silence are rare in Bulgarian literature. Pencho Slaveykov, around one hundred years before Ralin, created a precedent, but his silence was motivated by clearly stated social reasons. In the case of Ralin, the reasons are at best only alluded to, and this gives metaphysical overtones to his poetic inability to speak. The theme of the poetic silence has an interesting evolution in Ralin. In the early poem "Balada za zaginalata pesen" (A Ballad for the Perished Song, 1958), to destroy a poem out of cowardice is the greatest conceivable artistic and human sin, whereas later, in poems such as "Vsichko mi govori" (Everything Speaks to Me, 1964) and "Dochakan razriv" (Awaited-for Rupture, 1969), poetic silence symbolizes the abortiveness of a being. "Pepel" (Ashes) reads: "I have no verses. You have no verses as well. We are already not present from this moment on."

During Ralin's long poetic career his style changes: in the 1940s he started following the postsymbolist imagery and formal meters introduced in Bulgarian literature by Atanas Dalchev, whom Ralin has always admired, whereas from the 1960s on he wrote predominantly free verse that is often meditative and employs the paradoxical juxtapositions that are also characteristic of his satire.

Ralin's first humorous writings appeared in the newspapers *Burgaski far* (Burgas Lighthouse) and *Zarya* (Dawn) in 1939 and 1940. His humorous and satiric works utilize many genres and cover a wide thematic range. The major target of Ralin's satire, however, is those whose youth was spent struggling against fascism in the name of high social ideals, but who, once in power, became bureaucrats who use the slogans of freedom and equality as a cover for mercenary deeds. These works strike at the very core of socialist ideology and contrast it with socialist practice. The popularity of Ralin's satire comes not from its references to the minor issues of everyday life, which were the main province of the satire during the time of socialism and which he himself treats in many of his writings, but from the incessant interest in the problems of political power, social justice, ideological manipulation, and the split between ideals and reality. This holds true for both his socialist and post-socialist satire. Ralin is the most consistent, powerful, and stentorian political satirist in Bulgarian literature after World War II, one who excels in politically colored short stories, satiric poems, and, above all, political epigrams.

A noteworthy event, crucial for the semilegendary status of Ralin and representative of the atmosphere in which satire existed in socialist Bulgaria, happened in 1968, when Ralin's collection of epigrams, *Lyuti chushki* (Hot Peppers) appeared. Dimovski, the illustrator of all the satiric books of Ralin, had drawn a pig whose tail was reminiscent of the signature of the party and state leader at that time, Todor Zhivkov. *Lyuti chushki* was banned, and a campaign against Ralin, Dimovski, and other satirists was opened in which the Communist Party taught the writers and the artists what and how to criticize. Ralin was put under house arrest and later interned in the city of Silistra for his book and for sympathizing with the writers in Czechoslovakia during the events in 1968. The campaign had an unexpected effect: *Lyuti chushki* became immensely popular, and so did Ralin and Dimovski.

Eskimoski plazh (Eskimo Beach, 1993) gives an indication of Ralin's truthfulness to the ideals of social justice after the breakdown of socialism. The time after the communist "Glacial Period" is ironically presented as an Eskimo Beach, or, as in the poem "Pos[t]leditsi" (Post-Ice-Age Period /Consequences), as a deluge caused by the sudden thaw that destroys the world. The book is a collection of socialist and postsocialist epigrams and satiric poems that, in a similar way, castigate the incompetence, greediness, servility, and superciliousness of the rulers, both old and new. The message of *Eskimoski plazh* is that between these two eras in Bulgarian history a sad continuity exists, one that undermines the hope for positive historical development, or, as the epigram "Telegrama" (A Telegram) reads, "They again lied to us."

The unifying principle behind the many themes and styles of Ralin's satiric writings is found in the bonds between his satire and the mental, verbal, and poetic patterns of ordinary, everyday discourse. It is not by chance that *Lyuti chushki* has the genre subtitle *Narodni epigrami* (People's Epigrams). The semilegendary status of Ralin as a sort of witty folklore histrion who, despite his weak social position, always succeeds in laying bare any injustice forced by the powerful, would have been unthinkable without Ralin's gift for spelling out and playing upon popular, commonsense social feelings. The wisdom of Ralin's satire is not bookish, but colloquial; its viability comes not from erudition, but from praxis. In this respect Ralin takes over a long and strong humorous and satiric tradition in Bulgarian literature, that of Elin Pelin and Chudomir. This ex-

Portrait of Ralin by Boris Dimonski, used as an illustration in Ralin's novel Eskimoski plazh *(Eskimo Beach, 1993)*

plains why, on the one hand, Ralin's writings so easily transfer from the realm of literature into the province of contemporary folklore, and why, on the other hand, the vast majority of his best satiric works are based on traditional plots and sayings. *Lyuti chushki* contains many epigrams that are, in fact, well-known proverbs; Ralin's contributions are the titles that breathe contemporary meanings into the wisdom of yore. Many of Ralin's tales follow a similar principle: "Dyado na pazar" (An Old Man at the Market), "Shturetsŭt i mravkata" (The Cricket and the Ant), and "Lŭzhlivoto ovcharche" (The Little Lying Shepherd) are contemporary variations of popular Bulgarian folktales. Time and again Ralin rewrites well-known narratives from world literature and history: "Khamlet" (Hamlet), "Bibleyska legenda" (A Biblical Legend), "Srebŭrnata svatba na imperator Yustinian" (The Silver Wedding of Emperor Justinian), "Kroyki za novite drekhi na tsarya" (Patterns for the New Clothes of the King), and so on. The same is true of stories derived from Bulgarian literature and history: "Prikazka za stŭlbata" (A Tale for the Staircase), "Istina za stŭlbata" (Truth for the Staircase), and "Zavetŭt na Kubrata" (The Precept of Kubrat). A favorite genre of Ralin is the "mistake"; in it, proverbs and popular aphorisms, by changing one or two phonemes in them, are unexpectedly remodeled. Ralin is also the author of hundreds of neologisms that express in a condensed way substantial social truths and that contain ingenious verbal collages; a few of these words have become very popular. Some of Ralin's plays are also parodic reworkings of folktales like *Zlatnata ribka* (The Little Golden Fish, 1982), or of myths, like *Zlatnoto runo* (The Golden Fleece, 1990). The clash of high literature and colloquial wisdom is extremely effective in Ralin's apostrophizing well-known works by Bulgarian writers from the nineteenth and twentieth centuries: meanings that seem cast in stone suddenly, when apostrophized, start shining with new light. A similar effect is achieved in *Kadrovikŭt Teofrast* (Theophrastus, the Personnel Director, 1987), a collection of thirty-three satiric essays written from 1959 to 1982. Here, drawing on Theophrastus's *Characters* (319 B.C.), Ralin juxtaposes the tradition of the erudite philosophical essay and everyday chitchat: each essay starts as a treatise on a vice but ends as a sharing of family or friendly gossip. In Ralin's satiric works socialist clichés are incessantly used in traditional narratives; in this way the hackneyed stories are rejuvenated, whereas the clichés are parodied. The pompous official language of socialism is satirized in many short stories.

Utesheniyata na Vasil Chertovenski (The Consolations of Vasil Chertovenski, 1994), a "novel of anecdotes," is another example of how deeply Ralin is immersed in the dynamics of ordinary language. The major character is Vasil Chertovenski, a real-life humorist who recently passed away; he is a gourmand, his opinions are bizarre, and his amorous comments are indecent. The topics of the anecdotes are Bohemian, and the language is licentious; in this respect, the novel is part and parcel of the rediscovery of the low, even vulgar, layers in Bulgarian language after 1989, layers that the socialist language practice had suppressed.

Az sŭm Levski (I Am Levski, 1994) is Ralin's only lengthy work. Neither poetry nor satire, it is a "movie-novel" that was written between 1971 and 1974, initially as a film script. This solidly documented book depicts the life and death of Vasil Levski (1837–1873), the revolutionary who is considered the quintessence of Bulgarian national spirit. The novel, which at first sight seems to stand apart from anything else written by Ralin, is in reality connected with some of the deepest characteristics of his work. First, it is a historical concretization of the poetic theme of personal time and especially of its existentially most profound variant, that of self-reliance and of finding the meaning of one's life here and now. (Levski preached that the Bulgarians, instead of waiting for their freedom from Russia or from the West, had to fight for their liberation.) Second, Levski traditionally epitomizes the revolutionary who never misuses his power; he incarnates the ideal leader who selflessly serves his people and dies on their behalf. Levski, implicitly, is the measuring rod for every Bulgarian politician; he also provides the absolute criterion by which Ralin the satirist passes his judgments. Finally, Levski, despite his brilliant intelligence, was not a highly educated person, but one whose practical wisdom drew its strength from its immediate connections with the common people. In other words, he is one of the great role models for Ralin's satiric stance, in which Ralin voices, on the borderline between literature and folklore, the feelings of the ordinary people in their own ordinary language.

His enduring literary and cultural importance consists not so much in the thematics of his diverse and politically courageous writings but rather in his lifelong adherence to a deeper principle guiding both his depicting the world and his acting in the world. Ralin, in literature as well as in real life, plays the role of the idealist who, although occupying a weak social and political position, always tests through his suspicious laughter any ready and allegedly obvious truth inherited either from a cultural tradition or imposed by those who hold power.

References:

Zhel'o Avdzhiev, "Mladezhkite stikhove na Radoy Ralin," *Ezik i literatura*, 4 (1983): 131–149;

Vikhren Chernokozhev, "Ima li satirata dobri sezoni?," *Plamŭk*, 12 (1988): 156–160;

Boris Delchev, "Vŭzmŭzhavaneto no tvoretsa," *Literaturna misŭl*, 5 (1962): 39–70;

Chavdar Dobrev, "Za lirikata na Radoy Ralin," *Septemvri*, 7 (1976): 207–233;

Veselin Khanchev, " 'Nepredvideni chuvstva,' " *Plamŭk*, 1 (1960): 86;

Stefan Kolarov, "Radoy Ralin: liricheskoto mu tvorchestvo," *Literaturna misŭl*, 3 (1977): 70–82;

Minko Nikolov, "Stikhotvoreniyata na Radoy Ralin," *Septemvri*, 7 (1950): 146–152;

Bogomil Raynov, "Satirata-partiyno orŭzhie," *Literaturen front*, 48 (21 November 1968);

Pen'o Rusev, " 'Planinata se srina,' " *Septemvri*, 2 (1955): 184–188.

Tomaž Šalamun
(4 July 1941 -)

Michael Biggins
University of Washington

BOOKS: *Poker* (Ljubljana: Privately printed, 1966; second edition, with a new introduction by Tomaž Brejc, Ljubljana: Cankarjeva založba, 1989);
Namen pelerine (Ljubljana: Privately printed, 1968);
Romanje za Maruško (Ljubljana: Cankarjeva založba, 1971);
Amerika (Maribor: Obzorja, 1972);
Bela Itaka (Ljubljana: Državna založba Slovenije, 1972);
Arena (Koper: Lipa, 1973);
Sokol (Ljubljana: Mladinska knjiga, 1974);
Druidi (Koper: Lipa, 1975);
Imre (Ljubljana: Državna založba Slovenije, 1975);
Turbine (Maribor: Obzorja, 1975);
Praznik (Ljubljana: Cankarjeva založba, 1976);
Zvezde (Ljubljana: Državna založba Slovenije, 1976);
Metoda angela (Ljubljana: Mladinska knjiga, 1978);
Po sledeh divjadi (Koper: Lipa, 1979);
Zgodovina svetlobe je oranžna (Maribor: Obzorja, 1979);
Maske (Ljubljana: Mladinska knjiga, 1980);
Pesmi (Ljubljana: Državna založba Slovenije, 1980);
Balada za Metko Krašovec (Ljubljana: Državna založba Slovenije, 1981);
Analogije svetlobe (Ljubljana: Cankarjeva založba, 1982);
Glas (Maribor: Obzorja, 1983);
Sonet o mleku (Ljubljana: Mladinska knjiga, 1984);
Soy realidad (Koper: Lipa, 1985);
Ljubljanska pomlad (Ljubljana: Državna založba Slovenije, 1986);
Mera časa (Ljubljana: Cankarjeva založba, 1987);
Živa rana, živi sok (Maribor: Obzorja, 1988);
Otrok in jelen (Salzburg: Wieser, 1990);
Wal: Gedichte slowenisch und deutsch, selected and translated by Fabjan Hafner (Graz: Droschl, 1990).

Tomaž Šalamun in 1991 (courtesy of Tomaž Šalamun)

Collections in English: *Snow,* translated by Anselm Hollo, Bob Perelman, Michael Waltuch, and others (West Branch, Iowa: Toothpaste Press, 1973);
Turbines, translated by Šalamun, Hollo, and Elliott Anderson (Iowa City: Windhover Press, University of Iowa, 1973);
The Selected Poems of Tomaž Šalamun, translated by Charles Simic and others, edited by Simic, with an introduction by Robert Hass (New York: Ecco Press, 1988);
Painted Desert: Poems, translated by Michael Biggins, Perelman, and Šalamun, edited by Richard Seehus (Chattanooga, Tenn.: Poetry Miscellany, 1991);
The Four Questions of Melancholy: New and Selected Poems, translated by Michael Biggins and

others (Fredonia, N.Y.: White Pine Press, 1997).

TRANSLATIONS: Alexandre Dumas, père, *Dvajset let pozneje,* translated by Šalamun and David Senar (Maribor: Obzorja, 1969);

Ho Chi Minh, *Spisi, pisma, govori, 1920–1967,* translated by Šalamun and others (Ljubljana: Cankarjeva založba, 1969);

Simone de Beauvoir, *Mandarini,* translated by Šalamun (Ljubljana: Cankarjeva založba, 1971);

André Maurois, *Hugo: olimpijec in lovek,* translated by Šalamun, Severin Sali, and Branko Rudolf (Maribor: Obzorja, 1973).

OTHER: *57 pesmi od Murna do Hanžka,* edited by Šalamun and Tomaž Brejc (Maribor: Obzorja, 1970).

Recent treatments of Slovene literature generally recognize the year 1966 as a watershed. What came before is seen as flowing with all due dignity into literary history. What comes after, almost statutorily, qualifies as contemporary writing in the strictest sense. That this is so is largely to the credit of Tomaž Šalamun, whose first book of poetry, *Poker,* still holds the honor of signaling that change of direction. Šalamun's poetry, like its predecessors for nearly a hundred years, proceeds from the poetic "I" as its center of focus; but, unlike the meditative, mostly passive lyric subject well established in Slovenia until then, Šalamun's is an assertive self that actively creates and molds its poetic environment with total disregard for convention, producing worlds that bear little resemblance to the one that traditional categories of thought–spatial, logical, and ethical–allow the greater part of humanity to re-create on waking each morning. Critics have characterized this shift of focus as a "Copernican revolution," the kind of 360-degree spiral upward that occurs only once in an era. While Šalamun's revolution has had particular importance within its Slovene context, its intent is nothing if not universal, and that in the most literal sense.

Born in Zagreb, Croatia, on 4 July 1941, only three months after Axis forces seized Yugoslavia, Šalamun spent his early childhood in Ljubljana, the once and future Slovene capital that in the course of the war passed from Italian into German hands. In 1949 the family lived for a year in Mostar, Herzegovina, and from 1950 to 1960 they lived in Koper on the Slovenian coast, where his father, Branko Šalamun, a well-known pediatrician, held a key position in public health service. His mother, Dagmar Šalamun, née Gulič, worked as a librarian and pursued art history as an avocation, an interest that she passed on to her son. By all accounts, Tomaž and his three younger siblings had a happy, active, and privileged childhood at the crossroads of three diverse cultures–Central European, Mediterranean, and Balkan.

In 1960 Šalamun enrolled at the University of Ljubljana to study history and art history. In 1964 he was elected editor in chief of the literary journal *Perspektive* (Perspectives), where some of his first poems were published. Perceiving the journal as a threat to the public order, the authorities shut *Perspektive* down almost immediately. Because of his leading role in the journal and his contributions that were perceived as provocative, Šalamun was arrested, but a clamor of protest by leading Slovene intellectuals brought about his release within a few days. From his new position as political renegade and cause célèbre he continued to write poetry as a sideline while completing his university degree.

Despite occasional pogroms, poetry was one of the few relatively untouched preserves of the imagination in post-1945 Eastern European societies, perhaps because it appealed to a narrower audience than other genres or perhaps because its subversive meanings were often well disguised to both censor and reader. A rich modern poetry developed inside Yugoslavia beginning in the 1950s, once the country had overcome its initial flirtation with Soviet bloc membership and the attendant cultural trappings such as socialist realism. Yet, even within the bounds of this relative freedom, authentic poetry from the 1950s to 1980 used two filters to refract the world in which it originated–it could tend toward philosophical resignation, registering that world's flaws in fairly ambiguous terms, always to conclude with a fatalistic shrug (Zbigniew Herbert in Poland being a conspicuous practitioner); or it could rebel against the official parameters in pursuit of larger, usually quite grim existential truths.

From the mid 1950s, important young Slovene writers such as Gregor Strniša and Dane Zajc reintroduced poetry of mythological dimensions that dared to reject the aesthetic and ethical parameters still fostered by the ministries of culture. These poets drew on traditional mythologies (Strniša on Dante Alighieri and ancient Greece) or created new ones to depict and as-

Dust jacket for Šalamun's 1987 collection of poems. The jacket reproduces a painting by Šalamun's wife.

suage the divisions of the modern psyche, particularly as these had been deepened by the recent experience of war. Although they initiated a revolt, the alternatives they offered were largely an opposite reaction to the reality they faced, and deeply rooted in it. The world their poetry evoked was steadily collapsing on itself, the poet a helpless but observant bystander confronted with a blank, insurmountable wall.

Enter–and exit–Šalamun. In the opening lines on the first page of *Poker* he proclaimed: "I've grown weary of the image of my tribe / and departed," a terse, no-excuses declaration of his unwillingness to abide by rules imposed on his domain from without. Rules that his fellows, in a sense victims all, grudgingly accepted as a priori, Šalamun shrugged off in a phrase, setting the new boundaries, or antiboundaries, of what would follow over the next three decades. His break with meaning in poetry is best understood in this historical context: Slovenia had been supersaturated with meaning for decades, in the form of millions of pages commissioned to represent the ethical, moral, or aesthetic values of the political establishment, to manipulate words and concepts in support of preconceived conclusions.

His solution was to cut loose from meaning completely, refusing to play the victim of outside ideological agendas, and to create from scratch. The referent for his "tribe" is characteristically elastic: is it the Slovenes, with their fabled lethargy and self-perpetuating status as victims?; artists, caught in a vicious circle by an excess of logic?; or the thinking reed itself, hopelessly out of touch with its reedness? The proclamation continued:

> With long nails
> I will forge the limbs of a new body.
> Rags will be the guts.
> A cape of rotting carrion
> will be the cloak of my solitude.
> I will pluck an eye from the swamp's depths.
> Worm-eaten slabs of revulsion
> will be the halo I put on.

It was a direct, if outrageously overstated, poetic program: here one would revel in every kind of phenomenon, even the cast-offs and offal normally shoved into waste bins and carted off to the curbside. The Gothic-novel lexical field that he drew on for these seamy props had just been intensively mined by the existentially alien-

others' dualistic refuse. His early experiments in conceptual art, with its junkyard constructions of disparate materials, also had much to do with his poetry. The sculptor's fascination with textures, contours, and dimensions leads to poems that are almost tactile. The emblematic poem in *Poker* concludes with an abrupt shift in texture: "Mine will be a sharp-edged world, / cruel and permanent." The new rules were set. The poetic imagination would be sovereign within this world. Its ability to mold, create, and surprise would have full rein.

Throughout the rest of *Poker*, Šalamun demolishes one extra-artistic concept after another. He parodies:

> responsibility responsibility
> world without nature
> world without discourse
> trees, while still growing, are not responsible
> the sun doesn't need it for setting
> nor the sky which is sheer blueness and nothing more[.]

When he does this, he targets a whole range of related meanings, from the concept totalitarian regimes had perverted beyond recognition into a mandate for personal betrayal, to the concept as any authority uses it to assert its control, and especially the presumption that art should be obliged to intersect with responsiblity at any level. Above all he assaults the twentieth century's mythic image of the poet as mediator of higher truths—a sort of agnostic seeker's guide to the absolute—by launching into statements pregnant with the promise of revelation, only to deflate all grandiose expectations with incongruous detours into the everyday and banal:

> On the subject of god briefly
> he never said very much
> never said rosemary
> never said peace-loving
> if there were ants in the corners
> the ants stayed in the corners.

Poker, as all of Šalamun's most successful collections, is propelled by a felicitous combination of rebelliousness, antic wit, willful opacity, and perfect timing. Its delphic pronouncements briskly mutate into vaudeville shtick, just as its most farcical passages can modulate abruptly into tragedy or mystery. His random oscillations prevent the poet from being trapped in any one discursive pose for too long—from becoming the victim of narrative conventions and sacrificing spontaneity to them. In the process of negotiating these close calls and shifting moods he generates enormous verbal energy, not only from page to page but from one phrase to the next. His penchant for colloquial speech, macaronics, and occasional scatalogical vocabulary introduced Slovene poetry to a whole new lower register of diction. Conscious of the variety of changing voices and faces that he brings to the book, he closes *Poker* with a series of paradoxical observations in prose that provide some hint of how to interpret the title and offer as much of a skeleton key to the work as one is likely to find.

The critical reception of *Poker* was varied, ranging from reserved and scattered applause to a veritable din of shouts of "heretic" and "nihilist." Academic criticism found it expedient to coin two "-isms" to categorize the new phenomenon—reism, to take in its fascination with the life of objects, and ludism, to account for its apparently pointless capriciousness. Both terms, when applied, carried vaguely denigrating connotations, as though their very use apologized for what was unconventional and inexplicable in the new poetry. But Šalamun's long chains of creative non sequiturs were by no means a wholly new phenomenon. In a monographic essay, Vladimir Nabokov once pointed to a similar trait in Nikolay Gogol, Russia's unconventional nineteenth-century novelist, whose rambling, illogical digressions were a fundamental element of his style. Russian futurist and absurdist writers such as Velimir Khlebnikov and Daniil Kharms enjoyed a brief but powerful efflorescence in the 1920s, concurrently with dadaists and surrealists in Europe. Witold Gombrowicz and Stanislaw Witkiewicz were the main exponents of a similar current in prewar Poland, while experimental writing after 1945 developed under the signs of Samuel Beckett and Eugène Ionesco in Europe and of the Beat poets in America. Šalamun continued a well-established tradition of rebellion against the *Logos,* even if it had not yet become a Slovenian one.

In the late 1960s Šalamun used his specialized knowledge of art history in a variety of professional positions—first as an assistant curator at the Gallery of Modern Art, then as a lecturer at the Academy of Fine Arts, both in Ljubljana. From 1969 to 1970 he also participated with his brother Andraž and three other young artists in the conceptualist art group OHO (an amalgam of the Slovene words for "eye" and "ear"). In 1970 Kyneston McShine, curator of the Museum of Modern Art in New York, invited the group to have a monthlong exhibit there after he had seen and admired the catalogue of one of OHO's Zagreb exhibits. Šalamun was positively overwhelmed by this first exposure to the United States, and by a lucky chance the following year he received an invitation to the International Writing Program at the University of Iowa. There he worked closely with Finnish American poet Anselm Hollo, the first to help him translate his work into English, and he befriended many other Americans, among them Elliott Anderson and then-student Bob Perelman, who would later gain prominence as a proponent of West Coast Language poetry. Šalamun also became conversant with modern American poetry through the works of Ezra Pound, William Carlos Williams, Wallace Stevens, John Ashberry, and others.

His second and third collections of poems, *Namen pelerine* (The Purpose of the Cloak, 1968) and *Romanje za Maruško* (Pilgrimage for Maruška, 1971), the last ones published before his extended journeymanship in the United States, both pursued idioms at sharp variance with the one he had exploited in *Poker* to free himself from dominant Slovene traditions. *Namen pelerine,* self-published like *Poker,* appeared in an oversized format with a front cover that reproduced the playing board of the popular European game "Mensch, ärgere dich nicht" (Man, don't get riled), a preemptive admonishment to critics. Its tone is subdued and meditative in an absurdist way, and while high points are achieved, the dynamism of *Poker* is conspicuously missing. Following three years later, *Romanje za Maruško* is a concerted exploration of a different current, aiming at a renewed vitality in poems constructed around long chains of briefly glimpsed scenes; fragments of exotic, bizarre, and everyday images; philosophical and mystical concepts; and literary allusions that typically effervesce for no more than the space of a noun phrase, propelled by the force of the poet's ecstatic receptivity:

Lord, how I rise
how I am strong, terrible and wise
how I undress, peel and migrate
it's done by you god, I kill ...

... blessed fuck, sovereign, your food is ours,
peach trees, bodies, mountains, smoke,
the dead, their skin, necklaces,
I pluck golden teeth, sell them for bread

angels stand up from the sea, cherubim flutter
my verses are like splitting rocks
crushing jaws and shouting, let me eat lord,

let me be your supreme law all the way to the end.

—translation by Anselm Hollo

Yet even to say that these scenes are glimpsed bypasses a central point concerning their ostensible genesis. Šalamun is aware of this risk, and to relocate his readers in the proper perceptual framework he occasionally steps back to deliver a briefly digressive *ars poetica,* to make clear that he is not a mere observer of this process but the source itself: "I am not the subject. / I am God's strongbox. / I make no decision to look / either down or up."

Although *Romanje za Maruško* served as the proving ground for a visionary style that became a Šalamun trademark, its high-pitched intensity and unrelenting circling around a single target were unsustainable in the long run. It may be that his immersion in contemporary American literature at Iowa provided a solution to this problem. The longer narrative poems of *Amerika* (1972), his fourth book, are a new feature in his work, perhaps ascribable to the influence of American poetry, in which narrative is a dominant form. A new, winningly naive and amiably seductive dimension to the poetic self develops here, thanks to the broader personal space that the narrative form allows. The poet's wife, daughter, parents, friends from America and Yugoslavia, and even a few personal nemeses all make appearances in *Amerika*. The narrative provides relief from the peculiar intensity of his other well-established forms and introduces the possibility of dramatic development within the framework of a single book. Šalamun is careful, though, not to fall into the narrative as a trap; he remakes it after his own alogical and hectic image as yet another tactic of self-mythologizing. Frequently, narrative takes the form of a dream transcript, conveying in vivid yet dispassionate terms surreal events direct from the subconscious, devoid of any conventional points of reference. At other times it takes conventional settings and characters as its backdrop but transposes these elements into the realm of the fantastic, real, or imagined episodes from the poet's ongoing autobiography, becoming the pretext for enormous creative leaps. With this repertory of ecstatic, parodic, narrative, and oracular modes, Šalamun's polyphonic voice reached maturation in the early 1970s.

The image of America resonates through the collections published over the next few years. *Arena* (1973), *Sokol* (Hawk, 1974), *Turbine* (Tur-

bines, 1975), and *Imre* (1975) were written largely during his yearlong tenure at Iowa. Encounters with North American topoi worlds apart from anything known in Central Europe—the western deserts, the jungles of the Yucatan—often serve as metaphors for the final word of the universe on the subject of civilization. Šalamun's imagination seems stimulated yet at ease in vast expanses without a trace of man's imprint, as though, like blank paper, these provided the ideal medium in which to create. In one ebullient poem he strips naked and is on the verge of racing out toward the desert horizon, much to the consternation of his traveling companions, who think he has gone insane. In another he aims for the conceptual difference between the minimal landscape of flat earth/overarching sky and the more cultivated one of Europe:

> We eat the landscape in a different way, at a distance.
> The logos doesn't need to grind at the stomach walls from
>   inside,
> because it came in parts and was never
> fully assembled.
> The parts were arranged as gas pumps and fields....
> If you take a gallon along, you'll use three hundred
> to California, you could even die of drought
> if you have a thousand gallons in the tank. It vanishes.
>   You're infinitely smaller in the landscape. It hums[.]

America as mythic topos represents great creative freedom and a high level of unhampered energy. If Šalamun sometimes appears to go native in these surroundings, he does so with the intention that Slovenia should benefit from the experience. And if America betokens freedom, it is sadly also a place of exile from a home country seemingly immune to his message, even if desperately in need of it. From this distance Šalamun addresses alternately loving or scathing jeremiads to his fellow Slovenes and to Central Europe, "all those malnourished and mouldering nations / in their crumpled coats." His initial claims in *Poker* to have rejected his native milieu notwithstanding, Šalamun remains a decidedly national poet, as most Slovene poets before him have been. His unconventional poeses and many extended sojourns abroad have afforded his Slovene readers with a broad perspective otherwise rare within the confines of a small, socially stratified, and historically traumatized country.

Despite his attempts to break through these limitations in his writing, for most of the decade after 1972 Šalamun was drawn back into the vortex of Slovenia's increasingly harsh political reality. After a nearly decade-long period of liberali-

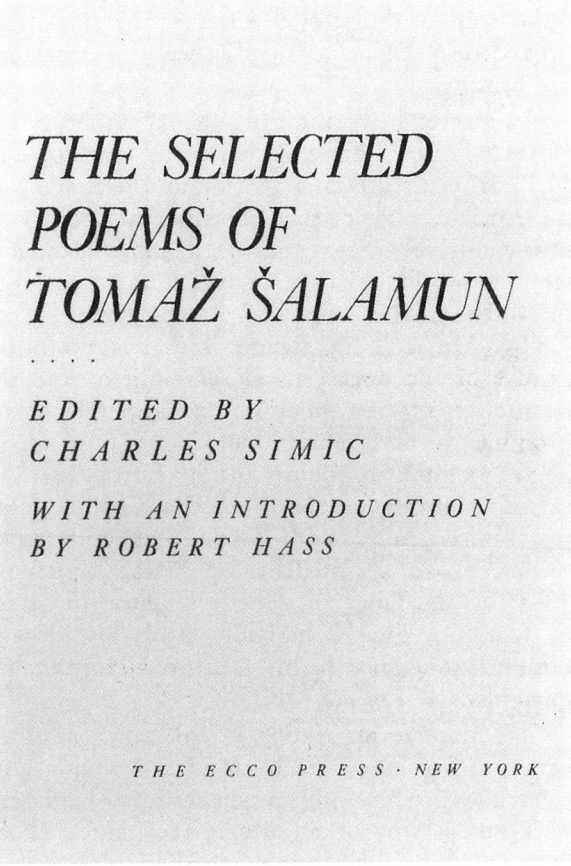

Cover for a 1989 translation of Šalamun's poems

zation that *Perspektive* had helped signal in the early 1960s, the regional governments were forced in 1972 to cede much of their hard-won autonomy to the Communist central government in Belgrade. The shift of power away from Slovenia and the other republics had a marked effect in the cultural sphere as censorship was reintroduced, and uncompliant writers and artists were subjected to systematic, thinly disguised harassment. In 1975, entirely by coincidence, Šalamun published a poem dedicated to Edvard Kocbek precisely at the moment when Kocbek began to draw the regime's fire head-on. The unfortunate timing cost Šalamun untold opportunities over the next few years. He continued to publish, though largely from the reserves of work he had brought back with him from America. To support himself he translated from English and French and accepted odd jobs such as selling encyclopedias door to door. His internal exile came to an end in 1979 when he was invited for a two-month residency at Yaddo, an artists' colony in upstate New York. Then followed a successful application for a two-year Yugoslav government fellowship to Mexico, a shot in the dark that proved to be of major significance as he regained his bearings.

Šalamun's work during the 1980s bears the clear imprint of his experiences in Mexico. The Mexican years are an extension and deepening of his American experience, opening his poetry to new fields of energy and a still more elemental worldview that proved to be in harmony with the directions his work was already taking in the 1970s. Mexico's landscape, Indian mythology, echoes of the poetry of Cesar Vallejo, and the mysticism of San Juan de la Cruz all figure prominently in a setting that juxtaposes elements of pre-Columbian culture and its European overlay. The autobiographical current becomes more pronounced in *Maske* (Masks, 1980) and *Balada za Metko Krašovec* (Ballad for Metka Krašovec, 1981), as the power of Mexico's appeal threatens to win him over completely from his already tenuous allegiance to his Central European origins.

A notable innovation in Šalamun's most recent writing takes the form of a dialogue conducted with the younger generation of Slovene poets—those who began to gain recognition in the early 1980s and represented the first serious challenge to Šalamun's twenty-year primacy in Slovene letters. Educated in the spirit of deconstructionism and Jacques Lacan, they produced work that is an eloquent exploration of the essential artificiality of the creative act, of its function as an attractive veneer on the surface of a random world offering no real prospect of divination. What surely is Šalamun's admiration for their mastery of language and form is evident in the new formalism of his own verses. Yet, perhaps sensing that their poetry constituted a return to the premises of the writing he had rebelled against twenty years earlier, he has also responded with a series of poetic tractates that seek to refute their assumptions by example. He argues with them, for instance, that the poem is a litmus paper that, when dipped into the universe's solution, registers its shapes and qualities:

> Where did the fire come from that visited
> Pascal? Or how do shivers crush your spine (do they rack it?) if you have the gift of sensing out the right word
> buried at just the right angle? As though you'd excavate three
> inches of the earth that lies atop that mountain. The rocks that
> lie there do that with a purpose. This sky's blue is meant to bind and gag. Like terrorists, and Beuys: whiteness, blood,
> stench, little eyes. What does a bee know of pollination?

Or, more to the point, he rejects their work out of hand, as in this three-line notification: "Too narrow. / That's why it rips at the seams. / You're much too squeezed between death and effect."

Šalamun himself is squeezed between nothing. His expansive poetry continues to encompass the most disparate phenomena with its intimations of cataclysmic violence and all-embracing agape standing at what one might conventionally perceive to be two extremes. But no extremes are implied here, only an integral whole in which the reader may briefly recollect how the world appeared to pre-Manichaean eyes.

Interviews:

France Pibernik, "Tomaž Šalamun," in *Med modernizmom in avantgardo* (Ljubljana: Slovenska matica, 1981), pp. 140–146;

Richard Jackson, "A Conversation with Tomaž Šalamun," *Poetry Miscellany*, 20 (1988): 7–9;

Christopher Buckley, "What Kind of Grace Will Come: An Interview with Tomaž Šalamun," *Denver Quarterly*, 25, no. 1 (Summer 1990): 110–120;

Tea Stoka, "Jezik je ena najnevarnejših drog: intervju, Tomaž Šalamun," *Literatura*, 9 (1990): 47–65.

References:

Ivan Cesar, "In the Beginning Was the Sign: Contemporary Slovene Poetry," *Slovene Studies*, 7, no. 1-2 (1985): 13–22;

Cesar, "Od riječi do znaka: novo u slovenskoj pjesničkoj avangardi," in his *Od riječi do znaka* (Zagreb: Globus, 1990), pp. 81–102;

Taras Kermauner, *Avantgardni pesnik pred sodiščem* (Ljubljana: Scena, 1972);

Kermauner, "Samovolja do niča," in his *Na poti k niču in reči: porajanje reizma v povojni slovenski poeziji* (Maribor: Obzorja, 1968), pp. 49–78.

Petar Šegedin
(8 July 1909 -)

Cynthia Simmons
Boston College

Petar Šegedin

BOOKS: *Djeca božja* (Zagreb: Matica hrvatska, 1946);
Osamljenici (Zagreb: Društvo književnika Hrvatske, 1947);
Na putu (Zagreb: Zora, 1953);
Mrtvo more (Zagreb: Kultura, 1953);
Proza (Belgrade: Novo pokoljenje, 1953);
Eseji (Zagreb: Kultura, 1955);
Essai o obliku i sadržaju (Zagreb: JAZU, 1955);
Čovjek u riječi (Zagreb: JAZU, 1956);
Susreti (Zagreb: JAZU, 1962);
Na istom putu (Zagreb: Naprijed, 1963);
Orfej u maloj bašti (Sarajevo: Svjetlost, 1964);
Sveti vrag (Zagreb: Naprijed, 1966);
Crni smiješak (Zagreb: Matica hrvatska, 1969);
Izvještaj iz pokrajine (Zagreb: Zora, 1969);
Riječi o riječi (Zagreb: Naprijed, 1969);
Svjetovi (Belgrade: Rad, 1969)
Svi smo mi odgovorni? (Zagreb: Matica hrvatska, 1971);
Petar Šegedin, Pet stoljeća hrvatske književnosti, no. 128, 2 volumes (Zagreb: Matica hrvatska, 1977); volume 1: *Pripovijetke, Djeca božja;* volume 2: *Pripovijetke, Crni smiješak; Putopisi;*
Getsemanski vrtovi (Zagreb: Liber, 1981);
Tišina: Novele (Zagreb: Matica hrvatska, 1982);
Vjetar (Zagreb: Globus, 1986);
Licem u lice (Zagreb: Naprijed, 1987);
Krug što skamenjuje (Zagreb: Globus, 1988);
Pričanje: Kratke proze (Zagreb: August Cesarec, 1991);
Izdajnik (Zagreb: Matica hrvatska, 1993);
Svijetle noći (Zagreb: Naprijed, 1993);
Frankfurtski dnevnik, ili, Priča o pobožnom pustolovu (Zagreb: Ceres, 1994).
Collection: *Odabrana djela,* 4 volumes (Rijeka: Otokar Keršovani, 1964).
Editions In English: "Life Is Not So Simple," *Some Yugoslav Novelists,* no. 5 (Belgrade, n.d.), pp. 29-48;
"The Marriage of Figaro," translated by Branko Brusar, *The Bridge,* no. 8-9 (1967-1968): 12-224; also translated by Donald Davenport in *Introduction to Yugoslav Literature,* edited by Branko Mikasinovich and others (New York: Twayne, 1973), pp. 474-490;

"His Window," translated by Brusar in *An Anthology of Yugoslav Short Stories,* edited by Augustin Stipčević (New Delhi: Indian Council for Cultural Relations, 1969), pp. 126-139;

"Holy Devil," translated by Celia Williams, *The*

Bridge, no. 23-24 (1970): 123-131;

"A Feeder of Pigeons," translated by Mario Suško and Edward J. Czerwinski, *Slavic and East European Arts*, 2, no. 2 (1984): 87-92.

Along with Vladan Desnica and Vjekoslav Kaleb, Petar Šegedin is one of a generation of Dalmatian-born Croatian writers whose works filter the cataclysm of world war and the particularly Balkan upheavals of wartime and postwar Yugoslavia through the reality of provincial Roman Catholic Adriatic culture. The wartime context of his first published prose is transfigured but preserved elsewhere in his writing by the atmosphere of confrontation between ignorance and enlightenment, moral lassitude and rectitude, and tradition and innovation. His creative writing, as opposed to his essays, usually formulates an argument without imposing a solution. Šegedin's philosophical questing and modern narrative technique offered an alternative to the aesthetically and intellectually crude tenets of socialist realism. During the years when literature in the former Yugoslavia was expected to be tendentious, writing such as Šegedin's served to hold Croatia afloat in the current of modern world literature.

Šegedin was born on 8 July 1909 in Žrnovo, a town on the Dalmatian island of Korčula. He studied in Dubrovnik to be a teacher, then continued his education in the Croatian capital. Eventually, he graduated from the philosophy faculty of the University of Zagreb. He taught in Kula Norinska, Račišće, and returned finally to teach in Zagreb. His debut as a writer came relatively late. His first published work, *Odlomak proze* (A Fragment of Prose), appeared in 1939 in Miroslav Krleža's magazine *Pečat*, under the pseudonym of Petar Kružić. (The work was aptly titled; prompted by his dissatisfaction with the work, Šegedin had earlier destroyed most of his manuscript.) It was only after the war and the publication of his novels *Djeca božja* (God's Children, 1946) and *Osamljenici* (The Lonely Ones, 1947) that he attracted serious critical attention. Šegedin's work, often naturalistic and pessimistic, did not fare well with the literary hard-liners. Nonetheless, the author remained true to his convictions. At the Second Congress of Yugoslav Writers in Zagreb in 1949, Šegedin, in a speech titled "On Our Criticism," spoke out against the exclusivity of socialist realism. This preceded by three years Miroslav Krleža's renowned speech in the same spirit at the Third Congress in Ljubljana in 1952.

Like several other writers of his generation, Šegedin managed to dovetail his literary career with public service. He was twice appointed president of the Society of Croatian Writers, and from 1946 to 1947 he served as secretary of the publishing house Matica hrvatska. From 1956 to 1960 Šegedin held the post of cultural attaché in the Yugoslav Embassy in Paris. After leaving the diplomatic service, he became a full-time professional writer. He was elected to the Yugoslav Academy of Arts and Sciences (Jugoslavenska akademija znanosti i umjetnosti) in 1964.

Šegedin's first novel, *Djeca božja*, recalls the Dalmatian-island atmosphere and mentality invoked by the celebrated Croatian writer Vladimir Nazor a generation earlier. The story is set in Žrnovo, Šegedin's native village on the island of Korčula, and corresponds chronologically to the author's boyhood during World War I. As Nazor does in his tales of provincial Dalmatian life, Šegedin maintains a tension throughout his narrative between the near-claustrophobic boundedness of village life, with its ignorance, boredom, and pettiness, and the limitless sense of wonder at the majesty of nature and the mystery of the Roman Catholic Church. Although the story is told in the third person, the reigning consciousness of the narrative is that of eight-year old Stakan. His ruminations on good and evil and his own sinfulness are conveyed in a narrated first person (erlebte Rede) that earmarks the work as stylistically modern. And the young boy's belief that the devil is literally "afoot," and the priest Don Petar's faith in divine intervention on the most mundane level of human existence, invoke the twentieth-century tradition of magical realism that has come to be recognized in Latin American fiction.

The characters in *Djeca božja* are at once a pitiful and an amazing lot. They can be astonishingly cruel. The women of Žrnovo gossip unmercifully, and few hesitate to chastise transgressors publicly. They attribute the world war to the general decline in morality. The relatively wealthy villagers, those who have macaroni to eat, flaunt their good fortune before their hungry neighbors. Even Stakan, who is repelled by his friends' inclination to torture small animals, carries his own burden of transgressions: stealing the priest's eucharists, destroying a bird's nest, and inadvertently knocking his mother from her chair. However, true to the modernist tendency to hint at salvation, Šegedin offers, if not a counterbalance, then at least a glimmer of hope. On his deathbed, Stakan's Uncle Antun doubts his faith; yet he is concerned that the pages of his memoir are preserved and make their way to his nephew and kindred spirit. The priest Don Petar also has moments of doubt and is plagued by vanity and temptation; yet, at the core, he is a believer, and that certainty is conveyed to his parishioners.

Most amazing in the novel is the characterization of Stakan. The late-twentieth-century reader wonders how best to analyze this young protagonist. He is painfully sensitive (the son of a victim of tuberculosis, he is the object of prejudice), with a vivid imagination. His guilt is embodied at every turn in visions of the devil. Most startling is his decision to be crucified to expiate sins—his own and those of the slayers of animals, and especially the original sin of the unbaptized children who languish in purgatory. Stakan never expects to suffer physically as a martyr. He believes he will be rescued at the last moment by an angel. Yet Stakan's act of religious hysteria is undercut at the end of the novel when his friends renege on their promise to nail him to the cross. He interprets their laughter as ridicule, although it may have been elicited by fear or embarrassment, and to regain their respect Stakan nails his own hand to the cross. It is not clear whether this last action of the novel is meant to represent an act of faith on the part of Stakan or, in the boy's need to impress his friends, another example of the detrimental influence on him of the sinful inhabitants of Žrnovo.

In a general comparison to *Djeca božja,* Šegedin's second novel, *Osamljenici,* is distinguished by an urban, though still provincial, locale, and perhaps consequently an even gloomier atmosphere. Here conscience and belief do not become incarnated in angels and devils. Church dicta and dogma are not the impetus to "soul-searching." Internal monologue, which revealed the consciousness of Stakan in *Djeca božja,* is a more prominent narrative mode, but it represents the solitary ruminations of the alienated protagonists of modernist literature. The characters represent a different stratum of society: the professor, Arturo; the failed writer, Srećko; and the medical student, Silvije, are all members of a provincial intelligentsia. Although one might debate the salutary influence of the Catholic Church in *Djeca božja,* in *Osamljenici,* without the constant reminder of spiritual life, there is certainly greater despair. The inhabitants of Žrnovo gossip, philander, and steal; in the provincial city of The Lonely Ones, they commit murder and rape. These novels exemplify the rapid shift from pro-

Title page of Šegedin's first novel, which evokes the experiences of an eight-year-old boy in a village on a Dalmatian island during World War I

vincial social organization (where authority lay in the hands of the church or the village community) to an urban, isolated, and secular existence that characterized post–World War II industrial development in Croatia and many other regions of the Western world. The psychologist and self-analysis have replaced religious instruction and the confessor.

The questions of material rather than spiritual existence, urban versus rural life, and the cerebral isolation of the intellectual were revisited in subsequent volumes of short stories. *Na istom putu* (On the Same Road), the title story of a collection published in 1963, is a simple tale about a young boy's move from village to town to attend school. Kuzmić, as he is called, is taken by his uncle to live with his aunt Rosalija. On the way they meet the old man Luporon, who, although once a judge, has fallen into disgrace and who is now harassed by the boy's friends. Kuzmić cries when his uncle leaves him. Rosalija's son wants nothing to do with the "peasant boy" who has come to live with them. In his loneliness he daydreams of his mother, his village, his favorite cherry tree, and the rainbows he would often see over them all. He is finally comforted when he envisions himself, his uncle, and the old judge Luporon all "on the same road." In his dream they are young and then old. The boy perceives the cycle of life and, it may be assumed, finds solace or acceptance in realizing that his journey from home and loved ones out into the world is one that has been experienced by others, and will be through eternity.

Stylistically, Šegedin's most unusual collection of stories is *Crni smiješak* (The Black Smile, 1969). In a series of letters to "my dear G.," the main protagonist, Charles, writes to his friend sporadically and from various locales. From his liminal vantage point in the period after World War II he ponders isolation, fear of intimacy, and the arbitrariness of fate.

The letter "Figarov pir" (translated as The Marriage of Figaro, 1967–1968) is itself a tale within a tale. Charles writes from an unnamed, presumably Croatian, island. There he is living like an animal in a stone hut and eating only what his landlords bring him. He admits that he is ill, but he is "content" to the degree that his physical isolation corresponds to his emotional state. Charles relates to G. the story of a fellow traveler whom he met on a train leaving Paris. An elderly Russian named Arkadievich is on his way to Basel to declare his love to a woman he betrayed thirty years ago. The old Russian speaks of his regret at having made this terrible mistake and of the futility of visiting his former love; she will never forgive him and is sure to reject him again. And yet he has decided to try once more. Charles is shaken by the denouement of this life story. After telling his story, the old man lies down on his seat to take a nap, has a heart attack, and dies. He never gets to Basel, and the last flicker of hope is extinguished. It is in response to this event that Charles retires to his island isolation.

"Figarov pir" is rife with intertextual allusions that provide a key to this story. Arkadievich tells Charles that he was born in Petrograd in 1867. Charles immediately makes the association to "White Nights," alluding to Fyodor Dostoyevsky's story by that name. In that work one of Dostoyevsky's dreamers contents himself with a few fleeting moments of happiness that are in fact unreal. During those magical days surrounding the summer solstice, the hero of "White Nights" (1848) imagines the possibility of Nastenka's love. When it turns out to be an illusion, he is not bitter. His dreaming encouraged him to hope. In Šegedin's story Arkadievich also allows himself to dream, and his hopes are also dashed. Charles reacts to fate's trick by rejecting society and reality. He describes himself as an insect and a fly, who writes from down under. The reader is meant to associate him with Dostoyevsky's "underground man" in *Notes from the Underground* (1864), who may represent an embittered version of the dreamer in "White Nights."

Indications that Charles suffers more from his own psychic malady and that his cynical reaction to life's vagaries is unjustified may lie in his comment that sometimes he feels that his meeting with Arkadievich never really happened at all, and also in Arkadievich's recurring reference to the fact that he was born in Petrograd in 1867. Arkadievich is referred to as an old man, and he tells Charles that he is eighty years old. The city he was born in had to be Saint Petersburg, and his reference to that city in 1947 would have to be to Leningrad. Thus, it is possible that Arkadievich and the cruel twist of his fate may be only a bad dream of Charles's. Even if this "trick" was not what the author intended, the reader can interpret this story within the context of Šegedin's other works. Like Dostoyevsky, Šegedin was skeptical about the forces that motivated humans, and he was often disappointed by human conduct. Like Dostoyevsky's characters, Šegedin's characters are often dreamers who willfully withdraw from society. But in the works of both authors, utter cynicism and alienation lead to spiritual death.

Šegedin published another novel in 1969, *Izvještaj iz pokrajine* (Report from the Province). The war serves here as the liminal locale that it is—a seedbed for morally ambivalent actions. The hero questions his responsibility in the execution of Mark, the man who was once his wife Matilda's husband. He wonders where his own guilt lies if Mark did not in fact commit treason, as had been supposed, and he questions what drew him to Mark's wife after the war. Typical of Šegedin's urban tales, the moral questions of right and wrong in this novel are not defined by the church; rather, they are questions that are confronted, although not necessarily determined, by the individual conscience.

In his fiction Šegedin mixes elements of the traditional and the modernist perspectives when he switches his stories from provincial to urban locales; he also crosses the form of the Bildungsroman with the themes of isolation and alienation; the techniques in his stories move from conventional first-person narration to interior monologues. Šegedin's work serves in Croatian literature as a bridge between the Dalmatian writers of a realistic bent who focus on describing local color and the influence of Roman Catholicism and the twentieth-century modernist writers who focus on stylistic innovation and on the repercussions of secularized urban life and the complexities of modern existence.

Šegedin has further contributed to the cultural life of the former Yugoslavia and of Croatia in his published collections of literary criticism and political essays. Included in *Riječi o riječi* (Conversation on the Word, 1969) are essays on the modern novel and poetry as well as on individual writers such as Ksaver Šandor Djalski, Vladan Desnica, and Šime Vučetić. In *Svi smo mi odgovorni* (We Are All Responsible, 1971), which contains such essays as "Problems of Our Culture," "Questions Concerning the Croatian Literary Language," and "Language and Our Reality," Šegedin speaks out for Croatian democratization. However, from his current position as an "elder statesman," he opposes the excesses of virulent nationalism that have afflicted the states of the former Yugoslavia.

Interviews:

Petar Šegedin (in conversation with Vlatko Pavletić), "Nema spasa od života ili doktor Zero nasuport pravom čoveku," *Forum*, 12 (1970): 908-944;

"An Interview of Petar Šegedin," *So Speak Croatian Dissidents* (Toronto: Zirval, 1983), pp. 63-67.

References:

Miloš I. Bandić, "Izmedju jezika i govora (Petar Šegedin)," *Letopis Matica srpske,* 4 (1971): 382-389;

Miodrag Bogićević, "Život izvan života," *Izraz,* 3 (1962): 293-297;

Branka Brlenić-Vujić, "Narativna struktura Šegedinove novele *Sveti vrag,*" *Forum,* 40 (1980): 1136-1144;

Nikola Disopra, "Dvije knjige proze Petra Šegedina," *Mogućnosti,* 1 (1970): 79-95;

Disopra, "Šegedin izmedju Zorića i Jeličića," *Mogućnosti,* 5 (1970): 520-533;

Branimir Donat, "Meditacije i krajolici," *Putevi,* 2 (1963): 193-198;

Petar Džadžić, "Šegedinov mit," *Književnost,* 10 (1954): 315-322;

Miroslav Egerić, "*Osamljenici* Petra Šegedina," *Delo,* 3 (1962): 396-401;

Dragan M. Jeremić, "Teoriski pokušaj Petra Šegedina," *Savremenik,* 1 (1956): 99-103;

Milan Mišković, "Desnicina sumnja: Kritika pjesničke vizije romana Proleća Ivan Galeba," *Izraz,* 37 (1975): 23-43;

Krešimir Nemec, "Izmedju regionalnog i univerzalnog: *Zimsko ljetovanje* Vladana Desnice," *Radovi Zavoda za slavenksu filologiju* (RZSF), 21 (1986): 57-75;

Boško Novaković, "Pripovetke Petra Šegedina," *Letopis Matica srpske,* 6 (1965): 264-268;

Bruno Popović, "Sezona u paklu," *Kritika,* 11 (1970): 225-232;

Popović, "Strah gradi čovjeka," *Mogućnosti,* 9 (1961): 925-944;

Popović, "Živjeti za pravu riječ," *Razlog,* nos. 38-39-40 (1965): 521-542;

Leona Strinić, "Svijet Petra Šegedina," *Kolo,* 9 (1971): 498-508;

Risto Trifković, "Tragovima Šegedinove pripovijetke," *Izraz,* 10 (1964): 362-366;

Pavle Zorić, "Svet bola i samoće," *Savremenik,* 6 (1959): 635-645.

Slobodan Selenić
(7 June 1933 – 27 October 1995)

Nadežda Obradović
University of Belgrade

BOOKS: *Avangardna drama* (Belgrade: Srpska književna zadruga, 1964);

Angažman u dramskoj formi (Belgrade: Prosveta, 1965);

Memoari Pere Bogalja (Belgrade: Prosveta, 1968);

Dramski pravci XX veka (Belgrade: Umetnička akademija, 1971);

Antologija savremene srpske drame (Belgrade: Srpska književna zadruga, 1977);

Prijatelji (Novi Sad: Matica srpska, 1980); republished as *Prijatelji sa Kosančićevog venca 7* (Belgrade: BIGZ, 1986);

Pismo, glava (Belgrade: Prosveta, 1982);

Očevi i oci (Belgrade: Prosveta, 1985);

Timor Mortis (Sarajevo: Svjetlost, 1989);

Ubistvo s predumišljajem (Belgrade: Prosveta, 1993).

Collection: *Drame* (Belgrade: BIGZ, 1990)—contains *Kosančićev venac*, *Ruženje naroda u dva dela,* and *Knez Pavle.*

Editions in English: *Fathers and Forefathers,* excerpt of *Očevi i oci,* translated by Ellen Elias-Bursac, *Relations,* no. 4 (1989); *North Dakota Quarterly,* 61, no. 1 (1993): 175–170;

Premeditated Murder, translated by Jelena Petrović (London: Harvill Press, 1996).

PLAY PRODUCTIONS: *Kosančićev venac 7,* Belgrade, Atelje 212, 2 March 1982;

Kosančićev venec, Skopje, Dramski teatar, 15 November 1982;

Ruženje naroda u dva dela, Belgrade, Jugoslovensko dramsko pozorište, 25 December 1987;

Knez Pavle, Belgrade, Jugoslovensko dramsko pozorište, 7 April 1991.

Slobodan Selenić is one of the most prominent contemporary Serbian writers, a novelist and playwright whose contribution to Serbian literature is indelible. In the historic year 1968, in his celebrated first novel, *Memoari Pere Bogalja* (Memoirs of Pera the Cripple), Selenić's severe criticism of his country's social order surprised

Slobodan Selenić

his readers, who were unaccustomed to such open, rigorous, sincere, and merciless critique.

Selenić was born on 7 June 1933 in Pakrac, Western Slavonia. His father, Sava, and mother, Vera, were both professors and ran a private school in Belgrade until 1941. Selenić attended the school in Belgrade and in 1956 graduated with a degree in English language and literature from Belgrade University. At that time he started reviewing theater productions and books. After graduation he also wrote theater critiques in the daily paper *Borba* (Struggle) from 1957 to 1968. In 1961 he received a scholarship and completed one year of postgraduate study in the drama department of the University of Bristol. He became the art director of Avala Film in 1963 and joined the Belgrade Drama Academy in 1965, where he was a professor for nearly thirty years and served as dean from 1981 to 1983. In 1968 and 1969, with a Ford Foundation grant, he studied playwriting. He lectured on creative writing in England and Scotland in 1979 and repeated the same course in the United States as a visiting professor in 1984. From 1988 to 1990 Selenić was president of the Federation of Yugoslav Writers prior to its demise; he resigned complaining that "the effort and time which he as a citizen of Yugoslavia invested so that one of its institutions would function, was in vain" and that "cooperation is obviously not possible with those who do not wish to cooperate." He died on 27 October 1995, leaving several unfinished works, including an unfinished novel.

Selenić first appeared on the literary scene in 1958 with a lengthy short story, "Ko je stranac?" (Who Is the Stranger?). The story has an interesting plot. A man comes to a crossroad and flips a coin to see which direction to take. On the one side, marriage and children await him; on the other side, the same. Thus, regardless of which road he takes, his destiny is predetermined.

Selenić's first novel, *Memoari Pere Bogalja*, appeared ten years later, in 1968, the historic year of student revolts against the "red bourgeoisie" all over Western and Eastern Europe, when students were demanding human rights and democracy and were rising against injustice, party privileges, lies, brainwashing, and political divisions. The novel offers a severe criticism of the new order established after World War II, of the "new class" of newcomers and former villagers who took over Belgrade after the war and assumed high positions and power. They became a privileged class who swept away the bourgeois stratum in the cities. Parvenus, an erosion of morality, and a loss of ethical values characterized these newcomers. To quote Predrag Palavestra in his *Književnost-kritika ideologije* (1991), "Selenić's bourgeois world is destroyed by opponents of the patriarchal morality and family values, by people from lower ranks and from the world without God, by a dreary, tormented, famished and cruel man who in his struggle for a bigger morsel and less deprivation is encouraged to become arrogant and thereby is transformed from a wretch into a crude revenger."

The protagonist and narrator, Pera, lost his legs as a child. His Serbian family was driven out of their home one night, along with other Serbs of the village, and their homes were burned down by the Croatian *Ustasha*. After the Serbs fled into the forest, Pera's father became their leader. The main action of the novel starts much later, after World War II, when Pera's

Cover for Selenić's novel Ubistvo s predumišljajem *(Premeditated Murder), which interweaves two love stories against the background of the 1990s civil war in the former Yugoslavia*

family moves to Belgrade. His father becomes a general in the new army. Pera, who had spent the entire war years on the back of his mother, is obsessed with the world of the "legged." He becomes an enthusiastic advocate of new ideas, values, and aims, seeing in his father—the experienced communist—a torchbearer of idealism. Then Draga appears, a daughter of the former government's minister who, as a young girl of sixteen, had fled the country with the king. She and Pera diligently study all the holy books of Marxism and Leninism. She lives in his household. Pera's first suspicions of the idealistic world of the new order coincide with the discovery of his father's affair with Draga, which makes him conscious of his own deep love for her. Draga becomes pregnant, and to prevent the child from being born out of wedlock, and to protect his father, Pera marries Draga and is sent abroad, leaving Draga behind. She becomes the center of the household. The big flat gradually becomes the showcase of the new class, with period furniture, expensive carpets, maids, cars, and travels abroad. The novel ends tragically. Pera's mother commits suicide because the happenings in her house clash with her moral beliefs. The boy also commits suicide by drowning, never accepting Pera's claim that he is the father. Pera's father is destroyed by the events, and Pera's suppressed love for his mother, to whom he always referred as "Stinker," emerges.

The novel *Prijatelji* (Friends, 1980) also shows the conflict between the old ways and the new. On the one hand, there is Vladan Hadžislavković, the last member of an affluent merchant family, a book-oriented, self-examining intellectual steeped in English literature and language, a sickly Belgrade bourgeois with a peculiar weakness (suppressed homosexuality). On the other hand there is an Albanian, Istref Veri, a strong, healthy, dynamic, ambitious boy. A most unlikely friendship develops between Vladan, a proprietor of a sumptuous house at Kosancic Circle 7, and Istref, the woodsawer living in the coal cellar. Vladan leads Istref with a gentle hand, educating him by teaching him how to behave, how to speak, and what to read, and he pays for his education. Under Vladan's guidance and helped by circumstances, Istref completes his schooling and becomes a man of the new order. Vladan's spacious home is nationalized and inhabited by shameless, selfish, rude, mean, petty, envious, career-loving, ambitious newcomers from many nationalities. Their misbehavior, deficiencies, and greediness are contrasted with Vladan's old-fashioned, patriarchal, high values. Vladan, rejected as an old glove by the tenants of his own house and by his beloved Istref, who joined the crowd, flees the house, his soul wounded by his pupil. At the end Istref becomes an engineer, the father of seven children, and a deputy.

The language used in *Prijatelji* is worth noting. At the beginning Istref speaks Albanian and very little Serbian, but through his companionship with Vladan and his night courses after a hard day's work, he masters the language of his new surroundings. The parlance of the other tenants of the house is nationally colored: Macedonian, Slovenian, rural Serbian, slang, and the language of uneducated people. In contrast, Vladan's speech is concise, accurate, sophisticated, and enriched by English phrases. Selenić adapted his novel into a play, *Prijatelji sa Kosančićevog venca 7* (Friends from the Kosančić Circle 7), and all subsequent editions of the novel carry that title.

The next novel, *Pismo, glava* (Head, Tails, 1982), continues in the same vein, criticizing the new order and lamenting the passing of the old. Using four narrators who all speak in the first person, Selenić juxtaposes the past and the present. The past is embodied in Maximilian–"Maki," an offspring of a well-to-do Belgrade family, a sensitive, educated, intelligent, but sickly young man suffering from juvenile diabetes. The present is represented by his antipode, Radiša, son of a milkman, a strong, energetic, rough young man who joins the new order and becomes one of its strongmen. The plot covers the years immediately prior to World War II, then the occupation and the crucial year of 1948, when the break with Joseph Stalin occurs. In the home of Maximilian's father, an affluent Belgrade intellectual, lives, along with his own family, Zlata, a relative, and Radiša, whom the family took in to educate. The calm, loving family life is interrupted by the arrival of Slišković, a communist who by his firm belief in the new ideology affects the father, who also accepts the communist ideology, for which he pays later with his own life. A deep, sincere comradeship and love develop between Maximilian and Zlata. The years of well-being prior to the war are followed by occupation, poverty, and hardships. Radiša, who joined the liberation struggle, works after the war as a secret service agent. In 1948, when the breach in the Communist Party occurs, Slišković, a high political official, approaches Maximilian in an attempt to attract Radiša to the Soviet faction. This leads to the imprisonment of Maki and his hearings, tortures, and death from the lack of insulin. It also sends Slišković to the notorious political labor camp, from which he returns a changed, broken man. From a fanatical communist he becomes a religious fanatic, living in extreme poverty. Radiša and Zlata marry, but their marriage is permanently haunted by the image of the dead Maki. Even after twenty years he is very much alive in both of them through their son, whom they have named Maki. They live an estranged, taciturn, distanced life. Her son takes after his father and sides with him amid the marital intolerance of two entirely different people. Zlata commits suicide. In a way her life ended with Maki's death, for which she blames herself.

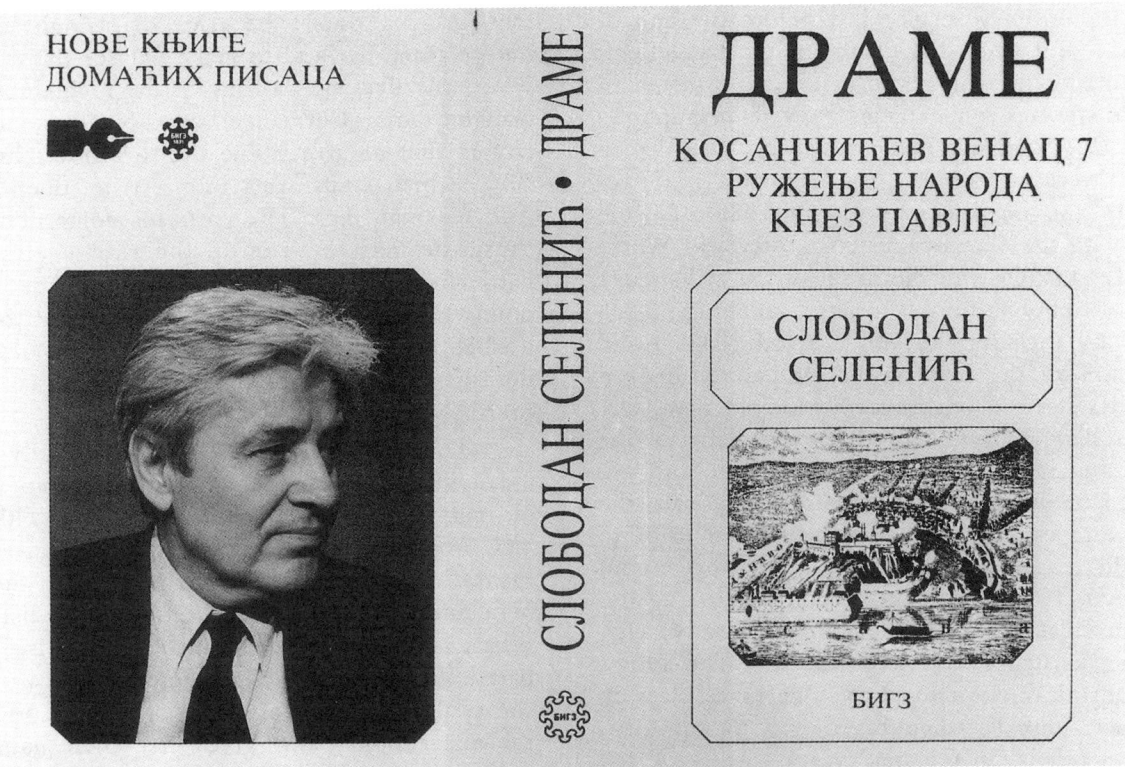

Dust jacket for Drame, a collection of Selenić's plays that includes Kosančić Venac (Konsančić Circle), Ruženje naroda u dva dela (Reprimanding of People in Two Parts), and Knez Pavle (Prince Paul)

The novel *Očevi i oci* (Fathers and Forefathers, 1985), perhaps Selenić's best work, depicts the disappearance of a Serbian bourgeois class that is unable to oppose the totalitarian ideologies of bolshevism and fascism. The demise is embodied in Stevan Medaković, a Belgrade University professor trained in England, married to an Englishwoman, and accepting English customs and manners, with connections to the highest strata of Serbian society. Before the war he had access to the royal court, drank tea with Prince Pavle and with foreign diplomats, and attended receptions and balls, yet he rejected political identification with the regime. By keeping himself aloof from the actual political happenings in Serbia, he and others like him allowed their opponents to take the helm of history. In Medaković's unwillingness to be involved in political affairs Selenić sees the roots of the destruction of their class.

The backdrop of the novel is the comparison of two cultures, Western Protestantism and Balkan Orthodoxy. At the beginning the reader sees a young, diligent, curious student, Stevan, attending an English university, strangely affected by foreign mores and customs that clash with his strict patriarchal upbringing; he has been brought up in the spirit of great historical events, and he has been imbued with the suffering of his people. His wet nurse, a simple woman from the people, instilled with patriarchal values and traditions and permeated with the spirit of patriotism and national poetry, sees herself as a guardian of the national ancestry and customs and was strict in bringing up the young boy in the same spirit, so that Stevan observes Englishmen and their way of life through her eyes. But Selenić brings in another actor—an intelligent English girl, Elizabeth, who, once married to Stevan, cannot understand either his language or his customs. She gradually learns the language of her new country and accepts the mores of her surroundings, yet she views her husband critically; he has opinions about everything and knows everything but does not act, though aware of pernicious political events, to right wrongs. Their only son clearly sees that he differs from others by his looks, education, and manners. To blend with his surroundings and to be one with his friends, he rejects his former values instilled by his parents and adopts the values of his new environment. To prove that he is "like them," he volunteers for military service just before the end of the war and finds his death on the battlefield, condemning his parents to a life encapsulated in their memories while trying in vain to suppress them. *Očevi i oci* was made into a play and had a great success.

In the novel *Timor Mortis* (1989), Selenić deals with the occupation of Yugoslavia in World War II, starting with the death of the protagonist Dragan's parents during the first bombing of Belgrade by the Germans on 6 April 1941. Amid the ruins of the mass grave Dragan, a medical student, meets a one-hundred-year-old man, Slobodan Blagojević, a retired lawyer. Between the meek student and the old man a close and unusual friendship grows. Together they pass the three and one-half years of occupation prior to the old man's death. Through the story about this man Selenić presents the history, tragedy, and survival of the inhabitants of his native city, Pakrac, located in Western Slavonia. The author skillfully develops two plots. One takes place in the last century, when Blagojević, a prominent Serbian official in Croatia, was a witness of and a participant in the parliamentary skirmishes in Zagreb during the largely successful attempts to erase the Serbian name, language, and population. From the news clippings quoted in the novel one sees the roots of the misfortune that befell the Serbs from the areas under Croatian control, as when, for example, Serbs attending church were slaughtered and thrown into a pit or when a whole household of Blagojević's cousins were gunned down because their neighbor, a member of the Ustasha, coveted their nice house. The years of occupation, famine, cold, public hanging of the partisans in the center of Belgrade, everyday predicaments, and the struggle for sheer survival are presented without pathos. The change in the lives of the two men occurs when Bilja, a young peasant woman, comes to their house. At the beginning she is the object of spite, contempt, and hate by both men, because she is satisfying the German soldiers; but soon a friendship develops and they help each other, spending hours together.

The author's sympathies are with Bilja, a naive, rural harlot, almost a child, good-hearted and resourceful, who seems as if she wanted to atone for her sexual favors with the occupation officers through her good intentions and deeds. Through her goodness and generosity many children from her neighborhood were able to have heat to survive the severe winters of the occupation. Dragan's feelings toward Bilja are ambivalent. At the outset he tries to straighten her out—to teach her and to make her see the mud in which she lives by dancing in the nightclubs and bringing home German officers; but he soon discovers that an irresistible desire attracts him to Bilja, which transforms into a true, deep love. The old man dies. The partisans come. The enthusiastic masses clear up the rubble after the battle for the liberation of Belgrade. Bilja is denounced and is to be taken to prison, but the unleashed mob intercepts her on the street and kills her brutally, proving once again that violence breeds violence.

The language in the novel is carefully studied, giving each character a distinct flavor. The old man, a polyglot, enriches his speech with foreign words, so that Dragan refers to him as "Illustrissimus," the most illustrious, while the old man addresses him as "Auditore," the listener. Bilja's language is the most colorful; it is syncopated, the language of an uneducated woman; she swallows the initial letters of a word, uses rural expressions, and gives her own name to every person with whom she becomes acquainted. All this enhances the artistic quality and the attractiveness of the work.

The novel *Ubistvo s predumišljajem* (1993, translated as *Premeditated Murder*, 1996) is set in the early 1990s. Unlike previous works by Selenić, it interweaves two love stories, separated by some fifty years, of two Jelenas, one the present-day heroine and the other her grandmother. The contemporary Jelena, a student of dramatic arts with dreams of becoming a writer, finds in a cupboard a diary of her grandmother, Jelena, and some other writings. The writings are interesting; the heroine sees in them material for a book; and she starts looking for people who knew her relatives. She learns that her grandmother was brought up in the home of her stepfather, together with his son, Jovan, with whom she later had a three-year sexual relationship. She also had an affair with the police colonel, Krsman, a conceited representative of the new privileged class. This first Jelena becomes pregnant, but who fathered her child, Jovan or Krsman, remains a mystery. Emulating her grandmother, the younger Jelena has a love affair with a university graduate who is a wounded veteran of the 1993 civil war; the affair grows into a deep mutual love. The book ends in a typical Selenić fashion—tragically: Jovan rapes Jelena, kills Krsman, and commits suicide. The granddaughter's beloved student perishes on the battlefield, after which she leaves everything behind and goes to her mother in New Zealand.

The innovation in this novel is its subject matter—the civil war of the 1990s. Distance, considered by many indispensable in treating historical events, is dispensed with, and the news and information about the actual war and its casualties permeate the book. The description of the recent civil war provides a strong element of authenticity in that Selenić skillfully relates the present conflict to the killings of fifty years before, thus demonstrating that history moves in circles and repeats itself. The differentiation of characters' speech was drawn here even more saliently than in the previous novels. The younger Jelena uses the Belgrade slang, replete with abuses and curses; Krsman uses the new language of the victorious uneducated class; the older Jelena uses the standard parlance of the educated bourgeoisie of her time.

Almost all of Selenić's works have been rewritten for the stage, with some showing greater differences from their novel sources than others. Selenić has also written two original plays. *Ruženje naroda u dva dela* (Reprimanding of People in Two Parts, 1987) uses the unity of place to achieve its purpose. Selenić places in one prison cell the state's enemies who fought as the nationalists, or *Chetniks,* in World War II, together with some partisans who had committed offenses. In the limited space of a cell all kinds of characters are brought together: high intellectuals and peasants, assassins condemned to long terms, womanizers, drunk party officers, and a prison director. They debate and argue, scold and fight, trying to get an insight into the past, to find reasons for their own behavior and that of the people around them, and for their misfortune. All of them blame the Serbian people for their characteristic intolerance and their disagreements among themselves. The play ends tragically and surprisingly: the high intellectual kills the assassin who had killed many people and who had humiliated the intellectual by accusing him of being a police denouncer.

The play *Knez Pavle* (Prince Paul, 1990) differs in several ways from his previous plays. While in the earlier ones the protagonists are ordinary people, in *Knez Pavle* the main characters are high personages—the kings of Serbia and England and high officials of Croatia and Germany. The plot evolves during the crisis of 1939–1941, when Yugoslavia faced a crucial dilemma: sign the treaty with Nazi Germany and save hundreds of thousands of lives, or subject the country to war and devastation. Prince Paul opted for the first solution, but the people rose up, bringing about war and the flight of the king and his family to England. The country and its people were left to their tragic destiny.

With his six novels and five plays Selenić has become a well-known and widely read author. Almost all his works have gone through several editions. His fiction and his plays feature a wealth of topics, a boldness in grappling with taboo subjects, the viewing of history in new ways and of everyday life from unusual angles, a sharpness of focus, a vivacity, a novelty in composition, and a realistic creation of a variety of types of speech—all of which have contributed to the writer's outstanding reputation. The value of his creativity was confirmed by his receiving several literary awards: in 1969 he was awarded the October Prize of Belgrade for *Memoari Pere Bogalja;* in 1980 he received the NIN Award for the novel of the year, *Prijatelji;* in 1981 he won the National Library of Serbia Award for the most widely read book, *Prijatelji;* in 1988 he won the Sterija Prize for the best play for his *Ruženje naroda u dva dela;* and in 1989 he won the Meša Selimović Prize for the book of the year, *Timor Mortis.*

Selenić took upon himself the role of a chronicler of Belgrade, the city where nearly all his novels and plays are set. At the time when Borghesian literature, avant-garde writings, magic realism, and, later, minimalism and postmodernism were in vogue, Selenić opted for a traditional and realistic approach to his subjects. He is also a political writer who explores ideas and taboo subjects. His novels serve as a platform from which he presents his views, opinions, political stances, and especially his strong, unswerving criticism of the new social order that dominated in his country after World War II up to the 1990s. He deeply and openly regrets the disappearance of the middle-class stratum of his country. His lament over the toppling of the bourgeoisie in Serbia by the liberation struggle from 1941 to 1945 is genuine.

Selenić's background in dramatic theory is reflected in his fiction, which has an eminently theatrical structure. He portrays two worlds in conflict: the disappearing old world and the new world that is unmercifully imposing itself. The author's sympathies are obviously with the old world. As if to soften his subjective preferences, Selenić brands his protagonists: one is crippled; one is a suppressed homosexual; another has been a diabetic from his childhood; yet another is uprooted from his people; and one is lame. A further feature of Selenić's books is the tragic ending of his characters, be it by suicide, killing by a mob, death in prison, or perishing on the battlefield. But his heroes and heroines are not to blame for their destinies; they are victims of historical circumstances and, as such, are passive, helpless, and hopeless. Selenić, however, does not use his works solely to voice his own ideas; instead, he explores in them a range of ideas. Eschewing experimentation, Selenić became a leading writer in contemporary Serbian literature. As Predrag Palavestra writes, "Selenić is a writer who brings back the belief in the story and who appreciates the action, relations and characters in the novel."

References:
Miloš I. Bandić, "Roman i romansijeri u godini 1968: Slobodan Novak, Slobodan Selenić, Dragoslav Mihailović," *Letopis Matice srpske,* 403, no. 3 (1969): 320-336;

Snežana Brajović, "Staro i novo: Slobodan Selenić, *Prijatelji,*" *Književnost,* 71, nos. 5-6 (1981): 1035-1039;

Petar Džadžić, "Čisti i prljavi: *Memoari Pere Bogalja,*" in his *Kritike i ogledi* (Belgrade: Srpska književna zadruga, 1973), pp. 151-154;

Džadžić, "Romani Slobodana Selenića: Svet promene i vraćanja," in his *Homo Balcanicus, Homo Heroicus* (Belgrade: BIGZ, 1987), pp. 296-346;

Miroslav Egerić, "Ispovest jednog koji je verovao," in his *Ljudi, knjige, datumi* (Novi Sad: Matica srpska, 1971), pp. 147-154;

Ivan V. Lalić, "Jedan dan života i smrti kentaura: *Memoari Pere Bogalja,*" *Književnost,* 48, no. 3 (1969): 308-311;

Mateja Matejić, "On the Contemporary Yugoslav Novel," *Canadian Slavic Studies,* 5 (1971): 362-382;

Borislav Mihajlović-Mihiz, "Slobodan Selenić: *Memoari Pere Bogalja,*" in his *Književni razgovori* (Belgrade: Srpska književna zadruga, 1971), pp. 241-246;

Predrag Palavestra, *Književnost—kritika ideologije* (Belgrade: Srpska književna zadruga, 1991), pp. 166-190;

Feliks Pašić, "Serbian Divisions: Slobodan Selenić, *Ruženje naroda u dva dela,*" *Scena,* no. 12 (1989): 10-15.

Meša Selimović
(26 April 1910 – 11 July 1982)

Thomas J. Butler
Cambridge, Massachusetts

BOOKS: *Prva četa* (Zagreb: Zora, 1950);
Tišine (Sarajevo: Svjetlost, 1961);
Tudja zemlja (Sarajevo: Veselin Masleša, 1962);
Magla i mjesečina (Sarajevo: Svjetlost, 1965);
Eseji i ogledi (Sarajevo: Veselin Masleša, 1966);
Derviš i smrt (Sarajevo: Svjetlost, 1966);
Za i protiv Vuka (Novi Sad: Matica srpska, 1967);
Tvrdjava (Sarajevo: Svjetlost, 1970);
Djevojka crvene kose (Sarajevo: Svjetlost, 1970);
Ostrvo (Belgrade: Prosveta, 1974);
Sjećanja (Belgrade/Rijeka: Sloboda/Otokar Keršovani, 1976).

Collections: *Sabrana dela* (Belgrade/Rijeka: Sloboda/Otokar Keršovani, 1975);
Sabrana dela, 1–10 (Belgrade: Sloboda, 1979).

Editions in English: *The Island,* translated by Jeanie Shaterian (Toronto: Serbian Heritage Academy, 1983);
Death and the Dervish, translated by Bogdan Rakić and Stephen M. Dickey (Evanston: Northwestern University Press, 1996).

Meša Selimović was born on 26 April 1910 in Tuzla, Bosnia. His father, a merchant, was of the upper, or *aga,* class, so Meša and his siblings knew neither want nor hardship during their early years. It was probably from his father that Meša absorbed a certain noblesse that he carried with him throughout his life. In his memoir, *Sjećanja* (Memories, 1976), a book full of simplicity and wisdom, Selimović makes it clear that his was an extremely dysfunctional family in which the son obtained an "audience" with his dissipated, womanizing father only during special religious feasts such as Bajram, when all six children would line up outside their father's study, waiting their turn to go in and kiss his hand. Selimović, who suffered before, during, and after such meetings, suggests that this was the beginning of his lifelong hatred of authority. Selimović also mentions that once, when his illness happened to coincide with that of one of his father's

Meša Selimović

favorite dogs, his father was full of solicitude about the dog but never came to inquire about his son. On the other hand, Selimović provides a loving portrait of his mother, who kept the family together through "thick and thin." In spite of the family's upper-class status, Selimović was not shielded from the proletariat of Tuzla. He claims he learned from his father's coachmen and stable boys a more earthly Serbo-Croatian than he heard at home. He also associated with the sons of miners who lived in ramshackle huts in the village of Tušanj.

Selimović both praises and condemns his

early education. He seems to have loved and respected most of his high-school teachers and emphasizes that his school was no ordinary provincial school. He says: "If we their students have accomplished anything in life, we owe it to these brave and gifted people." On the other hand, he has nothing good to say about his religion teacher, a certain Tribo, a Moslem doctoral graduate of Al-Azhar University in Cairo, who was a tyrant and a hypochondriac. This man made a substantial contribution to Selimović's rebelliousness, helping engender in him an atheism he evidently preserved to the end of his life.

One incident nearly spelled the end to Selimović's high-school education. He had written a paper questioning the doctrine of free will, basing his conclusions on the ideas of the French writer, Jean-Baptiste Lamarck. Some of his teachers wanted to expel him, including Tribo, but the Catholic priest, Drago D., argued successfully for his reinstatement. Of Father Drago, Selimović writes: "He was always our intercessor, always on our side, even when we were guilty, and we didn't forget it, even though he scolded us afterwards when we were alone." The future novelist portrays the priest's tolerance in terms that would have pleased the eighteenth-century French philosophe: "He spoke well of all religions—they are all good and noble, God is always of the same essence."

It was this same Drago D. whose behavior during World War II provided Selimović with insight into the inscrutability of the human mind and the inconsistency of human behavior, as he became the local *Ustaša* (Croatian Fascist Party) chief, sending Serbs and Jews to their deaths at the concentration camp of Jasenovac. One of Drago D.'s victims was a colleague, Danilo Salom, a Jewish teacher of mathematics. Young *Ustaša* students of Salom were sent to get him, beating him in his home and on the street. Drago D. was executed by the partisans at the end of the war. "He was shot one dark October morning when our units liberated Tuzla, in 1944.... That inglorious wartime end to a life, which until 1941 had seemed completely pure, troubled me considerably."

Selimović moved to Belgrade in 1929 to begin his studies at the University of Belgrade. He worked little his first year, spending his evenings in *kafanas* (coffeehouses) and bars and losing money at cards. But the world economic crisis bankrupted his father, destroying the family wealth and forcing the young Meša to give up his carefree ways. He became a boarder at a Moslem student dormitory, appropriately called *Gajret* (Arabic for "zeal"), supported by a charitable Bosnian society of the same name. Selimović praises his literature teachers, Pavle and Bogdan Popović, who helped create the "Belgrade style" of writing, modeled on literary French. But he admits that he was not a particularly diligent student; he found the political scene far more exciting. It was here that he came to grips with his own inhibitions toward public debate—an excessive fear that pained him throughout his life. Yet in spite of his inhibition, Selimović claims he was normal in every other way, a good athlete, "in love with girls, in love with Belgrade, in love with life!" It was also during his college years that Selimović became a communist fellow traveler, associating with Milovan Djilas and the Moslem Hasan Brkić, also from Bosnia. Brkić instructed Selimović to join key student organizations and to get elected to leadership positions so the party could influence their policies. Yet the same distrust of authority that attracted him to the revolutionary movement in the first place also kept him from joining the party at that time. When Brkić asked him to become a member, Selimović declined, noting that he did not want to lose his independence:

> That's what I said to Hasan Brkić. Hasan remembered that during the War, he didn't forgive or forget my youthful vagary, even though we were good friends. Whether for this remark, or because others too saw my peculiarities, there was always in my party file, from 1941 to 1951, that I was an intellectual and an individualist—a totally negative characterization.

After receiving his degree in Serbo-Croatian literature from Belgrade University in 1934, Selimović returned to his native Tuzla, where he began to teach literature in his old high school. He taught there for seven years, during which time he was the only support of his family. All of the Selimović children, including his two brothers and three sisters, were either members of the Communist Party or *skojevci* (Communist Youth). When war between Germany and the Soviet Union broke out in June 1941, they quickly became involved in the resistance against the Nazis and the Croatian fascist state that had taken over Bosnia. Selimović says they felt obliged to become active because of the *Ustaša* genocide against the Serbs and Jews in Bosnia. With his brothers and sisters Selimović smuggled supplies to the partisans, listened to foreign radio broadcasts, and disseminated news from the Eastern front. Their house became a safe house for communist "illegals" on the run. Eventually Selimović and his sisters were imprisoned, narrowly escaping being sent to the death camp at Jasenovac. Selimović has stated about this period: "My strongest impressions of the war are connected with my imprisonment, and it is them I remember most often."

Selimović left Tuzla in 1943 to join the Partisan resistance in the field. He was assigned to Brkić, who was head of agitprop for Eastern Bosnia. Selimović tells how Brkić burst out laughing when he read a propaganda leaflet he had prepared. Selimović had tried to be original, quoting the Russian poet Demjan Bednyj and avoiding clichés like "workers, peasants, honored intelligentsia." But Brkić explained to him that "repetition means security—it instills calm in the person who reads or listens, training him to move within a circle of recognized concepts. It is very important for psychological conviction."

"When I told him," says Selimović, "that this was the technique and psychology of prayer, he answered that this was correct, and I shouldn't be ironic about it." Selimović claims that he never heard the psychology of propaganda explained so convincingly, as by Brkić that day in the hills of eastern Bosnia. Their discussion, related in *Sjećanja,* highlights a crucial difference in the attitudes of these two men toward human individuality. After the war Brkić rose to positions of power in the new government, while for Selimović another rebellion lay ahead.

In November 1944, as the war in Yugoslavia drew toward its close, Šefkija Selimović, Meša's older brother and battalion commander, was executed by a Partisan firing squad for having removed a few pieces of furniture from a public warehouse. He had intended to replace his own furniture, stolen by the *Ustaša*. It was publicly announced that Šefkija was shot to set an example, because he was from a well-known communist family. The news of his brother's execution stunned Selimović, but it did not prevent him from giving a scheduled political lecture a few days later. It was this fanatical adherence to duty, in the face of deep personal sorrow, that Selimović could not forgive himself later, when it seemed to him that he had placed party loyalty above love for his brother. In a real sense he had temporarily become the kind of reflexive automaton Brkić wanted him to be. It is this moment of self-degradation that Selimović has in mind when he writes in *Derviš i smrt* (Death and the Dervish, 1966): "What am I now? Stunted brother or unsure dervish? Have I lost my human love or have I weakened my faith, thus losing everything?"

Selimović gives few details of Šefkija's death, but it does seem possible that his brother had exhibited some of that same individualism and patrician nonchalance that were characteristic of Selimović himself. He had evidently made enemies who finished him off when they saw their chance. It was this confrontation with the old Balkan tribal mores that struck Selimović to the quick, when he was forced to accept not only the loss of his brother but the shattering of the ideals on which he had based his life for fifteen years.

At the end of 1944 Selimović moved to Belgrade, where he was assigned to the War Crimes Commission as head of its publications unit. He also helped establish a new magazine, *Naša književnost* (Our Literature), in which he published a few short stories about the war, including his first story "Pjesma u oluji" ("Song in the Storm"). He married a *partizanka,* in what was perhaps an impetuous attempt to keep from breaking with his Communist past. This marriage lasted less than a year; Selimović then left his pregnant wife for Darka, the daughter of a prewar Serbian general who had died at Dachau. Darka was the writer's salvation. As he told one interviewer: "I can say that without her I wouldn't have written anything."

Selimović's rejection of a *partizanka* for the daughter of a royalist general was certainly among the most politically incorrect things he could have done, according to the code of morality prevailing in Yugoslavia after the war, a code later described by Djilas in his *Anatomija jednog morala* (Anatomy of a Morality, 1954). Selimović was fired from his job and dismissed from the party, and in 1947 he and Darka set out for Sarajevo to begin a new life.

Like Ivo Andrić's forced exile to Bosnia during World War I, Selimović's return to his native soil was crucial to his development as a writer. For the next ten years he, Darka, and their two little girls lived from hand to mouth, with Selimović borrowing from his friend Risto Trifković every month before payday. Selimović worked at a variety of jobs and wrote at night. His first volume of short stories was lost at the publisher's (it was the only copy he had), yet with Darka's encouragement he kept writing, and in 1950 he published his first collection, *Prva četa* (First Company).

From the beginning Selimović worked at developing his own style, his own voice, shunning the dictates of socialist realism. The early stories

Dust jacket for the translation of Selimović's 1974 novel, Ostrvo, which contains meditations on life, aging, and death

are reminiscent of Ernest Hemingway and Erich Maria Remarque: short sentences with beautiful, careful description and dialogue without circumstantial details to interrupt the flow of words. But Selimović was not satisfied. After the publication of his first book, he spent most of the next decade studying the novel form while continuing to search for his own voice. During this quest he seems to have been particularly influenced by Albert Camus, Jean-Paul Sartre, Thomas Wolfe, and Fyodor Dostoyevsky. Meanwhile, he was appointed editor of *Svjetlost* (Light) publishing house, where he published editions of the poetry of Branko Radičević, Jovan Dučić, and T. S. Eliot, the plays of Anton Chekhov, and the folk songs of the First and Second Serbian Uprisings.

In 1961 Selimović's first novel, *Tišine* (Silences), appeared. This is the first work in which the theme of his lost brother appears, although it is partly muffled. The novel opens near the end of the war as an unnamed partisan soldier is on his way back to Belgrade. He wonders whether his brother is still alive. Boarding a darkened train with his friend Duško, he thinks:

> Maybe my brother is among these people. He had been in prison, in a camp ... but now I can't find him. I only hear rumors. I know what Duško is asking me–Do you really think you will find him? Yes, I think I will. It's impossible that I won't find him. I loved him more than myself, or at least as much as myself. He is too good, too handsome, too dear not to be any more.

He and Duško walk through the aisles of the train, calling for his brother in the dark. This illogical but sad stunt, typical of young men suddenly released from extreme pressure, emphasizes how deeply Selimović was troubled by the injustice of his brother's death seventeen years earlier. Elsewhere in the novel the hero interrogates himself regarding his brother's death:

> And your brother? How did your brother die?
> He died in battle. He was a battalion commander.
> He perished, he died, he disappeared, he was shot during a charge, he fell into an enemy ambush, he was killed by a mine, slaughtered with a knife, as though he had ten lives and had lost them one by one. There were rumors that our forces had shot him, somewhere at the other end of our country, because of some insubordination, because of his stubbornness. I had barely heard those unsure reasons. I won't believe that, I can't, he's better than I,

and thousands of others on our side, no, not at all, that is madness, he died in battle, or he's still alive, I'll find him perhaps.

He was headstrong, they say. Yes, that's him. But you don't shoot a man for that. I'll find him if he's alive, I'll find his grave if he died, in an attack.

Reworked in 1965 and given more plot, *Tišine* is noteworthy for its lack of partisan chest-beating and for its honesty about returning veterans—their difficulty in expressing and accepting love, their cynicism toward civilians. One is reminded of Hemingway's lost generation, but this is not imitation: the details and atmosphere are consistent with Belgrade after World War II. Because it is written in first person, unlike his earlier short stories, this novel represents a big step toward the kind of inner psychological exploration, akin at times to the Bosnian *zanos* (ecstasy) that characterizes Selimović's later style.

Selimović's next major work, *Magla i mjesečina* (Fog and Moonlight, 1965), was an experimental novel in which he tried to present the psychological totality of a situation by viewing it through the simultaneous inner monologues of the main characters: a partisan commander, a farmer (his brother), the farmer's wife, and a young city-bred partisan with whom the wife falls in love. In the end the farmer and the young partisan are killed by the Germans, and the woman buries them together. There is no illumination, no increase in understanding, no epiphany in this work, but a nagging sense that this partisan activity is disjointed and meaningless in the eyes of the civilian bystanders who are anchored to real life. The grimness of the story is mitigated by the beautiful writing, the descriptions of countryside, and the sensitive shadings of feeling one would not expect to find in a novel about war, written in a land with a heroic epic tradition.

None of Selimović's stories and novels about war inspired more than a modest response from the reading public. This can be partly explained by his own fears of personal disclosure, as well as by the fact that by comparison to more-popular war writers such as Mihailo Lalić and Dobrica Ćosić he was psychologically ahead of his time. But when his next novel, *Derviš i smrt*, appeared in 1966, the Yugoslav public was ready for him. The novel was an instantaneous success, with four editions in the first two years. Set in eighteenth-century Sarajevo, *Derviš i smrt* transcends its time frame as Selimović tries once again to treat the pain of his brother's death.

The main protagonist, Ahmed Nurudin, whose name means "light of the faith," is the sheikh or chief dervish of a branch of the Mawlawi sect of whirling dervishes. Nurudin learns that his brother has been imprisoned and visits the local (*kadi*, judge), (*muselim*, police chief), and mufti, trying to effect his release. Each time he meets with either indifference or threat. The sheikh's faith in the Ottoman system gradually weakens until finally he learns that his brother has been executed. As he says:

> Twenty years I've been a dervish. I went away to school as a little child, and all I know is what they chose to teach me.... I always knew what I was supposed to do–the dervish order thought for me.... And you see, it happened that misfortune struck my brother. I don't like violence, I think it's a sign of weakness. But when it was done to others I kept silent, I refused to condemn, even admitting that sometimes evil must be done for the greater good. But when the whip of power struck my brother, it also cut me to the quick.... I know that boy, he is incapable of crime. But you see, I don't defend him strongly enough, and I don't justify them; it only seems to me that they have done evil to me, too, almost equally hurt me, confronted me with life outside my true orbit, forced me to take a stand.

One is never certain whether it is grief for his brother or anger at the insult to his position, or a combination of the two, that forces the dervish to act. He plants the seeds of a local rebellion; the *kadi* is killed; and he takes over as judge. In time, under the influence of traditional procedures, such as the use of spies and informers, he becomes like his ruthless predecessor, falls victim to intrigue, and as the novel ends he is waiting in prison to be garroted.

Derviš i smrt is the story of the conflict between ideology and life, between power and love. For Selimović the eighteenth-century setting is only a stage on which he shows what would have happened to him if he had been able to take the road to power and had waited to take revenge on his brother's murderers. (He surely must have had moments when he wrestled with the idea of seeking some form of retaliation.) Yet he demonstrates through his art that had he been capable of following in his agitprop mentor Brkić's footsteps and had he been able to reach a position of power, he would have surely become in the end like those he despised and died spiritually, if not physically, like the dervish. In this sense *Derviš i smrt* was a catharsis, not only for Selimović but for all Yugoslavs who suffered injustice during the war and after. This fact, along with the beauty of its style and its contemporary, existential mood, helps explain why the novel won universal acclaim, its author gaining the coveted Njegoš Prize in 1969, which is awarded only once every three years.

Selimović's second major novel, *Tvrdjava* (The Fortress, 1970), is about modern-day alienation and its healing through the power of love. The author himself states, in an epilogue to the novel:

> The fortress is every man, every society, every state, every ideology. The main hero wants to find a bridge to other people, to come out of the fortress, because he knows we are being split apart and destroyed by hatred, and only love will sustain us, or at least the faith that some sort of understanding is possible between individuals and society. Guided by that faith and desire ... he remains morally pure.

Just as *Derviš i smrt* narrates Selimović's personal experience of the loss of his brother, his grief, and symbolic death, so *Tvrdjava* expresses Selimović's resurrection through his love for Darka. Set in seventeenth-century Sarajevo, the story uses names and details from Mula Mustafa Bašeskija's *Ljetopis* (Chronicle, 1746–1804) while mirroring Selimović's own move to Sarajevo with Darka in 1947 and their struggle to survive. His hero, Ahmet Šabo, is a returned veteran who marries a Christian (Tijana) and is refused work because of his criticism of the local ruling circles. He is helped to survive by his friend Mulla Ibrihim, a scribe, whose life he had saved during the battle of Khotin.

Like *Derviš i smrt*, *Tvrdjava* is written in first person, which gives the novel a different tone from that provided by the omniscient narrator in Andrić's works. Selimović's Ahmet Šabo has a tortured sensitivity to the evil that is happening around him and a stubborn unwillingness to accept Evil as a cosmic force on a parity with Good. Thus in this novel Selimović transcends the absurd, restores a redemptive power to the universe (love), and thereby meaning, while rejecting the fatalism and autochthonous Manicheism of Andrić.

Selimović's final novel, *Ostrvo* (The Island, 1974), written after the author had experienced his first heart attack, is a series of meditations on the meaning of life, aging, and death. The story is set in contemporary Yugoslavia. The chief protagonists, Ivan and his wife Katarina, have relinquished their apartment in the city to a married son and moved to a little house on an island. There they find the same problems of alienation they experienced in the city. As Selimović writes:

> They didn't notice any difference between life in the city and in the country so far as personal relations were concerned. In both places people lived for themselves, or no longer knew how to get along with others. As if they were living between the past and future, in a time which doesn't exist: between the warm homogeneity of patriarchal society, where all individuality must be surrendered to the group, and the cold alienation of modern urbanism, where every man must fend for himself.

Katarina and Ivan are antipodal figures: she believes in God, goes to church, and fantasizes about a time past when she held promise as a pianist; he, on the other hand, is an atheist, completely cynical about his fellowman, and desperately seeks reconciliation with life. Their pensioners' drama is played out in a series of incidents, each one a separate chapter, with the protagonists' quest for meaning being the one unifying force. In the most brilliant chapter, "Da li da umre stari mandarin?" (Should the Old Mandarin Die?) Selimović forces Ivan and Katarina to ask themselves whether the death of any one individual can ever be justified in terms of the common good. Bold and explicit, the story leaves no question as to the author's position. It is a final, civilized answer to men like Hasan Brkić.

As *homo duplex,* novelist and critic, Selimović has also written some fascinating pieces about other writers, particularly about the psychology of creativity. Some of his longer articles, on Stevan Sremac, Hasan Kikić, August Cesarec, and Jovan Dučić, have been published in his collected works as part of a separate volume, *Pisci, Mišljenja, Razgovori* (Writers, Thoughts, Conversations). Selimović has also written *Za i protiv Vuka* (Pro and Contra Vuk, 1967), in which he reexamines the Serbian language reform instituted by Vuk Stefanović Karadžić in the nineteenth century. In the process he also refutes some statements by his erstwhile teacher from Belgrade University, the noted linguist Professor Aleksandar Belić.

Selimović contends that the Serbian literary language is too concrete, inadequately stocked with abstract terminology, and not easily molded in imagery. He attributes this inadequacy to Vuk, who based the new literary idiom on the finite language of the peasantry. Selimović cites Gavrilo Stefanović Venclović and Petar Petroviæ Njegoš II as two poets whose works pointed to an alternative direction for the evolving Serbian literary language, one that was not followed. He admires in both these writers their ability to circumvent the concreteness of the language by suggesting the relationship between the external world and the inner mood, establishing what he calls "the double landscape, physical and spiritual, always in a figurative sense as metaphor and allegory." Beneath these words, one suspects, there lies hidden a deeper debate between Selimović and his predecessors, including Ivo Andrić, who typify the "Vukovian" stream of language.

Ever the iconoclast, Selimović contests the conventional wisdom concerning the perfection of Vuk's reform and the "backwardness" of his nineteenth-century opponents, including Milovan Vidaković and Jovan Hadžić, just as in his own life he had dared to reject the totalitarian ideology that controlled his youth. Thus, what his Russian translator L. Aninskij has stated about Selimović's writing of Derviš i smrt can be applied to Selimović's life and works overall: "A sense of the indomitability of the spiritual man is stirred in us by the fact that this novel was written."

Selimović died on 11 July 1982 in Belgrade after an extended illness.

Bibliography:

Zumreta Zahirović, "Prilog bibliografiji Meše Selimovića," Sabrana djela Meše Selimovića, Magla i mjesečina (Sarajevo: Svjetlost, 1970), pp. 151–209.

References:

Danica Andrejević, Poetika Meše Selimovića (Belgrade: Prosveta, 1993);

L. Aninskij, "Meša Selimović: njegova knjiga o čoveku," Savremenik, 5 (1975): 441–447;

Midhat Begić, "Meša Selimović: Derviš i smrt," Izraz, 12 (1967): 1171–1178;

Miodrag Bogičević, "Derviš i smrt Meše Selimovića," Izraz, 1 (1967): 59–66;

Branka Brlenić-Bujić, "Derviš i smrt Meše Selimovića u dilemi duha i dilemi bivanja," Revija, 4 (1978): 45–58;

Thomas J. Butler, "Literary Style and Poetic Function in Meša Selimović's The Dervish and Death," Slavonic and East European Review, 52 (1974): 533–547;

Thomas Eekman, Thirty Years of Yugoslav Literature (1945–1975) (Ann Arbor: Michigan Slavic Studies, 1978), pp. 104–110;

Miroslav Egerić, "Čovjek i sudbina u Tvrdjavi Meše Selimovića," Delo, 10 (1973): 1161–1176;

Nedjeljko Fabrio, "Spisateljski profil Meše Selimovića," Život, 2 (1974): 191–207;

Radomir Ivanović, "Doprinos Meše Selimovića nauci o književnosti," in his Studije i ogledi (Belgrade: Sloboda, 1984), pp. 112–124;

Razija Lagumdžija, Kritčari o Meši Selimoviću (Sarajevo: Svjetlost, 1973);

Lagumdžija, "Lični bol Ahmeda Nurudina i njegovo prerastanje u opšteljudsku patnju," Prilozi nastavi srpskohrvatskog jezika i književnosti (Banja Luka, 1969–1970), pp. 46–56;

Ivan V. Lalić, "Roman o čoveku i smrti. Meša Selimović: Derviš i smrt," Letopis Matice srpske, 4 (1967): 376–380;

Slavko Leovac, "Meša Selimović: Tudja zemlja," in his Metamorfoze (Sarajevo, 1965), pp. 159–164;

Ante Pedišić, "Beznadje Selimovićevog Derviša," Mogućnosti, 8 (1967): 872–884;

Muharem Pervić, "Derviš i pesnik," in Selimović's Derviš i smrt (Belgrade: SKZ, 1969), pp. vii–xxvi;

Miodrag Petrović, Roman Meše Selimovića (Niš: Gradina, 1981);

Kasim Prohić, Činiti i biti. Roman Meše Selimovića (Sarajevo: Svjetlost, 1972);

Muhsin Rizvić, "Tri faze u razvitku psihološke proze Meše Selimovića," Izraz, 6 (1964): 653–666;

Janež Rotar, "Misaoni i narativni slojevi u strukturi Selimovićeve Tvrdjave," Izraz (1971): 507–514;

Radoslav Stojković, "Priča o škrtom ostrvu," Stremljenja, 5 (1975): 645–657;

Nikolaj Timčenko, "Ponor koji zjapi," Savremenik, 5 (1975): 418–425;

Slobodan Tomović, "Ahmed Nurudin," Književnost i jezik, XXIII, 1–2 (1976): 21–36;

Risto Trifković, "Čitajući djela Meše Selimovića," Život, XX, 1–2 (1971): 116–123;

Trifković, "Meša Selimović: Tišine," Život, XI, 3 (1962): 178–184;

Radovan Vučković, "Meša Selimović," Život, XXXI, 3–4 (1982): 199–220.

Ljubomir Simović
(2 December 1935 -)

Dubravka Juraga
University of Arkansas

BOOKS: *Slovenske elegije* (Titovo Užice: Klub studenata, 1958);

Veseli grobovi (Belgrade: Nolit, 1961);

Poslednja zemlja (Belgrade: Prosveta, 1964);

Šlemovi (Belgrade: Prosveta, 1967);

Uoči trećih petlova (Belgrade: Srpska književna zadruga, 1972);

Čudo u Šarganu (Belgrade: Atelje 212, 1975);

Hasanaginica (Novi Sad: Sterijino pozorje, 1976);

Subota: poema (Belgrade: Prosveta, 1976);

Vidik na dve vode (Belgrade: Nolit, 1980);

Um za morem (Belgrade: Privately printed by L. Simović and M. Josić-Višnjić, 1982);

Deset obraćanja Bogorodici trojeručici hilandarskoj (Belgrade: Privately printed by L. Simović and M. Josić-Višnjić, 1983);

Duplo dno: eseji o srpskim pesnicima (Belgrade: Prosveta, 1983);

Istočnice (Belgrade: Književne novine, 1983);

Drame: Hasanaginica i Čudo u Šarganu (Belgrade: BIGZ, 1984);

Hleb i so: izabrane pesme (Belgrade: Srpska književna zadruga, 1985);

Gornji grad (Belgrade: BIGZ, 1985);

Putujuće pozorište Šopalović (Belgrade: Biblioteka "Ars dramatica" Jugoslovenskog dramskog pozorišta, 1985);

Snevnik, Delo, 1-2 (1987): 123-171;

Savremena drama I (Čudo u Šarganu i Putujuće pozorište Šopalović) (Belgrade: Nolit, 1988);

Boj na Kosovu (Belgrade: Srpska književna zadruga, 1989);

Kovačnica na Čakovini: razgovori, pisma, eseji 1981-1989 (Niš: Gradina, 1990);

Dela u pet knjiga (Belgrade: Srpska književna zadruga/BIGZ/Prosveta/Dečje novine, 1991);

Igla i konac (Belgrade: Srpska književna zadruga, 1992);

Galop na puževima: Srbi u jugoslovenskom ratu (Gornji Milanovac: Dečje novine / Belgrade: Prosveta, 1994);

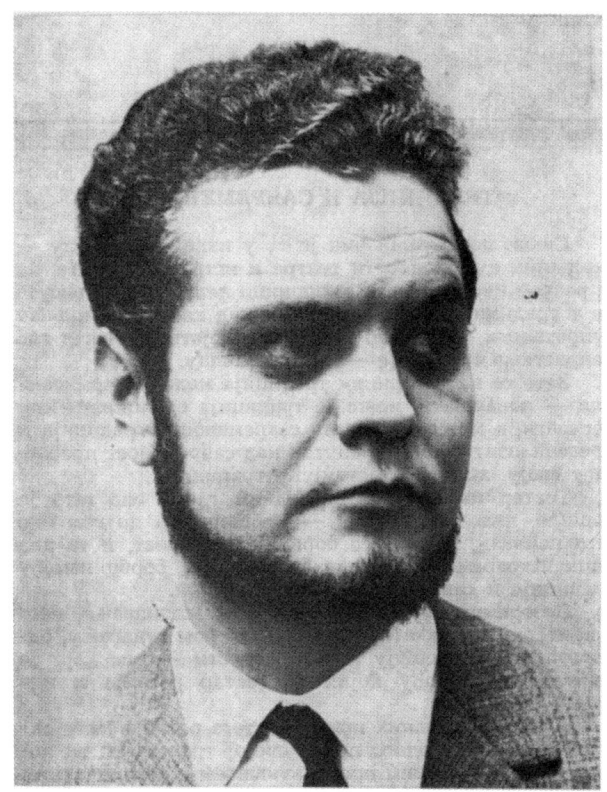

Ljubomir Simović

Učenje u mraku: izabrane i nove pesme (Belgrade: Srpska književna zadruga, 1995).

Collection: *Izabrane pesme* (Belgrade: Slovo ljubve/Narodna knjiga, 1980);

Editions in English: *Four Yugoslav Poets: Ivan V. Lalić, Branko Miljković, Milorad Pavić, Ljubomir Simović,* translated by Charles Simic (Northwood Narrows, N.H.: Lillabulero Press, 1970);

Poems, translated by Bernard Johnson, in *New Yugoslav Writing,* edited by Johnson (Baltimore: Penguin, 1970), pp. 133-135;

Poems, translated by Simic, in *Contemporary Yugoslav Poetry,* edited by Vasa D. Mihailovich

(Iowa City: University of Iowa Press, 1977), pp. 168–73;

Poems, translated by Vera Tošić, *Relations*, nos. 2–3 (1984): 11–14;

"Hasanaga's Wife," translated by Tim Bowen, *Scena*, no. 8 (1985): 32–53;

Poems, translated by Karolina Udovički, *Relations*, no. 3 (1985): 15–29;

"The Travelling Troupe Šopalović," translated by Alan McConnel-Duff, *Scena*, no. 9 (1986): 241–272;

Poems, translated by various translators, in *Serbian Poetry from the Beginnings to the Present*, edited by Milne Holton and Mihailovich (New Haven, Conn.: Yale Center for International and Area Studies, 1988), pp. 356–358;

"The Battle of Kosovo," excerpt translated by Mirela Djokić, *Relations*, no. 1–3 (1989): 125–137;

Poems, translated by Simic, in *The Horse Has Six Legs: An Anthology of Serbian Poetry*, edited by Simic (Saint Paul, Minn.: Graywolf's Press, 1992), pp. 125–137.

PLAY PRODUCTIONS: *Hasanaginica*, Belgrade, Narodno pozorište, 19 May 1974;

Čudo u Šarganu, Belgrade, Atelje 212, 24 October 1975;

Putujuće pozorište Šopalović, Belgrade, Jugoslovensko dramsko pozorište, 10 October 1985.

MOTION PICTURE: *Boj na Kosovu*, Feniks Film, Centar Film, and Television Belgrade, 1989.

TELEVISION: *Hasanaginica*, Television Belgrade, 1983.

OTHER: *Đuroa Jakšić: Pesme*, selected and with a foreword by Simović (Belgrade: Mlado pokolenje, 1966; Belgrade: Nolit, 1976);

Miodrag Pavlović: Velika Skitija i druge pesme, selected and with a foreword by Simović (Belgrade: Srpska književna zadruga, 1972);

Dušan Vasiljev: Izabrane pesme, selected and with an afterword by Simović (Belgrade: Rad, 1975);

Laza Kostić: Pesme, selected and with a foreword by Simović (Belgrade: Slovo ljubve, 1979);

Momčilo Nastasijević: Pet lirskih krugova + Magnovenja + Odjeci, selected and with a foreword by Simović (Belgrade, 1981);

Jovan Jovanović Zmaj: Izabrane pesme, selected and with a foreword by Simović (Belgrade: Srpska književna zadruga, 1982);

Miodrag Pavlović: Bezazlenstva, izabrane pesme, selected and with a foreword by Simović (Valjevo: Milan Rakić, 1988);

Milovan Danojlić: Tačka otpora, izabrane pesme, selected and with a foreword by Simović (Belgrade: Srpska književna zadruga, 1990).

Ljubomir Simović is a major contemporary Serbian poet, dramatist, and essayist. His poetry, which he began writing during the 1950s, addresses issues that gained a new urgency in the turmoil in the 1990s that has afflicted the states of the former Yugoslavia. Moreover, his poetry attempts to help create a viable contemporary Serbian cultural identity from the tradition of early Serbian feudal history and the centuries-long Serbian resistance to the Ottoman Empire. Like his poetry, his plays address the issues of art and its relevance for oppressed people exhausted and impoverished by their long servitude. However, besides the tragic vision that often colors Simović's work, many of his poems express an appreciative and even joyous acceptance of life. Some of his poems acclaim the vitality and the fantastic side of life and nature. Simović is fully aware of the transient nature of human existence, and his poetry often celebrates the sensual and material manifestation of the present moment.

Simović was born on 2 December 1935 in Užice, in the Serbian heartland. His father, Dragiša Simović, was a shoemaker from Užice, while his mother, Radojka Cvijić, was from Sarajevo. She was from a somewhat unusual family: her father, Đorđe Cvijić, was a stonecutter who as a young man went to Germany to improve his craft. He returned from Germany with Ana Klara Walter, who converted to Orthodox Christianity, married Đorđe, and had five children with him. The youngest child was Ljubomir's mother, Radojka. When her sons Ljubomir and Predrag were little, Radojka told them many stories and adventures from her own Sarajevo childhood. The young Ljubomir used these stories (with his own experiences on trips to the "exotic" Sarajevo) to construct fantastic tales of "Bukhara and Baghdad," which he narrated to his childhood friends in Užice. Ljubomir's imagination was further stirred by the stories he heard from his grandmother's second husband, the Russian émigré Andrei Kosjukov, a Cossack whose whole family was killed during the Russian Revolution.

Many of the early memories Simović has from his childhood are of war and soldiers of various nationalities who occupied or fought for

Scene from Simović's 1974 play Hasanaginica *(Hasanaga's Wife), winner of the Sterija Prize for drama*

Užice during World War II. The Simović family lived relatively peacefully during the war, though suffering great poverty. Ljubomir attended the King Peter II elementary school in Užice where, already an avid reader, he was impressed to learn that the husband of his first teacher was a writer. His first "literary love" was Mark Twain's *Huckleberry Finn* (1884), which he reread many times. Besides Mark Twain, he read novels of the American West by Karl May, James Fenimore Cooper, and others. He also liked to read detective novels and novels about Chicago gangsters.

Simović was also influenced during his early years in Užice by his mother's involvement in the local theater, where she was an amateur actress popular among the Užice audience. She actively encouraged her son's interest in theater. As a high school student Simović frequented the local theater to see plays by William Shakespeare, Moliére, Carlo Goldoni, Lope de Vega, Pierre-Augustin Caron de Beaumarchais, Anton Chekhov, Aleksandr Ostrovsky, Nikolay Gogol, Maksim Gorky, George Bernard Shaw, Arthur Miller, and Tennessee Williams. Yugoslav playwrights such as Marin Držić, Miroslav Krleža, Borisav Stanković, and Branislav Nušić were also frequently staged.

Because of the war, Simović's education was often interrupted. The school was open irregularly—when the army or the air raids allowed. Like other people from Užice, he and his family often had to flee into the nearby forests, as the German (and later British) airplanes frequently flew over the town. Also, German raids on the local population were frequent, and Simović's father was caught several times and held as a hostage or taken to provide forced labor. After Simović graduated from the elementary school, he continued his education in a local gymnasium. Because of a difficult financial situation, Simović had to transfer to a secondary school for primary-school teachers despite his desire to finish gymnasium and go to college. In school Simović started writing poetry and was soon known among his fellow students as a young poet. Because of his talents, he was also much favored by many of his teachers. While in gymnasium and later in teachers' school, Simović participated in the work of literary clubs, where the students actively discussed literature and, particularly, poetry. Russian poets such as Mikhail Lermontov and Aleksandr Pushkin were especially popular.

Simović published his first poems in 1952. "Jutro" (A Morning) was published in the journal *Učiteljska iskra* (Teachers' Spark), and "Putevi" (Roads) and "Novembar" (November) were published in the Belgrade *Omladina* (Youth). However, Simović himself considers his actual literary beginning the publication of "Balada o običnom čoveku" (A Ballad about an Ordinary Man) in *Mlada kultura* (Young Culture) in 1953 and "Epitafi sa karanskog groblja" (Epitaphs from the Karan Cemetery) in 1957 in *Vidici* (Horizons). These were the first poems in which Simović found the distinctive poetic voice that he continued to develop later. His first collection of poems, *Slovenske elegije* (Slavic Elegies), was published in Užice in 1958.

In 1955 Simović graduated from the teachers' school and, despite the still difficult financial situation of his family, he decided to continue his university education in Belgrade. He became a student in the department of Yugoslav literatures, majoring in the history of Yugoslav literature and in the Serbo-Croatian language. He studied the Italian language as his third major. To support himself, Simović became a correspondent of *Vesti* (News), a journal from Užice to which he had often contributed articles as a high school student. In 1958 Simović married Nadežda Karadžić and began to work part time at Radio Belgrade in programming for young people. He worked on the preparation of the program "Radio–The Merriest of All Towns," which was produced live in various cities in Yugoslavia. Simović traveled with the rest of the staff, usually at night, and worked during the day. He needed the job to support his college education, but the job was so exhausting that it left little time for study.

During Simović's college years the contemporary Belgrade literary scene was exceptionally lively, with a host of debates between the realists and the modernists. Simović was very much aware of these debates, although he did not participate in them. He closely followed the rich Yugoslav literary production of the 1950s and eventually became active in the literary world of his time. As a student he was a contributor to the well-known student literary journal *Vidici*, which promoted modernist and avant-garde art, painting, and literature. Simović was only one among the many now-celebrated contributors to *Vidici*, such as Nikola Koljević, Ljuba Popović, Leonid Šejka, Matija Bećković, Miloš Stambolić, Mića Danojlić, and Miroslav Egerić. In 1958 Simović became a member of the editorial board of *Vidici*, actively participating in the creation and production of the journal. He worked with Danilo Kiš, Nikola Koljević, Slobodan Mašić, and other young lions of Yugoslav literature. Simović eventually became chief editor of *Vidici*.

After graduation in 1962 Simović was offered a teaching position at Belgrade University. Although tempted, he did not accept the job, fearing that it would distract him from creative writing. He served a year in the army, and then in 1963 became chief editor of the art program of Radio Belgrade's "First Program." Simović did not particularly welcome this demanding and politically sensitive job; he preferred to create single programs like "A Thousand Years of Lyric Poetry," in which he explored the Yugoslav poetic heritage, or "Poetry and Music." He therefore transferred to a less important position as a contributor, which left him time to write his own poetry. His career with Radio Belgrade then came to a halt after he signed the manifesto "Predlog za razmišljanje" (A Suggestion for Consideration), which almost caused him to be expelled from the Communist Party. A beneficial side effect of this disruption of his career was that he then had much more time for writing. At the time of this writing, Simović still works for the literary program of Radio Belgrade.

His second book of poetry, *Veseli grobovi* (Merry Tombs), was published in 1961. The next collection of his poetry, *Poslednja zemlja* (The Last Land), appeared in 1964. The collection *Šlemovi* (Helmets) appeared in 1967. In 1968 Simović was awarded two prizes for his poetry: he received the "Đorđe Jovanović" award and the "Isidora Sekulić" award for the collection *Šlemovi*. Despite these public acknowledgments, Simović was not fully satisfied with his poetry. In one of his interviews in 1992 Simović explained that these early collections reflect a certain confusion and disorientation that he felt at the time. He noted that he had briefly found his own voice in the first collection, *Slovenske elegije,* but that he did not recognize it at the time, losing it and finding it again only after years of search. *Uoči trećih petlova* (Before the Third Cock Crowing), published in 1972, was the collection in which Simović created a distinctive poetic style that he has maintained throughout his later creative output. The poems in the first two segments of the collection deal with the realities of war and Serbian national destiny in an inhospitable world, while those in the later two segments are phantasmagoric invocations of the world, much in the vein of Marc Chagall's paintings. In 1973 Simović received the renowned Matica srpska award, "Zmajeva nagrada" (Zmaj Award), for this collection.

Simović is also an important dramatist, though he sees himself primarily as a poet who accidentally ventured into drama. He attributes his success in playwriting to his ability to maintain his own poetic voice and to address important issues that he explores primarily in his poetry. His first play, *Čudo u Šarganu* (Miracle in Šargan), was performed by Belgrade's prestigious Atelje 212 in 1975. The play became one of the most popular Yugoslav plays ever staged; it was performed for thirteen sell-out seasons. The most important Yugoslav prize for drama, the Sterija's Prize, was awarded to Simović in 1975 for his play *Hasanaginica* (Hasanaga's Wife). The poem *Subota* (Saturday), published in 1976, is one of Simović's most important poems. It is a polyphonic rendition of life on a Saturday in a pub. Through the voices of different people in the pub, Simović good-naturedly and somewhat humorously presents and comments on various points of view, attitudes, stereotypes, clichés, and conventionalities that color contemporary life in Serbia.

In 1980 Simović received the Branko Miljković award for his collection of poems called *Vidik na dve vode* (A Gable Roof View), published that same year. He also received the Milan Rakić award from the Writers' Association of Serbia in 1982 for his collection of poetry *Um za more* (Mind Behind the Sea), published that year. In 1983 Simović published *Duplo dno* (False Bottom), a collection of essays on Serbian poets such as Dositej Obradović, Dorđe Marković Koder, Laza Kostić, Vojislav Ilić, Stanislav Vinaver, Desanka Maksimović, Dušan Vasiljev, Milovan Danojlić, and Matija Bećković. Simović uses his own poetic experience to present a distinctive point of view of Serbian poetry and its historical development. That same year saw the publication of Simović's controversial collection, *Istočnice* (Sources). It includes the powerful poem "Na tridesetosmogodišnjicu bitke između partizana i četnika na Jelovoj Gori meseca septembra godine 1944" (On the Thirty-eighth Anniversary of the Battle between the Partisans and Četniks on the Jelova Gora in September of the Year 1944), which notes the tragic fact that the war between the partisans and the Chetniks was a civil war among brothers and neighbors. *Istočnice* was banned from publication in the literary journal *Gradina* on the eve of its publication. The poems were nevertheless published that same year in the *Književne novine* (Literary Gazette), leading to a strident public debate and to widespread and blistering official criticism of them as nationalistic, anticommunist, and destructive. Some denounced Simović as an enemy of the people and even demanded that he be tried for treason. His books disappeared from libraries, and there were suggestions that he should be fired from his post at Radio Belgrade. But many Yugoslav writers and intellectuals came to Simović's defense. The attack eventually subsided, and Simović ultimately maintained his position as an important poet and playwright.

The play *Putujuće pozorište Šopalović* (The Traveling Troupe Šopalović) was first performed in Belgrade in 1985. It addresses such issues as the relationship between art and reality, especially in situations of crisis such as wartime. The play shows a traveling troupe arriving in Užice, which has been occupied by the German forces during World War II. The citizens are astonished and insulted that the troupe can seem to ignore reality and live playfully in the shadow of gallows. But the citizens radically change their opinion about the artists after the actor Filip Trnavac is executed following his inadvertent confession (when he thinks that he is acting a part in a play) to a terrorist attack of which a local youth had been accused. Meanwhile, Milun, an official torturer whose future victims choose death by suicide rather than by his torture, becomes enchanted with an actress in the troupe. Her trust in him and belief in his humanity cause him to be so revolted by his former acts of cruelty that he hangs himself, thus sparing the community his violence. Simović thus suggests that art can be of great value in times of crisis and can have a crucial role in the life of a community even though that role might not be obvious. *Putujuće pozorište Šopalović* was widely acclaimed as one of the most important theatrical achievements of its time in the Yugoslav theater. In 1986 Simović again received the Sterija's Prize while the Yugoslav Drama Theater from Belgrade won the Sterija Award for the best performance for its production of the play. The play also received the Sterija Critics Award for the best play that year.

Besides his poetry, plays, and essays, Simović has published translations of poetry into Serbo-Croatian from Russian, Italian, Polish, and Slovak. He also collaborated with other translators and poets in the translation of William Blake, William Wordsworth, Johann Wolfgang von Goethe, and Adam Mickiewicz. For his distinguished contributions to Serbian culture Simović was elected an adjunct member of the Serbian Academy of Arts and Sciences in 1988. The next year he received the prominent October Award of the City of Belgrade for his play *Boj na Kosovu* (The Battle of Kosovo). In 1990 Simović received the "7 July" award for his outstanding lifelong creative work. That year he also received the BIGZ (Belgrade Publishing Company) award for his collection of poems *Gornji grad* (Upper Town). He also published *Kovačnica na Čakovini* (A Blacksmith's Forge on Čakovina), a collection of his previously published essays, interviews, and speeches. In these essays Simović analyzes the themes that are a constant preoccupation in all of his work. These include poetry, art, theater, history, and Serbian cultural traditions.

In 1992 he received the "Zlatan krst kneza Lazara" award ("The Golden Cross of Prince Lazar"), and in 1993 he received his third Sterija's Prize for the play *Čudo u Šarganu*. The production by the Srpsko narodno pozorište from Novi Sad received the Sterija Prize for the best performance that year. In 1994 Simović was elected a full member of the Serbian Academy of Arts and Sciences. That same year he was the first to receive the newly established Desanka Maksimović award, given to outstanding poets for their lifetime poetic achievement. The same year Simović published *Galop na puževima* (Galloping at a Snail's Pace), a collection of interviews, speeches, commentaries, and essays written during the late 1980s and the early 1990s. He analyzes the contemporary state of the Serbian nation and the political situation in Serbia and concludes that the present time is one of the lowest moments in Serbian history. He suggests that one of the most important problems the Serbian nation faces in the 1990s is its regime, whose legality has been unequivocally compromised by its oppressive and totalitarian methods. Simović argues that these methods have been inherited from the previous Yugoslav communist regime. He suggests that the communist regime also shaped the Serbian nation into one susceptible to undemocratic and totalitarian rule. Simović denies the claim of the 1990s regime that it represents the interests of the Serbian people. He charges that the sole aim of the regime led by Slobodan Milošević is to maintain its own power, in the interest of which it is willing to employ all methods of terror and tyranny and to plunge the Serbian people into the depths of war, poverty, despair, hopelessness, primitivism, and even national annihilation.

In these essays Simović emphasizes the urgency of the creation of a new, democratic Serbia, whose people will be able to restore the legitimacy of the state, create opportunities for the Serbian people to live peacefully and prosperously, and regain the respect of the world community. He also emphasizes the importance of a viable political opposition, liberal and democratic, which must continue to fight against the present Serbian regime at all costs. He sees the Serbian national tradition, with its central symbol of the Battle of Kosovo, as a basis for the creation of a positive cultural identity for a new and democratic Serbia. Simović believes that the restoration of Serbia's "lost history," in particular the history that has been repressed or concealed by the previous communist regime, is an urgent task for contemporary Serbian intellectuals. Indeed, he is himself currently working to recover just such a lost past by preparing an extensive book about his hometown in Serbia, *Užice (hronika, koja je povremeno roman, ili roman, koji je povremeno hronika)* (Užice [A Chronicle Which is at Times a Novel, or a Novel Which is at Times a Chronicle]).

Simović's art is rich and full of life. He sees the world as being full of various elements: fantastic and mundane, carnivalesque and prosaic, violent and gentle. A poet of everyday life and a poet of war, he attempts to understand, depict, and describe human life in its quotidian splendor. His concerns are broad, and he focuses on such large issues as the fundamental role of art in society and the reconstruction of a Serbian national identity from the elements of its past. His writing has made him one of the most important literary figures in Serbia after World War II.

Bibliography:
Dela, volume 5 (Belgrade: Srpska književna zadruga, 1991), pp. 211-213.

References:
Zdenka Aćin, ed., "Razgovor o najnovijim pesmama Ljubomira Simovića: Istočnice dobra i zla," *Savremenik,* 58 (1983): 200-228;

Jovan Ćirilov, "Simović's *The Šopalović's Abroad,*" *Relations,* 2-4 (1990): 103-104;

Časlav Đorđević, *Pesnički vidici Ljubomira Simovića* (Belgrade: Naučna knjiga, 1982);

Jovan Hristić, "*About the Travelling Troupe Šopalović* by Ljubomir Simović," *Scena,* 10 (1987): 268-272;

Miloš Jevtić, *Tri večeri sa Simovićem* (Belgrade: Naučna knjiga, 1990);

Radoman Kordić, "Poistovećenje s jezikom," *Savremenik,* 52 (1980): 352-369;

Zvonimir Kostić, "Pesnik gorke vedrine," *Savremenik,* 52 (1980): 370-392;

Ivan V. Lalić, "Talent i zrelost," in his *Kritika i delo* (Belgrade: Nolit, 1971), pp. 184-190;

Mirko Magarašević, "Aveti boga Marsa," *Savremenik,* 52 (1980): 337-351;

Petar Marjanović, "Ljubomir Simović: *Hasanaga's Wife*," *Scena*, no. 8 (1985): 55-60, 228-30;

Radivoje Mikić, "Ljubomir Simović, pesnik preokreta," in his *Jezik poezije* (Belgrade: BIGZ, 1990), pp. 76-91;

Vidan Nikolić "Psiholingvistički i mikrosociolingvistički osvrt na drame Ljubomira Simovića," *Savremenik,* 56 (1982): 302-312;

Miodrag Petrović, "Eksplicitna poetika Ljubomira Simovića," *Letopis Matice srpske* (October 1990): 549-553;

Petrović, "Poezija Ljubomira Simovića," *Izraz,* 32 (1988): 217-247;

Predrag Protić, "Stilizacija ljudskog govora u poemi *Subota,*" *Savremenik,* 52 (1980): 393-396;

Pavle Zorić, "Ljubomir Simović ili trijumf poetske slike," in his *Vrhovi: Miodrag Pavlović, Ljubomir Simović, Matija Bećković* (Belgrade: Srpska književna zadruga, 1991), pp. 59-114;

Slobodan Zubanović and Mihajlo Pantić, "Ljubomir Simović, 'gost iz oblaka,' " in their *Deset pesama–deset razgovora* (Novi Sad: Matica srpska, 1992), pp. 123-146.

Ivan Slamnig
(24 June 1930 -)

Thomas Eekman
University of California, Los Angeles

BOOKS: *Aleja poslije svečanosti* (Zagreb: Matica hrvatska, 1956);
Odron (Zagreb: Lykos, 1956);
Neprijatelj (Zagreb: Zora, 1959);
Naronska sijesta (Zagreb: Razlog, 1963);
Povratnik s mjeseca (Zagreb: Zora, 1964);
Monografija (Kruševac: Bagdala, 1965);
Disciplina mašte (Zagreb: Matica hrvatska, 1965);
Limb (Zagreb: Razlog, 1965);
Analecta (Zagreb: Razlog, 1971);
Bolja polovica hrabrosti (Zagreb: Znanje, 1972);
Dronta (Zagreb: Znanje, 1981);
Hrvatska versifikacija. Narav, povijest, veze (Zagreb: Liber, 1981);
Sedam pristupa pjesmi (Rijeka: Izdavački centar Rijeka, 1986);
Jedanaest drama (Rijeka: Izdavački centar Rijeka, 1986);
Relativno naopako (Zagreb: Iros, 1987);
Sed scholae (Zagreb: Mladost, 1987);
Tajna (Zagreb: Naprijed, 1988).

Editions and Collections: *Pjesme,* selected by Slobodan Novak (Zagreb: Znanje, 1973);
Izabrana djela, "Pet stoljeća hrvatske književnosti" (Zagreb: Matica hrvatska, 1983);
Sabrane pjesme (Zagreb: Grafički zavod Hrvatske, 1990);
Sabrana kratka proza (Zagreb: Grafički zavod Hrvatske, 1992).

Editions in English: Poems translated by various translators in *The Bridge,* no. 19-20 (1970): 60-63;
Poems translated by Ivan V. Lalic and Bernard Johnson in *New Writing in Yugoslavia,* edited by Johnson (Baltimore, Md.: Penguin, 1970), pp. 139-142;
Poems by various translators in *Contemporary Yugoslav Poetry,* edited by Vasa D. Mihailovich (Iowa City: University of Iowa Press, 1977), pp. 129-133;
The Birthday, translated by Andriana Hewitt (Zagreb: Radio Zagreb, 1979);

Ivan Slamnig

Poems translated by Slobodan Drenovac in *Bridge,* no. 2 (1986): 22, 54-60;
Poems translated by Milka Lukic in *Exile,* 17, no. 1 (1993): 66-71.

OTHER: *Američka lirika,* edited by Slamnig and Antun Šoljan (Zagreb: Zora, 1952);
Suvremena engleska poezija, edited by Slamnig and Šoljan (Zagreb: Lykos, 1956);
Antologija hrvatske poezije od najstarijih zapisa do kraja XIX. stoljeća (Zagreb: Lykos, 1959);
Suvremena nordijska poezija, edited by Slamnig and Šoljan (Sarajevo: Veselin Masleša, 1961);
Hrvatska poezija 17. stoljeća (Zagreb: Matica hrvatska, 1964);
Svjetska književnost zapadnoga kruga, by Slamnig, Aleksandar Flaker, and S. Slamnig (Zagreb: Školska knjiga, 1973);
Antologija hrvatske poezije od A. Kačića Miošića do A. G. Matoša (Zagreb: Školska knjiga, 1974).

With his original and multifaceted productivity, Ivan Slamnig is a writer and scholar who made his distinctive mark on post–World War II Croatian literature (both poetry and prose) and on literary life and scholarship in Croatia.

Born on 24 June 1930 in Metković, Croatia, on the Neretva River not far from the Adriatic coast, Slamnig attended school in Metković and Dubrovnik; he later attended high school in the Croatian capital, Zagreb. At the University of Zagreb he enrolled in 1948 as a student of Slavic languages and literatures, graduating in 1955. He obtained his Ph.D. in 1980 with a dissertation on Croatian versification that, in a revised form, was published as a book the following year. He became a teacher in the Department of Slavic Studies at Zagreb University but spent several years teaching Serbo-Croatian abroad: in Florence, Italy; Bloomington, Indiana; Chicago, Illinois; Amsterdam; and Uppsala, Sweden. In addition to the main Slavic languages he learned German, Italian, English, Dutch, and Swedish. He was then appointed a full professor of comparative literature at Zagreb University, until for health reasons he took an early retirement in the 1980s after suffering two strokes.

As a young man Slamnig became an active member of a group of talented young writers and poets concentrated in Zagreb. He cofounded the magazine *Krugovi* (Circles), which played a leading role in the movement created by these artists. It was partly a reaction to the preceding period of obligatory "socialist realism," although it was not a political or ideological movement; the members aspired to a renewal of literature without an overarching doctrine. The prose of the group, and partly also their verse, was characterized by a predominantly light, mocking tone, humor, and a playful type of realism (that in some cases changed into the fantastic). These young writers were influenced to some extent by James Joyce, and even more by Jorge Luis Borges.

Slamnig's first publication was *Američka lirika* (American Lyrics, 1952), an anthology of American lyrical poetry compiled with his friend and fellow student Antun Šoljan. They also collaborated on a volume of contemporary English poetry in 1956 and a volume of contemporary Scandinavian poetry in 1961. Slamnig also prepared an anthology of classical Croatian poetry in 1959, of seventeenth-century Croatian poetry in 1964, and of eighteenth- and nineteenth-century Croatian poetry in 1974. Slamnig and Šoljan also translated some English prose works, and Slamnig translated from Italian and Swedish.

His early original literary production consisted of poems, two collections of which were published in 1956. In the course of the 1960s, 1970s, and 1980s nine more volumes appeared, and then, in 1990, *Sabrane pjesme,* a volume of his collected poems, was published. The majority of these poems could be designated as "light verse": they are sometimes humorous, derisive, or serious, but never heavy, elegiac, or moralizing. When he was fourteen he wrote the poem "In Front of the Wheels," included in the volume *Aleja poslije svečanosti* (The Boulevard after the Ceremony, 1956):

> Watch out, young lady,
> you were almost run over by a streetcar.
> Or did you do that purposely?
> Oh no—what an idea!
> But of course, there's no answer,
> and who am I?
> —The streetcar driver.

His later poetry likewise usually consists of rather short, mostly witty, and often tongue-in-cheek poems with puns, multiple rhymes, and assonances; still, some poems are serious, lyrical, and personal. A reflection of the years of political oppression and persecution can be noted at the end of the poem "Udarac" (The Slap, 1956):

> On the sidewalk people merge with people,
> Wet spots have evaporated
> under dead yellow leaves. Thirstily
> the canal laps up the melting brown puddles.
> The thin glaze on the asphalt is drying up.
> A one-eyed streetcar waddles like a pup.
> Suddenly someone hits me on the back.
> I don't turn around, although I am surprised.
> Maybe it is some friend, I think,
> Or maybe I am recognized.

His volumes of short stories, *Neprijatelj* (The Enemy, 1959) and *Povratnik s mjeseca* (The Returner From the Moon, 1964), were extremely successful. In the former volume the most substantial stories are the eponymous first one and "Putovotkinja" (The Tour Guide). In "The Enemy" the story is set in Zagreb under the German-ustaše occupation. The narrator is a high-school boy who decides he has to kill Marko, a *ustaša* (a member of the secret police), who sometimes comes to visit his parents. Together with a friend he plans to poison him; however, news comes that Marko has been killed somewhere in Bosnia. The story is interrupted by fragments in italics in which the same narrator is talking or writing, but on subjects which are not directly connected to the main plot. "The Tour Guide" also starts out as a story told in the first person, but in the third chapter the "I" is not the young man of the first two chapters, but the Swedish girl he has met, who works as a tour-bus guide on a trip in Dalmatia. The first narrator then makes love with another girl ("she raped me"), but returns to his Swedish girlfriend; he even takes over the tourist group to show them the town, giving her a day off with his younger brother. There is no plot and no real story; the narrative presents a summer folly in which the narrator-hero's lust for sex is the main motif and the moving force. "The Story of Zvezdana" has an interesting structure. In this story a girl meets three boys (one of whom is the narrator) and tells them about her problem: she is entitled to a sum of money because of her father's death, but there is a lot of red tape and it turns out that she will receive the money only if she has sex with a powerful bureaucrat. The three young men each give their advice, but the girl has already made up her mind: she will not succumb. "How powerful am I," the narrator ends his story, "being able to provide happy endings!"

"Unprovable Murder," in structure somewhat similar to "The Story of Zvezdana," is much more suspenseful and contains elements of the crime novel. The narrator is visited by his friend Karlo, who admits that he has killed their mutual acquaintance, Marin. The narrator divulges this shocking news to the small group of friends to which he and Karlo belong. One friend does not believe Karlo actually murdered Marin; he supposes that, instead, he has killed Silva, the young woman who had created jealousy between the two young men. Another member of the group believes that Karlo has committed suicide. A third accuses the narrator of killing Karlo. A meeting of the group is agreed upon, where Karlo will also be present; but when the narrator comes to the designated place, at the time agreed upon, nobody appears. Thus, the story ends mysteriously. "Maybe I have been killed. Maybe this is not a square in a coastal city. Maybe this is the gate of hell." Most of these stories (including those remaining: "Lost," "A Night on a Ship," and "Teacher of Latin") have an erotic theme, or at least a strong erotic component.

In *Povratnik s mjeseca* Slamnig collected ten stories. The first, "The Refrigerator," is a story of jealousy. The narrator is portrayed as a rather petit-bourgeois, pedestrian, and not-too-bright person. The whole story, the entire plot, is actually somewhat pedestrian, but it is well presented. A liaison begins between the narrator's wife, Erika, and a visiting friend, Karlo (an artist and a more interesting man than the husband); this relationship develops. At the end Erika proves victorious: she has had an adventure, but keeps her husband; her marriage remains intact; and she also received a nice present (a refrigerator). The short text about "the returner from the moon" tells how the first-person narrator of the story meets his friend Stjepo, who initiates, as a kind of game, a collective story. It is about six men (one a Croatian) who flew to the moon; after his return the Croatian decides he wants to go to his birthplace. Stjepo and the narrator build on this story; then two young women add their episodes to the story and introduce their ideas. The story ends with the moon traveler in an embrace with his beloved, and "in his imagination he sees a big green disk hanging over the moon mountains: the earth." Thus, a topical, scientific, and even somewhat lofty theme is connected with "pedestrian" people, surroundings, and conversations.

The remaining stories are also about students. "The Celebrator" focuses on a table in the student cafeteria, where "we" are sitting every day with other students—this time with an inconspicuous girl, a middle-aged student-teacher, and two southerners. One of them, celebrating his birthday, produces a bottle of *dingač* (Dalmatian wine), followed by another bottle; he talks, tells a story, and the group feels like "a patriarchal family circle," even though they know they will probably never sit together again and may hardly even recognize each other the next day. A similar story of inaction is "Sparina" (Sultriness), in which the narrator and five other young men sit together and talk about assembling a car and traveling; but they just talk; the theme switches to a summer cottage that will be easy to build; and it is mentioned that last year they had been talking the same way about a ship. It is hot, and, as the last sentence says, "too muggy to distinguish one thing from another." "The Rest Is Silence" is the only story that is not written completely in first-person narration: in the beginning the "I" of the story mentions that he will reconstruct the story "with the help of what my best friend Marko told me"; the narrator is no more than an eyewitness of part of the action.

Ivan Slamnig in 1996

Slamnig's first scholarly publication in book form was *Disciplina mašte* (The Discipline of Fancy, 1965), which contains fourteen essays on Croatian poets and poetry, mostly from the past, and one essay that deals with prose. The first essay, "The Poem as a Factor of Collective Consciousness," discusses the nature and essence of a poem and its building block: the word; the difference of a word in poetry and in scientific language; and the importance of poetry, and art in general, for the community. In the essay "National Literature and Comparative Studies" he states: "To deal with Serbian and Croatian literature separately during the entire course of their development is impossible: in certain periods and certain fields there was literary activity that we can only call Yugoslav. To Yugoslav literature belongs, for example, that oral literature that developed richly in the central areas of the Serbo-Croatian linguistic territory." There is also an essay on the comparative study of popular or folk poetry and the contacts and mutual influences of "official," published poetry and anonymous folk poetry. Slamnig argues in his conclusion that "Comparative studies have their legitimate place in the study of oral poetry and, moreover, contribute essentially to the clarification of some principal problems of the study of oral poetry."

In "The Rhythm of Language and Verse Rhythm" Slamnig offers interesting observations on intonation, vowel length, and similar phonetic questions that pertain to many European languages. The basic differences between Romance, Germanic, and Slavic versification (notably in Croatian folk poetry) are discussed in "Our Old Verse As Compared To Roman Verse," which also deals with the connection between verse and melody: as a rule, old Croatian poetry (both art and folk poetry) was sung. The essay "The Verse of Modern Poetry" is about various Croatian nineteenth- and early twentieth-century poets and their meters and rhymes. Slamnig then returns to the theme of the oral poetry tradition in "The Metrical Basis of Our Decasyllable"; this is a polemic with a poet and verse theoretician, Marin Franičević, whose claims that Croatian verse is, in general, tonic, and that the folksinger-poet prefers stresses on odd syllables are disputed. "Verse As Form and Material" contains interesting and important deliberations on poetry in general, poetic language, stress, free verse (old and new), and distinctions between Croatian and foreign free verse. He states that "free verse is both an eternal form and an innovator's banner." In "On the Versification of Translations" Slamnig addresses various questions about poetry translations and concedes that "the ideal transmission of a poem from culture to culture, from one language to the other, one nation to the other is impossible." But he points out that the modern Croatian practice of accepting both the tonic and syllabic principle facilitates verse translation; he also gives examples of successful translations from the works of William Shakespeare and Dante Alighieri.

Two essays are dedicated to the sixteenth-century Dubrovnik poet Marisn Držić. Slamnig pleads for a commentary on Držić's works that would reconstruct the original, old meanings of the text—the meanings that the words and expressions had in his world and his time. There is an essay on Stanko Vraz, the early-nineteenth-century Slovene-Croatian poet; on the German, Polish, and Czech influences on his work; his fluctuation between Slovene and Croatian-štokavian; and his relation to Dubrovnik poetry and to Slovene folk poetry. Slamnig argues that Vraz's "folksiness" was not a mannerism or imitation, but his genuine expression within the traditions and manners of his time.

Much more closely related to his own time is "An Approach to Contemporary Poetry," in which he says: "Everything in the language that is fresh and impressive, that attracts the eye and the ear, in a word, everything that is creative—all that is poetical, and when, in addition, it is structurally solid, and not merely raw poetic material, then it is a poem, no matter how short it is."

The final essay in the book deals with prose. It is titled "The People within the Human," subtitled "Notes About Contemporary Prose," and divided into twelve chapters. Slamnig deliberates upon the difficulties of writing about prose because it is in constant fluctuation and development, even within the work of one author. As innovators in the field of contemporary Croatian prose he mentions Slobodan Novak, Vojislav Jelić, and Vjekoslav Kaleb—the latter being the author of two short novels, or "long short stories," more or less in the vein of Ernest Hemingway, Albert Camus, or Françoise Sagan. Slamnig tries to distinguish between a real literary work and a fragment or sketch, even if it contains some good observations or witty remarks. He notices that contemporary prose (especially short prose) is generally written in the first person, so it consists of soliloquies. He calls "a tendency toward sincerity" one of the most evident characteristics of the new prose (referring to himself and his generation, but even more to the younger generation). As an example, he analyzes the story "Zagrljaj" (The Embrace) by the prominent Croatian fiction writer Ranko Marinković, in which new conceptions were introduced.

Closely connected with this theoretical volume is Slamnig's *Hrvatska versifikacija* (Croatian Versification, 1981), which deviates from the standard versification handbooks in its fresh, novel approach; independent ideas; and original arrangement of the material. At the beginning, for example, Slamnig polemicizes with Roman Jakobson, who believed in the genealogical continuity of verse elements in the poetry of all the Slavs; he concludes that "the community of various peoples is of greater weight than the common ancestry of a group of peoples." He points to the great importance of Latin versification and the spreading of Christianity for the proliferation of metrical forms and patterns all over Europe. The book contains a chronological survey of the development of Croatian verse from 1100 to 1980, with references to other national literatures and illustrative examples. As for contemporary poetry, Slamnig concludes: "The versification of the great majority of contemporary Croatian poets is based on the steadiness of the accent unit, which, therefore, is equivalent to the verse foot of regular metric verse." He observes "a greater and greater importance of the stress in contemporary Croatian poetry." He focuses, too, on translating verse (a whole chapter on the subject) and on the difference between traditional and free verse.

Sedam pristupa pjesmi (Seven Approaches to the Poem, 1986) belongs to the same category of works; it consists of seventeen papers published in the years from 1955 to 1985. They are preceded by a general introduction in which Slamnig lists various traditional approaches to poetry, including the functional and the acoustic method. In the rest of the book he hardly works with or mentions these terms. The first essay, "Mediterranean Location and Northern Visions of the Croats," presents a succinct overview of the peoples around the Mediterranean and their history: it is Predrag Matvejević's well-known *Mediterranean Breviary* in a nutshell. In "Croatian Literature Prior to the Renaissance As an Organic Part of the European Literary Movement" and in other essays Slamnig places Croatian literature in the context of international European literary developments, currents, movements, and phenomena, a valuable analysis that in many instances points to connections that were not clear before. He discusses the type of folk poetry called *bugarštica*, which is a term he derives from the Latin *vulgaris* (a relation to Bulgaria, in Serbo-Croatian Bugarska, is not even considered or mentioned), and he states: "There exists the opinion—and it is the most generally accepted one—that bugarštica verse is a Slavic, Serbian variant of the Byzantine *political verse*. I think it is more likely that the bugarštica verse should be explained by the coexistence, and at the same time opposition of Slavic and Latin poetry writing; as the place of origin I would indicate the Duklja area" (that is, in Montenegro).

In his essay on Ivan Mažuranić and his epic *Smrt Smail-age Čengijića* (Smail Aga Čengijić's Death, 1846), Slamnig offers some useful observations about this work, claiming that Mažuranić combined the people's *deseterac* (decasyllable line) with the octosyllable of Dubrovnik, the verse of Ivan Gundulić's *Osman* (circa 1651). In the next essay, on the rhymes of the Serbian poet Jovan Jovanović Zmaj, he makes observations about and comments on rhyme in the European tradition and, especially, its tradition on Yugoslav territory. He discusses Zmaj's versification forms and his use of imperfect rhymes. Arriving at the poets of his own century Slamnig writes about the term and phenomenon of the "secession" in Croatian poetry, which lasted from approximately 1897 to 1920, when the avant-garde appeared. Slamnig discusses the verse of Jure Kaštelan, who felt a strong kinship to Walt Whitman, although he modified his style, and who "has a good knowledge of the theory of constructing a poem." However, Slamnig adds, "he never published a poem written in strict traditional tonic rhythm or in whatever consistent, existing form. He is hindered by the mechanical character of such poetry—he simply has no use for it." Slamnig also discusses Josip Pupačić.

Slamnig's only novel is *Bolja polovica hrabrosti* (The Better Half of Courage, 1972), which was translated into Hungarian and Polish. As in many of his story lines, Slamnig takes the reader to his student years; again, the reader is introduced to a group of university students, classmates, and friends. The work is written, especially in the beginning, in a light style, and the atmosphere is recognizable from his short stories. Slamnig loves to interweave his text with English, German, and other foreign words and expressions. As could be expected, this work, too, is written in first-person narration. Several threads run through the novel: there are the narrator's relations to two young women, Zeta and Anita, and to some other students. Above all, there is Zeta's aunt (never called by her name), with whom the narrator has personal contact but who is primarily important because of her manuscript, her life, and her love story, which is inserted (in italics) in the text in four fragments. This character enables the author to introduce the years of World War II into his novel. Another element in "The Better Half of Courage" is the students' archeological interest, their expeditions to remote Croatian villages, and their discovery of an epitaph from 1828 (the text, apparently authentic, is reproduced here and, in a scholarly context, in one of the papers in *Seven Approaches to the Poem*).

Bibliographies:
Savremeni književni prevodioci Jugoslavije (Belgrade: Savez književnih prevodilaca Jugoslavije, 1970);

Vasa D. Mihailovich and Mateja Matejić, *A Comprehensive Bibliography of Yugoslav Literature in English, 1593–1980* (Columbus, Ohio: Slavica, 1984), p. 172; second supplement, p. 123.

References:
Dalibor Cvitan, *Ironični narcis* (Zagreb: Matica hrvatska, 1971), pp. 54, 252;

Cvitan, "Narcisoidnost i ironija Ivana Slamniga," *Književnik*, no. 6 (1959);

Branimir Donat, "Bolja polovica hrabrosti," *Teka* (1972);

Donat, "Liričar parafraze [limb]," *Kritika*, no. 4 (1969);

Thomas Eekman, "Disciplina mašte," *International PEN Bulletin of Selected Books*, 17 (1966): 110–111; *Books Abroad*, 41 (1967): 361;

Aleksandar Flaker, "Bolja polovica romana," *Zbornik zagrebačke slavističke škole*, no. 3 (1975);

Boško Ivkov, "*Disciplina mašte* od Ivana Slamniga," *Letopis Matice srpske*, no. 5 (1966);

Stanko Lasić, *Problemi narativne strukture* (Zagreb: Liber, 1977), pp. 85–92;

Igor Mandić, *Uz dlaku* (Zagreb: Mladost, 1970), pp. 34, 228;

Branko Mikasinovich, "Limb," *Books Abroad*, 43 (1969): 625–626;

Pavao Pavličić, "Ivan Slamnig, 'When I Am Fed up with Everything,'" *Bridge*, no. 2 (1986): 22–31;

Dušan Puvačić, "Bolja polovica hrabrosti," *Books Abroad*, 43 (1973): 586–587;

Draško Redjep, "Novele Ivana Slamniga," *Letopis Matice srpske*, no. 1 (1964);

Miroslav Šicel, *Pregled novije hrvatske književnosti* (Zagreb: Liber, 1979), p. 182; bibliography, p. 239;

Ivo Smoljan, *Ćudi knjige* (Zagreb: August Cesarec, 1972), p. 71;

Miroslav Vaupotić, *Hrvatska suvremena književnost / Contemporary Croatian Literature* (Zagreb: PEN Club Centre, 1966), pp. 78–79, 146–149, 194–195;

Vaupotić, "Pripovjedanje kao svjesna igra (*Povratnik s mjeseca*)," *Republika*, no. 12 (1965);

Stojan Vučićević, "Zavičajni dnevnik Ivana Slamniga," *Mogućnosti*, no. 4 (1966).

Milivoj Slaviček
(24 October 1929 -)

Aida Vidan
Harvard University

BOOKS: *Zaustavljena pregršt* (Zagreb: Mladost, 1954);
Daleka pokrajina (Zagreb: Lykos, 1957);
Modro veče (Zagreb: Zora, 1959);
Predak (Zagreb: Naprijed, 1963);
Noćni autobus ili naredni dio cjeline (Zagreb: Zora, 1964);
Soneti, pjesme o ljubavi i ostale pjesme (Čakovec: Ogranak Matice hrvatske, 1967);
Purpurna pepeljara, naime to i to (Zagreb: Naprijed, 1969);
Poglavlje (Zagreb: Razlog, 1970);
Naslov što ga nikad neću zaboraviti (Sarajevo: Veselin Masleša, 1974);
Otvoreno radi (eventualnog) preuredjenja (Zagreb: Alfa-August Cesarec, 1978);
Pjesme neke buduće knjige (Split: Čakavski sabor, 1979);
Trinaesti pejzaž (Zagreb: Znanje, 1981);
Teror/Terror (Zagreb: Biblioteka Biškupić, 1981);
Sjaj ne/svakodnevnice (Zagreb: Naprijed, 1987);
Nastanjen uvijek (Zagreb: Kršćanska sadašnjost, 1990).
Collections: *Izmedju. Izbor pjesama* (Kruševac: Bagdala, 1965);
Izabrane pjesme (Zagreb: Nakladni zavod Matice hrvatske, 1987).
Editions in English: Poems, translated by Vasa D. Mihailovich, Ronald Moran, Charles David Wright, and Sonia Bićanić, *The Bridge,* no. 19-20 (1970): 52-54;
Poems, translated by Vasa D. Mihailovich and Ronald Moran, in *Contemporary Yugoslav Poetry,* edited by Mihailovich (Iowa City: Iowa University Press, 1977), pp. 93-97;
"The Story of the Belt of the Earth" and "An Encounter with Križanić (with the Memorial Tablet in His Honor) in Warsaw," translated by Antun Nizeteo and G. Marvin Tatum, *Journal of Croatian Studies,* no. 22 (1981): 128-130;
"Some Huge Flag of Mine" and "My Dog and I,"

Milivoj Slaviček

translated by Mihailovich, *The Bridge,* no. 3 (1982): 59-60;
Silent Doors, selected poems translated by Branko Gorjup and Jeannette Lynes (Toronto: Exile Editions, 1988);
Poems, translated by Branko Gorjup and Jeannette Lynes, *Exile,* 14, no. 3 (1990): 42-45; *Exile,* 16, no. 4 (1992): 124.

OTHER: *A Collection of Modern Croatian Verse,* edited by Slaviček (Zagreb: Hrvatski centar P.E.N. Cluba, 1965);

Wewnetrzne morze. Antologia poezji chorwackiej XX wieku, edited by Slaviček (Krakow: Wydawnictwo Literackie, 1982).

Milivoj Slaviček's first public appearance as a poet occurred in January 1947, while he was a high-school student. As the youngest member of the *Omladinski literarni kružok* (Youth Literary Circle), established at the University of Zagreb in the fall of 1946, he participated in a literary evening organized by this group of young literary enthusiasts. Important names of modern Croatian literature, such as Jure Kaštelan, Slobodan Novak, Živko Jeličić, and Vesna Parun, all engaged in the activities of the *Kružok,* which quickly gained attention because of the talent of its members as well as their willingness to experiment with the themes and forms of their works. However, it was precisely the challenging spirit of Parun's and Slaviček's respective poems, as different as they are, that provoked official criticism at the literary evening in 1947. In the postwar period of renovation and pragmatism, Slaviček's individualistic, experimental verse, with its shrewd commentary on society, was not welcome. The criticism that he received at the literary evening caused fluctuations in the quality and the orientation of Slaviček's early works, but it did not prevent his eventually developing an authentic, highly recognizable poetic voice.

Slaviček was born on 24 October 1929 in Čakovec, in the northern Croatian region of Medjimurje. His father, Mato, a lawyer by profession, was from Medjimurje as well, while the poet's mother, Dragica, came from Slavonija. After Slaviček finished elementary school in Prelog, he moved to Zagreb, where he completed his secondary education. He obtained his bachelor of arts degree from the College of Philosophy, University of Zagreb, in 1954. After graduation, in addition to his uninterrupted activity as a poet, he held a variety of jobs: he was a collector of commercial announcements for telephone directories, a salesman, a teacher, and a librarian. Besides writing poetry, he has also worked as an editor of several literary publications and made contributions in the field of literary criticism. His translations from several Slavic languages have brought him wide recognition. The various important literary awards he has won in Croatia, as well as the numerous translations of his works into other European languages, have established Slaviček's central position in contemporary Croatian poetry. Since 1969 he has divided his time between Zagreb and Warsaw.

Slaviček belongs to the "*Krugovi* generation," the group of young Croatian writers that established the literary publication *Krugovi* (Circles) in 1952. In critical analyses of postwar Croatian poetry his name is usually connected with those of Slavko Mihalić and Ivan Slamnig and opposed to the more traditional expression of Vesna Parun and Jure Kaštelan. Although Slaviček's first verses announced the arrival of a potentially interesting contributor to the Croatian literary scene, it should be noted that not all of his early poems are of equal quality. The pressure of political factors in Yugoslavia in the 1950s and the demand for an optimistic, collective viewpoint in literature made Slaviček occasionally succumb to themes and forms not well suited to his talent. The meanderings of a young poet are thus most obvious in his early collections, *Zaustavljena pregršt* (The Restrained Armful, 1954), and *Daleka pokrajina* (A Far Away Province, 1957), although even in these one can find poems such as "Pušim lulu, držim je prstima, i gledam u dim" (I smoke my pipe, hold it in my fingers, and look at the smoke) that announce Slaviček's typical simplicity, or cycles such as "Vode" (Waters), a group of six sonnets in which the author experiments with this traditional form.

One of Slaviček's main contributions to contemporary Croatian poetry is undoubtedly his unique understanding and use of language. Already in his first poems one sees his preoccupation with colloquial elements and the desire to bring a prosaic quality to poetry. This tendency deepens and becomes more prominent as Slaviček matures, gradually transforming the somewhat sentimental overtones of his early poems into the tongue-in-cheek attitude or even openly voiced sarcasm and irony in his later works. Some critics have seen this approach as a deliberate statement, stressing Slaviček's conscious and (in the later period) consistent avoidance of both poetic devices and poetic language. This tendency toward a "democratic" expression in verse has its roots in the Croatian *moderna* and is apparent also in the works of Antun Branko Šimić and Dragutin Tadijanović, the latter of whom is often regarded as the poet who had the greatest influence on Slaviček.

Slaviček, however, does not follow his predecessors in terms of sound experimentation, something that remains for the most part foreign to his style. As a result much of his poetry comes close to "spilling" into prose, and it is only in the correlation and juxtaposition of phrases and syntactic units that one can recognize poetic principles at work. The opening of an untitled poem from his collection *Daleka pokrajina* is typical: "The city loves me so when it's deserted and white / and the dear places sleep under the snow as if non-existent / they only kiss me softly with silence and silence." On the lexical level it is not only that Slaviček brings urban colloquial expressions into his verse, but that he also refuses to use romantically colored nature vocabulary in the fashion typical for most of his predecessors and contemporaries. Nature, in its concrete manifestations, is absent from Slaviček's poetry. On the rare occasions when it is mentioned, it is mostly viewed from an urban environment as something distant, almost symbolic.

The only contact between Slaviček's lyric persona and nature happens in the city parks, and even then it remains superficial. Because Slaviček's primary concern is with humanity, he observes nature exclusively in relation to human existence, to which it remains secondary. As specific as Slaviček can be about urban landscapes, he remains distant and abstract in his rare evocations of images from nature. This can be observed, for example, in the poem "Rijeka i ja smo u neprijateljstvu" (The River and I Are in a State of Enmity) from the collection *Modro veče* (Blue Evening, 1959). In eleven rebellious verses, in which Slaviček calls for and celebrates individuality, the motif of the river is used as a metaphor for everything that is mainstream, obedient, and unchallenging. Throughout the poem the river remains an abstract notion and is stripped of any specific attributes.

It is in this collection that Slaviček comes to terms with his inclinations as a poet and more courageously discards traditional frameworks. In addition, his preoccupation with the position of the common person in the alienating conditions of twentieth-century civilization clearly takes a central position in this book. Even the title of one of its poems, "Vrijeme je da se dogadja napokon Čovjek" (It Is Time for the Man to Finally Happen), is enough to indicate this concern. In the opening verses of an untitled poem from the same collection Slaviček essentially states his unwritten poetics and underscores the thematic range that is to recur in his poetry for decades: "It is necessary to write an entirely everyday poem / simply express it as a conversation as a meeting as melancholy / between the small things after the working hours and before the working hours." In the same way in which Slaviček deintellectualized the language of his poems and freed his style from the burden of tradi-

Cover for a 1969 collection of Slaviček's poems that demonstrate the poet's technique of focusing on small objects as a way of illuminating large issues

tion, he introduced the apparently banal particulars of everyday existence as a legitimate subject of poetry.

As Antun Šoljan observes in his essay "Tri aspekta suvremenosti u poeziji Milivoja Slavičeka" (Three Aspects of Contemporaneity in the Poetry of Milivoj Slaviček, *Forum*, 1979), Slaviček's orientation toward the colloquial and everyday was a way of avoiding the prescribed formulaic language and narrow thematic scope of officially propagated literature. "Aspiration towards the everyday spoken language," Šoljan writes, "is at the same time the aspiration towards live, unpetrified, ungovernable, and unmanipulated (as opposed to axiomatic, normative, impoverished, formulaic) language which took over not only in the domain of the discursive, but also in that of poetry." Slaviček's nonchalant linguistic attitude thus masks his desire for liberation; it is a sign of protest and, to use Šoljan's words, "a repository of common sense" that reveals the absurdity of any closed system, political, linguistic, or poetic. This is clearly stated in his poem "Naknadni predgovor" (Subsequent Foreword) from the collection *Naslov što ga nikad neću zaboraviti* (The Title I Will Never Forget, 1974): "Do not look for philosophy (philosophical system, philosophical treatise) in this poem / For philosophy has (for a long time already) been 'a discipline,' while poetry is not 'a discipline' / ... / Mine is the oldest poetics: non-existent / It is as man is."

Slaviček's poetry can be regarded as a diary of quotidian urban minutiae that nevertheless has a much more ambitious task than mere description. In a spontaneous and straightforward fashion the author uncovers "between the small things" the problems and anxieties of the individual in the street who is equally concerned with the political and social schemes peculiar to this century and with the problems of human existence in general. Critics have viewed this humanistic line in Slaviček's poetry as his "criticism of practical living," or as the poet's "practical mission in the world." A good illustration of this is his often-quoted poem "Mašta (U dubini XX. stoljeća n.e.)" (Imagination [In the Depth of the XXth Century A.D.]), from the collection *Predak* (The Ancestor, 1963):

> With sweat on my face I turn from side to side
> prostrated on my back: magicians and founders of religions spoke of it
> showing it as fate and punishment. Philosophers and psychologists wrote about it
> ......
> the thing got more and more complicated
> even the revolutionaries came to say their word
> ......
> It would be high time for them to celebrate my patience, too.

Slaviček's ironic use of trivial phrases, his intensely realistic and simplified language, reflects the reasoning of a common person who, exasperated and embittered by the way the world is, tries to find some reason for the current state of affairs and to voice his protest.

In many poems Slaviček simply lists events and observations that are invariably rooted in a modest individual experience. This perspective "from the bottom" connects these poems with those in which the rebellious tones are more obvious. "Recitativ iz jednog četvrtka" (Recitative from a Thursday), in the same collection, contrasts the nonevents in the experiences of a common person with the seemingly significant events brought by the newspapers:

> ...mid-December in some express restaurant
> where people stand and sip and chat and eat something
> and look at some tiny spot outside these rooms
> And the popular songsters hum through the small loudspeakers
> and it's smoky and the cash registers are busy
> ......
> that day when you waited for the newspapers
> (those days many things were happening).

The "important" events from the newspapers are announced but never elaborated, while the insignificant particulars observed by the lyric persona are given in full. It could be argued that Slaviček's poetics is grounded in "the pragmatics of insignificance," to borrow the title of Cathy Popkin's book (1993) in which she attributes this principle to prose works by Nikolay Gogol, Anton Čexov, and Mikhail Zoščenko. Indeed, Slaviček's perception of what is significant and deserves to enter literature has much in common with the views of the three great Russian authors. The reasons behind his choices of what is significant are different, but ultimately what connects them is that they are made in relation to someone else's definition of what is relevant or important. Thus, writing about what is considered unimportant becomes a political statement that comments on the views in a given literature or society, or both.

Slaviček's poetry is dialogic in its nature and makes every attempt to involve the reader, which is quite often achieved by addressing him directly. In his poem "Kompleksni i šarmirajući putovi prema katastrofi" (Complex and Charming Paths Toward Catastrophe), from the collection *Pjesme neke buduće knjige* (Poems from Some Future Book, 1979), the end is left open, and it is the reader who is supposed to supply it. The reader is already involved in the first verse by means of the first-person plural:

> Of course we are going towards a catastrophe
> Listening to the singers, singing, working, swearing; being elated less and less
> (and the cohorts of politicians pose more and more)
> ......
> Everyone has to eat better and more scientifically, everyone has to have (at least) two children
> Everyone has to have (also) a so-called automobile (telephone, television), and has to fly as well.

Having named in a lengthy list at least some activities typical for a reader who belongs to modern Western civilization, and having questioned at the same time his choice of the significant, Slaviček leaves the future choices and final decision about the priorities in one's life precisely to the reader: "The continuation of the poem is in your hands / I just collect the data / (and in this or that way compress them) / (or just sort them)." In this way the reader becomes both the author's collaborator and his fellow participant in the creative process of writing and living.

Conversation is at the crux of many of Slaviček's poems, not only lexically but also structurally. Frequently the poet selects what appear to be random utterances and uses them as the basic material of the poem. Examples of this technique occur in the cycle "Tri pjesme o rečenicama" (Three Poems on Sentences), from *Predak,* as well as in the poems "Pjesma o riječi nikad" (Poem About the Word Never), from *Purpurna pepeljara, naime to i to* (The Purple Ashtray, Namely That and That, 1969), and in "Preozbiljna pjesma" (A Too Serious Poem), from *Otvoreno radi (eventualnog) preuredjenja* (Open Due to [a Possible] Renovation, 1978). In these poems the lyric persona introduces the main theme only to withdraw into the background and let the other (undefined, but clearly quoted) voices provide statements related to the main theme. The lyric persona reappears at the end to make a concluding point. This multiplicity of voices intensifies the impression of dialogue and, in a sense, underscores the prose orientation of Slaviček's poetry. In this organization of the poems, the lyric persona can be perceived as a narrator, while a series of juxtaposed utterances can be viewed as representations of characters' voices. This quality is yet another proof that Slaviček is a poet of polyphony and openness rather than of monologue and closed systems.

From Slaviček's first book of poetry to the most recent, certain themes and techniques recur. Moreover, the author quite often brings the works of previous years into his new collections, thereby encouraging the reader to disregard the chronology and to read his poems not as separate entities but rather in relation to one another. It could even be argued that they are to be perceived as different chapters of a single text whose logic does not depend on a temporal sequence. The tone that connects different chapters of Slaviček's oeuvre is one of simplicity, resistance, and protest, which is what makes this poetry "with a mission" or "poetry of detail" so recognizable.

References:

Branko Gorjup and Jeannette Lynes, Afterword to *Silent Doors,* by Milivoj Slaviček (Toronto: Exile Editions, 1988), pp. 117-121;

Vlatko Pavletić, Foreword to Slaviček's *Izabrana djela* (Zagreb: Nakladni zavod Matice hrvatske, 1987), pp. 7-46;

Toma Podrug, "Jednostavno o jednostavnom," *Republika,* nos. 2-3 (1971): 253-254;

Petar Šegedin, "Uz trinaest pjesama Milivoja Slaviček," *Forum,* no. 6 (1964): 839-843;

Antun Šoljan, "Tri aspekta suvremenosti u poeziji Milivoja Slavičeka," *Forum,* no. 12 (1979): 1016-1036;

Ante Stamać, "Otisci pred vratima," *Razlog,* nos. 52-53 (1967): 281-285.

Antun Šoljan
(1 December 1932 - 9 July 1993)

Ellen Elias-Bursać
Harvard University

BOOKS: *Na rubu svijeta* (Zagreb: Matica hrvatska, 1956);

Specijalni izaslanici (Zagreb: Naklada Društva književnika Hrvatske, 1957);

Izvan fokusa (Zagreb: Lykos, 1957);

Izdajice (Zagreb: Zora, 1961);

Kratki izlet (Belgrade: Prosveta, 1965);

Trogodišnja kronika poezije hrvatske i srpske 1960-1962: kritike poezije iz tjednika Telegram (Zagreb: Naprijed, 1965);

Ganlic za čas kratiti (Kruševac: Bagdala, 1965);

Deset kratkih priča za moju generaciju (Novi Sad: Matica srpska, 1966);

Devet drama (Zagreb: Matica hrvatska, 1970);

Gazela i druge pjesme (Zagreb: Matica hrvatska, 1970);

Zanovijetanje iz zamke; Deset godina podlistaka, 1960-1970; feljtoni (Zagreb: Znanje, 1972);

Luka (Zagreb: Znanje, 1974);

Ovo i druga mora (Zagreb: Školska knjiga, 1975);

Obiteljska večera i druge priče (Zagreb: Naprijed, 1975);

Čitanje Ovidijevih Metamorfoza/Rustichello (Zagreb: Biblioteka Studentskog centra Sveučilišta u Zagrebu, 1976);

Drugi ljudi na Mjesecu (Zagreb: Znanje, 1978);

Bacač kamena (Zagreb: Matica hrvatska, 1985);

Hrvatski Joyce i druge igre (Zagreb: Grafički zavod Hrvatske, 1989);

Sloboda čitanja (Zabreb: Graficki Zarod Hrvatske, 1991);

Prošlo nesvršeno vrijeme (Zagreb: Hrvatska sveučilišna naklada, 1992);

Prigovori (Zagreb: Durieux, 1993).

Editions and Collections: *Izabrane pjesme* (Novi Sad: Matica srpska, 1976);

Antun Šoljan: Izabrana djela I and II (Zagreb: Matica hrvatska, 1987);

Izabrana djela Antuna Šoljana (Zagreb: Grafički zavod Hrvatske, 1991).

Antun Šoljan

Editions in English: "King," and "Travelling," translated by Charles Simic, *Confrontation*, 7 (1973): 32-33;

"The Man Who Throws Stones," translated by Simic, *Confrontation*, 8 (1974): 21-22;

"Ship in a Bottle," translated by Antun Šoljan, *New England Review*, 1, no. 4 (1979): 445-450;

The Stone Thrower and Other Poems, translated by Simic and others (Toronto: Exile Publications, 1990);

"The Bard," translated by William E. Yuill, *Most/The Bridge*, 1-2 (1992): 7-80;

"The Mannheim Story," translated by Ellen Elias-Bursać, *North Dakota Quarterly*, (Fall/Winter 1993): 182-185; *Most/The Bridge*, 3 (1994): 17-18;

"Rhinoceroses," translated by Maja Šoljan, *Most/The Bridge*, 3 (1994): 25;

"Shrapnel," translated by Vera Andrassy, *Most/The Bridge*, 3 (1994): 15–16;

The Other People on the Moon: An Adventure Story, translated by Graham McMaster (Zagreb: Croatian Writers' Association, 1994).

PLAY PRODUCTIONS: *Lice*, Zagreb, Mala scena Hrvatskog narodnog kazališta, 19 April 1966;

Brdo, Zagreb, Teatar ITD, 29 April 1967;

Galilejevo uzašašće, Zagreb, Teatar ITD, 29 April 1967;

Dioklecijanova palača, Zagreb, Teatar ITD, 22 February 1969;

Tarampesta; Mototor, Zagreb, Teatar ITD, 12 April 1974;

Romanca o tri ljubavi, Zagreb, Teatar ITD, 10 May 1977;

Bard, Zagreb, Hrvatsko narodno kazalište, 19 May 1987.

TELEVISION: *Sova*, RTV Belgrade, 1965;

Ledeno ljeto, RTV Belgrade, 1968;

Potop, RTV Belgrade, 1969.

RADIO: *Dobre vijesti, gospo*, Radio Zagreb, 1968;

Klopka, Radio Zagreb, 1969;

Starci, Radio Zagreb, 1972;

Tarampesta, Radio Zagreb, 1973;

Čovjek koji je spasio Nizozemsku, Radio Zagreb, 1983.

Throughout his life Antun Šoljan took an activist role in defining the tasks of the writer and the writer's relation to society. Many threads make up his creative work: fiction, essays, translations, poetry, and plays. His written works place him among the most significant of the postwar Croatian writers, but his importance as a writer and cultural figure transcends his writing. Šoljan was, from 1974 to 1993, the éminence grise of the Croatian cultural scene and, because he dissented from the Communist political line, a persona non grata in public life who was prevented from appearing in the media, in interviews, or in person. His forced absence, however, guaranteed a ubiquitous presence for his ideas and views. After 1990 Šoljan's was an impassioned public voice until his death.

Šoljan was born in Belgrade on 1 December 1932. Only nine years old when World War II spilled over into Yugoslavia, he spent the war years in Slavonski Brod. After the war he moved to Zagreb, where he studied German and English literature. In later years he divided his time between Zagreb and Rovinj. He became editor first of the short-lived journal *Medutim* (However) in 1953, then of *Krugovi* (Circles) from 1955 to 1958, and of *Književnik* (Writer) from 1959 to 1961. From 1970 to 1973 he was president of the Croatian P.E.N. He died in Zagreb on 9 July 1993, survived by his wife, two daughters, and two grandchildren. Šoljan's family originally came from Dalmatia, and his family ties to the Dalmatian coast are perhaps the source of his profound attachment to things maritime. The language he uses when he writes, however, rarely reflects the dialect of his Dalmatian heritage but is rather an excellent example of standard urban Croatian usage.

Even a cursory glance at a few of Šoljan's titles suggests that his work is an exploration of the political role of the writer: *Izdajice* (Traitors, 1961), *Bacač kamena* (The Stone Thrower, 1985), *Zanovijetanje iz zamke* (Grumbling from a Trap, 1972), *Sloboda čitanja* (The Freedom of Reading, 1991), and *Prigovori* (Objections, 1993). Influenced by T. S. Eliot and Jean-Paul Sartre, he was maturing as a writer during the 1940s and early 1950s when the debate on engagement in literature was raging. Out of this emerged his lifelong dedication to the notion of an active role for the writer in society, but rather than the engagement envisaged by the socialist leadership of the time, his was one committed to individual expression, mercilessly candid literary criticism, and a literature of true spiritual values.

Šoljan speaks most directly of his thoughts on being a writer in his verse. His poems are only rarely addressed to others; most are either implicitly or explicitly in the first person. The poems are mostly on the nature of art and writing. He enjoys rhyme and uses it for its musicality, levity, and impact, but his poems are governed more by the rhythms of speech than by fixed rhyme schemes.

Šoljan wrote fifteen plays for theater, radio, and television. Unlike his poetry, his plays are not structured around a Šoljan-like character. They employ a small cast and use the framework of theatrical discourse to explore, in essaylike fashion, the twists of human nature, the struggle of the individual against authority, and the interaction of human frailty and historical myth. Two of his plays stand out from the rest for their complexity and narrative plots. One, *Bard* (1987), is a portrayal of the relationship between a writer from a fictitious Central American country, Costa Mala, who has been living abroad, and his government, which is pressuring him to return home on its terms. The other, *Čovjek koji je spasio Nizozemsku* (The Man Who Saved the Netherlands, 1983), describes the plight of a guest worker in the Netherlands who comes across a hole in a dike and plugs it with his finger. The dike he is plugging has been abandoned for some time, but, nevertheless, he is certain that he is saving the Netherlands. This play, written for radio, has been translated into fourteen languages and was awarded the Prix Futura award in Berlin in 1985.

Šoljan is best known for his novels and short stories. He brings to his writing a stylistic clarity and linguistic control unusual among his predecessors. Šoljan's first book of fiction, the short-story collection *Specijalni izaslanici* (Special Envoys), appeared in 1957. In it he inaugurates a nihilistic voice new to Croatian prose. Take, for example, the closing lines of "Kiša" (Rain):

> The rain was still coming down from above, from nowhere, falling nowhere, and I was dangling like a dead bat and women feared me, passersby sidestepped around me carefully. It seemed to me, that I could remember myself in similar situations. I must have experienced this before. The rain kept falling. I stood there and did not leave. I wouldn't leave. At least not too soon. Perhaps not even tomorrow. Perhaps not even the day after tomorrow. Perhaps not this whole week.

Šoljan's fictional writing is narrated, with few exceptions, in the first person. He uses elements of fantasy: a diabolical, plague-ridden gypsy holding the narrator in her thrall; a narrator who finds himself on board a ship in a bottle; a choral ensemble that arrives at a town to hold a concert only to end up buried all together in a single grave in the town's cemetery; and the madonna of the freeway, a woman standing on a bridge over a highway, her spectral silhouette sending people hurtling into the setting sun, into fatal accidents.

There are stories that demonstrate the same acerbic social commentary found in his poems and plays. In *Obiteljska večera* (A Family Dinner, 1975) the narrator, a writer, has spent his adult life eluding his nemesis, a fellow student from university days who is an aggressive political and social climber. The two men run into each other on the waterfront in Split:

> I knew that I really ought to hightail it out of there. But he had already begun, with his boisterous exclamations, to let the entire waterfront know he had bumped into an old friend; with elbows jabbing my ribs and a fist at my back he steered toward his hospitable home. People turned, uncertain whether they were witnessing an overflowing of heartfelt congeniality, or an arrest. And though I strained my gray matter to engineer a getaway, I was hooked like a fish on a line, and delivered straight to the dinner table.

The first of Šoljan's four novels, *Izdajice,* is a loosely knit string of short stories revolving around a crew of artists and writers fixing up a summer house in the town of Rovinj, on the Istrian coast. Even this early writing demonstrates Šoljan's technique of starting with comic, often poignant vignettes and moving from them to stark images of barren landscapes or lives headed nowhere.

His second novel, *Kratki izlet* (Brief Excursion, 1965), a picaresque allegorical adventure of a group of art historians seeking frescoes in Istrian towns, also moves between these two poles. Typically, his characters are stirred to action by the chimera of something they covet, something often obscured by the mists of the past, only to find themselves faced, in the end, with nothing. In *Kratki izlet* the chimera is the sought-for frescoes: a tantalizing hint of hidden riches and forgotten beauty. In the end the narrator arrives, alone, at nowhere:

> I found myself in a vast, gray rolling stony landscape which stretched off into the distance. The sky was covered with the curtain of a cloud and the diffuse moonlight illuminated the landscape phantasmagorically. There was nothing in that landscape, no houses, no vegetation, no man or beast, only bare rock and a pale gray moonlight, poisonous as mercury. The sky was lower than it ever had been. I stepped into that world, but I couldn't hear my own step. I felt as if I were walking not on rocks, but on heaps of wool, in ankle-deep fog. It was like some phantom-like birth on deaf ground. Nothing. Nothing. Nothing.

Šoljan invariably moves between these two extremes in his fiction: the poignant beauty of a lost world and the ultimate, unpeopled void. In his two later novels, *Luka* (The Port, 1974) and *Drugi ljudi na Mjesecu* (The Other People on the Moon, 1978), he refines the dynamic. The latter, an adventure story about two men traveling by raft up the Adriatic Coast to Istria in search of amphoras, starts with the poignant image of a map the narrator had inherited from his fisherman father, which has marked on it the sites of shipwrecks and amphoras in a faded, nearly illegible hand. The one perfect amphora they do wrest from the deep disappears when their raft is torn apart in a storm. They find themselves on board a cruising ship with Italian cigarette smugglers, assisting unintentionally in the smugglers' capture and ending the story, as always, empty-handed.

Luka is the most starkly cynical of all Šoljan's fiction. The protagonist, an engineer, is selected to oversee the construction of a port to service recently discovered petroleum wells. The town he has been assigned to transform into an industrial port is the town from which his family came. The politicos in charge of the project inform him that he must set an example for the recalcitrant local inhabitants by relinquishing his family home to eminent domain. He agrees to this, compromising his relationship with the townspeople, only to discover that the petroleum has run out. The project is abandoned, and he has burned the bridges to his past. In 1992 *Luka* was made into a film by director Tomislav Radić.

Šoljan's more recent writing further describes the movement from poignancy to nothingness. He opens his story "Mont Blanc" (1986) with the words:

> I bought myself a new fountain pen the other day–Mont Blanc–and I wanted to try it out, to write something with it at once. I could no longer write anything with the old one: it had been worn down dragging across all manner of paper, and with abuse: I'd used it to poke around a clogged drain, to clean finger nails, to punch holes in my belt. I could no longer recognize my own handwriting: it had warped, it kept getting stuck on the paper as if gasping. Great hopes were placed on the new fountain pen. With the new fountain pen at least I'd recover my old handwriting, if not some other, greater successes. But it didn't work. I had nothing to say.

In "Mannheimska priča" (The Mannheim Story, 1990) he tells of an old boat he had had with a motor retooled from the motor of a cement mixer. As a younger man he had notified the manufacturer in Mannheim that their motor was still working in hopes that they might consider placing it in their museum. From them he receives a disappointing, though courteous, reply. He ends the story musing, amidst a talk he is holding years later in Mannheim:

> Perhaps there is a factory here with spare parts in stock for me, perhaps here is the place where I can undergo a general overhaul, and afterward maybe I'll feel re-tooled, like new, ready to ply the seas with replenished vigor while in me pounds, if not a new heart, at least a brand new *pacemaker*. . . .

> But I don't know whom to turn to, I never seem to know the address I'm supposed to write to, and I fear that all the addresses where I keep sending my secret, sly calls for help will stay silent as usual, and should they reply, that their response will be, as usual, a polite, perfectly reasonable but rather disappointing answer.

There are satiric moments in all of Šoljan's writing, but the most purely satiric piece he wrote is a spoof published in 1989: *Hrvatski Joyce i druge igre* (The Croatian Joyce), a takeoff on academic scholarship. He provides an introduction to the work of fictitious author Šimun Freudenreich, then presents the author's invented work: *Budjenje Smail-age* (The Awakening of Smail-Aga), followed by an array of footnotes. The piece is a hodgepodge of satiric arrows aimed at local scholars, English literary scholarship, and, of course, political innuendo.

Over the years Šoljan translated into Croatian verse by Aleksandr Blok, T. S. Eliot, Edgar Allan Poe, Ezra Pound, and Mark Strand; he co-edited two anthologies of American and English poetry; and he translated the prose of Lewis Carroll, Joseph Heller, Ernest Hemingway, Norman Mailer, Henry Miller, George Orwell, and F. Scott Fitzgerald, and plays by William Shakespeare, Bertolt Brecht, Harold Pinter, Eugene O'Neill, and Tom Stoppard. Šoljan often worked in tandem with writer Ivan Slamnig. Their coupled names, Šoljan/Slamnig, became synonymous with a playful, innovative approach to translation.

Essays are yet another form that Šoljan often used. He represents a profoundly personal point of view in his essays, writing with an emotional rationality. After 1990, when Šoljan was again able to participate in public life, he did so most frequently through his essays, which appeared in the daily papers. One essay in particular, "Glagoljanje nad gelerom" (Talking Over Shrapnel, 1992), a reflection inspired by a bomb shard that smashed through the window of Šoljan's study and lodged in the wall directly behind his desk chair in October 1991, is perhaps the most articulate crystallization of the bitterness and rage he and other Croatian intellectuals felt concerning the betrayal, as they perceived it, by Serbian intellectuals who either openly provoked the war or did not do enough to stop it.

The earlier critiques of Šoljan's works were either book reviews as his work appeared or attacks on his politics. In a raging polemic Goran Babić accuses him in 1976 of subverting virtually all of Croatian culture. He claims that Šoljan, with his literature of emptiness, is whining; that the entire "Krugovi" generation is a chorus of whiners; and that with their vocal discontent they, led by Šoljan, succeeded in poisoning the minds of the younger generation and leading them astray in the unrest of the early 1970s. Indeed, both those benevolent toward and those inimical to Šoljan's writing focused on his nihilism. Šoljan himself had the following to say in the article "Kratka povijest 'Kratkog izleta' " (Brief History of *Brief Excursion,* 1990):

> Deep in my soul, I somehow believe that a person by the very nature of his constitution can not confess to or speak of a genuine nihilism. But well-informed people do know that cautious, tentative nihilism is a plausible position, before which they mustn't close their eyes, and against which they still have found no convincing, let alone defensible, arguments. Which does not suggest, of course, that there is no further need to continue seeking such arguments. Each of us, when we run into this position in life or writing, does so instinctively.

In articles after his death critics concur on the crucial role he played both within the sphere of literature and beyond it. Aleksandar Flaker comments: "We do not know what to emphasize more: his ridicule, his angst or his wisdom." Kušan, in an article in *The Bridge,* "The Secret of Success" (1994), concludes that the secret of Šoljan's success was his courage: "Šoljan always kept his head above the morass. They pushed him in, pushed him under, slapped him, but he always surfaced cleaner and newer." Hrvoje Pejaković, in "The Sailor's Cheerful Testament" in the same issue of *The Bridge,* notes that Šoljan maintained a critical, skeptical attitude toward reality, never trading the right to his own opinion for the ostensible advantages resulting from compliance to the herd.

The poem "Nipošto, kada umrem," from the book of verse *Prigovori* (Objections, 1993), is Šoljan's last poem in his last book. It addresses the question of his own death, a subject he had ten years to think about while he lived with throat cancer. In these lines he confronts a lifetime of uncompromising landscapes and moves the attention from them to the protagonist. The writer is returned, time and time again, by the stark, unwelcoming beauty of his surroundings to his own, human resources:

> By no means, when I die, would I
> Be star or stone, any thing everlasting,
> Better I be of stuff that is joyously spent
> Muscle and sinew, flank and shoulder.
>
> So that once more in a time of no time,
> So that somewhere in a placeless place,
> I will know naught but of breathing air,
> But of living and rejoicing.

Bibliography:

Branimir Donat, "Bibliografija," in his *Pet stoljeća Hrvatske književnosti* 174/I (Zagreb: Matica hrvatska, 1987), pp. 41–46.

References:

Goran Babić, "Strašno lice ništavila," *Oko,* 124 (1976): 4–5;

Branimir Donat, "Antun Šoljan," in his *Pet stoljeća Hrvatske književnosti* 174/I (Zagreb: Matica hrvatska, 1987), pp. 7–40;

Donat, *Bogatstvo vrta: studija o književnom djelu Antuna Šoljana* (Zagreb: Durieux, 1993);

Donat, "From Disembodied Voice to the Stage: Antun Šoljan as a Playwright," *Most/The Bridge,* 1-2 (1992): 84–89;

Aleksandar Flaker, "I na početku bijaše Šoljan," *Republika,* 1–3 (1994): 75–78;

Ivan Kušan, "The Secret of Success," *Most/The Bridge* (1994);

Marina Gatti Lipovac, "Rustichello," *Uomimi e libri,* 111 (Milano, 1986);

Igor Mandić, "Nesporazumi oko mučeništva," *Vjesnik* (21 December 1968);

Tonko Maroević, "Podrugljivi trubadur," *Slobodna Dalmacija* (10 December 1970);

Vladimir Ognev, "Ekho boljšoj vojny," foreword to the anthology *Poslednaja vysota* (Moscow: Khudožestvennaja literatura, 1970);

Hrvoje Pejaković, "The Sailor's Cheerful Testament," *Most/The Bridge,* 3 (1994): 29–30;

Vjeran Zuppa, "Uvod u Šoljana," *Telegram* (27 March 1970).

Papers:

At present Šoljan's papers, letters, manuscripts, and other private effects are held by family members.

Aco Šopov
(20 December 1923 - 20 April 1982)

Graham W. Reid
University of Skopje

BOOKS: *Pesni* (Belgrade & Kumanovo: Tipografi omladinci Srbije, 1944);
Pruga na mladost, by Šopov and Slavko Janevski (Skopje: Glaven odbor na Narodnata mladina na Makedonija, 1947);
Na Gramos (Skopje: NOPOK, 1950);
So naši race (Skopje: Državno knjigoizdatelstvo na Makedonija, 1950);
Stihovi za makata i radosta (Skopje: Kočo Racin, 1952);
Slej se so tišinata (Skopje: Kočo Racin, 1955);
Vetrot nosi ubavo vreme (Skopje: Kočo Racin, 1957);
Nebidnina (Skopje: Kočo Racin, 1963);
Ragjanje na zborot (Skopje: Misla, 1966);
Jus-univerzum (Skopje: Misla, 1968);
Izbor (Skopje: Makedonska kniga, 1968);
Zlaten krug na vremeto (Skopje: Misla, 1969);
Gledač vo pepellu (Skopje: Makedonska kniga, 1972);
Pesni (Skopje, 1974);
Pesna za crnata žena (Skopje: Misla, 1976);
Okeanot e mal, čovekot golem (Skopje: Centar za kultura i informacii, 1977);
Drvo na ridot (Skopje: Misla, 1980);
Luzna (Skopje: Misla, 1980);
Nebo na tišinata (Skopje: Kultura, 1990).
Collection: *Odbrani dela,* 5 volumes (Skopje: Misla, 1976).

TRANSLATIONS: Eduard Bagricki, *Pesna za Apanasa,* translated by Šopov and Slavko Janevski (1951);
Oton Župančič, *Ciciban* (1951);
I. A. Krilov, *Basani* (1953);
Gustav Krklec, *Telegrafski basni* (1954);
Jovan Jovanović Zmaj, *Pesni* (1954);
Pierre Corneille, *Le Cid* (1958);
Grigor Vitez, *Pesna na cuculigata* (1959);
William Shakespeare, *Hamlet* (1960);
Miroslav Krleža, *Pesni/Izbor* (1963);
Izet Sarajlić, *Poezija* (1965);

Aco Šopov

Dragutin Tadijanović, *Vecer nad gradot* (1966);
Shakespeare, *Sonnets* (1970).

Aco Šopov is one of the most important Macedonian poets. He was born on 20 December 1923 in Štip, in eastern Macedonia, where he attended both primary and secondary school. Influenced by his mother, a schoolteacher who herself wrote love lyrics, Šopov's poetic debut took the form of writing for a wall newspaper in his high school. Various societies there provided a focus for people of a literary bent, and to one of these, Vančo Prke–himself a budding poet strongly influenced by Miroslav Krleža–Šopov showed his first notebooks containing poems inspired by cur-

Title page of Šopov's 1976 collection of poems, Pesna za crnata žena (Song for a Black Woman)

rent events. As a young man caught up in the enthusiasm of a revolutionary situation, Šopov wrote his first poems in social protest, as a revolt against injustice.

On the eve of Yugoslavia's involvement in World War II, which began in 1941, Sopov wrote the poem "Anovite" (Inns), describing the fate of the last soldiers to be drafted into the army of prewar Yugoslavia. Soon engaged in the partisan resistance to the Nazi occupying forces, he continued writing poetry in the lulls between fighting. Such are the poems "Ljubov" (Love), written in his army notebook immediately after an engagement, and "Partizanska prolet" (Partisan Spring) written during an attack on the town of Kratovo. These first poems showed Šopov to be a highly personal poet even when he was chronicling events of a social or patriotic nature. They showed a lyrical individuality and an autobiographical intimacy. He found his subject matter in his own experience, as when writing of a much-loved woman who was a fellow partisan, and yet he succeeded in avoiding too great a preoccupation with the self and the clichés of a falsely sentimental intimacy. In the same way his poems of social protest avoid the cheap and easy use of the slogans and catch phrases that were then in vogue.

Šopov's poetry of this period, closely bound with his own experience of a war of national liberation, serves to illustrate his rejection, from the outset, of a utilitarian style with a narrow social or political purpose. This is not to say that these poems do not have a clear message. They treat the horrors of war, the traumas of a people finding itself, and the youthful awakening of consciousness throughout society, and they embody a vision of the future. Treating also the themes of love, struggle, and death, and employing imagery that conjures up an apocalyptic atmosphere, they also have overtones from folk poetry. Defiant and often action packed, they convey deep feeling and contain striking passages and images; nevertheless, these poems, published as *Pesni* (Poems) in Belgrade and Kumanovo in 1944 and in Štip the following year, are primarily of historical interest.

After the war Šopov graduated in philosophy from the University of Skopje and began work in the public sector. He had already been involved editorially in the youth publication *Ogin* (Fire) and from 1947 on was engaged in various literary undertakings: he founded the journal *Idnina* (Future) and at various times worked as editor of *Nov den* (New Day), *Sovremenost* (Contemporaneity) and *Horizont* (Horizon) and the satiric magazine *Osten* (Spur), to all of which he also contributed poems and translations. He then became director of the Makedonska kniga publishing house. His next three books of poetry, *Pruga na mladost* (The Youth's Railroad) (written with Slavko Janevski, 1947), *Na Gramos* (On Gramos, 1950), and *So naši race* (With Our Hands, 1950) developed the themes of his earlier poems and were a further organization of his experience of revolution and national liberation.

With *Stihovi za makata i radosta* (Verses of Suffering and Joy, 1952) and *Slej se so tišinata* (Merge with Silence, 1955) there came a turning point in Šopov's poetry and conceivably in Macedonian poetry at large. Consistently writing out of individual experience, Šopov now began to address his readers as individuals rather than as collectivized humankind. These largely confessional lyrics on romantic lines are poems of feelings, sensuous evocations permeated by the emotions of resignation, pain, sorrow, weariness, parting, and melancholy, while yet retaining a belief in human values. Šopov was writing affirmatively of beauty, love, and freedom in this transitional phase while also acknowledging the existence of ugliness, hatred, and slavery. In his third phase, that of the award-winning collection *Vetrot nosi ubavo vreme* (Winds Bring Nice Weather, 1957), Šopov was engaged in delving as deeply as possible in search of himself, and the resulting poetry was often tinged with a dark melancholy.

The periods of Šopov's poetry are not hermetically self-contained. What distinguishes them is a marked development at each stage in both range and complexity, with no loss of directness and with an increasingly sophisticated simplicity. If, overall, his first phase was one of a movement from the general to the personal and the second phase is marked by writing of a personal nature, the line of his third phase moves from the personal to the universal. These poems present the subject of love as their starting point and project a view of the world and its phenomena as essentially transitory. They present a more complex reality than his previous work, uncovering in the depths of the author's own being that nonbeing that threatens everyone and everything and that constantly hovers in the atmosphere of a world where unrest is unending. No longer either exclamatory or purely confessional, these poems are meditations on an unbeing that emerges not from unbeing as a transcendental system of ideas but from the poet's own experience and his feelings toward the world he inhabits. In these poems of love with a cosmic dimension Šopov employs a wealth of symbols and ideas, finding a place for intellectual experience as well.

The existential questions posed in the poems in *Nebidnina* (Nonbeing, 1963) are developed in the next two collections, *Gledač vo pepelta* (Looking into Ashes, 1972) and *Pesna za crnata žena* (Song for a Black Woman, 1976), written out of the experience of the years 1971 to 1975, when Šopov was the Yugoslav ambassador to Senegal. There is a fusion of content and spirit in a form that allows a certain ambiguity; the formal elements of rhythm and versification are not added decoration but are integral to the whole structure of the poetry as an organizing principle. The author's main concern here is the conflict between humanity and the nature of existence and a resolution of that conflict. He achieves this resolution through the metaphors that extend throughout these three collections. As a proven craftsman, he presents his own experience of life together with the wider drama of human destiny in a reflective synthesis that reaches out to the limits of existence and occasionally to the realm of the absurd. The confessional element is still found in these poems, but it has been rigorously refined. The verse is disciplined, highly organized, and taut, as he carries on an unsparing and at times terrible dialogue with himself, with his poetry, and with literature in general in a world that is often chaotic and indeed verges on the incomprehensible.

In Šopov's later writing unbeing came to represent not only the tragic aspect of human nature but also a Promethean heroism, a Faustian exhilaration, a torch of Heraclitean fire burning in humankind and after and beyond an individual's life. However fleeting human life, however tragic the history of the black peoples of Africa, however isolated the experiences of loss, sickness, and death, humankind is involved in an unceasing struggle through understanding to overcome transience, death, and nothingness. Šopov sees the transcendence of these conditions as a reconciliation of darkness with light, of unbeing with love, of mutability with lastingness, and of life with poetry. Thus, an individual's life and all upon which one has left his mark are transformed into symbols and memories that outlast him.

This is the substance of the poems of the poet's last book, *Drvo na ridot* (A Tree on a Bare Hill, 1980), and those included in the selection *Luzna* (1980). In these poems Šopov achieves a coherent construction with no redundant word or image and a lively and pregnant imagery that binds together the experience of the author and the reader. The language of these poems is penetrating, resonant, and melodic. Poetry is the tool with which the author explores life's mystery, whether this suffuses the beauty of Africa despite the shadow cast by slavery, the lone tree in a bare Macedonian landscape, or the reflections of a clochard in a Paris hospital.

From his earliest work Šopov speaks with his own voice, but his voice developed and was refined in part through his work as a translator. Working mainly from Serbo-Croatian, Russian, and French, he translated into Macedonian, over a period of twenty years, an impressive list of world classics by authors including Pierre Corneille, Edmond Rostand, William Shakespeare, Miroslav Krleža, Jovan Jovanović Zmaj, Izet Sarajlić, and Dragutin Tadijanović. In turn, his poems have been translated into many languages, including English. After a long illness Sopov died in Skopje on 20 April 1982.

References:

Miodrag Drugovac, "The Poetry of Aco Šopov," *Macedonian Review,* 5 (1975): 281-290;

Drugovac, "Umetnik pesme Aco Šopov," in his *Biographia litteraria* (Kruševac: Bagdala, 1970), pp. 70-90;

Milan Gjurčinov, "Refleksivna zrelost na intimata," in his *Kritički svedoštva (1953-1973)* (Skopje: Kultura, 1976), pp. 144-146;

Vojislav I. Ilić, "Aco Šopov–tišine i meditacije," in his *Tokovi makedonske književnosti* (Priština: Jedinstvo, 1976), pp. 273-278;

Radomir Ivanoviḱ, "Otkrivanje na ubavinata: Zapis za poezijata na Aco Šopov," *Razgledi,* 17 (1975): 127-141;

Dimitar Mitrev, "Poezija na trajni vrednosti," *Sovremenost,* 4 (1956): 275-291;

Duško Nanevski, "Lirika na crnata nebidnina," *Sovremenost,* 20 (1970): 387-400;

Georgi Stardelov, "Poetskoto iskustvo na Aco Šopov," *Sovremenost,* 17 (1967): 799-827.

Emiliyan Stanev
(28 February 1907 - 15 March 1979)

Cleo Protokhristova
University of Plovdiv, Bulgaria

BOOKS: *Primamlivi blyasŭtsi: Razkazi* (Sofia: Dobromir Chilingirov, 1938);

Mechtatel: Razkazi (Sofia: Sŭuz na bŭlgarskite pisateli, 1939);

Sami: Razkazi (Sofia: Khemus, 1940);

Vŭlchi noshti: Razkazi (Sofia: Khemus, 1943);

Posledna borba (Sofia: Lŭchezar Stanchev, Biblioteka geroy, 1943);

Prez vodi i gori: Priklyucheniya na edin taralezh i na edna kostenurka. Povest (Sofia: Perun, 1943); revised as *Prez vodi i gori, Lakomoto meche: Razkazi* (Sofia: Bŭlgarski pisatel, 1968);

Lakomoto meche (Sofia: Khemus, 1944); republished as *Slŭnchevoto zayche: Razkazi za detsa* (Sofia: Narodna mladezh, 1954);

Delnitsi i praznitsi: Razkazi (Sofia: Khemus, 1945);

Diva ptitsa: Povest (Sofia: Khemus, 1946);

V tikha vecher: novela (Sofia: Narodna kultura, 1948);

Kradetsŭt na praskovi: Povest (Sofia: Narodna kultura, 1948);

Tezhŭk zhivot: Razkazi (Sofia, 1948);

Povest za edna gora; Roman za yunoshi (Sofia: Narodna mladezh, 1948);

Kogato skrezhŭt se topi: Povest (Sofia: Fizkultura, 1950);

Yanuarsko gnezdo: Razkazi (Sofia: Bŭlgarski pisatel, 1953);

Gorski chudesa: Vesela prikazka za detsa (Sofia: Bŭlgarski pisatel, 1955);

Kŭshtichka pod snega: Prikazka (Sofia: Narodna mladezh, 1955);

Palavnitsa: Prikazka (Sofia: Bŭlgarski hudozhnik, 1955);

Ivan Kondarev: Roman v dva toma, volume 1 (Sofia: Bŭlgarski pisatel, 1958), volume 2 (Sofia: Bŭlgarski pisatel, 1962);

Kozelŭt: Razkazi (Sofia: Narodna mladezh, 1958);

Strashnata ptitsa: Prikazka (Sofia: Spisanie Slaveyche, 1958);

Sŭbi: Razkazi za detsa (Sofia: Bŭlgarski hudozhnik, 1965);

Emiliyan Stanev

Gorska kŭshtichka. Sbornik prikazki (Sofia: Bŭlgarski hudozhnik, 1968);

Legenda za Sibin, Preslavskiya knyaz: Povest (Sofia: Narodna mladezh, 1968);

Antikhrist: Roman (Sofia: Bŭlgarski pisatel, 1970);

Tŭrnovskata tsaritsa. Kradetsŭt na praskovi. Vŭlkŭt. Skot Reynolds i nepostizhimoto (Sofia: Bŭlgarski pisatel, 1973);

Nedovŭrsheni i nepublikuvani tvorbi, stsenarii, publitsistika (Sofia: Bŭlgarski pisatel, 1983).

Editions and Collections: *Chernishka: Izbrani povesti* (Sofia: Narodna kultura, 1950);

Sled lova: Izbrani razkazi (Sofia: Fizkultura, 1954);
Izbrani razkazi (Sofia: Bŭlgarski pisatel, 1957);
Izbrani razkazi povesti (Sofia: Bŭlgarski pisatel, 1965);
Razkazi i povesti (Sofia: Bŭlgarski pisatel, 1968);
Izbrani povesti razkazi (Sofia: Otechestven front, 1976);
Izbrani proizvedeniia, 3 volumes (Sofia: Bŭlgarski pisatel, 1977);
Sŭbrani sŭchineniia v sedem toma, 7 volumes (Sofia: Bŭlgarski pisatel, 1981–1983).

Editions in English: *Over Hill and Dale,* translated by Todor Kirov (Sofia: Foreign Languages Press, 1965);
The Stranger, and Other Short Stories, translated by Marguerite Alexieva and Zdravko Stankov (Sofia: Foreign Languages Press, 1967);
The Peach Thief and Other Bulgarian Stories (London: Cassel, 1968);
Wildlife Heroes and Villains, translated by Alexieva (Harrisburg, Pa.: Stackpole Books, 1969).

Emiliyan Stanev is one of the most characteristic and controversial talents in modern Bulgarian literature. He entered the literary scene in the 1930s and instantly staked his claim as a serious artistic presence. He created a wide range of works—from urban and animal short stories and novellas with profound psychological insight to a variety of novels, some with a strong philosophic fervor. He also wrote for children. Stanev is among the Bulgarian writers who are widely known abroad. His books have been published in England, Germany, Italy, France, Poland, the Czech Republic, Slovakia, Russia, Romania, Greece, the United States, Brazil, Japan, and other countries.

Emiliyan Stanev is the pseudonym of Nikolay Stoyanov Stanev, born in Veliko Tŭrnovo on 28 February 1907 to a clerk's family. Both of Stanev's parents came from families with long traditions, strong patriotic feelings, and an abundance of colorful characters. Stanev finished secondary school in his native city, then studied in Elena, where he finished sixth grade. In 1927 he enrolled in the Art Academy in Sofia, where his intended field was painting; he started his studies under the guidance of Professor Tseno Todorov. At the same time he made his first attempts in fiction. The next year he went to Vratsa to finish high school as a private student, then enrolled in the Free University in Sofia to study finance and trade. Stanev later married Nadezhda Staneva, a well-known translator of French.

His first publication was the short story "Sreshtu Velikden" (Easter Eve, 1931). In 1932 he started working as a minor clerk in the city hall, which remained his job for more than ten years. In 1934 he used the pseudonym "Emiliyan Stanev" for the first time for his short story "Kradetsŭt i kucheto" (The Thief and the Dog). During these years he contributed to the journals *Sŭdba* (Fate), *Zlatorog* (The Golden Horn), *Mlad kooperator* (The Young Cooperative Worker), *Izkustvo i kritika* (Art and Criticism), *Bŭlgarski misŭl* (Bulgarian Thought), and *Lovets* (The Hunter), and to the newspapers *Misŭl* (Thought), *Literaturen glas* (Literary Voice), *Literaturen Sviat* (Literary World), *Nova kambana* (The New Bell), *Literaturen zhivot* (Literary Life), and *Vestnik na zhenata* (The Women's Newspaper), among others.

Stanev's first book, published in 1938 under the title *Primamlivi blyasŭtsi* (Alluring Radiances), contains twelve short stories. Four are based on episodes characteristic of the atmosphere in the capital during the 1930s. Three are about animals; the rest depict life in small provincial cities poisoned by petty ambitions and prejudice. In this first book Stanev remained mainly within the tradition of the urban short story. His heroes are mediocre personalities with humble ambitions, whose only attempts to overcome the banality of their lives are their dreams. The book revealed a fully mature author, and it is no wonder that eight of these earlier stories would reappear in most of his later collections.

His next book, *Mechtatel* (The Dreamer, 1939), issued by the Bulgarian Writers' Union for a lottery, was an accidental edition. It includes only three short stories, two taken from the previous collection. In 1940 the Khemus publishing house offered the collection *Sami* (Alone), illustrated by the well-known painter Boris Angelushev, in which stories about animals dominated but still combined with other themes. An integrated collection did not come about until *Vŭlchi noshti* (Wolves' Night, 1943), a cycle of animal stories that represents one of the best accomplishments of the genre in Bulgarian literature. Being a passionate hunter himself, the writer had a subtle feeling for nature. Hence his description of the animals' world is marked with a profound understanding and sympathy. According to several interviews, Stanev considered *Vŭlchi noshti* his best book (along with the novel *Antikhrist,* 1970). The short story "Smŭrtta na edna ptitsa" (The Death of a Bird), from the same collection, was his favorite work.

Shortly after the coup of September 1944 Stanev was appointed to oversee the administration of hunting in Bukovetts in the Elena Balkans. From this time on he contributed to virtually all significant Bulgarian periodicals. His fifth book, *Delnitsi i praznitsi* (Workdays and Holidays, 1945), includes his urban short stories, half from his debut book, expressing a prominent tendency in Bulgarian fiction of that time–to depict life in the city with its social and moral conflicts, ever conscious of the characters' intimate psychological dimensions.

In the late 1940s Stanev entered a new period of his creative career. Having mastered the form of the short story, he abandoned it in favor of larger narratives. The two novellas written in 1946, *Diva ptitsa* (Wild Bird) and *Foker,* a story about a hunter's dog, are still connected with his animal short stories. A later one, "Chernishka" (1950), which relates the story of a fox, as well as a cycle of hunter's short stories, *Kogato skrezhŭt se topi* (When the White Frost Is Thawing)–both published in 1950–completed this thematic group. Meanwhile, the range of the author's artistic interests widened. His next two works, the novellas *Kradetsŭt na praskovi* (1948; translated as *The Peach Thief,* 1968) and *V tikha vecher* (On a Quiet Evening, 1948), made him a celebrated author. *Kradetsŭt na praskovi,* considered one of the best Bulgarian prose works, has been translated into many languages and included in several international anthologies. It is an account of a beautiful and tragic love affair between a Serbian prisoner of war and a Bulgarian woman, unhappy and alienated in her marriage to a high-ranking officer. *V tikha vecher* gives an original interpretation of the inner world of a participant in the antifascist movement. The accent is on the psychological dimensions of personal choice and on the moral issues involved in that choice.

From 1950 to 1955 Stanev headed the fiction section of the newspaper *Literaturen front* (Literary Front). This was his last formal job; from 1955 on he devoted himself entirely to literary activity. At this time he began contemplating the writing of his first novel, *Ivan Kondarev,* which he worked on for fourteen years, starting in October 1950. Its two volumes appeared in 1958 and 1962. In this novel the events surrounding the uprising of September 1923 are depicted by showing a wide panorama of social life in the country and a multitude of heroes. The plot concentrates on a period of several months, and a

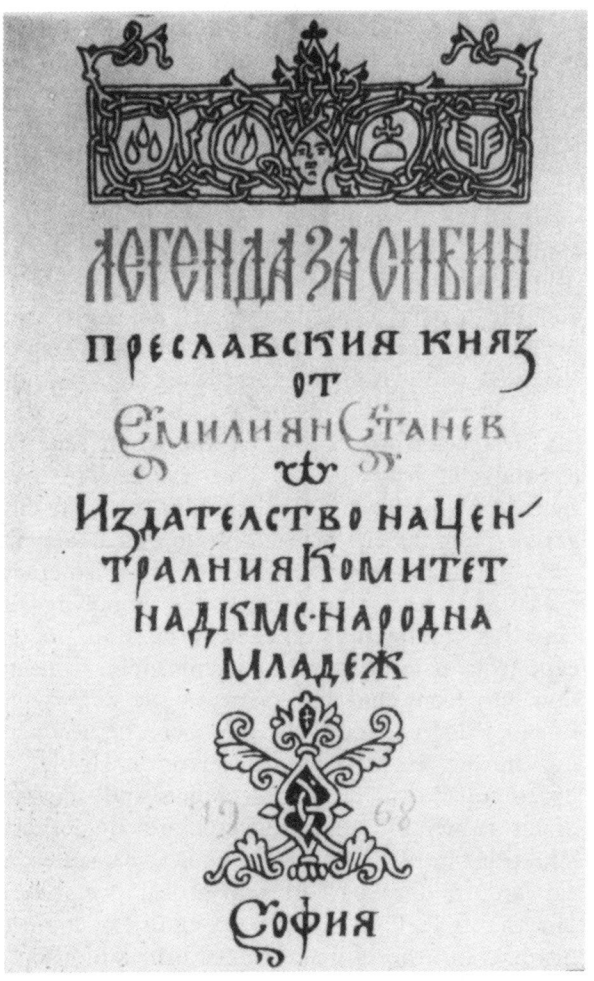

Cover for Stanev's 1968 historical novel Legenda za Sibin, Preslavskiya knyaz *(A Legend of Sibin, a Preslav Prince)*

dominating role is given to political themes. This includes the opposition between the characters Ivan Kondarev and Konstantin Dzhopuna, Kondarev and Khristakiev, and Kondarev and Khristina, all of them expressing a different position in the current political events. On a larger scale the novel is an attempt to explore morals and values in Bulgarian life during the first decades of the twentieth century, to reconsider Bulgarian national character and history, and to explore the recent social cataclysms in the country. Its first part stirred controversy. Many critics believed that the novel strayed too far from orthodox communist ideology. Later, however, the novel imposed its presence on the literary scene. Stanev was awarded various high prizes and honorary titles–the Dimitrov Prize in 1964 (especially for *Ivan Kondarev*), the title of People's Cultural Worker in 1966, and that of Hero of Socialist Labor in 1967.

Toward the end of the 1960s Stanev turned to the issues of Bulgarian history and wrote remarkable historical works. *Legenda za Sibin, Preslavskiya knyaz* (A Legend of Sibin, a Preslav Prince, 1968) is set at the beginning of the thirteenth century, the years of the early development of the Bogomil movement in Bulgaria. The ideological conflict is seen in a multidimensional perspective—as a rivalry between the Bogomils and the official Christian church as well as between monotheism and the rudimentary paganism still found among some Bulgarian people. Creating the leading figure as a beloved child of his own pagan world outlook, the writer searches for the characteristics of both the epoch (transient, controversial, and discordant) and the Bulgarian national character (diverse and contradictory). Sibin is a representative of the aristocracy; he comes from a neglected clan opposing the czar. An intellectual type, he gropes for an escape from painful moral and philosophical hesitation and from the clash between the mighty, influential dogmatism of the new heresy, the orthodox norms, and the pagan memories. His inability to cope with the inner conflicts and demands of his vulnerable youth makes him a tragic hero. The tragedy of Sibin is seen both as a metaphysical issue and as part of a historical perspective. His moral feelings happen to deny the logic of history, and the ultimate choice brings him to catastrophe. A somewhat more positive, but nevertheless tragic, alternative is found in the other central character, Father Silvester, whose denial of the official religion in favor of free human thought proves easy to destroy as well as to be historically doomed.

The novel *Antikhrist* (Antichrist) is set in the medieval period. The significance of the historical moment is seen in its projection onto an individual's fate. The events depicted in the narration are from the end of the fourteenth century when Bulgaria lost its independence. In the author's characteristic manner the main character, En'o-Teofil, is in quest of the ultimate truth in human existence—exploring God and evil, concentrating on the human soul, encountering the greatest personalities of the epoch, trying to rationalize his own place in national history and to perceive the moral demands of both the epoch and eternity. Making use of a specific form—a *zhitie* (a saint's life)—written as a first-person narrative, Stanev presents the sad confession of a divided person. In the past, En'o, the young boy, had lived a harmonious existence. Crippled by the church court, he becomes a rebel. Teofil goes through different phases, including self-denial, religious doubt, meditation, disputes with his teachers, and finally opposition to the Turkish invaders. *Antikhrist* is written in a remarkable style, combining a reflexive and imaginative narration that corresponds to the dual nature of human existence. The writer confessed to various interviewers and friends that *Antikhrist* was the work that best expressed his own personality and hence was to a large extent autobiographical.

In 1977 Stanev finished the sequel to *Sibin*, which is *Tikhik i Nazariy* (Tikhik and Nazariy), on which he had been working for years. It is a short narrative about Sibin's servant, Tikhik, who becomes the leader of the Bogomils, and the artist Nazariy, who is overwhelmed by personal doubts. In opposing these two characters the writer again comes to grips with basic philosophical issues concerning good and evil, the hierarchy of different types of knowledge—sensual and intellectual—and the meaning of art and its relationship to power.

While working on *Antikhrist* and *Tikhik i Nazariy,* Stanev also wrote the novella *Tŭrnovskata tsaritsa* (The Tsarina of Turnovo, 1973), which evoked his childhood memories from the time of the Balkan War. The hero, Dr. Stariradev, returns from France after receiving his degree only to face a boring and suffocating social environment. Marina, his assistant and later his lover, is a kind and simple person who has totally different morals and believes in the value of human relations. For Stariradev the affair with her is just a convenience that should be kept secret. The conflict becomes inevitable when he comes close to an engagement with a merchant's daughter, his own patient. When the scandal erupts, Marina leaves to become a nurse. While taking care of wounded soldiers, she is infected with cholera and dies. The doctor marries the wealthy woman, founds a private hospital, and forgets about the aspirations and anxieties of his youth. *Tŭrnovskata tsaritsa* forms a specific diptych with *Kradetsŭt na praskovi*. In both, the writer not only exploits memories from his childhood, but also makes use of the same narrative technique, shifting the point of view and finally introducing the child narrator.

During his last years Stanev returned again to his favorite form—the short story. His best achievements are "Vŭlkŭt" (The Wolf, 1970), "Skot Reynolds i nepostizhimoto" (Scott Reynolds and the Unattainable, 1971), "Yazovetsŭt" (The Badger, 1975), and "Lazar i Isus" (Lazarus and Jesus, 1977). The first story resulted from a decade-long project. Following the pattern of a hunter's story, it offers a deep insight into human nature and its impact on the social choices a present-day hero is forced to make. "Skot Reynolds i nepostizhimoto" explores the personal problems hidden behind the public image of a great scientist as well as moral responsibility and the challenges of consciousness. Nature versus intellect, human happiness versus the demands of a professional career, personal independence versus social patterns—these are the dimensions within which the writer locates his hero, a world-renowned physicist who has come to the Bulgarian seashore hoping to relax and make peace with himself. For all his efforts to overcome the inertia of thought and social behavior, he finally has to recognize his own moral impotence.

In "Yazovetsŭt" Stanev makes use of a similar plot. A French woman, the wife of a well-known professor and archeologist, is having her vacation at the Black Sea. Deathly bored and exhausted by her alienation, she meets a strange but talented artist who sells his paintings to a mediocre professional, thus giving away the fame he deserves, but who is also tormented by the "devil" of vanity and the damnation of his creativity. The portrait of the woman which the artist draws reveals the image of her better self, hidden far back in her past. She, however, is unable to trust in spiritual beauty. Her impulse to love the artist, to experience an enchanting and elevating intimacy, deteriorates to a habitual, primitive sexual lust. The encounter proves to be crucial for both of them. She will never be able to overcome the baseness of her life, while he is forced to give up the delusion of improving reality by means of art.

On 24 May 1974 Stanev was elected to the Bulgarian Academy of Science. He received his second Hero of Socialist Labor award in 1977. His last works, which remain unfinished, are the novella "Cherniyat monach" and the play "Nasŭn i nayave" (Black Monk). In the latter he returns to the issues of modern science, the moral responsibility of scientists, and the subject of human reason in general. Seriously ill, Stanev worked until his last hours, sincerely caring about the painful challenges of life and thought, about humankind and its future, and about his homeland, with its unsteady, tragic, but nevertheless inspiring, fate.

Interview:

Ivan Sarandev, *Emiliyan Stanev. Literaturna anketa* (Sofia: Bŭlgarska akademiya na naukite, 1977).

Bibliography:

Emiliya Barakovska, Nina Nikolova, *Emiliyan Stanev. Bio-bibliografiya* (Sofia: Dom na literaturata i izkustvata za detsa i yunoshi, 1977).

Biographies:

Nadezhda Staneva, *Dnevniks prodŭlzhenie* (Sofia: Profizdat, 1979);

Staneva, *Den sled den* (Sofia: Profizdat, 1985).

References:

Petŭr Dinekov, "Tvorcheskiyat pŭt na Emiliyan Stanev" and "Chovekŭt i pisatelyat," in his *V zhivota i literaturata* (Sofia: Nauka i izkustvo, 1982), pp. 177-189, 193-199;

Chavdar Dobrev, *Zabranenite plodove na poznanieto—Emiliyan Stanev* (Plovdiv: Khr. G. Danov, 1982);

Stoyan Karolev, *Neutolimiyat: Kniga za Emiliyan Stanev* (Sofia: Bŭlgarski pisatel, 1981);

Rozaliya Likova, "Sred taynite na bitieto i problemite na sŭvremennostta. 80 godini ot rozhdenieto na Emiliyan Stanev," *Septemvri*, no. 2 (1987): 228-235;

Mariya Masheva and Iliya Manev, *Az sŭm tuk. Kniga za Emiliyan Stanev* (Sofia: Otechestven front, 1990);

Khristo Mednikarov, *Po sledite na Emiliyanstanevite geroi* (Sofia: Otechestven front, 1982);

Boyan Nichev, "Emiliyan Stanev," in his *Literaturna klasika i sŭvremennost* (Sofia: Bŭlgarski pisatel, 1990), pp. 100-137;

Minko Nikolov, "Problemi i kharakteri v Ivan Kondarev," in his *Profili i problemi* (Sofia: Bŭlgarski pisatel, 1989), pp. 357-384;

Edvin Sugarev, "Krŭstopŭtishta na razuma i dushata. Za romana *Antikhrist* na Emiliyan Stanev," *Literaturna misŭl*, no. 3 (1987): 47-62;

Rumyana Yoveva, *Filosofsko-istoricheskite romani na Emiliyan Stanev: obrazi i kompozitsiya* (Sofia: Narodna prosveta, 1981);

Panteley Zarev, *Emiliyan Stanev: Izsledvane* (Sofia: Bŭlgarski pisatel, 1973);

Toncho Zhechev, "Uchastta choveshka u Emiliyan Stanev," in his *Istoriya i literatura* (Sofia: Bŭlgarski pisatel, 1979), pp. 534-543.

Goran Stefanovski
(27 April 1952 -)

George Mitrevski
Auburn University

BOOKS: *Divo meso,* includes *Jane Zadrogaz* (Skopje: Misla, 1981);
Let vo mesto (Skopje: Misla, 1982);
Bušava azbuka, with Dušan Petričić (Skopje: Detska radost, 1987);
Long Play (Skopje: Dom na mladi, 1988);
Černodrinski se vraka doma (Skopje: Magazin 21, 1992).

Collections: *Odbrani drami,* includes the plays *Divo meso, Let vo mesto, Hi-Fi, Duplo dno,* and *Tetovirani duši* (Skopje: Misla, 1987).

Editions in English: *Proud Flesh,* translated by Alan McConnell Duff in *Scena,* 4 (1981): 170–186; translated by Ralph Bogert, *Slavic and East European Arts,* 2, no. 1 (1983): 59–93;
Hi-Fi and *The False Bottom,* translated by Patricia Marsh-Stefanovska (Kansas City: Bookmark Press, University of Missouri, 1985).

PLAY PRODUCTIONS: *Jane Zadrogaz,* Skopje, Dramski teatar, 26 December 1974;
Divo meso, Skopje, Dramski teatar, 29 December 1979;
Let vo mesto, Skopje, Dom na mladi, 8 January 1982;
Hi-Fi, Sarajevo, Kamerni teatar, 28 December 1982;
Klinč, Štip, Dramsko studio, 17 June 1983;
Duplo dno, Sarajevo, Narodno pozorište, 17 December 1983;
Tetovirani duši, Skopje, Dramski teatar, 26 October 1985;
Crna dupka, Skopje, Makedonski naroden teatar, 10 February 1988;
Long Play, Subotica, Narodno pozorište, 3 June 1988;
Kula vavilonska, Skopje, Dramski teatar, 14 January 1990;
Černodrinski se vraka doma, Skopje, Dramski teatar, 31 January 1992.

MOTION PICTURE: *Hi-Fi,* screenplay by Stefanovski, Vardar Film, 1987.

Goran Stefanovski

TELEVISION: *Klinč,* script by Stefanovski, TV Skopje, 1975;
Soslušuvanyeto na železničarot, script by Stefanovski, TV Skopje, 1976;
Tome od benziskata pumpa, script by Stefanovski, TV Skopje 1979;
Naši godini, script by Stefanovski, series in 6 episodes, TV Skopje, 1979;
Tumba, tumba divina, script by Stefanovski, TV Skopje, 1982;
Bušava azbuka, script by Stefanovski, series in 31 episodes, screenplay by Stefanovski and Petrichic, TV Skopje, 1986.

RADIO: *Čirakot Šekspir,* script by Stefanovski, Radio Skopje, 1975.

OTHER: "Hi-Fi," in *Ka novoj drami,* 3 (Belgrade: Tribina, 1983), pp. 1–68;

"Long Play," in *YU Fest 1988* (Subotica: National Theater Subotica, 1988), pp. 170–205;

Traviata, Omladinski kulturni centar, Zagreb, June 1989;

Zodiak, Makedonski naroden teatar, Skopje, 21 January 1990.

Macedonian theater and drama came of age in the years immediately following World War II, after Macedonian was formally established as a literary language. The first generation of Macedonian playwrights writing in dialects close to contemporary literary Macedonian wrote in the period between the beginning of the twentieth century and the end of the Second World War. This group includes Voydan Chernodrinski, Vasil Ilyoski, Anton Panov, and Risto Krle. The second generation of Macedonian playwrights includes writers educated in the period before World War II who were actively writing for the theater from the end of the war through the 1960s and early 1970s. The most important dramatists in this group include Kole Čašule, Tome Arsovski, Branko Pendovski, and Živko Čingo. Almost exclusively, this group of writers gained their fame in the genres of the novel and the short story. Their work is significant in the development of Macedonian theater and drama because they helped establish modern theater in Macedonia and give it its national identity. It is fair to say, however, that no significant dramatic texts were produced by this generation, nor did they have much influence on the next generation of playwrights. The youngest generation of Macedonian playwrights was educated in the 1960s and early 1970s and was influenced by the styles and themes of contemporary Western theater and drama. Although they all write in other genres, the dramatic genre seems to be their favorite. Among the most prominent playwrights of this generation are Yordan Plevneš, Rusomir Bogdanovski, and Goran Stefanovski.

Stefanovski is perhaps the most significant and prolific playwright in the short history of Macedonian theater. Educated in the spirit of contemporary Western theater, he, together with a small group of actors and directors, elevated the quality of theater in Macedonia to world-class levels. In 1974, at the age of twenty-two, he appeared on the theater scene with his play *Jane Zadrogaz.* The play was directed by Slobodan Unkovski, who is of the same generation and was educated in the same Western tradition as Stefanovski. This play marks the beginning of the Stefanovski–Unkovski tandem. Unkovski has directed all except two of Stefanovski's plays, and the playwright's most recent work, *Černodrinski se vraḱa doma* (Černodrinski Comes Home, 1992), is dedicated to Unkovski. The tandem are joined by a group of equally dedicated young actors at the Skopje Drama Theater.

Stefanovski's plays have all enjoyed a high degree of popularity, and they have all been staged in theaters throughout Macedonia and other Yugoslav republics. Many have been staged abroad in the United States, Great Britain, Poland, Hungary, France, Germany, the republics of the former Soviet Union, Bulgaria, and Venezuela. *Divo meso* (Proud Flesh, 1979) and *Crna Dupka* (The Black Hole, 1988) were awarded the Play of the Year Prize in 1980 and 1988, respectively, at the Sterijino Pozorje Drama Festival in Novi Sad. Stefanovski's plays have been published in their original Macedonian and in various translations–both as separate editions and in literary magazines and anthologies–in Serbo-Croatian, English, Russian, French, Czech, and Polish.

Stefanovski was born on 27 April 1952 in Bitola, Macedonia, a city in the southwest part of the southernmost republic of Yugoslavia. His introduction to the theater came through his parents. His father, Mirko, was a theater director in Bitola, and his mother, Nada, was an actress. Both parents are deceased. There is a story told by Unkovski about how the theater in Bitola passed a resolution in 1952 that Nada Stefanovska was not "permitted" to give birth that year because the group was too busy rehearsing for the season. Contemporaries recount that it was not unusual to see Nada nursing young Goran during rehearsals and between scenes. Some of Stefanovski's earliest childhood memories are from life in the theater, watching his mother being killed on the stage night after night in the role of a tragic heroine.

Stefanovski spent his college years in Skopje, the capital and cultural center of Macedonia, studying in the Department of English Language and Literature at the University of Skopje, from which he graduated in 1974. During these formative years he became acquainted with English and American literature and began to read the original English-language texts of William Shakespeare, Samuel Beckett, and other British and American writers. The year 1974 is also important for Stefanovski because it is the year he met his future wife, Patricia, who at the time was

Scene from Dramski theater production of Stefanovski's Divo Meso *(Proud Flesh), about a family in Skopje on the eve of World War II*

a British lecturer of English at the University of Skopje. She is the English translator of his plays. Stefanovski and Patricia have two children.

The person most responsible for nurturing Stefanovski's talents as a dramatist during his early twenties was his uncle, Risto Stefanovski. He is a well-known theater historian, and for many years was the managing director of the Skopje Drama Theater where Stefanovski's first play was staged in 1974. At the Skopje Drama Theater, his uncle was instrumental in introducing Stefanovski to the theater craft and to two generations of theater professionals: the generation of his parents, and the younger generation of actors and directors, who at the time were eager to experiment and were looking for new and exciting texts. Stefanovski also received professional training as a dramatist during his one year at the Belgrade Theater Academy. At that time, the academy was the single most important place in Yugoslavia for the training of professionals in theater, film, drama, and television. Among the faculty at the academy were some of the most experienced and gifted Yugoslav directors, critics, and playwrights.

Outside the theater Stefanovski's strongest interest is American rock music. One can find thematic and stylistic influences of this genre in several of his plays. He has also worked closely with his younger brother, Vladko, who also joined the artistic world at an early age as a student at the University of Skopje. Together with two of his friends, Vladko formed a rock band, "Leb i sol" (Bread and Salt), which became popular among audiences in Macedonia and throughout Yugoslavia. Goran has written the lyrics for several of the band's songs, as well as the libretto for the rock opera *Zodiak,* which was performed by "Leb i sol" at the Macedonian National Theater in Skopje on 21 January 1990. "Leb i sol," in turn, performed the music for Goran's play *Let vo mesto* (Flying on the Spot, 1982).

From 1974 to 1977 Stefanovski worked as a dramaturge in the drama section of Skopje Television. It was during this period that he wrote several screenplays for television, two of which were directed by his friend and colleague Unkovski. From 1977 to 1986 he was a lecturer in English literature at Skopje University. In 1979 he received his master's degree from the

Faculty of Philology at Belgrade University. The title of his thesis was "Stage Directions as the Foundation of the Theatre of Samuel Beckett." Soon after receiving his M.A., Stefanovski began working on his Ph.D. The subject of his research was contemporary British drama and the playwright Edward Bond. He spent the 1979–1980 academic year at Manchester University in England, conducting research on this subject. While in Great Britain he wrote the screenplay for the television drama *Tumba, tumba divina* (1982).

Stefanovski has traveled to the United States several times. In the autumn of 1984 he spent three months as a guest of the Iowa International Writing Program. He also spent one semester in 1990 at Brown University on a five-month Fulbright Outstanding Artist Scholarship, where he taught a course, "Introduction to Dramatic Writing," in the Department of Theater, Speech, and Dance. While in the United States he also lectured at Harvard University, the University of California, Los Angeles, and the University of Missouri, Kansas City. He currently teaches playwriting and the theory of drama in the School of Dramatic Arts at the University of Skopje.

When Stefanovski's first play, *Jane Zadrogaz*, was staged at the Skopje Drama Theater in 1974, audiences were delighted by the playful and animated dialogue, the simple, folk-inspired plot elements, and the general theatrical approach to the production. Critics were unsure which direction this new, gifted playwright would take next, and they had to wait five years to see another play by him. It became apparent each new play would be a new experience.

Jane Zadrogaz marks the beginning of his career as a playwright, as well as the beginning of his association with the Skopje Drama Theater and with the director Unkovski. The subject for the play comes from Macedonian literature, specifically from folktales collected by Marko Cepenkov (1829-1920) in the nineteenth century. The story deals with an imaginary kingdom ruled by an evil queen. The kingdom is terrorized by a dragon that no one can kill. The queen is pregnant, and everyone is waiting for a prince to be born who will liberate them. The queen has been pregnant for nine years. She finally gives birth to three sons, and they attempt to kill the dragon. They are joined by Jane Zadrogaz, a small, weak mischief-maker. Jane Zadrogaz fights the dragon first, but in no time she is swallowed by him. The dragon convinces the three princes that he would like to be their father and to rule together with their mother. The queen and the princes agree to the arrangement, but the rest of the people will not hear of it. They kill the dragon, liberate Jane Zadrogaz from his belly, and chase the queen and the princes out of the kingdom.

The play consists of ten scenes and is framed by the historical character Marko Cepenkov, who in the prologue informs the audience that today is a holiday celebrated with songs, dances, and performances, and the people will put on a performance for their enjoyment. He comes onstage again at the end of the play to thank the audience. This play-within-a-play structure Stefanovski repeats in his latest play, *Černodrinski se vraka doma*. Theater critics were in a predicament in approaching the text and the performance of *Jane Zadrogaz*, perhaps because neither followed the classical structure of a play, and the subject matter, plot, and characters were too simple to require deep analysis. But it was exactly this "lightness" and theatricality that delighted the theater public the most. The plot and characters are subservient to the rich folklore elements, especially the language. It is obvious that before working on this play, Stefanovski carefully read Cepenkov's ten-volume collection of Macedonian folklore. From this material Stefanovski includes in this play elements from folktales, laments, prayers, beliefs, blessings, curses, secret languages, descriptions of trades, diseases, curses, and more. The language and dialogue were of the type that the spectator might have heard from grandparents archaic, yet familiar. The play is meant to be more of a theatrical piece than a dramatization of Cepenkov's folktales.

Stefanovski's second play, *Divo meso*, was written and staged a full five years after *Jane Zadrogaz*. The action in the play takes place in Skopje, the capital of Macedonia, in the 1930s, on the eve of World War II. At this time in its history Macedonia was a part of the Kingdom of Yugoslavia and Serbia's Vardar region. The play explores the social disintegration of the traditional urban family structure. Dimitriya, the family patriarch, is an invalid; he was a master bricklayer who fell and broke his legs while building his own house. Mariya, the mother, upon whom everyone depends to keep the family together, has lost her sanity. There are three sons in the family. Simon, the oldest, is a waiter and an alcoholic. He hates his job and detests his wife because she can not give him a child. Stefan works as an executive at a branch of a German automobile factory. He is the most ambitious of the three and looks to Europe for an exit from the depressing situation in Skopje. Andreya, the youngest, works as a salesclerk and is active in the labor movement.

The cataclysm begins with the arrival of Klaus, a representative of the German firm where Stefan works. He comes to Skopje to oversee the operations at the plant. The Skopje branch of the plant is run by Hercog, a Jew. Stefan is most excited about Klaus's arrival, because he looks to him for an opportunity to leave Skopje for a better life in Europe. Stefan and Klaus become friends, but Klaus is a homosexual and has different intentions for him. Stefan refuses his advances, and as a result loses his job and the opportunity to go to Europe. Andreya is arrested for organizing a strike. Stefan looks to Sivić, a Serb, and Klaus to help get him out, but they both refuse, and Andreya is sent to a labor camp. Simon is drafted into the army, from which he escapes; he is eventually found dead in the room of a prostitute.

In the final scene the total physical, social, and moral disintegration of the family is clear. The family house has been torn down to make room for an expansion of the automobile plant. The survivors—father, mother, Stefan, and Simon's wife—stand in the midst of the ruins. Mariya, the senile mother, has no concept of what has just taken place. She invites the workers who have demolished the house for some food and drink. The father plays some discordant tunes from a wooden flute that he has been carving during the entire play. Among the ruins, Stefan finds a gun that Andreya had hidden and fires it in the air.

The title of the play, *Divo meso* (more correctly translated as "wild flesh"), comes from an expression that Mariya uses to describe her belief that if one swallows hair, it gets stuck in the throat, where it takes root and grows to the point of choking the individual. The wild flesh metaphor has been interpreted by critics to stand for the outside forces that control the destiny of each individual in the Andréević family. Before his death, Simon tells his brother Stefan that he can already feel this flesh growing in his throat.

Most critics of this play agree that it is both a sociological and a political play. It shows the impact of the political and economic forces of the period on the relationships among the members of the Andréević family and their personal reactions to the same forces. Critics have noted that each family member represents the view of a different part of Macedonian urban society on the eve of World War II. Dimitriya, the invalid father, represents the old generation that is both resigned and ineffective. Stefan is the pragmatist and survivor, who will look even to his enemy to better his life. Andreya is the young Communist who sees revolutionary action as the only means to end the oppressive conditions. At the end, however, she realizes that her action is useless against forces of such great magnitude. On the political level the play depicts the political situation in Macedonia during this period. Macedonia is not yet an independent state, and the language spoken by the Macedonians is considered to be a southern dialect of Serbian. Both politically and economically the region is dominated by outsiders. They are the "wild flesh" that suffocate the aspirations of the new generation.

Let vo mesto (Flying on the Spot, 1982), Stefanovski's third play, is set in the year 1878. This is the year that Macedonia was expected to be given independence at the Berlin Congress after the Russo-Turkish War of that same year. Romania, Serbia, and Montenegro were granted independence, but Macedonia remained under Turkish political rule and under Serbian, Bulgarian, and Greek cultural domination. Macedonian schoolchildren were taught in Serbian; the economy was controlled by Greek merchants; and all of Macedonia's neighbors wanted control of its religion and churches.

The story centers around the fate of a Macedonian monastery and the individuals that have interest in it. In the priory of the monastery live two brothers, Mihaylo and Evto, Evto's wife and child, and their elderly mother, Sultana. The brothers, who are masons, are ordered by the Turkish governor and by Panaiotis, a Greek, to cover up the monastery's frescoes so that new ones can be painted in the Greek style. The conflict begins when the question is asked as to what should be the appropriate response to such an order. In the midst of this foreign political, economic, and cultural dominance, the frescoes on the walls of the monastery are the only tangible images that point to an independent Macedonian identity. Evto, a pragmatist and realist, is ready to do anything for his own survival and the survival of his family. The question of Macedonian national identity is too large for him to grasp or to be concerned with. For Mihaylo, covering up the frescoes is equivalent to wiping away Macedonian cultural history, an act that would allow foreigners to deny its existence. The characters in the play, and the conflicts among them, paint a complete picture of the political,

Scene from 1992 production by Dramski theater of Stefanovski's Černodrinski se vraḱa doma (Černodrinski Comes Home), a play about the father of Macedonian theater

cultural, and social conflicts of the time. When placed in the historical context of the period, the conflict is not always between Macedonians and outsiders, but among Macedonians and among outsiders as well. The conflicts among the outsiders are the result of their greed for power and domination. In Let vo mesto, as is characteristic for all of Stefanovski's plays, one finds no resolution to the conflict at the end of the play.

In Hi-Fi (1983) Stefanovski deals with the problem of oppression and with the conflicts among three generations of a contemporary family. The story in this play, as in all of Stefanovski's plays, is simple. Having spent five years in prison for murder, Boris, the grandfather, returns home to find chaos in the household. His apartment has been taken over by his grandson, Matey, who is obsessed with jazz and has long hair. He rebels against his mother and against all social order. Matey's mother represents the middle generation. She is a young widow, but her marriage had fallen apart even before her husband died in an automobile accident. Unable to deal with her son, she looks to Boris to bring order in the house. Boris's war and prison experiences have taught him that only through force and mental torture is it possible to change the behavior of an individual and to bring order in a social group. In the second part of the play Boris attempts to forcefully reeducate his grandson. At the end he realizes the futility of such an approach; Matey has become a transvestite and a spiritually empty, submissive individual.

Thematically the play is less about a conflict between generations than it is a depiction of what can happen when force is used in moral reeducation. The title of the play reveals its central theme. Boris notices the word Hi-Fi on Matey's stereo and wants to know its meaning. He perverts the meaning of the word *fidelity* (faithfulness, devotion, loyalty) and believes that these are exactly the things that are missing in Matey's lifestyle. The end of the play makes it obvious that a Hi-Fi existence cannot be forcefully imposed on an individual; force creates perverted characters such as Matey and Boris. Thematically, this play is one of Stefanovski's most universal pieces, which accounts for its immense popularity in Yugoslavia. Although the characters are Macedonian and the action is set in Macedonia, the themes are recognizable in any culture. The play was performed by fifteen theaters throughout Yugoslavia, and it was made into a feature film in 1988.

Duplo dno (False Bottom, 1983), Stefanovski's "confessional" play, deals with art and the role of the artist in a bureaucratized society. In a commentary about the play Stefanovski remarked: "A man who is truly alive can counteract the petrified world of oppression in three ways: through art, insanity, and revolution." The play is in three parts, labeled *Art, Insanity,* and *Revolution.* Each part is a play within a play. The action is set in three historical periods: part 1 is in the future, in the year 1999; part 2 takes place near the turn of the twentieth century, in 1911; and part 3 is set in the present.

Part 1 is set in a fallout shelter; an atomic war has just started. Hiding in the shelter are Božo (the minister of culture and a writer), his wife, Paraskeva, and their daughter, Kristina. They lead a monotonous existence until the entertainer, Yakov, arrives and offers to provide entertainment. Yakov asks Božo what the artist's role should be in these cataclysmic times. Božo tells him to keep taking the free sedatives that the government offers everyone. Yakov realizes that in this bureaucratized social order people are much happier in a spiritually dead existence. Although he recognizes the futility of the artist in such a world, at the end of part 1 he states that he refuses to be alive "by inertia," and he swears that he will use all his means to free the human spirit.

Part 2, *Insanity,* is set in the salon of Božo's expensively furnished house. In this part the same family appears along with Yakov, the artist, now tied in a straightjacket. Bozhin has just finished reading the manuscript of a play, which is actually part one of *Duplo dno.* Yakov asks him to comment on the characters and the action in the play. In this part Yakov withdraws from society into madness to save true art from bureaucracy. The other choice is to turn into a false artist, as did his school friend from the university, Nove. Nove, also a writer, is totally dedicated to conventional morality and order at any cost. As in part 1, Yakov fails in his attempt to show Božo that his life is spiritually empty and that bureaucracy destroys true art and individuality.

In the third part, *Revolution,* Yakov appears as an artist-revolutionary. The play begins just as Božo completes reading parts 1 and 2 of *Duplo dno,* written by Yakov the anarchist. Yakov comes to judge Božo for his crimes against art and the freedom of the artist. Although Božo has written volumes of artistic and scholarly works, Yakov accuses him of being functionally illiterate, since his works were created without consideration for true art. Through his revolutionary act Yakov wants to create a world where art is free of all dogma, bureaucratic restrictions, and political fears.

The play ends with a coda. Yakov appears on an empty stage and assumes the role of the playwright, Stefanovski. Holding the manuscript of *Duplo dno,* he addresses the audience. The artist realizes that any role he takes against bureaucratized art is futile, but he swears that he will continue working to free the human spirit by using all his means. He throws the manuscript up in the air and leaves the stage with the statement, "Nothing is like my play, and I don't know what is my reality." This three-part play did not enjoy the popularity of Stefanovski's earlier plays. It lacks the theatrical element necessary to move the action along; it also differs stylistically from earlier plays in that Stefanovski departs from the short-scene structure. *Duplo dno* is a play of ideas, and as such it is much more interesting as a text. Through the character of Yakov, one sees clearly Stefanovski's views about the function of art in society and about his own craft.

Stefanovski's next play, *Tetovirani duši* (Tattooed Souls, 1985), deals with the lives of Macedonian émigrés in a large American city, most likely New York. Voydan, a young Macedonian graduate student, comes to the United States to conduct ethnological research on Macedonian émigrés and to search for his father, whom he has not seen for many years. He becomes disoriented because the characters he encounters do not seem to fall into the stereotyped categories he imagined before his arrival. He meets people from many walks of life and believes that he knows everything about them and the forces that move them. From the time of his arrival his positivist, Marxist ideological preconceptions clash with the reality of everyday life in America.

At the beginning Voydan believes that he can discover everything about the individuals in question by having them fill out a questionnaire. He becomes disappointed and frustrated when he discovers that the questions he is asking are irrelevant to the people in the new reality. He can not figure out how some have assimilated totally into American society; some desperately want to assimilate but can not; some have joined the criminal world; some want to go back to their roots; some have brought their problems with them into the new world; and some have lost their sanity. His attempt to find his father ends without success. He is told by Altana, the owner of a small restaurant, that his father died in an automobile accident. Another person tells him that his father is in an insane asylum. When he meets the man from the asylum, who has his father's name, they do not recognize each other. Voydan leaves not knowing if he has really found his father.

Nothing in America seems to be like Voydan imagined; he must throw out the forms, become part of the chaos, and start his research from the beginning. In this play Stefanovski presents a picture in which reality has no recognizable definitions: it is foggy, imprecise, and moved by blind forces. The theme of the life of immigrants in America is a universal one. In this play Stefanovski avoids sentimental and nationalistic treatment of the subject, and in this sense the conflict between Voydan and his expatriates is recognizable among other émigré groups in America.

The play *Crna dupka* (Black Hole, 1988) was inspired by the folktale "Silyan the Stork," which is part of Cepenkov's collection of Macedonian folklore. The main character in *Crna dupka* is also named Silyan. Like the folktale character, he is a young man who does not care about family responsibilities. He refuses to take care of his father, his wife, and his children. He is unhappy with his job and his life, and decides to run to past and present girlfriends for comfort and pleasure. He is obsessed with sex and looks for new experiences in every encounter with a woman. In every sexual experience he looks for the ultimate pleasure. And since none of his lovers can provide it, he mistreats them.

In the second part of the play Silyan is hallucinating, and his late mother appears in his hallucination. She tells him the story of the two birds, Sive and Čule. Once upon a time they were one bird, but they were cursed by their mother to look for each other in the fields increasingly but never find each other. The scenes in the remainder of part 2 are repetitions and variations of those in part 1. Silyan watches each scene from part 1 repeat itself. He observes the characters but can not be seen by them. Various characters take the role of Silyan in each scene. From this position he can observe himself as others saw him; he can gaze at the misfortunes of those he could have loved.

Černodrinski se vraka doma (Černodrinski Comes Home, 1992) is Stefanovski's most recent play. Both structurally and thematically it is the most unique of all his plays. While *Duplo dno* was his homage to art, this latest play is Stefanovski's homage to the theater craft. It was dedicated to his friend and director, Unkovski, in appreciation of twenty years of cooperation. The play is about the "father" of Macedonian theater, Voydan Černodrinski. One can get a better grasp at Stefanovski's approach in this play by reading his notes in the introduction of the published text:

> We leave intentional and unintentional traces in the lives of strangers. With every action, word and mood, we touch others, strangers and acquaintances . . . In the theater these traces are thick and sticky. Every stage preserves the energy of the shadows of all those who have passed through it. In world theater, Shakespeare's traces are the deepest; in our theater, the traces left by Voydan Černodrinski . . . The play follows traces that have been covered up. Some are real and necessary, others probable and possible. . . . You make a doughnut by starting with a hole and building a ring around it with dough. The concept of the doughnut is in its organized empty middle. This play describes a circle using tangents.

The "dough" in this play consists of thirteen scenes. Each scene is actually a short play with its own plot and characters. They are all connected to the "global" text by the name *Černodrinski*. His name figures in each scene for various reasons. In scene 1, for example, a young student is trying to write an essay about Černodrinski, about whom he knows nothing. Scene 3 describes a love relationship between a married woman and a person who pretends to be a member of Černodrinski's acting group "Skrb i uteha." Each scene is a dramatization of the intentional or unintentional "traces" that Černodrinski may have left in the lives of acquaintances and strangers.

Above all, Stefanovski is an intellectual and a self-made philosopher who passionately questions, debates, and argues about any subject that deals with the unique individuality of people, with Macedonian history, and with the Macedonian psyche. Like many other Slavic intellectuals, he believes that it is much more interesting to raise the appropriate questions than to provide appropriate answers. Some of the most frequent questions and themes with which his plays are concerned include: how human beings react to forces over which they have no control; how a contemporary Macedonian understands history; what it means to be Macedonian; what causes the breakup of traditional family structures; and what the function of art is in a bureaucratized society. Dramatic dialogue and the theater stage seem to give Stefanovski the best means to express his philosophical and moral concerns.

The style in Stefanovski's plays shows the influence of Western dramatic traditions, namely Shakespeare, Edward Bond, Beckett, and vaudeville. Stefanovski gives up entirely on the traditional play structure of acts and prefers the short scene as the basic structural unit. Many scenes in his plays are only of several lines, and each one is framed in intense dialogue. This style is appropriate for Stefanovski's dramaturgy, because on the thematic level he believes that large philosophical, historical, and moral questions are faced by simple individuals that can react to them only from their own little microcosms. Such questions and problems are irrelevant outside the world of the individual. They become relevant only at the point when they leave the world of the abstract and enter the everyday life of the individual. In Stefanovski's plays one rarely finds scenes with masses of characters or ideas that are belabored through several scenes.

Because Stefanovski is closely involved with the staging of each of his plays (he is always present for rehearsals), he has learned much about the craft of acting and directing, and in his plays he gives both director and actors flexibility to experiment with the text. The short-scene structure and emotional dialogue contribute to this flexibility and to the wildly theatrical productions.

References:

Aleksandar Aleksiev, "Let kon sonceto i slobodata," in Stefanovski's *Let vo mesto* (Skopje: Misla, 1982), pp. 113–118;

Jovan Ćirilov, "Dramatičar posle zemljotresa," in his *Dramski pisci, moji savremenici* (Novi Sad: Sterijino Pozorje, 1989), pp. 155–175;

Ćirilov, "Visoka vernost Gorana Stefanovskog," in Stefanovski's *Tetovirane duše druge drame* (Belgrade: Narodna knjiga, 1987), pp. 201–220;

Dalibor Foretić, "Goran Stefanovski," in his *Nova drama* (Novi Sad: Sterijino Pozorje, 1989), pp. 252–277;

Blagoya Ivanov, "Dramskoto tvoreštvo na Goran Stefanovski," in *Spektar*, 10, no. 12 (1987): 29–42;

Georgi Stardelov, "Dramite na Goran Stefanovski," in Stefanovski's *Odbrani drami* (Skopje: Misla, 1987), pp. 333–353;

Gane Todorovski, "Podaleku od zanesot, poblizu do bolot! Beleški kon Divo meso," in Stefanovski's *Divo meso* (Skopje: Misla, 1981), pp. 133–148; translated as "Further from Passion, Closer to Pain!" in Stefanovski's *Proud Flesh* (Novi Sad: Sterijino Pozorje, 1980): 76–89;

Natalya Vagapova, "Dramičeskiy triptikh Gorana Stefanovskogo," in Stefanovski's *Polet na meste i drugie p'esy* (Moscow: Raduga, 1987), pp. 5–15.

Gregor Strniša
(18 November 1930 – 23 January 1987)

Tom Lozar
Vanier College

BOOKS: *Mozaiki* (Koper: založba Lipa, 1959);
Odisej (Ljubljana: Cankarjeva založba, 1963);
Zvezde (Ljubljana: Državna založba Slovenije, 1965);
Samorog (Maribor: Založba Obzorja, 1967);
Žabe (Maribor: Založba Obzorja, 1969);
Želod (Ljubljana: Državna založba Slovenije, 1972);
Ljudožerci, (Maribor: Založba Obzorja, 1972);
Mirabilia (Koper: Založba Lipa, 1973);
Oko (Ljubljana: Cankarjeva založba, 1973);
Škarje (Maribor: Založba Obzorja, 1975);
Jajce (Maribor: Založba Obzorja, 1975);
Driada (Ljubljana: Mladinska knjiga, 1976);
Rebrnik (Ljubljana: Državna založba Slovenije, 1976);
Kvadrat pa pika (Ljubljana: Mladinska knjiga, 1977);
Potovanje z bršljanom (Ljubljana: Mladinska knjiga, 1980);
Jedca mesca (Ljubljana: Mladinska knjiga, 1982);
Vesolje (Ljubljana: Cankarjeva založba, 1983);
Lučka regrat (Ljubljana: Mladinska knjiga, 1987);
Rhombos and "Relativnostna Pesnitev" (Ljubljana: Državna založba Slovenije, 1989).

Editions and Collections: *Severnica* (Maribor: Založba Obzorja, 1974);
Pesmi (Ljubljana: Državna založba Slovenije, 1978);
Svetovje (Ljubljana: Državna založba Slovenije, 1988);
Balade o svetovjih, edited, with commentary, by Peter Kolšek (Ljubljana: Mladinska knjiga, 1989).

PLAY PRODUCTIONS: *Samorog,* Ljubljana, Mestno Gledališče Ljubljansko, 1967–1968;
Žabe, Ljubljana, Slovensko Narodno Gledališče, 1970–1971;
Driada, Ljubljana, Slovensko Narodno Gledališče, 1976–1977;

Gregor Strniša

Ljudožerci, Ljubljana, Mestno Gledališče Ljubljansko, 1976–1977;
Žabe, Ljubljana, Akademija za Gledališče, radio, film i televizijo, 1979–1980;
Žabe, Ljubljana, Slovensko Narodno Gledališče, 1986–1987;
Ljudožerci, Nova Gorica, Primorsko Dramsko Gledališče, 1987–1988.

OTHER: *Pesmi,* by Strniša, Kajetan Kovič, and Dane Zajc (Ljubljana: Mladinska knjiga, 1976);

"Mavrična krila" and "Steklenica vode," in *Mavrična krila* (Ljubljana: Tehniška Založba Slovenije, 1979).

PERIODICAL PUBLICATIONS: "Svet in kozmos," *Nova Revija*, 6 (1987): 254–266;
"Spoznavati deželo in literaturo," *Nova Revija*, 7 (1988): 353–356.

When, in 1990, the influential *Nova Revija* (New Review) asked fourteen Slovenian poets to create an anthology of their favorite Slovenian poems, Josip Murn and Gregor Strniša led the list, with eleven selections each. The revered Edvard Kocbek and the legendary Srečko Kosovel were second. However, few of those who made the selections followed Strniša beyond his early work. Andrej Brvar admitted that, just as he prefers the Kocbek of *Zemlja* (Earth, 1934), so he only finds Strniša convincing until *Zvezde* (The Stars, 1965).

Not only is Strniša's poetry influential, but so was his stance. Because he deeply and literally believed in the importance of poetry for humanity's evolution, Strniša was always the poet. When he read, he read like a seer. But such a personality does not necessarily bring honor, and Strniša was difficult. Janez Menart, for instance, in *Med tradicijo in modernizmom* (Between Tradition and Modernism, 1978), though conceding that Strniša is a "good post-war poet," found unforgivable "his publicly proclaimed, self-centered arrogance." The positive view is what Jože Snoj wrote in his 1988 *Nova Revija* tribute: that Strniša was a poet of "an extinct, classically romantic kind . . . a text-book case . . . at odds with the present, entranced by the past, yearning for the lost paradise of pre-natal cosmic harmonies."

Gregor Strniša was born in Ljubljana on 18 November 1930 to Luiza (Alojzija) Paloutz and the writer Gustav Strniša, best known for his children's books. His son later wrote for children, too. Strniša attended the classical high school in Ljubljana. He did not graduate until he was twenty-two because, with his family, he had been sentenced to four years in prison for sheltering a cousin fleeing the political police. Strniša told *Književne novine* (Literary Gazette) in 1969, as Janez Stanek notes in his 1974 article in *Prostor in Čas* (Time and Place) that "the world . . . of creative work . . . is the immeasurable world of the great–a Brobdingnag–because it springs from truth and not merely the strength of this side, unlike the false Lilliputian world which functions because of illusory importance and momentary power." Strniša served two years and two months of his sentence. His eventually fatal alcoholism was exacerbated by real injustices suffered.

After prison Strniša studied in the Department of Germanic Languages at the University of Ljubljana, where he was greatly interested in historical linguistics. The chair of the department offered him a teaching assistantship, but Strniša was refused the necessary approval from, among others, the student association because of what were then all-important political reasons. He graduated deeply disappointed and became a full-time writer, taking a scholar's approach to hidden worlds. His choice did not make for a comfortable life. He lived in a huge universe, but the family house in Rožna dolina was forever crumbling around him. He was proud that he supplemented his meager artist's wages writing pop-song lyrics.

His poems began appearing in the late 1950s in *Nova obzorja* (New Horizons) and *Revija 57* (Review 57). At first glance his first collection, *Mozaiki* (Mosaics, 1959), appears somewhat old-fashioned. The title poem begins with this stanza:

> Gold mosaics, old mosaics
> staring at the dusk of churches,
> standing memories aloof,
> woof to shadows where the heart was.

But one can see, even in translation, that the young poet is a gifted pupil of Josip Murn, Alojz Gradnik, Simon Jenko, and Božo Vodušek. Peter Kolšek notes in *Balade o svetovjih* (Ballads about Universes, 1989) that Strniša's "Impressionism" found an official publisher, while Veno Taufer and Dane Zajc had to publish themselves.

But there was cosmic subversion already beginning in the poet. Strniša believed, as he says in the introduction to *Ljudožerci* (Cannibals, 1972), that "all our efforts in farming, trades, science, philosophy, and art are but a form of our desire to transcend this world." His art would not be that of an individual observing the world, but that of the world speaking in its own voice, under its own light. The "I" eventually disappears from his poems. But, as he says in *Driada* (Dryad, 1976), "human language is still a child," and *Mosaics* is the most childish of Strniša's books. Here he still occasionally says "I know" or "I hear," but the desire to transcend is already present. Thus, in "Ladja Duhov" (Ship of Spirits) someone has stepped from the poet's breast, and

Cover for Strniša's 1969 play patterned on the medieval mystery plays

"shadow midst shadows flees from me." Left behind in "Jesenka obala" (The Coast in Autumn) is a world "like dusty mirrors / in a great chamber where there is no one." Humanity's removal from the center of the universe does not diminish it, but rather makes it possible, as "Relativnostna Pesnitev" (The Poetry of Relativity) says, to look at "all living and non-living things as monads with their own laws and their legitimate presence in the hugeness of space and time."

In *Odisej* (Odysseus, 1963) and *Zvezde* (The Stars, 1965), the exploration of space and time begins on Earth. Snoj says that one finds in these volumes "the preserved soul of the romantically sensitive, erudite youth, full of youth's beauties and terrors, and its faith and doubts." He had been reading about Gulliver, odysseys, and cowboys and Indians and reading H. G. Wells, Jules Verne, H. Rider Haggard, and Edgar Allan Poe.

Like all odysseys these have inner journeys, too. In "Tuje bil tiger" (There Was a Tiger Here) the poet writes:

> So you live, are always off to distant places,
> down foggy seas, up snowy mountain ranges,
> you see so many new, so many foreign cities,
> in whose small quiet squares you love to sit.

Because the goal arrived at in this poem is metaphysical, the cityscapes are like Giorgio di Chirico's, to whom Strniša dedicated poems in *Škarje* (Scissors, 1975).

Sitting in that square, humanity is ready to evolve. In *Odisej* the greater vehicle of exploration is humanity's dreams, until in "Sanje Leta" (Dreams of the Year), the year itself is dreaming:

> Caught in the honeycomb of night, dreams
> each mind its bit of the communal dreams,

and the whole hive's mosaic dreams
softly grow into the cold spring dusk.

Notice the axiomatic sound of the poet as scientist. When in the poem one meets "the deer people," one learns that "from their brows like dreams / heavy antlers are sprouting." The dreamworld is so real that it may be useful to read Strniša, who himself wrote science fiction, in the light of Arthur C. Clarke's *Childhood's End* (1953), in which one meets the first children of the human race's next stage, born at humanity's childhood's end. The signs of their newness are dreams of places yet unseen, and unseeable to some.

In "Relativnostna pesnitev"–eventually appropriately collected in 1989 with *Rhombos,* his unfinished fantasy–Strniša specifically parallels the exploration of outer and inner space. Given humanity's evolution thus far, one can suppose, according to Strniša, that "the more deeply we push on into the great external space, the universe, the more deeply we will go into our own land of forms and ideas of the feeling and thinking inner world."

In *Zvezde* one name for the goal is "Brobdingnag." The road to it is endless; its beauty is the unknowability of its heart. Meanwhile in the Lilliputian world, communism in Slovenia was marching myriad-voiced into the future. Strniša's program reads as a marvelous ironic challenge to the official faith. He was a progressive to such a degree that no idealogue could possibly keep up with him.

Strniša did not begin his voyage beyond because of some Existentialist complaint, though that was in the air. His work seems sunny, almost naive. In "Tu je bil tiger," despite the fact that the tiger represents Death, the reader follows him with great equanimity through "mazy sleep, like gazing out the window / and beyond it softly snows and will not stop," and past "huge, snarling dogs / ... tearing at their chains outside in the gardens."

The apparent optimism in a terrible world is partly due to the form. Strniša does not engage in poetic experimentation. From Slovenian folk poetry he takes the lyrical ballad and stays for the rest of his poetic career almost exclusively with his five-part poems, each part having three four-line stanzas, with some rhyme but more assonance–lyrics with the reach of epics. The old forms say that the search is endless, and persistence the secret. Thus, the cosmic poet is also very Slovenian, and "Tu je bil tiger," for instance, is also printed on a series of postcards of Ljubljana.

In *Želod* (Acorn, 1972) one enters the "enchanted kingdom / of faithful Earth, of the stern stars." The proportions in "Vesolje" (The Universe) are appropriate for the inside of an acorn: "Mountains are drops of dew in the night," and the sun is one "you hear, you do not see." But there is plenty of room. In "Veseljak" (The Reveler) a pirate, rowing to the horizon in an acorn's cup, reports that "to the sea, there is no end / but there are cities in the middle." Appropriately, in "Vrba" (Willow), there is no death to speak of:

With the sun climbing the sky,
how should it ever die, the willow?
Not one leaf does autumn take.
Neither will you ever die.

Showing that he was no mere dreamer, Strniša in *Oko* (Eye, 1973), within his most prolific period, attempted a systematic view of his worlds. The subtitle, *Oris transcendentalne logike* (An Outline of Transcendental Logic), is Kantian. The eye of the title is the third eye. The collection is divided into PROLEGOMENA (PROLOGUE), ANALISIS (ANALYSIS), DIALEKTIKE (DIALECTICS), and ESHATOLOGIJA (ESCHATOLOGY). The divisions have subdivisions, and these have subdivisions. Under "Apparitions," for instance (which is under "Forgotten Carousel," under "Old Corners," under "Mirabilia," under ANALYSIS, all in the ken of the Eye), each planet gets a poem, but the first, just before "Mercury," is called "Meadow." This is a wonderful, serious game. Under "Invisibilia" sits a reminder of the all too real–"Delirium tremens."

In *Škarje,* subtitled *Zgodba o času* (A Tale about Time), "Svila" (Silk) is an excerpt from humanity's autobiography. One thousand apprentices led by a master weaver have made a silk with the texture of the surface of rivers:

One thread the scarlet of the deeps,
another, clear light from the sky,
the first, most deeply woven thread,
the blackness of the deep of night.

The voice of the master gazing into the distance is young, but his hands are wounded.

Jajce (Egg, 1975), subtitled *Slikanica o laži* (A Picture Book about Lying), contains the masterpiece, "Sneg" (Snow), dedicated to Thea Skinder, whom Strniša married in 1974. The couple's only child, Erna, was born in 1980. No Slovenian poet since Murn has created snow more evocatively—or, in the case of the snow in "Delirium tremens," more terrifyingly—though the only snow of "Snow" is eternity falling "one summer's day into the palm / like snow of a winter of yore." These are the concluding stanzas:

> They're not eternal, these heavens,
> these absent galaxies,
> and not eternal, this blue star forlorn—
> only we mourn.
>
> We mourn as a small creature
> in the hills will mourn away,
> except that maybe our hurt is deeper:
> will the memory stay?
>
> Will the two of you ever, in memory, here,
> as you did, live again—will the memory go?
> Will you be, at least, without the memory, together?
> Will she, will you know?

Strniša's last volume of poetry, *Vesolje* (Universe, 1983), is, according to his introduction, not "a chronological overview and summary of past work, but, according to the principles and demands of the theme itself, a newly arranged thematic selection." The theme is the universe, rearranged from the poet's new vantage point.

Strniša's plays are patterned on the medieval mystery plays. *Žabe* (The Frogs, 1969) is a morality play; *Ljudožerci* is a dance of death; *Driada*, a farce. As is especially clear in *Samorog* (Unicorn, 1967), their theme is the distance of this world from the truer world. In *Samorog*, Uršula, a holy fool, speaking to the executioner, sings of a world so beautiful that it hurts. Yet she knows that "this world—this time—this everything there is / is but a vision of that which isn't." It is clear in the plays that Strniša's characters were free to be much more sentimental than he. Some of their poems were collected in *Rebrnik* (Skeleton, 1976). The plays, however, are not about individual fates, but about the fate of the world.

In *Ljudožerci* Strniša broached something all too real for the authorities in his corner of the universe. The play includes the poem "O fantu ki je jedel fanta" (About a Boy Who Fed on a Boy), which refers to the postwar massacres by the Slovenian Communists of their opponents. Some ten thousand—in a population of less than two million—had been mowed down into mass graves, many buried alive. In the poem one young man survives by eating human flesh. Strengthened, he climbs out, is recaptured, and hanged. Another, who will not eat flesh, survives to tell the tale of "how a boy ate a boy / because the earth has a huge hole."

Given the enormity of the crime, Strniša countered with monumental blasphemy. But whereas, as Denis Poniž says in *Gledališki list* (Theater Journal, 1986-1987), a Werner Fassbinder would have staged the play in a slaughterhouse after the last shift of the day, when it was directed by Mile Korun it was, as Strniša judged from the rehearsals, reduced to mere satire about the dog-eat-dog world. Strniša tried, unsuccessfully, to stop the production, believing that the play had been purposely subverted. The politically correct critics praised the director and damned the playwright. In reaction Strniša destroyed the play he was then working on and vowed never to set foot in a theater again. When asked why he had destroyed the manuscript, Strniša is said to have replied that the play on paper was after all not the play. He had it in his head and could write it again at will.

The last installment of "Relativnostna Pesnitev"—which had been appearing in various forms in *Nova Revija* and *Med tradicijo in modernizmom*—was on Strniša's 1986 application for the Fulbright scholarship, in an addendum called "Discovering Your Land and Literature." One wonders what great work might have resulted had this voyager been allowed to discover the United States of America. He was never told why he had been passed over, but the Fulbright Strniša applied for was given to someone else, a not untypical fate for an applicant from what Belgrade regarded as the provinces.

Strniša was awarded the Greater Prešeren Prize in 1986. He died on 23 January 1987. He had overcome his alcoholism for many years but succumbed again toward the end of his life. In the introduction to *Vesolje* he had spoken of "the funny fear the individual has of his own death." This reminds one that his quest was ultimately ethical. Not at all morbidly, the poet of transcendence, in "Relativnostna Pesnitev," cites death as the basis for poetry: "Poetry grows directly out of death, as grass grows out of the soil and finally covers it over.... Thus the art of words stands with one foot outside reality and with the other in the grave of this world, and grows out of it, and takes on its qualities, and in its own way transforms them." As Death himself says in *Ljudožerci*:

> I stand behind every thing—I am Death.
> I am the garden behind the house.

I am the forest behind the tree.
I stand behind every man like his youth.

Refusing to follow poetic fashions, rejecting the poetry of the sensitive soul, Strniša sought not merely a way of saying, but also a way of knowing. His very choice of old forms underlined that he was part of a search that has been going on for a long time. Mere emotion or mere enthusiasm would not reach the unknown, the perhaps unknowable. It may be that he took his role too seriously. Certainly the theorizing, with its references to physics, sounds at times farfetched; and the chosen form, for all that he crowded into it, may indeed have limited him. But the long poetic silence before his death is deeply regrettable. He has, nevertheless, left behind veritable time machines and rockets. One enters a mere poem at one end and comes out fifteen stanzas and five minutes later a traveler back from the stars, feeling a certain amount of rocket lag. Thus, "Tu je bil tiger," "Odisej," "Inferno," "Zvezde," "Lutka," "Brobdingnag," "Svila," and "Sneg," for example, are Slovenian masterpieces. Though very translatable, they are for now still hidden masterpieces of world literature.

References:

Antologija slovenske poezije, Nova Revija, 9, no. 100 (1990);

Jože Koruza, "Gregor Strniša," *Le livre slovène,* 1-2 (1974): 42-44;

Janez Menart, letter quoted in *Med tradicijo in modernizmom,* edited by France Pibernik (Ljubljana: Slovenska Matica, 1978), pp. 95-130;

Denis Poniž, "Prolegomena v Strniševo metafiziko," *Gledališki list* (1986-1987): 164-166;

Jože Snoj, "Ptič feniks Strniševe poezije," *Nova Revija,* 7 (1988): 399-402;

Janez Stanek, "Pesništvo Gregorja Strniše," *Prostor in Čas,* 6 (1974): 542-551;

Stanek, "Na poti k etični umetnini," *Nova Revija,* 7 (1988): 407-416.

Dragutin Tadijanović
(4 November 1905 -)

Dasha Čulić Nisula
Western Michigan University

BOOKS: *Lirika šestorice* (Zagreb: Vlastita naklada, 1931);

Lirika (Zagreb: Vlastita naklada, 1931);

Sunce nad oranicama (Zagreb: Vlastita naklada, 1933);

Pepeo srca (Zagreb: Matica hrvatska, 1936);

Dani djetinjstva (Zagreb: Vlastita naklada, 1937);

Tuga zemlje (Zagreb: Hrvatski izdavalački bibliografski zavod, 1942);

Pjesme (Zagreb: Zora, 1951);

Intimna izložba crteža iz Raba (Zagreb: Jugoslavenska akademija znanosti i umjetnosti, 1955);

Pjesme i proza (Zagreb: Matica hrvatska, 1969);

Poezija (Zagreb: Mladost, 1973);

Vezan za zemlju (Zagreb: Društvo književnika Hrvatske, 1974);

Svjetiljka ljabavi (Zagreb: ALFA, 1984);

Moje djetinjstvo (Zagreb: Naša djeca, 1985);

Kruh svagdanji (Zagreb: Naprijed, 1986);

More u meni (Valjevo: Milić Rakić, 1987).

Editions and Collections: *Blagdan žetve* (Zagreb: Zora i Seljačka sloga, 1956);

Srebrne svirale (Zagreb: Školska knjiga, 1960);

Prsten (Zagreb: Matica hrvatska, 1963; second expanded edition, Zagreb: Arion, 1965);

Sabrane pjesme, poems from *1920-1975* (Zagreb: Mladost, 1975);

San, poems from *1973-1975* (Zagreb: Božo Biškupić, 1976);

Prijateljstvo riječi, poems from *1975-1987* (Zagreb: Liber, 1981);

Sabrana djela Dragutina Tadijanovića, five volumes, edited by Milan Mirić (Zagreb: Naprijed, 1988-1989).

Edition in English: *Selected Poems*, translated by Edward Goy and Dennis Ward (Zagreb: PEN, 1993).

OTHER: *Hrvatska moderna lirika,* edited by Tadijanović and Olinko Delorko (Zagreb: Zagrebačka privredna štamparija, 1933);

Dragutin Tadijanović (photograph by Dragutin Dumančić)

Ivan Kozarac, *Proza,* edited by Tadijanović (Zagreb: Nakladni zavod Matice hrvatske, 1947);

Silvije Strahimir Kranjčević, *Izabrane pjesme,* edited by Tadijanović (Zagreb: Matica hrvatska, 1956);

Petar Preradović, *Izabrane pjesme,* edited by Tadijanović (Zagreb: Matica hrvatska, 1956);

Janko Polić Kamov, *Sabrana djela,* edited by Tadijanović (Rijeka: Otokar Keršovani, 1956-1958);

Antologija hrvatskih pjesama u prozi, edited by Tadijanović and Zlatko Tomičić (Zagreb: Matica hrvatska, 1958);

August Cesarec, *Izabrane pjesme,* edited by Tadijanović (Zagreb: Matica hrvatska, 1961);

Zvonko Milković, *Izabrane pjesme,* edited by Tadijanović (Zagreb: Matica hrvatska, 1961);

Vladimir Nazor, *Izabrane pjesme,* edited by Tadijanović (Zagreb: Matica hrvatska, 1965);

Petar Preradović, *Pozdrav domovini,* edited by Tadijanović (Zagreb: Matica hrvatska, 1970);

Ivan Goran Kovačić, *Sabrana djela,* edited by Tadijanović (Zagreb: Nakladni zavod Matice hrvatske, 1983);

Zbornik radova o Marijanu Lanosoviću, edited by Tadijanović (Osijek: Jugoslavenska akademija znanosti i umjetnosti, 1985).

TRANSLATIONS: Johann Wolfgang von Goethe, *Knjiga poezije,* edited by Zdenko Škreb (Zagreb: Nakladni zarod Hrvatske, 1950);

Heinrich Heine, *Poezija,* edited by Ivo Hergešić (Zagreb: Zora, 1951);

Sabrane pjesme 1920-1975, includes Tadijanović's translations into Croatian of Vitězslav Nezval, Goethe, Friedrich Hölderlin, Friedrich von Hardenberg Novalis, Heine, Jakob van Hoddis, Ivan Cankar, and others (Zagreb: Mladost, 1975).

Spontaneity and simplicity characterize the poetry of one of the most important and best-loved Croatian poets, Dragutin Tadijanović, who has continued to write and publish into his nineties in a literary career that includes sixty years of writing. Much of his poetry is autobiographical, and it is from this personal perspective that the poet touches upon such universal themes as alienation, transience, and death. These, the poet suggests, can be overcome only through love.

Born in Rastušje in the region of Slavonia on 4 November 1905, Dragutin Tadijanović grew up in the village where his parents, Mirko and Manda, were farmers. He had two sisters, Franjka and Kata, and a brother, Đuro. From 1912 until 1916 he attended grade school in the neighboring village, making the daily trips on foot. Tadijanović attended junior high from 1916 until 1918 and then high school from 1918 until 1925, where he began writing during his third year, at the age of thirteen. By 1920 he had destroyed all of his earlier pieces; that year he also made his first trip to Zagreb. In the fall of 1920 until the spring of the following year he wrote ten poems that were published shortly thereafter under a pseudonym.

In 1922 he published under the pseudonym Margan Tadeon his poem "Tužna jesen" (Sad Autumn) in Zagreb's young people's journal *Omladina* (Youth). He repeated a year of high school after failing mathematics and graduated in 1925. He made his first trip abroad in 1924, traveling with his father to Vienna; after his graduation in 1925 he visited Sarajevo, Kotor, and the Dalmatian cities of Šibenik, Split, and Dubrovnik. In the fall of 1925 he enrolled at the University of Zagreb in the Department of Forestry. Two and one-half years later he switched to the Department of Croatian Studies in the College of Arts and Sciences.

It was not until 1930 that Tadijanović's poetry appeared in print under his own name. The following year eleven of his poems appeared in the collection *Lirika šestorice* (Lyrics of Six Poets). His first collection was also published in 1931 under the title *Lirika* (Lyrics). In 1932, the year of his father's death, Tadijanović graduated from the University of Zagreb. In the same year he received a stipend to study in Czechoslovakia, where he began to translate Vitězslav Nezval. His own poem, "Jutarnja zvijezda pozlaćen orah" (Morning Star, Gilded Walnut), was translated into Czech—his first poem to be translated into a foreign language. Tadijanović's second book of poetry, *Sunce nad oranicama* (Sunshine Over the Plow-Fields), appeared in April 1933. Because one poem offended some critics, this edition was banned, and later that month a second, revised version without the offending poem was released.

Early in 1934 the poet's brother died of tuberculosis in Zagreb. At the end of that year Tadijanović began working as an editor for the Zagreb journal *Slovo* (Word); he lost his job in April the following year because of job cuts but promptly found another position as a newspaper editor. In April 1936 he published his third collection, *Pepeo srca* (Ashes of the Heart). The same year several of his poems were translated into Esperanto. His fourth collection of poetry, *Dani djetinjstva* (Days of My Childhood), appeared in 1937. Two years later he married Jela Ljevaković, a professor. He was appointed an instructor of Croatian language and literature at the Arts Academy in Zagreb. Tadijanović's fifth collection of poetry, *Tuga zemlje* (The Sorrow of the Earth), appeared in 1942.

By 1945, after he stopped working at the Arts Academy in Zagreb, he started working as an editor for the printing house of Nakladni zavod Matice hrvatske and began editing a collection of works by Ivan Goran Kovačić, completing seven books by 1949. During the second half of the 1940s he also edited many editions of selected and collected works by such Croatian writers as Silvije Strahimir Kranjčević, Antun Gustav Matoš, Vladimir Vidrić, Janko Polić Kamov, Augustin "Tin" Ujević, and Goran Kovačić. At the same time he was working on a translation of Johann Wolfgang von Goethe's poetry, which was published in 1950.

During the next decade Tadijanović worked as an editor in the publishing house Zora. He edited numerous collections of works by Croatian writers such as Vidrić, Matoš, and Antun Branko Šimić for Matica hrvatska, a total of twenty-eight large volumes by 1958. At this time he was also translating Friedrich Hölderlin, Friedrich von Hardenberg Novalis, and Heinrich Heine. One of Tadijanović's own collections, *Pjesme* (Poems), was published in 1951. Two years later he was elected director of the Institute for Literature of the Yugoslav Academy of Arts and Sciences, working in this capacity until 1966, when he retired and served as an honorary director until 1973.

Health problems required the poet to spend time on the island of Rab, where in 1954 he wrote a collection of poetry, *Intimna izložba crteža iz Raba* (An Intimate Exhibit of Sketches from Rab), which appeared in 1955. The following year, along with Dobriša Cesarić and Šime Vučetić, he edited a volume of young Croatian lyricists, *Četrdesetorica* (Forty Poets). Another collection of his own poetry, *Blagdan žetve* (Harvest Holiday), was published in 1956. Two years later he and Zlatko Tomičić edited *Antologija hrvatskih pjesama u prozi* (An Anthology of Croatian Poetry in Prose).

A book that has had many editions (the sixteenth was published in 1987) is a selection of poems titled *Srebrne svirale* (Silver Pipes), published by in 1960. A year later Tadijanović was recognized with the Golden Wreath Award for his work. During the first half of the 1960s his work was included in a Polish anthology, and his poems also appeared in German, Italian, French, Russian, Hungarian, and English anthologies. His most popular collection of poetry, *Prsten* (Ring), appeared in

Cover for 1993 translation of Tadijanović's poems

1963. For this volume he received the Zmaj Award from Matica srpska in Novi Sad, as well as the City of Zagreb Award. His poetry was also included in an English translation in P.E.N.'s 1965 publication, *A Collection of Modern Croatian Verse*. The following year he published *Večer nad gradom* (Evening Over the City), selected poems that appeared in the Croatian, Macedonian, and Slovenian languages. His work also appeared in a Czech anthology, while he continued to publish collections of Croatian poetry, including a book on Kovačić, Vučetić, Ujević, Matoš, and Petar Preradović. This work culminated in a Vladimir Nazor Award in 1968 for his life's efforts. The end of the decade is marked by the appearance of his *Pjesme i proza* (Poetry and Prose) in 1969.

In the early 1970s he again traveled to Switzerland, Italy, Austria, and Belgium. In 1972 he received the Marko Marulić Award, and in 1973 he published a collection titled *Poezija* (Poetry). His next collection, *Vezan za zemlju* (Bound to the Earth), came out in 1974. In December of the same year a cycle of his short stories, "Slike is mog djetinjstva" (Pictures from My Childhood), appeared in the journal *Forum*. The following year, when he celebrated his seventieth birthday, his poetry was read; his books were exhibited in many cities throughout the country; and he received the Golden Star Award for his work. In 1975 he also submitted to the publisher his *Sabrane pjesme* (Collected Poems). His poetry continued to be translated into Hungarian, French, and other foreign languages throughout the 1970s. His last collection to be published in the 1970s was *San* (Dream, 1976).

He began the 1980s with the publication of *Lirika* (Lyrics) in Slovenian. For his seventy-fifth anniversary an important volume, edited by Jure Kaštelan, Marijan Matković, and Nedjeljko Mihanović, appeared: *Dragutin Tadijanović: Zbornik radova o pjesniku* (Dragutin Tadijanović: An Anthology of Works About the Poet). In 1981 he published a collection of poems from 1975 to 1981, *Prijateljstvo riječi* (Friendship of Words). Two years later he was awarded the Goran Wreath Award for his poetry and for his contributions to the preservation of works by Ivan Goran Kovačić. In 1983, under his direction, a five-volume collection of works by Goran Kovačić was produced.

Still another book, a collection of selected love poetry, *Svjetiljka ljubavi* (Lamp of Love) appeared in 1984, followed in 1985 by *Moje djetinjstvo* (My Childhood). Tadijanović's poems from 1982 to 1986 appeared in 1986 in his collection *Kruh svagdanji* (Daily Bread), with the second edition in 1987, for which he received the "Tin" Ujević Award. Another elaborate collection of the poet's selections appeared in 1987, *More u meni* (The Sea in Me). A noteworthy publication in five volumes, *Sabrana djela Dragutina Tadijanovića* (Collected Works of Dragutin Tadijanović), appeared in 1988 and 1989. These volumes were compiled by the poet himself, with Milan Mirić serving as editor in chief. The second volume of *Dragutin Tadijanović: Zbornik radova o pjesniku* was issued in 1991 under the direction of Ivo Frangeš.

The recollection of things past is the most enduring theme in Tadijanović's poetry. In recollecting the serenity and fascination of his own childhood and his hometown of Rastušje, the poet takes the reader back to his or her own childhood experiences. The poet does this in a clear language, with words that seem to have been freed from any bondage or servitude to ideological or political aims. In returning to his childhood Tadijanović goes back to a rich source that for many years has served as the well of his poetic inspiration. It is not surprising then that the titles of his collections all refer to childhood: *Dani djetinjstva* (1937), *Slike iz mog djetinjstva* (1974), and *Moje djetinjstvo*. Tadijanović's poetry is also his autobiography. His concern with the inconstancy of experience is contrasted with the permanence of his free verse. As far back as *Dani djetinjstva,* Tadijanović was already protesting the loss of childhood. In *Lirika* he writes about a return to one's "hearth," one's place of birth. These themes continue throughout his twenty-one books. In creating his free-verse style, he dropped rhyme but not rhythm. In fact, Tadijanović has a great feeling for rhythm in his poetry. He reminds the reader of Walt Whitman in that his poetic lines, too, begin with the rhythm of speech.

Tadijanović is a poet of remembrance, of details and their transience; a poet who, in poem after poem, arrests a moment of everyday experience. At a time when social autism appears to be a symptom in modern societies, Tadijanović attempts to shake up his readers and remind them that only memory can redeem and define an individual. In reading Tadijanović one realizes that, through his miniature and apparently insignificant details, the poet is defending the individual and the individual experience before the onslaught of collective forgetfulness.

Despite the simplicity that has been attributed to him, this poet is in reality a puzzling poet, not because he desires to be so, but because in the contemporary world words have lost their original clarity. In going back to his childhood Tadijanović hopes to cleanse words of their worldly baggage and have them stand as fresh in the reader's mind as they once stood before him or her in childhood. In so doing the poet offers the reader a source of remembrance in a world of forgetfulness.

For readers interested in specific and even minute details regarding the origins of a particular poem or work, Tadijanović has supplied ample information. The best source for this information is in his collected works, *Sabrana djela Dragutina Tadijanovića*. As for the critical articles about his work, of which there are more than five hundred, many are included in the two-volume *Dragutin Tadijanović: Zbornik radova o pjesniku* Anthology of Works About the Poet (volume 1, 1980; volume 2,

1991). The multiple editions of Tadijanović's collections and the sheer volume of articles about his work are evidence of the high regard in which the poet is held among scholars, critics, and the general public.

References:

Branimir Bošnjak, "Konkretizam kao sinteza poetike Dragutina Tadijanovića," *Mogućnosti,* 38 (1991): 341–344;

Ivo Frangeš, "Neprolaznost prolaznosti," *Forum,* 24 (1985): 578–588;

Frangeš, "Vječni život poezije," *Forum,* 30 (1991): 177–180;

Edward D. Goy, "The Poetry of Dragutin Tadijanović," in Tadijanović's *Selected Poems,* translated by Goy and Dennis Ward (Zagreb: PEN, 1993), pp. 235–239;

Jure Kaštelan, "Dragutin Tadijanović," in Tadijanović's *Pjesme i proza* (Zagreb: Matica hrvatska, 1969), pp. 7–28;

Kaštelan, Marijan Matković, and Nedjeljko Mihanović, eds., *Dragutin Tadijanović: Zbornik radova o pjesniku,* volume 1 (Zagreb: Mladost, 1980); volume 2, edited by Frangeš (Zagreb: Mladost, 1991);

Jasna Melvinger, "Prozodijske duljine u stihovima Dragutina Tadijanovića," *Jezik,* 2 (1982): 33–40;

Nedjeljko Mihanović, "Poezija Dragutina Tadijanovića," *Republika,* 36 (1980): 621–631;

Cvjetko Milanja, *Struktura i vizija Tadijanovićeve poezije* (Osijek: Revija, 1975);

Joža Skok, "Tadijanovićeva poezija i poetika djetinjstva," *Republika,* 47 (1991): 118–123;

Šime Vučetić, "Dragutin Tadijanović," *Forum,* 32 (1976): 545–560.

Dimitŭr Talev
(1 September 1898 - 20 October 1966)

Ivan Ruskov
University of Plovdiv

BOOKS: *Sŭlzite na mama* (Sofia: Knizharnitsa "Apolon," Pechatnitsa "Sŭglasie," 1925);

Usilni godini: Book I, *V drezgavinata na utroto* (Sofia: Knizharnitsa "Apolon," Pechatnitsa "Sŭglasie," 1928); Book II, *Podem* (Sofia: Izdanie na avtora, 1929); Book III, *Ilinden* (Sofia: Izdanie na avtora, 1930);

Zdravets i Iglika. Sŭrtseto tsvete (Sofia: Knizharnitsa Georgi T. Krŭstev, pechatnitsa "Sredets," 1930);

Proletta e magyosnitsa (Sofia: Knizharnitsa Georgi T. Krŭstev, Pechatnitsa P. Ovcharov, 1931);

Pod mrachno nebe (Sofia: Sŭyuz na makedonskite kulturno-prosvetni organizatsii v Bŭlgariya, Pechatnitsa Ovcharov, 1932);

Zlatniyat klyuch (Sofia: Pechatnitsa P. K. Ovcharov, 1935);

Velikiyat tsar (Sofia: Kazanlŭshka dolina, 1937);

Starata kŭshta (Sofia: Khemus, 1938);

Igra (Sofia: Sŭyuz na bŭlgarskite pisateli, Pechatnitsa "ABV," 1939);

Na zavoy (Sofia: Biblioteka "Zaveti," Pechatnitsa Poligrafiya, 1940);

Gotse Delchev (Sofia: Biblioteka "Brannik," Pechatnitsa "Izgrev," 1942);

Grad Prilep. Borbi za rod i svoboda (Sofia: Ministerstvo na narodnoto prosveshtenie, 1943);

Zavrŭshtane (Sofia: Perun, 1943);

Zhelezniyat svetilnik (Sofia: Bŭlgarski pisatel, 1952);

Ilinden (Sofia: Bŭlgarski pisatel, 1953);

Kiprovets vŭstana (Sofia: Narodna kultura, 1953);

Prespanskite kambani (Sofia: Bŭlgarski pisatel, 1954);

Ilindentsi (Sofia: Narodna mladezh, 1955);

Samuil (Sofia: Narodna kultura, 1958-1960): Book I, *Shtitove kamenni*—1958; Book II, *Pepelyashka i tsarskiyat sin*—1959; Book III, *Pogibel*—1960; revised edition, *Samuil. Roman-letopis za kraya na Pŭrvata bŭlgarska durzhava,* Books I-III (Sofia: Narodna kultura, 1965);

Bratyata ot Struga (Sofia: Bŭlgarski pisatel, 1962);

Hilendarskiyat monah (Sofia: Narodna mladezh, 1962);

Glasovete vi chuvam (Sofia: Bŭlgarski pisatel, 1966).

Editions and Collections: *Razkazi i povesti. 1927-1960* (Sofia: Bŭlgarski pisatel, 1962);

Sŭchineniya, 11 volumes, edited by Stoyan Karolev and others (Sofia: Bŭgarski pisatel, 1972-1978).

Editions in English: *The Iron Candlestick,* translated by Marguerite Alexevia (Sofia: Foreign Languages Press, 1964);

The Bells of Prespa, translated by Mihail Todorov (Sofia: Foreign Languages Press, 1966);

Ilinden: A Novel of the Macedonian Rebellion of 1903, translated by Nadya Kolin (Sofia: Foreign Languages Press, 1966).

Dimitŭr Talev is one of the most significant Bulgarian novelists in the years after World War II, a writer who provided a profound and many-sided portrait of the Macedonian people by evoking their complex and tragic history, their way of life, and their moral and spiritual values. The country of Macedonia was Talev's greatest and most constant love; its people and its land were lifelong inspirations both to the man and the artist.

Dimitŭr Talev Petrov was born on 1 September 1898 in the town of Prilep, Macedonia. His father, Tale Petrov Palislamov ("Palikupa" or "Palislama" was a derogatory name for the peasants who moved to town), came from the countryside and was a skillful blacksmith. He died in 1908, before Dimitŭr was ten. Talev's mother, Donka, came from Prilep. The writer later considered that his mother's personality was representative of the town, while his father personified the village. Talev admired his mother's intensive emotional and spiritual life and her strength of character, which was definitely greater than his

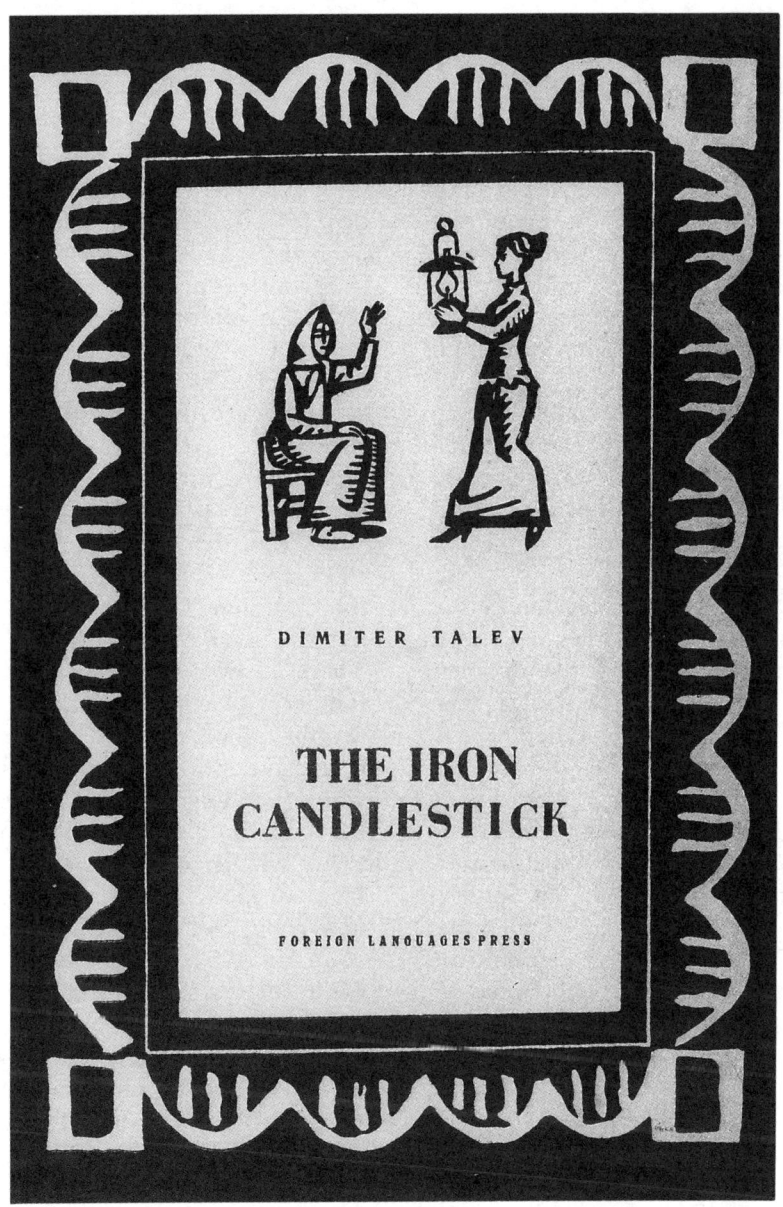

Cover for a translation of Dimitŭr Talev's 1952 novel, Zhelezniyat svetilnik, *considered by many critics to be his greatest artistic achievement*

father's, and embodied some of her features in Sultana, the richest, most imposing character in his novel *Zhelezniyat svetilnik* (1952; translated as *The Iron Candlestick*, 1964). Talev was the youngest son in his family and was nearsighted from birth. His eldest brother, Georgi, was a schoolteacher; his other brother, Alexi, was a blacksmith. Both of them (especially Georgi) took part in the activities of the VMRO—an organization struggling for the liberation of Macedonia. Their participation enabled Talev to make an early and close acquaintance with the underground resistance that he later depicted in his works. His only sister, Maria, died at an early age in 1935.

The Balkan Wars that began in 1912 had a great impact on Talev's life; they were also the reason that his education was irregular and unsystematic. After finishing the primary school in his hometown, he lived through an educational odyssey that took him from the Bulgarian high school in Thessaloníki (1912), to Bitolya (1913–1914), and then to Skopje (1916). His first short story was published in 1917 in the Skopje newspaper *Rodina* (Fatherland) and was never reprinted. It was titled "V ochakvane" (Waiting), and its plot was a variant of the celebrated short story "Ide li?" (Is He Coming?), by Ivan Vazov. In 1918, the last year of World War I, Talev was mobilized for a while in Sofia but continued his studies in Stara Zagora. In 1920 he graduated from a Serbian high school in Bitolya. In the same year he became a medical student at the University of Zagreb but left after the first semester. He then moved to the philosophy department at the University of Vienna, but his fascination with philosophy lasted only one semester, the spring of 1921. Finally he found his great love—the University of Sofia, where he majored in Slavic philology in 1925. During his studies he was helped financially by his brother Georgi, who, along with their mother, gave the writer constant moral and spiritual support.

Sofia was the place where Talev finally settled after graduation and started his career as a journalist and a writer. For the next two decades, until World War II ended in Bulgaria in September 1944, he wrote many books in different genres and on different subjects, but he was not considered a particularly important writer during these years. From 1923 to 1925 he wrote short stories, sketches, and essays on social issues: "Vampirŭt" (The Vampire); "Payak" (A Spider); "Na ulitsata" (In the Street); and "Golemiyat Petko i malkiyat Petko" (Big Petko and Little Petko), published in workers' and communist periodicals and newspapers, such as *Rabotnicheski vestnik* (Workers' Newspaper), *Rabotnichesko edinstvo* (Workers' Unity), *Lŭch* (A Ray), and the journal *Nov pŭt* (New Way). These works did not display great artistry; the author was still looking for the problems and themes that corresponded to his creative ambitions. The same is true about his three books for children: *Sŭlzite na mama* (Mama's Tears: Short Stories and Fairy Tales for Children, 1925), a debut book; *Zdravets i Iglika. Sŭrtseto tsvete* (Crane's Bill and Primrose: The Flower Heart, 1930), in which both texts are reprints from his first book; and *Proletta e magyosnitsa* (Spring Is a Magician, 1931).

From 1927 Talev worked as a proofreader at the newspaper *Makedonia;* then in 1929 he became a member of the editorial board. In addition to working at the newspaper and writing short stories, he also wrote his first novel, *Usilni godini* (Hard Years, 1928-1930). The work is in three parts: *V drezgavinata na utroto* (In the Twilight of the Morning, 1928), *Podem* (Uplift, 1929), and *Ilinden* (Saint Elija's Day, 1930). This novel marks the beginning of the basic issue in his work—the fate of Macedonia identified as a geographic and ethnocultural area, whose status and frontiers are determined by complicated political and ideological factors and are based on various multinational confrontations and the contradictory interests of local Balkan and European entities. The novel chronicles the dramatic events from the end of the Russo-Turkish War in 1878 until the suppression of the Ilinden uprising in 1903. Contemporary criticism, unlike some rather favorable evaluations in the past, has dismissed the novel as sketchy and conceptually weak. The same events that constitute the plot of *Usilni godini* were given a more successful artistic interpretation by the mature Talev in his novel *Ilinden* (1953; translated 1966).

From the second half of 1930 to September 1931 Talev was the editor in chief of *Makedonia;* then he left the newspaper and spent a few months in Paris in the winter of 1931-1932. There he wrote his only drama, *Pod mrachno nebe* (Under a Gloomy Sky, 1932), a rather unsuccessful illustration of the author's protest against the repressive attitude of the Serbian authorities toward the Bulgarians in Macedonia. His trip to Paris resulted in several short stories of little value written during the 1940s. After returning from France, Talev resumed his work at the newspaper and became its manager from 1933 to 1934. In 1934 a coup d'état took place in Bulgaria, after which *Makedonia* was banned and its publication stopped.

During the 1930s Talev's short stories, articles, and sketches appeared in the pro-Macedonian press—the newspapers *Makedonska tribuna* (Macedonian Tribune); *Vardar;* the underground *Svoboda ili smŭrt* (Freedom or Death); and the journal *Rodina*. After *Makedonia* was banned to mid 1944, almost all Talev's short stories appeared in the newspaper *Zora* (Dawn); these stories were collected in five books: *Zlatniyat klyuch* (The Gold Key, 1935); *Velikiyat tsar* (The Great Czar, 1937); *Starata kŭshta* (The Old House, 1938); *Igra* (A Game, 1939), consisting of only two long short stories; and *Zavrŭshtane* (Return, 1943). The short stories develop a main theme of Talev's works, the recounting of patriarchal country life, in *Zlatniyat klyuch* and *Starata kŭshta* (in which some of the short stories show the influence of Yordan Yovkov). Others base their plots on history and legends: the short stories in *Velikiyat tsar* are about old-time Bulgarian rulers; the last seven form a cycle of stories about King Samuil, and this cycle gives the title to the book. Many of the subjects, problems, and plots of the short stories are later used by Talev in his novels. After he had become a recognized writer, he somewhat underestimated his achievements in the short genres, considering them just "grains" or "passing steps" that made the way to the novel easier. In 1962 he made a selection of his earlier short stories and published them in his book *Razkazi i povesti. 1927–1960* (Short Stories and Novellas, 1927–1960).

In 1940 Talev's second novel, *Na zavoy* (At a Turn), was published. It takes place at the end of the 1920s in Bulgaria. This is the time when the wars have recently ended, leaving a tragic mark on the national consciousness; the wars were followed by a period of terrorism and repression from 1923 to 1925. In his book Talev suggests a way out of the conflicts by showing what turns an individual must make to save himself, his family, and his country. The novel depicts an interesting psychological conflict, but the author's solution is unconvincing: the only salvation seems to be a return to peasant labor and a simple way of life. The author's message is dispersed by many impressive but quite trivial and naive peripeties that conclude with a village idyll for the main character, Krum Kosherov, after his marriage with a rich girl.

For critics of the 1940s *Na zavoy* was an undoubted success; now the novel may be seen simply as an important stage in Talev's development as a novelist, in which he works with a contemporary setting that was not typical in his early work. Ironically, this book was later among the most objectionable of Talev's works and one of the main reasons for the sharp turn in his life after World War II. The novel, whose main character goes all the way from communism to complete rejection of any political engagement and, to make things worse, becomes a wealthy landowner, seems totally opposed to the economic doctrine and artistic criteria imposed by the postwar government.

Shortly before the government vetoed Talev's creative ambitions, he succeeded in having two books published, *Gotse Delchev* (1942) and *Grad Prilep. Borbi za rod i svoboda* (The Town of Prilep: Struggles for Kin and Freedom, 1943). The former is a biography of Gotse Delchev, a prominent activist of VMRO who perished for the freedom of Macedonia. The latter is an essay, a synthesis of many-sided perspectives on the life and history of the writer's native town of Prilep–a key place whose patriarchal atmosphere pervades many of Talev's works.

After the end of World War II on 9 September 1944, Talev found himself among those repressed by the new government, for reasons that were not clear. Probably his relations with VMRO and his work at *Makedonia*, as well as some of his ideas expressed in the novel *Na zavoy*, the collection *Velikiyat tsar*, and the books about Gotse Delchev and Prilep, along with the fact that he was born in Macedonia, made him a politically unreliable figure from the new government's ideological point of view. On 18 October 1944 Talev was arrested and jailed in the Central Prison in Sofia until the end of April 1945. The lack of any offense saved him from the so-called People's Court, but after prison he was sent to forced labor in the Bobovdol mine. In August 1945 he was released, but in the autumn of 1947 the visit to Bulgaria by the Yugoslav president, Josip Broz Tito, resulted in the arrests of many Macedonian activists.

Talev was then sent to the open-cast mine Kutziyan. On 20 December 1947 he was buried under a coal avalanche and discovered and saved only by chance. On 10 January 1948 he was moved to the Bogdanov mine. Inhumane living conditions–dirt, vermin, and undernourishment–were constantly his lot in those years of forced labor. After the intercession of influential people Talev, who was extremely sick, was released. Returning home in February 1948, he weighed only forty-six kilograms. Because he had been expelled from the Writers' Union, he could not find a job. On 8 August 1948 he and his family were interned at Lukovit. His life was extremely difficult, and his right of free movement around the country was limited. At the same time he was not given a chance to publish his novel *Zhelezniyat svetilnik*, finished on 4 September 1946 (extracts from it had appeared in 1944 in *Zora*), nor other works.

The physical intimidation of the writer then changed to political intimidation. Following their propaganda and their ideological aims, the political authorities forced Talev to make a declaration to "repent his mistakes," to censure VMRO and its leaders as well as some Yugoslav politicians. The declaration was published in the newspaper *Pirinsko delo* (Pirin Cause) on 28 January 1951. The headline created by the editors read: "Makedonskiyat pisatel Dimitŭr Talev razoblichava Ivan-Mihaylovata banda i Kolishevtsi" (The Macedonian Writer Dimitŭr Talev Unmasks Ivan Mihaylov's Band and the Kolishevs). What is remarkable in the headline and in the text itself is that Talev is presented as a Macedonian, not a Bulgarian. The amateurish language and the redundancy of vulgar ideological clichés indicate that this squib, typical of the Cold War, was dictated by someone other than Talev.

The declaration put an end to Talev's exile in Lukovit. In February 1952 he returned to Sofia. After all this, the publication of his works became possible and the first one, *Zhelezniyat svetilnik,* appeared in the same year. This novel marked the beginning of Talev's recognition and his remarkable writer's career. Along with that, however, one notices the growing influence of ideological prescriptions imposed during the 1950s and 1960s. The novels *Zhelezniyat svetilnik, Prespanskite kambani* (1954; translated as *The Bells of Prespa,* 1966), *Ilinden,* and *Glasovete vi chuvam* (Your Voices I Hear, 1966) form a tetralogy that is considered Talev's most significant work. It gives a multifaceted vision of life in Macedonia from the 1830s to the first decade of the twentieth century. The individual fate of the characters from three generations of the Glaushev clan is the prism through which typical individual and national features are viewed.

Zhelezniyat svetilnik is regarded as the best of the four novels and Talev's greatest artistic achievement. It is set in the town of Prespa (the literary name of Prilep) during the time of Turkish rule and just after the plague in 1833. The social conventions of the time are challenged by a nontraditional act: Sultana, the only granddaughter of a respected old clan, marries an obscure peasant newcomer, Stoyan Glaushev. Displaying great moral strength, Sultana repudiates the groundless accusations of immorality and even helps her husband win recognition as a master blacksmith and start his own business in the *tcharshiya* (market street). Later their son, Lazar Glaushev, becomes a leader of the youth and an organizer of the struggle for spiritual awakening in Prespa. Inspired by the idea of continuity between generations, Talev shows how the sons take up their fathers' cause and continue to struggle for the benefit of their people. In each novel of the tetralogy this struggle proceeds in accordance with the historical processes in the Revival and post-Revival eras in Macedonia. The author develops several plot lines that present different sides of the characters' lives. This enables him to be profound and convincing in the details of ethical and psychological analysis. The complicated relationship between family life and national history persists throughout the novel, but it is especially prominent in the conflicts between love and duty, between Sultana's maternal feelings and social morality, and between pragmatism and idealism. In Lazar's case the complicated accumulation of poligenetic imperatives is solved by the objective change of circumstances, but Sultana, the most tragic character in Talev's creation, faces a clash of opposing moral principles that cannot find a simple and painless solution. The most moving pages in the novel are the ones dedicated to this clash. The description of the psychological drama of Sultana, who, torn between maternal love and moral norms, causes the death of her daughter, Katerina, is among the masterpieces of Bulgarian literature. The novel starts with the marriage of Sultana and Stojan and ends with the marriage of their son Lazar. But the end of the novel is not a happy ending because between these two marriages there is one that remains unrealized—the tragic love story of Sultana's youngest daughter, seventeen-year-old Katerina, and Rafe Klintche, a master wood-carver, an artist in heart and soul, a wanderer who has come to Prespa to make a wonderful iconostasis for the newly built church.

Prespanskite kambani takes place from the mid 1860s to the early 1880s. The family tension here is focused on the aggravated relations between Lazar's wife, Niya, and Sultana. This tension is not eased until Niya, humiliated for many years because of her infertility, finally gives birth to Boris, her first and only child. Socially and historically, the most important event is the Russo-Turkish War of 1877–1878. At first Macedonia, being a part of Bulgaria, is a free territory, but after the interference of the "Great Powers" in Europe, Macedonia is left under Turkish rule. The revolutionary committee in Prespa organizes the struggle against the Turks and prepares an uprising. The leading figures are Lazar and the teacher Rayko Vardarski, a newcomer to the town. After an unsuccessful attempt at an uprising, Vardarski is hanged, and Lazar spends three years in a Turkish prison. The novel ends with the death of the old Glaushevs—first Stoyan, then Sultana.

In the novel *Ilinden* the narrative revolves around the preparation, outbreak, and suppression of the Ilinden uprising in 1903 (it was the fiftieth anniversary of this uprising that caused *Ilinden* to be printed before the second novel of the tetralogy, *Prespanskite kambani*). The author reveals the complicated character of the revolutionary movement: the fate of Macedonia is decided in the light of assimilative ambitions, as the terroristic and ideological confrontations among Bulgarians, Serbs, and Greeks heat up. Under these circumstances Boris, Lazar's son, nicknamed "Milostiviya" (the Merciful), joins the struggle. The author also portrays such historical figures as Gotse Delchev and Dame Gruev, promoting their idea of the autonomy of Macedonia.

In the novel *Glasovete vi chuvam* the main character is Boris Glaushev; the historical period is that of Macedonia between the suppression of the uprising in 1903 and the eve of the Balkan War in 1912. Total hatred separates the Christians of different ethnic identities as terrorism and assassinations become everyday occurrences. The author develops further his idea that only love can overcome the religious, ethnical, and social differences that divide people, that it should dominate people's lives. Especially faithful, but also victims of their love, are the women: Katerina (from *Zheleznijat svetilnik*); Niya; the teacher Ivanka Rumenova (from *Prespanskite kambani*); the teacher Dona Kraycheva (from *Ilinden*); and the Greek girl Angelika (from *Glasovete vi chuvam*), who commits suicide because of her love for Boris, thus protesting ethnic hatred between Bulgarians and Greeks.

In the men's world, however, weapons speak louder than the voice of the heart, and changes in the concept of homeland are painful. In *Zhelezniyat svetilnik,* which is dominated by the figure of the mother, the homeland is interpreted as an inseparable unity of territory, history, and ethnic community and is called Bulgaria. In the other novels of the tetralogy–those that evoke the world of the sons–the concept of homeland acquires ideological shades, and the population of Macedonia becomes the object of assimilative attacks from different Balkan states and nations. In this novel Talev presents the tragic and hopeless situation that resulted when the idea of ethnic community could not overcome the separatist and aggressive tendencies in the cultural and political life of the Balkans at the beginning of the twentieth century.

When Boris Milostiviya finds himself in the vortex of preposterous murders, he does not act out of conviction but succumbs to inertia because he is tortured by questions whose answers lay beyond the historically dominant idea of patriotism: "Isn't the love of your people a hatred of the other one?" In the end of the novel Boris's parents, Lazar and Niya Glaushevi, are alive but confused by the horror of the events and thankful that their son, thought to be dead, is alive and has been sent to Bulgaria to recover. Talev intended to follow Boris's further life in another novel but died before he was able to write the book. *Glasovete vi chuvam* is his last work.

During the 1950s and 1960s Talev wrote several other works that do not reach the artistic level of his tetralogy but are still comparatively interesting as educational readings, especially for children: *Kiprovets vŭstana* (Kiprovets Revolted, 1953); *Samuil* (Samuil, 1958–1960); *Bratyata ot Struga* (The Brothers from Struga, 1962); and *Hilendarskiyat monah* (The Monk of Hilendar, 1962). The novella *Kiprovets vŭstana* deals with the struggle of the Bulgarian people against their Turkish oppressors–the uprising in 1688 in Kiprovets (modern Tchiprovtzi, a small town northwest of Sofia). It is followed by *Ilindentsi* (1955), an unsuccessful juvenile adaptation of the novel *Ilinden*.

As his early short stories from *Velikiyat tsar* prove, Talev was deeply moved by the tragic glory of Czar Samuil. Fifteen thousand of Samuil's soldiers were blinded in 1014 by the victorious Byzantine emperor Vasiliy II, called "Bŭlgaroubiets" (the murderer of Bulgarians). These historical facts are reproduced in the novel *Samuil,* consisting of three parts: Book I, *Shtitove kamenni* (Shields of Stone, 1958); Book II, *Pepelyashka i tsarskiyat sin* (Cinderella and the Prince, 1959); and Book III, *Pogibel* (Destruction, 1960). The sight of the blinded soldiers broke Samuil, and soon afterward he died from a heart attack. The novel represents a broad picture of the Bulgarian people's many wars with Byzantium and the way of life, including religious and political conflicts in Bulgaria, that led to Bulgaria's falling under Byzantine rule.

The novella *Bratyata ot Struga* chronicles the lives of Dimitŭr and Konstantin Miladinovs, teachers and spiritual leaders during the Revival in Macedonia who eventually died in a Turkish prison. In *Razkazi i povesti. 1927–1960* (Short Stories and Novellas: 1927–1960, [1962]) Talev published his psychological novellas, "Posledno pŭtuvane" (Last Journey) and "Dva miliona" (Two Million), written during the 1940s. The former presents the last days of an old woman whom none of her three sons wants to look after; the latter tells the story of a rich pharmacist who has cancer and his greedy and hypocritical relatives who are waiting for his will. Another book that appeared in 1962 is *Hilendarskiyat monah*–a novel about the life of Paisiy Hilendarski, who wrote *Istoriya slavenobolgarskaya* (A Slavic Bulgarian History, 1762), a book that marks the beginning of the Bulgarian National Revival.

Talev died from stomach cancer on 20 October 1966. He left behind an imposing body of work on various themes, many of which powerfully evoke and interpret the historical ordeals of the Bulgarian people. For his writing he was awarded the Dimitrov Prize in 1959, as well as the titles Honored Cultural Worker (1963) and People's Cultural Worker (1966).

Interview:

Ganka Naydenova-Stoilova, "V tvorcheskata laboratoriya na pisatelya Dimitŭr Talev," *Literaturna misŭl,* 1, 2, 3 (1957): 93-102; 83-96; 88-103.

Bibliographies:

Magdalena Shishkova, "Bibliografiya za Dimitŭr Talev. (Izbrana)," in Talev's *Sŭchineniya v 11 toma,* volume 11 (Sofia: Bŭlgarski pisatel, 1978), pp. 453-457;

Shishkova, in *Rechnik na bŭlgarskata literatura,* volume 3, edited by Georgi Tsanev (Sofia: BAN, 1982), pp. 434-435.

Biographies:

Toncho Zhechev, ed., *Dimitŭr Talev, Svetoslav Minkov i Dimitŭr Dimov v spomenite na sŭvremennitsite si* (Sofia: Bŭlgarski pisatel, 1973);

Kosta Tsŭrnushanov, *Dimitŭr Talev v moite spomeni* (Sofia: Makedoniya, 1992).

References:

Georgi Konstantinov, "Dimitŭr Talev," in his *Moeto pokolenie v literaturata* (Sofia: Bŭlgarski pisatel, 1967), pp. 143-185;

Boiyan Nichev, *Dimitŭr Talev. Literaturnokriticheski ocherk* (Sofia: Bŭlgarski pisatel, 1961);

Nichev, "Kŭm tipologiyata na epichniya roman," "Stranitsi ot poetikata na bŭlgarskiya roman," and "Pŭtyat na istoricheskiya roman," in his *Sŭvremenniyat bŭlgarski roman* (Sofia: Bŭlgarski pisatel, 1978), pp. 108-156; 157-195; 237-263;

Nichev, "Milostiviyat i chetirite knigi na negoviya zhivot," in his *Kritika i literaturna istoriya* (Sofia: Bŭlgarski pisatel, 1980), pp. 85-96;

Aleksandŭr Spiridonov, *Dimitŭr Talev. Literaturnokriticheski ocherk* (Sofia: Narodna mladezh, 1986);

Valeri Stefanov, "Mezhdu Stsila i Xaribda (Uchastta na kontseptsiyata za istoriyata v tetralogiyata na Dimitŭr Talev)," in his *Tvorbata-bezkraen dialog* (Sofia: Sv. Kliment Ohridski, 1992);

Simeon Yanev, "Emotsionalno razmishlenie nad istoriyata," *Literaturen vestnik,* 7 (1993): 6;

Pantaley Zarev, "Dimitŭr Talev," in his *Bŭlgarska klasika,* volume 2 (Sofia: Nauka i izkustvo, 1987), pp. 379-424;

Toncho Zhechev, "Zagadkata na Dimitŭr Talev" and "Romanistut Dimitŭr Talev," in his *Istoriya i literatura* (Sofia: Bŭlgarski pisatel, 1979), pp. 507-533.

Veno Taufer
(19 February 1933 -   )

Marko Juvan
University of Ljubljana

BOOKS: *Svinčene zvezde* (Ljubljana: Published by the author, 1958);

Jetnik prostosti (Ljubljana: Cankarjeva založba, 1963);

Prometej ali tema v zenici sonca: Pesniška igra s prologom (Maribor: Obzorja, 1968);

Vaje in naloge (Maribor: Obzorja, 1969);

Ob londonskem gledališkem poldnevniku: Gledališki vtisi v petih aktih z odmori (Ljubljana: Mestno gledališče ljubljansko, 1970);

Podatki (Maribor: Obzorja, 1972);

Prigode (Ljubljana: Cankarjeva založba, 1973);

Pesmarica rabljenih besed (Ljubljana: Državna založba Slovenije, 1975);

Avantgardna in eksperimentalna gledališča (Ljubljana: Mestno gledališče ljubljansko, 1975);

Odrom ob rob (Ljubljana: DZS, 1977);

Ravnanje žebljev in druge pesmi (Ljubljana: Državna založba Slovenije, 1979);

Sonetje (Ljubljana: Mladinska knjiga, 1979);

Pesmi (Ljubljana: Državna založba Slovenije, 1980);

O jej krokodil (Ljubljana: Mladinska knjiga, 1983);

Tercine za obtolčeno trobento (Ljubljana: Mladinska knjiga, 1985);

Vodenjaki (Ljubljana: Državna založba Slovenije, 1986);

Kaj kdo je in kaj kdo kuha (Ljubljana: Mladinska knjiga, 1986);

Črepinje pesmi (Maribor: Obzorja, 1989);

Odisej & sin ali svet in dom (Ljubljana: Slovenska knjiga, 1990);

Nihanje molka: Izbrane pesmi (Ljubljana: Mladinska knjiga, 1994);

Še ode (Ljubljana: Cankarjeva založba, 1996).

TRANSLATIONS: T. S. Eliot: *Pesmi in pesnitve,* edited and translated by Taufer (Ljubljana: Državna založba Slovenije, 1966);

Eliot, *Umor v katedrali. Poezija in drama,* translated by Taufer (Maribor: Obzorja, 1967);

Veno Taufer

Ezra Pound, *Pound,* edited and translated by Taufer (Ljubljana: Mladinska knjiga, 1973);

Slavko Mihalić, *Zadnja večerja,* translated by Taufer (Ljubljana: Državna založba Slovenije, 1974);

A. B. Šimić, *Pesmi,* translated by Taufer (Maribor: Obzorja, 1975);

Augustin "Tin" Ujević, *Ujević,* edited by Taufer, translated by Taufer and Božo Vodušek (Ljubljana: Mladinska knjiga, 1975);

Vlada Urošević, *Neko drugo mesto*, translated by Taufer (Ljubljana: Državna založba Slovenije, 1975);

Afrika, mati moja: Črnska umetna lirika, translated by Aleš Berger and Taufer (Maribor: Obzorja, 1976);

T. S. Eliot, *Iz pesmi, dram in esejev*, edited and translated by Taufer (Ljubljana: Cankarjeva založba, 1977);

Miodrag Pavlović, *Svetli in temni prazniki*, translated by Taufer (Ljubljana: Državna založba Slovenije, 1977);

Radovan Pavlovski, *Rdeči in črni petelin*, translated by Taufer (Maribor: Obzorja, 1977);

Vesna Parun, *Pesmi*, translated by Taufer (Ljubljana: Državna založba Slovenije, 1978);

Branko Miljković, *S smrtjo nad smrt*, translated by Taufer (Ljubljana: Državna založba Slovenije, 1980);

T. S. Eliot, *Pesmi*, edited and translated by Taufer (Ljubljana: Mladinska knjiga, 1982);

W. B. Yeats, *Izbrano delo*, edited and translated by Taufer (Ljubljana: Cankarjeva založba, 1983);

Bogomil Džuzel, *Riba smisla*, translated by Taufer (Ljubljana: Državna založba Slovenije, 1985);

Ted Hughes, *Ted Hughes*, edited and translated by Taufer (Ljubljana: Mladinska knjiga, 1988);

Tomas Venclova, translated by Niko Jež and Taufer (Ljubljana: Društvo slovenskih pisateljev, 1991).

PLAY PRODUCTIONS: *Prometej ali tena v zenici sonca: Peniška igra s prologom*, Celje, Slovensko ljudsko gledališče, 1973;

Odisej & sin ali svet in dom, Ljubljana, Slovensko mladinsko gledališče, 1990.

OTHER: *Vilenica Desetnica: 1986–1995*, edited by Taufer (Ljubljana: Društvo slovenskih, pisateljev).

Veno Taufer is one of the founders of Slovene literary modernism, which began flourishing in the 1950s and the 1960s; he is also a precursor of postmodernism. He is a persistent innovator who has cultivated an intellectual, hermetic poetic style. As an avant-garde-oriented translator, critic, editor, playwright, and organizer, he has opened his country's literary horizons to the modern world and facilitated the promotion of Slovene literature internationally while also promoting exchange between modernist authors in the former Yugoslavia. As a member of dissident cultural and political groups in Slovenia he worked to enhance personal and artistic freedom and made an important contribution to the democratization and independence of Slovenia. He was a founder of the Vilenica International Writers' Conference and hence took part in the reaffirmation of the Central European identity.

Veno (Venčeslav) Taufer was born on 19 February 1933 in Ljubljana. His father, Venčeslav, was a teacher, and his mother, Marija (née Bizjak), was a clerk. An only child, he spent his childhood in Zasavje, a region on the Sava River. In 1939 he started school in the small mountain village of Dole; after the beginning of the war and the German occupation in 1941 he attended the elementary school in Gabrovka. In 1943 his father, a leftist and one of the first organizers of the uprising against the Nazi occupation in Zasavje, was killed in battle. In 1944 Veno began the college preparatory high school (gymnasium) in Ljubljana and graduated after the war, in 1952. That same year he enrolled in the Faculty of Arts in Ljubljana, in the Department of Comparative Literature and Literary Theory. He graduated in 1960, two years after his marriage to Jasna Škrinjar and a year after the birth of his first son. He wrote his thesis on the reception of Maksim Gorky's work in Slovenia. After making his first attempts at writing in high school, he entered literary life in his college years, in 1956 and 1957, publishing poems in *Beseda* (Word), *Tribuna* (Tribune), *Revija 57* (Review 57), and *Naši razgledi* (Our Views). He eventually became associated with the literary-cultural circle that played a leading role in the modernization of Slovene literature.

At the beginning of its literary career Taufer's generation was burdened by its experiences of both of the violence of World War II and of the ideological conflicts that resulted when the Slovene resistance against Nazi occupation became intertwined with the Communist revolution. As the son of a partisan killed in the war, Taufer was ethically divided between his loyalty to socialist ideals and his contempt for the ideologically oppressive postwar mechanisms and dogmas fostered by the Communist regime. Moreover, under the influence of existentialists such as Albert Camus and Jean-Paul Sartre and modern poets like Charles Baudelaire, Federico García Lorca, and Božo Vodušek, Taufer and his generation explored existential states of disgust, horror, and the experience of the absurd, and they confronted nihilism as a worldview. The writers who influenced them also raised their radical critical and rebellious consciousness and helped them develop a new poetic language that avoided sentimentalism and could express modern urban feelings or irrational and fantastic worlds.

Taufer, who in 1957 was editor of the literary supplement of the student newspaper *Tribuna* (Tribune), also became a literary editor of the pivotal journal *Revija 57* (Review 57) from 1957 to 1958, in which the younger generation attempted "to realize and arrange the world of new values of their own," as Vital Klabus wrote in *Naši razgledi* (10 August 1957) and continue the modernizing and pluralist tendencies of *Beseda* (1951–1957), which had been abolished for political reasons. Although it included some contributors from *Beseda,* the new, so-called critical generation was more radical in its modernism: unlike the slightly older poets from *Beseda,* they did not try to escape the collectivist socialist spirit by searching for refuge in personal intimacy and sentiment. *Revija 57* extended pluralism from the ideological and cultural spheres into politics, provoking the government to abolish the journal in 1958. Its contributors were interrogated, investigated, and some of them found guilty (Taufer spent more than a week in jail at the end of 1959).

The beginning of poetic modernism in Slovenia is marked by the fact that the first books by the two main poets of the critical generation, Dane Zajc (*Požgana trava* [Burned Grass]) and Veno Taufer (*Svinčene zvezde* [Leaden Stars]) in 1958, had to be published by the authors themselves because of the ideological interference in publishing. The critical generation also found an alternative to aesthetically ossified and ideologically controlled institutions—a non-institutional theater: it founded the avant-garde, experimental Oder 57 (which lasted from 1957 to 1964). This small theater, which was, like the journal *Revija 57,* intended to be a vehicle of public enlightenment, first staged some important new Slovene dramatic works and introduced modern theatrical genres such as antidrama, poetic drama, existentialist drama, and political drama. Taufer headed the theater from 1962 to 1964 from the office where he was editor of *Perspektive* (Perspectives). At the time he was without a full-time, permanent job: although in 1960 he had become a radio announcer and later a cultural editor at Ljubljana RTV, he quit in November 1961 and turned to freelancing because he could not tolerate political interference with his work.

After a year's hiatus, *Perspektive* (1960–1964) continued the movement started by *Revija 57* and its theater. Taufer was one of the most active and essential *Perspektive* contributors, although he was never a member of its editorial board. The more liberal Communist faction for some time tolerated the journal of the "court opposition" (as it was labeled by its opponents) as a laboratory of ideas. *Revija 57,* Oder 57, and *Perspektive* were the dynamic socializing media of a tightly knit group of artists, authors, sociologists, philosophers, and critics (among others, Primož Kozak, Dominik Smole, Dane Zajc, Gregor Strniša, Peter Božič, Marjan Rožanc, Rudi Šeligo, Lojze Kovačič, Janko Kos, Taras Kermauner, Veljko Rus, Jože Pučnik, and Vital Klabus) who were united by their basic orientation and strategies. They shared a profoundly existentialist view (shaped by Albert Camus, Jean-Paul Sartre, and Martin Heidegger), an ethical perspective that was early Marxist or influenced by Milovan Djilas, and a shared critical consciousness that worked to free Slovene society from ideological myths and inertia and renew it with open dialogue. In *Revija 57* and *Perspektive* Taufer published the central texts of his early literary production. *Perspektive,* a forum for the emerging cultural and political opposition, was abolished by the government in the spring of 1964; the event was accompanied by political trials. The same year (when Taufer's second son was born), following staged riots, Oder 57 was abolished as well. Hence the political-allegorical, poetic drama *Prometej ali tema v zenici sonca* (Prometheus or Darkness in the Pupil of the Sun), which Taufer wrote in 1963 and 1964 and placed in the repertoire of that theater, had to wait for its publication until 1966 in the journal *Problemi* (Problems).

In Taufer's life the abolishing of *Perspektive* meant the end of a collective, utopian project of the ethical renovation and pluralization of Slovene society. After the journal's demise he devoted much of his time to translating works by T. S. Eliot, Ezra Pound, and some Croatian and Serbian modernists; from his work in translation he derived impulses for his own literary creativity as well. From September 1966 to August 1969 he worked in London as an announcer for the Yugoslav section of the British Broadcasting Corporation. At the same time he followed the modern theater scene in London closely, publishing his critical impressions in the book *Ob londonskem gledališkem poldnevniku* (At the London Theatrical Meridian, 1970). After he again became employed in the cultural section of Ljubljana RTV (a position he held from 1969 to 1990), he attended writers' congresses and theater and poetry festivals in the former Yugoslavia and abroad, participating as a critic. In his book *Avantgardna in eksperimentalna gledališča* (The Avant-Garde and Experimental Theaters, 1975) he collected and commented on the published documents on the activities of Oder 57 and other noninstitutional theaters between 1955 and 1967. Later, he continuously and favorably dealt with Yugoslav as well as international modern theater trends. Reviews and essays on this topic are collected in *Odrom ob rob* (Marginalia Concerning Theaters, 1977), where he published his dialogic essay on ethical, ideological, and aesthetic dilemmas of the avant-garde theater, "Birnamski gozd" (Birnam Wood).

After the temporary warming of the social and political climate in 1965 when the liberal faction of the Slovene Communist Party came to power, Taufer and some of the former *Perspektive* contributors joined the journal *Problemi* (1962–). However, Taufer's ties with the journal were much looser than with *Perspektive,* and not just because he was living in London. At *Problemi* the younger generation was advancing, introducing the new French novel, concrete art, neo-avant-gardism, structuralism, neo-Marxism, sociological functionalism, liberal pragmatism, Martin Heidegger, and Jacques Derrida. In his *Jetnik prostosti* (Prisoner of Liberty, 1963) Taufer paved the way for two neo-avant-garde trends, ludism (the play of textual codes) and reism (the cataloguing of objects and signs), and then ethically revised them in *Vaje in naloge* (Exercises and Assignments, 1969) and *Podatki* (Data, 1972).

From 1958 to 1972 Taufer was considered one of the leading Slovene modernist poets. While he was highly regarded by the circles who shared his ideological and aesthetic orientation, the more conservative factions accused him of being cerebral, hermetic, and verbalistic. In this period Taufer introduced and radicalized modernist poetics, omitting punctuation and favoring the parallelist, iterative composition of texts. He avoided neo-Romantic sentiment and explicit personal confession by introducing nihilism, existentialism, and surrealism, and, finally, in his experimental playing with linguistic signifiers and perceptions he supplanted any communication of ideas.

As early as *Svinčene zvezde* (1958) the poet attempts to objectify through images the black-wave mixture of melancholy and the explosive, rebellious anger toward the oppressiveness and ideological monism of postwar socialist societies. Existential anxiety, fear of nothingness, urban indifference, and the absurd are evoked with animated countryside or urban scenes and with mythological and literary allusions. The cycle *Melanholija drugega ešalona* (The Second Echelon's Melancholy) that describes the sons being burdened by their fathers' war sacrifices is a confession by the critical generation. Taufer often surrealistically, grotesquely deforms motives and nihilistically overturns the official state poetic genres, Communist iconography, and journalistic embellishments of the facts. With the poet's self-reflective distancing from his own idealism and will for power, the absurd looses its heroic, tragic modulation and becomes playful. *Jetnik prostosti* is an allusion to Sartre's ethics of decision: should one, after the destruction of metaphysical and historical revolutionary visions, passively suffer like a prisoner the fear of nothingness, conform, be afraid of questionable authorities, and resort to illusions and privacy; or should he take risks and, with actions directed toward society, boldly realize his existence and inner freedom? Taufer mostly distances himself from the former inert possibility with humor or irony, exposing its misery in grotesque images, from which the acting characters often disappear (for example, the cycle *Slovenski sonetje* [The Slovene Sonnets]). Despite all his reflective skepticism, he perceives action as an authentic substitute for an eroded metaphysics, which gives the collection a confident sense of belonging to the rebellious, spiritually liberated generation of *Perspektive* and the archetype of the sower. The cycle of sonnets about wartime youth includes elements of stream of consciousness. In the shorter modernist long poems the realistic motive base is fantastically transformed or geometrically stylized with contrastive, Lorcan color symbolism and with ancient and biblical myths shining through the contemporary situations. As a sign of a rational formal distance Taufer introduced the sonnet and terza rima into the collection.

Taufer's *Prometej ali tema v zenici sonca* (1966, 1968) is by its genre (a "poetic play") as well as by its topic (the relationship of the intellectual versus authority) representative of *Perspektive* drama. With sometimes deliberately comical metaphors baroque in their richness, Taufer modernizes and travesties the Greek myth. Prometheus is an allegory of a humanistic intellectual's problem in a modern, socialist society where orthodox communism gives way to so-called self-management in the 1960s. Prometheus, as an engineer of spirits, is an heir of the revolution, a creator of ideas that are supposed to give meaning to the society as a whole and bring progress to it. However, his fanatic idealism is undermined by the crisis of values and the disintegration of the common interest into a host of private interests. Prometheus perishes mostly because of the nihilistic core hidden in his metaphysics, that is, the will to power.

Taufer's most virtuosic volume of poems, *Vaje in naloge* (1969), followed the forceful destruction of the *Perspektive* movement and his search for a new poetic identity in the context of the ludic and reistic neo-avant-gardes. In these poetic cycles and poems Taufer introduces expressive devices from concrete and visual poetry and collage; he combines myths with contemporary settings; he uses intertextuality, parody, and abstraction or registration of objects without subjective or editorial perspective. After the defeat of *Perspektive*, crisis situations (a sense of being lost, self-denial, and seeking refuge in intimacy and in memories, as well as thoughts of suicide) are the subjects in poems with various intertextual connections, particularly with France Prešeren's *Krst pri Savici* (The Baptism on the Savica, 1836) (the motive of defeat), with folklore, and with the Gospels (Peter's disavowal of Christ). The poet is extremely critical of the forces that render social and poetic authenticity impossible: he parodically burlesques the emblems, slogans, and diction of discourses embodying contemporary repression, ideology, and consumer inertia; in the same way he treats the burden of violent political history and the limits of literary traditions that were bound up with social, moral, and utilitarian roles.

In 1972 the ultramodernist *Podatki* is the highest point in Taufer's revolt against the mimetic tradition in literature and in his orientation toward language as autonomous poetic material. The sonnets as a traditionally high literary genre are internally undermined; they possess neither the subject's editorial perspective nor an evident idea. These poems are an abstract, hermetic montage of overlapping sensual impressions; memories; and artistic, journalistic, and mythological fragments from private and political reality. The poet in an associative way registers the days in which the sonnets were written. In the second part of the volume, in quatrains with folkloric connotation, the creative process is extremely innerlinguistic: the title words in poems simulating encyclopedic entries trigger a metaphoric, metonymic and phraseological-terminological game with linguistic signifiers.

In 1972, when Stane Kavčič, the main force behind liberalism, was forced into retirement by the orthodox Communist Party line, the political control and cultural oppression intensified anew (the so-called leaden 1970s). This year Taufer and some other undesirable contributors (among others, Taras Kermauner and the Heideggeran philosopher and literary theoretician Dušan Pirjevec) were forced to leave *Problemi*. Following this incident Taufer ceased to publish his poetry in Slovene journals for an entire decade, until the establishment of *Nova revija* (New Review, 1982). However, he continued publishing reviews and translations, and by 1980 he had published four books at the official Slovene publishing houses and even received two state awards for his poetry and translations, the Prešeren Fund Award (1974) and the Sovre Award (1975). In 1979 his third child was born.

In June of 1980 Taufer was among the initiators of a new journal intended to revive creative autonomy and ideological-aesthetic and political pluralism, and grounded already in the spirit of the postmodern era (end of metaphysics, ideologies, history, and the cult of innovation; they were supposed to be replaced by the coexistence of the tradition and modernity as well as of other differences). Taufer immediately became one of the leading poets of *Nova revija*. By the end of the 1980s he published three additional volumes of poetry. In 1987 he received the most prestigious award for poetry (the Jenko Award) from the Slovene Writers' Association for his volume of poems *Vodenjaki* (Waterlings, 1986). *Nova revija* grew to be one of the main fields of Slovene political democratization and national emancipation. It became involved in risky conflicts with the government, which, because of the crumbling Communist regimes, gradually became more open to dialogue. Between 1985 and 1989 Taufer occupied vulnerable positions as secretary of the Slovene Writers' Association and president of the Association's Committee for a Protection of Thought and Written Expression, which responded with statements, petitions, and public forums to the government's oppressive actions against various types of opposition. In the mid 1980s the majority of Slovene intellectuals became Central European–oriented as a reaction to Yugoslav unitarianism and revived Stalinist tendencies. Since 1985 Taufer has been organizing the annual Vilenica Central European Writers' Conference, editing its multilingual proceedings, and has been a member of the jury for the international literary award (it was awarded, among others, to Fulvio Tomizza, Peter Handke, Zbigniew Herbert, Milan Kundera, and Adolf Muschg). In 1987 Taufer's life and creativity were dealt a painful blow by the incomprehensible tragic death of his younger son, Matej, which marked some of the most touching elegies in his *Črepinje pesmi* (Shards of Poems, 1989) and was probably a motivation for his modern dramatic treatment of the motives of Odysseus roaming around the world, Telemachus's search and endangered family (*Odisej & sin ali Svet in dom* [Odysseum & Son or The World and Home] was staged and published in 1990). However, soon Taufer was again pulled into the stream of social developments, in other words, into the "Slovene spring." From 1988 he was a member of the Committee for the Protection of Human Rights, which protested against the military trial of the Slovene journalists and writers. This civil societal association grew into a movement for multiparty democracy and independence of Slovenia. From January 1991 (in April 1990 the noncommunist opposition won the first democratic elections) to April 1995 Taufer was a government adviser in the cultural ministry and ministry of foreign affairs of the newly independent Slovene state. Currently (1996) he serves as the director of Vilenica. In December 1995 he received the Central European Award in Vienna for his contribution to Vilenica and his involvement in the spiritual renaissance and democratization of Slovenia. In February 1996 he was awarded the Prešeren Award for his life's work. In 1996 his volume of poetry, *Še ode* (Ever Odes), was published.

In the 1970s and the 1980s Taufer's poetry gained a solid position in the canon of modern Slovene literature; it also became known in the former Yugoslavia and started to make its way abroad. Although the author became a well-known public figure, his work was never popular. In the 1980s reservations about its hermetic, intellectualist, thematically burdened character were coming not only from traditionalists but also from some younger, postmodernist critics. In his opus after 1975, the ideas, topics, and techniques indicating postmodernism are added to the modernist and avant-garde, experimental, poetical bases. Modernist elements remaining in his poetry are incoherence, indefinable semantics, fragmentation and reduction of expression, as well as acoustic tension and explosiveness. The poet does not make any attempt, like postmodernism, to please the reader, but wants "to feel the poem physically, like a mason building a house" (interview in *Razgledi*, 7 February 1996). The postmodernistic elements are Taufer's sense of "a fragmentariness / ... / of any truth" (interview in *Literatura* [Literature] 5/21, 1993), the emphasis on the intertextual "memory" of a poem, symbolizing nonmetaphysical being and reviving the presence of self as a person, a marginal voice.

Pesmarica rabljenih besed (A Songbook of Used Words, 1975) is conceived as a collection of contemporary, extremely modern variations on Slovene folk songs, particularly ballads. By his imagistic focusing on fragments of old originals, Taufer evokes ambiguity, elusiveness of truth, and existential and ontological themes based on Heidegger's philosophy: existence for death, abhorrence of nothingness, longing, and the destructive game of being. The philosopher Tine Hribar proclaimed Taufer's essay in the commentary "O rabi rabljenih besed" (On the Use of Used Words) one of the first programs of Slovene postmodernism.

Ravnanje žebljev in druge pesmi (Nail Straightening, 1979) to some extent redundantly deals with experimentation, particularly with the sonnet and tezra rima forms (for example, with constellations of verses or with poetization of grammatical words). However, the cyclic poem *Ravnanje žebljev in druge pesmi* crowns reistic registration of objects and minimalistic expression with extraordinary meaningfulness. Marginal, nonpoetic reality (nail pounding, pulling, and so forth) becomes a vehicle of a symbolism of a paradoxical personal or social existence (the relationship between an individual and the majority, between the pressure of the authorities and perseverance, resistance, sharpness, and cunning of the individual). One cycle was published in expanded form in the independent volume *Vodenjaki* (Waterlings, 1986). The title word is a neologism, denoting anthropomorphic creatures found on archaic excavations. The texts imitate mythic discourse and logic, stylize folklorist and sacral genres, and create their own mythological world, a modern equivalent of the Apocalypse. In minimalist techniques, the poems deal with chaos and the decay of a subject and of identity threatening anthropocentric civilization after the nuclear war. Some of the tercets in *Ravnanje žebljev in druge pesmi* direct the reader to the distinctly philosophical, reflective poetry, prevalent in the following three volumes.

The design of the volume *Tercine za obtolčeno trobento* (Tercets for a Dented Trumpet, 1985) is, despite variegated poems written between 1972 and 1984, conceptually and formally uniform. It is an homage to the poetry by the poets that, for Taufer, continue to be alive. Through the "memory" of his terza rima, here and there in a palimpsest manner, shine the motive fragments, stylemes, moods, value attitudes, or themes characteristic of Slovene romantic and modern tradition. The titles of the cycles are philosophical (for example, *Pesmi brez metafizike* [Poems without Metaphysics], *Pesmi o transcendenci* [Poems about Transcendence], *Dialektike* [Dialectics]), introducing the reader to dramatic and paradoxical events in an individual's mortal existence: the traces of metaphysical, religious, historical, or aesthetic transcendence clash with the profane invasion of a disenchanted world plagued by pollution, entropy, disease, and a disorientated value system. The poems with marginal appearance of first-person voice relativize and profane everything transcendent, but on the other hand they transcend the reality with hermetic symbols, mythological allusions, generalizations, and cosmic universalizations of personal experiences.

Črepinje pesmi, with more coherent and poetic expression, is devoted mostly to ontological and social actualizations of Greek myths and to vivid engrossments into war violence placed in indefinite history. Myths, which we "feed from a dead divine mouth," are indispensable for our survival in the monstrous machinery of nothingness. Amid a true exaltation of spleen and self-destructive grotesque, these are the purest elegiac poems, in which the poet, with extreme reservation but very powerfully, expresses the physical pain, horror, helplessness, and silence at the incomprehensible death of his younger son: reduced experiential, entirely concrete or imagistically symbolic motives (a candle, nightmares of Icarus's fall, a raging sea hidden in everything, or a white thistle among green blades of grass) are underscored with phonic and rhythmic instrumentation. The poet uses the same poetics to voice a hymn to beautiful, extraordinary moments in evanescent life.

The play *Odisej & sin ali svet in dom* retells Odysseus's and Telemachus's story. It employs whole sections of Homer's text as quotes, which are then complemented with Taufer's original poetic parts and dramaturgically divided into fragments in various genres (the work carries a subtitle ironic in a Shakespearean way, "tragical-comical-historical-pastoral"). The poet intervenes with poems and chansons which actualize the story as well as give it a social critical point and transfer it into the cosmic dimensions of metaphysical nihilism. The fundamental themes are Odysseus's duality (the tragic condemnation to eternal restlessness, but cruelty and rationality as well) and the crisis of the family, Telemachus's need for a father.

The 1996 volume *Še ode* contains mainly sonnets that formally come close to terza rima (3-3-3-3-2). Framing these sonnets are two engaged political poems in terza rima that condemn, with a fugue of evocative pictures, the barbaric destruction of Vukovar and Sarajevo during the war in the former Yugoslavia. By modernizing his sonnets (which in Slovenia represent a prestigious genre of high, encyclopedic confession), by alluding to Slovene traditions from the past one thousand years, and by employing symbolic and fragmentary texts, Taufer is able to intertwine several themes: the existential and artistic defiance of civilization's blind forces, the abhorrence of nothingness, the history of Slovenes during a period of the crumbling of transcendent values, post-Communist immorality, and the individual's relationship with God. The volume is marked by expressive lyric scenes from nature as well as by a distinctly reflective tone and personal moral pain. The poet treats the mass media with great irony; he explores the loss of people's sense of reality, entropy, and the ghettoization of beauty; most of all, he reflects on the experience of lethally dangerous pain. In the pain and mortal terror caused by the "dagger of language" as he searches for the authenticity of existence, Taufer discovers the riches, or the "crystal," of fleeting existence. Hence the title, indicating his skeptical persevering in the poetic mode.

Taufer's literary opus is the expression of an existence that faces being and nothingness (most often symbolized by an ocean) from the top of the ruins of metaphysics and historical eschatologies. Taufer is intensely aware of death and its mystery; he also knows that any truth is fragmentary, making it fragile but also combative and dynamic. Taufer attempts to express poetically the paradox of existence in the most authentic way, every time employing new poetic solutions that evolve spirally from early to late modernism with elements of postmodernism. As a modernist he requires the reader's effort and participation. In the name of existential authenticity, his poetry and drama nihilistically demythologize or humorously relativize the lifestyle that many people accept, the social and religious authorities, and the myths, ideologies, and conventions of the literary canon. Taufer's works disassemble the principles of traditional mimesis and confession and open the aesthetic roundedness of literary works to discussion. In the place of traditional conventions Taufer introduces into his writing ironic self-reflection, depersonalization, fragmentariness, intertextuality, asceticism and minimalism, incoherence, equivocal and semantic indeterminacy, montage, the grotesque and the profane, paradoxical and dramatic tensions in composition, acoustic explosiveness, and linguistic and formal experimentation. All these elements are blended and shaped by the author's incisive reflections and experiences.

Interviews:

Tine Hribar, "Pogovor z Venom Tauferjem," *Nova revija*, 26-27 (1984): 2991-3018;

Aleš Berger, "Kovana zmuzljivost jezika," *Literatura*, 21 (1993): 37-45;

Nela Malečkar and Tea Štoka, "Pesem moram čutiti fizično–kakor zidar, ki zida hišo," *Razgledi*, 3 (7 February 1996): 4-9.

Bibliography:

"Bibliografija," in Veno Taufer, *Nihanje molka: Izbrane pesmi,* edited by Matevž Kos (Ljubljana: Mladinska knjiga, 1994): 230-236.

Biography:

Jože Koruza, "Veno Taufer," in *Slovenski biografski leksikon,* volume 12 (Ljubljana, 1980), pp. 12-13.

References:

Marjan Dolgan, "Tauferjeva (neobrabljena) pesmarica rabljenih besed: Poskus interpretacije," *Sodobnost*, 1 (1976): 63-75;

Aleš Gabrič, *Socialistična kulturna revolucija: Slovenska kulturna politika 1953-1962* (Ljubljana: Cankarjeva založba, 1995), pp. 38-52, 58-76, 132-139, 174-184, 193-202, 222-228, 268-280;

Niko Grafenauer, "Branje nove (in stare) poezije: Prelomne razsežnosti v poezji Vena Tauferja," *Jezik in slovstvo,* 6 (1974/75): 145-155; extended version "Pesniški modernizem: o poeziji Vena Tauferja," in his *Izročenost pesmi* (Maribor: Obzorja, 1982), pp. 101-123;

Tine Hribar, "S pesmijo globoke rane," in Taufer's *Tercine za obtolčeno trobento* (Ljubljana: Mladinska knjiga, 1985), pp. 67-77;

Hribar, "Sodobna slovenska poezija," in his *Sodobna slovenska poezija* (Maribor: Obzorja, 1984), pp. 173-283;

Marko Juvan, "Književne odnosnice v poeziji Vena Tauferja," *Slavistična revija,* 1 (1985): 51-70;

Taras Kermauner, *Perspektivovci* (Ljubljana: Znanstveno in publicistično središče, 1995);

Kermauner, "Točka avtoblokade," in his *Od igre do telesa* (Ljubljana: Mestno gledališče ljubljansko, 1976), pp. 109-145;

Kermauner, "Žebljasta pesem," *Problemi,* 7 (1980): 43-53;

Janko Kos, "Sodobna slovenska lirika 1950-1980," *Sodobnost,* 12 (1982): 1098-1115; reprinted with the same title in his *Sodobna slovenska lirika 1950-1980* (Ljubljana: Mladinska knjiga, 1983), pp. 133-155;

Matevž Kos, "Razpokane besede," in Taufer's *Nihanje molka: Izbrane pesmi,* edited by M. Kos (Ljubljana: Mladinska knjiga, 1994), pp. 207-226;

Boris Paternu, "Drugi povojni val mladih med novim ekspresionizmom in nadrealizmom"; "Veno Taufer," in *Slovenska književnost 1945-65, 1: Lirika in proza,* edited by Paternu, Helga Glušič, and Matjaž Kmecl (Ljubljana: Slovenska matica, 1967), pp. 171-173; 182-190;

Paternu, "Tauferjev *Jetnik prostosti,*" *Problemi,* 11 (1963): 979-988;

Jože Pogačnik, "Eksistencializem in strukturalizem," in *Zgodovina slovenskega slovstva,* by Pogačnik and Franc Zadravec (Maribor: Obzorja, 1973), pp. 507-579;

Pogačnik, "Obrazi sodobnih slovenskih pesnikov II: Veno Taufer," *Sodobnost,* 2 (1972): 194-198;

Denis Poniž, "Jetnik besed, jetnik sveta: Utrinki o poeziji Vena Tauferja," in his *Molk in pisava* (Ljubljana, 1986);

Božo Repe, *Obračun s Perspektivami* (Ljubljana: Znanstveno in publicistično središče, 1990);

Ivo Svetina, ed., *Veno Taufer, Odisej & sin ali Svet in dom: Slovensko mladinsko gledališče: Program, sezona 1989/90, predstava 1* (Ljubljana, 1990);

Franc Zadravec, "Moderno gledališče in revija Perspektive," in *Slovenska književnost 1945-65, 2: Dramatika ter književna esejistika in kritika,* by Jože Koruza and Zadravec (Ljubljana: Slovenska matica, 1967), pp. 271-276.

Papers:

The manuscripts are kept by the author at his residence, Ilirska 4, SI-1000 Ljubljana, Slovenia.

Aleksandar Tišma
(16 January 1924 -)

Dubravka Juraga
University of Arkansas

BOOKS: *Naseljeni svet* (Novi Sad: Matica srpska, 1956);
Krčma (Novi Sad: Progres, 1961);
Krivice (Novi Sad: Budućnost, 1961);
Nasilje (Belgrade: Prosveta, 1965);
Drugde: putopisi (Belgrade: Nolit, 1969);
Za crnom devojkom (Belgrade: Prosveta, 1969); an excerpt translated by Alan McConnel as "In Search of the Dark Girl," *Relations*, no. 1-2 (1970): 50-63;
Knjiga o Blamu (Belgrade: Nolit, 1972);
Mrtvi ugao (Novi Sad: Radnički univerzitet "Radivoj Ćirpanov," 1973);
Upotreba čoveka (Belgrade: Nolit, 1976);
Škola bezboništva (Belgrade: Nolit, 1978);
Bez krika (Belgrade: Nolit, 1980);
Begunci (Titograd: Pobjeda, 1981);
Vere i zavere (Belgrade: Nolit, 1983);
Hiljadu i druga noć (Belgrade: Srpska književna zadruga, 1987);
Kapo (Belgrade: Nolit, 1987);
Naseljeni svet, Krčma i ostalo: pesme (Novi Sad: Književna zajednica Novog Sada, 1987);
Pre mita (Banja Luka: Glas, 1989);
Široka vrata (Belgrade: Nolit, 1989);
Dnevnik 1942-1951: Postajanje (Novi Sad: Matica srpska, 1990);
Koje volimo (Sarajevo: Svjetlost, 1990);
Iskušenja ljubavi (Belgrade: Vreme knjige, 1994).
Editions in English: "In Search of the Dark Girl," an excerpt translated by Alan McConnell, *Relations*, no. 1-2 (1970): 50-63;
"Personality," translated by Celia Williams, in *New Writing in Yugoslavia*, edited by Bernard Johnson (Harmondsworth: Penguin Books, 1970), pp. 145-162;
"The Vigil," translated by Maja Samolov, *Relations* (1976): 184-190;
"The School of Godlessness," translated by Dragan Monašević, in *The Serbian Short Story 1950-1982: Anthology*, edited by Radivoje Mikić, *Relations* (1983): 58-85;

Aleksandar Tišma

The Use of Man, translated by Johnson (New York: Harcourt Brace Jovanovich, 1988);
Kapo, translated by Richard Williams (New York: Harcourt Brace Jovanovich, 1993).

PLAY PRODUCTION: *Cena laži. Pozorišni komad u tri saslušanja*, Niš, Niško pozorište, 15 December 1953;

MOTION PICTURES: *Tragovi crne devojke*, screenplay by Tišma, 1972;
Život je lep, based upon the short story *Nasilje*, screenplay by Tišma, 1985.

Aleksandar Tišma belongs to a large group of European writers whose attention is intensely focused on the destruction and suffering caused by human violence and brutality. Tišma's work parallels that of writers from modernists such as James Joyce and Franz Kafka to postmodernists such as Peter Handke and Samuel Beckett in their treatment of the disintegration of identity of both individuals and societies in the modern world. But Tišma treats these issues specifically within his own historical and cultural context. Like Primo Levi, Tadeusz Borowski, Bertolt Brecht, Bruno Schultz, Thomas Mann, Elie Wiesel, and many others, he locates much of the difficulty of modern existence in the horrors of the Nazi devastation of Europe before and during World War II. Much of his work deals with various attempts, mainly unsuccessful, at psychological and social regeneration in the postwar Yugoslav socialist society.

Tišma's novels and short stories are frequently set in the northeastern Yugoslav province of Vojvodina and in his hometown, Novi Sad. He particularly focuses on the destruction of the Jewish community in Novi Sad during the pro-Nazi Hungarian regime and on the problems Jewish survivors faced trying to grasp the reality of the attempted annihilation of their world. The image of a lonely, isolated Jew unable to establish a meaningful relationship to the present embodies for Tišma, as for Danilo Kiš, a broader human condition in a twentieth century characterized by violent ruptures with the past and consequent alienation from the present. For many of his themes Tišma draws upon his own experience, and the lives of many of his characters resemble his own life in many ways.

Tišma was born on 16 January 1924 in the village of Horgoš, near Subotica. His mother, Olga Müller Tišma, was from a well-to-do Jewish family from Horgoš. His father, Gavra Tišma, came from a Serbian peasant family from Visuć, a village in Lika. After the end of World War I Gavra Tišma traveled to Horgoš as an employee of a trading company that sent him there to close down some of their unprofitable wine shops. It was during that trip that Gavra met Olga and her family. Gavra and Olga soon married and settled in Novi Sad. Olga's family, the Müllers, had been affluent and cultured. Her mother played the piano, read widely, and frequently attended theater performances. Olga later encouraged her only son, Aleksandar, to develop a love and respect for literature, art, and music. Already bilingual in Hungarian and Serbo-Croatian, Aleksandar began at the age of ten to study German with a private tutor; he later learned French and English as well. Even though the whole family was affected by the economic crisis of the late 1920s and the 1930s, Tišma's mother insisted that his education not suffer. Aleksandar's father was at that time an independent salesman. To help the family survive, Olga learned to sew corsets, and with this craft she supported the family for years to come.

In 1930 Aleksandar began his elementary education in the Nikolajevska School in Novi Sad. In 1941 Vojvodina was annexed by Hungary and the high school system, in which Tišma had been a student since 1934, was reorganized into separate Serbian and Hungarian high schools where the languages of instruction were Serbo-Croatian and Hungarian. Tišma attended the Serbian high school. One of the most traumatic and therefore memorable events of Tišma's youth occurred during his last year in high school in 1942. That January, to frighten the population of Vojvodina into obedience, the Hungarian regime organized pogroms in various villages and towns, killing many of the inhabitants. In Novi Sad, during a three-day raid, more than fourteen hundred Jews and Serbs were slaughtered in the streets of the town and on the shores of the Danube. Tišma and his parents were spared, possibly because their Hungarian neighbors did not denounce them to the Hungarian police when questioned. Many of Tišma's literary works refer to this traumatic event of his youth.

Tišma graduated from high school in June 1942 and moved to Budapest, where he lived with his maternal grandmother. There, amid the dangerous wartime environment of Miklós Horthy de Nagybánya's pro-Nazi regime, he enrolled in university classes (in the department of French language and literature) and intended to continue his schooling. However, he did not attend the lectures regularly nor pass any exams at the time. At the same time, to support himself, he worked at an import-export company, MAEK (Magyar àltalànos élelmiszer központ). The Hungarian occupation of Novi Sad ended in November 1944, though a large portion of Yugoslavia was still occupied by Axis troops. Tišma returned to Novi Sad from Budapest and enlisted in the new Yugoslav army. In November 1945 he was discharged from the army and returned to Novi Sad. This was the period when his literary and journalistic work began.

Tišma applied for a position as a journalist at the suggestion of his high school teacher, who worked at the time for the Novi Sad daily *Slobodna Vojvodina* (Free Vojvodina). In November 1945 he was hired at the daily, where he became a correspondent from Subotica and Sremska Mitrovica. In the summer of 1946 he started to write for the financial section of the newspaper and continued to write about economics after his transfer two years later to another daily, the Belgrade *Borba* (Struggle). In 1949, amid the turmoil caused by Josip Broz Tito's break with Joseph Stalin and the Soviet Union, Tišma decided to end his journalistic career. In November 1949 he returned to Novi Sad to a job as a publishing editor in the publishing company Matica srpska, where he would remain until his retirement in August 1980. While working full time as a journalist, he decided to finish his college education. He enrolled in the department of English literature and language at the University of Belgrade, from which he graduated in 1954. In January 1952 he married Sonja Drakulić, a librarian for Matica srpska. Their only child, Andrej, was born in November that same year.

Always surrounded by books and literature, Tišma had been interested in becoming a writer since the age of fifteen, but it took more than a decade before he was satisfied enough with his literary efforts to have them published. His search for his literary style and expression is described in a diary that he started writing in 1942. The diaries were later published as *Dnevnik 1942-1951: Postajanje* (Diary of Maturation, 1942-1951). Here Tišma records his development as a writer and discusses the importance of writing in his life: "Writing provides me a place in my society. It is the place of an independent intellectual, oriented toward the people (especially those of his generation) and trying to understand them and to draw upon them for his own life." The diary also illuminates current political events, especially the events of the Yugoslav break with the Soviet Union in 1948: it is an interesting record of the lives of ordinary people during that critical decade.

In 1956 Tišma published his first literary work, the collection of poems *Naseljeni svet* (The Populated World). His next collection of poems, *Krčma* (A Tavern), was published in 1961. He published the collections of stories *Krivice* (Cases of Guilt) in 1961 and *Nasilje* (Violence) in 1965. *Krivice* is a chronicle of life set in the provincial Novi Sad of the 1950s. Most of the stories offer a realistic, at times almost naturalistic, depiction of people, events, and moods. One of the best stories in *Krivice*, "Ibikina kuća" (Ibika's House), depicts the life and disintegration of an old madam and her "house" in Novi Sad. "Ibikina kuća" employs the Brechtian allegorical equation between prostitution and capitalism to portray the disintegration of the capitalist, prewar Yugoslavia at the end of World War II, when the communist partisans arrived in liberated Novi Sad and established a new socialist order. Another brilliant story from the collection is "Koncert" (A Concert), which powerfully depicts the survival of the old, prewar bourgeoisie and the early existence of a new petty bourgeoisie in the new socialist Yugoslavia.

In addition to the poetry and short stories in the 1950s, Tišma wrote one play, *Cena laži: Pozorišni komad u tri saslušanja* (The Price of a Lie: A Play in Three Hearings, 1953). The play is set in Prague during the trial of a government minister. The Communist Party pressures the son of the minister to testify falsely against his father. The son complies but, overcome with guilt, commits suicide. The play, which has not been published, was also performed in Niš, Yugoslavia, and in Iserlohn, Germany. Although invited to attend the German premiere, Tišma was unable to go because he was denied a passport. At the police headquarters of Vojvodina, Tišma was labeled a "Kominformist" in his dossier, and this label was sufficient for the police to prevent Tišma from traveling abroad. He then abandoned drama and returned to poetry.

Tišma's first published literary pieces were critical essays on contemporary Yugoslav writers such as Mihailo Lalić, Erih Koš, Gojko Banjević, and Vladan Desnica. Tišma was quite active as a journalist and literary editor for the renowned Yugoslav literary journal *Letopis Matice srpske* (Annals of the Serbian Cultural Society), to which he contributed a regular column, "Listajući časopise" (Leafing through Journals). From 1953 to 1965 he wrote reviews and commentaries on various artists, writers, and poets as well as on cultural and literary events from Yugoslavia and around the world. Topics addressed by Tišma include Franz Kafka, Sinclair Lewis, the Munich journal, *Welt und Wort* (World and Word), Miroslav Krleža, literary circles in Great Britain, *The Times Literary Supplement, The Nouvelle Revue Française* (New French Revue), Bertrand Russell, William Faulkner, German war novels, British postwar literary production, Alberto Moravia, Norman Mailer, the Chilean literary world, Heinrich Böll, Albert Camus, the literature of Adolf Hitler's Germany, Alfred Döblin, Bertolt Brecht, Erich Auerbach, *Les Temps Modernes* (Modern Times), Ivo Andrić, Boris Pasternak, T. S. Eliot, Richard Wright, Isaac Babel, Tobias Smollett, James Joyce, *Le Figaro Literaire* (The Figaro Literary Supplement), Nikos Kazantzakis, Jack Kerouac, Nadine Gordimer, Vladimir Nabokov, Theodore Dreiser, Robert Penn Warren, *Partisan Review, Tel Quel, Neue deutsche Hefte* (New German Notebook),

Title page for a translation of Tišma's 1987 novel that explores the psychic damage suffered by victims of the Nazi concentration camps

The London Magazine, Les Lettres Française (French Letters), the Pulitzer Prize, Stefan Zweig, Irwing Shaw, Klaus Mann, and Miklos Radnoti.

For his many literary and cultural achievements Tišma received the October Prize of the City of Novi Sad in 1966. In 1969 Tišma published a collection of essays, *Drugde: putopisi* (Elsewhere: Travelogues), describing his travels abroad after he finally obtained a Yugoslav passport in 1957. In his essays on France and Great Britain, where he went in 1957 and 1960, respectively, Tišma contemplates the differences in cultures and lifestyles between Eastern and Western Europe. In his essays on the divided Berlin and on Central Europe he examines culture, history, and politics, as well as the ideological positions that tied Poland, Czechoslovakia, and Hungary into the entity of Central Europe. The essay on his bicycle trip through the heartland of Serbia presents an intimate and warm picture of the land and its people. The essay about his trip to the United States in 1968 is an insightful description of the many cultural idiosyncrasies and conflicts that characterized the Untied States during the tumultuous 1960s. He also perceptively discusses the differences between Central European and American cultural paradigms.

Tišma's first novel, *Za crnom devojkom* (In Search of the Dark Girl), was also published in 1969. The unnamed protagonist is a young man whose life's ambitions and expectations are radically disrupted by World War II. After the war the protagonist is unable to organize his life meaningfully because he has no strength or energy to continue his disrupted education, despite his desire to do so. Instead he wastes his life on various unappealing jobs, inane relationships with women for whom he does not care, and tedious, everyday routines that he is unable to avoid. Eventually he comes to believe that his only chance at establishing a fulfilling life came in a brief encounter with a dark-haired girl he had met by chance one night in a small Vojvodina town. But he had discarded the girl unthinkingly the next morning, as he was greedily and vainly hoping for some other exciting adventure, which did not materialize, the following night. We follow his twenty-year search for the "dark girl," which comes to symbolize to him all the happiness and fulfillment that has eluded him. Thus, the novel depicts the failure to establish meaningful interpersonal relationships in the Yugoslav society disrupted by war.

Za crnom devojkom focuses on the failure of its protagonist within his personal world and on his individual inability to live a meaningful life. In his subsequent work Tišma shifts his attention to the much broader theme of the difficulty of the establishment of individual, particularly Jewish, identities and cultural identities in Central Europe after the devastations in World War II. Tišma focuses his explorations on various obstacles from the past and present that impede the establishment of cultural and individual identity in a postwar Yugoslav society, especially within the context of Vojvodina. His project becomes the exploration of the doomed efforts of various protagonists, quite often allegorical representatives, to emerge with a viable identity in a society that has rejected its own past identity and is struggling to construct a new one.

In 1972 *Knjiga o Blamu* (The Book of Blahm) was published. Set in Novi Sad after

World War II, it examines themes that Tišma frequently explores, including the suffering and destruction of the Jewish and Serbian people in the war and the attempts at reestablishing ordinary life in a situation where the past and its traumas render ordinary life unbearable and almost impossible. The novel poignantly captures the efforts of the eponymous protagonist, Miroslav Blahm, to come to terms with the past and to find his place in the present social and cultural context. Blahm is a man who has lost his identity in the turmoils and horrors of the war and whose existence (reminiscent of Robert Musil's *Der Mann ohne Eigenschaften* [1930-1932], translated into English as *The Man without Qualities* [1953–1960]) is, in Tišma's words in an interview, "problematic, vague, without solidity." Blahm is paralyzed by the fact that he is a survivor of a world that has disappeared. His keen sense of loss and disintegration reinforces his passivity and prevents him from establishing a meaningful relationship with the present. *Knjiga o Blamu* was followed by the story collection *Mrtvi ugao* (Blind Spot) in 1973. *Mrtvi ugao* again examines the problems of violence and destruction. The title story from this collection was later rewritten as a novel, published in 1981 as *Begunci* (The Fugitives).

In 1976 Tišma's major novel, *Upotreba čoveka* (The Use of Man), was published. Although he was already a well-known and respected writer, it was this novel that catapulted Tišma to the pinnacle of Yugoslav belles lettres. *Upotreba čoveka* again deals with his frequent theme of the wartime destruction of the Jewish community that had thrived in prewar Yugoslavia. The novel presents the attempts and failures of various protagonists to overcome the horrors they survived and the emptiness to which they have returned; it details the inability of these protagonists to reestablish or create a new identity for themselves by overcoming the past and finding some meaning in the present and the future. In *Upotreba čoveka* Tišma departs from his usual realistic mode of narration, employing several experimental techniques. Most importantly, he eschews linear narration and constructs the book from montagelike fragments. The reader must then piece together these fragments to make sense of the story, which thereby conveys the attempts of the protagonists to piece together their broken lives. The overall effect is much like that of the photographs of piles of eyeglasses or shoes discovered in Nazi concentration camps, from which the enormity of the destruction can be conceived.

Tišma's collection of short stories *Povratak miru* (Return to Peace) was published in 1977. In this diverse collection Tišma focuses on the portraits of various characters during brief interludes in their lives. Rather than focusing on plot development, Tišma chooses in most stories of this collection to depict a particular moment in a protagonist's life. He then enlarges this moment into an almost naturalistic "still photograph" of a particular mood, psychological state, or interpersonal relationship. Although most of the stories are narrated in a rather straightforward way, some stories, such as "Hiljadu i druga noć" (One Thousand and Second Night) and "Zemlja-vazduh" (Earth-Air), contain moments when Tišma departs from this technique, venturing into experimental styles reminiscent of Jorge Luis Borges, Kiš, and Kafka.

The collection *Škola bezboništva* (translated as "The School of Godlessness," 1983) appeared in 1978. It consists mostly of previously published stories, though it also includes several outstanding new ones. One of the new stories, "Stan" (The Apartment), is about a man, Čaković, a former partisan and orthodox communist, whose postwar life has been filled with failures. Because of his extreme (even fanatic) zealousness during the land appropriation soon after the war, Čaković was removed from his prominent position of power once the political climate became more moderate. The story, set in the 1960s, describes Čaković's attempts to obtain from the government a larger apartment for his growing family. In the government office where he goes to seek help Čaković is welcomed by an official who is a younger brother of one of his comrades who died in combat. In his dealings with the government Čaković discovers that the people in power are actually using that power quite freely and unashamedly to satisfy their own needs and desires. The old idealistic generation is either pushed aside and ignored, like him, or dead, like his old comrade. Because of the pressures of his family he resignedly accepts the apartment he is offered, although he is rather offended by the machinations he witnesses. Through the slow decline of the career of the protagonist, who is unable to adapt to the changing political situation in postwar Yugoslavia, Tišma depicts the gradual betrayal of the original beliefs of the communists and their transformation into "red bourgeoisie," which he also describes vividly in "Koncert."

The 1970s were successful for Tišma. In addition to his ample output of new literary material during this period, he was widely recognized in Yugoslavia for his work. He received many awards for his literary achievements. In 1977 he received the prestigious NIN and NOLIT awards, reserved for the most prominent Yugoslav writers; in the same year he also received the Kàroly Szirmai Prize, which is awarded in Vrbas (Vojvodina) in honor of the Vojvodina writer Kàroly Szirmai. In 1979 he also received another exceptionally prestigious award named after the only Yugoslav Nobel Prize winner, Ivo Andrić.

Tišma continued his prolific work in the 1980s. In 1980 he published *Bez krika* (Without a Cry), a collection of short stories, some of which had already appeared in *Krivice* and *Povratak miru*. The collection was followed by *Begunci* in 1981 and *Vere i zavere* (Faiths and Conspiracies) in 1983. In 1984 Tišma received the award of the steel mill company Sisak for his literary accomplishments. The collection of stories *Hiljadu i druga noć* was published in 1987 at the same time as Tišma's important novel *Kapo* (translated as *Kapo*, 1993), which again addresses the themes of World War II, the irrationality of violence and cruelty, and the problems of power, gender, oppression, and domination.

Kapo examines the problems of the suffering of various victimized groups—in particular Jews and Serbians—under the Nazis and Ustashas. The book also explores the psychic damage suffered by victims of the monstrous circumstances of the Nazi concentration camps. The novel depicts the "development" of the main character, Vilko Lamian, a Christianized Jew, from an isolated and alienated youth growing up in a small Croatian town in prewar Yugoslavia into an old, still-alienated man disintegrating under the pressures of his past. Lamian spent the years of World War II in the concentration camps in Jasenovac and Auschwitz. In order to survive he served the Nazis, helping them murder, plunder, and torture other prisoners. After the war Lamian retreats to a small town in Bosnia to hide from the world. Most of the novel is set some forty years after the war, when Lamian's sense of alienation reaches its climax and he finally comes out of hiding to set out on a quest to find someone who can help him reach a catharsis and purge himself of the feelings of paranoia, guilt, and alienation that overwhelm him. Lamian tries to track down one of his old victims, a Jewess, Helena Lifka, hoping that his former victim will grant him forgiveness or reject him with revulsion, in either case setting off a cathartic reaction that will free him from the emotional numbness that has become his lot.

Koje volimo (Those We Love), published in 1990, is a novella composed of brief realistic vignettes about the lives of a group of madams and their prostitutes trying to survive and even prosper by selling their sexual favors in Novi Sad during the 1950s. Tišma again weaves a narrative about the demimonde of Novi Sad in the years following World War II and gives a bleak picture of poverty, despair, petty bourgeois hypocrisy, and hopelessness. Though the novella is written as a fairly straightforward narrative, it departs from Tišma's customary realistic mode in several ways, employing many of the strategies used earlier in *Upotreba čoveka*. The narrative is fragmented and unfocused. Instead of a main character there are many different protagonists, most of them uneducated and unemployed women who resort to prostitution as a means of dealing with the problems of gender relations and alienation in a socialist society. It calls attention to the fact that the "new Yugoslavia" has not solved the gender problems it inherited from the prewar bourgeois regime. *Koje volimo* thus continues to explore the issues of gender and the relationship between sex and power that Tišma had already addressed in earlier works such as *Upotreba čoveka*, *Kapo*, and *Za crnom devojkom*.

Pre mita (Before the Myth, 1989) is a collection of Tišma's previously written essays on various themes from literature, politics, and culture. The collection also includes critical essays on the work of such writers as Erih Koš, Mihailo Lalić, Miklos Radnoti, and Vladan Desnica. In the first essay of the collection (written in 1956) Tišma explains his view that the function of literature is to purge its readers of the evil that has accumulated in the present. For Tišma, literature ought to describe or delineate this evil by providing it with an artistic representation that will, in the end, reveal the evil for what it really is. He suggests that to ignore the evil would necessarily allow it to exist as a potentiality that would eventually emerge again to kill, torture, and impose itself on a society again and again.

In addition to writing fiction and essays, Tišma is a prolific translator of both prose and poetry from several languages into Serbo-Croatian. He has translated works of Stefan Zweig, Leonard Frank, Sir Philip Sidney, Ben Jonson, Edmund Spenser, William Shakespeare, and François Villon. Tišma has been particularly active in the translation of contemporary Hungarian literature. He has translated from Hungarian authors such as Ferenz Molnar, Szirmai Károl, Tibor Déry, Mihal Babič, Pap József, and Laslo Vegel.

Prior to 1992 Tišma had spent most of his adult life in Novi Sad, though he did travel in Europe (as described in *Drugde*), and in 1972 he also traveled to India. But his last and longest absence from Vojvodina was from October 1992 to February 1995, when he went into exile in France. This last trip was closely related to his disagreement with the political situation in Yugoslavia in the early 1990s and the country's subsequent disintegration. As he often points out in his interviews, he was satisfied with Yugoslavia as a multinational community as it reflected his own multinational background, and the Yugoslav disintegration (for the second time in his life) was a major traumatic event for him. In 1994, while in exile in France, Tišma received the international award for the best European essay, awarded by the Writers' Association in Brno, Slovakia. In 1995, however, Tišma returned to Novi Sad, where he again resides.

Tišma's literary oeuvre is a distinctive testimony to an age and a city, Novi Sad, both of which have radically changed with the demise of Yugoslavia. His work is parallel to and continues the work of Kiš in the evocation of the Central European world of the twentieth century. Like Kiš's, Tišma's fictional recordings of the fates of the Jewish people in Yugoslavia before and after World War II offer characteristic documents of that time. Tišma's writing also offers a more general exploration of issues such as violence, gender, memory, and the paralyzing effects of the past. In addition, his work offers an interesting and intriguing window on the social conditions of the socialist Yugoslavia, pointing out the many controversies and conflicts of its short existence.

References:

Thomas Eekman, "Aleksandar Tišma," in *Thirty Years of Yugoslav Literature: 1945–1975* (Ann Arbor: Michigan Slavic Publication, 1978), pp. 189–190;

Eekman, "Aleksandar Tišma's Novel *The Use of Man*," *Serbian Studies*, no. 2 (1989): 81–87;

Miroslav Egerić, "'Egzistencijalni' realizam Aleksandra Tišme," in his *Dani i dela: Eseji i kritike*, volume 2 (Novi Sad: Matica srpska, 1982), pp. 219–231;

Egerić, "Etički ideal i stvarnost u romanu Aleksandra Tišme *Knjiga o Blamu*," in his *Dela i dani* (Novi Sad: Matica srpska, 1975), pp. 218–237;

Slavko Gordić, "Fascinantni prilozi dehumanizacije," *Dometi* (Sombor), 8 (1976): 143–144;

Božur Hajduković, "Draž dubinske perspektive," *Književnost*, no. 2–3 (1977): 282–289;

Hajduković, "Tišmina vizija ljudske sudbine," *Dometi*, 17 (1989): 71–77;

Barbara Heldt, "Aleksandar Tišma's 'Personality': A Feminist Critique," *Essays in Poetics: The Journal of the British Neo-Formalist School*, 12 (1987): 75–81;

Milivoje Marković, "Izazov životu," in his *Prostori: Realizma: Vladan Desnica, Meša Selimović, Ranko Marinković, Mihailo Lalić, Aleksandar Tišma* (Subotica: Minerva, 1981), pp. 299–356;

Čedomir Mirković, "Od kratke priče do složenog romana: Proza Aleksandra Tišme," *Savremenik*, 3 (1979): 259–264;

Mirković, "Senke Jasenovca i Aušvica," in his *Subotnji dnevnik: odabrane kritike* (Gornji Milanovac: Dečje novine, 1989), pp. 214–218;

Boško Novaković, "Nastanak i struktura *Begunaca* Aleksandra Tišme," *Savremenik*, 57 (1983): 49–56;

Novaković, "Obnovljeni realizam: Aleksandar Tišma," in his *Vihorno razdoblje* (Novi Sad: Matica srpska, 1985), pp. 262–285;

Danica Pejčić, "Geneza Tišminog romansijerskog postupka–ka muzikalizovanju romana," *Književna istorija*, no. 53 (1981): 69–89;

Branko Popović, "Svedočanstvo zloupotrebe čoveka," *Savremenik*, no. 5 (1980): 329–344;

Vladislava Ribnikar, "NIN-ova nagrada za roman godine. Aleksandar Tišma: *Upotreba čoveka*," *Treći program Radio-Beograda*, 32 (1977): 38–40;

Ribnikar, "Tišmina 'konstrukcija bezumlja,'" *Gradina*, 2 (1977): 31–34;

Risto Trifković, "Aleksandar Tišma–slikar ljudske sudbine," *Gradina*, no. 5 (1977): 98–102.

Dubravka Ugrešić
(27 March 1949 -)

E. Celia Hawkesworth
University of London

BOOKS: *Mali plamen* (Zagreb: Mladost, 1971);
Filip i Srećica (Zagreb: Mladost, 1976);
Poza za Prozu (Zagreb: CDD, 1978);
Nova ruska proza (Zagreb: Liber, 1980);
Štefica Cvek u raljama života (Zagreb: Grafički zavod Hrvatske, 1981, 1984; Ljubljana: Mladinska knjiga, 1990);
Život je bajka (Zagreb: Grafički zavod Hrvatske, 1983);
Kućni duhovi (Zagreb: August Cesarec, 1988);
Forsiranje romana-reke (Zagreb: August Cesarec, 1988-1989);
Američki fikcionar (Zagreb: Durieux, 1993);
Kultura laži (Arkzin, 1996).

Editions in English: "Life Is a Fable," translated by Mario Suško and Edward J. Czerwinski, *Slavic and East European Arts,* 2, no. 2 (1984): 109-122;
"A Hot Day in a Warm Bun," translated by Michael Henry Heim, *Formations,* 5, no. 2 (1989): 96-106;
Fording the Stream of Consciousness, translated by Heim (London: Virago Press, 1991; Evanston, Ill.: Northwestern University Press, 1993);
"Lend Me Your Character," translated by Celia Hawkesworth, *Cimarron Review,* 96 (1991): 57-66;
In the Jaws of Life, translated by Hawkesworth and Heim (London: Virago Press, 1992); republished as *In the Jaws of Life and Other Stories* (Evanston, Ill.: Northwestern University Press, 1993);
Out of Yugoslavia (Balkan Blues), translated by Hawkesworth, in *Storm* (London: Carcanet Press, 1994), pp. 3-35;
Have a Nice Day, translated by Hawkesworth (London: Cape, 1994; New York: Viking Penguin, 1995).

Dubravka Ugrešić is one of the most important writers of fiction in contemporary Croatian literature. Two related features dominate her work: parody and irony, which convey, respectively, the essentially postmodern content and the style of her work. The leitmotiv running through her fiction is that nothing is what it seems or is projected to be. Ugrešić's fiction is characterized by a thorough knowledge of her craft and of the literary heritage of the Western world and its most recent manifestations. She moves freely in this context, using parody and intertextual reference as her tools. The immediate surface impression of her works is their engaging wit, their playful mockery of the "high seriousness" of Literature with a capital *L*. The mockery is all-encompassing and therefore includes herself: she is present in most of her works as the author who is subjected to the same ironic treatment as her characters. But her humor is destructive only of pomposity; underlying it is a bedrock of compassion and humanity. Similarly, even her most serious comment on the political reality of the Croatia of the 1990s is characterized by her sharply intelligent sense of the absurd. In all her works genres and tones undermine each other and mix in an imaginative blend, reminding the reader always of the interaction of "reality" and the potential worlds of creative writing, of the limited power of the written word to render "truth," and the compelling power of cliché, gossip, and myth to create "reality."

Ugrešić was born on 27 March 1949 in Kutina. She studied comparative literature and Russian at the University of Zagreb and then continued to work at the university in the Institute for the Study of Literature, writing scholarly articles, editing anthologies of modern Russian prose and editions of individual writers, and working on a glossary of Russian avant-garde concepts with Alexsandar Flaker, until she resigned in 1993. Her first published works of fiction were novels for children, in which she began to develop the delight in fantasy and humor that characterize her later fiction. She was immediately recognized as an original voice; her earliest volume, *Mali plamen* (The Little Flame, 1971) was awarded the Grigor Vitez Prize for the best children's book of the year.

Ugrešić's works to date fall into two distinct parts separated by the outbreak of the Yugoslav wars in 1991. Her first fiction for adults may be seen as playing with ideas about the relationship of fiction to reality. The works written since 1991 are concerned with the reality of Croatia in wartime, including the projection of reality as fiction. In each case the single most striking characteristic of Ugrešić's work is her ironic distance, her refusal to be taken in either by the self-importance of the literary profession or by compelling appeals to patriotic emotion.

Like so many postmodern fiction writers, Ugrešić in her early works mixes elements from a range of literary genres, from the traditional canon of "high" literature to the "trivial" forms of romance, thriller, and fantasy. Features of all these collide with one another, undermining the coherence of the reader's anticipated response. The first of these works, *Poza za Prozu* (A Pose for Prose, 1978), represents a kind of hypothetical sketchbook for Ugrešić's future writing; here she tries out and rejects various possible styles and approaches colored by the ironic deflation of the title. The first part, titled "Love Story," is developed as a series of ideas and texts created by the first-person narrator in an effort to please her literary-critic lover. Because of the narrator's gender, her writing becomes simply another manifestation of women's destiny—the struggle for acceptance and approval by men. Thus, both material and narrator are objects of mockery: all the exchanges between the two characters on the nature and future of literature become allegories of a sexual game. This longest section is followed by "autobiographical" sketches of incidents during a visit to the Soviet Union with a friend. In these pieces the material is no longer mediated through a supposed narrator, but presented in the direct, personal tone that Ugrešić consistently adopts for such direct statements by the author, which are an essential part of her procedure. She rejects the conventions whereby a piece of writing has traditionally been given legitimacy by being considered factual and exposes the notions of document and diary equally to question and mockery.

Such a constant undermining of her material is inherently destructive and inhibits the creation of a sustained narrative. It is no sur-

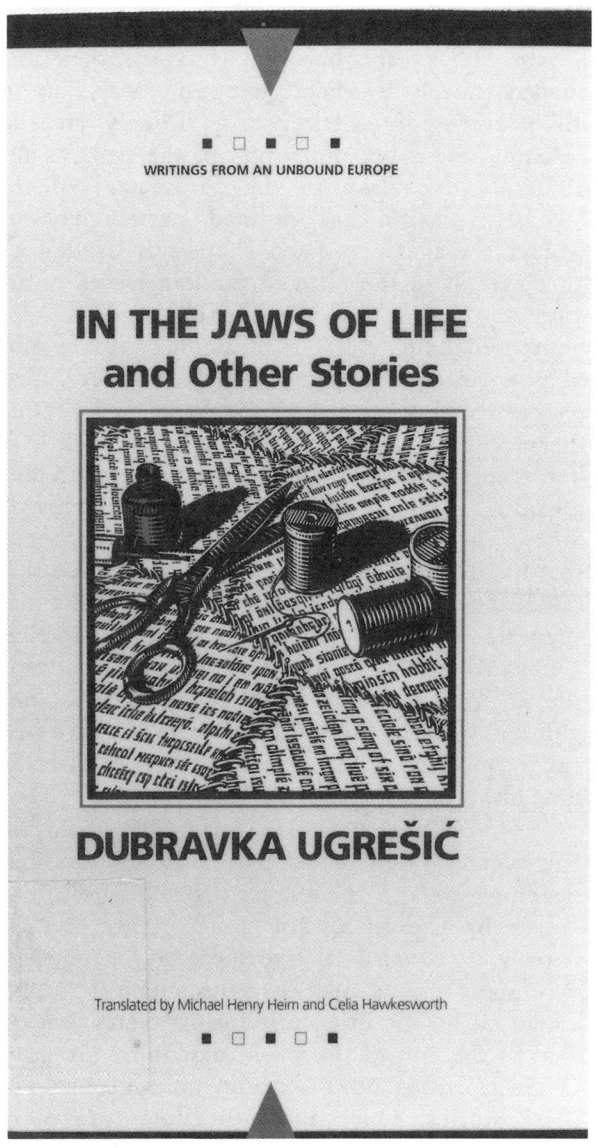

Cover for a translation of Ugrešić's 1981 short novel, Štefica Cvek u raljama života, *the story of a heroine trapped by the clichés of women's magazines*

prise, then, that Ugrešić's early works tend to be short: they have no physical substance to counteract the skepticism of their tone. It has also been observed that her writing is condensed; she tends to stop where other writers might have expanded the material. Where these short pieces are put together to form a longer whole, the clearly delineated components act as a kind of mosaic, giving scope for radical changes of tone.

This was the procedure adopted in the relatively long "Love Story," and it determines the form of Ugrešić's first short novel, *Štefica Cvek u raljama života* (Stefica Cvek [Steffie Speck] in the Jaws of Life, 1981). The focus of the work is a playful illustration of the extent to which human beings are trapped within fictions: the outward life of Steffie, the heroine, is constrained and shaped entirely by cliché, the basic story line being provided by a letter to a "Lonely Hearts" column. The other dimension of the work is the elaborate evocation of the parameters of the "woman's world" as defined particularly by women's magazines. Each chapter is headed by an epigraph in the form of random pieces of advice on health, beauty, cooking, and sundry household hints. But for all Steffie's surface simplicity, the fairy tales and trivialized, prepackaged solutions cannot touch the real person; the patches of advice that she tries to stick over her empty life fail to form a pattern with any meaning. The novel, subtitled "Patchwork Story," is given shape by the elaborate conceit that it is not being intellectually created but sewn. The manner of its presentation thus also suggests the stereotyped notion of a timeless "woman's world," one where women are firmly rooted in an enduring world of folklore that provides its inhabitants with ready-made formulae and responses as a substitute for real emotion or thought.

Ugrešić's next work, *Život je bajka* (Life is a Fairy Tale, 1983), develops one of the possibilities suggested in the earlier "sketch-book," and indeed by Ugrešić's whole ironic stance, notably parody. It consists of five pieces; each of these may stand on its own, but the whole is greatly enhanced by the brief introductory notes that appear at the end of the work, describing the point of transforming other writings or fragments into these stories. Once again the notes are themselves part of the text, beginning with a mock scholarly explanation in the style of Jorges Luis Borges of the origin of the word métaterxies, defined as metatextual-therapeutic tales.

One of the most successful of these pieces is based on Nikolay Gogol's story "Nos" (The Nose, 1836). It illustrates an essential feature of Ugrešić's technique in many of her "parodies": they do not function as negative caricatures, rather they adopt an attitude similar to that found in the original work. This tends to dictate the author's choice of source—her exploitation of the zany fantasy of Lewis Carroll's *Alice in Wonderland* (1865), for example. The last of the five stories represents perhaps the ultimate in parody. Titled "Posudi mi svog lika" (Lend Me Your Character), it subjects to scrutiny what has been and remains the author's own most fruitful procedure: the narrator describes how a writer friend asks her for permission to use one of her female characters in his story because his male character "needs a woman." The result is a text that may be seen as typifying Ugrešić's procedure: it can be read on its surface level as an account of an incident in the relationship between the two writers, with its implications of female subservience; it can be enjoyed for its unobtrusive technical manipulation of its different levels; and then it may be seen as exposing its author's own technique to question and gentle mockery.

Ugrešić's first extended prose work appeared in 1988: *Forsiranje romana-reke* (Forcing the 'Roman-Fleuve,' 1988–1989; translated as *Fording the Stream of Consciousness,* 1991). It was greeted with wide critical acclaim and awarded three prestigious literary prizes: the Ksaver Šandor Gjalski Award for the best Croatian novel of the year and the Meša Selimović and NIN awards for the best Yugoslav novel of the year. Like many of Ugrešić's other writings, the immediate appeal of this work consists in its elaborate playing with many aspects of writing, both from the inside, with the use of different styles, genres, references, and quotations, and also from the outside, with its account of all the paraphernalia of criticism, of commercialism, and of the international literary community—the whole elaborate world of literary activity. The setting is an international literary conference held in Zagreb, attended by writers and critics from Eastern and Western Europe and the United States. This focus reinforces the self-consciousness of postmodern literature and the ambiguous relationship of literary material to the daily life and experience of writers. Superficially, the work is shaped by the genre of the detective story, although there is no sense of progression toward an explanation for the many deaths that occur in the novel. There are additional elements from tales of espionage, with all that form's standard requisites of suspense, unsolved mysteries, and intrigue. The treatment of some of the characters belongs to other genres, from popular romance, crude socialist realism, and science fiction to what may be considered traditional "serious" literature. The representatives of different genres and cultures enable the author to treat each of them in the appropriate style, while at the same time undermining the reader's expectations as the characters fail to conform.

All of this is deftly controlled and highly entertaining. The whole work demonstrates the thoroughness with which Ugrešić handles her craft, emphasizing always the intricate and arbitrary relationship of fiction to "reality." Unlike those in a "real" detective story, the characters here have inner, everyday lives that are at variance with the public image presented to the conference. This highlights the fundamental characteristic of the work, which has been described by literary critic Jasmina Lukić as a series of Chinese boxes, each containing and commenting on both the one that contains it and the one it contains. One such "box" is the typically ambiguous framework that both beguiles and disturbs. The body of the work, with its clear composition shaped by the three days of the conference and set in a Zagreb hotel, is placed within two sets of "diary" entries that contain enough autobiographical detail to convince the reader that they refer at least to some extent to the author, and yet they are as much a part of the text as the "notes" accompanying her earlier works. While sharing much of the quality of gentle mockery present in all her works, they serve to remind the reader of the tenuous boundaries between "fact" and "fiction." Ugrešić uses them to emphasize the fluidity and ambiguity of any organized version of "reality" and the relativity of such notions as "truth" and "falsehood" in its projection.

Nevertheless, Ugrešić's works are not neutral in tone: one of their most engaging features is their emotional coloring, which counterbalances the process of intellectual deconstruction. While subject, as she is herself, to mockery, most of her characters are treated with a degree of the understanding and sympathy that is an important part of the flavor of her work. It has been suggested by critic Velimir Visković that this is the kind of quality associated with twentieth-century Czech writing, from Jaroslav Hašek to Vaclav Havel, and it is clear from many of Ugrešić's works that she feels a special affinity with this tradition.

In the autumn of 1991, when hostilities between Serbia and Croatia were intensifying, Ugrešić traveled to Holland for a week for the promotion of one of her books. From there she went to Connecticut to teach. Throughout the nine months she spent in the United States she wrote a regular column for an Amsterdam newspaper, commenting on her reactions to the situation in Croatia from her temporary exile and reflecting on her perception of America. On her return she collected these articles in *Američki ficionar* (My American Fictionary, 1993; translated as *Have a Nice Day,* 1994). The volume is permeated with the blend of "fear, despair, hopelessness and vague sense of shame" that she identifies as the frame of mind in which she left for the United States. In the introduction she describes the experience of trying to adjust to the violent transformation of the country in which she had grown up: "All of a sudden we had to change everything: address books and addresses, language and customs, identity.... With astounding speed everything had been turned into a lumber-room, without anyone having had time to stick catalogue labels onto anything. The whole country had shrunk, slipped into the *Dictionary of Imaginary Places.*" And she goes on to reflect:

> I think now that in this postmodern age the increasingly common genre of the *dictionary*–which has abandoned its linguistic framework and moved over into literature–has nothing to do with nostalgia as might at first sight seem. The practice of this genre seems rather to resemble the effort of patients with Alzeimer's disease to find their way in the world around them with the help of little bits of paper, notelets, labels, before they (or the world?) sink into complete oblivion. All the various *dictionaries* in this postmodern age are only an intimation of the chaos which leads to oblivion. Or the oblivion which leads to chaos.

The *Fictionary* is aptly named. Balanced on the dividing line between social and political comment and fiction, it mixes genres in a blend that is perceptive, poignant, always witty, and colored by Ugrešić's trademark of self-irony. There is, however, a new sharpness to her wit, a new undercurrent of black humor, revealing sudden shafts of anger. Her familiar skepticism, her witty sabotage of pretension, applied now not to the craft and business of literature but to the political reality of her times, is intensified in new, incisive forms.

This new approach is all the clearer in the writing on which she has been engaged since 1993, the writing that earned her, with several other women writers and journalists, the label of "witch." In these texts she is preoccupied with the discrepancy between the public projection of contemporary events and their reality. She is careful to refer to these articles, collected in *Kultura laži* (The Culture of Lies, 1996), and those published in her *Fictionary,* as literature. Her skepticism and denial of pretension prevent her from proposing anything other than a personal version of the "truth," but it is one that requires an equivalent clarity of vision from others around her in acknowledging that what is being constructed before their eyes as "truth" is at best a highly selective account of reality. Ugrešić's difficulty, perceived by supporters of the new

Croatian establishment as her profoundly unpatriotic stance, stems from her inability to see things in black and white. She belongs to a generation that has no voice and no place in the current scheme of things in what used to be her country. Her fundamental crime, at a time when the word *Yugoslavia* is being systematically erased from Croatian textbooks and maps, is said to be "Yugonostalgia." The accusation of self-delusion, leveled against someone of such pervasive skepticism, is far-fetched, but it is equally impossible for Ugrešić to recognize Yugoslavia, the country in which she grew up and in whose cultural life she participated fully, as a "prison of nations," as it is officially proclaimed in Croatia.

In the particularly concentrated text "Kultura laži," which gives its title to the volume of "antipolitical essays," Ugrešić sums up her experience of the birth of her new "homeland." She points out at the beginning and the end of the essay that she has focused on Croatia, not because similar if not identical processes are not at work "on the other side," but because Croatia is what she knows best. Written with characteristic wit and balance, the text draws attention both to facets of the specific situation of Croatia in the 1990s and to other phenomena of general relevance. She warns that the tragedy of Bosnia cannot be observed indifferently from the comfortable armchairs of Western Europeans without consequence: its specters will return to haunt the rest of Europe, perhaps where they are least expected. She describes the confusion of truth and reality, of fact and fiction that prevails on the surface of the civilized world as essentially "postmodern":

> In the former Yugoslav territories people are now living a postmodern chaos/order. Past, present and future are all lived simultaneously. In the circular temporal mish-mash suddenly everything we ever knew and everything we shall know has sprung to life and gained its right to existence.
>
> After exactly a round fifty years (1991-1941), by almost infernal symmetry, the Second World War has sprung up again, many of the same villages have been burned down again, many families have experienced a symmetrical fate, many children and grandchildren have lived through the fate of their fathers. Even the weapons are sometimes the same: stolen out of necessity from local 'museums of the revolution,' belonging to the Partisans in other words, or else taken down from attics and out of trunks, left there for fifty years by 'ustashas' or 'chetniks.'
>
> The newly created states are also 'museum pieces,' quotations, and the responses of the newly elected leaders are only references to those already uttered. [...] In the disintegrated Yugoslav territories we are also living simultaneously the future, that postapocalyptic one, the one that for others has yet to come.

This text sums up much of Ugrešić's thinking and writing about her experience of living in Croatia as it came into being as an independent country in wartime. As such it marks the end of the second phase of her writing. This period of "antipolitical essays" was forced on her by external circumstances: "in the circumstances of war, there simply is not time for anything else," as she has expressed it. But Ugrešić's first allegiance is to fiction. As a writer of rare intelligence and imagination, each of whose works has demonstrated new creative vigor, Ugrešić still has much to contribute to the literature of both Croatia and the Western world.

Interview:
Priscilla Meyer, "Scholarship and Art. Interview with Dubravka Ugrešić," *Cross Currents*, 12 (1993): 189-204.

References:
Neal Davis Anderson, "Un-Merging Realities. The Dilemmas of Dubravka Ugrešić," *Border Crossings. A Magazine of the Arts* (Fall 1993): 34-37;

Celia Hawkesworth, "Dubravka Ugrešić: the Insider's Story," *Slavonic and East European Review*, 68, no. 3 (July 1990): 436-446.

Dane Zajc
(26 October 1929 -   )

Marija Mitrović
University of Trieste

BOOKS: *Požgana trava* (Ljubljana: Privately printed, 1958);
Jezik iz zemlje (Ljubljana: Cankarjeva založba, 1961);
Otroka reke (Ljubljana: Cankarjeva založba, 1963);
Ubijavci kač (Maribor: Obzorja, 1968);
Glava sejavka (Maribor: Obzorja, 1971);
Kepa pepela (Ljubljana: Mladinska knjiga, 1974);
Potohodec (Ljubljana: Cankarjeva založba, 1974);
Rožengruntar (Maribor: Obzorja, 1974);
Voranc (Maribor: Obzorja, 1978);
Si videl (Ljubljana: Partizanska knjiga, 1979);
Pesmi (Ljubljana: Državna založba, 1979);
Zarotitve (Ljubljana: Mladinska knjiga, 1985);
Igre (Ljubljana: Mladinska knjiga, 1989);
Dane Zajc v petih knjigah (Ljubljana: Emonica, 1990).
Editions in English: Poems, translated by Veno Taufer and Michael Scammell, in *Contemporary Yugoslav Poetry,* edited by Vasa D. Mihailovich (Iowa City: University of Iowa Press, 1977), pp. 179-183;
Poems, by various translators, in *Le livre slovène,* 20, nos. 1-2 (1982): 50-55; no. 1-2 (1988): 112-115;
Ashes, translated by Michael Biggins and Scammell (Chattanooga, Tenn.: Poetry Miscellany Chapbooks, 1990).

PLAY PRODUCTIONS: *Otroka reke,* Ljubljana, Oder 57, 22 January 1962;
Potohodec, Ljubljana, Bekarna, 11 March 1972;
Voranc, Ljubljana Drama SNG, 16 January 1980;
Mlada Breda, Ljubljana, Drama SNG, 23 October 1982;
Kalevala, Ljubljana, Mali oder Drama SNG, 16 January 1986;
Medeja, Celje, Skovensko Lludško Gledalisče, 9 December 1988.

The poetry and the poetic plays of Dane Zajc brought a significant change into Slovene literature after World War II. Together with Gregor Strniša and Veno Taufer, at the end of the

Dane Zajc

1950s Zajc opted for poetry whose goal is not a sentimental or idealized picture of the world and man in it but a search for the deeper meanings of events and experiences and an attempt to understand the world as it is, without the help of ideological, philosophical, or religious principles. When the first books of these three poets were published, the critics characterized them as belonging to the "critical generation" of poets. Even later they were frequently spoken of as belonging to the same generation, even though each one developed his own distinctive voice and vision. All three are among the most important poets in modern Slovenian poetry.

Dane Zajc was born on 26 October 1929 in Javoršica pri Moravčah. His childhood was marked tragically by World War II. He lost his father and two brothers, and the home in which he was born and in which his family lived was burned down by the occupying army. His schooling was interrupted, but after the war he continued his education, moving from one boarding school to another in smaller Slovene towns such as Domžale, Kamnik, and Gornja Radgona. In 1947 he arrived in Ljubljana, where he met several young artists in the home for war orphans, with whom he began to publish his writings in the in-house newspaper *Mi mladi* (We, the Young). He published his first poem in 1948 in *Mladinska revija* (Youth Review), a journal that very early rejected the official socialist realist poetry. In 1951, because of a "verbal offense," Zajc was sentenced to three months in jail and thrown out of school in the eleventh grade. "My shipwreck began in 1951, when I was jailed because of a few publicly spoken words, sentenced, thrown out of high school, and sent to serve military duty.... A person can never again get rid of the pictures of his first solitary confinement in which, as a twenty-one-year old, he experienced the onset of his own powerlessness," Zajc said in a 1990 interview in *Nova revija*.

Even later, on several occasions, the poet fell into difficulties with the law because of the restrictions on freedom of speech. The book *Intervjui* (Interviews), contained in his collected works in *Dane Zajc v petih knjigah* (1990), begins with a series of letters titled "Dopisivanje sa sudom" (Correspondence with the Court). Zajc often appeared at literary evenings and public protests, but only to read his poetry. He has shied away from direct political engagement and political language, believing it is his duty as a poet to resist violence with his poetry and personal behavior and not with political manifestos. He has published many essays and interviews, but his medium is exclusively poetry—the art of the word. To the inevitable friction between the intellectuals and the authorities in a realist-socialistic society Zajc has always reacted with his poetic creativity and poetic gestures. The tyranny of the authorities, the irrational policy that passed for the basis of a better future but in reality destroyed people in the present, he answered by increasing his concentration on expressing what he saw in his private vision and by illuminating his immediate surroundings. Only by noting that Zajc has consistently lived in a manner worthy of a poet can one see clearly how deeply he was marked by the court, the trial, and his imprisonment. It becomes clear what a poet who expresses himself only in an artistic way or in his reflections about art wants to say when he places at the beginning of a book of his interviews his correspondence with a judge. In 1965 the judge penalized him monetarily for words expressed at a literary meeting.

In the middle of 1953, after serving in the military, Zajc worked at a post office; then in 1955 he was hired to work in a youth library. In the 1990 interview in *Nova revija* he recalled: "Five years I lived in a small room in a Workers' House which was hardly big enough for one person and yet there were three of us. I worked at the same place as today, and sometimes when I arrived 'home' the little room was so filled with cigarette smoke that you could cut it with a knife, and in it a group of passionate card-players. I turned around and went to an inn, from which I returned only in the morning, if I returned at all." In such difficult conditions Zajc completed evening high school in 1958, in addition to having to work. He worked in the library until his retirement in 1989. The library brought him inevitably into contact with the world of young people, a world that attracted him by its variety, its strict moral principles, and its surrealism. He devoted a large part of his creativity to writing for young people.

Zajc contributed to many of the leading Slovene literary journals in the former Yugoslavia, including *Beseda* (Word), *Revija 57* (Review 57), *Perspektive* (Perspectives), *Problemi* (Problems), and *Nova revija* (New Review). In 1957, when *Revija 57* started in Ljubljana, a journal that so deviated from the officially sanctioned policy in culture that it was banned after its sixth issue, Zajc served on its editorial board. He also worked on *Perspektive,* which carried on the struggle for democratization in both the society and the culture. In the beginning of 1964, when this journal was also banned, Zajc was its editor, along with Taras Kermauner. Zajc was then and remained a staunch supporter of individual freedom of speech and the freedom of relationships among people. He always came into conflict with the authorities and any official policy that imposed collectivization and negated the individual's personality. From his first collection of poetry he was a genuine and consistent political dissident, although he never wrote a "political" essay or proclamation. He never wrote a politically engaged poem, but always opposed the authorities with poetic means exclusively and with a maximally refined poetic language.

In 1981–1982 he spent a year at Columbia University in New York in the Fulbright program. He has received many awards for his poetic works, of which the most important are the "Goranov vijenac" (Goran's Wreath, 1980) and the Great Prešeren Award for his entire work, which he received in 1981. Modest and restrained in public communication, always separating poetry from politics, he accepted only in 1991 an important social role: the presidency of the Society of Slovene Writers, an office in which he served until 1995.

"No one will notice the change" is the concluding verse in Zajc's collection *Zarotitve* (Oaths, 1985). The change that no one will notice is not small: "Instead of a head, I will have a white, transparent turtle egg." The world of Zajc's poetry, already inhabited with absurd, grotesque figures and strange, surreal creatures, is the world of great metamorphoses, so that even such a wonder as a turtle egg in place of a head is not noticed, lost in the sea of strange images. From his first verses at the end of the 1940s to the present Zajc has persistently created a poetry of authentic rhythm and voice; but within that recognizable Zajcean poetry of a subdued voice and an almost monotonous rhythm, great changes took place, tracing the development of his views on the world and arts. Thus, *change* is a consistent and constituent word in Zajc's poetry. Just as central is the concept of constancy. Zajc believes that it is not a poet's duty to change the external world. The poet, rather, is a witness to the changes in a world that is both kind and cruel, full of love and hatred, Eros and Thanatos, beauty and ugliness, luxury and asceticism, splendor and poverty, yet is a world that is always the same in the sense that it expects individuals to accept, understand, live, and experience it the way it is—human, full of conflicts, and integral. The acceptance of the world as it is, its illumination by some inner eye of a poet, without glorification and elevation (a staple fare in the poetry and literature in Yugoslavia immediately after the war), without complaints or the sentimental self-pity of an individual released into the world—these are the characteristics of Zajc's poetry from the first poems in *Mladinska revija* (from 1948 to 1951), *Beseda, Revija 57,* and the collection *Požgana trava* (Burnt Grass, 1958), which he had to publish himself because the worldview it expressed did not conform to the officially sanctioned view.

At the time when the War of Liberation against the Nazi occupation was depicted as a heroic struggle with high goals, Zajc wrote in his poem "Jalova setev" (Barren Harvest), "It is senseless to sow / one's beautiful dark eyes / for a barren harvest. // I remember you, brother. / Our mother / thought of your beautiful teeth. / Your beautiful teeth / were the barren harvest." Since Zajc's brother was killed as a fighter in the War of Liberation, these verses were interpreted as a negation of the revolution. A collection with such verses could not obtain the green light from the so-called Council, a group of people whose duty was until the end of the communist reign to ensure politically correct writings and to give or deny permission for publication.

In Zajc's early poetry the romantic persona of the poet had a difficult time agreeing with the new circumstances in which it found itself (without God, ideology, or faith). The traces of the romantic yearning for the "beautiful soul" were still present, especially in the metaphors and the poetic language of the first collection, as attested by its title, "Burnt Grass." It is as though the poet is seeking an alliance with nature, with "The Tall Red Moon," with clouds, birds, and strong, large, dangerous animals—bulls, wolves, and hyenas; but there are no signs of collaboration ("the ice of fear fetters my legs," and "the sun in the east sharpens the shiny butcher's axe"). The world has conspired against humans and there is no help or ally. Still, there is no grumbling or scream, only fear and tension.

The focus in *Požgana trava* is on the description of the external world. The poetic persona is rarely the direct actor in the drama; he is seldom present on the huge, surrealistically conceived canvas of the grotesque picture. In the next collection, *Jezik iz zemlje* (Tongue of the Earth, 1961), the focus shifts from the descriptive to the contemplative and metaphysical categories, to explorations of the concept of human freedom, of the spirit and its relationship to the body, and of the relationships between names and things and words and objects. These explorations then touch and intertwine with emotions, the most dominant of which is love.

An overriding and finely wrought theme in Zajc's poetry is the infirmity of language. In the poem "Kepa pepela" (Heap of Ashes) the poet distinguishes between what he wants to say (calling it fire) and what he really says (which, in relation to fire, has the value of ashes). In the process of articulation energy and charge are lost, the value of the words changes, and a new value is acquired: instead of expressing fire, the words are able to say only what is left after coals—ashes. Like God, who has created man from clay, the poet, in order to overcome difficulties with words, creates his language ("And then you make a new language out of clay. / Language that speaks earthy words"). The picture of the world such language describes should be more material, concrete, diverse. But, just as the divine creation—man—has refused to obey his creator, the new language betrays the poet's expectations: he seeks ever-new answers; his vision of the world becomes richer, expands, and, at the end, dissipates. Dissipated and separated, the parts exclaim in "Pesem magla" (The Poem of the Fog): "We are free." Freedom exists only as an ideal; even when one is the freest, he cannot escape coercion of some external will to which he must subordinate himself. His existence is only an emergency stage, which by its nature is no advantage. As the poet writes in "Faith": "Then comes a beaten- up dog / and laps the rain water / from your open skull. / Lively mice gnaw / your ears. / Your lips. / The rats weave a nest / in your chest. // Then your bare teeth / laugh gaily. / You get up white, clean, emotionless. / You step on the threshold of a new day. / The sun places the horn on your mouth. / Hot brass horn. / You never fell."

In *Ubijavci kač* (Snake Killers, 1968) and *Glava sejavka* (Sowing Head, 1971), the same problem is postulated, but with greater urgency; the poet is forced to seek new exits and answers. Images are richer and more grotesque, fuller of contrasts of opposing qualities (holy and profane, sinful and sinless, sensual and spiritual), and metaphors increase, but the poet begins to notice the inefficiency and dangers from all those riches and saturation. Just as total freedom meant explosion and destruction, this saturation causes its opposite: a total quiet, reduction to contours and skeletons. In the poem "Glava sejavka," Zajc writes: "No one saw the head rolling on the hill / with the mask of earth patched up with the herbs of rotting: / I return for good. I return to freedom, she sang / and drunkenly cast around teeth / and happily lost her eyes on the wet grass. / She rolled down into the ditch / where she squatted / and for a long time melted toward perfection."

When he began to notice his difficulties with the expressive range of the language, Zajc set off toward the enrichment of his poetic language, especially of the metaphorical and visual features. In the autopoetic text "Igra besed intišin" (Play of Words and Silence, 1972), published soon after *Glava sejavka,* Zajc sees poetry as "approaching the atomic nucleus of oneself": "Of all the people, I am the greatest secret to myself after all." The uncovering of the secrets is the process at the root of poetry, its essence and the only legitimate point of departure; but that process is not without danger: "That which has been transformed into words destroys the experience of the poet." The poet senses that his security has been undermined; the worded experience is exhausted; and the rich picture has become untrue and unreal in relationship to the experience. Moreover, after describing his experience the poet knows no longer what is real and true: his fiction, the picture related by words, or his concrete experience.

The first collection after this autopoetic text, with its expressed doubts about the possibility of synchronizing experience with the representation of that experience, was *Rožengruntar* (1974), in many ways different from the previous collections. "Rožengruntar is a paradigm of folly which we have to endure from time to time, to which we succumb, and from which we sometimes luckily escape," the author explains in a commentary. By the title itself (*rožengruntar* is the poet's neologism for a creature which "tills," that is, a creature of deep yet primary, down-to-earth thoughts, like a landowner who thinks about roses), the author endeavors to say much with few words, to express in one word the concerns, the deep thinking of a fictitious being, his unreality, and his dependence on the earth, nature, and ownership. The poet's ideal becomes a poem that is sparing in its use of words but is permeated with a monotonous, prayerlike rhythm.

Zajc thus begins to muzzle words, condense description, and interrupt it constantly with repetitions and monotonous questions. In the cycle that gave the title to the collection, the protagonist, the rožengruntar, is a symbol of transformation, which represents the basic principle of human existence. Everything is contained in this person: he is both a slave and a master, a shadow and the truth, ugliness and beauty. The poetic persona—which appears in the plural, as "we"—feels as though he is in the hands of that strange, unreal being, but that he is also his master. The secret of the many grows ever larger, and he no longer resembles a living human being but a creature from dreams and lunacy where everything is possible—every change and every contradiction. "The path is in a circle. The path is the same. No distance disappears. No approach approaches. Some game repeats itself. Some always repeats itself"—these are the concluding verses of the collection. In the poem "Isti" (The Same), in an eternal, same circle the hoop of words and images tightens and begins to resemble a prayer and sorcery, relieving itself of everything superfluous: "He is in another world. The same. / Different in the same world. Same. / Same in the same world. Different in the different. / The same." The poem ends with the verses: "Woe, what a meaning. What a doublenothing. Hah! / (He babbles the same words. Rolls the same tongue.) The same."

The collection *Zarotitve* (Oaths) is the result of the author's concentration on the skewed relationship between the experienced and the written: the experienced remains forever a secret, no matter how much the poet tries to unravel the secret. If before this collection Zajc was a poet of powerful cognitive, gnostic function who attempted to discover the world, its laws and contradictions, its totality and his personal place and rhythm within that totality, now the poet no longer wishes to touch the secret; it has become for him something sacred and unattainable. He is now convinced that the secret can be neither expressed nor revealed. Now he only makes vows, endeavoring that the secret remain a secret: as long as the secret lasts, the world lasts. The secret is the world; the secret is sacred; it should not be named by its name. The poet communicates with the secret, conjures it (hence the rhythm of the prayer and sorcery), and counts on it, but does not disclose it. Zajc's poetry no longer wins over with its fantastic, surreal vision of the world, but rather with its sternness, its shutting down before danger. Now Zajc says only what he must, what is forced from inside. He says it as if he were afraid to say it "all," for he would then betray himself and the world's secret (which is also a sacred secret, a mythic deity with universal good and bad qualities). The secret would cease to be a secret; deity would be desecrated.

Much more consistently and radically than in his poetry, Zajc has expressed his vision of the world in his plays, which he began publishing in the 1960s but which gained recognition by both the critics and the public only in the 1980s. In the early 1960s, when his play *Otroka reke* (Children of the River, 1962) was staged, there was no understanding for a play that speaks about a mythical, timeless world and the omnipresence of evil. The play was obviously a reaction to the intoxication with victory and the faith in the future that dominated the ideology and literature during the practice of socialist realism. Another play, *Potohodec* (Traveler, 1972), is a much more complex drama about physical and psychological violence in society. The theme of the intertwining of the killer and the victim, introduced after World War II by Eduard Kocbek in his stories, Zajc now deepens and adapts to the philosophy of the absurd: all are murderers; evil is universal, but no one is excited because of

Zajc in his study, 1978

it; everything is quiet; emotions have disappeared along with all relationships and obligations; and no one is obligated to anyone. The goal of that unfeeling society, without motherly, conjugal, comradely, or any other relationships, is to become one of the mass.

Zajc based his most complex dramatic works on the historical event that most deeply marked him—World War II in Slovenia. Both the radio play *Likvidacija* (Liquidation, 1972) and the balladic drama *Voranc* (Voranc, 1980), which has brought the author the most recognition, are set in that period. The locale of both plays—with the rugged mountains and the last, isolated house—is the poet's native region. *Likvidacija* was written from the perspective of an honest, nonaggressive, simple mountain man, Možina, who cannot adapt to the world of animalistic cruelty, the utter dishonesty, and the sadistic drives released in war, so that the closest and the least guilty become victims; at the end, such a person has nothing left for him but, like Močina, to take a shovel and dig himself a grave. The play succeeds in bringing to life all the complexity of a war situation, in which one is guilty if he collaborates with the enemy but also if he helps his people. It is as though the play were written in the 1990s during the bloody Balkan war when there was so much cruelty toward those who were closest: neighbors and childhood friends.

In *Voranc,* Zajc adds to the war calamity and cruelty a family tragedy (the mountain people, who are often idealized in literature, are shown here as cruel: father and son behave toward each other as the greatest enemies), as well as the tragedy of poverty and the social catastrophe of the dying-out of isolated mountain households. The author himself confessed to the autobiographical nature of the play, and for some characters there were prototypes in his burned village. Everything in the play is intertwined: as in Jorge Luis Borges's fiction, deep tragedies, told in the lofty, festive language of a poem, come into contact with and complement a chronicle of crime expressed in a coarse, undeveloped, stiff peasant language. During the few hours covered in the play, Voranc and his wife, Neča, are tortured by memories of the past and by their fear about the future of their son, who has turned into a thief, as well as by their hopelessness concerning their speck of land. The value of the play is, above all, in the author's ability to bring all the protagonists to the edge of the precipice, where they are bent over many threatening dangers. In essence this primary human lives a harsh, timeless, emotionless life, taking in all the horrors and not believing in a better world.

The Finnish epic *Kalevala* serves as a basis for Zajc's 1986 drama by the same title; the characters in Zajc's play have the same names as the characters in the Finnish epic and they pass through the same countries, but the goal of the journey is different: the heroes do not conquer or liberate lands but try to satisfy their ecstatic moods, to fulfill their erotic dreams or, more often, some indistinct states, some strange yearnings for death. The play is significant for its specific dialogue with one of the most often used myths in Slovene literature, that of Beautiful Vida, as well as for the poetic language, which is in this play perhaps the most metaphoric. Zajc has used Greek mythology in the play *Medeja* (Medea, 1988), in which he remained faithful to the original story.

Zajc is also a popular writer of juvenile books. In his many poetic collections and picture books he neither infantilizes his poetic language nor does he approach his work for young people with schematized or preconceived notions about childhood. The principle prevalent in his literature for children is "making strange." At a proper moment Zajc distorts a picture more or less familiar to a child and illuminates it with an unexpected light. For Zajc, the juvenile world is full of endless imagination and surprise and a willingness to accept miracles and to "understand" a fairy tale. This openness Zajc wants to enlarge upon, to give it a "home" in his surreal poetry, stating that children are the only ones whose power of imagination has not been destroyed by life and school. This is why he so gladly communicates with the world of children.

No matter what form he uses—poem, play, poem for children, essay, or even the form of an interview—Zajc is a poet. The imagery and metaphors of his language, the rhythm of the narration by which he pulls the reader into the vortex of spoken words, and the melody of his phrases make Zajc an eloquent and important representative of modern poetry. Poetic beauty is offered in his plays as well. Relatively early, when literature was allocated an engaged, political role, Zajc realized—and openly confessed, which put him in difficulties with the ruling regime—that the basic role of a poet is to be, so to speak, a god of words: to create them, to open them, to make them a door into the world, and to tend, gather, and purify them. In a world in which both ideals and illusions have been destroyed, the poet has attached himself to the Word as his highest and only truth.

Interview:

Boris A. Novak, "Intervjui," in his *Dane Zajc v petih knjigah*, volume 5 (Ljubljana: Emonica, 1990).

References:

Aleš Berger, "Pet pesniških iger Daneta Zajca," in Zajc's *Igre* (Ljubljana: Mladinska knjiga, 1989), pp. 321-333;

Niko Grafenauer, "Smrtni dar ljubezni," in Zajc's *Zarotitve* (Ljubljana: Mladinska knjiga, 1985), pp. 65-89;

Grafenauer, "Ta roža je zate," *Otrok in knjiga*, 12 (1981): 5-15;

Richard Jackson, "Against Fear: The Poetry of Dane Zajc," *Poetry Miscellany*, 2 (1994);

Taras Kermauner, "Svet žive smrti (Premišljevanje ob pesniški zbirki *Jezik iz zemlje*)," *Problemi*, 3 (1965-1966): 1452-1490;

Boris A. Novak, "Pesem in človek (dvogovor s poezijo Daneta Zajca)," in Zajc's *Kepa pepela* (Ljubljana: Mladinska knjiga, 1984), pp. 136-151;

Novak, ed., *Interpretacije* (Ljubljana: Nova revija, 1995).

Vitomil Zupan
(18 January 1914 - 14 May 1987)

Peter Scherber
University of Göttingen

Vitomil Zupan

BOOKS: *Andante patetico* (Ljubljana: Slovenski umetniški klub, 1945);
Punt. Tri zaostale ure, by Zupan and Mile Klopčič (Ljubljana: Propagandna komisija pri IOOF, 1945);
Rojstvo v nevihti (Ljubljana: Propagandna komisija pri IOOF, 1945);
Stvar Jurija Trajbasa (Ljubljana: SKZ, 1947; Maribor: Obzorja, 1972);
Popotovanje v tisočera mesta, as "Langus" (Ljubljana: Mladinska knjiga, 1956, 1983);
Noč brez očiju (Zagreb: "Dramska biblioteka," 1967, in Croatian);
Vrata iz meglenega mesta (Maribor: Obzorja, 1968);
Sončne lise (Ljubljana: Cankarjeva založba, 1969);
Trije konji (Ljubljana: Mladinska knjiga, 1970);
Ladja brez imena (Maribor: Obzorja, 1972);
Klement (Ljubljana: Državna založba Slovenije, 1972);
Polnočno vino (Ljubljana: Državna založba Slovenije, 1973);
Bele rakete letijo na Amsterdam (Maribor: Obzorja, 1973);
Sholion (Maribor: Obzorja, 1973);
Zasledovalec samega sebe (Ljubljana: Državna založba Slovenije, 1973);
Angeli, ljudje, živali (Maribor: Obzorja, 1974);
Popotovanje na konec pomladi (Ljubljana: Cankarjeva založba, 1974);
Plašček za Barbaro (Ljubljana: Mladinska knjiga, 1974);
Menuet za kitaro (Ljubljana: Cankarjeva založba, 1975; Murska Sobota: Pomurska založba, 1980);
Duh po človeku (Ljubljana: Mladinska knjiga, 1976);
Mrtva mlaka (Koper: Lipa, 1976);
Igra s hudičevim repom (Murska Sobota: Pomurska založba, 1978);
Komedija človeškega tkiva, 2 volumes (Ljubljana: Cankarjeva založba, 1980);
Levitan (Ljubljana: Cankarjeva zalozba, 1982);
Gora brez Prometeja (Ljubljana: Mladinska knjiga, 1983);
Človek letnih časov (Maribor: Obzorja, 1987);
Apokalipsa vsakdanjosti (Ljubljana: Mladinska knjiga, 1988).

Edition: *Izbrana dela,* volumes 1-6 (Murska Sobota: Pomurska zalozba, 1985).

PLAY PRODUCTIONS: *Aki, Jelenov žleb,* Slovensko narodno gledalisce na osvobojenem ozemlju, 26 March 1944;

Punt, Slovensko narodno gledalisce na osvobojenem ozemlju, 11 April 1944;

Tri zaostale ure, Slovensko narodno gledalisce na osvobojenem ozemlju, 11 April 1944;

Aki, Slovensko narodno gledalisce na osvobojenem ozemlju, 16 May 1944;

Rojstvo v nevihti, Ljubljana, Slovensko narodno gledališče, 9 November 1945;

Andante patetico, Trieste, Slovensko narodno gledališče, 7 December 1945;

Aleksander praznih rok, Ljubljana, Oder 57, 3 December 1961;

Barbara Nives, Ljubljana, Mestno gledališče ljubljansko, 28 February 1962; revised, performed and published as *Angeli, Ljudje, Živali* (Maribor: Obzorja, 1974);

Če denar pade na skalo, Ljubljana, Slovensko narodno gledališče, 22 March 1963;

Crvi, Nova Gorica, Primorsko dramsko gledalisce, 23 April 1970.

TELEVISION: *V pričakovanju jutra,* script by Zupan, RTV Ljubljana, 1961;

Strup, RTV Ljubljana, 1961;

Sarabanda za obesence, RTV Ljubljana, 1968;

Atentator in kralj, RTV Ljubljana, 1971;

Ulica treh rodov, RTV Ljubljana, 1972;

Vest in pločevina, RTV Ljubljana, 1973.

RADIO: *Smrt luninega zraka,* script by Zupan, Radio Ljubljana, 1962;

S strahom in pilulo hrabrosti okrog sveta, script by Zupan, as "Vidas," Radio Ljubljana, 1968;

Upor črvov, script by Zupan, Radio Ljubljana, 1969;

Suženskij trg, script by Zupan, Radio Ljubljana, 1971;

Poplah na ladji Jutro, script by Zupan, Radio Ljubljana, 1973;

Odločitev, script by Zupan, Radio Ljubljana, 1976;

Ptici pojejo pesem, script by Zupan, Radio Ljubljana, 1977.

PERIODICAL PUBLICATIONS: "Aleksander praznih rok," *Perspektive,* 1 (1960–1962): 10–13;

"Preobrazbe brez poti nazaj," *Problemi,* 123–124 (1973): 176–202;

"Zapiski o sistemu," *Problemi,* 1–2 (1975): 119–144.

Although he was born just before the beginning of World War I, Vitomil Zupan did not achieve literary success until the end of the 1960s. In the following fifteen years he published the greater part of his writings. The reasons for his late appearance on the scene were both political and literary. For nearly two decades he was unable to publish because of an official ban against him; during this period he was also imprisoned for many years and ostracized from society. There were also literary reasons for the lateness of his recognition: his writings departed radically from what were for many years the officially accepted artistic standards and the predominant critical taste.

In the 1970s the Slovene literary milieu became more open to experimental and nonconformist styles of writing. In a succession of essays Taras Kermauner, the leading critic from the Slovene avant-garde, prepared the public to accept Zupan as an important contemporary author. Although he is now, after his death in 1987, recognized as one of the leading novelists and dramatists of postwar Slovenia, Zupan is still considered by some to have produced works that are "savage," and he is called a kind of "devil's pupil" by those who believe that his work veers too far from acceptable artistic standards. His strength is undoubtedly in his fiction and dramas; critics have not formed any consensus about his poems because only a small part of them have ever been published.

Zupan was born on 18 January 1914, shortly before World War I. His birthplace was Ljubljana, then called Laibach, the capital of the Austrian region of Krain. After Zupan's father, Ivan Zupan, was killed in the war, Zupan's mother, Ivanka, née Korban, married Adolf Robida, a minor dramatist and theater critic. After attending high school in Ljubljana, Zupan took his graduation examinations in 1932 and 1933. In 1933 he also published his first short story, "Črni šahovski konj" (Black Chess Horse, 1933) in the periodical *Mladika* (Fresh Branch). After a short time as an engineering student at the technical faculty of the University of Ljubljana, Zupan began a long, unsteady period during which he moved from job to job, both in his own country and abroad, working variously as a ski instructor, sailor, boxer, painter, fitter, and stoker, and traveling across Europe, North Africa, and the Near East. During this time he wrote poetry, fiction, and plays, without any chance of being published; in fact, all these writings remained unpublished until the 1970s.

In 1941, shortly after Yugoslavia was dragged into World War II, Zupan joined the liberation movement in his country. At the beginning of 1942 the Italian occupying forces arrested him and he was held in internment camps. In autumn of 1943 he was released and joined the partisans' army of Josip Broz Tito, working as a writer and announcer for the liberation army's broadcasting unit; he also worked at the outlawed Slovene National Theater. Some of his closest comrades of that time were Jože Brejc, later called Jože Javoršek; Filip Kalan, a playwright; and the philosopher and literary critic Dušan Pirjevec. Here, at the partisan theater in 1944, Zupan's first one-act plays were performed: *Aki, Jelenov žleb, Tri ostale ure* (Three Watches Being Slow), and *Punt* (The Rebellion). He also wrote reports and sketches on various occasions and his first piece of fiction, *Andante patetico*, published directly after the liberation in 1945, which bore the subtitle *Povest o panterju Dingo* (Novella of the Panter Dingo). "Panter Dingo" is the partisan nickname for the story's first-person narrator, the part-time leader of a partisan combat unit who is courageous and brave but has a mind of his own. He does his utmost for the salvation of his native country but does not deny the individual, subjective points of view on human and political matters. Dingo is a special kind of antihero, one outside the heroic presentation of partisans favored by the communist view of literature; orthodox critics soon defamed Zupan, claiming that his work was decadent and harmful. The novella tries to show a realistic, rather than a propagandistic, image of war. Some might argue that the ideology in the story is questionable, but the main thrust of the work is forward-looking, both literarily and aesthetically.

One of his dramas of partisan times, *Rojstvo v nevihti* (Birth in the Thunderstorm, 1945), was staged after the liberation and applauded by critics and the public. From 1945 to 1947 Zupan worked at the radio station in Ljubljana. In 1947 another drama, *Stvar Jurija Trajbasa* (The Case of Jurij Trajbas), was produced, a play written during the war in the dramatic tradition of the early-twentieth-century writer, Ivan Cankar. The ruling Italian censors had not allowed it to be performed during the war, and after the postwar performance of this drama Zupan was again charged with being a decadent author. All these accusations were harbingers of the legal proceedings against Zupan after the so-called Informbiro, the break between Tito and Joseph Stalin that was followed by a persecution mania against dissidents of every shade. In the process Zupan was accused of immorality, attempted homicide, betrayal of state secrets, propaganda for the enemy, and subversive activities. In February of 1949 he received a sentence of ten years; sometime later, in an appeal hearing, he was sentenced to eighteen years of prison and compulsory labor.

Zupan was not released until 1954. In later textbooks and literary histories critics euphemistically referred to these years as his "unintentional break of creativity"; in fact, Zupan was writing in a tremendous creative surge. His drama *Ladja brez imena* (Ship Unnamed, 1972), the novel *Levitan* (1982), and many other books, most of which were not published until at least two decades later, were written while he was in prison. After he was released he had almost no chance of his work being published and wrote for occasional periodical publications, radio, TV, and film. He wrote about fifty screenplays, most of which remained unproduced. He also finished his studies in Ljubljana and received his diploma as a construction engineer in 1958.

Under the pseudonym Langus, Zupan did publish one book, a story for children titled *Popotovanje v tisočera mesta* (Journey into a Thousand Places, 1956). This and the book *Trije konji* (Three Horses, 1970) and a later a book for children, *Plašček za Barbaro* (A Coat for Barbara, 1974), were Zupan's contributions to Slovene literature for young people. The first is a fantastic journey into a wondrous land, full of bizarre and magic adventures, and a mosaic of scenes, sometimes coupled together with no logical connections; all the fantasies are revealed at the end to be the feverish dreams of the main hero, the young boy Tek. *Trije konji* is a chain of fairy tales collected in a frame story and also motivated by dream events. Both books are regarded among the better works of children's literature from recent decades. In 1960 Serbian and Croatian theaters staged a play that remained unpublished and unperformed in Slovenia: *Noč brez oči* (Night without Eyes). From 1961 on Slovene theaters occasionally performed plays by Zupan.

The tragicomedy *Aleksander praznih rok* (Alexander Empty-handed, 1961), spoken in a Ljubljana dialect, was performed by the experimental theater Oder 57. The central theme of the play was based on the well-known story of Alexander the Great and the philosopher Diogenes, who lived in a barrel. At the end of their lives both characters are nothing more than poor and empty-handed human beings. A drama about the life of an actress, *Barbara Nives,* was first produced in 1962 and then revised and performed again in 1974 under the new title, *Angeli, ljudje, živali* (Angels, Humans, Animals). In 1963 there followed *Če denar pade na skalo* (If Money Falls on the Rocks), a play that received less attention.

Zupan's first book after his many years of being persona non grata was the novel *Vrata iz meglenega mesta* (The Gate out of the Misty City), published in 1968 but written years earlier. The novel presents a picture of the times just before World War II and then the war years from the point of view of the poor people living in the villages. From many autobiographical sources Zupan creates the individual passions, suffering, and heroism of typical inhabitants of the misty city, Ljubljana, which is located near a large marshland. *Sončne lise* (Sun Spots, 1969) is a collection of Zupan's short prose, beginning with pieces written in his youth. The radio play, *Upor črvov* (The Rebellion of the Worms, 1969), was revised for stage performance later under the title *Črvi* (Worms, 1970); the story presented a typical Yugoslav postwar generation gap between a father, a former partisan and member of the ruling class, and his son, who rebels against his father's values and is imprisoned.

In the following years Zupan published more and more of the many novels and plays that he had written earlier. One was the poetic play *Ladja brez imena* (1972), an allegorical and philosophical text written during his prison years. Also in 1972 one of his great novels appeared, *Popotovanje na konec pomladi* (Journey to the End of Springtime); written just before the war, it portrays the intellectual life and lifestyle of the prewar middle classes.

The year 1973 proved to be remarkably productive. Four of Zupan's books were published. His play *Bele rakete letijo na Amsterdam* (White Missiles Flying to Amsterdam) was one of the highlights of his dramatic oeuvre. Written for studio theater, it concentrates on three characters and exploits the dramatic unity of space and time to create its own microcosm of human relations and the everyday hell that may be suffered on earth. The literary journal *Problemi* (Problems) published another drama, "Preobrazba brez poti nazaj" (The Metamorphosis without Any Way Back). That year many of Zupan's poems and essays appeared in the main Slovene cultural journals, but he collected only one book of lyrical poetry, under the title *Polnočno vino* (Midnight Wine, 1973). The critics received this small book with respect and goodwill, but it was judged to be merely a sort of by-product of his work. Another book published in 1973, containing one long essay on the Slovene theater situation in 1972, was *Sholion*.

Klement (1972) was one of the novels written in the beginning of Zupan's literary career. It develops in a mingling of realistic events and imaginative dream images the inner portrait of its hero, the antiquarian Klement, in his existence as a stranger in a world of increasing alienation. The novel may be regarded as an early counterpart of Albert Camus's *Le Mythe de Sisyphe* (1942, translated as *The Myth of Sisyphus,* 1955), showing once more that Zupan's work anticipated certain trends of modern thinking and writing.

Zasledovalec samega sebi (The Persecutor of Himself, 1973) written in 1938, is a modern rewriting of Fyodor Dostoyevsky's *Crime and Punishment* (1866). Having killed the father of his girlfriend, the young Tah attempts suicide, but fails. Later, he resigns himself to remaining alive, but he punishes himself by wandering restlessly through the world. The moral of the story can be summarized: the guilty man persecutes and punishes himself more powerfully than earthly justice does. One of the most popular and successful of Zupan's novels was his *Menuet za kitaro* (Minuet for Guitar, 1975), a late work and one of his few works that explores the themes of World War II and the partisan resistance to German occupation. The book was reprinted several times and adapted for the screen in 1980; the movie version was titled *Na svidenje v naslednji vojni* (See You Again in the Next War) and produced by the Serbian director Živojin Pavlovič. The play "Zapiski o sistemu" (Notices about the System, 1975) was published in the magazine *Problemi*. It presents a group of experimental scientists and shows the bondage and violence that result from the alienation of people in modern societies.

In the last decade of Zupan's life his literary productivity was slowed by his advanced age and his increasingly severe illness. But some important works continued to appear in these years, including the novel, *Mrtva mlaka* (The Dead Puddle, 1976), also written years before. *Duh po človeku* (Odor of Human Being, 1976) and *Igra s hudičevim repom* (The Game with the Devil's Tail, 1978) are situated in surroundings of crime and depravity and are some of the most provoking and shocking works of modern Slovene fiction. The two-volume novel *Komedija človeškega tkiva* (Comedy of Human Tissue, 1980) is a kind of literary summary that is largely autobiographical. This novel was later adapted into a play.

Perhaps the most spectacular of Zupan's novels is *Levitan*. Written while he was in prison, it was supposed to appear at the end of the

1960s but was not published until 1982. Along with other contemporary books that criticized postwar censorship and the disregard of human rights in communist Yugoslavia, books such as Branko Hofman's *Noč do jutra* (From Night to Morning, 1975-1981), *Levitan* helped to prepare a literary climate that encouraged more tolerance and self-confidence and fewer political taboos. It is one of the works whose impact on intellectual life and the Slovene cultural and political landscape cannot be overlooked. In 1983 Zupan published novellas written in the preceding two decades in a collection titled *Gora brez Prometeja* (The Mountain without Prometheus). Two years later Kermauner, the critic largely responsible for the discovery and appreciation of Zupan's works, edited a reprint of his six most important novels as *Izbrana dela* (Selected Writings, 1985). Zupan died on 14 May 1987 after long years of suffering. Two posthumous works of prose soon came out: *Človek letnih časov* (The Man of the Seasons, 1987) and the fragment *Apokalipsa vsakdanjosti* (Apocalypse of Everyday Life, 1988), an autobiographical story about the experiences of illness and aging.

Zupan was awarded several prizes for his work. In 1947 he won the Preseren Award for his partisan drama *Rojstvo v nevihti*. In 1984 he won the same award for his life work. Some prizes for radio plays were given to Zupan, and, together with Ciril Kosmac, he won in 1947 an award for the screenplay "Sredotežnost" (Centripetal Force), which was never produced. In 1972 the drama *Bele rakete letijo na Amsterdam* won awards from Serbian theaters in Belgrade, Novi Sad, and Niš. The Župančič Award of the city of Ljubljana was given twice to Zupan, in 1973 for the novel *Popotovanje na konec pomladi* and in 1983 for *Levitan*. Most of Zupan's plays and prose writings have been translated into Serbo-Croatian. Only a few have been translated into other east or west European languages. Zupan once commented: "For the West I am too much Easterly, for the East I am too much Western." In fact, Zupan was an accurate witness of his times, nearly always biting and acidic, impolite and shocking, but always straight and upright concerning the ethical principles of authorship. His works exerted a great influence on Slovene literature and culture in the 1970s and 1980s.

Interviews:

Branko Hofman, "Interview with Vitomil Zupan," in *Pogovori s slovenskimi pisatelji* (Ljubljana: Cankarjeva založba, 1978), pp. 511-524;

France Pibernik, "Interview with Vitomil Zupan," in *Čas Romana. Pogovori s slovenskimi pisatelji* (Ljubljana: Cankarjeva založba, 1983), pp. 25-33.

References:

France Bernik and Marjan Dolgan, *Slovenska vojna proza 1941-1980* (Ljubljana: Slovenska matica, 1988);

Dolgan, "Hudičev učenec ali Vitomil Zupan," in *Seminar slovenskega jezika, literature in kulture*, XXV (Ljubljana: Univerza Edvarda Kardelja, 1989), pp. 147-154;

Helga Glušič-Krisper and Matjaž Kmecl, "Proza," in *Slovenska književnost 1945-1965*, volume 1 (Ljubljana: Slovenska matica, 1967), pp. 323-324;

Andrej Inkret, *Spomini na branje* (Maribor: Obzorja, 1977);

Inkret, "V. Zupan," in *Slovenski biografski leksikon*, volume 4 (Ljubljana: Slovenska akademija znanosti in umetnosti, 1980-1991), pp. 880-884;

Taras Kermauner, *Družbena razveza* (Ljubljana: Cankarjeva založba, 1982);

Kermauner, *Pomenske spremembe v sodobni slovenski dramatiki* (Ljubljana: Mladinska knjiga, 1975);

Kermauner, *Vračanje mita v sodobni slovenski dramatiki* (Ljubljana: Partizanska knjiga, 1988);

Kermauner, "Zapiski o občestvu polžev," in *Od igre do telesa* (Ljubljana: Knjižnica mestnega gledališča, 1976), pp. 215-225;

Kermauner, *Zgodba o živi zdajšnjosti* (Maribor: Obzorja, 1975);

Jože Koruža, "Dramatika," in *Slovenska književnost 1945-1965*, volume 2 (Ljubljana: Slovenska matica, 1967), pp. 126-133;

Janko Kos and others, *Vitomil Zupan* (Ljubljana: Nova revija, 1993);

Mitja Mejak, "Tri mladinska dela," in *Književna kronika* (Ljubljana: Državna založba Slovenije, 1961), pp. 132-138;

Denis Poniž, "Vitomil Zupan (1914-1987)," in *Črtomirovo Slovenstvo* (Ljubljana: Cankarjeva založba, 1993), pp. 140-151;

Dimitrij Rupel, *Branje* (Maribor: Obzorja, 1973);

Viktor Smolej, "Slovstvo v letih vojne," in *Zgodovina slovenskega slovstva*, volume 7 (Ljubljana: Slovenska matica, 1971), pp. 309-316;

Mirko Zupančič, "Aleksander praznih rok," in *Gledališki zapisi in eseji* (Maribor: Obzorja, 1972), pp. 109-110.

Checklist of Further Readings

Barac, Antun. *A History of Yugoslav Literature*. Ann Arbor: Michigan Slavic Publications, 1973.

Cronia, Arturo. *Storia della letteratura Serbo-Croata*. Milan: Nuova accadèmia editrice, 1956.

Deretić, Jovan. *Istorija srpske književnosti*. Belgrade: Nolit, 1983.

Deretić, *Srpski roman 1800–1950*. Belgrade: Nolit, 1981.

Eekman, Thomas. *Thirty Years of Yugoslav Literature (1945–1975)*. Ann Arbor: Michigan Slavic Publications, 1978.

Holton, Milne, and Vasa D. Mihailovich. *Serbian Poetry from the Beginnings to the Present*. New Haven: Yale Center for International and Areas Studies, 1988.

Igov, Svetlozar. *Istoriia na Bŭlgarska literatura (1878–1944)*. Sofia: Bŭlgarska akademiia na naukite, 1990.

Istoriia na Bŭlgarskata literatura. 4 volumes. Sofia: Bulgarska akademiia na naukite, 1962–1976.

Kadić, Ante. *Contemporary Croatian Literature*. The Hague: Mouton, 1960.

Kadić, *Contemporary Serbian Literature*. The Hague: Mouton, 1964.

Kermauner, Taras. *Dileme sodobnega slovenskega pesništva*. Ljubljana: Cankarjeva založba, 1971.

Koblar, F. *Dvajset let slovenske drame*. Ljubljana: Slovenska matica, 1964.

Koneski, Blaže. *Makedonska književnost*. Belgrade: Srpska književna zadruga, 1961.

Lasić, Stanko. *Sukob na književnoj ljevici 1928–1952*. Zagreb: Liber, 1970.

Legiša, Lino, ed. *Zgodovina slovenskega slovstva*, 7 volumes. Ljubljana: Slovenska matica, 1956–1971.

Lukić, Sveta. *Contemporary Yugoslav Literature*. Urbana: University of Illinois Press, 1972.

Maver, Giovanni. *Letteratura Slovena*. Milan, 1960.

Mihailovich and Mateja Matejić. *A Comprehensive Bibliography of Yugoslav Literature in English 1593–1980*. Columbus, Ohio: Slavica, 1984; First Supplement 1981–1985 (1988); Second Supplement 1986–1990 (1992).

Palavestra, Predrag. *Istorija moderne srpske književnosti*. Belgrade: Srpska književna zadruga, 1986.

Palavestra, *Posleratna srpska književnost 1945–1970*. Belgrade: Prosveta, 1972.

Pavletić, Vlatko. *Panorama hrvatske književnosti XX stoječa*. Zagreb: Stvarnost, 1965.

Peleš, Gajo. *Poetika suvremenog jugoslavenskog romana 1945-1961*. Zagreb: Naprijed, 1966.

Penev, Boian. *Istoriia na novata Bŭlgarska literatura*. 4 volumes. Sofia: Bŭlgarski pisatel, 1976-1978.

Rechnik na Bŭlgarskata literatura. 3 volumes. Sofia: Bŭlgarska akademiia na naukite, 1976-1982.

Šicel, Miroslav. *Pregled novije hrvatske književnosti*. Zagreb: Matica hrvatska, 1966.

Slodnjak, Anton. *Geschichte der slovenischen Literatur*. Berlin: De Gruyter, 1958.

Slodnjak, *Slovensko slovstvo*. Ljubljana: Mladinska knjiga, 1968.

Vaupotić, Miroslav. *Hrvatska suvremena književnost—Contemporary Croatian Literature*. Zagreb: Croatian PEN Club Centre, 1966.

Zadravec, Franc, and Jože Pogačnik, eds. *Zgodovina slovenskega slovstva*. 8 volumes. Maribor: Založba Obzorja, 1968-1972.

Živkovic, Dragiša. *Evropski okviri srpske književnosti*. 3 volumes. Belgrade: Prosveta, 1970-1983.

Contributors

Michael Biggins	University of Washington
Thomas J. Butler	Harvard University
Henry R. Cooper Jr.	Indiana University
Dasha Čulić Nisula	Western Michigan University
Savo Cvetanovski	University of Skopje
Edward J. Czerwinski	State University of New York at Stony Brook
Ljerka Debush	Harvard University
Roumiana Deltcheva	University of Alberta
Thomas Eekman	University of California–Los Angeles
Ellen Elias-Bursać	Harvard University
Helga Glušič	University of Ljubljana
Radmila J. Gorup	Columbia University
E. D. Goy	Cambridge University
E. Celia Hawkesworth	University of London
W. Milne Holton	University of Maryland
Bernard Johnson	London School of Economics
Francis R. Jones	University of Newcastle
Dubravka Juraga	University of Arkansas
Marko Juvan	University of Ljubljana
Christina Kramer	University of Toronto
Raia Kuncheva	Institute of Literature, Sofia
Anita Lekić	State University of New York at Stony Brook
Tomislav Z. Longinović	University of Wisconsin–Madison
Tom Lozar	Vanier College
Maria B. Malby	East Carolina University
Vasa D. Mihailovich	University of North Carolina–Chapel Hill
George Mitrevski	Auburn University
Marija Mitrović	University of Trieste
Nicholas Moravcevich	University of Illinois–Chicago
Nikita Nankov	Indiana University
Nadežda Obradović	University of Belgrade
Lyubomira Parpulova-Gribble	Ohio State University
Aleksandar Petrov	University of Pittsburgh
Branko Popović	Teachers' School, Belgrade, Serbia
Cleo Protokhristova	University of Plovdiv
Bogdan Rakić	Indiana University
Graham W. Reid	University of Skopje
Ivan Ruskov	University of Plovdiv
Peter Scherber	University of Göttingen
Cynthia Simmons	Boston College
Aldijana Šišić	University of London
Krinka Vidaković	University of Pittsburgh
Aida Vidan	Harvard University

Cumulative Index

Dictionary of Literary Biography, Volumes 1-181
Dictionary of Literary Biography Yearbook, 1980-1996
Dictionary of Literary Biography Documentary Series, Volumes 1-14

Cumulative Index

DLB before number: *Dictionary of Literary Biography,* Volumes 1-181
Y before number: *Dictionary of Literary Biography Yearbook,* 1980-1996
DS before number: *Dictionary of Literary Biography Documentary Series,* Volumes 1-14

A

Abbey Press DLB-49

The Abbey Theatre and Irish Drama, 1900-1945 . . . . DLB-10

Abbot, Willis J. 1863-1934 . . . . DLB-29

Abbott, Jacob 1803-1879 . . . . DLB-1

Abbott, Lee K. 1947- DLB-130

Abbott, Lyman 1835-1922 . . . . DLB-79

Abbott, Robert S. 1868-1940 . . . . DLB-29, 91

Abelard, Peter circa 1079-1142 . . . . . DLB-115

Abelard-Schuman DLB-46

Abell, Arunah S. 1806-1888 . . . . DLB-43

Abercrombie, Lascelles 1881-1938 . . . . DLB-19

Aberdeen University Press Limited DLB-106

Abish, Walter 1931- DLB-130

Ablesimov, Aleksandr Onisimovich 1742-1783 . . . . DLB-150

Abraham à Sancta Clara 1644-1709 . . . . DLB-168

Abrahams, Peter 1919- DLB-117

Abrams, M. H. 1912- DLB-67

Abrogans circa 790-800 . . . . DLB-148

Abschatz, Hans Aßmann von 1646-1699 . . . . DLB-168

Abse, Dannie 1923- DLB-27

Academy Chicago Publishers DLB-46

Accrocca, Elio Filippo 1923- DLB-128

Ace Books DLB-46

Achebe, Chinua 1930- DLB-117

Achtenberg, Herbert 1938- DLB-124

Ackerman, Diane 1948- DLB-120

Ackroyd, Peter 1949- DLB-155

Acorn, Milton 1923-1986 . . . . DLB-53

Acosta, Oscar Zeta 1935?- DLB-82

Actors Theatre of Louisville DLB-7

Adair, James 1709?-1783? DLB-30

Adam, Graeme Mercer 1839-1912 . . . . . DLB-99

Adame, Leonard 1947- DLB-82

Adamic, Louis 1898-1951 . . . . DLB-9

Adams, Alice 1926- Y-86

Adams, Brooks 1848-1927 . . . . DLB-47

Adams, Charles Francis, Jr. 1835-1915 . . . . DLB-47

Adams, Douglas 1952- Y-83

Adams, Franklin P. 1881-1960 . . . . . . DLB-29

Adams, Henry 1838-1918 . . . . DLB-12, 47

Adams, Herbert Baxter 1850-1901 . . . . DLB-47

Adams, J. S. and C. [publishing house] DLB-49

Adams, James Truslow 1878-1949 . . . . . DLB-17

Adams, John 1735-1826 . . . . DLB-31

Adams, John Quincy 1767-1848 . . . . . . DLB-37

Adams, Léonie 1899-1988 . . . . DLB-48

Adams, Levi 1802-1832 . . . . DLB-99

Adams, Samuel 1722-1803 . . . . . . DLB-31, 43

Adams, Thomas 1582 or 1583-1652 . . . . DLB-151

Adams, William Taylor 1822-1897 . . . . DLB-42

Adamson, Sir John 1867-1950 . . . . . . DLB-98

Adcock, Arthur St. John 1864-1930 . . . . DLB-135

Adcock, Betty 1938- DLB-105

Adcock, Betty, *Certain Gifts* DLB-105

Adcock, Fleur 1934- DLB-40

Addison, Joseph 1672-1719 . . . . DLB-101

Ade, George 1866-1944 . . . . DLB-11, 25

Adeler, Max (see Clark, Charles Heber)

Adonias Filho 1915-1990 . . . . DLB-145

Advance Publishing Company DLB-49

AE 1867-1935 . . . . DLB-19

Ælfric circa 955-circa 1010 . . . . . . DLB-146

Aeschines circa 390 B.C.-circa 320 B.C. DLB-176

Aeschylus 525-524 B.C.-456-455 B.C. DLB-176

Aesthetic Poetry (1873), by Walter Pater DLB-35

After Dinner Opera Company Y-92

Afro-American Literary Critics: An Introduction DLB-33

Agassiz, Jean Louis Rodolphe 1807-1873 . . . . DLB-1

Agee, James 1909-1955 . . . . . DLB-2, 26, 152

The Agee Legacy: A Conference at the University of Tennessee at Knoxville Y-89

Aguilera Malta, Demetrio 1909-1981 . . . . DLB-145

Ai 1947- DLB-120

Aichinger, Ilse 1921- DLB-85

Aidoo, Ama Ata 1942- DLB-117

Aiken, Conrad 1889-1973 . . . . . DLB-9, 45, 102

Aiken, Joan 1924- DLB-161

Aikin, Lucy 1781-1864 . . . . DLB-144, 163

Ainsworth, William Harrison 1805-1882 . . . . DLB-21

Aitken, George A. 1860-1917 . . . . . . DLB-149

Aitken, Robert [publishing house] . . . DLB-49

Akenside, Mark 1721-1770 . . . . DLB-109

Akins, Zoë 1886-1958 . . . . DLB-26

Akutagawa, Ryūnosuke 1892-1927 . . . . DLB-180

Alabaster, William 1568-1640 . . . . . DLB-132

Alain-Fournier 1886-1914 . . . . DLB-65

Alarcón, Francisco X. 1954- DLB-122

Alba, Nanina 1915-1968 . . . . DLB-41

Albee, Edward 1928- DLB-7

Albert the Great circa 1200-1280 . . . DLB-115

Alberti, Rafael 1902- DLB-108

Albertinus, Aegidius circa 1560-1620 . . . . DLB-164

Alcaeus born circa 620 B.C. DLB-176

Alcott, Amos Bronson 1799-1888 . . . . . DLB-1

Alcott, Louisa May 1832-1888 . . . . . . DLB-1, 42, 79; DS-14

Alcott, William Andrus 1798-1859 . . . . DLB-1

Alcuin circa 732-804 . . . . DLB-148

Alden, Henry Mills 1836-1919 . . . . . . DLB-79

Alden, Isabella 1841-1930 . . . . DLB-42

Alden, John B. [publishing house] . . . DLB-49

Alden, Beardsley and Company DLB-49

Aldington, Richard 1892-1962 . . . . . . DLB-20, 36, 100, 149

Aldis, Dorothy 1896-1966 . . . . DLB-22

Aldiss, Brian W. 1925- DLB-14

Cumulative Index

Aldrich, Thomas Bailey 1836-1907 . . . . DLB-42, 71, 74, 79

Alegría, Ciro 1909-1967 . . . . DLB-113

Alegría, Claribel 1924- DLB-145

Aleixandre, Vicente 1898-1984 . . . . . DLB-108

Aleramo, Sibilla 1876-1960 . . . . DLB-114

Alexander, Charles 1868-1923 . . . . . . DLB-91

Alexander, Charles Wesley [publishing house] DLB-49

Alexander, James 1691-1756 . . . . . . DLB-24

Alexander, Lloyd 1924- DLB-52

Alexander, Sir William, Earl of Stirling 1577?-1640 . . . . DLB-121

Alexie, Sherman 1966- DLB-175

Alexis, Willibald 1798-1871 . . . . . . DLB-133

Alfred, King 849-899 . . . . DLB-146

Alger, Horatio, Jr. 1832-1899 . . . . . . DLB-42

Algonquin Books of Chapel Hill DLB-46

Algren, Nelson 1909-1981 . . . . . DLB-9; Y-81, 82

Allan, Andrew 1907-1974 . . . . DLB-88

Allan, Ted 1916- DLB-68

Allbeury, Ted 1917- DLB-87

Alldritt, Keith 1935- DLB-14

Allen, Ethan 1738-1789 . . . . DLB-31

Allen, Frederick Lewis 1890-1954 . . . . DLB-137

Allen, Gay Wilson 1903-1995 . . . . DLB-103; Y-95

Allen, George 1808-1876 . . . . DLB-59

Allen, George [publishing house] DLB-106

Allen, George, and Unwin Limited DLB-112

Allen, Grant 1848-1899 . . . . DLB-70, 92, 178

Allen, Henry W. 1912- Y-85

Allen, Hervey 1889-1949 . . . . DLB-9, 45

Allen, James 1739-1808 . . . . DLB-31

Allen, James Lane 1849-1925 . . . . . . DLB-71

Allen, Jay Presson 1922- DLB-26

Allen, John, and Company DLB-49

Allen, Paula Gunn 1939- DLB-175

Allen, Samuel W. 1917- DLB-41

Allen, Woody 1935- DLB-44

Allende, Isabel 1942- DLB-145

Alline, Henry 1748-1784 . . . . DLB-99

Allingham, Margery 1904-1966 . . . . . DLB-77

Allingham, William 1824-1889 . . . . . DLB-35

Allison, W. L. [publishing house] DLB-49

The *Alliterative Morte Arthure* and the *Stanzaic Morte Arthur* circa 1350-1400 . . . . DLB-146

Allott, Kenneth 1912-1973 . . . . DLB-20

Allston, Washington 1779-1843 . . . . . DLB-1

Almon, John [publishing house] DLB-154

Alonzo, Dámaso 1898-1990 . . . . . . DLB-108

Alsop, George 1636-post 1673 . . . . . DLB-24

Alsop, Richard 1761-1815 . . . . DLB-37

Altemus, Henry, and Company DLB-49

Altenberg, Peter 1885-1919 . . . . DLB-81

Altolaguirre, Manuel 1905-1959 . . . . . DLB-108

Aluko, T. M. 1918- DLB-117

Alurista 1947- DLB-82

Alvarez, A. 1929- DLB-14, 40

Amadi, Elechi 1934- DLB-117

Amado, Jorge 1912- DLB-113

Ambler, Eric 1909- DLB-77

America: or, a Poem on the Settlement of the British Colonies (1780?), by Timothy Dwight DLB-37

American Conservatory Theatre DLB-7

American Fiction and the 1930s DLB-9

American Humor: A Historical Survey
East and Northeast
South and Southwest
Midwest
West DLB-11

The American Library in Paris Y-93

American News Company DLB-49

The American Poets' Corner: The First Three Years (1983-1986) Y-86

American Proletarian Culture: The 1930s DS-11

American Publishing Company DLB-49

American Stationers' Company DLB-49

American Sunday-School Union DLB-49

American Temperance Union DLB-49

American Tract Society DLB-49

The American Trust for the British Library Y-96

The American Writers Congress (9-12 October 1981) Y-81

The American Writers Congress: A Report on Continuing Business Y-81

Ames, Fisher 1758-1808 . . . . DLB-37

Ames, Mary Clemmer 1831-1884 . . . . DLB-23

Amini, Johari M. 1935- DLB-41

Amis, Kingsley 1922-1995 . . . . DLB-15, 27, 100, 139, Y-96

Amis, Martin 1949- DLB-14

Ammons, A. R. 1926- DLB-5, 165

Amory, Thomas 1691?-1788 . . . . . . DLB-39

Anaya, Rudolfo A. 1937- DLB-82

Ancrene Riwle circa 1200-1225 . . . . . DLB-146

Andersch, Alfred 1914-1980 . . . . . . DLB-69

Anderson, Margaret 1886-1973 . . . . DLB-4, 91

Anderson, Maxwell 1888-1959 . . . . . DLB-7

Anderson, Patrick 1915-1979 . . . . . . DLB-68

Anderson, Paul Y. 1893-1938 . . . . . . DLB-29

Anderson, Poul 1926- DLB-8

Anderson, Robert 1750-1830 . . . . . . DLB-142

Anderson, Robert 1917- DLB-7

Anderson, Sherwood 1876-1941 . . . . DLB-4, 9, 86; DS-1

Andreae, Johann Valentin 1586-1654 . . . . DLB-164

Andreas-Salomé, Lou 1861-1937 . . . . DLB-66

Andres, Stefan 1906-1970 . . . . DLB-69

Andreu, Blanca 1959- DLB-134

Andrewes, Lancelot 1555-1626 . . . . DLB-151, 172

Andrews, Charles M. 1863-1943 . . . . . DLB-17

Andrews, Miles Peter ?-1814 . . . . . . DLB-89

Andrian, Leopold von 1875-1951 . . . . DLB-81

Andrić, Ivo 1892-1975 . . . . DLB-147

Andrieux, Louis (see Aragon, Louis)

Andrus, Silas, and Son DLB-49

Angell, James Burrill 1829-1916 . . . . . DLB-64

Angell, Roger 1920- DLB-171

Angelou, Maya 1928- DLB-38

Anger, Jane flourished 1589 . . . . . . DLB-136

Angers, Félicité (see Conan, Laure)

Anglo-Norman Literature in the Development of Middle English Literature DLB-146

The Anglo-Saxon Chronicle circa 890-1154 . . . . DLB-146

The "Angry Young Men" DLB-15

Angus and Robertson (UK) Limited DLB-112

Anhalt, Edward 1914- DLB-26

Anners, Henry F. [publishing house] DLB-49

Annolied between 1077 and 1081 . . . . DLB-148

Anselm of Canterbury 1033-1109 . . . . DLB-115

Anstey, F. 1856-1934 . . . . DLB-141, 178

Anthony, Michael 1932- DLB-125

Anthony, Piers 1934- DLB-8

Anthony Burgess's *99 Novels*: An Opinion Poll Y-84

Antin, David 1932- DLB-169

Antin, Mary 1881-1949 . . . . Y-84

Anton Ulrich, Duke of Brunswick-Lüneburg 1633-1714 . . . . DLB-168

Antschel, Paul (see Celan, Paul)

Anyidoho, Kofi 1947- DLB-157

Anzaldúa, Gloria 1942- DLB-122

Anzengruber, Ludwig 1839-1889 . . . . DLB-129

Apess, William 1798-1839 . . . . DLB-175

Apodaca, Rudy S. 1939- DLB-82

Apollonius Rhodius third century B.C. DLB-176

Apple, Max 1941- DLB-130

Appleton, D., and Company DLB-49

Appleton-Century-Crofts DLB-46

Applewhite, James 1935- DLB-105

Apple-wood Books DLB-46

Aquin, Hubert 1929-1977 . . . . DLB-53

Aquinas, Thomas 1224 or 1225-1274 . . . . DLB-115

Aragon, Louis 1897-1982 . . . . DLB-72

Aralica, Ivan 1930- DLB-181

Aratus of Soli circa 315 B.C.-circa 239 B.C. DLB-176

Arbor House Publishing Company DLB-46

Arbuthnot, John 1667-1735 . . . . DLB-101

Arcadia House DLB-46

Arce, Julio G. (see Ulica, Jorge)

Archer, William 1856-1924 . . . . DLB-10

Archilochhus mid seventh century B.C.E. DLB-176

The Archpoet circa 1130?-? DLB-148

Archpriest Avvakum (Petrovich) 1620?-1682 . . . . DLB-150

Arden, John 1930- DLB-13

Arden of Faversham DLB-62

Ardis Publishers Y-89

Ardizzone, Edward 1900-1979 . . . . . DLB-160

Arellano, Juan Estevan 1947- DLB-122

The Arena Publishing Company DLB-49

Arena Stage DLB-7

Arenas, Reinaldo 1943-1990 . . . . . . DLB-145

Arensberg, Ann 1937- Y-82

Arguedas, José María 1911-1969 . . . . DLB-113

Argueta, Manlio 1936- DLB-145

Arias, Ron 1941- DLB-82

Arishima, Takeo 1878-1923 . . . . DLB-180

Aristophanes circa 446 B.C.-circa 446 B.C.-circa 386 B.C. DLB-176

Aristotle 384 B.C.-322 B.C. DLB-176

Arland, Marcel 1899-1986 . . . . DLB-72

Arlen, Michael 1895-1956 . . . . DLB-36, 77, 162

Armah, Ayi Kwei 1939- DLB-117

Der arme Hartmann ?-after 1150 . . . . DLB-148

Armed Services Editions DLB-46

Armstrong, Richard 1903- DLB-160

Arndt, Ernst Moritz 1769-1860 . . . . . DLB-90

Arnim, Achim von 1781-1831 . . . . . . DLB-90

Arnim, Bettina von 1785-1859 . . . . . . DLB-90

Arno Press DLB-46

Arnold, Edwin 1832-1904 . . . . DLB-35

Arnold, Edwin L. 1857-1935 . . . . . . DLB-178

Arnold, Matthew 1822-1888 . . . . DLB-32, 57

Arnold, Thomas 1795-1842 . . . . DLB-55

Arnold, Edward [publishing house] DLB-112

Arnow, Harriette Simpson 1908-1986 . . . . DLB-6

Arp, Bill (see Smith, Charles Henry)

Arpino, Giovanni 1927-1987 . . . . . . DLB-177

Arreola, Juan José 1918- DLB-113

Arrian circa 89-circa 155 . . . . DLB-176

Arrowsmith, J. W. [publishing house] DLB-106

Arthur, Timothy Shay 1809-1885 . . . . DLB-3, 42, 79; DS-13

The Arthurian Tradition and Its European Context DLB-138

Artmann, H. C. 1921- DLB-85

Arvin, Newton 1900-1963 . . . . DLB-103

As I See It, by Carolyn Cassady DLB-16

Asch, Nathan 1902-1964 . . . . DLB-4, 28

Ash, John 1948- DLB-40

Ashbery, John 1927- DLB-5, 165; Y-81

Ashendene Press DLB-112

Asher, Sandy 1942- Y-83

Ashton, Winifred (see Dane, Clemence)

Asimov, Isaac 1920-1992 . . . . . . DLB-8; Y-92

Askew, Anne circa 1521-1546 . . . . . DLB-136

Asselin, Olivar 1874-1937 . . . . DLB-92

Asturias, Miguel Angel 1899-1974 . . . . DLB-113

Atheneum Publishers DLB-46

Atherton, Gertrude 1857-1948 . . . . DLB-9, 78

Athlone Press DLB-112

Atkins, Josiah circa 1755-1781 . . . . . DLB-31

Atkins, Russell 1926- DLB-41

The Atlantic Monthly Press DLB-46

Attaway, William 1911-1986 . . . . . . DLB-76

Atwood, Margaret 1939- DLB-53

Aubert, Alvin 1930- DLB-41

Aubert de Gaspé, Phillipe-Ignace-François 1814-1841 . . . . DLB-99

Aubert de Gaspé, Phillipe-Joseph 1786-1871 . . . . DLB-99

Aubin, Napoléon 1812-1890 . . . . . . DLB-99

Aubin, Penelope 1685-circa 1731 . . . . . DLB-39

Aubrey-Fletcher, Henry Lancelot (see Wade, Henry)

Auchincloss, Louis 1917- DLB-2; Y-80

Auden, W. H. 1907-1973 . . . . . . DLB-10, 20

Audio Art in America: A Personal Memoir Y-85

Auerbach, Berthold 1812-1882 . . . . . DLB-133

Auernheimer, Raoul 1876-1948 . . . . . DLB-81

Augustine 354-430 . . . . DLB-115

Austen, Jane 1775-1817 . . . . DLB-116

Austin, Alfred 1835-1913 . . . . DLB-35

Austin, Mary 1868-1934 . . . . DLB-9, 78

Austin, William 1778-1841 . . . . DLB-74

Author-Printers, 1476–1599 . . . . . . DLB-167

The Author's Apology for His Book (1684), by John Bunyan DLB-39

An Author's Response, by Ronald Sukenick Y-82

Authors and Newspapers Association DLB-46

Authors' Publishing Company DLB-49

Avalon Books DLB-46

Avancini, Nicolaus 1611-1686 . . . . . DLB-164

Avendaño, Fausto 1941- DLB-82

Averroës 1126-1198 . . . . DLB-115

Avery, Gillian 1926- DLB-161

Avicenna 980-1037 . . . . DLB-115

Avison, Margaret 1918- DLB-53

Avon Books DLB-46

Awdry, Wilbert Vere 1911- DLB-160

Awoonor, Kofi 1935- DLB-117

Ayckbourn, Alan 1939- DLB-13

Aymé, Marcel 1902-1967 . . . . DLB-72

Aytoun, Sir Robert 1570-1638 . . . . . DLB-121

Aytoun, William Edmondstoune 1813-1865 . . . . DLB-32, 159

B

B. V. (see Thomson, James)

Babbitt, Irving 1865-1933 . . . . DLB-63

Babbitt, Natalie 1932- DLB-52

Babcock, John [publishing house] DLB-49

Babrius circa 150-200 . . . . DLB-176

Baca, Jimmy Santiago 1952- DLB-122

Bache, Benjamin Franklin 1769-1798 . . . . DLB-43

Bachmann, Ingeborg 1926-1973 . . . . . DLB-85

Bacon, Delia 1811-1859 . . . . DLB-1

Bacon, Francis 1561-1626 . . . . DLB-151

Bacon, Roger circa 1214/1220-1292 . . . . DLB-115

Bacon, Sir Nicholas circa 1510-1579 . . . . DLB-132

Bacon, Thomas circa 1700-1768 . . . . . DLB-31

Badger, Richard G., and Company DLB-49

Bage, Robert 1728-1801 . . . . DLB-39

Bagehot, Walter 1826-1877. . . . . DLB-55

Bagley, Desmond 1923-1983. . . . . . . DLB-87

Bagnold, Enid 1889-1981. . . . . . DLB-13, 160

Bagryana, Elisaveta 1893-1991. . . . . DLB-147

Bahr, Hermann 1863-1934. . . . . DLB-81, 118

Bailey, Alfred Goldsworthy 1905- DLB-68

Bailey, Francis [publishing house]. DLB-49

Bailey, H. C. 1878-1961. . . . . DLB-77

Bailey, Jacob 1731-1808. . . . . DLB-99

Bailey, Paul 1937- DLB-14

Bailey, Philip James 1816-1902. . . . . . DLB-32

Baillargeon, Pierre 1916-1967. . . . . . . DLB-88

Baillie, Hugh 1890-1966. . . . . DLB-29

Baillie, Joanna 1762-1851. . . . . DLB-93

Bailyn, Bernard 1922- DLB-17

Bainbridge, Beryl 1933- DLB-14

Baird, Irene 1901-1981. . . . . DLB-68

Baker, Augustine 1575-1641. . . . . . DLB-151

Baker, Carlos 1909-1987. . . . . DLB-103

Baker, David 1954- DLB-120

Baker, Herschel C. 1914-1990. . . . . DLB-111

Baker, Houston A., Jr. 1943- DLB-67

Baker, Samuel White 1821-1893 . . . . DLB-166

Baker, Walter H., Company ("Baker's Plays"). DLB-49

The Baker and Taylor Company DLB-49

Balaban, John 1943- DLB-120

Bald, Wambly 1902- DLB-4

Balde, Jacob 1604-1668. . . . . DLB-164

Balderston, John 1889-1954. . . . . . . DLB-26

Baldwin, James 1924-1987. . . . . . . DLB-2, 7, 33; Y-87

Baldwin, Joseph Glover 1815-1864. . . . . DLB-3, 11

Baldwin, Richard and Anne [publishing house]. DLB-170

Baldwin, William circa 1515-1563. . . . . DLB-132

Bale, John 1495-1563. . . . . DLB-132

Balestrini, Nanni 1935- DLB-128

Ballantine Books. DLB-46

Ballantyne, R. M. 1825-1894. . . . . . DLB-163

Ballard, J. G. 1930- DLB-14

Ballerini, Luigi 1940- DLB-128

Ballou, Maturin Murray 1820-1895. . . . . DLB-79

Ballou, Robert O. [publishing house]. DLB-46

Balzac, Honoré de 1799-1855. . . . . DLB-119

Bambara, Toni Cade 1939- DLB-38

Bancroft, A. L., and Company DLB-49

Bancroft, George 1800-1891. . . . . DLB-1, 30, 59

Bancroft, Hubert Howe 1832-1918. . . . . DLB-47, 140

Bangs, John Kendrick 1862-1922. . . . . DLB-11, 79

Banim, John 1798-1842. . . . . DLB-116, 158, 159

Banim, Michael 1796-1874. . . . . DLB-158, 159

Banks, John circa 1653-1706. . . . . . . DLB-80

Banks, Russell 1940- DLB-130

Bannerman, Helen 1862-1946. . . . . DLB-141

Bantam Books. DLB-46

Banti, Anna 1895-1985. . . . . DLB-177

Banville, John 1945- DLB-14

Baraka, Amiri 1934- DLB-5, 7, 16, 38; DS-8

Barbauld, Anna Laetitia 1743-1825. . . . . . DLB-107, 109, 142, 158

Barbeau, Marius 1883-1969. . . . . . . DLB-92

Barber, John Warner 1798-1885. . . . . DLB-30

Bàrberi Squarotti, Giorgio 1929- DLB-128

Barbey d'Aurevilly, Jules-Amédée 1808-1889. . . . . DLB-119

Barbour, John circa 1316-1395. . . . . DLB-146

Barbour, Ralph Henry 1870-1944. . . . . DLB-22

Barbusse, Henri 1873-1935. . . . . . . DLB-65

Barclay, Alexander circa 1475-1552. . . . . DLB-132

Barclay, E. E., and Company DLB-49

Bardeen, C. W. [publishing house]. DLB-49

Barham, Richard Harris 1788-1845. . . . . DLB-159

Baring, Maurice 1874-1945. . . . . . . DLB-34

Baring-Gould, Sabine 1834-1924. . . . DLB-156

Barker, A. L. 1918- DLB-14, 139

Barker, George 1913-1991. . . . . DLB-20

Barker, Harley Granville 1877-1946. . . . . DLB-10

Barker, Howard 1946- DLB-13

Barker, James Nelson 1784-1858. . . . . DLB-37

Barker, Jane 1652-1727. . . . . . . DLB-39, 131

Barker, Lady Mary Anne 1831-1911. . . . . DLB-166

Barker, William circa 1520-after 1576. . . . . . . DLB-132

Barker, Arthur, Limited. DLB-112

Barkov, Ivan Semenovich 1732-1768. . . . . DLB-150

Barks, Coleman 1937- DLB-5

Barlach, Ernst 1870-1938. . . . . . DLB-56, 118

Barlow, Joel 1754-1812. . . . . DLB-37

Barnard, John 1681-1770. . . . . DLB-24

Barne, Kitty (Mary Catherine Barne) 1883-1957. . . . . DLB-160

Barnes, Barnabe 1571-1609. . . . . . DLB-132

Barnes, Djuna 1892-1982. . . . . . DLB-4, 9, 45

Barnes, Jim 1933- DLB-175

Barnes, Julian 1946- Y-93

Barnes, Margaret Ayer 1886-1967. . . . DLB-9

Barnes, Peter 1931- DLB-13

Barnes, William 1801-1886. . . . . DLB-32

Barnes, A. S., and Company. DLB-49

Barnes and Noble Books. DLB-46

Barnet, Miguel 1940- DLB-145

Barney, Natalie 1876-1972. . . . . DLB-4

Barnfield, Richard 1574-1627. . . . . . DLB-172

Baron, Richard W., Publishing Company DLB-46

Barr, Robert 1850-1912. . . . . DLB-70, 92

Barral, Carlos 1928-1989. . . . . DLB-134

Barrax, Gerald William 1933- DLB-41, 120

Barrès, Maurice 1862-1923. . . . . . . DLB-123

Barrett, Eaton Stannard 1786-1820. . . . . DLB-116

Barrie, J. M. 1860-1937. . . . DLB-10, 141, 156

Barrie and Jenkins. DLB-112

Barrio, Raymond 1921- DLB-82

Barrios, Gregg 1945- DLB-122

Barry, Philip 1896-1949. . . . . DLB-7

Barry, Robertine (see Françoise)

Barse and Hopkins DLB-46

Barstow, Stan 1928- DLB-14, 139

Barth, John 1930- DLB-2

Barthelme, Donald 1931-1989. . . . . DLB-2; Y-80, 89

Barthelme, Frederick 1943- Y-85

Bartholomew, Frank 1898-1985. . . . . DLB-127

Bartlett, John 1820-1905. . . . . DLB-1

Bartol, Cyrus Augustus 1813-1900. . . . DLB-1

Barton, Bernard 1784-1849. . . . . DLB-96

Barton, Thomas Pennant 1803-1869. . . . . DLB-140

Bartram, John 1699-1777. . . . . DLB-31

Bartram, William 1739-1823. . . . . . . DLB-37

Basic Books. DLB-46

Basille, Theodore (see Becon, Thomas)

Bass, T. J. 1932- Y-81

Bassani, Giorgio 1916- DLB-128, 177

Basse, William circa 1583-1653. . . . . DLB-121

Bassett, John Spencer 1867-1928. . . . . DLB-17

Bassler, Thomas Joseph (see Bass, T. J.)

Bate, Walter Jackson 1918- DLB-67, 103
Bateman, Christopher [publishing house] DLB-170
Bateman, Stephen circa 1510-1584 ..... DLB-136
Bates, H. E. 1905-1974 ..... DLB-162
Bates, Katharine Lee 1859-1929 ..... DLB-71
Batsford, B. T. [publishing house] DLB-106
Battiscombe, Georgina 1905- DLB-155
The Battle of Maldon circa 1000 ..... DLB-146
Bauer, Bruno 1809-1882 ..... DLB-133
Bauer, Wolfgang 1941- DLB-124
Baum, L. Frank 1856-1919 ..... DLB-22
Baum, Vicki 1888-1960 ..... DLB-85
Baumbach, Jonathan 1933- Y-80
Bausch, Richard 1945- DLB-130
Bawden, Nina 1925- DLB-14, 161
Bax, Clifford 1886-1962 ..... DLB-10, 100
Baxter, Charles 1947- DLB-130
Bayer, Eleanor (see Perry, Eleanor)
Bayer, Konrad 1932-1964 ..... DLB-85
Baynes, Pauline 1922- DLB-160
Bazin, Hervé 1911- DLB-83
Beach, Sylvia 1887-1962 ..... DLB-4
Beacon Press DLB-49
Beadle and Adams DLB-49
Beagle, Peter S. 1939- Y-80
Beal, M. F. 1937- Y-81
Beale, Howard K. 1899-1959 ..... DLB-17
Beard, Charles A. 1874-1948 ..... DLB-17
A Beat Chronology: The First Twenty-five Years, 1944-1969 ..... DLB-16
Beattie, Ann 1947- Y-82
Beattie, James 1735-1803 ..... DLB-109
Beauchemin, Nérée 1850-1931 ..... DLB-92
Beauchemin, Yves 1941- DLB-60
Beaugrand, Honoré 1848-1906 ..... DLB-99
Beaulieu, Victor-Lévy 1945- DLB-53
Beaumont, Francis circa 1584-1616 and Fletcher, John 1579-1625 ..... DLB-58
Beaumont, Sir John 1583?-1627 ..... DLB-121
Beaumont, Joseph 1616–1699 ..... DLB-126
Beauvoir, Simone de 1908-1986 ..... DLB-72; Y-86
Becher, Ulrich 1910- DLB-69
Becker, Carl 1873-1945 ..... DLB-17
Becker, Jurek 1937- DLB-75
Becker, Jurgen 1932- DLB-75
Beckett, Samuel 1906-1989 ..... DLB-13, 15; Y-90
Beckford, William 1760-1844 ..... DLB-39

Beckham, Barry 1944- DLB-33
Becon, Thomas circa 1512-1567 ..... DLB-136
Bećković, Matija 1939- DLB-181
Beddoes, Thomas 1760-1808 ..... DLB-158
Beddoes, Thomas Lovell 1803-1849 ..... DLB-96
Bede circa 673-735 ..... DLB-146
Beecher, Catharine Esther 1800-1878 ..... DLB-1
Beecher, Henry Ward 1813-1887 ..... DLB-3, 43
Beer, George L. 1872-1920 ..... DLB-47
Beer, Johann 1655-1700 ..... DLB-168
Beer, Patricia 1919- DLB-40
Beerbohm, Max 1872-1956 ..... DLB-34, 100
Beer-Hofmann, Richard 1866-1945 ..... DLB-81
Beers, Henry A. 1847-1926 ..... DLB-71
Beeton, S. O. [publishing house] DLB-106
Bégon, Elisabeth 1696-1755 ..... DLB-99
Behan, Brendan 1923-1964 ..... DLB-13
Behn, Aphra 1640?-1689 ..... DLB-39, 80, 131
Behn, Harry 1898-1973 ..... DLB-61
Behrman, S. N. 1893-1973 ..... DLB-7, 44
Belaney, Archibald Stansfeld (see Grey Owl)
Belasco, David 1853-1931 ..... DLB-7
Belford, Clarke and Company DLB-49
Belitt, Ben 1911- DLB-5
Belknap, Jeremy 1744-1798 ..... DLB-30, 37
Bell, Clive 1881-1964 ..... DS-10
Bell, Gertrude Margaret Lowthian 1868-1926 ..... DLB-174
Bell, James Madison 1826-1902 ..... DLB-50
Bell, Marvin 1937- DLB-5
Bell, Millicent 1919- DLB-111
Bell, Quentin 1910- DLB-155
Bell, Vanessa 1879-1961 ..... DS-10
Bell, George, and Sons DLB-106
Bell, Robert [publishing house] DLB-49
Bellamy, Edward 1850-1898 ..... DLB-12
Bellamy, John [publishing house] DLB-170
Bellamy, Joseph 1719-1790 ..... DLB-31
Bellezza, Dario 1944- DLB-128
La Belle Assemblée 1806-1837 ..... DLB-110
Belloc, Hilaire 1870-1953 ..... DLB-19, 100, 141, 174
Bellow, Saul 1915- DLB-2, 28; Y-82; DS-3
Belmont Productions DLB-46
Bemelmans, Ludwig 1898-1962 ..... DLB-22
Bemis, Samuel Flagg 1891-1973 ..... DLB-17

Bemrose, William [publishing house] DLB-106
Benchley, Robert 1889-1945 ..... DLB-11
Benedetti, Mario 1920- DLB-113
Benedictus, David 1938- DLB-14
Benedikt, Michael 1935- DLB-5
Benét, Stephen Vincent 1898-1943 ..... DLB-4, 48, 102
Benét, William Rose 1886-1950 ..... DLB-45
Benford, Gregory 1941- Y-82
Benjamin, Park 1809-1864 ..... DLB-3, 59, 73
Benlowes, Edward 1602-1676 ..... DLB-126
Benn, Gottfried 1886-1956 ..... DLB-56
Benn Brothers Limited DLB-106
Bennett, Arnold 1867-1931 ..... DLB-10, 34, 98, 135
Bennett, Charles 1899- DLB-44
Bennett, Gwendolyn 1902- DLB-51
Bennett, Hal 1930- DLB-33
Bennett, James Gordon 1795-1872 ..... DLB-43
Bennett, James Gordon, Jr. 1841-1918 ..... DLB-23
Bennett, John 1865-1956 ..... DLB-42
Bennett, Louise 1919- DLB-117
Benoit, Jacques 1941- DLB-60
Benson, A. C. 1862-1925 ..... DLB-98
Benson, E. F. 1867-1940 ..... DLB-135, 153
Benson, Jackson J. 1930- DLB-111
Benson, Robert Hugh 1871-1914 ..... DLB-153
Benson, Stella 1892-1933 ..... DLB-36, 162
Bent, James Theodore 1852-1897 ..... DLB-174
Bent, Mabel Virginia Anna ?-? DLB-174
Bentham, Jeremy 1748-1832 ..... DLB-107, 158
Bentley, E. C. 1875-1956 ..... DLB-70
Bentley, Richard [publishing house] DLB-106
Benton, Robert 1932- and Newman, David 1937- DLB-44
Benziger Brothers DLB-49
Beowulf circa 900-1000 or 790-825 ..... DLB-146
Beresford, Anne 1929- DLB-40
Beresford, John Davys 1873-1947 ..... DLB-162; 178
Beresford-Howe, Constance 1922- DLB-88
Berford, R. G., Company DLB-49
Berg, Stephen 1934- DLB-5
Bergengruen, Werner 1892-1964 ..... DLB-56
Berger, John 1926- DLB-14
Berger, Meyer 1898-1959 ..... DLB-29

Berger, Thomas 1924- DLB-2; Y-80
Berkeley, Anthony 1893-1971 ...... DLB-77
Berkeley, George 1685-1753 .... DLB-31, 101
The Berkley Publishing
   Corporation DLB-46
Berlin, Lucia 1936- DLB-130
Bernal, Vicente J. 1888-1915 .... DLB-82
Bernanos, Georges 1888-1948 ...... DLB-72
Bernard, Harry 1898-1979 .... DLB-92
Bernard, John 1756-1828 .... DLB-37
Bernard of Chartres
   circa 1060-1124? DLB-115
Bernari, Carlo 1909-1992 .... DLB-177
Bernhard, Thomas
   1931-1989 .... DLB-85, 124
Bernstein, Charles 1950- DLB-169
Berriault, Gina 1926- DLB-130
Berrigan, Daniel 1921- DLB-5
Berrigan, Ted 1934-1983 ...... DLB-5, 169
Berry, Wendell 1934- DLB-5, 6
Berryman, John 1914-1972 .... DLB-48
Bersianik, Louky 1930- DLB-60
Berthelet, Thomas
   [publishing house] DLB-170
Berto, Giuseppe 1914-1978 ..... DLB-177
Bertolucci, Attilio 1911- DLB-128
Berton, Pierre 1920- DLB-68
Besant, Sir Walter 1836-1901 ..... DLB-135
Bessette, Gerard 1920- DLB-53
Bessie, Alvah 1904-1985 .... DLB-26
Bester, Alfred 1913-1987 .... DLB-8
The Bestseller Lists: An Assessment Y-84
Betham-Edwards, Matilda Barbara (see Edwards,
   Matilda Barbara Betham-)
Betjeman, John 1906-1984 ..... DLB-20; Y-84
Betocchi, Carlo 1899-1986 .... DLB-128
Bettarini, Mariella 1942- DLB-128
Betts, Doris 1932- Y-82
Beveridge, Albert J. 1862-1927 ..... DLB-17
Beverley, Robert
   circa 1673-1722 .... DLB-24, 30
Beyle, Marie-Henri (see Stendhal)
Bianco, Margery Williams
   1881-1944 .... DLB-160
Bibaud, Adèle 1854-1941 .... DLB-92
Bibaud, Michel 1782-1857 .... DLB-99
Bibliographical and Textual Scholarship
   Since World War II Y-89
The Bicentennial of James Fenimore
   Cooper: An International
   Celebration Y-89
Bichsel, Peter 1935- DLB-75
Bickerstaff, Isaac John
   1733-circa 1808 .... DLB-89

Biddle, Drexel [publishing house] DLB-49
Bidermann, Jacob
   1577 or 1578-1639 .... DLB-164
Bidwell, Walter Hilliard
   1798-1881 .... DLB-79
Bienek, Horst 1930- DLB-75
Bierbaum, Otto Julius 1865-1910 ..... DLB-66
Bierce, Ambrose
   1842-1914? DLB-11, 12, 23, 71, 74
Bigelow, William F. 1879-1966 ..... DLB-91
Biggle, Lloyd, Jr. 1923- DLB-8
Bigiaretti, Libero 1905-1993 ..... DLB-177
Biglow, Hosea (see Lowell, James Russell)
Bigongiari, Piero 1914- DLB-128
Billinger, Richard 1890-1965 ..... DLB-124
Billings, John Shaw 1898-1975 ..... DLB-137
Billings, Josh (see Shaw, Henry Wheeler)
Binding, Rudolf G. 1867-1938 ..... DLB-66
Bingham, Caleb 1757-1817 .... DLB-42
Bingham, George Barry
   1906-1988 .... DLB-127
Bingley, William
   [publishing house] DLB-154
Binyon, Laurence 1869-1943 ...... DLB-19
Biographia Brittanica DLB-142
Biographical Documents I Y-84
Biographical Documents II Y-85
Bioren, John [publishing house] DLB-49
Bioy Casares, Adolfo 1914- DLB-113
Bird, Isabella Lucy 1831-1904 ..... DLB-166
Bird, William 1888-1963 .... DLB-4
Birken, Sigmund von 1626-1681 .... DLB-164
Birney, Earle 1904- DLB-88
Birrell, Augustine 1850-1933 ...... DLB-98
Bisher, Furman 1918- DLB-171
Bishop, Elizabeth 1911-1979 ..... DLB-5, 169
Bishop, John Peale 1892-1944 ... DLB-4, 9, 45
Bismarck, Otto von 1815-1898 ..... DLB-129
Bisset, Robert 1759-1805 .... DLB-142
Bissett, Bill 1939- DLB-53
Bitzius, Albert (see Gotthelf, Jeremias)
Black, David (D. M.) 1941- DLB-40
Black, Winifred 1863-1936 .... DLB-25
Black, Walter J.
   [publishing house] DLB-46
The Black Aesthetic: Background DS-8
The Black Arts Movement, by
   Larry Neal DLB-38
Black Theaters and Theater Organizations in
   America, 1961-1982:
   A Research List DLB-38
Black Theatre: A Forum
   [excerpts] DLB-38

Blackamore, Arthur 1679-? DLB-24, 39
Blackburn, Alexander L. 1929- Y-85
Blackburn, Paul 1926-1971 .... DLB-16; Y-81
Blackburn, Thomas 1916-1977 ...... DLB-27
Blackmore, R. D. 1825-1900 .... DLB-18
Blackmore, Sir Richard
   1654-1729 .... DLB-131
Blackmur, R. P. 1904-1965 .... DLB-63
Blackwell, Basil, Publisher DLB-106
Blackwood, Algernon Henry
   1869-1951 .... DLB-153, 156, 178
Blackwood, Caroline 1931- DLB-14
Blackwood, William, and
   Sons, Ltd. DLB-154
Blackwood's Edinburgh Magazine
   1817-1980 .... DLB-110
Blair, Eric Arthur (see Orwell, George)
Blair, Francis Preston 1791-1876 ..... DLB-43
Blair, James circa 1655-1743 .... DLB-24
Blair, John Durburrow 1759-1823 .... DLB-37
Blais, Marie-Claire 1939- DLB-53
Blaise, Clark 1940- DLB-53
Blake, Nicholas 1904-1972 .... DLB-77
   (see Day Lewis, C.)
Blake, William
   1757-1827 .... DLB-93, 154, 163
The Blakiston Company DLB-49
Blanchot, Maurice 1907- DLB-72
Blanckenburg, Christian Friedrich von
   1744-1796 .... DLB-94
Blaser, Robin 1925- DLB-165
Bledsoe, Albert Taylor
   1809-1877 .... DLB-3, 79
Blelock and Company DLB-49
Blennerhassett, Margaret Agnew
   1773-1842 .... DLB-99
Bles, Geoffrey
   [publishing house] DLB-112
Blessington, Marguerite, Countess of
   1789-1849 .... DLB-166
The Blickling Homilies
   circa 971 .... DLB-146
Blish, James 1921-1975 .... DLB-8
Bliss, E., and E. White
   [publishing house] DLB-49
Bliven, Bruce 1889-1977 .... DLB-137
Bloch, Robert 1917-1994 .... DLB-44
Block, Rudolph (see Lessing, Bruno)
Blondal, Patricia 1926-1959 ...... DLB-88
Bloom, Harold 1930- DLB-67
Bloomer, Amelia 1818-1894 .... DLB-79
Bloomfield, Robert 1766-1823 ..... DLB-93
Bloomsbury Group DS-10
Blotner, Joseph 1923- DLB-111

Bloy, Léon 1846-1917 . . . . DLB-123	Bolton, Herbert E. 1870-1953 . . . . . DLB-17	Boswell, James 1740-1795 . . . . . DLB-104, 142
Blume, Judy 1938- DLB-52	Bonaventura DLB-90	Botev, Khristo 1847-1876 . . . . DLB-147
Blunck, Hans Friedrich 1888-1961 . . . . DLB-66	Bonaventure circa 1217-1274 . . . . . . DLB-115	Bote, Hermann circa 1460-circa 1520 . . . . DLB-179
Blunden, Edmund 1896-1974 . . . . DLB-20, 100, 155	Bonaviri, Giuseppe 1924- DLB-177	Botta, Anne C. Lynch 1815-1891 . . . . . DLB-3
Blunt, Lady Anne Isabella Noel 1837-1917 . . . . DLB-174	Bond, Edward 1934- DLB-13	Bottomley, Gordon 1874-1948 . . . . . . DLB-10
Blunt, Wilfrid Scawen 1840-1922 . . . . DLB-19, 174	Bond, Michael 1926- DLB-161	Bottoms, David 1949- DLB-120; Y-83
Bly, Nellie (see Cochrane, Elizabeth)	Bonnin, Gertrude Simmons (see Zitkala-Ša)	Bottrall, Ronald 1906- DLB-20
Bly, Robert 1926- DLB-5	Boni, Albert and Charles [publishing house] DLB-46	Boucher, Anthony 1911-1968 . . . . DLB-8
Blyton, Enid 1897-1968 . . . . DLB-160	Boni and Liveright DLB-46	Boucher, Jonathan 1738-1804 . . . . . . DLB-31
Boaden, James 1762-1839 . . . . DLB-89	Robert Bonner's Sons DLB-49	Boucher de Boucherville, George 1814-1894 . . . . DLB-99
Boas, Frederick S. 1862-1957 . . . . . DLB-149	Bonsanti, Alessandro 1904-1984 . . . . . DLB-177	Boudreau, Daniel (see Coste, Donat)
The Bobbs-Merrill Archive at the Lilly Library, Indiana University Y-90	Bontemps, Arna 1902-1973 . . . . . DLB-48, 51	Bourassa, Napoléon 1827-1916 . . . . . . DLB-99
The Bobbs-Merrill Company DLB-46	The Book Arts Press at the University of Virginia Y-96	Bourget, Paul 1852-1935 . . . . DLB-123
Bobrov, Semen Sergeevich 1763?-1810 . . . . DLB-150	The Book League of America DLB-46	Bourinot, John George 1837-1902 . . . . DLB-99
Bobrowski, Johannes 1917-1965 . . . . . DLB-75	Book Reviewing in America: I Y-87	Bourjaily, Vance 1922- DLB-2, 143
Bodenheim, Maxwell 1892-1954 . . . DLB-9, 45	Book Reviewing in America: II Y-88	Bourne, Edward Gaylord 1860-1908 . . . . DLB-47
Bodenstedt, Friedrich von 1819-1892 . . . . DLB-129	Book Reviewing in America: III Y-89	Bourne, Randolph 1886-1918 . . . . DLB-63
Bodini, Vittorio 1914-1970 . . . . DLB-128	Book Reviewing in America: IV Y-90	Bousoño, Carlos 1923- DLB-108
Bodkin, M. McDonnell 1850-1933 . . . . DLB-70	Book Reviewing in America: V Y-91	Bousquet, Joë 1897-1950 . . . . DLB-72
Bodley Head DLB-112	Book Reviewing in America: VI Y-92	Bova, Ben 1932- Y-81
Bodmer, Johann Jakob 1698-1783 . . . . DLB-97	Book Reviewing in America: VII Y-93	Bovard, Oliver K. 1872-1945 . . . . . . DLB-25
Bodmershof, Imma von 1895-1982 . . . DLB-85	Book Reviewing in America: VIII Y-94	Bove, Emmanuel 1898-1945 . . . . DLB-72
Bodsworth, Fred 1918- DLB-68	Book Reviewing in America and the Literary Scene Y-95	Bowen, Elizabeth 1899-1973 . . . . DLB-15, 162
Boehm, Sydney 1908- DLB-44	Book Reviewing and the Literary Scene Y-96	Bowen, Francis 1811-1890 . . . . DLB-1, 59
Boer, Charles 1939- DLB-5	Book Supply Company DLB-49	Bowen, John 1924- DLB-13
Boethius circa 480-circa 524 . . . . . . DLB-115	The Book Trade History Group Y-93	Bowen, Marjorie 1886-1952 . . . . DLB-153
Boethius of Dacia circa 1240-? DLB-115	The Booker Prize Y-96	Bowen-Merrill Company DLB-49
Bogan, Louise 1897-1970 . . . . . . DLB-45, 169	The Booker Prize Address by Anthony Thwaite, Chairman of the Booker Prize Judges Comments from Former Booker Prize Winners Y-86	Bowering, George 1935- DLB-53
Bogarde, Dirk 1921- DLB-14		Bowers, Claude G. 1878-1958 . . . . . . DLB-17
Bogdanovich, Ippolit Fedorovich circa 1743-1803 . . . . DLB-150		Bowers, Edgar 1924- DLB-5
Bogue, David [publishing house] DLB-106	Boorde, Andrew circa 1490-1549 . . . . DLB-136	Bowers, Fredson Thayer 1905-1991 . . . . DLB-140; Y-91
Böhme, Jakob 1575-1624 . . . . DLB-164	Boorstin, Daniel J. 1914- DLB-17	Bowles, Paul 1910- DLB-5, 6
Bohn, H. G. [publishing house] DLB-106	Booth, Mary L. 1831-1889 . . . . DLB-79	Bowles, Samuel III 1826-1878 . . . . . . DLB-43
Bohse, August 1661-1742 . . . . DLB-168	Booth, Philip 1925- Y-82	Bowles, William Lisles 1762-1850 . . . . DLB-93
Boie, Heinrich Christian 1744-1806 . . . . DLB-94	Booth, Wayne C. 1921- DLB-67	Bowman, Louise Morey 1882-1944 . . . . DLB-68
Bok, Edward W. 1863-1930 . . . . DLB-91	Borchardt, Rudolf 1877-1945 . . . . . . DLB-66	Boyd, James 1888-1944 . . . . DLB-9
Boland, Eavan 1944- DLB-40	Borchert, Wolfgang 1921-1947 . . . . DLB-69, 124	Boyd, John 1919- DLB-8
Bolingbroke, Henry St. John, Viscount 1678-1751 . . . . DLB-101	Borel, Pétrus 1809-1859 . . . . DLB-119	Boyd, Thomas 1898-1935 . . . . DLB-9
Böll, Heinrich 1917-1985 . . . . . . Y-85, DLB-69	Borges, Jorge Luis 1899-1986 . . . . DLB-113; Y-86	Boyesen, Hjalmar Hjorth 1848-1895 . . . . DLB-12, 71; DS-13
Bolling, Robert 1738-1775 . . . . DLB-31	Börne, Ludwig 1786-1837 . . . . DLB-90	Boyle, Kay 1902-1992 . . . . . . DLB-4, 9, 48, 86; Y-93
Bolotov, Andrei Timofeevich 1738-1833 . . . . DLB-150	Borrow, George 1803-1881 . . . . DLB-21, 55, 166	Boyle, Roger, Earl of Orrery 1621-1679 . . . . DLB-80
Bolt, Carol 1941- DLB-60	Bosch, Juan 1909- DLB-145	Boyle, T. Coraghessan 1948- Y-86
Bolt, Robert 1924- DLB-13	Bosco, Henri 1888-1976 . . . . DLB-72	Božić, Mirko 1919- DLB-181
	Bosco, Monique 1927- DLB-53	Brackenbury, Alison 1953- DLB-40
	Boston, Lucy M. 1892-1990 . . . . DLB-161	

Brackenridge, Hugh Henry
   1748-1816. . . . . DLB-11, 37
Brackett, Charles 1892-1969 . . . . DLB-26
Brackett, Leigh 1915-1978. . . . . . . DLB-8, 26
Bradburn, John
   [publishing house]. DLB-49
Bradbury, Malcolm 1932- DLB-14
Bradbury, Ray 1920- DLB-2, 8
Bradbury and Evans. DLB-106
Braddon, Mary Elizabeth
   1835-1915. . . . . DLB-18, 70, 156
Bradford, Andrew 1686-1742 . . . . DLB-43, 73
Bradford, Gamaliel 1863-1932 . . . . . . DLB-17
Bradford, John 1749-1830. . . . . DLB-43
Bradford, Roark 1896-1948. . . . . DLB-86
Bradford, William 1590-1657 . . . . DLB-24, 30
Bradford, William III
   1719-1791. . . . . DLB-43, 73
Bradlaugh, Charles 1833-1891 . . . . . . DLB-57
Bradley, David 1950- DLB-33
Bradley, Marion Zimmer 1930- DLB-8
Bradley, William Aspenwall
   1878-1939. . . . . DLB-4
Bradley, Ira, and Company DLB-49
Bradley, J. W., and Company. DLB-49
Bradstreet, Anne
   1612 or 1613-1672 . . . . DLB-24
Bradwardine, Thomas circa
   1295-1349 . . . . DLB-115
Brady, Frank 1924-1986. . . . . DLB-111
Brady, Frederic A.
   [publishing house]. DLB-49
Bragg, Melvyn 1939- DLB-14
Brainard, Charles H.
   [publishing house]. DLB-49
Braine, John 1922-1986 . . . . . DLB-15; Y-86
Braithwait, Richard 1588-1673 . . . . . DLB-151
Braithwaite, William Stanley
   1878-1962. . . . . DLB-50, 54
Braker, Ulrich 1735-1798. . . . . DLB-94
Bramah, Ernest 1868-1942 . . . . DLB-70
Branagan, Thomas 1774-1843 . . . . . . DLB-37
Branch, William Blackwell
   1927- DLB-76
Branden Press. DLB-46
Brant, Sebastian 1457-1521 . . . . DLB-179
Brassey, Lady Annie (Allnutt)
   1839-1887 . . . . DLB-166
Brathwaite, Edward Kamau
   1930- DLB-125
Brault, Jacques 1933- DLB-53
Braun, Volker 1939- DLB-75
Brautigan, Richard
   1935-1984 . . . . DLB-2, 5; Y-80, 84
Braxton, Joanne M. 1950- DLB-41

Bray, Anne Eliza 1790-1883. . . . . . . DLB-116
Bray, Thomas 1656-1730. . . . . DLB-24
Braziller, George
   [publishing house] DLB-46
The Bread Loaf Writers'
   Conference 1983. . . . . Y-84
The Break-Up of the Novel (1922),
   by John Middleton Murry. DLB-36
Breasted, James Henry 1865-1935 . . . . DLB-47
Brecht, Bertolt 1898-1956. . . . . . DLB-56, 124
Bredel, Willi 1901-1964. . . . . DLB-56
Breitinger, Johann Jakob
   1701-1776 . . . . DLB-97
Bremser, Bonnie 1939- DLB-16
Bremser, Ray 1934- DLB-16
Brentano, Bernard von
   1901-1964 . . . . DLB-56
Brentano, Clemens 1778-1842 . . . . . DLB-90
Brentano's DLB-49
Brenton, Howard 1942- DLB-13
Breton, André 1896-1966. . . . . DLB-65
Breton, Nicholas
   circa 1555-circa 1626 . . . . DLB-136
The Breton Lays
   1300-early fifteenth century DLB-146
Brewer, Warren and Putnam DLB-46
Brewster, Elizabeth 1922- DLB-60
Bridgers, Sue Ellen 1942- DLB-52
Bridges, Robert 1844-1930 . . . . . DLB-19, 98
Bridie, James 1888-1951 . . . . DLB-10
Briggs, Charles Frederick
   1804-1877. . . . . DLB-3
Brighouse, Harold 1882-1958. . . . . . . DLB-10
Bright, Mary Chavelita Dunne
   (see Egerton, George)
Brimmer, B. J., Company DLB-46
Brines, Francisco 1932- DLB-134
Brinley, George, Jr. 1817-1875 . . . . . DLB-140
Brinnin, John Malcolm 1916- DLB-48
Brisbane, Albert 1809-1890. . . . . DLB-3
Brisbane, Arthur 1864-1936. . . . . . . DLB-25
British Academy DLB-112
The British Library and the Regular
   Readers' Group Y-91
The British Critic 1793-1843. . . . . . . DLB-110
*The British Review and London
   Critical Journal* 1811-1825 . . . . . DLB-110
Brito, Aristeo 1942- DLB-122
Broadway Publishing Company DLB-46
Broch, Hermann 1886-1951. . . . . DLB-85, 124
Brochu, André 1942- DLB-53
Brock, Edwin 1927- DLB-40
Brockes, Barthold Heinrich
   1680-1747 . . . . DLB-168

Brod, Max 1884-1968. . . . . DLB-81
Brodber, Erna 1940- DLB-157
Brodhead, John R. 1814-1873 . . . . . DLB-30
Brodkey, Harold 1930- DLB-130
Broeg, Bob 1918- DLB-171
Brome, Richard circa 1590-1652 . . . . DLB-58
Brome, Vincent 1910- DLB-155
Bromfield, Louis 1896-1956 . . . . DLB-4, 9, 86
Broner, E. M. 1930- DLB-28
Bronk, William 1918- DLB-165
Bronnen, Arnolt 1895-1959 . . . . . . DLB-124
Brontë, Anne 1820-1849 . . . . DLB-21
Brontë, Charlotte 1816-1855 . . . . DLB-21, 159
Brontë, Emily 1818-1848. . . . . . . DLB-21, 32
Brooke, Frances 1724-1789 . . . . . DLB-39, 99
Brooke, Henry 1703?-1783. . . . . DLB-39
Brooke, L. Leslie 1862-1940 . . . . . . DLB-141
Brooke, Margaret, Ranee of Sarawak
   1849-1936 . . . . DLB-174
Brooke, Rupert 1887-1915 . . . . DLB-19
Brooker, Bertram 1888-1955 . . . . . . DLB-88
Brooke-Rose, Christine 1926- DLB-14
Brookner, Anita 1928- Y-87
Brooks, Charles Timothy
   1813-1883. . . . . DLB-1
Brooks, Cleanth 1906-1994 . . . . DLB-63; Y-94
Brooks, Gwendolyn
   1917- DLB-5, 76, 165
Brooks, Jeremy 1926- DLB-14
Brooks, Mel 1926- DLB-26
Brooks, Noah 1830-1903. . . . . DLB-42; DS-13
Brooks, Richard 1912-1992. . . . . . . DLB-44
Brooks, Van Wyck
   1886-1963 . . . . DLB-45, 63, 103
Brophy, Brigid 1929- DLB-14
Brossard, Chandler 1922-1993 . . . . . DLB-16
Brossard, Nicole 1943- DLB-53
Broster, Dorothy Kathleen
   1877-1950 . . . . DLB-160
Brother Antoninus (see Everson, William)
Brougham and Vaux, Henry Peter
   Brougham, Baron
   1778-1868. . . . . DLB-110, 158
Brougham, John 1810-1880. . . . . . . DLB-11
Broughton, James 1913- DLB-5
Broughton, Rhoda 1840-1920 . . . . . . DLB-18
Broun, Heywood 1888-1939 . . . . DLB-29, 171
Brown, Alice 1856-1948. . . . . DLB-78
Brown, Bob 1886-1959 . . . . DLB-4, 45
Brown, Cecil 1943- DLB-33
Brown, Charles Brockden
   1771-1810. . . . . DLB-37, 59, 73
Brown, Christy 1932-1981 . . . . DLB-14

Brown, Dee 1908- Y-80
Brown, Frank London 1927-1962 . . . . DLB-76
Brown, Fredric 1906-1972 . . . . DLB-8
Brown, George Mackay
  1921- DLB-14, 27, 139
Brown, Harry 1917-1986 . . . . DLB-26
Brown, Marcia 1918- DLB-61
Brown, Margaret Wise
  1910-1952 . . . . DLB-22
Brown, Morna Doris (see Ferrars, Elizabeth)
Brown, Oliver Madox
  1855-1874 . . . . DLB-21
Brown, Sterling
  1901-1989 . . . . DLB-48, 51, 63
Brown, T. E. 1830-1897 . . . . DLB-35
Brown, William Hill 1765-1793 . . . . . DLB-37
Brown, William Wells
  1814-1884 . . . . DLB-3, 50
Browne, Charles Farrar
  1834-1867 . . . . DLB-11
Browne, Francis Fisher
  1843-1913 . . . . DLB-79
Browne, Michael Dennis
  1940- DLB-40
Browne, Sir Thomas 1605-1682 . . . . DLB-151
Browne, William, of Tavistock
  1590-1645 . . . . DLB-121
Browne, Wynyard 1911-1964 . . . . . DLB-13
Browne and Nolan DLB-106
Brownell, W. C. 1851-1928 . . . . DLB-71
Browning, Elizabeth Barrett
  1806-1861 . . . . DLB-32
Browning, Robert
  1812-1889 . . . . DLB-32, 163
Brownjohn, Allan 1931- DLB-40
Brownson, Orestes Augustus
  1803-1876 . . . . DLB-1, 59, 73
Bruccoli, Matthew J. 1931- DLB-103
Bruce, Charles 1906-1971 . . . . DLB-68
Bruce, Leo 1903-1979 . . . . DLB-77
Bruce, Philip Alexander
  1856-1933 . . . . DLB-47
Bruce Humphries
  [publishing house] DLB-46
Bruce-Novoa, Juan 1944- DLB-82
Bruckman, Clyde 1894-1955 . . . . . . DLB-26
Bruckner, Ferdinand 1891-1958 . . . . DLB-118
Brundage, John Herbert (see Herbert, John)
Brutus, Dennis 1924- DLB-117
Bryant, Arthur 1899-1985 . . . . DLB-149
Bryant, William Cullen
  1794-1878 . . . . DLB-3, 43, 59
Bryce Echenique, Alfredo
  1939- DLB-145
Bryce, James 1838-1922 . . . . DLB-166

Brydges, Sir Samuel Egerton
  1762-1837 . . . . DLB-107
Bryskett, Lodowick 1546?-1612 . . . . . DLB-167
Buchan, John 1875-1940 . . . . DLB-34, 70, 156
Buchanan, George 1506-1582 . . . . . . DLB-132
Buchanan, Robert 1841-1901 . . . . . DLB-18, 35
Buchman, Sidney 1902-1975 . . . . . . DLB-26
Buchner, Augustus 1591-1661 . . . . . DLB-164
Büchner, Georg 1813-1837 . . . . DLB-133
Bucholtz, Andreas Heinrich
  1607-1671 . . . . DLB-168
Buck, Pearl S. 1892-1973 . . . . DLB-9, 102
Bucke, Charles 1781-1846 . . . . DLB-110
Bucke, Richard Maurice
  1837-1902 . . . . DLB-99
Buckingham, Joseph Tinker 1779-1861 and
  Buckingham, Edwin
  1810-1833 . . . . DLB-73
Buckler, Ernest 1908-1984 . . . . DLB-68
Buckley, William F., Jr.
  1925- DLB-137; Y-80
Buckminster, Joseph Stevens
  1784-1812 . . . . DLB-37
Buckner, Robert 1906- DLB-26
Budd, Thomas ?-1698 . . . . DLB-24
Budrys, A. J. 1931- DLB-8
Buechner, Frederick 1926- Y-80
Buell, John 1927- DLB-53
Buffum, Job [publishing house] DLB-49
Bugnet, Georges 1879-1981 . . . . DLB-92
Buies, Arthur 1840-1901 . . . . DLB-99
Building the New British Library
  at St Pancras Y-94
Bukowski, Charles
  1920-1994 . . . . DLB-5, 130, 169
Bulatović, Miodrag 1930-1991 . . . . . DLB-181
Bulger, Bozeman 1877-1932 . . . . . . DLB-171
Bullein, William
  between 1520 and 1530-1576 . . . . DLB-167
Bullins, Ed 1935- DLB-7, 38
Bulwer-Lytton, Edward (also Edward Bulwer)
  1803-1873 . . . . DLB-21
Bumpus, Jerry 1937- Y-81
Bunce and Brother DLB-49
Bunner, H. C. 1855-1896 . . . . DLB-78, 79
Bunting, Basil 1900-1985 . . . . DLB-20
Bunyan, John 1628-1688 . . . . DLB-39
Burch, Robert 1925- DLB-52
Burciaga, José Antonio 1940- DLB-82
Bürger, Gottfried August
  1747-1794 . . . . DLB-94
Burgess, Anthony 1917-1993 . . . . . . DLB-14
Burgess, Gelett 1866-1951 . . . . DLB-11
Burgess, John W. 1844-1931 . . . . . . DLB-47

Burgess, Thornton W.
  1874-1965 . . . . DLB-22
Burgess, Stringer and Company DLB-49
Burick, Si 1909-1986 . . . . DLB-171
Burk, John Daly circa 1772-1808 . . . . DLB-37
Burke, Edmund 1729?-1797 . . . . DLB-104
Burke, Kenneth 1897-1993 . . . . . DLB-45, 63
Burlingame, Edward Livermore
  1848-1922 . . . . DLB-79
Burnet, Gilbert 1643-1715 . . . . DLB-101
Burnett, Frances Hodgson
  1849-1924 . . . . . . DLB-42, 141; DS-13, 14
Burnett, W. R. 1899-1982 . . . . DLB-9
Burnett, Whit 1899-1973 and
  Martha Foley 1897-1977 . . . . . . DLB-137
Burney, Fanny 1752-1840 . . . . DLB-39
Burns, Alan 1929- DLB-14
Burns, John Horne 1916-1953 . . . . Y-85
Burns, Robert 1759-1796 . . . . DLB-109
Burns and Oates DLB-106
Burnshaw, Stanley 1906- DLB-48
Burr, C. Chauncey 1815?-1883 . . . . . DLB-79
Burroughs, Edgar Rice 1875-1950 . . . . DLB-8
Burroughs, John 1837-1921 . . . . DLB-64
Burroughs, Margaret T. G.
  1917- DLB-41
Burroughs, William S., Jr.
  1947-1981 . . . . DLB-16
Burroughs, William Seward
  1914- DLB-2, 8, 16, 152; Y-81
Burroway, Janet 1936- DLB-6
Burt, Maxwell S. 1882-1954 . . . . DLB-86
Burt, A. L., and Company DLB-49
Burton, Hester 1913- DLB-161
Burton, Isabel Arundell
  1831-1896 . . . . DLB-166
Burton, Miles (see Rhode, John)
Burton, Richard Francis
  1821-1890 . . . . DLB-55, 166
Burton, Robert 1577-1640 . . . . DLB-151
Burton, Virginia Lee 1909-1968 . . . . . DLB-22
Burton, William Evans
  1804-1860 . . . . DLB-73
Burwell, Adam Hood 1790-1849 . . . . . DLB-99
Bury, Lady Charlotte
  1775-1861 . . . . DLB-116
Busch, Frederick 1941- DLB-6
Busch, Niven 1903-1991 . . . . DLB-44
Bushnell, Horace 1802-1876 . . . . DS-13
Bussieres, Arthur de 1877-1913 . . . . . DLB-92
Butler, Juan 1942-1981 . . . . DLB-53
Butler, Octavia E. 1947- DLB-33
Butler, Robert Olen 1945- DLB-173
Butler, Samuel 1613-1680 . . . . . DLB-101, 126

Butler, Samuel 1835-1902. . . . DLB-18, 57, 174
Butler, William Francis 1838-1910 . . . . DLB-166
Butler, E. H., and Company. DLB-49
Butor, Michel 1926- DLB-83
Butter, Nathaniel [publishing house] DLB-170
Butterworth, Hezekiah 1839-1905 . . . . DLB-42
Buttitta, Ignazio 1899- DLB-114
Buzzati, Dino 1906-1972. . . . . DLB-177
Byars, Betsy 1928- DLB-52
Byatt, A. S. 1936- DLB-14
Byles, Mather 1707-1788 . . . . DLB-24
Bynneman, Henry [publishing house] DLB-170
Bynner, Witter 1881-1968 . . . . DLB-54
Byrd, William circa 1543-1623 . . . . . DLB-172
Byrd, William II 1674-1744 . . . . DLB-24, 140
Byrne, John Keyes (see Leonard, Hugh)
Byron, George Gordon, Lord 1788-1824 . . . . DLB-96, 110

C

Caballero Bonald, José Manuel 1926- DLB-108
Cabañero, Eladio 1930- DLB-134
Cabell, James Branch 1879-1958 . . . . DLB-9, 78
Cabeza de Baca, Manuel 1853-1915 . . . . DLB-122
Cabeza de Baca Gilbert, Fabiola 1898- DLB-122
Cable, George Washington 1844-1925. . . . . DLB-12, 74; DS-13
Cabrera, Lydia 1900-1991. . . . . DLB-145
Cabrera Infante, Guillermo 1929- DLB-113
Cadell [publishing house] DLB-154
Cady, Edwin H. 1917- DLB-103
Caedmon flourished 658-680 . . . . . . DLB-146
Caedmon School circa 660-899 . . . . . DLB-146
Cahan, Abraham 1860-1951 . . . . DLB-9, 25, 28
Cain, George 1943- DLB-33
Caldecott, Randolph 1846-1886 . . . . . DLB-163
Calder, John (Publishers), Limited. DLB-112
Caldwell, Ben 1937- DLB-38
Caldwell, Erskine 1903-1987 . . . . . DLB-9, 86
Caldwell, H. M., Company DLB-49
Calhoun, John C. 1782-1850 . . . . DLB-3
Calisher, Hortense 1911- DLB-2

A Call to Letters and an Invitation to the Electric Chair, by Siegfried Mandel DLB-75
Callaghan, Morley 1903-1990 . . . . . DLB-68
Callahan, S. Alice 1868-1894 . . . . . DLB-175
Callaloo Y-87
Callimachus circa 305 B.C.-240 B.C. DLB-176
Calmer, Edgar 1907- DLB-4
Calverley, C. S. 1831-1884. . . . . DLB-35
Calvert, George Henry 1803-1889 . . . . DLB-1, 64
Cambridge Press DLB-49
Cambridge Songs (Carmina Cantabrigiensia) circa 1050 . . . . DLB-148
Cambridge University Press. DLB-170
Camden, William 1551-1623 . . . . . . DLB-172
Camden House: An Interview with James Hardin. Y-92
Cameron, Eleanor 1912- DLB-52
Cameron, George Frederick 1854-1885 . . . . DLB-99
Cameron, Lucy Lyttelton 1781-1858 . . . . DLB-163
Cameron, William Bleasdell 1862-1951 . . . . DLB-99
Camm, John 1718-1778. . . . . DLB-31
Campana, Dino 1885-1932 . . . . . . DLB-114
Campbell, Gabrielle Margaret Vere (see Shearing, Joseph, and Bowen, Marjorie)
Campbell, James Dykes 1838-1895 . . . . DLB-144
Campbell, James Edwin 1867-1896 . . . . DLB-50
Campbell, John 1653-1728 . . . . DLB-43
Campbell, John W., Jr. 1910-1971. . . . . DLB-8
Campbell, Roy 1901-1957 . . . . DLB-20
Campbell, Thomas 1777-1844 . . . . DLB-93, 144
Campbell, William Wilfred 1858-1918 . . . . DLB-92
Campion, Edmund 1539-1581 . . . . DLB-167
Campion, Thomas 1567-1620 . . . . DLB-58, 172
Camus, Albert 1913-1960. . . . . DLB-72
The Canadian Publishers' Records Database Y-96
Canby, Henry Seidel 1878-1961 . . . . . DLB-91
Candelaria, Cordelia 1943- DLB-82
Candelaria, Nash 1928- DLB-82
Candour in English Fiction (1890), by Thomas Hardy DLB-18
Canetti, Elias 1905-1994 . . . . . DLB-85, 124
Canham, Erwin Dain 1904-1982 . . . . DLB-127

Canitz, Friedrich Rudolph Ludwig von 1654-1699 . . . . DLB-168
Cankar, Ivan 1876-1918 . . . . DLB-147
Cannan, Gilbert 1884-1955 . . . . DLB-10
Cannell, Kathleen 1891-1974 . . . . DLB-4
Cannell, Skipwith 1887-1957 . . . . . . DLB-45
Canning, George 1770-1827 . . . . . . DLB-158
Cannon, Jimmy 1910-1973 . . . . . . DLB-171
Cantwell, Robert 1908-1978 . . . . DLB-9
Cape, Jonathan, and Harrison Smith [publishing house] DLB-46
Cape, Jonathan, Limited. DLB-112
Capen, Joseph 1658-1725 . . . . DLB-24
Capes, Bernard 1854-1918. . . . . DLB-156
Capote, Truman 1924-1984 . . . . DLB-2; Y-80, 84
Caproni, Giorgio 1912-1990. . . . . . . DLB-128
Cardarelli, Vincenzo 1887-1959 . . . . . DLB-114
Cárdenas, Reyes 1948- DLB-122
Cardinal, Marie 1929- DLB-83
Carew, Jan 1920- DLB-157
Carew, Thomas 1594 or 1595-1640 . . . . DLB-126
Carey, Henry circa 1687-1689-1743 . . . . DLB-84
Carey, Mathew 1760-1839 . . . . . DLB-37, 73
Carey and Hart. DLB-49
Carey, M., and Company DLB-49
Carlell, Lodowick 1602-1675 . . . . . . DLB-58
Carleton, William 1794-1869 . . . . . . DLB-159
Carleton, G. W. [publishing house] DLB-49
Carlile, Richard 1790-1843 . . . . DLB-110, 158
Carlyle, Jane Welsh 1801-1866 . . . . . . DLB-55
Carlyle, Thomas 1795-1881 . . . . . DLB-55, 144
Carman, Bliss 1861-1929 . . . . DLB-92
Carmina Burana circa 1230 . . . . DLB-138
Carnero, Guillermo 1947- DLB-108
Carossa, Hans 1878-1956 . . . . DLB-66
Carpenter, Humphrey 1946- DLB-155
Carpenter, Stephen Cullen ?-1820? DLB-73
Carpentier, Alejo 1904-1980 . . . . . . DLB-113
Carrier, Roch 1937- DLB-53
Carrillo, Adolfo 1855-1926 . . . . . . DLB-122
Carroll, Gladys Hasty 1904- DLB-9
Carroll, John 1735-1815 . . . . DLB-37
Carroll, John 1809-1884 . . . . DLB-99
Carroll, Lewis 1832-1898 . . . . DLB-18, 163, 178
Carroll, Paul 1927- DLB-16
Carroll, Paul Vincent 1900-1968 . . . . . DLB-10
Carroll and Graf Publishers DLB-46

Carruth, Hayden 1921- DLB-5, 165
Carryl, Charles E. 1841-1920 ...... DLB-42
Carswell, Catherine 1879-1946 ...... DLB-36
Carter, Angela 1940-1992 .... DLB-14
Carter, Elizabeth 1717-1806 ...... DLB-109
Carter, Henry (see Leslie, Frank)
Carter, Hodding, Jr. 1907-1972 ..... DLB-127
Carter, Landon 1710-1778 .... DLB-31
Carter, Lin 1930- Y-81
Carter, Martin 1927- DLB-117
Carter and Hendee DLB-49
Carter, Robert, and Brothers DLB-49
Cartwright, John 1740-1824 ...... DLB-158
Cartwright, William circa
   1611-1643 .... DLB-126
Caruthers, William Alexander
   1802-1846 .... DLB-3
Carver, Jonathan 1710-1780 ...... DLB-31
Carver, Raymond
   1938-1988 .... DLB-130; Y-84, 88
Cary, Joyce 1888-1957 ...... DLB-15, 100
Cary, Patrick 1623?-1657 .... DLB-131
Casey, Juanita 1925- DLB-14
Casey, Michael 1947- DLB-5
Cassady, Carolyn 1923- DLB-16
Cassady, Neal 1926-1968 .... DLB-16
Cassell and Company DLB-106
Cassell Publishing Company DLB-49
Cassill, R. V. 1919- DLB-6
Cassity, Turner 1929- DLB-105
Cassius Dio circa 155/164-post 229
   .... DLB-176
Cassola, Carlo 1917-1987 .... DLB-177
The Castle of Perseverance
   circa 1400-1425 .... DLB-146
Castellano, Olivia 1944- DLB-122
Castellanos, Rosario 1925-1974 ... DLB-113
Castillo, Ana 1953- DLB-122
Castlemon, Harry (see Fosdick, Charles Austin)
Čašule, Kole 1921- DLB-181
Caswall, Edward 1814-1878 .... DLB-32
Catacalos, Rosemary 1944- DLB-122
Cather, Willa
   1873-1947 .... DLB-9, 54, 78; DS-1
Catherine II (Ekaterina Alekseevna), "The
   Great," Empress of Russia
   1729-1796 .... DLB-150
Catherwood, Mary Hartwell
   1847-1902 .... DLB-78
Catledge, Turner 1901-1983 ...... DLB-127
Cattafi, Bartolo 1922-1979 ...... DLB-128
Catton, Bruce 1899-1978 .... DLB-17
Causley, Charles 1917- DLB-27

Caute, David 1936- DLB-14
Cavendish, Duchess of Newcastle,
   Margaret Lucas 1623-1673 .... DLB-131
Cawein, Madison 1865-1914 ...... DLB-54
The Caxton Printers, Limited DLB-46
Caxton, William
   [publishing house] DLB-170
Cayrol, Jean 1911- DLB-83
Cecil, Lord David 1902-1986 ..... DLB-155
Celan, Paul 1920-1970 .... DLB-69
Celaya, Gabriel 1911-1991 ...... DLB-108
Céline, Louis-Ferdinand
   1894-1961 .... DLB-72
The Celtic Background to Medieval English
   Literature DLB-146
Celtis, Conrad 1459-1508 .... DLB-179
Center for Bibliographical Studies and
   Research at the University of
   California, Riverside Y-91
The Center for the Book in the Library
   of Congress Y-93
Center for the Book Research Y-84
Centlivre, Susanna 1669?-1723 ... DLB-84
The Century Company DLB-49
Cernuda, Luis 1902-1963 .... DLB-134
Cervantes, Lorna Dee 1954- DLB-82
Chacel, Rosa 1898- DLB-134
Chacón, Eusebio 1869-1948 ..... DLB-82
Chacón, Felipe Maximiliano
   1873-? DLB-82
Chadwyck-Healey's Full-Text Literary Data-bases:
   Editing Commercial Databases of
   Primary Literary Texts Y-95
Challans, Eileen Mary (see Renault, Mary)
Chalmers, George 1742-1825 ..... DLB-30
Chaloner, Sir Thomas
   1520-1565 .... DLB-167
Chamberlain, Samuel S.
   1851-1916 .... DLB-25
Chamberland, Paul 1939- DLB-60
Chamberlin, William Henry
   1897-1969 .... DLB-29
Chambers, Charles Haddon
   1860-1921 .... DLB-10
Chambers, W. and R.
   [publishing house] DLB-106
Chamisso, Albert von
   1781-1838 .... DLB-90
Champfleury 1821-1889 .... DLB-119
Chandler, Harry 1864-1944 ...... DLB-29
Chandler, Norman 1899-1973 .... DLB-127
Chandler, Otis 1927- DLB-127
Chandler, Raymond 1888-1959 ..... DS-6
Channing, Edward 1856-1931 ..... DLB-17
Channing, Edward Tyrrell
   1790-1856 .... DLB-1, 59

Channing, William Ellery
   1780-1842 .... DLB-1, 59
Channing, William Ellery, II
   1817-1901 .... DLB-1
Channing, William Henry
   1810-1884 .... DLB-1, 59
Chaplin, Charlie 1889-1977 ...... DLB-44
Chapman, George
   1559 or 1560 - 1634 .... DLB-62, 121
Chapman, John DLB-106
Chapman, William 1850-1917 ..... DLB-99
Chapman and Hall DLB-106
Chappell, Fred 1936- DLB-6, 105
Chappell, Fred, A Detail
   in a Poem DLB-105
Charbonneau, Jean 1875-1960 .... DLB-92
Charbonneau, Robert 1911-1967 .. DLB-68
Charles, Gerda 1914- DLB-14
Charles, William
   [publishing house] DLB-49
The Charles Wood Affair:
   A Playwright Revived Y-83
Charlotte Forten: Pages from
   her Diary DLB-50
Charteris, Leslie 1907-1993 ...... DLB-77
Charyn, Jerome 1937- Y-83
Chase, Borden 1900-1971 .... DLB-26
Chase, Edna Woolman
   1877-1957 .... DLB-91
Chase-Riboud, Barbara 1936- DLB-33
Chateaubriand, François-René de
   1768-1848 .... DLB-119
Chatterton, Thomas 1752-1770 ... DLB-109
Chatto and Windus DLB-106
Chaucer, Geoffrey 1340?-1400 ... DLB-146
Chauncy, Charles 1705-1787 ..... DLB-24
Chauveau, Pierre-Joseph-Olivier
   1820-1890 .... DLB-99
Chávez, Denise 1948- DLB-122
Chávez, Fray Angélico 1910- DLB-82
Chayefsky, Paddy
   1923-1981 .... DLB-7, 44; Y-81
Cheever, Ezekiel 1615-1708 ...... DLB-24
Cheever, George Barrell
   1807-1890 .... DLB-59
Cheever, John
   1912-1982 .... DLB-2, 102; Y-80, 82
Cheever, Susan 1943- Y-82
Cheke, Sir John 1514-1557 ...... DLB-132
Chelsea House DLB-46
Cheney, Ednah Dow (Littlehale)
   1824-1904 .... DLB-1
Cheney, Harriet Vaughn
   1796-1889 .... DLB-99
Cherry, Kelly 1940- Y-83

Cherryh, C. J. 1942- Y-80

Chesnutt, Charles Waddell
1858-1932. . . . . DLB-12, 50, 78

Chester, Alfred 1928-1971. . . . . DLB-130

Chester, George Randolph
1869-1924. . . . . DLB-78

The Chester Plays circa 1505-1532;
revisions until 1575 . . . . DLB-146

Chesterfield, Philip Dormer Stanhope,
Fourth Earl of 1694-1773. . . . . . DLB-104

Chesterton, G. K. 1874-1936
. . . . . DLB-10, 19, 34, 70, 98, 149, 178

Chettle, Henry
circa 1560-circa 1607 . . . . DLB-136

Chew, Ada Nield 1870-1945 . . . . . . DLB-135

Cheyney, Edward P. 1861-1947 . . . . . DLB-47

Chiara, Piero 1913-1986. . . . . DLB-177

Chicano History. DLB-82

Chicano Language DLB-82

Child, Francis James
1825-1896 . . . . DLB-1, 64

Child, Lydia Maria
1802-1880 . . . . DLB-1, 74

Child, Philip 1898-1978. . . . . DLB-68

Childers, Erskine 1870-1922 . . . . DLB-70

Children's Book Awards
and Prizes. DLB-61

Children's Illustrators,
1800-1880 . . . . DLB-163

Childress, Alice 1920-1994. . . . . . DLB-7, 38

Childs, George W. 1829-1894 . . . . . . DLB-23

Chilton Book Company DLB-46

Chinweizu 1943- DLB-157

Chitham, Edward 1932- DLB-155

Chittenden, Hiram Martin
1858-1917. . . . . DLB-47

Chivers, Thomas Holley
1809-1858. . . . . DLB-3

Chopin, Kate 1850-1904 . . . . . . DLB-12, 78

Chopin, Rene 1885-1953 . . . . DLB-92

Choquette, Adrienne 1915-1973 . . . . . DLB-68

Choquette, Robert 1905- DLB-68

The Christian Publishing
Company DLB-49

Christie, Agatha 1890-1976. . . . . DLB-13, 77

Christus und die Samariterin
circa 950. . . . . DLB-148

Chulkov, Mikhail Dmitrievich
1743?-1792. . . . . DLB-150

Church, Benjamin 1734-1778. . . . . . . DLB-31

Church, Francis Pharcellus
1839-1906. . . . . DLB-79

Church, William Conant
1836-1917. . . . . DLB-79

Churchill, Caryl 1938- DLB-13

Churchill, Charles 1731-1764 . . . . . . DLB-109

Churchill, Sir Winston
1874-1965 . . . . DLB-100

Churchyard, Thomas
1520?-1604. . . . . DLB-132

Churton, E., and Company. DLB-106

Chute, Marchette 1909-1994 . . . . . . DLB-103

Ciardi, John 1916-1986 . . . . . . DLB-5; Y-86

Cibber, Colley 1671-1757. . . . . DLB-84

Cima, Annalisa 1941- DLB-128

Čingo, Živko 1935-1987 . . . . DLB-181

Cirese, Eugenio 1884-1955 . . . . DLB-114

Cisneros, Sandra 1954- DLB-122, 152

City Lights Books. DLB-46

Cixous, Hélène 1937- DLB-83

Clampitt, Amy 1920-1994 . . . . DLB-105

Clapper, Raymond 1892-1944 . . . . . DLB-29

Clare, John 1793-1864 . . . . . . DLB-55, 96

Clarendon, Edward Hyde, Earl of
1609-1674 . . . . DLB-101

Clark, Alfred Alexander Gordon
(see Hare, Cyril)

Clark, Ann Nolan 1896- DLB-52

Clark, Catherine Anthony
1892-1977 . . . . DLB-68

Clark, Charles Heber
1841-1915 . . . . DLB-11

Clark, Davis Wasgatt 1812-1871. . . . . DLB-79

Clark, Eleanor 1913- DLB-6

Clark, J. P. 1935- DLB-117

Clark, Lewis Gaylord
1808-1873 . . . . DLB-3, 64, 73

Clark, Walter Van Tilburg
1909-1971. . . . . DLB-9

Clark, C. M., Publishing
Company DLB-46

Clarke, Austin 1896-1974 . . . . . . DLB-10, 20

Clarke, Austin C. 1934- DLB-53, 125

Clarke, Gillian 1937- DLB-40

Clarke, James Freeman
1810-1888 . . . . DLB-1, 59

Clarke, Pauline 1921- DLB-161

Clarke, Rebecca Sophia
1833-1906. . . . . DLB-42

Clarke, Robert, and Company. DLB-49

Clarkson, Thomas 1760-1846. . . . . . DLB-158

Claudius, Matthias 1740-1815 . . . . . . DLB-97

Clausen, Andy 1943- DLB-16

Claxton, Remsen and
Haffelfinger DLB-49

Clay, Cassius Marcellus
1810-1903 . . . . DLB-43

Cleary, Beverly 1916- DLB-52

Cleaver, Vera 1919- and
Cleaver, Bill 1920-1981. . . . . . . DLB-52

Cleland, John 1710-1789 . . . . DLB-39

Clemens, Samuel Langhorne
1835-1910 . . . . . . DLB-11, 12, 23, 64, 74

Clement, Hal 1922- DLB-8

Clemo, Jack 1916- DLB-27

Cleveland, John 1613-1658 . . . . DLB-126

Cliff, Michelle 1946- DLB-157

Clifford, Lady Anne 1590-1676. . . . . DLB-151

Clifford, James L. 1901-1978 . . . . . . DLB-103

Clifford, Lucy 1853?-1929 . . . . . DLB-135, 141

Clifton, Lucille 1936- DLB-5, 41

Clode, Edward J.
[publishing house]. DLB-46

Clough, Arthur Hugh 1819-1861 . . . . DLB-32

Cloutier, Cécile 1930- DLB-60

Clutton-Brock, Arthur
1868-1924. . . . . DLB-98

Coates, Robert M.
1897-1973 . . . . DLB-4, 9, 102

Coatsworth, Elizabeth 1893- DLB-22

Cobb, Charles E., Jr. 1943- DLB-41

Cobb, Frank I. 1869-1923 . . . . DLB-25

Cobb, Irvin S.
1876-1944. . . . . DLB-11, 25, 86

Cobbett, William 1763-1835 . . . . DLB-43, 107

Cobbledick, Gordon 1898-1969 . . . . . DLB-171

Cochran, Thomas C. 1902- DLB-17

Cochrane, Elizabeth 1867-1922 . . . . . DLB-25

Cockerill, John A. 1845-1896. . . . . . . DLB-23

Cocteau, Jean 1889-1963 . . . . DLB-65

Coderre, Emile (see Jean Narrache)

Coffee, Lenore J. 1900?-1984. . . . . . DLB-44

Coffin, Robert P. Tristram
1892-1955. . . . . DLB-45

Cogswell, Fred 1917- DLB-60

Cogswell, Mason Fitch
1761-1830 . . . . DLB-37

Cohen, Arthur A. 1928-1986 . . . . . . DLB-28

Cohen, Leonard 1934- DLB-53

Cohen, Matt 1942- DLB-53

Colden, Cadwallader
1688-1776. . . . . DLB-24, 30

Cole, Barry 1936- DLB-14

Cole, George Watson
1850-1939 . . . . DLB-140

Colegate, Isabel 1931- DLB-14

Coleman, Emily Holmes
1899-1974. . . . . DLB-4

Coleman, Wanda 1946- DLB-130

Coleridge, Hartley 1796-1849. . . . . . DLB-96

Coleridge, Mary 1861-1907 . . . . . DLB-19, 98

Coleridge, Samuel Taylor
1772-1834 . . . . DLB-93, 107

Colet, John 1467-1519 . . . . DLB-132

Colette 1873-1954 . . . . DLB-65

Colette, Sidonie Gabrielle (see Colette)
Colinas, Antonio 1946- DLB-134
Collier, John 1901-1980........... DLB-77
Collier, Mary 1690-1762 .... DLB-95
Collier, Robert J. 1876-1918 .... DLB-91
Collier, P. F. [publishing house] DLB-49
Collin and Small DLB-49
Collingwood, W. G. 1854-1932..... DLB-149
Collins, An floruit circa 1653...... DLB-131
Collins, Merle 1950- DLB-157
Collins, Mortimer 1827-1876..... DLB-21, 35
Collins, Wilkie 1824-1889 ... DLB-18, 70, 159
Collins, William 1721-1759 .... DLB-109
Collins, William, Sons and
 Company DLB-154
Collins, Isaac [publishing house] DLB-49
Collyer, Mary 1716?-1763?........ DLB-39
Colman, Benjamin 1673-1747 ...... DLB-24
Colman, George, the Elder
 1732-1794 .... DLB-89
Colman, George, the Younger
 1762-1836 .... DLB-89
Colman, S. [publishing house] DLB-49
Colombo, John Robert 1936- DLB-53
Colquhoun, Patrick 1745-1820 ..... DLB-158
Colter, Cyrus 1910- DLB-33
Colum, Padraic 1881-1972 .... DLB-19
Colvin, Sir Sidney 1845-1927 ...... DLB-149
Colwin, Laurie 1944-1992 .... Y-80
Comden, Betty 1919- and Green,
 Adolph 1918- DLB-44
Comi, Girolamo 1890-1968 .... DLB-114
The Comic Tradition Continued
 [in the British Novel]........ DLB-15
Commager, Henry Steele
 1902- DLB-17
The Commercialization of the Image of
 Revolt, by Kenneth Rexroth..... DLB-16
Community and Commentators: Black
 Theatre and Its Critics........ DLB-38
Compton-Burnett, Ivy
 1884?-1969 .... DLB-36
Conan, Laure 1845-1924 .... DLB-99
Conde, Carmen 1901- DLB-108
Conference on Modern Biography Y-85
Congreve, William
 1670-1729.............. DLB-39, 84
Conkey, W. B., Company......... DLB-49
Connell, Evan S., Jr. 1924- DLB-2; Y-81
Connelly, Marc 1890-1980 ..... DLB-7; Y-80
Connolly, Cyril 1903-1974 .... DLB-98
Connolly, James B. 1868-1957 ..... DLB-78
Connor, Ralph 1860-1937 .... DLB-92

Connor, Tony 1930- DLB-40
Conquest, Robert 1917- DLB-27
Conrad, Joseph
 1857-1924........ DLB-10, 34, 98, 156
Conrad, John, and Company DLB-49
Conroy, Jack 1899-1990 .... Y-81
Conroy, Pat 1945- DLB-6
The Consolidation of Opinion: Critical
 Responses to the Modernists DLB-36
Constable, Henry 1562-1613 ..... DLB-136
Constable and Company
 Limited................... DLB-112
Constable, Archibald, and
 Company DLB-154
Constant, Benjamin 1767-1830 .... DLB-119
Constant de Rebecque, Henri-Benjamin de
 (see Constant, Benjamin)
Constantine, David 1944- DLB-40
Constantin-Weyer, Maurice
 1881-1964.................. DLB-92
Contempo Caravan: Kites in
 a Windstorm............... Y-85
A Contemporary Flourescence of Chicano
 Literature Y-84
The Continental Publishing
 Company DLB-49
A Conversation with Chaim Potok..... Y-84
Conversations with Editors.......... Y-95
Conversations with Publishers I: An Interview
 with Patrick O'Connor Y-84
Conversations with Publishers II: An Interview
 with Charles Scribner III Y-94
Conversations with Publishers III: An Interview
 with Donald Lamm Y-95
Conversations with Publishers IV: An Interview
 with James Laughlin........... Y-96
Conversations with Rare Book Dealers I: An
 Interview with Glenn Horowitz..... Y-90
Conversations with Rare Book Dealers II: An
 Interview with Ralph Sipper Y-94
Conversations with Rare Book Dealers
 (Publishers) III: An Interview with
 Otto Penzler................ Y-96
The Conversion of an Unpolitical Man,
 by W. H. Bruford DLB-66
Conway, Moncure Daniel
 1832-1907................... DLB-1
Cook, Ebenezer
 circa 1667-circa 1732......... DLB-24
Cook, Edward Tyas 1857-1919..... DLB-149
Cook, Michael 1933- DLB-53
Cook, David C., Publishing
 Company DLB-49
Cooke, George Willis 1848-1923..... DLB-71
Cooke, Increase, and Company DLB-49
Cooke, John Esten 1830-1886 ...... DLB-3

Cooke, Philip Pendleton
 1816-1850 .... DLB-3, 59
Cooke, Rose Terry
 1827-1892............... DLB-12, 74
Cook-Lynn, Elizabeth 1930- DLB-175
Coolbrith, Ina 1841-1928 .... DLB-54
Cooley, Peter 1940- DLB-105
Cooley, Peter, Into the Mirror DLB-105
Coolidge, Susan (see Woolsey, Sarah Chauncy)
Coolidge, George
 [publishing house]............ DLB-49
Cooper, Giles 1918-1966 .... DLB-13
Cooper, James Fenimore 1789-1851.... DLB-3
Cooper, Kent 1880-1965 .... DLB-29
Cooper, Susan 1935- DLB-161
Cooper, William
 [publishing house]........... DLB-170
Coote, J. [publishing house]....... DLB-154
Coover, Robert 1932- DLB-2; Y-81
Copeland and Day DLB-49
Ćopić, Branko 1915-1984 .... DLB-181
Copland, Robert 1470?-1548 ..... DLB-136
Coppard, A. E. 1878-1957 .... DLB-162
Coppel, Alfred 1921- Y-83
Coppola, Francis Ford 1939- DLB-44
Copway, George (Kah-ge-ga-gah-bowh)
 1818-1869 .... DLB-175
Corazzini, Sergio 1886-1907....... DLB-114
Corbett, Richard 1582-1635....... DLB-121
Corcoran, Barbara 1911- DLB-52
Corelli, Marie 1855-1924 ..... DLB-34, 156
Corle, Edwin 1906-1956 .... Y-85
Corman, Cid 1924- DLB-5
Cormier, Robert 1925- DLB-52
Corn, Alfred 1943- DLB-120; Y-80
Cornish, Sam 1935- DLB-41
Cornish, William
 circa 1465-circa 1524 .... DLB-132
Cornwall, Barry (see Procter, Bryan Waller)
Cornwallis, Sir William, the Younger
 circa 1579-1614 .... DLB-151
Cornwell, David John Moore
 (see le Carré, John)
Corpi, Lucha 1945- DLB-82
Corrington, John William 1932- DLB-6
Corrothers, James D. 1869-1917 ..... DLB-50
Corso, Gregory 1930- DLB-5, 16
Cortázar, Julio 1914-1984 .... DLB-113
Cortez, Jayne 1936- DLB-41
Corvinus, Gottlieb Siegmund
 1677-1746 .... DLB-168
Corvo, Baron (see Rolfe, Frederick William)
Cory, Annie Sophie (see Cross, Victoria)

Cory, William Johnson 1823-1892 . . . . DLB-35

Coryate, Thomas 1577?-1617 . . . . DLB-151, 172

Ćosić, Dobrica 1921- DLB-181

Cosin, John 1595-1672 . . . . DLB-151

Cosmopolitan Book Corporation DLB-46

Costain, Thomas B. 1885-1965 . . . . . . DLB-9

Coste, Donat 1912-1957 . . . . DLB-88

Costello, Louisa Stuart 1799-1870 . . . DLB-166

Cota-Cárdenas, Margarita 1941- DLB-122

Cotter, Joseph Seamon, Sr. 1861-1949 . . . . DLB-50

Cotter, Joseph Seamon, Jr. 1895-1919 . . . . DLB-50

Cottle, Joseph [publishing house] DLB-154

Cotton, Charles 1630-1687 . . . . DLB-131

Cotton, John 1584-1652 . . . . DLB-24

Coulter, John 1888-1980 . . . . DLB-68

Cournos, John 1881-1966 . . . . DLB-54

Cousins, Margaret 1905- DLB-137

Cousins, Norman 1915-1990 . . . . . . DLB-137

Coventry, Francis 1725-1754 . . . . . . DLB-39

Coverdale, Miles 1487 or 1488-1569 . . . . DLB-167

Coverly, N. [publishing house] DLB-49

Covici-Friede DLB-46

Coward, Noel 1899-1973 . . . . DLB-10

Coward, McCann and Geoghegan DLB-46

Cowles, Gardner 1861-1946 . . . . . . DLB-29

Cowles, Gardner ("Mike"), Jr. 1903-1985 . . . . DLB-127, 137

Cowley, Abraham 1618-1667 . . . . DLB-131, 151

Cowley, Hannah 1743-1809 . . . . . . DLB-89

Cowley, Malcolm 1898-1989 . . . . DLB-4, 48; Y-81, 89

Cowper, William 1731-1800 . . . . DLB-104, 109

Cox, A. B. (see Berkeley, Anthony)

Cox, James McMahon 1903-1974 . . . . DLB-127

Cox, James Middleton 1870-1957 . . . . DLB-127

Cox, Palmer 1840-1924 . . . . DLB-42

Coxe, Louis 1918-1993 . . . . DLB-5

Coxe, Tench 1755-1824 . . . . DLB-37

Cozzens, James Gould 1903-1978 . . . . DLB-9; Y-84; DS-2

Crabbe, George 1754-1832 . . . . DLB-93

Crackanthorpe, Hubert 1870-1896 . . . . DLB-135

Craddock, Charles Egbert (see Murfree, Mary N.)

Cradock, Thomas 1718-1770 . . . . . . DLB-31

Craig, Daniel H. 1811-1895 . . . . DLB-43

Craik, Dinah Maria 1826-1887 . . . . DLB-35, 136

Cranch, Christopher Pearse 1813-1892 . . . . DLB-1, 42

Crane, Hart 1899-1932 . . . . DLB-4, 48

Crane, R. S. 1886-1967 . . . . DLB-63

Crane, Stephen 1871-1900 . . . . DLB-12, 54, 78

Crane, Walter 1845-1915 . . . . DLB-163

Cranmer, Thomas 1489-1556 . . . . . . DLB-132

Crapsey, Adelaide 1878-1914 . . . . . . DLB-54

Crashaw, Richard 1612 or 1613-1649 . . . . DLB-126

Craven, Avery 1885-1980 . . . . DLB-17

Crawford, Charles 1752-circa 1815 . . . . DLB-31

Crawford, F. Marion 1854-1909 . . . . . DLB-71

Crawford, Isabel Valancy 1850-1887 . . . . DLB-92

Crawley, Alan 1887-1975 . . . . DLB-68

Crayon, Geoffrey (see Irving, Washington)

Creamer, Robert W. 1922- DLB-171

Creasey, John 1908-1973 . . . . DLB-77

Creative Age Press DLB-46

Creech, William [publishing house] DLB-154

Creede, Thomas [publishing house] DLB-170

Creel, George 1876-1953 . . . . DLB-25

Creeley, Robert 1926- DLB-5, 16, 169

Creelman, James 1859-1915 . . . . DLB-23

Cregan, David 1931- DLB-13

Creighton, Donald Grant 1902-1979 . . . . DLB-88

Cremazie, Octave 1827-1879 . . . . . . DLB-99

Crémer, Victoriano 1909?- DLB-108

Crescas, Hasdai circa 1340-1412? DLB-115

Crespo, Angel 1926- DLB-134

Cresset Press DLB-112

Cresswell, Helen 1934- DLB-161

Crèvecoeur, Michel Guillaume Jean de 1735-1813 . . . . DLB-37

Crews, Harry 1935- DLB-6, 143

Crichton, Michael 1942- Y-81

A Crisis of Culture: The Changing Role of Religion in the New Republic DLB-37

Crispin, Edmund 1921-1978 . . . . . . DLB-87

Cristofer, Michael 1946- DLB-7

"The Critic as Artist" (1891), by Oscar Wilde DLB-57

"Criticism In Relation To Novels" (1863), by G. H. Lewes DLB-21

Crnjanski, Miloš 1893-1977 . . . . DLB-147

Crockett, David (Davy) 1786-1836 . . . . DLB-3, 11

Croft-Cooke, Rupert (see Bruce, Leo)

Crofts, Freeman Wills 1879-1957 . . . . DLB-77

Croker, John Wilson 1780-1857 . . . . DLB-110

Croly, George 1780-1860 . . . . DLB-159

Croly, Herbert 1869-1930 . . . . DLB-91

Croly, Jane Cunningham 1829-1901 . . . . DLB-23

Crompton, Richmal 1890-1969 . . . . . DLB-160

Crosby, Caresse 1892-1970 . . . . DLB-48

Crosby, Caresse 1892-1970 and Crosby, Harry 1898-1929 . . . . DLB-4

Crosby, Harry 1898-1929 . . . . DLB-48

Cross, Gillian 1945- DLB-161

Cross, Victoria 1868-1952 . . . . DLB-135

Crossley-Holland, Kevin 1941- DLB-40, 161

Crothers, Rachel 1878-1958 . . . . DLB-7

Crowell, Thomas Y., Company DLB-49

Crowley, John 1942- Y-82

Crowley, Mart 1935- DLB-7

Crown Publishers DLB-46

Crowne, John 1641-1712 . . . . DLB-80

Crowninshield, Edward Augustus 1817-1859 . . . . DLB-140

Crowninshield, Frank 1872-1947 . . . . . DLB-91

Croy, Homer 1883-1965 . . . . DLB-4

Crumley, James 1939- Y-84

Cruz, Victor Hernández 1949- DLB-41

Csokor, Franz Theodor 1885-1969 . . . . DLB-81

Cuala Press DLB-112

Cullen, Countee 1903-1946 . . . . DLB-4, 48, 51

Culler, Jonathan D. 1944- DLB-67

The Cult of Biography
Excerpts from the Second Folio Debate: "Biographies are generally a disease of English Literature"—Germaine Greer, Victoria Glendinning, Auberon Waugh, and Richard Holmes Y-86

Cumberland, Richard 1732-1811 . . . . . DLB-89

Cummings, Constance Gordon 1837-1924 . . . . DLB-174

Cummings, E. E. 1894-1962 . . . . . DLB-4, 48

Cummings, Ray 1887-1957 . . . . DLB-8

Cummings and Hilliard DLB-49

Cummins, Maria Susanna 1827-1866 . . . . DLB-42

Cundall, Joseph [publishing house] DLB-106

Cuney, Waring 1906-1976 .... DLB-51
Cuney-Hare, Maude 1874-1936 ..... DLB-52
Cunningham, Allan
 1784-1842. .... DLB-116, 144
Cunningham, J. V. 1911- DLB-5
Cunningham, Peter F.
 [publishing house]. DLB-49
Cunqueiro, Alvaro 1911-1981...... DLB-134
Cuomo, George 1929- Y-80
Cupples and Leon DLB-46
Cupples, Upham and Company DLB-49
Cuppy, Will 1884-1949. .... DLB-11
Curll, Edmund
 [publishing house] DLB-154
Currie, James 1756-1805. .... DLB-142
Currie, Mary Montgomerie Lamb Singleton,
 Lady Currie (see Fane, Violet)
Cursor Mundi circa 1300 .... DLB-146
Curti, Merle E. 1897- DLB-17
Curtis, Anthony 1926- DLB-155
Curtis, Cyrus H. K. 1850-1933 ..... DLB-91
Curtis, George William
 1824-1892 .... DLB-1, 43
Curzon, Robert 1810-1873 .... DLB-166
Curzon, Sarah Anne 1833-1898 .... DLB-99
Cynewulf circa 770-840 .... DLB-146
Czepko, Daniel 1605-1660. .... DLB-164

D

D. M. Thomas: The Plagiarism
 Controversy. Y-82
Dabit, Eugène 1898-1936......... DLB-65
Daborne, Robert circa 1580-1628 .... DLB-58
Dacey, Philip 1939- DLB-105
Dacey, Philip, Eyes Across Centuries:
 Contemporary Poetry and "That
 Vision Thing"............. DLB-105
Dach, Simon 1605-1659......... DLB-164
Daggett, Rollin M. 1831-1901 ..... DLB-79
D'Aguiar, Fred 1960- DLB-157
Dahl, Roald 1916-1990 .... DLB-139
Dahlberg, Edward 1900-1977...... DLB-48
Dahn, Felix 1834-1912. .... DLB-129
Dale, Peter 1938- DLB-40
Daley, Arthur 1904-1974 .... DLB-171
Dall, Caroline Wells (Healey)
 1822-1912................ DLB-1
Dallas, E. S. 1828-1879.......... DLB-55
The Dallas Theater Center DLB-7
D'Alton, Louis 1900-1951......... DLB-10
Daly, T. A. 1871-1948.......... DLB-11
Damon, S. Foster 1893-1971...... DLB-45

Damrell, William S.
 [publishing house]. DLB-49
Dana, Charles A. 1819-1897 ..... DLB-3, 23
Dana, Richard Henry, Jr
 1815-1882 .... DLB-1
Dandridge, Ray Garfield DLB-51
Dane, Clemence 1887-1965........ DLB-10
Danforth, John 1660-1730 .... DLB-24
Danforth, Samuel, I 1626-1674..... DLB-24
Danforth, Samuel, II 1666-1727 ... DLB-24
Dangerous Years: London Theater,
 1939-1945............... DLB-10
Daniel, John M. 1825-1865........ DLB-43
Daniel, Samuel
 1562 or 1563-1619 .... DLB-62
Daniel Press DLB-106
Daniells, Roy 1902-1979 .... DLB-68
Daniels, Jim 1956- DLB-120
Daniels, Jonathan 1902-1981 ..... DLB-127
Daniels, Josephus 1862-1948 ..... DLB-29
Dannay, Frederic 1905-1982 and
 Manfred B. Lee 1905-1971..... DLB-137
Danner, Margaret Esse 1915- DLB-41
Danter, John [publishing house]..... DLB-170
Dantin, Louis 1865-1945 .... DLB-92
Danzig, Allison 1898-1987........ DLB-171
D'Arcy, Ella circa 1857-1937 ..... DLB-135
Darley, George 1795-1846 .... DLB-96
Darwin, Charles 1809-1882..... DLB-57, 166
Darwin, Erasmus 1731-1802 ..... DLB-93
Daryush, Elizabeth 1887-1977 ..... DLB-20
Dashkova, Ekaterina Romanovna
 (née Vorontsova) 1743-1810 .... DLB-150
Dashwood, Edmée Elizabeth Monica
 de la Pasture (see Delafield, E. M.)
Daudet, Alphonse 1840-1897...... DLB-123
d'Aulaire, Edgar Parin 1898- and
 d'Aulaire, Ingri 1904- DLB-22
Davenant, Sir William
 1606-1668 .... DLB-58, 126
Davenport, Guy 1927- DLB-130
Davenport, Robert ?-?........... DLB-58
Daves, Delmer 1904-1977 .... DLB-26
Davey, Frank 1940- DLB-53
Davidson, Avram 1923-1993....... DLB-8
Davidson, Donald 1893-1968....... DLB-45
Davidson, John 1857-1909 .... DLB-19
Davidson, Lionel 1922- DLB-14
Davie, Donald 1922- DLB-27
Davie, Elspeth 1919- DLB-139
Davies, Sir John 1569-1626 ...... DLB-172
Davies, John, of Hereford
 1565?-1618................ DLB-121

Davies, Rhys 1901-1978.......... DLB-139
Davies, Robertson 1913- DLB-68
Davies, Samuel 1723-1761 .... DLB-31
Davies, Thomas 1712?-1785.... DLB-142, 154
Davies, W. H. 1871-1940...... DLB-19, 174
Davies, Peter, Limited........... DLB-112
Daviot, Gordon 1896?-1952 ...... DLB-10
 (see also Tey, Josephine)
Davis, Charles A. 1795-1867....... DLB-11
Davis, Clyde Brion 1894-1962....... DLB-9
Davis, Dick 1945- DLB-40
Davis, Frank Marshall 1905-? DLB-51
Davis, H. L. 1894-1960 .... DLB-9
Davis, John 1774-1854 .... DLB-37
Davis, Lydia 1947- DLB-130
Davis, Margaret Thomson 1926- DLB-14
Davis, Ossie 1917- DLB-7, 38
Davis, Paxton 1925-1994 .... Y-94
Davis, Rebecca Harding
 1831-1910 .... DLB-74
Davis, Richard Harding
 1864-1916 .... DLB-12, 23, 78, 79; DS-13
Davis, Samuel Cole 1764-1809...... DLB-37
Davison, Peter 1928- DLB-5
Davys, Mary 1674-1732 .... DLB-39
DAW Books DLB-46
Dawson, Ernest 1882-1947 ...... DLB-140
Dawson, Fielding 1930- DLB-130
Dawson, William 1704-1752 ..... DLB-31
Day, Angel flourished 1586....... DLB-167
Day, Benjamin Henry 1810-1889 ... DLB-43
Day, Clarence 1874-1935........ DLB-11
Day, Dorothy 1897-1980 .... DLB-29
Day, Frank Parker 1881-1950 ..... DLB-92
Day, John circa 1574-circa 1640..... DLB-62
Day, John [publishing house] DLB-170
Day Lewis, C. 1904-1972 ...... DLB-15, 20
 (see also Blake, Nicholas)
Day, Thomas 1748-1789 .... DLB-39
Day, The John, Company DLB-46
Day, Mahlon [publishing house]..... DLB-49
Deacon, William Arthur
 1890-1977................ DLB-68
Deal, Borden 1922-1985 .... DLB-6
de Angeli, Marguerite 1889-1987..... DLB-22
De Angelis, Milo 1951- DLB-128
De Bow, James Dunwoody Brownson
 1820-1867 .... DLB-3, 79
de Bruyn, Günter 1926- DLB-75
de Camp, L. Sprague 1907- DLB-8
The Decay of Lying (1889),
 by Oscar Wilde [excerpt] DLB-18

Dedication, *Ferdinand Count Fathom* (1753), by Tobias Smollett DLB-39

Dedication, *The History of Pompey the Little* (1751), by Francis Coventry DLB-39

Dedication, *Lasselia* (1723), by Eliza Haywood [excerpt] DLB-39

Dedication, *The Wanderer* (1814), by Fanny Burney DLB-39

Dee, John 1527-1609 . . . . DLB-136

Deeping, George Warwick 1877-1950 . . . . DLB 153

Defense of *Amelia* (1752), by Henry Fielding DLB-39

Defoe, Daniel 1660-1731 . . . . DLB-39, 95, 101

de Fontaine, Felix Gregory 1834-1896 . . . . DLB-43

De Forest, John William 1826-1906 . . . . DLB-12

DeFrees, Madeline 1919- DLB-105

DeFrees, Madeline, The Poet's Kaleidoscope: The Element of Surprise in the Making of the Poem DLB-105

de Graff, Robert 1895-1981 . . . . Y-81

de Graft, Joe 1924-1978 . . . . DLB-117

De Heinrico circa 980? DLB-148

Deighton, Len 1929- DLB-87

DeJong, Meindert 1906-1991 . . . . . . DLB-52

Dekker, Thomas circa 1572-1632 . . . . DLB-62, 172

Delacorte, Jr., George T. 1894-1991 . . . . DLB-91

Delafield, E. M. 1890-1943 . . . . DLB-34

Delahaye, Guy 1888-1969 . . . . DLB-92

de la Mare, Walter 1873-1956 . . . . DLB-19, 153, 162

Deland, Margaret 1857-1945 . . . . DLB-78

Delaney, Shelagh 1939- DLB-13

Delany, Martin Robinson 1812-1885 . . . . DLB-50

Delany, Samuel R. 1942- DLB-8, 33

de la Roche, Mazo 1879-1961 . . . . . . DLB-68

Delbanco, Nicholas 1942- DLB-6

De León, Nephtal 1945- DLB-82

Delgado, Abelardo Barrientos 1931- DLB-82

De Libero, Libero 1906-1981 . . . . . . DLB-114

DeLillo, Don 1936- DLB-6, 173

de Lisser H. G. 1878-1944 . . . . DLB-117

Dell, Floyd 1887-1969 . . . . DLB-9

Dell Publishing Company DLB-46

delle Grazie, Marie Eugene 1864-1931 . . . . DLB-81

Deloney, Thomas died 1600 . . . . . . DLB-167

Deloria, Ella C. 1889-1971 . . . . DLB-175

Deloria, Vine, Jr. 1933- DLB-175

del Rey, Lester 1915-1993 . . . . DLB-8

Del Vecchio, John M. 1947- DS-9

de Man, Paul 1919-1983 . . . . DLB-67

Demby, William 1922- DLB-33

Deming, Philander 1829-1915 . . . . . DLB-74

Demorest, William Jennings 1822-1895 . . . . DLB-79

De Morgan, William 1839-1917 . . . . DLB-153

Demosthenes 384 B.C.-322 B.C. DLB-176

Denham, Henry [publishing house] DLB-170

Denham, Sir John 1615-1669 . . . . DLB-58, 126

Denison, Merrill 1893-1975 . . . . DLB-92

Denison, T. S., and Company DLB-49

Dennie, Joseph 1768-1812 . . . . DLB-37, 43, 59, 73

Dennis, John 1658-1734 . . . . DLB-101

Dennis, Nigel 1912-1989 . . . . . . DLB-13, 15

Dent, Tom 1932- DLB-38

Dent, J. M., and Sons DLB-112

Denton, Daniel circa 1626-1703 . . . . DLB-24

DePaola, Tomie 1934- DLB-61

De Quincey, Thomas 1785-1859 . . . . DLB-110, 144

Derby, George Horatio 1823-1861 . . . . DLB-11

Derby, J. C., and Company DLB-49

Derby and Miller DLB-49

Derleth, August 1909-1971 . . . . DLB-9

The Derrydale Press DLB-46

Derzhavin, Gavriil Romanovich 1743-1816 . . . . DLB-150

Desaulniers, Gonsalve 1863-1934 . . . . DLB-92

Desbiens, Jean-Paul 1927- DLB-53

des Forêts, Louis-Rene 1918- DLB-83

Desnica, Vladan 1905-1967 . . . . . . DLB-181

DesRochers, Alfred 1901-1978 . . . . . DLB-68

Desrosiers, Léo-Paul 1896-1967 . . . . DLB-68

Dessì, Giuseppe 1909-1977 . . . . . . DLB-177

Destouches, Louis-Ferdinand (see Céline, Louis-Ferdinand)

De Tabley, Lord 1835-1895 . . . . . . DLB-35

Deutsch, Babette 1895-1982 . . . . . . DLB-45

Deutsch, Niklaus Manuel (see Manuel, Niklaus)

Deutsch, André, Limited DLB-112

Deveaux, Alexis 1948- DLB-38

The Development of the Author's Copyright in Britain DLB-154

The Development of Lighting in the Staging of Drama, 1900-1945 . . . . DLB-10

de Vere, Aubrey 1814-1902 . . . . . . DLB-35

Devereux, second Earl of Essex, Robert 1565-1601 . . . . DLB-136

The Devin-Adair Company DLB-46

De Voto, Bernard 1897-1955 . . . . . . DLB-9

De Vries, Peter 1910-1993 . . . . DLB-6; Y-82

Dewdney, Christopher 1951- DLB-60

Dewdney, Selwyn 1909-1979 . . . . . . DLB-68

DeWitt, Robert M., Publisher DLB-49

DeWolfe, Fiske and Company DLB-49

Dexter, Colin 1930- DLB-87

de Young, M. H. 1849-1925 . . . . . . DLB-25

Dhlomo, H. I. E. 1903-1956 . . . . . DLB-157

Dhuoda circa 803-after 843 . . . . . . DLB-148

The Dial Press DLB-46

Diamond, I. A. L. 1920-1988 . . . . . DLB-26

Di Cicco, Pier Giorgio 1949- DLB-60

Dick, Philip K. 1928-1982 . . . . DLB-8

Dick and Fitzgerald DLB-49

Dickens, Charles 1812-1870 . . . . DLB-21, 55, 70, 159, 166

Dickinson, Peter 1927- DLB-161

Dickey, James 1923-1997 . . . . . . DLB-5; Y-82, 93; DS-7

James Dickey, American Poet Y-96

Dickey, William 1928-1994 . . . . DLB-5

Dickinson, Emily 1830-1886 . . . . DLB-1

Dickinson, John 1732-1808 . . . . . . DLB-31

Dickinson, Jonathan 1688-1747 . . . . DLB-24

Dickinson, Patric 1914- DLB-27

Dickinson, Peter 1927- DLB-87

Dicks, John [publishing house] DLB-106

Dickson, Gordon R. 1923- DLB-8

Dictionary of Literary Biography Yearbook Awards Y-92, 93

The Dictionary of National Biography DLB-144

Didion, Joan 1934- DLB-2, 173; Y-81, 86

Di Donato, Pietro 1911- DLB-9

Die Fürstliche Bibliothek Corvey Y-96

Diego, Gerardo 1896-1987 . . . . . . DLB-134

Digges, Thomas circa 1546-1595 . . . . DLB-136

Dillard, Annie 1945- Y-80

Dillard, R. H. W. 1937- DLB-5

Dillingham, Charles T., Company DLB-49

The Dillingham, G. W., Company DLB-49

Dilly, Edward and Charles [publishing house] DLB-154

Dilthey, Wilhelm 1833-1911 . . . . . . DLB-129

Dimitrova, Blaga 1922- DLB-181

Dimov, Dimitŭr 1909-1966 . . . . . . DLB-181

Dingelstedt, Franz von 1814-1881 . . . . DLB-133

Dintenfass, Mark 1941- Y-84

Diogenes, Jr. (see Brougham, John)

Diogenes Laertius circa 200 . . . . DLB-176

DiPrima, Diane 1934- DLB-5, 16

Disch, Thomas M. 1940- DLB-8

Disney, Walt 1901-1966 . . . . DLB-22

Disraeli, Benjamin 1804-1881 . . . . DLB-21, 55

D'Israeli, Isaac 1766-1848 . . . . DLB-107

Ditzen, Rudolf (see Fallada, Hans)

Dix, Dorothea Lynde 1802-1887 . . . . . DLB-1

Dix, Dorothy (see Gilmer, Elizabeth Meriwether)

Dix, Edwards and Company DLB-49

Dixie, Florence Douglas 1857-1905 . . . . DLB-174

Dixon, Paige (see Corcoran, Barbara)

Dixon, Richard Watson 1833-1900 . . . . DLB-19

Dixon, Stephen 1936- DLB-130

Dmitriev, Ivan Ivanovich 1760-1837 . . . . DLB-150

Dobell, Sydney 1824-1874 . . . . DLB-32

Döblin, Alfred 1878-1957 . . . . DLB-66

Dobson, Austin 1840-1921 . . . . DLB-35, 144

Doctorow, E. L. 1931- DLB-2, 28, 173; Y-80

Documents on Sixteenth-Century Literature DLB-167, 172

Dodd, William E. 1869-1940 . . . . . . DLB-17

Dodd, Anne [publishing house] DLB-154

Dodd, Mead and Company DLB-49

Doderer, Heimito von 1896-1968 . . . . DLB-85

Dodge, Mary Mapes 1831?-1905 . . . . DLB-42, 79; DS-13

Dodge, B. W., and Company DLB-46

Dodge Publishing Company DLB-49

Dodgson, Charles Lutwidge (see Carroll, Lewis)

Dodsley, Robert 1703-1764 . . . . DLB-95

Dodsley, R. [publishing house] DLB-154

Dodson, Owen 1914-1983 . . . . DLB-76

Doesticks, Q. K. Philander, P. B. (see Thomson, Mortimer)

Doheny, Carrie Estelle 1875-1958 . . . . DLB-140

Domínguez, Sylvia Maida 1935- DLB-122

Donahoe, Patrick [publishing house] DLB-49

Donald, David H. 1920- DLB-17

Donaldson, Scott 1928- DLB-111

Doni, Rodolfo 1919- DLB-177

Donleavy, J. P. 1926- DLB-6, 173

Donnadieu, Marguerite (see Duras, Marguerite)

Donne, John 1572-1631 . . . . . DLB-121, 151

Donnelley, R. R., and Sons Company DLB-49

Donnelly, Ignatius 1831-1901 . . . . . . DLB-12

Donohue and Henneberry DLB-49

Donoso, José 1924- DLB-113

Doolady, M. [publishing house] DLB-49

Dooley, Ebon (see Ebon)

Doolittle, Hilda 1886-1961 . . . . DLB-4, 45

Doplicher, Fabio 1938- DLB-128

Dor, Milo 1923- DLB-85

Doran, George H., Company DLB-46

Dorgelès, Roland 1886-1973 . . . . . . DLB-65

Dorn, Edward 1929- DLB-5

Dorr, Rheta Childe 1866-1948 . . . . . DLB-25

Dorris, Michael 1945-1997 . . . . . . DLB-175

Dorset and Middlesex, Charles Sackville, Lord Buckhurst, Earl of 1643-1706 . . . . DLB-131

Dorst, Tankred 1925- DLB-75, 124

Dos Passos, John 1896-1970 . . . . DLB-4, 9; DS-1

John Dos Passos: A Centennial Commemoration Y-96

Doubleday and Company DLB-49

Dougall, Lily 1858-1923 . . . . DLB-92

Doughty, Charles M. 1843-1926 . . . . DLB-19, 57, 174

Douglas, Gavin 1476-1522 . . . . DLB-132

Douglas, Keith 1920-1944 . . . . DLB-27

Douglas, Norman 1868-1952 . . . . . . DLB-34

Douglass, Frederick 1817?-1895 . . . . . . DLB-1, 43, 50, 79

Douglass, William circa 1691-1752 . . . . DLB-24

Dourado, Autran 1926- DLB-145

Dove, Rita 1952- DLB-120

Dover Publications DLB-46

Doves Press DLB-112

Dowden, Edward 1843-1913 . . . . DLB-35, 149

Dowell, Coleman 1925-1985 . . . . . . DLB-130

Dowland, John 1563-1626 . . . . DLB-172

Downes, Gwladys 1915- DLB-88

Downing, J., Major (see Davis, Charles A.)

Downing, Major Jack (see Smith, Seba)

Dowriche, Anne before 1560-after 1613 . . . . . . DLB-172

Dowson, Ernest 1867-1900 . . . . . DLB-19, 135

Doxey, William [publishing house] DLB-49

Doyle, Sir Arthur Conan 1859-1930 . . . . . . DLB-18, 70, 156, 178

Doyle, Kirby 1932- DLB-16

Drabble, Margaret 1939- DLB-14, 155

Drach, Albert 1902- DLB-85

Dragojević, Danijel 1934- DLB-181

The Dramatic Publishing Company DLB-49

Dramatists Play Service DLB-46

Drant, Thomas early 1540s?-1578 . . . . DLB-167

Draper, John W. 1811-1882 . . . . DLB-30

Draper, Lyman C. 1815-1891 . . . . . . DLB-30

Drayton, Michael 1563-1631 . . . . . . DLB-121

Dreiser, Theodore 1871-1945 . . . . DLB-9, 12, 102, 137; DS-1

Drewitz, Ingeborg 1923-1986 . . . . . . DLB-75

Drieu La Rochelle, Pierre 1893-1945 . . . . DLB-72

Drinkwater, John 1882-1937 . . . . DLB-10, 19, 149

Droste-Hülshoff, Annette von 1797-1848 . . . . DLB-133

The Drue Heinz Literature Prize Excerpt from "Excerpts from a Report of the Commission," in David Bosworth's *The Death of Descartes* An Interview with David Bosworth Y-82

Drummond, William Henry 1854-1907 . . . . DLB-92

Drummond, William, of Hawthornden 1585-1649 . . . . DLB-121

Dryden, Charles 1860?-1931 . . . . . . DLB-171

Dryden, John 1631-1700 . . . DLB-80, 101, 131

Držić, Marin circa 1508-1567 . . . . . . DLB-147

Duane, William 1760-1835 . . . . DLB-43

Dubé, Marcel 1930- DLB-53

Dubé, Rodolphe (see Hertel, François)

Dubie, Norman 1945- DLB-120

Du Bois, W. E. B. 1868-1963 . . . . DLB-47, 50, 91

Du Bois, William Pène 1916- DLB-61

Dubus, Andre 1936- DLB-130

Ducharme, Réjean 1941- DLB-60

Dučić, Jovan 1871-1943 . . . . DLB-147

Duck, Stephen 1705?-1756 . . . . DLB-95

Duckworth, Gerald, and Company Limited DLB-112

Dudek, Louis 1918- DLB-88

Duell, Sloan and Pearce DLB-46

Duerer, Albrecht 1471-1528 . . . . . . DLB-179

Duff Gordon, Lucie 1821-1869 . . . . . DLB-166

Duffield and Green DLB-46

Duffy, Maureen 1933- DLB-14

Dugan, Alan 1923- DLB-5

Dugard, William
[publishing house] DLB-170

Dugas, Marcel 1883-1947 . . . . DLB-92

Dugdale, William
[publishing house] DLB-106

Duhamel, Georges 1884-1966 . . . . . . DLB-65

Dujardin, Edouard 1861-1949 . . . . . . DLB-123

Dukes, Ashley 1885-1959 . . . . DLB-10

Du Maurier, George
1834-1896 . . . . DLB-153, 178

Dumas, Alexandre, *père*
1802-1870 . . . . DLB-119

Dumas, Henry 1934-1968 . . . . DLB-41

Dunbar, Paul Laurence
1872-1906 . . . . DLB-50, 54, 78

Dunbar, William
circa 1460-circa 1522 . . . . . DLB-132, 146

Duncan, Norman 1871-1916 . . . . DLB-92

Duncan, Quince 1940- DLB-145

Duncan, Robert 1919-1988 . . . . . . DLB-5, 16

Duncan, Ronald 1914-1982 . . . . DLB-13

Duncan, Sara Jeannette
1861-1922 . . . . DLB-92

Dunigan, Edward, and Brother DLB-49

Dunlap, John 1747-1812 . . . . DLB-43

Dunlap, William
1766-1839 . . . . DLB-30, 37, 59

Dunn, Douglas 1942- DLB-40

Dunn, Stephen 1939- DLB-105

Dunn, Stephen, The Good,
The Not So Good DLB-105

Dunne, Finley Peter
1867-1936 . . . . DLB-11, 23

Dunne, John Gregory 1932- Y-80

Dunne, Philip 1908-1992 . . . . DLB-26

Dunning, Ralph Cheever
1878-1930 . . . . DLB-4

Dunning, William A. 1857-1922 . . . . DLB-17

Duns Scotus, John
circa 1266-1308 . . . . DLB-115

Dunsany, Lord (Edward John Moreton
Drax Plunkett, Baron Dunsany)
1878-1957 . . . . DLB-10, 77, 153, 156

Dunton, John [publishing house] DLB-170

Dupin, Amantine-Aurore-Lucile (see Sand, George)

Durand, Lucile (see Bersianik, Louky)

Duranty, Walter 1884-1957 . . . . DLB-29

Duras, Marguerite 1914- DLB-83

Durfey, Thomas 1653-1723 . . . . DLB-80

Durrell, Lawrence
1912-1990 . . . . DLB-15, 27; Y-90

Durrell, William
[publishing house] DLB-49

Dürrenmatt, Friedrich
1921-1990 . . . . DLB-69, 124

Dutton, E. P., and Company DLB-49

Duvoisin, Roger 1904-1980 . . . . DLB-61

Duyckinck, Evert Augustus
1816-1878 . . . . DLB-3, 64

Duyckinck, George L. 1823-1863 . . . . DLB-3

Duyckinck and Company DLB-49

Dwight, John Sullivan 1813-1893 . . . . DLB-1

Dwight, Timothy 1752-1817 . . . . DLB-37

Dybek, Stuart 1942- DLB-130

Dyer, Charles 1928- DLB-13

Dyer, George 1755-1841 . . . . DLB-93

Dyer, John 1699-1757 . . . . DLB-95

Dyer, Sir Edward 1543-1607 . . . . . . DLB-136

Dylan, Bob 1941- DLB-16

E

Eager, Edward 1911-1964 . . . . DLB-22

Eames, Wilberforce 1855-1937 . . . . . DLB-140

Earle, James H., and Company DLB-49

Earle, John 1600 or 1601-1665 . . . . . DLB-151

Early American Book Illustration,
by Sinclair Hamilton DLB-49

Eastlake, William 1917- DLB-6

Eastman, Carol ?- DLB-44

Eastman, Charles A. (Ohiyesa)
1858-1939 . . . . DLB-175

Eastman, Max 1883-1969 . . . . DLB-91

Eaton, Daniel Isaac 1753-1814 . . . . . DLB-158

Eberhart, Richard 1904- DLB-48

Ebner, Jeannie 1918- DLB-85

Ebner-Eschenbach, Marie von
1830-1916 . . . . DLB-81

Ebon 1942- DLB-41

Ebasis Captivi circa 1045 . . . . DLB-148

Ecco Press DLB-46

Eckhart, Meister
circa 1260-circa 1328 . . . . DLB-115

The Eclectic Review 1805-1868 . . . . . DLB-110

Edel, Leon 1907- DLB-103

Edes, Benjamin 1732-1803 . . . . DLB-43

Edgar, David 1948- DLB-13

Edgeworth, Maria
1768-1849 . . . . DLB-116, 159, 163

The Edinburgh Review 1802-1929 . . . . DLB-110

Edinburgh University Press DLB-112

The Editor Publishing Company DLB-49

Editorial Statements DLB-137

Edmonds, Randolph 1900- DLB-51

Edmonds, Walter D. 1903- DLB-9

Edschmid, Kasimir 1890-1966 . . . . . DLB-56

Edwards, Amelia Anne Blandford
1831-1892 . . . . DLB-174

Edwards, Jonathan 1703-1758 . . . . . DLB-24

Edwards, Jonathan, Jr. 1745-1801 . . . DLB-37

Edwards, Junius 1929- DLB-33

Edwards, Matilda Barbara Betham-
1836-1919 . . . . DLB-174

Edwards, Richard 1524-1566 . . . . . . DLB-62

Edwards, James
[publishing house] DLB-154

Effinger, George Alec 1947- DLB-8

Egerton, George 1859-1945 . . . . DLB-135

Eggleston, Edward 1837-1902 . . . . . . DLB-12

Eggleston, Wilfred 1901-1986 . . . . . . DLB-92

Ehrenstein, Albert 1886-1950 . . . . . . DLB-81

Ehrhart, W. D. 1948- DS-9

Eich, Günter 1907-1972 . . . . . . DLB-69, 124

Eichendorff, Joseph Freiherr von
1788-1857 . . . . DLB-90

1873 Publishers' Catalogues DLB-49

Eighteenth-Century Aesthetic
Theories DLB-31

Eighteenth-Century Philosophical
Background DLB-31

Eigner, Larry 1927- DLB-5

Eikon Basilike 1649 . . . . DLB-151

Eilhart von Oberge
circa 1140-circa 1195 . . . . DLB-148

Einhard circa 770-840 . . . . DLB-148

Eisenreich, Herbert 1925-1986 . . . . . DLB-85

Eisner, Kurt 1867-1919 . . . . DLB-66

Eklund, Gordon 1945- Y-83

Ekwensi, Cyprian 1921- DLB-117

Eld, George
[publishing house] DLB-170

Elder, Lonne III 1931- DLB-7, 38, 44

Elder, Paul, and Company DLB-49

Elements of Rhetoric (1828; revised, 1846),
by Richard Whately [excerpt] DLB-57

Elie, Robert 1915-1973 . . . . DLB-88

Elin Pelin 1877-1949 . . . . DLB-147

Eliot, George 1819-1880 . . . . . DLB-21, 35, 55

Eliot, John 1604-1690 . . . . DLB-24

Eliot, T. S. 1888-1965 . . . . DLB-7, 10, 45, 63

Eliot's Court Press DLB-170

Elizabeth I 1533-1603 . . . . DLB-136

Elizabeth of Nassau-Saarbrücken
after 1393-1456 . . . . DLB-179

Elizondo, Salvador 1932- DLB-145

Elizondo, Sergio 1930- DLB-82

Elkin, Stanley 1930- DLB-2, 28; Y-80

Elles, Dora Amy (see Wentworth, Patricia)

Ellet, Elizabeth F. 1818?-1877 . . . . . DLB-30

Elliot, Ebenezer 1781-1849 . . . . DLB-96

Elliot, Frances Minto (Dickinson) 1820-1898 .... DLB-166

Elliott, George 1923- DLB-68

Elliott, Janice 1931- DLB-14

Elliott, William 1788-1863 .... DLB-3

Elliott, Thomes and Talbot DLB-49

Ellis, Edward S. 1840-1916 .... DLB-42

Ellis, Frederick Staridge [publishing house] DLB-106

The George H. Ellis Company DLB-49

Ellison, Harlan 1934- DLB-8

Ellison, Ralph Waldo 1914-1994 .... DLB-2, 76; Y-94

Ellmann, Richard 1918-1987 .... DLB-103; Y-87

The Elmer Holmes Bobst Awards in Arts and Letters Y-87

Elyot, Thomas 1490?-1546 .... DLB-136

Emanuel, James Andrew 1921- DLB-41

Emecheta, Buchi 1944- DLB-117

The Emergence of Black Women Writers DS-8

Emerson, Ralph Waldo 1803-1882 .... DLB-1, 59, 73

Emerson, William 1769-1811 .... DLB-37

Emin, Fedor Aleksandrovich circa 1735-1770 .... DLB-150

Empedocles fifth century B.C. DLB-176

Empson, William 1906-1984 .... DLB-20

The End of English Stage Censorship, 1945-1968 .... DLB-13

Ende, Michael 1929- DLB-75

Engel, Marian 1933-1985 .... DLB-53

Engels, Friedrich 1820-1895 .... DLB-129

Engle, Paul 1908- DLB-48

English Composition and Rhetoric (1866), by Alexander Bain [excerpt] DLB-57

The English Language: 410 to 1500 .... DLB-146

The English Renaissance of Art (1908), by Oscar Wilde DLB-35

Enright, D. J. 1920- DLB-27

Enright, Elizabeth 1909-1968 .... DLB-22

L'Envoi (1882), by Oscar Wilde. DLB-35

Epictetus circa 55-circa 125-130 ..... DLB-176

Epicurus 342/341 B.C.-271/270 B.C. DLB-176

Epps, Bernard 1936- DLB-53

Epstein, Julius 1909- and Epstein, Philip 1909-1952. ...... DLB-26

Equiano, Olaudah circa 1745-1797 .... DLB-37, 50

Eragny Press DLB-112

Erasmus, Desiderius 1467-1536 .... DLB-136

Erba, Luciano 1922- DLB-128

Erdrich, Louise 1954- DLB-152, 178

Erichsen-Brown, Gwethalyn Graham (see Graham, Gwethalyn)

Eriugena, John Scottus circa 810-877 .... DLB-115

Ernest Hemingway's Toronto Journalism Revisited: With Three Previously Unrecorded Stories Y-92

Ernst, Paul 1866-1933 .... DLB-66, 118

Erskine, Albert 1911-1993 .... Y-93

Erskine, John 1879-1951 ...... DLB-9, 102

Ervine, St. John Greer 1883-1971 .... DLB-10

Eschenburg, Johann Joachim 1743-1820 .... DLB-97

Escoto, Julio 1944- DLB-145

Eshleman, Clayton 1935- DLB-5

Espriu, Salvador 1913-1985 .... DLB-134

Ess Ess Publishing Company DLB-49

Essay on Chatterton (1842), by Robert Browning DLB-32

Essex House Press DLB-112

Estes, Eleanor 1906-1988 .... DLB-22

Estes and Lauriat DLB-49

Etherege, George 1636-circa 1692 .... DLB-80

Ethridge, Mark, Sr. 1896-1981 ..... DLB-127

Ets, Marie Hall 1893- DLB-22

Etter, David 1928- DLB-105

Ettner, Johann Christoph 1654-1724 .... DLB-168

Eudora Welty: Eye of the Storyteller Y-87

Eugene O'Neill Memorial Theater Center DLB-7

Eugene O'Neill's Letters: A Review Y-88

Eupolemius flourished circa 1095 .... DLB-148

Euripides circa 484 B.C.-407/406 B.C. DLB-176

Evans, Caradoc 1878-1945 .... DLB-162

Evans, Donald 1884-1921 .... DLB-54

Evans, George Henry 1805-1856 .... DLB-43

Evans, Hubert 1892-1986 .... DLB-92

Evans, Mari 1923- DLB-41

Evans, Mary Ann (see Eliot, George)

Evans, Nathaniel 1742-1767 .... DLB-31

Evans, Sebastian 1830-1909 .... DLB-35

Evans, M., and Company DLB-46

Everett, Alexander Hill 790-1847 .... DLB-59

Everett, Edward 1794-1865 ..... DLB-1, 59

Everson, R. G. 1903- DLB-88

Everson, William 1912-1994 ..... DLB-5, 16

Every Man His Own Poet; or, The Inspired Singer's Recipe Book (1877), by W. H. Mallock DLB-35

Ewart, Gavin 1916- DLB-40

Ewing, Juliana Horatia 1841-1885 .... DLB-21, 163

The Examiner 1808-1881 .... DLB-110

Exley, Frederick 1929-1992 .... DLB-143; Y-81

Experiment in the Novel (1929), by John D. Beresford DLB-36

von Eyb, Albrecht 1420-1475 ...... DLB-179

Eyre and Spottiswoode DLB-106

Ezzo ?-after 1065 .... DLB-148

F

"F. Scott Fitzgerald: St. Paul's Native Son and Distinguished American Writer": University of Minnesota Conference, 29-31 October 1982 .... Y-82

Faber, Frederick William 1814-1863 .... DLB-32

Faber and Faber Limited DLB-112

Faccio, Rena (see Aleramo, Sibilla)

Fagundo, Ana María 1938- DLB-134

Fair, Ronald L. 1932- DLB-33

Fairfax, Beatrice (see Manning, Marie)

Fairlie, Gerard 1899-1983 .... DLB-77

Fallada, Hans 1893-1947 .... DLB-56

Falsifying Hemingway Y-96

Fancher, Betsy 1928- Y-83

Fane, Violet 1843-1905 .... DLB-35

Fanfrolico Press DLB-112

Fanning, Katherine 1927- DLB-127

Fanshawe, Sir Richard 1608-1666 .... DLB-126

Fantasy Press Publishers DLB-46

Fante, John 1909-1983 ...... DLB-130; Y-83

Al-Farabi circa 870-950 .... DLB-115

Farah, Nuruddin 1945- DLB-125

Farber, Norma 1909-1984 .... DLB-61

Farigoule, Louis (see Romains, Jules)

Farjeon, Eleanor 1881-1965 ...... DLB-160

Farley, Walter 1920-1989 .... DLB-22

Farmer, Penelope 1939- DLB-161

Farmer, Philip José 1918- DLB-8

Farquhar, George circa 1677-1707 .... DLB-84

Farquharson, Martha (see Finley, Martha)

Farrar, Frederic William 1831-1903 .... DLB-163

Farrar and Rinehart DLB-46

Farrar, Straus and Giroux DLB-46

Farrell, James T. 1904-1979 .... DLB-4, 9, 86; DS-2

Farrell, J. G. 1935-1979 .... DLB-14

Fast, Howard 1914- DLB-9

Faulkner, William 1897-1962 . . . . DLB-9, 11, 44, 102; DS-2; Y-86

Faulkner, George [publishing house] DLB-154

Fauset, Jessie Redmon 1882-1961 . . . . DLB-51

Faust, Irvin 1924- DLB-2, 28; Y-80

Fawcett Books DLB-46

Fearing, Kenneth 1902-1961 . . . . DLB-9

Federal Writers' Project DLB-46

Federman, Raymond 1928- Y-80

Feiffer, Jules 1929- DLB-7, 44

Feinberg, Charles E. 1899-1988 . . . . Y-88

Feind, Barthold 1678-1721 . . . . DLB-168

Feinstein, Elaine 1930- DLB-14, 40

Feldman, Irving 1928- DLB-169

Felipe, Léon 1884-1968 . . . . DLB-108

Fell, Frederick, Publishers DLB-46

Felltham, Owen 1602?-1668 . . . . DLB-126, 151

Fels, Ludwig 1946- DLB-75

Felton, Cornelius Conway 1807-1862 . . . . DLB-1

Fennario, David 1947- DLB-60

Fenno, John 1751-1798 . . . . DLB-43

Fenno, R. F., and Company DLB-49

Fenoglio, Beppe 1922-1963 . . . . DLB-177

Fenton, Geoffrey 1539?-1608 . . . . . . DLB-136

Fenton, James 1949- DLB-40

Ferber, Edna 1885-1968 . . . . . . DLB-9, 28, 86

Ferdinand, Vallery III (see Salaam, Kalamu ya)

Ferguson, Sir Samuel 1810-1886 . . . . . DLB-32

Ferguson, William Scott 1875-1954 . . . . DLB-47

Fergusson, Robert 1750-1774 . . . . . DLB-109

Ferland, Albert 1872-1943 . . . . DLB-92

Ferlinghetti, Lawrence 1919- DLB-5, 16

Fern, Fanny (see Parton, Sara Payson Willis)

Ferrars, Elizabeth 1907- DLB-87

Ferré, Rosario 1942- DLB-145

Ferret, E., and Company DLB-49

Ferrier, Susan 1782-1854 . . . . DLB-116

Ferrini, Vincent 1913- DLB-48

Ferron, Jacques 1921-1985 . . . . DLB-60

Ferron, Madeleine 1922- DLB-53

Fetridge and Company DLB-49

Feuchtersleben, Ernst Freiherr von 1806-1849 . . . . DLB-133

Feuchtwanger, Lion 1884-1958 . . . . . . DLB-66

Feuerbach, Ludwig 1804-1872 . . . . . DLB-133

Fichte, Johann Gottlieb 1762-1814 . . . . DLB-90

Ficke, Arthur Davison 1883-1945 . . . . DLB-54

Fiction Best-Sellers, 1910-1945 . . . . . . DLB-9

Fiction into Film, 1928-1975: A List of Movies Based on the Works of Authors in *British Novelists,* 1930-1959 . . . . . . DLB-15

Fiedler, Leslie A. 1917- DLB-28, 67

Field, Edward 1924- DLB-105

Field, Edward, The Poetry File DLB-105

Field, Eugene 1850-1895 . . . . . DLB-23, 42, 140; DS-13

Field, John 1545?-1588 . . . . DLB-167

Field, Marshall, III 1893-1956 . . . . . . DLB-127

Field, Marshall, IV 1916-1965 . . . . . . DLB-127

Field, Marshall, V 1941- DLB-127

Field, Nathan 1587-1619 or 1620 . . . . DLB-58

Field, Rachel 1894-1942 . . . . DLB-9, 22

A Field Guide to Recent Schools of American Poetry Y-86

Fielding, Henry 1707-1754 . . . . DLB-39, 84, 101

Fielding, Sarah 1710-1768 . . . . DLB-39

Fields, James Thomas 1817-1881 . . . . . DLB-1

Fields, Julia 1938- DLB-41

Fields, W. C. 1880-1946 . . . . DLB-44

Fields, Osgood and Company DLB-49

Fifty Penguin Years Y-85

Figes, Eva 1932- DLB-14

Figuera, Angela 1902-1984 . . . . DLB-108

Filmer, Sir Robert 1586-1653 . . . . . . DLB-151

Filson, John circa 1753-1788 . . . . . . DLB-37

Finch, Anne, Countess of Winchilsea 1661-1720 . . . . DLB-95

Finch, Robert 1900- DLB-88

Findley, Timothy 1930- DLB-53

Finlay, Ian Hamilton 1925- DLB-40

Finley, Martha 1828-1909 . . . . DLB-42

Finn, Elizabeth Anne (McCaul) 1825-1921 . . . . DLB-166

Finney, Jack 1911- DLB-8

Finney, Walter Braden (see Finney, Jack)

Firbank, Ronald 1886-1926 . . . . DLB-36

Firmin, Giles 1615-1697 . . . . DLB-24

Fischart, Johann 1546 or 1547-1590 or 1591 . . . . DLB-179

First Edition Library/Collectors' Reprints, Inc Y-91

First International F. Scott Fitzgerald Conference Y-92

First Strauss "Livings" Awarded to Cynthia Ozick and Raymond Carver An Interview with Cynthia Ozick An Interview with Raymond Carver Y-83

Fischer, Karoline Auguste Fernandine 1764-1842 . . . . DLB-94

Fish, Stanley 1938- DLB-67

Fishacre, Richard 1205-1248 . . . . . . DLB-115

Fisher, Clay (see Allen, Henry W.)

Fisher, Dorothy Canfield 1879-1958 . . . . DLB-9, 102

Fisher, Leonard Everett 1924- DLB-61

Fisher, Roy 1930- DLB-40

Fisher, Rudolph 1897-1934 . . . . . DLB-51, 102

Fisher, Sydney George 1856-1927 . . . . DLB-47

Fisher, Vardis 1895-1968 . . . . DLB-9

Fiske, John 1608-1677 . . . . DLB-24

Fiske, John 1842-1901 . . . . DLB-47, 64

Fitch, Thomas circa 1700-1774 . . . . . DLB-31

Fitch, William Clyde 1865-1909 . . . . . DLB-7

FitzGerald, Edward 1809-1883 . . . . . DLB-32

Fitzgerald, F. Scott 1896-1940 . . . . . DLB-4, 9, 86; Y-81; DS-1

F. Scott Fitzgerald Centenary Celebrations Y-96

Fitzgerald, Penelope 1916- DLB-14

Fitzgerald, Robert 1910-1985 . . . . Y-80

Fitzgerald, Thomas 1819-1891 . . . . . DLB-23

Fitzgerald, Zelda Sayre 1900-1948 . . . . . Y-84

Fitzhugh, Louise 1928-1974 . . . . DLB-52

Fitzhugh, William circa 1651-1701 . . . . DLB-24

Flanagan, Thomas 1923- Y-80

Flanner, Hildegarde 1899-1987 . . . . . DLB-48

Flanner, Janet 1892-1978 . . . . DLB-4

Flaubert, Gustave 1821-1880 . . . . . . DLB-119

Flavin, Martin 1883-1967 . . . . DLB-9

Fleck, Konrad (flourished circa 1220) DLB-138

Flecker, James Elroy 1884-1915 . . . DLB-10, 19

Fleeson, Doris 1901-1970 . . . . DLB-29

Fleißer, Marieluise 1901-1974 . . . . DLB-56, 124

Fleming, Ian 1908-1964 . . . . DLB-87

Fleming, Paul 1609-1640 . . . . DLB-164

The Fleshly School of Poetry and Other Phenomena of the Day (1872), by Robert Buchanan DLB-35

The Fleshly School of Poetry: Mr. D. G. Rossetti (1871), by Thomas Maitland (Robert Buchanan) DLB-35

Fletcher, Giles, the Elder 1546-1611 . . . . DLB-136

Fletcher, Giles, the Younger 1585 or 1586-1623 . . . . DLB-121

Fletcher, J. S. 1863-1935 . . . . DLB-70

Fletcher, John (see Beaumont, Francis)

Fletcher, John Gould 1886-1950 . . . DLB-4, 45

Fletcher, Phineas 1582-1650 . . . . . . DLB-121

Flieg, Helmut (see Heym, Stefan)

Flint, F. S. 1885-1960 . . . . DLB-19

Flint, Timothy 1780-1840 . . . . DLB-73

Florio, John 1553?-1625 . . . . DLB-172

Foix, J. V. 1893-1987 . . . . DLB-134

Foley, Martha (see Burnett, Whit, and Martha Foley)

Folger, Henry Clay 1857-1930 . . . . . DLB-140

Folio Society DLB-112

Follen, Eliza Lee (Cabot) 1787-1860 . . . DLB-1

Follett, Ken 1949- Y-81, DLB-87

Follett Publishing Company DLB-46

Folsom, John West [publishing house] DLB-49

Folz, Hans between 1435 and 1440-1513 . . . . DLB-179

Fontane, Theodor 1819-1898 . . . . . . DLB-129

Fonvisin, Denis Ivanovich 1744 or 1745-1792 . . . . DLB-150

Foote, Horton 1916- DLB-26

Foote, Samuel 1721-1777 . . . . DLB-89

Foote, Shelby 1916- DLB-2, 17

Forbes, Calvin 1945- DLB-41

Forbes, Ester 1891-1967 . . . . DLB-22

Forbes and Company DLB-49

Force, Peter 1790-1868 . . . . DLB-30

Forché, Carolyn 1950- DLB-5

Ford, Charles Henri 1913- DLB-4, 48

Ford, Corey 1902-1969 . . . . DLB-11

Ford, Ford Madox 1873-1939 . . . . DLB-34, 98, 162

Ford, Jesse Hill 1928- DLB-6

Ford, John 1586-? DLB-58

Ford, R. A. D. 1915- DLB-88

Ford, Worthington C. 1858-1941 . . . . DLB-47

Ford, J. B., and Company DLB-49

Fords, Howard, and Hulbert DLB-49

Foreman, Carl 1914-1984 . . . . DLB-26

Forester, Frank (see Herbert, Henry William)

Fornés, María Irene 1930- DLB-7

Forrest, Leon 1937- DLB-33

Forster, E. M. 1879-1970 . . . DLB-34, 98, 162, 178; DS-10

Forster, Georg 1754-1794 . . . . DLB-94

Forster, John 1812-1876 . . . . DLB-144

Forster, Margaret 1938- DLB-155

Forsyth, Frederick 1938- DLB-87

Forten, Charlotte L. 1837-1914 . . . . . DLB-50

Fortini, Franco 1917- DLB-128

Fortune, T. Thomas 1856-1928 . . . . . DLB-23

Fosdick, Charles Austin 1842-1915 . . . . DLB-42

Foster, Genevieve 1893-1979 . . . . . . DLB-61

Foster, Hannah Webster 1758-1840 . . . . DLB-37

Foster, John 1648-1681 . . . . DLB-24

Foster, Michael 1904-1956 . . . . DLB-9

Foulis, Robert and Andrew / R. and A. [publishing house] DLB-154

Fouqué, Caroline de la Motte 1774-1831 . . . . DLB-90

Fouqué, Friedrich de la Motte 1777-1843 . . . . DLB-90

Four Essays on the Beat Generation, by John Clellon Holmes DLB-16

Four Seas Company DLB-46

Four Winds Press DLB-46

Fournier, Henri Alban (see Alain-Fournier)

Fowler and Wells Company DLB-49

Fowles, John 1926- DLB-14, 139

Fox, John, Jr. 1862 or 1863-1919 . . . . DLB-9; DS-13

Fox, Paula 1923- DLB-52

Fox, Richard Kyle 1846-1922 . . . . . . DLB-79

Fox, William Price 1926- DLB-2; Y-81

Fox, Richard K. [publishing house] DLB-49

Foxe, John 1517-1587 . . . . DLB-132

Fraenkel, Michael 1896-1957 . . . . . . DLB-4

France, Anatole 1844-1924 . . . . . . DLB-123

France, Richard 1938- DLB-7

Francis, Convers 1795-1863 . . . . DLB-1

Francis, Dick 1920- DLB-87

Francis, Jeffrey, Lord 1773-1850 . . . . DLB-107

Francis, C. S. [publishing house] DLB-49

François 1863-1910 . . . . DLB-92

François, Louise von 1817-1893 . . . . DLB-129

Franck, Sebastian 1499-1542 . . . . . . DLB-179

Francke, Kuno 1855-1930 . . . . DLB-71

Frank, Bruno 1887-1945 . . . . DLB-118

Frank, Leonhard 1882-1961 . . . . DLB-56, 118

Frank, Melvin (see Panama, Norman)

Frank, Waldo 1889-1967 . . . . DLB-9, 63

Franken, Rose 1895?-1988 . . . . Y-84

Franklin, Benjamin 1706-1790 . . . . DLB-24, 43, 73

Franklin, James 1697-1735 . . . . DLB-43

Franklin Library DLB-46

Frantz, Ralph Jules 1902-1979 . . . . . . DLB-4

Franzos, Karl Emil 1848-1904 . . . . . DLB-129

Fraser, G. S. 1915-1980 . . . . DLB-27

Fraser, Kathleen 1935- DLB-169

Frattini, Alberto 1922- DLB-128

Frau Ava ?-1127 . . . . DLB-148

Frayn, Michael 1933- DLB-13, 14

Frederic, Harold 1856-1898 . . . . DLB-12, 23; DS-13

Freeling, Nicolas 1927- DLB-87

Freeman, Douglas Southall 1886-1953 . . . . DLB-17

Freeman, Legh Richmond 1842-1915 . . . . DLB-23

Freeman, Mary E. Wilkins 1852-1930 . . . . DLB-12, 78

Freeman, R. Austin 1862-1943 . . . . . DLB-70

Freidank circa 1170-circa 1233 . . . . DLB-138

Freiligrath, Ferdinand 1810-1876 . . . . DLB-133

French, Alice 1850-1934 . . . . . DLB-74; DS-13

French, David 1939- DLB-53

French, James [publishing house] DLB-49

French, Samuel [publishing house] DLB-49

Samuel French, Limited DLB-106

Freneau, Philip 1752-1832 . . . . . . DLB-37, 43

Freni, Melo 1934- DLB-128

Freshfield, Douglas W. 1845-1934 . . . . DLB-174

Freytag, Gustav 1816-1895 . . . . DLB-129

Fried, Erich 1921-1988 . . . . DLB-85

Friedman, Bruce Jay 1930- DLB-2, 28

Friedrich von Hausen circa 1171-1190 . . . . DLB-138

Friel, Brian 1929- DLB-13

Friend, Krebs 1895?-1967? DLB-4

Fries, Fritz Rudolf 1935- DLB-75

Fringe and Alternative Theater in Great Britain DLB-13

Frisch, Max 1911-1991 . . . . . . DLB-69, 124

Frischlin, Nicodemus 1547-1590 . . . . DLB-179

Frischmuth, Barbara 1941- DLB-85

Fritz, Jean 1915- DLB-52

Fromentin, Eugene 1820-1876 . . . . . DLB-123

From The Gay Science, by E. S. Dallas DLB-21

Frost, A. B. 1851-1928 . . . . DS-13

Frost, Robert 1874-1963 . . . . . . DLB-54; DS-7

Frothingham, Octavius Brooks 1822-1895 . . . . DLB-1

Froude, James Anthony 1818-1894 . . . . DLB-18, 57, 144

Fry, Christopher 1907- DLB-13

Fry, Roger 1866-1934 . . . . DS-10

Frye, Northrop 1912-1991 . . . . . DLB-67, 68

Fuchs, Daniel 1909-1993 . . . . DLB-9, 26, 28; Y-93

Fuentes, Carlos 1928- DLB-113

Fuertes, Gloria 1918- DLB-108

The Fugitives and the Agrarians: The First Exhibition Y-85

Fulbecke, William 1560-1603? DLB-172

Fuller, Charles H., Jr. 1939- DLB-38

Fuller, Henry Blake 1857-1929 . . . . . DLB-12

Fuller, John 1937- DLB-40

Fuller, Roy 1912-1991 . . . . DLB-15, 20

Fuller, Samuel 1912- DLB-26

Fuller, Sarah Margaret, Marchesa
   D'Ossoli 1810-1850 . . . . . . DLB-1, 59, 73

Fuller, Thomas 1608-1661. . . . . DLB-151

Fullerton, Hugh 1873-1945 . . . . . . DLB-171

Fulton, Len 1934- Y-86

Fulton, Robin 1937- DLB-40

Furbank, P. N. 1920- DLB-155

Furman, Laura 1945- Y-86

Furness, Horace Howard
   1833-1912 . . . . DLB-64

Furness, William Henry 1802-1896 . . . . DLB-1

Furthman, Jules 1888-1966 . . . . DLB-26

Futabatei, Shimei (Hasegawa Tatsunosuke)
   1864-1909 . . . . DLB-180

The Future of the Novel (1899), by
   Henry James DLB-18

Fyleman, Rose 1877-1957 . . . . DLB-160

G

The G. Ross Roy Scottish Poetry
   Collection at the University of
   South Carolina Y-89

Gadda, Carlo Emilio 1893-1973 . . . . DLB-177

Gaddis, William 1922- DLB-2

Gág, Wanda 1893-1946 . . . . DLB-22

Gagnon, Madeleine 1938- DLB-60

Gaine, Hugh 1726-1807 . . . . DLB-43

Gaine, Hugh [publishing house] DLB-49

Gaines, Ernest J.
   1933- DLB-2, 33, 152; Y-80

Gaiser, Gerd 1908-1976 . . . . DLB-69

Galarza, Ernesto 1905-1984 . . . . DLB-122

Galaxy Science Fiction Novels DLB-46

Gale, Zona 1874-1938 . . . . DLB-9, 78

Galen of Pergamon 129-after 210 . . . DLB-176

Gall, Louise von 1815-1855 . . . . DLB-133

Gallagher, Tess 1943- DLB-120

Gallagher, Wes 1911- DLB-127

Gallagher, William Davis
   1808-1894 . . . . DLB-73

Gallant, Mavis 1922- DLB-53

Gallico, Paul 1897-1976 . . . . DLB-9, 171

Galsworthy, John
   1867-1933 . . . . DLB-10, 34, 98, 162

Galt, John 1779-1839 . . . . DLB-99, 116

Galton, Sir Francis 1822-1911 . . . . . DLB-166

Galvin, Brendan 1938- DLB-5

Gambit DLB-46

Gamboa, Reymundo 1948- DLB-122

Gammer Gurton's Needle DLB-62

Gannett, Frank E. 1876-1957 . . . . . . DLB-29

Gaos, Vicente 1919-1980 . . . . DLB-134

García, Lionel G. 1935- DLB-82

García Lorca, Federico
   1898-1936 . . . . DLB-108

García Márquez, Gabriel
   1928- DLB-113

Gardam, Jane 1928- DLB-14, 161

Garden, Alexander
   circa 1685-1756 . . . . DLB-31

Gardiner, Margaret Power Farmer (see
   Blessington, Marguerite, Countess of)

Gardner, John 1933-1982 . . . . . DLB-2; Y-82

Garfield, Leon 1921- DLB-161

Garis, Howard R. 1873-1962 . . . . . . DLB-22

Garland, Hamlin
   1860-1940 . . . . DLB-12, 71, 78

Garneau, Francis-Xavier
   1809-1866 . . . . DLB-99

Garneau, Hector de Saint-Denys
   1912-1943 . . . . DLB-88

Garneau, Michel 1939- DLB-53

Garner, Alan 1934- DLB-161

Garner, Hugh 1913-1979 . . . . DLB-68

Garnett, David 1892-1981 . . . . DLB-34

Garnett, Eve 1900-1991 . . . . DLB-160

Garraty, John A. 1920- DLB-17

Garrett, George
   1929- DLB-2, 5, 130, 152; Y-83

Garrick, David 1717-1779 . . . . DLB-84

Garrison, William Lloyd
   1805-1879 . . . . DLB-1, 43

Garro, Elena 1920- DLB-145

Garth, Samuel 1661-1719 . . . . DLB-95

Garve, Andrew 1908- DLB-87

Gary, Romain 1914-1980 . . . . DLB-83

Gascoigne, George 1539?-1577 . . . . . DLB-136

Gascoyne, David 1916- DLB-20

Gaskell, Elizabeth Cleghorn
   1810-1865 . . . . DLB-21, 144, 159

Gaspey, Thomas 1788-1871 . . . . . . DLB-116

Gass, William Howard 1924- DLB-2

Gates, Doris 1901- DLB-22

Gates, Henry Louis, Jr. 1950- DLB-67

Gates, Lewis E. 1860-1924 . . . . DLB-71

Gatto, Alfonso 1909-1976 . . . . DLB-114

Gaunt, Mary 1861-1942 . . . . DLB-174

Gautier, Théophile 1811-1872 . . . . . DLB-119

Gauvreau, Claude 1925-1971 . . . . . . DLB-88

The Gawain-Poet
   flourished circa 1350-1400 . . . . . DLB-146

Gay, Ebenezer 1696-1787 . . . . DLB-24

Gay, John 1685-1732 . . . . DLB-84, 95

The Gay Science (1866), by E. S. Dallas [excerpt]
   . . . . DLB-21

Gayarré, Charles E. A. 1805-1895 . . . . DLB-30

Gaylord, Edward King
   1873-1974 . . . . DLB-127

Gaylord, Edward Lewis 1919- DLB-127

Gaylord, Charles
   [publishing house] DLB-49

Geddes, Gary 1940- DLB-60

Geddes, Virgil 1897- DLB-4

Gedeon (Georgii Andreevich Krinovsky)
   circa 1730-1763 . . . . DLB-150

Geibel, Emanuel 1815-1884 . . . . . . DLB-129

Geiogamah, Hanay 1945- DLB-175

Geis, Bernard, Associates DLB-46

Geisel, Theodor Seuss
   1904-1991 . . . . DLB-61; Y-91

Gelb, Arthur 1924- DLB-103

Gelb, Barbara 1926- DLB-103

Gelber, Jack 1932- DLB-7

Gelinas, Gratien 1909- DLB-88

Gellert, Christian Fürchtegott
   1715-1769 . . . . DLB-97

Gellhorn, Martha 1908- Y-82

Gems, Pam 1925- DLB-13

A General Idea of the College of Mirania (1753),
   by William Smith [excerpts] DLB-31

Genet, Jean 1910-1986 . . . . DLB-72; Y-86

Genevoix, Maurice 1890-1980 . . . . . DLB-65

Genovese, Eugene D. 1930- DLB-17

Gent, Peter 1942- Y-82

Geoffrey of Monmouth
   circa 1100-1155 . . . . DLB-146

George, Henry 1839-1897 . . . . DLB-23

George, Jean Craighead 1919- DLB-52

Georgslied 896? DLB-148

Gerhardie, William 1895-1977 . . . . . DLB-36

Gerhardt, Paul 1607-1676 . . . . DLB-164

Gérin, Winifred 1901-1981 . . . . DLB-155

Gérin-Lajoie, Antoine 1824-1882 . . . . DLB-99

German Drama 800-1280 . . . . DLB-138

German Drama from Naturalism
   to Fascism: 1889-1933 . . . . DLB-118

German Literature and Culture from
   Charlemagne to the Early Courtly
   Period DLB-148

German Radio Play, The DLB-124

German Transformation from the Baroque
   to the Enlightenment, The DLB-97

The Germanic Epic and Old English Heroic
   Poetry: Widsith, Waldere, and The
   Fight at Finnsburg DLB-146

Germanophilism, by Hans Kohn DLB-66

Gernsback, Hugo 1884-1967 . . . . . DLB-8, 137

Gerould, Katharine Fullerton
   1879-1944 . . . . DLB-78

Gerrish, Samuel [publishing house] . . . DLB-49

Gerrold, David 1944- DLB-8
The Ira Gershwin Centenary Y-96
Gersonides 1288-1344 .... DLB-115
Gerstäcker, Friedrich 1816-1872 ..... DLB-129
Gerstenberg, Heinrich Wilhelm von
   1737-1823 .... DLB-97
Gervinus, Georg Gottfried
   1805-1871 .... DLB-133
Geßner, Salomon 1730-1788 .... DLB-97
Geston, Mark S. 1946- DLB-8
Al-Ghazali 1058-1111. .... DLB-115
Gibbon, Edward 1737-1794 .... DLB-104
Gibbon, John Murray 1875-1952 .... DLB-92
Gibbon, Lewis Grassic (see Mitchell,
   James Leslie)
Gibbons, Floyd 1887-1939 .... DLB-25
Gibbons, Reginald 1947- DLB-120
Gibbons, William ?-? DLB-73
Gibson, Charles Dana 1867-1944 .... DS-13
Gibson, Charles Dana 1867-1944 .... DS-13
Gibson, Graeme 1934- DLB-53
Gibson, Margaret 1944- DLB-120
Gibson, Margaret Dunlop
   1843-1920 .... DLB-174
Gibson, Wilfrid 1878-1962 .... DLB-19
Gibson, William 1914- DLB-7
Gide, André 1869-1951 .... DLB-65
Giguère, Diane 1937- DLB-53
Giguère, Roland 1929- DLB-60
Gil de Biedma, Jaime 1929-1990 .... DLB-108
Gil-Albert, Juan 1906 .... DLB-134
Gilbert, Anthony 1899-1973 ...... DLB-77
Gilbert, Michael 1912- DLB-87
Gilbert, Sandra M. 1936- DLB-120
Gilbert, Sir Humphrey
   1537-1583 .... DLB-136
Gilchrist, Alexander
   1828-1861 .... DLB-144
Gilchrist, Ellen 1935- DLB-130
Gilder, Jeannette L. 1849-1916 ..... DLB-79
Gilder, Richard Watson
   1844-1909 .... DLB-64, 79
Gildersleeve, Basil 1831-1924 ..... DLB-71
Giles, Henry 1809-1882 .... DLB-64
Giles of Rome circa 1243-1316 .... DLB-115
Gilfillan, George 1813-1878 ...... DLB-144
Gill, Eric 1882-1940 .... DLB-98
Gill, William F., Company DLB-49
Gillespie, A. Lincoln, Jr.
   1895-1950 .... DLB-4
Gilliam, Florence ?-? DLB-4
Gilliatt, Penelope 1932-1993 ..... DLB-14
Gillott, Jacky 1939-1980 .... DLB-14

Gilman, Caroline H. 1794-1888 .... DLB-3, 73
Gilman, W. and J.
   [publishing house] DLB-49
Gilmer, Elizabeth Meriwether
   1861-1951 .... DLB-29
Gilmer, Francis Walker
   1790-1826 .... DLB-37
Gilroy, Frank D. 1925- DLB-7
Gimferrer, Pere (Pedro) 1945- DLB-134
Gingrich, Arnold 1903-1976 ...... DLB-137
Ginsberg, Allen 1926- DLB-5, 16, 169
Ginzburg, Natalia 1916-1991 ..... DLB-177
Ginzkey, Franz Karl 1871-1963 .... DLB-81
Gioia, Dana 1950- DLB-120
Giono, Jean 1895-1970 .... DLB-72
Giotti, Virgilio 1885-1957 .... DLB-114
Giovanni, Nikki 1943- DLB-5, 41
Gipson, Lawrence Henry
   1880-1971 .... DLB-17
Girard, Rodolphe 1879-1956 ...... DLB-92
Giraudoux, Jean 1882-1944 .... DLB-65
Gissing, George 1857-1903 .... DLB-18, 135
Giudici, Giovanni 1924- DLB-128
Giuliani, Alfredo 1924- DLB-128
Gladstone, William Ewart
   1809-1898 .... DLB-57
Glaeser, Ernst 1902-1963 .... DLB-69
Glancy, Diane 1941- DLB-175
Glanville, Brian 1931- DLB-15, 139
Glapthorne, Henry 1610-1643? DLB-58
Glasgow, Ellen 1873-1945 .... DLB-9, 12
Glaspell, Susan 1876-1948 .... DLB-7, 9, 78
Glass, Montague 1877-1934 ...... DLB-11
The Glass Key and Other Dashiell Hammett
   Mysteries Y-96
Glassco, John 1909-1981 .... DLB-68
Glauser, Friedrich 1896-1938 ..... DLB-56
F. Gleason's Publishing Hall DLB-49
Gleim, Johann Wilhelm Ludwig
   1719-1803 .... DLB-97
Glendinning, Victoria 1937- DLB-155
Glover, Richard 1712-1785 .... DLB-95
Glück, Louise 1943- DLB-5
Glyn, Elinor 1864-1943 .... DLB-153
Gobineau, Joseph-Arthur de
   1816-1882 .... DLB-123
Godbout, Jacques 1933- DLB-53
Goddard, Morrill 1865-1937 ..... DLB-25
Goddard, William 1740-1817 ..... DLB-43
Godden, Rumer 1907- DLB-161
Godey, Louis A. 1804-1878 ...... DLB-73
Godey and McMichael DLB-49
Godfrey, Dave 1938- DLB-60

Godfrey, Thomas 1736-1763 ...... DLB-31
Godine, David R., Publisher DLB-46
Godkin, E. L. 1831-1902 .... DLB-79
Godolphin, Sidney 1610-1643 ..... DLB-126
Godwin, Gail 1937- DLB-6
Godwin, Mary Jane Clairmont
   1766-1841 .... DLB-163
Godwin, Parke 1816-1904 ..... DLB-3, 64
Godwin, William
   1756-1836 .... DLB-39, 104, 142, 158, 163
Godwin, M. J., and Company DLB-154
Goering, Reinhard 1887-1936 ..... DLB-118
Goes, Albrecht 1908- DLB-69
Goethe, Johann Wolfgang von
   1749-1832 .... DLB-94
Goetz, Curt 1888-1960 .... DLB-124
Goffe, Thomas circa 1592-1629 .... DLB-58
Goffstein, M. B. 1940- DLB-61
Gogarty, Oliver St. John
   1878-1957 .... DLB-15, 19
Goines, Donald 1937-1974 .... DLB-33
Gold, Herbert 1924- DLB-2; Y-81
Gold, Michael 1893-1967 .... DLB-9, 28
Goldbarth, Albert 1948- DLB-120
Goldberg, Dick 1947- DLB-7
Golden Cockerel Press DLB-112
Golding, Arthur 1536-1606 ...... DLB-136
Golding, William 1911-1993 .... DLB-15, 100
Goldman, William 1931- DLB-44
Goldsmith, Oliver
   1730?-1774 .... DLB-39, 89, 104, 109, 142
Goldsmith, Oliver 1794-1861 ..... DLB-99
Goldsmith Publishing Company DLB-46
Gollancz, Victor, Limited DLB-112
Gómez-Quiñones, Juan 1942- DLB-122
Gomme, Laurence James
   [publishing house] DLB-46
Goncourt, Edmond de 1822-1896 ... DLB-123
Goncourt, Jules de 1830-1870 .... DLB-123
Gonzales, Rodolfo "Corky"
   1928- DLB-122
González, Angel 1925- DLB-108
Gonzalez, Genaro 1949- DLB-122
Gonzalez, Ray 1952- DLB-122
González de Mireles, Jovita
   1899-1983 .... DLB-122
González-T., César A. 1931- DLB-82
Goodbye, Gutenberg? A Lecture at
   the New York Public Library,
   18 April 1995 .... Y-95
Goodison, Lorna 1947- DLB-157
Goodman, Paul 1911-1972 ...... DLB-130
The Goodman Theatre DLB-7

Goodrich, Frances 1891-1984 and
   Hackett, Albert 1900- DLB-26
Goodrich, Samuel Griswold
   1793-1860 . . . . DLB-1, 42, 73
Goodrich, S. G. [publishing house] . . . DLB-49
Goodspeed, C. E., and Company DLB-49
Goodwin, Stephen 1943- Y-82
Googe, Barnabe 1540-1594 . . . . . . DLB-132
Gookin, Daniel 1612-1687 . . . . DLB-24
Gordon, Caroline
   1895-1981 . . . . DLB-4, 9, 102; Y-81
Gordon, Giles 1940- DLB-14, 139
Gordon, Lyndall 1941- DLB-155
Gordon, Mary 1949- DLB-6; Y-81
Gordone, Charles 1925- DLB-7
Gore, Catherine 1800-1861 . . . . DLB-116
Gorey, Edward 1925- DLB-61
Gorgias of Leontini circa 485 B.C.-376 B.C.
   . . . . DLB-176
Görres, Joseph 1776-1848 . . . . DLB-90
Gosse, Edmund 1849-1928 . . . . . DLB-57, 144
Gosson, Stephen 1554-1624 . . . . . . DLB-172
Gotlieb, Phyllis 1926- DLB-88
Gottfried von Straßburg
   died before 1230 . . . . DLB-138
Gotthelf, Jeremias 1797-1854 . . . . . . DLB-133
Gottschalk circa 804/808-869 . . . . . . DLB-148
Gottsched, Johann Christoph
   1700-1766 . . . . DLB-97
Götz, Johann Nikolaus
   1721-1781 . . . . DLB-97
Gould, Wallace 1882-1940 . . . . DLB-54
Govoni, Corrado 1884-1965 . . . . . . DLB-114
Gower, John circa 1330-1408 . . . . . . DLB-146
Goyen, William 1915-1983 . . . . . DLB-2; Y-83
Goytisolo, José Augustín 1928- DLB-134
Gozzano, Guido 1883-1916 . . . . . . DLB-114
Grabbe, Christian Dietrich
   1801-1836 . . . . DLB-133
Gracq, Julien 1910- DLB-83
Grady, Henry W. 1850-1889 . . . . DLB-23
Graf, Oskar Maria 1894-1967 . . . . . . DLB-56
Graf Rudolf between circa 1170
   and circa 1185 . . . . DLB-148
Grafton, Richard
   [publishing house] DLB-170
Graham, George Rex
   1813-1894 . . . . DLB-73
Graham, Gwethalyn 1913-1965 . . . . . DLB-88
Graham, Jorie 1951- DLB-120
Graham, Katharine 1917- DLB-127
Graham, Lorenz 1902-1989 . . . . DLB-76
Graham, Philip 1915-1963 . . . . DLB-127

Graham, R. B. Cunninghame
   1852-1936 . . . . DLB-98, 135, 174
Graham, Shirley 1896-1977 . . . . DLB-76
Graham, W. S. 1918- DLB-20
Graham, William H.
   [publishing house] DLB-49
Graham, Winston 1910- DLB-77
Grahame, Kenneth
   1859-1932 . . . . DLB-34, 141, 178
Grainger, Martin Allerdale
   1874-1941 . . . . DLB-92
Gramatky, Hardie 1907-1979 . . . . . . DLB-22
Grand, Sarah 1854-1943 . . . . DLB-135
Grandbois, Alain 1900-1975 . . . . . . DLB-92
Grange, John circa 1556-? DLB-136
Granich, Irwin (see Gold, Michael)
Grant, Duncan 1885-1978 . . . . DS-10
Grant, George 1918-1988 . . . . DLB-88
Grant, George Monro 1835-1902 . . . . DLB-99
Grant, Harry J. 1881-1963 . . . . DLB-29
Grant, James Edward 1905-1966 . . . . DLB-26
Grass, Günter 1927- DLB-75, 124
Grasty, Charles H. 1863-1924 . . . . . . DLB-25
Grau, Shirley Ann 1929- DLB-2
Graves, John 1920- Y-83
Graves, Richard 1715-1804 . . . . DLB-39
Graves, Robert
   1895-1985 . . . . DLB-20, 100; Y-85
Gray, Asa 1810-1888 . . . . DLB-1
Gray, David 1838-1861 . . . . DLB-32
Gray, Simon 1936- DLB-13
Gray, Thomas 1716-1771 . . . . DLB-109
Grayson, William J. 1788-1863 . . . . DLB-3, 64
The Great Bibliographers Series Y-93
The Great War and the Theater, 1914-1918
   [Great Britain] DLB-10
Greeley, Horace 1811-1872 . . . . . . DLB-3, 43
Green, Adolph (see Comden, Betty)
Green, Duff 1791-1875 . . . . DLB-43
Green, Gerald 1922- DLB-28
Green, Henry 1905-1973 . . . . DLB-15
Green, Jonas 1712-1767 . . . . DLB-31
Green, Joseph 1706-1780 . . . . DLB-31
Green, Julien 1900- DLB-4, 72
Green, Paul 1894-1981 . . . . . . DLB-7, 9; Y-81
Green, T. and S.
   [publishing house] DLB-49
Green, Timothy
   [publishing house] DLB-49
Greenaway, Kate 1846-1901 . . . . . . DLB-141
Greenberg: Publisher DLB-46
Green Tiger Press DLB-46
Greene, Asa 1789-1838 . . . . DLB-11

Greene, Benjamin H.
   [publishing house] DLB-49
Greene, Graham 1904-1991
   . . . DLB-13, 15, 77, 100, 162; Y-85, Y-91
Greene, Robert 1558-1592 . . . . . DLB-62, 167
Greenhow, Robert 1800-1854 . . . . . . DLB-30
Greenough, Horatio 1805-1852 . . . . . DLB-1
Greenwell, Dora 1821-1882 . . . . DLB-35
Greenwillow Books DLB-46
Greenwood, Grace (see Lippincott, Sara Jane
   Clarke)
Greenwood, Walter 1903-1974 . . . . . DLB-10
Greer, Ben 1948- DLB-6
Greflinger, Georg 1620?-1677 . . . . . DLB-164
Greg, W. R. 1809-1881 . . . . DLB-55
Gregg Press DLB-46
Gregory, Isabella Augusta
   Persse, Lady 1852-1932 . . . . DLB-10
Gregory, Horace 1898-1982 . . . . . . DLB-48
Gregory of Rimini
   circa 1300-1358 . . . . DLB-115
Gregynog Press DLB-112
Greiffenberg, Catharina Regina von
   1633-1694 . . . . DLB-168
Grenfell, Wilfred Thomason
   1865-1940 . . . . DLB-92
Greve, Felix Paul (see Grove, Frederick Philip)
Greville, Fulke, First Lord Brooke
   1554-1628 . . . . DLB-62, 172
Grey, Lady Jane 1537-1554 . . . . DLB-132
Grey Owl 1888-1938 . . . . DLB-92
Grey, Zane 1872-1939 . . . . DLB-9
Grey Walls Press DLB-112
Grier, Eldon 1917- DLB-88
Grieve, C. M. (see MacDiarmid, Hugh)
Griffin, Bartholomew
   flourished 1596 . . . . DLB-172
Griffin, Gerald 1803-1840 . . . . DLB-159
Griffith, Elizabeth 1727?-1793 . . . . DLB-39, 89
Griffith, George 1857-1906 . . . . . . DLB-178
Griffiths, Trevor 1935- DLB-13
Griffiths, Ralph
   [publishing house] DLB-154
Griggs, S. C., and Company DLB-49
Griggs, Sutton Elbert
   1872-1930 . . . . DLB-50
Grignon, Claude-Henri 1894-1976 . . . . DLB-68
Grigson, Geoffrey 1905- DLB-27
Grillparzer, Franz 1791-1872 . . . . . . DLB-133
Grimald, Nicholas
   circa 1519-circa 1562 . . . . DLB-136
Grimké, Angelina Weld
   1880-1958 . . . . DLB-50, 54
Grimm, Hans 1875-1959 . . . . DLB-66

Grimm, Jacob 1785-1863 . . . . DLB-90

Grimm, Wilhelm 1786-1859 . . . . DLB-90

Grimmelshausen, Johann Jacob Christoffel von
   1621 or 1622-1676 . . . . DLB-168

Grimshaw, Beatrice Ethel
   1871-1953 . . . . DLB-174

Grindal, Edmund
   1519 or 1520-1583 . . . . DLB-132

Griswold, Rufus Wilmot
   1815-1857 . . . . DLB-3, 59

Gross, Milt 1895-1953 . . . . DLB-11

Grosset and Dunlap. DLB-49

Grossman Publishers DLB-46

Grosseteste, Robert
   circa 1160-1253 . . . . DLB-115

Grosvenor, Gilbert H. 1875-1966 . . . . DLB-91

Groth, Klaus 1819-1899 . . . . DLB-129

Groulx, Lionel 1878-1967 . . . . DLB-68

Grove, Frederick Philip 1879-1949 . . . DLB-92

Grove Press DLB-46

Grubb, Davis 1919-1980 . . . . DLB-6

Gruelle, Johnny 1880-1938 . . . . DLB-22

von Grumbach, Argula
   1492-after 1563? DLB-179

Grymeston, Elizabeth
   before 1563-before 1604 . . . . . . DLB-136

Gryphius, Andreas 1616-1664 . . . . . . DLB-164

Gryphius, Christian 1649-1706 . . . . . DLB-168

Guare, John 1938- DLB-7

Guerra, Tonino 1920- DLB-128

Guest, Barbara 1920- DLB-5

Guèvremont, Germaine
   1893-1968 . . . . DLB-68

Guidacci, Margherita 1921-1992 . . . . DLB-128

Guide to the Archives of Publishers, Journals, and
   Literary Agents in North American Libraries
   . . . . Y-93

Guillén, Jorge 1893-1984 . . . . DLB-108

Guilloux, Louis 1899-1980 . . . . DLB-72

Guilpin, Everard
   circa 1572-after 1608? DLB-136

Guiney, Louise Imogen 1861-1920 . . . DLB-54

Guiterman, Arthur 1871-1943 . . . . . . DLB-11

Günderrode, Caroline von
   1780-1806 . . . . DLB-90

Gundulić, Ivan 1589-1638 . . . . DLB-147

Gunn, Bill 1934-1989 . . . . DLB-38

Gunn, James E. 1923- DLB-8

Gunn, Neil M. 1891-1973 . . . . DLB-15

Gunn, Thom 1929- DLB-27

Gunnars, Kristjana 1948- DLB-60

Günther, Johann Christian
   1695-1723 . . . . DLB-168

Gurik, Robert 1932- DLB-60

Gustafson, Ralph 1909- DLB-88

Gütersloh, Albert Paris 1887-1973 . . . DLB-81

Guthrie, A. B., Jr. 1901- DLB-6

Guthrie, Ramon 1896-1973 . . . . DLB-4

The Guthrie Theater DLB-7

Guthrie, Thomas Anstey (see Anstey, FC)

Gutzkow, Karl 1811-1878 . . . . DLB-133

Guy, Ray 1939- DLB-60

Guy, Rosa 1925- DLB-33

Guyot, Arnold 1807-1884 . . . . DS-13

Gwynne, Erskine 1898-1948 . . . . DLB-4

Gyles, John 1680-1755 . . . . DLB-99

Gysin, Brion 1916- DLB-16

H

H. D. (see Doolittle, Hilda)

Habington, William 1605-1654 . . . . . DLB-126

Hacker, Marilyn 1942- DLB-120

Hackett, Albert (see Goodrich, Frances)

Hacks, Peter 1928- DLB-124

Hadas, Rachel 1948- DLB-120

Hadden, Briton 1898-1929 . . . . DLB-91

Hagedorn, Friedrich von
   1708-1754 . . . . DLB-168

Hagelstange, Rudolf 1912-1984 . . . . . DLB-69

Haggard, H. Rider
   1856-1925 . . . . . . DLB-70, 156, 174, 178

Haggard, William 1907-1993 . . . . . . Y-93

Hahn-Hahn, Ida Gräfin von
   1805-1880 . . . . DLB-133

Haig-Brown, Roderick 1908-1976 . . . DLB-88

Haight, Gordon S. 1901-1985 . . . . . . DLB-103

Hailey, Arthur 1920- DLB-88; Y-82

Haines, John 1924- DLB-5

Hake, Edward
   flourished 1566-1604 . . . . DLB-136

Hake, Thomas Gordon 1809-1895 . . . DLB-32

Hakluyt, Richard 1552?-1616 . . . . . . DLB-136

Halbe, Max 1865-1944 . . . . DLB-118

Haldane, J. B. S. 1892-1964 . . . . DLB-160

Haldeman, Joe 1943- DLB-8

Haldeman-Julius Company DLB-46

Hale, E. J., and Son DLB-49

Hale, Edward Everett
   1822-1909 . . . . DLB-1, 42, 74

Hale, Janet Campbell 1946- DLB-175

Hale, Kathleen 1898- DLB-160

Hale, Leo Thomas (see Ebon)

Hale, Lucretia Peabody
   1820-1900 . . . . DLB-42

Hale, Nancy 1908-1988 . . . . DLB-86; Y-80, 88

Hale, Sarah Josepha (Buell)
   1788-1879 . . . . DLB-1, 42, 73

Hales, John 1584-1656 . . . . DLB-151

Haley, Alex 1921-1992 . . . . DLB-38

Haliburton, Thomas Chandler
   1796-1865 . . . . DLB-11, 99

Hall, Anna Maria 1800-1881 . . . . . . DLB-159

Hall, Donald 1928- DLB-5

Hall, Edward 1497-1547 . . . . DLB-132

Hall, James 1793-1868 . . . . DLB-73, 74

Hall, Joseph 1574-1656 . . . . DLB-121, 151

Hall, Samuel [publishing house] DLB-49

Hallam, Arthur Henry 1811-1833 . . . . DLB-32

Halleck, Fitz-Greene 1790-1867 . . . . . DLB-3

Haller, Albrecht von 1708-1777 . . . . . DLB-168

Hallmann, Johann Christian
   1640-1704 or 1716? DLB-168

Hallmark Editions DLB-46

Halper, Albert 1904-1984 . . . . DLB-9

Halperin, John William 1941- DLB-111

Halstead, Murat 1829-1908 . . . . DLB-23

Hamann, Johann Georg 1730-1788 . . . DLB-97

Hamburger, Michael 1924- DLB-27

Hamilton, Alexander 1712-1756 . . . . . DLB-31

Hamilton, Alexander 1755?-1804 . . . . DLB-37

Hamilton, Cicely 1872-1952 . . . . DLB-10

Hamilton, Edmond 1904-1977 . . . . . . DLB-8

Hamilton, Elizabeth 1758-1816 . . . . DLB-116, 158

Hamilton, Gail (see Corcoran, Barbara)

Hamilton, Ian 1938- DLB-40, 155

Hamilton, Patrick 1904-1962 . . . . . . DLB-10

Hamilton, Virginia 1936- DLB-33, 52

Hamilton, Hamish, Limited DLB-112

Hammett, Dashiell 1894-1961 . . . . . . DS-6

Dashiell Hammett:
   An Appeal in *TAC* Y-91

Hammon, Jupiter 1711-died between
   1790 and 1806 . . . . DLB-31, 50

Hammond, John ?-1663 . . . . DLB-24

Hamner, Earl 1923- DLB-6

Hampton, Christopher 1946- DLB-13

Handel-Mazzetti, Enrica von
   1871-1955 . . . . DLB-81

Handke, Peter 1942- DLB-85, 124

Handlin, Oscar 1915- DLB-17

Hankin, St. John 1869-1909 . . . . DLB-10

Hanley, Clifford 1922- DLB-14

Hannah, Barry 1942- DLB-6

Hannay, James 1827-1873 . . . . DLB-21

Hansberry, Lorraine 1930-1965 . . . . DLB-7, 38

Hapgood, Norman 1868-1937 . . . . . . DLB-91

Happel, Eberhard Werner
   1647-1690 . . . . DLB-168

Harcourt Brace Jovanovich DLB-46
Hardenberg, Friedrich von (see Novalis)
Harding, Walter 1917- DLB-111
Hardwick, Elizabeth 1916- DLB-6
Hardy, Thomas 1840-1928 . . . . DLB-18, 19, 135
Hare, Cyril 1900-1958 . . . . DLB-77
Hare, David 1947- DLB-13
Hargrove, Marion 1919- DLB-11
Häring, Georg Wilhelm Heinrich (see Alexis, Willibald)
Harington, Donald 1935- DLB-152
Harington, Sir John 1560-1612 . . . . . DLB-136
Harjo, Joy 1951- DLB-120, 175
Harlow, Robert 1923- DLB-60
Harman, Thomas
 flourished 1566-1573 . . . . DLB-136
Harness, Charles L. 1915- DLB-8
Harnett, Cynthia 1893-1981 . . . . DLB-161
Harper, Fletcher 1806-1877 . . . . DLB-79
Harper, Frances Ellen Watkins
 1825-1911 . . . . DLB-50
Harper, Michael S. 1938- DLB-41
Harper and Brothers DLB-49
Harraden, Beatrice 1864-1943 . . . . . . DLB-153
Harrap, George G., and Company
 Limited DLB-112
Harriot, Thomas 1560-1621 . . . . DLB-136
Harris, Benjamin ?-circa 1720 . . . . DLB-42, 43
Harris, Christie 1907- DLB-88
Harris, Frank 1856-1931 . . . . DLB-156
Harris, George Washington
 1814-1869 . . . . DLB-3, 11
Harris, Joel Chandler
 1848-1908 . . . . . DLB-11, 23, 42, 78, 91
Harris, Mark 1922- DLB-2; Y-80
Harris, Wilson 1921- DLB-117
Harrison, Charles Yale
 1898-1954 . . . . DLB-68
Harrison, Frederic 1831-1923 . . . . . . DLB-57
Harrison, Harry 1925- DLB-8
Harrison, Jim 1937- Y-82
Harrison, Mary St. Leger Kingsley (see Malet, Lucas)
Harrison, Paul Carter 1936- DLB-38
Harrison, Susan Frances
 1859-1935 . . . . DLB-99
Harrison, Tony 1937- DLB-40
Harrison, William 1535-1593 . . . . . DLB-136
Harrison, James P., Company DLB-49
Harrisse, Henry 1829-1910 . . . . DLB-47
Harsdörffer, Georg Philipp
 1607-1658 . . . . DLB-164
Harsent, David 1942- DLB-40

Hart, Albert Bushnell 1854-1943 . . . . . DLB-17
Hart, Julia Catherine 1796-1867 . . . . . DLB-99
The Lorenz Hart Centenary Y-95
Hart, Moss 1904-1961 . . . . DLB-7
Hart, Oliver 1723-1795 . . . . DLB-31
Hart-Davis, Rupert, Limited DLB-112
Harte, Bret 1836-1902 . . . . DLB-12, 64, 74, 79
Harte, Edward Holmead 1922- DLB-127
Harte, Houston Harriman 1927- DLB-127
Hartlaub, Felix 1913-1945 . . . . DLB-56
Hartlebon, Otto Erich
 1864-1905 . . . . DLB-118
Hartley, L. P. 1895-1972 . . . . . . DLB-15, 139
Hartley, Marsden 1877-1943 . . . . . . DLB-54
Hartling, Peter 1933- DLB-75
Hartman, Geoffrey H. 1929- DLB-67
Hartmann, Sadakichi 1867-1944 . . . . . DLB-54
Hartmann von Aue
 circa 1160-circa 1205 . . . . DLB-138
Harvey, Gabriel 1550?-1631 . . . . . . DLB-167
Harvey, Jean-Charles 1891-1967 . . . . DLB-88
Harvill Press Limited DLB-112
Harwood, Lee 1939- DLB-40
Harwood, Ronald 1934- DLB-13
Haskins, Charles Homer
 1870-1937 . . . . DLB-47
Hass, Robert 1941- DLB-105
The Hatch-Billops Collection DLB-76
Hathaway, William 1944- DLB-120
Hauff, Wilhelm 1802-1827 . . . . DLB-90
A Haughty and Proud Generation (1922),
 by Ford Madox Hueffer DLB-36
Haugwitz, August Adolph von
 1647-1706 . . . . DLB-168
Hauptmann, Carl
 1858-1921 . . . . DLB-66, 118
Hauptmann, Gerhart
 1862-1946 . . . . DLB-66, 118
Hauser, Marianne 1910- Y-83
Hawes, Stephen
 1475?-before 1529 . . . . DLB-132
Hawker, Robert Stephen
 1803-1875 . . . . DLB-32
Hawkes, John 1925- DLB-2, 7; Y-80
Hawkesworth, John 1720-1773 . . . . . DLB-142
Hawkins, Sir Anthony Hope (see Hope, Anthony)
Hawkins, Sir John
 1719-1789 . . . . DLB-104, 142
Hawkins, Walter Everette 1883-? DLB-50
Hawthorne, Nathaniel
 1804-1864 . . . . DLB-1, 74
Hay, John 1838-1905 . . . . DLB-12, 47
Hayashi, Fumiko 1903-1951 . . . . . . DLB-180
Hayden, Robert 1913-1980 . . . . . . DLB-5, 76

Haydon, Benjamin Robert
 1786-1846 . . . . DLB-110
Hayes, John Michael 1919- DLB-26
Hayley, William 1745-1820 . . . . . DLB-93, 142
Haym, Rudolf 1821-1901 . . . . DLB-129
Hayman, Robert 1575-1629 . . . . . . DLB-99
Hayman, Ronald 1932- DLB-155
Hayne, Paul Hamilton
 1830-1886 . . . . DLB-3, 64, 79
Hays, Mary 1760-1843 . . . . . . DLB-142, 158
Haywood, Eliza 1693?-1756 . . . . . . DLB-39
Hazard, Willis P. [publishing house] DLB-49
Hazlitt, William 1778-1830 . . . . DLB-110, 158
Hazzard, Shirley 1931- Y-82
Head, Bessie 1937-1986 . . . . DLB-117
Headley, Joel T. 1813-1897 . . . DLB-30; DS-13
Heaney, Seamus 1939- DLB-40
Heard, Nathan C. 1936- DLB-33
Hearn, Lafcadio 1850-1904 . . . . . DLB-12, 78
Hearne, John 1926- DLB-117
Hearne, Samuel 1745-1792 . . . . DLB-99
Hearst, William Randolph
 1863-1951 . . . . DLB-25
Hearst, William Randolph, Jr
 1908-1993 . . . . DLB-127
Heath, Catherine 1924- DLB-14
Heath, Roy A. K. 1926- DLB-117
Heath-Stubbs, John 1918- DLB-27
Heavysege, Charles 1816-1876 . . . . . DLB-99
Hebbel, Friedrich 1813-1863 . . . . . . DLB-129
Hebel, Johann Peter 1760-1826 . . . . . DLB-90
Hébert, Anne 1916- DLB-68
Hébert, Jacques 1923- DLB-53
Hecht, Anthony 1923- DLB-5, 169
Hecht, Ben 1894-1964
 . . . . DLB-7, 9, 25, 26, 28, 86
Hecker, Isaac Thomas 1819-1888 . . . . . DLB-1
Hedge, Frederic Henry
 1805-1890 . . . . DLB-1, 59
Hefner, Hugh M. 1926- DLB-137
Hegel, Georg Wilhelm Friedrich
 1770-1831 . . . . DLB-90
Heidish, Marcy 1947- Y-82
Heißenbüttel 1921- DLB-75
Hein, Christoph 1944- DLB-124
Heine, Heinrich 1797-1856 . . . . DLB-90
Heinemann, Larry 1944- DS-9
Heinemann, William, Limited DLB-112
Heinlein, Robert A. 1907-1988 . . . . . . DLB-8
Heinrich Julius of Brunswick
 1564-1613 . . . . DLB-164
Heinrich von dem Türlîn
 flourished circa 1230 . . . . DLB-138

Heinrich von Melk
  flourished after 1160 . . . . DLB-148
Heinrich von Veldeke
  circa 1145-circa 1190 . . . . DLB-138
Heinrich, Willi 1920- DLB-75
Heiskell, John 1872-1972 . . . . . . DLB-127
Heinse, Wilhelm 1746-1803 . . . . . DLB-94
Heinz, W. C. 1915- DLB-171
Hejinian, Lyn 1941- DLB-165
Heliand circa 850 . . . . DLB-148
Heller, Joseph 1923- DLB-2, 28; Y-80
Heller, Michael 1937- DLB-165
Hellman, Lillian 1906-1984 . . . . . DLB-7; Y-84
Hellwig, Johann 1609-1674 . . . . . DLB-164
Helprin, Mark 1947- Y-85
Helwig, David 1938- DLB-60
Hemans, Felicia 1793-1835 . . . . . DLB-96
Hemingway, Ernest 1899-1961
  . . . . . DLB-4, 9, 102; Y-81, 87; DS-1
Hemingway: Twenty-Five Years
  Later Y-85
Hémon, Louis 1880-1913 . . . . DLB-92
Hemphill, Paul 1936- Y-87
Hénault, Gilles 1920- DLB-88
Henchman, Daniel 1689-1761 . . . . DLB-24
Henderson, Alice Corbin
  1881-1949 . . . . DLB-54
Henderson, Archibald
  1877-1963 . . . . DLB-103
Henderson, David 1942- DLB-41
Henderson, George Wylie
  1904- DLB-51
Henderson, Zenna 1917-1983 . . . . DLB-8
Henisch, Peter 1943- DLB-85
Henley, Beth 1952- Y-86
Henley, William Ernest
  1849-1903 . . . . DLB-19
Henniker, Florence 1855-1923 . . . . DLB-135
Henry, Alexander 1739-1824 . . . . DLB-99
Henry, Buck 1930- DLB-26
Henry VIII of England
  1491-1547 . . . . DLB-132
Henry, Marguerite 1902- DLB-22
Henry, O. (see Porter, William Sydney)
Henry of Ghent
  circa 1217-1229 - 1293 . . . . . . DLB-115
Henry, Robert Selph 1889-1970 . . . DLB-17
Henry, Will (see Allen, Henry W.)
Henryson, Robert
  1420s or 1430s-circa 1505 . . . . DLB-146
Henschke, Alfred (see Klabund)
Hensley, Sophie Almon 1866-1946 . . . DLB-99
Henson, Lance 1944- DLB-175
Henty, G. A. 1832?-1902 . . . . . DLB-18, 141

Hentz, Caroline Lee 1800-1856 . . . . DLB-3
Heraclitus flourished circa 500 B.C.
  . . . . DLB-176
Herbert, Agnes circa 1880-1960 . . . . DLB-174
Herbert, Alan Patrick 1890-1971 . . . . DLB-10
Herbert, Edward, Lord, of Cherbury
  1582-1648 . . . . DLB-121, 151
Herbert, Frank 1920-1986 . . . . DLB-8
Herbert, George 1593-1633 . . . . . . DLB-126
Herbert, Henry William
  1807-1858 . . . . DLB-3, 73
Herbert, John 1926- DLB-53
Herbert, Mary Sidney, Countess of Pembroke
  (see Sidney, Mary)
Herbst, Josephine 1892-1969 . . . . . DLB-9
Herburger, Gunter 1932- DLB-75, 124
Hercules, Frank E. M. 1917- DLB-33
Herder, Johann Gottfried
  1744-1803 . . . . DLB-97
Herder, B., Book Company DLB-49
Herford, Charles Harold
  1853-1931 . . . . DLB-149
Hergesheimer, Joseph
  1880-1954 . . . . DLB-9, 102
Heritage Press DLB-46
Hermann the Lame 1013-1054 . . . . DLB-148
Hermes, Johann Timotheus
  1738-1821 . . . . DLB-97
Hermlin, Stephan 1915- DLB-69
Hernández, Alfonso C. 1938- DLB-122
Hernández, Inés 1947- DLB-122
Hernández, Miguel 1910-1942 . . . . DLB-134
Hernton, Calvin C. 1932- DLB-38
"The Hero as Man of Letters: Johnson,
  Rousseau, Burns" (1841), by Thomas
  Carlyle [excerpt] DLB-57
The Hero as Poet. Dante; Shakspeare (1841),
  by Thomas Carlyle DLB-32
Herodotus circa 484 B.C.-circa 420 B.C.
  . . . . DLB-176
Heron, Robert 1764-1807 . . . . . . DLB-142
Herrera, Juan Felipe 1948- DLB-122
Herrick, Robert 1591-1674 . . . . . DLB-126
Herrick, Robert 1868-1938 . . . DLB-9, 12, 78
Herrick, William 1915- Y-83
Herrick, E. R., and Company DLB-49
Herrmann, John 1900-1959 . . . . . DLB-4
Hersey, John 1914-1993 . . . . DLB-6
Hertel, François 1905-1985 . . . . . DLB-68
Hervé-Bazin, Jean Pierre Marie (see Bazin, Hervé)
Hervey, John, Lord 1696-1743 . . . . DLB-101
Herwig, Georg 1817-1875 . . . . . . DLB-133
Herzog, Emile Salomon Wilhelm (see Maurois, André)

Hesiod eighth century B.C. DLB-176
Hesse, Hermann 1877-1962 . . . . . DLB-66
Hessus, Helius Eobanus
  1488-1540 . . . . DLB-179
Hewat, Alexander
  circa 1743-circa 1824 . . . . DLB-30
Hewitt, John 1907- DLB-27
Hewlett, Maurice 1861-1923 . . . DLB-34, 156
Heyen, William 1940- DLB-5
Heyer, Georgette 1902-1974 . . . . . DLB-77
Heym, Stefan 1913- DLB-69
Heyse, Paul 1830-1914 . . . . DLB-129
Heytesbury, William
  circa 1310-1372 or 1373 . . . . . DLB-115
Heyward, Dorothy 1890-1961 . . . . DLB-7
Heyward, DuBose
  1885-1940 . . . . DLB-7, 9, 45
Heywood, John 1497?-1580? DLB-136
Heywood, Thomas
  1573 or 1574-1641 . . . . DLB-62
Hibbs, Ben 1901-1975 . . . . DLB-137
Hichens, Robert S. 1864-1950 . . . . DLB-153
Hickman, William Albert
  1877-1957 . . . . DLB-92
Hidalgo, José Luis 1919-1947 . . . . . DLB-108
Hiebert, Paul 1892-1987 . . . . DLB-68
Hieng, Andrej 1925- DLB-181
Hierro, José 1922- DLB-108
Higgins, Aidan 1927- DLB-14
Higgins, Colin 1941-1988 . . . . . . DLB-26
Higgins, George V. 1939- DLB-2; Y-81
Higginson, Thomas Wentworth
  1823-1911 . . . . DLB-1, 64
Highwater, Jamake 1942? DLB-52; Y-85
Hijuelos, Oscar 1951- DLB-145
Hildegard von Bingen
  1098-1179 . . . . DLB-148
Das Hildesbrandslied circa 820 . . . . DLB-148
Hildesheimer, Wolfgang
  1916-1991 . . . . DLB-69, 124
Hildreth, Richard
  1807-1865 . . . . DLB-1, 30, 59
Hill, Aaron 1685-1750 . . . . DLB-84
Hill, Geoffrey 1932- DLB-40
Hill, "Sir" John 1714?-1775 . . . . . DLB-39
Hill, Leslie 1880-1960 . . . . DLB-51
Hill, Susan 1942- DLB-14, 139
Hill, Walter 1942- DLB-44
Hill and Wang DLB-46
Hill, George M., Company DLB-49
Hill, Lawrence, and Company,
  Publishers DLB-46
Hillberry, Conrad 1928- DLB-120
Hilliard, Gray and Company DLB-49

Cumulative Index

Hills, Lee 1906- DLB-127

Hillyer, Robert 1895-1961 . . . . DLB-54

Hilton, James 1900-1954 . . . . . . DLB-34, 77

Hilton, Walter died 1396 . . . . DLB-146

Hilton and Company. DLB-49

Himes, Chester
1909-1984. . . . . DLB-2, 76, 143

Hindmarsh, Joseph
[publishing house] DLB-170

Hine, Daryl 1936- DLB-60

Hingley, Ronald 1920- DLB-155

Hinojosa-Smith, Rolando
1929- DLB-82

Hippel, Theodor Gottlieb von
1741-1796 . . . . DLB-97

Hippocrates of Cos flourished circa 425 B.C.
. . . . DLB-176

Hirabayashi, Taiko 1905-1972. . . . . DLB-180

Hirsch, E. D., Jr. 1928- DLB-67

Hirsch, Edward 1950- DLB-120

The History of the Adventures of Joseph Andrews
(1742), by Henry Fielding
[excerpt] DLB-39

Hoagland, Edward 1932- DLB-6

Hoagland, Everett H., III 1942- DLB-41

Hoban, Russell 1925- DLB-52

Hobbes, Thomas 1588-1679. . . . . . DLB-151

Hobby, Oveta 1905- DLB-127

Hobby, William 1878-1964 . . . . . . DLB-127

Hobsbaum, Philip 1932- DLB-40

Hobson, Laura Z. 1900- DLB-28

Hoby, Thomas 1530-1566. . . . . . . DLB-132

Hoccleve, Thomas
circa 1368-circa 1437 . . . . DLB-146

Hochhuth, Rolf 1931- DLB-124

Hochman, Sandra 1936- DLB-5

Hodder and Stoughton, Limited DLB-106

Hodgins, Jack 1938- DLB-60

Hodgman, Helen 1945- DLB-14

Hodgskin, Thomas 1787-1869 . . . . . DLB-158

Hodgson, Ralph 1871-1962. . . . . . . DLB-19

Hodgson, William Hope
1877-1918 . . . . . . DLB-70, 153, 156, 178

Hoffenstein, Samuel 1890-1947. . . . . DLB-11

Hoffman, Charles Fenno
1806-1884. . . . . DLB-3

Hoffman, Daniel 1923- DLB-5

Hoffmann, E. T. A. 1776-1822 . . . . . DLB-90

Hoffmanswaldau, Christian Hoffman von
1616-1679 . . . . DLB-168

Hofmann, Michael 1957- DLB-40

Hofmannsthal, Hugo von
1874-1929 . . . . DLB-81, 118

Hofstadter, Richard 1916-1970 . . . . . DLB-17

Hogan, Desmond 1950- DLB-14

Hogan, Linda 1947- DLB-175

Hogan and Thompson DLB-49

Hogarth Press DLB-112

Hogg, James 1770-1835 . . . . DLB-93, 116, 159

Hohberg, Wolfgang Helmhard Freiherr von
1612-1688 . . . . DLB-168

von Hohenheim, Philippus Aureolus
Theophrastus Bombastus (see Paracelsus)

Hohl, Ludwig 1904-1980 . . . . DLB-56

Holbrook, David 1923- DLB-14, 40

Holcroft, Thomas
1745-1809 . . . . DLB-39, 89, 158

Holden, Jonathan 1941- DLB-105

Holden, Jonathan, Contemporary
Verse Story-telling DLB-105

Holden, Molly 1927-1981. . . . . DLB-40

Hölderlin, Friedrich 1770-1843 . . . . . DLB-90

Holiday House DLB-46

Holinshed, Raphael died 1580 . . . . DLB-167

Holland, J. G. 1819-1881. . . . . DS-13

Holland, Norman N. 1927- DLB-67

Hollander, John 1929- DLB-5

Holley, Marietta 1836-1926. . . . . . . DLB-11

Hollingsworth, Margaret 1940- DLB-60

Hollo, Anselm 1934- DLB-40

Holloway, Emory 1885-1977 . . . . . DLB-103

Holloway, John 1920- DLB-27

Holloway House Publishing
Company DLB-46

Holme, Constance 1880-1955. . . . . . DLB-34

Holmes, Abraham S. 1821?-1908 . . . . DLB-99

Holmes, John Clellon 1926-1988. . . . DLB-16

Holmes, Oliver Wendell
1809-1894. . . . . DLB-1

Holmes, Richard 1945- DLB-155

Holroyd, Michael 1935- DLB-155

Holst, Hermann E. von
1841-1904. . . . . DLB-47

Holt, John 1721-1784 . . . . DLB-43

Holt, Henry, and Company DLB-49

Holt, Rinehart and Winston DLB-46

Holthusen, Hans Egon 1913- DLB-69

Hölty, Ludwig Christoph Heinrich
1748-1776 . . . . DLB-94

Holz, Arno 1863-1929 . . . . DLB-118

Home, Henry, Lord Kames (see Kames, Henry
Home, Lord)

Home, John 1722-1808 . . . . DLB-84

Home, William Douglas 1912- DLB-13

Home Publishing Company DLB-49

Homer circa eighth-seventh centuries B.C.
. . . . DLB-176

Homes, Geoffrey (see Mainwaring, Daniel)

Honan, Park 1928- DLB-111

Hone, William 1780-1842 . . . . DLB-110, 158

Hongo, Garrett Kaoru 1951- DLB-120

Honig, Edwin 1919- DLB-5

Hood, Hugh 1928- DLB-53

Hood, Thomas 1799-1845 . . . . DLB-96

Hook, Theodore 1788-1841. . . . . . DLB-116

Hooker, Jeremy 1941- DLB-40

Hooker, Richard 1554-1600. . . . . . DLB-132

Hooker, Thomas 1586-1647 . . . . . . DLB-24

Hooper, Johnson Jones
1815-1862 . . . . DLB-3, 11

Hope, Anthony 1863-1933. . . . . DLB-153, 156

Hopkins, Gerard Manley
1844-1889. . . . . DLB-35, 57

Hopkins, John (see Sternhold, Thomas)

Hopkins, Lemuel 1750-1801 . . . . . . DLB-37

Hopkins, Pauline Elizabeth
1859-1930. . . . . DLB-50

Hopkins, Samuel 1721-1803 . . . . . . DLB-31

Hopkins, John H., and Son DLB-46

Hopkinson, Francis 1737-1791 . . . . . DLB-31

Horgan, Paul 1903- DLB-102; Y-85

Horizon Press DLB-46

Horne, Frank 1899-1974 . . . . DLB-51

Horne, Richard Henry (Hengist)
1802 or 1803-1884 . . . . DLB-32

Hornung, E. W. 1866-1921 . . . . . . DLB-70

Horovitz, Israel 1939- DLB-7

Horton, George Moses
1797?-1883? DLB-50

Horváth, Ödön von
1901-1938 . . . . DLB-85, 124

Horwood, Harold 1923- DLB-60

Hosford, E. and E.
[publishing house] DLB-49

Hoskyns, John 1566-1638 . . . . DLB-121

Hotchkiss and Company DLB-49

Hough, Emerson 1857-1923 . . . . DLB-9

Houghton Mifflin Company DLB-49

Houghton, Stanley 1881-1913 . . . . . DLB-10

Household, Geoffrey 1900-1988 . . . . DLB-87

Housman, A. E. 1859-1936. . . . . . . DLB-19

Housman, Laurence 1865-1959. . . . . DLB-10

Houwald, Ernst von 1778-1845 . . . . DLB-90

Hovey, Richard 1864-1900 . . . . DLB-54

Howard, Donald R. 1927-1987 . . . . DLB-111

Howard, Maureen 1930- Y-83

Howard, Richard 1929- DLB-5

Howard, Roy W. 1883-1964 . . . . . . DLB-29

Howard, Sidney 1891-1939 . . . . . DLB-7, 26

Howe, E. W. 1853-1937 . . . . . . DLB-12, 25

Howe, Henry 1816-1893 .... DLB-30
Howe, Irving 1920-1993 .... DLB-67
Howe, Joseph 1804-1873 .... DLB-99
Howe, Julia Ward 1819-1910 ..... DLB-1
Howe, Percival Presland
   1886-1944 .... DLB-149
Howe, Susan 1937- DLB-120
Howell, Clark, Sr. 1863-1936 ...... DLB-25
Howell, Evan P. 1839-1905 ...... DLB-23
Howell, James 1594?-1666 .... DLB-151
Howell, Warren Richardson
   1912-1984 .... DLB-140
Howell, Soskin and Company DLB-46
Howells, William Dean
   1837-1920 .... DLB-12, 64, 74, 79
Howitt, William 1792-1879 and
   Howitt, Mary 1799-1888 ...... DLB-110
Hoyem, Andrew 1935- DLB-5
Hoyers, Anna Ovena 1584-1655 ... DLB-164
Hoyos, Angela de 1940- DLB-82
Hoyt, Palmer 1897-1979 .... DLB-127
Hoyt, Henry [publishing house] DLB-49
Hrabanus Maurus 776?-856 ...... DLB-148
Hrotsvit of Gandersheim
   circa 935-circa 1000 .... DLB-148
Hubbard, Elbert 1856-1915 ...... DLB-91
Hubbard, Kin 1868-1930 .... DLB-11
Hubbard, William circa 1621-1704 ... DLB-24
Huber, Therese 1764-1829 .... DLB-90
Huch, Friedrich 1873-1913 ...... DLB-66
Huch, Ricarda 1864-1947 .... DLB-66
Huck at 100: How Old Is
   Huckleberry Finn? Y-85
Huddle, David 1942- DLB-130
Hudgins, Andrew 1951- DLB-120
Hudson, Henry Norman
   1814-1886 .... DLB-64
Hudson, W. H.
   1841-1922 .... DLB-98, 153, 174
Hudson and Goodwin DLB-49
Huebsch, B. W.
   [publishing house] DLB-46
Hughes, David 1930- DLB-14
Hughes, John 1677-1720 .... DLB-84
Hughes, Langston
   1902-1967 .... DLB-4, 7, 48, 51, 86
Hughes, Richard 1900-1976 ..... DLB-15, 161
Hughes, Ted 1930- DLB-40, 161
Hughes, Thomas 1822-1896 .... DLB-18, 163
Hugo, Richard 1923-1982 .... DLB-5
Hugo, Victor 1802-1885 .... DLB-119
Hugo Awards and Nebula Awards ... DLB-8
Hull, Richard 1896-1973 .... DLB-77

Hulme, T. E. 1883-1917 .... DLB-19
Humboldt, Alexander von
   1769-1859 .... DLB-90
Humboldt, Wilhelm von
   1767-1835 .... DLB-90
Hume, David 1711-1776 .... DLB-104
Hume, Fergus 1859-1932 .... DLB-70
Hummer, T. R. 1950- DLB-120
Humorous Book Illustration DLB-11
Humphrey, William 1924- DLB-6
Humphreys, David 1752-1818 .... DLB-37
Humphreys, Emyr 1919- DLB-15
Huncke, Herbert 1915- DLB-16
Huneker, James Gibbons
   1857-1921 .... DLB-71
Hunold, Christian Friedrich
   1681-1721 .... DLB-168
Hunt, Irene 1907- DLB-52
Hunt, Leigh 1784-1859 .... DLB-96, 110, 144
Hunt, Violet 1862-1942 .... DLB-162
Hunt, William Gibbes 1791-1833 ... DLB-73
Hunter, Evan 1926- Y-82
Hunter, Jim 1939- DLB-14
Hunter, Kristin 1931- DLB-33
Hunter, Mollie 1922- DLB-161
Hunter, N. C. 1908-1971 .... DLB-10
Hunter-Duvar, John 1821-1899 ..... DLB-99
Huntington, Henry E.
   1850-1927 .... DLB-140
Hurd and Houghton DLB-49
Hurst, Fannie 1889-1968 .... DLB-86
Hurst and Blackett DLB-106
Hurst and Company DLB-49
Hurston, Zora Neale
   1901?-1960 .... DLB-51, 86
Husson, Jules-François-Félix (see Champfleury)
Huston, John 1906-1987 .... DLB-26
Hutcheson, Francis 1694-1746 .... DLB-31
Hutchinson, Thomas
   1711-1780 .... DLB-30, 31
Hutchinson and Company
   (Publishers) Limited DLB-112
von Hutton, Ulrich 1488-1523 .... DLB-179
Hutton, Richard Holt 1826-1897 ... DLB-57
Huxley, Aldous
   1894-1963 .... DLB-36, 100, 162
Huxley, Elspeth Josceline 1907- DLB-77
Huxley, T. H. 1825-1895 .... DLB-57
Huyghue, Douglas Smith
   1816-1891 .... DLB-99
Huysmans, Joris-Karl 1848-1907 ... DLB-123
Hyman, Trina Schart 1939- DLB-61

I

Iavorsky, Stefan 1658-1722 ...... DLB-150
Ibn Bajja circa 1077-1138 .... DLB-115
Ibn Gabirol, Solomon
   circa 1021-circa 1058 .... DLB-115
Ibuse, Masuji 1898-1993 .... DLB-180
The Iconography of Science-Fiction
   Art DLB-8
Iffland, August Wilhelm
   1759-1814 .... DLB-94
Ignatow, David 1914- DLB-5
Ike, Chukwuemeka 1931- DLB-157
Iles, Francis (see Berkeley, Anthony)
The Illustration of Early German
   Literary Manuscripts,
   circa 1150-circa 1300 .... DLB-148
Imbs, Bravig 1904-1946 .... DLB-4
Imbuga, Francis D. 1947- DLB-157
Immermann, Karl 1796-1840 ..... DLB-133
Inchbald, Elizabeth 1753-1821 .... DLB-39, 89
Inge, William 1913-1973 .... DLB-7
Ingelow, Jean 1820-1897 ...... DLB-35, 163
Ingersoll, Ralph 1900-1985 ...... DLB-127
The Ingersoll Prizes Y-84
Ingoldsby, Thomas (see Barham, Richard
   Harris)
Ingraham, Joseph Holt 1809-1860 .... DLB-3
Inman, John 1805-1850 .... DLB-73
Innerhofer, Franz 1944- DLB-85
Innis, Harold Adams 1894-1952 ..... DLB-88
Innis, Mary Quayle 1899-1972 ..... DLB-88
International Publishers Company DLB-46
An Interview with David Rabe Y-91
An Interview with George Greenfield,
   Literary Agent Y-91
An Interview with James Ellroy Y-91
An Interview with Peter S. Prescott ... Y-86
An Interview with Russell Hoban ... Y-90
An Interview with Tom Jenks Y-86
Introduction to Paul Laurence Dunbar,
   Lyrics of Lowly Life (1896),
   by William Dean Howells DLB-50
Introductory Essay: Letters of Percy Bysshe
   Shelley (1852), by Robert
   Browning DLB-32
Introductory Letters from the Second Edition
   of Pamela (1741), by Samuel
   Richardson DLB-39
Irving, John 1942- DLB-6; Y-82
Irving, Washington
   1783-1859 .... DLB-3, 11, 30, 59, 73, 74
Irwin, Grace 1907- DLB-68
Irwin, Will 1873-1948 .... DLB-25

Isherwood, Christopher 1904-1986 . . . . DLB-15; Y-86

The Island Trees Case: A Symposium on School Library Censorship
An Interview with Judith Krug
An Interview with Phyllis Schlafly
An Interview with Edward B. Jenkinson
An Interview with Lamarr Mooneyham
An Interview with Harriet Bernstein Y-82

Islas, Arturo 1938-1991 . . . . DLB-122

Ivanišević, Drago 1907-1981 . . . . . . DLB-181

Ivers, M. J., and Company DLB-49

Iwano, Hōmei 1873-1920 . . . . DLB-180

Iyayi, Festus 1947- DLB-157

Izumi, Kyōka 1873-1939 . . . . DLB-180

J

Jackmon, Marvin E. (see Marvin X)

Jacks, L. P. 1860-1955 . . . . DLB-135

Jackson, Angela 1951- DLB-41

Jackson, Helen Hunt 1830-1885 . . . . DLB-42, 47

Jackson, Holbrook 1874-1948 . . . . . . DLB-98

Jackson, Laura Riding 1901-1991 . . . . DLB-48

Jackson, Shirley 1919-1965 . . . . DLB-6

Jacob, Piers Anthony Dillingham (see Anthony, Piers)

Jacobi, Friedrich Heinrich 1743-1819 . . . . DLB-94

Jacobi, Johann Georg 1740-1841 . . . . . DLB-97

Jacobs, Joseph 1854-1916 . . . . DLB-141

Jacobs, W. W. 1863-1943 . . . . DLB-135

Jacobs, George W., and Company . . . DLB-49

Jacobson, Dan 1929- DLB-14

Jaggard, William [publishing house] DLB-170

Jahier, Piero 1884-1966 . . . . DLB-114

Jahnn, Hans Henny 1894-1959 . . . . DLB-56, 124

Jakes, John 1932- Y-83

James, C. L. R. 1901-1989 . . . . DLB-125

James, George P. R. 1801-1860 . . . . . DLB-116

James, Henry 1843-1916 . . . . . . DLB-12, 71, 74; DS-13

James, John circa 1633-1729 . . . . DLB-24

The James Jones Society Y-92

James, M. R. 1862-1936 . . . . DLB-156

James, P. D. 1920- DLB-87

James Joyce Centenary: Dublin, 1982 . . . . Y-82

James Joyce Conference Y-85

James VI of Scotland, I of England 1566-1625 . . . . DLB-151, 172

James, U. P. [publishing house] DLB-49

Jameson, Anna 1794-1860 . . . . DLB-99, 166

Jameson, Fredric 1934- DLB-67

Jameson, J. Franklin 1859-1937 . . . . . DLB-17

Jameson, Storm 1891-1986 . . . . DLB-36

Jančar, Drago 1948- DLB-181

Janés, Clara 1940- DLB-134

Janevski, Slavko 1920- DLB-181

Jaramillo, Cleofas M. 1878-1956 . . . . DLB-122

Jarman, Mark 1952- DLB-120

Jarrell, Randall 1914-1965 . . . . . DLB-48, 52

Jarrold and Sons DLB-106

Jasmin, Claude 1930- DLB-60

Jay, John 1745-1829 . . . . DLB-31

Jefferies, Richard 1848-1887 . . . . DLB-98, 141

Jeffers, Lance 1919-1985 . . . . DLB-41

Jeffers, Robinson 1887-1962 . . . . . . DLB-45

Jefferson, Thomas 1743-1826 . . . . . . DLB-31

Jelinek, Elfriede 1946- DLB-85

Jellicoe, Ann 1927- DLB-13

Jenkins, Elizabeth 1905- DLB-155

Jenkins, Robin 1912- DLB-14

Jenkins, William Fitzgerald (see Leinster, Murray)

Jenkins, Herbert, Limited DLB-112

Jennings, Elizabeth 1926- DLB-27

Jens, Walter 1923- DLB-69

Jensen, Merrill 1905-1980 . . . . DLB-17

Jephson, Robert 1736-1803 . . . . DLB-89

Jerome, Jerome K. 1859-1927 . . . . DLB-10, 34, 135

Jerome, Judson 1927-1991 . . . . DLB-105

Jerome, Judson, Reflections: After a Tornado DLB-105

Jerrold, Douglas 1803-1857 . . . . DLB-158, 159

Jesse, F. Tennyson 1888-1958 . . . . . . DLB-77

Jewett, Sarah Orne 1849-1909 . . . . DLB-12, 74

Jewett, John P., and Company DLB-49

The Jewish Publication Society DLB-49

Jewitt, John Rodgers 1783-1821 . . . . DLB-99

Jewsbury, Geraldine 1812-1880 . . . . . DLB-21

Jhabvala, Ruth Prawer 1927- DLB-139

Jiménez, Juan Ramón 1881-1958 . . . . DLB-134

Joans, Ted 1928- DLB-16, 41

John, Eugenie (see Marlitt, E.)

John of Dumbleton circa 1310-circa 1349 . . . . DLB-115

John Edward Bruce: Three Documents DLB-50

John O'Hara's Pottsville Journalism Y-88

John Steinbeck Research Center Y-85

John Webster: The Melbourne Manuscript Y-86

Johns, Captain W. E. 1893-1968 . . . . DLB-160

Johnson, B. S. 1933-1973 . . . . . . DLB-14, 40

Johnson, Charles 1679-1748 . . . . DLB-84

Johnson, Charles R. 1948- DLB-33

Johnson, Charles S. 1893-1956 . . . DLB-51, 91

Johnson, Denis 1949- DLB-120

Johnson, Diane 1934- Y-80

Johnson, Edgar 1901- DLB-103

Johnson, Edward 1598-1672 . . . . . . DLB-24

Johnson E. Pauline (Tekahionwake) 1861-1913 . . . . DLB-175

Johnson, Fenton 1888-1958 . . . . . DLB-45, 50

Johnson, Georgia Douglas 1886-1966 . . . . DLB-51

Johnson, Gerald W. 1890-1980 . . . . . DLB-29

Johnson, Helene 1907- DLB-51

Johnson, James Weldon 1871-1938 . . . . DLB-51

Johnson, John H. 1918- DLB-137

Johnson, Linton Kwesi 1952- DLB-157

Johnson, Lionel 1867-1902 . . . . DLB-19

Johnson, Nunnally 1897-1977 . . . . . DLB-26

Johnson, Owen 1878-1952 . . . . Y-87

Johnson, Pamela Hansford 1912- DLB-15

Johnson, Pauline 1861-1913 . . . . DLB-92

Johnson, Ronald 1935- DLB-169

Johnson, Samuel 1696-1772 . . . . DLB-24

Johnson, Samuel 1709-1784 . . . . . . DLB-39, 95, 104, 142

Johnson, Samuel 1822-1882 . . . . DLB-1

Johnson, Uwe 1934-1984 . . . . DLB-75

Johnson, Benjamin [publishing house] DLB-49

Johnson, Benjamin, Jacob, and Robert [publishing house] DLB-49

Johnson, Jacob, and Company DLB-49

Johnson, Joseph [publishing house] DLB-154

Johnston, Annie Fellows 1863-1931 . . . DLB-42

Johnston, Basil H. 1929- DLB-60

Johnston, Denis 1901-1984 . . . . DLB-10

Johnston, George 1913- DLB-88

Johnston, Sir Harry 1858-1927 . . . . DLB-174

Johnston, Jennifer 1930- DLB-14

Johnston, Mary 1870-1936 . . . . DLB-9

Johnston, Richard Malcolm 1822-1898 . . . . DLB-74

Johnstone, Charles 1719?-1800? DLB-39

Johst, Hanns 1890-1978 . . . . DLB-124

Jolas, Eugene 1894-1952 . . . . DLB-4, 45

Jones, Alice C. 1853-1933 . . . . DLB-92

Jones, Charles C., Jr. 1831-1893 . . . . DLB-30

Jones, D. G. 1929- DLB-53

Jones, David 1895-1974 . . . . DLB-20, 100

Jones, Diana Wynne 1934- DLB-161

Jones, Ebenezer 1820-1860 . . . . DLB-32

Jones, Ernest 1819-1868. . . . . DLB-32

Jones, Gayl 1949- DLB-33

Jones, Glyn 1905- DLB-15

Jones, Gwyn 1907- DLB-15, 139

Jones, Henry Arthur 1851-1929 . . . . . DLB-10

Jones, Hugh circa 1692-1760. . . . . . . DLB-24

Jones, James 1921-1977. . . . . . . DLB-2, 143

Jones, Jenkin Lloyd 1911- DLB-127

Jones, LeRoi (see Baraka, Amiri)

Jones, Lewis 1897-1939 . . . . DLB-15

Jones, Madison 1925- DLB-152

Jones, Major Joseph (see Thompson, William Tappan)

Jones, Preston 1936-1979. . . . . DLB-7

Jones, Rodney 1950- DLB-120

Jones, Sir William 1746-1794 . . . . . . DLB-109

Jones, William Alfred 1817-1900. . . . . DLB-59

Jones's Publishing House DLB-49

Jong, Erica 1942- DLB-2, 5, 28, 152

Jonke, Gert F. 1946- DLB-85

Jonson, Ben 1572?-1637. . . . . . DLB-62, 121

Jordan, June 1936- DLB-38

Joseph, Jenny 1932- DLB-40

Joseph, Michael, Limited DLB-112

Josephson, Matthew 1899-1978 . . . . . DLB-4

Josephus, Flavius 37-100. . . . . DLB-176

Josiah Allen's Wife (see Holley, Marietta)

Josipovici, Gabriel 1940- DLB-14

Josselyn, John ?-1675 . . . . DLB-24

Joudry, Patricia 1921- DLB-88

Jovine, Giuseppe 1922- DLB-128

Joyaux, Philippe (see Sollers, Philippe)

Joyce, Adrien (see Eastman, Carol)

Joyce, James
1882-1941. . . . . . . DLB-10, 19, 36, 162

Judd, Sylvester 1813-1853 . . . . DLB-1

Judd, Orange, Publishing Company DLB-49

Judith circa 930 . . . . DLB-146

Julian of Norwich
1342-circa 1420. . . . . DLB-1146

Julian Symons at Eighty Y-92

June, Jennie (see Croly, Jane Cunningham)

Jung, Franz 1888-1963 . . . . DLB-118

Jünger, Ernst 1895- DLB-56

Der jüngere Titurel circa 1275 . . . . . DLB-138

Jung-Stilling, Johann Heinrich
1740-1817 . . . . DLB-94

Justice, Donald 1925- Y-83

The Juvenile Library (see Godwin, M. J., and Company)

K

Kacew, Romain (see Gary, Romain)

Kafka, Franz 1883-1924. . . . . DLB-81

Kahn, Roger 1927 . . . . DLB-171

Kaiser, Georg 1878-1945 . . . . DLB-124

Kaiserchronik circa 1147 . . . . DLB-148

Kaleb, Vjekoslav 1905- DLB-181

Kalechofsky, Roberta 1931- DLB-28

Kaler, James Otis 1848-1912 . . . . DLB-12

Kames, Henry Home, Lord
1696-1782 . . . . DLB-31, 104

Kandel, Lenore 1932- DLB-16

Kanin, Garson 1912- DLB-7

Kant, Hermann 1926- DLB-75

Kant, Immanuel 1724-1804. . . . . DLB-94

Kantemir, Antiokh Dmitrievich
1708-1744 . . . . DLB-150

Kantor, Mackinlay 1904-1977 . . . . DLB-9, 102

Kaplan, Fred 1937- DLB-111

Kaplan, Johanna 1942- DLB-28

Kaplan, Justin 1925- DLB-111

Kapnist, Vasilii Vasilevich
1758?-1823 . . . . DLB-150

Karadžić, Vuk Stefanović
1787-1864 . . . . DLB-147

Karamzin, Nikolai Mikhailovich
1766-1826 . . . . DLB-150

Karsch, Anna Louisa 1722-1791 . . . . . DLB-97

Kasack, Hermann 1896-1966. . . . . . . DLB-69

Kasai, Zenzō 1887-1927 . . . . DLB-180

Kaschnitz, Marie Luise 1901-1974 . . . . DLB-69

Kaštelan, Jure 1919-1990 . . . . DLB-147

Kästner, Erich 1899-1974 . . . . DLB-56

Kattan, Naim 1928- DLB-53

Katz, Steve 1935- Y-83

Kauffman, Janet 1945- Y-86

Kauffmann, Samuel 1898-1971 . . . . . DLB-127

Kaufman, Bob 1925- DLB-16, 41

Kaufman, George S. 1889-1961 . . . . . . DLB-7

Kavanagh, P. J. 1931- DLB-40

Kavanagh, Patrick 1904-1967 . . . . DLB-15, 20

Kawabata, Yasunari 1899-1972 . . . . . DLB-180

Kaye-Smith, Sheila 1887-1956. . . . . . . DLB-36

Kazin, Alfred 1915- DLB-67

Keane, John B. 1928- DLB-13

Keary, Annie 1825-1879 . . . . DLB-163

Keating, H. R. F. 1926- DLB-87

Keats, Ezra Jack 1916-1983 . . . . DLB-61

Keats, John 1795-1821 . . . . DLB-96, 110

Keble, John 1792-1866 . . . . DLB-32, 55

Keeble, John 1944- Y-83

Keeffe, Barrie 1945- DLB-13

Keeley, James 1867-1934 . . . . DLB-25

W. B. Keen, Cooke
and Company DLB-49

Keillor, Garrison 1942- Y-87

Keith, Marian 1874?-1961 . . . . DLB-92

Keller, Gary D. 1943- DLB-82

Keller, Gottfried 1819-1890 . . . . . . DLB-129

Kelley, Edith Summers 1884-1956. . . . . DLB-9

Kelley, William Melvin 1937- DLB-33

Kellogg, Ansel Nash 1832-1886 . . . . . DLB-23

Kellogg, Steven 1941- DLB-61

Kelly, George 1887-1974 . . . . DLB-7

Kelly, Hugh 1739-1777 . . . . DLB-89

Kelly, Robert 1935- DLB-5, 130, 165

Kelly, Piet and Company DLB-49

Kelmscott Press DLB-112

Kemble, Fanny 1809-1893 . . . . DLB-32

Kemelman, Harry 1908- DLB-28

Kempe, Margery
circa 1373-1438 . . . . DLB-146

Kempner, Friederike 1836-1904 . . . . . DLB-129

Kempowski, Walter 1929- DLB-75

Kendall, Claude
[publishing company] DLB-46

Kendell, George 1809-1867 . . . . DLB-43

Kenedy, P. J., and Sons DLB-49

Kennedy, Adrienne 1931- DLB-38

Kennedy, John Pendleton 1795-1870 . . . . DLB-3

Kennedy, Leo 1907- DLB-88

Kennedy, Margaret 1896-1967 . . . . . . DLB-36

Kennedy, Patrick 1801-1873 . . . . . . DLB-159

Kennedy, Richard S. 1920- DLB-111

Kennedy, William 1928- DLB-143; Y-85

Kennedy, X. J. 1929- DLB-5

Kennelly, Brendan 1936- DLB-40

Kenner, Hugh 1923- DLB-67

Kennerley, Mitchell
[publishing house] DLB-46

Kenny, Maurice 1929- DLB-175

Kent, Frank R. 1877-1958 . . . . DLB-29

Kenyon, Jane 1947- DLB-120

Keough, Hugh Edmund 1864-1912. . . DLB-171

Keppler and Schwartzmann DLB-49

Kerner, Justinus 1776-1862 . . . . DLB-90

Kerouac, Jack 1922-1969 . . . . DLB-2, 16; DS-3

The Jack Kerouac Revival Y-95

Kerouac, Jan 1952- DLB-16

Kerr, Orpheus C. (see Newell, Robert Henry)

Kerr, Charles H., and Company DLB-49

Kesey, Ken 1935- DLB-2, 16

Kessel, Joseph 1898-1979 . . . . DLB-72

Kessel, Martin 1901- DLB-56

Kesten, Hermann 1900- DLB-56

Keun, Irmgard 1905-1982. . . . . DLB-69

Key and Biddle DLB-49

Keynes, John Maynard 1883-1946 . . . . . DS-10

Keyserling, Eduard von 1855-1918 . . . DLB-66

Khan, Ismith 1925- DLB-125

Khaytov, Nikolay 1919- DLB-181

Khemnitser, Ivan Ivanovich
   1745-1784 . . . . DLB-150

Kheraskov, Mikhail Matveevich
   1733-1807 . . . . DLB-150

Khristov, Boris 1945- DLB-181

Khvostov, Dmitrii Ivanovich
   1757-1835 . . . . DLB-150

Kidd, Adam 1802?-1831 . . . . DLB-99

Kidd, William
   [publishing house] DLB-106

Kiely, Benedict 1919- DLB-15

Kieran, John 1892-1981 . . . . DLB-171

Kiggins and Kellogg DLB-49

Kiley, Jed 1889-1962 . . . . DLB-4

Kilgore, Bernard 1908-1967 . . . . . . DLB-127

Killens, John Oliver 1916- DLB-33

Killigrew, Anne 1660-1685 . . . . . . DLB-131

Killigrew, Thomas 1612-1683 . . . . . DLB-58

Kilmer, Joyce 1886-1918 . . . . DLB-45

Kilwardby, Robert
   circa 1215-1279 . . . . DLB-115

Kincaid, Jamaica 1949- DLB-157

King, Clarence 1842-1901 . . . . DLB-12

King, Florence 1936 . . . . Y-85

King, Francis 1923- DLB-15, 139

King, Grace 1852-1932 . . . . DLB-12, 78

King, Henry 1592-1669 . . . . DLB-126

King, Stephen 1947- DLB-143; Y-80

King, Thomas 1943- DLB-175

King, Woodie, Jr. 1937- DLB-38

King, Solomon [publishing house] DLB-49

Kinglake, Alexander William
   1809-1891 . . . . DLB-55, 166

Kingsley, Charles
   1819-1875 . . . . . . DLB-21, 32, 163, 178

Kingsley, Mary Henrietta
   1862-1900 . . . . DLB-174

Kingsley, Henry 1830-1876 . . . . . . DLB-21

Kingsley, Sidney 1906- DLB-7

Kingsmill, Hugh 1889-1949 . . . . . . DLB-149

Kingston, Maxine Hong
   1940- DLB-173; Y-80

Kingston, William Henry Giles
   1814-1880 . . . . DLB-163

Kinnell, Galway 1927- DLB-5; Y-87

Kinsella, Thomas 1928- DLB-27

Kipling, Rudyard
   1865-1936 . . . . . DLB-19, 34, 141, 156

Kipphardt, Heinar 1922-1982 . . . . . DLB-124

Kirby, William 1817-1906 . . . . DLB-99

Kircher, Athanasius 1602-1680 . . . . DLB-164

Kirk, John Foster 1824-1904 . . . . . . DLB-79

Kirkconnell, Watson 1895-1977 . . . . DLB-68

Kirkland, Caroline M.
   1801-1864 . . . . . . DLB-3, 73, 74; DS-13

Kirkland, Joseph 1830-1893 . . . . . . DLB-12

Kirkman, Francis
   [publishing house] DLB-170

Kirkpatrick, Clayton 1915- DLB-127

Kirkup, James 1918- DLB-27

Kirouac, Conrad (see Marie-Victorin, Frère)

Kirsch, Sarah 1935- DLB-75

Kirst, Hans Hellmut 1914-1989 . . . . DLB-69

Kiš, Danilo 1935-1989 . . . . DLB-181

Kitcat, Mabel Greenhow
   1859-1922 . . . . DLB-135

Kitchin, C. H. B. 1895-1967 . . . . . . DLB-77

Kizer, Carolyn 1925- DLB-5, 169

Klabund 1890-1928 . . . . DLB-66

Klaj, Johann 1616-1656 . . . . DLB-164

Klappert, Peter 1942- DLB-5

Klass, Philip (see Tenn, William)

Klein, A. M. 1909-1972 . . . . DLB-68

Kleist, Ewald von 1715-1759 . . . . . . DLB-97

Kleist, Heinrich von 1777-1811 . . . . DLB-90

Klinger, Friedrich Maximilian
   1752-1831 . . . . DLB-94

Klopstock, Friedrich Gottlieb
   1724-1803 . . . . DLB-97

Klopstock, Meta 1728-1758 . . . . . . DLB-97

Kluge, Alexander 1932- DLB-75

Knapp, Joseph Palmer 1864-1951 . . . DLB-91

Knapp, Samuel Lorenzo
   1783-1838 . . . . DLB-59

Knapton, J. J. and P.
   [publishing house] DLB-154

Kniazhnin, Iakov Borisovich
   1740-1791 . . . . DLB-150

Knickerbocker, Diedrich (see Irving, Washington)

Knigge, Adolph Franz Friedrich Ludwig,
   Freiherr von 1752-1796 . . . . DLB-94

Knight, Damon 1922- DLB-8

Knight, Etheridge 1931-1992 . . . . . DLB-41

Knight, John S. 1894-1981 . . . . . . DLB-29

Knight, Sarah Kemble 1666-1727 . . . DLB-24

Knight, Charles, and Company DLB-106

Knight-Bruce, G. W. H.
   1852-1896 . . . . DLB-174

Knister, Raymond 1899-1932 . . . . . DLB-68

Knoblock, Edward 1874-1945 . . . . . DLB-10

Knopf, Alfred A. 1892-1984 . . . . Y-84

Knopf, Alfred A.
   [publishing house] DLB-46

Knorr von Rosenroth, Christian
   1636-1689 . . . . DLB-168

Knowles, John 1926- DLB-6

Knox, Frank 1874-1944 . . . . DLB-29

Knox, John circa 1514-1572 . . . . . . DLB-132

Knox, John Armoy 1850-1906 . . . . . DLB-23

Knox, Ronald Arbuthnott
   1888-1957 . . . . DLB-77

Kobayashi, Takiji 1903-1933 . . . . . DLB-180

Kober, Arthur 1900-1975 . . . . DLB-11

Kocbek, Edvard 1904-1981 . . . . . . DLB-147

Koch, Howard 1902- DLB-26

Koch, Kenneth 1925- DLB-5

Kōda, Rohan 1867-1947 . . . . DLB-180

Koenigsberg, Moses 1879-1945 . . . . DLB-25

Koeppen, Wolfgang 1906- DLB-69

Koertge, Ronald 1940- DLB-105

Koestler, Arthur 1905-1983 . . . . Y-83

Kokoschka, Oskar 1886-1980 . . . . . DLB-124

Kolb, Annette 1870-1967 . . . . DLB-66

Kolbenheyer, Erwin Guido
   1878-1962 . . . . DLB-66, 124

Kolleritsch, Alfred 1931- DLB-85

Kolodny, Annette 1941- DLB-67

Komarov, Matvei
   circa 1730-1812 . . . . DLB-150

Komroff, Manuel 1890-1974 . . . . . . DLB-4

Komunyakaa, Yusef 1947- DLB-120

Koneski, Blaže 1921-1993 . . . . DLB-181

Konigsburg, E. L. 1930- DLB-52

Konrad von Würzburg
   circa 1230-1287 . . . . DLB-138

Konstantinov, Aleko 1863-1897 . . . . DLB-147

Kooser, Ted 1939- DLB-105

Kopit, Arthur 1937- DLB-7

Kops, Bernard 1926?- DLB-13

Kornbluth, C. M. 1923-1958 . . . . . . DLB-8

Körner, Theodor 1791-1813 . . . . . . DLB-90

Kornfeld, Paul 1889-1942 . . . . DLB-118

Kosinski, Jerzy 1933-1991 . . . . . DLB-2; Y-82

Kosmač, Ciril 1910-1980 . . . . DLB-181

Kosovel, Srečko 1904-1926 . . . . . . DLB-147

Kostrov, Ermil Ivanovich
   1755-1796 . . . . DLB-150

Kotzebue, August von 1761-1819 . . . DLB-94

Kotzwinkle, William 1938- DLB-173

Kovačić, Ante 1854-1889 . . . . DLB-147

Kovič, Kajetan 1931- DLB-181

Kraf, Elaine 1946- Y-81

Kranjčević, Silvije Strahimir
   1865-1908 . . . . DLB-147

Krasna, Norman 1909-1984 . . . . DLB-26

Kraus, Karl 1874-1936 . . . . DLB-118

Krauss, Ruth 1911-1993 . . . . DLB-52

Kreisel, Henry 1922- DLB-88

Kreuder, Ernst 1903-1972 . . . . DLB-69

Kreymborg, Alfred 1883-1966 . . . . DLB-4, 54

Krieger, Murray 1923- DLB-67

Krim, Seymour 1922-1989 . . . . DLB-16

Krleža, Miroslav 1893-1981 . . . . DLB-147

Krock, Arthur 1886-1974 . . . . DLB-29

Kroetsch, Robert 1927- DLB-53

Krutch, Joseph Wood 1893-1970 . . . . DLB-63

Krylov, Ivan Andreevich
   1769-1844 . . . . DLB-150

Kubin, Alfred 1877-1959 . . . . DLB-81

Kubrick, Stanley 1928- DLB-26

Kudrun circa 1230-1240 . . . . DLB-138

Kuffstein, Hans Ludwig von
   1582-1656 . . . . DLB-164

Kuhlmann, Quirinus 1651-1689 . . . . . DLB-168

Kuhnau, Johann 1660-1722 . . . . DLB-168

Kumin, Maxine 1925- DLB-5

Kunene, Mazisi 1930- DLB-117

Kunikida, Doppo 1869-1908 . . . . . . DLB-180

Kunitz, Stanley 1905- DLB-48

Kunjufu, Johari M. (see Amini, Johari M.)

Kunnert, Gunter 1929- DLB-75

Kunze, Reiner 1933- DLB-75

Kupferberg, Tuli 1923- DLB-16

Kürnberger, Ferdinand
   1821-1879 . . . . DLB-129

Kurz, Isolde 1853-1944 . . . . DLB-66

Kusenberg, Kurt 1904-1983 . . . . DLB-69

Kuttner, Henry 1915-1958 . . . . DLB-8

Kyd, Thomas 1558-1594 . . . . DLB-62

Kyffin, Maurice
   circa 1560?-1598 . . . . DLB-136

Kyger, Joanne 1934- DLB-16

Kyne, Peter B. 1880-1957 . . . . DLB-78

L

L. E. L. (see Landon, Letitia Elizabeth)

Laberge, Albert 1871-1960 . . . . DLB-68

Laberge, Marie 1950- DLB-60

Lacombe, Patrice (see Trullier-Lacombe,
   Joseph Patrice)

Lacretelle, Jacques de 1888-1985 . . . . DLB-65

Lacy, Sam 1903- DLB-171

Ladd, Joseph Brown 1764-1786 . . . . DLB-37

La Farge, Oliver 1901-1963 . . . . DLB-9

Lafferty, R. A. 1914- DLB-8

La Flesche, Francis 1857-1932 . . . . . DLB-175

La Guma, Alex 1925-1985 . . . . DLB-117

Lahaise, Guillaume (see Delahaye, Guy)

Lahontan, Louis-Armand de Lom d'Arce,
   Baron de 1666-1715? DLB-99

Laing, Kojo 1946- DLB-157

Laird, Carobeth 1895- Y-82

Laird and Lee DLB-49

Lalić, Ivan V. 1931-1996 . . . . DLB-181

Lalić, Mihailo 1914-1992 . . . . DLB-181

Lalonde, Michèle 1937- DLB-60

Lamantia, Philip 1927- DLB-16

Lamb, Charles
   1775-1834 . . . . DLB-93, 107, 163

Lamb, Lady Caroline 1785-1828 . . . . DLB-116

Lamb, Mary 1764-1874 . . . . DLB-163

Lambert, Betty 1933-1983 . . . . DLB-60

Lamming, George 1927- DLB-125

L'Amour, Louis 1908?- Y-80

Lampman, Archibald 1861-1899 . . . . DLB-92

Lamson, Wolffe and Company DLB-49

Lancer Books DLB-46

Landesman, Jay 1919- and
   Landesman, Fran 1927- DLB-16

Landolfi, Tommaso 1908-1979 . . . . . DLB-177

Landon, Letitia Elizabeth 1802-1838 . . . DLB-96

Landor, Walter Savage
   1775-1864 . . . . DLB-93, 107

Landry, Napoléon-P. 1884-1956 . . . . DLB-92

Lane, Charles 1800-1870 . . . . DLB-1

Lane, Laurence W. 1890-1967 . . . . . DLB-91

Lane, M. Travis 1934- DLB-60

Lane, Patrick 1939- DLB-53

Lane, Pinkie Gordon 1923- DLB-41

Lane, John, Company DLB-49

Laney, Al 1896-1988 . . . . DLB-4, 171

Lang, Andrew 1844-1912 . . . . . . DLB-98, 141

Langevin, André 1927- DLB-60

Langgässer, Elisabeth 1899-1950 . . . . DLB-69

Langhorne, John 1735-1779 . . . . . . DLB-109

Langland, William
   circa 1330-circa 1400 . . . . DLB-146

Langton, Anna 1804-1893 . . . . DLB-99

Lanham, Edwin 1904-1979 . . . . DLB-4

Lanier, Sidney 1842-1881 . . . . DLB-64; DS-13

Lanyer, Aemilia 1569-1645 . . . . DLB-121

Lapointe, Gatien 1931-1983 . . . . . . DLB-88

Lapointe, Paul-Marie 1929- DLB-88

Lardner, John 1912-1960 . . . . DLB-171

Lardner, Ring
   1885-1933 . . . . DLB-11, 25, 86, 171

Lardner, Ring, Jr. 1915- DLB-26

Lardner 100: Ring Lardner
   Centennial Symposium Y-85

Larkin, Philip 1922-1985 . . . . DLB-27

La Roche, Sophie von 1730-1807 . . . . DLB-94

La Rocque, Gilbert 1943-1984 . . . . . DLB-60

Laroque de Roquebrune, Robert (see Roquebrune,
   Robert de)

Larrick, Nancy 1910- DLB-61

Larsen, Nella 1893-1964 . . . . DLB-51

Lasker-Schüler, Else
   1869-1945 . . . . DLB-66, 124

Lasnier, Rina 1915- DLB-88

Lassalle, Ferdinand 1825-1864 . . . . . DLB-129

Lathrop, Dorothy P. 1891-1980 . . . . . DLB-22

Lathrop, George Parsons
   1851-1898 . . . . DLB-71

Lathrop, John, Jr. 1772-1820 . . . . . . DLB-37

Latimer, Hugh 1492?-1555 . . . . DLB-136

Latimore, Jewel Christine McLawler
   (see Amini, Johari M.)

Latymer, William 1498-1583 . . . . . . DLB-132

Laube, Heinrich 1806-1884 . . . . DLB-133

Laughlin, James 1914- DLB-48

Laumer, Keith 1925- DLB-8

Lauremberg, Johann 1590-1658 . . . . DLB-164

Laurence, Margaret 1926-1987 . . . . . DLB-53

Laurentius von Schnüffis
   1633-1702 . . . . DLB-168

Laurents, Arthur 1918- DLB-26

Laurie, Annie (see Black, Winifred)

Laut, Agnes Christiana 1871-1936 . . . . DLB-92

Lavater, Johann Kaspar 1741-1801 . . . . DLB-97

Lavin, Mary 1912- DLB-15

Lawes, Henry 1596-1662 . . . . DLB-126

Lawless, Anthony (see MacDonald, Philip)

Lawrence, D. H.
   1885-1930 . . . . DLB-10, 19, 36, 98, 162

Lawrence, David 1888-1973 . . . . DLB-29

Lawrence, Seymour 1926-1994 . . . . . . Y-94

Lawson, John ?-1711 . . . . DLB-24

Lawson, Robert 1892-1957 . . . . DLB-22

Lawson, Victor F. 1850-1925 . . . . . . DLB-25

Layard, Sir Austen Henry
   1817-1894 . . . . DLB-166

Layton, Irving 1912- DLB-88

LaZamon flourished circa 1200 . . . . . DLB-146

Lazarević, Laza K. 1851-1890 . . . . . DLB-147

Lea, Henry Charles 1825-1909 . . . . . DLB-47

Lea, Sydney 1942- DLB-120
Lea, Tom 1907- DLB-6
Leacock, John 1729-1802 .... DLB-31
Leacock, Stephen 1869-1944 ...... DLB-92
Lead, Jane Ward 1623-1704 ...... DLB-131
Leadenhall Press DLB-106
Leapor, Mary 1722-1746 .... DLB-109
Lear, Edward 1812-1888 ... DLB-32, 163, 166
Leary, Timothy 1920-1996 .... DLB-16
Leary, W. A., and Company DLB-49
Léautaud, Paul 1872-1956 .... DLB-65
Leavitt, David 1961- DLB-130
Leavitt and Allen DLB-49
Le Blond, Mrs. Aubrey
   1861-1934 .... DLB-174
le Carré, John 1931- DLB-87
Lécavelé, Roland (see Dorgeles, Roland)
Lechlitner, Ruth 1901- DLB-48
Leclerc, Félix 1914- DLB-60
Le Clézio, J. M. G. 1940- DLB-83
Lectures on Rhetoric and Belles Lettres (1783),
   by Hugh Blair [excerpts]....... DLB-31
Leder, Rudolf (see Hermlin, Stephan)
Lederer, Charles 1910-1976........ DLB-26
Ledwidge, Francis 1887-1917...... DLB-20
Lee, Dennis 1939- DLB-53
Lee, Don L. (see Madhubuti, Haki R.)
Lee, George W. 1894-1976....... DLB-51
Lee, Harper 1926- DLB-6
Lee, Harriet (1757-1851) and
   Lee, Sophia (1750-1824) DLB-39
Lee, Laurie 1914- DLB-27
Lee, Li-Young 1957- DLB-165
Lee, Manfred B. (see Dannay, Frederic, and
   Manfred B. Lee)
Lee, Nathaniel circa 1645 - 1692 .... DLB-80
Lee, Sir Sidney 1859-1926........ DLB-149
Lee, Sir Sidney, "Principles of Biography," in *Elizabethan and Other Essays*........ DLB-149
Lee, Vernon
   1856-1935.... DLB-57, 153, 156, 174, 178
Lee and Shepard DLB-49
Le Fanu, Joseph Sheridan
   1814-1873 .... DLB-21, 70, 159, 178
Leffland, Ella 1931- Y-84
le Fort, Gertrud von 1876-1971 ..... DLB-66
Le Gallienne, Richard 1866-1947 .... DLB-4
Legaré, Hugh Swinton
   1797-1843 .... DLB-3, 59, 73
Legaré, James M. 1823-1859 ...... DLB-3
The Legends of the Saints and a Medieval
   Christian Worldview DLB-148
Léger, Antoine-J. 1880-1950........ DLB-88

Le Guin, Ursula K. 1929- DLB-8, 52
Lehman, Ernest 1920- DLB-44
Lehmann, John 1907- DLB-27, 100
Lehmann, Rosamond 1901-1990..... DLB-15
Lehmann, Wilhelm 1882-1968 ..... DLB-56
Lehmann, John, Limited. DLB-112
Leiber, Fritz 1910-1992........... DLB-8
Leibniz, Gottfried Wilhelm
   1646-1716 .... DLB-168
Leicester University Press DLB-112
Leinster, Murray 1896-1975 .... DLB-8
Leisewitz, Johann Anton
   1752-1806 .... DLB-94
Leitch, Maurice 1933- DLB-14
Leithauser, Brad 1943- DLB-120
Leland, Charles G. 1824-1903 ..... DLB-11
Leland, John 1503?-1552 .... DLB-136
Lemay, Pamphile 1837-1918 ...... DLB-99
Lemelin, Roger 1919- DLB-88
Lemon, Mark 1809-1870 .... DLB-163
Le Moine, James MacPherson
   1825-1912................ DLB-99
Le Moyne, Jean 1913- DLB-88
L'Engle, Madeleine 1918- DLB-52
Lennart, Isobel 1915-1971 ...... DLB-44
Lennox, Charlotte
   1729 or 1730-1804 .... DLB-39
Lenox, James 1800-1880........ DLB-140
Lenski, Lois 1893-1974 .... DLB-22
Lenz, Hermann 1913- DLB-69
Lenz, J. M. R. 1751-1792 .... DLB-94
Lenz, Siegfried 1926- DLB-75
Leonard, Elmore 1925- DLB-173
Leonard, Hugh 1926- DLB-13
Leonard, William Ellery
   1876-1944 .... DLB-54
Leonowens, Anna 1834-1914 .... DLB-99, 166
LePan, Douglas 1914- DLB-88
Leprohon, Rosanna Eleanor
   1829-1879 .... DLB-99
Le Queux, William 1864-1927 ..... DLB-70
Lerner, Max 1902-1992........ DLB-29
Lernet-Holenia, Alexander
   1897-1976............... DLB-85
Le Rossignol, James 1866-1969..... DLB-92
Lescarbot, Marc circa 1570-1642..... DLB-99
LeSeur, William Dawson
   1840-1917 .... DLB-92
LeSieg, Theo. (see Geisel, Theodor Seuss)
Leslie, Frank 1821-1880 ...... DLB-43, 79
Leslie, Frank, Publishing House DLB-49
Lesperance, John 1835?-1891 ...... DLB-99
Lessing, Bruno 1870-1940 .... DLB-28

Lessing, Doris 1919- DLB-15, 139; Y-85
Lessing, Gotthold Ephraim
   1729-1781................ DLB-97
Lettau, Reinhard 1929- DLB-75
Letter from Japan............... Y-94
Letter from London Y-96
Letter to [Samuel] Richardson on *Clarissa*
   (1748), by Henry Fielding DLB-39
Lever, Charles 1806-1872......... DLB-21
Leverson, Ada 1862-1933 .... DLB-153
Levertov, Denise 1923- DLB-5, 165
Levi, Peter 1931- DLB-40
Levi, Primo 1919-1987 .... DLB-177
Levien, Sonya 1888-1960......... DLB-44
Levin, Meyer 1905-1981 .... DLB-9, 28; Y-81
Levine, Norman 1923- DLB-88
Levine, Philip 1928- DLB-5
Levis, Larry 1946- DLB-120
Levy, Amy 1861-1889.......... DLB-156
Levy, Benn Wolfe
   1900-1973............. DLB-13; Y-81
Lewald, Fanny 1811-1889 .... DLB-129
Lewes, George Henry
   1817-1878 .... DLB-55, 144
Lewis, Agnes Smith 1843-1926 ..... DLB-174
Lewis, Alfred H. 1857-1914 ...... DLB-25
Lewis, Alun 1915-1944 ...... DLB-20, 162
Lewis, C. Day (see Day Lewis, C.)
Lewis, C. S. 1898-1963 .... DLB-15, 100, 160
Lewis, Charles B. 1842-1924....... DLB-11
Lewis, Henry Clay 1825-1850........ DLB-3
Lewis, Janet 1899- Y-87
Lewis, Matthew Gregory
   1775-1818 .... DLB-39, 158, 178
Lewis, R. W. B. 1917- DLB-111
Lewis, Richard circa 1700-1734 ..... DLB-24
Lewis, Sinclair
   1885-1951 .... DLB-9, 102; DS-1
Lewis, Wilmarth Sheldon
   1895-1979 .... DLB-140
Lewis, Wyndham 1882-1957 ..... DLB-15
Lewisohn, Ludwig
   1882-1955......... DLB-4, 9, 28, 102
Lezama Lima, José 1910-1976..... DLB-113
The Library of America DLB-46
The Licensing Act of 1737........ DLB-84
Lichfield, Leonard I
   [publishing house] DLB-170
Lichtenberg, Georg Christoph
   1742-1799 .... DLB-94
Lieb, Fred 1888-1980 .... DLB-171
Liebling, A. J. 1904-1963 ...... DLB-4, 171
Lieutenant Murray (see Ballou, Maturin
   Murray)

Lighthall, William Douw
1857-1954 . . . . DLB-92

Lilar, Françoise (see Mallet-Joris, Françoise)

Lillo, George 1691-1739 . . . . DLB-84

Lilly, J. K., Jr. 1893-1966 . . . . DLB-140

Lilly, Wait and Company DLB-49

Lily, William circa 1468-1522 . . . . . DLB-132

Limited Editions Club DLB-46

Lincoln and Edmands DLB-49

Lindsay, Jack 1900- Y-84

Lindsay, Sir David
circa 1485-1555 . . . . DLB-132

Lindsay, Vachel 1879-1931 . . . . DLB-54

Linebarger, Paul Myron Anthony (see Smith, Cordwainer)

Link, Arthur S. 1920- DLB-17

Linn, John Blair 1777-1804 . . . . DLB-37

Lins, Osman 1924-1978 . . . . DLB-145

Linton, Eliza Lynn 1822-1898 . . . . . DLB-18

Linton, William James 1812-1897 . . . DLB-32

Lintot, Barnaby Bernard
[publishing house] DLB-170

Lion Books DLB-46

Lionni, Leo 1910- DLB-61

Lippincott, Sara Jane Clarke
1823-1904 . . . . DLB-43

Lippincott, J. B., Company DLB-49

Lippmann, Walter 1889-1974 . . . . . DLB-29

Lipton, Lawrence 1898-1975 . . . . . . DLB-16

Liscow, Christian Ludwig
1701-1760 . . . . DLB-97

Lish, Gordon 1934- DLB-130

Lispector, Clarice 1925-1977 . . . . . DLB-113

The Literary Chronicle and Weekly Review
1819-1828 . . . . DLB-110

Literary Documents: William Faulkner
and the People-to-People
Program Y-86

Literary Documents II: *Library Journal*
Statements and Questionnaires from
First Novelists Y-87

Literary Effects of World War II
[British novel] DLB-15

Literary Prizes [British] DLB-15

Literary Research Archives: The Humanities
Research Center, University of
Texas Y-82

Literary Research Archives II: Berg
Collection of English and American
Literature of the New York Public
Library Y-83

Literary Research Archives III:
The Lilly Library Y-84

Literary Research Archives IV:
The John Carter Brown Library . . . Y-85

Literary Research Archives V:
Kent State Special Collections Y-86

Literary Research Archives VI: The Modern
Literary Manuscripts Collection in the
Special Collections of the Washington
University Libraries Y-87

Literary Research Archives VII:
The University of Virginia
Libraries Y-91

Literary Research Archives VIII:
The Henry E. Huntington
Library Y-92

"Literary Style" (1857), by William
Forsyth [excerpt] DLB-57

Literatura Chicanesca: The View From Without
. . . . DLB-82

Literature at Nurse, or Circulating Morals (1885),
by George Moore DLB-18

Littell, Eliakim 1797-1870 . . . . DLB-79

Littell, Robert S. 1831-1896 . . . . . . DLB-79

Little, Brown and Company DLB-49

Littlewood, Joan 1914- DLB-13

Lively, Penelope 1933- DLB-14, 161

Liverpool University Press DLB-112

The Lives of the Poets DLB-142

Livesay, Dorothy 1909- DLB-68

Livesay, Florence Randal
1874-1953 . . . . DLB-92

Livings, Henry 1929- DLB-13

Livingston, Anne Howe
1763-1841 . . . . DLB-37

Livingston, Myra Cohn 1926- DLB-61

Livingston, William 1723-1790 . . . . . DLB-31

Livingstone, David 1813-1873 . . . . . DLB-166

Liyong, Taban lo (see Taban lo Liyong)

Lizárraga, Sylvia S. 1925- DLB-82

Llewellyn, Richard 1906-1983 . . . . . DLB-15

Lloyd, Edward
[publishing house] DLB-106

Lobel, Arnold 1933- DLB-61

Lochridge, Betsy Hopkins (see Fancher, Betsy)

Locke, David Ross 1833-1888 . . . . DLB-11, 23

Locke, John 1632-1704 . . . . DLB-31, 101

Locke, Richard Adams 1800-1871 . . . DLB-43

Locker-Lampson, Frederick
1821-1895 . . . . DLB-35

Lockhart, John Gibson
1794-1854 . . . . DLB-110, 116, 144

Lockridge, Ross, Jr.
1914-1948 . . . . DLB-143; Y-80

Locrine and *Selimus* DLB-62

Lodge, David 1935- DLB-14

Lodge, George Cabot 1873-1909 . . . . DLB-54

Lodge, Henry Cabot 1850-1924 . . . . DLB-47

Lodge, Thomas 1558-1625 . . . . DLB-172

Loeb, Harold 1891-1974 . . . . DLB-4

Loeb, William 1905-1981 . . . . DLB-127

Lofting, Hugh 1886-1947 . . . . DLB-160

Logan, James 1674-1751 . . . . . . DLB-24, 140

Logan, John 1923- DLB-5

Logan, William 1950- DLB-120

Logau, Friedrich von 1605-1655 . . . . DLB-164

Logue, Christopher 1926- DLB-27

Lohenstein, Daniel Casper von
1635-1683 . . . . DLB-168

Lomonosov, Mikhail Vasil'evich
1711-1765 . . . . DLB-150

London, Jack 1876-1916 . . . . . DLB-8, 12, 78

The London Magazine 1820-1829 . . . . DLB-110

Long, Haniel 1888-1956 . . . . DLB-45

Long, Ray 1878-1935 . . . . DLB-137

Long, H., and Brother DLB-49

Longfellow, Henry Wadsworth
1807-1882 . . . . DLB-1, 59

Longfellow, Samuel 1819-1892 . . . . . DLB-1

Longford, Elizabeth 1906- DLB-155

Longinus circa first century DLB-176

Longley, Michael 1939- DLB-40

Longman, T. [publishing house] DLB-154

Longmans, Green and Company DLB-49

Longmore, George 1793?-1867 . . . . . DLB-99

Longstreet, Augustus Baldwin
1790-1870 . . . . DLB-3, 11, 74

Longworth, D. [publishing house] . . . DLB-49

Lonsdale, Frederick 1881-1954 . . . . . DLB-10

A Look at the Contemporary Black Theatre
Movement DLB-38

Loos, Anita 1893-1981 . . . . . DLB-11, 26; Y-81

Lopate, Phillip 1943- Y-80

López, Diana (see Isabella, Ríos)

Loranger, Jean-Aubert 1896-1942 . . . DLB-92

Lorca, Federico García 1898-1936 . . . DLB-108

Lord, John Keast 1818-1872 . . . . . . DLB-99

The Lord Chamberlain's Office and Stage
Censorship in England DLB-10

Lorde, Audre 1934-1992 . . . . DLB-41

Lorimer, George Horace
1867-1939 . . . . DLB-91

Loring, A. K. [publishing house] DLB-49

Loring and Mussey DLB-46

Lossing, Benson J. 1813-1891 . . . . . DLB-30

Lothar, Ernst 1890-1974 . . . . DLB-81

Lothrop, Harriet M. 1844-1924 . . . . DLB-42

Lothrop, D., and Company DLB-49

Loti, Pierre 1850-1923 . . . . DLB-123

Lotichius Secundus, Petrus
1528-1560 . . . . DLB-179

Lott, Emeline ?-? DLB-166

The Lounger, no. 20 (1785), by Henry
Mackenzie DLB-39

Lounsbury, Thomas R. 1838-1915. . . . DLB-71

Louÿs, Pierre 1870-1925. . . . . DLB-123

Lovelace, Earl 1935- DLB-125

Lovelace, Richard 1618-1657 . . . . . . DLB-131

Lovell, Coryell and Company DLB-49

Lovell, John W., Company DLB-49

Lover, Samuel 1797-1868 . . . . DLB-159

Lovesey, Peter 1936- DLB-87

Lovingood, Sut (see Harris, George Washington)

Low, Samuel 1765-? DLB-37

Lowell, Amy 1874-1925 . . . . DLB-54, 140

Lowell, James Russell 1819-1891 . . . . DLB-1, 11, 64, 79

Lowell, Robert 1917-1977 . . . . . . DLB-5, 169

Lowenfels, Walter 1897-1976 . . . . . . DLB-4

Lowndes, Marie Belloc 1868-1947 . . . . DLB-70

Lownes, Humphrey [publishing house] DLB-170

Lowry, Lois 1937- DLB-52

Lowry, Malcolm 1909-1957 . . . . DLB-15

Lowther, Pat 1935-1975 . . . . DLB-53

Loy, Mina 1882-1966 . . . . DLB-4, 54

Lozeau, Albert 1878-1924 . . . . DLB-92

Lubbock, Percy 1879-1965 . . . . DLB-149

Lucas, E. V. 1868-1938 . . . . DLB-98, 149, 153

Lucas, Fielding, Jr. [publishing house] DLB-49

Luce, Henry R. 1898-1967 . . . . DLB-91

Luce, John W., and Company DLB-46

Lucian circa 120-180 . . . . DLB-176

Lucie-Smith, Edward 1933- DLB-40

Lucini, Gian Pietro 1867-1914 . . . . . DLB-114

Luder, Peter circa 1415-1472 . . . . . . DLB-179

Ludlum, Robert 1927- Y-82

Ludus de Antichristo circa 1160 . . . . . . DLB-148

Ludvigson, Susan 1942- DLB-120

Ludwig, Jack 1922- DLB-60

Ludwig, Otto 1813-1865 . . . . DLB-129

Ludwigslied 881 or 882 . . . . DLB-148

Luera, Yolanda 1953- DLB-122

Luft, Lya 1938- DLB-145

Luke, Peter 1919- DLB-13

Lupton, F. M., Company DLB-49

Lupus of Ferrières circa 805-circa 862 . . . . DLB-148

Lurie, Alison 1926- DLB-2

Luther, Martin 1483-1546 . . . . DLB-179

Luzi, Mario 1914- DLB-128

L'vov, Nikolai Aleksandrovich 1751-1803 . . . . DLB-150

Lyall, Gavin 1932- DLB-87

Lydgate, John circa 1370-1450 . . . . . DLB-146

Lyly, John circa 1554-1606 . . . . . DLB-62, 167

Lynch, Patricia 1898-1972 . . . . DLB-160

Lynch, Richard flourished 1596-1601 . . . . DLB-172

Lynd, Robert 1879-1949 . . . . DLB-98

Lyon, Matthew 1749-1822 . . . . DLB-43

Lysias circa 459 B.C.-circa 380 B.C. DLB-176

Lytle, Andrew 1902-1995 . . . . . DLB-6; Y-95

Lytton, Edward (see Bulwer-Lytton, Edward)

Lytton, Edward Robert Bulwer 1831-1891 . . . . DLB-32

M

Maass, Joachim 1901-1972 . . . . DLB-69

Mabie, Hamilton Wright 1845-1916 . . . . DLB-71

Mac A'Ghobhainn, Iain (see Smith, Iain Crichton)

MacArthur, Charles 1895-1956 . . . . DLB-7, 25, 44

Macaulay, Catherine 1731-1791 . . . . . DLB-104

Macaulay, David 1945- DLB-61

Macaulay, Rose 1881-1958 . . . . DLB-36

Macaulay, Thomas Babington 1800-1859 . . . . DLB-32, 55

Macaulay Company DLB-46

MacBeth, George 1932- DLB-40

Macbeth, Madge 1880-1965 . . . . DLB-92

MacCaig, Norman 1910- DLB-27

MacDiarmid, Hugh 1892-1978 . . . . . DLB-20

MacDonald, Cynthia 1928- DLB-105

MacDonald, George 1824-1905 . . . . DLB-18, 163, 178

MacDonald, John D. 1916-1986 . . . . DLB-8; Y-86

MacDonald, Philip 1899?-1980 . . . . . DLB-77

Macdonald, Ross (see Millar, Kenneth)

MacDonald, Wilson 1880-1967 . . . . . DLB-92

Macdonald and Company (Publishers) DLB-112

MacEwen, Gwendolyn 1941- DLB-53

Macfadden, Bernarr 1868-1955 . . . . DLB-25, 91

MacGregor, John 1825-1892 . . . . . . DLB-166

MacGregor, Mary Esther (see Keith, Marian)

Machado, Antonio 1875-1939 . . . . . DLB-108

Machado, Manuel 1874-1947 . . . . . . DLB-108

Machar, Agnes Maule 1837-1927 . . . . DLB-92

Machen, Arthur Llewelyn Jones 1863-1947 . . . . DLB-36, 156, 178

MacInnes, Colin 1914-1976 . . . . DLB-14

MacInnes, Helen 1907-1985 . . . . DLB-87

Mack, Maynard 1909- DLB-111

Mackall, Leonard L. 1879-1937 . . . . . DLB-140

MacKaye, Percy 1875-1956 . . . . DLB-54

Macken, Walter 1915-1967 . . . . DLB-13

Mackenzie, Alexander 1763-1820 . . . . . DLB-99

Mackenzie, Compton 1883-1972 . . . . DLB-34, 100

Mackenzie, Henry 1745-1831 . . . . . . DLB-39

Mackey, Nathaniel 1947- DLB-169

Mackey, William Wellington 1937- DLB-38

Mackintosh, Elizabeth (see Tey, Josephine)

Mackintosh, Sir James 1765-1832 . . . . DLB-158

Maclaren, Ian (see Watson, John)

Macklin, Charles 1699-1797 . . . . . . DLB-89

MacLean, Katherine Anne 1925- DLB-8

MacLeish, Archibald 1892-1982 . . . . DLB-4, 7, 45; Y-82

MacLennan, Hugh 1907-1990 . . . . . DLB-68

Macleod, Fiona (see Sharp, William)

MacLeod, Alistair 1936- DLB-60

Macleod, Norman 1906-1985 . . . . . . DLB-4

Macmillan and Company DLB-106

The Macmillan Company DLB-49

Macmillan's English Men of Letters, First Series (1878-1892) DLB-144

MacNamara, Brinsley 1890-1963 . . . . . DLB-10

MacNeice, Louis 1907-1963 . . . . . DLB-10, 20

MacPhail, Andrew 1864-1938 . . . . . . DLB-92

Macpherson, James 1736-1796 . . . . . DLB-109

Macpherson, Jay 1931- DLB-53

Macpherson, Jeanie 1884-1946 . . . . . DLB-44

Macrae Smith Company DLB-46

Macrone, John [publishing house] DLB-106

MacShane, Frank 1927- DLB-111

Macy-Masius DLB-46

Madden, David 1933- DLB-6

Maddow, Ben 1909-1992 . . . . DLB-44

Maddux, Rachel 1912-1983 . . . . Y-93

Madgett, Naomi Long 1923- DLB-76

Madhubuti, Haki R. 1942- DLB-5, 41; DS-8

Madison, James 1751-1836 . . . . DLB-37

Maginn, William 1794-1842 . . . . DLB-110, 159

Mahan, Alfred Thayer 1840-1914 . . . . DLB-47

Maheux-Forcier, Louise 1929- DLB-60

Mahin, John Lee 1902-1984 . . . . DLB-44

Mahon, Derek 1941- DLB-40

Maikov, Vasilii Ivanovich 1728-1778 . . . . DLB-150

Mailer, Norman
   1923- DLB-2, 16, 28; Y-80, 83; DS-3

Maillet, Adrienne 1885-1963 . . . . DLB-68

Maillet, Antonine 1929- DLB-60

Maillu, David G. 1939- DLB-157

Main Selections of the Book-of-the-Month Club, 1926-1945 . . . . DLB-9

Main Trends in Twentieth-Century Book Clubs DLB-46

Mainwaring, Daniel 1902-1977 . . . . . DLB-44

Mair, Charles 1838-1927 . . . . DLB-99

Mais, Roger 1905-1955 . . . . DLB-125

Major, Andre 1942- DLB-60

Major, Clarence 1936- DLB-33

Major, Kevin 1949- DLB-60

Major Books DLB-46

Makemie, Francis circa 1658-1708 . . . . DLB-24

The Making of a People, by J. M. Ritchie DLB-66

Maksimović, Desanka 1898-1993 . . . . DLB-147

Malamud, Bernard
   1914-1986 . . . . . DLB-2, 28, 152; Y-80, 86

Malet, Lucas 1852-1931 . . . . DLB-153

Malleson, Lucy Beatrice (see Gilbert, Anthony)

Mallet-Joris, Françoise 1930- DLB-83

Mallock, W. H. 1849-1923 . . . . . DLB-18, 57

Malone, Dumas 1892-1986 . . . . DLB-17

Malone, Edmond 1741-1812 . . . . . . DLB-142

Malory, Sir Thomas
   circa 1400-1410 - 1471 . . . . DLB-146

Malraux, André 1901-1976 . . . . DLB-72

Malthus, Thomas Robert
   1766-1834 . . . . DLB-107, 158

Maltz, Albert 1908-1985 . . . . DLB-102

Malzberg, Barry N. 1939- DLB-8

Mamet, David 1947- DLB-7

Manaka, Matsemela 1956- DLB-157

Manchester University Press DLB-112

Mandel, Eli 1922- DLB-53

Mandeville, Bernard 1670-1733 . . . . . DLB-101

Mandeville, Sir John
   mid fourteenth century DLB-146

Mandiargues, André Pieyre de
   1909- DLB-83

Manfred, Frederick 1912-1994 . . . . . . DLB-6

Mangan, Sherry 1904-1961 . . . . DLB-4

Mankiewicz, Herman 1897-1953 . . . . DLB-26

Mankiewicz, Joseph L. 1909-1993 . . . . DLB-44

Mankowitz, Wolf 1924- DLB-15

Manley, Delariviére
   1672?-1724 . . . . DLB-39, 80

Mann, Abby 1927- DLB-44

Mann, Heinrich 1871-1950 . . . . . DLB-66, 118

Mann, Horace 1796-1859 . . . . DLB-1

Mann, Klaus 1906-1949 . . . . DLB-56

Mann, Thomas 1875-1955 . . . . DLB-66

Mann, William D'Alton
   1839-1920 . . . . DLB-137

Manning, Marie 1873?-1945 . . . . DLB-29

Manning and Loring DLB-49

Mannyng, Robert
   flourished 1303-1338 . . . . DLB-146

Mano, D. Keith 1942- DLB-6

Manor Books DLB-46

Mansfield, Katherine 1888-1923 . . . . . DLB-162

Manuel, Niklaus circa 1484-1530 . . . . DLB-179

Manzini, Gianna 1896-1974 . . . . DLB-177

Mapanje, Jack 1944- DLB-157

March, William 1893-1954 . . . . . . DLB-9, 86

Marchand, Leslie A. 1900- DLB-103

Marchant, Bessie 1862-1941 . . . . DLB-160

Marchessault, Jovette 1938- DLB-60

Marcus, Frank 1928- DLB-13

Marden, Orison Swett
   1850-1924 . . . . DLB-137

Marechera, Dambudzo
   1952-1987 . . . . DLB-157

Marek, Richard, Books DLB-46

Mares, E. A. 1938- DLB-122

Mariani, Paul 1940- DLB-111

Marie-Victorin, Frère 1885-1944 . . . . . DLB-92

Marin, Biagio 1891-1985 . . . . DLB-128

Marinković, Ranko 1913- DLB-147

Marinetti, Filippo Tommaso
   1876-1944 . . . . DLB-114

Marion, Frances 1886-1973 . . . . DLB-44

Marius, Richard C. 1933- Y-85

The Mark Taper Forum DLB-7

Mark Twain on Perpetual Copyright Y-92

Markfield, Wallace 1926- DLB-2, 28

Markham, Edwin 1852-1940 . . . . . . DLB-54

Markle, Fletcher 1921-1991 . . . . DLB-68; Y-91

Marlatt, Daphne 1942- DLB-60

Marlitt, E. 1825-1887 . . . . DLB-129

Marlowe, Christopher 1564-1593 . . . . . DLB-62

Marlyn, John 1912- DLB-88

Marmion, Shakerley 1603-1639 . . . . . DLB-58

Der Marner
   before 1230-circa 1287 . . . . DLB-138

The Marprelate Tracts 1588-1589 . . . . DLB-132

Marquand, John P. 1893-1960 . . . . DLB-9, 102

Marqués, René 1919-1979 . . . . DLB-113

Marquis, Don 1878-1937 . . . . . . DLB-11, 25

Marriott, Anne 1913- DLB-68

Marryat, Frederick 1792-1848 . . . . DLB-21, 163

Marsh, George Perkins
   1801-1882 . . . . DLB-1, 64

Marsh, James 1794-1842 . . . . DLB-1, 59

Marsh, Capen, Lyon and Webb DLB-49

Marsh, Ngaio 1899-1982 . . . . DLB-77

Marshall, Edison 1894-1967 . . . . DLB-102

Marshall, Edward 1932- DLB-16

Marshall, Emma 1828-1899 . . . . DLB-163

Marshall, James 1942-1992 . . . . DLB-61

Marshall, Joyce 1913- DLB-88

Marshall, Paule 1929- DLB-33, 157

Marshall, Tom 1938- DLB-60

Marsilius of Padua
   circa 1275-circa 1342 . . . . DLB-115

Marson, Una 1905-1965 . . . . DLB-157

Marston, John 1576-1634 . . . . . . DLB-58, 172

Marston, Philip Bourke 1850-1887 . . . . DLB-35

Martens, Kurt 1870-1945 . . . . DLB-66

Martien, William S.
   [publishing house] DLB-49

Martin, Abe (see Hubbard, Kin)

Martin, Charles 1942- DLB-120

Martin, Claire 1914- DLB-60

Martin, Jay 1935- DLB-111

Martin, Johann (see Laurentius von Schnüffis)

Martin, Violet Florence (see Ross, Martin)

Martin du Gard, Roger 1881-1958 . . . DLB-65

Martineau, Harriet
   1802-1876 . . . . DLB-21, 55, 159, 163, 166

Martínez, Eliud 1935- DLB-122

Martínez, Max 1943- DLB-82

Martyn, Edward 1859-1923 . . . . DLB-10

Marvell, Andrew 1621-1678 . . . . DLB-131

Marvin X 1944- DLB-38

Marx, Karl 1818-1883 . . . . DLB-129

Marzials, Theo 1850-1920 . . . . DLB-35

Masefield, John
   1878-1967 . . . . DLB-10, 19, 153, 160

Mason, A. E. W. 1865-1948 . . . . DLB-70

Mason, Bobbie Ann
   1940- DLB-173; Y-87

Mason, William 1725-1797 . . . . DLB-142

Mason Brothers DLB-49

Massey, Gerald 1828-1907 . . . . DLB-32

Massinger, Philip 1583-1640 . . . . DLB-58

Masson, David 1822-1907 . . . . DLB-144

Masters, Edgar Lee 1868-1950 . . . . . . DLB-54

Mastronardi, Lucio 1930-1979 . . . . . . DLB-177

Matevski, Mateja 1929- DLB-181

Mather, Cotton
   1663-1728 . . . . DLB-24, 30, 140

Mather, Increase 1639-1723 . . . . DLB-24

Mather, Richard 1596-1669. . . . . DLB-24

Matheson, Richard 1926- DLB-8, 44

Matheus, John F. 1887- DLB-51

Mathews, Cornelius
1817?-1889. . . . . DLB-3, 64

Mathews, John Joseph
1894-1979 . . . . DLB-175

Mathews, Elkin
[publishing house]. DLB-112

Mathias, Roland 1915- DLB-27

Mathis, June 1892-1927. . . . . DLB-44

Mathis, Sharon Bell 1937- DLB-33

Matković, Marijan 1915-1985. . . . . . DLB-181

Matoš, Antun Gustav 1873-1914. . . . DLB-147

The Matter of England
1240-1400 . . . . DLB-146

The Matter of Rome
early twelfth to late fifteenth
century. DLB-146

Matthews, Brander
1852-1929. . . . . DLB-71, 78; DS-13

Matthews, Jack 1925- DLB-6

Matthews, William 1942- DLB-5

Matthiessen, F. O. 1902-1950 . . . . . . DLB-63

Maturin, Charles Robert
1780-1824 . . . . DLB-178

Matthiessen, Peter 1927- DLB-6, 173

Maugham, W. Somerset
1874-1965. . . . . DLB-10, 36, 77, 100, 162

Maupassant, Guy de 1850-1893 . . . . DLB-123

Mauriac, Claude 1914- DLB-83

Mauriac, François 1885-1970 . . . . . . DLB-65

Maurice, Frederick Denison
1805-1872 . . . . DLB-55

Maurois, André 1885-1967 . . . . DLB-65

Maury, James 1718-1769 . . . . DLB-31

Mavor, Elizabeth 1927- DLB-14

Mavor, Osborne Henry (see Bridie, James)

Maxwell, William 1908- Y-80

Maxwell, H. [publishing house] DLB-49

Maxwell, John [publishing house]. . . . DLB-106

May, Elaine 1932- DLB-44

May, Karl 1842-1912 . . . . DLB-129

May, Thomas 1595 or 1596-1650 . . . . DLB-58

Mayer, Bernadette 1945- DLB-165

Mayer, Mercer 1943- DLB-61

Mayer, O. B. 1818-1891. . . . . DLB-3

Mayes, Herbert R. 1900-1987. . . . . . DLB-137

Mayes, Wendell 1919-1992. . . . . . . DLB-26

Mayfield, Julian 1928-1984. . . . . DLB-33; Y-84

Mayhew, Henry 1812-1887 . . . . . DLB-18, 55

Mayhew, Jonathan 1720-1766 . . . . . . DLB-31

Mayne, Jasper 1604-1672 . . . . DLB-126

Mayne, Seymour 1944- DLB-60

Mayor, Flora Macdonald
1872-1932. . . . . DLB-36

Mayrocker, Friederike 1924- DLB-85

Mazrui, Ali A. 1933- DLB-125

Mažuranić, Ivan 1814-1890 . . . . . . DLB-147

Mazursky, Paul 1930- DLB-44

McAlmon, Robert 1896-1956 . . . . DLB-4, 45

McArthur, Peter 1866-1924. . . . . . . DLB-92

McBride, Robert M., and
Company DLB-46

McCaffrey, Anne 1926- DLB-8

McCarthy, Cormac 1933- DLB-6, 143

McCarthy, Mary 1912-1989 . . . . DLB-2; Y-81

McCay, Winsor 1871-1934. . . . . DLB-22

McClane, Albert Jules 1922-1991. . . . DLB-171

McClatchy, C. K. 1858-1936. . . . . . . DLB-25

McClellan, George Marion
1860-1934 . . . . DLB-50

McCloskey, Robert 1914- DLB-22

McClung, Nellie Letitia 1873-1951. . . . DLB-92

McClure, Joanna 1930- DLB-16

McClure, Michael 1932- DLB-16

McClure, Phillips and Company. DLB-46

McClure, S. S. 1857-1949 . . . . DLB-91

McClurg, A. C., and Company DLB-49

McCluskey, John A., Jr. 1944- DLB-33

McCollum, Michael A. 1946. . . . . Y-87

McConnell, William C. 1917- DLB-88

McCord, David 1897- DLB-61

McCorkle, Jill 1958- Y-87

McCorkle, Samuel Eusebius
1746-1811 . . . . DLB-37

McCormick, Anne O'Hare
1880-1954. . . . . DLB-29

McCormick, Robert R. 1880-1955. . . . DLB-29

McCourt, Edward 1907-1972. . . . . . . DLB-88

McCoy, Horace 1897-1955 . . . . DLB-9

McCrae, John 1872-1918 . . . . DLB-92

McCullagh, Joseph B. 1842-1896. . . . . DLB-23

McCullers, Carson
1917-1967 . . . . DLB-2, 7, 173

McCulloch, Thomas 1776-1843 . . . . . DLB-99

McDonald, Forrest 1927- DLB-17

McDonald, Walter
1934- DLB-105, DS-9

McDonald, Walter, Getting Started:
Accepting the Regions You Own—
or Which Own You DLB-105

McDougall, Colin 1917-1984. . . . . . . DLB-68

McDowell, Obolensky DLB-46

McEwan, Ian 1948- DLB-14

McFadden, David 1940- DLB-60

McFall, Frances Elizabeth Clarke
(see Grand, Sarah)

McFarlane, Leslie 1902-1977 . . . . . . DLB-88

McFee, William 1881-1966 . . . . . . DLB-153

McGahern, John 1934- DLB-14

McGee, Thomas D'Arcy
1825-1868. . . . . DLB-99

McGeehan, W. O. 1879-1933 . . . DLB-25, 171

McGill, Ralph 1898-1969 . . . . DLB-29

McGinley, Phyllis 1905-1978. . . . . DLB-11, 48

McGirt, James E. 1874-1930 . . . . . . DLB-50

McGlashan and Gill. DLB-106

McGough, Roger 1937- DLB-40

McGraw-Hill. DLB-46

McGuane, Thomas 1939- DLB-2; Y-80

McGuckian, Medbh 1950- DLB-40

McGuffey, William Holmes
1800-1873 . . . . DLB-42

McIlvanney, William 1936- DLB-14

McIlwraith, Jean Newton
1859-1938 . . . . DLB-92

McIntyre, James 1827-1906. . . . . . . DLB-99

McIntyre, O. O. 1884-1938 . . . . DLB-25

McKay, Claude
1889-1948 . . . . DLB-4, 45, 51, 117

The David McKay Company DLB-49

McKean, William V. 1820-1903 . . . . . DLB-23

The McKenzie Trust. Y-96

McKinley, Robin 1952- DLB-52

McLachlan, Alexander 1818-1896 . . . . DLB-99

McLaren, Floris Clark 1904-1978 . . . . DLB-68

McLaverty, Michael 1907- DLB-15

McLean, John R. 1848-1916 . . . . DLB-23

McLean, William L. 1852-1931 . . . . . DLB-25

McLennan, William 1856-1904. . . . . . DLB-92

McLoughlin Brothers DLB-49

McLuhan, Marshall 1911-1980 . . . . . DLB-88

McMaster, John Bach 1852-1932. . . . . DLB-47

McMurtry, Larry
1936- DLB-2, 143; Y-80, 87

McNally, Terrence 1939- DLB-7

McNeil, Florence 1937- DLB-60

McNeile, Herman Cyril
1888-1937 . . . . DLB-77

McNickle, D'Arcy 1904-1977 . . . . . DLB-175

McPherson, James Alan 1943- DLB-38

McPherson, Sandra 1943- Y-86

McWhirter, George 1939- DLB-60

McWilliams, Carey 1905-1980 . . . . . DLB-137

Mead, L. T. 1844-1914 . . . . DLB-141

Mead, Matthew 1924- DLB-40

Mead, Taylor ?- DLB-16

Meany, Tom 1903-1964. . . . . DLB-171

Mechthild von Magdeburg
circa 1207-circa 1282 . . . . DLB-138

Medill, Joseph 1823-1899 . . . . DLB-43

Medoff, Mark 1940- DLB-7

Meek, Alexander Beaufort
1814-1865 . . . . DLB-3

Meeke, Mary ?-1816? DLB-116

Meinke, Peter 1932- DLB-5

Mejia Vallejo, Manuel 1923- DLB-113

Melanchton, Philipp 1497-1560 . . . . . DLB-179

Melançon, Robert 1947- DLB-60

Mell, Max 1882-1971 . . . . DLB-81, 124

Mellow, James R. 1926- DLB-111

Meltzer, David 1937- DLB-16

Meltzer, Milton 1915- DLB-61

Melville, Elizabeth, Lady Culross
circa 1585-1640 . . . . DLB-172

Melville, Herman 1819-1891 . . . . . DLB-3, 74

Memoirs of Life and Literature (1920),
by W. H. Mallock [excerpt] DLB-57

Menander 342-341 B.C.-circa 292-291 B.C.
. . . . DLB-176

Menantes (see Hunold, Christian Friedrich)

Mencke, Johann Burckhard
1674-1732 . . . . DLB-168

Mencken, H. L.
1880-1956 . . . . . . DLB-11, 29, 63, 137

Mencken and Nietzsche: An Unpublished Excerpt
from H. L. Mencken's *My Life
as Author and Editor* Y-93

Mendelssohn, Moses 1729-1786 . . . . . DLB-97

Méndez M., Miguel 1930- DLB-82

The Mercantile Library of
New York Y-96

Mercer, Cecil William (see Yates, Dornford)

Mercer, David 1928-1980 . . . . DLB-13

Mercer, John 1704-1768 . . . . DLB-31

Meredith, George
1828-1909 . . . . . . DLB-18, 35, 57, 159

Meredith, Louisa Anne
1812-1895 . . . . DLB-166

Meredith, Owen (see Lytton, Edward Robert Bulwer)

Meredith, William 1919- DLB-5

Mergerle, Johann Ulrich
(see Abraham ä Sancta Clara)

Mérimée, Prosper 1803-1870 . . . . . . DLB-119

Merivale, John Herman
1779-1844 . . . . DLB-96

Meriwether, Louise 1923- DLB-33

Merlin Press DLB-112

Merriam, Eve 1916-1992 . . . . DLB-61

The Merriam Company DLB-49

Merrill, James
1926-1995 . . . . DLB-5, 165; Y-85

Merrill and Baker DLB-49

The Mershon Company DLB-49

Merton, Thomas 1915-1968 . . . . . DLB-48; Y-81

Merwin, W. S. 1927- DLB-5, 169

Messner, Julian [publishing house] DLB-46

Metcalf, J. [publishing house] DLB-49

Metcalf, John 1938- DLB-60

The Methodist Book Concern DLB-49

Methuen and Company DLB-112

Mew, Charlotte 1869-1928 . . . . DLB-19, 135

Mewshaw, Michael 1943- Y-80

Meyer, Conrad Ferdinand
1825-1898 . . . . DLB-129

Meyer, E. Y. 1946- DLB-75

Meyer, Eugene 1875-1959 . . . . DLB-29

Meyer, Michael 1921- DLB-155

Meyers, Jeffrey 1939- DLB-111

Meynell, Alice
1847-1922 . . . . DLB-19, 98

Meynell, Viola 1885-1956 . . . . DLB-153

Meyrink, Gustav 1868-1932 . . . . DLB-81

Michaels, Leonard 1933- DLB-130

Micheaux, Oscar 1884-1951 . . . . DLB-50

Michel of Northgate, Dan
circa 1265-circa 1340 . . . . DLB-146

Micheline, Jack 1929- DLB-16

Michener, James A. 1907?- DLB-6

Micklejohn, George
circa 1717-1818 . . . . DLB-31

Middle English Literature:
An Introduction DLB-146

The Middle English Lyric DLB-146

Middle Hill Press DLB-106

Middleton, Christopher 1926- DLB-40

Middleton, Richard 1882-1911 . . . . . DLB-156

Middleton, Stanley 1919- DLB-14

Middleton, Thomas 1580-1627 . . . . . DLB-58

Miegel, Agnes 1879-1964 . . . . DLB-56

Mihailović, Dragoslav 1930- DLB-181

Mihalić, Slavko 1928- DLB-181

Miles, Josephine 1911-1985 . . . . DLB-48

Miliković, Branko 1934-1961 . . . . . . DLB-181

Milius, John 1944- DLB-44

Mill, James 1773-1836 . . . . . . DLB-107, 158

Mill, John Stuart 1806-1873 . . . . . . DLB-55

Millar, Kenneth
1915-1983 . . . . DLB-2; Y-83; DS-6

Millar, Andrew
[publishing house] DLB-154

Millay, Edna St. Vincent
1892-1950 . . . . DLB-45

Miller, Arthur 1915- DLB-7

Miller, Caroline 1903-1992 . . . . DLB-9

Miller, Eugene Ethelbert 1950- DLB-41

Miller, Heather Ross 1939- DLB-120

Miller, Henry 1891-1980 . . . . . DLB-4, 9; Y-80

Miller, J. Hillis 1928- DLB-67

Miller, James [publishing house] DLB-49

Miller, Jason 1939- DLB-7

Miller, May 1899- DLB-41

Miller, Paul 1906-1991 . . . . DLB-127

Miller, Perry 1905-1963 . . . . DLB-17, 63

Miller, Sue 1943- DLB-143

Miller, Vassar 1924- DLB-105

Miller, Walter M., Jr. 1923- DLB-8

Miller, Webb 1892-1940 . . . . DLB-29

Millhauser, Steven 1943- DLB-2

Millican, Arthenia J. Bates
1920- DLB-38

Mills and Boon DLB-112

Milman, Henry Hart 1796-1868 . . . . . DLB-96

Milne, A. A.
1882-1956 . . . . . . DLB-10, 77, 100, 160

Milner, Ron 1938- DLB-38

Milner, William
[publishing house] DLB-106

Milnes, Richard Monckton (Lord Houghton)
1809-1885 . . . . DLB-32

Milton, John 1608-1674 . . . . . DLB-131, 151

The Minerva Press DLB-154

Minnesang circa 1150-1280 . . . . DLB-138

Minns, Susan 1839-1938 . . . . DLB-140

Minor Illustrators, 1880-1914 . . . . . . DLB-141

Minor Poets of the Earlier Seventeenth
Century DLB-121

Minton, Balch and Company DLB-46

Mirbeau, Octave 1848-1917 . . . . DLB-123

Mirk, John died after 1414? DLB-146

Miron, Gaston 1928- DLB-60

A Mirror for Magistrates DLB-167

Mitchel, Jonathan 1624-1668 . . . . . . DLB-24

Mitchell, Adrian 1932- DLB-40

Mitchell, Donald Grant
1822-1908 . . . . DLB-1; DS-13

Mitchell, Gladys 1901-1983 . . . . DLB-77

Mitchell, James Leslie 1901-1935 . . . . . DLB-15

Mitchell, John (see Slater, Patrick)

Mitchell, John Ames 1845-1918 . . . . . DLB-79

Mitchell, Joseph 1908-1996 . . . . Y-96

Mitchell, Julian 1935- DLB-14

Mitchell, Ken 1940- DLB-60

Mitchell, Langdon 1862-1935 . . . . . . DLB-7

Mitchell, Loften 1919- DLB-38

Mitchell, Margaret 1900-1949 . . . . . . DLB-9

Mitchell, W. O. 1914- DLB-88

Mitchison, Naomi Margaret (Haldane) 1897- DLB-160

Mitford, Mary Russell 1787-1855. .... DLB-110, 116

Mittelholzer, Edgar 1909-1965. .... DLB-117

Mitterer, Erika 1906- DLB-85

Mitterer, Felix 1948- DLB-124

Mitternacht, Johann Sebastian 1613-1679 .... DLB-168

Miyamoto, Yuriko 1899-1951 .... DLB-180

Mizener, Arthur 1907-1988 .... DLB-103

Modern Age Books DLB-46

"Modern English Prose" (1876), by George Saintsbury DLB-57

The Modern Language Association of America Celebrates Its Centennial Y-84

The Modern Library DLB-46

"Modern Novelists – Great and Small" (1855), by Margaret Oliphant DLB-21

"Modern Style" (1857), by Cockburn Thomson [excerpt] DLB-57

The Modernists (1932), by Joseph Warren Beach DLB-36

Modiano, Patrick 1945- DLB-83

Moffat, Yard and Company DLB-46

Moffet, Thomas 1553-1604 .... DLB-136

Mohr, Nicholasa 1938- DLB-145

Moix, Ana María 1947- DLB-134

Molesworth, Louisa 1839-1921 .... DLB-135

Möllhausen, Balduin 1825-1905 .... DLB-129

Momaday, N. Scott 1934- DLB-143, 175

Monkhouse, Allan 1858-1936 .... DLB-10

Monro, Harold 1879-1932 .... DLB-19

Monroe, Harriet 1860-1936 .... DLB-54, 91

Monsarrat, Nicholas 1910-1979 .... DLB-15

Montagu, Lady Mary Wortley 1689-1762 .... DLB-95, 101

Montague, John 1929- DLB-40

Montale, Eugenio 1896-1981 .... DLB-114

Monterroso, Augusto 1921- DLB-145

Montgomerie, Alexander circa 1550?-1598 .... DLB-167

Montgomery, James 1771-1854 .... DLB-93, 158

Montgomery, John 1919- DLB-16

Montgomery, Lucy Maud 1874-1942 .... DLB-92; DS-14

Montgomery, Marion 1925- DLB-6

Montgomery, Robert Bruce (see Crispin, Edmund)

Montherlant, Henry de 1896-1972 .... DLB-72

The Monthly Review 1749-1844 .... DLB-110

Montigny, Louvigny de 1876-1955 .... DLB-92

Montoya, José 1932- DLB-122

Moodie, John Wedderburn Dunbar 1797-1869 .... DLB-99

Moodie, Susanna 1803-1885 .... DLB-99

Moody, Joshua circa 1633-1697 .... DLB-24

Moody, William Vaughn 1869-1910 .... DLB-7, 54

Moorcock, Michael 1939- DLB-14

Moore, Catherine L. 1911- DLB-8

Moore, Clement Clarke 1779-1863 .... DLB-42

Moore, Dora Mavor 1888-1979 .... DLB-92

Moore, George 1852-1933 .... DLB-10, 18, 57, 135

Moore, Marianne 1887-1972 .... DLB-45; DS-7

Moore, Mavor 1919- DLB-88

Moore, Richard 1927- DLB-105

Moore, Richard, The No Self, the Little Self, and the Poets DLB-105

Moore, T. Sturge 1870-1944 .... DLB-19

Moore, Thomas 1779-1852 .... DLB-96, 144

Moore, Ward 1903-1978 .... DLB-8

Moore, Wilstach, Keys and Company DLB-49

The Moorland-Spingarn Research Center DLB-76

Moorman, Mary C. 1905-1994 .... DLB-155

Moraga, Cherríe 1952- DLB-82

Morales, Alejandro 1944- DLB-82

Morales, Mario Roberto 1947- DLB-145

Morales, Rafael 1919- DLB-108

Morality Plays: *Mankind* circa 1450-1500 and *Everyman* circa 1500 .... DLB-146

Morante, Elsa 1912-1985 .... DLB-177

Morata, Olympia Fulvia 1526-1555 .... DLB-179

Moravia, Alberto 1907-1990 .... DLB-177

Mordaunt, Elinor 1872-1942 .... DLB-174

More, Hannah 1745-1833 .... DLB-107, 109, 116, 158

More, Henry 1614-1687 .... DLB-126

More, Sir Thomas 1477 or 1478-1535 .... DLB-136

Moreno, Dorinda 1939- DLB-122

Morency, Pierre 1942- DLB-60

Moretti, Marino 1885-1979 .... DLB-114

Morgan, Berry 1919- DLB-6

Morgan, Charles 1894-1958 .... DLB-34, 100

Morgan, Edmund S. 1916- DLB-17

Morgan, Edwin 1920- DLB-27

Morgan, John Pierpont 1837-1913 .... DLB-140

Morgan, John Pierpont, Jr. 1867-1943 .... DLB-140

Morgan, Robert 1944- DLB-120

Morgan, Sydney Owenson, Lady 1776?-1859 .... DLB-116, 158

Morgner, Irmtraud 1933- DLB-75

Morhof, Daniel Georg 1639-1691 .... DLB-164

Mori, Ōgai 1862-1922 .... DLB-180

Morier, James Justinian 1782 or 1783?-1849 .... DLB-116

Mörike, Eduard 1804-1875 .... DLB-133

Morin, Paul 1889-1963 .... DLB-92

Morison, Richard 1514?-1556 .... DLB-136

Morison, Samuel Eliot 1887-1976 .... DLB-17

Moritz, Karl Philipp 1756-1793 .... DLB-94

Moriz von Craûn circa 1220-1230 .... DLB-138

Morley, Christopher 1890-1957 .... DLB-9

Morley, John 1838-1923 .... DLB-57, 144

Morris, George Pope 1802-1864 .... DLB-73

Morris, Lewis 1833-1907 .... DLB-35

Morris, Richard B. 1904-1989 .... DLB-17

Morris, William 1834-1896 .... DLB-18, 35, 57, 156, 178

Morris, Willie 1934- Y-80

Morris, Wright 1910- DLB-2; Y-81

Morrison, Arthur 1863-1945 .... DLB-70, 135

Morrison, Charles Clayton 1874-1966 .... DLB-91

Morrison, Toni 1931- DLB-6, 33, 143; Y-81

Morrow, William, and Company DLB-46

Morse, James Herbert 1841-1923 .... DLB-71

Morse, Jedidiah 1761-1826 .... DLB-37

Morse, John T., Jr. 1840-1937 .... DLB-47

Morselli, Guido 1912-1973 .... DLB-177

Mortimer, Favell Lee 1802-1878 .... DLB-163

Mortimer, John 1923- DLB-13

Morton, Carlos 1942- DLB-122

Morton, John P., and Company DLB-49

Morton, Nathaniel 1613-1685 .... DLB-24

Morton, Sarah Wentworth 1759-1846 .... DLB-37

Morton, Thomas circa 1579-circa 1647 .... DLB-24

Moscherosch, Johann Michael 1601-1669 .... DLB-164

Moseley, Humphrey [publishing house] DLB-170

Möser, Justus 1720-1794 .... DLB-97

Mosley, Nicholas 1923- DLB-14

Moss, Arthur 1889-1969 .... DLB-4

Moss, Howard 1922-1987 .... DLB-5

Moss, Thylias 1954- DLB-120

The Most Powerful Book Review in America [*New York Times Book Review*] Y-82

Motion, Andrew 1952- DLB-40	Munro, George [publishing house]. DLB-49	Nabokov, Vladimir 1899-1977 . . . . . DLB-2; Y-80, Y-91; DS-3
Motley, John Lothrop 1814-1877 . . . . DLB-1, 30, 59	Munro, Norman L. [publishing house]. DLB-49	Nabokov Festival at Cornell. Y-83
Motley, Willard 1909-1965 . . . . . DLB-76, 143	Munroe, James, and Company. DLB-49	The Vladimir Nabokov Archive in the Berg Collection Y-91
Motte, Benjamin Jr. [publishing house] DLB-154	Munroe, Kirk 1850-1930 . . . . DLB-42	Nafis and Cornish DLB-49
Motteux, Peter Anthony 1663-1718 . . . . DLB-80	Munroe and Francis DLB-49	Nagai, Kafū 1879-1959 . . . . DLB-180
Mottram, R. H. 1883-1971 . . . . DLB-36	Munsell, Joel [publishing house] DLB-49	Naipaul, Shiva 1945-1985 . . . . . DLB-157; Y-85
Mouré, Erin 1955- DLB-60	Munsey, Frank A. 1854-1925 . . . . DLB-25, 91	Naipaul, V. S. 1932- DLB-125; Y-85
Mourning Dove (Humishuma) between 1882 and 1888?-1936 . . . . DLB-175	Munsey, Frank A., and Company DLB-49	Nancrede, Joseph [publishing house]. DLB-49
Movies from Books, 1920-1974 . . . . . . DLB-9	Murav'ev, Mikhail Nikitich 1757-1807 . . . . DLB-150	Naranjo, Carmen 1930- DLB-145
Mowat, Farley 1921- DLB-68	Murdoch, Iris 1919- DLB-14	Narrache, Jean 1893-1970. . . . . DLB-92
Mowbray, A. R., and Company, Limited. DLB-106	Murdoch, Rupert 1931- DLB-127	Nasby, Petroleum Vesuvius (see Locke, David Ross)
Mowrer, Edgar Ansel 1892-1977 . . . . . DLB-29	Murfree, Mary N. 1850-1922 . . . . DLB-12, 74	Nash, Ogden 1902-1971 . . . . DLB-11
Mowrer, Paul Scott 1887-1971 . . . . . . DLB-29	Murger, Henry 1822-1861. . . . . DLB-119	Nash, Eveleigh [publishing house] DLB-112
Moxon, Edward [publishing house] DLB-106	Murger, Louis-Henri (see Murger, Henry)	Nashe, Thomas 1567-1601? DLB-167
Moxon, Joseph [publishing house] DLB-170	Murner, Thomas 1475-1537. . . . . . . DLB-179	Nast, Conde 1873-1942. . . . . DLB-91
Mphahlele, Es'kia (Ezekiel) 1919- DLB-125	Muro, Amado 1915-1971 . . . . DLB-82	Nastasijević, Momčalo 1894-1938 . . . . DLB-147
Mtshali, Oswald Mbuyiseni 1940- DLB-125	Murphy, Arthur 1727-1805 . . . . DLB-89, 142	Nathan, George Jean 1882-1958 . . . . DLB-137
	Murphy, Beatrice M. 1908- DLB-76	Nathan, Robert 1894-1985 . . . . DLB-9
Mucedorus DLB-62	Murphy, Emily 1868-1933 . . . . DLB-99	The National Jewish Book Awards Y-85
Mudford, William 1782-1848 . . . . . . DLB-159	Murphy, John H., III 1916- DLB-127	The National Theatre and the Royal Shakespeare Company: The National Companies DLB-13
Mueller, Lisel 1924- DLB-105	Murphy, John, and Company DLB-49	
Muhajir, El (see Marvin X)	Murphy, Richard 1927-1993 . . . . . . DLB-40	Natsume, Sōseki 1867-1916 . . . . DLB-180
Muhajir, Nazzam Al Fitnah (see Marvin X)	Murray, Albert L. 1916- DLB-38	Naughton, Bill 1910- DLB-13
Mühlbach, Luise 1814-1873 . . . . DLB-133	Murray, Gilbert 1866-1957 . . . . DLB-10	Naylor, Gloria 1950- DLB-173
Muir, Edwin 1887-1959 . . . . . DLB-20, 100	Murray, Judith Sargent 1751-1820 . . . . DLB-37	Nazor, Vladimir 1876-1949 . . . . DLB-147
Muir, Helen 1937- DLB-14	Murray, Pauli 1910-1985 . . . . DLB-41	Ndebele, Njabulo 1948- DLB-157
Mukherjee, Bharati 1940- DLB-60	Murray, John [publishing house] DLB-154	Neagoe, Peter 1881-1960 . . . . DLB-4
Mulcaster, Richard 1531 or 1532-1611 . . . . DLB-167	Murry, John Middleton 1889-1957 . . . . DLB-149	Neal, John 1793-1876 . . . . DLB-1, 59
Muldoon, Paul 1951- DLB-40	Musäus, Johann Karl August 1735-1787 . . . . DLB-97	Neal, Joseph C. 1807-1847 . . . . DLB-11
Müller, Friedrich (see Müller, Maler)		Neal, Larry 1937-1981 . . . . DLB-38
Müller, Heiner 1929- DLB-124	Muschg, Adolf 1934- DLB-75	The Neale Publishing Company DLB-49
Müller, Maler 1749-1825 . . . . DLB-94	The Music of Minnesang DLB-138	Neely, F. Tennyson [publishing house]. DLB-49
Müller, Wilhelm 1794-1827. . . . . DLB-90	Musil, Robert 1880-1942 . . . . . DLB-81, 124	
Mumford, Lewis 1895-1990 . . . . DLB-63	Muspilli circa 790-circa 850 . . . . . . DLB-148	Negri, Ada 1870-1945 . . . . DLB-114
Munby, Arthur Joseph 1828-1910 . . . . DLB-35	Mussey, Benjamin B., and Company DLB-49	"The Negro as a Writer," by G. M. McClellan. DLB-50
Munday, Anthony 1560-1633. . . . DLB-62, 172	Mutafchieva, Vera 1929- DLB-181	"Negro Poets and Their Poetry," by Wallace Thurman DLB-50
Mundt, Clara (see Mühlbach, Luise)	Mwangi, Meja 1948- DLB-125	
Mundt, Theodore 1808-1861 . . . . . . DLB-133	Myers, Gustavus 1872-1942 . . . . DLB-47	Neidhart von Reuental circa 1185-circa 1240 . . . . DLB-138
Munford, Robert circa 1737-1783 . . . . DLB-31	Myers, L. H. 1881-1944 . . . . DLB-15	Neihardt, John G. 1881-1973 . . . . . DLB-9, 54
Mungoshi, Charles 1947- DLB-157	Myers, Walter Dean 1937- DLB-33	Neledinsky-Meletsky, Iurii Aleksandrovich 1752-1828 . . . . DLB-150
Munonye, John 1929- DLB-117		
Munro, Alice 1931- DLB-53	**N**	Nelligan, Emile 1879-1941 . . . . DLB-92
Munro, H. H. 1870-1916 . . . . . DLB-34, 162	Nabbes, Thomas circa 1605-1641 . . . . DLB-58	Nelson, Alice Moore Dunbar 1875-1935 . . . . DLB-50
Munro, Neil 1864-1930 . . . . DLB-156	Nabl, Franz 1883-1974 . . . . DLB-81	Nelson, Thomas, and Sons [U.S.] DLB-49
		Nelson, Thomas, and Sons [U.K.] . . . DLB-106

Nelson, William 1908-1978 . . . . . . DLB-103
Nelson, William Rockhill
   1841-1915 . . . . DLB-23
Nemerov, Howard 1920-1991 . . . DLB-5, 6; Y-83
Nesbit, E. 1858-1924 . . . . . DLB-141, 153, 178
Ness, Evaline 1911-1986 . . . . DLB-61
Nestroy, Johann 1801-1862 . . . . DLB-133
Neukirch, Benjamin 1655-1729 . . . . . DLB-168
Neugeboren, Jay 1938- DLB-28
Neumann, Alfred 1895-1952 . . . . . . DLB-56
Neumark, Georg 1621-1681 . . . . DLB-164
Neumeister, Erdmann 1671-1756 . . . . DLB-168
Nevins, Allan 1890-1971 . . . . DLB-17
Nevinson, Henry Woodd
   1856-1941 . . . . DLB-135
The New American Library DLB-46
New Approaches to Biography: Challenges
   from Critical Theory, USC Conference
   on Literary Studies, 1990 . . . . Y-90
New Directions Publishing
   Corporation DLB-46
A New Edition of *Huck Finn* Y-85
New Forces at Work in the American Theatre:
   1915-1925 . . . . DLB-7
New Literary Periodicals:
   A Report for 1987 . . . . Y-87
New Literary Periodicals:
   A Report for 1988 . . . . Y-88
New Literary Periodicals:
   A Report for 1989 . . . . Y-89
New Literary Periodicals:
   A Report for 1990 . . . . Y-90
New Literary Periodicals:
   A Report for 1991 . . . . Y-91
New Literary Periodicals:
   A Report for 1992 . . . . Y-92
New Literary Periodicals:
   A Report for 1993 . . . . Y-93
The New Monthly Magazine
   1814-1884 . . . . DLB-110
The New *Ulysses* Y-84
The New Variorum Shakespeare Y-85
A New Voice: The Center for the Book's First
   Five Years Y-83
The New Wave [Science Fiction] DLB-8
New York City Bookshops in the 1930s and
   1940s: The Recollections of Walter
   Goldwater Y-93
Newbery, John
   [publishing house] DLB-154
Newbolt, Henry 1862-1938 . . . . DLB-19
Newbound, Bernard Slade (see Slade, Bernard)
Newby, P. H. 1918- DLB-15
Newby, Thomas Cautley
   [publishing house] DLB-106
Newcomb, Charles King 1820-1894 . . . . DLB-1

Newell, Peter 1862-1924 . . . . DLB-42
Newell, Robert Henry 1836-1901 . . . . DLB-11
Newhouse, Samuel I. 1895-1979 . . . . DLB-127
Newman, Cecil Earl 1903-1976 . . . . . DLB-127
Newman, David (see Benton, Robert)
Newman, Frances 1883-1928 . . . . Y-80
Newman, John Henry
   1801-1890 . . . . DLB-18, 32, 55
Newman, Mark [publishing house] DLB-49
Newnes, George, Limited DLB-112
Newsome, Effie Lee 1885-1979 . . . . . DLB-76
Newspaper Syndication of American
   Humor DLB-11
Newton, A. Edward 1864-1940 . . . . . DLB-140
Ngugi wa Thiong'o 1938- DLB-125
Niatum, Duane 1938- DLB-175
The *Nibelungenlied* and the *Klage*
   circa 1200 . . . . DLB-138
Nichol, B. P. 1944- DLB-53
Nicholas of Cusa 1401-1464 . . . . . . DLB-115
Nichols, Dudley 1895-1960 . . . . DLB-26
Nichols, Grace 1950- DLB-157
Nichols, John 1940- Y-82
Nichols, Mary Sargeant (Neal) Gove 1810-11884
   . . . . DLB-1
Nichols, Peter 1927- DLB-13
Nichols, Roy F. 1896-1973 . . . . DLB-17
Nichols, Ruth 1948- DLB-60
Nicholson, Norman 1914- DLB-27
Nicholson, William 1872-1949 . . . . . DLB-141
Ní Chuilleanáin, Eiléan 1942- DLB-40
Nicol, Eric 1919- DLB-68
Nicolai, Friedrich 1733-1811 . . . . . . DLB-97
Nicolay, John G. 1832-1901 and
   Hay, John 1838-1905 . . . . DLB-47
Nicolson, Harold 1886-1968 . . . . DLB-100, 149
Nicolson, Nigel 1917- DLB-155
Niebuhr, Reinhold 1892-1971 . . . . . DLB-17
Niedecker, Lorine 1903-1970 . . . . . . DLB-48
Nieman, Lucius W. 1857-1935 . . . . . DLB-25
Nietzsche, Friedrich 1844-1900 . . . . . DLB-129
Niggli, Josefina 1910- Y-80
Nightingale, Florence 1820-1910 . . . . . DLB-166
Nikolev, Nikolai Petrovich
   1758-1815 . . . . DLB-150
Niles, Hezekiah 1777-1839 . . . . DLB-43
Nims, John Frederick 1913- DLB-5
Nin, Anaïs 1903-1977 . . . . . . DLB-2, 4, 152
1985: The Year of the Mystery:
   A Symposium Y-85
Nissenson, Hugh 1933- DLB-28
Niven, Frederick John 1878-1944 . . . . DLB-92
Niven, Larry 1938- DLB-8

Nizan, Paul 1905-1940 . . . . DLB-72
Njegoš, Petar II Petrović
   1813-1851 . . . . DLB-147
Nkosi, Lewis 1936- DLB-157
Nobel Peace Prize
The 1986 Nobel Peace Prize
   Nobel Lecture 1986: Hope, Despair and Memory
   Tributes from Abraham Bernstein,
   Norman Lamm, and
   John R. Silber Y-86
The Nobel Prize and Literary Politics . . . Y-86
Nobel Prize in Literature
The 1982 Nobel Prize in Literature
   Announcement by the Swedish Academy
   of the Nobel Prize Nobel Lecture 1982:
   The Solitude of Latin America Excerpt
   from *One Hundred Years of Solitude* The
   Magical World of Macondo A Tribute
   to Gabriel García Márquez Y-82
The 1983 Nobel Prize in Literature
   Announcement by the Swedish Academy Nobel Lecture 1983 The Stature of
   William Golding Y-83
The 1984 Nobel Prize in Literature
   Announcement by the Swedish Academy
   Jaroslav Seifert Through the Eyes of the
   English-Speaking Reader
   Three Poems by Jaroslav Seifert Y-84
The 1985 Nobel Prize in Literature
   Announcement by the Swedish Academy
   Nobel Lecture 1985 . . . . Y-85
The 1986 Nobel Prize in Literature
   Nobel Lecture 1986: This Past Must Address
   Its Present Y-86
The 1987 Nobel Prize in Literature
   Nobel Lecture 1987 . . . . Y-87
The 1988 Nobel Prize in Literature
   Nobel Lecture 1988 . . . . Y-88
The 1989 Nobel Prize in Literature
   Nobel Lecture 1989 . . . . Y-89
The 1990 Nobel Prize in Literature
   Nobel Lecture 1990 . . . . Y-90
The 1991 Nobel Prize in Literature
   Nobel Lecture 1991 . . . . Y-91
The 1992 Nobel Prize in Literature
   Nobel Lecture 1992 . . . . Y-92
The 1993 Nobel Prize in Literature
   Nobel Lecture 1993 . . . . Y-93
The 1994 Nobel Prize in Literature
   Nobel Lecture 1994 . . . . Y-94
The 1995 Nobel Prize in Literature
   Nobel Lecture 1995 . . . . Y-95
Nodier, Charles 1780-1844 . . . . DLB-119
Noel, Roden 1834-1894 . . . . DLB-35
Nogami, Yaeko 1885-1985 . . . . DLB-180
Nogo, Rajko Petrov 1945- DLB-181
Nolan, William F. 1928- DLB-8
Noland, C. F. M. 1810?-1858 . . . . . . DLB-11
Nonesuch Press DLB-112

Noonday Press DLB-46
Noone, John 1936- DLB-14
Nora, Eugenio de 1923- DLB-134
Nordhoff, Charles 1887-1947 . . . . . . DLB-9
Norman, Charles 1904- DLB-111
Norman, Marsha 1947- Y-84
Norris, Charles G. 1881-1945 . . . . . . DLB-9
Norris, Frank 1870-1902 . . . . DLB-12
Norris, Leslie 1921- DLB-27
Norse, Harold 1916- DLB-16
North, Marianne 1830-1890 . . . . . . DLB-174
North Point Press DLB-46
Nortje, Arthur 1942-1970 . . . . DLB-125
Norton, Alice Mary (see Norton, Andre)
Norton, Andre 1912- DLB-8, 52
Norton, Andrews 1786-1853 . . . . DLB-1
Norton, Caroline 1808-1877 . . . . DLB-21, 159
Norton, Charles Eliot 1827-1908 . . . DLB-1, 64
Norton, John 1606-1663 . . . . DLB-24
Norton, Mary 1903-1992 . . . . DLB-160
Norton, Thomas (see Sackville, Thomas)
Norton, W. W., and Company DLB-46
Norwood, Robert 1874-1932 . . . . . . DLB-92
Nossack, Hans Erich 1901-1977 . . . . DLB-69
Notker Balbulus circa 840-912 . . . . . DLB-148
Notker III of Saint Gall
  circa 950-1022 . . . . DLB-148
Notker von Zweifalten ?-1095 . . . . . DLB-148
A Note on Technique (1926), by
  Elizabeth A. Drew [excerpts] DLB-36
Nourse, Alan E. 1928- DLB-8
Novak, Slobodan 1924- DLB-181
Novak, Vjenceslav 1859-1905 . . . . . . DLB-147
Novalis 1772-1801 . . . . DLB-90
Novaro, Mario 1868-1944 . . . . DLB-114
Novás Calvo, Lino 1903-1983 . . . . . DLB-145
"The Novel in [Robert Browning's] 'The Ring and
  the Book' " (1912), by
  Henry James DLB-32
The Novel of Impressionism,
  by Jethro Bithell DLB-66
Novel-Reading: The Works of Charles Dickens,
  The Works of W. Makepeace Thackeray
  (1879), by Anthony Trollope DLB-21
The Novels of Dorothy Richardson (1918),
  by May Sinclair DLB-36
Novels with a Purpose (1864), by
  Justin M'Carthy DLB-21
Noventa, Giacomo 1898-1960 . . . . . DLB-114
Novikov, Nikolai Ivanovich
  1744-1818 . . . . DLB-150
Nowlan, Alden 1933-1983 . . . . DLB-53
Noyes, Alfred 1880-1958 . . . . DLB-20

Noyes, Crosby S. 1825-1908 . . . . . . DLB-23
Noyes, Nicholas 1647-1717 . . . . DLB-24
Noyes, Theodore W. 1858-1946 . . . . DLB-29
N-Town Plays circa 1468 to early
  sixteenth century DLB-146
Nugent, Frank 1908-1965 . . . . DLB-44
Nugent, Richard Bruce 1906- DLB-151
Nušić, Branislav 1864-1938 . . . . . . DLB-147
Nutt, David [publishing house] DLB-106
Nwapa, Flora 1931- DLB-125
Nye, Edgar Wilson (Bill)
  1850-1896 . . . . DLB-11, 23
Nye, Naomi Shihab 1952- DLB-120
Nye, Robert 1939- DLB-14

O

Oakes, Urian circa 1631-1681 . . . . . . DLB-24
Oates, Joyce Carol
  1938- DLB-2, 5, 130; Y-81
Ober, William 1920-1993 . . . . Y-93
Oberholtzer, Ellis Paxson
  1868-1936 . . . . DLB-47
Obradović, Dositej 1740?-1811 . . . . DLB-147
O'Brien, Edna 1932- DLB-14
O'Brien, Fitz-James 1828-1862 . . . . . DLB-74
O'Brien, Kate 1897-1974 . . . . DLB-15
O'Brien, Tim
  1946- DLB-152; Y-80; DS-9
O'Casey, Sean 1880-1964 . . . . DLB-10
Occom, Samson 1723-1792 . . . . . . DLB-175
Ochs, Adolph S. 1858-1935 . . . . DLB-25
Ochs-Oakes, George Washington
  1861-1931 . . . . DLB-137
O'Connor, Flannery
  1925-1964 . . . . DLB-2, 152; Y-80; DS-12
O'Connor, Frank 1903-1966 . . . . . . DLB-162
Octopus Publishing Group DLB-112
Odell, Jonathan 1737-1818 . . . . . . DLB-31, 99
O'Dell, Scott 1903-1989 . . . . DLB-52
Odets, Clifford 1906-1963 . . . . DLB-7, 26
Odhams Press Limited DLB-112
O'Donnell, Peter 1920- DLB-87
O'Donovan, Michael (see O'Connor, Frank)
O'Faolain, Julia 1932- DLB-14
O'Faolain, Sean 1900- DLB-15, 162
Off Broadway and Off-Off Broadway . . DLB-7
Off-Loop Theatres DLB-7
Offord, Carl Ruthven 1910- DLB-76
O'Flaherty, Liam
  1896-1984 . . . . DLB-36, 162; Y-84
Ogilvie, J. S., and Company DLB-49

Ogot, Grace 1930- DLB-125
O'Grady, Desmond 1935- DLB-40
Ogunyemi, Wale 1939- DLB-157
O'Hagan, Howard 1902-1982 . . . . . DLB-68
O'Hara, Frank 1926-1966 . . . . . . DLB-5, 16
O'Hara, John 1905-1970 . . . . DLB-9, 86; DS-2
Okara, Gabriel 1921- DLB-125
O'Keeffe, John 1747-1833 . . . . DLB-89
Okes, Nicholas
  [publishing house] DLB-170
Okigbo, Christopher 1930-1967 . . . . DLB-125
Okot p'Bitek 1931-1982 . . . . DLB-125
Okpewho, Isidore 1941- DLB-157
Okri, Ben 1959- DLB-157
Olaudah Equiano and Unfinished Journeys:
  The Slave-Narrative Tradition and
  Twentieth-Century Continuities, by
  Paul Edwards and Pauline T.
  Wangman DLB-117
Old English Literature:
  An Introduction DLB-146
Old English Riddles
  eighth to tenth centuries DLB-146
Old Franklin Publishing House DLB-49
Old German Genesis and Old German Exodus
  circa 1050-circa 1130 . . . . DLB-148
Old High German Charms and
  Blessings DLB-148
The Old High German Isidor
  circa 790-800 . . . . DLB-148
Older, Fremont 1856-1935 . . . . DLB-25
Oldham, John 1653-1683 . . . . DLB-131
Olds, Sharon 1942- DLB-120
Olearius, Adam 1599-1671 . . . . DLB-164
Oliphant, Laurence
  1829?-1888 . . . . DLB-18, 166
Oliphant, Margaret 1828-1897 . . . . . DLB-18
Oliver, Chad 1928- DLB-8
Oliver, Mary 1935- DLB-5
Ollier, Claude 1922- DLB-83
Olsen, Tillie 1913?- DLB-28; Y-80
Olson, Charles 1910-1970 . . . . . . DLB-5, 16
Olson, Elder 1909- DLB-48, 63
Omotoso, Kole 1943- DLB-125
"On Art in Fiction "(1838),
  by Edward Bulwer DLB-21
On Learning to Write Y-88
On Some of the Characteristics of Modern
  Poetry and On the Lyrical Poems of
  Alfred Tennyson (1831), by Arthur
  Henry Hallam DLB-32
"On Style in English Prose" (1898), by
  Frederic Harrison DLB-57
"On Style in Literature: Its Technical
  Elements" (1885), by Robert Louis
  Stevenson DLB-57

"On the Writing of Essays" (1862),
 by Alexander Smith DLB-57
Ondaatje, Michael 1943- DLB-60
O'Neill, Eugene 1888-1953. . . . . DLB-7
Onetti, Juan Carlos 1909-1994 . . . . . DLB-113
Onions, George Oliver
 1872-1961 . . . . DLB-153
Onofri, Arturo 1885-1928 . . . . DLB-114
Opie, Amelia 1769-1853 . . . . . DLB-116, 159
Opitz, Martin 1597-1639 . . . . DLB-164
Oppen, George 1908-1984 . . . . . DLB-5, 165
Oppenheim, E. Phillips 1866-1946 . . . . DLB-70
Oppenheim, James 1882-1932 . . . . . DLB-28
Oppenheimer, Joel 1930- DLB-5
Optic, Oliver (see Adams, William Taylor)
Orczy, Emma, Baroness
 1865-1947 . . . . DLB-70
Origo, Iris 1902-1988 . . . . DLB-155
Orlovitz, Gil 1918-1973 . . . . DLB-2, 5
Orlovsky, Peter 1933- DLB-16
Ormond, John 1923- DLB-27
Ornitz, Samuel 1890-1957 . . . . . DLB-28, 44
Ortese, Anna Maria 1914- DLB-177
Ortiz, Simon J. 1941- DLB-120, 175
Ortnit and *Wolfdietrich*
 circa 1225-1250 . . . . DLB-138
Orton, Joe 1933-1967 . . . . DLB-13
Orwell, George 1903-1950 . . . . . DLB-15, 98
The Orwell Year Y-84
Ory, Carlos Edmundo de 1923- . . . DLB-134
Osbey, Brenda Marie 1957- DLB-120
Osbon, B. S. 1827-1912 . . . . DLB-43
Osborne, John 1929-1994 . . . . DLB-13
Osgood, Herbert L. 1855-1918 . . . . . DLB-47
Osgood, James R., and
 Company DLB-49
Osgood, McIlvaine and
 Company DLB-112
O'Shaughnessy, Arthur
 1844-1881 . . . . DLB-35
O'Shea, Patrick
 [publishing house] DLB-49
Osipov, Nikolai Petrovich
 1751-1799 . . . . DLB-150
Oskison, John Milton 1879-1947 . . . . DLB-175
Osofisan, Femi 1946- DLB-125
Ostenso, Martha 1900-1963 . . . . . . DLB-92
Ostriker, Alicia 1937- DLB-120
Osundare, Niyi 1947- DLB-157
Oswald, Eleazer 1755-1795 . . . . DLB-43
Oswald von Wolkenstein
 1376 or 1377-1445 . . . . DLB-179
Otero, Blas de 1916-1979 . . . . DLB-134

Otero, Miguel Antonio
 1859-1944 . . . . DLB-82
Otero Silva, Miguel 1908-1985 . . . . DLB-145
Otfried von Weißenburg
 circa 800-circa 875? DLB-148
Otis, James (see Kaler, James Otis)
Otis, James, Jr. 1725-1783 . . . . DLB-31
Otis, Broaders and Company DLB-49
Ottaway, James 1911- DLB-127
Ottendorfer, Oswald 1826-1900 . . . . DLB-23
Ottieri, Ottiero 1924- DLB-177
Otto-Peters, Louise 1819-1895 . . . . . DLB-129
Otway, Thomas 1652-1685 . . . . DLB-80
Ouellette, Fernand 1930- DLB-60
Ouida 1839-1908 . . . . DLB-18, 156
Outing Publishing Company DLB-46
Outlaw Days, by Joyce Johnson DLB-16
Overbury, Sir Thomas
 circa 1581-1613 . . . . DLB-151
The Overlook Press DLB-46
Overview of U.S. Book Publishing,
 1910-1945 . . . . DLB-9
Owen, Guy 1925- DLB-5
Owen, John 1564-1622 . . . . DLB-121
Owen, John [publishing house] DLB-49
Owen, Robert 1771-1858 . . . . DLB-107, 158
Owen, Wilfred 1893-1918 . . . . DLB-20
Owen, Peter, Limited DLB-112
The Owl and the Nightingale
 circa 1189-1199 . . . . DLB-146
Owsley, Frank L. 1890-1956 . . . . . . DLB-17
Oxford, Seventeenth Earl of, Edward de Vere
 1550-1604 . . . . DLB-172
Ozerov, Vladislav Aleksandrovich
 1769-1816 . . . . DLB-150
Ozick, Cynthia 1928- DLB-28, 152; Y-82

P

Pace, Richard 1482?-1536 . . . . DLB-167
Pacey, Desmond 1917-1975 . . . . . . DLB-88
Pack, Robert 1929- DLB-5
Packaging Papa: *The Garden of Eden* Y-86
Padell Publishing Company DLB-46
Padgett, Ron 1942- DLB-5
Padilla, Ernesto Chávez 1944- DLB-122
Page, L. C., and Company DLB-49
Page, P. K. 1916- DLB-68
Page, Thomas Nelson
 1853-1922 . . . . DLB-12, 78; DS-13
Page, Walter Hines 1855-1918 . . . DLB-71, 91
Paget, Francis Edward
 1806-1882 . . . . DLB-163

Paget, Violet (see Lee, Vernon)
Pagliarani, Elio 1927- DLB-128
Pain, Barry 1864-1928 . . . . DLB-135
Pain, Philip ?-circa 1666 . . . . DLB-24
Paine, Robert Treat, Jr. 1773-1811 . . . DLB-37
Paine, Thomas
 1737-1809 . . . . DLB-31, 43, 73, 158
Painter, George D. 1914- DLB-155
Painter, William 1540?-1594 . . . . . . DLB-136
Palazzeschi, Aldo 1885-1974 . . . . . . DLB-114
Paley, Grace 1922- DLB-28
Palfrey, John Gorham
 1796-1881 . . . . DLB-1, 30
Palgrave, Francis Turner
 1824-1897 . . . . DLB-35
Palmer, Joe H. 1904-1952 . . . . DLB-171
Palmer, Michael 1943- DLB-169
Paltock, Robert 1697-1767 . . . . DLB-39
Pan Books Limited DLB-112
Panamaa, Norman 1914- and
 Frank, Melvin 1913-1988 . . . . . . DLB-26
Pancake, Breece D'J 1952-1979 . . . . DLB-130
Panero, Leopoldo 1909-1962 . . . . . DLB-108
Pangborn, Edgar 1909-1976 . . . . . . DLB-8
"Panic Among the Philistines": A Postscript,
 An Interview with Bryan Griffin Y-81
Panneton, Philippe (see Ringuet)
Panshin, Alexei 1940- DLB-8
Pansy (see Alden, Isabella)
Pantheon Books DLB-46
Paperback Library DLB-46
Paperback Science Fiction DLB-8
Paquet, Alfons 1881-1944 . . . . DLB-66
Paracelsus 1493-1541 . . . . DLB-179
Paradis, Suzanne 1936- DLB-53
Pareja Diezcanseco, Alfredo
 1908-1993 . . . . DLB-145
Pardoe, Julia 1804-1862 . . . . DLB-166
Parents' Magazine Press DLB-46
Parise, Goffredo 1929-1986 . . . . . . DLB-177
Parisian Theater, Fall 1984: Toward
 A New Baroque Y-85
Parizeau, Alice 1930- DLB-60
Parke, John 1754-1789 . . . . DLB-31
Parker, Dorothy
 1893-1967 . . . . DLB-11, 45, 86
Parker, Gilbert 1860-1932 . . . . DLB-99
Parker, James 1714-1770 . . . . DLB-43
Parker, Theodore 1810-1860 . . . . . . DLB-1
Parker, William Riley 1906-1968 . . . . DLB-103
Parker, J. H. [publishing house] DLB-106
Parker, John [publishing house] DLB-106

Parkman, Francis, Jr.
1823-1893 . . . . DLB-1, 30

Parks, Gordon 1912- DLB-33

Parks, William 1698-1750. . . . . . . DLB-43

Parks, William [publishing house] DLB-49

Parley, Peter (see Goodrich, Samuel Griswold)

Parmenides late sixth-fifth century B.C.
. . . . DLB-176

Parnell, Thomas 1679-1718. . . . . . . DLB-95

Parr, Catherine 1513?-1548 . . . . . . DLB-136

Parrington, Vernon L.
1871-1929. . . . . DLB-17, 63

Parronchi, Alessandro 1914- DLB-128

Partridge, S. W., and Company DLB-106

Parton, James 1822-1891 . . . . DLB-30

Parton, Sara Payson Willis
1811-1872. . . . . DLB-43, 74

Parun, Vesna 1922- DLB-181

Pasinetti, Pier Maria 1913- DLB-177

Pasolini, Pier Paolo 1922- DLB-128, 177

Pastan, Linda 1932- DLB-5

Paston, George 1860-1936. . . . . . . DLB-149

The Paston Letters 1422-1509. . . . . . DLB-146

Pastorius, Francis Daniel
1651-circa 1720 . . . . DLB-24

Patchen, Kenneth 1911-1972. . . . DLB-16, 48

Pater, Walter 1839-1894 . . . . . DLB-57, 156

Paterson, Katherine 1932- DLB-52

Patmore, Coventry 1823-1896 . . . . DLB-35, 98

Paton, Joseph Noel 1821-1901 . . . . . DLB-35

Paton Walsh, Jill 1937- DLB-161

Patrick, Edwin Hill ("Ted")
1901-1964 . . . . DLB-137

Patrick, John 1906- DLB-7

Pattee, Fred Lewis 1863-1950 . . . . . DLB-71

Pattern and Paradigm: History as
Design, by Judith Ryan DLB-75

Patterson, Alicia 1906-1963 . . . . . . DLB-127

Patterson, Eleanor Medill
1881-1948. . . . . DLB-29

Patterson, Eugene 1923- DLB-127

Patterson, Joseph Medill
1879-1946. . . . . DLB-29

Pattillo, Henry 1726-1801. . . . . DLB-37

Paul, Elliot 1891-1958 . . . . DLB-4

Paul, Jean (see Richter, Johann Paul Friedrich)

Paul, Kegan, Trench, Trubner and Company
Limited. DLB-106

Paul, Peter, Book Company DLB-49

Paul, Stanley, and Company
Limited. DLB-112

Paulding, James Kirke
1778-1860. . . . . DLB-3, 59, 74

Paulin, Tom 1949- DLB-40

Pauper, Peter, Press. DLB-46

Pavese, Cesare 1908-1950 . . . . . DLB-128, 177

Pavić, Milorad 1929- DLB-181

Pavlov, Konstantin 1933- DLB-181

Pavlović, Miodrag 1928- DLB-181

Paxton, John 1911-1985. . . . . DLB-44

Payn, James 1830-1898 . . . . DLB-18

Payne, John 1842-1916 . . . . DLB-35

Payne, John Howard 1791-1852 . . . . DLB-37

Payson and Clarke DLB-46

Peabody, Elizabeth Palmer
1804-1894. . . . . DLB-1

Peabody, Elizabeth Palmer
[publishing house]. DLB-49

Peabody, Oliver William Bourn
1799-1848 . . . . DLB-59

Peace, Roger 1899-1968 . . . . DLB-127

Peacham, Henry 1578-1644? DLB-151

Peacham, Henry, the Elder
1547-1634 . . . . DLB-172

Peachtree Publishers, Limited. DLB-46

Peacock, Molly 1947- DLB-120

Peacock, Thomas Love
1785-1866 . . . . DLB-96, 116

Pead, Deuel ?-1727 . . . . DLB-24

Peake, Mervyn 1911-1968 . . . . DLB-15, 160

Pear Tree Press DLB-112

Pearce, Philippa 1920- DLB-161

Pearson, H. B. [publishing house] DLB-49

Pearson, Hesketh 1887-1964. . . . . . DLB-149

Peck, George W. 1840-1916 . . . . DLB-23, 42

Peck, H. C., and Theo. Bliss
[publishing house]. DLB-49

Peck, Harry Thurston
1856-1914. . . . . DLB-71, 91

Peele, George 1556-1596 . . . . . DLB-62, 167

Pegler, Westbrook 1894-1969 . . . . . DLB-171

Pekić, Borislav 1930-1992 . . . . . . DLB-181

Pellegrini and Cudahy DLB-46

Pelletier, Aimé (see Vac, Bertrand)

Pemberton, Sir Max 1863-1950 . . . . DLB-70

Penguin Books [U.S.]. DLB-46

Penguin Books [U.K.] DLB-112

Penn Publishing Company DLB-49

Penn, William 1644-1718. . . . . DLB-24

Penna, Sandro 1906-1977 . . . . DLB-114

Penner, Jonathan 1940- Y-83

Pennington, Lee 1939- Y-82

Pepys, Samuel 1633-1703 . . . . DLB-101

Percy, Thomas 1729-1811. . . . . . . DLB-104

Percy, Walker 1916-1990 . . . . DLB-2; Y-80, 90

Percy, William 1575-1648. . . . . . . DLB-172

Perec, Georges 1936-1982. . . . . . . DLB-83

Perelman, S. J. 1904-1979 . . . . . DLB-11, 44

Perez, Raymundo "Tigre"
1946- DLB-122

Peri Rossi, Cristina 1941- DLB-145

Periodicals of the Beat Generation. . . . DLB-16

Perkins, Eugene 1932- DLB-41

Perkoff, Stuart Z. 1930-1974 . . . . . . DLB-16

Perley, Moses Henry 1804-1862. . . . . DLB-99

Permabooks DLB-46

Perrin, Alice 1867-1934 . . . . DLB-156

Perry, Bliss 1860-1954 . . . . DLB-71

Perry, Eleanor 1915-1981 . . . . DLB-44

Perry, Sampson 1747-1823 . . . . . . DLB-158

"Personal Style" (1890), by John Addington
Symonds. DLB-57

Perutz, Leo 1882-1957 . . . . DLB-81

Pesetsky, Bette 1932- DLB-130

Pestalozzi, Johann Heinrich
1746-1827 . . . . DLB-94

Peter, Laurence J. 1919-1990 . . . . . . DLB-53

Peter of Spain circa 1205-1277 . . . . DLB-115

Peterkin, Julia 1880-1961. . . . . DLB-9

Peters, Lenrie 1932- DLB-117

Peters, Robert 1924- DLB-105

Peters, Robert, Foreword to
Ludwig of Bavaria. DLB-105

Petersham, Maud 1889-1971 and
Petersham, Miska 1888-1960. . . . . DLB-22

Peterson, Charles Jacobs 1819-1887 . . . DLB-79

Peterson, Len 1917- DLB-88

Peterson, Louis 1922- DLB-76

Peterson, T. B., and Brothers DLB-49

Petitclair, Pierre 1813-1860 . . . . DLB-99

Petrov, Aleksandar 1938- DLB-181

Petrov, Gavriil 1730-1801 . . . . . . DLB-150

Petrov, Vasilii Petrovich
1736-1799 . . . . DLB-150

Petrov, Valeri 1920- DLB-181

Petrović, Rastko 1898-1949 . . . . . . DLB-147

Petruslied circa 854? DLB-148

Petry, Ann 1908- DLB-76

Pettie, George circa 1548-1589 . . . . DLB-136

Peyton, K. M. 1929- DLB-161

Pfaffe Konrad
flourished circa 1172 . . . . DLB-148

Pfaffe Lamprecht
flourished circa 1150 . . . . DLB-148

Pforzheimer, Carl H. 1879-1957 . . . . DLB-140

Phaer, Thomas 1510?-1560 . . . . . . DLB-167

Phaidon Press Limited. DLB-112

Pharr, Robert Deane 1916-1992 . . . . DLB-33

Phelps, Elizabeth Stuart
1844-1911 . . . . DLB-74

Philander von der Linde
(see Mencke, Johann Burckhard)

Philip, Marlene Nourbese
1947- DLB-157

Philippe, Charles-Louis
1874-1909 . . . . DLB-65

Philips, John 1676-1708 . . . . DLB-95

Philips, Katherine 1632-1664 . . . . . DLB-131

Phillips, Caryl 1958- DLB-157

Phillips, David Graham
1867-1911 . . . . DLB-9, 12

Phillips, Jayne Anne 1952- Y-80

Phillips, Robert 1938- DLB-105

Phillips, Robert, Finding, Losing,
Reclaiming: A Note on My
Poems DLB-105

Phillips, Stephen 1864-1915 . . . . DLB-10

Phillips, Ulrich B. 1877-1934 . . . . DLB-17

Phillips, Willard 1784-1873 . . . . DLB-59

Phillips, William 1907- DLB-137

Phillips, Sampson and Company DLB-49

Phillpotts, Eden
1862-1960 . . . . . . DLB-10, 70, 135, 153

Philo circa 20-15 B.C.-circa A.D. 50
. . . . DLB-176

Philosophical Library DLB-46

"The Philosophy of Style" (1852), by
Herbert Spencer DLB-57

Phinney, Elihu [publishing house] DLB-49

Phoenix, John (see Derby, George Horatio)

PHYLON (Fourth Quarter, 1950),
The Negro in Literature:
The Current Scene DLB-76

Physiologus
circa 1070-circa 1150 . . . . DLB-148

Piccolo, Lucio 1903-1969 . . . . DLB-114

Pickard, Tom 1946- DLB-40

Pickering, William
[publishing house] DLB-106

Pickthall, Marjorie 1883-1922 . . . . . . DLB-92

Pictorial Printing Company DLB-49

Piel, Gerard 1915- DLB-137

Piercy, Marge 1936- DLB-120

Pierro, Albino 1916- DLB-128

Pignotti, Lamberto 1926- DLB-128

Pike, Albert 1809-1891 . . . . DLB-74

Pilon, Jean-Guy 1930- DLB-60

Pinckney, Josephine 1895-1957 . . . . . . DLB-6

Pindar circa 518 B.C.-circa 438 B.C.
. . . . DLB-176

Pindar, Peter (see Wolcot, John)

Pinero, Arthur Wing 1855-1934 . . . . . DLB-10

Pinget, Robert 1919- DLB-83

Pinnacle Books DLB-46

Piñon, Nélida 1935- DLB-145

Pinsky, Robert 1940- Y-82

Pinter, Harold 1930- DLB-13

Piontek, Heinz 1925- DLB-75

Piozzi, Hester Lynch [Thrale]
1741-1821 . . . . DLB-104, 142

Piper, H. Beam 1904-1964 . . . . DLB-8

Piper, Watty DLB-22

Pirckheimer, Caritas 1467-1532 . . . . DLB-179

Pirckheimer, Willibald
1470-1530 . . . . DLB-179

Pisar, Samuel 1929- Y-83

Pitkin, Timothy 1766-1847 . . . . DLB-30

The Pitt Poetry Series: Poetry Publishing Today
. . . . Y-85

Pitter, Ruth 1897- DLB-20

Pix, Mary 1666-1709 . . . . DLB-80

Plaatje, Sol T. 1876-1932 . . . . DLB-125

The Place of Realism in Fiction (1895), by
George Gissing DLB-18

Plante, David 1940- Y-83

Platen, August von 1796-1835 . . . . . . DLB-90

Plath, Sylvia 1932-1963 . . . . . DLB-5, 6, 152

Plato circa 428 B.C.-348-347 B.C.
. . . . DLB-176

Platon 1737-1812 . . . . DLB-150

Platt and Munk Company DLB-46

Playboy Press DLB-46

Playford, John
[publishing house] DLB-170

Plays, Playwrights, and Playgoers DLB-84

Playwrights and Professors, by
Tom Stoppard DLB-13

Playwrights on the Theater DLB-80

Der Pleier flourished circa 1250 . . . . DLB-138

Plenzdorf, Ulrich 1934- DLB-75

Plessen, Elizabeth 1944- DLB-75

Plievier, Theodor 1892-1955 . . . . DLB-69

Plomer, William 1903-1973 . . . . DLB-20, 162

Plotinus 204-270 . . . . DLB-176

Plumly, Stanley 1939- DLB-5

Plumpp, Sterling D. 1940- DLB-41

Plunkett, James 1920- DLB-14

Plutarch circa 46-circa 120 . . . . . . DLB-176

Plymell, Charles 1935- DLB-16

Pocket Books DLB-46

Poe, Edgar Allan
1809-1849 . . . . DLB-3, 59, 73, 74

Poe, James 1921-1980 . . . . DLB-44

The Poet Laureate of the United States
Statements from Former Consultants
in Poetry Y-86

Pohl, Frederik 1919- DLB-8

Poirier, Louis (see Gracq, Julien)

Polanyi, Michael 1891-1976 . . . . . . DLB-100

Pole, Reginald 1500-1558 . . . . DLB-132

Poliakoff, Stephen 1952- DLB-13

Polidori, John William
1795-1821 . . . . DLB-116

Polite, Carlene Hatcher 1932- DLB-33

Pollard, Edward A. 1832-1872 . . . . . DLB-30

Pollard, Percival 1869-1911 . . . . DLB-71

Pollard and Moss DLB-49

Pollock, Sharon 1936- DLB-60

Polonsky, Abraham 1910- DLB-26

Polotsky, Simeon 1629-1680 . . . . . . DLB-150

Polybius circa 200 B.C.-118 B.C. DLB-176

Pomilio, Mario 1921-1990 . . . . DLB-177

Ponce, Mary Helen 1938- DLB-122

Ponce-Montoya, Juanita 1949- DLB-122

Ponet, John 1516?-1556 . . . . DLB-132

Poniatowski, Elena 1933- DLB-113

Ponsonby, William
[publishing house] DLB-170

Pony Stories DLB-160

Poole, Ernest 1880-1950 . . . . DLB-9

Poole, Sophia 1804-1891 . . . . DLB-166

Poore, Benjamin Perley
1820-1887 . . . . DLB-23

Popa, Vasko 1922-1991 . . . . DLB-181

Pope, Abbie Hanscom
1858-1894 . . . . DLB-140

Pope, Alexander 1688-1744 . . . . DLB-95, 101

Popov, Mikhail Ivanovich
1742-circa 1790 . . . . DLB-150

Popović, Aleksandar 1929-1996 . . . . DLB-181

Popular Library DLB-46

Porlock, Martin (see MacDonald, Philip)

Porpoise Press DLB-112

Porta, Antonio 1935-1989 . . . . DLB-128

Porter, Anna Maria
1780-1832 . . . . DLB-116, 159

Porter, Eleanor H. 1868-1920 . . . . . . DLB-9

Porter, Gene Stratton (see Stratton-Porter, Gene)

Porter, Henry ?-? DLB-62

Porter, Jane 1776-1850 . . . . . . DLB-116, 159

Porter, Katherine Anne
1890-1980 . . . . DLB-4, 9, 102; Y-80; DS-12

Porter, Peter 1929- DLB-40

Porter, William Sydney
1862-1910 . . . . DLB-12, 78, 79

Porter, William T. 1809-1858 . . . . DLB-3, 43

Porter and Coates DLB-49

Portis, Charles 1933- DLB-6

Posey, Alexander 1873-1908 . . . . . . DLB-175

Postans, Marianne
circa 1810-1865 . . . . DLB-166

Postl, Carl (see Sealsfield, Carl)

Poston, Ted 1906-1974 . . . . DLB-51

Postscript to [the Third Edition of] *Clarissa* (1751), by Samuel Richardson DLB-39

Potok, Chaim 1929- DLB-28, 152; Y-84

Potter, Beatrix 1866-1943 . . . . DLB-141

Potter, David M. 1910-1971 . . . . . . DLB-17

Potter, John E., and Company DLB-49

Pottle, Frederick A. 1897-1987 . . . . DLB-103; Y-87

Poulin, Jacques 1937- DLB-60

Pound, Ezra 1885-1972 . . . . . DLB-4, 45, 63

Povich, Shirley 1905- DLB-171

Powell, Anthony 1905- DLB-15

Powers, J. F. 1917- DLB-130

Pownall, David 1938- DLB-14

Powys, John Cowper 1872-1963 . . . . DLB-15

Powys, Llewelyn 1884-1939 . . . . . . DLB-98

Powys, T. F. 1875-1953 . . . . . DLB-36, 162

Poynter, Nelson 1903-1978 . . . . . . DLB-127

The Practice of Biography: An Interview with Stanley Weintraub Y-82

The Practice of Biography II: An Interview with B. L. Reid Y-83

The Practice of Biography III: An Interview with Humphrey Carpenter Y-84

The Practice of Biography IV: An Interview with William Manchester Y-85

The Practice of Biography V: An Interview with Justin Kaplan Y-86

The Practice of Biography VI: An Interview with David Herbert Donald Y-87

The Practice of Biography VII: An Interview with John Caldwell Guilds Y-92

The Practice of Biography VIII: An Interview with Joan Mellen Y-94

The Practice of Biography IX: An Interview with Michael Reynolds Y-95

Prados, Emilio 1899-1962 . . . . . . DLB-134

Praed, Winthrop Mackworth 1802-1839 . . . . DLB-96

Praeger Publishers DLB-46

Praetorius, Johannes 1630-1680 . . . . DLB-168

Pratolini, Vasco 1913–1991 . . . . . . DLB-177

Pratt, E. J. 1882-1964 . . . . DLB-92

Pratt, Samuel Jackson 1749-1814 . . . . . DLB-39

Preface to *Alwyn* (1780), by Thomas Holcroft DLB-39

Preface to *Colonel Jack* (1722), by Daniel Defoe DLB-39

Preface to *Evelina* (1778), by Fanny Burney DLB-39

Preface to *Ferdinand Count Fathom* (1753), by Tobias Smollett DLB-39

Preface to *Incognita* (1692), by William Congreve DLB-39

Preface to *Joseph Andrews* (1742), by Henry Fielding DLB-39

Preface to *Moll Flanders* (1722), by Daniel Defoe DLB-39

Preface to *Poems* (1853), by Matthew Arnold DLB-32

Preface to *Robinson Crusoe* (1719), by Daniel Defoe DLB-39

Preface to *Roderick Random* (1748), by Tobias Smollett DLB-39

Preface to *Roxana* (1724), by Daniel Defoe DLB-39

Preface to *St. Leon* (1799), by William Godwin DLB-39

Preface to Sarah Fielding's *Familiar Letters* (1747), by Henry Fielding [excerpt] DLB-39

Preface to Sarah Fielding's *The Adventures of David Simple* (1744), by Henry Fielding DLB-39

Preface to *The Cry* (1754), by Sarah Fielding DLB-39

Preface to *The Delicate Distress* (1769), by Elizabeth Griffin DLB-39

Preface to *The Disguis'd Prince* (1733), by Eliza Haywood [excerpt] DLB-39

Preface to *The Farther Adventures of Robinson Crusoe* (1719), by Daniel Defoe . . . DLB-39

Preface to the First Edition of *Pamela* (1740), by Samuel Richardson DLB-39

Preface to the First Edition of *The Castle of Otranto* (1764), by Horace Walpole DLB-39

Preface to *The History of Romances* (1715), by Pierre Daniel Huet [excerpts] DLB-39

Preface to *The Life of Charlotta du Pont* (1723), by Penelope Aubin DLB-39

Preface to *The Old English Baron* (1778), by Clara Reeve DLB-39

Preface to the Second Edition of *The Castle of Otranto* (1765), by Horace Walpole DLB-39

Preface to *The Secret History, of Queen Zarah, and the Zarazians* (1705), by Delariviere Manley DLB-39

Preface to the Third Edition of *Clarissa* (1751), by Samuel Richardson [excerpt] DLB-39

Preface to *The Works of Mrs. Davys* (1725), by Mary Davys DLB-39

Preface to Volume 1 of *Clarissa* (1747), by Samuel Richardson DLB-39

Preface to Volume 3 of *Clarissa* (1748), by Samuel Richardson DLB-39

Préfontaine, Yves 1937- DLB-53

Prelutsky, Jack 1940- DLB-61

Premisses, by Michael Hamburger DLB-66

Prentice, George D. 1802-1870 . . . . . DLB-43

Prentice-Hall DLB-46

Prescott, Orville 1906-1996 . . . . Y-96

Prescott, William Hickling 1796-1859 . . . . DLB-1, 30, 59

The Present State of the English Novel (1892), by George Saintsbury DLB-18

Prešeren, France 1800-1849 . . . . . . DLB-147

Preston, Thomas 1537-1598 . . . . . . DLB-62

Price, Reynolds 1933- DLB-2

Price, Richard 1723-1791 . . . . DLB-158

Price, Richard 1949- Y-81

Priest, Christopher 1943- DLB-14

Priestley, J. B. 1894-1984 . . . . DLB-10, 34, 77, 100, 139; Y-84

Primary Bibliography: A Retrospective Y-95

Prime, Benjamin Young 1733-1791 . . . DLB-31

Primrose, Diana floruit circa 1630 . . . . DLB-126

Prince, F. T. 1912- DLB-20

Prince, Thomas 1687-1758 . . . . . DLB-24, 140

The Principles of Success in Literature (1865), by George Henry Lewes [excerpt] . . . DLB-57

Printz, Wolfgang Casper 1641-1717 . . . . DLB-168

Prior, Matthew 1664-1721 . . . . DLB-95

Prisco, Michele 1920- DLB-177

Pritchard, William H. 1932- DLB-111

Pritchett, V. S. 1900- DLB-15, 139

Procter, Adelaide Anne 1825-1864 . . . . DLB-32

Procter, Bryan Waller 1787-1874 . . . . DLB-96, 144

The Profession of Authorship: Scribblers for Bread Y-89

The Progress of Romance (1785), by Clara Reeve [excerpt] DLB-39

Prokopovich, Feofan 1681?-1736 . . . . DLB-150

Prokosch, Frederic 1906-1989 . . . . . . DLB-48

The Proletarian Novel DLB-9

Propper, Dan 1937- DLB-16

The Prospect of Peace (1778), by Joel Barlow DLB-37

Protagoras circa 490 B.C.-420 B.C. DLB-176

Proud, Robert 1728-1813 . . . . DLB-30

Proust, Marcel 1871-1922 . . . . DLB-65

Prynne, J. H. 1936- DLB-40

Przybyszewski, Stanislaw 1868-1927 . . . . DLB-66

Pseudo-Dionysius the Areopagite floruit circa 500 . . . . DLB-115

The Public Lending Right in America
Statement by Sen. Charles McC.
Mathias, Jr. PLR and the Meaning
of Literary Property Statements on
PLR by American Writers Y-83

The Public Lending Right in the United Kingdom
Public Lending Right: The First Year in the
United Kingdom Y-83

The Publication of English
Renaissance Plays DLB-62

Publications and Social Movements
[Transcendentalism] DLB-1

Publishers and Agents: The Columbia
Connection Y-87

A Publisher's Archives: G. P. Putnam . . . Y-92

Publishing Fiction at LSU Press Y-87

Pückler-Muskau, Hermann von
1785-1871 . . . . DLB-133

Pufendorf, Samuel von
1632-1694 . . . . DLB-168

Pugh, Edwin William 1874-1930 . . . . DLB-135

Pugin, A. Welby 1812-1852 . . . . DLB-55

Puig, Manuel 1932-1990 . . . . DLB-113

Pulitzer, Joseph 1847-1911 . . . . DLB-23

Pulitzer, Joseph, Jr. 1885-1955 . . . . . DLB-29

Pulitzer Prizes for the Novel,
1917-1945 . . . . DLB-9

Pulliam, Eugene 1889-1975 . . . . DLB-127

Purchas, Samuel 1577?-1626 . . . . . . DLB-151

Purdy, Al 1918- DLB-88

Purdy, James 1923- DLB-2

Purdy, Ken W. 1913-1972 . . . . DLB-137

Pusey, Edward Bouverie
1800-1882 . . . . DLB-55

Putnam, George Palmer
1814-1872 . . . . DLB-3, 79

Putnam, Samuel 1892-1950 . . . . DLB-4

G. P. Putnam's Sons [U.S.] DLB-49

G. P. Putnam's Sons [U.K.] DLB-106

Puzo, Mario 1920- DLB-6

Pyle, Ernie 1900-1945 . . . . DLB-29

Pyle, Howard 1853-1911 . . . . DLB-42; DS-13

Pym, Barbara 1913-1980 . . . . . . DLB-14; Y-87

Pynchon, Thomas 1937- DLB-2, 173

Pyramid Books DLB-46

Pyrnelle, Louise-Clarke 1850-1907 . . . . DLB-42

Pythagoras circa 570 B.C.-? DLB-176

Q

Quad, M. (see Lewis, Charles B.)

Quarles, Francis 1592-1644 . . . . DLB-126

The Quarterly Review
1809-1967 . . . . DLB-110

Quasimodo, Salvatore 1901-1968 . . . . DLB-114

Queen, Ellery (see Dannay, Frederic, and
Manfred B. Lee)

The Queen City Publishing House . . . DLB-49

Queneau, Raymond 1903-1976 . . . . . DLB-72

Quennell, Sir Peter 1905-1993 . . . . . DLB-155

Quesnel, Joseph 1746-1809 . . . . DLB-99

The Question of American Copyright
in the Nineteenth Century
Headnote
Preface, by George Haven Putnam
The Evolution of Copyright, by Brander
Matthews
Summary of Copyright Legislation in
the United States, by R. R. Bowker
Analysis of the Provisions of the
Copyright Law of 1891, by
George Haven Putnam
The Contest for International Copyright,
by George Haven Putnam
Cheap Books and Good Books,
by Brander Matthews DLB-49

Quiller-Couch, Sir Arthur Thomas
1863-1944 . . . . DLB-135, 153

Quin, Ann 1936-1973 . . . . DLB-14

Quincy, Samuel, of Georgia ?-? DLB-31

Quincy, Samuel, of Massachusetts
1734-1789 . . . . DLB-31

Quinn, Anthony 1915- DLB-122

Quintana, Leroy V. 1944- DLB-82

Quintana, Miguel de 1671-1748
A Forerunner of Chicano
Literature DLB-122

Quist, Harlin, Books DLB-46

Quoirez, Françoise (see Sagan, Francçise)

R

Raabe, Wilhelm 1831-1910 . . . . . . DLB-129

Rabe, David 1940- DLB-7

Raboni, Giovanni 1932- DLB-128

Rachilde 1860-1953 . . . . DLB-123

Racin, Kočo 1908-1943 . . . . DLB-147

Rackham, Arthur 1867-1939 . . . . . . DLB-141

Radcliffe, Ann 1764-1823 . . . . . DLB-39, 178

Raddall, Thomas 1903- DLB-68

Radichkov, Yordan 1929- DLB-181

Radiguet, Raymond 1903-1923 . . . . . DLB-65

Radishchev, Aleksandr Nikolaevich
1749-1802 . . . . DLB-150

Radványi, Netty Reiling (see Seghers, Anna)

Rahv, Philip 1908-1973 . . . . DLB-137

Raičković, Stevan 1928- DLB-181

Raimund, Ferdinand Jakob
1790-1836 . . . . DLB-90

Raine, Craig 1944- DLB-40

Raine, Kathleen 1908- DLB-20

Rainolde, Richard
circa 1530-1606 . . . . DLB-136

Rakić, Milan 1876-1938 . . . . DLB-147

Ralegh, Sir Walter 1554?-1618 . . . . . DLB-172

Ralin, Radoy 1923- DLB-181

Ralph, Julian 1853-1903 . . . . DLB-23

Ralph Waldo Emerson in 1982 . . . . . Y-82

Ramat, Silvio 1939- DLB-128

Rambler, no. 4 (1750), by Samuel Johnson
[excerpt] DLB-39

Ramée, Marie Louise de la (see Ouida)

Ramírez, Sergío 1942- DLB-145

Ramke, Bin 1947- DLB-120

Ramler, Karl Wilhelm 1725-1798 . . . DLB-97

Ramon Ribeyro, Julio 1929- DLB-145

Ramous, Mario 1924- DLB-128

Rampersad, Arnold 1941- DLB-111

Ramsay, Allan 1684 or 1685-1758 . . . DLB-95

Ramsay, David 1749-1815 . . . . DLB-30

Ranck, Katherine Quintana
1942- DLB-122

Rand, Avery and Company DLB-49

Rand McNally and Company DLB-49

Randall, David Anton
1905-1975 . . . . DLB-140

Randall, Dudley 1914- DLB-41

Randall, Henry S. 1811-1876 . . . . . . DLB-30

Randall, James G. 1881-1953 . . . . . . DLB-17

The Randall Jarrell Symposium: A Small
Collection of Randall Jarrells
Excerpts From Papers Delivered at
the Randall Jarrell
Symposium Y-86

Randolph, A. Philip 1889-1979 . . . . . DLB-91

Randolph, Anson D. F.
[publishing house] DLB-49

Randolph, Thomas 1605-1635 . . . DLB-58, 126

Random House DLB-46

Ranlet, Henry [publishing house] DLB-49

Ransom, John Crowe
1888-1974 . . . . DLB-45, 63

Ransome, Arthur 1884-1967 . . . . . . DLB-160

Raphael, Frederic 1931- DLB-14

Raphaelson, Samson 1896-1983 . . . . DLB-44

Raskin, Ellen 1928-1984 . . . . DLB-52

Rastell, John 1475?-1536 . . . . . . DLB-136, 170

Rattigan, Terence 1911-1977 . . . . . . DLB-13

Rawlings, Marjorie Kinnan
1896-1953 . . . . DLB-9, 22, 102

Raworth, Tom 1938- DLB-40

Ray, David 1932- DLB-5

Ray, Gordon Norton
1915-1986 . . . . DLB-103, 140

Ray, Henrietta Cordelia
 1849-1916 .... DLB-50
Raymond, Henry J. 1820-1869 ... DLB-43, 79
Raymond Chandler Centenary Tributes
 from Michael Avallone, James Elroy, Joe Gores,
 and William F. Nolan Y-88
Reach, Angus 1821-1856 .... DLB-70
Read, Herbert 1893-1968 ...... DLB-20, 149
Read, Herbert, "The Practice of Biography," in
 The English Sense of Humour and Other Essays DLB-149
Read, Opie 1852-1939 .... DLB-23
Read, Piers Paul 1941- DLB-14
Reade, Charles 1814-1884 .... DLB-21
Reader's Digest Condensed
 Books DLB-46
Reading, Peter 1946- DLB-40
Reading Series in New York City Y-96
Reaney, James 1926- DLB-68
Rebhun, Paul 1500?-1546 .... DLB-179
Rèbora, Clemente 1885-1957 ..... DLB-114
Rechy, John 1934- DLB-122; Y-82
The Recovery of Literature: Criticism in the
 1990s: A Symposium Y-91
Redding, J. Saunders
 1906-1988 .... DLB-63, 76
Redfield, J. S. [publishing house] DLB-49
Redgrove, Peter 1932- DLB-40
Redmon, Anne 1943- Y-86
Redmond, Eugene B. 1937- DLB-41
Redpath, James [publishing house] DLB-49
Reed, Henry 1808-1854 .... DLB-59
Reed, Henry 1914- DLB-27
Reed, Ishmael
 1938- DLB-2, 5, 33, 169; DS-8
Reed, Sampson 1800-1880 .... DLB-1
Reed, Talbot Baines 1852-1893 .... DLB-141
Reedy, William Marion 1862-1920 ... DLB-91
Reese, Lizette Woodworth
 1856-1935 .... DLB-54
Reese, Thomas 1742-1796 .... DLB-37
Reeve, Clara 1729-1807 .... DLB-39
Reeves, James 1909-1978 .... DLB-161
Reeves, John 1926- DLB-88
Regnery, Henry, Company DLB-46
Rehberg, Hans 1901-1963 .... DLB-124
Rehfisch, Hans José 1891-1960 ... DLB-124
Reid, Alastair 1926- DLB-27
Reid, B. L. 1918-1990 .... DLB-111
Reid, Christopher 1949- DLB-40
Reid, Forrest 1875-1947 .... DLB-153
Reid, Helen Rogers 1882-1970 .... DLB-29
Reid, James ?-? DLB-31

Reid, Mayne 1818-1883 .... DLB-21, 163
Reid, Thomas 1710-1796 .... DLB-31
Reid, V. S. (Vic) 1913-1987 .... DLB-125
Reid, Whitelaw 1837-1912 .... DLB-23
Reilly and Lee Publishing
 Company DLB-46
Reimann, Brigitte 1933-1973 ..... DLB-75
Reinmar der Alte
 circa 1165-circa 1205 .... DLB-138
Reinmar von Zweter
 circa 1200-circa 1250 .... DLB-138
Reisch, Walter 1903-1983 .... DLB-44
Remarque, Erich Maria 1898-1970 .. DLB-56
"Re-meeting of Old Friends": The Jack
 Kerouac Conference Y-82
Remington, Frederic 1861-1909 .... DLB-12
Renaud, Jacques 1943- DLB-60
Renault, Mary 1905-1983 .... Y-83
Rendell, Ruth 1930- DLB-87
Representative Men and Women: A Historical
 Perspective on the British Novel,
 1930-1960 .... DLB-15
(Re-)Publishing Orwell Y-86
Rettenbacher, Simon 1634-1706 ... DLB-168
Reuchlin, Johannes 1455-1522 .... DLB-179
Reuter, Christian 1665-after 1712 ... DLB-168
Reuter, Fritz 1810-1874 .... DLB-129
Reuter, Gabriele 1859-1941 ...... DLB-66
Revell, Fleming H., Company DLB-49
Reventlow, Franziska Gräfin zu
 1871-1918 .... DLB-66
Review of Reviews Office DLB-112
Review of [Samuel Richardson's] *Clarissa* (1748),
 by Henry Fielding DLB-39
The Revolt (1937), by Mary Colum
 [excerpts] DLB-36
Rexroth, Kenneth
 1905-1982 ...... DLB-16, 48, 165; Y-82
Rey, H. A. 1898-1977 .... DLB-22
Reynal and Hitchcock DLB-46
Reynolds, G. W. M. 1814-1879 ... DLB-21
Reynolds, John Hamilton
 1794-1852 .... DLB-96
Reynolds, Mack 1917- DLB-8
Reynolds, Sir Joshua 1723-1792 .... DLB-104
Reznikoff, Charles 1894-1976 ... DLB-28, 45
"Rhetoric" (1828; revised, 1859), by
 Thomas de Quincey [excerpt] ... DLB-57
Rhett, Robert Barnwell 1800-1876 ... DLB-43
Rhode, John 1884-1964 .... DLB-77
Rhodes, James Ford 1848-1927 .... DLB-47
Rhys, Jean 1890-1979 ..... DLB-36, 117, 162
Ricardo, David 1772-1823 ..... DLB-107, 158
Ricardou, Jean 1932- DLB-83

Rice, Elmer 1892-1967 .... DLB-4, 7
Rice, Grantland 1880-1954 .... DLB-29, 171
Rich, Adrienne 1929- DLB-5, 67
Richards, David Adams 1950- DLB-53
Richards, George circa 1760-1814 .... DLB-37
Richards, I. A. 1893-1979 .... DLB-27
Richards, Laura E. 1850-1943 ..... DLB-42
Richards, William Carey
 1818-1892 .... DLB-73
Richards, Grant
 [publishing house] DLB-112
Richardson, Charles F. 1851-1913 ... DLB-71
Richardson, Dorothy M.
 1873-1957 .... DLB-36
Richardson, Jack 1935- DLB-7
Richardson, John 1796-1852 ...... DLB-99
Richardson, Samuel
 1689-1761 .... DLB-39, 154
Richardson, Willis 1889-1977 .... DLB-51
Riche, Barnabe 1542-1617 ...... DLB-136
Richler, Mordecai 1931- DLB-53
Richter, Conrad 1890-1968 .... DLB-9
Richter, Hans Werner 1908- DLB-69
Richter, Johann Paul Friedrich
 1763-1825 .... DLB-94
Rickerby, Joseph
 [publishing house] DLB-106
Rickword, Edgell 1898-1982 ..... DLB-20
Riddell, Charlotte 1832-1906 ... DLB-156
Riddell, John (see Ford, Corey)
Ridge, John Rollin 1827-1867 .... DLB-175
Ridge, Lola 1873-1941 .... DLB-54
Ridge, William Pett 1859-1930 .... DLB-135
Riding, Laura (see Jackson, Laura Riding)
Ridler, Anne 1912- DLB-27
Ridruejo, Dionisio 1912-1975 ... DLB-108
Riel, Louis 1844-1885 .... DLB-99
Riemer, Johannes 1648-1714 ..... DLB-168
Riffaterre, Michael 1924- DLB-67
Riggs, Lynn 1899-1954 .... DLB-175
Riis, Jacob 1849-1914 .... DLB-23
Riker, John C. [publishing house] DLB-49
Riley, John 1938-1978 .... DLB-40
Rilke, Rainer Maria 1875-1926 .... DLB-81
Rimanelli, Giose 1926- DLB-177
Rinehart and Company DLB-46
Ringuet 1895-1960 .... DLB-68
Ringwood, Gwen Pharis
 1910-1984 .... DLB-88
Rinser, Luise 1911- DLB-69
Ríos, Alberto 1952- DLB-122
Ríos, Isabella 1948- DLB-82
Ripley, Arthur 1895-1961 .... DLB-44

Ripley, George 1802-1880..... DLB-1, 64, 73
The Rising Glory of America:
 Three Poems DLB-37
The Rising Glory of America: Written in 1771
 (1786), by Hugh Henry Brackenridge and
 Philip Freneau............. DLB-37
Riskin, Robert 1897-1955......... DLB-26
Risse, Heinz 1898-............ DLB-69
Rist, Johann 1607-1667 .... DLB-164
Ritchie, Anna Mowatt 1819-1870 ..... DLB-3
Ritchie, Anne Thackeray
 1837-1919 .... DLB-18
Ritchie, Thomas 1778-1854........ DLB-43
Rites of Passage
 [on William Saroyan] Y-83
The Ritz Paris Hemingway Award Y-85
Rivard, Adjutor 1868-1945 .... DLB-92
Rive, Richard 1931-1989 .... DLB-125
Rivera, Marina 1942- DLB-122
Rivera, Tomás 1935-1984 .... DLB-82
Rivers, Conrad Kent 1933-1968 ..... DLB-41
Riverside Press DLB-49
Rivington, James circa 1724-1802 .... DLB-43
Rivington, Charles
 [publishing house].......... DLB-154
Rivkin, Allen 1903-1990 .... DLB-26
Roa Bastos, Augusto 1917- DLB-113
Robbe-Grillet, Alain 1922- DLB-83
Robbins, Tom 1936- Y-80
Roberts, Charles G. D. 1860-1943.... DLB-92
Roberts, Dorothy 1906-1993 .... DLB-88
Roberts, Elizabeth Madox
 1881-1941............ DLB-9, 54, 102
Roberts, Kenneth 1885-1957....... DLB-9
Roberts, William 1767-1849....... DLB-142
Roberts Brothers DLB-49
Roberts, James [publishing house] ... DLB-154
Robertson, A. M., and Company DLB-49
Robertson, William 1721-1793 ..... DLB-104
Robinson, Casey 1903-1979 .... DLB-44
Robinson, Edwin Arlington
 1869-1935................ DLB-54
Robinson, Henry Crabb
 1775-1867 .... DLB-107
Robinson, James Harvey
 1863-1936................ DLB-47
Robinson, Lennox 1886-1958...... DLB-10
Robinson, Mabel Louise
 1874-1962 .... DLB-22
Robinson, Mary 1758-1800 .... DLB-158
Robinson, Richard
 circa 1545-1607 .... DLB-167
Robinson, Therese
 1797-1870 .... DLB-59, 133

Robison, Mary 1949- DLB-130
Roblès, Emmanuel 1914- DLB-83
Roccatagliata Ceccardi, Ceccardo
 1871-1919 .... DLB-114
Rochester, John Wilmot, Earl of
 1647-1680 .... DLB-131
Rock, Howard 1911-1976........ DLB-127
Rodgers, Carolyn M. 1945- DLB-41
Rodgers, W. R. 1909-1969........ DLB-20
Rodríguez, Claudio 1934- DLB-134
Rodriguez, Richard 1944- DLB-82
Rodríguez Julia, Edgardo
 1946- DLB-145
Roethke, Theodore 1908-1963...... DLB-5
Rogers, Pattiann 1940- DLB-105
Rogers, Samuel 1763-1855 .... DLB-93
Rogers, Will 1879-1935.......... DLB-11
Rohmer, Sax 1883-1959 .... DLB-70
Roiphe, Anne 1935- Y-80
Rojas, Arnold R. 1896-1988 ...... DLB-82
Rolfe, Frederick William
 1860-1913 .... DLB-34, 156
Rolland, Romain 1866-1944 ...... DLB-65
Rolle, Richard
 circa 1290-1300 - 1340 ...... DLB-146
Rölvaag, O. E. 1876-1931......... DLB-9
Romains, Jules 1885-1972........ DLB-65
Roman, A., and Company........ DLB-49
Romano, Lalla 1906- DLB-177
Romano, Octavio 1923- DLB-122
Romero, Leo 1950- DLB-122
Romero, Lin 1947- DLB-122
Romero, Orlando 1945- DLB-82
Rook, Clarence 1863-1915 ...... DLB-135
Roosevelt, Theodore 1858-1919 .... DLB-47
Root, Waverley 1903-1982......... DLB-4
Root, William Pitt 1941- DLB-120
Roquebrune, Robert de 1889-1978.... DLB-68
Rosa, João Guimarães
 1908-1967 .... DLB-113
Rosales, Luis 1910-1992......... DLB-134
Roscoe, William 1753-1831 ...... DLB-163
Rose, Reginald 1920- DLB-26
Rose, Wendy 1948- DLB-175
Rosegger, Peter 1843-1918........ DLB-129
Rosei, Peter 1946- DLB-85
Rosen, Norma 1925- DLB-28
Rosenbach, A. S. W. 1876-1952 ... DLB-140
Rosenberg, Isaac 1890-1918....... DLB-20
Rosenfeld, Isaac 1918-1956....... DLB-28
Rosenthal, M. L. 1917- DLB-5
Ross, Alexander 1591-1654 ...... DLB-151

Ross, Harold 1892-1951......... DLB-137
Ross, Leonard Q. (see Rosten, Leo)
Ross, Martin 1862-1915......... DLB-135
Ross, Sinclair 1908- DLB-88
Ross, W. W. E. 1894-1966 .... DLB-88
Rosselli, Amelia 1930-.......... DLB-128
Rossen, Robert 1908-1966 .... DLB-26
Rossetti, Christina Georgina
 1830-1894............. DLB-35, 163
Rossetti, Dante Gabriel 1828-1882.... DLB-35
Rossner, Judith 1935- DLB-6
Rosten, Leo 1908- DLB-11
Rostenberg, Leona 1908-......... DLB-140
Rostovsky, Dimitrii 1651-1709 ..... DLB-150
Bertram Rota and His Bookshop...... Y-91
Roth, Gerhard 1942- DLB-85, 124
Roth, Henry 1906?-............ DLB-28
Roth, Joseph 1894-1939......... DLB-85
Roth, Philip 1933- DLB-2, 28, 173; Y-82
Rothenberg, Jerome 1931- DLB-5
Rotimi, Ola 1938- DLB-125
Routhier, Adolphe-Basile
 1839-1920................ DLB-99
Routier, Simone 1901-1987........ DLB-88
Routledge, George, and Sons..... DLB-106
Roversi, Roberto 1923- DLB-128
Rowe, Elizabeth Singer
 1674-1737............. DLB-39, 95
Rowe, Nicholas 1674-1718 .... DLB-84
Rowlands, Samuel
 circa 1570-1630 .... DLB-121
Rowlandson, Mary
 circa 1635-circa 1678.......... DLB-24
Rowley, William circa 1585-1626 .... DLB-58
Rowse, A. L. 1903- DLB-155
Rowson, Susanna Haswell
 circa 1762-1824............. DLB-37
Roy, Camille 1870-1943 .... DLB-92
Roy, Gabrielle 1909-1983......... DLB-68
Roy, Jules 1907- DLB-83
The Royal Court Theatre and the English
 Stage Company............ DLB-13
The Royal Court Theatre and the New Drama
 .... DLB-10
The Royal Shakespeare Company
 at the Swan Y-88
Royall, Anne 1769-1854 .... DLB-43
The Roycroft Printing Shop DLB-49
Royster, Vermont 1914- DLB-127
Royston, Richard
 [publishing house] DLB-170
Ruark, Gibbons 1941- DLB-120
Ruban, Vasilii Grigorevich
 1742-1795 .... DLB-150

460

Rubens, Bernice 1928- DLB-14
Rudd and Carleton DLB-49
Rudkin, David 1936- DLB-13
Rudolf von Ems
  circa 1200-circa 1254 .... DLB-138
Ruffin, Josephine St. Pierre
  1842-1924 .... DLB-79
Ruganda, John 1941- DLB-157
Ruggles, Henry Joseph 1813-1906 .... DLB-64
Rukeyser, Muriel 1913-1980 ...... DLB-48
Rule, Jane 1931- DLB-60
Rulfo, Juan 1918-1986 .... DLB-113
Rumaker, Michael 1932- DLB-16
Rumens, Carol 1944- DLB-40
Runyon, Damon 1880-1946 . . DLB-11, 86, 171
Ruodlieb circa 1050-1075 .... DLB-148
Rush, Benjamin 1746-1813 .... DLB-37
Rusk, Ralph L. 1888-1962 .... DLB-103
Ruskin, John 1819-1900 ...... DLB-55, 163
Russ, Joanna 1937- DLB-8
Russell, B. B., and Company DLB-49
Russell, Benjamin 1761-1845 ..... DLB-43
Russell, Bertrand 1872-1970 ..... DLB-100
Russell, Charles Edward
  1860-1941 .... DLB-25
Russell, George William (see AE)
Russell, R. H., and Son DLB-49
Rutherford, Mark 1831-1913 ...... DLB-18
Ryan, Michael 1946- Y-82
Ryan, Oscar 1904- DLB-68
Ryga, George 1932- DLB-60
Rymer, Thomas 1643?-1713 .... DLB-101
Ryskind, Morrie 1895-1985 .... DLB-26
Rzhevsky, Aleksei Andreevich
  1737-1804 .... DLB-150

S

The Saalfield Publishing
  Company DLB-46
Von Saaz, Johannes (see von Tepl, Johannes)
Saba, Umberto 1883-1957 .... DLB-114
Sábato, Ernesto 1911- DLB-145
Saberhagen, Fred 1930- DLB-8
Sacer, Gottfried Wilhelm
  1635-1699 .... DLB-168
Sachs, Hans 1494-1576 .... DLB-179
Sackler, Howard 1929-1982 .... DLB-7
Sackville, Thomas 1536-1608 ..... DLB-132
Sackville, Thomas 1536-1608
  and Norton, Thomas
  1532-1584 .... DLB-62

Sackville-West, V. 1892-1962 ..... DLB-34
Sadlier, D. and J., and Company ... DLB-49
Sadlier, Mary Anne 1820-1903 .... DLB-99
Sadoff, Ira 1945- DLB-120
Saenz, Jaime 1921-1986 .... DLB-145
Saffin, John circa 1626-1710 ..... DLB-24
Sagan, Françoise 1935- DLB-83
Sage, Robert 1899-1962 .... DLB-4
Sagel, Jim 1947- DLB-82
Sagendorph, Robb Hansell
  1900-1970 .... DLB-137
Sahagún, Carlos 1938- DLB-108
Sahkomaapii, Piitai (see Highwater, Jamake)
Sahl, Hans 1902- DLB-69
Said, Edward W. 1935- DLB-67
Saiko, George 1892-1962 .... DLB-85
St. Dominic's Press DLB-112
Saint-Exupéry, Antoine de
  1900-1944 .... DLB-72
St. Johns, Adela Rogers 1894-1988 . . . DLB-29
St. Martin's Press DLB-46
St. Omer, Garth 1931- DLB-117
Saint Pierre, Michel de 1916-1987 . . . DLB-83
Saintsbury, George
  1845-1933 .... DLB-57, 149
Saki (see Munro, H. H.)
Salaam, Kalamu ya 1947- DLB-38
Šalamun, Tomaž 1941- DLB-181
Salas, Floyd 1931- DLB-82
Sálaz-Marquez, Rubén 1935- DLB-122
Salemson, Harold J. 1910-1988 .... DLB-4
Salinas, Luis Omar 1937- DLB-82
Salinas, Pedro 1891-1951 .... DLB-134
Salinger, J. D. 1919- DLB-2, 102, 173
Salkey, Andrew 1928- DLB-125
Salt, Waldo 1914- DLB-44
Salter, James 1925- DLB-130
Salter, Mary Jo 1954- DLB-120
Salustri, Carlo Alberto (see Trilussa)
Salverson, Laura Goodman
  1890-1970 .... DLB-92
Sampson, Richard Henry (see Hull, Richard)
Samuels, Ernest 1903- DLB-111
Sanborn, Franklin Benjamin
  1831-1917 .... DLB-1
Sánchez, Luis Rafael 1936- DLB-145
Sánchez, Philomeno "Phil"
  1917- DLB-122
Sánchez, Ricardo 1941- DLB-82
Sanchez, Sonia 1934- DLB-41; DS-8
Sand, George 1804-1876 .... DLB-119
Sandburg, Carl 1878-1967 ...... DLB-17, 54

Sanders, Ed 1939- DLB-16
Sandoz, Mari 1896-1966 .... DLB-9
Sandwell, B. K. 1876-1954 .... DLB-92
Sandy, Stephen 1934- DLB-165
Sandys, George 1578-1644 .... DLB-24, 121
Sangster, Charles 1822-1893 ..... DLB-99
Sanguineti, Edoardo 1930- DLB-128
Sansom, William 1912-1976 ..... DLB-139
Santayana, George
  1863-1952 .... DLB-54, 71; DS-13
Santiago, Danny 1911-1988 ...... DLB-122
Santmyer, Helen Hooven 1895-1986 .... Y-84
Sapidus, Joannes 1490-1561 ..... DLB-179
Sapir, Edward 1884-1939 .... DLB-92
Sapper (see McNeile, Herman Cyril)
Sappho circa 620 B.C.-circa 550 B.C.
  .... DLB-176
Sarduy, Severo 1937- DLB-113
Sargent, Pamela 1948- DLB-8
Saro-Wiwa, Ken 1941- DLB-157
Saroyan, William
  1908-1981 .... DLB-7, 9, 86; Y-81
Sarraute, Nathalie 1900- DLB-83
Sarrazin, Albertine 1937-1967 .... DLB-83
Sarris, Greg 1952- DLB-175
Sarton, May 1912- DLB-48; Y-81
Sartre, Jean-Paul 1905-1980 ..... DLB-72
Sassoon, Siegfried 1886-1967 .... DLB-20
Sata, Ineko 1904- DLB-180
Saturday Review Press DLB-46
Saunders, James 1925- DLB-13
Saunders, John Monk 1897-1940 .... DLB-26
Saunders, Margaret Marshall
  1861-1947 .... DLB-92
Saunders and Otley DLB-106
Savage, James 1784-1873 .... DLB-30
Savage, Marmion W. 1803?-1872 . . . DLB-21
Savage, Richard 1697?-1743 ..... DLB-95
Savard, Félix-Antoine 1896-1982 .... DLB-68
Saville, (Leonard) Malcolm
  1901-1982 .... DLB-160
Sawyer, Ruth 1880-1970 .... DLB-22
Sayers, Dorothy L.
  1893-1957 .... DLB-10, 36, 77, 100
Sayles, John Thomas 1950- DLB-44
Sbarbaro, Camillo 1888-1967 .... DLB-114
Scannell, Vernon 1922- DLB-27
Scarry, Richard 1919-1994 ...... DLB-61
Schaeffer, Albrecht 1885-1950 ... DLB-66
Schaeffer, Susan Fromberg 1941- DLB-28
Schaff, Philip 1819-1893 .... DS-13
Schaper, Edzard 1908-1984 ..... DLB-69

Scharf, J. Thomas 1843-1898 . . . . . . DLB-47

Schede, Paul Melissus 1539-1602 . . . . DLB-179

Scheffel, Joseph Viktor von
  1826-1886 . . . . DLB-129

Scheffler, Johann 1624-1677 . . . . . . DLB-164

Schelling, Friedrich Wilhelm Joseph von
  1775-1854 . . . . DLB-90

Scherer, Wilhelm 1841-1886 . . . . . . DLB-129

Schickele, René 1883-1940 . . . . DLB-66

Schiff, Dorothy 1903-1989 . . . . DLB-127

Schiller, Friedrich 1759-1805 . . . . . . DLB-94

Schirmer, David 1623-1687 . . . . DLB-164

Schlaf, Johannes 1862-1941 . . . . DLB-118

Schlegel, August Wilhelm
  1767-1845 . . . . DLB-94

Schlegel, Dorothea 1763-1839 . . . . . . DLB-90

Schlegel, Friedrich 1772-1829 . . . . . . DLB-90

Schleiermacher, Friedrich
  1768-1834 . . . . DLB-90

Schlesinger, Arthur M., Jr. 1917- DLB-17

Schlumberger, Jean 1877-1968 . . . . . DLB-65

Schmid, Eduard Hermann Wilhelm (see Edschmid, Kasimir)

Schmidt, Arno 1914-1979 . . . . DLB-69

Schmidt, Johann Kaspar (see Stirner, Max)

Schmidt, Michael 1947- DLB-40

Schmidtbonn, Wilhelm August
  1876-1952 . . . . DLB-118

Schmitz, James H. 1911- DLB-8

Schnabel, Johann Gottfried
  1692-1760 . . . . DLB-168

Schnackenberg, Gjertrud 1953- DLB-120

Schnitzler, Arthur 1862-1931 . . . . DLB-81, 118

Schnurre, Wolfdietrich 1920- DLB-69

Schocken Books DLB-46

Scholartis Press DLB-112

The Schomburg Center for Research
  in Black Culture DLB-76

Schönbeck, Virgilio (see Giotti, Virgilio)

Schönherr, Karl 1867-1943 . . . . DLB-118

Schoolcraft, Jane Johnston
  1800-1841 . . . . DLB-175

School Stories, 1914-1960 . . . . DLB-160

Schopenhauer, Arthur 1788-1860 . . . . DLB-90

Schopenhauer, Johanna 1766-1838 . . . DLB-90

Schorer, Mark 1908-1977 . . . . DLB-103

Schottelius, Justus Georg
  1612-1676 . . . . DLB-164

Schouler, James 1839-1920 . . . . DLB-47

Schrader, Paul 1946- DLB-44

Schreiner, Olive 1855-1920 . . . . DLB-18, 156

Schroeder, Andreas 1946- DLB-53

Schubart, Christian Friedrich Daniel
  1739-1791 . . . . DLB-97

Schubert, Gotthilf Heinrich
  1780-1860 . . . . DLB-90

Schücking, Levin 1814-1883 . . . . . . DLB-133

Schulberg, Budd
  1914- DLB-6, 26, 28; Y-81

Schulte, F. J., and Company DLB-49

Schulze, Hans (see Praetorius, Johannes)

Schupp, Johann Balthasar
  1610-1661 . . . . DLB-164

Schurz, Carl 1829-1906 . . . . DLB-23

Schuyler, George S. 1895-1977 . . . DLB-29, 51

Schuyler, James 1923-1991 . . . . . . DLB-5, 169

Schwartz, Delmore 1913-1966 . . . . DLB-28, 48

Schwartz, Jonathan 1938- Y-82

Schwarz, Sibylle 1621-1638 . . . . DLB-164

Schwerner, Armand 1927- DLB-165

Schwob, Marcel 1867-1905 . . . . DLB-123

Sciascia, Leonardo 1921-1989 . . . . . . DLB-177

Science Fantasy DLB-8

Science-Fiction Fandom and
  Conventions DLB-8

Science-Fiction Fanzines: The Time
  Binders DLB-8

Science-Fiction Films DLB-8

Science Fiction Writers of America and the
  Nebula Awards DLB-8

Scot, Reginald circa 1538-1599 . . . . . DLB-136

Scotellaro, Rocco 1923-1953 . . . . . . DLB-128

Scott, Dennis 1939-1991 . . . . DLB-125

Scott, Dixon 1881-1915 . . . . DLB-98

Scott, Duncan Campbell
  1862-1947 . . . . DLB-92

Scott, Evelyn 1893-1963 . . . . DLB-9, 48

Scott, F. R. 1899-1985 . . . . DLB-88

Scott, Frederick George
  1861-1944 . . . . DLB-92

Scott, Geoffrey 1884-1929 . . . . DLB-149

Scott, Harvey W. 1838-1910 . . . . . . DLB-23

Scott, Paul 1920-1978 . . . . DLB-14

Scott, Sarah 1723-1795 . . . . DLB-39

Scott, Tom 1918- DLB-27

Scott, Sir Walter
  1771-1832 . . . . DLB-93, 107, 116, 144, 159

Scott, William Bell 1811-1890 . . . . . DLB-32

Scott, Walter, Publishing
  Company Limited DLB-112

Scott, William R.
  [publishing house] DLB-46

Scott-Heron, Gil 1949- DLB-41

Scribner, Charles, Jr. 1921-1995 . . . . . Y-95

Charles Scribner's Sons DLB-49; DS-13

Scripps, E. W. 1854-1926 . . . . DLB-25

Scudder, Horace Elisha
  1838-1902 . . . . DLB-42, 71

Scudder, Vida Dutton 1861-1954 . . . . DLB-71

Scupham, Peter 1933- DLB-40

Seabrook, William 1886-1945 . . . . . . DLB-4

Seabury, Samuel 1729-1796 . . . . DLB-31

Seacole, Mary Jane Grant
  1805-1881 . . . . DLB-166

The Seafarer circa 970 . . . . DLB-146

Sealsfield, Charles 1793-1864 . . . . . . DLB-133

Sears, Edward I. 1819?-1876 . . . . . . DLB-79

Sears Publishing Company DLB-46

Seaton, George 1911-1979 . . . . DLB-44

Seaton, William Winston
  1785-1866 . . . . DLB-43

Secker, Martin, and Warburg
  Limited DLB-112

Secker, Martin [publishing house] DLB-112

Second-Generation Minor Poets of the
  Seventeenth Century DLB-126

Sedgwick, Arthur George
  1844-1915 . . . . DLB-64

Sedgwick, Catharine Maria
  1789-1867 . . . . DLB-1, 74

Sedgwick, Ellery 1872-1930 . . . . DLB-91

Sedley, Sir Charles 1639-1701 . . . . . DLB-131

Seeger, Alan 1888-1916 . . . . DLB-45

Seers, Eugene (see Dantin, Louis)

Segal, Erich 1937- Y-86

Šegedin, Petar 1909- DLB-181

Seghers, Anna 1900-1983 . . . . DLB-69

Seid, Ruth (see Sinclair, Jo)

Seidel, Frederick Lewis 1936- Y-84

Seidel, Ina 1885-1974 . . . . DLB-56

Seigenthaler, John 1927- DLB-127

Seizin Press DLB-112

Séjour, Victor 1817-1874 . . . . DLB-50

Séjour Marcou et Ferrand, Juan Victor (see Séjour, Victor)

Selby, Hubert, Jr. 1928- DLB-2

Selden, George 1929-1989 . . . . DLB-52

Selected English-Language Little Magazines
  and Newspapers [France,
  1920-1939] DLB-4

Selected Humorous Magazines
  (1820-1950) DLB-11

Selected Science-Fiction Magazines and
  Anthologies DLB-8

Selenić, Slobodan 1933-1995 . . . . . . DLB-181

Self, Edwin F. 1920- DLB-137

Seligman, Edwin R. A. 1861-1939 . . . . DLB-47

Selimović, Meša 1910-1982 . . . . DLB-181

Selous, Frederick Courteney
  1851-1917 . . . . DLB-174

Seltzer, Chester E. (see Muro, Amado)

Seltzer, Thomas
 [publishing house]............ DLB-46
Selvon, Sam 1923-1994 .... DLB-125
Senancour, Etienne de 1770-1846.... DLB-119
Sendak, Maurice 1928- DLB-61
Senécal, Eva 1905- DLB-92
Sengstacke, John 1912- DLB-127
Senior, Olive 1941- DLB-157
Šenoa, August 1838-1881 .... DLB-147
"Sensation Novels" (1863), by
 H. L. Manse DLB-21
Sepamla, Sipho 1932- DLB-157
Seredy, Kate 1899-1975.......... DLB-22
Sereni, Vittorio 1913-1983...... DLB-128
Seres, William
 [publishing house]........... DLB-170
Serling, Rod 1924-1975.......... DLB-26
Serote, Mongane Wally 1944- DLB-125
Serraillier, Ian 1912-1994 .... DLB-161
Serrano, Nina 1934- DLB-122
Service, Robert 1874-1958 .... DLB-92
Seth, Vikram 1952- DLB-120
Seton, Ernest Thompson
 1860-1942............. DLB-92; DS-13
Settle, Mary Lee 1918- DLB-6
Seume, Johann Gottfried
 1763-1810................ DLB-94
Seuse, Heinrich 1295?-1366....... DLB-179
Seuss, Dr. (see Geisel, Theodor Seuss)
The Seventy-fifth Anniversary of the Armistice:
 The Wilfred Owen Centenary and the Great
 War Exhibit at the University of
 Virginia.................... Y-93
Sewall, Joseph 1688-1769 .... DLB-24
Sewall, Richard B. 1908- DLB-111
Sewell, Anna 1820-1878.......... DLB-163
Sewell, Samuel 1652-1730. .... DLB-24
Sex, Class, Politics, and Religion [in the
 British Novel, 1930-1959] DLB-15
Sexton, Anne 1928-1974 .... DLB-5, 169
Seymour-Smith, Martin 1928- DLB-155
Shaara, Michael 1929-1988........... Y-83
Shadwell, Thomas 1641?-1692...... DLB-80
Shaffer, Anthony 1926- DLB-13
Shaffer, Peter 1926- DLB-13
Shaftesbury, Anthony Ashley Cooper,
 Third Earl of 1671-1713 ...... DLB-101
Shairp, Mordaunt 1887-1939 ...... DLB-10
Shakespeare, William
 1564-1616............. DLB-62, 172
The Shakespeare Globe Trust........ Y-93
Shakespeare Head Press........ DLB-112
Shakhovskoi, Aleksandr Aleksandrovich
 1777-1846............... DLB-150

Shange, Ntozake 1948- DLB-38
Shapiro, Karl 1913- DLB-48
Sharon Publications DLB-46
Sharp, Margery 1905-1991 ...... DLB-161
Sharp, William 1855-1905....... DLB-156
Sharpe, Tom 1928- DLB-14
Shaw, Albert 1857-1947......... DLB-91
Shaw, Bernard 1856-1950 ..... DLB-10, 57
Shaw, Henry Wheeler 1818-1885 .... DLB-11
Shaw, Joseph T. 1874-1952....... DLB-137
Shaw, Irwin 1913-1984 .... DLB-6, 102; Y-84
Shaw, Robert 1927-1978 ...... DLB-13, 14
Shaw, Robert B. 1947- DLB-120
Shawn, William 1907-1992 ...... DLB-137
Shay, Frank [publishing house]...... DLB-46
Shea, John Gilmary 1824-1892..... DLB-30
Sheaffer, Louis 1912-1993........ DLB-103
Shearing, Joseph 1886-1952...... DLB-70
Shebbeare, John 1709-1788 ...... DLB-39
Sheckley, Robert 1928- DLB-8
Shedd, William G. T. 1820-1894 ... DLB-64
Sheed, Wilfred 1930- DLB-6
Sheed and Ward [U.S.]......... DLB-46
Sheed and Ward Limited [U.K.] ... DLB-112
Sheldon, Alice B. (see Tiptree, James, Jr.)
Sheldon, Edward 1886-1946...... DLB-7
Sheldon and Company DLB-49
Shelley, Mary Wollstonecraft
 1797-1851..... DLB-110, 116, 159, 178
Shelley, Percy Bysshe
 1792-1822.......... DLB-96, 110, 158
Shelnutt, Eve 1941- DLB-130
Shenstone, William 1714-1763 ..... DLB-95
Shepard, Ernest Howard
 1879-1976 .... DLB-160
Shepard, Sam 1943- DLB-7
Shepard, Thomas I,
 1604 or 1605-1649 .... DLB-24
Shepard, Thomas II, 1635-1677 .... DLB-24
Shepard, Clark and Brown....... DLB-49
Shepherd, Luke
 flourished 1547-1554 .... DLB-136
Sherburne, Edward 1616-1702 .... DLB-131
Sheridan, Frances 1724-1766 .... DLB-39, 84
Sheridan, Richard Brinsley
 1751-1816................ DLB-89
Sherman, Francis 1871-1926 ..... DLB-92
Sherriff, R. C. 1896-1975......... DLB-10
Sherry, Norman 1935- DLB-155
Sherwood, Mary Martha
 1775-1851 .... DLB-163
Sherwood, Robert 1896-1955 .... DLB-7, 26
Shiel, M. P. 1865-1947 .... DLB-153

Shiels, George 1886-1949........ DLB-10
Shiga, Naoya 1883-1971 .... DLB-180
Shillaber, B.[enjamin] P.[enhallow]
 1814-1890 .... DLB-1, 11
Shimazaki, Tōson 1872-1943 ..... DLB-180
Shine, Ted 1931- DLB-38
Ship, Reuben 1915-1975 .... DLB-88
Shirer, William L. 1904-1993 ...... DLB-4
Shirinsky-Shikhmatov, Sergii Aleksandrovich
 1783-1837 .... DLB-150
Shirley, James 1596-1666 .... DLB-58
Shishkov, Aleksandr Semenovich
 1753-1841 .... DLB-150
Shockley, Ann Allen 1927- DLB-33
Short, Peter
 [publishing house]........... DLB-170
Shorthouse, Joseph Henry
 1834-1903 .... DLB-18
Showalter, Elaine 1941- DLB-67
Shulevitz, Uri 1935- DLB-61
Shulman, Max 1919-1988........ DLB-11
Shute, Henry A. 1856-1943 .... DLB-9
Shuttle, Penelope 1947- DLB-14, 40
Sibbes, Richard 1577-1635....... DLB-151
Sidgwick and Jackson Limited DLB-112
Sidney, Margaret (see Lothrop, Harriet M.)
Sidney, Mary 1561-1621......... DLB-167
Sidney, Sir Philip 1554-1586 ...... DLB-167
Sidney's Press DLB-49
Siegfried Loraine Sassoon: A Centenary Essay
 Tributes from Vivien F. Clarke and
 Michael Thorpe Y-86
Sierra, Rubén 1946- DLB-122
Sierra Club Books DLB-49
Siger of Brabant
 circa 1240-circa 1284 .... DLB-115
Sigourney, Lydia Howard (Huntley)
 1791-1865 .... DLB-1, 42, 73
Silkin, Jon 1930- DLB-27
Silko, Leslie Marmon
 1948- DLB-143, 175
Silliman, Ron 1946- DLB-169
Silliphant, Stirling 1918- DLB-26
Sillitoe, Alan 1928- DLB-14, 139
Silman, Roberta 1934- DLB-28
Silva, Beverly 1930- DLB-122
Silverberg, Robert 1935- DLB-8
Silverman, Kenneth 1936- DLB-111
Simak, Clifford D. 1904-1988 ...... DLB-8
Simcoe, Elizabeth 1762-1850 ..... DLB-99
Simcox, George Augustus
 1841-1905 .... DLB-35
Sime, Jessie Georgina 1868-1958 .... DLB-92

Simenon, Georges 1903-1989 . . . . DLB-72; Y-89

Simic, Charles 1938- DLB-105

Simic, Charles, Images and "Images" DLB-105

Simmel, Johannes Mario 1924- DLB-69

Simmes, Valentine [publishing house] DLB-170

Simmons, Ernest J. 1903-1972 . . . . . DLB-103

Simmons, Herbert Alfred 1930- DLB-33

Simmons, James 1933- DLB-40

Simms, William Gilmore 1806-1870 . . . . DLB-3, 30, 59, 73

Simms and M'Intyre DLB-106

Simon, Claude 1913- DLB-83

Simon, Neil 1927- DLB-7

Simon and Schuster DLB-46

Simons, Katherine Drayton Mayrant 1890-1969 . . . . Y-83

Simović, Ljubomir 1935- DLB-181

Simpkin and Marshall [publishing house] DLB-154

Simpson, Helen 1897-1940 . . . . DLB-77

Simpson, Louis 1923- DLB-5

Simpson, N. F. 1919- DLB-13

Sims, George 1923- DLB-87

Sims, George Robert 1847-1922 . . . . DLB-35, 70, 135

Sinán, Rogelio 1904- DLB-145

Sinclair, Andrew 1935- DLB-14

Sinclair, Bertrand William 1881-1972 . . . . DLB-92

Sinclair, Catherine 1800-1864 . . . . DLB-163

Sinclair, Jo 1913- DLB-28

Sinclair Lewis Centennial Conference Y-85

Sinclair, Lister 1921- DLB-88

Sinclair, May 1863-1946 . . . . . . DLB-36, 135

Sinclair, Upton 1878-1968 . . . . DLB-9

Sinclair, Upton [publishing house] DLB-46

Singer, Isaac Bashevis 1904-1991 . . . . DLB-6, 28, 52; Y-91

Singmaster, Elsie 1879-1958 . . . . DLB-9

Sinisgalli, Leonardo 1908-1981 . . . . . DLB-114

Siodmak, Curt 1902- DLB-44

Sissman, L. E. 1928-1976 . . . . DLB-5

Sisson, C. H. 1914- DLB-27

Sitwell, Edith 1887-1964 . . . . DLB-20

Sitwell, Osbert 1892-1969 . . . . DLB-100

Skármeta, Antonio 1940- DLB-145

Skeffington, William [publishing house] DLB-106

Skelton, John 1463-1529 . . . . DLB-136

Skelton, Robin 1925- DLB-27, 53

Skinner, Constance Lindsay 1877-1939 . . . . DLB-92

Skinner, John Stuart 1788-1851 . . . . . DLB-73

Skipsey, Joseph 1832-1903 . . . . DLB-35

Slade, Bernard 1930- DLB-53

Slamnig, Ivan 1930- DLB-181

Slater, Patrick 1880-1951 . . . . DLB-68

Slaveykov, Pencho 1866-1912 . . . . . DLB-147

Slaviček, Milivoj 1929- DLB-181

Slavitt, David 1935- DLB-5, 6

Sleigh, Burrows Willcocks Arthur 1821-1869 . . . . DLB-99

A Slender Thread of Hope: The Kennedy Center Black Theatre Project DLB-38

Slesinger, Tess 1905-1945 . . . . DLB-102

Slick, Sam (see Haliburton, Thomas Chandler)

Sloane, William, Associates DLB-46

Small, Maynard and Company DLB-49

Small Presses in Great Britain and Ireland, 1960-1985 . . . . DLB-40

Small Presses I: Jargon Society Y-84

Small Presses II: The Spirit That Moves Us Press Y-85

Small Presses III: Pushcart Press Y-87

Smart, Christopher 1722-1771 . . . . . DLB-109

Smart, David A. 1892-1957 . . . . . . DLB-137

Smart, Elizabeth 1913-1986 . . . . . . DLB-88

Smellie, William [publishing house] DLB-154

Smiles, Samuel 1812-1904 . . . . DLB-55

Smith, A. J. M. 1902-1980 . . . . DLB-88

Smith, Adam 1723-1790 . . . . DLB-104

Smith, Alexander 1829-1867 . . . . . DLB-32, 55

Smith, Betty 1896-1972 . . . . Y-82

Smith, Carol Sturm 1938- Y-81

Smith, Charles Henry 1826-1903 . . . . DLB-11

Smith, Charlotte 1749-1806 . . . . . DLB-39, 109

Smith, Chet 1899-1973 . . . . DLB-171

Smith, Cordwainer 1913-1966 . . . . . . DLB-8

Smith, Dave 1942- DLB-5

Smith, Dodie 1896- DLB-10

Smith, Doris Buchanan 1934- DLB-52

Smith, E. E. 1890-1965 . . . . DLB-8

Smith, Elihu Hubbard 1771-1798 . . . . DLB-37

Smith, Elizabeth Oakes (Prince) 1806-1893 . . . . DLB-1

Smith, F. Hopkinson 1838-1915 . . . . . DS-13

Smith, George D. 1870-1920 . . . . . DLB-140

Smith, George O. 1911-1981 . . . . . . DLB-8

Smith, Goldwin 1823-1910 . . . . DLB-99

Smith, H. Allen 1907-1976 . . . . . . DLB-11, 29

Smith, Hazel Brannon 1914- DLB-127

Smith, Henry circa 1560-circa 1591 . . . . DLB-136

Smith, Horatio (Horace) 1779-1849 . . . . DLB-116

Smith, Horatio (Horace) 1779-1849 and James Smith 1775-1839 . . . . DLB-96

Smith, Iain Crichton 1928- DLB-40, 139

Smith, J. Allen 1860-1924 . . . . DLB-47

Smith, John 1580-1631 . . . . DLB-24, 30

Smith, Josiah 1704-1781 . . . . DLB-24

Smith, Ken 1938- DLB-40

Smith, Lee 1944- DLB-143; Y-83

Smith, Logan Pearsall 1865-1946 . . . . . DLB-98

Smith, Mark 1935- Y-82

Smith, Michael 1698-circa 1771 . . . . . DLB-31

Smith, Red 1905-1982 . . . . DLB-29, 171

Smith, Roswell 1829-1892 . . . . DLB-79

Smith, Samuel Harrison 1772-1845 . . . . DLB-43

Smith, Samuel Stanhope 1751-1819 . . . . DLB-37

Smith, Sarah (see Stretton, Hesba)

Smith, Seba 1792-1868 . . . . DLB-1, 11

Smith, Sir Thomas 1513-1577 . . . . . DLB-132

Smith, Stevie 1902-1971 . . . . DLB-20

Smith, Sydney 1771-1845 . . . . DLB-107

Smith, Sydney Goodsir 1915-1975 . . . . DLB-27

Smith, Wendell 1914-1972 . . . . DLB-171

Smith, William flourished 1595-1597 . . . . DLB-136

Smith, William 1727-1803 . . . . DLB-31

Smith, William 1728-1793 . . . . DLB-30

Smith, William Gardner 1927-1974 . . . . DLB-76

Smith, William Henry 1808-1872 . . . . DLB-159

Smith, William Jay 1918- DLB-5

Smith, Elder and Company DLB-154

Smith, Harrison, and Robert Haas [publishing house] DLB-46

Smith, J. Stilman, and Company DLB-49

Smith, W. B., and Company DLB-49

Smith, W. H., and Son DLB-106

Smithers, Leonard [publishing house] DLB-112

Smollett, Tobias 1721-1771 . . . . . DLB-39, 104

Snellings, Rolland (see Touré, Askia Muhammad)

Snodgrass, W. D. 1926- DLB-5

Snow, C. P. 1905-1980 . . . . DLB-15, 77

Snyder, Gary 1930- DLB-5, 16, 165

Sobiloff, Hy 1912-1970 . . . . DLB-48

The Society for Textual Scholarship and
   TEXT Y-87
The Society for the History of Authorship, Reading and Publishing Y-92
Soffici, Ardengo 1879-1964 . . . . . . DLB-114
Sofola, 'Zulu 1938- DLB-157
Solano, Solita 1888-1975 . . . . DLB-4
Soldati, Mario 1906- DLB-177
Soljan, Antun 1932-1993 . . . . DLB-181
Sollers, Philippe 1936- DLB-83
Solmi, Sergio 1899-1981 . . . . DLB-114
Solomon, Carl 1928- DLB-16
Solway, David 1941- DLB-53
Solzhenitsyn and America Y-85
Somerville, Edith Œnone
   1858-1949 . . . . DLB-135
Song, Cathy 1955- DLB-169
Sontag, Susan 1933- DLB-2, 67
Sophocles 497/496 B.C.-406/405 B.C.
   . . . . DLB-176
Šopov, Aco 1923-1982 . . . . DLB-181
Sorge, Reinhard Johannes
   1892-1916 . . . . DLB-118
Sorrentino, Gilbert
   1929- DLB-5, 173; Y-80
Sotheby, William 1757-1833 . . . . . . DLB-93
Soto, Gary 1952- DLB-82
Sources for the Study of Tudor and Stuart Drama DLB-62
Souster, Raymond 1921- DLB-88
The *South English Legendary*
   circa thirteenth-fifteenth
   centuries DLB-146
Southerland, Ellease 1943- DLB-33
Southern Illinois University Press Y-95
Southern, Terry 1924- DLB-2
Southern Writers Between the
   Wars DLB-9
Southerne, Thomas 1659-1746 . . . . . DLB-80
Southey, Caroline Anne Bowles
   1786-1854 . . . . DLB-116
Southey, Robert
   1774-1843 . . . . DLB-93, 107, 142
Southwell, Robert 1561?-1595 . . . . . DLB-167
Sowande, Bode 1948- DLB-157
Sowle, Tace
   [publishing house] DLB-170
Soyfer, Jura 1912-1939 . . . . DLB-124
Soyinka, Wole 1934- DLB-125; Y-86, 87
Spacks, Barry 1931- DLB-105
Spalding, Frances 1950- DLB-155
Spark, Muriel 1918- DLB-15, 139
Sparke, Michael
   [publishing house] DLB-170
Sparks, Jared 1789-1866 . . . . DLB-1, 30

Sparshott, Francis 1926- DLB-60
Späth, Gerold 1939- DLB-75
Spatola, Adriano 1941-1988 . . . . . . DLB-128
Spaziani, Maria Luisa 1924- DLB-128
The Spectator 1828- DLB-110
Spedding, James 1808-1881 . . . . . . DLB-144
Spee von Langenfeld, Friedrich
   1591-1635 . . . . DLB-164
Speght, Rachel 1597-after 1630 . . . . DLB-126
Speke, John Hanning 1827-1864 . . . DLB-166
Spellman, A. B. 1935- DLB-41
Spence, Thomas 1750-1814 . . . . . . DLB-158
Spencer, Anne 1882-1975 . . . . . DLB-51, 54
Spencer, Elizabeth 1921- DLB-6
Spencer, Herbert 1820-1903 . . . . . . DLB-57
Spencer, Scott 1945- Y-86
Spender, J. A. 1862-1942 . . . . DLB-98
Spender, Stephen 1909- DLB-20
Spener, Philipp Jakob 1635-1705 . . . DLB-164
Spenser, Edmund circa 1552-1599 . . . DLB-167
Sperr, Martin 1944- DLB-124
Spicer, Jack 1925-1965 . . . . DLB-5, 16
Spielberg, Peter 1929- Y-81
Spielhagen, Friedrich 1829-1911 . . . . DLB-129
"*Spielmannsepen*"
   (circa 1152-circa 1500) DLB-148
Spier, Peter 1927- DLB-61
Spinrad, Norman 1940- DLB-8
Spires, Elizabeth 1952- DLB-120
Spitteler, Carl 1845-1924 . . . . DLB-129
Spivak, Lawrence E. 1900- DLB-137
Spofford, Harriet Prescott
   1835-1921 . . . . DLB-74
Squibob (see Derby, George Horatio)
The St. John's College Robert Graves Trust
   . . . . Y-96
Stacpoole, H. de Vere
   1863-1951 . . . . DLB-153
Staël, Germaine de 1766-1817 . . . . . DLB-119
Staël-Holstein, Anne-Louise Germaine de
   (see Staël, Germaine de)
Stafford, Jean 1915-1979 . . . . . . DLB-2, 173
Stafford, William 1914- DLB-5
Stage Censorship: "The Rejected Statement"
   (1911), by Bernard Shaw
   [excerpts] DLB-10
Stallings, Laurence 1894-1968 . . . . DLB-7, 44
Stallworthy, Jon 1935- DLB-40
Stampp, Kenneth M. 1912- DLB-17
Stanev, Emiliyan 1907-1979 . . . . . . DLB-181
Stanford, Ann 1916- DLB-5
Stanković, Borisav ("Bora")
   1876-1927 . . . . DLB-147

Stanley, Henry M. 1841-1904 . . . . . . DS-13
Stanley, Thomas 1625-1678 . . . . . . DLB-131
Stannard, Martin 1947- DLB-155
Stansby, William
   [publishing house] DLB-170
Stanton, Elizabeth Cady 1815-1902 . . . DLB-79
Stanton, Frank L. 1857-1927 . . . . . . DLB-25
Stanton, Maura 1946- DLB-120
Stapledon, Olaf 1886-1950 . . . . DLB-15
Star Spangled Banner Office DLB-49
Starkey, Thomas circa 1499-1538 . . . DLB-132
Starkweather, David 1935- DLB-7
Statements on the Art of Poetry DLB-54
Stationers' Company of
   London, The DLB-170
Stead, Robert J. C. 1880-1959 . . . . . DLB-92
Steadman, Mark 1930- DLB-6
The Stealthy School of Criticism (1871), by
   Dante Gabriel Rossetti DLB-35
Stearns, Harold E. 1891-1943 . . . . . . DLB-4
Stedman, Edmund Clarence
   1833-1908 . . . . DLB-64
Steegmuller, Francis 1906-1994 . . . . DLB-111
Steel, Flora Annie
   1847-1929 . . . . DLB-153, 156
Steele, Max 1922- Y-80
Steele, Richard 1672-1729 . . . . . DLB-84, 101
Steele, Timothy 1948- DLB-120
Steele, Wilbur Daniel 1886-1970 . . . . DLB-86
Steere, Richard circa 1643-1721 . . . . DLB-24
Stefanovski, Goran 1952- DLB-181
Stegner, Wallace 1909-1993 . . . . . DLB-9; Y-93
Stehr, Hermann 1864-1940 . . . . . . DLB-66
Steig, William 1907- DLB-61
Stein, Gertrude 1874-1946 . . . . . DLB-4, 54, 86
Stein, Leo 1872-1947 . . . . DLB-4
Stein and Day Publishers DLB-46
Steinbeck, John 1902-1968 . . . DLB-7, 9; DS-2
Steiner, George 1929- DLB-67
Steinhoewel, Heinrich
   1411/1412-1479 . . . . DLB-179
Stendhal 1783-1842 . . . . DLB-119
Stephen Crane: A Revaluation Virginia
   Tech Conference, 1989 . . . . Y-89
Stephen, Leslie 1832-1904 . . . . . DLB-57, 144
Stephens, Alexander H. 1812-1883 . . . DLB-47
Stephens, Ann 1810-1886 . . . . . . DLB-3, 73
Stephens, Charles Asbury
   1844?-1931 . . . . DLB-42
Stephens, James
   1882?-1950 . . . . DLB-19, 153, 162
Sterling, George 1869-1926 . . . . . . DLB-54
Sterling, James 1701-1763 . . . . DLB-24

Sterling, John 1806-1844 . . . . DLB-116

Stern, Gerald 1925- DLB-105

Stern, Madeleine B. 1912- DLB-111, 140

Stern, Gerald, Living in Ruin DLB-105

Stern, Richard 1928- Y-87

Stern, Stewart 1922- DLB-26

Sterne, Laurence 1713-1768 . . . . DLB-39

Sternheim, Carl 1878-1942 . . . . . DLB-56, 118

Sternhold, Thomas ?-1549 and
    John Hopkins ?-1570 . . . . DLB-132

Stevens, Henry 1819-1886 . . . . DLB-140

Stevens, Wallace 1879-1955 . . . . DLB-54

Stevenson, Anne 1933- DLB-40

Stevenson, Lionel 1902-1973 . . . . . . DLB-155

Stevenson, Robert Louis 1850-1894
    . . . . . DLB-18, 57, 141, 156, 174; DS-13

Stewart, Donald Ogden
    1894-1980 . . . . DLB-4, 11, 26

Stewart, Dugald 1753-1828 . . . . DLB-31

Stewart, George, Jr. 1848-1906 . . . . . DLB-99

Stewart, George R. 1895-1980 . . . . . . DLB-8

Stewart and Kidd Company DLB-46

Stewart, Randall 1896-1964 . . . . . . DLB-103

Stickney, Trumbull 1874-1904 . . . . . DLB-54

Stieler, Caspar 1632-1707 . . . . DLB-164

Stifter, Adalbert 1805-1868 . . . . . . DLB-133

Stiles, Ezra 1727-1795 . . . . DLB-31

Still, James 1906- DLB-9

Stirner, Max 1806-1856 . . . . DLB-129

Stith, William 1707-1755 . . . . DLB-31

Stock, Elliot [publishing house] DLB-106

Stockton, Frank R.
    1834-1902 . . . . DLB-42, 74; DS-13

Stoddard, Ashbel
    [publishing house] DLB-49

Stoddard, Richard Henry
    1825-1903 . . . . DLB-3, 64; DS-13

Stoddard, Solomon 1643-1729 . . . . . DLB-24

Stoker, Bram 1847-1912 . . . . DLB-36, 70, 178

Stokes, Frederick A., Company DLB-49

Stokes, Thomas L. 1898-1958 . . . . . . DLB-29

Stokesbury, Leon 1945- DLB-120

Stolberg, Christian Graf zu
    1748-1821 . . . . DLB-94

Stolberg, Friedrich Leopold Graf zu
    1750-1819 . . . . DLB-94

Stone, Herbert S., and Company DLB-49

Stone, Lucy 1818-1893 . . . . DLB-79

Stone, Melville 1848-1929 . . . . DLB-25

Stone, Robert 1937- DLB-152

Stone, Ruth 1915- DLB-105

Stone, Samuel 1602-1663 . . . . DLB-24

Stone and Kimball DLB-49

Stoppard, Tom 1937- DLB-13; Y-85

Storey, Anthony 1928- DLB-14

Storey, David 1933- DLB-13, 14

Storm, Theodor 1817-1888 . . . . DLB-129

Story, Thomas circa 1670-1742 . . . . . DLB-31

Story, William Wetmore 1819-1895 . . . . DLB-1

Storytelling: A Contemporary
    Renaissance Y-84

Stoughton, William 1631-1701 . . . . . DLB-24

Stow, John 1525-1605 . . . . DLB-132

Stowe, Harriet Beecher
    1811-1896 . . . . DLB-1, 12, 42, 74

Stowe, Leland 1899- DLB-29

Stoyanov, Dimit"r Ivanov (see Elin Pelin)

Strabo 64 or 63 B.C.-circa A.D. 25
    . . . . DLB-176

Strachey, Lytton
    1880-1932 . . . . DLB-149; DS-10

Strachey, Lytton, Preface to Eminent
    Victorians DLB-149

Strahan and Company DLB-106

Strahan, William
    [publishing house] DLB-154

Strand, Mark 1934- DLB-5

The Strasbourg Oaths 842 . . . . DLB-148

Stratemeyer, Edward 1862-1930 . . . . DLB-42

Strati, Saverio 1924- DLB-177

Stratton and Barnard DLB-49

Stratton-Porter, Gene 1863-1924 . . . . DS-14

Straub, Peter 1943- Y-84

Strauß, Botho 1944- DLB-124

Strauß, David Friedrich
    1808-1874 . . . . DLB-133

The Strawberry Hill Press DLB-154

Streatfeild, Noel 1895-1986 . . . . . . DLB-160

Street, Cecil John Charles (see Rhode, John)

Street, G. S. 1867-1936 . . . . DLB-135

Street and Smith DLB-49

Streeter, Edward 1891-1976 . . . . DLB-11

Streeter, Thomas Winthrop
    1883-1965 . . . . DLB-140

Stretton, Hesba 1832-1911 . . . . DLB-163

Stribling, T. S. 1881-1965 . . . . DLB-9

Der Stricker circa 1190-circa 1250 . . . DLB-138

Strickland, Samuel 1804-1867 . . . . . . DLB-99

Stringer and Townsend DLB-49

Stringer, Arthur 1874-1950 . . . . DLB-92

Strittmatter, Erwin 1912- DLB-69

Strniša, Gregor 1930-1987 . . . . DLB-181

Strode, William 1630-1645 . . . . DLB-126

Strother, David Hunter 1816-1888 . . . . DLB-3

Strouse, Jean 1945- DLB-111

Stuart, Dabney 1937- DLB-105

Stuart, Dabney, Knots into Webs: Some Autobiographical Sources DLB-105

Stuart, Jesse
    1906-1984 . . . . . . DLB-9, 48, 102; Y-84

Stuart, Lyle [publishing house] DLB-46

Stubbs, Harry Clement (see Clement, Hal)

Stubenberg, Johann Wilhelm von
    1619-1663 . . . . DLB-164

Studio DLB-112

The Study of Poetry (1880), by
    Matthew Arnold DLB-35

Sturgeon, Theodore
    1918-1985 . . . . DLB-8; Y-85

Sturges, Preston 1898-1959 . . . . DLB-26

"Style" (1840; revised, 1859), by
    Thomas de Quincey [excerpt] DLB-57

"Style" (1888), by Walter Pater DLB-57

Style (1897), by Walter Raleigh
    [excerpt] DLB-57

"Style" (1877), by T. H. Wright
    [excerpt] DLB-57

"Le Style c'est l'homme" (1892), by
    W. H. Mallock DLB-57

Styron, William 1925- DLB-2, 143; Y-80

Suárez, Mario 1925- DLB-82

Such, Peter 1939- DLB-60

Suckling, Sir John 1609-1641? . . . DLB-58, 126

Suckow, Ruth 1892-1960 . . . . . . DLB-9, 102

Sudermann, Hermann 1857-1928 . . . . DLB-118

Sue, Eugène 1804-1857 . . . . DLB-119

Sue, Marie-Joseph (see Sue, Eugène)

Suggs, Simon (see Hooper, Johnson Jones)

Sukenick, Ronald 1932- DLB-173; Y-81

Suknaski, Andrew 1942- DLB-53

Sullivan, Alan 1868-1947 . . . . DLB-92

Sullivan, C. Gardner 1886-1965 . . . . . DLB-26

Sullivan, Frank 1892-1976 . . . . DLB-11

Sulte, Benjamin 1841-1923 . . . . DLB-99

Sulzberger, Arthur Hays
    1891-1968 . . . . DLB-127

Sulzberger, Arthur Ochs 1926- DLB-127

Sulzer, Johann Georg 1720-1779 . . . . . DLB-97

Sumarokov, Aleksandr Petrovich
    1717-1777 . . . . DLB-150

Summers, Hollis 1916- DLB-6

Sumner, Henry A.
    [publishing house] DLB-49

Surtees, Robert Smith 1803-1864 . . . . . DLB-21

A Survey of Poetry Anthologies,
    1879-1960 . . . . DLB-54

Surveys of the Year's Biographies

A Transit of Poets and Others: American
    Biography in 1982 . . . . Y-82

The Year in Literary Biography . . . Y-83–Y-96

Survey of the Year's Book Publishing

The Year in Book Publishing Y-86

Survey of the Year's Children's Books

The Year in Children's Books Y-92–Y-96

Surveys of the Year's Drama

The Year in Drama
. . . . Y-82–Y-85, Y-87–Y-96

The Year in London Theatre Y-92

Surveys of the Year's Fiction

The Year's Work in Fiction:
A Survey Y-82

The Year in Fiction: A Biased View Y-83

The Year in
Fiction Y-84–Y-86, Y-89, Y-94–Y-96

The Year in the
Novel Y-87, Y-88, Y-90–Y-93

The Year in Short Stories Y-87

The Year in the
Short Story Y-88, Y-90–Y-93

Survey of the Year's Literary Theory

The Year in Literary Theory Y-92–Y-93

Surveys of the Year's Poetry

The Year's Work in American
Poetry Y-82

The Year in Poetry Y-83–Y-92, Y-94–Y-96

Suso, Henry (see Seuse, Heinrich)

Sutherland, Efua Theodora
1924- DLB-117

Sutherland, John 1919-1956 . . . . DLB-68

Sutro, Alfred 1863-1933 . . . . DLB-10

Swados, Harvey 1920-1972 . . . . DLB-2

Swain, Charles 1801-1874 . . . . DLB-32

Swallow Press DLB-46

Swan Sonnenschein Limited DLB-106

Swanberg, W. A. 1907- DLB-103

Swenson, May 1919-1989 . . . . DLB-5

Swerling, Jo 1897- DLB-44

Swift, Jonathan
1667-1745 . . . . DLB-39, 95, 101

Swinburne, A. C. 1837-1909 . . . . . DLB-35, 57

Swineshead, Richard floruit
circa 1350 . . . . DLB-115

Swinnerton, Frank 1884-1982 . . . . . . DLB-34

Swisshelm, Jane Grey 1815-1884 . . . . . DLB-43

Swope, Herbert Bayard 1882-1958 . . . . DLB-25

Swords, T. and J., and Company DLB-49

Swords, Thomas 1763-1843 and
Swords, James ?-1844 . . . . DLB-73

Sykes, Ella C. ?-1939 . . . . DLB-174

Sylvester, Josuah
1562 or 1563 - 1618 . . . . DLB-121

Symonds, Emily Morse (see Paston, George)

Symonds, John Addington
1840-1893 . . . . DLB-57, 144

Symons, A. J. A. 1900-1941 . . . . . DLB-149

Symons, Arthur
1865-1945 . . . . DLB-19, 57, 149

Symons, Julian
1912-1994 . . . . DLB-87, 155; Y-92

Symons, Scott 1933- DLB-53

A Symposium on *The Columbia History of
the Novel* Y-92

Synge, John Millington
1871-1909 . . . . DLB-10, 19

Synge Summer School: J. M. Synge and the Irish
Theater, Rathdrum, County Widow, Ireland
. . . . Y-93

Syrett, Netta 1865-1943 . . . . DLB-135

Szymborska, Wisława 1923- Y-96

T

Taban lo Liyong 1939?- DLB-125

Taché, Joseph-Charles 1820-1894 . . . . . DLB-99

Tadijanović, Dragutin 1905- DLB-181

Tafolla, Carmen 1951- DLB-82

Taggard, Genevieve 1894-1948 . . . . . . DLB-45

Tagger, Theodor (see Bruckner, Ferdinand)

Tait, J. Selwin, and Sons DLB-49

Tait's Edinburgh Magazine
1832-1861 . . . . DLB-110

The Takarazaka Revue Company Y-91

Talander (see Bohse, August)

Talev, Dimitŭr 1898-1966 . . . . DLB-181

Tallent, Elizabeth 1954- DLB-130

Talvj 1797-1870 . . . . DLB-59, 133

Tan, Amy 1952- DLB-173

Tanizaki, Jun'ichirō 1886-1965 . . . . . DLB-180

Tapahonso, Luci 1953 . . . . DLB-175

Taradash, Daniel 1913- DLB-44

Tarbell, Ida M. 1857-1944 . . . . DLB-47

Tardivel, Jules-Paul 1851-1905 . . . . . . DLB-99

Targan, Barry 1932- DLB-130

Tarkington, Booth 1869-1946 . . . . DLB-9, 102

Tashlin, Frank 1913-1972 . . . . DLB-44

Tate, Allen 1899-1979 . . . . . . DLB-4, 45, 63

Tate, James 1943- DLB-5, 169

Tate, Nahum circa 1652-1715 . . . . . . DLB-80

Tatian circa 830 . . . . DLB-148

Taufer, Veno 1933- DLB-181

Tavčar, Ivan 1851-1923 . . . . DLB-147

Taylor, Ann 1782-1866 . . . . DLB-163

Taylor, Bayard 1825-1878 . . . . DLB-3

Taylor, Bert Leston 1866-1921 . . . . . . DLB-25

Taylor, Charles H. 1846-1921 . . . . . . DLB-25

Taylor, Edward circa 1642-1729 . . . . . DLB-24

Taylor, Elizabeth 1912-1975 . . . . . . DLB-139

Taylor, Henry 1942- DLB-5

Taylor, Sir Henry 1800-1886 . . . . . . DLB-32

Taylor, Jane 1783-1824 . . . . DLB-163

Taylor, Jeremy circa 1613-1667 . . . . . DLB-151

Taylor, John
1577 or 1578 - 1653 . . . . DLB-121

Taylor, Mildred D. ?- DLB-52

Taylor, Peter 1917-1994 . . . . Y-81, Y-94

Taylor, William, and Company DLB-49

Taylor-Made Shakespeare? Or Is
"Shall I Die?" the Long-Lost Text
of Bottom's Dream? Y-85

Teasdale, Sara 1884-1933 . . . . DLB-45

The Tea-Table (1725), by Eliza Haywood [excerpt]
DLB-39

Telles, Lygia Fagundes 1924- DLB-113

Temple, Sir William 1628-1699 . . . . . DLB-101

Tenn, William 1919- DLB-8

Tennant, Emma 1937- DLB-14

Tenney, Tabitha Gilman
1762-1837 . . . . DLB-37

Tennyson, Alfred 1809-1892 . . . . DLB-32

Tennyson, Frederick 1807-1898 . . . . . DLB-32

von Tepl, Johannes
circa 1350-1414/1415 . . . . DLB179

Terhune, Albert Payson 1872-1942 . . . . DLB-9

Terhune, Mary Virginia 1830-1922 . . . . DS-13

Terry, Megan 1932- DLB-7

Terson, Peter 1932- DLB-13

Tesich, Steve 1943- Y-83

Tessa, Delio 1886-1939 . . . . DLB-114

Testori, Giovanni 1923-1993 . . . . DLB-128, 177

Tey, Josephine 1896?-1952 . . . . DLB-77

Thacher, James 1754-1844 . . . . DLB-37

Thackeray, William Makepeace
1811-1863 . . . . . . DLB-21, 55, 159, 163

Thames and Hudson Limited DLB-112

Thanet, Octave (see French, Alice)

The Theater in Shakespeare's
Time DLB-62

The Theatre Guild DLB-7

Thegan and the Astronomer
flourished circa 850 . . . . DLB-148

Thelwall, John 1764-1834 . . . . . . DLB-93, 158

Theocritus circa 300 B.C.-260 B.C.
. . . . DLB-176

Theodulf circa 760-circa 821 . . . . . . DLB-148

Theophrastus circa 371 B.C.-287 B.C.
. . . . DLB-176

Theriault, Yves 1915-1983 . . . . DLB-88

Thério, Adrien 1925- DLB-53

Theroux, Paul 1941- DLB-2

Thibaudeau, Colleen 1925- DLB-88

Thielen, Benedict 1903-1965 . . . . . . DLB-102

Thiong'o Ngugi wa (see Ngugi wa Thiong'o)

Third-Generation Minor Poets of the Seventeenth Century........ DLB-131

Thoma, Ludwig 1867-1921........ DLB-66

Thoma, Richard 1902- DLB-4

Thomas, Audrey 1935- DLB-60

Thomas, D. M. 1935- DLB-40

Thomas, Dylan 1914-1953.......... DLB-13, 20, 139

Thomas, Edward 1878-1917.......... DLB-19, 98, 156

Thomas, Gwyn 1913-1981........ DLB-15

Thomas, Isaiah 1750-1831...... DLB-43, 73

Thomas, Isaiah [publishing house].... DLB-49

Thomas, Johann 1624-1679....... DLB-168

Thomas, John 1900-1932 .... DLB-4

Thomas, Joyce Carol 1938- DLB-33

Thomas, Lorenzo 1944- DLB-41

Thomas, R. S. 1915- DLB-27

Thomasîn von Zerclære circa 1186-circa 1259 .... DLB-138

Thomasius, Christian 1655-1728 .... DLB-168

Thompson, David 1770-1857....... DLB-99

Thompson, Dorothy 1893-1961 ..... DLB-29

Thompson, Francis 1859-1907 ..... DLB-19

Thompson, George Selden (see Selden, George)

Thompson, John 1938-1976 ...... DLB-60

Thompson, John R. 1823-1873 .... DLB-3, 73

Thompson, Lawrance 1906-1973 .... DLB-103

Thompson, Maurice 1844-1901............. DLB-71, 74

Thompson, Ruth Plumly 1891-1976 .... DLB-22

Thompson, Thomas Phillips 1843-1933 .... DLB-99

Thompson, William 1775-1833..... DLB-158

Thompson, William Tappan 1812-1882 .... DLB-3, 11

Thomson, Edward William 1849-1924............. DLB-92

Thomson, James 1700-1748 ..... DLB-95

Thomson, James 1834-1882 ..... DLB-35

Thomson, Joseph 1858-1895 ..... DLB-174

Thomson, Mortimer 1831-1875 ..... DLB-11

Thoreau, Henry David 1817-1862 .... DLB-1

Thorpe, Thomas Bangs 1815-1878 .... DLB-3, 11

Thoughts on Poetry and Its Varieties (1833), by John Stuart Mill DLB-32

Thrale, Hester Lynch (see Piozzi, Hester Lynch [Thrale])

Thucydides circa 455 B.C.-circa 395 B.C. DLB-176

Thümmel, Moritz August von 1738-1817 .... DLB-97

Thurber, James 1894-1961 .... DLB-4, 11, 22, 102

Thurman, Wallace 1902-1934 ..... DLB-51

Thwaite, Anthony 1930- DLB-40

Thwaites, Reuben Gold 1853-1913............... DLB-47

Ticknor, George 1791-1871........... DLB-1, 59, 140

Ticknor and Fields DLB-49

Ticknor and Fields (revived)...... DLB-46

Tieck, Ludwig 1773-1853......... DLB-90

Tietjens, Eunice 1884-1944........ DLB-54

Tilney, Edmund circa 1536-1610.... DLB-136

Tilt, Charles [publishing house]..... DLB-106

Tilton, J. E., and Company DLB-49

Time and Western Man (1927), by Wyndham Lewis [excerpts]............ DLB-36

Time-Life Books............. DLB-46

Times Books DLB-46

Timothy, Peter circa 1725-1782 ..... DLB-43

Timrod, Henry 1828-1867......... DLB-3

Tinker, Chauncey Brewster 1876-1963 .... DLB-140

Tinsley Brothers DLB-106

Tiptree, James, Jr. 1915-1987 .... DLB-8

Tišma, Aleksandar 1924- DLB-181

Titus, Edward William 1870-1952 .... DLB-4

Tlali, Miriam 1933- DLB-157

Todd, Barbara Euphan 1890-1976 .... DLB-160

Tofte, Robert 1561 or 1562-1619 or 1620 .... DLB-172

Toklas, Alice B. 1877-1967 .... DLB-4

Tokuda, Shūsei 1872-1943 .... DLB-180

Tolkien, J. R. R. 1892-1973 .... DLB-15, 160

Toller, Ernst 1893-1939 .... DLB-124

Tollet, Elizabeth 1694-1754....... DLB-95

Tolson, Melvin B. 1898-1966 .... DLB-48, 76

Tom Jones (1749), by Henry Fielding [excerpt] DLB-39

Tomalin, Claire 1933- DLB-155

Tomasi di Lampedusa, Giuseppe 1896-1957 .... DLB-177

Tomlinson, Charles 1927- DLB-40

Tomlinson, H. M. 1873-1958 ... DLB-36, 100

Tompkins, Abel [publishing house] ... DLB-49

Tompson, Benjamin 1642-1714...... DLB-24

Tonks, Rosemary 1932- DLB-14

Tonna, Charlotte Elizabeth 1790-1846 .... DLB-163

Tonson, Jacob the Elder [publishing house].......... DLB-170

Toole, John Kennedy 1937-1969 ..... Y-81

Toomer, Jean 1894-1967 .... DLB-45, 51

Tor Books.................. DLB-46

Torberg, Friedrich 1908-1979...... DLB-85

Torrence, Ridgely 1874-1950....... DLB-54

Torres-Metzger, Joseph V. 1933- DLB-122

Toth, Susan Allen 1940- Y-86

Tottell, Richard [publishing house].......... DLB-170

Tough-Guy Literature DLB-9

Touré, Askia Muhammad 1938- DLB-41

Tourgée, Albion W. 1838-1905 ..... DLB-79

Tourneur, Cyril circa 1580-1626..... DLB-58

Tournier, Michel 1924- DLB-83

Tousey, Frank [publishing house] DLB-49

Tower Publications DLB-46

Towne, Benjamin circa 1740-1793 .... DLB-43

Towne, Robert 1936- DLB-44

The Townely Plays fifteenth and sixteenth centuries DLB-146

Townshend, Aurelian by 1583 - circa 1651 .... DLB-121

Tracy, Honor 1913- DLB-15

Traherne, Thomas 1637?-1674 ..... DLB-131

Traill, Catharine Parr 1802-1899..... DLB-99

Train, Arthur 1875-1945 .... DLB-86

The Transatlantic Publishing Company DLB-49

Transcendentalists, American.......... DS-5

Translators of the Twelfth Century: Literary Issues Raised and Impact Created................ DLB-115

Travel Writing, 1837-1875 .... DLB-166

Travel Writing, 1876-1909 .... DLB-174

Traven, B. 1882? or 1890?-1969?........ DLB-9, 56

Travers, Ben 1886-1980 .... DLB-10

Travers, P. L. (Pamela Lyndon) 1899- DLB-160

Trediakovsky, Vasilii Kirillovich 1703-1769 .... DLB-150

Treece, Henry 1911-1966........ DLB-160

Trejo, Ernesto 1950- DLB-122

Trelawny, Edward John 1792-1881.......... DLB-110, 116, 144

Tremain, Rose 1943- DLB-14

Tremblay, Michel 1942- DLB-60

Trends in Twentieth-Century Mass Market Publishing DLB-46

Trent, William P. 1862-1939....... DLB-47

Trescot, William Henry 1822-1898 .... DLB-30

Trevelyan, Sir George Otto 1838-1928 .... DLB-144

Trevisa, John circa 1342-circa 1402 .... DLB-146
Trevor, William 1928- DLB-14, 139
Trierer Floyris circa 1170-1180 ...... DLB-138
Trilling, Lionel 1905-1975 ...... DLB-28, 63
Trilussa 1871-1950 .... DLB-114
Trimmer, Sarah 1741-1810 .... DLB-158
Triolet, Elsa 1896-1970 .... DLB-72
Tripp, John 1927- DLB-40
Trocchi, Alexander 1925- DLB-15
Trollope, Anthony 1815-1882 .... DLB-21, 57, 159
Trollope, Frances 1779-1863 .... DLB-21, 166
Troop, Elizabeth 1931- DLB-14
Trotter, Catharine 1679-1749 ...... DLB-84
Trotti, Lamar 1898-1952 .... DLB-44
Trottier, Pierre 1925- DLB-60
Troupe, Quincy Thomas, Jr. 1943- DLB-41
Trow, John F., and Company DLB-49
Truillier-Lacombe, Joseph-Patrice 1807-1863 .... DLB-99
Trumbo, Dalton 1905-1976 .... DLB-26
Trumbull, Benjamin 1735-1820 ...... DLB-30
Trumbull, John 1750-1831 .... DLB-31
Tscherning, Andreas 1611-1659 ..... DLB-164
T. S. Eliot Centennial Y-88
Tsubouchi, Shōyō 1859-1935 ...... DLB-180
Tucholsky, Kurt 1890-1935 .... DLB-56
Tucker, Charlotte Maria 1821-1893 .... DLB-163
Tucker, George 1775-1861 ..... DLB-3, 30
Tucker, Nathaniel Beverley 1784-1851 .... DLB-3
Tucker, St. George 1752-1827 ...... DLB-37
Tuckerman, Henry Theodore 1813-1871 .... DLB-64
Tunis, John R. 1889-1975 ..... DLB-22, 171
Tunstall, Cuthbert 1474-1559 ...... DLB-132
Tuohy, Frank 1925- DLB-14, 139
Tupper, Martin F. 1810-1889 ...... DLB-32
Turbyfill, Mark 1896- DLB-45
Turco, Lewis 1934- Y-84
Turnbull, Andrew 1921-1970 ...... DLB-103
Turnbull, Gael 1928- DLB-40
Turner, Arlin 1909-1980 .... DLB-103
Turner, Charles (Tennyson) 1808-1879 .... DLB-32
Turner, Frederick 1943- DLB-40
Turner, Frederick Jackson 1861-1932 .... DLB-17
Turner, Joseph Addison 1826-1868 .... DLB-79

Turpin, Waters Edward 1910-1968 .... DLB-51
Turrini, Peter 1944- DLB-124
Tutuola, Amos 1920- DLB-125
Twain, Mark (see Clemens, Samuel Langhorne)
Tweedie, Ethel Brilliana circa 1860-1940 .... DLB-174
The 'Twenties and Berlin, by Alex Natan DLB-66
Tyler, Anne 1941- DLB-6, 143; Y-82
Tyler, Moses Coit 1835-1900 .... DLB-47, 64
Tyler, Royall 1757-1826 .... DLB-37
Tylor, Edward Burnett 1832-1917 .... DLB-57
Tynan, Katharine 1861-1931 ...... DLB-153
Tyndale, William circa 1494-1536 .... DLB-132

U

Udall, Nicholas 1504-1556 .... DLB-62
Ugrešić, Dubravka 1949- DLB-181
Uhland, Ludwig 1787-1862 .... DLB-90
Uhse, Bodo 1904-1963 .... DLB-69
Ujević, Augustin ("Tin") 1891-1955 .... DLB-147
Ulenhart, Niclas flourished circa 1600 .... DLB-164
Ulibarrí, Sabine R. 1919- DLB-82
Ulica, Jorge 1870-1926 .... DLB-82
Ulizio, B. George 1889-1969 ..... DLB-140
Ulrich von Liechtenstein circa 1200-circa 1275 .... DLB-138
Ulrich von Zatzikhoven before 1194-after 1214 .... DLB-138
Unamuno, Miguel de 1864-1936 .... DLB-108
Under the Microscope (1872), by A. C. Swinburne DLB-35
Unger, Friederike Helene 1741-1813 .... DLB-94
Ungaretti, Giuseppe 1888-1970 ..... DLB-114
United States Book Company DLB-49
Universal Publishing and Distributing Corporation DLB-46
The University of Iowa Writers' Workshop Golden Jubilee Y-86
The University of South Carolina Press Y-94
University of Wales Press DLB-112
"The Unknown Public" (1858), by Wilkie Collins [excerpt] DLB-57
Uno, Chiyo 1897-1996 .... DLB-180
Unruh, Fritz von 1885-1970 .... DLB-56, 118
Unspeakable Practices II: The Festival of Vanguard Narrative at Brown University Y-93

Unwin, T. Fisher [publishing house] DLB-106
Upchurch, Boyd B. (see Boyd, John)
Updike, John 1932- DLB-2, 5, 143; Y-80, 82; DS-3
Upton, Bertha 1849-1912 .... DLB-141
Upton, Charles 1948- DLB-16
Upton, Florence K. 1873-1922 ..... DLB-141
Upward, Allen 1863-1926 .... DLB-36
Urista, Alberto Baltazar (see Alurista)
Urzidil, Johannes 1896-1976 .... DLB-85
Urquhart, Fred 1912- DLB-139
The Uses of Facsimile Y-90
Usk, Thomas died 1388 .... DLB-146
Uslar Pietri, Arturo 1906- DLB-113
Ustinov, Peter 1921- DLB-13
Uttley, Alison 1884-1976 .... DLB-160
Uz, Johann Peter 1720-1796 ..... DLB-97

V

Vac, Bertrand 1914- DLB-88
Vadianus, Joachim 1484-1551 ..... DLB-179
Vail, Laurence 1891-1968 .... DLB-4
Vailland, Roger 1907-1965 .... DLB-83
Vajda, Ernest 1887-1954 .... DLB-44
Valdés, Gina 1943- DLB-122
Valdez, Luis Miguel 1940- DLB-122
Valduga, Patrizia 1953- DLB-128
Valente, José Angel 1929- DLB-108
Valenzuela, Luisa 1938- DLB-113
Valeri, Diego 1887-1976 .... DLB-128
Valgardson, W. D. 1939- DLB-60
Valle, Víctor Manuel 1950- DLB-122
Valle-Inclán, Ramón del 1866-1936 .... DLB-134
Vallejo, Armando 1949- DLB-122
Vallès, Jules 1832-1885 .... DLB-123
Vallette, Marguerite Eymery (see Rachilde)
Valverde, José María 1926- DLB-108
Van Allsburg, Chris 1949- DLB-61
Van Anda, Carr 1864-1945 .... DLB-25
Van Doren, Mark 1894-1972 ...... DLB-45
van Druten, John 1901-1957 ...... DLB-10
Van Duyn, Mona 1921- DLB-5
Van Dyke, Henry 1852-1933 .... DLB-71; DS-13
Van Dyke, Henry 1928- DLB-33
van Itallie, Jean-Claude 1936- DLB-7
Van Loan, Charles E. 1876-1919 .... DLB-171
Van Rensselaer, Mariana Griswold 1851-1934 .... DLB-47

Cumulative Index

Van Rensselaer, Mrs. Schuyler (see Van Rensselaer, Mariana Griswold)
Van Vechten, Carl 1880-1964 . . . . . DLB-4, 9
van Vogt, A. E. 1912- DLB-8
Vanbrugh, Sir John 1664-1726 . . . . . . DLB-80
Vance, Jack 1916?- DLB-8
Vane, Sutton 1888-1963 . . . . DLB-10
Vanguard Press DLB-46
Vann, Robert L. 1879-1940 . . . . DLB-29
Vargas, Llosa, Mario 1936- DLB-145
Varley, John 1947- Y-81
Varnhagen von Ense, Karl August 1785-1858 . . . . DLB-90
Varnhagen von Ense, Rahel 1771-1833 . . . . DLB-90
Vásquez Montalbán, Manuel 1939- DLB-134
Vassa, Gustavus (see Equiano, Olaudah)
Vassalli, Sebastiano 1941- DLB-128
Vaughan, Henry 1621-1695 . . . . . . DLB-131
Vaughan, Thomas 1621-1666 . . . . . DLB-131
Vaux, Thomas, Lord 1509-1556 . . . . DLB-132
Vazov, Ivan 1850-1921 . . . . DLB-147
Vega, Janine Pommy 1942- DLB-16
Veiller, Anthony 1903-1965 . . . . DLB-44
Velásquez-Trevino, Gloria 1949- DLB-122
Veloz Maggiolo, Marcio 1936- DLB-145
Venegas, Daniel ?-? DLB-82
Vergil, Polydore circa 1470-1555 . . . . DLB-132
Veríssimo, Erico 1905-1975 . . . . . . DLB-145
Verne, Jules 1828-1905 . . . . DLB-123
Verplanck, Gulian C. 1786-1870 . . . . . DLB-59
Very, Jones 1813-1880 . . . . DLB-1
Vian, Boris 1920-1959 . . . . DLB-72
Vickers, Roy 1888?-1965 . . . . DLB-77
Victoria 1819-1901 . . . . DLB-55
Victoria Press DLB-106
Vidal, Gore 1925- DLB-6, 152
Viebig, Clara 1860-1952 . . . . DLB-66
Viereck, George Sylvester 1884-1962 . . . . DLB-54
Viereck, Peter 1916- DLB-5
Viets, Roger 1738-1811 . . . . DLB-99
Viewpoint: Politics and Performance, by David Edgar DLB-13
Vigil-Piñon, Evangelina 1949- DLB-122
Vigneault, Gilles 1928- DLB-60
Vigny, Alfred de 1797-1863 . . . . . . DLB-119
Vigolo, Giorgio 1894-1983 . . . . DLB-114
The Viking Press DLB-46
Villanueva, Alma Luz 1944- DLB-122
Villanueva, Tino 1941- DLB-82

Villard, Henry 1835-1900 . . . . DLB-23
Villard, Oswald Garrison 1872-1949 . . . . DLB-25, 91
Villarreal, José Antonio 1924- DLB-82
Villegas de Magnón, Leonor 1876-1955 . . . . DLB-122
Villemaire, Yolande 1949- DLB-60
Villena, Luis Antonio de 1951- DLB-134
Villiers de l'Isle-Adam, Jean-Marie Mathias Philippe-Auguste, Comte de 1838-1889 . . . . DLB-123
Villiers, George, Second Duke of Buckingham 1628-1687 . . . . . DLB-80
Vine Press DLB-112
Viorst, Judith ?- DLB-52
Vipont, Elfrida (Elfrida Vipont Foulds, Charles Vipont) 1902-1992 . . . . . DLB-160
Viramontes, Helena María 1954- DLB-122
Vischer, Friedrich Theodor 1807-1887 . . . . DLB-133
Vivanco, Luis Felipe 1907-1975 . . . . DLB-108
Viviani, Cesare 1947- DLB-128
Vizenor, Gerald 1934- DLB-175
Vizetelly and Company DLB-106
Voaden, Herman 1903- DLB-88
Voigt, Ellen Bryant 1943- DLB-120
Vojnović, Ivo 1857-1929 . . . . DLB-147
Volkoff, Vladimir 1932- DLB-83
Volland, P. F., Company DLB-46
Volponi, Paolo 1924- DLB-177
von der Grün, Max 1926- DLB-75
Vonnegut, Kurt 1922- DLB-2, 8, 152; Y-80; DS-3
Voranc, Prežihov 1893-1950 . . . . . . DLB-147
Voß, Johann Heinrich 1751-1826 . . . . DLB-90
Vroman, Mary Elizabeth circa 1924-1967 . . . . DLB-33

W

Wace, Robert ("Maistre") circa 1100-circa 1175 . . . . DLB-146
Wackenroder, Wilhelm Heinrich 1773-1798 . . . . DLB-90
Wackernagel, Wilhelm 1806-1869 . . . . DLB-133
Waddington, Miriam 1917- DLB-68
Wade, Henry 1887-1969 . . . . DLB-77
Wagenknecht, Edward 1900- DLB-103
Wagner, Heinrich Leopold 1747-1779 . . . . DLB-94
Wagner, Henry R. 1862-1957 . . . . . DLB-140
Wagner, Richard 1813-1883 . . . . . . DLB-129
Wagoner, David 1926- DLB-5

Wah, Fred 1939- DLB-60
Waiblinger, Wilhelm 1804-1830 . . . . DLB-90
Wain, John 1925-1994 . . . . DLB-15, 27, 139, 155
Wainwright, Jeffrey 1944- DLB-40
Waite, Peirce and Company DLB-49
Wakoski, Diane 1937- DLB-5
Walahfrid Strabo circa 808-849 . . . . DLB-148
Walck, Henry Z. DLB-46
Walcott, Derek 1930- DLB-117; Y-81, 92
Waldegrave, Robert [publishing house] DLB-170
Waldis, Burkhard circa 1490-1556? DLB-179
Waldman, Anne 1945- DLB-16
Waldrop, Rosmarie 1935- DLB-169
Walker, Alice 1944- DLB-6, 33, 143
Walker, George F. 1947- DLB-60
Walker, Joseph A. 1935- DLB-38
Walker, Margaret 1915- DLB-76, 152
Walker, Ted 1934- DLB-40
Walker and Company DLB-49
Walker, Evans and Cogswell Company DLB-49
Walker, John Brisben 1847-1931 . . . . DLB-79
Wallace, Dewitt 1889-1981 and Lila Acheson Wallace 1889-1984 . . . . DLB-137
Wallace, Edgar 1875-1932 . . . . DLB-70
Wallace, Lila Acheson (see Wallace, Dewitt, and Lila Acheson Wallace)
Wallant, Edward Lewis 1926-1962 . . . . DLB-2, 28, 143
Waller, Edmund 1606-1687 . . . . . . DLB-126
Walpole, Horace 1717-1797 . . . . DLB-39, 104
Walpole, Hugh 1884-1941 . . . . DLB-34
Walrond, Eric 1898-1966 . . . . DLB-51
Walser, Martin 1927- DLB-75, 124
Walser, Robert 1878-1956 . . . . DLB-66
Walsh, Ernest 1895-1926 . . . . DLB-4, 45
Walsh, Robert 1784-1859 . . . . DLB-59
Waltharius circa 825 . . . . DLB-148
Walters, Henry 1848-1931 . . . . DLB-140
Walther von der Vogelweide circa 1170-circa 1230 . . . . DLB-138
Walton, Izaak 1593-1683 . . . . DLB-151
Wambaugh, Joseph 1937- DLB-6; Y-83
Waniek, Marilyn Nelson 1946- DLB-120
Warburton, William 1698-1779 . . . . DLB-104
Ward, Aileen 1919- DLB-111
Ward, Artemus (see Browne, Charles Farrar)
Ward, Arthur Henry Sarsfield (see Rohmer, Sax)

Ward, Douglas Turner 1930- DLB-7, 38	Waugh, Auberon 1939- DLB-14	Wells, Robert 1947- DLB-40
Ward, Lynd 1905-1985......... DLB-22	Waugh, Evelyn 1903-1966 ..... DLB-15, 162	Wells-Barnett, Ida B. 1862-1931 ..... DLB-23
Ward, Lock and Company...... DLB-106	Way and Williams DLB-49	Welty, Eudora 1909- DLB-2, 102, 143; Y-87; DS-12
Ward, Mrs. Humphry 1851-1920 .... DLB-18	Wayman, Tom 1945- DLB-53	Wendell, Barrett 1855-1921........ DLB-71
Ward, Nathaniel circa 1578-1652 .... DLB-24	Weatherly, Tom 1942- DLB-41	Wentworth, Patricia 1878-1961...... DLB-77
Ward, Theodore 1902-1983 .... DLB-76	Weaver, Gordon 1937- DLB-130	Werder, Diederich von dem 1584-1657 .... DLB-164
Wardle, Ralph 1909-1988 .... DLB-103	Weaver, Robert 1921- DLB-88	Werfel, Franz 1890-1945 ..... DLB-81, 124
Ware, William 1797-1852 .... DLB-1	Webb, Frank J. ?-? DLB-50	The Werner Company.......... DLB-49
Warne, Frederick, and Company [U.S.]............ DLB-49	Webb, James Watson 1802-1884..... DLB-43	Werner, Zacharias 1768-1823....... DLB-94
Warne, Frederick, and Company [U.K.]........... DLB-106	Webb, Mary 1881-1927 .... DLB-34	Wersba, Barbara 1932- DLB-52
Warner, Charles Dudley 1829-1900 .... DLB-64	Webb, Phyllis 1927- DLB-53	Wescott, Glenway 1901- DLB-4, 9, 102
Warner, Rex 1905- DLB-15	Webb, Walter Prescott 1888-1963 .... DLB-17	Wesker, Arnold 1932- DLB-13
Warner, Susan Bogert 1819-1885 .... DLB-3, 42	Webbe, William ?-1591 .... DLB-132	Wesley, Charles 1707-1788........ DLB-95
Warner, Sylvia Townsend 1893-1978 .... DLB-34, 139	Webster, Augusta 1837-1894...... DLB-35	Wesley, John 1703-1791......... DLB-104
Warner, William 1558-1609....... DLB-172	Webster, Charles L., and Company............ DLB-49	Wesley, Richard 1945- DLB-38
Warner Books................ DLB-46	Webster, John 1579 or 1580-1634? DLB-58	Wessels, A., and Company DLB-46
Warr, Bertram 1917-1943 .... DLB-88	Webster, Noah 1758-1843....... DLB-1, 37, 42, 43, 73	Wessobrunner Gebet circa 787-815............. DLB-148
Warren, John Byrne Leicester (see De Tabley, Lord)	Weckherlin, Georg Rodolf 1584-1653 .... DLB-164	West, Anthony 1914-1988 .... DLB-15
Warren, Lella 1899-1982......... Y-83	Wedekind, Frank 1864-1918 ...... DLB-118	West, Dorothy 1907- DLB-76
Warren, Mercy Otis 1728-1814 ..... DLB-31	Weeks, Edward Augustus, Jr. 1898-1989 .... DLB-137	West, Jessamyn 1902-1984 ..... DLB-6; Y-84
Warren, Robert Penn 1905-1989 ..... DLB-2, 48, 152; Y-80, 89	Weems, Mason Locke 1759-1825........... DLB-30, 37, 42	West, Mae 1892-1980........... DLB-44
Die Wartburgkrieg circa 1230-circa 1280 .... DLB-138	Weerth, Georg 1822-1856........ DLB-129	West, Nathanael 1903-1940 .... DLB-4, 9, 28
Warton, Joseph 1722-1800..... DLB-104, 109	Weidenfeld and Nicolson DLB-112	West, Paul 1930- DLB-14
Warton, Thomas 1728-1790.... DLB-104, 109	Weidman, Jerome 1913- DLB-28	West, Rebecca 1892-1983 ..... DLB-36; Y-83
Washington, George 1732-1799 ..... DLB-31	Weigl, Bruce 1949- DLB-120	West and Johnson DLB-49
Wassermann, Jakob 1873-1934...... DLB-66	Weinbaum, Stanley Grauman 1902-1935............. DLB-8	Western Publishing Company DLB-46
Wasson, David Atwood 1823-1887 .... DLB-1	Weintraub, Stanley 1929- DLB-111	The Westminster Review 1824-1914 .... DLB-110
Waterhouse, Keith 1929- DLB-13, 15	Weise, Christian 1642-1708....... DLB-168	Weston, Elizabeth Jane circa 1582-1612 ...... DLB-172
Waterman, Andrew 1940- DLB-40	Weisenborn, Gunther 1902-1969 .... DLB-69, 124	Wetherald, Agnes Ethelwyn 1857-1940 .... DLB-99
Waters, Frank 1902- Y-86	Weiß, Ernst 1882-1940.......... DLB-81	Wetherell, Elizabeth (see Warner, Susan Bogert)
Waters, Michael 1949- DLB-120	Weiss, John 1818-1879.......... DLB-1	Wetzel, Friedrich Gottlob 1779-1819 .... DLB-90
Watkins, Tobias 1780-1855........ DLB-73	Weiss, Peter 1916-1982 .... DLB-69, 124	Weyman, Stanley J. 1855-1928............. DLB-141, 156
Watkins, Vernon 1906-1967 .... DLB-20	Weiss, Theodore 1916- DLB-5	Wezel, Johann Karl 1747-1819...... DLB-94
Watmough, David 1926- DLB-53	Weisse, Christian Felix 1726-1804.... DLB-97	Whalen, Philip 1923- DLB-16
Watson, James Wreford (see Wreford, James)	Weitling, Wilhelm 1808-1871...... DLB-129	Whalley, George 1915-1983 .... DLB-88
Watson, John 1850-1907 .... DLB-156	Welch, James 1940- DLB-175	Wharton, Edith 1862-1937 ..... DLB-4, 9, 12, 78; DS-13
Watson, Sheila 1909- DLB-60	Welch, Lew 1926-1971? DLB-16	Wharton, William 1920s?- Y-80
Watson, Thomas 1545?-1592...... DLB-132	Weldon, Fay 1931- DLB-14	Whately, Mary Louisa 1824-1889 .... DLB-166
Watson, Wilfred 1911- DLB-60	Wellek, René 1903- DLB-63	What's Really Wrong With Bestseller Lists................... Y-84
von Watt, Joachim (see Vadianus, Joachim)	Wells, Carolyn 1862-1942 .... DLB-11	Wheatley, Dennis Yates 1897-1977 .... DLB-77
Watt, W. J., and Company DLB-46	Wells, Charles Jeremiah circa 1800-1879 .... DLB-32	
Watterson, Henry 1840-1921....... DLB-25	Wells, Gabriel 1862-1946 .... DLB-140	Wheatley, Phillis circa 1754-1784 ...... DLB-31, 50
Watts, Alan 1915-1973 .... DLB-16	Wells, H. G. 1866-1946 ...... DLB-34, 70, 156, 178	
Watts, Franklin [publishing house].... DLB-46		
Watts, Isaac 1674-1748 .... DLB-95		

Wheeler, Anna Doyle 1785-1848? DLB-158

Wheeler, Charles Stearns 1816-1843 .... DLB-1

Wheeler, Monroe 1900-1988 .... DLB-4

Wheelock, John Hall 1886-1978 ..... DLB-45

Wheelwright, John circa 1592-1679 .... DLB-24

Wheelwright, J. B. 1897-1940 ..... DLB-45

Whetstone, Colonel Pete (see Noland, C. F. M.)

Whetstone, George 1550-1587 ..... DLB-136

Whicher, Stephen E. 1915-1961 .... DLB-111

Whipple, Edwin Percy 1819-1886 .... DLB-1, 64

Whitaker, Alexander 1585-1617 ..... DLB-24

Whitaker, Daniel K. 1801-1881 ..... DLB-73

Whitcher, Frances Miriam 1814-1852 .... DLB-11

White, Andrew 1579-1656 .... DLB-24

White, Andrew Dickson 1832-1918 .... DLB-47

White, E. B. 1899-1985 .... DLB-11, 22

White, Edgar B. 1947- DLB-38

White, Ethel Lina 1887-1944 ...... DLB-77

White, Henry Kirke 1785-1806 ..... DLB-96

White, Horace 1834-1916 .... DLB-23

White, Phyllis Dorothy James (see James, P. D.)

White, Richard Grant 1821-1885 .... DLB-64

White, T. H. 1906-1964 .... DLB-160

White, Walter 1893-1955 .... DLB-51

White, William, and Company DLB-49

White, William Allen 1868-1944 .... DLB-9, 25

White, William Anthony Parker (see Boucher, Anthony)

White, William Hale (see Rutherford, Mark)

Whitechurch, Victor L. 1868-1933 .... DLB-70

Whitehead, Alfred North 1861-1947 .... DLB-100

Whitehead, James 1936- Y-81

Whitehead, William 1715-1785 .... DLB-84, 109

Whitfield, James Monroe 1822-1871 .... DLB-50

Whitgift, John circa 1533-1604 ..... DLB-132

Whiting, John 1917-1963 .... DLB-13

Whiting, Samuel 1597-1679 .... DLB-24

Whitlock, Brand 1869-1934 .... DLB-12

Whitman, Albert, and Company DLB-46

Whitman, Albery Allson 1851-1901 .... DLB-50

Whitman, Alden 1913-1990 .... Y-91

Whitman, Sarah Helen (Power) 1803-1878 .... DLB-1

Whitman, Walt 1819-1892 ...... DLB-3, 64

Whitman Publishing Company DLB-46

Whitney, Geoffrey 1548 or 1552?-1601 .... DLB-136

Whitney, Isabella flourished 1566-1573 .... DLB-136

Whitney, John Hay 1904-1982 ..... DLB-127

Whittemore, Reed 1919- DLB-5

Whittier, John Greenleaf 1807-1892 .... DLB-1

Whittlesey House DLB-46

Who Runs American Literature? Y-94

Wickram, Georg circa 1505-circa1561 .... DLB-179

Wideman, John Edgar 1941- ... DLB-33, 143

Widener, Harry Elkins 1885-1912 .... DLB-140

Wiebe, Rudy 1934- DLB-60

Wiechert, Ernst 1887-1950 .... DLB-56

Wied, Martina 1882-1957 .... DLB-85

Wiehe, Evelyn May Clowes (see Mordaunt, Elinor)

Wieland, Christoph Martin 1733-1813 .... DLB-97

Wienbarg, Ludolf 1802-1872 ...... DLB-133

Wieners, John 1934- DLB-16

Wier, Ester 1910- DLB-52

Wiesel, Elie 1928- DLB-83; Y-87

Wiggin, Kate Douglas 1856-1923 .... DLB-42

Wigglesworth, Michael 1631-1705 .... DLB-24

Wilberforce, William 1759-1833 ..... DLB-158

Wilbrandt, Adolf 1837-1911 .... DLB-129

Wilbur, Richard 1921- DLB-5, 169

Wild, Peter 1940- DLB-5

Wilde, Oscar 1854-1900 .... DLB-10, 19, 34, 57, 141, 156

Wilde, Richard Henry 1789-1847 .... DLB-3, 59

Wilde, W. A., Company DLB-49

Wilder, Billy 1906- DLB-26

Wilder, Laura Ingalls 1867-1957 ..... DLB-22

Wilder, Thornton 1897-1975 .... DLB-4, 7, 9

Wildgans, Anton 1881-1932 .... DLB-118

Wiley, Bell Irvin 1906-1980 .... DLB-17

Wiley, John, and Sons DLB-49

Wilhelm, Kate 1928- DLB-8

Wilkes, George 1817-1885 .... DLB-79

Wilkinson, Anne 1910-1961 .... DLB-88

Wilkinson, Sylvia 1940- Y-86

Wilkinson, William Cleaver 1833-1920 .... DLB-71

Willard, Barbara 1909-1994 .... DLB-161

Willard, L. [publishing house] DLB-49

Willard, Nancy 1936- DLB-5, 52

Willard, Samuel 1640-1707 .... DLB-24

William of Auvergne 1190-1249 .... DLB-115

William of Conches circa 1090-circa 1154 .... DLB-115

William of Ockham circa 1285-1347 .... DLB-115

William of Sherwood 1200/1205 - 1266/1271 .... DLB-115

The William Chavrat American Fiction Collection at the Ohio State University Libraries Y-92

Williams, A., and Company DLB-49

Williams, Ben Ames 1889-1953 ..... DLB-102

Williams, C. K. 1936- DLB-5

Williams, Chancellor 1905- DLB-76

Williams, Charles 1886-1945 .... DLB-100, 153

Williams, Denis 1923- DLB-117

Williams, Emlyn 1905- DLB-10, 77

Williams, Garth 1912- DLB-22

Williams, George Washington 1849-1891 .... DLB-47

Williams, Heathcote 1941- DLB-13

Williams, Helen Maria 1761-1827 .... DLB-158

Williams, Hugo 1942- DLB-40

Williams, Isaac 1802-1865 .... DLB-32

Williams, Joan 1928- DLB-6

Williams, John A. 1925- DLB-2, 33

Williams, John E. 1922-1994 ...... DLB-6

Williams, Jonathan 1929- DLB-5

Williams, Miller 1930- DLB-105

Williams, Raymond 1921- DLB-14

Williams, Roger circa 1603-1683 ..... DLB-24

Williams, Samm-Art 1946- DLB-38

Williams, Sherley Anne 1944- DLB-41

Williams, T. Harry 1909-1979 ..... DLB-17

Williams, Tennessee 1911-1983 .... DLB-7; Y-83; DS-4

Williams, Ursula Moray 1911- DLB-160

Williams, Valentine 1883-1946 ..... DLB-77

Williams, William Appleman 1921- DLB-17

Williams, William Carlos 1883-1963 .... DLB-4, 16, 54, 86

Williams, Wirt 1921- DLB-6

Williams Brothers DLB-49

Williamson, Jack 1908- DLB-8

Willingham, Calder Baynard, Jr. 1922- DLB-2, 44

Williram of Ebersberg circa 1020-1085 .... DLB-148

Willis, Nathaniel Parker 1806-1867 ..... DLB-3, 59, 73, 74; DS-13

Willkomm, Ernst 1810-1886. . . . . . . DLB-133
Wilmer, Clive 1945- DLB-40
Wilson, A. N. 1950- DLB-14, 155
Wilson, Angus 1913-1991 . . . . DLB-15, 139, 155
Wilson, Arthur 1595-1652 . . . . DLB-58
Wilson, Augusta Jane Evans 1835-1909 . . . . DLB-42
Wilson, Colin 1931- DLB-14
Wilson, Edmund 1895-1972 . . . . DLB-63
Wilson, Ethel 1888-1980 . . . . DLB-68
Wilson, Harriet E. Adams 1828?-1863? DLB-50
Wilson, Harry Leon 1867-1939 . . . . . . DLB-9
Wilson, John 1588-1667 . . . . DLB-24
Wilson, John 1785-1854 . . . . DLB-110
Wilson, Lanford 1937- DLB-7
Wilson, Margaret 1882-1973 . . . . DLB-9
Wilson, Michael 1914-1978 . . . . DLB-44
Wilson, Mona 1872-1954 . . . . DLB-149
Wilson, Thomas 1523 or 1524-1581 . . . . DLB-132
Wilson, Woodrow 1856-1924 . . . . . . DLB-47
Wilson, Effingham [publishing house] DLB-154
Wimpfeling, Jakob 1450-1528 . . . . . DLB-179
Wimsatt, William K., Jr. 1907-1975 . . . . DLB-63
Winchell, Walter 1897-1972 . . . . DLB-29
Winchester, J. [publishing house] DLB-49
Winckelmann, Johann Joachim 1717-1768 . . . . DLB-97
Winckler, Paul 1630-1686 . . . . DLB-164
Wind, Herbert Warren 1916- DLB-171
Windet, John [publishing house] DLB-170
Windham, Donald 1920- DLB-6
Wingate, Allan [publishing house] . . . DLB-112
Winnemucca, Sarah 1844-1921 . . . . DLB-175
Winnifrith, Tom 1938- DLB-155
Winsloe, Christa 1888-1944 . . . . . . DLB-124
Winsor, Justin 1831-1897 . . . . DLB-47
John C. Winston Company DLB-49
Winters, Yvor 1900-1968 . . . . DLB-48
Winthrop, John 1588-1649 . . . . . DLB-24, 30
Winthrop, John, Jr. 1606-1676 . . . . . DLB-24
Wirt, William 1772-1834 . . . . DLB-37
Wise, John 1652-1725 . . . . DLB-24
Wiseman, Adele 1928- DLB-88
Wishart and Company DLB-112
Wisner, George 1812-1849 . . . . DLB-43
Wister, Owen 1860-1938 . . . . . . DLB-9, 78
Wither, George 1588-1667 . . . . . . DLB-121
Witherspoon, John 1723-1794 . . . . . DLB-31

Withrow, William Henry 1839-1908 . . . . DLB-99
Wittenwiler, Heinrich before 1387-circa1414? DLB-179
Wittig, Monique 1935- DLB-83
Wodehouse, P. G. 1881-1975 . . . . DLB-34, 162
Wohmann, Gabriele 1932- DLB-75
Woiwode, Larry 1941- DLB-6
Wolcot, John 1738-1819 . . . . DLB-109
Wolcott, Roger 1679-1767 . . . . DLB-24
Wolf, Christa 1929- DLB-75
Wolf, Friedrich 1888-1953 . . . . . . DLB-124
Wolfe, Gene 1931- DLB-8
Wolfe, John [publishing house] DLB-170
Wolfe, Reyner (Reginald) [publishing house] DLB-170
Wolfe, Thomas 1900-1938 . . . . . DLB-9, 102; Y-85; DS-2
Wolfe, Tom 1931- DLB-152
Wolff, Helen 1906-1994 . . . . Y-94
Wolff, Tobias 1945- DLB-130
Wolfram von Eschenbach circa 1170-after 1220 . . . . DLB-138
Wolfram von Eschenbach's Parzival: Prologue and Book 3 . . . . DLB-138
Wollstonecraft, Mary 1759-1797 . . . . DLB-39, 104, 158
Wondratschek, Wolf 1943- DLB-75
Wood, Benjamin 1820-1900 . . . . . . DLB-23
Wood, Charles 1932- DLB-13
Wood, Mrs. Henry 1814-1887 . . . . . DLB-18
Wood, Joanna E. 1867-1927 . . . . . . DLB-92
Wood, Samuel [publishing house] . . . DLB-49
Wood, William ?-? DLB-24
Woodberry, George Edward 1855-1930 . . . . DLB-71, 103
Woodbridge, Benjamin 1622-1684 . . . DLB-24
Woodcock, George 1912- DLB-88
Woodhull, Victoria C. 1838-1927 . . . DLB-79
Woodmason, Charles circa 1720-? . . . DLB-31
Woodress, Jr., James Leslie 1916- DLB-111
Woodson, Carter G. 1875-1950 . . . . DLB-17
Woodward, C. Vann 1908- DLB-17
Woodward, Stanley 1895-1965 . . . . DLB-171
Wooler, Thomas 1785 or 1786-1853 . . . . DLB-158
Woolf, David (see Maddow, Ben)
Woolf, Leonard 1880-1969 . . . DLB-100; DS-10
Woolf, Virginia 1882-1941 . . . . . DLB-36, 100, 162; DS-10
Woolf, Virginia, "The New Biography," New York Herald Tribune, 30 October 1927 . . . . DLB-149

Woollcott, Alexander 1887-1943 . . . . DLB-29
Woolman, John 1720-1772 . . . . DLB-31
Woolner, Thomas 1825-1892 . . . . . . DLB-35
Woolsey, Sarah Chauncy 1835-1905 . . . . DLB-42
Woolson, Constance Fenimore 1840-1894 . . . . DLB-12, 74
Worcester, Joseph Emerson 1784-1865 . . . . DLB-1
Worde, Wynkyn de [publishing house] DLB-170
Wordsworth, Christopher 1807-1885 . . . . DLB-166
Wordsworth, Dorothy 1771-1855 . . . . DLB-107
Wordsworth, Elizabeth 1840-1932 . . . . DLB-98
Wordsworth, William 1770-1850 . . . . DLB-93, 107
The Works of the Rev. John Witherspoon (1800-1801) [excerpts] DLB-31
A World Chronology of Important Science Fiction Works (1818-1979) DLB-8
World Publishing Company DLB-46
World War II Writers Symposium at the University of South Carolina, 12–14 April 1995 . . . . Y-95
Worthington, R., and Company DLB-49
Wotton, Sir Henry 1568-1639 . . . . . DLB-121
Wouk, Herman 1915- Y-82
Wreford, James 1915- DLB-88
Wren, Percival Christopher 1885-1941 . . . . DLB-153
Wrenn, John Henry 1841-1911 . . . . DLB-140
Wright, C. D. 1949- DLB-120
Wright, Charles 1935- DLB-165; Y-82
Wright, Charles Stevenson 1932- DLB-33
Wright, Frances 1795-1852 . . . . DLB-73
Wright, Harold Bell 1872-1944 . . . . . DLB-9
Wright, James 1927-1980 . . . . . DLB-5, 169
Wright, Jay 1935- DLB-41
Wright, Louis B. 1899-1984 . . . . . . DLB-17
Wright, Richard 1908-1960 . . . . DLB-76, 102; DS-2
Wright, Richard B. 1937- DLB-53
Wright, Sarah Elizabeth 1928- DLB-33
Writers and Politics: 1871-1918, by Ronald Gray DLB-66
Writers and their Copyright Holders: the WATCH Project Y-94
Writers' Forum Y-85
Writing for the Theatre, by Harold Pinter DLB-13
Wroth, Lady Mary 1587-1653 . . . . . DLB-121
Wurlitzer, Rudolph 1937- DLB-173

Wyatt, Sir Thomas
   circa 1503-1542 . . . . DLB-132

Wycherley, William 1641-1715. . . . . . DLB-80

Wyclif, John
   circa 1335-31 December 1384 . . . DLB-146

Wylie, Elinor 1885-1928. . . . . DLB-9, 45

Wylie, Philip 1902-1971 . . . . DLB-9

Wyllie, John Cook 1908-1968 . . . . . DLB-140

X

Xenophon circa 430 B.C.-circa 356 B.C.
   . . . . DLB-176

Y

Yates, Dornford 1885-1960 . . . . . DLB-77, 153

Yates, J. Michael 1938- DLB-60

Yates, Richard 1926-1992. . . . DLB-2; Y-81, 92

Yavorov, Peyo 1878-1914. . . . . DLB-147

Yearsley, Ann 1753-1806 . . . . DLB-109

Yeats, William Butler
   1865-1939. . . . . . . DLB-10, 19, 98, 156

Yep, Laurence 1948- DLB-52

Yerby, Frank 1916-1991 . . . . DLB-76

Yezierska, Anzia 1885-1970. . . . . . . DLB-28

Yolen, Jane 1939- DLB-52

Yonge, Charlotte Mary
   1823-1901 . . . . DLB-18, 163

The York Cycle
   circa 1376-circa 1569 . . . . DLB-146

A Yorkshire Tragedy DLB-58

Yoseloff, Thomas
   [publishing house]. DLB-46

Young, Al 1939- DLB-33

Young, Arthur 1741-1820 . . . . DLB-158

Young, Dick 1917 or 1918 - 1987. . . DLB-171

Young, Edward 1683-1765 . . . . DLB-95

Young, Stark 1881-1963 . . . . . . DLB-9, 102

Young, Waldeman 1880-1938 . . . . . DLB-26

Young, William [publishing house]. . . DLB-49

Young Bear, Ray A. 1950- DLB-175

Yourcenar, Marguerite
   1903-1987. . . . . DLB-72; Y-88

"You've Never Had It So Good," Gusted by
"Winds of Change": British Fiction in the
1950s, 1960s, and After DLB-14

Yovkov, Yordan 1880-1937 . . . . DLB-147

Z

Zachariä, Friedrich Wilhelm
   1726-1777 . . . . DLB-97

Zajc, Dane 1929- DLB-181

Zamora, Bernice 1938- DLB-82

Zand, Herbert 1923-1970. . . . . DLB-85

Zangwill, Israel 1864-1926 . . . . . DLB-10, 135

Zanzotto, Andrea 1921- DLB-128

Zapata Olivella, Manuel 1920- DLB-113

Zebra Books. DLB-46

Zebrowski, George 1945- DLB-8

Zech, Paul 1881-1946. . . . . DLB-56

Zepheria DLB-172

Zeidner, Lisa 1955- DLB-120

Zelazny, Roger 1937-1995 . . . . DLB-8

Zenger, John Peter 1697-1746 . . . . DLB-24, 43

Zesen, Philipp von 1619-1689. . . . . . DLB-164

Zieber, G. B., and Company DLB-49

Zieroth, Dale 1946- DLB-60

Zigler und Kliphausen, Heinrich Anshelm von
   1663-1697 . . . . DLB-168

Zimmer, Paul 1934- DLB-5

Zingref, Julius Wilhelm
   1591-1635 . . . . DLB-164

Zindel, Paul 1936- DLB-7, 52

Zinzendorf, Nikolaus Ludwig von
   1700-1760 . . . . DLB-168

Zitkala-Ša 1876-1938. . . . . DLB-175

Zola, Émile 1840-1902. . . . . DLB-123

Zolotow, Charlotte 1915- DLB-52

Zschokke, Heinrich 1771-1848 . . . . . DLB-94

Zubly, John Joachim 1724-1781 . . . . DLB-31

Zu-Bolton II, Ahmos 1936- DLB-41

Zuckmayer, Carl 1896-1977 . . . . DLB-56, 124

Zukofsky, Louis 1904-1978 . . . . DLB-5, 165

Zupan, Vitomil 1914-1987. . . . . . . DLB-181

Župančič, Oton 1878-1949 . . . . DLB-147

zur Mühlen, Hermynia 1883-1951 . . . . DLB-56

Zweig, Arnold 1887-1968. . . . . DLB-66

Zweig, Stefan 1881-1942 . . . . . . DLB-81, 118

Zwingli, Huldrych 1484-1531 . . . . . . DLB-179

ISBN 0-7876-1070-4

90000